S0-BAG-983

COLERIDGE

DARKER REFLECTIONS

1804-1834

ALSO BY RICHARD HOLMES

One for Sorrow (poems)

Shelley: The Pursuit

Gautier: My Fantoms (translations)

Shelley on Love

Coleridge

Footsteps: Adventures of a Romantic Biographer

Nerval: The Chimeras (with Peter Jay)

Mary Wollstonecraft and William Godwin:
A Short Residence in Sweden and *Memoirs*

Kipling: Something of Myself (with Robert Hampson)

De Feministe en de Filosoof

Coleridge: Early Visions, 1772-1804

Dr. Johnson & Mr. Savage

Coleridge: Selected Poems

COLERIDGE

DARKER REFLECTIONS

1804-1834

RICHARD HOLMES

Pantheon Books • New York

 Published in the United States by Pantheon Books, a division of Random House, Inc., New York. Originally published in Great Britain by HarperCollins Publishers, London, in 1998. Originally published in hardcover in the United States by Pantheon Books, a division of Random House, Inc., New York, in 1999.

Pantheon Books and colophon are registered trademarks of Random House, Inc.

Library of Congress Cataloging-in-Publication Data

Holmes, Richard, 1945–
Coleridge / Richard Holmes.
p. cm.
Includes bibliographical references and index.
Contents: v. 1. Early visions, 1772–1804 — v. 2. Darker reflections, 1804–1834.
ISBN 0-375-70838-3 (v. 2)
1. Coleridge, Samuel Taylor, 1772–1834. 2. Poets, English—19th century—Biography. 3. Critics—Great Britain—Biography. I. Title.
PR4483.H57 1999 821'.7—dc21 [B] 98-30501 CIP

Random House Web Address: www.randomhouse.com

Printed in the United States of America

First Pantheon Paperback Edition 2000
2 4 6 8 9 7 5 3 1

To Rose, with love

Contents

Illustrations

Portrait Gallery, London)
Crabb Robinson from a drawing by Masquerier, date unknown
William Hazlitt by William Bewick, 1825 (*National Portrait Gallery, London*)
Nineteenth-century laudanum bottles (*Science and Society Picture Library*)
Frontispiece to *The Rime of the Ancient Mariner*, 1837, designed and etched by David Scott (*Wordsworth Trust, Dove Cottage*)
Perce Bysshe Shelley by Amelia Curran, 1819 (*National Portrait Gallery, London*)
Thomas Love Peacock by Roger Jean, 1805 (*National Portrait Gallery, London*)
John Keats by Charles Armitage Brown, 1819 (*National Portrait Gallery, London*)
Lord Byron by Richard Westall, 1813 (*National Portrait Gallery, London*)
James Gillman from a sketch by C. R. Leslie, 1816
Ann Gillman from an oil painting by Maria Spilsbury
Coleridge's daughter Sara by Charlotte Jones, 1827
Hartley Coleridge, anon, *c.* 1850 (*Highgate Literary and Scientific Institution*)
The Grove, Highgate (*Highgate Literary and Scientific Institution*)
Aerial view of Highgate Village (*London Aerial Photo Library*)
Illustration from *The Ancient Mariner* engraved by Gustave Doré, 1877
'Samuel Taylor Coleridge Table-Talking' by Max Beerbohm from *The Poet's Corner*, 1904 (*Wordsworth Trust, Dove Cottage/© The Estate of Max Beerbohm, reprinted by permission of London Management*)

Maps

(drawn by John Gilkes)

COLERIDGE

DARKER REFLECTIONS

1804-1834

1

Adrift in the Mediterranean

1

"Signals, Drums, Guns, Bells, & the sound of Voices weighing up & clearing Anchors". So Coleridge fled south aboard the *Speedwell*, expecting to die but half-hoping to be reborn. "Monday April 9th, 1804, really set sail . . . No health or Happiness without Work."[1]

Behind him he left his family under Southey's care in the Lake District; he left the Wordsworths and his love Sara Hutchinson; he left Charles Lamb and Daniel Stuart and all his London friends; each of them anxiously speculating about his future. "Far art thou wandered now," wrote Wordsworth in *The Prelude*, "in search of health,/And milder breezes . . . Speed thee well".[2]

Ahead of him lay the glittering Mediterranean, the legendary outposts of Gibraltar, Malta and Sicily, a war-zone of fleets and harbour-fortresses, where he would fight his own battles against opium and despair. "Do we not pity our past selves?" he reflected in his new Notebook, using a special metallic pencil designed to withstand sea-salt. "Is not this always accompanied by Hope? It makes the Images of the Past vivid . . . Are not vivid Ideas themselves a sort of pleasure, as Music whether sad or lively, is always Music?"[3]

Down in his cabin on the first night, he watched the lights of England recede along the Cornish coast through the brass porthole above his narrow berth. The 130-ton ship moved uneasily, not rolling on its beam, but rocking sharply from stem to stern, "as a cruel Nurse rocks a screaming baby".[4] Coleridge lay with his eyes closed, thirty-one years old, but hearing childhood music. "Thought of a Lullaby song, to a Child on a Ship: great rocking Cradle . . . creak of main top Irons, rattle of Ropes, & squeak of the Rudder . . . And so play Bo-peep with the Rising Moon, and the Lizard Light. 'There is thy native country, Boy! Whither art thou going to . . .' "[5]

2

Coleridge's ship the *Speedwell* was a two-masted merchant brig, lightly armed with fourteen guns, but carrying a heavy cargo of eighty-four cannons in her hold destined for Trieste.[6] Smartly trimmed in silver and gold, she was one of the fastest merchants in the fleet, commanded by a thoughtful Scotsman, Captain John Findlay, from whom Coleridge gradually extracted much sea-lore, sailor's yarns and sea-shanties.

She was part of the spring-time convoy of thirty-five ships, escorted by ten men-o'-war and the flagship HMS *Leviathan*, going to join Nelson's fleet in the Mediterranean and carrying supplies to British and allied ports in the war against France and Spain. Having finally left Spithead on 9 April 1804, the first leg of their journey ran through the Bay of Biscay and round Cape St Vincent to Gibraltar.

As the French fleet under Villeneuve was bottled up by Nelson's squadron off Toulon, the greatest danger came from privateers and corsairs operating out of Spanish and North African ports. So Captain Findlay cheerfully instructed Coleridge: "in a calm [they] will run out, pick up a merchant Vessel under the very stern of the Commodore, as a Fox will a Fowl when the Wolf dog that guards the poultry yard can only bark at him from his Chain".[7] Coleridge kept a close eye on the wind throughout their voyage, as he did on all other maritime matters, so the whole imagery of the sea journey came to possess him.

3

By the second day he had found his sea-legs, and with hair flying and double-waistcoats flapping, he patrolled the deck agog with excitement, questioning and noting. Nothing seemed to escape his attention. If a merchantman lagged behind or failed to obey signals, the seventy-four-gun *Leviathan* fired warning shots at her – "Commodore's strengthening *Pills* for the Memory", and a fine of five shillings.[8] Down in the first hold, a sheep abandoned its hay, "kneeling its poor face to the Deck, its knees black, worn and sore . . . alas! it came from flat peaceable meadows".[9] At victuals, a ship's boy ran up the rigging to the main top "with a large Leg of Mutton swung, Albatross-fashion about his neck".[10]

Always there was "great sea-Savannah" rolling unpastured about them, in all its changing lights and sounds. "The beautiful bright Slate, & the Soap stone colour by the Vessel's side, in a brisk gale, immediately under the mast in a froth-cream, that throws itself into network, with its *brisk* sound, which the word brisk itself may be made to imitate by hissing on the 'isk' . . ."[11] These observations went on constantly, by day and night, and several were later incorporated into the 1817 edition of the "Mariner", such as the eerie light of the compass and rudder-man's lamp "reflected with forms on the Main Sail".[12]

Along with the crated ducks, three pigs, the melancholy sheep and a ship's cat with kittens, Coleridge had two fellow passengers. They shared the cabin in increasingly pungent intimacy as the voyage progressed. One was a purple-faced lieutenant on half pay, who largely restricted his attentions to the ship's claret; the other was a plump and garrulous merry widow, a Mrs Ireland, "who would have wanted elbow-room on Salisbury Plain".[13] Mrs Ireland's conversation was confined to food, and she dwelt lovingly on the roast potatoes, pickles and apricot tart to be expected in Malta.[14]

The cabin conditions were extremely cramped, and probably not improved by Coleridge's tendency "in very gusty weather" to vomit up his food without warning. The process intrigued him, as it was never accompanied by seasickness: "it was an action as mechanical seemingly as that by which one's glass or teacup is emptied by a thwart blow of the Sea".[15] Surprisingly, the merry "Mrs Carnosity" accepted this with good grace, and much worse which was to follow, after Gibraltar, when the mephitic stench from the bilge became overpowering.

Coleridge drew up a daily schedule for work in "a perseverant Spirit of industry": it began with ginger tea and journal-writing, proceeded with a study of Wordsworth's precious manuscript of the *Prelude* before dinner, and in the afternoon relaxed into Italian lessons and Dante; finally the night-watch was assigned to poetry and the completion of "Christabel". But after the ginger tea and journal, Coleridge usually found that he flagged and spent his time up on deck,[16] or dozing uneasily on his bunk under a pile of books. These included, besides Dante and a portable Italian dictionary, a technical work on mineralogy, the meditations of Marcus Aurelius, and the complete works of Sir Thomas Browne, together with a mutinous crew of fresh lemons that he chewed to protect against scurvy.

He has much exercised by the bunk, which his large frame swaddled in double coats and double trousers, reduced to a precarious "mantel". On inspection it measured five and a half feet long by twenty inches wide. It was fine for sitting, eating, drinking, writing, even shaving: "it fails only in its original purpose, that of lying & sleeping: like a great Genius apprenticed to a wrong Trade".[17] But above it was the brass porthole upon which he lavished all his ingenuity. Finding it edged with small iron rings he laced these with cords to form a net, and stacked the bottom half with books to make a flat shelf for his kit. Inside this seamanlike cupboard he carefully arranged his shaving things, teacup and soup plate, supply of lemons and portable inkstand, whose unmoving pool of black ink seemed a suggestive contrast to the ceaseless lurching of the ship. 'By charm and talismanic privilege: one of those Smooth places in the Mediterranean, where the breakers foam in a circle around, yet send in no wrinkles upon the mirror-bright, mirror-smooth *Lacus in mare*."

Like the charmed pool of the imagination, the steady inkwell amidst the churning sea was "Imperium in Imperio", a realm within a realm.[18] This is what he hoped to become himself. To get all ship-shape, he also opened up the little escritoire that Lady Beaumont had given him, and found each drawer packed with comforts, which seized him "by a hundred Tentacula of Love and affection & pleasurable Remembrances".[19]

4

Up on deck, he chatted to the sailors he always admired – "a neat handed Fellow who could shave himself in a storm without drawing blood"[20] – and recorded sextant readings, compass-bearings, cloud formations, star patterns and semaphore messages through the squadron. Above all he recorded the huge, beautiful complexity of the ship's sails. They were constantly re-set throughout the fleet to form an endless series of visual harmonies. On Saturday, 14 April, he made no less than eleven pages of notes on these sail shapes. What interested him was their aesthetic values, their painterly suggestions of form and function, of energy transferred between curve and straight line. "The harmony of the Lines – the ellipses & semicircles of the bellying Sails of the Hull, with the variety of the one and the contingency of the other."

He puzzled over their "obscure resemblance" to human shapes, to gestures of mental alertness, determination and attention. "The height of the naked mast above the sails, connected however with them by Pennant & Vane, associated I think, with the human form on a watch-tower: a general feeling – e.g. the *Men* on the tops of conical mountains . . . in Cumberland and Westmoreland."[21] This idea of the symbolic "watch-tower" haunted Coleridge. He later found that Nelson had described the navy in Malta as "the watch-tower of the Mediterranean". Later still he used the image to describe Wordsworth's dominance of the poetic horizon: "From the dread watch-tower of man's absolute self".[22] Wordsworth indeed, as a man-o'-war, in full sail.

But Coleridge's notes press further. "Every one of these sails is *known* by the Intellect to have a strict & necessary action & reaction on all the rest, and the whole is made up of parts . . ." This technical knowledge of the complementary function of the sails produces the sense of unity which we call beauty: "this phantom of complete visual wholeness in an object, which visually does not form a whole, by the influence *ab intra* of the sense of its perfect Intellectual Beauty or Wholeness".[23] This subtle aesthetic emerged on the deck of the *Speedwell* in the Bay of Biscay. From it Coleridge dashed into a bracket a formulation which would become central to his *Biographia Literaria*: "all Passion unifies as it were by natural Fusion".

It is evident from such notes that Coleridge was recovering fast from the mood of helpless despondency that had beset him in past months. At night, down in the cabin, he still had his "Dreams of Terror & obscure forms",[24] and sometimes awoke screaming as in the old, bad times at Keswick. In low moments he still thought mournfully of Asra too: "Why ain't you here? This for ever: I have no rooted thorough thro feeling – & never exist wholly present to any Sight, to any sound, to any Emotion . . . feeling of yearning, that at times passes into Sickness."[25] His poem to her, "Phantom", dates from this part of the voyage.

All look and likeness caught from earth,
All accident of kin and birth,
Had pass'd away. There was no trace
Of aught on that illumined face,
Uprais'd beneath the rifted stone
But of one spirit all her own;
She, she herself, and only she,
Shone through her body visibly.[26]

But his sense of excitement and stimulation was unmistakable. On 16 April the look-out "hailed the beautiful Coast of Portugal, & Oporto", and Coleridge swarmed up on deck in his greatcoat, without bothering to put on his shoes. He began a long, enthusiastic letter to Robert Southey, sitting at his desk on the rudder case with the quacking ducks at his feet. He filled it with beautiful descriptions of the coastline and jokes about Mrs Carnosity. "We sail on at a wonderful rate, & considering we are in a Convoy, all have made a most lucky Voyage to Gibraltar if we are not becalmed, & taken in the Gut . . ."[27]

His main complaint was his bunk at night, "Dejection & Discomfort", and the wallowing motion of the following sea. "*This damned* Rocking . . . is troublesome & impertinent . . . like the presence & gossip of an old Aunt."[28] But the magic of the ships made up for everything: "Oh with what envy I have gazed at our Commodore, the Leviathan of 74 guns, the majestic & beautiful creature: sailing right before us . . . upright, motionless, as a church with its Steeple – as tho it moved by its will, as tho its speed were spiritual . . ."[29]

Three nights later he was sitting at his post under a bright moon – "how hard to describe that sort of Queen's metal plating, which the Moonlight forms on the bottle-green Sea" – with Spain on his left hand and the Barbary Coast on his right. "This is Africa! That is Europe! There is division, sharp boundary, abrupt change! and what are they in Nature – two Mountain banks, that make a noble River of the interfluent Sea . . . no division, no Change, no Antithesis."[30]

As the *Speedwell* slipped into the Mediterranean, he mused on this strange difference between human and natural geography, how human associations form our landscapes and boundaries far more than Nature herself. The power of human association with physical places and objects was perhaps the foundation of biography – "a Pilgrimage to see a great man's Shin Bone found unmouldered in his Coffin". Yet surely in this biography was a form of stupid superstition. "A Shakespeare, a Milton, a Bruno, exist in the mind as *pure Action*, defecated of all that is material & passive." He could look at the fabled mulberry tree that Shakespeare planted without emotion. Yet as he gazed out into the moonlit path between two continents, Coleridge recognized deeper feelings of connection within himself. "At certain times, uncalled and sudden, subject to no bidding of my own or others, these Thoughts would come upon me, like a Storm, & fill the Place with something more than Nature."[31]

Coleridge planned to put his meditations into a traveller's anthology, "Comforts and Consolations",[32] which was aimed at those who suffered from "speculative Gloom". Perhaps partly inspired by Marcus Aurelius, it enshrined the significant idea that depression could be treated by stoic self-analysis, and the application of "the Reason, the Imagination, and the moral Feelings" to our own mental processes and mood-shifts. But writing to Southey he also mentioned the cheerfulness of unaccustomed abstemiousness: he was eating no meat, and despite his crate of fine wines, "marvellous Brandy, & Rum 20 years old" provided by Sir George Beaumont, was drinking nothing but lemonade. The abstinence also included opium, at least for the first fortnight.[33]

5

At dawn on 19 April, Coleridge's telescope picked out the great brown rock of Gibraltar's "famous Apes Hill" detaching itself from the limestone sweeps and ridges of the Spanish coast. By the evening they were anchored under Europa Point and awaiting quarantine clearance – a rigid requirement in a zone of rapidly transmitted plagues and fevers, which killed off far more men than actual combat.

Coleridge was now entering a new world: colourful, hot, violent, polyglot, dominated by war and the rumours of war. People of every race and degree thronged the island – Jews, Arabs, Spaniards, Italians, Greeks. His first expedition along the quayside yielded a muleteer with the face of a monkey, a learned Jew in university dress, a Greek woman with earrings the size of "chain rings on a landing place for mooring boats", a senior English officer with an "angel Face" woman on his arm, and "Soldiers of all Regiments & Runaway Sailors" of every nation.[34]

Taken by Captain Findlay to Griffith's Hotel, through a stinking labyrinth of backstreets, he found himself plunged into the active-service culture of the British navy abroad: patriotic, punctilious, hard-drinking, with its endless yarns about weather, battles and promotion. The first news he heard was of the previous Portsmouth convoy, largely wrecked in a foul-weather passage to the West Indies; and of Nelson's dispatches intercepted by a French frigate.

He delivered letters of introduction to the navy chaplain, and to Major Adye, a young gunnery officer. Adye was a one-time pupil of his brother George's, who sportingly volunteered to act as his guide to the rock. Then he spent the afternoon climbing over Europa Point, pleased to see the homely pink geraniums clinging to the walls among the exotic prickly pears. 'Reluctantly I returned to a noisy Dinner of 17 Sea Captains, indifferent food, and burning Wines."

Much discussion turned on Nelson's Mediterranean strategy, and the importance of Malta for securing the trade routes into the eastern Mediterranean, the *casus belli* of 1803. "Struggle in the minds of the (native) inhabitants between their Dislike of English manners & their Dread of French Government. I find it a common opinion that if the Peace had continued the French would have monopolized the Commerce of the Levant."[35] This was to become a topic of dominant importance during his time in Malta. Coleridge finally escorted Captain Findlay – "my now very tipsy Capt" – back to the *Speedwell*, and left him drinking with three other merchant masters in his cabin.

They spent five hectic days at Gibraltar. Coleridge togged himself out in sailor's nankeen trousers and canvas shirt, and roamed all over the island, basking in the heat, drinking beer, making notes on plants, racial types, architecture, naval gossip and Mediterranean politics. In a packed letter to his newspaper editor Daniel Stuart, he leaped from subject to subject with all his old ebullience. The island was worth "a dozen plates by Hogarth". The climate of the south would "re-create" him. Whole days were spent "scrambling about on the back of the Rock among the Monkeys: I am a match for them in climbing, but in Hops & flying leaps they beat me."[36]

Meanwhile Major Adye briefed him on military matters, and sent a Corporal to escort him round the cliff-side gun emplacements – "The Noise so deafening in these galleries on the discharge of Guns, that the Soldiers' Ears have bled." By contrast, he scrambled alone into the deep silence of St Michael's Cave, with its massy natural pillars and huge stalactites "the models of Trees in stone", and wondered at the subterranean chambers (an old fascination) where men had descended three or four hundred feet "till the Smoke of their torches became intolerable".[37]

Sitting high up at Signal House, the very summit of Gibraltar, "which looks over the blue Sea-lake to Africa", the magic of the Mediterranean south rose up to him in sight and sound and smell (the crushed tansy under his shoe). He thought how many mountains he had stood on in his life, and how the Rock was something profoundly new and mysterious, in all its warlike nameless shapes and intimations. "What a complex Thing! At its feet mighty ramparts establishing themselves in the Sea with their huge artillery – hollow trunks of Iron where Death and Thunder sleep; the gardens in deep Moats between lofty and massive walls; a Town of All Nations & all languages; . . . fences of the prickly aloe, strange Plant that does not seem to be alive, but to have been a thing fantastically carved in wood & coloured, some Hieroglyph or temple Ornament of undiscovered meaning."[38]

Coleridge was deeply excited by the Mediterranean, and his whole body responded to the physical impact of sun and sea. Moving easily among the soldiers and sailors, picking up their talk and laughter, he saw himself once again as footloose adventurer, poetic traveller, special correspondent for Daniel Stuart's newspaper. His letter gives detailed naval "intelligence" of Nelson's lost dispatches, and the *Hindoostan* burnt out with only four survivors and the loss of fifty guns and £300,000 of cargo, "chiefly of naval Stores of all kinds for Malta with a hundred Artificers". Malta would be in "great Distress" for these losses, and he thought this would be the first crucial chance to get the news to London, by the return convoy: "after Letters will be better worth the postage".[39]

But, of course, beneath breathless activity, the manly sweating extraversion of the new self, older feelings stirred. "What change of place, Country, climate, company, situation, health – of Shrubs,

Flowers, Trees – moving Seasons: & ever is that one feeling at my heart, felt like a faint Pain, a spot which it seems I could lay my finger on." It was Asra, of course; and everything she represented of the Wordsworths, the Lakes, lost love.

The past self stood like a ghostly reflection in every company; the remembered hills rose up behind every sunlit cliff and rock. "I talk loud or eager, or I read or meditate the abstrusest Researches; or I laugh, jest, tell tales of mirth; & ever as it were, within & behind, I think & image you; and while I am talking of Government or War or Chemistry, there comes ever into my bodily eye some Tree, beneath which we have rested, some Rock where we have walked together, or on the perilous road edging high above the Crummock Lake, where we sat beneath the rock, & those dear Lips pressed my forehead."[40] This was the cargo of memory that could not be sunk or abandoned or burnt; the secret self that crouched below the waterline.

Coleridge's last day on Gibraltar was spent on a "long & instructive walk" with Major Adye round the entire defences, from the gun emplacements to the brewery, discussing British strategy in the Mediterranean. They visited St Michael's Cave again, and Coleridge was more and more struck by its mysterious rock formations, "the obelisks, the pillars, the rude statues of strange animals" like some cathedral of half-created forms and monuments.[41]

They planned to meet again in Malta, and Adye promised to carry home to England whatever letters and journals Coleridge had prepared. Back on the *Speedwell*, they discussed the dangers of the voyage ahead, and sailors' superstitions about dates and positions of the moon which reminded Coleridge of his Mariner. Captain Findlay said briskly, "Damn me! I have no superstition", but then revealed that he thought "Sunday is a really lucky day to sail on." They were interrupted by a huge cargo-ship, which nearly rammed them as they lay at anchor, and were only saved by Findlay shouting directions to the lubberly crew to go about. "Myself, the Capt. and the Mate all confessed, that our knees trembled under us," for the towering forecastle threatened to strike them amidships and sink them instantly. This at any rate was not a good omen.[42]

6

The *Speedwell* got under weigh from Gibraltar on 25 April 1804, now escorted by HMS *Maidstone*, and hoping to make the second leg of their journey in a week. In the event it took twenty-eight days, alternately beaten by storms and transfixed by calms, which took a terrible toll on Coleridge's health and spirits. Initially his journal records the continuing beauty of the seascape, the excitement of a turtle hunt, hornpipe dancing on the deck, and long grog sessions in Captain Findlay's cabin.

To beguile the time he began an essay on Superstition, "taken in its philosophical and most comprehensive Sense", as it affects men of action – soldiers, sailors, fishermen, farmers, even lovers and gamblers – who are placed "in an absolute Dependence on Powers & Events, over which they have no Control".[43] He noted how the patterns of "an old Idolatry" rose in response to physical fear, and fixed themselves angrily on scapegoats or astronomical signs, like the star which dogs a crescent moon. There began to be talk of a "Jonas in the Fleet", and he dryly remarked that this was one advantage of sailing in a convoy. "On a single Vessel the Jonas must have been sought among ourselves."

Conditions aboard the *Speedwell* steadily deteriorated. The "Mephitis of the bilge burst forth, like a fury" filling the cabins with nauseous stench, turning the gold paintwork red and black and covering everything with a kind of "silvery grease" which stank of sulphur. (Coleridge made a note to ask Humphry Davy about the chemistry of this effect.)[44] He became incapable of holding down food, and began to resort to opium: "desperately sick, ill, abed, one deep dose after another".[45] His unhappy dreams of Asra returned, mixed up with memories of schoolboy bullying and deprivation, "Christ Hospitalized the forms & incidents".[46]*

* Coleridge had been reliant on opium since the winter of 1801. He drank it in the form of laudanum, that is tincture of opium diluted in wine or brandy. Opium was also available in powdered form, and in many popular patent medicines such as Kendal Black Drop, Dover's Powder and Godfrey's Cordial. The drug was easily obtainable from pharmacists, druggists and physicians as an analgesic and antispasmodic, cheaply and without prescription. There was no medical concept of "addiction" (physical dependency), and the most advanced laboratory research at Edinburgh University and Göttingen (injecting dogs and frogs) had yet to agree if it was a stimulant, a hallucinogen, or a depressant. (See Andreas-Holhger Maehle, "Pharmacological

footnote continued overleaf

On 1 May, in wet, foggy, oppressive weather, they had drifted back towards the Barbary coast off Carthagina. "We are very nearly on the spot, where on Friday last about this same hour we caught the Turtles – And what are 5 days' toiling to windward just not to lose ground, to almost *5 years*. Alas! alas! what have I been doing on the Great Voyage of Life since my return from Germany but fretting upon the front of the wind – well for me if I have indeed kept my ground even!"[47]

On 4 May, a wind got up, and Coleridge composed a grateful sea-shanty for Captain Findlay, "who foretold a fair wind/ Of a constant mind", though "neither Poet, nor Sheep" could yet eat.[48] But the wind turned into a squall, and then a storm, which carried away their foremost yard-arm on 6 May. He sank further into opium, besieged by "these Sleeps, these Horrors, these Frightful Dreams of Despair". He could no longer get up on deck, and was now seriously ill, with violent stomach pains and humiliating flatulence. A flowered curtain was rigged round his bunk, and he began to hallucinate, seeing "yellow faces" in the cloth. The ship was again becalmed, and he thought the flapping sails were fish dying on the deck.[49] Mr Hardy, the surgeon of the *Maidstone*, was alerted and the rumour went round the convoy that one of the *Speedwell*'s passengers was dying. Coleridge knew he had become the Jonas of the fleet.

The opium doses had completely blocked his bowels. The shame,

---

footnote continued

Experimentation with Opium in the Eighteenth Century", in *Drugs and Narcotics in History*, edited Roy Porter, CUP 1995) In fact *Papaver somniferum* (the opium poppy) has all these properties, since it contains Nature's richest cocktail of drugs, from which nineteenth-century chemists would eventually derive morphine, heroin, nepenthe and codeine. Evidence for the strength, frequency and cost of Coleridge's habit will emerge later in my story. (For fellow-addicts, including Crabbe, Wilberforce, De Quincey, Poe, and Wilkie Collins see Alethea Hayter, *Opium and the Romantic Imagination*, 1968.) It is remarkable that nowhere in Coleridge's later *Notebooks* are there descriptions of the "pleasures" of opium, only of the agonizing physical and psychological effects of "withdrawal". His addiction can also be considered an emotional state which throws light on his extraordinary imaginative "dependency" on certain close, human relationships such as those with Wordsworth and Sara Hutchinson (Asra), and even more strangely, on their substitutes. Love and Opium are sometimes interchangeable substances in Coleridge's mind and body.

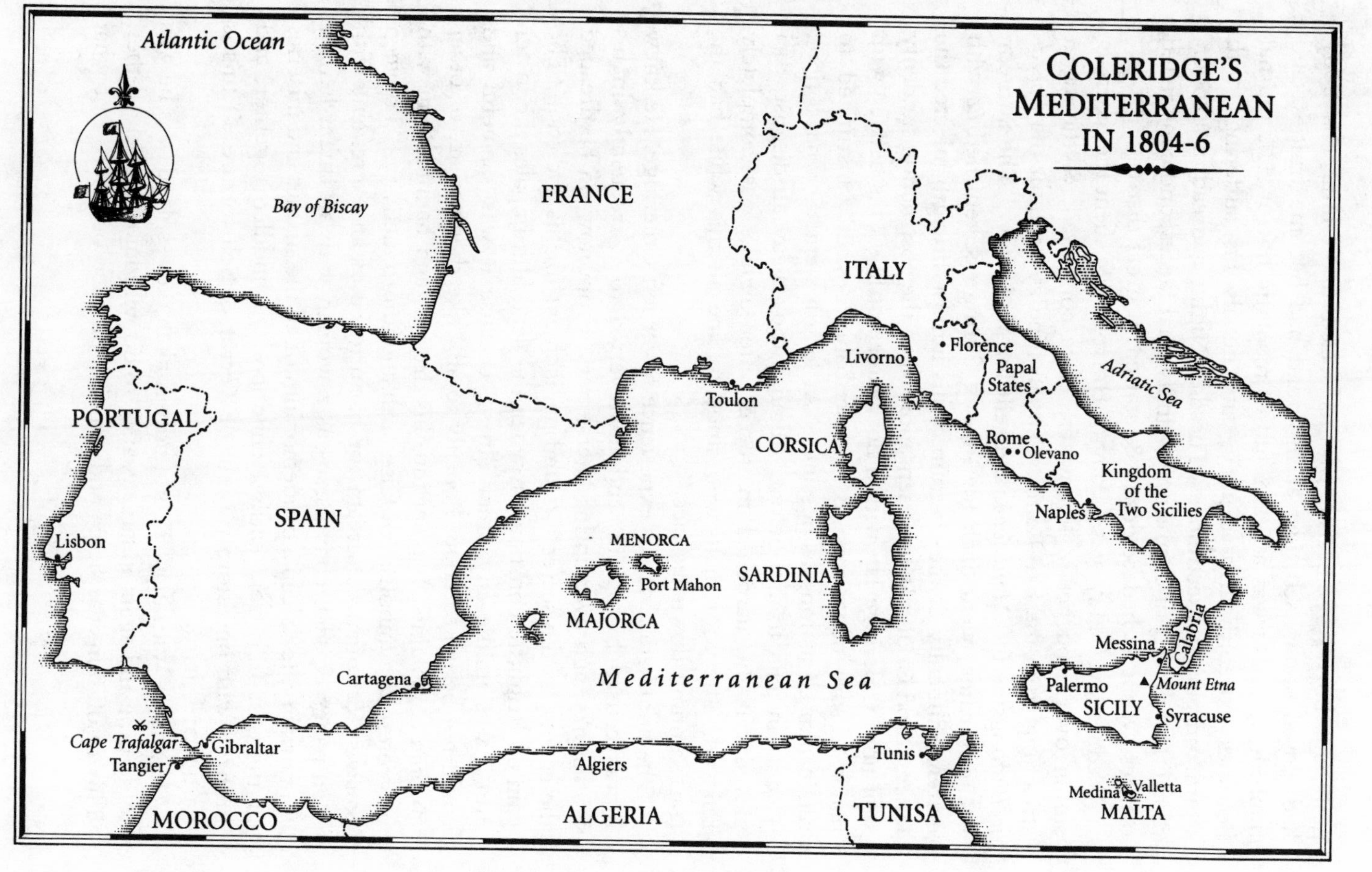
COLERIDGE'S MEDITERRANEAN IN 1804-6
Atlantic Ocean
Bay of Biscay
FRANCE
ITALY
PORTUGAL
SPAIN
Lisbon
Cape Trafalgar
Gibraltar
Tangier
MOROCCO
Cartagena
MENORCA
Port Mahon
MAJORCA
Mediterranean Sea
Algiers
ALGERIA
Toulon
CORSICA
SARDINIA
Livorno
Florence
Papal States
Rome
Olevano
Adriatic Sea
Kingdom of the Two Sicilies
Naples
Calabria
Messina
Palermo
Mount Etna
SICILY
Syracuse
Tunis
TUNISA
Medina
Valletta
MALTA

guilt and horrid symbolism of this seized upon him. His body had closed upon itself, just as his mind had become fruitless and unproductive. He was a vessel full of mephitic horror. His journal becomes extraordinarily explicit, and details his sufferings with weird, unsparing exactitude. "Tuesday Night, a dreadful Labour, & fruitless throes, of costiveness – individual faeces, and constricted orifices. Went to bed & dozed & started in great distress."[50]

Wednesday, 9 May was "a day of Horror". He spent the morning sitting over a bucket of hot water, "face convulsed, & the sweat streaming from me like Rain". Captain Findlay brought the *Speedwell* alongside the *Maidstone*, and sent for Mr Hardy. "The Surgeon instantly came, went back for Pipe & Syringe & returned & with extreme difficulty & the exertion of his utmost strength injected the latter. Good God! – What a sensation when the obstruction suddenly shot up!" Coleridge lay with a hot water bottle on his belly, "with pains & sore uneasiness, & indescribable desires", instructed to retain himself as long as possible. "At length went: O what a time! – equal in pain to any before. Anguish took away all disgust, & I picked out the hardened matter & after awhile was completely relieved. The poor mate who stood by me all this while had the tears running down his face."[51]

The humiliation of this experience never left Coleridge. He knew it was caused by opium, and he reverted to it frequently in his Notebooks, and even in his later letters. From now on he dreaded the enema, as the secret sign and punishment for his addiction. The pain of "frightful constipation when the dead filth impales the lower Gut", was unlike any other illness, because it was shameful and could not be talked about "openly to all" like rheumatism, or other chronic complaints. It crept into his dreams, and haunted him with its grotesque symbolism of false birth and unproductivity. "To weep & sweat & moan & scream for parturience of an excrement with such pangs & such convulsions as a woman with an Infant heir of Immortality: for Sleep a pandemonium of all the shames and miseries of the past Life from earliest childhood all huddled together, and bronzed with one stormy Light of Terror & Self-torture. O this is hard, hard, hard."[52]

It was "a Warning". Profoundly shaken, he resolved – as he was to do time and again in later years – to do without opium altogether. This resolution was fierce and genuine on each occasion. But what

Coleridge could not know was that by now complete withdrawal from the drug was physiologically a virtual impossibility without skilled medical aid. He could no longer do it alone, by a simple effort of will. So each time his will was broken, he suffered and lost confidence in his own powers. This terrible repetition of resolution and failure – like one of the endless, circular punishments of Dante's *Inferno* – shaped much of what happened in the second part of his life. Yet he never stopped resolving, and this dogged determination to battle on also became characteristic and took him through experiences that few of his contemporaries shared or even remotely understood.

Aboard the *Speedwell*, at midnight on 13 May, he turned towards his Creator for help: "O dear God! give me strength of Soul to make one thorough trial – if I land at Malta – spite all horrors to go through one month of unstimulated Nature – yielding to nothing but manifest danger of Life – O great God! Grant me grace truly to look into myself, & to begin the serious work of Self-amendment. Have Mercy on me Father & God! . . . who with undeviating Laws Eternal yet carest for the falling of the feather from the Sparrow's wing."[53]

Crawling back on deck, he found they were in sight of Sardinia. A hawk with battered plumage flew overhead, and settled on the bowsprit, until the sailors shot at it. It flew off heavily among the other ships, and Coleridge listened to the firing from further and further away, as each crew refused it hospitality in turn. "Poor Hawk! O strange Lust of Murder in Man! – It is not cruelty: it is mere non-feeling from non-thinking."[54] He ate rhubarb for his bowels, and was cosseted by "the good Mrs Ireland", never again referred to as "Mrs Carnosity".

Gradually his thoughts grew calmer. "Scarcely a day passes but something new in fact or illustration rises up in me, like Herbs and Flowers in a Garden in early Spring; but the combining Power, the power to do, the manly effective Will, that is dead or slumbers most diseasedly – Well I will pray for the Hour when I 'may quit the tiresome sea & dwell on Shore' . . ." He sat at the rudder-case and wrote notes on the moon, the notion of Sublimity, and the nature of poetry. "Poetry – a rationalized Dream – dealing out to manifold Forms our own Feelings – that never perhaps were attached by us consciously to our own Personal Selves".[55]

7

By 17 May Coleridge was quite restored, "uncommonly well", and observing the noble blue peak of Mount Etna rising out of the eastern waters. By dawn on the 18th the *Speedwell* was in clear sight of Malta, and Mrs Ireland was confiding in him that she expected to be met by her lover.[56] Captain Findlay put on all sail, and by 4 p.m. they were sliding under the huge sandstone fortifications of Valletta harbour ahead of the *Maidstone*. Observing the great battlements and citadel, originally built by the Knights of Malta to withstand the Great Siege of 1565, Coleridge felt like Aeneas arriving at Carthage.

Leaving his boxes to be unloaded, he disembarked in the first cutter and clambered breathlessly up the long stairs of Old Bakery Street, feeling like his own Mariner, "light as a blessed Ghost". He was glad to be alive. He made straight for the Casa de St Foix, the house of John Stoddart, the Chief Advocate of Malta. It stood at the top of the street, a large building in orange freestone, with brightly painted wooden casements and enclosed balconies, commanding a dramatic view over the Marsamxett harbour. Round it spread a labyrinth of tilting streets, enclosed by huge bastions, which echoed with the bustle and shout of Maltese street-vendors, the barking of dogs, the clanging of church bells and rumble of donkey-carts. Music poured from the taverns, as the innkeepers and prostitutes prepared to welcome the new influx of British sailors.

Coleridge was stunned by the noise and activity. "They are the noisiest race under Heaven . . . sudden shot-up explosive Bellows – no cries in London would give you the faintest idea of it. When you pass by a fruit stall, the fellow will put his Hand like a speaking trumpet to his mouth & shoot such a Thunder bolt of Sound full at you."[57]

After two hours of confusion and delay among the servants, Stoddart finally appeared and greeted him with a further "explosion of surprise and welcome". He was given rooms and promised introductions. So began Coleridge's sixteen-month sojourn on the tiny, rocky, Mediterranean outpost.

Initially, Coleridge's plans were uncertain. He would restore his health, travel to Sicily perhaps, keep a journal, maybe find a temporary post in the colonial administration. He would write essays on art or politics, and send articles to Stuart. He would let the Mediterranean sun bleach out his heartache and his opium sickness. What actually fixed these plans was his meeting with the civilian governor of Malta, Sir Alexander Ball. It was, Coleridge later wrote, "that daily and familiar intercourse with him, which made the fifteen months from May 1804 to October 1805, in many respects, the most memorable and instructive period of my life".[58] It was also, perhaps, the most unlikely of all his friendships, for Ball was, *par excellence*, the man of action, a wartime admiral, confidant of Nelson, hero of the battle of Aboukir Bay, and forceful administrator and strategist.

Coleridge first met Ball on 20 May, when he called officially at the Governor's palace, to deliver letters of recommendation to him and General Villettes, the military commander. The great palace with its huge shadowy inner courtyard, planted with palm trees, rather overawed him. The meeting in a vast chamber hung with crimson silk and Italian religious pictures was coldly formal. "A very polite man; but no hopes, I see clearly, of any situation."[59] Ball was a tall, avuncular figure, with a high domed forehead and small observant eyes, who said little. But the following day Coleridge was invited out to his country palace at San Antonio.

Coleridge rode out with unaccustomed punctuality at 6 a.m., and breakfasted with Ball in a garden full of orange and lemon trees. This time, a Mr Lane, the tutor of Ball's son, was present and the conversation became more general. It was later that Ball, riding back alone with Coleridge to Valletta through the little stony lanes overlooking the harbour, began to talk of the role of luck in naval actions and life generally.

Turning to his visitor, Ball suddenly asked if he thought the old proverb was true, that "Fortune Favours Fools". It could have been meant as a joke, but to his surprise Coleridge launched into a brilliant monologue on notions of chance, accident, contingency and superstition; and contrasted these with the underlying patterns of scientific law and human skills. In what sense, he asked, could it be said that Humphry Davy's discoveries in chemistry were lucky? In what sense that a great commander's victories were fortunate?[60]

Ball was impressed, and probably also amused. He began to tell Coleridge his own life story, and on this conversation Coleridge later felt was founded "the friendship and confidence, with which he afterwards honoured me". It was one of the "most delightful mornings" he ever passed. Very soon he was riding with the Governor over most of the island, and the Coleridgean floodgates were opened, day after day in June. But Coleridge also listened, and Ball's anecdotes and opinions came to fill his Malta Notebooks. Years later, in 1809, they became the basis for a biographical study – both of Ball and Nelson – in which the notion of leadership and courage, of command and self-command, is philosophically examined.[61]

Besides dealing with the civil administration of Malta, most pressing being the matters of law decrees and corn supplies, Ball was also engaged in a continuous debate with Nelson off Toulon, and the War Office in London, over the exact objectives of British strategy in the Mediterranean, as the war unfolded. Ball's central idea was that Britain should permanently occupy both Malta and Sicily, with a view to controlling the sea-routes via Egypt to India. By mid-June he had enlisted Coleridge in this top-level and highly confidential discussion, commissioning him to draft a series of "position papers" setting forth arguments with the addition of whatever Coleridge could glean from books, pamphlets or newspapers.

This was work well adapted to Coleridge's experience as a leader writer for Daniel Stuart on the *Courier*. Over the next weeks he produced four long papers, the first of which, "The French in the Mediterranean", was dispatched to Nelson on 7 July 1804. Others followed on "Algeria", "Malta", and "Egypt", which were forwarded to Granville Penn in Downing Street, for presentation to the secretary of state for war, during the summer. A fifth paper on "Sicily" was completed in September.[62] It was evidently this work which convinced Ball of Coleridge's real abilities; not merely a poet of genius, he would crisply inform the British Ambassador in Naples. Coleridge was given official rooms in the Governor's palace and a salary, all within five weeks of his arrival in Malta.

On 5 July he wrote triumphantly to Sotheby, "I have hitherto lived with Dr Stoddart, but tomorrow shall take up residence at the Palace, in a suite of delightfully cool & commanding Rooms which Sir Alexander was so kind as not merely to offer me but to make me feel that he wished me to accept the Offer . . . Sir A.B. is a very extraordinary man – indeed a great man. And he is really the abstract Idea of a wise & good Governor."[63]

As Coleridge got into the new routine of his work, his health improved and his spirits soared. He breakfasted, dined and took evening coffee with the Governor, meeting foreign diplomats and navy staff, and making contact with leading Maltese figures like Vittorio Barsoni, the influential editor of the *Malta Gazette*. "I have altered my whole system," he wrote to his wife in July: he was getting up to swim before sun-rise, eating regular meals, spending a few shillings on summer clothes and ice-creams, and filling his Notebooks with Italian lessons and Ball's table-talk.

With ceaseless, extrovert activity he was able to keep opium at bay, avoid depression, and even stop longing so obsessively for Asra to be with him – a shift of feeling he hoped to put into "a poem in 2 parts".[64] He found "Salvation in never suffering myself to be idle ten minutes together; but either to be actually *composing*, or walking, or in Company. – For the moment I begin to think, my feelings drive me almost to agony and madness; and then comes on the dreadful *Smothering* on my chest etc."[65]

To Stuart he wrote, that "after being near death, I hope I shall return in Spirit a regenerated Creature"; and also with his finances much improved. He started sending confidential copies of the "position papers" for the *Courier* to publish anonymously (a rather daring form of unofficial "leaks"): "some Sibylline Leaves, which I wrote for Sir A.B. who sent them to the Ministry – they will give you my Ideas on the importance of the Island . . . you will of course take them – only not in the same words." If he survived, he would become "a perfect man of business", and already he considered himself "a sort of diplomatic Understrapper hid in Sir Alexander's Palace". In the rocky, sun-beaten island ("86 in the Shade"), he was starting to flourish again.

8

In mid-July 1804 Sir Alexander moved his family and staff four miles inland, to the summer residence at San Antonio, with its high cool rooms, exotic gardens, and magnificent panoramas over Citta Vecchia (Medina) and the eastern approaches. The diplomatic understrapper went with them, now admitted to real intimacy, and was given a fine room immediately under the tower from where he could turn his telescope over much of the island.[66]

There was a holiday atmosphere, and in the early mornings he wandered for hours in the high stony pastures, never out of the sound of "Steeple Clock and Churchbells", chewing the pods of locust trees "full of an austere dulcacid Juice, that reminds me of a harsh Pear". He was continually amazed by the gorgeous variety of trees and shrubs in the San Antonio garden, a sort of oasis among the rocky landscape, where he sat making notes. He listed pomegranate, prickly pear, pepper tree, oleander, date ("with its Wheel of Plumage"), myrtle, butterfly-flower, walnut, mulberry, orange and lemon.[67] He wished he had a copy of Linnaeus to look them all up in.

Coleridge was happier at San Antonio in the summer of 1804 than he had been for many months. He had "manifest strength and spirits".[68] Beside the work for Sir Alexander, he wrote the long-promised letter to Wordsworth laying out the philosophical structure for "The Recluse", completed a travel journal of the Malta voyage for the Beaumonts (which he later intended to publish), and laid his plans for an autumn expedition to Sicily and Naples.

His Notebooks contain exquisite observations on wildlife, such as his description of the brilliantly coloured green lizards with their bright gold spots and "darting and angular" movements. Some of these approach the condition of prose-poems, meditations on the relations between man and animal, which foreshadow the poems of D. H. Lawrence. The lizard's attentive posture, "the Life of the threddy Toes . . . his head & innocent eye sidelong towards me, his side above the forepaw throbbing with a visible pulse", becomes an emblem of Nature's mysterious and fragile beauty. One "pretty fellow" lying frozen under Coleridge's gaze in a network of sun and shade, seems to summon up a protective power to save him from all human interference: ". . . then turned his Head to me, depressed it, & looked up half-watching, half-imploring; at length taking advantage of a brisk breeze that made all the Network dance & toss, & darted off as if an Angel of Nature had spoken in the breeze: – Off! I'll take care, he shall not hurt you."[69]

9

On 10 August Coleridge set sail for Sicily, in the company of Major Adye who had now arrived from Gibraltar. Sir Alexander Ball generously retained him on his Private Secretary's salary of

£25 per month, and supplied him with a letter of introduction to the honorary consul at Syracuse, G. F. Leckie. But first Coleridge and Adye struck out for Catania along the coast, and made a strenuous ascent of Mount Etna, with local guides. They camped at one of the *casina* or shelters just above the tree-line, where the ground "scorched" their feet, and dined off meat barbecued over an open fire and drank the local wine, chatting in bad Italian to some beautiful local peasant girls: "voices shrill but melodious, especially the 21 years old wheedler & talker, who could not reconcile to herself that I did not understand her: yet in how short a time a man living so would understand a language".[70] Around them stretched the desolate lava field, purple in the shadows, with a "smoke-white Bloom upon it".[71]

Coleridge seems to have made two ascents to the crater itself, though curiously there is no description in his Notebooks of the bleak, ashy lip or of his impressions from the top. Yet he seems to have reached it, for ten years later the image came surging back to him in the time of his worst opium struggles when his religious faith was threatened by a dark pit of despair.[72] "I recollect when I stood on the summit of Etna, and darted my gaze down the crater; the immediate vicinity was discernible, till lower down, obscurity gradually terminated in total darkness. Such figures exemplify many truths revealed in the Bible. We pursue them until, from the imperfection of our faculties, we are lost in impenetrable night."[73]

At the time he recalled only the blessed cool of the Benedictine monastery at Nicolsai as they returned, and the next day the sun on Etna rising "behind Calabria out of the midst of the Sea . . . deep crimson . . . skies coloured with yellow a sort of Dandelion".[74] On the way down he copied a Latin inscription from the monastery gardens. "Here under Black Earth, Ashes of Holy Monks lie Hid. Marvel not. Sterile sand of Sacred Bones, everywhere becomes Fruit, And loads the fruit-Tree Branches . . . Go on your road, All things will be well."[75]

At the ancient port of Syracuse, made famous by Thucydides's account of the Greek Expedition and its catastrophic defeat, Coleridge was given rooms by Leckie in his idyllic villa on the site of the Timoleon antiquities overlooking the bay. For two months it was his base for a series of rambles round the island, with Leckie often acting as his guide. Leckie was a formidable figure. A classical scholar and adventurer, he had farmed in India, knocked about the Mediterranean, and finally settled with a beautiful wife in Sicily, where his money and fluency in Italian and French set him on equal terms with the local aristocracy. His hospitality, his pungent views, and the flirtatiousness of his glamorous wife, made the Villa Timoleon a popular port of call among numerous English travellers and naval officers, and he remained in regular contact with Sir Alexander. Coleridge's admiration of Mrs Leckie was expressed in a subtle appreciation of her jewellery: "Mrs Leckie's opal surrounded with small brilliants: grey blue & the wandering fire that moves about it; and often usurps the whole."[76]

The air of voluptuous enchantment which descended over this Sicilian sojourn was oddly disturbing to Coleridge. As he walked and rode between the classical ruins, he was haunted by the discovery that the fields were full of poppies cultivated for opium. Leckie described to him the process in expert detail. "The white poppy seed, sown in the months of October & November, the plants weeded to 8 inches distance, & well watered till the plants are about ½ a foot high, when a compost of dung, without Earth, & Ashes is spread over the beds – a little before the flowers appear, again watered profusely, till the capsules are half-grown, at which time the opium is collected."[77]

Leckie showed him how each pod was incised with a knife, and Coleridge pulled out the grains with his thumb. Later he learnt that Indian hemp was also grown extensively, and that the whole island was a paradise of narcotics. Leckie, an experienced farmer, reckoned the opium crop was worth over £50 a square foot. The place where Coleridge had once dreamed of settling with Asra and the Wordsworths in an ideal Mediterranean Pantisocracy, was in reality for him one of the most dangerous places on earth.

Sicily held other temptations. On 26 September the opera season opened at Syracuse, and Coleridge first saw the young Italian prima donna Anna-Cecilia Bertozzi.[78] He was immediately captivated by her singing of Metastasio's aria, "Amo Te Solo" ("I love none but Thee"). He was swept by "a phantom of memory", and experienced the "meeting soul" of music, for Cecilia (named after the patron saint of music) fatally reminded him of a younger version of Asra.[79]

By 11 October he had met her backstage, and had made the first of a series of secret assignations, though "the voice of Conscience whispered to me, concerning myself & my intent of visiting la P[rima] D[onna] tomorrow".[80] These assignations continued through October and early November, becoming a source of both guilt and delight, so that the green lane with its long line of softly swaying trees up to the Opera House began to haunt him with its "aromatic Smell of Poplars". His "cruelly unlike Thoughts" would come upon him at each return, with gathered force: "What recollections, if I were worthy of indulging them."[81]

Cecilia's singing could be heard outside in the Opera House yard and the street, and the "ragged boys & girls" would learn her songs after a couple of performances, so that even during the day the back-alleys of Syracuse rang with the sound of urchins mimicking her "with wonderful accuracy & agility of Voice".[82] He also saw Cecilia dancing at the public balls, and perhaps danced with her, at least in imagination: "Dancing, when poor human Nature lets itself loose from bondage & circumstances of anxious selfish care: it is Madness."[83]

He was invited to her dressing-rooms, and on at least one occasion to her bedroom. A single tiny fragment of verse about Cecilia survives in his Notebooks, though almost obliterated by a later hand: ". . . the Breeze, And let me float & think on Asra/Thee, And . . . Body . . . myself in suffering . . . applied spiritually."[84] Perhaps he was also thinking of Cecilia when he described the quintet singing at the Syracuse Opera, with voices that "leave, seek, pursue, oppose . . . and embrace each other again", as the sweet image of "wayward yet fond lovers" who quarrel and make up and achieve "the total melting union".[85]

It would not be surprising if, after five months alone in the Mediterranean, cut off from those he loved, immersed in the wine and languors of the South, and looking for hope and "regeneration", the 32-year-old Coleridge had embarked on an affair with the enticing Cecilia. One might even hope that he did, if only to release him from the ghost of Asra. During a violent autumnal thunderstorm at the Villa Timoleon, which broke like "an explosion of artillery" and set the dogs barking throughout Syracuse, Coleridge suddenly recalled another femme fatale he had created: "Vivid flashes in mid day, the terror without the beauty. A ghost by day time: Geraldine."[86]

But the evidence of the Notebooks is very thin at the time, and

Cecilia herself remains a mystery. She was evidently young, probably in her early twenties, for her first recorded performances were at Rome in 1798–9.[87] She was also talented, because she became the prima donna at Palermo by 1809. Coleridge's later recollections also suggest that she was beautiful, naive and vivacious, and fully prepared to take him to bed. In these recollections of 1808 Coleridge admitted how much he longed for Cecilia during those dreamy weeks: "the outworks of my nature [were] already carried by the sweetness of her Temper, the child-like Simplicity of her Smiles, and the very great relief to my Depression and deathly Weighing-down of my heart (and the Bladder) from her Singing & Playing, so that I began to crave after her society." There was sexual attraction, he felt, on her side too. "Neither her Beauty, with all her power of employing it, neither her heavenly Song, were as dangerous as her sincere vehemence of attachment to me . . . it was not mere Passion, & yet Heaven forbid that I should call it Love."

But paradoxically it was the directness of Cecilia's feelings, her sunny Italian spontaneity, that seemed to frighten him. It was too simple, too sexual, for Coleridge's anxious sense of self and religious conscience to accept. He craved, but he could not give way. When it actually came to the point, he could not deliver himself up into the arms of the warm South. "Remorse and the total loss of Self-Esteem would have been among the Knots of the Cords by which I should have been held." What was offered to him as a joyful release, came to seem like a terrible trap, a bondage. That is why, it seems, Coleridge finally refused Cecilia.

Coleridge explained this to himself as Asra's triumph, a triumph of his better nature. He was saved by a vision of Asra which came to him even in Cecilia's bedroom. "When I call to mind the heavenly Vision of her Face, which came to me as the guardian Angel of my Innocence and Peace of Mind, at Syracuse, at the bedside of the too fascinating Siren, against whose witcheries Ulysses' Wax would have proved but a Half-protection, poor Cecilia Bertozzi . . . I was saved by that vision, wholly & exclusively by it, and sure I am, that nothing on earth but it could at that time have saved me."[88]

But was he saved? Or had he delivered himself up into a far more subtle bondage, the cords of his old English dreams which he had hoped to break? There is no mention of more conventional loyalties, his marriage vows, his feelings for his children. It was almost as if Asra had prevented him from discovering something vital about his own sexual nature, had saved him not from sin but from self-knowledge. She had preserved his "Innocence and Peace of Mind", not his purity.

Perhaps Coleridge no longer wanted real women at all, or only in his opium dreams, singing like Abyssinian maids of Mount Abora. Were these his "cruelly unlike Thoughts" on the way to visit Cecilia? He wrote gloomily: "I tremble to think what I was at that moment on the very brink of being surprised into – by the prejudices of the shame of sex, as much as by the force of its ordinary Impulses."[89] Perhaps those ordinary impulses were being destroyed.

Whatever really happened between Coleridge and Cecilia Bertozzi, the end of October 1804 marked a turning point in Sicily. His birthday entry of 21 October was miserable, lamenting his "habit of bedrugging the feelings, & bodily movements, & habit of dreaming". He had "fled like a cowed Dog" from the thought of his age, "so completely has a whole year passed, with scarcely the fruits of a month . . . I am not worthy to live . . . I have done nothing! Not even layed up any material, any inward stores – of after action!"[90]

In fact he had just sent off the large packet of work to Wordsworth and Sir George Beaumont (including now a Sicilian journal) in the care of Major Adye, who was returning to England via Gibraltar. And he was planning a trip to Messina and Naples. Daniel Stuart was beginning to use his Malta papers for leaders in the *Courier* in London, while Wordsworth was tracing his journeys in imagination in Book X of *The Prelude*, re-dedicating the poem to Coleridge the wanderer.

> Oh! Wrap him in your Shades, ye Giant Woods,
> On Etna's side, and thou, O flowery Vale
> Of Enna! Is there not some nook of thine,
> From the first playtime of the infant earth
> Kept sacred to restorative delights?

Wordsworth was blissfully imagining Coleridge, "a Visitant on Etna's top", a "lonely wanderer" with "a heart more ripe" for pleasure, drawing inspiration from Aresthusa's fountain (on the quayside at Syracuse) and "divine" nourishment from Theocritus's bees who fed the exiled Comates.[91] He hoped he would linger there as a happy votary, "and not a Captive, pining for his home". Nonetheless, Wordsworth also expected Coleridge to return as promised by the following spring, and sort out his marriage and his domestic arrangements.

Coleridge clambered over the ruins of the Greek amphitheatre above Leckie's villa, but was most drawn to the area of caves and limestone quarries with its famous "Ear of Dionysus" and the "Quarry of the Capuchins", which with its groves and flowering cliffs appeared a sort of miniature garden of Eden. (Yet it was here that 7,000 captive Athenian soldiers died in a kind of concentration camp in 413 BC.)[92] Serious archaeology did not begin until a generation later, but in this autumn of 1804 the most beautiful of all Sicilian statues, the headless Landolina Venus with her shining marble breasts and large voluptuous limbs, was dug out of the earth like a spirit returning from the underworld.

Coleridge described the ruins and the caves in detail, with Etna's cone hovering above the Epipoli ridge in its "floating mantle of white smoke"; and he took a boat to Tremiglia where Neptune was buried under a bay tree, "with vines wreathing about it: Sleep, Shade, & Quiet!"[93] Standing high above the bay of Syracuse, surrounded by these buried antiquities and strange portents, he watched the sun go down into the sea, and wrote one of his most haunting Mediterranean fragments, "A Sunset". Its thirteen lines end with a shiver of Delphic prophesy, as if the classically haunted landscape would soon release its violent gods and heroes once again as the sun disappears.

> Abrupt, as Spirits vanish, he is sunk!
> A soul-like breeze possesses all the wood.
> The boughs, the sprays have stood
> As motionless as stands the ancient trunk!
> But every leaf through all the forest flutters,
> And deep the cavern of the fountain mutters.[94]

10

Despite the affair with Cecilia Bertozzi, or perhaps because of it, Coleridge was now anxious to press on to Naples. He was restless in Syracuse, decayed and baroque, with its corruption and gossip, and the oppressive omnipresence of its Catholic priests. "I found no one native with whom I could talk of anything but the weather and the opera: ignorant beyond belief – the churches take up the third part of the whole city, & the Priests are numerous as the Egyptian Plague."[95]

On 23 October, Sir Alexander sent him a letter of recommendation to Hugh Elliott, the British Minister at the Court of King Ferdinand in Naples. It shows that Coleridge was already held in high esteem, and puts his private feelings of worthlessness in a more generous perspective.

> My dear Sir, I beg to introduce to your Excellency Mr Coleridge whose literary fame I make no doubt is well known to you. He possesses great genius, a fine imagination and good judgement, and these qualities are made perfect by an excellent heart and good moral character. He has injured his health by intense study, and he is recommended to travel for its re-establishment. You will have much pleasure in his conversation . . .[96]

But on 5 November, just as he was preparing to board a carriage for Messina, Coleridge was dramatically drawn back into his new role as public servant and all further wanderings were cut short. A diplomatic incident took place in Syracuse harbour, and Leckie deputed Coleridge, as Sir Alexander's personal emissary, to deal with it. As unexpected as it might seem, Coleridge became part of the British naval war machine.

Four days previously a French privateer had sailed into Syracuse with two captured British merchantmen, claiming the rights of a neutral port to unload its prizes. A British navy cutter, *L'Hirondelle*, was immediately dispatched from Valletta to dispute the claim, and anchored alongside the privateer with broadside cannons run out, "tompions" uncovered and trained on the French ship. Both captains appealed to the Sicilian Governor, while threatening to blow each other out of the water. Officially the matter turned on the validity of the privateer's papers, and whether it had the right to take prizes on the high seas under the normal articles of war between the two sovereign states, or whether it was simply a pirate flying the French flag for its own convenience. Unofficially, as so often in these incidents, everything depended on what political pressure could be brought to bear.

Leckie seems to have realized early on that the privateer's papers were in fact valid, so he took Coleridge with him to make the best of a bad job. The priority was to defuse an ugly situation at the harbour front, where the British Captain Skinner soon found himself surrounded by a hostile crowd. When Leckie and Coleridge arrived at seven in the evening, bloodshed seemed imminent. "On stepping out of the carriage I found by the Torches that about 300 Soldiers were drawn up on the shore opposite the English Cutter, and that the walls etc. were manned: Mr Skinner and two of his Officers were on the rampart, and the Governor and a crowd of Syracusan nobles with him at the distance of two or three yards from Mr Skinner."[97] The Governor "talked, or rather screamed, indeed incessantly".

Coleridge was surprised to discover that he himself remained calm. "I never witnessed a more pitiable scene of confusion, & weakness, and manifest determination to let the French escape." The French privateer captain hurled abuse from a nearby wall, but was stoically ignored. Leckie and Coleridge insisted that nothing should be done until the privateer's papers were translated (from Italian) and properly examined the following day. At last order was restored, the French crew were put under guard at the Lazaretto, and Captain Skinner was removed to the safety of Leckie's house.

Over the next two days Coleridge visited the Syracuse Governor, and disputed the privateer's papers. He also drew up a long and vividly circumstantial account of the whole incident for Sir Alexander. It was soon clear that the prize and ransom money would not be released: the Governor "will acquit the Crew of Piracy, and suffer them to escape, and probably make a complaint against Mr Skinner".

Coleridge quickly realized that it was now Captain Skinner who was in difficulties, having failed in his mission and being liable to reprimand in Malta. He therefore heavily weighted his report in Skinner's favour, and volunteered to return to Valletta on *L'Hirondelle* to deliver the report in person. He wrote firmly: "It is but justice however to notice the coolness, dignity and good sense, with which Mr Skinner acted throughout the whole Business, and which formed an interesting Contrast to the noisy Imbecility of the

Governor, and the brutal Insolence of the Commander of the Privateer."[98]

This supportive action of Coleridge for the young captain, in such an unenviable situation, was never forgotten. It not only impressed Sir Alexander, it made him lasting friends among the whole circle of British naval officers on the Malta station for the rest of his stay. He was accepted, in their tight-knit circle, as "a friend in need", who could be counted on. It was also noted among several American naval officers, temporarily stationed at Syracuse, among whom was the gallant Captain Stephen Decatur, famed for his recent exploit in blowing up the captured *Philadelphia* in Tripoli harbour (and later for his saying, "my country right or wrong").

Decatur became one of Coleridge's warmest admirers. Thus began a connection with Americans in the Mediterranean which had a lasting impact on his stay. Coleridge was back in Valletta on 8 November, and while in quarantine (for plague had been declared) completed his report, with nine documents annexed, for Sir Alexander. He concluded: "of course nothing further was to be done . . . and instead of going to Messina have returned to Malta, thinking, that I might be of some service perhaps to Captain Skinner in the explanation of the Business."[99]

He returned to Sir Alexander's congratulations, and glorious autumn weather, the trees "loaded with Oranges" and his health "very greatly improved in this heavenly climate".[100] He was paid four months' back-salary of £100, and given a new set of rooms in the garrets of the Treasury building (now the Casino Maltese) with a decorated ceiling and huge windows "commanding a most magnificent view" of Valletta harbour. The ceiling depicted the Four Winds as baroque, curly-headed angels "spewing white smoke", and whirling around a mariner's compass in the middle.[101] Coleridge would spend many hours in the coming months contemplating their navigational symbolism, and then gazing out over the sea with all its possible voyages.

11

The first of these was no less than a trip to Russia and the Black Sea. One of Sir Alexander's primary duties in the defence of Malta was to obtain corn supplies, and each spring he sent a special

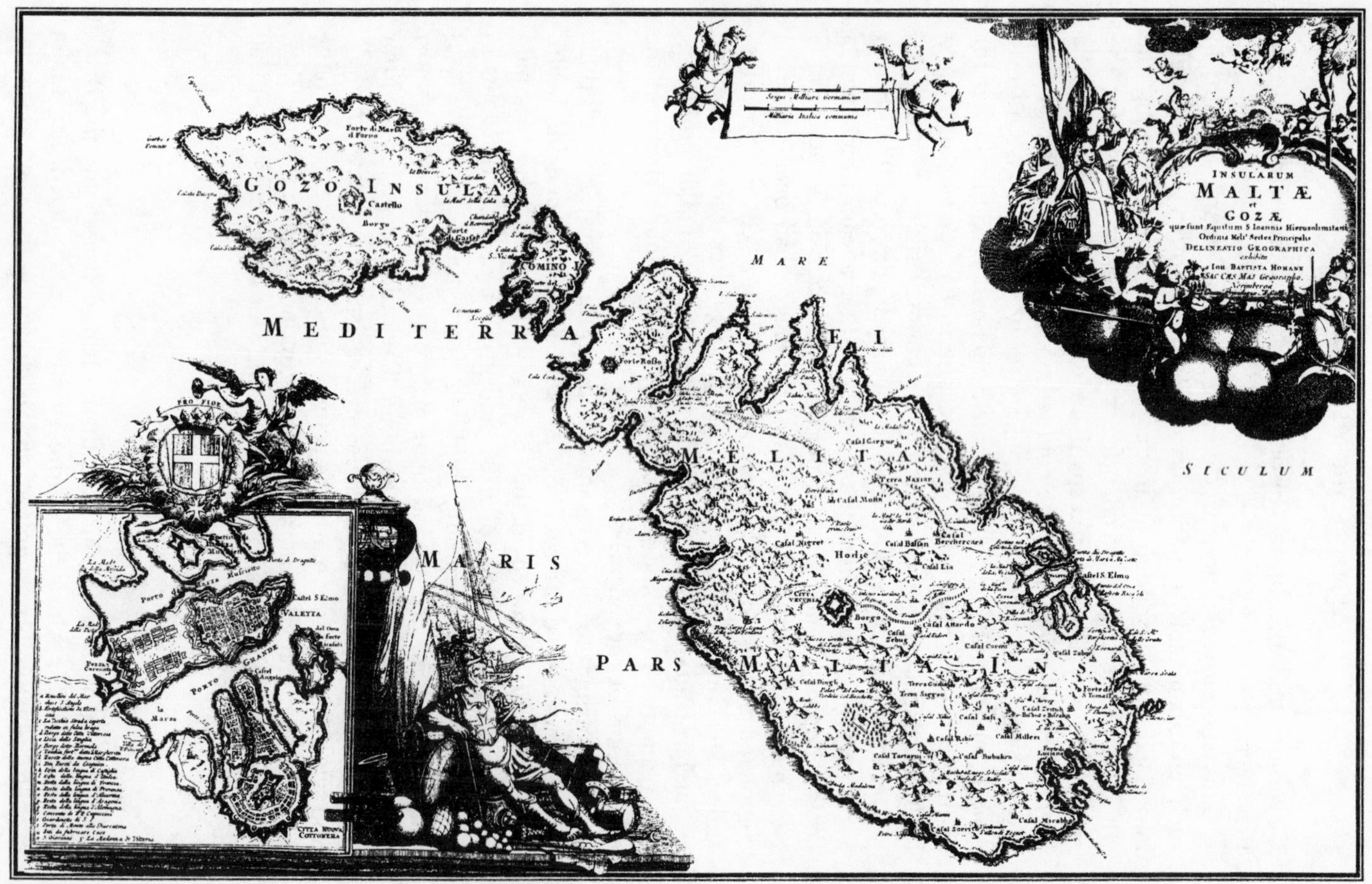

INSULARUM
MALTÆ
et
GOZÆ
quæ sunt Equitum S. Ioannis Hierosolimitani
Ordinis Melit. Sedes Principalis
DELINEATIO GEOGRAPHICA
exhibita
a IOH. BAPTISTA HOMANN
SAC. CÆS. MAJ. Geographo.
Norimbergæ
MEDITERRANEI MARIS PARS
MARE SICULUM
GOZO INSULA
Castello di Borgo
COMINO
MELITA
MALTA INS.
Forte Rosso
Citta Vecchia
Borgo
Castel S. Elmo
Casal Nigret
Casal Bassan
Casal Bercheraca
Casal Lia
Casal Attardo
Casal Zebug
Casal Gargur
Terra Naxiar
Casal Mosta
Casal Dingli
Casal Tartarni
Casal Rabio
Casal Bubakra
Casal Millers
Casal Zorrico
Casal Micabba
PRO FIDE
Porto Muscetto
VALETTA
PORTO GRANDE
Castel Angelo
CITTA NUOVA COTTONERA

mission to purchase corn in Greece, Turkey and the Crimea. He now requested Coleridge to consider undertaking the 1805 mission, in company with a Captain Leake, departing in January for a round trip of three or four months. "The confidence placed in me by Sir A. Ball is unlimited . . . but it will be a most anxious business – as shall have the trust and management of 70, or 80 thousand pounds, while I shall not have for my toils & perils more than 3 or 4 hundred pounds, exclusive of all my expenses in travelling etc." For the moment he was undecided.[102]

The Russian proposal finally forced Coleridge to turn to the question he had been avoiding for many months, not least at the bedside of Cecilia Bertozzi. What was he really doing in the Mediterranean? Did he intend to make a new life out there, to abandon once and for all the difficulties of his marriage, the affections of his children, the ambiguous dreams of happiness with Asra and the Wordsworths? Could he remake his career as a civil servant and diplomat, writing poetry and political reports, following Sir Alexander's wartime star, drawing an ever-increasing salary, and settling in some exotic country villa shrouded in orange and lemon groves, waited upon by servants and some dusky, voluptuous Italian muse? Could this be a rebirth, a second life; or an ultimate self-abandonment, with the alluring demon of opium ever at his side?

It is clear that the answer hung in the balance for many weeks in the winter of 1804–5, and was not fully resolved until the following summer. But now for the first time he faced it. In a long letter of 12 December to his wife Sara, he set out the position. His health was radically improved, his work for the government was valuable and well paid, he could guarantee her an allowance of £100 a year and a continuance of his life assurance policy in her favour, as well as the £150 Wedgwood annuity. "I remain faithful to you and to my own Honour in all things." He was "tranquil", though never happy – "no visitations of mind or of fancy" – and he agonized always over his children – "My children! – my children!" – sometimes in "a flood of tears". He had only agreed to consider the Russian mission "in a fit of Despair, when Life was a burthen to me", and he would refuse it "on the whole, if I could get off with honour". Yet all the same, he might stay in the Mediterranean, in Malta or Sicily or Sardinia. He admitted this in a sudden burst of explanation and self-contradiction, which well expressed his divided feelings.

> If I could make up my mind to stay here, or to follow Sir A.B. in case that circumstances & changes in the political world should lead him to Sardinia, no doubt, I might have about £500 a year, & live mainly at the Palace. But O God! O God! if that, Sara! which we both know too well, were not unalterably my Lot, how gladly would I prefer the mere necessaries of Life in England, & these obtained by daily Effort. But since my Health has been restored to me, I have felt more than ever how unalterable it is![103]

One wonders how Sara Coleridge would have understood this. Her wayward husband's "unalterable lot" could be taken as simply a reference to his opium addiction, which had been known to her ever since 1801. Or it could be a darker admission, of Coleridge's depression and unhappiness, his emotional incompatibility with her, and still obsessive love for Asra which made any true return and reunion impossible. Perhaps indeed the two elements were inextricably involved for him, and he was trying to get her to accept this. He concluded his letter with a formal assurance that "whatever & wherever I am" he would make it his "first anxiety and prominent Duty" to contribute to her happiness; and signed "most anxiously and affectionately, your Friend and more than Friend, S. T. Coleridge". But it could not have been a reassuring letter to receive.[104]

Sitting up in his garret in the Treasury, gazing out at the "beautifully white sails of the Mediterranean (so carefully when in port put up into clean bags)", Coleridge considered the same problem in the privacy of his Notebooks. He felt the "Quietness, Security within & without in Malta".[105] He valued the regularity, the naval comradeship among the officers, the smooth sequence of time and command, "the rings of Russet smoke from the evening Gun, at Valletta".[106] He was working; he was content; he saw a possible future for himself.

But was he happy? In a long, calm, reflective entry he considered it. "Days & weeks & months pass on; and now a year; and the sun, the Sea, the Breeze has its influences on me, and good and sensible men. – And I feel a pleasure upon me, & I am to the outward view of all cheerful, & have myself no distinct consciousness of the contrary; for I use my faculties, not indeed as once, yet freely. – But oh [Asra]! I am never happy, – never deeply gladdened – I know not, I have forgotten what the Joy is of which the Heart is full as of a deep & quiet fountain overflowing insensibly; or the gladness of Joy, when the fountain overflows ebullient – STC."[107]

That absence, surely, was his unalterable lot; and for the moment he rested within it, waiting upon events. Through the long nights he read deeply, Thomas More on Utopia, Sir Thomas Browne on religion, Harrington on government. No letters reached him from England.[108]

On 18 January 1805, the eighty-year-old Public Secretary of Malta, Mr Macauley, died in his sleep in a thunderstorm. Coleridge was immediately offered and accepted the post of Acting Public Secretary, the second in diplomatic rank to the Governor, with a salary of £600 a year. The Russian mission was put aside, and Coleridge agreed to remain with Sir Alexander in Malta for the next three months or until the arrival of the new Public Secretary, Mr Chapman, on the springtime convoys in March or April. The post was distinguished but laborious, requiring regular work in Sir Alexander's cabinet, the drafting of a steady stream of *bandi* or civil decrees, and attendance in the law courts.[109]

Coleridge was pleased, for though it curtailed the opportunities for further travel and writing, it would sort out his finances, and give him valuable experience of public affairs. It also put off the problematic question of his return from the Mediterranean. He wrote cheerfully to Southey, who had become in effect the guardian of his children at Greta Hall: "I am and some 50 times a day subscribe myself, Segretario Publico dell'Isole di Malta, Gozo, e delle loro dipendenze. I live in a perfect Palace, & have all my meals with the Governor; but my profits will be much less, than if I had employed my time & efforts in my own literary pursuits. However, I gain new Insights; & if (as I doubt not, I shall) I return, having expended nothing, having paid all my prior debts . . . with Health, & some additional knowledge in Things & Languages, I shall surely not have lost a year."[110]

But as he settled into his work, letters did begin to reach him from England, and the news that they brought was bad and began to throw his plans into disarray. First was the rumour that Mr Jackson, the landlord of Greta Hall, was considering selling the house in his absence, leaving his family and Southey's without a home. Second was the bitter intelligence that his friend Major Adye had died of plague in Gibraltar and all his effects were burnt by quarantine officers. Thus one by one, most of Coleridge's literary papers of the previous year had been destroyed. He had lost the entire travel journal for Beaumont, the letter to Wordsworth on "The Recluse", an extended political essay for Stuart, and several long family letters. All back-up copies of these had also been lost from the frigates *Arrow* and *Acheron*, thrown overboard according to navy regulations during pursuit by French privateers.[111]

Thus almost all his literary work in the first year at Malta (except for the four strategic papers) had been useless. Among them, incidentally, must have been the missing account of climbing Mount Etna. Later he felt that he was being "punished" for all his previous neglect, by "writing industriously to no purpose" for months on end. "No one not absent on a dreary Island so many leagues of sea from England can conceive the effect of these Accidents on the Spirits & inmost Soul. So help me Heaven! they have nearly broken my Heart."[112]

So more and more Coleridge turned now to his Notebooks. They are extraordinarily rich for the winter and spring of 1804–5, despite the daily pressures of his duties as Public Secretary. While there are only six letters home between January and August 1805, there are over 300 Notebook entries for a similar period, amounting to several hundred manuscript pages, mainly in four leather or metal-clasp pocket-books, much worn from carrying.[113] Coleridge recorded his external life, visits to hospitals, workhouses, the theatre, and his regular talks with Sir Alexander about government, diplomacy and warfare. Even more vividly he recorded his inner life: dreams, psychological analysis, theories of perception, religious beliefs, superb visions of the Mediterranean landscape and skyscape, and long disquisitions on opium-taking and sexual fantasies.

Coleridge turned to these Notebooks in Malta, as consciously as he had done during the dark winters of the Lake District, as witnesses to his trials for the after times. "If I should perish without having the power of destroying these & my other pocket books, the history of my own mind for my own improvements: O friend! Truth! Truth! but yet Charity! Charity! I have never loved evil for its own sake; no! nor ever sought pleasure for its own sake, but only as the means of escaping from pains that coiled round my mental powers, as a serpent around the body & wings of an Eagle."[114]

12

Coleridge was in a lively mood throughout the Christmas of 1804, planning to write "300 volumes", allowing ten years for each. "You have ample Time, my dear fellow! . . . you can't think of living less than 4,000 years, & that would nearly suffice for your present schemes."[115]

He analysed his talkativeness as producing a "great Blaze of colours" that dazzled bystanders by containing too many ideas in two few words. "My illustrations swallow up my thesis – I feel too intensely the omnipresence of all in each, platonically speaking." His brain-fibres glittered with "spiritual Light" like the phosphorescence "in sundry rotten mackerel!" Once started on a subject he went on and on, "from circle to circle till I break against the shore of my Hearer's patience, or have any Concentricals dashed to nothing by a Snore".

Yet at Malta he had tried to restrain himself and had earned, he believed, "the general character of being a quiet well-meaning man, rather dull indeed – & who would have thought, that he had been a *Poet* 'O a very wretched Poetaster, Ma'am'".[116]

If by day Coleridge gave the impression of a busy, punctilious bureaucrat, bustling between the Treasury, the palace and the Admiralty Court (where he argued cases in a wig and gown), dining cheerfully with the Governor and gossiping with senior clerks like Mr Underwood in the corridors, his night life was another existence altogether. It was solitary, introspective, and often intoxicated. On 27 December he started using cipher in his Notebooks, and entered bleakly: "No night without its guilt of opium and spirits."[117]

After his autumn débâcle with Cecilia Bertozzi, he was much preoccupied with sexual matters. He dwelt on the link between mental and physical arousal, the sexual stimulation of dreams, the different sense of "Touch" in lips and fingers, and operations of "the mem(brum) virile in acts of (Es)sex". He brilliantly intuited a whole modern theory of "erogenous zones" existing outside the genital area, which respond to sexual excitement. "Observe that in certain excited states of feeling the knees, ankle, side & soles of the feet, become organic. Query – the nipple in a woman's breast, does that ever become the seat of a particular feeling, as one would guess by its dormancy & sudden awakings."[118] Most strikingly, he linked sexual confidence and fulfilment with more general feelings of well-being and spiritual optimism in life:

"Important metaphysical Hint: the influence of bodily vigour and strong Grasp of Touch facilitating the passion of Hope: eunuchs – in all degrees even to the full ensheathment and the both at once."[119] (This last entry was also in cipher, and might suggest a personal anxiety about impotence caused by opium.) Later in the spring he countered this in a beautiful entry about his own children, as proof of sexual power and as part of a living resource of social amelioration: "the immense importance of young Children to the keeping up the stock of Hope in the human species: they seem as immediately the secreting-organ of Hope in the great organized Body of the whole Human Race, in all men considered as component Atoms of Man, as young Leaves are the organs of supplying vital air to the atmosphere."[120]*

In January 1805 these night-speculations led to a devastating piece of psychological self-analysis, examining the patterns of hope and dread which had dominated his early life. "It is a most instructive part of my Life the fact, that I have been always preyed on by some Dread, and perhaps all my faulty actions have been the consequence of some Dread or other on my mind: from fear of Pain, or Shame, not from prospect of Pleasure."

Coleridge ran through his boyhood horrors at Christ's Hospital, his adolescent "short-lived Fit of Fears from sex", his wholly

---

* Coleridge's intuition of the whole world as a single organic system (like a tree) ascending towards some kind of spiritual unity becomes one of his most importants beliefs, derived from his beautiful letters on "the one Life" in 1802. (See *Early Visions*, pp. 324–7.) It reflects both a homely Burkean view of "organic" human society, and the remote metaphysics of German *Naturphilosophie* propounding an "Absolute" unity and a "World Soul" (*Geist*) developed in the dialectical philosophy of Schelling, Fichte and later Hegel. (See Alan White, "The System of Identity" in *Schelling: An Introduction to the System of Freedom*, 1983.) This intuition, with its characteristic use of organic metaphors and its emphasis on spiritual "Hope", regularly recurs in modern scientific-mystical speculation, such as Pierre Teilhard de Chardin's *The Phenomenon of Man* (1959) and, with an environmentalist appeal, in James Lovelock's *Gaia* (1991): "the Earth might in certain ways be alive – not as the ancients saw her, a sentient goddess with purpose and foresight – more like a tree. A tree that exists, never moving except to sway in the wind, yet endlessly conversing with the sunlight and the soil."

"imaginative and imaginary Love" for Mary Evans. Then came the "stormy time" of Pantisocracy when "America really inspired Hope", and his increasingly unhappy marriage. "Constant dread in my mind respecting Mrs Coleridge's Temper, etc. – and finally stimulants in the fear & prevention of violent Bowel-attacks from mental agitation." Finally came the "almost epileptic night-horrors in my sleep: & since then every error I have committed, has been the immediate effect of these bad most shocking Dreams – anything to prevent them."

He summed it up in an extraordinary, domestic image of food: of a child's comfort-food, sticky and enticing, but which is also red and bleeding like a wound. "All this interwoven with its minor consequences, that fill up the interspaces – the cherry juice running in between the cherries in a cherry pie: procrastination in the dread of this – & something else in consequence of that procrastination etc." The entry ends with a desperate thought of Asra, how he had "concentred" his soul on a woman "almost as feeble in Hope as myself".[121] Self-pity and self-knowledge were finely balanced in these reflections, and the sinister percolating cherry juice gleams dark red like laudanum splashing into a wine glass and running down his throat.

But on other nights in January and February, Coleridge was also making superb, lucid entries on subjects as diverse as aesthetics, politics, theology or philosophy. Notes on Ball's talk of Mediterranean strategy mix with discussion of the Platonic fathers, etymology, astronomy versus astrology, Roman Catholic superstitions, Captain Decatur's naval adventures, the symbolism of wood-fires, the spring flora of Malta, or the attempt to assassinate the Bey of Tunis. Many of these topics would later appear in Coleridge's books and lectures, so that this whole period of reading and self-immersion served a purpose not immediately evident to Coleridge and yet vital to his intellectual expansion and development.

Coleridge's power to draw analogies and cross-references is continually astonishing. Reading Samuel Horsey's critique of the Greek philosopher Athenagoras on the subject of childbirth (in *A Charge Delivered to the Clergy of the Archdeaconry of St Albans*, *1783*, a book he had picked up on the secondhand stalls of Queen's Square in Valletta), Coleridge emerges with the concept of "organic form" which was to shape years of lecturing back in London. "Wherein then would Generation differ from Fabrication, or a child from a Statue or a Picture? It is surely the inducement of a Form on pre-existing material in consequence of the transmission of a Life . . . The difference therefore between Fabrication and Generation becomes clearly inducible: the Form of the latter is *ab intra*, evolved; the other *ab extra*, impressed."[122] From this distinction, as from his earlier observations on sailing-ships, a whole theory of imaginative "generation" would come.

One of his most persistent night-themes is the huge Mediterranean moon viewed from his garret window across Valletta harbour. To Coleridge it was still the magic moon of the "Ancient Mariner", but now he turned to it with a new intensity, as a witness to his own sufferings. One midnight it was "blue at one edge from the deep utter Blue of the Sky, a mass of pearl-white Cloud below, distant and travelling to the Horizon." He found himself praying to it, as to a divinity. "Consciously I stretched forth my arms to embrace the Sky and in a trance I had worshipped God in the Moon: the Spirit not the Form. I felt in how innocent a feeling Sabeism might have begun: O not only the Moon, but the depth of the Sky!" He recognized in this a profoundly religious instinct that was to grow with ever-greater force in the coming years: that he was not spiritually self-sufficient, and that he had a primitive, almost pagan, need for an external power. "O yes! – Me miserable! O yes! – Have Mercy on me, O something *out* of me! For there is no power (and if that can be, less strength) in aught within me! Mercy! Mercy!'[123]

On another, calmer night the same feeling emerged more philosophically. Now the moon presaged a whole theory of poetic language, which would take its authority from the same recognition of transcendent human need deep within the spirit. Now it was language itself – the divine *logos* – which impelled Coleridge from a pagan Pantheism to the rebirth of a fundamental Christianity. The moon at Malta provided Coleridge with a religious revelation about divine power radiating through the natural universe. It was for him, with his fundamental and never-abandoned identity as a poet, essentially an *articulating* power, an expressive *fiat* as in the opening of the Book of Genesis.

> In looking at objects of Nature while I am thinking, as at yonder moon dim-glimmering thro' the dewy window-pane, I

seem rather to be seeking, as it were *asking*, a symbolical language for something within me that already and forever exists, than observing any thing new. Even when the latter is the case, yet still I have always an obscure feeling as if that new phenomenon were the dim Awaking of a forgotten or hidden Truth of my inner Nature. It is still interesting as a Word, a Symbol! It is LOGOS, the Creator! and the Evolver![124]

13

All this time Coleridge continued his daylight work as Public Secretary. In February he was inspecting the hospital, every wall covered with grotesque crucifixes, and in the ward for venereal diseases a child of twelve in the same bed as an old man of seventy.[125] In March he was sailing round the harbour to inspect the defences with Lieutenant Pasley. Spain had now declared war against Britain, and the French fleet had broken out of Toulon. The convoy system was in shambles, and Nelson was making a sweep to the Azores. Communications were disrupted, and there was no sign of Mr Chapman (Coleridge's replacement) who was somewhere in the Black Sea. The plague, which had carried off Major Adye at Gibraltar, now threatened Valletta and beach landings were expected imminently in Sicily or southern Italy.

Back in England the Wordsworths were deeply worried. They had planned to leave Grasmere in 1805, and settle wherever they could persuade Coleridge to join them on his return, which they expected in the spring. But they had had no news for three months, "no tidings of poor Coleridge, for Heaven's sake", and feared the worst from war or pestilence.[126] Daniel Stuart had gazetted Coleridge's appointment as Public Secretary in the *Courier*, but waited in vain for further dispatches from him.

But the disaster that struck came from a wholly unexpected quarter. At one o'clock on 31 March 1805 Coleridge was summoned from the Treasury by Sir Alexander to attend a diplomatic reception. As he entered the packed drawing-room, Lady Ball turned to him and asked if he knew Captain John Wordsworth. "Is he not a Brother of Mr Wordsworth, you so often talk of?" John Wordsworth's ship, the *Abergavenny*, had been wrecked in a storm off Weymouth, with the loss of all cargo, three hundred men and the captain himself. Lady Ball faltered, as she saw Coleridge go pale. "Yes, it is his brother," he replied, and staggered from the room. He walked back to his garret, supported by the Sergeant-at-Arms and pursued by Sir Alexander. As he got to his door, he collapsed. Later he would say that the shock was so great that he "fell down on the ground in a convulsive fit" in front of fifty people in the "great Saloon of the Palace" itself.[127]

It was an expressive exaggeration. He was ill for a fortnight, and shaken in a way that only the Wordsworths could have understood. William wrote to Sir George Beaumont: "We have had no tidings of Coleridge. I tremble for the moment when he is to hear of my brother's death; it will distress him to the heart, – and his poor body cannot bear sorrow. He loved my brother, and he knows how we at Grasmere loved him."[128] For the Wordsworths, who had also invested heavily in John's ship, his death was to change all their plans for the future and tighten the little Grasmere circle, "the Concern", in ways that subtly affected their commitment to Coleridge.

For Coleridge himself it was news that haunted and terrified him, with intimations of failure, loss and physical horror. "O dear John: and so ended thy dreams of Tarns & mountain Becks, & obscure vales in the breasts and necks of Mountains. So thy dream of living with or among thy Brother and *his*. – O heavens! Dying in all its Shapes, shrieks; and confusion; and mad Hope; and Drowning more deliberate than Suicide; – these, these were the Dorothy, the Mary, the Sara Hutchinson, to kiss the cold drops from thy Brow, & to close thy Eyes! – Never yet has any Loss gone so far into the Life of Hope, with me. I now only fear."[129]

The violence of his reaction can also be explained by the role he had sometimes imagined for John, as his own alter ego in Asra's heart, capable of bringing her one day a solid, companionable love, which he could not match. If this seems a strange, almost masochistic displacement, it was genuine and indeed typical of Coleridge. "O blessed Sara, you whom in my imagination at one time I so often connected with him, by an effort of agonizing Virtue, willing it with cold sweat-drops on my Brow!"[130] At some level, Coleridge felt it should have been him who had died in John's place.

The news of John Wordsworth's death also brought to a head

the question of Coleridge's return to England. William confidently expected that it would be immediate: "he has engagements with the Governor: if these do not prevent him I am sure he will return the first minute he can after hearing the news. I am as sure of this as if I heard him say so."[131] But he could not hear the silent night-voice of Coleridge's Notebooks, which was more than ever uncertain. "Lord Nelson is pursuing the French Fleet & the Convoy is to be deferred. I felt glad – how can I endure that it should depart without me? Yet if I go, wither am I to go? Merciful Providence! what a cloud is spread before me: a cloud is my only guide by day and by night: I have no pillar of Fire . . ."[132]

It was the same "procrastination" that had greeted the news of the death of his child, little Berkeley, long ago in Germany. But now it was his whole future life that seemed at issue. Part of him longed to go back to his children, to Asra and the Wordsworths; part of him would do anything to avoid a reunion with Mrs Coleridge; and part of him simply luxuriated in the easy, expansive living of the Mediterranean, the orange trees coming into blossom ("a prodigality of beauty"), the talkative dinners with Ball and the navy officers, the guilty opium sessions at night, the drowsy sexual dreams, the endless reading and philosophizing. Above all, perhaps, his suspended exile in Malta allowed him to fantasize about Asra: "O Sara! gladly if my miserable Destiny would relax, gladly would I think of thee and me, as of two Birds of passage, reciprocally resting on each other in order to support the long flight, the awful Journey."[133]

Throughout April his opium-taking increased, and he struggled with boils and fever. Sometimes his thoughts turned to suicide – "Die my Soul, die! – Suicide – rather than this, the worst state of Degradation! –"[134]; and sometimes he even beat himself, "hands, breast or forehead, in the paroxysms of Self-reproof".[135] Eventually the convoy left without him, and he resumed work as Public Secretary more busily than ever. The note of pure pleasure quickly returned, as on the afternoon he walked up to join Sir Alexander for a weekend at San Antonio in the gardens. "Having had showers (23 April) I smelt the orange blossom long before I reached St Antonio. When I entered it was overpowering: the Trees were indeed oversnowed with Blossoms, and the ground snowed with the fallen leaves: the Bees on them, & the golden ripe fruit on the inner branches glowing."[136]

He wrote to Stuart that his work occupied him "from 8 o'clock in the morning to 5 in the afternoon, having besides the most anxious duty of writing public Letters and Memorials". He was bitterly disappointed at having missed the spring convoy, and all sea-voyages were now perilous; but he was planning to return overland by Naples, Trieste and Germany, to outflank the French armies now pressing down on Austria and northern Italy. "I have resolved, let the struggle cost what it may, & even at the forfeiture of Sir A. Ball's Good will, to return home at the latter end of May." He wrote similarly to Wordsworth: "O dear Friends! Death has come amongst us! . . . I mean to return in the latter end of May at all events, and have wept like a child that the convoy is off without me, but my office of Public Secretary makes it impossible."[137]

But in fact this resolution was not to be carried out for a further year. Perhaps the only hint of his divided feelings came in his evident attachment to Ball and the satisfaction in working for him. "Sir A. B. behaves to me with really personal fondness, and with almost fatherly attention – I am one of his Family, whenever my Health permits me to leave my own House."[138]

14

From now on, Coleridge's letters home become few and erratic, and none has survived until the end of July. Mr Chapman did not return, and the increasing gravity of the strategic situation in the Mediterranean put great pressures on the Malta administration, with problems of supply, unrest among the local population (including demonstrations against the Jews, which Coleridge issued proclamations to suppress),[139] counterfeit passports, and preparations for a huge naval expedition under General Sir James Craig. Nelson was now hastening back from the West Indies, looking for a major confrontation with the French and Spanish fleets under Villeneuve.

Coleridge was continually riding around the island, being bitten by dogs; dealing with local disputes, transport and medical problems; and working hard and late at the Treasury on *bandi* and official letters. On one occasion, working in the "Saloon built for Archives & Library, & now used as the Garrison Ballroom", and probably well-dosed with laudanum, he fell into a doze and awoke to see the ghostly figure of another secretary, Mr Dennison, sitting in a chair opposite him, although the man had retired to bed ten minutes previously.

He wrote a long note on this interesting apparition, "that of a person seen thro thin smoke, distinct indeed but yet a sort of distinct *Shape & Colour* – with a diminished Sense of *Substantiality* – like a Face in a clear Stream." He remarked that he had often had similar experiences, the product of nerves and exhaustion, "and therefore resolved to write down the Particulars whenever any new instance should occur: as a weapon against Superstition, and an explanation of *Ghosts* – Banquo in Macbeth – the very same Thing." These notes eventually reappeared in 1809 in a brilliant essay on Luther's vision of the devil. He felt no fear, and recalled: "I once told a Lady, the reason why I did not believe in the existence of Ghosts etc. was that I had seen too many of them myself."[140]

Despite the tense fortress atmosphere, and the pressure of work, Coleridge spent many weekends up at San Antonio, where he was given his own room high up above the gardens, and was able to walk on the palace roof with a telescope. He copied and translated Italian madrigals and sonnets by Marino; and made extensive botanical notes, and weird medical cocktails using aconite, angostura and "German Leopard's Bane".[141]

His sexual dreams continued, sometimes on an epic scale and gloriously free from guilt. One, in June, was "a long Dream of my Return, Welcome, etc. full of Joy & Love", which was full of curious "images and imagined actions" free from desire but implying "awakened Appetite". In this dream which clearly featured Asra in some form of tropical paradise, Coleridge found himself in a primitive state of society "like that of those great Priests of Nature who formed the Indian worship in its purity, when all things, strictly of Nature, were reverenced according to their importance, undebauched by associations of Shame and Impudence".[142]

It was probably now, in the summer gardens of San Antonio, that he began his unfinished poem to Asra, "The Blossoming of the Solitary Date-Tree". It was suggested by a fact "mentioned by Linnaeus, of a date tree in a nobleman's garden which year after year had put forth a full show of blossoms, but never produced fruit, till a branch from another date-tree had been conveyed from a distance of some hundred leagues". It opens with the image of huge frosty mountain peaks "beneath the blaze of a tropical Sun", an image of unreflected or unrequited love. "What no-one with us shares, scarce seems our own." In one stanza it catches his mood of renewed hopefulness and the richness of the Mediterranean landscape offering him an "overflow" of gifts; and in the next shadows this with a sense of exile, of living in a "lonesome tent", far away from the voice that can inspire him.

Coleridge lost the manuscript in his subsequent journeyings, but years later was able to reconstruct a rough version of the third and fourth stanzas. The first of these was a projection of his ideal poetic self, dedicated to the highest view of his life's vocation and gratefully conscious of Nature's gifts to him in Italy:

> Imagination; honourable aims;
> Free commune with the choir that cannot die;
> Science and song; delight in little things,
> The buoyant child surviving in the man;
> Fields, forests, ancient mountains, ocean, sky,
> With all their voices – O dare I accuse
> My earthly lot as guilty of my spleen,
> Or call my destiny niggard! O no! no!
> It is her largeness, and her overflow,
> Which being incomplete, disquieteth me so!

The second, by contrast, was a vision of his solitary wandering self, rootless and exiled, adrift from Asra's love and hallucinating her voice:

> For never touch of gladness stirs my heart,
> But tim'rously beginning to rejoice
> Like a blind Arab, that from sleep doth start
> In lonesome tent, I listen for thy voice.
> Belovéd! 'tis not thine; thou art not there!
> Then melts the bubble into idle air.
> And wishing without hope I restlessly despair.[143]

The poem continues with a counter-image of satisfied love, a child basking in its mother's gaze, which has an almost Italianate, Madonna-like intensity. But it ends with Coleridge's poignant question, to be repeated again and again in the coming years, "Why was I made for Love and Love denied to me?"[144]

These moments of dreamy pleasure and sudden despondency seemed to alternate at San Antonio as Coleridge hovered in a kind of weightless trance in his Maltese exile, frantically busy and yet curiously passive, floating and yet marooned. There are no true rivers anywhere on the island, only wells and thin water-courses, but the image of a dried-up stream – perhaps inspired by the hesitant plashing of the Eagle Fountain (1623) in the gardens – produced one of Coleridge's most memorable images of that summer. He is no longer a bird, but a fish. "STC – The Fish gasps on the glittering mud, the mud of this once full stream, now only moist enough to be glittering mud. The tide will flow back, time enough to lift me up with straws & withered sticks and bear me down into the ocean. O me! that being what I have been I should be what I am!"[145]

The heat began to increase in July, and at 4 a.m. one morning there was an earthquake, which seemed to him like the premonition of some great battle. Typically, Coleridge was awake, and saw his old friend the moon above the Garrison Battery, almost at the full, but very strange with a "reddish smoke-colour" like a god of war.[146] With the heat came increasing noise, or at least sensitivity to it and Coleridge was regularly woken in the Treasury by trumpets of the "accursed Reveille" in the square below and the "malignant torture" of the parade drums, which attacked his head "like a party of yelling drinking North American Indians attacking a Crazy Fort with a tired Garrison".[147]

The Public Secretary's temper frayed even with the ordinary Maltese, whose carts thundered down the steps of Valletta, whose children screamed ("horrid fiendliness – for fun!"), and whose boatmen howled. "But it goes through everything – their Street-Cries, their Priests, their Advocates: their very Pigs yell rather than squeak." The dogs howled all night, and the "Cats in their amours" were like imps in hell. "He who has only heard cater-wauling on English Roofs can have no idea of a cat-serenade in Malta."

This note of comic exasperation suggests perhaps the real, underlying stresses of Coleridge's daily work, and the typically drawn state of bureaucratic nerves in wartime. It led to various frictions in the Treasury. Mr Underwood, in particular, was irritated beyond measure by Coleridge's ceaseless literary talk and maddening tendency to produce exquisite Italian sonnets from his pile of official paper, innocently repeating the same translation to every visitor, as something "he had just thrown off".[148]

The heat also produced lugubrious stories, such as the one about the consul's clerk in Tripoli, who got out of bed in the middle of the night to drink water, remembered with horror the danger of scorpions when walking in the dark with bare feet, "went back & slipped his feet into his Shoes, in one of which a Scorpion was, & bit him mortally". Coleridge thought this narrative so neat, that it was actually an "invention".[149]

Relations nevertheless remained generally good. Vittori Barzoni discussed each edition of the *Malta Gazette* with the Public Secretary, and later described Coleridge as an outstanding personality with whom he had "the closest intimacy".[150] Captain Decatur of the US navy relished his company, and when he was about to sail to a new Mediterranean station, sent from his ship outside Valletta harbour a warm note of farewell which also captures the urgency of these months: "I am extremely near the shore, & have not time to be lengthy, & have only to beg you will believe me since whom [sic] I assure there is no man's good opinion whom I would set a higher value on. PS. Should you come out, make a sign & I shall heave to immediately."[151]

By the end of July 1805, Coleridge was able to send his wife a draft for £110 from his accumulated salary, which with the Wedgwood annuity put Sara in the best financial position she had been in for some time. The threatened loss of the family home at Greta Hall had also dissolved, since the prospective buyer had withdrawn.

Coleridge's actual return to England remained as problematic as ever, though he tried to appear more decisive than he felt. "I have been hoping and expecting to get away from England for 5 months past, and Mr Chapman not arriving, Sir Alexander's Importunities have always overpowered me, tho my gloom has increased at each disappointment. I am determined however to go in less than a month."[152] By contrast he emphasized the importance of his work in the wartime administration. "My office, as Public Secretary, the next civil dignity to the Governor, is at times a very busy one . . . I often subscribe my name 150 times a day . . . & administer half as many Oaths, besides which I have the public memorials to write, & worse than all constant matters of Arbitration." Sir Alexander, despite his importunities, is still described as "indeed exceedingly kind to me". From his point of view, of course, Coleridge was sticking honourably to his post.

In August the heat went up to 88° in the shade and 140° in full sunlight. The buildings were full of sweating men and splitting furniture, with cracking boards and exploding tea-chests. "Captain Lamb's tea chest went off, as loud as a Pistol . . . the Cooper's shop (where there is at present a large quantity of Mahogany & English oak) presents to the Ear a successive Let-off of Fireworks." Up at San Antonio all the floorboards in Sir Alexander's beautiful new dining-room split, one by one, with startling cracks, as they sat at dinner.

Curiously the heat suited Coleridge, and once again he found himself wishing that Asra, and all the Wordsworths and his children, were with him. "I have the prickly Heat on my Body, but without . . . annoying me, & I am better than I have been in a long time. In short, if my mind & heart were at ease, if my children + SH + WDMW were with me, & they were well, I should be more than well. I should luxuriate, like a Negro, in the Oven of the Shade and the Blaze of the Sunshine."[153]

Assuming that Coleridge had already left Malta, Wordsworth in fact was expecting Coleridge to appear at any moment in London, probably at Daniel Stuart's *Courier* offices. He scotched a "rumour" that the appointment as Public Secretary was permanent, and was making a first tentative plan for them all to reunite at Sir George Beaumont's new estate in Leicestershire. He had finished the *Prelude* and was anxious for Coleridge's opinion.[154]

But as August progressed a new mood of despondency descended on Coleridge. He walked at 5 a.m. on the roof of San Antonio, "deeply depressed", and gazed out at the pitiless beauty of the sea, "the Horizon dusky crimson" and the many boats swaying at anchor. He watched the wild dogs "reviving in the moonlight, & playing & gamboling in flocks". Boils returned on his arm, and he drank "Castor oil in Gin & Water", and had an "epileptic" return of his sexual dreams – "alas! alas! the consequences – *stimulos*".[155]

On 21 August he wrote to Mrs Coleridge, and this time the tone of exhaustion and disenchantment is unmistakable. "Malta, alas! it is a barren Rock: the Sky, the Sea, the Bays, the buildings are all beautiful. But no rivers, no brooks, no hedges, no green fields, almost no trees, & the few that are unlovely." He now felt it would have been better if he had remained "independent", and continued with his own writing. His position seemed ridiculous rather than important: "for the living in a huge palace all to myself, like a mouse in a Cathedral on a Fair on Market day, and the being hailed 'Most Illustrious Lord, the Public Secretary' are no pleasures to me who have no ambition."

Sir Alexander had always "contrived, in one way or another" to prevent his return, but now it was assured for September. He had the Governor's "solemn promise" that as soon as he had completed a series of public Letters "& examined into the Law-forms of the Island", he would be sent home on a convoy via Naples. Sir Alexander would also use his best interest with Hugh Elliott, the British Ambassador in Naples, to send him back officially with dispatches, which would "frank him home" free of charge. Nevertheless he would retain a further £120 of his salary in case he had to travel overland.

Even so the dream of some permanent post in the Mediterranean was not entirely abandoned. Now the moment of departure really approached, Coleridge began wondering if he might not after all return and settle permanently. The possibilities held forth by the Governor still promised the enchantments of the South. "Sir Alexander Ball's Kindness & Confidence in me is unlimited. He told a Gentleman a few days ago, that were he a man of Fortune he would gladly give me £500 a year to dine with him twice a week for the mere advantage which he received from my Conversation. And for a long time past he has been offering me different places to induce me to return. He would give me a handsome House, Garden, Country House, & a place of £600 a year certain. I thank him cordially – but neither accept nor refuse." Even more galling for Mrs Coleridge, perhaps, was an airy mention of "a fine Opening in America" that he had lately received – probably through Captain Decatur. "I was much inclined to accept; but my knowledge of Wordsworth's aversion to America stood in my way."[156]

It would be easy to dismiss much of this as Coleridge's optimistic fantasy of some perfect state of exile, and perhaps even as a provocation or warning to his wife. But Sir Alexander did in fact recommend Coleridge to the War Office for just such a posting, which would have provided very much the situation and the salary he describes. In a letter dated 18 September 1805, he wrote to Granville

Penn, chief assistant to the Secretary of State at Downing Street. In it he suggested that Coleridge combine the largely formal post of Superintendent of Quarantine (as applied to ships), with the much more interesting job of turning the *Malta Gazette* into an influential wartime newspaper to be distributed across the Mediterranean. The terms of this letter, despite its measured official tones, were a remarkable endorsement of Coleridge's unlikely success as a wartime bureaucrat. It also suggests Coleridge's continuing power to throw his spell over even the most rigorous executive mind.

The Governor first mentioned Coleridge's "literary Talents", political principles and moral character, and confirmed that he had fulfilled the Public Secretaryship "seven months to my satisfaction". He could also provide "the fullest information" on the Malta government to the Foreign Office. He then added: "As the climate agrees with Mr Coleridge he would accept Mr Eton's situation [as Superintendent] and allow him three hundred Pound a year, and as the business of the office would occupy but little of his time he could assist Mr Barzoni in making the *Malta Gazette* a powerful political engine besides rendering other services to this Government." He asked Penn to approach the head of department, persuaded "of deriving great public good from his appointment".[157] A similar note of private recommendation went to Ball's brother back in England. As Coleridge already possessed the recommendation to Hugh Elliot of the previous autumn, praising his imagination, judgement, and goodness of heart, he could feel pleasingly well documented by officialdom, as he prepared to leave.

When Mr Chapman finally arrived in Valletta on 9 September, Coleridge prepared to leave, depositing many of his books and papers with John Stoddart to be forwarded by convoy. None of these would he see again. There is no record of his farewells, though he noted "Tears & misery at the Thought of not returning" on one occasion after a talk with Captain Pasley. He prepared himself by reading Italian poets of the fifteenth century, and noted their "pleasing" confusion of heathen and Christian mythology. The layerings of classical myth, of Renaissance Latin upon Greek, as he hoped to study in Italy this autumn, also produced a characteristic word-coinage. It required "a strong imagination as well as an accurate *psycho-analytical* understanding" to conceive "the passion of those Times for Jupiter, Apollo etc.; & the nature of the Faith (for a

Faith it was . . .)".[158] The bureaucrat was to become the independent, wandering scholar once more.

15

Coleridge finally left Valletta a little after midnight on 4 September 1805, making a night crossing to Sicily under a shower of shooting stars. He could not make up his mind to sleep and, in an expressive gesture, left it to the stars to decide. "I was standing gazing at the starry Heaven, and said, I will go to bed at the next star that shoots." He knew that this tiny moment symbolized much about his long Mediterranean sojourn, and the self-knowledge that he had gained. "Observe this in counting fixed numbers previous to doing anything etc. etc. & deduce from man's own unconscious acknowledgement man's dependence on some thing out of him, on something apparently & believedly subject to regular and certain Laws other than his own Will & Reason."[159]

Coleridge's wanderings now became so uncertain that they are barely traceable until he arrived unexpectedly in Rome on 31 December, some three months later. He wrote no letters, and kept the barest record of dates and places in his Notebooks. On 26 September he was at Syracuse with the Leckies, and he visited Cecilia Bertozzi for the last time. On 4 October he was at Messina, and made the "melancholy observation" that he was growing fat. Perhaps Cecilia had pointed it out to him as a gesture of farewell.

Sometime after 15 October he abandoned the plan to sail to Trieste and return overland, perhaps on hearing news of the defeat, on 20 October, of the Austrian army at the Ulm. By mid-November he had sailed to Naples, probably on a troop ship belonging to General Craig's convoy, and dined with Hugh Elliott at the British Embassy.

All the news then was of the Battle of Trafalgar, which had been fought on 21 October (Coleridge's 33rd birthday), achieving a great strategic victory. But when news of Nelson's death reached Naples, Coleridge walked through the streets and found many Englishmen openly in tears, coming up to him to shake hands and completely overcome with an emotion which he instinctively shared.[160] Ball had received a final dispatch from Nelson at Valletta four days before the engagement, describing his daring battle plan to cut through the centre of the huge French squadron in a double line astern. Nelson told Ball that his young officers had christened it "the Nelson touch", and added with a characteristic insouciance, "I hope it is touch and taken!" The only record of this dispatch remained unpublished in Ball's private papers, but similar stories circulated widely, the kind of thing that made all Nelson's officers adore him and filled Coleridge with admiration.[161]

There was now much confusion in Naples, and Coleridge was not after all "franked home" with official papers by Elliot. So instead he made a leisurely expedition into Calabria with Captain Pasley. He visited Virgil's tomb and contemplated Vesuvius. In late December he was offered a carriage-trip to Rome, for a fortnight as he supposed, and leaving his boxes of books and papers with an embassy friend, set out on Christmas Day. Almost immediately on his arrival, he heard from Mr Jackson, the English consul, of the battle of Austerlitz and the French armies sweeping southwards into Italy. "To stay, or not to stay?" he noted calmly. He decided to stay, and once again found himself marooned by circumstances. He made no attempt to continue his journey until the spring, and still he wrote no letters home.

The absence of news frightened the Wordsworths and infuriated Southey. Dorothy wrote to Lady Beaumont on Christmas Day: "Poor Coleridge was with us two years ago at this time . . . We hear no further tidings of him, and I cannot help being very uneasy and anxious: though without any evil, many causes might delay him; yet it is a long time since he left Malta. The weather is dreadful for a sea voyage. O my dear friend, what a fearful thing a windy night is now at our house! I am too often haunted with dreadful images of Shipwrecks and the Sea when I am in bed and hear a stormy wind, and now that we are thinking so much of Coleridge it is worse than ever."[162]

The truth seems to be that Coleridge, with plenty of money and several letters of recommendation and credit, was embarked on a leisurely tour of the Roman sites and galleries.* One long note on

---

* Coleridge's surprisingly prudent handling of his finances give another indication of his half-formed plan to remain in the Mediterranean. He had earned £150 as Ball's Private Secretary by December 1804, and a further £325 as Acting Public Secretary by the end of August 1805, giving him a total salary of £525, the most he had ever earned. Of this, he managed to send

footnote continued overleaf

the Spanish Steps suggests that he was staying in the English quarter beneath the Trinita dei Monti (where Keats would die of tuberculosis sixteen years later). Rather than face the prospect of England, he had decided to risk capture by the French armies who were steadily descending through northern Italy. While most English visitors fled back to Naples, and General Craig's expedition sailed ignominiously back to Sicily, Coleridge was quietly making notes on the Last Judgement in the Sistine Chapel. "Ideal = the subtle hieroglyphical felt-by-all, though not without abstruse and difficult analysis detected & understood . . . Take as an instance of the true Ideal Michel Angelo's despairing Woman at the bottom of the Last Judgement."[163]

Captain Pasley, who had also pulled back with his regiment to Sicily, wrote to a fellow-officer, "I was happy to meet our friend Coleridge at Naples, certainly few men are more interesting. He is now at Rome, where he stayed. Not withstanding advices of the English Resident there [Jackson] to retire, I hope the poet's eye in a fine frenzy rolling may never contemplate the roof of a French prison: but from his natural indolence I cannot be too sanguine of his taking himself off in time."[164] Coleridge's book box was also shipped back, and eventually finished up where it had started, in Valletta with Stoddart. Coleridge was alone with his shirts, his guidebooks, and two remaining notebooks, in the Eternal City.

It seems to have suited him very well. Within a matter of days he had introduced himself with great success into the circle of two notable expatriate groups, one literary and the other painterly, who frequented the artistic quarter round the Spanish Steps. The first was a group of German writers who gathered at the splendid residence of Wilhelm von Humboldt, directly overlooking the Trinita dei Monti. Humboldt was a distinguished young diplomat in his mid-thirties, brother of the famous South American traveller. He had been appointed Prussian Minister to the Court of Pius

footnote continued
£160 to his wife (£50 in December 1804, and a further £110 in August 1805) and also repaid borrowings of £75 to Stoddart before leaving Malta. He managed to put aside £120 for his journey through Italy, but his expenses evidently increased in Rome, as he had effectively spent all his remaining savings in the six months to June 1806, and did not even have the price of a sea-passage home. There is a clear suggestion that he only finally left Italy because he was penniless, and had found no other work. (See Donald Sultana, *Samuel Taylor Coleridge in Malta and Italy*, 1969.)

VII, and held a salon with many German university visitors where Coleridge, an honorary graduate of Göttingen, immediately felt in his element.

Humboldt had formed a life-long friendship with Schiller at Jena University, and developed advanced theories of linguistics and philology, publishing learned papers on Basque and Javanese dialects. His notion of a "language world" was calculated to appeal to Coleridge, and his famous binary concept of "the Dual" (as opposed to two singulars and/or a plural) was much in Coleridge's metaphysical style. Humboldt later championed ideals of "academic freedom", and helped to found Berlin University. He was a patron of both arts and sciences, and among his protégés at the Trinita dei Monti was the brilliant young Romantic poet and critic, Johann Ludwig Tieck.

Coleridge formed an animated friendship with Tieck, discussing Goethe and A. W. Schlegel, and the latest philosophical work of Schelling (who had also been a professor at Jena) which they compared with that of the mystic Jacob Boehme. It was probably now that Coleridge first came to grips with Schelling's *System of Transcendental Idealism* (1800), which rekindled his ambition to write his own general philosophical treatise at some later date. Tieck's sister, Sophie Bernhardi, later wrote to Schlegel of the remarkable Englishman at Rome, who knew so much current German literature and who admired Schlegel's own work on Shakespeare "unbelievably so". Coleridge in turn admired Tieck, translated one of his poems,[165] greatly valued his hospitality and "kindness", and met him again years later in London with fond recollections of their Roman hours together.[166]

But Coleridge's real intimacies were formed in the more bohemian circle of the painters. At the Cafe Greco on Strada de' Condotti he fell in with a group that included George Wallis, Thomas Russell, and the 27-year-old American artist Washington Allston. Russell was an art student from Exeter, and Wallis a Scottish landscape painter travelling through Italy with his family, including a ten-year-old son grandly named Trajan Wallis, who delighted Coleridge with his precociousness. But it was Washington Allston, a dreamy young man, elegant and aristocratic, with wild black hair framing a pale abstracted face, to whom he most instinctively warmed.

Allston had grown up on a cotton plantation in South Carolina, and had the slow finesse of a Southern gentleman. Moneyed and leisurely, he had attended Harvard and gone on to study art in Paris and at the Royal Academy in London, where he knew Fuseli and Benjamin West. Melancholy and amusing, he said he had received his imaginative education through the stories of the black plantation workers, tales of "barbaric magic and superstition . . . ghosts and goblins . . . myths and legends to startle and alarm".[167] He had a "tendency towards the marvellous" and loved to stay up all night talking. A friend said Allston could never paint the reflections of dawn sunlight on water, because he had never seen a sunrise.

Naturally, Allston espoused the Sublime school of painting, with its brooding landscapes and dramatic subjects. He preferred Gothic to Greek, and his beau-ideal was Titian and Veronese with their rich colours and mysterious allegories. He had painted scenes from Schiller's plays, Mrs Radcliffe's novels, Milton's *Paradise Lost*, and the Bible. The latter characteristically included "St Peter When He Heard the Cock Crow". Leaving a fiancée behind in Boston, he had come to Rome in 1805, renting a studio by the Borghese Gardens, and a rustic summer lodging up in the Roman hills at Olevano.

One of the first things Coleridge ever heard him say was that a fellow-painter was too realistic and down to earth. "He works too much with the Pipe in his mouth – looks too much at the particular Thing, instead of overlooking – *ubersehen*." Allston valued the ideal above all else, and Nathaniel Hawthorne would later put him into a short story to illustrate this quality pursued to excess, "The Artist of the Beautiful". Like Coleridge, he had trouble finishing his work, and he was to spend over twenty-five years on his last canvas, a monumental picture of "Belshazzar's Feast", which was unfinished at his death.

He had just completed a large mythological canvas, "Diana and Her Nymphs in the Chase", which appears to be much influenced by Claude Lorraine. Coleridge wrote a minute prose description of it, treating it in a way that delighted Allston, as a real landscape through which he could wander at will, slipping on the perilous bridge of moss-covered tree-trunk over a chasm – "take care, for heaven's sake" – and watching the graceful undulations of a huge umbrella-pine "exhaling" movement, "for it rises indeed, even as smoke in calm weather".[168]

Allston and Coleridge were soon walking all over Rome together

– to the Forum, the Castello San Angelo, the Borghese Gardens – talking and comparing notes. In between the Sublime, Coleridge was careful to keep an eye on the grotesque, like the stallholder in the Roman market who twisted the necks of some two hundred goldfinches, one after another, leaving them fluttering and gasping in a box, "meantime chit-chatting with a neighbour stallman, throwing his Head about, and sometimes using the neck-twisting gesture in help of his Oratory".[169]

Years later Allston would say that he owed more "intellectually" to Coleridge than to any other man in Italy. "He used to call Rome the *silent* city; but I never could think of it as such, while with him; for, meet him when or where I would, the fountain of his mind was never dry, but like the far-reaching aqueducts that once supplied this mistress of the world, its living streams seemed especially to flow for every classic ruin which we wandered. And when I recall some of our walks under the pines of the Villa Borghese, I am almost tempted to dream that I once listened to Plato, in the groves of the Academy."[170]

This was Allston in the American Sublime style perhaps, but it suggests why Coleridge found him congenial company. When the French army arrived at the outskirts of Rome in February, the two men simply sauntered off to Allston's bucolic retreat up at Olevano under the trees. They remained there for some five weeks, sketching, talking, sampling the Albano wine, and discussing art history and aesthetics. Coleridge's sketches were verbal ones, describing the green panorama of the Olevano valley – "a Labyrinth of sweet Walks, glens, green Lanes, with Hillsides" – much as it still is. While Allston painted, Coleridge lounged, making notes on chiaroscuro, painter's easels, goddesses, ruins and harmony.

16

In March, primroses came out and it snowed on the blossom of the almond trees.[171] Coleridge seems to have been perfectly happy, suspended briefly from all sense of duty or guilt; and Allston asked him to sit for a half-length portrait, relaxed and meditative, in a window overlooking the valley. His face looks puffy and pale, yet handsome and almost raffish, with an extravagant tangle of silk scarves knotted casually round his neck. The mouth is full, and the eyes gaze into the distance with the hint of a smile. The Public Secretary has reverted to his persona of footloose artist on his travels. Coleridge later said it was one of his best likenesses, perhaps partly because it was unfinished.[172]

But Allston felt he had not captured his friend's animation, and some ten years after he would try again. He would also try to describe Coleridge in verse, comparing his nightlong talks to a great ship, launched out into the dark of "the Human Soul" but radiating light over the shadowy waters:

> . . . For oft we seemed
> As on some starless sea, – all dark above,
> All dark below, – yet, onward as we drove,
> To plough up light that ever round us streamed.[173]

They returned to Rome in March for the Easter celebrations, and found the city now occupied by the French army. But Napoleon had not yet ordered the expulsion of English nationals, and Coleridge continued to visit the galleries and the Sistine Chapel, making notes on Michelangelo, Raphael and the Apollo Belvedere, apparently unperturbed. He regarded the French with increasing contempt. On one occasion, he was delivering a learned analysis of the monumental statue of Moses by Michelangelo, which is part of Julius II's tomb in San Pietro. Coleridge observed that the Moses was remarkable for its beard and horns, which could be interpreted as an ancient sun-sign from Greek, Abyssinian and Middle Eastern mythologies, symbolizing a "darker power than the conscious intellect of man", and the equivalent to the horned figure of Pan.

At this juncture, two elegant French officers swaggered into the church, and leeringly remarked that Moses wore the beard of a goat and the horns of a cuckold. Coleridge thought this a typical example of "degraded" French wit, not only because it exhibited their taste for "burlesque and travesty", but because it indicated an inability to grasp a "unified" symbolic pattern as opposed to vulgar and fragmentary "generalizations". The French were "passive Slaves of Association". That was why they would never match German literary criticism, or British naval strategy. They saw everything in fixed "parts" without a sense of the fluid "whole": they had fancy without imagination, wit without intuition.[174]

He had the same criticism of Bernini's baroque hemisphere of Papal statues outside St Peter's: "a great genius bewildered – and lost by an excess of fancy over imagination".[175] Other entries in his Notebooks show him trying to forge a new language of art criticism, obviously in conversation with Allston. How can one use terms like "truth", "beauty" the "ideal" with proper philosophical accuracy; "without possibility of misconception"?[176] And why were direct images from nature always so symbolically powerful? There was a shopkeeper's sign near the Castello St Angelo, advertising "Aqua Vita, Rosoli, Spiriti, e Tabacchi", but broken off its wall and "more than half veiled by tall nettles". Why did this produce the exact image "of a deserted City"?[177]

But Coleridge was now running short of funds. He gave up his lodgings, and moved in with Wallis's family, borrowing money from Thomas Russell. Russell would later recall his "destitute condition" and increasing moods of depression.[178] Bad dreams and opium returned, and the sense of indecision. "A Kettle is on the slow Fire; & I turn from my Book, & loiter from going to my bed, in order to see whether it will boil: & on that my Hope hovers – on the Candle burning in the socket – or will this or that Person come this evening."[179] Once again he was being forced to meet the necessity of returning home. But still he did not write, and back in England it was only through Stoddart's letters that there were rumours of him in Rome, being "much noticed" among the German and American colony.

17

On 18 May 1806, Coleridge finally set out with Russell for the port of Livorno, making a leisurely journey by vetturino, and stopping off to visit the waterfall at Terni and the galleries of Perugia and Florence. At Pisa he saw the leaning tower by moonlight, "something of a supernatural look", but was more interested by "the perfect cleanliness & good order" of the two hospitals for men and women. He contemplated the "great door of open iron work" to the wards, through which all must pass.

He was transfixed by the huge fresco in the Camposanto at Pisa, said to be by Giotto and his pupils, "The Triumph of Death". The faded condition of the tempera, the flat glimmering of human forms without colour or perspective, all processing towards inevitable death, impressed him even more than Dante. He was haunted by it, and over a decade later recalled his impressions at length in a set of Philosophical Lectures. The frescoes presented that sense of inexhaustible and hypnotic power, "which we are reminded of when in the South of Europe we look at the deep blue sky . . . The same unwearied form presents itself, yet still we look on, sinking deeper and deeper, and therein offering homage to the infinity of our souls which no mere form can satisfy."[180]

At Pisa he had less Platonic detachment, and felt that he was now drifting into Death's cortège. By the time he reached Livorno on 7 June, he was in a mood of "black" despair equal to any experienced in Malta. While Russell looked for a ship to take them back, Coleridge plunged into a suicidal state of gloom, dreading the dangers of the voyage, and dreading even more its safe completion. Nothing could more clearly reveal his reluctance to leave the South, which he had so long half-hidden from himself, disguising it as his duty to Ball, or the difficulties of travel, or his new friendship with Allston. Now all his thoughts turned to his children, the one thing he felt he could not abandon. "O my Children, my Children! I gave you life once, unconscious of the Life I was giving; and you as unconsciously have given Life to me . . . Many months past I should have essayed whether Death is what I groan for, absorption and transfiguration of Consciousness . . . Even this moment I could commit Suicide but for you, my Darlings."[181]

Even the thought of returning to the Wordsworths and Asra was no comfort. "Of Wordsworths – of Sara Hutchinson: that is passed – or of remembered thoughts to make a Hell of." He felt racked with pain and self-disgust: "no other Refuge than Poisons that degrade the Being, while they suspend the torment".[182] Grimly, he went out and purchased a brass enema and pipe.

It was not easy to find a ship, as the navy had suspended its operations off Italy, and neutral merchantmen were nervous of taking British nationals. They shuttled between inns at Livorno, Pisa and Florence, making enquiries and spending the last of their money. Allston's recommendation to Pietro Benevuti, the Professor of Painting at the Florentine Academy, came to nothing as Coleridge was for once beyond the point of projecting his charm in bad Italian. But at last they found an American sailor, Captain Derkheim of "the Gosport", and Coleridge summoned sufficient energy to convince the Captain that they were cargo worthy of passage on credit. Captain Derkheim later said he had heard nothing like Coleridge since leaving the Niagara Falls.[183]

The effort of it all was so great that Coleridge awoke the next day screaming and trying to vomit, his right arm paralysed. It gradually wore off, but he believed he had suffered a "manifest stroke of Palsy". Trying to calm himself, he finally sat and wrote a long letter to Allston at the Cafe Greco in Rome. He did not mention opium, but wrote frankly about his depression, his dangerous illness, and his thoughts of his children.

"But for them I would try my chance. But they pluck out the wingfeathers from the mind." He praised young Russell for his "Kindness & tender-heartedness to me"; and worried about the Wallis family still in Rome. His farewell to Allston expressed passionate friendship, and a sense of star-crossed destiny as he prepared to leave. "My dear Allston! somewhat from increasing age, but much more from calamity & intense pre-affections my heart is not open to more than kind good wishes in general; to you & to you alone since I have left England, I have felt more; and had I not known the Wordsworths, should have loved & esteemed you *first* and *most*: and as it is, next to them I love & honour you. Heaven knows, a part of such a Wreck as my Head & Heart is scarcely worth your acceptance."[184]

By 22 June, Coleridge and Russell were back at Pisa, waiting at the Globe Inn for a storm to disperse before boarding. It seems that it was too dangerous to linger in Livorno itself, because of possible arrest by French troops, and Captain Derkheim had already had to pass them off as American nationals. Coleridge would later embroider a much more dramatic story that Napoleon had issued a personal warrant for his arrest, and his "escape" from Rome to Livorno had been arranged through "the kindness of a noble Benedictine, and the gracious connivance of that good old man, the present Pope".[185]

A warrant had certainly been issued for the British consul in Rome, Mr Jackson, and a general order to expel British nationals from Italy in May, which was why Coleridge was worried about the Wallis family. But the tale of a hectic personal pursuit was really a fiction, designed to cover up the otherwise inexplicable time he had remained in Italy with Allston, undecided about returning to England at all.[186]

Coleridge would soon present this whole latter part of his sojourn in the Mediterranean as a sequence of events almost entirely beyond his control: "retained" against his will by Sir Alexander Ball, "duped" by the consul at Naples Mr Elliot, and forced to live in hiding among the bohemians of Rome while pursued by Napoleon's vengeful officers. In truth, he had acted much more wilfully, delaying and taking casual risks which would have appalled his family and friends.

The true chaos of his existence over the past eighteen months came to a head at Pisa. He was holed up in a cheap inn with an art student, virtually penniless, having a few books and presents in an old box, a supply of opium and an enema, and two precious Notebooks. He was in imminent danger of arrest, disguised as an American, and deeply uncertain if he wanted to return to England to take up his old life and identity. Once again he felt the best solution would have been if he had died in John Wordsworth's place. "O dear John Wordsworth! Ah that I could but have died for you: & you have gone home, married S. Hutchinson, & protected my Poor little ones. O how very, very gladly would I have accepted the conditions.'[187]

On the night before their final departure for Livorno, he wrote a hymn to death, sitting in the window of the inn and watching the bolts of lightning crash down over the river Arno. "Sunday, June 22nd 1806. Globe, Pisa . . . Repeatedly during this night's storm have I desired that I might be taken off, not knowing when or where. But a few moments past a vivid flash passed across me, my nerves thrilled, and I earnestly wished, so help me God! like a Love-longing, that it would pass through me!"[188]

Yet this Coleridgean death was no ordinary extinction. It was more like a transfiguration, a complete transformation of the terms of his existence. It would "take him off" to some other dimension. It was: "Death without deformity, or assassin-like self-disorganization; Death, in which the mind by its *own* wish might seem to have caused its own purpose to be performed, as instantaneously and by an instrument almost as spiritual, as the Wish itself!" It was Death which seemed almost like re-birth, Death which seemed like an act of love, preparing for something new, blowing away the old self:

Come, come, thou bleak December wind,
And blow the dry Leaves from the Tree!
Flash, like a love-thought, thro' me, Death!
And take a life, that wearies me.[189]

The imagery of winter, with its dead leaves, still promised the possibility of some other springtime, with the buds and blossoms of another life.

It would be easy to misjudge Coleridge's mood of temporary despair on departing from Italy. Years later he would remember the "heavenly" valley of the Arno with affection, and put it into his poetry. He would write and lecture on Italian art, and recall the work of Michelangelo and Giotto as "deeply interesting to me . . . having a life of its own in the spirit of that revolution of which Christianity was effect, means and symbol". He would fix on Italy as an ideal place of retreat, and an image of spiritual resurrection from the dead. "Were I forced into exile . . . I should wish to pass my summers at Zurich, and the remaining eight months alternately at Rome and in Florence, so to join as much as I could German depth, Swiss ingenuity, and the ideal genius of Italy; that, at least, which we cannot help thinking, almost feeling, to be still there, be it but as the spirit of one departed hovering over his own tomb, the haunting breeze of his own august, desolate mausoleum."[190]

As he and Russell rattled along in the coach to Livorno, he looked tenderly on a group of "beggar children" running alongside and calling to them with a strange "shudder-whistle" of farewell. The *Gosport* set sail for England on 23 June 1806.

18

The passage took fifty-five days – almost twice the outward voyage – and lived up to Coleridge's worst expectations. He spent much of his time in his cabin, sick and constipated, and for once kept no journal at all of his impressions. They were boarded by a Spanish privateer, but Captain Derkheim talked them free, after throwing official papers (including some of Coleridge's Malta notes) into the sea. Coleridge submitted to twelve enemas, "my dread of and antipathy increased every time", each administered by Derkheim in conditions of pain and humiliation. The sense of violation and punishment horrified him, as he later admitted to Southey. "Tho' the Captain was the strongest man on board – it used to take all the force of his arm, & bring the blood up in his face before he could finish. Once I brought off more than a pint of blood – & three times he clearly saved my Life."[191]

Both Derkheim and Russell continued to behave with "every possible Tenderness", though their own feelings can only be imagined. For the rest it was a battering, claustrophobic voyage: "working up against head winds, rotting and sweating in calms, or running under hard gales, with the dead lights secured". Russell later wrote home of their grim experience, saying that Coleridge had nearly died. Coleridge himself wrote that "no motive on earth" would make him venture on another sea-voyage of more than three days: "I would rather starve in a hovel".

Confined in his quarters, he grew fat and pallid, and his Mediterranean tan faded away. Gazing out through the closed porthole, he thought distractedly of Asra at Grasmere. It was perhaps now that the first images of his fine, bleak meditative poem on their love, "Constancy to an Ideal Object" began to coalesce.

> . . . Home and Thou are one.
> The peacefull'st cot, the moon shall shine upon,
> Lulled by the thrush, and wakened by the lark,
> Without thee were but a becalméd bark,
> Whose Helmsman on an ocean waste and wide
> Sits mute and pale his mouldering helm beside.[192]

But it would be many years before the verse were completed.

The *Gosport* finally sighted Portsmouth in early August, where it was quarantined, and then allowed to continue eastwards into the Thames estuary. Here Coleridge took the earliest chance of disembarking at the little quayside and customs post of Stangate Creek, on the edge of the Medway. He "leaped on land" on the afternoon of 17 August 1806. Leaving his box of books and papers in Captain Derkheim's care, to be taken on up to Wapping, he hurried to "a curious little Chapel" by the quayside at Lower Halstow, which still exists, overlooking the mournful expanse of the Kentish marshes towards Sheerness. He found it open and empty, and dropping to his knees "offered, I trust, as deep a prayer as ever without words or thoughts was sent up by a human Being".

Going outside again, he surveyed the lapping waters and the tide running up through the baked mud and yellowing bulrushes of his native land. "Almost immediately after landing Health seemed to flow in upon me, like the mountain waters upon the dry stones of a vale-stream after Rains."[193] The following morning he was in London, at the Bell Inn in the Strand, wondering if he had enough money for a "decent Hat" and a pair of shoes.

2

The Sense of Home

1

Now he had returned home after two and a half years of wandering, Coleridge suddenly felt that he had no real home to return to. He walked down the Strand in a dirty shirt, full of dismay, hearing everyone talk of the death of Pitt and the illness of Charles James Fox, the political era of his youth sliding into the past. Now the news was of blockades, war shortages, conscription, unrest in the country. Like all exiles, he felt he had come back to a changed world which had moved on without him. Should he stay in London, go north to Keswick and his wife, agree to meet the Wordsworths in Leicestershire, or even return to his old family haunts in the West Country?

In the event he would try all these over the next twelve months. For the moment he needed work, money and advice. The one thing he could not face was an immediate confrontation with Sara Coleridge, and he did not write to her directly for a month. Instead he sent messages round to his old editor Daniel Stuart at the *Courier* offices, and to Charles Lamb at India House, and dashed off letters to Southey and Wordsworth announcing his return to England rather like a piece of flotsam washed up by a lucky tide.

'I am now going to Lamb's – Stuart is at Margate; all are out of town; I have no one to advise me – I am shirtless & almost penniless . . . My MSS are all – excepting two pocket-books – either in the Sea or . . . carried back to Malta." He had not settled "any rational plan", but he could write "more tranquilly" to them than to Mrs Coleridge (but they should pass on his news).[1]

It was Stuart who replied immediately with a credit for £50, kind enquiries about his health, and a businesslike suggestion for articles about the careers of Pitt and Fox, the Mediterranean war, the Continental blockade, or anything else Coleridge liked to turn his hand to. He also invited him to Margate, simply to talk about his life and his future.

2

Stuart was not an intimate friend, but he was a man of the world, and a newspaperman who understood writers, even writers like Coleridge. They would talk of his marriage, of his career, of his prospects. Over the next two years, Coleridge would try to re-establish himself as a professional man of letters, with a steady determination that was often disguised by the lurid chaos of his emotional entanglements and the regular descents into opium. His struggles to separate from his wife, to look after his children, to resolve his relationship with Asra, and above all to find a way of living, or not living, within the overpowering sphere of Wordsworth's magnetic influence, would consume much of his energies. Frequently they would appear to reduce him to a kind of passive despair, a mere hulk upon the stream of circumstance, "rudderless and hopeless" as he so often said himself, washed from one temporary harbour to the next. But in reality the struggle and the determination always continued. The record of it still bursts out of his Notebooks, letters and poetry.

He was living out what many people experience, in the dark disorder of their hidden lives, but living it on the surface and with astonishing, even alarming candour that many of his friends found unendurable or simply ludicrous. Moreover he continued to write about it, to witness it, in a way that makes him irreplaceable among the great Romantic visionaries. His greatness lies in the understanding of these struggles, not (like Wordsworth perhaps) in their solution. So it was, talking to Stuart in these first weeks back in England (as he later recalled), that he first glimpsed the crisis that would close round him in these middle years. With his peculiar mixture of comedy and pathos, he projected out of his private chaos an universal dilemma. He was only thirty-four that October, but he felt that somewhere in the Mediterranean he had imperceptibly crossed a shadowline into darker waters.

Stuart had made the "important remark" that there was a middle period in a man's life, "varying in various men, from 35 to 45", when for no evident reason he began to feel the "vanity of his pursuits" and to ask "what is all this *for*?". Coleridge felt this sudden undermining of the self, this panicky self-questioning of the grounds of life, was especially acute in lonely men – in bachelors, widowers or "Unhappy Husbands". Such a man "becomes half-melancholy, gives in to wild dissipation, or self-regardless Drinking" and might even deliberately destroy himself. He would leave his "ingenious female, or female-minded friends, to fish out some *motive* for an act which . . . would have acted even without a motive even as the Terror in Nightmairs".[2]

Such a crisis would burst upon a man from whatever casual cause, as surely as "gunpowder in a Smithy" would eventually be ignited by some chance spark or other. "I had *felt* this Truth; but never saw it before so clearly; it came upon me at Malta, under the melancholy dreadful feeling of finding myself to be a *Man*, by a distinct division from Boyhood, Youth, and 'Young Man' – Dreadful was the feeling – before that Life had flown on so that I had always been *a Boy*, as it were – and this sensation had blended in all my conduct . . ." If men survived this period, "they commonly become cheerful again – that is a comfort – for mankind – *not for me*!"[3] It was this sense of crisis, the entry into Dante's "dark wood" of middle age, that haunted Coleridge quite as much as opium in these restless years.

3

Some practical prospects slowly took shape in London during September. The Royal Institution proposed a series of Lectures on the Fine Arts for the autumn. The First Lord of the Admiralty, Lord Howick, agreed to an interview about a possible civil service post, in response to Sir Alexander Ball's recommendations to Downing Street. Charles and Mary Lamb fed him with meat and porter and puns, and discussed his marriage. He and Charles tried smoking "segars". Very gradually things fell into place. He even grappled with the opium problem, making an analytic list of the repeated pattern of his relapses. "1. Uncomfortable [feelings]. 2. Opium + Brandy. 3. Increased N.E. [Nervous Energy]. 4. Positive body pain. 5. Remorse & Despondency . . . Try little by little . . ."[4]

He sketched a beautiful, haunting new stanza for the *Mariner*, a sort of nightmare souvenir of his time on the *Gosport*:

. . . And stifled words & groans of pain
Mix'd on each murmuring lip,
We look'd round & we look'd up
And Fear at our hearts as at a Cup
The Life-blood seem'd to sip.
The Sky was dull & dark the Night
The Helmsman's face by his lamp gleam'd bright,
From the Sails the Dews did drip –
Till clomb above the eastern bar
The horned Moon, with one bright Star
Within its nether tip."[5]

So these early weeks of autumn 1806 became a time of stocktaking and confidences about his life. Ostensibly Coleridge was delayed by an absurd series of confusions about his book box, which was lost at Wapping, with its precious cargo of books, papers, old shirts, Roman pearls and attar of roses perfume. Coleridge suspected Captain Derkheim of purloining the latter (the Captain had suddenly married and even more suddenly returned to sea, an object-lesson in American promptitude) and he spent days frantically combing the warehouses around Tower Hill in the rain.[6] It was not till October that everything was found safely packed away in a box labelled "Thomas Russell". Similar confusion attended his attempts to wait on Lord Howick, who finally dismissed him in the best bureaucratic manner, with a non-committal message left with the doorman. But by this time another government posting was far from Coleridge's mind.[7]

He wrote to Stuart a measured reflection on his Mediterranean adventures. "Though no emolument could ever force me again to the business, intrigue, form and pomp of a public situation, yet beyond all doubt I have acquired a great variety of useful knowledge, quickness in discovering men's characters, and adroitness in dealing with them. I have learnt the inside character of many eminent living men . . . In short, if I recover a steady tho' imperfect Health, I perhaps should have no reason to regret my long Absence, not even my perilous detention in Italy." He thought that his friendship with Allston and other "Artists of acknowledged highest reputation" had done more for his insight into the fine arts, in three months in Rome, than had twenty years in England.[8]

He also wrote, in less measured tones, about his marriage. Stuart later destroyed most of this confession, marking the gap grimly "Coleridge 1806 wife". What has remained is a memorable passage of special pleading, heightened by the vivid imagery of his "Dejection" ode to Sara Hutchinson. Coleridge claimed that his unhappy marriage was the source of all his difficulties. "This, this perpetual Struggle, and endless *heart-wasting*, was at the bottom of all my irresolution, procrastination, languor, and former detestable habit of poison-taking –: this turned me away so long from political and moral disquisition, poetry, and all the flowers & herbs that grow in the Light and Sunshine, to be meanwhile a Delver in the unwholesome quick-silver mines of abstruse Metaphysics . . ."[9]

He had said it before, and he would say it again, endlessly, and with great poetic conviction. Certainly he believed now that his marriage had always been ill-destined, and it had long been beyond his powers to save it. Every divorce lawyer is familiar with such retrospective statements. Yet the strangest claim was not that his "former" opium habit was the product of his marriage; or that his wife had "turned him away" from a literary career. Even their mutual friends (even Southey) saw that they had long been unable to live on productive, or even tranquil terms. It was the claim that metaphysics, which in reality he loved passionately and to which he would dedicate so much of his later life, was somehow shameful and "unwholesome". For these "quick-silver mines" were also his magic caverns "measureless to man", the dimension that gave his poetry and all his writing its unique resonance. Why should he deny these to Stuart, unless they were inextricably associated in his mind with the guilt and deception of his opium underworld?

While Coleridge lurked in London, anxious messages beamed out from Grasmere. Dorothy wrote to Mary Lamb, and Wordsworth to Sir George Beaumont. The planned autumn move to Beaumont's estate at Coleorton was in suspense, until Coleridge had decided on his "settled rational plan" and this seemed less and less forthcoming. A single sonnet appeared in the pages of the *Courier* of 27 September, like a distant distress flare. It was entitled "Farewell to Love", a beautiful adaptation of a piece by Fulke Greville. But to whom was it addressed – to which Sara? To Asra or to Mrs Coleridge? (And did it contain a reproach to Wordsworth in its seventh line?)

Farewell, sweet Love! Yet blame you not my truth;
More fondly ne'er did mother eye her child
Than I your form: *yours* were my hopes of youth,
And as *you* shaped my thoughts I sighed or smiled.

While most were wooing wealth, or gaily swerving
To pleasure's secret haunts, and some apart
Stood strong in pride, self-conscious of deserving,
To you I gave my whole weak wishing heart.

And when I met the maid that realised
Your fair creations, and had won her kindness,
Say, but for her if aught on earth I prized!
Your dreams alone I dreamt, and caught your blindness.

O grief! – but farewell, Love! I will go play me
With thoughts that please me less, and less betray me.[10]

Wordsworth wrote impatiently to Beaumont: "What shall I say of Coleridge? . . . he dare not go home, he recoils so much from the thought of domesticating with Mrs Coleridge . . . he is so miserable that he dare not encounter it. What a deplorable thing! I have written to him to say that if he does not come down immediately I must insist on seeing him somewhere. If he appoints London, I shall go."[11]

In the end it was Mary Lamb who convinced Coleridge that he must write to his wife. She believed a separation was inevitable, but she sounded exhausted with the discussions and delays. "You must write here, that I may know you write, or you must come and dictate a letter for me to write to her . . . but yet a letter from me or you *shall go today*." Yet she never regretted his presence, and reminded him that "a few cheerful evenings spent with you serves to bear up our spirits many a long & weary year".[12]

In the event, Coleridge's letter was subdued and suspiciously practical. He did not speak of a separation as such, but proposed a schedule of work commitments which would quickly bring him back to London. His wife and Hartley could join him if they wished. "On Friday Sennight, please God! I shall quit Town, and trust to be at Keswick on Monday, Sept. 29th. If I finally accept the Lectures,

I must return by the midst of November; but propose to take you and Hartley with me, as we may be sure of Rooms either in Mr Stuart's House at Knightsbridge, or in the Strand. – My purpose is to divide my time steadily between my 'Reflections Moral and Political grounded on Information obtained during two years Resident in Italy and the Mediterranean'; and the Lectures on the Principles common to all the Fine Arts." He reminded her of the £110 sent from Malta, spoke of his tenderness to his "dear children" and assured her of his "deep tho' sad affection" towards her.[13]

In the event, Coleridge did not set out for Keswick until 12 October, but from now on he kept his wife regularly informed of his movements, emphasizing the financial importance to both of them of the lecture scheme. One further possibility was a combined series of winter lectures, at both the Royal Institution and the London Institution, which would make "a respectable annuity of perhaps £400 a year". When he heard that Southey "strongly disapproved" of the scheme, he added indignantly: "Something (he knows) I must do, & that immediately, to get money . . . And if I should die, as soon as I feel probable, it seems the most likely mode of distinguishing myself so as to leave Patrons for you & my Children."[14]

Perhaps it should have been clear to Sara Coleridge that her husband had come back from the Mediterranean with a new vision of his future. That future lay essentially in London, where he could find work as a writer and some help for his opium addiction. He was not prepared to live permanently with her again at Keswick, but he wanted to see his children, help with their education, and support the whole family with the Wedgwood annuity and his own literary earnings. He wanted the two boys, especially Hartley who had just turned ten years old, to spend time with him and perhaps attend London schools for part of the year. "The opportunity of giving Hartley opportunities of Instruction, he would not otherwise have, weighed a great deal with me."[15] Given the "unconquerable Difference of Temper" which he referred to both in his letters and private Notebooks, it did not seem an unreasonable compromise.[16]

The lecture scheme, which both Southey and soon Wordsworth would discourage, was a perfectly realistic one. Public lectures had begun to flourish in the city (itself a wartime phenomenon, like increased newspaper reading) and several new lecture institutions had been founded. Humphry Davy had achieved an extraordinary popular following at the Royal Institution, making Albemarle Street notorious for its traffic jams. The first of his great Bakerian lectures also began at the Royal Society in November 1806. Indeed it was Davy, with his passionate belief in Coleridge's potential as a public educator, who now sought him out and introduced him to Thomas Bernard, the Committee Member and secretary of the Royal Institution, who was commissioning lecture series on a wide range of arts and science subjects.

As Coleridge informed his wife on 3 October: "Davy has been for many days urging me, with an eagerness and importunity not common to him, to go with him to Mr Bernard's at Roehampton . . . the business is really important."[17] Davy, backed by Stuart, would persist with his encouragement for the whole of the next year, finally bringing Coleridge to the lecture dais in the winter of 1807–8. From then on, public lectures would provide Coleridge with an income, and sometimes even a *raison d'être*, for more than a decade. Indeed it was lecturing, and the sense of a continuing audience, that may partly have saved Coleridge's life in the dark years to come.

4

Coleridge's last weeks before the dreaded marital confrontation at Keswick were not entirely spent in prevarication. Sara's wayward brother, young George Fricker, had turned to Methodism in a crisis of nerves and unemployment after his disastrous adventures at sea. Coleridge introduced him to the kindly Lambs, and wrote him long soothing letters about his faith, and had many patient talks with him. Coleridge was at his best and most tender with lost young men of this kind (as he had shown years before with Hazlitt). He opened his own heart with directness and sympathy. "I am far from surprised that, having seen what you have seen, and suffered what you have suffered, you should have opened your soul to a sense of our fallen nature; and the incapability of man to heal himself. My opinions may not be in all points the same as yours; but I have experienced a similar alteration."

His Mediterranean journeys had forced him to "look into himself" in a new way. "Ill health, and disappointment in the only deep wish I ever cherished" had led him to reread the New Testament in a new light. He felt that the proof of God from the design of the natural world, as argued by Paley and other eighteenth-century theologians, was producing "infidels" in the new mechanistic culture. Thinking men needed habitually "to look into their own souls, instead of always looking out, both of themselves and of their nature".[18]

He discussed the Trinitarian view of Christianity, but felt that his own "living Faith" was still uncertain on such questions. "Alas! my moral being is too untranquil, too deeply possessed by one lingering passion after earthly good withheld . . . to be capable of being that, which its own 'still small voice' tells me, even in my dreams, that it ought to be . . ."[19]

His grief over his marriage, and his impossible love for Asra, is evidently referred to in these asides; as well as his guilt over opium. Philosophically it marked the continuation of a long path of religious self-enquiry which would culminate in the *Aids to Reflection* twenty years later. George Fricker responded by joining in the search for his sea-box at Wapping.

The time was also used to renew his contacts with Thomas Clarkson, the evangelical who was writing a history of the slave trade. This, too, produced some striking reflections on religious matters. When Coleridge finally set out for Keswick, he immediately broke his journey at Clarkson's house at Bury St Edmund's, and wrote for Clarkson a brilliant 3,000-word essay on the nature of theological belief. Clarkson had set him three fundamental questions: what is God? what is the Soul? and what is the difference between Kantian higher "Reason" (*Vernunft*) and logical, scientific thought or "Understanding" (*Verstandt*)?

Once again, he argued against mechanistic conceptions. God must be considered as a Platonic idea, "the Archetype" of all living things, expressed in a personal trinity whose presence had direct impact on each individual. Otherwise, "God becomes a mere power in darkness, even as Gravitation, and instead of a moral Religion of practical Influence we shall have only a physical Theory to gratify ideal curiosity." Similarly, the soul must be conceived not as a mechanistic entity, but as a progression "of reflex consciousness" arising through the hierarchy of Nature.

This idea, clearly developed from his reading in Schelling, would profoundly affect Coleridge's later grapplings with the scientific theory of evolution. The human soul differed from all other levels of animal consciousness, first by its ability to reflect upon itself, thereby producing a "continuous" moral conscience; but second by its power to be "modified" by other human beings and to move towards some greater unity or spiritual identity. This ultimately mystical idea could be seen as an intensification of his earlier poetic conception of "the One Life", so beautifully set out in his Conversation Poems and his letters to Sotheby of 1802. It is a vivid mixture of his old Pantheism, now combined with the traditional Christian doctrine of spiritual unity in the body of Christ.

Coleridge formulated this in a strikingly untheological way. "A male & female Tiger is neither more or less whether you suppose them only existing in their appropriate wilderness, or whether you suppose a thousand Pairs. But man is truly altered by the co-existence of other men; his faculties cannot be developed in himself alone, & only himself. Therefore the human race not by a bold metaphor, but in sublime reality, approach to, & might become, one body whose Head is Christ (the Logos)".[20] In anthropological language, "the whole Species is capable of being regarded as one Individual".*

The essay contained much else, speculative and self-questioning. It was not least remarkable for demonstrating Coleridge's ability to withdraw into his cave of metaphysics with Olympian calm at the very moment when the crisis of his marriage pressed upon him. Perhaps the image of paired tigers alone betrayed his worldly terrors.

During Coleridge's absence in Malta, Clarkson had published his *Portraiture of Quakerism*, and resumed his campaigning work on the Abolition Committee which sponsored a series of successful bills against the slave trade in 1805–6 championed by Wilberforce. His wife Catherine had become intimate with Dorothy Wordsworth, and now Coleridge also opened his heart to Catherine, remaining with her at Bury St Edmund's for nearly a week. One result of this stop-over was that Catherine and Dorothy now began a confidential

---

* This whole passage points towards Wittgenstein's famous aside that "if a lion could talk, we could not understand him". (*Philosophical Investigations*, 1953, p. 223.) Coleridge believed that the human language-world depends upon an entire structure of perceptions, which is generated by human social experience and ultimately by religious beliefs. So language, like the soul, was a unique form of unifying human consciousness and collectivity which animals could not share. In what sense it had "evolved" from Nature, or was a gift of God ("the Logos"), or perhaps both, constantly shifted in Coleridge's thinking and was often expressed differently in his poetry and his philosophic prose. On the whole he wsa most orthodox in his letters of consolation to others, as here; and most speculative in his private Notebooks. (See Mary Anne Perkins, *Coleridge's Philosophy: The Logos as Unifying Principle*, 1994.)

correspondence about Coleridge's health and marriage which provided an inexhaustible topic for gossip over the next four years.

Coleridge's anxieties did not preclude a flying visit to the Newmarket races, where he was particularly struck by the mahogany-topped dicing tables, deeply indented by the circular heels of dice-boxes banged down by the players in their excitement or disappointment, so that the imprinted table-tops were "truly a written History of the fiendish Passions of Gambling".[21] Another expedition took him to Cambridge, the first return since undergraduate days twelve years previously, where the young men all looked just the same in the university pubs and "the only alteration" was in himself. He dropped into Trinity College library, where he found his old Professor of Greek, Richard Porson, who failed to recognize him, though this could have been because Porson was in a "pitiable State" of drunkenness. These visions of excess were not reassuring, and he wondered gloomily what impression he himself would make at Keswick under the penetrating gaze of Southey and Mrs Coleridge.

5

On 26 October he finally committed himself to the Carlisle stagecoach. But on the way he formed a plan to find Sara Hutchinson where she was staying at Penrith, before going on to his family at Greta Hall. His legs and face swelled during the journey, as he blanketed himself in opium and brandy. At Penrith, he found that Wordsworth had forestalled him. Sara had left half an hour previously with the whole Grasmere household, who had at last set out for their winter stay at Coleorton. They were now stopping over with friends at Kendal. Notes flew between Penrith and Kendal, Coleridge refusing to go on, and the Wordsworths refusing to go back, hampered by their trunks and three small children. It was a chaotic reunion. In the end Coleridge appeared at Kendal at seven in the evening, but took rooms at an inn in a curious gesture of independence, bidding William to join him for supper. Of course they all came hurrying round at once.

They had been apart for nearly three years. Coleridge the Romantic traveller, Coleridge the imagined confidant of the *Prelude*, Coleridge the tragic exile, had grown to mythical proportions in their minds. But it was far from the emotional reunion they had all imagined. He was physically unrecognizable: pallid, overweight, ill at ease, his mind still drifting somewhere in the Mediterranean.

It was Dorothy who recorded their dismay at the strange, distracted wanderer whom they found in place of their old, long-lost friend. She wrote to Mrs Clarkson: "We all went thither to him and never did I feel such a shock as the first in sight of him. We all felt in the same way . . . He is utterly changed; and yet sometimes, when he was in animated conversation concerning things removed from him, I saw something of his former self. But never when we were alone with him. He then scarcely ever spoke of anything that concerned him, or us, or our common friends nearly, except we forced him to it; and immediately he changed the conversation to Malta, Sir Alexander Ball, the corruptions of government, anything but what we were yearning after . . . that he is ill I am well assured, and must sink if he does not grow more happy." Only once or twice did Dorothy catch a shadow, a transitory gleam, of that "divine expression of his countenance" they all remembered.[22]

They remained with him from Sunday evening till Tuesday morning; "his misery has made him so weak". They supported his plan to separate from Mrs Coleridge, though fearing he would never have the resolution to go through with it. Wordsworth criticized the London lecture scheme, and offered instead to cancel the whole Coleorton plan and rent a large house near Hawkshead so they could all winter together again in the Lakes. Coleridge in turn rejected this, as compromising all hope of financial independence. Finally Wordsworth sent his whole party on to Leicestershire, and remained behind for a third night at the inn alone with Coleridge.

Alone, that is, except for Sara Hutchinson, who also stayed behind unchaperoned with the two men. This was an unconventional move, with some risk of scandal. There is no record of what the three of them discussed or decided on that momentous night of 29 October 1806 at Kendal, but it was to affect Coleridge's life for the next four years. One immediate result was that, despite all his resolutions and reflections in Italy, Coleridge found that he was still desperately in love with Asra, and he believed the feeling was reciprocated.

He later entered in his Notebook what was perhaps his most open declaration of love for Asra; and not merely love, but undeniable sexual passion: "I know, you love me! – My reason knows it, my heart feels it; yet still let your eyes, your hands tell me; still say,

O often & often say, 'My Beloved! I love you'; indeed I love you: for why should not my ears, and all my outward Being share in the Joy – the fuller my inner Being is of the sense, the more my outward organs yearn & crave for it. O bring my whole nature into balance and harmony."[23]

Wordsworth's role as friend and confidant, and go-between with Asra, is not entirely easy to understand. His private letters (as well as Dorothy's) certainly show that he believed Coleridge's marriage was already wrecked, and that he alone could provide the stable household that could bring Coleridge's drinking and opium-taking under control. "If anything good is to be done for him, it must be done by me."[24] But he also wanted Coleridge's help and advice with *The Prelude*, and perhaps unconsciously did everything he could to forestall Coleridge's embarking on a new literary career in London.

Sara Hutchinson thus became crucial to the future life Wordsworth envisioned for Coleridge, as the one woman, besides his own sister Dorothy, who could respond to Coleridge's emotional needs. But was Wordsworth prepared for Sara to become Coleridge's mistress under his own roof at Coleorton? Or did he believe that Sara herself really wished this? It is very hard to tell. Certainly Coleridge himself would soon be agonizing over his friend's ambiguity in these matters.

Sara Hutchinson's own feelings remain as mysterious as ever, though there are some clues. She would write to Coleridge from Coleorton, but these letters have all been destroyed. She evidently shared Dorothy's sense of shock at Coleridge's physical appearance and emotional disarray. It seems that she was still deeply attached to him, admired him, and wished to help him as far as possible. But it would gradually emerge that his physical passion was not requited. During Coleridge's long absence in the Mediterranean, she had settled into an increasingly domestic role in Wordsworth's household, caring for the Wordsworth children, and sharing with Dorothy the arduous role of Wordsworth's secretary and amanuensis. As Coleridge would soon discover, she had become less of a free spirit and more of a universal aunt, relied on for her wit and practicality, and dedicated to Wordsworth himself. The death of John Wordsworth had not freed her as Coleridge supposed, but drawn her more tightly into the family circle. His "Moorish maid" – like his Abyssinian maid – had disappeared.

Perhaps they all felt, in their genuine anxiety to help their old friend, that they could "manage" his passion as they could manage his brandy-drinking and opium-taking. This at any rate was what Dorothy seemed to imply in a long, circumspect letter to Lady Beaumont, describing in great detail the breakdown of his health and his marriage: "if he is not inclined to manage himself, we can manage him . . ."[25] The repeated emphasis on "managing" did not bode well. Yet all agreed that the great object was to get Coleridge safely to Coleorton, and it was with this promise that Wordsworth and Asra continued south, and Coleridge turned his face, if not his heart, towards Keswick again.

6

Coleridge arrived at Greta Hall on 30 October 1806. He had been away for very nearly three years, but the children at least – Hartley, Derwent and little Sara – greeted him with raptures. Derwent, then six, remembered years later the excitement, and how he had surrendered his pillow to make his father's bed comfortable: "I would lie on a straw for my father".[26] Sara Coleridge seemed welcoming, and bustled around him as though he were an invalid. Southey greeted him with cordiality, but very much as the master of the house. For a few days there was something like harmony, and long talks about his adventures in the Mediterranean. But the moment Coleridge raised the question of separation, all the old antagonisms burst out, and for night after night there were scenes of "outrageous passions", exactly as Coleridge had feared, and indeed as he must have expected.

During the day he walked uneasily with Southey, and sank himself in the works of Fulke Greville, upon which he made copious notes. In the evenings he returned to the fray, and then made himself incoherent with opium. He felt exposed in all his "human weakness", but convinced that his wife felt nothing for him and only feared the social scandal of a divorce. She was motivated by "mere selfish desire to have a rank in life". He wrote bitterly to the Wordsworths of Sara's "temper, and selfishness, her manifest dislike of me (as far as her nature is capable of a positive feeling) and her self-encouraged admiration of Southey as a vindictive feeling in which she delights herself as satirizing me etc. etc . . ."[27]

There was much in this that exposed Coleridge's own guilt and sense of inadequacy as a husband, especially with the ever-present example of his brother-in-law's shining virtues. Southey's literary career was driving ahead, a popular poet, a respected reviewer (soon to be thundering from the *Quarterly Review*), an acknowledged expert on Spain and Portugal who was embarking on his massive *History of Brazil*. Mrs Coleridge's admiration for Southey went back to her early Bristol days: he was prompt, hard-working, self-disciplined and reliable, where Coleridge was merely brilliant, erratic and now increasingly self-destructive. Nothing seemed to be gained by the long Mediterranean absence. To be rejected by such a man, after those long months of holding his household together, must have seemed a terrible humiliation and betrayal. Little wonder that she fought him, made scenes, and appealed to Southey.

Southey tried to appear the voice of reason. He upbraided Coleridge for his submission to the Wordsworths, yet he counselled Sara that a separation on proper terms was advisable. But underneath his moderation lay the old, self-righteous scorn that reduced Coleridge and all his difficulties to a mere monster of self-indulgence. Gossiping to his friend John Rickman of the affair, with cruel indiscretion, he seemed to take perverse delight in the whole, sad business. "The separation is a good thing – his habits are so murderous of all domestic comfort that I am only surprised Mrs C. is not rejoiced at being rid of him. He besots himself with opium, or with spirits, till his eyes look like a Turks who is half reduced to idiotcy by the practice – he calls up the servants at all hours of the night to prepare food for him – he does in short all things at all times except the proper time – does nothing that he ought to do, and everything which he ought not.

"His present scheme is to live with Wordsworth – it is from idolatry of that family that this had begun – they have always humoured him in all his follies, listened to his complaints of his wife, and when he complained of his itch, helped him to scratch, instead of covering him with brimstone ointment, and shutting him up by himself."[28]

Despite everything that Southey implied, Coleridge in fact brought the situation round with remarkable swiftness. Within a fortnight he entered in his notebook: "Keswick, finally resolved, Wednesday 15 November 1806."[29] What almost certainly transformed the position was his fondness for the children, and his determination to care for them and Sara financially. The Wedgwood annuity of £150 would remain with her; he would contribute what he could to the boys' education; Hartley would go with him to Coleorton, but Derwent and little Sara ("sweet Squirrel") could stay at Greta Hall, until they all met up together again in the spring in London.

This last provision caused Coleridge particular heart-searching as he wrote to the Wordsworths: "If I go away without them [Hartley and Derwent] I am a Bird who has struggled himself from off a Bird-lime twig, & then finds a string round his leg pulling him back . . ."[30] But he acquiesced, and hoped for the best. In his study, he opened the sash window where his old Aeolian harp lay, and at once let in "music and sweet air" that seemed to purify and delight the whole room. At night he sat with his candle, watching how the "amber-edged" inner flame seemed to combine with the blue outer one, which made him think of his love for Asra.[31]

Instead of preparing his Royal Institution lectures, Coleridge began teaching Hartley Greek. He started to compile a Greek grammar, dedicated to his son, on 4 November 1806, which eventually ran to ninety-three pages in a special leather-bound notebook. It ranged from simple, humorous mnemonics to a philosophical defence of grammar itself, as teaching "Habits of attention, and the power of self-control".[32] There are amusing notes on poetic metre, and some curious sequences of vocabulary for learning, including this list of fifth-declension nouns: "Rook – Dewdrop – Lyre – Lynx – Furrow – Flesh – Starling – Wife – Liver – Louse – Sky – Saviour – Heart – Witness – Water."[33] Later he turned the metrical notes into a poem, which he also sent to Derwent from Coleorton. It ended:

Could you stand upon Skiddaw, you would not from its whole Ridge
See a man who so loves you, as your fond S.T. Coleridge.[34]

This could perhaps be described as a galloping anapaest, momentarily hobbled by a little spondee.

He remained at Greta Hall for a further month, still coping with delayed-fuse explosions from his wife, and coming out in a sympathetic crop of boils. He was exhausted. But he still managed to leave with Hartley in time for Christmas at Coleorton. Hartley, now ten years old, would later recall this as the start of an "annus mirabilis" with his father.[35]

7

Coleridge and Hartley arrived at Coleorton on 22 December, where they were greeted with "an uproar of sincere Joy". Hartley's parting from his mother had passed off easily: "he behaved very well indeed", but on the coach south he suddenly disappeared at the coaching inn outside Derby while the horses were being changed. He was finally found by his frantic father, standing by the margin of a nearby river, a small solitary figure looking down into the swiftly flowing waters. This piece of "field-truantry", a disquieting echo of Coleridge's own boyhood disappearance by the river Otter, was explained as his "hatred of confinement".

Coleridge found him "a very good, and sweet child", yet also strange and fantastical. He had invented an entire imaginary world called "Ejuxria", to which he flew on the back of a "great bird" borrowed from the Arabian Nights. Tiny for his age, brilliantly clever at his lessons, and mischievous at play, he caused chaos among the three Wordsworth children, with pixyish freaks and ingenious make-believe. Coleridge adored him, though he worried about his fibs and "sophisim", his indiscipline, and his "logical false-dice in the game of Excuses".

But in trying to reassure his wife of how well Hartley was being looked after, Coleridge made an extravagantly tactless reference to Sara Hutchinson's good influence. To Hartley's mother it can only have appeared deliberately wounding. "All here love him most dearly: and your name sake takes upon her all the duties of his Mother & darling Friend, with all the Mother's love and fondness. He is very fond of her." If this was not vindictiveness, it was certainly wishful thinking: for Sara Hutchinson was the one member of the Wordsworth household whom Hartley never liked. Like his son, Coleridge could live in imaginary worlds.[36]

The descent of Coleridge *père et fils* on the tranquil Coleorton household was magnificently disruptive. Hitherto the worst they had had to suffer was whooping cough among the children, and rainstorms cutting off the road to Ashby de la Zouche. The Beaumonts' vast estate, perched on the edge of Charnwood Forest, was being rebuilt from the profits of the local coalmines which criss-crossed the villages to the south. Coleorton Hall itself, secluded on an eminence amidst trees, was being redesigned in the gothic style by the architect George Dance the Younger, with polygonal turrets and medieval fluted windows, like a stage-set for the unfinished "Christabel". There was a family chapel, and extensive eighteenth-century grounds, part of which Wordsworth was helping to redesign as a winter garden on picturesque principles with cedar trees, holly-groves and bucolic monuments. (When the painters Haydon and Wilkie visited two years later, they found a cenotaph to Sir Joshua Reynolds at the end of one tree-lined alley, a bust of Wordsworth at another, and various stone seats and arbors carved with Wordsworthian couplets at each vantage point.)[37]

As the Hall itself was full of workmen, the Wordsworths were quartered in Coleorton Farm, ten minutes' walk across the fields to the west, a "roomy", comfortable, rambling old building with beamed ceilings and large fireplaces, offering fine views to Ashby and Coleorton village. "The sitting room," enthused Dorothy, "where by the fireside we have seen some glorious sunsets, we far more than like – we already love it." The Hall and its mysterious turrets looked "exceedingly well by moonlight".[38]

Both Coleridge and Wordsworth had writing-rooms, but some doubling-up was required: the children shared a nursery, Wordsworth slept with Mary, Dorothy with Sara Hutchinson, and Coleridge with Hartley, who was still frightened of the dark. Coleridge recalled touchingly how Hartley used to hug him in his sleep, "between sleeping and waking", and talk endlessly of Derwent and little Sara "before his eyes are fully open in the morning, and while he is closing them at Night".[39]

Despite the Greek lessons, pursued each day, paternal discipline was not very strict. To Dorothy, the boy appeared a "restless, whirling, self-sufficing creature" and they had trouble keeping him "silent and still" in the sitting-room. Like his father, he was perfectly undomesticated: "he is absolutely in a dream when you tell him to do the simplest things – his Books, his Slate, his Pencils, he drops them just where he finds them no longer useful." Yet his sweet temper made her forgive him everything.

Similarly Coleridge needed much organizing, especially at mealtimes (which he often missed) and at night when he went rambling or drinking at the local taverns or stayed up till dawn. She thought he had almost completely cut out his brandy, but there was "some danger in the strong beer" which he found in the nearby inns at Ashby and Thringston village. There is no overt mention of opium, but of course he was still taking it: "Stimulants to keep him in spirits while he is talking", as she tactfully put it to Lady Beaumont.[40]

The atmosphere at Coleorton Farm was very strange throughout the winter. Outwardly, the three women were running a thoroughly domestic household, largely dominated by the children: Mary was weaning little Tom, Dorothy was managing cooking and laundry, Asra was schooling and copying manuscripts. But the two men were engaged in a subliminal battle of wills of extraordinary intensity. It involved not only the whole question of their future careers and poetical precedence, but also Coleridge's drinking and opium-taking, and what were clearly disputed claims on Asra's affections.

For Wordsworth, Coleridge's return to their ancient comradeship meant that the *Prelude* could now be worked over in great detail. A grand formal reading in the sitting-room at Coleorton was planned for the New Year. For Coleridge there was the pressing matter of the London lectures. But Wordsworth finally persuaded him to postpone them, after a long discussion over Christmas. He thought him in too "dreamy and miserable state of mind" to undertake any regular work, and better off at Coleorton where they could "manage" him and keep him from the temptations of brandy and company.[41] There was still the plan for the Mediterranean travel book – "not *formal* Travels, but certain remarks and reflections which suggested themselves to him during his residence abroad".[42] But any immediate chance of financial income in the spring, as Coleridge had promised his wife, was thereby abandoned. This led on to talks about Coleridge's separation, in which Asra was again closely involved.

There were long rambles through the estate woodlands together, and an all-day expedition to visit Grace Dieu Abbey, a romantic ruin (once the home of the Jacobean dramatist Francis Beaumont) beneath the lowering crags of Charnwood Forest. Asra rode there on a little ass, which the men took turns to lead "over the dirty places".[43] All this time Coleridge seems to have been tortured by his feelings for Asra. Perhaps he was remembering that strange vow of sexual fidelity he had made at the bedside of Cecilia Bertozzi, the siren of Syracuse, two years before. His Notebook entries show the terrible contradiction of his emotions, which he could not express to her. "I should feel myself as much as fallen and unworthy of her Love in any tumult of Body indulged towards her, as if I had roamed (like a Hog) in the rankest Lanes of a (prostitute) city . . ." Yet at the same time he felt this love heaving within him, "like a Volcano beneath a sea always burning, tho' in silence . . ."[44]

8

It is very difficult to reconstruct what followed. Two days after Christmas, early in the morning, there was some sort of confrontation between him and Asra and Wordsworth. (Possibly Coleridge had been up all night, and gone into her room, but this is speculation.) Coleridge seems to have run out across the fields to the local inn, the Queen's Head, in a mood of despair and started drinking the "strong ale" that Dorothy had feared. He stayed alone at the inn most of the morning, drinking and writing in his Notebook. At the inn, Coleridge emblazoned into his Notebook, in huge, drunken capital letters, two portentous words, "THE EPOCH", followed by three pages of frantic scrawl. Later he tore out all these pages, leaving only the Delphic explanation: "Saturday, 27th December, 1806 – Queen's Head, Stringston, ½ a mile from Coleorton Church, 50 minutes after 10."[45]*

Though he destroyed his original Notebook entry, Coleridge reverted quite explicitly to this moment of confrontation in a series of painful subsequent notes. In September 1807 he wrote: "O agony! O the vision of that Saturday morning – of the Bed – O cruel! is he not beloved, adored by two – & two such Beings. – And must

* Coleridge often dated and located his most important entries in this very precise way. The phrase "half a mile from Coleorton Church" also curiously resembles the way he located the composition of "Kubla Khan", which was written at the farmhouse "a quarter of a mile from Culbone Church". He frequently visited Coleorton and Ashby churchyards, and copied down the tomb inscriptions there. One includes this verse on the death of a child: "The Babe was sucking at the Breast,/When God did call him to his Rest." On this particular morning of emotional revelation he may have gone to the churchyard first, and then hurried on over the fields to the Queen's Head inn to write in his Notebook. Dorothy later noted his habit of disappearing into "pot houses" when upset, at Penrith in 1809–10.

I not be beloved *near* him except as a Satellite? – But O mercy, mercy! is he not better, greater, more *manly*, & altogether more attractive to any but the purest Woman? And yet . . . he does not pretend, he does not wish, to love you as I love you, Sara!"[46]

Again, in May 1808, he broke out: "O that miserable Saturday morning! The thunder-cloud had long been gathering, and I had now been gazing, and now averting my eyes, from it, with anxious fears, of which I scarcely dared be conscious . . . But a minute and a half with ME and all the time evidently *restless & going* – An hour and more with Wordsworth – [in Greek code] *in bed* – O agony!"[47] Several of the poems he wrote at Coleorton over the next three months all touch, more or less obliquely, on this sense of Wordsworth's and Asra's devastating betrayal.

Was this "vision" of Wordsworth and Asra in bed together real then? Or was it part of some drunken, jealous delusion? Coleridge himself never seemed to be quite sure. Years later, he would be able to explain it away as a "horrid phantasm" on his part, and "intellectually" reject any idea of an actual sexual relationship between the two. Yet the bed scene itself, so repeatedly described, seems difficult to dismiss.

Coleridge himself had once cuddled with Asra and Mary on the sofa at Gallow Hill, and this form of tenderness was once current, almost indiscriminately, in their shared household. One might almost suspect Asra of still teasing and flirting with her two poets, perhaps unconscious of the perils of what she was doing. For Wordsworth, so confident in his emotional life, this offered no threat and might even be a way of asserting his power – not merely over Asra, but also over Coleridge. Asra, one might conclude, was as a patriarchal gift that he might bestow or withhold.

If this seems extravagant, it was nonetheless very much what Coleridge feared in his worst moments, especially when in the grip of opium or drink. His love for Asra was not weakened, as events showed; but his jealousy of Wordsworth – still his greatest friend – was much intensified. He feared Wordsworth's power over her, and that she would "learn from W. – to pity & withdraw herself from my affections".[48]

Years later, he was still brooding on that "dreadful Saturday Morning, at Coleorton". By then he saw more clearly the true psychological nature of the drama enacted. "Did I *believe* it? Did I not even *know*, that it *was* not so, *could* not be so? . . . Yes! Yes! I *knew* the horrid phantasm to be a mere phantasm and yet what anguish, what gnawings of despair, what throbbings and lancinations of positive Jealousy! – even to this day the undying worm of distempered sleep or morbid Day-Dreams."[49] Yet despite this rationalization, Coleridge would still recall more than a decade later (and still in Greek code) Asra's "beautiful breasts uncovered" that morning at Coleorton farmhouse.[50]

9

Even harder to understand, normal life seems to have continued at Coleorton. The following Sunday, 2 January 1807, Wordsworth began his planned reading from the thirteen books of *The Prelude*. Each evening after supper, Coleridge and the three women gathered solemnly round him in the firelit parlour. His deep, Cumbrian voice filled the room, and swept them into the mighty vision of his own life, hour after hour. The readings continued over several nights. As Coleridge sat there he was overwhelmed by the conviction that his friend had completed a masterpiece. He viewed him "with steadfast eye . . . in the choir of ever-enduring men".

Immediately after the last reading, Coleridge went to his study and spent most of the night drafting a reply, what is in effect the last of the Conversation Poems, "To William Wordsworth". There is not a word of doubt, not a hint of reproach. It is a poem of unstinting affirmation and praise, and the most passionate celebration of their friendship which Coleridge ever put into words. But at the same time it is a lament for his own failures, his sense of lost genius, characteristically orchestrated in images of such striking energy and beauty that they demonstrate the opposite: that his genius was still very much alive, despite everything.

> Comfort from thee, and utterance of thy love
> Came with such heights and depth of harmony,
> Such sense of wings uplifting, that the storm
> Scattered and whirl'd me, till my thoughts became
> A bodily tumult . . .
> Keen pangs of Love, awakening as a babe
> Turbulent, with an outcry in the heart . . .

In silence listening, like a devout child,
My soul lay passive, by thy various strain
Driven as in surges now beneath the stars,
With momentary stars of my own birth,
Fair constellated foam, still darting off
Into the darkness; now a tranquil sea,
Outspread and bright, yet swelling to the moon.[51]

In these contrasted metaphors of passivity and power, of childlike submission and elemental force, Coleridge defined some essential paradox in his relations with Wordsworth. The poem also celebrated the "dear tranquil time" of their evenings together, and the "sweet sense of Home" he had found at Coleorton, in that "happy vision of beloved faces" sitting round the room. Yet it ends, unlike the previous Conversation Poems so long ago in the Quantocks, with a movement of withdrawal into himself, the feeling of spiritual struggles yet to come.

And when O Friend! my comforter and guide!
Strong in thyself, and powerful to give strength! –
Thy long sustained Song finally closed,
And thy deep voice had ceased – yet thou thyself
Wert still before my eyes, and round us both
That happy vision of beloved faces –
Scarce conscious, and yet conscious of its close
I sate, my being blended in one thought
(Thought was it? or aspiration? or resolve?)
Absorbed, yet hanging still upon the sound –
And when I rose, I found myself in prayer.[52]

Neither Wordsworth nor Dorothy left any record of their reactions to Coleridge's poem, though four years later Wordsworth would try to prevent its publication. What made him uneasy was not Coleridge's praise, but the extremely emotional nature of Coleridge's description of their friendship. Rightly, perhaps, he felt that it left him vulnerable. Coleridge himself had no such qualms, regarding it as leaving a great deal unsaid, as his Notebooks would show.

But Wordsworth did measure the transformation that was coming over their friendship in a short, cruelly effective, lyric entitled "A

Complaint". In it, he uses the image of the fountain of love, which Coleridge had originally addressed to Asra in his sonnet of 1804. But now it is the love directed towards Wordsworth which is in question.

> There is a change – and I am poor;
> Your Love hath been, nor long ago,
> A Fountain at my fond Heart's Door,
> Whose only business was to flow . . .
> Now for this consecrated Fount
> Of murmuring, sparkling, living Love,
> What have I? Shall I dare to tell?
> A comfortless and hidden WELL.[53]

Wordsworth did not hesitate to publish his poem only four months later. Indeed this was a highly productive time for him at Coleorton, during which he prepared the most important collection of his lifetime, the *Poems in Two Volumes*, issued by Longman in May 1807. Coleridge encouraged him with this, also writing detailed notes and editorial suggestions for Book VI of *The Prelude*, and stiffening Wordsworth's resolve against anticipated criticism. When he received destructive reviews later in the summer, Wordsworth was able to write with lofty confidence to Lady Beaumont: "never forget what I believe was observed to you by Coleridge, that every great and original writer, in proportion as he is great or original, must himself create the taste by which he is to be relished. My flesh is as insensible as iron to these petty stings."[54]

But Coleridge, driven by opium and unhappiness, was as sensitive as water. "If I appear *little* (fretful and sullen concerning Trifles)," he confided to his Notebook, "O! consider Asra that this is only, because my intense Love makes even Trifles that relate to Wordsworth (= the Tree that fixes its root even deeper than the grave) so great to me, that Wealth & Reputation, become trifles compared to it."[55]

In a series of short poems written during January and February, most of them not published until after his death, Coleridge agonized over his feelings for Wordsworth and Asra, which were now inextricably involved. One, composed in Latin, "Ad Vilmum Axilogum", asked bitterly why Wordsworth should command him to endure Asra's neglect. "Why do you not also command me, William, to suffer my bowels to be pierced with a sword and then to pretend that it does not hurt?"[56]

In another, "The Tropic Tree", he appears to use the image of Wordsworth as the rooted tree by a river bank to summon up some nameless act of submission and worship:

As some vast Tropic tree, itself a wood,
That crests its head with clouds, beneath the flood
Feeds its deep roots, and with the bulging flank
Of its wide base controls the fronting bank –
(By the slant current's pressure scoop'd away
The fronting bank becomes a foam-piled bay)
High in the Fork the uncouth Idol knits
His channel'd brow; low murmurs stir by fits
And dark below the horrid Faquir sits . . .[57]

But there were also several pure love-lyrics to Asra, which suggest moments of great tenderness and intimacy in the gardens at Coleorton. One, "An Angel Visitant", describes them sitting together within the "circling hollies woodbine-clad" on the estate. Another, "You mould my Hopes", evokes her as the "love-throb" in his heart and the revivifying light of dawn. In these poems he "blessed" the destiny that had made him fall in love with her.[58]

. . . You lie in all my thoughts like Light,
Like the fair Light of Dawn, or summer Eve,
On rippling stream, or cloud-reflecting lake;
And looking to the Heaven that bends above you,
How oft! I bless the lot that made me love you.[59]

Listening to the hesitant birdsong of early spring, he found an image for these precious fragments of poetry.

The spruce and limber Yellow Hammer
In dawn of Spring, in the sultry Summer,
In hedge, or tree his hours beguiling
With notes, as of one that Brass is filing.[60]

When snow fell in mid-February he stood by the gate on the

Ashby road, looking back at Coleorton Farm, and noted the icicles in the hedge, "the cavernlets of Snow", and the marks of the wind like "eagle's claws" brushed across the white fields. "Can even the Eagle soar without Wings? And the wings given by thee to my soul – what are they, but the Love and Society of that Beloved?" In a long meditation on Asra's power to inspire his work, as he hoped, he summoned up a memory from his West Country days, to produce a beautiful image of psycho-sexual potency. "I have, like the Exeter Cathedral Organ, a pipe of far-sounding Music in its construction, yet it is dumb, a gilded Tube, till the Sister pipe be placed in correspondence. O Beloved! Beloved! – ah! what are Words but air? & impulses of air?"[61]

At night, he fell asleep dreaming of Asra; or sometimes went out to wander through the moonlit grounds, to look back at her window. On one occasion, plunging into the pitch blackness under some low trees, a "sudden flash of Light darted down as it were, upon the path close before me, with such rapid and indescribable effect, that my whole life seem snatched away from me". For a moment it seemed as if the moon itself had struck him "a Violent Blow" of admonition. But glancing up he found it was caused by "some very large Bird, who, scared by my noise, had suddenly flown upwards, and by the spring of his feet or body had driven down the branch on which he was a-perch," so letting in the terrifying semaphore of admonitory light.[62]

10

To the outside world, the old Lake District circle had re-established itself and Coleridge was being successfully "managed". Dorothy wrote at length to Mrs Clarkson of country walks and fireside study. Wordsworth wrote meticulous pages of horticultural advice to Sir George Beaumont. Even Coleridge wrote to Southey: "I am considerably better in health; and as one proof of it, have written between 4 and 500 verses, since I have been here; besides going on with my Travels. I felt as a man revisited by a familiar Spirit the first morning, that I felt that sort of stirring warmth about the Heart, which is with me the robe of incarnation of my genius, such as it is."[63] But much of this, like the number of Coleridge's verses, was an illusion.

With his plans for the London lectures still suspended, and the future of his children unclear, Coleridge cast around for some new shape to his life. Believing that Southey intended to leave Greta Hall, he wrote to his wife asking if she too intended to return to Bristol, only to receive a "frantic" reply that no such move could be contemplated. Dorothy was "called up stairs" to read this letter, and was secretly relieved that the idea of them all moving back together to Keswick was now "out of the question". But she realized that Mrs Coleridge had still not really accepted the separation: "as to poor Mrs Coleridge, I cannot but pity her, because she does suffer; though I feel and know that wounded pride and the world's remarks, are all that give her pain."[64]

Some time in March Coleridge received "a most affectionate Letter" from his brother George at Ottery, who had heard of his Italian adventures from young Russell. George knew nothing of the separation, and hearing of Coleridge's residence at Sir George's country estate, assumed his brother was now living well and happily with a wealthy patron. George himself was in grave difficulties with the Ottery school, and now wondered if Coleridge could come down to help him the following summer. This letter was to be the cause of much misunderstanding and bitterness subsequently within the family.

As Coleridge recalled, George wrote of himself as "distressed by the desertion of my Brother Edward with regard to his School – & dwelt on the hope & idea of my coming to him & being an aid & comfort to him in such affecting language that I was exceedingly moved – being at that time very unhappy at Coleorton from causes, I cannot mention, after a thousand painful struggles I wrote to him to say, that I would come & should be happy to assist him for any number of months that might be of service to his Health."[65]

This letter was sent on 2 April 1807, after long discussions with Wordsworth. Coleridge believed that he and his brother could take on "50 scholars at 50 guineas a year", and that Hartley and Derwent could now be educated at the Ottery school.[66] It was not an unreasonable plan, though it suggests how low Coleridge's professional expectations had fallen at Coleorton. He was now prepared to "strike root in my native place", working as a simple country schoolmaster, and "pour his whole Heart" into George. But Coleridge also felt he must first explain his own domestic situation to George: "I could not bear to come into his presence and bring my wife with me, with such a load of concealment on my heart." Accordingly, he described the "Trial" of his marriage, and how despite Mrs Coleridge's "many excellent qualities, of strict modesty, attention to her children, and economy", it was now "wholly incompatible with an endurable life".[67]

He also wished George to help smooth the parting from his wife, by receiving them all on a family visit in the early summer. "Mrs Coleridge wishes – & very naturally – to accompany me in to Devonshire that our separation may appear free from all shadow of suspicion of any other cause than that of unfitness and unconquerable difference of Temper." He added that the resolution to settle himself so far from the Wordsworths had occasioned "one of the two or three very severe struggles of my life".[68]

But Coleridge's fraternal letter contained some notable omissions. He did not mention that he was virtually penniless. He dropped no hint of ill-health, or opium; let alone Sara Hutchinson. Nor did he explain that on his instructions Mrs Coleridge, with Derwent and little Sara, were immediately setting out from Keswick for Bristol, on the assumption that George would acquiesce to this scheme.

In the event, George was nervous of the potential scandal of this new situation, and loath to compound his own family difficulties, abruptly changed his mind, and on 6 April wrote a confused and painful letter of refusal. But this was sent, on Coleridge's own instructions, to Josiah Wade's in Bristol where it awaited collection for the next two months.[69] This absurd and painful confusion was to become typical of Coleridge's practical arrangements in the coming years, when unopened letters and delayed meetings would cause havoc among even his staunchest friends and supporters.

At Coleorton it was decided that the whole household would go down to London in April for the publication of Wordsworth's *Poems in Two Volumes*, while Coleridge and Hartley prepared for Bristol. Only Dorothy and the children remained behind, planning a return to the Lake District. Now, she did not regret Coleridge's departure: "we had long experience at Coleorton, that it was not in our power to make him happy," she wrote sadly to Mrs Clarkson.[70]

Coleridge, in anticipation of the diplomatic visit to "Uncle G. Coleridge", wrote some instructions for Hartley to be read over "every two or three days", so that his behaviour at Ottery would be "such as to do yourself, and me and your dear Mother, credit". They reflect equally upon the anxious father and the brilliant, but unruly son, and show Coleridge slowly accepting the unaccustomed role of paterfamilias.

He wrote not in anger, but "on the contrary with great Love". He felt Hartley's nature was "very kind and forgiving, and wholly free from Revenge and Sullenness"; but equally he had "a very active & self-gratifying fancy, and such a high tide & flood of pleasurable feelings, that all unpleasant and painful Thoughts and events are hurried away upon it". This led Hartley into "bad Habits" and a refusal to accept discipline. He stole food, picked and snatched up things he liked, interrupted his elders, spoke too loudly, and had a maddening way of standing in half-opened doors. "Come in – or go out – & always speak and listen with the door shut."

He was a clever boy – Coleridge was immensely proud of this – but alas his cleverness led to lies and fantasies and false excuses. "Excuses may show your ingenuity, but they make your honesty suspected. We may admire a man for his cleverness; but we love and esteem him only for his goodness – and a strict attachment to Truth . . ." Hartley must do what he was told at once – "No procrastination – no self-delusion". If he took a little trouble, "everyone will be delighted with you". Coleridge added, "I have not spoken about your mad passions, and frantic Looks & pout-mouthing; because I trust, that is all over."

What worried Coleridge most about Hartley was a quality he knew now that he himself had bequeathed to his eldest son. "This power, which you possess, of shoving aside all disagreeable reflections, or losing them in a labyrinth of day-dreams, which saves you from present pain, has on the other hand interwoven into your nature a habit of procrastination, which unless you correct them in time (and it will require all your best exertions to do it effectually) – must lead you into lasting Unhappiness."

Not even Southey could have put this more acutely. It was the perfect device, that neither father nor son would ever quite accept. Coleridge had found a mirror in Hartley, and the reflections would haunt him, sometimes with laughter but more often with tears. He signed himself, "my dear, my very dear Hartley, most anxiously, Your fond Father, S.T. Coleridge".[71]

11

The trip to London was planned for a week, but lasted a month. They stayed with the Montagus, met up with Walter Scott, and took Hartley to visit the great sights of the capital. He was deliriously happy and excited. They saw the animals in the Tower of London, Humphry Davy's laboratories at the Royal Institution, and a pantomime at Covent Garden. In one of his earliest memories, Hartley recalled "the tiered boxes, the almost stupendous galleries, and the novelty of the sliding-scenes" which caught his young poet's imagination. He also remembered an oddly deflating remark of Sara Hutchinson's, who laughed at his astonishment at the wonderful stage-moon descending on a wire and compared it dismissively "to a copper warming-pan".[72]

Coleridge enjoyed showing off his son, but was much concerned with finances for the year ahead. He borrowed £50 from Wordsworth to pay his life assurance, and a further £50 from his old friend Sotheby to pay for the West Country expedition. He talked again with Davy about lecturing, and wrote to Godwin in search of the manuscript of his play *Osorio* which he suddenly thought of reviving for the new generation of actor-managers who seemed much taken with elaborate staging and exotic tales. Amazingly – but typically – he had kept no copy.

He wondered if Godwin "would take the trouble of rescuing it from any chance rubbish-corner, in which it may have been preserved. It is not merely a work which employed 8 months of my life from 23 to 24, it is interesting to me in the history of my own mind." Godwin did indeed find the manuscript in his meticulous filing system, and much later it would bring Coleridge the greatest financial success he had ever known.

He invited Godwin to the unlikely event of a Coleridgean breakfast at half past nine in the morning, but added that he was ill and much abed. "I am so unwell & so languid from – no matter what – other's follies and my own – from hopelessness without rest, & restlessness without hope – that I dare scarcely promise to *go* any where."[73] He also saw Stuart at the *Courier* office, discussed articles, and promised to repay his debts "by regular instalments" from the fees he happily assumed he would earn at Ottery. As a last quixotic throw (and no doubt encouraged by Wordsworth's example) he contracted with Longman for 100 guineas on a two-volume collection of poems – "these are all ready, but two" – to be delivered in two months provided "death & sickness" did not intervene.

The continuing dream of finishing "Christabel", and filling out the new volume with his Asra poems (dating right back to the "Dejection" ode) obviously inspired this idea. But it would involve a degree of literary self-exposure from which he shrank more than ever. Against this was the provoking fact that Walter Scott had achieved a resounding success with his "Lay of the Last Minstrel" (1805), which had now sold 15,000 copies, cleverly imitating the free syllabic metre of "Christabel", copying its gothic themes, and openly plagiarizing some of its most memorable phrasing. Coleridge was aware of this though he would not refer to it in print for many years.[74] In the event, the collection was not assembled for another decade, and Longman's guineas never materialized at any time. How far Coleridge's reputation would have altered, had he seriously tried to match Wordsworth's two volumes in 1807, is a subject he himself bitterly thought about in later years.

Coleridge hung on in London till the first week in May, when he and Hartley saw Asra off on the stagecoach to the Clarksons'. There is no record of their parting. But the following day Coleridge nearly collapsed in a Bedford Street on the way to visit Sotheby, and fled back in a horse-cab to the Lambs. Mary Lamb, one of the shrewdest and kindest of Coleridge's nurses, dosed him with brandy and strong broth, and stiffened his resolution for the next encounter with Mrs Coleridge.[75] Father and son departed on the Bristol mail about 10 May 1807 – "No procrastination – no self-delusion". Ahead of them lay an angry woman and an unpalatable letter, neither of which baleful objects should have been kept waiting in a well-ordered and rational universe.

Coleridge remained in the West Country for the next six months, and the Wordsworths did not hear from him again until November. But Asra secretly kept in touch from Bury St Edmund's, though all her letters have been destroyed. The first indication of Coleridge's arrival in Bristol – where he stayed with Josiah Wade in Queen's Square, while Mrs Coleridge remained at her sister Martha's – was the use of Greek cipher in his Notebooks.

An entry of 22 May, written in a curious pale red ink, which might be his "gout medicine" or even laudanum, suggests the marital rows over money and the children which now engulfed him. "As usual even the epoch of a pocket book must be marked with agitation . . . Mrs Coleridge this morning first planted in Hartley's mind the pang of divided duty: & left me stormy & miserable – The same day received the second letter from Sara [Asra]."[76]

Other Greek entries mention anger and jealousy, the hope of "reconciliation", and the continuing obsession of his unfulfilled love. "My love blazeth in presence: in absence it glows with a deep melancholy consuming flame. The walls, the window panes, the chair, the very *air* seems to sympathize with it!"[77] These almost hallucinatory sensations would be later transmuted into a tender, Platonic poem, "Recollections of Love".

But all the other work which he had so hopefully planned – the play, the collected poems, the Mediterranean travels – slid into oblivion. Even the letter from George remained unopened. As he wrote to another old Bristol friend, the publisher Joseph Cottle: "I will certainly give you the right hand of old-fellowship: but, alas! You will find me, rolling rudderless . . . Pain I have enough of, but that is indeed to me, a mere trifle, but the almost unceasing, overpowering sensations of wretchedness: aching in my limbs, with an indescribable restlessness, that makes action to any available purpose, almost impossible . . ."[78] But this was surely the effect of opium, as much as Mrs Coleridge.

It was Tom Poole, still a great favourite of both husband and wife, who now came to Coleridge's aid, inviting the whole family down to stay at Nether Stowey for the summer. They moved in early June. The children had the run of the large garden, the fun of haymaking, and the pungent fascination of the tanning yard. Mrs Coleridge had many old friends in the village, and Coleridge the hallowed retreat of Poole's now famous bookroom (it had been used by Wordsworth, Davy, Hazlitt, and Lamb), with its discreet external staircase providing an escape into the orchard. Poole's avuncular kindness and methodical efficiency were now directed briskly at Coleridge's ill-health, taking him out on long walks, encouraging him to write to friends, and helping him analyse his own feelings.

On one evening Coleridge noted with simple pleasure: "Blue Sky through the glimmering interspaces of the dark Elms at Twilight rendered a lovely deep yellow green."[79] On another he recorded Poole's characteristic and "affecting" remark, "How much the feelings of happy Childhood, when summer days appeared 20 times as long as now, may be produced by effective Industry – monuments of Time well spent."[80] Coleridge read agricultural textbooks, studies of astronomy (he had a brief fantasy of setting up his own observatory), and the poetry of the seventeenth-century religious mystic Richard Crashaw, whose Edenic images he compressed into tiny mottoes of hope: "Sunrise – As all the Trees of Paradise reblossoming in the East."[81]

Poole also began the painful task, pursued throughout the summer, of substituting country ale for brandy, and trying to wean Coleridge off his high level of opium intake. Coleridge's Notebooks become more and more explicit about actual physiological addiction – "all my Vitals are possessed by an unremitting Poison" – and now for the first time contain medically accurate descriptions of withdrawal symptoms. They produced pain in all his joints, especially the thighs and knees. But "the evil seems rather in the exceeding Unquiet, than in the pain – a cruel sweat on the brow, & on the chest – windy sickness at the Stomach – and in the mind a strong Temptation to . . . a reprobate Despair, that snatches at the known Poison . . ." He described the moment before succumbing to the next dose unforgettably, as "like the pause in the balancing of the Javelin".[82]

Even the act of analytical introspection itself became destructive. "Meanwhile the habit of inward Brooding daily makes it harder to confess the Thing, I am, to any one – least of all to those, whom I most love & who most love me – & thereby introduces and fosters a habit of negative falsehood, & multiplies the Temptations to positive Insincerity." Again for the first time, he acknowledged the need for professional help and made the first of innumerable resolutions to seek a medical cure, in this instance from his old friend Dr Beddoes of the Bristol Pneumatic Institute: "O God! let me bare my whole Heart to Dr B. or some other Medical Philosopher – if I could know there was no *Relief*; I might then *resolve* on something."[83]

While Coleridge battled these mental coils, Poole brought him round to face other, practical duties. Coleridge's patron Tom Wedgwood, upon whom half his annuity depended, had died during Coleridge's absence in Malta. Tom's brother, Josiah, had written asking for a memorial essay but Coleridge had simply failed to reply, leaving this letter too not merely unanswered but unopened for many weeks. Poole forced Coleridge to write a long, explanatory letter to Josiah from Stowey on 25 June, first smoothing the way with his own tactful missive.

"I admire and pity him more than ever," he wrote to Josiah. "His information is much extended, the great qualities of his mind heightened and better disciplined; but alas: his health is weaker, and his great failing, procrastination, or the incapability of acting agreeably to his wish and will, much increased."[84] This was the nearest that the loyal Poole would get to opium.

Coleridge's own explanation to Josiah mentioned "Ill-health, Despondency, domestic Distractions", adding that he had indeed previously written a paper on Tom Wedgwood's system of philosophy and "opinions in psychology" and had drawn at full "a portrait of my friend's mind & character", but this manuscript had been lost with his other Malta papers.[85]

As Sir James Mackintosh – now Josiah's son-in-law – was editing Tom Wedgwood's unpublished work, Coleridge did not offer to resurrect this paper from memory: "too great pain has baffled my attempts in going over again the detail of past times". In the event Mackintosh did not fulfil his promise either, and it was left to Coleridge to insert a short but beautiful tribute to Tom in a footnote to *The Friend* in 1809. "He is gone, my Friend! my munificent Co-patron, and not less the Benefactor of my Intellect! – He who beyond all other men known to me, added a fine and ever-wakeful sense of Beauty to the most patient Accuracy in experimental Philosophy . . ."[86]

Coleridge particularly credited Tom with a "Theory of Perception" based on self-analytic notes of his own abnormal mental states and hallucinations, calmly and empirically pursued, "even during the wretched nights of sickness, in watching and instantly recording these experiences of the world within us . . ." Tom's theory emphasized, in a new way, the subjective influence of memory and imagination on apparently inexplicable phenomena like ghosts and hallucinations. It was evidently of great importance to Coleridge, and his awkward protestations to Josiah – "O Sir! if you knew, what I suffer, and am this moment suffering, in thinking of him" – were heartfelt. Yet there was also a degree of calculation, since Coleridge "suspected & feared" his annuity would be discontinued.[87]

But Josiah Wedgwood, a large-minded man who had much

experience of literary "hypochondria" was prepared to be mollified. "I was truly glad to hear from him," he confided to Poole. "His letter removed all those feelings of anger which occasionally, but not permanently, existed in my mind towards him. I am very sorry for him."[88] It might also have calmed Coleridge to know that half the annuity was actually secured by the terms of Tom Wedgwood's will, and in practice Josiah could not touch it; but this only became clear later.

Not even Tom Poole's diplomacy could resolve the misunderstanding with George Coleridge. His letter of 6 April was still unopened at the end of June, when Coleridge was intending to go down to Ottery in less than a week, "from a sense of Duty as it affects myself, & from a promise made to Mrs Coleridge, as far as it affects her".[89] His folly in leaving it so long would be incredible if he had not openly admitted such procrastination to Josiah Wedgwood: "I have sunk under such a strange cowardice of Pain, that I have not unfrequently kept Letters from persons dear to me for weeks together unopened."[90] Southey would later observe that, in practical terms, this was perhaps the most damaging of all the symptoms of Coleridge's opium addiction, leading to endless business confusions, personal affronts and family chaos for over a decade. But it is also a revealing one, for it suggests that Coleridge knew instinctively where "Pain" and censure would come from, and unconsciously sought to protect himself by refusing to conform to civilized norms of behaviour. If the real world promised to be too harsh, he simply ignored it as long as possible, and tried to live in the breathing space. One is tempted to believe that he knew very well that George's letter would bring bad news. If so, Coleridge was not disappointed when he finally opened it in July.

George was overwhelmed with his own family difficulties – illness at the school, the frailty of their "poor aged mother", the "hereditary" despondency of Mrs James Coleridge – and could not possibly receive them. "To come to Ottery for such a purpose would be to create a fresh expense for yourself and to load my feelings with what they could not bear without endangering my life – I pray you therefore do not do so." He could not take on the children at the school, though he might be able to help financially. He thought Mrs Coleridge's friends might make "a settlement", but he strongly disapproved of the separation. (Later he would say it was "an irreligious act . . . which the New Testament forbids".) He upbraided Coleridge in the old paternal tones of his Cambridge days: "For God's sake strive to put on some fortitude and do nothing rashly."[91]

The whole Ottery plan thus collapsed in a storm of mutual reproaches. Mrs Coleridge not unnaturally blamed her husband. Coleridge with far less reason blamed not only George but all his Ottery brothers. Coleridge's anger was surprising and curiously refreshing to him. Though so largely unjustified, it left him free to dramatize himself as an outcast in a cruel world. Paradoxically, it made him feel better about himself, by embracing the worst that the respectable world could do to him. He wrote to Josiah Wade in a kind of satisfied fury at the ruin of his reputation and prospects. George had betrayed him.

> His pride & notion of character took alarm and he made public to all my Brothers, & even to their Children, [my] most confidential Letter, & so cruelly that while I was ignorant of all this Brewing, Colonel Coleridge's eldest son (a mere youth) had informed Mr King that *he* should not call on me (his Uncle) for that "*The Family*" had resolved not to receive me. These people are rioting in Wealth & without the least feeling add another £100 to my already most embarrassed circumstance . . . So that at the age of 35 I am to be penniless, resourceless, in heavy debt – my health & spirits absolutely broken down – & with scarce a friend in the world.[92]

Coleridge's sustaining anger against George would rumble on for another two years, when after a further outburst (which George described as "your downright red hot letter"), it was abruptly dispelled. But from July 1807 he began to feel steadily stronger, to write and plan, and cultivate his circle of friends, both old and new. Mrs Coleridge had announced that she would return to Bristol, much to Coleridge's relief, but first some social visits were to be paid in Bridgwater. Coleridge meekly accompanied her, noting laconically: "All the Linen at the Bridgwater Arms mark'd 'Stolen from the Bridgwater Arms.'"[93]

12

While staying at Thomas Chubb's house, Coleridge was taking the afternoon air at the gate, when he was approached by a diminutive figure leading a large horse. The shy, elfin young man introduced himself as an unknown admirer who had pursued him from London, to Bristol, to Stowey, and thence to Bridgwater. This pilgrim was the 22-year-old Thomas De Quincey. He later claimed to have recognized Coleridge by the "peculiar haze or dreaminess" in his large, softly gazing eyes. "He was in a deep reverie; for I had dismounted, made two or three trifling arrangements at an inn door, and advanced close to him, before he had apparently become conscious of my presence."[94]

After some difficulty in "recovering his position amongst daylight realities", Coleridge turned all his "gracious" attentions on the young traveller, invited him in for drinks, sat him down, urged him to stay for dinner, and began talking about the difference between the philosophies of David Hartley and Immanuel Kant, and continued easily for three hours. De Quincey was simply dazzled, just as young Hazlitt had been ten years before on hearing him preach. His description, elaborated like Hazlitt's many years after, shows Coleridge overwhelming the young Oxford student (De Quincey was in his third year at Worcester College) like an irresistible force of nature. The dinner arrangement being settled, "Coleridge, like some great river, the Oreallana or the St Lawrence, that, having been checked and fretted by rocks or thwarting islands, suddenly recovers its volume of waters and its mighty music swept at once, as if returning to his natural business, into a continuous strain of eloquent dissertation, certainly the most novel, the most finely illustrated, and traversing the most spacious fields of thought by transitions the most just and logical, that it was possible to conceive."

This display continued until abruptly interrupted by a woman's entrance. "Coleridge paused . . . in a frigid tone he said, while turning to me, 'Mrs Coleridge'; in some slight way he then presented me to her: I bowed; and the lady almost immediately retired. I gathered, what I afterwards learned redundantly, that Coleridge's marriage had not been a happy one."[95]

Even more than Hazlitt, De Quincey was to find his whole literary life shaped and directed by the consequences of this memorable first encounter. It led to his introduction into the Lake District circle that autumn (he had previously corresponded with Wordsworth, but had never dared to meet him); it confirmed his lifelong fascination with German philosophy and psychological criticism; and it gave him courage to explore his great autobiographical theme – opium addiction. His *Confessions of an English Opium Eater* made his name as a writer when published in 1821, and all his subsequent journalism was signed "The English Opium Eater". De Quincey made the subject fashionable, and his work was translated in France by Alfred de Musset. Thirty years of subsequent commentaries on and additions to the *Confessions* are inextricably involved with Coleridge's private experiences and may be taken as a lengthy (and often barbed) tribute to the older man and pioneer addict. Coleridge continuously haunts De Quincey's pages, as a sort of battered Virgilian guide to the opium Inferno.

At the time of meeting Coleridge in Chubb's gateway, De Quincey was still an aimless, Romantic young gentleman-vagabond very typical of his post-revolutionary university generation. He had no ambitions in business, science, church or politics. Brought up and spoiled by a widowed mother, educated at Manchester Grammar School (from which he ran away), he had spent his summer vacations living rough in Wales and experimenting with opium in London. Here he had his famous encounter with the teenage prostitute, "Anne of Oxford Street".

This formative affair, and his sexual fantasies of the embracing exotic woman "Levana" (one of the three "Our Ladies of Sorrows" who dominate the *Confessions'* great dream-sequences) he would later assign to the summers of 1802–4. Yet they suggest curious parallels with what De Quincey later learned of Coleridge's Asra obsession, and they may have been retrospectively shaped and coloured.

That summer of 1807 he had abandoned university, like Coleridge before him, without taking his final degree, and had determined on introducing himself to the authors of the *Lyrical Ballads*. He regarded them as the intellectual and spiritual authorities of their age. Brilliantly clever, but emotionally damaged and dependent (not least by his tiny size, which painfully recalls Hartley Coleridge), De Quincey was like some darting, changeling child seeking giant parents to worship and quarrel with. Over the next ten years (when he would settle at Grasmere and play almost daily with the children) Wordsworth would be his father and mentor. But Coleridge, the great river-god of words and opium, would be something more dangerous and elemental, a demonic elder brother or *doppelgänger*, easier to understand and far easier to despise.

De Quincey would claim that at Bridgwater Coleridge almost immediately brought up the subject of addiction: "for already he was under the full dominion of opium, as he himself revealed to me, and with a deep expression of horror at the hideous bondage, in a private walk of some length which I took with him about sunset."[96]

This, like many of De Quincey's colourful reconstructions (which he first published in *Tait's Magazine* in the year of Coleridge's death), has been largely doubted. But it seems quite possible, given the confessional tone of Coleridge's Notebooks at Coleorton and Stowey, and the openness with which he increasingly talked to the younger generation, far less censorious than his own contemporaries. Certainly, after his return to Bristol, De Quincey soon put in hand two schemes which were of immense practical aid to Coleridge. The first was to use £500 of his family inheritance as an "anonymous" long-term loan to Coleridge through Joseph Cottle. The second was to offer himself in Coleridge's stead as an escort to Mrs Coleridge and the children when they eventually returned, as now planned, to Keswick.

In retrospect one might accuse De Quincey of "buying" his way into the Lake District circle. Yet he was only twenty-two, and the awed tone of his letters at this date (especially to Wordsworth) suggest genuine and idealistic hero-worship. He spoke of himself as one "who bends the knee" before them. "And I will add that, to no man on earth except yourself," he wrote to Wordsworth, "and *one* other (a friend of yours), would I thus lowly and suppliantly prostrate myself."[97] After that first meeting at Bridgwater, De Quincey rode back the same night to Bristol, forty miles along the turnpike road under the stars, thinking rapturously of "the greatest man that has ever appeared".[98]

13

By August, Coleridge was blessedly alone with Poole at Stowey, and a note of bucolic and unaccustomed content crept into his difficult convalescence. "The Hayfield in the close hard by the Farm House: babe, and totterer little more; old cat with her eyes blinking in the Sun, & little kittens leaping and frisking over the Hay-lines."[99]

Coleridge made long notes on the planting of oak trees for the new generation, on the cultivation of sunflowers, and the predicting of weather. He walked with Poole to see the Cruikshanks at Enmore, to see Brice at Aisholt, and the fishermen at Combwich. He dined with Lord Egremont, and drank mead all night with Brice, explaining that "the second bottle became associated with the idea, & afterwards with the body, of S.T.C. – by necessity of metaphysical Law".[100]

He attended the opening of the Female Friendly Society of Stowey (another of Poole's philanthropic foundations, like the Stowey Bank) and unblushingly supplied the motto for its banner: "Foresight and Union, linked by Christian Love".[101] He wrote comic verses on their "georgo-episcopal Meanderings" (a combination of Virgilian nature-rambling and stately pilgrimage) which were so slow and digressive under Poole's guidance, stopping at every field-gate and hill-top, that Coleridge claimed they would avoid Purgatory because "the Last Day will have come" before they arrived anywhere. Their circuitous routes would require "a new road Map of the country" between Stowey and the sea.[102]

Coleridge even imagined settling in some perfect farmhouse in the Quantocks, which would contain among other things "two Staircases" at each end of the building to aid domestic harmony, and a brewhouse, a dairy, a cellar, a pigsty, and a "Palace of meditation" for his poetry.[103] "We set Spies and Watches on the Sun," he wrote thoughtfully. "We make Time give an account of itself, & shall we not give an account of Time?"[104]

All this while the opium struggle continued. Coleridge listed medical compounds for enema injections, and invented a new dilute laudanum solution using five pounds of quince juice to a quarter of a pound of opium, infused with a spice cocktail of cinnamon, nutmeg, cloves and saffron to aid digestion. "When in Malta, I might easily have tried it with Lemon Juice, instead of Quinces."[105]

There were of course moments of strain, even with Tom Poole: on one occasion a row about Coleridge's "unreasonable expectation" of being supplied with pen and ink; on another a "warm conversation" about miracles.[106] No doubt opium lay behind these. When urged by Poole to "exert himself", Coleridge replied with his old image of the eagle bidding the "Tortoise sunward soar", which Poole meticulously noted and filed without comment.[107]

But in fact Coleridge was secretly writing poetry again. One fragment, "A Dark Sky" (Coeali Ennarant) suggests agonizing religious doubts, as he sat one night in Poole's garden watching the stars overcome by racing storm-clouds. Those stars, once so friendly and companionable in the days of "Frost at Midnight", now seemed like a "conven'd conspiracy of spies" winking out some message of doubt and betrayal. The book of Heaven, in which he had promised Hartley one could read God's message of comfort and benevolence, now seemed blank and cruel:

> No constellations alphabet the sky:
> The Heavens one large Black Letter only shew,
> And as a child beneath its master's blow
> Shrills out at once its task and its affright –
> The groaning world now learns to read aright,
> And with its Voice of Voices cries out, O!"[108]

The harsh, metaphysical nature of this poem (drawing its image from the old Black Letter Bible which Coleridge recalled from his own painful schooldays under Bowyer) set the tone for much confessional poetry to come. But another more tender piece, "Recollections of Love" also took Coleridge back to more soothing memories of the early Quantock days, now infused with thoughts of Asra which haunted him like half-heard music.

> Eight springs have flown, since last I lay
> On sea-ward Quantock's healthy hills,
> Where quiet sounds from hidden rills
> Float here and there, like things astray,
> And high o'er head the sky-lark shrills.

No voice as yet had made the air
Be music with your name; yet why
That asking look? that yearning sigh?
That sense of promise every where?
Belovéd! flew your spirit by?[109]

The song-like beauty and simplicity of this poem also hides a complex metaphysical speculation about the nature of time in matters of the heart. It is entitled "Recollections", but it is equally about anticipations of love. For Coleridge, Asra's "spirit" already inhabited the hills and streams of the Quantocks in 1799. Emotional time stretched and flowed and doubled-back, fluid like a river, linking spots of happiness in a mysterious present-tense of place and season. "My Felicity", Coleridge wrote in another Notebook fragment, was "Like Milk that . . . in its easy stream Flows ever . . . in the Babe's murmuring Mouth".[110]

In returning to his old rambles over the Quantocks, crossing and recrossing the familiar tracks and combs, he was almost physically re-weaving the network of his youthful happiness, like a spider re-making a web of sights, sounds and associations:

. . . Time drew out his subtle
Threads so quick, That the long
Summer's Eve was one whole web,
A Space on which I lay commensurate –
For Memory & all undoubting Hope
Sang the same note & in the selfsame
Voice . . .[111]

The richness of the Quantocks' earth at harvest-time made him grateful to "magna mater, Diana multimammalia" – the great Mother, Diana the many-breasted.[112] Yet Time was still fleeting, a perilous river on which all human achievements of outward form were swept away. The counter-speculation, as old as Heraclitus, produced a series of "Kubla Khan"-like prose fragments which answered the lyric poetry in a grander, more openly philosophical manner. "Our mortal existence a stoppage in the blood of Life – a brief eddy in the everflowing Ocean of pure Activity . . . who beholds Pyramids, yea, Alps and Andes (giant Pyramids the work of Fire) raising monuments like a generous Victor, o'er its own conquests, tombstones of a world destroyed – yet, these too float adown the Sea of Time, & melt away, Mountains of floating ice."[113]

Lying on his back in the Quantocks' heather, gazing up at the English sky, Coleridge recalled his Malta meditations on the eternal blue of the Mediterranean, and reached towards some answering impulse in himself. "O I could annihilate in a deep moment all possibility of the needlepoint pinshead System of the Atomists by one submissive Gaze! . . . Thought formed not fixed, – the molten Being never cooled into a Thing, tho' begotten into the vast adequate Thought."[114] All these meditations on Time and Form, Love and Perception, would gradually be brought to bear on the nature of the poet's Imagination – "whose essence is passionate order" – which he would explore in the long-planned lectures of 1808.

If Poole thought Coleridge was not "exerting" himself this summer, one might ask how much hard work a writer may do lying on a hill in the sun.

3

The Lecture Shirt

1

Coleridge did not lie undisturbed for very long. At the end of August 1807, Poole received an urgent letter from Davy on the subject of the lectures in London. "The Managers of the Royal Institution are very anxious to engage him; and I think he might be of material service to the public, and of benefit to his own mind, to say nothing of the benefit his purse might receive. In the present condition of society, his opinions in matters of taste, literature, and metaphysics must have a healthy influence; and unless he soon becomes an actual member of the living world, he must expect to be brought to judgment 'for hiding his light' . . ."[1]

This time there was no Wordsworth to dissuade him, and no Asra to distract him (though both had been the subject of painful Notebook entries at Stowey, one of them about the bedroom incident, ending "Awakened from a dream of Tears, & anguish of involuntary Jealousy, ½ past 2 . . .").[2]

Coleridge wrote back to Davy with surprising promptitude on 9 September, accepting the proposal on a revised plan. After helpful discussions with Poole, he had decided to abandon the visual art aspect of the lectures (his Mediterranean materials still lying marooned with Stoddart at Malta) and to concentrate purely on the literary side. His subject would be "the Principles of Poetry". He would try to do something largely new in English criticism: to isolate and define the psychology of the creative imagination on systematic, philosophical grounds.

He would illustrate his theory with a grand sweep through the history of English literature: Chaucer, Shakespeare, Spenser, Milton, Dryden, Pope and the Moderns. Everything would be subordinated to his central concept, elaborated over many years, of the dynamic connection between the structure of poetry and the structure of the human mind. "In the course of these I shall have said, all I know, the whole result of many years' continued reflection on the subjects of Taste, Imagination, Fancy, Passion, the source of our pleasures in the fine Arts in the *antithetical* balance-loving nature of man, & the connections with moral excellence."[3]

At the heart of Coleridge's thesis would emerge a concept of the poetic imagination which acted as a single unifying force within all creative acts. This idea, which was to become a defining doctrine of Romanticism, may well have been partly triggered by Davy's own scientific theories about the nature of energy and matter, which he too was exploring that autumn at the Royal Society in a series of brilliant lectures and demonstrations. Coleridge wrote later that Davy's "own great discovery, of the identity of electricity and chemical attraction", had opened the way to a unified theory of energy in the universe. "Davy supposes that there is only one power in the world of the senses; which in particles acts as chemical attractions, in specific masses as electricity, & on matter in general, as planetary Gravitation . . . When this has been proved, it will then only remain to resolve this into some Law of vital Intellect – and all human Knowledge will be Science and Metaphysics the only Science."[4]

This was an early premonition of the modern physicist's search for a "Grand Unified Theory" applicable to the entire cosmos. Coleridge's fascination with the idea of "the one power in the world of the senses", led him to seek for an equivalent unifying dynamic within the human mind, the "one power" of Imagination. Certainly it encouraged him to believe that his "experimental" knowledge of poetry, and his endless private reflections in the Notebooks on his own mental processes, were no longer to be lost or wasted, but could be mounted into a general body of critical theory. This belief that all was not lost, that he still had a role to play as a poet and thinker, and that his light might not in the end be hidden, proved one of the most sustaining visions of his life. Out of all his dark sufferings and failures, some brightness might still be salvaged. As he observed of a battered peacock picking quietly around Tom Poole's yard: "The molting Peacock with only two of his long tail-feathers remaining, & those sadly in tatters, yet proudly as ever spreading out his ruined fan in the Sun & Breeze."[5]

Much of the rest of Coleridge's long and grateful letter to Davy was, of course, a lament over his troubles – among which Mrs Coleridge and the Ottery family débâcle featured in "wearying Detail", and his own "bodily derangement" with a medical exactitude that nonetheless excluded opium. The decision to send his wife and children back to Keswick is given without regret, and one wonders how Coleridge had explained this to Hartley, the abrupt end to his "annus mirabilis" with his father. Perhaps this was one of the "far crueller Calamities" that he did not explain to Davy either.

But in general Coleridge felt his time in the Quantocks had been immensely restoring. He had received "such manifest benefit from horse exercise, a gradual abandonment of fermented & total abstinence from spirituous liquors, & by being alone with Poole & the renewal of old times by wandering about among my dear old walks, of Quantock & Alfoxden, that I have now seriously set about composition . . ."[6]

Work in hand still included the Mediterranean "Travels", though the Longman two-volume edition of "all my poetic scraps" would be held over – as it turned out for nearly a decade. It was his serious determination "not to give a single Lecture till I have in fair writing at least one half of the whole course". Either at Stowey, or at Bristol, he began a new Notebook[7] which sketched out his preliminary themes, especially with reference to Shakespeare's "endless activity of Thought" as the primary example of "poetic Power" exercised through language.[8]

Coleridge returned to Bristol in late September, hoping to be with Davy in London by the end of the month, where concentrated work could begin. But first he had to arrange for his family's departure north, which instantly revived all the old frictions. Here young De Quincey's reappearance as willing acolyte at College Street smoothed Coleridge's passage. Sara Coleridge, writing privately to Poole (as she would do increasingly in coming years), gave her own wifely account of Coleridge's exasperating behaviour. "When he at length joined us in Bristol in such excellent health and improved looks, I thought of days 'lang syne' and hoped and prayed it might continue. Alas! in three or four days it was all over. He said he must go to town immediately about the Lectures, yet he stayed three weeks without another word about removing, and I durst not speak lest it should disarrange him. Mr De Quincey, who was a frequent visitor to C. in College Street, proposed accompanying me and the children into Cumberland, as he wished much to pay Wordsworth and Southey a visit. This was a pleasant scheme to me . . ."[9]

Sara's brisk practicality, which affords no mention of Coleridge's profound professional doubts or deep anxieties about the future of those children, suggests the gulf of misunderstanding which now divided husband and wife. Yet her impatience at Coleridge's apparent vagaries – was it really the husband or the wife who "durst not speak" about the departure? – also suggests at a deeper level some abiding, loyal affection. For her it is evident that the "separation" could not easily be acknowledged, and this too was to remain a source of pain and resentment.

Coleridge's delay in Bristol was partly caused by the delicate negotiations, undertaken through Cottle, over De Quincey's anonymous loan, which continued through October. Coleridge was concerned that his "unknown Benefactor" should not "transgress" his other duties; and also wanted his identity revealed "at the expiration of one year". De Quincey told Cottle that he was drawing on an expected inheritance of £2,600, at which Cottle urged a lower sum of £300.[10] This figure was eventually made over on 12 November.[11]

Coleridge was immediately able to pay off his debts to Wordsworth and Sotheby, and for the first time since returning from Italy to look with some calm at his future finances. He was immensely grateful, especially as Cottle had led him to believe that the benefactor was a man of suitable wealth and standing, not an undergraduate mortgaging his prospects. "I must tell you," Cottle assured him, "that there is not a man in the Kingdom of whom you would rather accept a favour . . ."[12] De Quincey meanwhile delivered Mrs Coleridge to Keswick, and became an immediate favourite with Hartley, Derwent and the Wordsworth children.

The other reason for delay was medical. Coleridge was again suffering from chronic stomach problems – the symptoms, "acrimony in the bowels", sounds like Irritable Bowel Syndrome brought on by a mixture of stress and opium-taking. On 13 October he walked over to Clifton to consult Dr Beddoes. However, he still did not have the courage to make the full confession of his addiction, as he had determined with Poole at Stowey. The following February he was still resolving "instantly to put myself under Dr Beddoes, & to open to him the whole of my case".[13]

In late October, on the very eve of departure, he was taken violently ill with vomiting and diarrhoea, while dining out with friends. "I was therefore a prisoner to the House, which was luckily Mr Morgan's; where had I been a child or favourite Brother, I could not have received more affectionate attentions and indulgences."[14] Coleridge took up residence on the Morgans' spare sofa for the next four weeks, where he was deliciously nursed and cosseted. No one outside Bristol – Poole, Davy, Mrs Coleridge, or Wordsworth – heard from him until the end of November.

2

Coleridge's abrupt disappearance into the bosom of the Morgan household in autumn 1807 was as significant as his descent upon the Wordsworths at Grasmere in 1800. He had discovered a new adoptive family, and all his cuckoo-like propensities were at once aroused. John Morgan was a Bristol lawyer in his early thirties, a one-time pupil of Christ's Hospital, and a friend of Charles Lamb's. After practising briefly in the City of London (he seems to have worked at the Blackfriars office of Coleridge's life assurance company), he had recently married a Miss Mary Brent, the wealthy daughter of a Hatton Garden silversmith. Together the young couple had moved back to an elegant house in St James's Square, Bristol, where they were joined by Mary's very attractive younger sister, Charlotte Brent.

The family was vivacious, fun-loving and, as events were to show, improvident. They were also childless, and had much time for books, theatre and pets (one of their favourites being a dog called "Vision"). John Morgan was a sensitive and intelligent man, having been brought up as a Unitarian, and frequently subject to relapses into religious gloom, which Coleridge was able to alleviate. He was to write of Coleridge's first, momentous residence: "Amongst other obligations to you I feel strongly that of making me able to defend at least in my own mind the Orthodox religion against the Unitarian philosophy."[15]

In return, Morgan had an unshakable admiration for Coleridge's literary gifts, a deep sympathy for his marital predicament, and an unusual understanding of his opium addiction which seems to have been revealed from the outset of their friendship. Less organizing than Tom Poole, less censorious than George Coleridge, and far less demanding than Wordsworth, John Morgan slipped unconsciously into the role of Coleridge's ideal and long-sought brother. Loyal, generous and naive, he became Coleridge's unfailing anchor-point in the dark years ahead.

Morgan's naivety extended from financial to emotional matters. It was never clear quite how far he realized the extraordinary mirror-image that Coleridge projected on to his triangular household. John, Mary and Charlotte became youthful substitutes for Wordsworth, Mary and Asra; and Coleridge orchestrated them into this sentimental pattern with alarming rapidity. When he eventually arrived in London, he wrote immediately to Dorothy Wordsworth of this fateful revelation, sounding both excited and guilty. "I never knew two pairs of human beings so alike, as Mrs Morgan & her Sister, Charlotte Brent, and Mary and Sara. I was reminded afresh of the resemblance every hour – & at times felt a self-reproach, that I could not love two such amiable, pure & affectionate Beings for their own sakes. But there is a time in Life, when the Heart stops growing."[16]

But Coleridge's heart, and his fantasies, were actually in a most active state. He had started a poem on the subject, and he was already recalling a host of tender moments at St James's Square: gifts, keepsakes, pet-names and shared jokes. In his mirror-universe, even the famous sofa scene with Mary and Asra at Gallow Hill (the subject of his Keswick poem, "A Day-Dream") had been re-enacted in Bristol. He would recall it fondly to Mary Morgan, as a token of their new-found intimacy: "that evening, when dear Morgan was asleep in the Parlour, and you and beloved Caroletta asleep at opposite Corners of the Sopha in the Drawing Room, of which I occupied the centre in a state of blessed half-consciousness, as a drowsy Guardian of your Slumbers . . ."[17]

3

Coleridge finally roused himself from these dreamy delights on 22 November, riding up on the night mail to London, sustained by a wing of chicken and a flask of rum laid in with his lecture papers. "If very, very affectionate thoughts, wishes, recollections, anticipations, can serve instead of *Grace* before & after meat, mine was a very religious Meal."[18] Daniel Stuart gave him a set of rooms above the *Courier* offices at No. 348, the Strand.

His mood was now buoyant. "My Lectures will be profitable – and I have rewritten my play [*Osorio*] – & about doubled the length of Christabel – 2 thirds are finished." This latter claim, which seems so definite (especially when added to similar statements of progress at Coleorton) remains one of the great mysteries of Coleridge's bibliography. No Part III of "Christabel" has ever been found among his papers, except for a possible eleven-line fragment, "The Knight's Tomb". Could it have been dreamt in an opium "reverie", like the missing 250 lines of "Kubla Khan"? or could it – as *Osorio* so nearly was – have been lost in some "lumber-room" or newspaper wastebin? The possibilities are tantalizing.

The lectures were due to begin in a fortnight, after Davy's were complete; but now it was Davy who fell dangerously ill after six weeks of brilliant but exhausting demonstrations, his "March of Glory" as Coleridge called it. (The illness was gaol fever, contracted while inspecting the ventilation problems at Newgate Prison.) The Literary Series was put back to January 1808, and Coleridge beguiled the time by taking Stuart back to Bristol to meet his new supporters, the Morgans, and by publishing his poem in their honour in the *Courier*.

The poem was entitled "To Two Sisters, A Wanderer's Farewell", and appeared on 10 December under the pen-name "Siesti" (an expressive amalgam of "STC" and "Siesta"). It is openly and even brazenly confessional, describing his longing "for some abiding place of love", and the Morgans' soothing tenderness as like the unexpected glow of winter sun "on unthaw'd ice". It casts himself as a homeless exile, and comes very close to admitting the "poison" of his opium addiction:

> Me disinherited in form and face
> By nature, and mishap of outward grace;
> Who, soul and body, through one guiltless fault
> Waste daily with the poison of sad thought . . .[19]

Coleridge goes on through fifty lines to explore the unsettling comparison between the two sets of women that he had pointed out to Dorothy: "Two dear, dear Sisters, prized all price above,/ Sisters, like you, with more than sisters' love . . ." In the younger Morgan household, "My best-beloved regain'd their youth in you". He ends by imagining all four sitting together round the same peaceful firelit hearth, while he remains apart "in solitude" content to dream of them – "ah: dream and pine!" in proud renunciation of all worldly happiness.

The sentimentality of the poem, flooded with pain and self-pity, is so powerful that it almost disguises its strange metaphysical argument about the nature of love. The two pairs of sisters are presented as almost literal reincarnations of each other, in "statures, tempers, looks, and mien". The memory of the one imposes itself, physically, on the vision of the other:

> Sight seem'd a sort of memory, and amaze
> Mingled a trouble with affection's gaze.

For Coleridge at this moment, all hopes of love and acceptance seem caught up in a fatal cycle of repetition, the past doomed to re-enact itself in the present.* This pattern, both soothing and imprisoning, suggests some original childlike state of emotional dependence from which he cannot escape. So the undertone of the poem is fretful, reproachful, even angry. One wonders, most of all, what Asra would have made of it, for her love still seems Coleridge's hidden theme. As he confided to his Notebooks at this time: "It is not the Wordsworths' knowledge of my frailties that prevents my entire Love of them: No! it is their Ignorance of the Deep place of my Being – and O! the cruel misconception of that which is purest in me, which alone is indeed pure – My Love of Asra . . ."[20]

If this publication was intended as a signal of reproach, or even

---

* These ideas of memory and repetition ultimately go back to Plato's belief that all knowledge is a form of rediscovery. In a philosophical (Kantian) sense, Coleridge believed that all perceptions were a combination of immediate sense-impressions, a priori mental forms (such as space, time, causality) and memory ("associations"). But in an emotional sense he believed that the perception of our most intense relationships could be cyclical, and symbols of some deeper unity of desire, revealed by such phenomena as "déja-vu" and the mysteriously repeated imagery of dreams. The belief can be found frequently among Romantic writers, perhaps in its most intense form in the work of Gérard de Nerval, whose wandering life and worship of the imaginary "Aurelia" has many parallels with Coleridge's experiences. (See Richard Holmes, "Dreams", in *Footsteps*, 1985.)

defiance, to those in the Lake District, it did not go unnoticed. Mrs Coleridge and Southey (who knew Morgan) were indignant; while Dorothy was resigned to his "very unsteady" behaviour in all things.[21] The Wordsworths at this very moment were planning their move to Allan Bank, a larger house west of Grasmere around the margins of the lake, partly so Coleridge and his children could be accommodated. But Dorothy did not now think he would have "the resolution" to come north again. Yet she still recognized his incalculable powers of self-renewal: "how Coleridge does rise up, as it were, almost from the dead!". She hoped his lectures would be of service to him, "especially as his exertions for the cause of human nature (such I may call them) will be animated by his strong sentiments of friendship and veneration for my Brother".[22]

4

Coleridge was due to begin his weekly lectures on Friday 15 January 1808. He made one more dash to Bristol, came back to attend the noisy celebrations of "a sort of Glee or Catch Club, composed wholly of professional singers – and was much delighted", and sailed into the Royal Institution the following afternoon at 2 p.m. But there was some bravado in this.

The Royal Institution, founded by private subscription in 1799, had quickly achieved a prestige second only to the Royal Society's. Its splendid buildings, with a frontage of fourteen Doric columns, dominated the top end of Albemarle Street with John Murray's publishing house at the other (Piccadilly end). Its lecture programmes, originally dedicated to both arts and sciences, achieved international status when Davy began his demonstrations there in 1802, with an increasingly spectacular series of chemical experiments. "The globules often burnt at the moment of their formation, and sometimes violently exploded and separated into smaller globules, which flew with great velocity through the air in a state of vivid combustion, producing a beautiful effect of continued jets of fire."[23] Coleridge hoped to do something similar with verbal pyrotechnics.

The popularity of the Institution's lectures so often jammed Albemarle Street with carriages that it eventually became the first one-way thoroughfare in London. The programme of 1808 included Davy on chemistry, Coleridge on poetry, and other experts on botany, architecture, German music, mechanics, and Persian literature.[24]

Though dogged by financial difficulties, the Institution's founder Count Rumford had entirely refurbished the Great Lecture Room in 1802, to become "the most beautiful and convenient in Europe", with superb acoustics so that even "a whisper may be distinctly heard". It held up to 500 people in a hemisphere of steeply tiered seats, with a gallery above and a circle of gas lamps, creating an atmosphere both intimate and intensely theatrical. It was a setting that demanded the speakers not merely to lecture, but to perform. (When Sydney Smith lectured on moral philosophy the previous year, it was said that the laughter could be heard outside in the street.) The attention of the audience was sustained by various creature comforts: green cushioned seating, green baize floor coverings, and the latest in central heating systems using copper pipes.

Albemarle Street was crowded with carriages, and the seats were packed. Coleridge launched into the concept of "Taste" in poetry before a large and attentive audience: "What is there in the primary sense of the word, which may give to its metaphorical meaning an import different from that of Sight or Hearing on the one hand, and of Touch or Feeling on the other?"[25] It went well, Coleridge felt, and "made an impression far beyond its worth or my expectation".

But on returning to his lodgings in the Strand, he immediately collapsed with sickness and continuous agonizing pain "of Stomach & Bowels". He postponed the next two lectures – "I disappoint hundreds" – and tried again on Friday, 5 February, but again collapsed with "acrid scalding evacuations, and if possible worse Vomitings".[26]

It was this lecture that De Quincey witnessed, when he came down to London on business for Wordsworth. He reported that Mr Coleridge was "exceedingly ill" and gave only "one extempore illustration" in his talk. But twenty years later his memories of Coleridge at the dais had ripened. "His appearance was generally that of a person struggling with pain and overmastering illness. His lips were baked with feverish heat, and often black in colour; and, in spite of water which he continued drinking through the whole course of the lecture, he often seemed to labour under an almost paralytic inability to raise the upper jaw from the lower."

There was "no heart, no soul" in anything he said. When he failed to appear for any of the remaining lectures in February,

Albemarle Street was blocked each Friday with smart carriages and scurrying footmen, as the news of his continued illness first excited "concern" and then increasing "disgust". The whole series, concluded De Quincey, was an inevitable disaster: ill-prepared, badly illustrated with quotations (except for "two or three, which I put ready marked into his hands") and unevenly delivered. He later thought no written record of it survived, and implied that Coleridge had offended the Institution managers and did not fulfil his contract.[27]

The original contract had specified twenty-five lectures, twice weekly in the winter season, from January to March, for a fee of £140 with a £60 advance. In fact Coleridge eventually delivered twenty lectures, largely postponed to the spring season from 30 March to 30 May, and these De Quincey did not attend. The disaster lay at the beginning, as was perhaps inevitable, for Coleridge had to establish a form of public address which was appropriate to his gifts.

Coleridge treated the management with great respect and always tried to warn them of impending disruptions to his series through illness. At least one unpublished letter survives in the Institution's archives, informing the Secretary of his imminent collapse in February – being "unable to stand in a public room" and "most cheerfully" offering to pay for the cost of informing subscribers and advertising the postponement. He also obtained a proper medical opinion of his state. "I have sent for [Dr] Abernethie, & shall learn from him whether this be only an interruption or a final farewell. Either myself or my medical attendant will write to Mr Bernard."[28] A first advance of £40 was given in late February, with an addition of £20 in late April. But the outstanding balance was not settled for over a year, and it was reduced at Coleridge's own suggestion to a further £60.[29]

Coleridge's collapse into opium at the outset of his lectures suggests that the strain and anxiety of performing in public was much greater than any of his friends had supposed. As he was already famed for his private talk, and had youthful experience of lecturing and preaching in Bristol in the 1790s, Davy and Bernard imagined he would quickly find his feet in front of the Royal Institution audience. But this was not the case. The Royal Institution was not a provincial meeting hall: its large mixed audience from the City and the West End was fashionable, sophisticated and easily bored.

Tickets were expensive, expectations were high, and the Institution management required a fully written text to be declaimed in a formal manner.

Coleridge was alarmed by these requirements, which inhibited his natural lecture style. Far from being unprepared, his notes (for years scattered in the British Library and the New York Public Library) show that he had written out his texts for the two early lectures in numbing detail. He had chosen to begin with relatively conventional eighteenth-century theoretical topics: the aesthetics of Taste and the theory of Imitation, with a complex background of reading in Johnson, Blair, Herder, Dennis, Schlegel and Erasmus Darwin.[30] The first lecture, for example, included a 2,000-word citation from Richard Payne Knight's *An Analytical Enquiry into the Principles of Taste* (1806), which evidently exhausted both lecturer and audience.

Coleridge only slowly realized he needed to be much more innovative and intimate – to be much more himself. Herein lay the terror of self-exposure which took him weeks to surmount. He needed in effect to create a new style of lecturing, dramatic and largely extempore, which took risks, changed moods, digressed and doubled back, and played with his own eccentricities. He needed, above all, to enact the imaginative process of the poet in his own person, to demonstrate a poet at work in the laboratory of his ideas.

Coleridge's efforts to face up to the demands of his lectures cost him almost two months of continuous illness and opium excess. From the middle of February till the end of March 1808 his life was suspended, much as it had been at Keswick in the terrible winter of 1801. His stomach problems were so severe that he sometimes thought he would die, and he wildly added doses of hensbane, rhubarb and magnesia to his laudanum. In his worst moments he thought he had kidney stones or bladder cancer.[31]

His rooms at the *Courier* office, immediately above the printing press which started at four each morning, were thunderously noisy and chaotic.[32] He stayed in bed most mornings, and was so disorganized he could not even muster a clean shirt for lecturing. On one occasion he started with six shirts, lost three in the laundry, found he had been sleeping in the fourth, and had inadvertently used the fifth as a floormat while washing. The sixth and last shirt, when he put it on, had no draw-strings to do up at the neck.[33] His landlady,

Mrs Brainbridge, was old and deaf and could not cope with his visitors. She turned away one, the distinguished painter John Landseer, with the explanation to Coleridge that he was "a sort of a Methody Preacher at that *Un*stitution, where you goes to spout, Sir". Coleridge counted this as a rare compliment.[34]

Charles Lamb wrote to his friend Manning in mid-February: "Coleridge has delivered two Lectures at the Royal Institution; two more were attended, but he did not come. It is thought he has gone sick upon them. He ain't well that's certain – Wordsworth is coming to see him. He sits up in a two pair of stairs room at the Courier Office, & receives visitors on his close-stool [commode]."[35]

Davy, himself recovering from the near lethal dose of gaol fever, was appalled by what he had witnessed from the gallery of the Great Lecture Room. He felt he had observed a great mind in operation, but undergoing a process of self-destruction. Using imagery that Coleridge had himself used of Shakespeare's mind, he saw his friend being overwhelmed by a jungle of disorder. "He has suffered greatly from Excessive Sensibility – the disease of genius. His mind is a wilderness in which the cedar & oak which might aspire to the skies are stunted in their growth by underwood, thorns, briars and parasitical plants. With the most exalted genius, enlarged views, sensitive heart & enlightened mind, he will be the victim of want of order, precision and regularity. I cannot think of him without experiencing mingled feelings of admiration, regard & pity."[36]

By contrast, De Quincey gleefully recalled the "philosopher's" abject state like the scene from a comic opera. "I often saw him, picturesquely enveloped in nightcaps, surmounted by handkerchiefs indorsed upon handkerchiefs, shouting from the attics of the *Courier* office, down three or four flights of stairs, to a certain 'Mrs Brainbridge', his sole attendant, whose dwelling was in the subterranean regions of the house . . . until I expected to hear the Strand and distant Fleet Street, take up the echo of 'Brainbridge!'."[37]

Besides being ill, Coleridge was intensely lonely. Throughout February and March, his letters flew out in every direction – to Asra, the Wordsworths, Lamb, De Quincey, Southey, Mrs Coleridge, and above all to the Morgans, seeking some form of solace. It was not easily to be found. To Mary Morgan he wrote of what seemed to him an inexplicably cruel reply from his wife: "from beginning to end it is in a strain of dancing, frisking high spirits – jokes about the Itch . . . and she notices my illness, the particulars of which and the strong & fearful suspicions entertained of the Stone, in these words – neither more nor less – '*Lord! how often you are ill! You must be MORE careful about Colds!*' "[38]

When John Morgan kindly suggested he retreat again to Bristol, Coleridge felt he could not abandon his lectures. Besides, he asked, "what right have I to make your House my Hospital – how am I justified in bringing Sickness, & Sorrow, and all the disgusts and all the troublesomeness of Disease, into your quiet Dwelling. Ah! whither else can I go? – To Keswick? The sight of that Woman would destroy me. To Grasmere? – They are still in their Cottage . . . & they have not room scarcely for a Cat."[39]

In a wild attempt to lift his gloom, Coleridge now pursued a postal flirtation with Mary and Charlotte, with strange suggestive sallies and opium-inspired fancies. He wore locks of their hair round his neck, and carried Charlotte's profile miniature in his pocket like a lucky charm. When he lost the "pretty Shirt Pin" Charlotte had sent him (another sign of chaos) he swore that he would never wear another one as long as he lived: "The sense of its real Absence shall make a sort of Imaginary Presence to me."[40]

He concocted an extraordinary scheme of having Mary and Charlotte purchase dresses in Bristol, measured to fit them, but intended to be sent on as presents for Asra and Mary Wordsworth in the Lake District. This was the "Two Sisters" fantasy brought alarmingly to life. Astonishingly, John Morgan allowed this to proceed, the dresses were bought and cut and posted north, while Coleridge gallantly disputed the price, pretending they had charged him too little. Coleridge's amorous protestations were couched in nursery endearments of the most deliberately blush-making kind. "As to my lovely Mantua-makers, if a beautiful Lady with a fine form, a sweet Chin and Mouth and black eyes will tell an *Eff-I-Bee*, about 14 shillings instead of at least £5, and another sweet young Lady with dear meek eyes, as sweet a chin & mouth, & a general *Darlingness* of Tones, manners, & Person, will join with her Sister & swear to the same Fib, what can a gallant young Gentleman do but admit that his Memory is the Fibster, tho' he should tell another Fib in so Doing?"[41]

When further fuelled by opium, this coy dalliance got increasingly out of hand and confused. Coleridge in one letter imagined an alternative life in which he might have been married to Charlotte, or for that matter to Mary Morgan, or either of the Hutchinson sisters. His actual marriage was a crucifixion. "Neither wonder nor be wounded, if in this transient Infirmity of Soul I gave way in my agony, and *causelessly* & almost *unknowing what I did*: cried out from my *Cross*, Eli lama sabachthani! My friends! My Sisters! Why have you forsaken me!"[42]

This was too much, even for the Morgans, as Coleridge quickly realized. He hastily apologized: "I intreat dear Miss Brent to think of what I wrote as the mere *light-headedness* of a diseased Body, and a heart sore-stricken – and fearing all things from every one."[43] Yet there is little doubt that these dreams did possess and torture him. He felt he had "played the fool, and cut the throat of my Happiness, of my genius, of my utility" in marrying Sara Coleridge.

Underneath all this still lay the haunting, seductive image of Asra. Besides the symbolic dress, he sent her a copy of Chapman's *Homer* (used in his lecture preparations), plaintively remarking that its battered jacket properly represented its sender's state: "to quote from myself – A Man disinherited, in form & face/ By nature & mishap, of outward Grace!'[44] He talked endlessly about her to Daniel Stuart – still his great confidant in this crisis – and wrote as well: "Would to God I had health & liberty! – If Sense, Sensibility, sweetness of Temper, perfect Simplicity and an unpretending Nature, joined to shrewdness & entertainingness, make a valuable Woman, Sara H. is so." He added bitterly that in marriage he saw no middle way "between great happiness and thorough Misery".[45]

Still seeking to reach Asra's heart, he roused himself from his sickbed to champion the cause of her sailor brother, Henry Hutchinson, who was trying to buy himself out of the navy. His story was typical of the times, and gives another view of Nelson's service. Henry had originally been taken by a wartime press gang, nearly wrecked in the Gulf of Mexico, and imprisoned for four months in Vera Cruz. He now languished in the man-of-war *Chichester*, anchored off the Essex marshes, which was about to set sail on another enforced voyage.

Coleridge organized food and clothes, and wrote an impassioned plea to Thomas Clarkson and Sir George Beaumont, begging them to intervene in the case. He dramatized Henry (whom he had never actually met) as an Ancient Mariner and even, one might think, as an alter ego. "This man's whole Life has been one dream-like Tale of Sufferings – of repeated Imprisonments, of Famine, of Wounds – and twice he has had the Yellow Fever – & escaped each time from among a charnel-house of Corpses. He has done enough – he has suffered enough. And to me it is as if it were my own child – far more than if it were myself – for he is the Brother of the two Beings, whom of all on Earth I most highly honour, most fervently love."[46] Henry Hutchinson's release was eventually obtained through the Admiralty the following year.

It was now that Wordsworth came south, as Lamb had prophesied, reaching London on 24 February. He was genuinely concerned by Coleridge's illness and mental state, and wild reports that he was dying. He had always disapproved of the lectures, and he determined to take Coleridge back to the safety of the Lakes, "to prevail on him to return" as Dorothy put it.[47] He also wished to consult Coleridge about his new poem, "The White Doe of Rylstone", and arrange for its publication by Longman. He remained in London, with several much needed relief-visits to the Clarksons at Bury, until 4 April.

Rather to his surprise, Coleridge initially made difficulties about seeing him, and he could never get entry to his *Courier* rooms until four in the afternoon. But after several evenings together, he began to feel that Coleridge had simply given way to opium and could easily recover himself.[48] His suspicions were deepened when Coleridge gave an animated tea-party in his rooms on 3 March, receiving his guests – Wordsworth, Godwin, Lamb and De Quincey – like an oriental potentate, swathed in blankets, and throned on his bed, thoroughly enjoying the fuss. Lamb was amused by the situation, a case of the Mountain coming to Mahomet. He joked about Wordsworth's grand descent upon the Strand. "Wordsworth, the great poet, is coming to Town; he is to have apartments in the Mansion House. He says he does not see much difficulty in writing like Shakespeare . . . Even Coleridge is a little checked by this hardihood of assertion."[49]

Wordsworth also brought news that Asra was ill, with a mysterious "broken blood vessel"; news which according to Dorothy would prevent Coleridge from brooding over his own misfortunes. Wordsworth continued to rally him: they went to see Sir Thomas Lawrence's collection of pictures, and later dined with Longman to discuss "The White Doe". It was a dull evening, "saving that we had some good haranguing – talk I cannot call it – from Coleridge."[50] It was now clear that Coleridge was indeed recovering, and determined to restart his lectures. Wordsworth, though gloomily apprehensive, loyally remained in London to attend the third and fourth of the relaunched series, delivered on 30 March and 2 April.

5

When Coleridge recommenced with his third lecture on Friday, 30 March, his approach had altered. His notes had become compact, and more like a prompt script. There were no long quotations from aesthetic theory. He began with an eloquent personal apology that immediately caught up his audience in the drama of his own struggles. "I could not but be conscious to how severe a trial I had put your patience and candour in my last Lecture . . . still lingering bodily indisposition . . . my Faculties too confused . . . too weak to recite aloud . . . my mind gradually regained its buoyancy . . ." This appeal was immediately followed by an amusing definition of types of listeners: sponges, sand-glasses, straining-bags, "and lastly, the Great-Moguls Diamond Sieves" who retain everything that is valuable and forget the rest.[51]

He then launched directly into one of his great psychological explorations of the poetic principle, as illustrated by Shakespeare's *Venus and Adonis*. Even before Shakespeare became a great dramatist, Coleridge argued, he had shown eight essential "Instances of the poetic Power of making everything present to the Imagination". His notes number these off with effective brevity, and some indications of extempore development.

1. Sense of Beauty . . . good sign-painter who begins with old men's and old women's faces –
2. With things remote from his own feeling . . .
3. Love of Natural objects – quote "The Hare" . . .
4. Fancy, or the aggregative Power – "Full gently now she takes him by the hand,/ A lily prison'd in a gaol of snow"
5. That power & energy of what a living poet has grandly &

appropriately – "To flash upon the inward eye/ Which is the Bliss of solitude" – & to make everything present by a Series of Images . . .

6. Imagination: power of modifying one image or feeling by the precedent or following one . . .
7. The describing natural objects by clothing them appropriately with human passions "Lo, here the gentle lark" . . .
8. Energy, depth and activity of Thought without which a man may be a pleasing and effective poet; but never a great one. Here introduce Dennis's "The Grounds of Criticism in Poetry" . . . & end with Chapman's "Homer"[52]

He wound up the lecture by leaving his audience with a single, striking image of Shakespeare's godlike creative power to transform himself into other forms of being: "to become by power of Imagination another Thing – Proteus, a river, a lion, yet still the God felt to be there".*

In his fourth lecture, which followed promptly on Friday, 2 April, he turned to analyse in greater detail the visionary gift and power of the Imagination. It was "the power of so carrying the eye of the Reader as to make him almost lose the consciousness of words – to make him see every thing . . . without any anatomy of description". The effect was achieved by converting a series of visual details into a single, unified impression or feeling: "by a sort of fusion to force many into one".

Here the Imagination, "this greatest faculty of the human mind", used language to imitate a shaping principle within the natural world

* Coleridge saw this power of displacement of the self into the other, of self-projection or self-metamorphosis, as central to the workings of the Imagination. He had already described it in a wonderful letter from Greta Hall in July 1802, which he may well have recalled in this public lecture. "It is easy to cloathe Imaginary Beings with our own Thoughts & Feelings; but to send ourselves out of ourselves, to *think* ourselves in to the Thoughts and Feelings of Beings in circumstances wholly & strangely different from our own: hoc labor, hoc opus: and who has achieved it? Perhaps only Shakespeare . . . A great Poet must be, implicite if not explicite, a profound Metaphysician. He may not have it in logical coherence, in his Brain & Tongue; but he must have it by *Tact*: for all sounds, & forms of human nature he must have the *Ear* of a wild Arab listening in the silent Desert; the *Eye* of a North American Indian tracing the footsteps of an Enemy upon the Leaves that strew the Forest; the *Touch* of a Blind Man feeling the face of a darling Child." (*Letters*, II, p.810; and discussed in *Early Visions*, pp. 324–7.)

itself. It created an interior landscape within the mind's eye, with a unifying perspective. Poetry worked "even as Nature, the greatest of Poets, acts upon us when we open our eyes upon an extended prospect". Coleridge here returned to Shakespeare's "Venus and Adonis", to give one of his most brilliant re-enactments of the imaginative process in the reader's mind. It is based on a single couplet from the poem, an evocation of the emotions of separation and departure.

> Thus the flight of Adonis from the enamoured Goddess in the dusk of evening:
>
> "Look! How a bright star shooteth from the Sky
> So glides he in the night from Venus' Eye"
>
> How many Images & feelings are here brought together without effort & without discord – the beauty of Adonis – the rapidity of his flight – the yearning yet hopelessness of the enamoured gazer – and a shadowy ideal character thrown over the whole – or it acts by impressing the stamp of human feeling, over inanimate Objects . . .[53]

Wordsworth was witnessing Coleridge lecture in public for the first time, and listening to a historic declaration of the Romantic principle of the Imagination. He had also had the peculiar satisfaction of hearing Coleridge quote his own lines on "Daffodils" in the third lecture (themselves adapted from an entry in Dorothy's *Journal*), as a signal illustration of that power. Yet he was dry in his praise to Sir George Beaumont, though he now seemed to accept the physical and mental struggle of Coleridge's undertaking. "I heard Coleridge lecture twice and he seemed to give great satisfaction; but he was not in spirits, and suffered much during the course of the week both in body and mind."[54]

Nonetheless Wordsworth did not think Coleridge too ill to leave him without several important commissions, concerning his own work, to fulfil in London. He was to undertake entire charge of the "White Doe" manuscript; to show it to Lamb for comments and present it to Sir George Beaumont, and negotiate the financial terms of its publication with Longman. He also hoped that Coleridge would puff it when he came to lecture on "The Moderns".

Dorothy was particularly anxious that William would not change his mind about immediate publication, despite the likelihood of a hostile reception from reviewers, as they needed the money for Allan Bank – "what matter, if you get your 100 guineas in your pocket?"[55] Later she wrote herself to Coleridge: "Our main reason (I speak in the name of the Females) for wishing that the Poem may be speedily published, is that William may get it out of his head; but further we think that it is of the utmost importance that it should come out before the Buzz of your Lectures is settled."[56]

Wordsworth spent the entire Saturday night after this fourth lecture in Coleridge's rooms in the Strand. They talked over its themes, the concept of the Imagination, and the use Coleridge had made of Wordsworth's poem "Daffodils" to illustrate the "fifth instance of poetic power", that of producing visual images in the mind. It was quite like old times, and their friendship was much restored by this all-night vigil together on purely literary matters.

Wordsworth left at seven o'clock on Sunday morning to catch the mail coach north from the City. It was snowing lightly, and his thoughts were very full, of Coleridge and poetry and the Imagination they both worshipped. He described his sensations in a most beautiful passage to Sir George Beaumont, which he later turned into a blank-verse poem. It can be taken as a tribute to their ancient comradeship, even as their paths and destinies were dividing; the one left to struggle in the great city, the other returning to his native stronghold.

"You will deem it strange," he told Beaumont "but really some of the imagery of London has since my return hither been more present to my mind, than that of this noble Vale. I will tell you how this happens to be. – I left Coleridge at 7 o'clock on Sunday morning; and walked towards the City in a very thoughtful and melancholy state of mind; I had passed through Temple Bar and by St Dunstans, noticing nothing, and entirely occupied by my own thoughts, when looking up, I saw before me the avenue of Fleet Street, silent, empty, and pure white with a sprinkling of new fallen snow, not a cart or carriage to obstruct the view . . . and beyond and towering above it was the huge and majestic form of St Paul's, solemnized by a thin veil of falling snow. I cannot say how much I was affected at this un-thought of sight, in such a place and what a blessing I felt there is in habits of exalted Imagination."[57] It was precisely this gift of poetic vision that Coleridge had been analysing in his fourth lecture.

6

Coleridge continued lecturing twice weekly, mainly using Shakespeare and Milton, until the end of May. He rarely stuck to his programme, but noted: "Illustration of principles my main Object, am therefore not so digressive as might appear."[58] The records of the remaining sixteen lectures are very scattered, but Crabb Robinson, the newly appointed Foreign Correspondent to *The Times*, was particularly struck by the combination of close textual readings of English poetry, with sudden upward flights into dizzy philosophical speculations from Kant, Schiller and Herder. He also observed that the digressions could be the most valuable and moving part of a session.[59] Later Coleridge would pride himself on the risky, but electrifying effect of seeming to have no text, like a high-wire artist working without a net.

The diarist Joseph Farrington recorded one characteristic opening gambit: "When Coleridge came into the Box there were several Books laying. He opened two or three of them silently and shut them again after a short inspection. He then paused, & leaned his head on his hand, and at last said, He had been thinking for a word to express the distinct character of Milton as a Poet, but not finding one that would express it, He should make one – '*Ideality*'. He spoke extempore."[60]

The shorthand reporter, J. P. Collier, who covered the later 1811 lecture series, recalled how Coleridge had learned his technique in 1808 by painful trial and error, finally claiming to hold his audience by complete spontaneity. "The first lecture he prepared himself and when it was finished received many high flown frigid compliments, which had evidently been before studied. For the next lecture he prepared himself less, and was much admired; for the third lecture, and for the remainder, he did not prepare himself at all, and was most enthusiastically applauded and approved, and the Theatre completely filled. The reason to his mind was obvious, for what he said came warm from the heart . . ."[61] Of course it was certainly not as simple as that (the second lecture had been De Quincey's memorable disaster), but it was a true reflection of Coleridge's method as it painfully evolved.

A twelve-year-old girl, Katherine Byerly (daughter of the manager of the Wedgwood potteries) recalled years later: "He came unprepared to lecture. The subject was a literary one, and the poet had either forgotten to write, or left what he had written at home. His locks were now trimmed, and a conscious importance gleamed in his eloquent eyes, as he turned then towards the fair and noble heads which bent to receive his apology. Every whisper (and there were some hundreds of ladies present) was hushed, and the poet began. I remember there was a stateliness in his language, and . . . I began to think, as Coleridge went on, that the lecture had been left at home on purpose; he was so eloquent – there was such a combination of wit and poetry in his similes . . ."[62]

The journalist Edward Jerningham was rather harder to please. Nonetheless he recorded grudging praise in a letter to his niece, Lady Bedingfield. Jerningham's evident disapproval of Coleridge's highly personal style makes his witness account particularly intriguing. "My opinion as to the Lecturer is that he possesses a great reach of mind; that he is a wild Enthusiast respecting the objects of his elogium; that he is sometimes very eloquent, sometimes paradoxical, sometimes absurd. His voice has something in it particularly plaintive and interesting. His person is short, thick, his countenance not inspirited with any animation. He spoke without assistance from a manuscript, and therefore said several things suddenly, struck off from the Anvil, some of which were entitled to high Applause and others incurred mental disapprobation. He too often interwove Himself into the texture of his Lecture."

The last trait was exactly what appealed to other listeners. Even Jerningham, seeing Coleridge's wild and dishevelled figure among so many judges, bishops, and "ladies of the first fashion", was prompted to compare him to the great medieval lecturer Peter Abelard, in the fashionable Schools of Paris.[63]

Coleridge found ways of charming and engaging his audience, even in the midst of his most obscure flights. Crabb Robinson recalled: "I came in late one day and found him in the midst of a deduction of the origin of the fine arts from the necessities of our being, which a friend who accompanied me could make neither head nor tail of, because he had not studied German metaphysics. The first 'free art' of man (architecture) arose from the impulse to make his habitation beautiful; 2nd arose from the instinct to provide himself food; the 3rd the love of dress. Here C. atoned for his metaphysics by his gallantry: he declared that the passion for dress in females has been the cause of the civilization of mankind. 'When I behold the ornaments which adorn a beautiful woman, I see that instinct which leads man not to be content with what is necessary or useful, but impels him to the beautiful.'"[64]

Again and again in the lectures he returned to the psychology of the Imagination, often finding both original and homely analogies. In one he examined the accounts of ghosts and apparitions, comparing them with the effects of stage illusion. A "trick" ghost was quite different from an internalized hallucination, which worked by a process of imaginative association very similar to poetry. The one merely stunned with painful shock, while the other gradually took over the mind like a dream or a fairytale, holding rational laws at bay. He had often experienced the latter himself in Malta.[65]

In another lecture, one attended by Sir George Beaumont, he developed the same central idea of the imaginative power suspending rational law, by analogy with children's modes of thinking. Here he "interwove" not himself, but his son Hartley. Taking the example of stage illusion, he used child psychology to explore a new Romantic doctrine of perception. The eighteenth-century French critics had claimed that theatre produced "actual Delusion" in an adult audience; while Dr Johnson had championed the English empiricist or common-sense tradition by denying "altogether" that any real delusion took place. Coleridge disagreed with both positions, and argued for a more subtle, dynamic account of what actually occurs. The mind does not stand passively outside its experience, registering and recording. It is more like an electrical current, pulsing between objective and subjective polarities.

This example was calculated to appeal to his audience:

> As Sir George Beaumont was showing me a very fine engraving from Rubens, representing a storm at sea (without a Vessel or Boat introduced), my little Boy (then about 5 years old) came dancing & singing into the room, and all at once (if I may dare use so low a phrase) *tumbled in* upon the print. He instantly started, stood silent and motionless, with the strongest

expression first of wonder & then of Grief in his eyes and countenance, and at length said "And where is the Ship? But that is sunk! – and the men all drowned!" – still keeping his eye fixed upon the Print. Now what Pictures are to little Children, Stage-Illusion is to Men, provided they retain any part of the Child's sensibility: except that in the latter instance, this suspension of the Act of Comparison, which permits this sort of Negative Belief, is somewhat more assisted by the Will, than in that of the Child respecting a picture.[66]

This argument proclaims the enduring, childlike part of the creative sensibility. But it also first uses the striking idea of "Negative Belief" (the metaphor drawn from positive and negative electrical polarities). He would later apply this doctrine of the "suspended state" of Imagination to poetry as a whole, in the *Biographia Literaria*, to produce one of the most influential of all his critical formulations, the "willing suspension of disbelief". In other lectures he drew similar analogies with dream states and nightmares.*

The most talked-about lecture of the whole series took place on 3 May 1808, and was a single digression from beginning to end. Still anxious to make good the casual impression of his postponements, Coleridge volunteered to give a free "supernumerary" double lecture on a subject of topical debate. His lecture was scheduled to last over two hours. The theatre and even the gallery were packed out with fashionable figures, and among his supporters were Davy, William Sotheby, Godwin, Basil Montagu, William Rogers, and Crabb Robinson (still busily taking notes).[67]

The subject he chose was intensely controversial, and bound to

---

* Coleridge originally applied this to his own presentation of "characters supernatural, or at least romantic" in the *Lyrical Ballads*. ". . . So as to transfer from our inward nature a human interest and semblance of truth sufficient to procure for these shadows of imagination that willing suspension of disbelief for the moment which constitutes poetic faith." (See the general discussion in *Biographia*, Chapter 14.) But seized upon by Keats in his Letters as "Negative Capability", and by Shelley in *The Defence of Poetry* (1821), it gradually emerged as perhaps the single, most influential phrase and critical concept that Coleridge ever produced. (See I.A. Richards, *Coleridge on Imagination*, 1934.) In one week in 1997 I recorded seven separate uses of the phrase in newspaper articles and radio programmes variously describing films, books, drama, and scientific theories (though, characteristically, none credited it to Coleridge). Part of its power lies in its memorable description of imaginative receptivity, a hospitable freedom or playfulness of mind, rather than a fixed and perhaps premature intellectual judgement.

be popular. Two educationalists, Dr Andrew Bell and Mr Joseph Lancaster, had recently published rival schemes to expand national schools by using a "monitor" system, in which older pupils were trained to teach younger ones. (By 1815 over 500 schools were using their methods.) Bell was an Anglican and saw his schools as state foundations, while Lancaster was a Quaker and saw them as independent institutions. Coleridge believed passionately that education, especially in poorer areas, should be the responsibility of the state, and supported Bell's "Madras System" (so-called because it had been pioneered in India). But what most engaged his attention was Lancaster's enforcement of rote-learning by an elaborate system of punishment and penalties. These particularly outraged Coleridge, who was otherwise a great admirer of the Quaker philosophy. They included an astonishing panoply of cruelties and humiliations: makeshift pillories, shackling of the leg with wooden logs, trussing up in a sack, walking backwards through the corridors, and being suspended in a "punishment basket" from the classroom ceiling.[68]

Southey later reported an eyewitness account of how Coleridge had riveted his audience by "throwing down" Lancaster's book with "contempt and indignation", and exclaiming: "No boy who has been subject to punishments like these will stand in fear of Newgate, or feel any horror at the thought of a slave ship!"[69] Coleridge bitterly attacked these practices, not merely as inhumane, but as an essential perversion of the educational principle, which was to "lead forth" by love and imagination, not to instil by rivalry and terror. Instead he proposed three cardinal rules for early education. "These are 1. to work by love and so generate love; 2. to habituate the mind to intellectual accuracy or truth; 3. to excite power."[70]

"He enforced a great truth strikingly," noted Robinson, taking down his words verbatim. "My experience tells me that little is taught or communicated by contest or dispute, but everything by sympathy and love. Collision elicits truth only from the hardest heads." He said that the text, "he that spareth the rod, spoileth the child", was the "source of much evil". He was against cramming, severe religious observance, or an atmosphere of "quiet and gloom" in the classroom. Everything should be done to draw out each child, most especially those from poor and deprived backgrounds.

What really moved his audience was, once again, Coleridge's "inter-weaving" of his own experiences. He retold the story of John Thelwall in the weed-covered garden at Stowey: "'What is this? . . . Only a garden educated according to Rousseau's principles.'" And according to Robinson, he deeply moved his audience with recollections of his sufferings at Christ's Hospital, leaving an image which remained with them long after. "On disgraceful punishments . . . he spoke with great indignation and declared that even now his life is embittered by the recollection of ignominious punishment he suffered when a child. It comes to him in disease and when his mind is dejected. – This part was delivered with fervour. Could all the pedagogues of the United Kingdom have been before him!"[71]

Crabb Robinson summarized the impact of this remarkable performance in a letter to Mrs Clarkson. "The extraordinary lecture on Education was most excellent, delivered with great animation and extorting praise from those whose prejudices he was mercilessly attacking. And he kept his audience on the rack of pleasure and offence two whole hours and 10 minutes, and few went away during the lecture . . ."

But the lecture also caused a scandal. Supporters of Lancaster threatened Coleridge, and talked of a prosecution for libel. The management of the Royal Institution complained that he had exceeded his functions as a literary lecturer, and eventually passed a motion of censure.[72] When accounts reached the Lake District, Wordsworth was troubled and Southey astounded. No one had expected such an explosive return of Coleridge's energy and daring.

The lecture on education established the controversial reputation of the entire series. Coleridge was regarded as brilliant, unorthodox, uneven, and prone to plunge without warning between metaphysics and melodrama. No one could tell from one performance to the next if he would be inspired or obscure, rambling or provocative. But he tasted a new kind of fame, and even notoriety, in London. His rooms in the Strand were besieged by smart visitors (seven in one evening); he dined with the Bishop of Durham; went to fashionable routs in Portman Square; was insulted publicly by Sir Henry Englefield; was jostled in the streets by "Bullies of Lancaster's Faction"; was praised by Sir George Beaumont; was invited to a celebration dinner by the Literary Fund and by "a very droll mistake" dined at the Whig Club instead.[73]

He was asked to sit for his portrait by the society painter Matilda Betham, but, on the way to her studio across the Thames, fell out of the boat ("two mere children were my Charons") and knocked himself out on the landing stage.[74] His next lecture began with a vivid account of this accident, which rather characteristically no one believed. He was now at last able to write to Mrs Coleridge, with an account of his activities: "Now, my dear! I leave it to you to judge whether I can do more than I do – having besides all this to prepare William's Poem for the Press."[75]

He had found time to conclude the negotiations with Longman for Wordsworth's "White Doe", to go over the text in detail, and write Wordsworth a long appreciation of the poem.[76] But by contrast he spoke deprecatingly of his lectures, and the stir they had caused: "whole Hods full of plaister of Paris – flatteries about as pleasant to me as rancid large Spanish Olives – these on the one side – & permanent hatred, & the most cruel public Insults on the other".[77] He found it difficult to boast of any success to Wordsworth.

His fame in London, besides helping to renew old friendships with Godwin, Sotheby, Montagu and others, brought him one unexpected and strangely upsetting encounter. At the end of one lecture, a plump, anxious, middle-aged woman appeared at his dais and introduced herself as Mrs Mary Todd. It took Coleridge several agonizing seconds to realize that he was talking to his old love from Cambridge days, Mary Evans – the woman whose rejection had led to his marriage to Sara Coleridge in 1795.[78]

Mary Todd invited him to supper with her husband, and Coleridge spent an exquisitely embarrassing evening with them, soon realizing that the poor, worn-out-looking woman was deeply unhappy in her own marriage and regretted the past even more than he. He lay awake that night in his Strand rooms, weeping. Later he told Stuart that Mary had suffered "the very worst parts of my own Fate, in an exaggerated Form". Mary Todd separated from her husband three years later.[79]

Talking over these matters with Stuart in May, he felt a growing urge to reassert himself, and prevent life slipping through his fingers. It was now that he wrote his long entries on the mid-life crisis, and "for the first time suffered murmurs, & more than murmurs, articulate Complaints, to escape from me, relatively to Wordsworth's conduct towards me . . ."[80] At his Strand rooms, in the midst of his lectures and dinners, Coleridge felt the awful gap between his busy public existence and his private isolation. "Ah! dear Book!" he sighed, "Sole Confidant of a breaking Heart, whose social nature compels *some* Outlet. I write more unconscious that I am writing, than in my most earnest modes I talk."[81]

Somewhere across the street, when the rumble of carriages fell silent, he could hear a caged canary singing from a hidden attic window. "O that sweet Bird! Where is it – it is encaged somewhere out of sight – but from my bedroom at the *Courier* office, from the windows of which I look out on the walls of the Lyceum, I hear it, early Dawn – often alas! then lulling me to late Sleep – again when I awake – and all day long. It is in Prison – all its instincts ungratified – yet it feels the influence of Spring – & calls with unceasing Melody to the Loves, that dwell in Fields and Greenwood bowers –; unconscious perhaps that it calls in vain. – O are they the Songs of a happy enduring Day-dream? Has the Bird Hope? Or does it abandon itself to the Joy of its Frame – a living Harp of Eolus? – O that I could do so."[82] The very self-consciousness of the symbolism, so plangent and so beautiful, was its own reproach.

But other symbols, uglier and more accusing, also haunted him and were strong enough to become verse. If he was a caged bird, Coleridge was also a caterpillar emerging in the spring, insatiable and devouring in the hunger of his heart. If his soul was the "Psyche" of Greek mythology, a butterfly free to take flight; his body was a more sinister and repulsive creature, perhaps even a monster of emotional greed:

> . . . For in this earthly frame
> Ours is the reptile's lot, much toil, much blame,
> Manifold motions making little speed,
> And to deform and kill the things whereon we feed.[83]

Yet he also wondered if the Greek doctrine of the separation of soul and body implied that his mind could never be truly corrupted, even by opium. Indeed, perhaps opium was the source of his inspiration, despite its terrible physical effects. "Need we wonder at Plato's opinions concerning the Body; at least, need that man wonder whom a pernicious Drug shall make capable of conceiving & bringing forth Thoughts, hidden in him before, which shall call forth the deepest feelings of his best, greatest & sanest Contemporaries? . . . That the dire poison for a delusive time has made the body, the unknown somewhat, a fitter Instrument for the all-powerful Soul."[84]

His Notebooks ("alas, my only Confidants")[85] of May and June are full of such questioning, about the nature of love, genius, imaginative power and self-destruction. As he lay "musing" on his sofa, his literary speculations from the lectures feeding back into his private ruminations, he often felt overwhelmed by the sheer activity of his mind: "My Thoughts crowd each other to death".[86] He was never free of painful broodings on Wordsworth, shimmering memories of Asra, or "fantastic pangs of imagination" about Charlotte Brent, either.[87]

7

Meanwhile the Royal Institution lectures came to an end as dramatically as they had begun. Coleridge was due to close the series with a final five lectures in the first fortnight of June on "Contemporary Poets", and most notably on Wordsworth. Whether he ever gave this one, or any of them, is wrapped in mystery. According to his own account, he became violently ill again at the beginning of June, and also suffered the loss of his crucial Notebook containing all his headings and quotations. He postponed, and then extemporized for at least one lecture, probably on 10 June, and then abruptly the whole series was terminated. What exactly occurred, and why, is problematic.

Edward Jerningham gave one sufficiently theatrical explanation, though without revealing if Wordsworth was ever mentioned. "He looked sullen and told us that He previously had prepared and written down Quotations from different Authors to illustrate the present Lecture. These Quotations he had put among the leaves of his Pocket Book which was stolen as he was coming to the Institution. This narrative was not indulgently received, and he went through his Lecture heavily and without advancing anything that was spirited or animated. The next day he received an

Intimation from the Managers that his Lectures were no longer expected."[88]

The theft, though, really did occur. De Quincey, down from Oxford for the summer, told his sister shortly afterwards: "This day week he lectured at the Institution, and had his pocket picked as he walked from the Strand; but, having notes, he managed to get through it very well."[90] Moreover, the Institution was keen for him to continue. It was only when the Secretary received a desperate note from Coleridge on 13 June, that they regretfully accepted his demission on the grounds of ill-health.

The Secretary took the highly unusual step of recording the letter in full in the Institution minutes. "I find my health in such a state as to make it almost death to me to give any further Lectures. I beg that you would acquaint the Managers that instead of expecting any remuneration, I shall, as soon as I can, repay the sum I have received. I am indeed more likely to repay it by my executors than myself. If I could quit my Bed-room, I would have hazarded everything rather than not have come, but I have such violent Fits of Sickness and Diarrhoea that it is literally impossible."[89]

The Committee, headed by Thomas Bernard, refused to accept Coleridge's gallant offer to return the £40 advance, but instead voted to make "a proportional payment" for the twenty lectures actually given, a sum calculated at £60. It was unfortunate that owing to the Institution's own financial difficulties, this was not made until ten months later in April 1809. Coleridge remained in friendly touch with Bernard, who clearly admired his work, and later advised him on a journalistic scheme. But later literary lectures were thereafter placed in more conventional hands (the Reverend Mr Dibdin and John Campbell, otherwise unknown to fame).

It was not till long after that the Institution came to regard Coleridge's series as one of the most remarkable it had ever sponsored, and commissioned retrospective lectures to celebrate it in the same theatre. It came to be seen as a historic linkage between philosophies of poetry and science, as essentially experimental disciplines "performed with the passion of Hope". It was the series that launched Coleridge into a new career as lecturer over the next decade, and always connected him in the public mind with the star scientific performer of the age, Humphry Davy. Indeed Davy, after his grim forebodings of February, was inspired to write a celebratory poem on the subject.*

But the puzzle of Coleridge's collapse in June 1808 remains. The real explanation seems to have been personal unhappiness, increased to the pitch of paranoia by opium-taking. In these weeks he wrote a series of dangerously emotional letters, not only to Wordsworth, but to his brother George Coleridge, reproaching them for their behaviour over the past months. To Wordsworth he wrote of Asra, and to George of the unfeeling cruelty of the Ottery Coleridges. To both he was bitter in his reproaches with an intensity he had never previously expressed.

To George he said it was his last ever communication: "when Brothers can exert themselves against an Orphan Brother, the latter must be either a mere monster, or the former must be warped by some improper Passion." He now asked merely for a copy of his birth certificate, so he could increase his life assurance policy so that all his family debts could be paid off on his death.[90]

What exactly he wrote to Wordsworth is not known, because Wordsworth destroyed the letter. Coleridge's feelings are, however, partly revealed in his Notebooks. He was overwhelmed with anger and self-pity; he felt that none of his friends or family understood the efforts he had made, or the loneliness of his situation in London.

---

* Coleridge inspired Davy to write one of his best poems at this time, which connects science and Poetry as methods of investigating the eternal laws of the universe.

> All speaks of change: the renovated forms
> Of long-forgotten things arise again;
> The light of suns, the breath of angry storms,
> The everlasting motions of the main.
> These are but engines of the Eternal will . . .
> Without whose power, the whole of mortal things
> Were dull, inert, an unharmonious band,
> Silent as are the Harp's untuned strings
> Without the touches of the Poet's hand.

(See David Knight: *Humphry Davy: Science and Power*, 1992, p. 69.) The Royal Institution took some seventy years to recover from Coleridge's appearance, but then began commissioning lectures in his honour, among which have been those by Leslie Stephen, "Coleridge" (1879); Katherine Coburn, "Coleridge: A Bridge between Science and Poetry" (1973); and Richard Holmes, "The Coleridge Experiment" (1996), all published in *The Proceedings of the Royal Institution of Great Britain*. For the fascinating links between Romantic science and poetry, see Trevor H. Levere, *Poetry Realized in Nature: Coleridge and Early Nineteenth-Century Science*, 1981.

He felt isolated, rejected and disapproved of, by people who were far happier and better established than he would ever be.

Driven on, no doubt by opium dosing late at night, he surrendered to lament and wild accusation. "In short, I have summoned courage *sfogarmi* to give vent to my poor stifled Heart – to let in air upon it: Cruelly have I been treated by almost everyone – by T. Poole, all my Brothers, by the Wedgwoods, by Southey . . . but above all by [the Fates] and by Wordsworth . . . A blessed Marriage for him & for her it has been! But O! wedded Happiness is the intensest sort of Prosperity, & all Prosperity, I find, hardens the Heart – and happy people become so very prudent & far-sighted . . . O human Nature! – I tremble, lest my own tenderness of Heart, my own disinterested enthusiasm for others, and eager Spirit of Self-sacrifice, should be owing almost wholly to my being & ever having been an unfortunate unhappy Man."[91]

Coleridge's complaints were hysterical and self-pitying, and could easily be dismissed as wholly unjustified, the paranoia of opium addiction. (It is difficult to see what he could have held against the faithful T. Poole.) But the envious cry against Wordsworth had its meaning, and probably lay at the root of his outburst. It was triggered by a strictly practical matter. After all his efforts over the "White Doe", Longman suddenly informed him that Wordsworth had withdrawn the poem and that Coleridge had "misunderstood" his commission to negotiate its publication. Coleridge was "painfully surprised", having heard nothing direct from Wordsworth about it, only Dorothy's urgings to forward the sale of the work with the "buzz" of his last lectures on contemporary poetry.[92]

In a first letter he pointed all this out, remarking that neither Wordsworth's nor Dorothy's judgement should be warped by "money-motives". He should publish without regard to criticism or financial disadvantage, considering only the "steady establishment of your classical Rank". Indeed Coleridge had written "a little preface" to help sell the poem if required, and even planned a publishing scheme which would bring in regular money to support Wordsworth if he needed it.

This last, apparently quixotic plan, was mentioned in terms that might have alerted Wordsworth to the coming explosion. "Indeed before my Fall etc. etc. etc. I had indulged the Hope, that by a division of Labour you would have no occasion to think about [money] – as if I had been to live, with very warm & zealous patronage, I was fast ripening a plan, which secures from 12 to 20£ a week – (the Prospectus indeed going to the Press, as soon as Mr Sotheby and Sir G. Beaumont has read it)."[93] This was Coleridge's first reference to his newspaper *The Friend*, originally conceived in the flush of his lecturing success, as a plan partly to help Wordsworth.

All these offers were swept aside, and Wordsworth did not publish "The White Doe" until 1815. He may have had his own sound literary reasons (Coleridge had himself suggested some 200 lines of rewriting), but his peremptory treatment of Coleridge's efforts and advice was humiliating. He now received a second letter, of shaking intensity, "an outcry at the heart" going back over months of frustration and suppressed hostility, but concentrating on the struggle over Asra's affections. This had become the symbol of their threatened friendship. It was, noted Wordsworth in his draft reply, "the keystone of our offences viz. our cruelty, a hope in infusing into Sara's mind the notion that your attachment to her has been the curse of all your happiness".[94]

Wordsworth tried to refute Coleridge's accusations point by point, and thus some idea of what Coleridge had actually written to him emerges. It is a series of most intimate reproaches: they had supervised Asra's letters; they had regarded his influence as "poison entering into her mind"; they had told Asra that she was "the cause" of all his misery.

It is clear that Wordsworth was shocked. The draft of his reply is several pages long, laborious and unusually rambling, its tone veering between outrage and pained rebuttal. Coleridge's accusations were made "in a lamentably insane state of mind". His obsession with Asra, and suspicions over Wordsworth's own conduct towards her, his "transports of passion", were all "unmanly and ungentlemanly" and the product of a perverted sexual imagination. It seems clear that Coleridge had mentioned, among other things, the bedroom vision at Coleorton.

> There is more than one sentence in your letter which I blushed to read, and which you yourself would have been unable to write, could never have thought of writing, nay, the matter of which could never even have passed through your mind, had

> you not acquired a habit, which I think a very pernicious one, of giving by voice and pen to your most lawless thoughts, and to your wildest fancies, an external existence . . . and finding by insensible reconcilement fair and attractive bosom-inmates in productions from which you ought to have recoiled as monsters.[95]*

It is revealing that Wordsworth did not question his own behaviour, or accept that Coleridge's feelings might have been genuinely wounded. Perhaps it was more than he could afford to do. Instead he is fiercely dismissive, and loftily confident in the purity of his own motives. "[Sara] is 34 years of age and what have I to do with overlooking her letters: It is indeed my business to prevent poison entering into her mind and body from any quarter, but it would be an extreme case in which I should solicit permission to explore her letters to know whether such poison were contained in them."[96] The implication of the word "body" seems deliberate.

Equally, there is no consideration of the obvious effect of opium on Coleridge's outburst, though if there was "the possibility of some matter of truth" in Coleridge's deplorable letter then it was the sort of truth conjured up in "the phrenzy of wine". For Wordsworth it served to show Coleridge's weakness of temperament by comparison with his own. "I am not fond of making myself hastily beloved and admired, you take more delight in it than a wise man ought. I am naturally slow to love and to cease loving, you promptitude. Here lies the inconsistency."

It is the sort of exchange of letters that could have ended their friendship forever. But Wordsworth's great strength, and indeed loyalty, is shown in the fact that having unburdened himself, he did not send his reply. No doubt with Dorothy's help, the matter was somehow smoothed over, and the invitation for Coleridge to join them later in the summer at Allan Bank still stood. But the whole episode is more than enough to explain Coleridge's collapse in

* Wordsworth's fear of Coleridge's "monsters" is highly suggestive of their relationship at this time. Monsters and "daemonic" eruptions (often with sexual significance) are also an important and connected presence in Coleridge's poetry, both in the early ballads and the later poems of self-analysis, and Keats would record them as one of the characteristic topics of his conversation in 1819. See Ted Hughes's fine speculative essay, "The Snake in the Oak", in *Winter Pollen* (1994).

London. Moreover the emotional hostilities, tacit at Coleorton, now rumbled perilously just beneath the surface of their literary relations, and were almost bound – sooner or later – to explode.

8

Meanwhile Coleridge was rescued from his Strand rooms once again by Daniel Stuart, who summoned him from his sickbed to convalesce at Margate. The sea air blew away some of his self-absorbed miseries. Relieved from the strain of lecturing and the tortuous solitude of his thoughts, he recovered steadily, and in early July went to join the Clarksons in Essex to talk over some of the knottier points of an *Edinburgh Review* article. At the end of May he had taken the surprising step of writing to Francis Jeffrey, the editor of the *Edinburgh Review*, offering to undertake a major review of Thomas Clarkson's *History* of the campaign against the slave trade. The *Edinburgh*, with its Whiggish views and polemical style, was badly disposed towards both Coleridge and Clarkson, and for this very reason Coleridge – rather in the spirit of his education lecture – sought to engage the enemy on their own ground.

Coleridge had already praised the book to Clarkson when he first saw the proofs in March, though he regretted the absence of his own name from the famous illustrated "map" of the English reformers who had contributed to the passing of the Abolition Bill in 1807. "By the bye, your book, and your little map were the only publication I ever wished to see my name in . . . my first public Effort was a Greek Ode against the Slave Trade . . . and [I] published a long Essay in the *Watchman* against the Trade in general . . ."[97]

Coleridge still felt passionately committed to the campaign, and threw down the gauntlet to Jeffrey with a clever mixture of challenge and apology. "I write to you now merely to intreat – for the sake of mankind – an honourable review of Mr Clarkson's *History of the Abolition of the Slave Trade* – I know the man – and if you knew him, you, I am sure, would revere him . . . It would be presumptuous in me to offer to write the Review of his Work – yet I should be glad were I permitted to submit to you the many thoughts, which occurred to me during its perusal."[98] Jeffrey was too astute an editor to let this chance of controversy pass, and commissioned the piece for £20. The essay went off promptly to Jeffrey on 16 July.

Charles Lamb was relieved by Coleridge's resurrection, and did not believe executors would really be required. Though Mary Lamb felt that Coleridge "in a manner gave us up when he was in Town", Charles took his usual genial line on his old friend's vagaries and disappearances. "It is true that he is *Bury'd*, though not dead; to understand this quibble, you must know that he is at Bury St Edmund's, relaxing, after the fatigues of lecturing and Londonizing."[99]

But at Allan Bank they heard nothing, until Mrs Clarkson sent news of his recovery. Dorothy returned a message obviously intended to reassure him that the explosion over Asra was, in her mind at least, all forgotten. "Give my fondest love to dear Coleridge – Tell him that we have anxiously expected to hear from him, and were very uneasy till we heard from you that his health was tolerable. Whether he be with you or not, pray tell him all that I have told you respecting Sara . . . persuade Coleridge to write if you can . . ."[100]

But for the time being Coleridge contented himself with writing to Francis Jeffrey about the slave trade. He accepted some alterations in his essay, but insisted that Clarkson's flat, unliterary style – "a sort of scriptural simplicity" – should not be held against him. "He, if ever human Being did it, listened exclusively to his Conscience, and obeyed its voice at the price of all his Youth & manhood, at the price of his Health, his private Fortune, and the fairest prospects of honourable ambition. Such a man I cannot regard as a mere author. I cannot read or criticize such a work as a mere literary production."

The essay draws particular attention to the kind of "conversion experience" that Clarkson had undergone as a young man just down from Cambridge, when a Latin prize essay on the slave trade, written originally for academic honours, had come to possess his mind as the spiritual summons to a personal crusade. Coleridge was deeply interested in the psychology of this conversion, characteristic of the best elements of the Quaker culture from which it sprang.[101] It led to Clarkson's incredible perseverance in procuring evidence" against the trade, in one instance interviewing sailors "from above a hundred and sixty vessels of war" to obtain a single eyewitness account of slavery in the Calabar.[102] It also led to Clarkson's mental breakdown, from which he was saved by his marriage to Catherine.

All this was of intense personal significance to Coleridge, especially since his Malta experiences, illustrating the motivation and drive of the man of action whom nothing will deflect from his goal. He later described Clarkson to Stuart as "the Moral Steam-Engine, or the Giant with one Idea".[103] It was, of course, the very opposite of his own psychological make-up, and for that very reason of the greatest analytic interest. He wrote with passion, and Jeffrey later insisted on modulating his "too rapturous style".[104]

The other changes that Jeffrey made, though without Coleridge's permission, were politically slanted against the Ministry. But he accepted the alterations, and the £20 fee, with some murmuring and denied that the article could be described as "shamefully mutilated".[105] Yet it left an impression of political trimming which embarrassed him; and he never again risked writing for the *Edinburgh Review*. Instead he turned back to his idea for *The Friend*, his own paper in which he hoped to be free of party politics and editorial interference.

Clarkson expressed his gratitude by turning his steam engine powers on to Coleridge's professional problems, and allowing his wife Catherine to administer to the emotional ones. Catherine, now partially an invalid, had already entered sympathetically into Coleridge's most private difficulties, corresponding with Dorothy, having had Asra to stay in the summer of 1807, and having encouraged Henry Crabb Robinson to report on the lectures. She had also consulted Dr Beddoes about her own illness, and seems to have had a shrewd estimate of Coleridge's troubles. He told Robinson that he had grown to love Catherine "even as my very own Sister, whose Love for me with that of Wordsworth's Sister, Wife, & Wife's Sister, form almost the only Happiness I have on earth".[108] Perhaps this was an example of what Wordsworth termed his "promptitude" to love; or perhaps it was simple gratitude.

The large, comfortable, yellow-brick house at St Mary's Square became his base for the next month. Discussions centred on the setting up of *The Friend*, and Coleridge's long-delayed plan to seek an opium cure under a doctor. Both were put in hand. Coleridge also corresponded with John Morgan, who was at Hatton Garden winding up his mother's estate, and had some £1,500 of capital to invest. But if this was offered to underwrite *The Friend*, Coleridge took Clarkson's and Stuart's advice to launch his paper by subscription.[107] Clarkson also suggested that Longman should be the publisher, while Davy and Thomas Bernard negotiated with the Royal Institution's printer, Savage, on Coleridge's behalf. The first task would be to define the aims and scope of the paper, and issue a prospectus.[108]

Coleridge embarked on his opium cure with equal vigour. It is not known what doctor he consulted, since Beddoes had died in December 1808, causing Coleridge temporarily to despair of ever finding a physician he could trust – "Beddoes's Departure has taken more hope out of my Life than any former Event except perhaps T. Wedgwood's".[109] But it seems that Clarkson found a Quaker doctor to begin treatment, starting with some attempt to regulate the daily laudanum doses. The process was slow and painful, continuing with relapses into September.

One immediate result was the new openness with which Coleridge admitted his addiction, writing to many friends in the autumn of the struggles he had undergone. This public admission of addiction is now regarded as the first, and indispensable step, of any real cure in cases of either alcoholism or drug dependency.[110] Coleridge seems to have understood this intuitively, and confessed himself with almost religious extravagance. Many of these confessions would be written, with deliberately dramatic effect, on the back of printed copies of his prospectus, as if sin and restitution were being offered in the same package.

With the opium cure, and the plans for *The Friend*, underway by August 1808, everything suggested that Coleridge would now settle in London, where all the professional help he required was easily available. In particular, the logistics of a weekly paper – in terms of research, printing and circulation – demanded the resources of the capital city. Coleridge now made one of the most critical decisions of his career. He determined once more to return to the Lake District, and to try once again to make his home and relaunch his writing in the North. He went back to the Wordsworths and Asra and his children, drawn by a power far greater than literary ambition. He entered in his Notebook one phrase: "Plucked up my Soul from its Root."[111]

4

The Friend in Need

1

When Coleridge left Bury St Edmund's in August 1808, he performed one of his characteristic disappearing acts, and did not arrive at Grasmere for a month. This time it seems that he went on a kind of "retreat", part religious and part medical, before embarking on the great gamble of his newspaper enterprise. His Notebooks suggest that he went to ground at Leeds, staying with some of Clarkson's Quaker friends. Here he underwent the worst pains of an opium-withdrawal regime. Clarkson wrote to him secretly at the Golden Sun Inn; and John Broadhead, a Quaker bookseller, furnished him with grocery supplies and more spiritual nourishment.[1]

Coleridge talked at length with the Friends (the title of his paper may have been inspired partly by their unworldly sympathy) and even visited one of their schools at nearby Ackworth, noting that the "Girls' Playground" was grassed but the Boys' worn "perfectly bare", a sign of their different capacities for play and aggression.[2] He discussed the inward spirituality of the great Quaker teachers William Law and George Fox, and envied the Quakers' simple confidence in prayer, so unlike his own.

"The habit of psychological Analysis makes additionally difficult the act of true Prayer. Yet as being a good Gift of God it may be employed as a guard against Self-delusion, tho' used *creaturely* it is too often the means of Self-delusion . . . O those who speak of Prayer, of deep, inward, sincere Prayer, as sweet and easy, if they have the Right to speak thus, O how enviable in their Lot!"[3] The struggle to renew his religious faith went hand in hand with the struggle against opium, each relapse felt like a "Savage Stab" piercing both "Health and Conscience".[4] He experienced as never before a sense of personal sin, of the "Fall" he had mentioned to Wordsworth, but now as an absolute condition of his life. The idea of redemption, both as religious and psychological need, came to possess his thinking "O for the power to cry out for mercy from the inmost: That would be Redemption!"[5]

Philosophically this placed the concept of Evil, as a fundamental and inescapable fact of nature, back at the centre of all his thought. Poetically, it had been there since the days of "The Ancient Mariner". But now it had returned as a personal conviction, connecting his religious views with those on art and politics. When he came to write the opening number of *The Friend*, he startled his readers with the declaration of this as an *a priori* truth of experience. "I give it merely as an article of my own faith, closely connected with all my hopes of amelioration in man . . . that there is Evil distinct from Error and from Pain, an Evil in human nature which is not wholly grounded in the limitations of our understandings. And this too I believe to operate equally in the subjects of Taste, as in the higher concerns of Morality."[6] It was a dark reflection, born out of personal sufferings, and articulating the spiritual "witness" that the anonymous Quakers had encouraged during this phase of his regeneration.

2

By the time Coleridge reached Grasmere on 1 September 1808, much of his old physical energy was miraculously returning. He made one of his spectacular arrivals at 11.30 at night, waking the whole household, booming down the tall, newly painted corridors of Allan Bank, admiring and greeting. Wordsworth thought him "in tolerable health and better spirits than I have known him to possess for some time".[7] Southey, when he saw him, declared him offensively noisy and fat, "about half as big as the house".[8]

But Coleridge's feelings were delicate and silent. The sight of Asra filled him with secret, trembling delight. "For Love, passionate in its deepest tranquillity, Love unutterable fills my whole Spirit, so that every fibre of my Heart, nay, of my whole frame seems to tremble under its perpetual touch and sweet pressure, like the string of a Lute . . . O well may I be grateful – She loves me."[9]

Domestic matters quickly engulfed him. Mary Wordsworth was about to give birth to her fourth child, rooms were still being decorated, De Quincey was expected, the Coleridge children were longing to see their father. Coleridge marched over Dunmail Raise with Wordsworth, and stayed a week with Mrs Coleridge, a visit that passed off with unexpected goodwill on all sides. Southey had now moved into Coleridge's old rooms at the front of Greta Hall, and plans were agreed to send Hartley and Derwent to the local school at Ambleside. Coleridge felt the Keswick household was running smoothly in his absence, and was pleased and not a little astonished when his wife tranquilly gave permission for his daughter, little six-year-old Sara, to stay with him for a month at Allan Bank, and the boys to visit at weekends. A degree of reconciliation was in the autumn air.

"Be assured, my dear Sara!" Coleridge told his wife gently, "that your kind behaviour has made a deep impression on my mind – Would to God, it had been always so on both sides – but the Past is past – & my business now is to recover the Tone of my Constitution if possible & to get money for you and our Children."[10] Mrs Coleridge expressed her approval by sorting out his shirts and making "a pair or two of Drawers for the thighs and seat" of her husband, which had mysteriously expanded under his new health regime.[11]

Allan Bank was large, with tall windows looking north, and east over Grasmere lake, and the towering shape of Silver Howe Fell enclosing it to the south. It had none of the charm of Dove Cottage (which Dorothy always regretted), or the comforts of Greta Hall. Bleak and exposed, the down-winds from the fell filled it with draughts in summer, and chimney-smoke in the winter, so that food and books were often dusted with soot. Coleridge had a large study and separate bedroom on the first floor, but there was little sense of peace or space. Wordsworth was determined to be self-sufficient, and the three women were endlessly busied with cooking, laundry, vegetable-gardening, baking, and looking after the children – as well as a cow and two piglets.[12] Visitors were frequent, including Hartley and Derwent, De Quincey and his friend John Wilson, and Dorothy records that there were often more than a dozen round the table at meals.

Little Sara's visit to Allan Bank with her father remained one of her earliest memories: a mixture of awkwardness, enchantment and homesickness. She felt overshadowed by the Wordsworth children, especially the angelic Dora, her blonde locks dressed with paper curlers, and all of whom seemed able to play with Coleridge much more freely than herself, making "enough racket for twenty". Though she slept in her father's bedroom, she felt lonely and inhibited at first. "My father reproached me, and contrasted my coldness with the childish caresses of the little Wordsworths. I slunk away, and hid myself."[13]

But Coleridge was delighted with his daughter, and understood her fears as he had understood Hartley's. He told her stories, kept a candle burning in the bedroom, took her for walks to make her "rosier and hardier", and encouraged her childish romance with little John Wordsworth. He also realized that she was extremely bright and bookish, in a quieter less fantastical way than Hartley, and had inherited the extraordinary Coleridge eyes. "Verily, Sara is a deal cleverer than I supposed. She is indeed a very sweet unblameable Darling. And what elegance of Form and Motion – her dear Eyes too! as I was telling a most wild Story to her & John, her large eyes grew almost as large again with wonderment."[14]

Sara remembered those stories ever after. "I slept with him, and he would tell me fairy stories when he came to bed at twelve and one o'clock. I remember his telling me a wild tale, too, in his study, and my trying to repeat it to the maids afterwards."

Sara was also aware, in the acute way of a child, of the mysterious bond between her father and Asra. But, like Hartley, she felt uneasy with it and could not understand the attraction. She saw Asra through her mother's disapproving eyes. "My father used to talk to me with much admiration and affection of Sara Hutchinson . . . She had fine, long, light brown hair, I think her only beauty, except a fair skin, for her features were plain and contracted, her figure dumpy, and devoid of grace and dignity. She was a plump woman, of little more than five feet. I remember my father talking to me admiringly of her long light locks, and saying how mildly she bore it when the baby pulled them hard."[15]

This tiny observation of Asra's willingness to suffer, perhaps out of a frustrated maternal instinct, and Coleridge's curious, almost erotic fascination with it, shows little Sara's perception. She also saw, at least in retrospect, that Coleridge wanted to beguile her affections away from Greta Hall. "I think my dear father was anxious that I should learn to love him and the Wordsworths and their children, and not cling so exclusively to my mother, and all around me at home." Like many children from a divided family she was to feel torn and guilty about this long into adulthood.

Coleridge himself was both excited and troubled by his new domestic arrangements. His outward family life, apparently now stabilized between Allan Bank and Greta Hall, brought a new sense of purpose which he would pour into *The Friend*. But his proximity to Asra, living and sleeping in the same house, always on the other side of a door or a wall, and always under Wordsworth's commanding eye, haunted him as it had done at Coleorton. He entered a tense, anxious little love-lyric in his Notebooks:

> Two wedded hearts, if e'er were such,
> Imprisoned in adjoining cells,
> Across whose thin partition-wall
> The Builder left one narrow rent,
> And where, most content in discontent,
> A joy with itself at strife –
> Die into an intenser Life.[16]

Wordsworth was obviously keen to avoid any such "intenser life", but chose an unexpected way to defuse the situation. In mid-September he took Coleridge and Asra on a week's walking tour along the river Duddon, just the three of them together, striding over the fells and staying at local inns. At Seathwaite Vale, Coleridge noted with a shiver of delight: "W. Wordsworth, Sara, & I – the Cottage, Hollinghouse!! all, all . . ."[17] But there is no further record of what was discussed, or what decided. Amid the landscape observations – the ferns changing from green to gold, "harbinger of our autumnal splendours", and the dark valley mists below Capel Crag ('Sara's most appropriate phrase at the Head of Wastdale: how DEEP it is!") – there was a strange silence on all matters of the heart. But there were stray glimpses, which suggest that once again Coleridge was being forced to renounce all expression of his love.

There was "something incomprehensible in Sara's feelings concerning [Wordsworth]". If she still felt "a real preference of Love" for himself, how could he explain "her evidently greater pleasure in gazing on" his friend?[18] Why was she now so uneasy in his physical company? "You never sat with me or near me ten minutes in your life without showing a restlessness, & a thought of going, etc., for at least five minutes out of the ten."[19] Why did she dart away from any expression of warmth or feeling: "she shines and is cold, as the tropic Firefly"?

The terrible thought again came to Coleridge that Asra's love might have become mere loyalty to him, out of pity for his sufferings. "But how much of her Love is Pity? Humane dread of inflicting Anguish? Dignified sense of Consistency & Faith?"[20] Yet he still saw her beauty burning in everything around him, even an autumn rose on the table at the inn. "How have I looked at a full-blown Rose, bending or drooping from its own weight over the edge of the Glass or Flower Pot, and seeming to spy Sara and at last even a countenance."[21]

Back at Allan Bank in October, Asra took to covering the long hair that Coleridge so admired with a cotton mob-cap. It took away the youthful softness of her face, and emphasized her bony nose and prominent chin. Coleridge was shocked by the transformation: "astonishing effect of an unbecoming Cap on Sara. It in the strictest sense of the word frightened me . . . producing a painful startle whenever she turned her face suddenly round on me . . ." He urged her not to "play these tricks with her angel countenance", but she refused to take it off. It was a clear assertion of her new domestic role and independence.

Coleridge wrote sorrowfully of the "heavenly Vision of her Face" which had saved him from Cecilia Bertozzi in Syracuse. Now he felt Asra was deliberately breaking the sacred chain of his memories and associations. It was "morally culpable", and cruel; but might one day make the subject for a poem. "What if on my Death-bed her Face, which had hovered before me as my soothing and beckoning Seraph, should all at once flash into that new face . . . ?" Over twenty years later the "distressing", dreamlike image of love's metamorphosis did indeed appear in his poem, "Phantom or Fact".[22]

Yet it seems likely from Asra's behaviour that the proximity that was so tantalizing to him was for her largely oppressive. Asra sought distance and homely practicality in their relations, reflecting the Wordsworths' own fears of Coleridge's emotional claims on the entire household. She would support him with his children, with his struggles against opium, above all with his work on *The Friend*. But she no longer wanted to be the object of his dreams, his love, his tortuous secret passion. If this was indeed her attitude (and if the heart can ever be quite steady in such circumstances), it was a not unreasonable or unkindly one. But of course it would have been a profound rejection of the very impulse that had brought Coleridge north again in the first place.

3

Coleridge's initial response was to embrace the practical, and to plunge headlong into the business of *The Friend*. For the next three months he worked with furious energy on every detail of the proposed paper: prospectus, subscriptions, printing arrangements, distribution, financing, and the provision of stamped paper (which was required by government regulations for weekly publications). Letters flew out to all his friends: Humphry Davy, Tom Poole, Daniel Stuart, Sir George Beaumont, Basil Montagu, John Monkhouse, and even brother George at Ottery and slippery Francis Jeffrey at the *Edinburgh Review*.

His rousing letter to Poole was typical of the rest:

> My dear Poole, I will make a covenant with you. Begin to count my Life, as a Friend of yours, from January 1809 . . . I promise you on my honour, that *The Friend* shall be the main Pipe thro' which I shall play off the whole reservoir of my collected Knowledge and of what you are pleased to believe Genius. It is indeed Time to be doing something for myself. Hitherto I have layed my Eggs with Ostrich carelessness & Ostrich oblivion – most indeed have been crushed under foot – yet not a few have crawled forth into Light to furnish Feathers for the Caps of others, and some too to plume the shafts in the Quivers of my Enemies. My first essay (and what will be at the BOTTOM of all the rest) is on the nature and importance of *Principles*.[23]

Coleridge's plan to produce a weekly paper was extraordinarily ambitious in itself. But to write, edit and publish it single-handedly from Grasmere seemed almost crazily so. Most of his friends, with the signal exception of his old Fleet Street editor Daniel Stuart, thought it could never succeed. Charles Lamb voiced the general view when he wrote wryly to Hazlitt in December: "There came this morning a printed Prospectus from S. T. Coleridge, Grasmere, of a Weekly Paper to be called *The Friend*. A flaming Prospectus,

I have no time to give the heads of it. To commence first Saturday in January [1809]. There came also Notice of a Turkey from Mr Clarkson, which I am more sanguine in expecting the accomplishment of than I am of Coleridge's prophesy."[24]

Wordsworth, Southey and Tom Poole were all secretly of the same opinion. Coleridge's disorganization, his unbusinesslike routine, his legendary prevarication over deadlines, his philosophical introspection, and above all his ill-health and opium addiction would surely destroy any chance of journalistic success. Only a man as optimistically naive as John Morgan could possibly write: "I think this plan of yours most admirably calculated for your habits of thinking . . . with a trifling effort you must succeed."[25]

Moreover Coleridge was not planning a conventional paper, with topical or polemical appeal. He distinguished his aims sharply from the regular pro-government papers, the fashionable radicalism of the newly-launched *Examiner*, the brilliant literary partisanship of the *Edinburgh Review*, or the racy political populism of William Cobbett's *Weekly Register* (his nearest rival as a one-man operation, but of "undigested passionate Monologues").

Coleridge intended to eschew all current affairs, literary novelties, personalities or political scandals. Indeed he rejected the very idea of journalistic appeal and popularity itself, even though Jeffrey and Cobbett had discovered a huge new readership for such material in an angry and discontented wartime England, disillusioned with its leadership and restless with economic deprivations. Coleridge wanted to challenge and provoke in a far deeper, more thoughtful way, and his readership would be deliberately restricted.

"My Purposes are widely different," he wrote to Humphry Davy. "I do not write in this Work for the *Multitude*; but for those who by Rank, or Fortune, or official Situation, or Talents or Habits of Reflection, are to *influence* the Multitude. I write to found true PRINCIPLES, to oppose false PRINCIPLES, in Criticism, Legislation, Philosophy, Morals, and International Law."[26]

These great "principles" were supposed to emerge as the work unfolded: there was no declaration of an initial ideology or campaign motto. But Coleridge wanted to write as an opinion-former, to create a philosophical intelligentsia in a new way. His work was to be deliberately elitist: exclusive and intellectually demanding. He made no apology for this. He was not producing a set of "Labourers' pocket knifes" for cutting bread and cheese, but a "Case of Lancets" for dissecting the anatomy of a national condition.[27] His target was what he came to call the "Heresy" of expediency, of short-term aims, superficial thinking; it was also the intellectual partisanship of British journalism itself.

4

There were various versions of his Prospectus, the first two printed at Kendal, and a third in London. They were circulated also as commercial advertisements by friends and booksellers in Oxford, Cambridge, Bristol, Bath, York and Leeds, with the initial intention of securing one thousand subscribers.

This relatively high circulation target was crucial to the financial viability of the project. Yet the tone of the Prospectus was far from commercial. It deliberately called attention to Coleridge's working habits, his reputation for "unrealized schemes", his vast and eccentric reading, and most significantly of all, the existence of his private Notebooks. This decision to make the paper a personal testament from the outset, with strong elements of intellectual autobiography, was the key to Coleridge's journalistic approach. Like the whole venture, it was a high-risk strategy, and the one that most alarmed his friends. But in the Prospectus he committed himself from the start, with all the perilous promises of self-exposure.

> At different Periods of my Life I have not only planned, but collected Material for many Works on various and important Subjects: so many indeed, that the Number of unrealized Schemes, and the Mass of my miscellaneous fragments, have often furnished my friends with a Subject of Raillery, and sometimes Regret and Reproof . . . I am inclined to believe, that this Want of Perseverance has been produced by Over-activity of Thought, modified by a Constitutional Indolence . . . I was still tempted onward by an increasing Sense of the Imperfection of my knowledge, and by the Conviction, that, in order to fully comprehend and develop any one Subject, it was necessary that I should make myself Master of some other, which again as regularly involved a third, and so on, with an ever-widening Horizon. Yet one Habit, formed during long

> Absences from those, with whom I converse with full Sympathy, has been of Advantage to me – that of daily noting down, in my Memorandum or Common-place Books, both Incidents and Observations; whatever had occurred to me from without, and all the Flux and Reflux of my Mind within itself. The Number of these Notices, and their Tendency, miscellaneous as they were, to one common End (*what we are and what we are born to become*) first encouraged me to undertake the Weekly Essay . . .[28]

This declaration was followed by a fabulous list of possible essay subjects. They ranged from the elevated and philosophical – "Ground of Morality as distinguished from Prudence", or "Origins of the Moral Impulses"; through the cultural aspects of Politics, Poetry, Painting, Gardening, Music, Foreign Literatures, Education and Travel; to the chatty "Characters met with in real Life". All these did eventually appear at some point in *The Friend*. Coleridge also added a mysterious final paragraph, hinting at the metaphysical depths he had plumbed in Malta. *The Friend* would provide: "Sources of Consolation to the Speculative Gloom afflicted in Misfortune, or Disease, or Dejection of Mind, from the Exertion and right Application of Reason, the Imagination, and the Moral Sense; and new Sources of Enjoyment opened out . . ."[29]

He received much correspondence in reaction to the Prospectus. Jeffrey objected to the phrase "Speculative Gloom"; Southey thought there was an "affectation of Humility in the Style"; and others simply doubted that he could possibly sustain a weekly publication. But Coleridge persisted, writing cheerfully to Davy on 7 December: "My Health and Spirits are improved beyond my boldest Hopes. A very painful Effort of moral Courage has been remunerated by Tranquillity – by Ease from the Sting of Self-disapprobation. I have done more for the last 10 weeks than I had done for three years before."[30]

In this and other letters he also again talked of his conquest of opium addiction, writing to Stuart's partner T. G. Street: "if I entirely recover, I shall deem it a sacred Duty to publish my Case, though without my name – for the practice of taking Opium is dreadfully spread." He now realized it was a common addiction among working people "throughout Lancashire and Yorkshire", and a local chemist told him he sold "three Pound of Opium, & a Gallon of Laudanum" each market day. He thought he might even campaign for "legislative Interference".[31]

5

The Friend was due to start publication in January 1809, and Coleridge felt "a quickening and throb in the pulse of Hope".[32] But around him at Allan Bank doubts were hardening. Wordsworth was embarked on a quite different journalistic venture, a long political pamphlet attacking the Convention of Cintra (August 1808), by which the government had "shamefully" allowed Napoleon to evacuate the Spanish peninsula. He wanted Coleridge's help with this, and wrapped up in parliamentary reports and party political debates, regarded *The Friend* as something of a dilettante distraction. He recommended it to Walter Scott and others, but without much enthusiasm.[33]

Dorothy hoped for success, but shrewdly observed Coleridge's erratic preparations. "Dear Coleridge is well and in good spirits, writing letters to all his friends and acquaintances, dispatching Prospectuses, and fully prepared to begin his work. Nobody, surely, but himself would have ventured to send forth this Prospectus, with not one essay written, no beginning made but yet I believe it was the only way for him." She also saw the shadow of opium darkening again in the long winter nights. "I cannot, however, be without hauntings of fear, seeing him so often obliged to lie in bed more than half of the day – often so very poorly as to be utterly unable to do anything whatever. Today, though he came down to dinner at three perfectly well, he did not rise till near two o'clock."

Yet Coleridge's Notebooks suggest he was reading hard through these solitary nights, and making "Hints for *The Friend*".[34] However ill he seemed in the mornings, he was "cheerful and comfortable at night", and had persuaded Asra to work alongside him sometimes in his study. Dorothy blessed the tranquillity of these evenings, when something of the old harmony had returned, and Coleridge had rejoined the circle. "Sara and he are sitting together in his parlour, William and Mary (alas! all involved in smoke) in William's study, where she is writing for him (he dictating) . . . Mr De Quincey is beside me, quietly turning over the leaves of a Greek book . . ."[35]

6

But this studious calm was short-lived, and Coleridge was soon plunged into a labyrinthine series of problems concerning the technical production of *The Friend*. These threatened to bring the whole enterprise to a halt, exactly as the sceptics had predicted. Much energy and persistence over the next six months was required to overcome them, involving dozens of letters and endless visits to printers. They turned on three essential questions: how should the paper be financed, where should it be printed, and how should it be distributed?

Coleridge originally thought that all these had been solved by his agreement with William Savage, the London printer for the Royal Institution. Savage would finance and handle the production, distribute through booksellers, and take 5 per cent of the profits.[36] But in mid-December he received a letter from Savage outlining an entirely different plan. Savage wanted a monthly, mass circulation paper, selling for sixpence, advertised by "at least 1,000" prospectuses, and with a distinctly political character. Moreover he wanted 50 per cent of the profits, "and the power of printing it . . . in any subsequent editions".[37]

All these terms went against Coleridge's conception of *The Friend*, and Daniel Stuart advised that the financial conditions "would have led you into a gulph of debt or obligation; they are most ruinous . . . You would have been like a Young Girl who gets into a Bawdy House."[38] Savage was dismissed, and the first postponement of the launch date, to February 1809, followed.

The next scheme, following Stuart's advice, was to find a local printer at Kendal. But this would involve distributing the paper by direct post, which required the purchase of government stamped paper, and the lodging of financial sureties. It took over a month to investigate these matters. Coleridge took a brief break with Hartley over the New Year, visiting the Lloyd family at Old Braithay.

Here seventeen-year-old Agatha Lloyd observed father and son with a candid, teenage eye. Coleridge was clearly a "genius", with strong paternal affections and "extraordinary" powers of mind and conversation. "But in his domestic habits I do not wonder at his being a very trying husband." Hartley, upon whom his father doted blindly, was actually very odd: "painfully out of the common way both in mind and constitution". Their visit was exciting but disruptive, and made Miss Agatha long for the return of the "quiet fireside" of their own family life.[39]

When Coleridge returned to Allan Bank, he found Asra ill and Wordsworth deep in a deadline crisis with his *Cintra* pamphlet, a synopsis of which was being serialized in the *Courier*. Stuart had asked for immediate rewrites, and Coleridge worked from eleven in the morning till 3 a.m. the next day producing an expanded text, which was posted at dawn and published on 13 January 1809.[40] This journalistic feat convinced Stuart of Coleridge's unshaken powers to produce the fast copy that *The Friend* would require, just as it brought home to Coleridge the extreme impracticality of the scheme without rapid and regular communications with London.

"It is not once in ten times, that we can answer by the same post, that brings the Letter . . . the bitterness of the raw frosty wind made it impracticable for me to walk three miles to & three miles back again so as to meet the Letter-carrier at Rydale, at ten o'clock at night . . . [Wordsworth] has twice walked out to the Carrier's House after two in the morning . . ."[41]

He now pinned his hopes on getting the paper printed by Matthew Pennington, "the worthy old Bookseller and Printer of Kendal", who had produced the original Prospectus. Stuart, who was now completely committed to the project, agreed to obtain supplies of stamped paper, and carried an advertisement for *The Friend* to begin in March 1809. Wordsworth and Southey, seeing Coleridge's determination, agreed to pledge £200 each as sureties.[42]

Coleridge wrote triumphantly to Poole that all was now prepared, despite "vexations, hindrances, scoundrelisms, disappointments". Though the stamped paper would make "a most villainous diminution of my profits", the basic mechanics of the paper were set up. "The Friend will be stamped as a Newspaper, and under the Newspaper Act – which will take 3½d from each Shilling but enable the Essay to pass into all parts & corners of the Empire without expence or trouble – it will be so published as to appear in London every Saturday Morning, and be sent off from the Kendal Post to every part of the Kingdom by the Thursday Morning's Post . . . The money is to be paid to the Bookseller, the agent, in the next town, once in twenty weeks."[43]

On 3 February he rode over to Kendal to finalize the arrangements. Here old Mr Pennington announced that he had decided to retire from business, and there was no one nearer than Liverpool who could take over the work.[44] Coleridge postponed his launch date till 1 April 1809.

7

Within a week he had conceived his next plan. He would set up his own press at Grasmere, print *The Friend* and also a luxury edition of the classics. De Quincey, who had now moved into Dove Cottage, would be co-opted on to the scheme, as a particularly suitable assistant. "Besides his erudition, he has a great turn for manual operations, and is even to something of old bachelor preciseness accurate, and regular in all he does. It is his determination to have printed under his own Eye immaculate Editions of such of the eminently great Classics, English and Greek as most needs it – and to begin with the Poetic Works of Milton."

Old Pennington – whom Coleridge still spoke of with great fondness, "a Genius, and mighty indifferent to the affairs of this Life" – had already costed the plan at £100 for "the Fonts of Type, the Press, and the Fitting-up etc."[45] Another long letter shot off to Stuart about typefaces, letter-founders and press makers. "I assure you, dear Stuart! that I am faint and sick at Heart with these Alps upon Alps of Hindrances, and Uncertainties." But he would cross them yet.[46]

The idea of Coleridge running the Grasmere Press (a strange avatar of Leonard Woolf's Hogarth Press) is historically intriguing, and not altogether unlikely. He had been closely involved with the print production of the *Watchman* in Bristol thirteen years before; and Sir Alexander Ball had asked him to do something similar with the *Gazette* in Malta. But the scheme was not favourably received at Allan Bank, where De Quincey was increasingly involved with proof-corrections to the *Cintra* pamphlet which would take him to London for most of the spring. Stuart thought it delightful but unwise, and wondered if they should fall back on a monthly publication issued by Longman in London.[47] But Coleridge insisted on the "weighty arguments" that required a weekly format.[48] He had now heard of an alternative printer, a young man called Brown, who had just started business at Penrith.

Half-way through a letter of 11 February, he abruptly broke off to follow up this new scheme, rushing off through the snow over Kirkstone Pass. The first part of the journey took him five hours on foot, including a bad fall on the ice. He took up his letter again five days later. "While writing the last sentence, I received a letter from Penrith, that Brown was both able & willing to print and publish *The Friend* – in consequence on Sunday I walked from Grasmere over the Mountains (O *Heaven*! what a *Journey*!) hither – and arrived at last limping, having sprained my knee in leaping a Brook . . . However I am perfectly satisfied with Brown's character, proposals, & capability."[49] The only slight difficulty remaining was that John Brown had no suitable typeface to print the paper. But this was a mere detail. Coleridge instantly sent to Wilson's of Glasgow for "a small Pica font", which cost him £38 less £2 discount.[50]

Coleridge now shifted his base of operations to Penrith, to deal with the final hurdle of the stamped paper. Dorothy regretted the move at such a "critical moment", fearing illness or opium: "If he had been able to stay quietly here the trial would have been a fair one . . . but then there is the affair of the Stamps, and what plague besides I know not, and he is so easily overturned – made ill by the most trifling vexations or fatigue."[51]

Yet by 17 March Coleridge was able to write to Stuart: "Every thing here is ready – the Printer, the Publisher, the Type, the Bonds etc. – I have more than 300 subscribers, tho there have been no advertisements – and eagerly have I hope to hear from you concerning the paper . . ." He hoped this could be obtained on credit from Fourdrinier Stationers in Lombard Street, but wrote to Bernard at the Royal Institution to have the £60 balance on his lectures (still unpaid) transferred direct to Stuart's account. "O dear friend! on this business my whole Prospect is set – I pray you, do set me going – I am ready with Essays full & written out – I can begin whenever the paper arrives . . ." Stuart duly dispatched 1,250 sheets "by the wagon for Penrith" on 25 March, expecting it to arrive in eight days.

Coleridge now set his launch date for 1 May 1809.[52]

8

Meanwhile he hoped to increase his subscribers to 500. Stuart had given him a rough estimate of his financial margins: 250 subscribers would cover his costs; 500 would bring him a profit of £300 at the twentieth issue; 1,000 would bring £800.[53] *The Friend* looked financially viable, and Coleridge wrote to Wordsworth that he should not involve himself in further journalism after the *Cintra* pamphlet for the sake of money. Wordsworth should not "withdraw himself from poetry", since he could "get money enough" for both of them.[54] However, Wordsworth confided bleakly to Poole: "I cannot say that Coleridge has been managing himself well; and therefore would not have you disappointed if *The Friend* should not last long; but do not hint a word of this to any body, as any thing of that kind should it come to his ears would completely dash him."[55]

But Coleridge was dashed by problems other than the increasing pessimism at Allan Bank. The Penrith wagon service, a rustic affair designed for local grocers rather than London journalists, did not deliver its precious cargo of paper for five weeks. In the interval, Coleridge went down with mumps, which prostrated him for much of April. Significantly, he retired not to Allan Bank but to Greta Hall, where Mrs Coleridge nursed him and Southey was unexpectedly encouraging.

Coleridge wrote to Poole with intense frustration: "just as I was beginning to enjoy the delight of composing the Numbers (& delightful I really did find it, compared with the misery of writing and reading letters of business, of travelling to & fro & hither & thither) but I was seized with a complaint in my Left Ear, heat, confusion, dull throbbing, turbid echo, & deafness, with the most intolerable dejection – utter despondency."

Once diagnosed, however, he cheered up again, moved his launch date to mid-May, and suggested that Poole contribute an essay to *The Friend* on the "delightful" subject of how to live happily on an income of £20,000 a year.[56] Then he crawled off to convalesce on the country estate of the local member of parliament, J. C. Curwen, whom he somehow convinced to lend free parliamentary franking on all business letters associated with the paper.

Still worried by the prospect of financing his first twenty issues, he also took the extreme step of offering the "absolute copyright" in all his poems – including the "Mariner" – to Longman for the derisory sum of £120.[57] Nothing could better show his complete, and even reckless, commitment to *The Friend* at this stage; especially bearing in mind that he had recently negotiated with Longman for a £100 payment on a single edition of just one of Wordsworth's poems. Longman replied on 4 May that his publishing house was "fearful that £120 is rather more than can be afforded", and the ruinous counter-offer of £100 was rejected by Coleridge after much heart-searching.[58] Meanwhile Stuart reassured him that the Royal Institution's £60 (paid at long last) would cover further supplies of stamped paper, and Coleridge's outstanding debts of £100 could wait.

The subscribers' list now stood at 500, including no less than twenty-eight members of parliament (among them the Foreign Secretary, George Canning), several bishops, many university dons, and a solid phalanx of the professional middle-class – doctors, lawyers, architects, bankers, businessmen, soldiers, clerics and schoolmasters.* Notable names among the literary and artistic world also included Walter Savage Landor, Benjamin Robert Haydon, William Bowles, Francis Jeffrey, Walter Scott, James Montgomery, Thomas De Quincey, Henry Crabb Robinson, and, rather suitably, the pioneer of aviation Sir George Cayley. And of course there were numerous old friends: Captain Pasley from Malta days; John Morgan; Sir George Beaumont; Thomas Clarkson; Josiah Wedgwood; John Prior Estlin; and even Coleridge's two brothers George and James at Ottery.

The launch date was set definitely for 1 June 1809.

At the end of May Coleridge secretly retired to the cottage of one of his Quaker friends, Thomas Wilkinson, who lived at Yanwarth just outside Penrith. Here he abstained from all opium and alcohol for a week, and made the final preparations for his first three essays. Dorothy later called Wilkinson, "even at the last, the Father of *The Friend*".[59]

* It has been suggested that nearly a fifth of Coleridge's original subscribers were Quakers, many of them gathered by Thomas Clarkson. See Deirdre Coleman, *Coleridge and The Friend*, 1988. But there is a more general problem of identifying Coleridge's readership, because in a sense he was trying to create what did not yet exist, a cross-party and inter-denominational "intelligenstia". This challenge of creating an appropriate audience, and finding a prose style to engage them, affects much of his later work. (See Marilyn Butler, "The Rise of the Man of Letters: Coleridge", in *Romantics, Rebels and Reactionaries*, 1981.)

9

Wordsworth had not seen Coleridge for nearly three months. He now wrote him an immensely long letter, largely about the editing of his own poems, "if they are ever republished during my lifetime". He also tendered some firm advice about *The Friend*. "You should always be beforehand with your work. On the general question of your health, one thing is obvious, that health of mind, that is, resolution, self-denial, and well-regulated conditions of feeling, are what you must depend upon; and that Doctors can do you little or no good, and that Doctors' stuff has been one of your greatest curses; and of course, of ours through you." He ended with a note of encouragement: "Sara is, I think, full as well as usual."[60] Coleridge did not reply.

At the end of May, Wordsworth also wrote to Coleridge's two staunchest supporters to give his measured assessment of his old friend's efforts. He did not of course know of all the struggles at Penrith, but he felt able to gauge the overall position, and felt duty-bound to be realistic. To Daniel Stuart he wrote: "Of *The Friend* and Coleridge, I hear nothing, and am sorry to say I hope nothing. It is I think too clear that Coleridge is not sufficiently master of his own efforts to execute anything which requires a regular course of application to one object. I fear so – indeed I am assured that it is so – to my great sorrow."[61]

To Thomas Poole at Stowey, he was rather more expansive. He pronounced on Coleridge's whole future, his career, his family life and his literary gifts. It was very sad, but there was no hope, no possibility of achievement, no second act.

> I am sorry to say that nothing appears more desirable than that his periodical essay should never commence. It is in fact *impossible* – utterly impossible – that he should carry it on; and therefore, better never begin it; far better, and if begun, the sooner it stop, also the better – the less will be the loss, and not greater the disgrace. You will consider me now as speaking to you in the most sacred confidence, and as under a strong sense of duty . . . I give it to you as my deliberate opinion, formed upon proofs which have been strengthening for years, that he neither will nor can execute any-

> thing of important benefit either to himself, his family or mankind. Neither his talents nor his genius mighty as they are, nor his vast information will avail him anything; they are all frustrated by a derangement in his intellectual and moral constitution . . .

Wordsworth added that nothing remained but to make some arrangements for Coleridge's children, "in the case of his death"; and that it was now useless for his wife or any of his friends to remonstrate with him. He concluded by asking Poole to burn the letter.[62] Such was the opinion of Coleridge's most valued and intimate companion, his literary comrade in arms for over a decade, at this crucial moment in May 1809.

A week later, on 1 June 1809, the first issue of *The Friend* arrived at Allan Bank. It opened with a quotation from Petrarch's *On the Life of Solitude*. "Believe me, it requires no little Confidence, to promise Help to the Struggling, Counsel to the Doubtful, Light to the Blind, Hope to the Despondent, Refreshment to the Weary . . . But it is my earnest wish, I confess, to employ my understanding and acquirements in that mode and direction, in which I may be enabled to benefit the largest number possible of my fellow-creatures."

The second issue followed on 8 June; and a week later Coleridge himself came into Grasmere, having climbed over Helvellyn by the Grisedale Tarn route, "our most perilous & difficult Alpine Pass".[63]

10

The history of *The Friend* that followed, over the next ten months from June 1809 to March 1810, is a pure expression of Coleridge's wayward genius. "I have been giving," he wrote towards the end, "the History of my own mind."[64]

Committed to weekly issues, pinned down to the "Procrustes bed" of sixteen pages – about 6,000 words per essay – and harassed to the end by printing difficulties and shortages of stamped paper, the production was chaotic and the great "exposition of Principles" continuously confused and sidetracked. Many issues ended with an unfinished sentence ("To be continued"), and many footnotes (often containing poetry) threatened to engulf the main text. Subscribers – eventually over 600 – were maddened by its obscurity. The impracticality of the subscription system, held over till the twentieth issue, involved Coleridge in a grave financial loss. From a journalistic and commercial point of view, *The Friend* was a disaster, exactly as Wordsworth had predicted.

But from a literary perspective, *The Friend* was a unique achievement and sustained in a way that astonished Coleridge's severest critics. In the end it ran for twenty-eight weekly issues (the *Watchman* had lasted ten issues), for which Coleridge wrote over 140,000 words of original copy (the equivalent of two modern novels), Exactly like his talk, it became a digressive masterpiece of learning, poetic insight, and thought-provoking asides and suggestions. Within its Amazonian jungle of tangled, unparagraphed, discursive prose, lay limpid pools of story-telling, criticism, memoir-writing and philosophic reflection.

For all its apparent lack of structure, it adapted and developed as Coleridge steadily responded to his readers. Three movements became evident as the weeks progressed. For the first ten issues, Coleridge concentrated largely on his original programme of political philosophy, dealing with themes as diverse as the concept of language and truth-telling in society, the freedom of the press, the function of taxation, and the Burkean notion of an organic community of reciprocal "rights and duties". He mounted a sustained attack on the Jacobin concept of the "Rights of Man", as a form of totalitarianism, and looked back at the English liberal reaction to the French Revolution and the rise of Napoleon.

11

For the next eleven issues, from November 1809, he attempted to make the paper more popular by introducing a whole range of miscellaneous subjects: travel-writing, tales of the paranormal, reflections on education and childhood, and much poetry. Broadly speaking, these illustrated his views on the psychology of the Imagination.

Finally, in the last seven issues, from January 1810, he tried to pull together his political and psychological themes, in a biographical study of wartime leadership as illustrated by the careers of Nelson and Sir Alexander Ball. But by this time he was exhausted, and the control of his materials became increasingly erratic. Nevertheless, the final issues of *The Friend* contain some of its most vivid and memorable writing, on what may be called his "title motif": friendship, courage, human solidarity amidst disaster.

Throughout *The Friend* Coleridge tried to remain true to his original, underlying purpose of pressing beneath the topical issues of the day, to examine what he saw as the animating principles and verities of human behaviour in society. His conscious rival was Cobbett's weekly *Political Register* (with five times his circulation and perhaps twenty times his readership), a forerunner of the modern tabloid packed with "news" and radical commentary. In this he was taking issue with the very notion of journalism itself, the cult of "novelty", personality and current affairs, which he felt destroyed the true, inner life of the mind.

To understand the world, his readers must look into themselves. To avoid superficiality, partisanship, and ultimately fanaticism, *The Friend* urged self-reflection and self-understanding. In this Coleridge wrote, as always at his best, as a poet who was bringing his own internal life to bear on the loud, exterior clamour of events.

Many of his most radiant and memorable passages expand this central thesis, paradoxically acknowledging that this was precisely why *The Friend* was doomed to failure in journalistic terms. As so often in his actual poetry, he took failure itself as his most liberating and radical subject. In issue No. 5, he wrote:

> But how shall I avert the scorn of those Critics who laugh at the oldness of my Topics, Evil and Good, Necessity and Arbitrement, Immortality and the Ultimate Aim. By what shall I regain their favour? My themes must be new, a French Constitution; a Balloon; a change of Ministry; a fresh Batch of Kings on the Continent, or of Peers in our happier Island; or who had the best of it of two Parliamentary Gladiators, and whose Speech, on the subject of Europe bleeding at a thousand wounds, or our own country struggling for herself and all human nature, was cheered by the greatest Number of *Laughs, loud Laughs, and very loud Laughs*: (which, carefully marked by italics, form most conspicuous and strange parenthesis in the Newspaper Reports) . . . Something new, however

> it must be, quite new and quite out of themselves: for whatever is within them, whatever is deep within them, must be as old as the first dawn of human Reason.

Against this parody of contemporary journalism and its heartless immediacy, Coleridge sought to champion "the blessed machinery of language" and its powers to "support, to kindle, to project the Spirit". His essays would seek to renew what was eternally fresh and questioning in the hearts of his readers, and to make them think like poets rather than like men and women of the world.

> But to find no contradiction in the union of old and new, to contemplate the ANCIENT OF DAYS with feelings as fresh as if they sprang forth at his own fiat, this characterizes the minds that feel the Riddle of the World, and may help to unravel it! To carry on the feelings of Childhood into the powers of Manhood, to combine the Child's sense of wonder and novelty with the Appearances which every day for perhaps forty years had rendered familiar,
>
> With Sun and Moon and Stars throughout the year,
> And Man and Woman –
>
> this is the character and privilege of Genius, and one of the marks which distinguish Genius from Talents.[65]

Thus he stated the central Romantic doctrine of *The Friend*, the inwardness of Truth, and its power as a Platonic revelation of what exists – or pre-exists – eternally within us all.

12

The early issues of *The Friend* remained irregular, until Stuart sent a second large batch of stamped paper in September. There were two in June, none in July, and one in August. But with No. 4 and No. 5 on 7 and 14 September, Coleridge got into his stride and continued weekly until January 1809. From No. 5 Asra became his trusted amanuensis, taking the essays from his dictation, some of them completed in hectic bursts of forty-eight hours' almost unbroken work.

The initial subject of "The Communication of Truth and the Rightful Liberty of the Press", expanded to an attack on the whole totalitarian nature of the Napoleonic regime. In this the wartime character of the paper was much in evidence (Coleridge reprinted a long extract from his "Fears in Solitude" in No. 2).

But his real object was a philosophical critique of Jacobinism itself, characterized as a government of abstract Reason denying all human continuity and tradition. Coleridge was driving towards a psychological as well as a historical analysis of the Jacobin spirit. This was revealed in Nos 8 and 9 in brilliantly original series of paired portraits, of Erasmus versus Voltaire, and Luther versus Rousseau.

The portrait of Luther is certainly one of the early triumphs of *The Friend* (No. 8, 5 October). Coleridge was attempting to define the inward, fanatical personality of the revolutionary spirit, the man whose private visions will be projected on to society around him, to bring forth angels or monsters. Luther, though a fundamentally religious man, was an archetype of the secular visionary like Rousseau, who would inflame an entire civilization with his dreams. The fundamental principle, as Coleridge analysed it, was a form of hysteria. It was exemplified by his famous vision of the Devil in his study at Warteburg. Coleridge presented this scene with poetic force, and drawing on what were clearly his own experiences with opium.

> It is evident from his Letters that he suffered under great irritability of his nervous System, the common effect of deranged Digestion in men of sedentary habits, who are at the same time intense thinkers: and his irritability added to, and revivifying the impressions made upon his early life, and fostered by the theological Systems of his Manhood, is abundantly sufficient to explain all his Apparitions and his nightly combats with evil Spirits. I see nothing improbable in the supposition, that in one of those unconscious half-sleeps, or rather those rapid alternations of the sleeping with the half-waking state, which is the true witching-time,
>
> "... the season
> Wherein the spirits hold their wont to walk"
>
> the fruitful matrix of Ghosts – I see nothing improbable, that in some one of those momentary Slumbers, into which the suspension of all Thought in the perplexity of intense thinking so often passes; Luther should have had a full view of the Room in which he was sitting, of his writing Table and all the Implements of his Study, as they really existed, and at the

same time a brain-image of the Devil, vivid enough to have acquired apparent Outness, and a distance regulated by the proportion of its distinctness to that of the objects really impressed on the outward sense.[66]

To this vividly realized scene, Coleridge attached a typically dazzling series of further speculations. He had viewed similar phenomena in his own study at Keswick, when at the moment of twilight his windows became partial mirrors, holding the night sky and the interior reflections of his firelit library in a simultaneous image: "my Books on the side shelves of the room were lettered, as it were, on their backs with Stars . . ."

This beautiful, and yet homely, poetic image provides the key to the mechanism of Luther's hallucinations. "Now substitute the Phantom from the brain for the Images of reflected light (the Fire for instance) and the Forms of the room and its furniture for the transmitted rays, and you have a fair resemblance of an Apparition, and a just conception of the manner in which it is seen together with real objects."*

He drew further analogies with Shakespeare's dramatic techniques of inward imagery ("for in certain sorts of dreams the dullest Wight becomes a Shakespeare"), and also added the long footnote on Tom Wedgwood's principles of psychological self-observation. He promised a further dissertation on the subject of "Dreams, Visions, Ghosts, Witchcraft etc.", and linked this with his ballad of "The Three Graves" and its study of obsession, already published in issue No. 6.

Finally, he brought the whole discussion back to Luther's obsessive religious temperament, and argued in a superb closing passage that if he had been born into a later, secular age, his dreams and fantasies would have become political, like Rousseau's.

---

* This combination of projected and reflected perceptions is characteristic of Coleridge's poetic and psychological approach to more general problems of Romantic epistemology. This whole passage could be seen as a demonstration of the Kantian concept of the "subjective" imposing itself on the "objective" view of reality. See Roger Scruton, *Kant*, 1985; or for that matter Jostein Gaarder's *Sophie's World*, 1995, pp. 268–79, which uses a very similar illustration. M.H. Abrams has examined the more literary implications of the Romantic doctrine of "vision" in a classic study, *The Mirror and the Lamp*, 1953. But the example of Luther also raises the issue of the moral ambiguity of Imagination: could it be demonic and dangerous under certain conditions? How far can it, or ought it to be, subjected to the Will?

> Conceive him a Citizen of Geneva, and a contemporary of Voltaire . . . His impetuous temperament, his deep-working mind, his busy and vivid Imagination – would they not have been a trouble to him in a World where nothing was to be altered, where nothing was to obey his power . . . ? His Pity, that so easily passed into Rage, would it not have found in the inequalities of Mankind, in the oppression of Governments, and the miseries of the Governed, an entire instead of a divided object? And might not a perfect Constitution, a Government of Pure Reason, a renovation of the social Contract, have easily supplied the place of the reign of Christ in the new Jerusalem . . . ?[67]

Charles Lamb, having followed Coleridge's struggles from London, now recognized that something extraordinary was emerging from the tentative and uncertain progress of the paper, and wrote urging Coleridge on. "The account of Luther in Warteburg is as fine as anything I ever read. God forbid that a Man who has such things to say should be silenced for want of £100. This Custom & Duty Age, would have made the *Preacher* on the Mount take out a License, and St Paul's Epistle *not* admissible without a Stamp."[68]

In his highly original and digressive way, Coleridge was building towards a central philosophic principle of *The Friend*, what he called in No. 10 (19 October) "The Errors of Party Spirit: or Extremes Meet". It was a larger and more subtle argument than the simple political revisionism that he would later be accused of by Hazlitt and other critics. It was an ideological and psychological critique of the extremist *mentality* itself. Coleridge identified this in the increasing polarization of English politics. "If the Jacobins ran wild with the Rights of Man, and the abstract Sovereignty of the People, their Antagonists flew off as extravagantly from the sober good sense of our Forefathers and idolized as pure an abstraction in the Rights of Sovereigns."[69]

Coleridge could also bring the point home with personal anecdote. "During the last War, an acquaintance of mine (least of all men a political Zealot) had christened a Vessel he had just built – 'The Liberty'; and was seriously admonished by his aristocratic Friends to change it for some other name. What? – replied the Owner very innocently – should I call it 'The Freedom'? That (it was replied) would be far better, as people might then think only of Freedom of Trade; whereas 'Liberty' has a *jacobinical* sound with it! Alas! . . . is there no medium between an Ague-fit and a Frenzy-fever?"[70]

He even took the risk in No. 11 (26 October) of recounting his own youthful flirtation with Jacobinism, in the Pantisocratic scheme of 1794. "I was a sharer in the general vortex, though my little World described the path of its Revolution in an orbit of its own." It was a defensive account, passing off his passionate and millennial beliefs as "air-built Castles" of the day, hot air balloons of "youthful Enthusiasm".[71]

This version particularly incensed Southey, who thought that if Coleridge himself had not once been a Jacobin, he did not know "who the devil" was. At the same time he was alarmed by Coleridge's increasing degree of political self-exposure in *The Friend*, in an attempt to hold his readers. Indeed the account is still historically fascinating, containing as it does what is probably the first recorded description of the phenomenon of the political "fellow-traveller". "We had been travelling with the crowd of less imaginative malcontents, through the dark lanes and foul bye-roads of ordinary Fanaticism. But Oh! There were thousands as young and innocent as myself who . . . were driven along with the general current!"[72]

13

Coleridge's coat-trailing into controversy (which Southey interpreted as coat-turning) was partly a response to widespread criticism of the undoubted obscurity of many of the early numbers. He was convinced that he had to do more to appeal to his readers. In late September, *The Friend* had reached another crisis point in its production. Stuart thought he was not holding his subscribers, and made it clear that he would not supply stamped paper after the first ten issues, when Coleridge had originally hoped for the first twenty.

He wrote in desperation to Stuart on 27 September: "I have waited & hoped till my heart is sick for a Letter from you – I print weekly 644 . . . & there is now only enough remaining for another number. For God's sake do not abandon me now – need I say that one of my great Objects in carrying on this work is to enable me to repay by degrees what I owe you–? . . . Do pray let me hear from you. I am fully aware that the Numbers hitherto are in too bad and laborious a style; but I trust you will find Nos 7, 8, 9, & 10 greatly improved & that every No. after these will become more and more entertaining."[73]

Stuart had in fact supplied over £130 worth of paper, for which Coleridge had only been able to advance his £60 lecture fees.[74] It appeared that no more was forthcoming, and much of October was spent looking for alternative backers. The Ottery Coleridges again turned him down, but eventually City money came from Richard Sharp (£46), business money from Tom Poole (£36), and farming money from Asra's brother Thomas Hutchinson (£53). This was a good indication of the broad spectrum of support that *The Friend* had found. The total investment was substantial: £137.16s.5d; with Thomas Hutchinson, perhaps significantly, providing the most generous share. Stuart also finally relented, and sent a last free batch of paper in November, to show that he still admired Coleridge's efforts.[75]

None of this eased the immense impracticality of printing at Penrith, where Coleridge had to carry copy often on foot, over the increasingly wintry hills. The opening of No. 9 was eaten by rats at the printers.

While struggling with these production problems, Coleridge was also seeking to broaden the appeal of *The Friend* by a shift in editorial approach. He decided that the philosophical sections must be "lighter and shorter"; that stories, poems and "amusements" should be more frequent; and that he should use letters and contributions from his readers.[76]

Surprisingly, there had been few objections to the political content of his essays, except from Southey and Wordsworth. Southey could not understand why he should risk bringing up the perilous topic of their youthful Jacobinism. And ironically, Wordsworth had suddenly grown extremely sensitive about political subjects, having been "haunted" for several weeks by the fear of being prosecuted for seditious libel over his *Cintra* pamphlet. (There was a rare glimpse of Asra here, when she remarked mockingly to De Quincey of this: "We females . . . have not the least fear of Newgate – if there was but a garden to walk in, we think we should do very nicely.")[77]

The objections to *The Friend* were largely stylistic: long, involved sentences; disorganized topics; and much "obscurity" of thought and references. As John Morgan wrote from London in October:

"Many people are complaining of its obscurity . . . But 'tis easier to fool than to think."[78] Poole's friend Samuel Purkis (a self-educated tanner) thought it "caviar to the Multitude". Dorothy summed it up well when she praised many "beautiful passages", and found that "everywhere the power of thought and the originality of a great mind are visible, but there is wanting a happiness of manner". In general, she too thought it "certainly very obscure".[79]

This word "obscurity" would settle on Coleridge like an albatross. The question of a "difficult" style was crucial to him, for he believed that the brief, punchy, short-sentenced and epigrammatic style of journalism was itself a form of superficiality. It lacked what he called "the cement of thought", and – in a vivid phrase – "the hooks-and-eyes of memory".[80] But he wanted *The Friend* to be demanding, and this was central to his editorial position. He wrote to Southey on 20 October that he suspected that ordinary readers had an "aversion to all energy of thinking"; in consequence, "I am like a physician who, for a patient paralytic in both arms, prescribes as the only possible cure, the use of dumb-bells."[81]

As part of his new editorial policy, he decided to present this problem of style directly to his readers, in the form of a letter in No. 11. Initially he asked Southey to write it: "chiefly urging, in a humorous manner, my Don Quixotism in expecting that the public will ever pretend to understand my lucubrations . . ."[82] He would then answer this with an editorial "on the nature of obscurity etc."

Southey agreed, impressed by what Coleridge had already achieved against all expectation: "*The Friend* is faulty in nothing but its mode of publication . . . it would be better to intersperse numbers of amusement . . . give them sugar plums so that they may be ready to swallow a tonic bolus every now & then before they are aware of what is coming." Reading over the last eight numbers, Southey was unexpectedly moved: "they left me in no heart for jesting or for irony. In time they will do their work . . . Insert a few more poems . . . and [show] the people what grounds they have for hope. God bless you!"[83]

14

Coleridge's shift in editorial approach, with its more varied and controversial touch, is immediately evident from No. 11, which appeared on 26 October, onwards. His revisionist account of Pantisocracy was followed by a strikingly well chosen extract from Wordsworth's unpublished *Prelude*, also describing youthful responses to the French Revolution, "Bliss was it in that dawn to be alive, But to be young was very heaven! . . .", a passage that has subsequently become famous.

Next came the editorial letter on prose style and intellectual difficulty, but written by Coleridge himself (not Southey after all) and turned into a clarion declaration rather than an apologia: "I must of necessity require the attention of my Reader to become my fellow-labourer . . . to retire *into themselves* and make their own minds the objects of their steadfast attention . . . No real information can be conveyed, no important errors rectified, no widely injurious prejudices rooted up, without requiring some effort of thought on the part of the Reader. But the obstinate (and towards a contemporary Writer, the contemptuous) aversion to all intellectual effort is the mother evil of which I had proposed to war against, the Queen Bee in the Hive of our errors and misfortunes, both private and national."[84]

No. 11 closed with two "Specimens of Rabbinical Wisdom", proverbial tales from the Jewish tradition; and Coleridge's own poem, "Hymn Before Sunrise, in the Vale of Chamouny", adapted from the German of Fredericka Brun. It could be described as an international issue.

A tonic bolus of a more patriotic kind followed in No. 12, "On the Vulgar Errors Respecting Taxes", in which Coleridge ingenuously argued that the National Debt had become, in time of war, an instrument of "political Strength and circumstantial Prosperity", unifying all classes. Even this found its supporters, notably Daniel Stuart who considered it "a most brilliant one", and reprinted extracts in both the *Courier* and the *Morning Post*.[85]

Then in No. 13 came a plum of sorts, though without much sugar, the grotesque "Tale of Maria Eleonora Schöning". This was a case of rape and infanticide, which had occurred in Nuremberg at the time of Coleridge's visit to Germany. He skilfully combined a number of newspaper accounts he had gathered, dramatically retold the story, and centred it on the passionate friendship of the teenage Maria with her sole friend and confidante Anna, which ends in an attempted suicide pact between the two young women. The narrative has the tragic inevitability of a folk-tale, and takes them first to prison and then to the scaffold. Coleridge linked it to his own ballad of witchcraft and possession, "The Three Graves", and the theme of friendship under extreme duress, even to the point of madness.

Further travellers' tales from Germany enlivened the next seven issues, together with more poetry and verse translations from Wordsworth. So as winter 1809 drew on, Coleridge steered *The Friend* on its more open editorial course; but he was still aware that the full statement of his "Principles" was not yet achieved. He was working more than ever from week to week, and from hand to mouth, with no guarantee that his 600 readers would ever pay off his debts, when subscriptions fell due at the twentieth issue, early in January 1810.

15

One purpose of the travel letters (which evidently drew on materials abandoned at Coleorton) was to give Coleridge a second, and more humorous, editorial voice. To do this he invented an eccentric "friend", the talkative companion of his early voyages in Germany, whom he introduced in No. 14 as "Satyrane". Named after the knight-errant in Spenser's *Faerie Queene*, Satyrane was a deliberately quixotic figure who tilted at the windmills of received opinion wherever he went, mixing shrewd observation of foreign customs with comic adventures and mishaps. He was clearly intended as a self-portrait, using a style of broad caricature familiar from the *Spectator* columns. Voluble, "sufficiently paradoxical", learned but faintly ludicrous, he is a revealing projection of what Coleridge felt was the more acceptable side of his public persona.

> His extensive erudition, his energetic and all too subtle intellect, the opulence of his imagination, and above all his inexhaustible store of anecdotism which always appeared to us the most interesting when of himself, and his passionate love of mountain scenery . . . will for ever endear the remembrance of that Tour to the survivors.

The tone of self-mockery was set by an early encounter with a foolish Danish merchant on the boat to Hamburg, who drunkenly perceives that Satyrane is "un Philosophe". Addressing him in "the most magnific style", he announces: "Vat Imagination! vat Language! vat vast Science! and vat Eyes! vat a milk-vite Forehead! – O my Heafen! vy, you're a Got!"[86] This was indeed how many enthusiasts had spoken of Coleridge in his youth (not least, Dorothy, Davy and Hazlitt); and it curiously foreshadows the more cutting caricatures of Coleridge in the novels of Peacock a decade later.

But Satyrane is also intended as a figure of pathos, for though "the sun never shone on a more joyous being", Coleridge says that he later fell into despondency in his middle years. "When he was at length compelled to see and acknowledge the true state of the morals and intellect of his contemporaries, his disappointment was severe, and his mind, always thoughtful, became pensive and gloomy: for to love and sympathize with mankind was a necessity of his nature."[87] Indeed Satyrane is now dead, killed off in his prime by some unexplained sickness or grief, against which he had struggled bravely but to no avail. This is described in a long verse epitaph, which Coleridge carefully adapted from one of the famous "Epitafi" of the seventeenth-century Italian poet Chiabrera:

> . . . Sickness, 'tis true,
> Whole years of weary days, besieg'd him close
> Even to the gates and inlets of his life!
> But it is true, no less, that strenuous, firm,
> And with a natural gladness, he maintained
> The Citadel unconquer'd, and in joy
> Was strong to follow the delightful Muse.

Coleridge also added one particular image, not in his Italian original, which took Satyrane right back to the sacred caves of "Kubla Khan", and even further, to the mysterious "Pixies' parlour" by the river Otter into which he had climbed as a child. This poignant memory of his boyhood was now invested with high, retrospective symbolism, as if his whole life (or rather, Satyrane's) had been a lonely process of subterranean exploration, of clambering into caverns, and potholing deep into the mysteries of knowledge.

. . . Yea oft alone
Piercing the long-neglected holy cave,
The haunt obscure of old Philosophy,
He bade with lifted torch its starry walls.
Sparkle, as erst they sparkled to the flame
Of odorous lamps tended by Saint and Sage.[88]

So the figure of Satyrane, Coleridge's tragi-comic double, was offered up to appease the readers of *The Friend*.

16

By this stage Coleridge was dictating every issue directly to Sara Hutchinson, closeted in his study, so that if the mouth was his then the hand was Asra's. Work went on usually at night, and frequently up to the last possible moment for the printer's deadline. Dorothy was alarmed by the way he would appear to be doing nothing for most of the week, and then suddenly rush off a whole essay in twenty-four hours.[89] But this has always been time-honoured journalistic practice, and the very pressure of the deadline was what Coleridge needed, especially to keep opium at bay.

By mid-November Allan Bank was sunk in snow, but still Coleridge ploughed over to Keswick (sixteen miles) or Penrith (twenty-eight miles by Kirkstone Pass) to deliver copy, using farmer's gig or grocer's cart where he could. Up to Christmas, only one issue was delayed. Dorothy was astonished, and sometimes even a little frightened by Coleridge's intensity and self-absorption in his imaginative world. "Coleridge is pretty well, as you will judge by the regularity of his work. The tale of Maria Schöning is beautifully told; but I wish it had not been the first tale in *The Friend*, for there is something so horrid in it that I cannot bear to think of the story. Sarah [H] is grown quite strong . . . Frost and snow we have had, but now the weather is milder. Coleridge goes on with his work briskly. How do you like William's sonnets?"[90]

Coleridge now had that daily, and even nightly, intimacy with Asra that he had so long and so passionately desired. But it was not easy for either of them. The shared pressure, and even excitement, of the literary work (often witnessed by Asra's breathless notes to

Coleridge in Bristol, aged twenty-two by Pieter van Dyke, 1795

Coleridge in Germany, aged twenty-six. Artist unknown, 1799

Coleridge, shortly before his journey to the Mediterranean, aged thirty-one.
After a portrait by James Northcote, 1804

Coleridge in Rome, aged thirty-three by Washington Allston, 1806

Coleridge at the time of his London Lectures, aged thirty-nine.
A sketch after George Dawe, 1811

Coleridge, established at Highgate, aged forty-five by Thomas Phillips, 1818

S. T. Coleridge
Mr Coleridge sat to me for this sketch about 182

Coleridge in his early fifties, sketched by C. R. Leslie, *c.* 1824

Coleridge aged sixty-one, from a pencil sketch by J. Kayser, late 1833

Brown the printer, reporting on progress) hid far deeper emotions and conflicts. Initially Asra had doubted, like Wordsworth, Coleridge's ability to sustain the essays, and her agreement to act as his amanuensis – itself rather puzzling – was taken with a certain scepticism. In August she had reported to her friend Mary Monkhouse that she had "some hopes" of Coleridge as he had materials prepared and was "quite in a writing cue", but that he liked to write "any thing but what he ought, & yet he always pretends he is doing his duty".[91] The scolding tone makes him sound almost like Hartley.

But Asra's governessy side was a help to Coleridge, not least in the matter of opium, which he resolved to limit to a single dose taken at midnight. "O then for her sake, Coleridge, the sake so dear above all other, & for which all others are chiefly dear – O do resolve on 12–12 – none between . . . OPIUM *at night only* – no morning – wine nor Spirits: no."[92]

As he fell into the pattern of working with her, this resolution held good into the winter, though privately he had no illusions about the addiction he was trying to control. "Chained by a darling passion or *tyrannic* Vice," he confided to his Notebooks, "Opium in Hell, yet with the Telescope of an unperverted Understanding descrying and describing Heaven and the Road thereto to my companions, the Damn'd! O fearful fate!"[93]

But the darling passion was also his love for Asra, and this was no easier to control. His Notebooks ranged back obsessively to memories of Coleorton in 1807, and even further back to the Sockburn drawing-room of 1799 where he had first met her. He thought of inserting an essay "On Love" in *The Friend*; trying to distinguish between the "irresistible" impulse of falling in love (as described by Sterne) and his own notion of love as "an act of the will", a "primary" expression of our highest nature. If it was not this, he observed bleakly, "Love itself is all a romantic Hum, a mere connection of Desire with a form appropriated to that form by accident, or the mere repetition of a Day-dream."[94] But he could not dictate such an essay to Asra, and it was only written long after.

Indeed, perhaps because of their very physical proximity, Coleridge could never speak openly to Asra of his feelings at Allan Bank. Closeted together for hours in his study, Coleridge – the great talker – was tortured by his own silence on this single, most vital subject. He could only speak to her in his Notebooks. "I appear cheerful to my acquaintance, on them bestow my life & my lively powers – to you, my friend! am dull & despondent? – O it is too true! but why? – because with those others I can forget myself, what I have been, am, might have been – but with you I cannot do this – You are my better Self."[95]

Instead he secretly harboured his fantasies, telling himself that if *The Friend* was a success, if his opium addiction was truly cured, somehow he would make Asra his wife and they would have children. In agonized entries, much of them written in his Greek cipher, he played guiltily with the tantalizing schemes, always promising himself that they were free of sexual impurity, that they were acts of will not of impulse.

> Again: as Mother of my children – how utterly improbable dared I hope it: How impossible for me (most pure indeed are my heart & fancy from such a thought) even to think of it, much less desire it! And yet at the encouraging prospect of emancipation from narcotics, of health & activity of mind & body, at the heavenly hope of becoming, as much as is possible, worthy of the unutterably Dear One, it is felt within me like an ordinance of adamantine Destiny!

He identified them too, with childlike dreams of innocence, as if he were indeed like Hartley beneath Asra's gaze. "Sweet Hartley! What did he say, speaking of some Tale & wild Fancy of his Brain? – 'It is not yet, but it will be – for it is – & it cannot stay always in here (pressing one hand on his forehead . . .) – and then it *will be* because it is not nothing.' O wife thou art! O wife thou *wilt be*!"[96]

But the idea that these fantasies might come into being, by the sheer power of their existing in his head, because they were "not nothing", may itself have been the product of opium, as much as childishness. Coleridge's awareness of his own uncontrollable fantasy-life, working at many levels, also fed directly into his psychological theorizing in *The Friend*. So there was an unbroken line between his observations of Hartley, his dreams of Asra, and his analysis of Luther and Maria Schöning.

Later he went back and annotated this "wife to be" entry with a sober Greek couplet: "Persons living in the same house/ Persons living in the same grave". Walking out in the snow below Allan Bank, he thought of his enforced silence like a river in winter:

Mountain snow whose hanging weight
Archeth some sullen river, that for fear
Steals underneath unmurmuring.[97]

The Wordsworths were aware of the tension in the household, but treated it rather like the smoking chimneys, as an unavoidable domestic nuisance, which might improve in the spring. Grudgingly impressed by the progress of *The Friend*, Wordsworth allowed more of his poetry to appear in its pages, and arranged for an exchange of essays on childhood education with John Wilson, to appear in the December issues (Nos 17–20), which were well received.

Coleridge was grateful, but felt more than ever the oppression of Wordsworth's patriarchal presence at Allan Bank. All the women, he thought, showed "too exclusive admiration" for his talents; and no other writer was "either thought or spoken of but with cold indifference". The old freedom of discussion was sadly curtailed compared to the early Grasmere days. "No literature at all is talked of with love, no books read – & William himself at length listened to as a duty with manifest distraction – only compare Dorothy with Dorothy of ten years ago – and just the same process has taken place with Mary and Sara."[98]

Perhaps as some remedy to this stultifying atmosphere, Coleridge concocted a scheme with his printer John Brown to publish cheap new "Lake" editions of Wordsworth's, Southey's and his own poetry, and tried to interest them in the plan. He wrote cheerfully to Brown in early December that they had "no passion for book-finery", and would be "far more flattered by seeing our poems in a shilling Edition on the same paper etc. as 'Reading Made Easy', in the Shelves of Country Booksellers and Stationers, than arrayed in all the Silks and Satins of Mr Ballantyne's Wardrobe, with engravings to boot." As to his own poems, he would "neither need nor shall ask the opinions of any".[99] In fact he had been considering publishing all his new poems since the first issue of *The Friend*. But in the event Wordsworth was not enthusiastic, and the scheme gradually faded from view.

Yet Coleridge never considered escape from Allan Bank, even for the most justifiable reasons. Shortly before Christmas he received news from his brother George that their old mother was terminally ill at Ottery, and dying of cancer in great pain. She wanted to see all her sons, but Coleridge was the only one who refused to go. It was clear that he still felt rejected and humiliated by the Ottery Coleridges, but he rationalized his refusal on the grounds of expense. That at any rate is what he wrote to Southey, in a transparently guilty letter.

"My poor Mother is near her end, and dying in great torture, death eating her piecemeal, her vital stamen is so very vigorous – & she wishes to see me before her death – But tho' my Brother knows I am penniless, not an offer of a Bank note to en[able] me to set off. In truth, I know not what to do – for [there] is not a shilling in our whole House."[100] He then changed the subject abruptly to the success of his German travel-letters in recent issues of *The Friend*. "You will grin at my modest account of Satyrane, the Idoloclast . . . but what can I do? – I must wear a mask."

17

It was news of a quite different death that now occupied him. On 20 October 1809, his old friend and mentor Sir Alexander Ball had suddenly died in Malta at the age of fifty-two. The reports reached Allan Bank in mid-December, and Coleridge immediately wrote an account of their memorable conversation on riding to San Antonio in 1804, "Does Fortune favour Fools?", which he rushed into issue No. 19 of *The Friend* on 28 December.

He now decided to embark on a full-length memoir, "Fragments and Sketches of the Life of the Late Admiral Sir Alexander Ball", which would mark the third distinctive stage of his paper into the spring of 1810. Ball would be presented as "the abstract Idea of a wise & good Governor", and thus draw together many of the political themes of *The Friend*.[101] "He was a Man above his Age: but for that very reason the Age has the more need to have the master features of his character portrayed and preserved . . . For he was indeed a living confutation of the assertion attributed to the Prince of Condé, that no Man appeared great to his Valet de Chambre."[102] Coleridge said – what he so signally did not say of his own mother – that he wept at the news of Ball's death.[103]

As Christmas celebrations filled the house at Allan Bank, and De Quincey masterminded a spectacular fireworks display for the children of Grasmere, Coleridge plunged back into his memories of Malta.[104] His thoughts filled the next four issues of *The Friend*, describing a distant world of sunlight and action, of patriotism and good fellowship, of courage and endurance, as far removed from his wintry existence on the edge of Grasmere lake as it was possible for him to imagine.

It was perhaps now, with his mind running on the Mediterranean, the ships and islands, the talk of sailors and the tales of heroism and disaster, that he wrote in his Notebook a magnificent extended entry comparing the whole of life to the experience of shipwreck.[105]

What is striking about this shipwreck is that it is not a disaster. It is presented far more as an existential adventure, a challenge to find one's significance and location in a world without maps or bearings, without certainties or sure information. All noble minds, wrote Coleridge, must eventually ask themselves the "great questions" – Where am I? What am I *for*? What are my duties? What are my relations with "futurity" and the present world? The answer came in an extended simile, drawn from his own voyages on the high seas, and as if the Ancient Mariner had suddenly begun a new tale, and momentarily found his voice again in prose.

> I would compare the human Soul to a Ship's Crew cast on an unknown Island (a fair simile: for these questions could not suggest themselves unless the mind had previously felt convictions, that the present World was not its whole destiny and abiding Country). What would be their first business? surely, to enquire what the Island was? in what Latitude? what ships visited the Island? when? and whither they went? . . . to think, how they should maintain and employ themselves during their stay – & how best stock themselves for the expected voyage, & procure the means of inducing the Captain to take them to the Harbour, which they wished to go to? The moment, when the Soul begins to be sufficiently self-conscious, to ask concerning itself, & its relations, is the first moment of its *intellectual* arrival in the World. Its *Being* – enigmatic as it must seem – is posterior to its *Existence*. Suppose the shipwrecked man stunned, & for many weeks in a state of Idiocy or utter loss of Thought and Memory. And then gradually awakened.[106]

What this memorable entry seemed to insist on, in the very midst of Coleridge's own shipwreck at Allan Bank, was that the state of struggle and self-enquiry, of "awakening", was the essential quality of being human. What kept his soul alive was the very act of self-consciousness, of continuous questioning of purpose and destiny.*

18

On 4 January 1810 *The Friend* reached its twentieth issue, when the 600 or so £1 subscriptions were due to be remitted. The minimum target was about £400. Because of the chaos of the collection system, some relying on local agents like the London bookseller George Ward, others on district postmasters, and many more on direct remittance to Coleridge himself at Kendal, it was not immediately clear what money had come in or how many readers Coleridge had retained. At all events, the subscriptions arrived slowly and piecemeal. Ward's accounts, for example, showed £9.15s.4d. on 3 January; a further £9.10s.0d. on 10 January; and a rather more promising but very late addition of £102.6s.0d. by 5 March. Mrs Coleridge also forwarded £10 that had somehow arrived at Greta Hall.[107] It seems very unlikely that the final subscription raised reached more than £300, or that Coleridge retained more than half his readership. This disappointing result – though by no means a catastrophe – did not emerge for several weeks.

In the meantime Coleridge issued a free, "Supernumerary" issue, in which he promised to continue the life of Ball, embark on a psychological analysis of the "Character of Bonaparte" (somewhat delayed, as he had originally promised it in the *Morning Post* in 1800, as he mildly pointed out), and launch into "a philosophical examination of the British Constitution in all its branches separately and collectively".[108] He felt this "first Series" of *The Friend* would now run to twenty-eight or thirty issues, when he would then consider starting a "second".

Publicly he took the high ground, admitting the difficulty of his style and subject-matter, but challenging his readers to stay the course. "For a living Writer is yet sub judice: and if we cannot

* The image of the shipwreck, a development of the Ancient Mariner's experience and John Wordsworth's tragic fate, was of cardinal importance to Coleridge and feeds into a rich 19th century tradition of such metaphysical disasters, from Géricault's painting "The Raft of the Medusa" (1819) to Rimbaud's poem "Le Bateau Ivre" (1871). For the image of the fateful sea-voyage, see also *Early Visions*, pp. 173–4.

follow his conceptions or enter into his feelings, it is more consoling to our Pride, as well as agreeable to our ignorance, to consider him as lost beneath, than as soaring out of our sight above us."[109]

Privately, Coleridge was bitterly disappointed, but far from ready to abandon his great venture. He now owed a total of over £200 to Stuart, Hutchinson, Poole and his other backers; and feared that he would lose "three in four" of his subscribers in the coming month. But he felt he might battle on if he could sustain a core of faithful readers. He postponed the next issue while he took stock, writing to Tom Poole on 12 January with a realistic assessment of his debts and prospects.

He told Poole that he felt angry and frustrated. He knew that *The Friend* was described everywhere as "an unreadable work, dry, obscure, fantastical, paradoxical, and God knows what else – according to each man's taste, and as if they wished to revenge themselves on me for the loss of their Shillings". On the other hand, many individual subscribers had written with "the warmest acknowledgments, and assurances that if *The Friend* were more generally known, its circulation would become considerable".[110]

His files bear him out, containing for example this typical note from one William Wray, an attorney at Maldon. "That such a work must eventually succeed with all serious and meditative Minds I think cannot be well doubted, but of this Class comparatively few I am afraid have hitherto become acquainted with its Merits: it has you know been little advertised and it would have many prejudices to encounter. The Extracts however from Time to Time given in the *Courier* – must have been of great service to its circulation."[111]

Poole himself had received an appreciative letter from John Rickman, the businesslike census-taker in London, who was usually most critical of Coleridge's efforts. "Of Coleridge, however, I think the better for his Friendly productions; there is writing of a high order thickly interspersed . . ."[112]

All in all, Coleridge felt honour-bound to go on, at least to the end of the first series. "My purpose is not to give up *The Friend* till it gives up itself – & I will go on tho' it should only barely pay its expenses, till I have brought it to some kind of completeness – however short of my wishes – and enable myself to do it by working over hours for the Newspapers."[113]

If taking on extra journalism to support *The Friend* at this juncture seemed a piece of quixotism worthy of Satyrane, it was in fact exactly what Coleridge had just done in an effort to reduce his debts with Stuart. Between 7 December and 20 January he contributed eight long articles to the *Courier* on the Spanish Peninsular War. These "Letters on the Spaniards" make a densely argued and well-informed case for the support of Spain against Napoleon, and draw a picture in depth of Britain's historic role in defending the cause of independent nation-states in Europe. The series was substantial, an off-shoot of the work he had put in on Wordsworth's *Cintra* pamphlet, and ran to well over twenty thousand words. He dismissed it as mere topical journalism, but it was the equivalent of writing three or four extra issues of *The Friend* in a month.[114] The series was unpaid, but set against his debts to the value of some £50. Coleridge was genuinely determined to battle on in this way.

Wordsworth's attitude to *The Friend* had gradually become more positive. It had, after all, become something of a showcase for his poetry. Coleridge had published two long extracts from *The Prelude*, including the famous skating episode which appeared to fine advantage in the Christmas issue (No. 19). He had also published about a dozen new sonnets, and Wordsworth's own translations from Chiabrera's *Epitafi*. Dorothy was particularly proud of these, and the fine "Essay on Epitaphs" (No. 25), in which Wordsworth for the first time wrote about his Pantheistic experiences as a child, as part of a prose autobiography. These publications brought back his confidence after the débâcle over the "White Doe", and sometime in mid-February Wordsworth returned to his great poem "The Recluse", cast aside in 1806, and began composing at the rate of fifty lines a day.[115] Spring 1810 was to be one of his great periods of sustained poetry writing.

At the same time, Coleridge's increasingly moody presence at Allan Bank was becoming a great burden on the domestic household. His nocturnal hours, his financial worries, his demands on Asra, his fluctuations between supine despondency on his sofa and hectic activity at his desk, produced an atmosphere of brooding crisis. Even Dorothy found his demands irksome. "There is his parlour to clean, fire to light – sometimes gruel – toast and water – eggs – his bed always to be made at an unreasonable time . . ."[116]

Hartley and Derwent came over from Greta Hall each weekend, filling the house with bustle and noise, while the two men shut themselves away in their ground-floor studies at either end of Allan Bank's freezing corridor. Wordsworth actually had to abandon his for several weeks, while their landlord put in a new bow window and tried once more to cure the smoking chimney. Coleridge on the other hand retreated into his study for longer and longer hours, taking more opium again as the pressures on him increased, and trying to imagine himself in some remote paradise with Asra.

In this fantasy, everything was perfect and love seemed to flow through his room like water, so their unspeaking silence was not tension but a rippling harmony. "So deeply do I now enjoy your presence, so totally possess you in myself, myself in you. The very sound would break the union, and separate *you-me* into you and me. We both, and this sweet Room, its books, its pictures & the shadows on the Wall slumbering with the how quiet Fire are all *our* Thought, a harmonious imagery of Forms distinct on the still substance of one deep Feeling, Love & Joy – a Lake – or if a stream, yet flowing so softly, so unwrinkled, that its flow is *Life* not Change."[117]

At these times, blissfully ignoring the anxiety and disruption he caused all around him, Coleridge imagined the Wordsworths would take him and Asra off to live in some bucolic retreat together, recreating the simple, tender life of the Dove Cottage years. He told Poole: "All, whom you know here, are pretty well. It is our intention, as soon as we must quit this House, i.e. before next Winter – to retire to some cheaper part of the Country . . . and live in the cottage style in good earnest – i.e. exactly as Cottagers live . . . with only one country Maid." Their only luxury was tea, which for him at breakfast was "an absolute necessary, if not of Life, yet of literary exertion". Otherwise none of them drank anything but water.[118] There was no mention of laudanum.

By contrast, Dorothy's account, though diplomatically worded to Lady Beaumont, reveals the strain of Coleridge's presence and profound anxieties about the future:

> I have daily put off writing till the next day in the hope of having more leisure and a quiet time for the free exercise of my thoughts . . . Coleridge's spirits have been irregular of late. He was damped after the 20th Number by the slow arrival of payments, and half persuaded himself that he ought not to go

on. We laboured hard against such a resolve, and he seems determined to fight onwards . . . You will hardly believe me when I tell you that there have been weeks and weeks when he has not composed a line. The fact is that he either does a great deal or nothing at all; and that he composes with a rapidity truly astonishing . . . He has written a whole Friend more than once in two days. They are never re-transcribed, and he generally has dictated to Miss Hutchinson, who takes the words down from his mouth.[119]

19

Coleridge now launched into his life of Sir Alexander Ball, which began in No. 21 on 25 January 1810, and continued for three more issues, despite increasing difficulties and discouragements. He opened with an attack on "Modern Biography" which had become, he thought, "a trade in the silliest anecdotes, in unprovoked abuse and senseless eulogy".

The rage for fame had attracted a negative form of "garrulous Biography" which did nothing but satisfy "worthless curiosity" in telling petty stories about great men. "In the present age (emphatically the age of personality!) there are more than ordinary motives for withholding all encouragement from this mania with busying ourselves with the names of others." Sir Alexander's own contempt of gossip would be his "Socratic Demon to warn and check" against such modish frivolity.

Nonetheless the example of a truly great man, both in his struggles and his achievements, could be an invaluable revelation of some general truth about life. It was therefore "the duty of an honest Biographer, to portray the prominent imperfections as well as the excellencies of his Hero"; but he should never forget "how mean a thing a mere Fact is, except as seen in the light of some comprehensive Truth".[120]

Coleridge's Life of Ball is indeed very sketchy with facts. It is said, for example, that Ball was attracted to the navy by "the deep impression and vivid images" left on his mind by reading Defoe's *Robinson Crusoe* in boyhood. But almost nothing is recorded about the actual events of his early service.[121] Instead, the biography is built up impressionistically, from a series of memorable anecdotes which Coleridge had himself heard in Malta. Many of them concern Ball's reputation for justice and humanity as a civilian governor, and his shrewd appreciation of the tyranny inherent in Napoleon's schemes for the Mediterranean. In this Ball is presented, with strong patriotic emphasis, as the beau ideal of the British colonial law-giver and wartime diplomat: shrewd, pragmatic, kindly, but with an inflexible sense of political principle and public duty. "Duty" – enshrined in Nelson's last signal before Trafalgar – is intended as the central theme, the "comprehensive Truth" of Ball's life, in Coleridge's biographic scheme.

But something else emerges with far more power and psychological conviction, in the most striking of his anecdotes. This is Ball's courage, both physical and moral, in moments of action and crisis; and more than this, Ball's intuitive ability to inspire courage in others and earn their undying loyalty. It was this quality that Coleridge really idealized and indeed idolized in Ball, and several of his stories have an allegorical element as well as a dramatic one. It is as if they were shadowy versions of the crisis of courage in his own life. His "Sketches" become not so much a study of duty in the abstract, but of the courage needed to carry out one's duty in extreme and particular circumstances.

Two of the stories concern Ball's cool behaviour in action, one under fire, and the other during a storm at sea. They have a subtly different emphasis. The first is directed towards a junior midshipman, the second towards a senior officer; but both are presented as acts of supreme friendship.

The first was told to Coleridge by a young naval officer, who had caught his attention during a large reception in the Governor's Palace. The young man continually gazed on Ball with a "mixed expression of awe and affection", though very rarely speaking. Coleridge later talked to this officer in confidence, and was given a memorable account of his first open-boat expedition under fire when he was only fourteen. Ball – then a lieutenant – was his new commander. Coleridge gives the story in the officer's own words, but skilfully drawing out the dramatic effect.

> As we were rowing up to the Vessel which we were to attack, amid a discharge of musketry, I was overpowered by fear, my

> knees trembled under me, and I seemed on the point of fainting away. Lieutenant Ball, who saw the condition I was in, placed himself close beside me, and still keeping his countenance directed towards the enemy, took hold of my hand, and pressing it in the most friendly manner, said in a low voice, "Courage, my dear Boy! don't be afraid of yourself! you will recover in a minute or so – I was just the same, when I first went out in this way." Sir, added the officer to me, it was as if an Angel had put a new Soul into me. With the feeling, that I was not yet dishonoured, the whole burthen of agony was removed; and from that moment I was as fearless and forward as the oldest of the boat crew, and on our return the Lieutenant spoke highly of me to our Captain.[122]

Much of the power and psychological acuity of this incident lies in its unexpectedness. Advancing under sustained fire is widely acknowledged as one of the most demanding of all battle experiences.[123] In the midst of action, both the boy and the man are required to be passive in the fearful moments before boarding and fighting. Coleridge perceives the peculiar terror in this, and shows how Ball is still capable of acting with fatherly tenderness under conditions of extreme violence, and the prospect of imminent death.

Moreover, Ball empathizes imaginatively with the boy – "I was just the same" – and pays him the sustaining compliment of assuming his fear is not of the enemy, but only of his own barely controllable reactions: "don't be afraid of yourself!" A more conventional officer, observes Coleridge, might have "scoffed, threatened, or reviled". Instead, the bond of courage formed between the young midshipman and the experienced officer becomes an example of Ball's capacity for bravery and humane leadership.

The second story concerns Ball, now promoted to the captaincy of a ship of the line, and his fleet commander Nelson. Here Ball's action is directed towards a senior officer, and is again highly unexpected and unconventional. Coleridge emphasizes that Ball and Nelson had previously met only on leave, that Ball had taken a dislike to Nelson's flamboyant manners and that there was "a coldness" between the two men, "in consequence of some punctilio". But this mutual antipathy was to be transformed in action.

Some years later Ball joined up with Nelson's fleet in the Mediterranean off Menorca, and during a violent storm Nelson's flagship was dismasted and driven towards a lee-shore near Port Mahon. Night fell and the storm intensified. While the rest of the fleet made for safety, Ball came alongside the flagship and took it in tow, but conditions worsened and shipwreck seemed inevitable. In the ensuing crisis both men displayed the courage that was peculiar to their characters.

"The difficulties and the dangers increased. Nelson considered the case of his own Ship as desperate, and that unless she was immediately left to her own fate, both Vessels would inevitably be lost. He, therefore, with the generosity natural to him, repeatedly requested Captain Ball to let him loose; and on Captain Ball's refusal, he became impetuous, and enforced his demands with passionate threats." It has to be understood at this juncture that Ball was refusing a direct command from his senior officer, and displaying the gravest form of insubordination – precisely the sort of insubordination for which Nelson had himself become famous in action.

"Captain Ball then himself took the speaking Trumpet, which the fury of the wind and waves rendered necessary, and with great solemnity and without the least disturbance of temper, called out in reply: 'I feel confident that I can bring you in safe; I therefore must not, and by the help of Almighty God! will not leave you.' What he promised he performed; and after they were safety anchored, Nelson came on board of Ball's ship, and embracing him with all the ardour of acknowledgement, exclaimed – 'A Friend in need is a Friend indeed.' "[124] From this time Ball was accepted as one of Nelson's famous "Band of Brothers", and referred to (with Admiral Troubridge) as one of Nelson's "three right arms" (the real arm, of course, having been lost in battle). An indissoluble bond of friendship had again been formed through shared courage in action.

Ball's bravery is again shown by Coleridge to be unexpected: his loyalty is shown precisely in disobedience, and in standing up not merely to the fury of the storm, but even more perhaps to the fury, the "passionate threats", of his superior officer. Ball's outstanding calm in the midst of this double onslaught, "without the least disturbance of temper", is presented as the epitome of both physical and moral courage, the heart of Coleridge's biographic portrait. This incident indeed became famous in Nelson's own biography, and was eventually enshrined in the *Dictionary of National Biography* in

Coleridge's own words.[125] (The exact location and circumstances have been questioned, and it may have occurred off the Atlantic coast of Spain.)

Coleridge was undoubtedly drawn to these stories, in a way frequently characteristic of biographic narration, by some degree of self-identification with the participants. Having used the images of storm, shipwreck, the dismasted ship, so often in his Notebooks to describe his own state, his battles with depression and opium, his terror of passivity and uncontrolled emotion, they came to him with all the force and conviction of his own psychic dramas. The trembling midshipman who finds a fatherly hand behind his back, the storm-tossed, disabled commander who finds a "Friend in Need" to tow him away from the lethal rocks: these were undoubtedly aspects of his own situation at Allan Bank in the spring of 1810.

The "Sketches" of Ball's life produced some of the most compelling and effective writing in the entire *Friend* series. By recounting matters so close to his own heart, Coleridge seemed to have recovered something of his stride and confidence by the end of January 1810. In the following three issues (Nos 22–4) he wrote stirring, patriotic pieces about Malta's role in the Mediterranean, and about the "Law of Nations" which governed Britain's wartime naval strategy of blockade in the Baltic and the Atlantic.

Refuting Dr Johnson's famous dismissal of an earlier naval campaign to defend the Falkland Islands, Coleridge insisted on the duty or "positive Right" of a sovereign power to defend its offshore possessions, however distant, small or insignificant they might seem. "To surrender, in our national character, the merest trifle, that is strictly our Right, the merest Rock on which the waves will scarcely permit the Sea-fowl to lay its Eggs, at the demand of an insolent and powerful Rival, on a shop-keeper's calculation of Loss and Gain, is in its final and assuredly not very distant consequences, a Loss of everything – of national Spirit, of national Independence, and with these of the very wealth, for which the low calculation was made."[126]

Here Coleridge was beginning to mount a powerful case against the growing tendency in Whig and radical circles towards a policy of appeasement, in the face of Napoleon's daunting military successes on land. (He had captured Vienna in May 1809, and would annex Holland in July 1810; and these advances would continue unchecked until the fateful Russian campaign of 1812.) The ironic mask of Satyrane was cast aside for a new voice in *The Friend*: the valiant rhetoric of the heroes Ball and Nelson. He told Poole that he knew it would lose him his Quaker subscribers, but he no longer cared.[127] "Above all, do not forget, that these are AWFUL TIMES!"[128]

20

Then suddenly in mid-February he faltered. The promised continuation of the "Sketches" was delayed, and instead Wordsworth's "Essay on Epitaphs" was thrown in to fill No. 25, "sadly misprinted", and with absolutely no logical connection with the new patriotic theme.

Dorothy explained to Lady Beaumont on 24 February: "The Essay of this week is by my Brother. He did not intend to publish it now; but Coleridge was in such bad spirits that when the time came he was utterly unprovided, and besides, had been put out of his regular course by waiting for books to consult respecting Duty . . ." Dorothy never wrote facetiously about Coleridge, but that last phrase may well have echoed her brother. She added, "I fear that people would be disappointed, having framed their expectations for the conclusions of Sir Alexander's history; and here I must observe that we have often cautioned Coleridge against making promises . . ."[129]

What had happened was simple and devastating. Asra had decided that she would leave Allan Bank, and go to live on her brother Tom's new farm in Wales. When Tom Hutchinson's partner, John Monkhouse, rode over to Grasmere (on the way, noted Coleridge feelingly, sustaining a fractured jaw from his horse's hoof), Asra announced that she would accompany him on his return to Radnorshire, in the first week of March.

Coleridge recorded a sinister dream. "I ate a red Herring for Supper, & had a dreadful night in consequence. Before I fell asleep, I had a spectrum of the fish's back-bone which immediately & perceptibly formed itself by lengthening & curving the cross bone threads into a sort of Scorpion."[130] Dorothy was aware of the blow that had befallen Coleridge, but she received it with resignation. "We shall find a great loss in her, as she has been with us more than four years; but Coleridge most of all will miss her . . ."

But Coleridge felt he had been stung to death. He finished just two more issues of *The Friend*, on 1 and 15 March (having broken off for one week). The last issue, No. 27, described, in one of his most moving passages, how he had heard of the death of Nelson while at Naples in 1805. "Numbers stopped and shook hands with me, because they had seen the tears on my cheeks, and conjectured, that I was an Englishman; and several, as they held my hand, burst into tears."[131] This issue ended in a bracket: "(To be concluded in the next Number.)" But it never appeared, though Coleridge pretended for weeks that he was writing it, and No. 27 was still lying on his desk two months later in May. He could not write it without Asra.

On the eve of Asra's departure on 5 March 1810, Coleridge sat up all night writing a long, philosophic entry in his Notebook. The subject was the psychological "Law of Association", by which memories are held together and produce the notion of identity. "I began strictly and as a matter of fact to examine that subtle Vulcanian Spider-web Net of Steel – strong as Steel yet subtle as Ether, in which my soul flutters inclosed with the Idea of yours."

He passed "rapidly as in a catalogue" the thousand images with which he associated his life with Asra: the farm at Gallow Hill, the ride to Scarborough, the walks on the fells, the study at Keswick – the meals, the books, the letters, the fireside talks, the nights under the stars. Gradually this careful list of precious associations turned into a terrible lament, grief-stricken and self-lacerating. It was like the April night at Greta Hall in 1802 on which he had written the first, great version of the ode "Dejection" (as "A Letter to Sara Hutchinson"), but now there was no storm to relieve his feelings or poetry to order them by. The "catalogue" was merely a litany of pain and regret.

> A candle in its socket, with its alternate fits & dying flashes of lingering Light – *O God! O God!* – Books of abstruse Knowledge – the Thomas Aquinas & Suarez from the Durham Library – a peony-faced cottage Girl (little Jane) – all articles of female dress – music – the opening of a Street door when you first came to Keswick – of a Bed room door – with what thoughts you would nightly open your own, when I was far away – & that sweet blessed Letter – Letters, yea, the very paper on which one might be written – or from the habit of

> half unconsciously writing your name or its Symbol invented by me to express it [ASRA] – all Travels – my yearning Absence – All books of natural History – O if I had been blest & had lived with you in the country, the continual food of conversation by watching & explaining the Heavens – your name in those bright Stars, or an M or W recalling those Stars – Aurora borealis – at Keswick by the corner parlour window – Waterfalls – that at Scale Force when Dorothy laughed at me & at you thro me, as the Lovers . . . any eye fixed kindly on me when I am talking – my own face in the . . .[132]

Here the entry breaks off, exactly as if Coleridge had raised his head to look at his own solitary reflection in the window of his study, and thrown down his pen in despair.

21

There is no other record of their parting. Sara Hutchinson did not write for five weeks, and then it was only an open letter to the household, in which she said she was "very comfortable" in Radnorshire, had given up "animal foods", and was a little bored in the evenings by the fireside as Tom and John were "sleepy before supper time" and only talked about "farming concerns".[133]

Coleridge would later write of Asra's "cruel neglect & contemptuous silence ever since", but at the time he said almost nothing. He laboured "under a depression of spirits, little less than absolute Despondency", refused to go out with the Wordsworths on early spring walks, and spent more and more time sleeping and reading.[134] Mrs Coleridge was surprised to receive a series of affectionate notes about the children, and the mild remark that he required "a change of scene" and would soon "unrust my toes and perform a walk to Greta Hall".[135] But he did not go until May.

News of Sara Hutchinson's departure did, however, spread quickly to Coleridge's friends in London, and of course they linked it to the abrupt silencing of *The Friend*. At the end of March Catherine Clarkson wrote breathlessly to Dorothy, asking how they were managing without her. Dorothy wrote back after some delay on 12 April. It was a long letter which gathered force as she gradually unburdened herself. She began with family news – Mary was expecting another baby, little Catherine Wordsworth had been ill, Wordsworth was talking of going to Coleorton in the summer, and Coleridge was talking of Keswick. "I hope he will choose the time of Mary's confinement for his journey, as though he does not require near so much waiting upon as formerly, he makes a great difference."

After these preliminaries, she began to write with greater candour and urgency.

> I need not tell you how sadly we miss Sara – but I must add the truth that we are all glad that she is gone. True it is she was the cause of the continuance of *The Friend* so long; but I am far from believing that it would have gone on if she had stayed. He was tired, and she had at last no power to drive him on; and now I really believe that *he* also is glad that she is not here, because he has nobody to tease him. His spirits have certainly been more equable, and much better. *Our* gladness proceeds from a different cause. He harassed and agitated her mind continually, and we saw that he was doing her health perpetual injury. I tell you this, that you may no longer lament her departure.

It was a severe judgement, even an impatient one, and suggests that the Wordsworths had had to cope with many emotional scenes between the two in the various parlours of Allan Bank. But it is also convincingly objective: Coleridge was "teased", Asra was "harassed".

But now Dorothy found she had much more to say, and she broke out to her confidante in her old, impetuous style. At last she could speak out, and she did so with an astonishing mixture of anger, disappointment and disillusion. It is one of the fiercest letters of her whole life, and it clearly echoes her brother's feelings about Coleridge too. It is a revelation of passionate disenchantment with their old friend.

> As to Coleridge, if I thought I should distress you, I would say nothing about him; but I hope that you are sufficiently prepared for the worst. We have no hope of him – none that he will ever do anything more than he has already done. If he were not under our Roof, he would be just as much the slave of stimulants as ever; and his whole time and thoughts,

> (except when he is reading, and he reads a great deal), are employed in deceiving himself, and seeking to deceive others. He will tell me that he has been writing, that he *has* written half a *Friend*; when I *know* he has not written a single line. This Habit pervades all his words and actions, and you feel perpetually new hollowness and emptiness. I am loath to say this, and burn this letter, I entreat you. I am loath to say it, but it is the truth. He lies in bed, always till after 12 o'clock, sometimes much later; and never walks out. Even the finest spring day does not tempt him to seek the fresh air; and this beautiful valley seems a blank to him. He never leaves his own parlour except at dinner and tea, and sometimes supper, and then he always seems impatient to get back to his solitude – he goes the moment his food is swallowed. Sometimes he does not speak a word, and when he does talk it is always very much and upon subjects as far aloof from himself and his friends as possible.[136]

Deception, hollowness, sloth, silence and aloofness: it is a terrible indictment, and Dorothy evidently intended it as such. But it is also a description of a depressed and lonely man at the end of his tether: facing professional disaster, opium addiction, financial debts, and unrequited love in middle age. Dorothy ended her letter by remarking that "William goes on writing industriously".

But the following morning she opened the letter again, puzzled and exasperated. "Coleridge is just come down stairs, ½ past 12 o'clock. He is in great spirits and says to me that he is going to work in good earnest. I replied, it [*The Friend*] cannot be out this week. 'No' said he, 'but we will get it out as fast as possible.'" She did not remark on his use of the word "we", but she turned once more to the subject of Sara Hutchinson, which evidently haunted and perplexed her.

Now finally she wrote with great bitterness, refusing to accept that Coleridge's "love" had – or had ever had – any reality. To her it all seemed, after ten years' intimacy, something that could be dismissed as a selfish, obsessive fantasy. "With respect to Coleridge, do not think it is his love for Sara which has stopped his work – do not believe it: his love for her is no more than a fanciful dream – otherwise he would prove it by a desire to make her happy. No!

He likes to have her about him as his own, as one devoted to him, but when she stood in the way of other gratifications it was all over. I speak this very unwillingly, and again I beg, *burn* this letter. I need not add, keep its contents to yourself alone."[137]

That Dorothy wrote what she believed can barely be doubted (though what exactly she meant by "other gratifications" – opium, alcohol, sexual tenderness – is not clear, as perhaps she intended). That she was in many ways still the most perceptive and generous human observer in the Allan Bank household also remains true. Yet there now stands a gulf between what she perceived, and what Coleridge actually experienced and recorded in his Notebooks and poetry. To conclude in some common-sense way, that she was right and he was wrong, is to deny the infinite involutions of the human heart.

It is also to refuse to face what Coleridge himself came to see as the profound philosophic problem posed by the nature of human love itself; and by extension, of all intensely subjective experience. Was love a self-created, self-referring illusion? Or was it "some dear embodied Good"? Was Asra in the end nothing more than "a fanciful dream", or was she genuinely a projection of his own best self, his conscience, his sense of beauty and power and hope?

This was the problem he faced again and again in his Notebooks in the succeeding months and years, and gradually in the slow accretions of his Confessional Poems, like "Constancy to an Ideal Object". This was the questioning poem he had begun in Malta, but it may well have been now that he added the stanza that best answers Dorothy's sad but memorable accusations, though he knew nothing of them at the time. It is, ironically, one of the most beautiful verses he ever wrote.

> . . . And art thou nothing? Such thou art, as when
> The woodsman winding westward up the glen
> At wintry dawn, where o'er the sheep-track's maze
> The viewless snow-mist weaves a glist'ning haze,
> Sees full before him, gliding without tread,
> An image with a glory round its head;
> So the enamoured rustic worships its fair hues,
> Nor knows he makes the shadow, he pursues![138]

5

In the Dark Chamber

1

What Coleridge did know is that he was no longer a welcome guest at Allan Bank in 1810. His thoughts turned briefly to London, from where he had received a kindly letter from John Morgan. "You ought to have had 4 or 500 pounds capital before you began to Work. I wish to God you would come to Town, if the *Friend* does not succeed, I am confident your Talents would here find satisfactory Employment – by Satisfactory I mean in point of money; as to comfort, somewhat of that must be sacrificed to Duty. – When you come, if not better provided for, you are [to be] with us."[1] Coleridge kept this offer in the back of his mind.

In the first week of May, he walked over as he had promised to Greta Hall on a short visit, ostensibly to see the children. It was not, to begin with, an official departure, but Dorothy's relief was palpable as she wrote in her next news report to Catherine Clarkson. "Coleridge went to Keswick about a week ago. As he said, to stay about ten days, but as he did not intend to return till our bustle with Mary should be over, it might probably be much longer, if his own irresolute habits had no influence in keeping him there, or preventing his return."[2] As the summer wore on, the books and manuscripts connected with *The Friend* followed in a desultory series of hay carts, making his removal a fact by accumulation.

Mrs Coleridge, sensing the crisis that had occurred at Allan Bank, as she had long predicted, was inclined to be magnanimous, and let him bury himself away in a study overlooking Bassenthwaite lake that she had kept prepared for the eventuality. "The last No. of *The Friend* lies on his Desk, the sight of which fills my heart with grief, and my eyes with tears; but I am obliged to conceal my trouble as much as possible, as the slightest expression of regret never fails to excite resentment – Poor Man! – I have not the least doubt but he is the most unhappy of the two; and the reason is too obvious to need any explanation."[3]

Southey, now completing his great *History of Brazil*, and reviewing hard for the *Quarterly*, was also in an equitable mood. He perhaps of all Coleridge's circle best understood the strain of working to journalistic deadlines, and felt that *The Friend* had been an honourable and productive effort: "there is so much got out of him which would never otherwise have come out".[4]

Both Dorothy, and now Mrs Coleridge, were convinced that Coleridge spent all his time reading and day-dreaming, and his "repeated assurances" that he was still writing for *The Friend* were mere camouflage. Certainly nothing further was published at this time. But in fact Coleridge's Notebooks contain over 250 pages of material – sketches of subjects, short essays, memoranda, timetables, reading-notes, philosophic reflections – intended for a continuation of the paper, and all written in the six months between March and August 1810.

These included the outline for an essay on the British constitution, a study of education, a defence of Christianity, and a long philosophic disquisition on the distinction between love and lust. Most striking was the beginnings of a detailed examination of the psychology of religious mysticism, as revealed in the life of St Theresa of Avila. He would continue this throughout the summer, clearly intending to develop some of the themes from his admired "Luther" issue of No. 8.

He also returned to his project of publishing a new collection of all his poems. He clung to some idea of steady, organized effort. One early timetable reads: "*The Friend* – 3 days, Sat. Sun. Mon. The Poems till finished – Tues. Wed. Thurs. *Courier* – Friday."[5] Asra's loss also seems to have strangely rekindled the idea of completing "Christabel", and he wrote one of his most suggestive fragments for her "lament" in the unknown Part III of the poem. "Christabel – My first cries mingled with my Mother's death-groan – and she beheld the vision of Glory ere I the earthly Sun – when I first looked up to Heaven, consciously, it was to look up after or for my Mother – etc. etc." This was also connected in his mind with St Theresa's experiences.[6]

At the same time he began to take new pleasure and interest in his children. Remarking on little Sara's early gift for languages –

he delighted in "Sariola's kalligraphical Initiations" – he began to give her regular lessons in Italian, which Mrs Coleridge joined in the parlour. He wrote them a "Dialogue on the Italian Language", headed "Sara and her Mama", and by the following year the nine-year-old girl was reading "French tolerably and Italian fluently".[7]

He also spent more time with the two boys, especially after the Ambleside school broke up for the summer. Hartley, now aged thirteen, was growing up fast and inclined to quarrel with "Lil' Darran" (or "Stumpy Canary") and Coleridge thought it was high time to consider his "profession or trade" for the future.[8] He was more brilliant and eccentric than ever (father and son discussed Eichhorn's critique of the Old Testament together), and his head-master Mr Dawes offered to take him for free extra tuition with an eye to Cambridge. Coleridge had no idea how university could be paid for, but he looked upon his eldest with a fond and partial gaze, and thought him "really handsome, at least, as handsome as a face so original & intellectual can be".

He regarded little Derwent, plain and puddingey, and struggling fruitlessly with his Greek, with a different kind of protective tenderness. He rejoiced in Stumpy Canary's enthusiasm for drawing triangles, and took pleasure in his less sophisticated view of the Bible. When talking about the animals in Noah's ark, Derwent gravely corrected his father about the insects missing from the role call. "'O yes, indeed, Father! – there were – there was a Grasshopper in the Ark – I saw it myself very often – I remember it very well.'"[9] Coleridge delighted in such anecdotes, and retold them to Mrs Coleridge as part of a normal family life which they could still share.

Indeed whenever Coleridge emerged from his study, his wife was astonished at his friendliness and good humour, and by August was giving Poole an account that differs so markedly from Dorothy's in the spring that one might easily conclude that she had been right, after all, about the relief of Asra's departure to him. She told Poole that he had been "in almost uniform kind disposition towards us all during his residence here; and all Southey's friends who have been here this Summer have thought his presence a great addition to the society here; and have all been uniformly great admirers of his conversation." She thought his spirits far happier than she had known them "for years", and was only puzzled that he was still publishing nothing. (What would happen to "these Lads" – fast approaching manhood – if he did not exert himself?)[10]

Southey reported the same to John Rickman – "better health than usual, and excellent spirits, and reading very hard and to no purpose". He added that Coleridge occasionally talked of going to London to start work again, but he would believe this when he saw it.[11] Meanwhile the Wordsworths had slipped gratefully away to Coleorton, going on in June to visit the Clarksons. Here Dorothy stayed for some weeks, while Wordsworth – as Coleridge later discovered – went on alone to see Tom Hutchinson, John Monkhouse and Asra at the farm in Radnorshire. So Coleridge gave every appearance of tranquillity at Greta Hall in the summer of 1810.

2

Yet all these appearances were painfully deceptive. Release from the weekly deadline of *The Friend* made him calmer and more sociable, and the presence of his children soothed and comforted him. Outwardly life seemed more normal, but inwardly his turmoil was as great as ever. His Notebooks, at first sight packed with reading-notes and sketches for *The Friend*, reveal on closer inspection terrible moments of rage and despair. His thoughts turned to suicide with an intensity not recorded since his last months in Italy in 1806, their power driving him towards poetry. Sometime in late May or June he wrote two entries which show how little either his wife or Southey understood his state of mind. The first struggles into blank verse of ghastly bleakness, and turns on his loss of Asra, but does not dare to name her:

. . . I have experienced
The worst, the World can wreak on me; the worst
That can make Life indifferent, yet disturb
With whisper'd discontents the dying prayer.
I have beheld the whole of all, wherein
My Heart had any interest in this Life,
To be disrent and torn from off my Hopes,
That nothing now is left. Why then live on?[12]

The clumsiness of the verse has its own peculiar horror, as if Coleridge could no longer find his own voice. In the intimacy of his own Notebook, he rants and postures like a bad actor on an empty stage. No one is listening so he shouts and rages against himself, threatening the deed which he will not really perform:

> . . . "Well may I break this Pact, this League, of Blood
> That ties me to myself – and break I shall"

This last sentence is placed in inverted commas, like a speech given to someone else, his other self, his opium-self perhaps.

The second entry tries a different voice, no longer grandiose, but low and small and oddly compulsive. Though taking the form of a lyric, it is written out as prose, (which led all Coleridge's subsequent editors to overlook it for his collected poems). Yet it is clearly a poem, and begins with an arresting, though apparently inexplicable, phrase: "When I was white . . ." What it records is indeed a physical compulsion, closely connected with the guilt of his opium-taking, which required him repeatedly to wash himself during the day, and to feel disgust at the slightest sensation of dirt anywhere on his body.

This repeated, obsessive washing had begun in Malta, no doubt in response to the sweat and heat of Mediterranean life. He had noted in April 1805: "I cannot endure the least atom or imagination of dirt on my person; but wash my body all over 20 times, where 8 or 9 years I washed half of it once."[13] But now it had become ritualized, a symbolic form of reassurance, which proved that he had not entirely lost control of his body, and somehow guaranteed the purity of his love for Asra. To wash and to weep for her had become forms of spiritual discipline.

It combined both voluptuous comfort and humiliating penance. This at any rate is what the strange and touching little poem (here printed as verse) seems to suggest.

> When I was white . . .
> Care had I to feel and know
> That all my body high and low
> Even parts that never met men's Eye
> Were pure of stain as new-fallen Snow.

When absent soon to meet again
That morning & that last Employ
Had only so much Pain
As the fears of Hope detract from certain Joy.
And now – O then I am least opprest
When with the cleansing Stream
I mix my tears –
And oft I'd fain neglect myself
Such anguish & such sinking down of Heart
Comes over me – yet never can I.
For neither death, nor absence, nor demerit
Can free the love-enchanted spirit –
And I seem always in her eye,
And she will never more appear to mine.[14]

The central parts of this poem are still unformed; but the morning of "that last Employ" seems to refer to the last issue of *The Friend* and Asra's departure; while the temptation to "neglect myself" indicates Coleridge's subsequent struggle with personal hygiene at Greta Hall.

Certainly Mrs Coleridge had a long battle with filthy shirts and spilt snuff throughout the summer, and sometimes Coleridge could see the funny side of this as well. "Sarah Coleridge says, on telling me of the universal Sneeze produced in the Lasses while shaking my Carpet, that she wishes my Snuff would grow: as I sow it so plentifully."[15]

As Coleridge received no letters from Asra in Wales, his sense of being abandoned and betrayed by her grew. The more he reflected on it, the more he blamed the Wordsworths, never once considering that his own demands and fantasies might have driven her away. He began to suspect that there was a secret plan for her to marry John Monkhouse, and when he heard of Wordsworth's trip to Radnorshire in June, he had a terrible dream "that W.W. and M. were going down to Wales to give her away". He awoke sweating and screaming at this "prophetic" thought. "O no! no! no! let me die – in the rack of the [kidney] Stone – only let me die before I suspect it, broad-awake! Yet, the too, too! evident, the undeniable joining in the conspiracy with W. and D. to deceive me, & her *cruel neglect & contemptuous silence ever since*!"[16]

All these dreams, demons and compulsions threatened to turn the night-life of his study into a mere madhouse, a pure opium-den of malignant fantasies and hysterical obsessions. Yet Coleridge battled through to emerge each morning – or rather, early afternoon – to be charming to his guests, cheerful with his children, and to spar gently with his wife. Sometimes there were jokes about a particularly bad night, Mrs Coleridge asking quizzically as he made his dishevelled appearance, "Have you taken too much or too little Opium?"[17] Sometimes Coleridge burst upon the children in the parlour with some outrageous doggerel:

> The little Birds shoot out their *gushes* round
> Mellow the shrill, an Oxymel of Sound:
> As if with sweet confusion sway'd,
> The thirsty Ear drank Lemonade.[18]

(While Hartley might just be able to identify the Greek roots of "Oxymel" as bitter-sweet music, Stumpy Canary would certainly recognize the properties of Lemonade – even if taken aurally rather than orally.)

Always the Notebooks continued to fill with his vast reading and scholarly reflections. Even Southey was impressed, and began to siphon off sketches and scraps that Coleridge brought him for an annual anthology, *Omniana* (first published in 1812). But what haunted Southey was that all would be wasted, and neither money for his family nor reputation for himself would ever be gained. Coleridge was producing "an accumulation of knowledge equal to that of any man living and a body of sound philosophy superior to what any man either of this or any former age has possessed – all of which will perish with him".[19]

In fact, as Coleridge told Tom Poole and Lady Beaumont, he was now planning to produce a corrected *Friend* in volume form, and to add a supplement with additional materials. His reading for this included Kant and Spinoza, Gibbon and Clarendon, Harrington and Blackstone, Chillingworth, Fulke Greville and George Herbert: philosophy, history, law, politics, religion, poetry.

Subjects sprout up with the tropical speed and variety of jungle plants: "Why is true Love like a Tree?";[20] "Essay in Defence of Punning";[21] "What was the origin of philosophy?";[22] "When did

Time begin?";[23] "Just distinction between certainly knowing and clearly knowing";[24] "Had the Christians failed, a kind of Christianity would and must have prevailed";[25] "Property clearly natural to man . . . manifest in animals – the Swans on Hawkshead Lake";[26] "Absolute Truth is always a mystery".[27]

What links this bewildering range of enquiries seems to be Coleridge's fascination with origins, with the grounds of knowledge and belief. His notes most frequently come back to religious questions – miracles, revelation, the origins of moral law, the notion of a personal God and a Trinity – but they perform vast circuits on the way. Their special quality resides perhaps in their psychological acuity, the way the individual mind grows and alters in its perception of truth, inevitably changed by age and experience.

Many such entries have strong autobiographical undertones. Coleridge proposed for example that belief in a personal God did not rest in an abstract notion of "the divine", but followed from the personal discovery of evil in the world, of failure that required forgiveness.[28] For this reason young people were naturally, and almost inevitably, both materialists and idealists.

His own experience of Pantisocracy shadows this argument. "Young men ignorant of the corruption & weakness of their own hearts, & therefore always prone to substitute the glorious *Ideal* of human nature for the existing reality. – This may be most affectingly shown by the fervent friendships & bitter quarrels of young men, each expecting the other to be an Angel, & taking their generous wishes in their most generous moods for Virtue. – Hence no need is felt of Redemption.'[29]

Equally he felt the insistent materialism of scientific theory, by its reductive rationalism, closed off the vital sense of knowledge itself as a process of growth and exploration carried on from one generation to the next. The recognition of mystery, like the recognition of evil, was essential to progressive understanding of the world in a psychological sense.

Thus an essay on the theory of lightning as the product of atmospheric friction begins with a characteristic qualification. "I do not like that presumptuous philosophy which in its rage of explanation allows no XYZ, no symbol representative of the vast Terra Incognita of Knowledge, for the Facts and Agencies of Mind and Matter reserved for future Explorers, while the ultimate grounds of all must remain inexplorable or Man cease to be progressive. Our Ignorance, with all the intermediates of obscurity, is the condition of our ever-increasing Knowledge."[30]*

He felt his own Notebooks should also have this open, provisional status, and that if he "should die without having destroyed this & my other Memorandum Books" they should be understood as "Hints & first Thoughts" and not as "fixed opinions". They were "acts of obedience to the apostolic command of Try all things: hold fast to that which is good."[31]

3

Coleridge began the remarkable group of entries concerning St Theresa of Avila at the end of June. He borrowed a two-volume edition of her *Life and Works* (divided as "The History of her Life", 1671; and "The History of her Foundations", 1675) from Southey's library, and annotated it in great detail. "Monday June 25 1810 Keswick – Began to read the deeply interesting Life & Works of St Teresa. She was indeed framed by nature & favoured by a very hot-bed in a hot-house of Circumstance, to become a mystic Saint of the first magnitude, a mighty Mother of spiritual transports, the materia prestabilita of divine Fusions, Infusions, and Confusions."[32]

Despite his initially ironic tone – he had learned to despise the excesses of Mediterranean Catholicism in Malta – he became more and more fascinated by the mixture of spiritual and erotic mysticism in her visions. As with Luther, he accepted them as psychological fact, but sought to explain them biographically in the peculiar circumstances of her upbringing.

He examined the influence of her parents, her early reading in

* The notion that certain kinds of knowledge can only be gained by a slow transitional passage through mystery and doubt, as opposed to a rapid logical unfolding, was one of Coleridge's most suggestive ideas for his later Victorian readers. "For how can we gather strength but by exercise? How can a truth, new to us, be made our own without examination and self-questioning – any new truth, I mean, that relates to the properties of the mind, and its various faculties and affections! But whatever demands effort, requires time. Ignorance seldom *vaults* into knowledge, but passes into it through an intermediate state of obscurity, even as Night into Day through Twilight." (Footnote to the 1812 edition, in *The Friend*, II, p.81.) A similar idea is pursued in Cardinal Newman's *An Essay in Aid of A Grammar of Assent*, 1870.

the lives of saints and martyrs, her passion for "Spanish Romance and Chivalry", and the guilt of her adolescent sexual experience. He saw her intense, romantic spirituality as formed from earliest childhood. "At about 8 years old She & her brother were engaged to run away & go to Africa in order to obtain the crown of Martyrdom. She regarded the Martyrs with more envy than Admiration: they were so very lucky in getting an eternal Heaven at so easy a price."[33] There are distant echoes here of his own childhood truancies – and Hartley's perhaps – to a beckoning, magical river. But the conscious connection he made was with the yearning, innocent character of Christabel, who like Theresa, had the "force of suppressed Instincts stirring in the heart & bodily frame".

All these conditions of "Religion, Manners, Climate, Constitution" quite naturally formed her visions which she accepted with complete conviction. "You will see how almost impossible it was, that young Spanish Maiden so innocent, & so susceptible, of an imagination so lively by nature & so fever-kindled by disease, & thus so well-furnished with the requisite images and preconceptions, should not mistake, & often, the less painful and in such a frame the sometimes pleasurable approaches to bodily Deliquium, and her imperfect Fainting-fits for divine Transports, & momentary Union with God."[34]

Initially Coleridge's biographic and psycho-pathological approach to St Theresa appears to be a sceptical one. But his tenderness towards her – an "innocent and loving Soul" – is empathetic, almost fraternal. Much of the "superstition" surrounding her is the fault of Dominican apologists writing twelve years afterwards at the height of the Inquisition.[35]

Her spiritual insights struck him as profound and moving, often expressed in imagery very close to his own poems. Her "elucidation" of the four states of prayer is given in water metaphors which strongly recall the experience of the Ancient Mariner. Prayer begins as an act of "seemingly unassisted poor labouring Will", like water drawn up painfully from a well in a bucket "by mere force of the arm"; later it is assisted "by the wheel & pulley"; thirdly it becomes easier like "the drawing off streamlets from a River & great Fountain"; and lastly it becomes the effortless pouring down of "copious rains from Heaven".

This is powerfully reminiscent of the wonderful description of the Mariner's release from spiritual drought in Part V of the ballad, where "By the grace of the Holy Mother, the Ancient Mariner is refreshed with rain":

> My lips were wet, my throat was cold,
> My garments all were dank;
> Sure I had drunken in my dreams,
> And still my body drank.[36]

For all her ecstasies, St Theresa also "judiciously" counselled against hysterical emotions. "The true Love of God doth not consist in having Tears, or Tenderness, or Spiritual Gusts"; we must always remain "Lords of ourselves".

All this spoke with great immediacy to Coleridge in his study at Greta Hall, and his notes are intercut with further reflections on his agonized longings for Asra. "June 25 1810. Keswick. – I most commonly do not *see* her with my imagination – have no visual image: but she is present to me, even as two persons at some small distance in the same dark room: they know that the one is present, & act & feel under that knowledge – & a subtler kind of sigh seems to confirm & enliven the knowledge. SARA (*in Greek*)."[37]

The image of the dark, solitary room containing some transcendent possibility of light and blissful communion, seized upon Coleridge. In some way his opium visions of Asra were connected with St Theresa in her monastic cell, and the experience of all other mystics like Luther, or St Francis de Sales, or Jakob Boehme.[38] He felt such visionary premonitions of happiness lay at the root of all religious feeling, and were universal in all times, all societies, and "Under all forms of Religion".[39]

These "Epiphanies & Incarnations", though they might be a mistake of "the sensuous imagination relatively to Place and to Space", were yet truths of "the moral Being". In a long, complex and ecstatic entry Coleridge analysed this "instinctive craving, dim & blind tho it may be, of the moral being after this unknown Bliss, or Blessedness". Though such blessedness might only be felt by its absence, "known only & anticipated by the Hollowness where it is", it was nevertheless a spiritual fact.

Seeking to express his own experience of this reassuring light, glimpsed in the metaphysical dark of his study, he returned to one of his familiar images from the natural world, perfectly balanced between hope and despair. (Characteristically, he placed it in a bracket.) "The Plant in its dark Chamber turns & twists its stem & grows toward the Light-Cranny, the sensation of the want supplying the sense of the Object wanted!"[40]

4

All these entries emphasized his feeling of deepening solitude at Greta Hall, as the summer wore on. External matters occasionally intrude – conversations with Southey, worries about keeping up his life assurance payments, notes on birdsong inspired by Gilbert White ("Owls hoot in 3 different keys, G Flat (Or F sharp) in B flat & in A Flat").[41] But the prevailing note is one of loneliness, with its familiar lament: "Alas, to no one dare I speak or even look my griefs & heart-wastings! Dear Book! now my only Confidant, my only faithful Friend."[42] The term has surely taken on a certain irony.

He was still gathering materials for the supplement to *The Friend* itself, but he knew that he could not put off for much longer the pressing need to publish, pay off some of his extensive debts, and earn money for his family. His thoughts turned increasingly to London, or Edinburgh, and the unavoidable necessity of topical journalism.

One idea was to write a long review of Scott's *Lady of the Lake*, which had been published in May 1810 with great success. Scott had told Jeffrey at the *Edinburgh Review* that it was greatly indebted to the unpublished "Christabel", and Coleridge's views were naturally of controversial interest.[43] Perhaps for this reason a copy had lain on Coleridge's desk "week after week till it cried shame to me for not opening it". He finally roused himself to do so in September, putting his first thoughts in a long letter to Wordsworth, who had returned to Grasmere. They had not met since May, and Scott's ballad provided relatively safe, neutral ground to reopen communications.

Coleridge avoided all personal reference, except to say he was "curious" to see Mary's new baby. Instead he adopted an easy tone to pour cheerful scorn on Scott's ballad, whose languid progress was "between a sleeping Canter and a Marketwoman's trot". He felt it was clearly derivative, "not without its peccadilloes against the 8th Commandment", with borrowings from Wordsworth's "Ruth" and "Hart Leap Well", as well as a "miserable copy" of Bracy the Bard from "Christabel".

"In short, what I felt in Marmion, I feel still more in the Lady of the Lake – viz. that a man accustomed to cast words in metre and familiar with descriptive Poets & Tourists . . . must be troubled with a mental Strangury, if he could not lift up his leg six times at six different Corners, and each time p – a canto."[44]

Coleridge's jocular ribaldry disguised an acute literary perception. A new generation of poets had arrived, and were taking over the revolutionary achievements of the *Lyrical Ballads* and making them commercially popular. The narrative verse-romance was to prove the bestselling form of the new decade. Scott's *Lady of the Lake* would sell 30,000 copies in 1810; and in 1812 Byron would double the figure on his return from Greece with *The Bride of Abydos* (written in a week), *The Corsair*, and *Lara*, all of which sold spectacularly well. Indeed the previous autumn of 1809, Byron had recorded in his journals his rapt reading of "The Ancient Mariner" on board ship sailing through the Mediterranean on his way to Greece.

Faced with this rising tide of imitation and popularizing, Coleridge sought to call back Wordsworth to their old literary comradeship. He did it in the light-hearted style of the old Quantock days. "In short, my dear William! – it is time to write a Recipe for Poems of this sort – I amused myself a day or two ago on reading a Romance in Mrs Radcliffe's style with making out a scheme, which was to serve for all romances a priori – only varying the proportions – A Baron or a Baroness ignorant of their Birth, and in some dependent situation – Castle – on a Rock – a Sepulchre – at some distance from the Rock – Deserted Rooms – Underground Passages – Pictures – a ghost, so believed – or – a written record – blood on it! – a wonderful Cut throat – etc. etc. etc. – Now I say, it is time to make out the component parts of the Scottish Minstrelsy . . ."

This recipe for a bestseller would include in addition "a vast string of patronymics", hunting, heraldry, falconry, "some pathetic moralizing on old times"; and of course a Bard ("that is absolutely necessary").[45]

Though Wordsworth had been back at Grasmere for a month ("he gives me grand accounts of Sara's good looks", Dorothy had noted), there is no evidence that he responded to this overture. Nor did Coleridge publish the review of Scott, though he had prepared for it extensively in his Notebooks, observing that as art criticism spoke of "schools" ("The Flemish School – The Venetian School") there was now a tendency to do the same in literary criticism – "but now! The Southeyian School, the Wordsworthian etc.". He did not mention a Coleridgean School.[46]

The review, so eagerly awaited and so financially necessary, was prevented by two unfortunate circumstances. The first was an attack on Scott's "imitations" from earlier authors, published in the *Courier* on 15 September, and inexplicably signed "STC". In fact it was written by Edward Dubois, the editor of the *Monthly Mirror* who had become a critic of the original "Lake School" and wished to stir up a literary war. Coleridge was forced to publish a denial in the paper, while Southey wrote to Scott assuring him that the article had nothing to do with anyone at Greta Hall.

Coleridge's hands were then further tied, when Scott graciously replied with a promise to review Southey's new ballad "The Curse of the Kehema" favourably in the *Quarterly Review*. As Southey was anxious that his own poem should receive good notices, he was understandably keen not to antagonize Scott any further through Coleridge. Besides, he was himself continuing to contribute to the *Quarterly* for handsome fees (they soon rose to £100 an article). In all these circumstances, Coleridge felt it was no longer possible to publish a critical review of Scott, and the chance to defend the true originality of "Christabel" in public was delayed for the next six years. Southey meanwhile went on to establish himself on the *Quarterly*, which became his main source of income for the next twenty years; and also to secure his friendship with Scott. When Scott was offered the Poet Laureateship three years later in 1813, he passed it up in favour of Southey.

5

By October, with his boys back at Ambleside School, and Asra as silent as ever, Coleridge became desperate to migrate for the winter from the increasingly chilly comforts of Greta Hall. He turned and twisted in his dark chamber. An income, an opium cure, a renewal of admiring company, must all be found before it was too late.

At length a means of escape appeared with the last of the season's visitors to the Lakes. Wordsworth's old and loquacious admirer Basil Montagu arrived on a late tour, proudly displaying a new carriage and a new wife, a handsome and managing widow with a taste for literary celebrities. Montagu, while retaining his Rousseauist ideal of the simple life, had managed to combine this with a brilliant career as a London barrister and a fine town house at 4 Gray's Inn Place, Holborn, where he kept a lively dinner table.[47]

After spending several days at Greta Hall, and sensing the domestic tensions, he invited Coleridge to join him in London for the winter. The invitation was obviously well meant, an opportunity for Coleridge to revive his health and literary prospects in the great city. For Mrs Montagu it may also have seemed something of a social catch, a decorative addition to the silverware of their soirées. Montagu evidently knew something, if not all, of Coleridge's opium problem; but like others before him felt that it could be "managed". He was a Unitarian, eschewed strong liquors, and believed in hard work and early rising. He was also a notorious gossip, one of the pleasures he shared with his new wife, a lady, as Coleridge observed, with a "Black eye & blue – both bright".[48]

To Coleridge the idea seemed like a godsend, both eminently practical and subtly flattering. He would travel down in Montagu's own chaise, be an honoured guest at Montagu's comfortable house, and be given an introduction to Mrs Montagu's personal physician, the fashionable London doctor Anthony Carlisle, renowned for his silver tongue and bedside manner.

Mrs Coleridge approved, though privately Southey was sceptical, writing to Rickman: "I do not know any other motive that he has for going to London, than that he becomes daily more and more uneasy at having done nothing for so long, and therefore flies away to avoid the sight of persons, who he knows must be grieved by his misconduct, tho they refrain from all remonstrance."[49] His book-box was packed, and he prepared for a dawn departure on 18 October, making first for Grasmere where the Montagus were paying a last call on Wordsworth.

It was during this brief interval that, unknown to Coleridge, Wordsworth intervened. What exactly he said to the Montagus will never be known exactly, and would become the subject of bitter dispute over the next two years. What he had previously written to Tom Poole, and what Dorothy had written to Catherine Clarkson, certainly explains his motives and gives some idea of the severity with which he may have spoken to Montagu. But whether he mentioned Asra, as well as opium and alcohol, is not clear. At all events he felt it his duty to warn Montagu about Coleridge's true condition as he saw it, and to advise Montagu strongly against putting up Coleridge in his house.

Coleridge was unaware that any such conversation had taken place as he set out for Grasmere, and nothing was mentioned by Wordsworth as he took his place in the chaise. When he told Wordsworth he already felt better in the head, he was only surprised that Wordsworth replied with a curious joke about Schiller's death, "that when he was opened his entrails were, as it were, eaten up, while his brain was sound".[50] But Coleridge put this down to the awkwardness of parting from his old friend; an awkwardness that they surely both felt.

It was Dorothy who gave the first circumstantial account of what had passed, several months later in a long letter to Catherine Clarkson. Wordsworth had felt that Coleridge's presence would be "a serious injury" to Montagu and his household, and that his "habits" would be intolerable to him. She elaborated this at some length.

> William used many arguments to persuade M. that his purpose of keeping Coleridge comfortable could not be answered by their being in the same house together – but in vain. Montagu was resolved. "He would do all that could be done for him and have him at his house." After this William spoke out and told M. the nature of C.'s habits (nothing in fact which everybody whose house he has been in for two days has not seen of themselves) and Montagu then perceived that it would be better for C. to have lodgings near him. William intended giving C. advice to the same effect; but he had no opportunity of talking with him when C. passed through Grasmere on his way to London. Soon after they got to London Montagu wrote to William that on their road he had seen so much of C.'s habits that he was convinced he should be miserable under the same roof with him, and that he had repeated to C. what William had said to him and that C. had been very angry.[51]

In fact Dorothy had not been at Allan Bank on the day of Coleridge's departure. Her account must have been taken from William himself, and it may have omitted or softened several details. But it is enough to suggest why Coleridge was now approaching one of the great emotional crises of his life.

By his own account, he was completely unsuspecting. As the coach rolled southwards through Yorkshire and Lincolnshire, he wrote a delighted appreciation of the grounds of Bolton Abbey, and admired a painting by Ciro Ferri at Stamford, "The Marriage of Boas and Ruth". The tender figure of Ruth, languorously wilting in a pale blue silk dress with her mass of auburn hair tied up in a band behind her head, inevitably reminded him of Asra. ("Were Sara here, even the adored here, enjoying it with me – then, then, it would be Heaven possessed!")[52]

6

The chaise arrived in London at 10 o'clock on the evening of Friday, 26 October. But it drew up outside No. 55 Frith Street, Soho, rather than Montagu's own house in Gray's Inn Place. (This appears to have been Mrs Montagu's family address, a rather less substantial residence, among printshops and many small businesses belonging to immigrant Italians in flight from Napoleon.) At some point Coleridge was informed of the new arrangements, which understandably dismayed him.

Then, on the following evening, there was a row over the serving of sufficient wine for dinner, when Coleridge's old Malta friend Captain Pasley – who had recently published a book on his Mediterranean experiences – came for the evening and expected a carouse with his old mess mate. Afterwards Coleridge confronted Montagu, and the whole story of Wordsworth's remarks came out in the open. There were "angry" words, perhaps even tears on Coleridge's part. He remembered bursting out: "O this is cruel! This is *base*!"[53]

In the heat of the moment Montagu said something to the effect that Wordsworth had "authorized" or even "commissioned" him to pass on his views to Coleridge. Whether this is true or not, or whether Coleridge misunderstood what the flurried Montagu was saying to cover his own embarrassment, the particular words entered into his soul with terrible conviction.

Coleridge fled to his room, and made a series of desperate notes over the weekend, swinging wildly between grief and fury. "Of this accursed analysis or rather anatomy of a friend's Character, as if a human Soul were made like a watch, or loved for this & that tangible and verbally expressible quality! W. authorized M. to tell me, he had no Hope of me! O God! what good reason for saying this? The very belief takes away all excuse, because all kind purpose for the declaration. W. once – was unhappy, dissatisfied, full of craving, then what Love & Friendship, now all calm & attached – and what contempt for the moral comforts of others."[54]

Coleridge strove to make sense of what had happened, and to put it in some sort of perspective. But Wordsworth's actual words, as reported by Montagu, kept coming back to him, with a sense of overwhelming betrayal. "Sunday Night. No Hope of me! absolute Nuisance! God's mercy it is a Dream!"[55] This is what he put in his Notebook that weekend, but there were obviously many other phrases that burned into his heart, and which he later repeated to his friends.

Montagu had said that "Wordsworth *has commissioned* me to tell you, first, that he has no Hope of you."[56] Wordsworth had said that "for years past [I] had been an ABSOLUTE NUISANCE in the Family".[57] Wordsworth had said he was a "rotten drunkard", or a drunkard who was "rotting out his entrails by intemperance". Wordsworth had said he was "in the habit of running into debt at little Pot-houses for Gin".[58] At one point, as the supreme irony, Mrs Montagu had apparently interjected in her bright-eyed way: "I thought it not friendly in Mr Wordsworth to go into such a detail."[59]

Outwardly Coleridge attempted to regain his composure. The next morning he informed Montagu, with as much calm as he could muster, that he thought it best in all the circumstances that he should remove to a hotel. Nonetheless, he would consult Dr Carlisle as had been arranged. But inwardly he felt as if his whole world had fallen apart, and out of control. "Whirled about without a centre – as in a nightmare – no gravity – a vortex without a centre." It was his old image of the flock of starlings in screaming flight, that he had observed so long ago, when lying isolated and trapped on the remote peak of Scaffel, not knowing how to go on or go back.[60]

By Wednesday, 31 October he was established in a little upper room at Hudson's Hotel, King Street, just behind Covent Garden. It was like his lonely return from Italy, four years previously. But this time he felt the journey of his whole life had been wasted and rendered meaningless. He felt "a compressing and strangling Anguish, made up of Love, and Resentment, and Sorrow – quarrelling with all the Future & refusing to be consoled for the Past".[61]

He wandered the streets, not daring to contact any friends, beset by "faintness & universal Trembling".[62] Finally he staggered round to the Lambs at 34 Southampton Buildings, just off Chancery Lane. Charles was still out at work in East India House, but Mary welcomed him in as usual. She told him that she had suffered a return of her nervous illness, and that she and Charles had given up alcohol, and were trying to replace it with a rhubarb diet, "not pleasant *to* you . . . but good *for* you".[63]

Coleridge let her prattle on, and tried to conceal his news. But the "wildness & paleness" of his face soon gave him away. Mary "entreated" him to tell her what was troubling him. "In the first attempt to speak, my feelings overpowered me, an agony of weeping followed, & then . . . I brought out convulsively some such words as – Wordsworth – Wordsworth has given me up. *He* has no hope of me – I have been an absolute Nuisance in his family."[64] Mary Lamb listened silently to her old friend, and then gave him a very large brandy.

7

Coleridge sat alone in his upstairs room at Hudson's Hotel for the first three wintry days of November 1810. Silently he surveyed the wreckage of his hopes – Wordsworth, Asra, *The Friend* – and tried to take stock of what was left. It was one of the bleakest moments of his life.

Initially he revealed his devastated feelings to no one. The obvious course of writing directly to Wordsworth for an explanation seemed impossible to him. In one note to John Monkhouse of 1 November he mentioned "a very painful affair with which I need not trouble you"; but then quickly went on to praise Mrs Montagu's "winning kind-heartedness" and to express his confidence in Dr Carlisle's abilities.[65] Indeed he had so smoothed things over with the Montagus that nothing seriously amiss was suspected at Grasmere. "We heard no more of this, or of C. in any way," wrote Dorothy later, "except soon after his arrival in Town, by Mrs Montagu, that he was well in health, powdered etc. and talked of being busy."[66] Powdered hair and a fashionable doctor indicated all was well.

But Coleridge was acting a part, and nothing was what it seemed. Anthony Carlisle quickly abandoned his case, evidently shocked by the extremity of his addiction. Breaking his Hippocratic oath, he then gossiped of it in London, and wrote indiscreetly to Southey at Keswick. Within a fortnight Southey was stoking the fires to his friend Charles Danvers. "Coleridge is in London – gone *professedly* to be cured of opium and drinking spirits by Carlisle – *really* because he was tired of being here, and wanted to do both more at his ease elsewhere. I have had a dismal letter about him from Carlisle. The case is utterly hopeless."[67] But of course Southey knew nothing about the Wordsworth affair either.

At Hudson's Hotel, Coleridge sat up late into the night making a series of long notes about his situation. "My Griefs and Sorrows passed all before my *Love*, and like the Birds & Beasts before Adam, receive their names – nay, their natures too – from it."[68] The large sprawling hand, the unrolling syntax and the moments of paranoia and self-pity, suggest that he was often very drunk. None the less the entries are perfectly coherent, and represent a tremendous concentrated effort to get some sort of bearings on his past life and find the grounds of his "moral being" for the future.

There were three main notes. The first was a confirmation of his love for Asra, now expressed with religious intensity.[69] The second was a "*Confessio Fidei*", or statement of his Christian faith, in carefully numbered propositions and asserting the reality of a spiritual life beyond the wreckage of his physical one.[70] The third was an "Ego-ana", or psychological self-analysis of his emotional predicament.[71]

The intense inwardness of these entries seems to promise a searing, unflinching examination of conscience. Yet many elements, many levels of self-awareness, are missing or suppressed. Coleridge made no attempt at this point to grapple with the fact of his opium addiction, to consider why his "habits" might have made him an "absolute nuisance" in any family he stayed with. Indeed the only specific mention of his addiction comes in an oblique, though intriguing, reference to the "Kubla Khan" autumn of 1797 in the Quantocks, and "the retirement between Linton and Porlock" which was "the first occasion of my having recourse to Opium".[72]

The love-note concerning Asra – virtually a hymn, a psalmic Song of Songs – is so idealized as to leave the actual figure of Sara Hutchinson far below in some mundane sphere. The woman in distant Radnorshire, even the tender auburn-haired Ruth in her Italian landscape, these have been subsumed and transformed into a divine presence. "My love of Asra is not so much in my Soul, as my Soul in it. It is my whole Being wrapt up in one Desire, all the Hopes & Fears, Joys & Sorrows, all the Powers, Vigour & Faculties of my Spirit abridged into one perpetual Inclination. To bid me not to love you were to bid me to annihilate myself – for to love you is all I know of Life, as far as my Life is an object of my Consciousness or my free Will."

Dorothy Wordsworth would instantly have identified this as Coleridge's opium fantasy, careless of all living relations and responsibilities. In any real, domestic world, this vision itself would have been an "absolute nuisance", an impossible demand. Yet for Coleridge alone in London, barely clinging to his own identity, drifting amidst the inner storms, drunk and weeping and hopeless, Asra still represented the spiritual force that he needed, the duty to exist, and the right to be happy. If his note is understood as a prayer as much as a vision, it represents courage in extremity, as much as delusion in despair.

> God is our Being, but thro his works alone doth he reveal himself . . . I hold it therefore neither Impiety on the one hand, nor Superstition on the other, that you are the God within me, even as the best & most religious of men have called their Conscience the God within them . . . In what form, with what voice, under what modification can I imagine God to work upon me, in which *you* have not worked? – All evil has kept aloof – you have worked ceaselessly every where, at all times – and the sum of your influence & Benignant Grace has been, Horror of whatever is base . . . fervent aspirations after good, & great, honourable & beautiful things – and the unconquerable necessity of making myself worthy of being happy as the one indispensable condition of possessing the one only happiness – your Love, your Esteem, and You.[73]

The exalted tone of all this is considerably modified in Coleridge's "*Confessio Fidei*". He states his belief in God, in free will, in the life to come, and the "Spiritual State of Being". Yet none of these is susceptible of "Scientific Demonstration" or can be proved by "Understanding or discursive Faculty". They are simply the universal assumptions of "Natural Religion" which all men, "all finite rational Beings", have a duty to believe. But his specifically Christian faith has a much darker ground, which effectively challenges the notion of free will or any inherent goodness in the natural human condition.

The doctrine of the "fallen state" or "Original Sin" was of course perfectly orthodox Christian teaching, based on Adam's disobedience as described in the Book of Genesis. Coleridge had restated it in the opening of *The Friend*. But now it seemed to be taking on an increasingly personal intensity, which clearly reflected the terrors of his addiction and the sense of powerlessness to control his own life. To him the "Fall" had become a recognizable event in his own autobiography. "I believe, and hold it as the fundamental article of Christianity, that I am a fallen creature; that I am myself capable of moral evil, but not of myself capable of moral good, and that Guilt is justly imputable to me prior to any given act, or assignable moment of time, in my Consciousness. I am born a child of Wrath. This fearful Mystery I pretend not to understand . . . but I know that it is so!"[74] Thus Coleridge struggled to come to terms with his guilt and dependency as a spiritual fact, an inescapable part of the human condition.

Coleridge's mood altered again with his self-analysis or "Egoana". Here, suddenly and startlingly, he saw himself as blameless, innocent and betrayed. He wrote about his marriage, his friendship for Wordsworth, and once again his love for Asra. In each case he felt he had offered unconditional love, which had never really been returned. For twenty-five years he had confused "two things essentially different" – the first, being "beloved by a person"; the second "a person's being highly pleased with being loved and admired by me".

Mrs Coleridge had never been a wife "in the purest, holiest sense of the word". His fourteen years of "consummate Friendship" for Wordsworth, "a man whose welfare never ceased to be far dearer to me than my own, and for whose Fame I have been enthusiastically watchful, even at the price of alienating the affections of my Benefactors", had always been based on a "reverential admiration" that was never truly reciprocated. Likewise his ten years of love for Asra, such as "I should feel no shame to describe to an Angel", had never really been understood. "One human Being, *entirely* loving me (this, of course must have been a Woman)" would have satisfied "all my Hopes". Everything was now clear to him. "The events of last year, and emphatically of the last month, have now forced me to perceive – No one on earth has ever LOVED me."

Whatever truths this might contain, it was hardly an objective self-analysis. It was an accusation, angry and self-pitying, in the voice of a hurt child – "turbulent, with an outcry at the heart" – as he had written in the poem "To William Wordsworth" at Coleorton. Coleridge's one attempt to impose an adult voice, to ask in what way *he* might be to blame for these failings, was sulky and unconvincing. "Doubtless, the fault must have been partly, perhaps chiefly, in myself. The want of reliability in little things, the infliction of little pains, the trifling with hope, in short, all that renders the idea of a person recall more pains than pleasures – these would account for the loss of Friendship." Perhaps, he mused, his one true fault was his "voluntary self-humiliation, my habitual abasement of my self & my talents".[75]

Yet for all this, the "Ego-ana" is a curiously spirited document. In the mournful recitation of wrongs and rejections, there is a stirring of self-assertion, a confused feeling of facing up to the worst. If Coleridge was cruelly, crazily, unjust to all the patience and years of loving support he had received at Grasmere and Keswick, he was also courageous in accepting the reality of his rejection from that world. If they had "no Hope" of him, very well then, he would have no hope of them.

Somehow he would recover his own sources of hope, and once again find his own independence in London. At Hudson's Hotel, the prospect appeared suicidally bleak and confused. He felt he was "looking forward upon Life, & down into the grave (on the brink of which I am now probably tottering)".[76] But the very fact that he could examine and describe his feelings and his beliefs held out some possibility of a future. It was some time now that he wrote one of his darkest and most unflinching poems, "The Visionary Hope". In it he described his sensation of his whole life being trapped, as if he were "some captive guest, some royal prisoner at his conqueror's feast".

That Hope, which was his inward bliss and boast,
Which waned and died, yet ever near him stood,
Though changed in nature, wander where he would –
For Love's Despair is but Hope's pining Ghost! –
For this one Hope he makes his hourly moan,
He wishes and can wish for this alone! . . .[77]

8

It was John Morgan who came to his rescue, appearing unannounced at the door of his room on Sunday night. Morgan had heard something from a friend of the Montagus, and quickly grasped the gravity of the situation. He hurried Coleridge away in a carriage to his own house at No. 7 Portland Place, Hammersmith (now Addison Bridge Place). Here he was fed, soothed and put to bed. Coleridge entered the names of Mary Morgan and Charlotte Brent in large ciphered letters in his Notebook, and later wrote with profound gratitude: "He came to me instantly, told me that I had enemies at work against my character, & pressed me to leave the Hotel & come home with him . . . If it be allowed to call anyone on earth Saviour, Morgan & his Family have been my Saviours, Body and Soul."[78]

6

Hamlet in Fleet Street

1

John Morgan's house at Hammersmith, then a leafy village on the western turnpike road out of London, became Coleridge's base and beloved haven for the next eighteen months. His stay there was not always tranquil: there were drunken scenes, periods of extreme depression, and a return of his nightmares and screaming fits. Several times Coleridge fled away to temporary lodgings around Fleet Street, fearful that he was "depressing" their spirits by his behaviour, "and in spite of myself gradually alienating your esteem & chilling your affection toward me". He was particularly worried that in these desperate, opium-confused nights at Hammersmith he had offended "dear dear Mary! dearest Charlotte!", with behaviour that was "unlike" himself.[1]

What exactly he may have done or said at these times is not clear, but entries in his Notebook suggest ghastly outbursts, troubling sexual fantasies, paranoid intervals and nightmare experiences in his bedroom. One note, heavily crossed out and ciphered in Greek, reads frantically: "The *painful* Disgust felt by every good mind, male or female, at certain things & Images (semen compared to urine) is itself a proof and effect of the natural union of Love and Lust, Thoughts and Sensations being so exceedingly dissimilar from the vehicle – As if a beloved Woman vanishing in our arms should leave a huge Toad – or worse."[2]

But the Morgans – kindhearted, unshockable, deeply convinced of Coleridge's fundamental genius, and themselves rather chaotic in domestic matters – were proof against these "habits" and aberrations. In every case Morgan hurried back into London, tracked Coleridge down, and prevailed upon him to return. Coleridge never forgot these flights and rescues by Morgan, "Intervals when from the bitter consciousness of my own infirmities & increasing inequality of Temper I took lodgings against his will, & was always by his zealous friendship brought back again."[3]

While these private dramas unfolded at Hammersmith, Coleridge eased himself back into London social life and the literary circle of his old friends, hoping to appear as much like his old self as possible. He did this with extraordinary effect, so that sometimes he appears to be two quite different men leading two quite different lives. Few had any idea of the performance he was putting on. A fortnight after leaving the Montagus, he was visiting Lamb regularly at Southampton Buildings, arguing with Hazlitt, dining with William Godwin in Skinner Street, planning political articles with Stuart at the *Courier* offices in the Strand, and dazzling Henry Crabb Robinson with his philosophical talk.

Charles Lamb sent one of his deliberately mischievous reports to Grasmere on 13 November. "Coleridge has powdered his head, and looks like Bacchus, Bacchus ever sleek and young. He is going to turn sober, but his Clock has not struck yet, meantime he pours down goblet after goblet, the 2d to see where the 1st is gone, the 3d to see no harm happens to the second, a fourth to say there's another coming, and a 5th to say he's not sure he's the last." Mary contented herself with saying that if she had not known "how ill" Coleridge was, she would have "no idea of it, for he has been very cheerful".[4] She did not think he had begun his "course of medicine & regimen" under Dr Carlisle; and she made no mention of his outburst about Wordsworth.

If these reports reassured the Wordsworths, they continued to exasperate Southey, as he wrote to Grosvenor Bedford. "When he is tired of his London and Hammersmith friends he will come back again as if he has done nothing amiss or absurd . . . he will destroy himself with self-indulgence . . . O Grosvenor what a mind is here overthrown!"[5] The last phrase was from *Hamlet*.

2

Henry Crabb Robinson had rather a different impression of Coleridge's mind in November 1810. Robinson had first heard Coleridge in the lectures of 1808, but he had never met him personally, until introduced this winter by Lamb. In the interval he had been abroad again, acting as *The Times*'s special correspondent in the Peninsular

War. He had returned with a considerable reputation as a war reporter, and at the age of thirty-six was settling down to practise at the Bar.

His early studies at the University of Jena had given him an unusual appreciation of German Romanticism, and an abiding fascination with literary personalities. In his spare time, he had set himself to report on London society in his diary, meeting everyone he could, gathering gossip, estimating reputations, and analysing movements on the literary battlefield.

These *Diaries*, not fully published until after his death in 1867, contain vivid accounts of Blake, Southey, Hazlitt, Godwin, Shelley, Lamb, Sydney Smith, Mrs Barbauld and Walter Scott. But, like Lamb, he already considered that Wordsworth and Coleridge were the master-spirits of the age, though his preference was for Wordsworth. "We spoke of Wordsworth and Coleridge, Lamb, to my surprise, asserted Coleridge to be the greater man. He preferred the *Mariner* to anything Wordsworth had written. Wordsworth, he thought, is narrow and confined in his views compared with him."[6]

On meeting Coleridge "for the first time in private" on 14 November, he was greatly impressed, writing to his brother of an epic encounter. "He kept me on the stretch of attention and admiration from half-past three till twelve o'clock. On politics, metaphysics and poetry, more especially on the Regency, Kant and Shakespeare, he was astonishingly eloquent."

There was no mention of drunkenness or confusion, only an unexpected inability to sustain his arguments. "Though he practises all sorts of delightful tricks and shows admirable skill in riding his hobbies, he may be easily unsaddled. I was surprised to find how easy it is to obtain from him concessions which lead to gross inconsistencies." Though Coleridge could hold a drawing-room entranced, as "an incomparable declaimer", Crabb Robinson thought he "would never have succeeded at the Bar". He lacked logical clarity and intellectual aggression, despite all his learning.

Yet Robinson warmed to this quality, which made Coleridge unusually accessible and irresistibly stimulating. He concluded with a shrewd distinction, contrasting his manner with Dr Johnson's reputation as a fearsome talker: though he felt "a sense of inferiority that makes me humble in his presence, I do not feel in the least afraid of him".[7]

Coleridge evidently found these social engagements at Lamb's an enormous relief to his private feelings. He could expand and perform, in admiring company, unbottling his ideas and kite-flying his theories, in a way that had been denied him for two long years in the Lakes. Old friends and new acquaintances were gradually drawn into the convivial circle at Southampton Buildings – John Rickman from the House of Commons, Sergeant Rough from the Bar, Godwin from his publishing house in Skinner Street, John Collier (with whom Robinson lodged in Hatton Garden) from *The Times*, William Hazlitt (also lodging in Southampton Buildings) with his increasingly radical views, and of course the Lambs themselves (still clinging with decreasing conviction to their water regime).

In their genial, though not uncritical, company Coleridge unfolded like some huge exotic plant, rustling and unbending in the unaccustomed light and warmth. Characteristically he was aware of this effect on himself, and simultaneously its effect on those around him, and captured it in a delightful paragraph in his Notebooks back at Hammersmith, a startling contrast to the grief-stricken entries that surround it.

> Man of genius places things in *a new light* – this trivial phrase better expresses the appropriate efforts of Genius than Pope's celebrated Distich – What oft was thought but ne'er so well exprest. It had been *thought* DISTINCTLY, but only possessed, as it were, unpacked & unsorted – the poet not only *displays* what tho often seen in its unfolded mass had never been opened out, but he likewise adds something, namely, Lights & Relations. – who has not seen a Rose, or a sprig of Jasmine, of Myrtle, etc. etc.? – But behold these same flowers in a posy or flowerpot, painted by a man of genius – or assorted by the hand of a woman of fine Taste & instinctive sense of Beauty?[8]

In December Robinson recorded how they compared their experiences of Germany and the Mediterranean. They talked widely of warfare, politics and religious beliefs, and particularly of German authors: of Tieck (whom Coleridge had met in Rome), of Schiller and Goethe (whom Robinson had met at Jena); of Kant's philosophy and its recent developments by Fichte and Schelling. Robinson was struck by how Coleridge's wide reading was constantly modulated by his own personal experiences, without any touch of the academic, but as matters deeply lived through and felt. The most obscure German metaphysics were continuously subjected to imaginative testing.

One of Coleridge's favoured methods was to "unpack" a philosophical proposition in terms of its psychological or religious truth. Discussing Kant's theory of the "categorical imperative", he thought it inadequate as a motive for moral action in daily life. "Mere knowledge of the right, we find by experience, does not suffice to ensure the performance of the Right – for mankind in general." Men were inevitably "sick & weak in their moral Being". The recognition of "Duty exclusively" was not a sufficient "motive to the performance". "Much less shall we be led to our Duty by calculation of pleasant or harmful consequences."

A wealth of personal suffering lay behind that remark, but Coleridge made it universal. "Selfish Promises & Threats" were the very grounds that destroyed true altruism. To behave altruistically towards someone else, one must first behave generously towards oneself. In a striking imaginative leap, Coleridge combined the two. "The more the selfish principle is set into fermentation, the more imperious & despotic does the Present Moment become – till at length to love our future Self is almost as hard as to love our Neighbour – it is indeed only a difference of Space & Time. My Neighbour is my other Self, *othered* by Space – my old age is to my youth and other Self, *othered* by Time."

Coleridge concluded that there must be a psychological "medium" between "mere conviction & resolve", and "suitable action". Since there was no medium in nature, it must be found in the spiritual world. "This medium is found in Prayer, & religious Intercommunion between Man & his Maker. – Hence the necessity of Prayer."[9]

Throughout these early encounters at Lamb's, Robinson was struck by Coleridge's fantastic range of intellectual reference – they talked of Kant, Goethe, Shakespeare, Spinoza, Newton, Voltaire, Locke, Hartley, Milton, Bentham, Jeremy Taylor, Fuseli and Wordsworth ("warm praise"). But he was also surprised by the originality of his views, when once they were unfolded.

In a discussion of religion, Coleridge "was apparently arguing in favour of Christianity" in a perfectly orthodox way, but when further prompted revealed the most challenging, metaphysical opinion. Christ was "a Platonic philosopher", miracles were not "essential" to the Christian system, "historic evidence" could never prove a religious faith, and religious belief was "an act not of the understanding but of the will". Yet despite what Robinson saw as "the sceptical tendency of such opinions", Coleridge affirmed passionate belief in the spirit of Christianity "in conformity with his own philosophy".[10]

In politics, Robinson also found strange contradictions between Coleridge's liberal instincts and his sudden, irrational prejudices. Coleridge hated the slave trade, but was "vehement" against Irish civil rights. "The catholic spirit, said C., is incorrigible." Yet though he abused the Irish, he had "no dislike to Jews or Turks". Coleridge criticized government corruption and the handling of the war in Spain, yet he was contemptuous of the Whig opposition, and despised Cobbett and the populist radicals. He admired Hazlitt's writing, but mocked "his morbid views of society, & his *Jacobin* character".[11]

On one notable occasion, 23 December, the discussion of moral action took a significantly literary turn. Robinson was fascinated by Goethe's theory of *Hamlet*, which had become one of the great cruxes of German Romantic criticism. In the novel *Wilhelm Meister's Apprenticeship* (1796), in a famous scene among a group of actors, Goethe put forward the idea that Hamlet's failure to avenge his father's death was the consequence of the weakness of youthful idealism. Hamlet was too young, too romantically self-obsessed, to grapple with political realities.

Questioned by Robinson, Coleridge put forward a darker, more intensely psychological interpretation. It was clearly the fruit of years of reflection in his Notebooks, the paralysing problem of his opium addiction, and the long train of thought that connected the inner visionary worlds of Luther and St Theresa with his own. It would become, the following year, one of the great set-pieces of his lectures, expanded and minutely filled out to encompass the entire dramatic unfolding of the play, its soliloquies, its image-patterns and even its stage directions.

"Hamlet, said C., is one whose internal images (ideas) are so vivid, that all actual objects are faint & dead to him; hence his soliloquies on the nature of man, his disregard of life & hence his vacillations & convulsive energies." For Coleridge, it was not Hamlet's youth, but his introverted nature and intense inwardness of imagination (a type of the Romantic artist) which defined his character and also dictated the subtle series of prevarications in the play's plot structure.

Robinson, shrewdly guessing the autobiographical force of this interpretation, then remarked that it was "unaccountable why Shakespeare did not make Hamlet destroy himself". Coleridge shook his head and observed that even suicide could be considered as a form of decisive moral action of which Hamlet was incapable. "C. said that Shakespeare meant to show that even such a character was forced to be the slave of chance – a salutary moral lesson. He remained to the last inept & immovable; not even the spirit of his father could rouse him to action."[12]

3

While Coleridge could hold forth freely in this largely sympathetic circle, his arrival in London caused less friendly ripples in the wider world. Both his poetry and his politics were becoming subjects of debate, and his opium addiction had become a satisfactory scandal. From September to November, the *Monthly Mirror* had run a popular series ridiculing, stanza by stanza, the ballad of "The Three Graves" which he had published in *The Friend*. Leigh Hunt's radical opposition paper the *Examiner*, reflecting the increasingly polarized state of British politics and journalism, greeted Coleridge's proposed return to the columns of the *Courier* with an ironic fanfare.

> Mr Coleridge, once a republican and a follower of Tom Paine, is now a courtier and a follower of Spencer Perceval. Not succeeding in persuading the public to read the crampt and courtly metaphysics of his lately deceased paper *The Friend*, he takes his revenge by writing against the popular judgement in hireling daily prints. – But here he is as harmless as ever; for what with the general distaste for such writings, and what with the difficulty of getting at Mr Coleridge's meaning, he obtains but very few readers.[13]

In fact the *Courier*, London's main evening newspaper, under the new management of Stuart's hard-headed partner T. G. Street, had gained the largest circulation in the country after *The Times* (estimated at 7,000 copies daily, with perhaps ten times that readership). Hunt had good reason to believe that it had become closely identified with the government under Spencer Perceval, and suffered personally from its attacks when he was tried for political libel in February 1811.[14] That Coleridge, the erstwhile firebrand of Bristol days, should apparently throw in his lot with this establishment, gave the younger generation of editorial writers a fine opportunity for sarcasm. "Extremes Meet", the *Examiner* announced jubilantly.

In fact the *Examiner*'s article was a pre-emptive strike. Coleridge did not begin writing regularly for the *Courier* until the following spring of 1811, and then with grave doubts about its political impartiality. But such attacks as these (soon to be followed by Cobbett in the *Political Register*) indicated that he was now stepping back on to the public stage as a figure of controversy. Over the next two years he was to become a recognized "lion" of Regency London, an object of unceasing curiosity, his doings and sayings widely recorded in diaries, memoirs, letters and newspaper articles. Adrift in his private life, he proved surprisingly resilient and stubborn in this public role, facing down criticism and personal hostility that would have destroyed many men. At some level controversy sustained him.

Nevertheless, Coleridge's return to public affairs in London was painful and uncertain. At Christmas time, overcome with family memories, he collapsed further into opium and deep depression over the Wordsworth "betrayal". For a month there is no record of him at the Lambs, or with Crabb Robinson; nor was he with the Morgans in Hammersmith. They had received a note saying that he was putting his case under the celebrated Dr John Abernethie, an "old bear" of a physician renowned for his severe methods and curt manner.[15] He would walk over from his new Fleet Street lodgings to spend a few days with them before he entered on this dread ordeal – "as some kind-hearted Catholics have taught, that the Soul is carried slowly along close by the walls of Paradise on its way to Purgatory".[16]

He was desperately worried by money, and still trying to scrape together outstanding subscriptions from *The Friend*. He begged them to send "all my Books & Papers with such of my Linen as may be clean, in my Box, by the *errand Cart* . . . a couple of Nails & a

Rope will sufficiently secure the Box."[17] And by implication, his coffin. In the event, Morgan tracked him down again and took him home to Hammersmith at the end of January 1811, the purgatory of Dr Abernethie's "fiery Trial" apparently having been postponed till the soul was better prepared.

The Notebooks continue to be full of grotesque nightmares: a "great pig" leaping on his legs; a "claw-like talon-nailed hand" coming through the bed-curtains and grasping his stomach; and "dreadful Trembling of my whole body" which led him to wake with "piercing out-cries". Typically these terrors are followed by careful, daylight "elucidations". He thought that they were not strictly speaking "dreams", but forms of half-directed "Reveries", very close to the state in which poetry is composed. Physical pain in the stomach, arm or leg became objectified as Monsters and Apparitions. "The Imagination therefore, the true inward Creatrix, instantly out of the chaos or shattered fragments of Memory puts together some form to fit it . . ."*

His analysis is very close to modern theories of "hypnagogic

* It was Montaigne who first observed that sleeping dogs and cats made eye and body movements that indicated the existence of a dream world in all higher animals. (*Essays*, 1595, Book One, No. 21, "On the Power of the Imagination".) But neither the work of Freud (*On the Interpretation of Dreams*, 1900), nor modern Consciousness Theory - with its analogies from computer processes – have yet produced a satisfactory explanation of the mechanism and function of dreams, of the kind that Coleridge thought desirable. (See Daniel C. Dennett, *Consciousness Explained*, 1992.) Coleridge suggested, before Freud, that a certain universal symbolic language might be employed in the "Night World"; and speculated that there were several levels of human dreaming. (See *Notebooks* III, 4409, "The Language of Dreams".) Though sadly he never produced the systematic treatise "On Dreams, Visions, Ghosts, Witchcraft" promised in *The Friend* (II, p. 117), my narrative shows him recording and carefully classifying various "genera and species" of them: "nightmares" characterized by a continually frustrated sense of rational control; half-conscious "reveries"; dreams produced by physiological impulses in the body; dreams connected with forms of "passive" memory-association; dreams actively directed by a "dramatizing" and creative power apparently still awake in the mind; and dreams entering a deeper and more mysterious world of "divination". (See *The Statesman's Manual*, 1816, Appendix C; and *Table Talk* 1 pp. 52–4.) Opium-dreams, or dreams in general, were analogies of the creative act whenever the poet was writing freely from his inspiration. Thus, in a marginal note on the theologian Eichhorn, Coleridge insisted on the "inspired character" of the Book of Ezekiel, "from the analogy of Dreams during an excited state of Nerves, which I myself have experienced, and the wonderful intricacy, and yet clarity of the visual Objects". (*Marginalia*, 3, p. 38.) For a general discussion see my "Preface to the Visionary Fragments" in *Selected Poems*, 1996; and Patricia Adair, *The Waking Dream: A Study of Coleridge's Poetry*, 1967.

images", which have been identified as occurring between the conditions of drowsiness and full dream-sleep. Coleridge felt just such a theory was required, which would emphasize the active symbol-making productions of the brain in "reverie", as opposed to its purely passive, associative functions in dream-sleep. "To explain & classify these strange sensations, the organic material Analogons (Ideas, *materiales* as the Cartesians say) of Fear, Hope, Rage, Shame, & strongest of all Remorse, forms at present the most difficult & at the same time the most interesting Problem of Psychology . . . The solution of this Problem would, perhaps, throw great doubt on this present dogma, that the Forms & Feelings of Sleep are always the reflections & confused Echoes of our waking Thoughts, & Experiences."[18]

Thus Coleridge continued to use his analytic powers to cling to his sanity, though he later described these weeks as "a frenzy of the heart" which produced "some of the effects of a derangement of the brain".[19] Through it all, the Morgans coped with him and also paid for him.

No news reached Keswick directly, and in January 1811 Southey wrote three upbraiding letters which he suspected were left unopened. If Coleridge opened the first, it is not surprising that he left the others closed. Southey wished to prevent him from "the ultimate shame of his applying to Abernethie". He urged him to return to the Lakes, "beseeching him to let me be his task-master for three months in which time, if he would only submit to the performance of as much daily work as I should require (and I would require but little) I would engage that he should lie down at night with a heart at ease . . . Something too I said about his children."[20]

Southey's attempts to organize Coleridge's life, as if he could be disciplined like a child, had one curiously tragic outcome. It concerned the fate of their old Pantisocratic friend George Burnett, who was also adrift in London this winter, even deeper in debt and opium than Coleridge. Burnett wrote to Coleridge for help, proposing "some schemes of authorship which C.'s name would enable him to effect with the booksellers". But the letter was sent to Keswick, and instead of forwarding it, Southey opened it himself. Only when he next wrote to Coleridge did he mention it, suggesting that Coleridge should persuade Burnett to find "a situation in the army or navy" and he would then "willingly contribute £20 towards equipping him for it".

As Coleridge was not opening Southey's letters, he learned nothing of Burnett's fate until too late. Burnett "died wretchedly in a workhouse" at the Marylebone Infirmary in February, believing himself abandoned by all his friends. Coleridge was the one person who would have understood George Burnett's predicament, and would undoubtedly have tried to help. When he heard the news in March at Lamb's he burst into tears. Southey dryly remarked that Coleridge's "wretched practice" of not opening letters made him "deaf and dumb to all who have any claims either of affection and duty upon him". He himself had often given Burnett good advice, and had he listened "he might at this hour have been alive and happy, a useful and a worthy member of society". Southey had "nothing" for which to blame himself in the affair.[21]

In fact Coleridge was far from incommunicado at Hammersmith, but the only letters he answered now were from London friends. In February he embarked on a detailed correspondence with the young writer Mary Russell Mitford, and meticulously revised the proof-sheets of her poem "Christina, The Maid of the South Seas". Her father, George Mitford, thanked him with the present of a jugged hare.[22]

Crabb Robinson sent him a copy of his translation of a German fairy-tale, *Amatonda*, which Coleridge reviewed at length in a letter of six pages, leading on to a discussion of Jean-Paul Richter's *Geist* and German theories of romantic love. Here Coleridge's private meditations on Asra were transformed into a philosophic essay on the universal nature of "true human Love". It contained many terms that he would later use in his lecture on *Romeo and Juliet*. He likened love to the positioning of two hearts, "like two correspondent concave mirrors, having a common focus, while each reflects and magnifies the other".

He insisted that love was a primary element, in the chemical sense, and not a compound of other emotions like friendship or sexual attraction. "There is such a passion, as Love – which is no more a compound, than Oxygen; tho' like Oxygen, it has an almost universal affinity, and a long & finely graduated Scale of elective Attractions. It combines with Lust – but how? – Does Lust call forth or occasion Love? – Just as much as the reek of the marsh calls up the Sun." However, he believed that "long & deep Affection" could sometimes, in a single moment, be "flash-transmuted into Love". These images of fire and sunlight produced a magnificently extended simile on the experience of falling in love.

> In short, I believe that *Love* . . . is always the abrupt creation of a moment – tho' years of *Dawning* may have preceded. I said, *Dawning* – for often as I have watched the Sun-rising, from the thinning, diluting Blue to the Whitening, to the fawn-coloured, the pink, the crimson, the glory, yet still the Sun itself has always *started* up, out of the Horizon – ! between the brightest Hues of the Dawn and the first Rim of the Sun itself there is a *chasm* – all before were Differences of Degrees, passing & dissolving into each other – but this is a difference of *Kind* – a chasm of Kind in a continuity of Time. – And as no man who has never watched for the rise of the Sun, could understand what I mean, so can no man who has not been in Love, understand what Love is – tho' he will be sure to imagine & believe, that he does.[23]

Here was Coleridge deliberately writing like one of the young, impassioned authors of the Romantic *sturm und drang*. This passage was a bid for Robinson's sympathy and a prelude to many intimacies to come. Coleridge, as so often, had set out to enchant his new friend with a revelation of his inner feelings, and to gather him into the fold of his admirers. He instinctively cast himself in the role that Robinson would respond to most immediately: the solitary man of intense feeling, the Germanic idealist of *Naturphilosophie*, the lonely watcher of the dawn skies alone at his study window.

Robinson could now see him like a figure in a landscape by Caspar David Friedrich. ("It has just come into my head", he prompted, "that this Scrawl is very much in the Style of Jean-Paul.") He was simultaneously the poet who had enumerated the colour-gradations of the dawn sky, and the philosopher who had distinguished "a chasm of Kind in a continuity of Time". This could hardly fail to fascinate the man who was also drawn to William Blake.

He also seems to have wanted Robinson to distinguish between his own Romantic sensibility, and that of Wordsworth. This accounts for the sudden, rather surprising, direction in which Coleridge's meditation on love finally turned. "Thus, Wordsworth is by nature incapable of being in Love, tho' no man more tenderly attached – hence he ridicules the existence of any other passion, than a compound of Lust with Esteem & Friendship, confined to one Object ... Now this will do very well – it will suffice to make a good Husband ... but still it is not *Love*."[24]

Later he would speak approvingly of Wordsworth's "brotherly love" for Dorothy, saying he envied it and that "his own character had suffered from the want of a sister".[25] But it is suggestive that Coleridge had no inkling of the real depth of marital love that Wordsworth would later reveal in passionate, private letters to Mary in 1812.[26] Coleridge wanted Robinson to prefer the figure adrift in London, lonely and undomesticated, with his unappeased longings of the heart.

4

By mid-March Coleridge was sufficiently recovered to be visiting Southampton Buildings again, and staying for several days at a time with the Lambs. Mary Lamb had one of her periodic breakdowns, and had to be taken by Charles to the asylum. Before she collapsed she wrote to Dorothy Wordsworth saying that she knew there was "a coldness" between Coleridge and her brother. She exhorted Wordsworth to come to London, and told Dorothy that Coleridge's mind was "seriously unhinged" by the affair. Lamb tried to prevent this letter being sent, although Coleridge may have been glad of it. But even so it produced no words of comfort from Grasmere.[27]

In May, Coleridge himself wrote to his wife saying he had been "injured unprovoked" by Wordsworth, and that Montagu's revelations had burst upon him like "a thunder clap". He asked for all his manuscripts to be packed and sent to London.[28] This letter was also passed on to Grasmere, and for first time there was some realization of the seriousness of the breach. But the Wordsworths' attitude had hardened: they could not understand why Coleridge did not write directly, if he was so hurt, and they felt he was exaggerating and making mischief against them in London. Dorothy put it down to "his miserable weakness", his opium-taking and his desire to attract sympathy.

On 12 May she wrote angrily to Catherine Clarkson: "when I

read all this my soul burned with indignation that William should thus (by implication) be charged with having caused disarrangement in his friend's mind. A pretty story to be told. 'Coleridge has been driven to madness by Wordsworth's cruel or unjust conduct towards him.' Would not anybody suppose that he had been guilty of the most atrocious treachery or cruelty? but what is the sum of all he did? he privately warned a common friend disposed to serve C. with all his might, that C. had one or two habits which might disturb his tranquillity . . ."[29]

Wordsworth wrote an explanation to Mrs Coleridge, and asked her to "transcribe" it for her husband; but Sara Coleridge in turn refused to embroil herself with the deepening quarrel. There the matter was left in the spring of 1811, with Dorothy hopefully supposing that Coleridge's "fancies will die away of themselves".

But they did not do so. Evidently there were now gulfs of misunderstanding on both sides, and the stubborn refusal of both men to communicate with each other directly told its own story of long-standing resentment, wounded pride and subtle jealousies. Perhaps too it suggested that at some level both were glad, or at least relieved, by the breach. Wordsworth had become exhausted by Coleridge's emotional demands; Coleridge had finally rebelled against Wordsworth's emotional domination of all those dependent on him. As writers, both were moving apart on separate paths. If the quarrel was tragic, it was also probably necessary.

But as in all divorces it was the rejected partner, Coleridge, who suffered the most and had to cope with the overwhelming sense of failure. While Wordsworth drew back into his domestic kingdom and calmly began work, as Dorothy noted, "on his great poem" "The Excursion", Coleridge cast around London for new forms of existence and hope. Wandering down the Strand amidst the rumble of coaches, he felt himself being swept out into the open sea:

> As when the new or full moon urges
> The high, long, large, unbreaking surges
> Of the Pacific Main.[30]

Watching the twilight settle over the rooftops of Fleet Street, and the stars come out behind the church spires along the Strand, he thought of the sunsets of the Lake District, and was carried back to his earliest memories of summer evenings at Christ's Hospital school when he had played truant to go bathing in the New River beyond Clerkenwell.

"I have never seen the evening Star set behind the mountains but it was as if I had lost a Hope out of my Soul – as if a Love were gone & a sad memory only remained. – O it was my earliest affection, the Evening Star. – One of my first utterances in verse was an address to it as I was returning from the New River, and it looked newly-bathed as well as I. – I remember the substance of the Sonnet was that the woman whom I could ever love, would surely have been emblemed in the pensive serene brightness of that Planet – that we were both constellated to it, & would after death return thither."[31] His memory was of a poem of 1790, "To the Evening Star", inspired by the "loveliest, 'mid the daughters of the night". It was never published in his lifetime.[32]

In coming back to London he wondered if his life had come full circle, his star was setting, he had no future and he was being swept away into the dark. His Notebooks show that he thought a lot about death. Sometimes they were apocalyptic visions. "Suppose the Earth gradually to approach nearer the Sun or to be scorcht by a close Comet – & still rolling on – with Cities menless – Channels riverless – 5 mile deep."[33] Sometimes they were uneasy dreams, half-awakened by the sounds of the city at night: "A low dead Thunder muttered thro' the Night,/ As twere a Giant angry in his Sleep."[34] Sometimes they were childlike longings for a kindly, tender parent to take away all his pains. "Nature! sweet Nurse! O take me in thy Lap – And tell me of my Father yet unseen Sweet Tales & True, that lull me into Sleep, & leave me dreaming."[35]

Sometimes they took the explicit form of suicidal urgings, which he addressed in a grim, self-lacerating little poem later entitled "The Suicide's Argument". The first, broken stanza describes his bleak misery with a life forced upon him, with "no question" ever asked whether he accepted its conditions in the first place, "if I wished it or no". Now he only wants to refuse it, throwing it back in Nature's face like a worthless gift.

Coleridge imagines Nature responding to this gesture of despair, not with sympathy but with anger. Here she is neither benign nor understanding. She is severe and impatient, like many of Coleridge's friends. She addresses him curtly, as if life was not a gift at all, but a commercial transaction in which he has failed to abide by the business terms. She accuses him of breach of contract and bad faith:

Nature's Answer
Is't returned as 'twas sent? Is it no worse for the wear!
Think first, what you are! Recollect, what you were!
I gave you Innocence, I gave you Hope,
Gave Power, and genius, and ample Scope;
Send you me back Guilt, Lethargy, Despair!
First, make out th' Invent'ry! Inspect! Compare!
Then die, if die you dare!
Be thy own heart our common arbiter.[36]

Assailed by these voices and visions, Coleridge struggled on at Southampton Buildings, trying to find new purpose and order, and the courage to start again. The Morgans begged him to return to Hammersmith, but for the time being he preferred to face his own demons, living from hand to mouth. He listed his expenses for "Tea, Sugar, Candles, Milk, Dinners, Fruit", and gave the maid a tip of 5s. 6d. "for encouragement".[37]

He dined out as often as he could, frequently with Lamb, Hazlitt and Crabb Robinson; sometimes with William Godwin at Skinner Street where he met the radical Irish statesman Henry Grattan and listened to arguments in favour of Catholic Emancipation; and once with Lady Jerningham where he sat in agony through a long piano recital. On one occasion he was delighted by the prima donna Angelica Catalana. She reminded him of Cecilia Bertozzi, for he noted afterwards, "What has all my Existence been since then but an Amo te Solo . . ."[38]

Often he got very drunk at these evenings, burst into weeping fits – which he explained as grief for George Burnett's death and Mary Lamb's madness – and returned to his lodgings to spend several days in bed, sunk in opium.[39] The painter Matilda Betham made several attempts to get him to sit for a portrait, but each time he failed to appear – apparently delayed at a party, lost in a coach, walking in the moonlight "with Mrs Morgan & her Sister to meet Mr Morgan", or suddenly back again at his lodgings sick in bed. "The more I force away my attention from my inward distress," he confided in Miss Betham, "the worse it becomes after – &

what I keep out of my mind or rather *keep down* in a state of under-consciousness, is sure to act meanwhile with its whole power of poison on my Body."[40]

5

Gradually, through it all, new schemes were slowly forming: for journalism, for lecturing, for continuing *The Friend*. At the end of April he wrote decisively to Daniel Stuart, after an evening of cathartic drunkenness at his old editor's house in Brompton. (He vowed never to drink another glass of wine at dinner, except "as a medicine", but this was a liberal prescription.)

Would Stuart recommend him to T. J. Street, the managing editor, as a salaried journalist at the *Courier*? He proposed a six-month contract as a "political Writer", with a month's trial to prove his "steadiness", in case Street had doubts. He was very specific about his duties and timetable. "I could be at the office every morning by ½ past 9, to read over all the Morning Papers etc., & point out whatever seemed noticeable to Mr Street." He could then write the "leading Paragraph" [leader] if Street was called to the City on business, as well as supplying a series of two-column articles on foreign affairs, and "small paragraphs, poems etc." to accumulate as space-fillers for less busy times. He would also be prepared to work as a simple "assistant" and proof-reader.

It was a turbulent time to be writing for any English newspaper. The war had produced deepening divisions in British society, without any notable statesmen (since the death of Pitt and Fox) to lead either government or opposition. With the appointment of a despised, extravagant and unpopular Prince Regent in February 1811 (in recognition of King George III's insanity), there was widespread suspicion of corruption and nepotism throughout the court, parliament and the armed forces. The humiliating fiasco of the Walcheren expedition, planned by the incompetent Duke of York against French forces in Holland, seemed to symbolize the bankruptcy of national institutions. (This was the Regent's brother and none other than "The Grand Old Duke of York" who in the nursery rhyme "had ten thousand men, marched them up to the top of the hill, and marched them down again.")

The Prime Minister Spencer Perceval's conduct of the war against

Napoleon was widely regarded as weak and vacillating. There was growing poverty and discontent in the working population, and more troops were stationed in the North of England and the Midlands than the Duke of Wellington (who would emerge as one of the few respected national figures) commanded in the Spanish Peninsula. Journalists and cartoonists were increasingly outspoken and scabrous in their criticisms, and many were prepared to go to prison for their cause (like Burdett in 1810, Cobbett in 1811 and Hunt in 1812). In the universities, many young men like Percy Bysshe Shelley (the son of a Whig MP and baronet) were utterly disaffected, and looked back to the revolutionary ideals of the 1790s for inspiration.[41]

Coleridge did not respond to this new wave of popular radicalism. He saw himself as an independent commentator, who was known to have challenged both government and opposition in *The Friend*. To set out his position, he submitted to Street a long, 6,000-word article on "The Regent and Mr Perceval" in which he acknowledged the need for political reforms, but questioned the popular cry of universal government corruption. As in *The Friend*, he argued for a measured and non-partisan approach in a time of national peril, and called for a spirit of national consensus.

"Nothing human can remain stationary. If we are not progressive, we must be retrograde. But the *feeling*, with which we enter on the work of reform and improvement, this is indeed of great moment; and to render it what it ought to be, no more effectual discipline can be recommended, than honestly to compare our own state (all grievances included) with that of former times at home, and of other countries at the present day . . ." He concluded by retelling a story about Sir Alexander Ball in Malta (from his unfinished biography). When approached by a Maltese nobleman for political favours at Valletta, Ball had calmly observed that he "would most certainly kick him down stairs" for making such an attempt.[42]

The whole article could be read as both an attack on corruption, and simultaneously an endorsement of the natural probity of British statesmen. Street was delighted with the piece, though twice as long as his normal leaders, and printed it over Coleridge's initials STC on 19 April. By 3 May, against all expectation, Coleridge was in daily harness at the newspaper office in the Strand.

Over the next five months, Coleridge produced ninety-one articles for the *Courier*, his pieces appearing virtually without a break every second or third day. His favoured topics were foreign policy, taxation, the heroic conduct of the war, the tyrannies of Napoleon, and the pandering to the "mob" by popular radicals such as William Cobbett and Sir Francis Burdett. Much of it was frankly little more than wartime propaganda, if not specifically pro-government, then solidly conservative and patriotic to the point of jingoism.

Probably his most successful series was a sequence of satirical articles, in which he gravely canvassed the idea of whether it was politically, morally, philosophically, ethically, or metaphysically justified to *assassinate* Napoleon. In these he paradoxically mocked the British sense of fair play. "This free people are fighting against the greatest tyranny that ever scourged mankind, and yet we ought not to speak of it but with coolness and moderation! We are fighting against the man who respects no treaties, who employs treachery and fraud, midnight assassinations, tortures, and every other cruelty as his engines, and yet we must not mark him as a murderer and villain! . . ."[43]

There were a few exceptional pieces. He mounted a passionate attack on a shameful case of judicial cruelty at a County Sessions, in which a young woman was sentenced to be whipped for stealing six loaves of bread. He was amazed that the legal punishment of "scourging females" was not obsolete, and urged that it should be struck from the penal code, on the grounds of humanity alone. But he also argued that it debased those who inflicted the "unmanly" punishment, and created such intense shame in the victim that it destroyed her sense of moral identity.

The way he framed this last argument was characteristic of Coleridge's use of his own private sufferings as a measure of common experience. As an opium addict he could empathize with the "fallen" woman. "O never let it be forgotten either by the framers or dispensers of criminal law, that the stimulus of shame, like other powerful medicines, if administered in too large a dose, becomes a deadly narcotic poison to the moral patient!"

He ended this unusually effective piece with an appeal to Shakespeare, "who alone of all Dramatic Poets possessed the power of combining the profoundest general morality with the wildest states of passion, and the truest workings of individual character under specific sufferings . . ." Shakespeare had damned such a "debasement of our common nature" in *King Lear*: "Thou rascal Beadle, hold thy bloody hand!/ Why dost thou whip that *woman*?"[44] Coleridge was to develop this empathetic approach with great brilliance in his lectures.

Yet Coleridge's resort to patriotic journalism in 1811, though it lasted less than a year, probably did more damage to his contemporary reputation than anything else he ever wrote. Some, like Crabb Robinson, thought it a tragic waste of his "powers of mind".[45] Mrs Clarkson thought it "a humiliation".[46] Others like Hazlitt, a lifelong admirer of Napoleon, considered it a profound and unforgivable betrayal of the radical cause, which he had once represented. He would later write: "Alas! 'Frailty, thy name is *Genius*!' – What is become of all this mighty heap of hope, of thought, of learning and humanity? It has ended in swallowing doses of oblivion and in writing paragraphs in the *Courier*. Such and so little is the mind of man!"[47]

At Grasmere, Dorothy dismissed it as "servile", and there was blank incomprehension as to why Coleridge should have returned to journalism at all. "I only grieve at the waste and prostitution of his fine genius," she wrote painfully, "at the sullying and perverting of what is lovely and tender in human sympathies, and noble and generous; and I do grieve whenever I think of him. His resentment to my Brother hardly ever comes into my thoughts. I feel perfectly indifferent about it."[48]

Coleridge felt far from indifferent. His determination to re-establish his professional independence in London, toiling in Fleet Street, was almost defined by his painful sense of the loss of the Grasmere circle. To combat his grief, to control his opium-induced sloth and horrors, he chose deliberately to tie himself to deadlines, to commute to an office. Otherwise he felt that the quarrel with Wordsworth would destroy him, and to crawl back to the Lakes (as Southey never ceased to urge) would be the real intellectual humiliation.

He had put this with great emotion to his old confidant Stuart in a letter of April:

> So deep and so rankling is the wound, which Wordsworth has wantonly and without the slightest provocation inflicted in return for a 15 years' most enthusiastic, self-despising & alas! self-injuring Friendship . . . that I cannot return to Grasmere

> or its vicinity – where I must often see & always be reminded of him. Every man must take the measure of his own strength. I may, I do, regret my want of fortitude; but so it is, that incurable depression of Spirits, Brooding, Indolence, Despondence, thence Pains & nightly Horrors, & thence the Devil & all his Imps to get rid of them or rather to keep them just at arm's length, would be infallibly the result. Even to have thought of Wordsworth, while writing these Lines, has, I feel fluttered & disordered my whole Inside . . .[49]

In such a maelstrom of feeling, to live by himself in London would be "almost equally dangerous". The "alternative" still in his power, was to pursue "any regular situation" with the newspaper and make a new home at Hammersmith "with perfect propriety, as a member of Morgan's Family".

This is exactly what Coleridge did. From early May he was rising at 6.30 a.m. each morning, and catching the 8 o'clock public coach from Hammersmith to the Strand. Later in the summer he even tried to cut down on his travel expenses (which the *Courier* paid) by returning on foot in the afternoon, "which will reduce my Coach-hire for the week from 18s to 9". He only begged not to be required to walk in as well, a distance of three miles, as it would "take all the blossom & fresh fruits of my Spirits".[50] Coleridge was hardly a natural commuter, and sometimes he did not appear before midday. But Street seems to have been satisfied with his time-keeping for most of the summer, and when friction did arise it was from other causes.

Financial dependence weighed on him. The Wedgwood annuity was still being paid faithfully to Mrs Coleridge, though now reduced by property tax to £135 per annum.[51] His newspaper salary – not recorded, but probably in the region of £4 or £5 per week – largely went to the Morgans, though no doubt reduced by opium expenses. His debts to Stuart were beyond his means to repay, though he hoped a republication of *The Friend* in augmented volume form might eventually produce a capital sum to draw on.[52]

There was the annual panic over his life assurance premium in May (with Mrs Coleridge continuing as the sole beneficiary in the event of his death), which he solved by offering the entire copyright in all his poems to Thomas Longman, as he had done in 1808. This time he promised a 360-page manuscript to be delivered in "a fortnight", for which Longman proposed the same shameful figure of £100. Coleridge accepted an advance of £22, which went immediately to pay the premium. But he was so angry with the terms that he called it, quite uncharacteristically, "a Jew Bargain", and never supplied the promised manuscript. He seemed quite cheerful about breaking this contract.[53] Seven years later he denied that he had "cheated" Longman, and calmly announced that in all the circumstances he considered it "my own money".[54]

The problems that emerged with Street concerned editorial compromises at the *Courier*. Coleridge was content to defend the government's wartime policy abroad, and he did it with genuine conviction. With Wellington pinned down against huge odds in the Spanish Peninsula, and Marshal Soult menacing the allied forces besieging Badajoz and Cuidad Rodrigo, the military situation was indeed critical and would remain so until 1812. Coleridge wrote rallying pieces entitled "Light in the Political Sky" and "The Spirit Unbroken".[55] But at home, with Perceval's administration refusing all liberal measures (a Reform Bill had been defeated the previous year), discontent with the government had reached a violent pitch, which would soon flare up in the Luddite riots of November 1811. The *Courier* was regarded increasingly as a government mouthpiece, and several times "hissing" mobs gathered outside its offices.[56]

Coleridge could not ignore the fact that his "independent" position looked increasingly compromised and isolated. For some time he tried to maintain his honour, at least in his own eyes, by refusing to write for Street on subjects which he privately condemned. As he told Stuart, with rather forced bravado: "while Cabbage-stalks rot on Dunghills, I will never write what, or for what, I do not think right – all that Prudence can Justify, is *not* to write what at certain times one may yet think."[57] But he knew that this came lamely from the author of *The Friend*, who had insisted precisely on the need for principle over prudence in public matters; let alone from the once daring young radical author of the *Watchman* who had declared that "the Truth shall make us Free". Many of his shorter articles were unsigned.

Yet Coleridge did try to challenge Street. In mid-June he drafted a long, critical article attacking the re-appointment of the Duke of York – the Prince Regent's brother – as Supreme Commander of the British Armed Forces. The appointment had been ratified by a parliamentary majority of over 200 votes, but was clearly the result of nepotism.[58] Coleridge seized this opportunity to go on the offensive, and his article was announced on Saturday, 9 June to run as the leader the following Monday.

Street read it over the weekend and, evidently alarmed, postponed its appearance. On 11 June Coleridge read his copy to Crabb Robinson, who described it as "very beautiful" in construction, and Coleridge as restless and "dissatisfied with his situation".[59] Street prevaricated and postponed for a month. Finally he appeared to yield to Coleridge, and set up the piece in type for the edition of Friday, 14 July. Coleridge left the office that afternoon assuming he had gained his point.

But meanwhile Street had arranged for a senior Treasury official, Mr Arbuthnot, to call privately on Daniel Stuart at Brompton and ask for it to be withdrawn. "Stuart resisted a long time," according to Crabb Robinson, "but at last yielded, and the greater number of the copies were cancelled." Apparently about 2,000 copies – a quarter of the normal *Courier* print-run – reached the City distributors, but the article did not go into general circulation and had no effect.[60] Coleridge now had irrefutable evidence that his position was compromised, and that Street was in regular contact with the Ministry, and would yield to its wishes. Moreover, Stuart was too "lazy" to back him against Street.[61]

Coleridge knew he should resign on the spot. Instead he hesitated, and secretly applied for a position on *The Times*, now regarded as a liberal voice. Crabb Robinson took a detailed set of proposals to the great editor John Walter in July. Coleridge offered to work at the office "any six hours of the Day, from 8 of the morning to 8 o'clock of the evening"; to supply "any number required" of small news paragraphs and leading articles; and to produce two major three-column essays each week "on the great Interests of the Time". His only stipulation was that the newspaper should be "truly independent, 1. of the Administration, & 2. of the populace."[62] There was no request about salary.

Negotiations continued for some days, but it is significant that Walter had doubts about Coleridge's compromised reputation, and besides already had a distinguished leader-writer, Fraser, under contract. There is also some evidence that Stuart heard of the discussions, and warned Walter off in a classic Fleet Street manoeuvre, by saying Coleridge was too unreliable to employ.[63] By the end of July Coleridge was still at the *Courier*, writing long articles about the political situation in America and Ireland, and about the overweening power of the East India Company. These were relatively non-controversial topics (though Catholic Emancipation would soon become a fiery one), and Street contented himself with publishing occasional retractions and disclaimers after Coleridge's articles.[64]

The moment for a heroic gesture had slipped away. Coleridge sweated on through the summer on what was now generally regarded as "a hireling newspaper". Even Stuart would later admit that by the end of 1811 the *Courier* under Street had become virtually an "official" organ of the Ministry.[65] The young radicals – Hazlitt, Leigh Hunt – never forgot this piece of political "apostasy" and would take their revenge in due course.

6

Yet the *Courier* job, however demeaning, brought a vital new stability into Coleridge's life at Hammersmith. He was happy with the Morgans, and sustained by a household atmosphere much easier and less demanding than Allan Bank. There were visits to new plays, art exhibitions, and frequent supper parties. Coleridge's renewed flirtation with Charlotte Brent, and "sisterly" confidences with Mary Morgan, softened the pain of his loss of Asra. Several of Asra's long, chatty letters to her cousin Mary Monkhouse written from Radnorshire have survived, and though full of talk of the Wordsworths and their children, it is rather chilling to observe that they make not a single mention of Coleridge, or enquiry about his health, until she returned to Grasmere in October.[66]

Coleridge also found an opportunity to reopen family communication with the Ottery Coleridges. Ever since the cancelled visit of summer 1807, relations had been strained, his brother George disapproving of the separation from Mrs Coleridge, and his military brother Colonel James making scathing observations about his journalism and his lectures. Coleridge had become, in effect, the black sheep of the family and a proverb among his brothers for profligacy and lack of discipline. But among the younger generation of Coleridges, perhaps for that very reason, he was a figure of fascination and worldly glamour. When two of Colonel James's sons – Henry aged twelve, and John aged twenty – came up to London for the summer vacation to stay with family friends, the Mays, in Richmond, a weekend invitation was tentatively sent over to Hammersmith.

Coleridge leaped at the chance of seeing his nephews, crossed the river, and tactfully took rooms at the local inn. For two days he breakfasted and dined in their company, and was the guest of honour at several large parties given by the Mays. Evidently he set out to win their hearts, and succeeded. Henry was entranced by his uncle, and John, who was in his third year at Oxford and had just won the Chancellor's Prize for Latin verse, was intellectually dazzled. He had never met "so delightful and astonishing a man".

John reported back to his father, with a certain undisguised triumph, that the black sheep was very different from his family reputation. "He made a conquest of all the men and women at Richmond, gave us analyses of long works which are to come out, told stories of his youth and travels, never sparing himself at all, and altogether made the most powerful impression on my mind of any man I ever saw." Though there were "some things" which John did not quite like – a certain extravagance and exhibitionism it would seem, and not least a promise to write to him about his prize poem, which was never fulfilled – he was largely won over.

John Taylor Coleridge was a brilliant boy, of great intellectual capacity and considerable social sophistication. After Eton and Oxford, where he took a first in Classics (he was an almost exact contemporary of Shelley's), he went on to read for the Bar, to contribute to the powerful *Quarterly Review*, and become a High Court judge. He wrote a life of his friend Keble, was appointed a privy councillor, and was knighted – though he always preferred to be known as Mr Justice Coleridge.[67] In his first encounter with his uncle, he listened and watched with judicial care, and later wrote a detailed account which Henry – to be even more closely associated with his uncle – published in an influential volume to be entitled *Table Talk* (1836).[68] Unlike so many later, spellbound listeners, John remembered and recorded what Coleridge actually said, and gave the most vivid impression of his huge range and revolving conversational style, as understood by an undergraduate.

The weekend began with talk of politics, Perceval's relations with the Prince Regent, the war in the Peninsula, and General Sir John

Moore's courage on the battlefield contrasted with his fearfulness of political opinion at home. These were evidently subjects drawn from Coleridge's *Courier* journalism. Then without apparent transition, he was suddenly racing into "German topics": Luther, High and Low German, Klopstock, Wieland and the German Romantic sense of the Sublime.

This dauntingly obscure subject was made vivid with a single illustration: German sublimity was produced by comparing something very great with something very small, and thereby "elevating" it. "Thus, for example, Klopstock says, – 'As the gardener goes forth, and scatters from his basket seed into the garden; so does the Creator scatter worlds with his right hand.' Here *worlds*, a large object, are made small in the hands of the Creator; consequently, the Creator is very great." But Coleridge regarded this technique as mechanical – he contrasted it with Edward Young's *Night Thoughts* – and therefore not poetical "in the very highest sense", which required an imaginative transformation of scale and feeling.

Yet the Germans were good metaphysicians and critics: "they criticized on principles previously laid down; thus, though they might be wrong, they were in no danger of being self-contradictory, which was too often the case with English critics." From there Coleridge spun on to the new German Biblical criticism – "he found professors in the universities lecturing against the most material points in the Gospel" – with an amusing aside about Catholic superstition and the "worship of saints" in Sicily. So "glancing off to Aristotle", he was on to Francis Bacon and Locke's attacks on the medieval Schoolmen, and the concepts of "quality", "quantity" and "quiddity" which he regarded as valuable counters to Locke's "sneering" materialism.

For John Coleridge this intellectual *tour d'horizon* would have much the same impact as for an English undergraduate in the 1850s first hearing of Hegelianism, or in the 1950s of French Existentialism. Coleridge added that he would be writing a "History of Speculative Philosophy" in due course, and then went on without pause to praise Southey's new poem "The Curse of the Kehema", which was the talk of the literary season, and "the art displayed in the employment of Hindu monstrosities". In the evening John walked Coleridge home to his inn, and was advised about his Oxford essay which he thought might be on the corruption of prose style, contrasting modern journalism with Apuleius and Cicero.[69]

The next morning, a Sunday, Coleridge appeared before breakfast, and was found in Mr May's "delightful bookroom", surrounded by open volumes, and gazing out in "silent admiration" at the beautiful garden. They all went to church, and Coleridge observed that tombstones in a peaceful Sunday churchyard always reminded him of re-birth rather than death: "it struck him as if God had given to man fifty-two springs in every year". But he was impatient of the sermon which was conventionally pious, "and invidious in its tone towards the poor".

Walking out through the meadows towards Twickenham, he talked about Gray's "Elegy in a Country Church Yard", and contrasted the sententiousness of Gray and Johnson as poets, with Milton and Dryden. "He thought Collins had more genius than Gray, who was a singular instance of a man of taste, poetic feeling, and fancy, without imagination." Surprisingly, he did not mention Wordsworth at this point. Instead he veered off on to his Mediterranean adventures again, talked of Nelson and Ball, criticized British foreign policy and "lamented the haughtiness with which Englishmen treated all foreigners abroad, and the facility with which our government had always given up any people which had allied itself to us, at the end of a war . . . These two things, he said, made us universally disliked on the Continent; though, as a people, most respected."

Then he talked of the United States, which he admired, though fearing the American Declaration of Independence had been "premature" and might lead to war with Britain (which it did in 1812). He felt America lacked a European social structure, a landed middle class who could give stability and tradition, and an intelligentsia or "learned class" which would provide political progress and regulate "the feelings of the people".[70]*

* Coleridge's hopes and fears about the political developments in American society are similar to the later views of Alexis de Tocqueville in *Democracy in America* (1835). Though Tocqueville saw America as the great world-cradle of liberalism, like Coleridge he feared the possible "tyranny" and "apathy" of an uneducated majority. "If ever freedom is lost in America, that will be due to the omnipotence of the majority driving the minorities to desperation and forcing them to appeal to physical force." (Book I, Part II, Chapter 7.) Here again Coleridge makes early reference to his notion of an "intelligenstia", a "National clerisy" or thinking class of educated men from many backgrounds, who would be capable of guiding and mediating the various forces and special-interests that drove social change. (See Henry Coleridge, Preface (1839) to Coleridge's *Church and State*, 1829, Appendix A.)

At dinner in the mid-afternoon, Coleridge became wrapped in scientific conversation with another guest, Professor Stephen Rigaud, who was Director of the Royal Observatory at Greenwich. But when the Mays' little children were allowed in to join the adults, he instantly broke off. To John's amusement, "he was in raptures with them, and descanted upon the delightful mode of treating them now, in comparison with what he had experienced in childhood" at Ottery and Christ's Hospital. John was greatly struck by Coleridge's quick rapport with the children, becoming noisy and playful, even to the point of embarrassment.

But the most extraordinary effect was produced afterwards at tea in the parlour. Coleridge and Professor Rigaud launched into a "discussion of Kant's System of Metaphysics". Respectful silence fell over the "little knots of company", the tea things were removed, and John expected to see the women slipping away from such abstruse and exclusively male talk, as "Mr C.'s voice grew louder". But something about Coleridge's voice held them back – it was "so ready, so energetic and so eloquent" – and his explanations of the famous "subjective" and "objective" became "so very neat and apposite", that they were gradually drawn in, engaged, and finally transfixed, hovering behind his chair and settling at his feet.

The Oxford undergraduate could scarcely believe it: "they were really entertained with Kant's Metaphysics!" In retrospect it seemed almost the most memorable moment of the whole weekend, particularly as there were several pretty young women among them, these ladies "loitering most attentively, and being really uncommonly entertained with a long discussion of two hours on the deepest metaphysics . . ."

When finally the candles were being lit, John pulled one of the ladies to the pianoforte, and as she was "a very sweet singer", whispered to her to end the evening with some Italian airs in Coleridge's honour. He was obviously delighted, the Italian music touching off memories and emotions that his nephew could not have guessed. The young woman was happy to charm the great metaphysician in her turn. "She was anxious to please him, and he was enraptured. His frame quivered with emotion, and there was a titter of uncommon delight on his countenance. When it was over, he praised the singer warmly, and prayed she might finish those strains in heaven!"[71]

The word "titter" did not carry the mockery that it would indicate nowadays. Yet there is a clear and interesting suggestion here, as earlier, that young John Coleridge sometimes found his extraordinary uncle to be embarrassingly expressive and emotional. Nonetheless, the family weekend was counted a great success, and most signally with the younger generation. Coleridge noted wistfully: "O what wisdom I could talk to a YOUTH of Genius & genial-heartedness! O how little could I teach! . . . especially if a woman . . ."[72]

7

At Hammersmith, some sort of calm gradually settled over Coleridge's nightly meditations. The daily regularity of the *Courier* work checked the opium-taking, and the agonizing over Wordsworth and Asra became less frequent for a while, though in August he noted briefly: "Why SARA alone? – Coleridge is no more!"[73]

Recalling Hamlet on the battlements of Elsinore at dawn, he wrote, "Every mere Passion, like Spirits, and Apparitions, have their hour of Cock-crow, in which they must vanish. But pure Love is therefore no *mere* Passion: & it is a test of its being Love, that no reason can be assigned *why* it should disappear. Shall we not always in this Life at least, remain *Animae dimidiatae* [Souls divided in two]?"[74]

The terrible nightmares also diminished, though Coleridge often could not sleep at all. He pulled back his bedroom curtains to watch anxiously for the summer sunrise to slide over the City rooftops in the east: "The sick and sleepless Man after the Dawn of the fresh Day watching the Smoke now from this, & then from the other chimney of the Town from his Bedchamber". The sight of so many ordinary households waking up was strangely soothing, allowing him "to borrow from others that sense of a new Day, of a discontinuity between the Yesterday and the ToDay".[75]

But sometimes those summer nights seemed endless, a purgatorial place of continuous twilight, in which his whole life seemed suspended outside time. He turned for consolation to his old friend the Moon, and it was now he began one of the most haunting and enigmatic of all his later poems, which he eventually entitled "Limbo":

'Tis a strange place, this Limbo! – not a Place,
Yet name it so; – where Time and weary Space
Fettered from flight, with night-mare sense of fleeing,
Strive for their last crepuscular half-being, –
Lank Space, and scytheless Time with branny hands
Barren and soundless as the measuring sands,
Not mark'd by flit of Shades, – unmeaning they
As moonlight on the dial of the day! . . .

The flitting, insubstantial figures of Time and Space (in a first version Time has "scytheless hands") could be seen as conventional personifications. But they also carry a metaphysical weight, being the two Kantian categories by which the human mind normally structures reality. Without them, Coleridge's normal world dissolves into a "crepuscular" half-reality, the limbo described by both Christian theologians and mystics like Jakob Boehme.

But a third figure survives. Old, worn, blind, and yet mysteriously heroic, he stands beneath the attendant moon, which for Coleridge is always the symbol of the Imagination. Some healing impulse, some promise of salvation, seems to pass between the two: "His whole face seemeth to rejoice in light!" But what this might be, or how a blind man might see it, is left as a riddle.

But that is lovely – looks like Human Time, –
An Old Man with a steady look sublime,
That stops his earthly task to watch the skies;
But he is blind – a statue hath such eyes; –
Yet having moonward turn'd his face by chance,
Gazes the orb with moon-like countenance,
With scant white hairs, with foretop bald and high,
He gazes still, – his eyeless face all eye; –
As 'twere an organ full of silent sight,
His whole face seemeth to rejoice in light! –
Lip touching lip, all moveless, bust and limb –
He seems to gaze at that which seems to gaze on him![76]

8

Coleridge drew much consolation from a curious German book of spiritual meditations which Crabb Robinson had given him, Jean-Paul Richter's *Geist, oder Chrestomathie*. Later translated into English as *Spirit*, it had originally been published in Leipzig in 1801. Jean-Paul (1763–1825), as his name became familiarized in England and France, was one of the finest introspective writers of German Romanticism. He was a man obsessed by the fragile, melancholy beauty of the natural world. His master-theme was that of God's reluctant departure from his Creation: the abandoning of modern man to intimations of a lost Paradise of faith. Writing equally in prose and verse, he became the great lyricist of spiritual loss, of autumnal emotions, and half-glimpsed revelations of ancient splendours.[77]

He would remain untranslated and unknown in England until taken up by De Quincey and Thomas Carlyle in the 1820s. But through Crabb Robinson, Coleridge discovered in him a spiritual brother, perfectly apt to his mood in 1811. He drew comfort from Jean-Paul's aphorisms and meditations in a particular way. He did not merely read and reflect on them, but incorporated them into his Notebooks in various forms of translation, imitation and reworked versions.

"The giant Shadows sleeping amid the wan yellow Light of the December morning like Wrecks & scattered Ruins of the long, long Night." So reads one particularly haunting Notebook fragment, which seems peculiarly Coleridgean, with its suggestion of dreams and shipwrecks.[78] In fact this is a condensed translation, or intensification, of aphorism No. 386 from Jean-Paul's *Geist*. "The December Sun, which hangs at Midday as low as the June Sun at Eventide, spreads its Deathly yellow light like burning methylated Spirits over the pale withered Meadows; and everywhere the long gigantic Shadows, like the Ruins and Ashes of the equally long Night, lie stretched out and slumbering in the Eventide of Nature and the Year."[79]

This method of privately translating and anthologizing Jean-Paul throws some light on the psychology of Coleridge's later plagiarisms. He had consciously used adapted translations in some of his earlier poetry, such as the "Hymn before Sunrise in the Vale of Chamouni" (from Fredericka Brun) in 1802; and more recently "A Tombless Epitaph" (from Chiabrera) in 1809. But his prose translations from Jean-Paul suggest a less deliberate, more internalized process at work in his private Notebooks. It was almost as if, in "the long, long Nights" of his study-bedroom at Hammersmith, he was holding a silent conversation with his confrère or brother-spirit in Leipzig.

Like Coleridge, Jean-Paul had thought a lot about worldly hope and spiritual despair. (One of his novels – *Palingenesien* (1798) – studies three kinds of unhappy marriage.) He had turned towards a poetic evocation of the immortal longings which seize upon unhappy people. Thus another aphorism from *Geist* (No. 4) spoke particularly to Coleridge, and is marked in the copy he borrowed from Robinson. "Strangers born in the *Mountains* are consumed in the *Lowlands* by an incurable homesickness. We are made for a Higher Place, and that is why we are gnawed by an Eternal Longing, and all the music we hear is the Cowbell that reminds us of our Alpine Home . . ."[80]

Coleridge clearly recognized himself in this, its poignant imagery reminding him of his own experience of leaving the Lake District. So his translation takes up the theme, expanding it with his own imagery, and developing it with a botanical analogy which comes from his poem "Psyche" (and which has no equivalent in Jean-Paul's text). "We are born in the mountains, in the Alps – and when we hire ourselves out to the Princes of the Lower Lands, sooner or later we feel an incurable Home-sickness – & every Tune that recalls our native Heights, brings on a relapse of that Sickness. – I seem to myself like a Butterfly who having foolishly torn or bedaubed his wings, is obliged to crawl like a Caterpillar with all the restless Instincts of the Butterfly."[81]

The "conversation" between Coleridge and Jean-Paul does not end here. The German author goes on to ask, what is the true significance of these "Eternal Longings"? He writes: "And what are we to conclude from this? Not that we are Unhappy, but that we are Immortal, and that the *second* world *within* us demands and demonstrates a second world *outside* us."[82] Coleridge takes up this idea in his translation (the "world *within*" clearly relating to his interpretation of *Hamlet*), but now moves away to follow his own completely original botanical analogy to explain the intimations of a "second" spiritual world.

> In short, all the organs of Sense are framed for a corresponding World of Sense: and we have it. All the organs of Spirit are framed for a corresponding World of Spirit: & we cannot but believe it. The Infidel proves only that the latter organs are not yet developed in him . . . And what is Faith? – it is to the Spirit of Man the same instinct, which impels the chrysalis of the horned fly to build its involucrum as long again as itself to make room for the Antennae, which are to come, tho' they never yet have been. – O the *Potential* works *in* us even as the Present mood works *on* us![83]

This notion of the spiritual world, and spiritual longing, being somehow programmed into Nature in an evolutionary sense, was to become of central importance to Coleridge. He had already written about it in April. "Just as much reason for affirming the future State as for denying that Nature ever *tells a Lie generically* – never makes animals have milk, when they are never to have sucklings etc."[84] But reading and translating Jean-Paul had concentrated and refined his own thoughts.

Yet he did not accept Jean-Paul uncritically. Praising him to Crabb Robinson, he also questioned Jean-Paul's florid use of analogies: "You admire, not the things combined, but the act of combination."[85] Annotating the passage from *Geist*, he identified its philosophical weakness as an actual logical *proof* of any spiritual "second world" beyond the physical. His own metaphor is characteristically vivid and forceful. "All these poetico-philosophical Arguments strike and shatter themselves into froth against that stubborn rock, the fact of *Consciousness*, or rather its dependence on the body."[86]

It would be absurd to describe Coleridge's entries as any kind of plagiarism. But at the same time it is easy to see how, in other circumstances, use of such "adapted" material could open him to such a charge. Coleridge was soon to find other German authors – notably A. W. Schlegel and Schelling – with whom he developed the same brotherly or symbiotic relationship. He read, translated, refined and expanded in his own way. But when he left the privacy of his study and published or lectured on the resulting text (without acknowledging his source) he inevitably opened himself to the charge of plagiarism.

Crabb Robinson was to be the first to observe this problem, being a German specialist in his own right, and the man who supplied Coleridge with several of his German authors initially. Significantly he did not in fact consider it plagiarism, being fully aware of Coleridge's vast background reading in German and British philosophy and criticism, and the originality of his particular interpretations. Moreover Coleridge was almost never dominated by his sources. Except in the particular case of Schelling, he never stole slavishly. His disagreements with German thought – most notably with Schlegel in the lectures – produced his great originality of emphasis, those sudden developments of psychological insight, and vivid metaphorical explanation. He was always inspired to outdo his originals, to speculate further, to enquire more closely. But the charge of plagiarism would eventually become a pressing and highly damaging one. It already shadows the lectures he began in the winter of 1811. Four years later, when Coleridge came to write the *Biographia*, using entire passages of Schelling rendered word for word and without anything like a proper acknowledgement, it would become inescapable.

It cannot be a coincidence that this period corresponds to the worst time of his opium addiction, the extreme sense of his loss of Wordsworth, and the severest lack of professional self-confidence and feelings of almost paralysing failure. At one level, then, plagiarism was a response to profound, almost disabling anxiety and intellectual self-doubt. His German authors gave him support and comfort: in a metaphor he often used himself, he twined round them like ivy round an oak.

But the early example of Jean-Paul Richter shows how subtle and perplexing this process was, at its roots. It involved a genuine act of intellectual discovery, of tracking down the new movements in European writing and thought. The very condition of Coleridge's desperation and self-doubt kept him intellectually receptive, raw and curiously youthful, in a way that many of his contemporaries had lost. He responded to new ideas because they still challenged him, still hurt him almost. His expansions of Jean-Paul express excitement, self-recognition, and spiritual pain.

The chaotic and spontaneous appearance of his Notebooks at this period do give a striking impression of some living and consoling dialogue between two brother authors actually taking place. They start at nightfall and break off at dawn. Sandwiched between dreams, domestic bills, fragments of poetry, addresses, journalistic notes, and prayers, the communings with Jean-Paul are like a continuous background murmur of conversation which suddenly rises into perfect audibility. In their loops and digressions, their journeys out and back, they have some distant correspondence with the earlier form of the Conversation Poems. They display, above all perhaps, Coleridge's haunted solitariness in London, and the desperate need for company. One might say that his plagiarisms began that summer in the sense of lost friendships, of loneliness, of intellectual isolation.

9

All sorts of strange shapes entered Coleridge's night-time world at Hammersmith, and not all of them were human. One of the oddest was a spider. Coleridge had been talking with Lamb about a set of Hogarth prints of "The Rake's Progress", which Lamb had hung in his new lodgings at the Middle Temple, to celebrate Mary Lamb's return from the asylum. Such topics were inclined to produce elaborate, and frequently drunken fantasies (which Hazlitt later said were liable to over-excite and "injure" the Lambs, though they themselves seemed to relish them).[87] They had alighted on one tiny detail from "The Rake's Marriage", which showed the poor-box in the church covered with a spider's web. It was one of Hogarth's inspired pieces of realistic observation, an emblem of poverty and callousness, expressing the entire theme of the picture in a single image. It delighted them with its sinister economy, Lamb observing that such graphic images had "the teeming, fruitful, suggestive meaning of *words*".[88]

Coleridge expanded the same idea: "everything in Hogarth is to be translated into *Language* – words – & to act as words, not as Images". So the spider could be understood as part of a larger, ever-expanding system of symbolic representation. Back in his study at Hammersmith, Coleridge's mind turned to the symbolism of the poor-box, and the way the spider's presence made its emptiness not merely palpable but repulsive. The spider seemed to gloat over an accumulation of human meanness.

As Coleridge played with this idea, a grotesque new image floated into his mind, recalling another spider he had seen spinning its web over the garden privy at Allan Bank. He rendered it with a surreal touch of comic disgust in his Notebook. "For so in a small House of frequent Resort I have seen in an autumn morning the *circular means to an end* completely covered by a Web, and the fat dumpy Spinster in the centre, like a Heathen Paged snuffing up the Incense."[89] He made no further comment, but his night thoughts had translated a church poor-box into a privy, a spider into a "dumpy" spinster, and a spinster into a pagan idol. Years later he would return to the spider in a poem about loss of feeling and the encroachments of old age, "The World that Spidery Witch".[90]

10

As the autumn arrived, Coleridge felt increasingly restless about his paragraph-writing for the *Courier*, which seemed to be leading nowhere. Southey visited London, still urging him to return to the Lakes, and haranguing Crabb Robinson about his fecklessness. "Of Coleridge, Southey spoke as I expected he would," Robinson noted evenly. "'With a strong sense of duty,' he said, 'he has neglected it in every relation of his life.'" Southey's recommendation was that Coleridge should give up opium and journalism, and write a Greek Grammar.[91]

At the end of September, there was a new crisis in connection with the newspaper. Coleridge abruptly left the Morgans after some painful scenes, and lodged alone again at No. 6 Southampton Buildings. He spent his mornings at a desk in the Westminster Library, trying to write a special series of articles for Street. In a desperate effort to escape the hackwork of topical journalism, and increase his salary, he had promised a substantial set of political essays on Pitt, Fox, Napoleon, Wellington, Ball and several other leading statesmen. These were based on his old idea of historical "Character Sketches", years ago promised to Stuart and also trailed in *The Friend*.[92] But everything depended on meeting the *Courier*'s deadlines in the second week of October.

On Friday, 5 October he announced categorically to Street that the first "Characters" were ready, and that they would open with a grand historical essay on Biography, "on the nature and uses of character-writing, relatively to the Lives of Plutarch". This he would write over the weekend. "I will give it to you on Monday Morning by a quarter after nine, together with Pitt's & Fox's – and you may rely on having the whole set given in so as never to delay the publication . . ." Street duly announced the series in a front-page banner-headline in the Friday evening edition, with the general essay for the Monday following, and "The Character of Bonaparte on Tuesday".[93]

Coleridge took a deep breath, opened his laudanum decanter, and collapsed. None of the essays was ever delivered. Stuart proved philosophical, and no doubt Walter at *The Times* was amused. But Street was understandably furious, terminated his contract, and ever afterwards spoke disparagingly of his vaunted contributor. Yet for Coleridge the disaster, as so often, was eventually liberating. Out of it emerged his idea for the first of his great series of Shakespeare lectures, and also an important new understanding with the Morgans.

In fact it seems likely that he was already disillusioned with the *Courier*. One of the last pieces he published there, on 21 September, seemed to prophesy his departure, by sending an ironic greeting to his journalistic arch-rival, William Cobbett. Describing one of his daily journeys over to the *Courier* office (he seems to have hired, or perhaps conveniently invented, a horse for the occasion), he recounts an exchange which would have delighted the editor of the radical *Weekly Register*:

> It has often struck me, as a peculiarity of this enlightened age, that in all classes we meet with critics and disputants; from Parliament to the Common Council, from the Crown and Anchor to the Chequers in St Giles's, nothing but discussion! A fellow in rags, who held my horse for the few moments that I had occasion to dismount, expressed his thanks for a shilling in these words: – Bless your honour! I have not had a pint of beer, or seen the *Register*, for a week past. The *Register*? quoth I. – Aye, replies he, with a grin, Cobbett's the man, Sir! He has *Ideas* – A man's nothing without *Ideas*.[94]

Coleridge remained at No. 6 Southampton Buildings for the rest of the month. He was often prostrate with opium and frequently very drunk, but his London friends rallied round. On 12 October he first spoke to Lamb of his idea for the lectures, and on 17 October John Payne Collier records him with "spreading canvas", sailing away majestically on the subject of Shakespeare's dramatic powers.[95]

It was not easy for even the sharpest observers to assess Coleridge's physical or mental state. Crabb Robinson had been taught a lesson by Lamb, when shaking his head over Coleridge's difficulties he had inadvertently let fall the phrase "poor Coleridge". The ever-faithful Lamb rounded on him. "He corrected me not angrily, but as if really pained by the expression . . . 'He is a fine fellow, in spite of all his faults and weaknesses. Call him Coleridge – I hate "*poor* Coleridge". I can't bear to hear pity applied to such a one.' "[96]

On the day after the *Courier* débâcle, 9 October, Robinson took evening tea with Catherine Clarkson to discuss what might be done. Much was said about the problem of Coleridge's work finding an appropriate form and audience. They thought he had neither the popular appeal of Walter Scott nor the journalistic vulgarity of Cobbett. How would he ever find a readership, or make a living? Mrs Clarkson then produced a manuscript of the unpublished "Christabel", which Robinson had never heard, and read it through to him in the candlelight. Robinson was astonished and delighted. "It has great beauties and interests me more than any so small a fragment I ever met with, and that purely by the force of poetic painting . . . the verse is very fine . . ."[97]

This led Robinson on to compare the reception of his work with Wordsworth's. Wordsworth's poetry, "inspired by the true spirit of contemplation", and directly combining "the great elements of natural scenery . . . with the noblest and best feelings of the heart", was now being read increasingly by his contemporaries. But this was not true for Coleridge. It was only the serious young of the next generation who would discover his powers and value his intellectual subtleties. "The mystical sentimentality of Coleridge, however adorned by original imagery, can never interest the gay and frivolous . . . and for the same reason, the deep glances into the innermost nature of man and the original views of the relations of things which Coleridge's works are fraught with, are a stumbling block and offence to the millions, not a charm."[98]

When Robinson next saw Coleridge himself at Lamb's, he was prevailed upon towards midnight to recite "Christabel" himself. The company fell silent, and Coleridge launched out in his chanting voice. Then he faltered and stopped: he was too drunk to remember his own masterpiece. Robinson recorded the humiliation in his diary, tactfully in German. But he did not write, poor Coleridge. Instead, they all began to talk about the new series of lectures.[99]

11

Once again, it was the Morgans who rescued Coleridge from Southampton Buildings and supported him in this new venture. Morgan had been horrified by his "disappearance" in early October, and had written persistently, gently asking for a meeting to put matters right. Coleridge at first refused, writing on 12 October that he must "either get thro, or sink under" on his own.[100]

The exchange that ensued was revealing. Initially Coleridge dramatized his situation for Morgan's benefit, much as he used to do in his letters to his brother George. He was abandoned, he was penniless, he was dying. He had been treated dishonestly by Street, disgracefully by Stuart ("a *Meacenas* worth £50,000"), and was tortured by "clamorous Letters [from Mrs Coleridge]".[101]

He suspected his behaviour over "the last 8 months" at Hammersmith had alienated Mary and Charlotte – though "Heaven knows how!" Few men had ever regretted their "own infirmities" more deeply than he had. He could not return to them telling "falsehoods" about his opium and drinking. He had never been guilty of "extravagance, or self-indulgence". He was suffering from the "never-closing, festering Wound of Wordsworth and his Family". Morgan must leave him to his fate: send round his "Books & other *paucities*" to No. 6 Southampton Buildings, and think of him "as one deceased who *had been* your sincere Friend". He concluded dramatically: "*Burn this after you have read it.*"[102]

But having finished this pyrrhic missive, with all its satisfactory and poignant self-justifications, Coleridge did something new and highly complimentary to the Morgans. He did not send it. He waited for three days, and then wrote again in chastened mood. "I entreat (and beg you to entreat for me) Mrs Morgan's and Charlotte's Forgiveness for the gross disrespect, which my absence & silence render me guilty of. I am truly and to my very heart sensible, that it has been such behaviour, as they & you had little merited from me – and that the rudeness is a trifle compared with the apparent Ingratitude."

He did indeed want to return to Hammersmith, but had felt that it was intolerable "to bring back to your Home of Peace & Love a spirit so disquieted". He had "solemnly vowed" never to be ill from opium "24 hours together in your House", and to demonstrate how bad his "state of mind" had been in this respect, he humbly enclosed the original letter which had "a great deal of peevish feeling in it". He begged their forgiveness, again urged Morgan to burn it, and signed himself their "affectionate & grateful" friend.[103] Ten days later he had returned to Hammersmith, full of his new lecture scheme. By 30 October, he had issued one of his famous prospectuses.

This important reconciliation marked a new degree of emotional commitment and frankness on both sides. Knowing very well how deeply Coleridge felt about his loss of the Wordsworths, the Morgans had determined that he should not suffer such a loss again, and that they would patiently weather all his storms as he struggled to make a new career. They had already endured for a year what the Montagus could not endure for a week. They assumed it was Coleridge at his worst (though it was not), and they concluded that they could cope.

On his side, Coleridge recognized them as his saviours. He could never love them like the Wordsworths (though he would try to recover Asra in Charlotte) or find the old intellectual companionship of Grasmere. But he found loyalty, affection and a kind of easy playfulness that was immensely reassuring. While John Morgan was practical, kindly and endlessly forgiving, his wife Mary was teasing and often outspoken. She was the force in the household, with Charlotte as her faithful satellite: pretty, shy and enigmatic, and perhaps rather dominated by her older sister. When Coleridge had occasion to apologize, which he did very often, it was always in the first place to the two women, with Charlotte as his intercessor.

Living with the Morgans through the summer of 1811 had made Coleridge aware of his domestic shortcomings, in a way never evident at Grasmere. In his "peevish" letter of 12 October, he had enumerated his own faults as a house-companion with considerable accuracy. He had always been good at self-portraits, and this one of a clever, voluble, over-emotional and frequently exhausting man, is alarmingly acute. There were, he said, *two* views of his character, which the Morgans could choose to read either way, depending on whether they were pleased or aggravated with him:

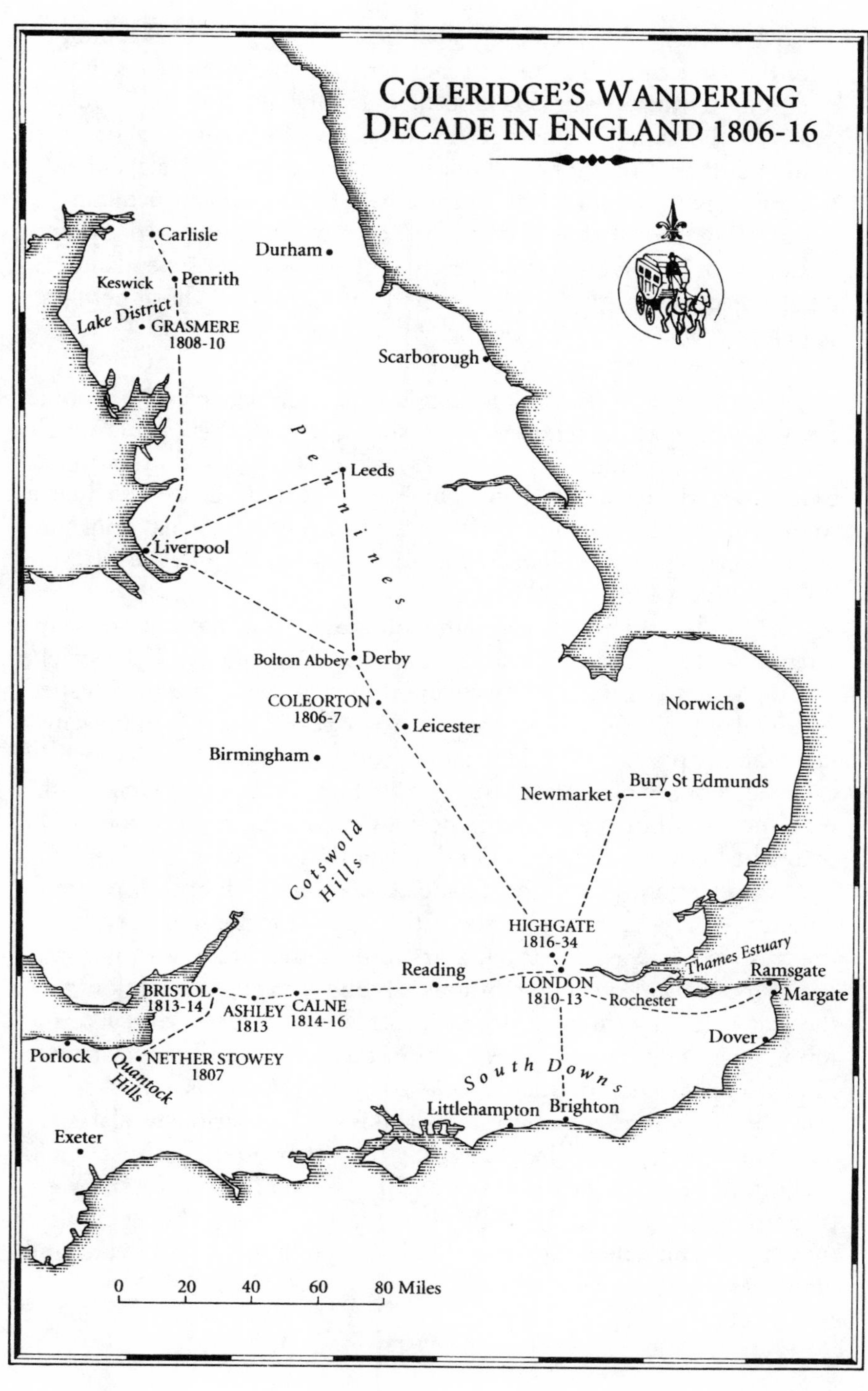
COLERIDGE'S WANDERING DECADE IN ENGLAND 1806-16
Carlisle
Durham
Keswick
Penrith
Lake District
GRASMERE 1808-10
Scarborough
Pennines
Leeds
Liverpool
Bolton Abbey
Derby
COLEORTON 1806-7
Leicester
Norwich
Birmingham
Newmarket
Bury St Edmunds
Cotswold Hills
HIGHGATE 1816-34
Thames Estuary
Reading
Ramsgate
BRISTOL 1813-14
ASHLEY 1813
CALNE 1814-16
LONDON 1810-13
Rochester
Margate
Dover
Porlock
NETHER STOWEY 1807
Quantock Hills
South Downs
Littlehampton
Brighton
Exeter
0 20 40 60 80 Miles

> Love a man, & his Talking shall be Eloquence – dislike him, & the same thing becomes Preaching. His quickness of Feeling & the starting Tear, shall be at one time natural sensibility – . . . the same at another time shall be loathsome maudlin unmanliness. Activity of Thought scattering itself as jests, puns, & sportive nonsense, shall in the bud & blossom of acquaintanceship be amiable playfulness, & met or anticipated by a Laugh or a correspondent Jest –: in the wane of Friendship, an object of Disgust, and a ground of warning to those better beloved, *not to get into that way*.[104]

Both these aspects of Coleridge's character had clearly become evident to the Morgans at Hammersmith, and this was Coleridge's way of acknowledging it. He was asking them to bear with his excesses, and never to "wane" in his support. If it seemed like a reproach, it was really intended as a plea. The Morgans would go on responding to it, gallantly and to some degree inexplicably, for the next five years.

Quite why they put up with Coleridge – if not out of pure affection – was always puzzling, not least to his family at Keswick, where Mrs Coleridge in particular always expressed astonished approval at their heroic endurance. "Mrs Coleridge seems quite satisfied with my plans," Coleridge later wrote to Morgan, "& abundantly convinced of my obligations to your & Mary's kindness to me. Nothing (she said) but the circumstances of my residing with you could reconcile her to my living in London. Southey is the semper idem."[105]

It was certainly not for financial reasons – though Coleridge would one day, against all expectation, prove to be their cavalry in this respect. It was not for literary ones either, like Wordsworth, for Morgan had no such ambitions beyond a vague fascination with the stage. If they intended to bask in his intellectual glory, like the Montagus, the glow was very fitful in these years and would hardly have compensated for the terrible trials (for them as much as for him) of his opium addiction and drinking. The curiously elaborate and humorously ritualized courting of Charlotte – whose main accomplishments, apart from her beauty and similarity to Asra, were (according to Coleridge) silent blushing and abominable spelling – may have enlivened the household. But it also caused tears and embarrassments.

The Morgans themselves left little record of their stewardship. There are no journals like Dorothy's, no memoirs like Crabb Robinson's, no essays like Lamb's, no gossip like Mrs Clarkson's. John Morgan's letters are few and punctilious, Mary's are lost, and Charlotte's were so inexpressive that Coleridge sometimes hinted that she had abjured the burden of literacy altogether. ("I hope, Charlotte was not offended at my Joke," he once wrote to Morgan, "in directing my Letter to her, as the great philo-letterist.")[106]

Charles Lamb innocently suggested that they fed Coleridge very well. Once in 1811 he conjured up a prospective Sunday lunch at Hammersmith: there would be no "expensive luxuries" such as green peas, but merely "a plate of plain Turtle, another of Turbot, with good roast Beef in the rear".[107] Southey, more gravely, acknowledged that they handled Coleridge's opium-taking with more practical kindness and effect, than any previous household, including his own. They continually battled to reduce it, but never held his lapses against him.[108] One concludes that the Morgans were simply and essentially kind; while Coleridge was still capable of exercising his ancient powers of enchantment. Amidst the chaos and disarray, the bewitching light still shone.

Most elusive of all the elements which held them together, was what Coleridge fleetingly described as "jests, puns & sportive nonsense". Coleridge simply had fun with the Morgans, in a way not really evident since his days with the undergraduates at Göttingen. (Indeed a certain adolescent or bohemian atmosphere always surrounds the Morgan household like a faint whiff of patchouli.) Coleridge could make them laugh at life. His later letters reveal their private world of ludicrous pet names, deliberately appalling puns (the worse he could make them, the better they were rated), imitated voices, imaginary household characters, running gag-lines, and messages in doggerel.

One of the main characters he adopted for their benefit was a Devonshire yokel, garrulous and fantastical, who held forth at metaphysical length on such significant subjects as snuff or fleas. On one occasion a long diatribe about *lice* in a stage-coach ended, in rustic persona and accent, with an exquisitely bad pun on telling *lies* and speaking sense. "Don't spake to henny wun, if u plaze, about them thare two Lousses, as I caut [on] my nek – becaze they may take the *License* to zay, has h[ow] I has more of the first sillybull in my 'ed, than the last."[109]

On another occasion he asked Morgan to buy a learned German tome for his lectures, J. J. W. Heinse's *Ardinghello* (1787), from a bookshop at 201 Piccadilly, in the following rhyming note:

My dear Morgan
I wish you would be my Organ
And when you pass down Piccadilly
To call in at Escher's, who sells books wise and silly.
But chiefly in a Lingo by the Learned called German,
And who himself looks less like a Man than a Mer-man–
Ask him if he still has a work called Ardinghello,
It was in his Catalogue, I am sure, and of course to sell o–
And if it is, to buy it for me. Don't forget it, my dear
Fellow![110]

Pretty bad, of course, though that was the point. Such absurdities could co-exist with the serious business of life.

Indeed Morgan would eventually prove his organ powers in the most vital way as Coleridge's amanuensis, taking over where Asra had left off. Already he was helping to draw up the Prospectus to the lectures, and on 29 October accompanied Coleridge to a business meeting with John Rickman about setting up subscription tickets and finding a suitable venue in the City.

Morgan helped Coleridge organize his lecture notes, supplied Shakespeare texts for quotation marked with red cards, and most vital of all packed up and delivered Coleridge by coach punctually on time for every single lecture from the end of November till the end of January. With this unlikely combination of frivolity and practicality, the Morgans transformed Coleridge's life and perhaps even saved it.

12

Unlike the 1808 series, the lectures of winter 1810–11 were arranged with great speed and efficiency. They were first advertised on 11 November, begun a week later on Monday, 18 November, and continued twice weekly for seventeen sessions, starting promptly at 7.30 each evening. They were sponsored by the newly founded Philosophical Institution which had taken over the old premises of the Royal Society at the Scot's Corporation Hall off Fetter Lane, Fleet Street. This was an area of London back-alleys and courtyards long associated with Dr Johnson. It was a location, observed Coleridge innocently, "renowned exclusively for pork and sausages".[111]

Passing the ancient Cheshire Cheese Inn in Fleet Street, it was approached down a narrow, insalubrious covered passageway, which debouched into Fleur de Luce Court. But the Institution was distinguished – set up by a group of City doctors and lawyers, with the Dukes of Kent and Sussex as its patrons. The Hall itself had, to Coleridge's eye, an almost comical splendour. "A spacious handsome room with an academical Stair-case & the Lecture room itself fitted up in a very grave authentic poetico-philosophical Style with Busts of Newton, Milton, Shakespeare, Pope & Locke behind the Lecturer's Cathedra."[112] These marbled worthies seemed to gaze down on him with pleasing expectation.[112]

The Prospectus announced succinctly "A Course of Lectures on Shakespeare and Milton, in Illustration of the Principles of Poetry", given by Mr Coleridge. It was more organized and sharply focused than the 1808 series. There would be an opening lecture on "False Criticism". This would be followed by a twofold exegesis of the plays in terms of dramatic psychology, and then aesthetic structure. First, "a philosophic Analysis and Explanation of the principal *Characters* of our great Dramatist" (Othello, Richard III, Falstaff and Hamlet were specified); and second "a critical *Comparison* of Shakespeare, in respect of Diction, Imagery, management of the Passions, Judgement in the construction of his Dramas . . . with his contemporaries". The whole would reveal what was "peculiar to his own Genius".[113] It was Coleridge back on track.

Tickets were sold in Fleet Street, Chancery Lane, Hatchard's Piccadilly, and Godwin's bookshop, at two guineas for the series or three guineas for gentlemen accompanied by a female guest – clearly aiming at a mixed audience. Each forthcoming lecture was advertised in *The Times*, and reporters from the *Morning Chronicle*, the *Sun* (then a literary broadsheet), and various smaller journals attended regularly. Most important of all, at least half the lectures were covered by shorthand reporters organized and apparently paid for by Morgan and Crabb Robinson, with encouragement from Southey who had urged that Coleridge should at last be recorded for posterity, "as a duty which he owes to himself, his friends and his family and the world".[114]

Robinson co-opted the young John Payne Collier from his lodgings at Hatton Garden who covered seven lectures, and a certain J. Tomalin covered a further eight. Everything was done to make the series a permanent landmark in Coleridge's new career.*

He was intensely nervous, and worked hard on his notes (scores of pages of which have survived quite separate from the transcripts) while determining to speak extempore as far as he could. Twelve days before the start, he wrote urgently to Robinson begging him to find a copy of A. W. Schlegel's three-volume set of newly published lectures, *Über dramatische Kunst und Litteratur, Vorlesungen* (Heidelberg, 1809–1811), *On Dramatic Art and Literature*.[115] These covered the Greek sources of Western drama, and gave a critical overview of Shakespeare's plays.

Nine days before the start his bowels seized up (the usual indication of increased opium), and he lay about his room in a dressing-gown with his trousers off, hoping to encourage an instant explosion with "strong aperient medicines".[116]

Four days before the start, still undetonated, he sent out a last flurry of complimentary tickets, including one to Godwin and extending the invitation to Godwin's children – especially the fourteen-year-old Mary (future author of *Frankenstein*) – who might "receive amusement".

Two days before the start, now altogether prone on his sofa and feeling like "a trunk which Nature had first locked, and then thrown away the Key", he received a supportive visit from Stuart and promise of newspaper coverage. Crabb Robinson also assured him that *The Times* would carry an article, though Walter did this grudgingly.[117]

Finally, on the last day before the start, Coleridge took the dread

* This would have been virtually a complete set of lecture transcripts for the first and only time in Coleridge's life, except for a later fatality, when his grandson, the meticulous and faithful editor Ernest Hartley Coleridge, somehow lost the Tomalin copies on the Great Western Railway during a train journey from Torquay, consigning them to the limbo of British Rail Lost Property where they were eventually joined by the first manuscript of T. E. Lawrence's *Seven Pillars of Wisdom*, lost on the South Eastern Line. One wonders what Lady Bracknell would have said about these derelictions, and how much Coleridge would have enjoyed Wilde's sense of perfect fatality.

step of summoning an ancient nurse with a stomach pump. The effect was better than instantaneous, and produced an operatic result which Coleridge orchestrated gleefully for Crabb Robinson's benefit.

> The *reality* of an old Woman added to the *idea* of a Clyster proved so vehement a stimulus to my morbid delicacy, that flash! like lightning, and roar & rumble! like thunder, it (i.e. the proximate cause) plunged down thro' me – & to the Music loud and visceral and cataractic I sang out, "I do not want the old Lady! – Give her half a crown & send her away!" – just as I heard her aged feet's plump and tardy echoes from the Stairs.[118]

He thought the psychology of this treatment, a pure case of mind over matter, extremely interesting: "marvellous Beings are we!"[118] The symbolism of the episode did not escape him either: physically unblocked he was now mentally freed for the flow of metaphysical inspiration. The "Music loud and visceral" had been a conscious echo of "Kubla Khan" with its "music loud and long".

The Corporation Hall was packed with some hundred and fifty people for the first two lectures, on Monday, 18th and Thursday, 21st November. Despite later assaults of "fog and snow", they remained well attended throughout the winter. The *Courier* noted "several Fashionables" from the Royal Institution series, but the audience was now mainly from the London literary world – "the young men of the City", as the newspaper put it, come "to hear a Poet discuss the principles of his art".

They included at various times (besides the faithful inner circle of Morgan, Lamb, Crabb Robinson and Godwin), Hazlitt, Rickman, Campbell, Humphry Davy and his smart young wife, George Dyer, Miss Mitford, Mrs Inchbald, and on at least two occasions the young Lord Byron recently returned from Greece. The two most noticeable absentees (from a modern viewpoint) were the seventeen-year-old John Keats, who had just begun attending surgical lectures at St Thomas's Hospital, across the river by Westminster Bridge; and the nineteen-year-old Percy Bysshe Shelley, who had just eloped with his first wife Harriet to Edinburgh.

The first lecture on "False Criticism" was judged eccentric and disappointing. The second, on "true definitions" of poetry, was thought brilliant and provocative. Subsequent lectures, with their numerous unannounced digressions, fluctuated between these two assessments, but always seemed to hold their audience. The general impression was that Coleridge got better and better as he proceeded.

Crabb Robinson's first report in *The Times*, which Walter had insisted should not be a puff but "dry and cold", caught the uncertain opening very well. Coleridge's initial targets, the rage for literary gossip and politicized reviewing, as epitomized by the *Edinburgh* and the *Quarterly Review*, seemed to Robinson rather odd and contentious: "viz. the excessive stimulus produced by the wonderful political events of the age; – the facilities afforded to general and indiscriminate reading; – the rage for public speaking, and the habit consequently induced of requiring instant intelligibility; – periodical criticism, which teaches those to fancy they can judge who ought to be content to learn; – the increase of cities, which has put an end to the old-fashioned village gossiping, and substituted literary small-talk in its place . . . From such topics it will be seen that Mr Coleridge is original in his views."[119]

J. P. Collier made it sound slightly more lively: "he contended that the present was 'an age of personality & political gossip' where insects, as in Egypt, were worshipped and valued in proportion to their sting". Yet he too thought the delivery was "not dazzling" as he expected, and the *Sun* urged Coleridge "to *speak* as much, and to *read* as little as possible".[120]

But by the second lecture, expectation was fulfilled. Young Collier thought it "not only beyond my praise but beyond the praise of any man, but himself . . . All others seem so contemptible in comparison. I . . . blessed my stars that I could comprehend what he had the power to invent."[121]

Coleridge opened with his witty definition of the four classes of poetry readers, went on to speak of true poetry as "a representation of Nature and the human affections". He insisted on its ancient origins in man's universal need for heightened perceptions and "pleasurable excitement", and found its beginnings in "the celebrations of the feasts of Bacchus". It was therefore a product of liberated natural energies rather than disciplined cultural forms.

He attacked the narrow, polite moralism of eighteenth-century Augustan criticism, the formal correctness of French theory and the earthbound limitations of Johnsonian common-sense. Such critics reminded Coleridge of "frogs croaking in a ditch or bog involved in darkness, but the moment a lantern was brought near the scene of their disputing society they ceased their discordant harangues".[122] They had not seen the light: that true poetry was never a formal game (metrical rules, dramatic unities, didactic, ideas dressed "in silks & satins") but always an imaginative expression of inward knowledge: "nor would it be otherwise until the idea were exploded that knowledge can be easily taught, & until we learnt the first great truth that to conquer ourselves is the only true knowledge".[123] He illustrated this theme with a spectacular array of references, from *Gulliver's Travels*, Erasmus Darwin's *Botanic Garden* and Pope's *Epistles*, to Catullus's love poetry, Sophocles's *Oedipus Rex*, and Shakespeare's *King Lear* and *Hamlet*.

Finally he promised to champion Shakespeare and Milton, with detailed readings from their works, as the great masters of imaginative power against which all "Young Poets" must match their desire for "glorious immortality". He ended with a characteristically challenging image of King Lear on the wild heath in his agony, "complaining to the Elements" in the highest poetical language that tragedy could afford, while simultaneously "mocked by the mimicry of the Fool" in the lowest language common to men, the "only attendant in his calamity". This was the richness of Nature that great poetry brought forth.[124] It was the first of his many oblique self-dramatizations. The audience left in a buzz of excitement.

Crabb Robinson approved: "a vast improvement on the first. It was delivered with ease, was popular, and contained interesting matter on that which his audience wished to hear about."[125] He went down to Hammersmith to congratulate Coleridge, and found him still "not quite well, but very eloquent", talking of Schelling's theory of the opposition between Art (as Consciousness) and Nature (as the Unconscious). He also compared Shakespeare and Calderon as imaginative poets, but there was no mention of Schlegel's *Lectures* at this point. "He observed of poetry that it united passion with order, and he very beautifully illustrated the nature of the human mind, which seeks to gratify contrary propensities (as sloth and the horror of vacancy) at the same time . . ." He rejoiced to find him safely "mounted on his hobby horse", and hurried away before he fell off.[126]

The third and fourth lectures took place, as advertised in *The Times*, punctually on 25 and 27 November. Coleridge was now more confident, and consequently more digressive and speculative. He worked back over his definitions of poetry, constantly throwing out provocations and new analogies. "Poetry is a species of composition opposed to Science, as having intellectual pleasure for its Object, and not Truth."[127] "Physicians asserted that each Passion has its proper pulse – So it is with metre when rightly used."[128] In writing of human affections, the poet "shall bring within the bounds of pleasure that which otherwise would be painful".[129]

The first (prose) chapter of the Book of Isaiah could be "reduced to complete hexameters" with only minor shifts in word-order, "so true it is that wherever Passion was, the language became a sort of metre".[130] Poetry responded to our "yearnings" to be something, or someone, other than ourselves: "we wish to have a shadow, a sort of prophetic existence present to us, which tells us what we are not . . ."[131]

Shakespeare was the great imaginative creator of this *otherness*, not "like a Dutch painter" in external details, but in a sort of passionate transmigration of the soul. "In the meanest character it was still Shakespeare, it was not the mere Nurse in *Romeo and Juliet*, or the blundering Constable in *Measure for Measure*, but it was this great & mighty Being changing himself into the Nurse or the blundering Constable that gave delight . . . He might compare it to Proteus who now flowed, a river; now raged, a fire; now roared; a lion – he assumed all changes, but still in the stream, in the fire, in the beast . . . it was the Divinity that appeared in it, & assumed the character."[132]

On and on Coleridge poured, spun and cataracted over his audience. References, asides and illustrations broke over them like foam: Newton, Milton, Handel, Michelangelo. Analogies of literary form might be found in a single American maple leaf, a wax doll, a mirror-image, or "a low lazy Mist on a Lake". They might consider Pope's *Essay on Man*, the Psalms, Homer's *Odyssey*, Richardson's novels, Burns's *Tam O'Shanter*, Shakespeare's Sonnet 113, "Venus and Adonis", and "The Rape of Lucrece" (all quoted from the passages marked with Morgan's red cards).

The great idols of eighteenth-century criticism – poetry as imitation, the dramatic unities of time and place, the belief in stage-illusion, the idea of Shakespeare as a "Child of Nature" – were all swept away like so much antiquarian flotsam. Again and again

Coleridge reverted to his central theme with wave-like repetition: the principle of poetry was an imaginative force, a power of the mind that generated its own forms and linguistic energies, a primordial "excitement", passion united with order.

At the end of the fourth lecture, he calmly dismissed a century of learned scholastic debate over the order of composition of Shakespeare's plays. "In examining the dramatic works of Shakespeare, Mr Coleridge said he should rather pursue the psychological, than the chronological order which had been so warmly disputed."[133]

The *Sun* newspaper was now vaguely aware that something historic was taking place in the obscure court off Fleet Street. "The critical appearance of this Gentleman in public constitutes a prominent feature in the Literature of the times . . ." But Coleridge had hardly begun.

Crabb Robinson was torn between admiration and frustration. "They have been brilliant; that is, in passages; but I doubt much his capacity to render them popular." What audience would follow his "musing over conceptions and imaginings beyond the reach of the analytic faculty"? Worse was Coleridge's maddening habit of "apologizing, anticipating and repeating" instead of pressing forward into his subject: after four lectures they were still "in the prolegomena" and chewing over definitions of poetry. Yet Robinson always "left the room with satisfaction", and was impressed by the large, philosophic approach.

Indeed he now had a German friend with him, a Herr Bernard Krusve, "who is delighted to find the logic & the rhetoric of his Country delivered in a foreign language. There is no doubt that Coleridge's mind is much more German than English. My friend has pointed out striking analogies between C. & German authors whom he has never seen."[134] This was the first shadowy reference to the influence of A. W. Schlegel, which was soon to receive less welcome attention.

On 27 November, Lamb hosted a lively evening of port and post-mortems on the lectures so far. Hazlitt (who was about to start his own rival lectures at the Russell Institute) seemed particularly grudging at first: Coleridge's definitions were "not distinct & clear"; his concept of "excitement" was unsatisfactory; his criticism of the dramatic unities had been partly anticipated by "Dr Sam Johnson of Lichfield"; and the best of his Shakespeare quotations had been supplied by Hazlitt himself. Rickman thought Coleridge didn't always understand his own definitions. Lamb gently insisted on his originality, and was intrigued by the idea of Shakespeare "transferring himself" in spirit to the Nurse. Dyer thought he was "the fittest man for a Lecturer he had ever known", particularly as he was always lecturing in private. Then Hazlitt, with one of his characteristic switches from witty criticism to ironic praise, said Coleridge still had "more ideas" than any other person he had ever known, but always "pushed matters" so far that he "became obscure to every body but himself".[135]

The next four lectures (Nos 5–8) were based on *Love's Labours Lost* and *Romeo and Juliet*, and Shakespeare's subtle exploration of the varieties of love. He made particularly fine presentations of the character and psychology of Romeo, Mercutio and the Nurse. Of Romeo Coleridge observed with feeling: "Love is not like hunger: Love is an associative quality . . . What was the first effect of love, but to associate the feeling with every object in nature: the trees whisper, the roses exhale their perfumes, the nightingales sing . . . Romeo became enamoured of the ideal he had formed in his own mind & then as it were christened the first real being as that which he desired. He appeared to be in love with Rosaline, but in truth he was only in love with his own idea."[136]

Mercutio, whose death was the structural key to "the whole catastrophe of the Play", was also a subtle variation on the psychological theme of ardent youth. He was a man "possessing all the elements of a Poet: high fancy; rapid thoughts; the whole world was as it were subject to his law of association . . ."[137] The Nurse, on the other hand, provided the tender counter-point of love in old age, and demonstrated Shakespeare's astonishing ability to orchestrate varied characters around a single emotional theme. "Thus in the Nurse you had all the garrulity of old age and all its fondness, which was one of the great consolations of humanity." Then Coleridge added one of those gentle, pensive comments with which he could always transfix his audience. "He had often thought what a melancholy world it would be without children, and what an inhuman world without the aged."[138]

As Coleridge grew more confident with his audience, assured of holding their attention and making them laugh, he developed one of his most characteristic traits as a lecturer: the brilliantly suggestive aside. They are rarely in his Notes, and the shorthand reporters had to work hard to catch them, particularly as they often depend on a spontaneous flash of poetic imagery. But a few were successfully caught on the wing. Of Shakespeare's puns, with their innocent energy, he suddenly observed: "they seemed as it were the first openings of the mouth of Nature".[139] Shakespeare's wit was "like the flourishing of a man's stick when he is walking along in the full flow of animal spirits. It was a sort of overflow of hilarity . . ."[140]

Homer's epics were "like a ship that had left a train of glory in its wake".[141] French poetry attained its effects "by peculiar turns of phrase, which like the beautiful coloured dust on the wings of a butterfly must not be judged of by touch".[142] The natural talent for poetry first showed in exuberance and linguistic extravagance, "it would be a hopeless symptom if he found a young man with perfect taste".[143]

The mature poet remained in some sense "unsubdued, unshackled by custom": he combined "the wonder of a child" with the "inquisitive powers of his manhood". "The Poet is not only the man made to solve the riddle of the Universe, but he is also the man who feels where it is *not* solved, and [this] continually awakens his feelings . . . What is old and worn out, not in itself but from the dimness of the intellectual eye brought on by worldly passions, he makes new: he pours upon it the dew that glistens, and blows round us the breeze which cooled us in childhood."[144]

With the conclusion of Lecture 8 on 12 December, Coleridge had reached the half-way point in the series, though he had hardly touched on more than a handful of plays. The problem was his old habit of digression, which sometimes led him spectacularly astray. In Lecture 6 he was diverted for half an hour on to the Bell–Lancaster controversy and his débâcle at the Royal Institution, in the middle of which Lamb leaned across and whispered to Robinson: "this is not so much amiss. Coleridge said in his advertisement he would speak about the Nurse in *Romeo and Juliet*, and so he is delivering the lecture in the character of the Nurse." Robinson agreed, "the man is absolutely incorrigible. But his vitia are indeed, *splendida*."[145]

By contrast Lecture 7 was "incomparably the best" since No. 2. "C. declaimed with great eloquence on Love, without wandering from his subject, *Romeo and Juliet*. He was spirited for the greater part, intelligible though profound. And he was methodical . . ."[146] In Lecture 8 he was thrown off track again, this time by an interminable disquisition on the "natural morality" of sexual passion, "brotherly and sisterly affections", and the ancient taboo against incest and "the law preserved in the Temple of Isis".[147] Some familiar demons from the Grasmere days stirred behind this "rhapsody", but Robinson thought it the "worst" so far, and for once "lost all power of attending him any longer".[148]

Yet the gathering impact of the lectures was formidable, and news of the series began to spread in various influential quarters. Sir George Beaumont sent a gift of money and announced that he would be directing his carriage towards Fleet Street. Lord Byron, who had heard rousing gossip of the "reformed schismatic" in the St James's clubs, decided to get up a party with the banker-poet Sam Rogers – if he could fit it in between play-going and dinners.[149]

The painter George Dawe, newly appointed Associate of the Royal Academy, decided to make Coleridge and his work the theme of his submission to the annual Spring Exhibition at the Academy's galleries in Piccadilly. He took a plaster life-mask (a process which Coleridge endured without "any expression of Pain or Uneasiness" despite the enforced silence for several hours), made the cast for a bust, drew a crayon portrait, and began work on a large painting to illustrate one of Coleridge's ballads. It is interesting that his choice fell on "Love" (which he titled "Genevieve") rather than "The Ancient Mariner", suggesting how little Coleridge's poetry was still known to the general public. "Love" had last been published almost a decade previously in Wordsworth's 1802 edition of the *Lyrical Ballads*. But Coleridge was delighted, considering the picture "very beautiful", and the crayon portrait "far more like than any former attempt, excepting Allston's".[150]

Yet it was hardly flattering, showing a fat and melancholy personage surrounded by his books, eyes raised to heaven and waistcoat bulging, slumped in thought with one arm over the back of an easy chair. It was difficult to imagine this indolent, supine, suffering creature delivering what Robinson called his "immethodical rhapsodies . . . abounding in brilliant thoughts, fine flashes of rhetoric, ingenious paradoxes . . ."[151] But perhaps that was why Coleridge liked it: it still suggested that "indolence capable of energies" he had described to John Thelwall nearly fifteen years before.

13

At this half-way point in the series, one other signal event occurred. Coleridge finally got hold of a German copy of Schlegel's *Lectures*. At the same moment, in the most delicate manner possible, he was first accused of plagiarism: the spectre that would haunt the rest of his career.

A revealing account appeared in a letter which Coleridge hastily drafted on the weekend before his ninth lecture. The draft was written on the back of a handbill advertising his 21 November lecture, and later annotated "intended to have been copied and sent to Lord B[yron]", though this may have been an afterthought. Coleridge wrote:

> After the close of my Lecture on Romeo and Juliet [No. 8], a German Gentleman, a Mr Bernard Krusve, introduced himself to me, and after some courteous Compliments said, Were it not almost impossible, I must have believed that you had either heard or read my Countryman Schlegel's Lecture on this play, given at Vienna: the principles, thought, and the very illustrations are so nearly the same – But the Lectures were but just published as I left Germany, scarcely more than a week since – and the only two Copies of the Work in England I have reason to think, that I myself brought over. One I retain: the other is at Mr Boosy's [bookseller] – I replied that I had not even heard of these Lectures, nor had indeed seen any work of Schlegel's except a volume of translations from Spanish Poetry, which the Baron von Humboldt had lent me when I was at Rome.[152]

This circumstantial account is a fine amalgam of truth and falsehood. From all the notes and shorthand reports of the first eight lectures, it is clear that Coleridge had not yet seen Schlegel's lectures as such. But he certainly knew of their existence, and it is nonsense to suggest that he was not aware of Schlegel's Shakespeare criticism in general. He had very probably read Schlegel's famous essay on *Romeo and Juliet*, published in 1798 (there are echoes of it in Lecture No. 8). He had praised Schlegel's work on Shakespeare to Von Humboldt in 1806, and urgently asked Robinson to obtain the new Schlegel Lectures on 6 November 1811. He was more familiar with the new German Romantic criticism than anyone else in England. Even in the 1808 lectures Crabb Robinson had noted with admiration his specific references to Herder, Lessing, Schiller and Kant – and indeed he had openly championed the revolutionary German approach as superior to the Shakespeare criticism of Johnson or Pope.[153] Part of his claim to originality (as a good deal of the charges of "obscurity and paradox") lay precisely in his daring interpretations of German theory, combined with his own uniquely poetic and psychological approach. He was "anxious" to read Schelgel as the latest advance in "Continental" criticism, and he fully intended to use him in forthcoming lectures, which he did in a way already suggested by his private adaptations of Jean-Paul Richter.

What seems so puzzling is not the question of Schlegel's influence at all, but Coleridge's panic and mendacity when challenged about it. Instead of proclaiming his knowledge and intentions, he hid them. This guilty reflex suggests an almost pathological failure of self-confidence. He felt all his work would be shown up as valueless by a hostile critic, and that he would be shown to have done nothing, thought nothing, written nothing on his own account.

According to the letter, Mr Krusve called round to Hammersmith the following morning and "made him a present" of Schlegel. Coleridge read it avidly over the weekend, and found it full of "anticipations" of his own work. This he stated quite openly, giving the reasonable explanation that as they had both studied Kant, their criticism had developed not merely on parallel lines but on closely overlapping ones, outside the English tradition. He freely admitted that it looked astonishingly as if he had plagiarized Schlegel. "Not in one Lecture, but in all the Lectures that related to Shakespeare, or to Poetry in general, the Grounds, Train of Reasoning etc. were different in language only – & often not even in that – The Thoughts too were so far peculiar, that to the best of my knowledge they did not exist in any prior work of Criticism."

Yet Coleridge still firmly denied plagiarism. He explained, with every appearance of conviction, that he had "anticipated" Schlegel in the 1808 and the first half of the 1811 series. "Yet I was far more flattered, or to speak more truly, I was more confirmed, than surprised. For Schlegel and myself had both studied deeply and perseverantly the philosophy of Kant, the distinguishing feature of which is to treat every subject in reference to the operation of the mental Faculties, to which it specially appertains . . ." They drew the "same trains of reasoning from the same principles", and they wrote "to one purpose & with one spirit".[154]

This part of the letter seems an admirable statement of his position. For the rest, he expanded into a general discussion of plagiarism in poetry, and made a generous defence of Scott's apparent borrowings from "Christabel". He summed up: "He who can catch the Spirit of an original, has it already." There is no evidence that Coleridge ever sent this letter to Byron, or anyone else. But it was perhaps a preparation of his defence, and the question was how he would now use it in public.

Lecture No. 9 followed on 16 December, and was based on *The Tempest*. Byron attended and seems to have been amused, since he came at least once again. Crabb Robinson criticized the 'desultory" opening, which repeated "old remarks" on classical drama, but thought the later parts "beautifully" handled and "most excellent".[155]

In fact the "old remarks" drew on Schlegel's twelfth lecture on the ancient drama, and show the first clear evidence of phrases and concepts partly drawn from his texts.[156] It is significant that Robinson did not think they represented a new line in Coleridge's thought. Coleridge then openly and publicly raised the question of his "anticipations" of German criticism. Collier reported his statement as follows: "Yesterday afternoon a friend had left for him a Work by a German writer of which Coleridge had had time only to read a small part but what he had read he approved & he should praise the book much more highly were it not that in truth it would be praising himself, as the sentiments contained in it were so coincident with those Coleridge had expressed at the Royal Institution."[157] This account was essentially the same as the letter, except that it contained two protective devices: it implied Coleridge had received the book at the end of the weekend, rather than the beginning (with much less time to read); and it signally failed to mention Schlegel by name.

Coleridge then went on to praise German criticism of Shakespeare, as he had done in 1808, and attacked English criticism for failing to appreciate properly "Shakespeare's mighty genius". He added an interesting sociological explanation for the theoretical advances in Germany. In the great struggle against Napoleon, that "evil Genius of the Planet", the British mind was attuned to action and the defence of traditional values. But the German mind, forced into inactivity by the Napoleonic occupations, had been driven inward "into speculation" and a reinterpretation of "ancient philosophy". All national feelings had been "forced back into the thinking and reasoning mind". They had developed the line of Kantian idealism: "incapable of acting outwardly, they have acted internally".

This intriguing suggestion also contained an autobiographical shadow. It aligned Coleridge's private experiences in the study with those of German thinkers in a subjected Europe. Both had existed and developed under conditions of intellectual siege. Both had undergone an enforced period of intense introversion (the parallel with Hamlet is implicit), and their thought had developed accordingly. In this he and Schlegel (like Richter) were spiritual soul-mates. But for all this, Coleridge again failed to mention Schlegel by name, and gave no further hint that he would draw directly upon his texts. Had he once done so, the question of plagiarism might never have arisen. But he did not do so.[158]

Interestingly, Crabb Robinson, who would have known all the details of the Schlegel saga, made no criticism. When later in February 1812 he read Schlegel for himself, after the lectures were over, his comment was: "read, in the evening, Schlegel's *Lectures on Shakespeare*. Coleridge, I find, did not disdain to borrow observations from Schlegel, though the coincidences between the two lectures are, for the greater part, coincidences merely and not the one caused by the other."[159]

Coleridge's "borrowings" in Lecture 9, one of the most fully recorded of the series, were characteristic of everything that came later and present typical problems of interpretation. They show vividly how his mind was working, with its extraordinary mixture of recognizing what he already knew, expropriating what he had not exactly thought himself, and beautifully developing what was entirely original.

In the middle of the lecture he suddenly announced, with a clarity that he had never previously found, the theory of "organic form". Collier recorded: "Coleridge here explained the difference between what he called mechanic and organic regularity. In the former the copy must be made as if it had been formed in the same mould as the original. – In the latter there is a law which all the parts obey conforming themselves to the outward symbols & manifestations of the essential principle. He illustrated this distinction by referring to the growth of Trees . . ."[160] Apart from the reference to trees, this was taken virtually word for word from Schlegel's twelfth lecture.

There can be no doubt that Coleridge was conscious of the German source for the passage, for he later translated Schlegel even more fully in his written notes for subsequent lectures in 1813. In these written notes he assigned it to "a Continental critic", but still without mentioning Schlegel's name. When published nearly a hundred years later, it came to be regarded as the classic statement of "organic" theory, and was accepted as essentially Coleridge's. Here was plagiarism.[161]

Or was it? Coleridge had been discussing the "organic" nature of poetic forms for years, ever since his letters to Sotheby of 1802 on the "one Life" of the Imagination.[162] At Valletta in 1805 he had made the long note (from the Greek philosopher Athenagoras) distinguishing between "Fabrication" and "Generation" in the birth of a child, and the consequent distinction between mechanically "imposed" forms and organically "evolved" ones.[163] It was clear that he instantly recognized the point of Schlegel's distinction, and felt he had anticipated it. What he had not done was express it so succinctly in a public lecture.

Moreover the illustration from the life of trees was his own, and took the argument further. (Schlegel had referred to flowers and crystalline salts.) Coleridge explained that the organic "principle" was not merely an internal evolution, but a response to environmental conditions outside. Poems were like "Trees, which from peculiar circumstances of soil, air or position differed from trees of the same kind – but every man was able to decide at first sight which was an ash or a poplar." So a poem or play was both "generated" from within by the poet's imagination to become a unique form, and yet also responded to external "circumstances" of social reality to become a type. Shakespeare's genius lay in combining the two.

The same ambiguity applied to Coleridge's use of Schlegel's remarks on *The Tempest*. The difference in style and development is shown by their contrasted treatment of Caliban. Schlegel made the suggestive, but very general point that while Ariel's name implies air, Caliban implies earth, and together they represent an opposition of nature's two fundamental elements in the play. "Caliban signifies the heavy element of earth." But for Coleridge Shakespeare's genius lay in what he did with the earth element, somehow making it both heavy ("brutish") and yet simultaneously noble. Caliban has the power to excite human sympathy. The miracle lay in creating an earth-monster (as Johnson saw him) who was also profoundly touching. How did Shakespeare do it?

In his reply Coleridge anticipated a long line of monstrous creations from Mary Shelley's outcast creature in *Frankenstein*, to Hollywood's King Kong. "The character of Caliban is wonderfully conceived: he is a sort of creature of the earth partaking of the qualities of the brute and distinguished from them . . ." He has understanding, but "without moral reason"; and at the same time he is "a noble being: a man in the sense of the imagination". All his images "are drawn from nature & are all highly poetical . . . Caliban gives you images from the Earth – Ariel images from the air." There is nothing mean in his "animal passions", only the "sense of repugnance at being commanded", by Prospero. We sympathize with Caliban because we feel he is enslaved.[164] This was a crucial, and characteristically psychological advance over Schlegel's reading.

The lecture concluded with a line-by-line analysis of Prospero's "solemnity of phraseology", showing how Shakespeare gave him the language of "the Magician, whose very art seems to consider all objects in nature in a mysterious point of view".[165] This notion of Prospero as essentially a poet, recreating the island-world of *The Tempest* for Miranda's benefit, was also entirely original. It was this part that Robinson thought "most excellent".[166]*

---

* There is always more to be said on this subject (see *Early Visions*, pp. 231–2; pp. 334–5), but it needs most of all a sense of perspective. In an age much concerned with "the originality" of genius, there were many disputes about plagiarism, most of which have now been forgotten. Chatterton was accused of plagiarising the medieval Rowley (though he invented him); Walter Scott was accused of plagiarising Coleridge in his ballads; Wordsworth of plagiarizing Walter Savage Landor in a poem; even Byron of plagiarizing Coleridge in "The Maid of Corinth" (rather exquisitely, he made the accusation himself).

But Coleridge was a special case. It is perfectly clear that between 1811 and 1816 he incorporated dozens of unacknowledged passages from German authors, either literally translated or freely adapted, in his lectures and published works. The most significant of these are A. W. Schlegel in the Shakespeare Lectures, Kant in "An Essay on Genial Criticism" (1814), and Schelling and Maass in the *Biographia Literaria* (1817). His contemporaries were aware of this, and there are published comments by Crabb Robinson, Hazlitt, Wordsworth, De Quincey ("Coleridge", *Tait's Magazine*, 1835), and J. F. Ferrier ("The Plagiarisms of S. T. Coleridge",

footnote continued overleaf

14

On 2 January 1812 Coleridge began his great lecture on *Hamlet*, which became the focus and highlight of the entire series. Crabb Robinson immediately hailed it as "perhaps his very best", and

---

footnote continued

Blackwood's Magazine, 1840); as well as a detailed record and defence of his borrowings in the edition published by his faithful daughter Sara Coleridge (1847).

But for nearly a hundred years academic criticism ignored the problem, or sidelined it, until two notably damning studies: René Wellek, *A History of Modern Criticism* (volume 2, 1955); and Norman Fruman, *Coleridge, the Damaged Archangel* (1971). The pendulum then swung the other way, and for some twenty years it became customary to treat much of Coleridge's critical prose (as well as some of the minor poetry) as a tissue of plagiarisms: exactly what Coleridge had most feared. However, some balanced view has now emerged among scholars, championed by Thomas McFarland in *Coleridge and the Pantheist Tradition* (1969), and lucidly confirmed by Rosemary Ashton in *Samuel Taylor Coleridge: A Critical Biography* (1996). With the publication of Coleridge's *Notebooks* for this period (notably volume 3, 1973); a new edition of the *Biographia* (2 vols, 1983); and a much more detailed record of the *Literary Lectures* (2 vols, 1987) it has become clear that the issue is extremely subtle.

Coleridge undoubtedly stole from the German writers, and lied about doing so. For a man of such originality and intellectual brilliance this is itself an acute problem in psychological terms, obviously connected with the mendacious habits of his drug-addiction, his astonishing lack of self-worth, and the moral humiliations of his private life – not least in the relationship with the Wordsworth circle. This is an area in which biography can, I hope, throw some sympathetic light into the lonely darkness of his solitary study and the endless, sometimes desperate, "night-conversations" with his fellow authors.

But from a historical viewpoint, the process is challenging and significant in a quite different way. Coleridge championed the new German criticism and idealist philosophy, adapted it and developed it in an English context, and successfully made it part of the Romantic movement. His intellectual heirs are De Quincey, Thomas Carlyle, J. S. Mill, and Matthew Arnold. It is impossible to imagine a modern view of literary form, creativity and the unconscious, or poetry itself, without Coleridge. Many of the specific concepts he was supposed to have plagiarized – such as the notion of "organic form", the attack on the "dramatic unities", the "fusing" power of the imagination, the role of the dream and the symbol – have a long and complex intellectual history in 18th century criticism, German, French and English. As in the physical sciences (with concepts like Evolution, Magnetism or Polarity, all of great interest to Coleridge) one can say they were afloat in the *Zeitgeist* throughout Europe. But time and time again it is Coleridge who formulates them most subtly and most memorably in his generation.

Where he stole – and one repeats, he did steal – he also transformed, clarified and made resonant. He brought ideas to life in a unique way. Moreover, far more than any of his German sources, he always wrote as a poet. His exquisite sensitivity to language, his psychological acuity, his metaphors and extended images of explanation (as well as his sudden asides) have no equivalent in his German sources, not even in Schlegel. It is this aspect of his work that has proved most enduring, as we shall see. To sum up: one can say that Coleridge plagiarized, but that no one plagiarized like Coleridge.

recognized the deliberately autobiographical theme of introversion and inaction.[167]

Coleridge's strategy was to show that eighteenth-century criticism, both English and German, had fundamentally underestimated the play through an inadequate psychological conception of Hamlet's character. Instead he proposed a brilliant and subtle reading of Hamlet's introversion, and argued that this was carefully explored throughout the entire structure of the play, giving it exceptional dramatic unity. Not merely the great soliloquies, but the plotting of the court intrigue, the revenge theme, the use of the ghost, the ambiguities of madness, and Hamlet's relations with both Ophelia and Gertrude, all served a deliberate and complex dramatic purpose.

His essential argument was that Shakespeare had consciously transformed the old, crude convention of the Elizabethan Revenge Play – a violent, extroverted and garish form – into a supremely poetic meditation on the inner workings of the imaginative mind and the tragedy of inaction. Shakespeare's genius had turned an action-drama into a study of moral paralysis. In so doing, he had created an archetypal Romantic hero – Hamlet as Everyman – who also seemed extraordinarily like Coleridge himself. Coleridge would elaborate on this theme in at least half-a-dozen *Hamlet* lectures over the next two years, and his Notes to the play became fuller than for any other Shakespearean subject.[168]

At the time he spoke, *Hamlet* was not regarded as an outstanding tragedy in the canon, but rather as an "irregular" melodrama with many objectionable and inexplicable scenes. When Coleridge opened by referring to the "general prejudices against Shakespeare" in his handling of the play, he was dismissing a vast body of previous criticism which would have been broadly familiar to his audience.

Voltaire had given the classical account in his *Letters on the English Nation* (1727): "Shakespeare is a sublime *natural* genius, without the least spark of good taste or the slightest understanding of the dramatic rules . . . *Hamlet* is a monstrous farce, haphazardly scattered with terrible soliloquies." Dr Johnson in his famous *Notes to the Complete Edition of Shakespeare* (1765) had been impressed by the power of the play, but felt it was full of "wanton cruelty" and insufficiently motivated: "Of the feigned madness of Hamlet there appears no adequate cause . . ." Goethe, in his influential chapter from *Wilhelm Meister* (1796), had argued that Hamlet was simply a weak man incapable of rising to the demands of historical destiny. "A lovely, pure and most moral nature, without the strength of nerve which forms a Hero, sinks beneath a Burden which it cannot bear . . . Impossibilities have been required of him."

Most significantly of all, Schlegel in his twelfth lecture (which Coleridge had now certainly read), while calling the play in the Kantian style "a tragedy of the reflection-process", had concentrated on the idea that Hamlet was not merely weak, but morally corrupt. His interpretation was surprisingly hostile. "Hamlet has a natural inclination to devious behaviour. He is a hypocrite towards himself. His far-fetched scruples are often mere pretexts to cover his want of resolution . . . He loses himself in labyrinths of thought . . . He has no compassion for others. He takes malicious joy in his schemes."[169]

Coleridge, by contrast, produced an interpretation so sympathetic and penetrating that it has shaped *Hamlet* criticism ever since (and is still sometimes reprinted in modern editions of the play).[170] He began by asking his audience to consider the play from the dramatist's point of view. "The first question was – What did Shakespeare mean when he drew the character of Hamlet? . . . What was the point to which Shakespeare directed himself? He meant to portray a person in whose view the external world and all its incidents and objects were comparatively dim . . . Hamlet beheld external objects in the same way that a man of vivid imagination who shuts his eyes, sees what has previously made an impression on his sight."

Coleridge then emphasized the paradoxically action-driven nature of the plot, in a masterly summary of the opening scenes. "Shakespeare places [Hamlet] in the most stimulating circumstances that a human being can be placed in: he is the heir apparent to the throne; his father dies suspiciously; his mother excludes him from the throne by marrying his uncle. This was not enough but the Ghost of his murdered father is introduced to assure the son that he was put to death by his own brother. What is the result? Endless reasoning and urging – perpetual solicitation of the mind to act, but as constant an escape from action – ceaseless reproaches of himself for his sloth, while the whole energy of his resolution passes away in those reproaches."

But this paralysis of the will cannot be dismissed as moral corruption, or a mere dreamy failure to grasp the realities around him. "This, too, not from cowardice, for he is made one of the bravest of his time; – not from want of forethought or quickness of apprehension, for he sees through the very souls of all who surround him. But merely from that aversion to action which prevails among such as have – as it were – a world within themselves."[171]

Coleridge pressed on to analyse the great dramatic confrontations of the play, as perfect theatrical expressions of this psychological theme. The Ghost is produced not once, but three times, each apparition being dramatically unexpected, but so as to generate a terrifying "accrescence of objectivity" for the audience. At the same time, belief in the Ghost reveals "a fearful subjectivity" in Hamlet. "The *front* of the mind, the whole consciousness of the speaker, is filled by the solemn apparition."[172]

When in the bedroom scene with Gertrude (Act III, scene 4), the Queen *cannot* see the Ghost, Shakespeare has moved the apparition into Hamlet's own psyche, telling him what he already unconsciously suspects. Gertrude is an adulteress, but she may also be a murderess. "Was Gertrude, or was she not, conscious of the fratricide?"[173] At the same time, Hamlet's earlier refusal to question Gertrude prepares us for the hysterical outbursts of this scene. As Coleridge put it in one of the most inspired of all his asides – which could be said to anticipate all Freud – "Suppression prepares for Overflow."[174]

Coleridge was equally penetrating on Hamlet's madness, which Johnson had found so inexplicable, and Schlegel viewed as purely manipulative and cruel. The revenge play had a long tradition of mad scenes, but also of *feigned* madness, used to produce grotesque comic-horror exchanges in which the audience could confidently share in the secret duplicity of the protagonist. For Coleridge, Shakespeare deliberately challenges this confident certainty, and thereby transforms the whole convention.

The ambiguity between acting and truly feeling, between "seeming" and actually "being", animates Hamlet's entire character. When the Player King weeps for Hecuba, Hamlet "breaks out into a delirium of rage against himself" – which may itself be partly an act.[175] When Hamlet feigns madness in front of Ophelia – who will actually go mad as a result – he himself may be closer to insanity than he (or we the audience) realize. His "antic disposition" may itself be genuinely unbalanced. "Terror is closely connected to the ludicrous. The latter is the common mode by which the mind tries to emancipate itself from Terror . . . Add to this, that Hamlet's wildness is but *half-false*. O! that subtle trick to *pretend* the acting, when we are very near *being* what we act. And this explanation is the same with Ophelia's vivid images of Hamlet's desperation in love: nigh akin to, and productive of, temporary mania."[176]

The skill with which Shakespeare elaborates and enters into this shifting "world within" of Hamlet's character creates an interior life – a Coleridgean life – of hypnotic power and complexity. He has "perfect knowledge of his own character", yet he "still yields to the same retiring from all reality" and is incapable of "carrying into effect his most obvious duty". So we believe in Hamlet precisely because we cannot be certain of him. He "mirrors" our own doubts about the nature of reality.[177]

Coleridge insisted that far from being weak, Hamlet has an imaginative power that makes him stronger than anyone else in the play, and one of Shakespeare's greatest creations. He becomes a kind of Everyman, whose soliloquies – on suicide, revenge, betrayal, world-weariness, destiny and death – are of "universal interest". They produce "a communion with the *heart*, that belongs to, or ought to belong, to all mankind".[178]

At the same time, his great soliloquies are those of a poet. "How [Hamlet's] character develops itself in these speeches . . . The aversion to externals, the betrayed habit of brooding over the world within him, and the prodigality of beautiful *words*. They are, as it were, the half-embodying of his thoughts, that give them an Outness, a reality *sui generis*. Yet they retain their correspondence and shadowy approach to the images and movements within."[179]

Coleridge's identification of himself with Hamlet gave this whole lecture a particular resonance, and would deepen in all his subsequent treatments of the play. He made Hamlet a Romantic and contemporary figure to his audience, but he did not hesitate to place him within a frame of unflinching ethical judgement. His summary was clear and monumental. "In Hamlet I conceive [Shakespeare] to have wished to exemplify the moral necessity of a due balance between our attention to outward objects and our meditation on inward thoughts – a due balance between the real and the imaginary world. In Hamlet this balance does not exist . . . Hence great, enormous, intellectual activity, and a consequent proportionate aversion to real action, with all its symptoms and accompanying qualities."[180]

Crabb Robinson was moved by the whole performance, and wrote in confidence to Catherine Clarkson about it. "Last night he concluded his fine development of the Prince of Denmark by an eloquent statement of the moral of the play. 'Action,' he said, 'is the great end of all – No intellect however grand is valuable if it draw us from action & lead us to think & think till the time of action is passed by, and we can do nothing.' Somebody said to me, this is a Satire on himself; No, said I, it is an Elegy. A great many of his remarks on Hamlet were capable of a like application."[181] To the end of his life, Coleridge would mildly claim, "I have a smack of Hamlet myself, if I may say so."[182]

15

The series continued until the end of January, but few records have remained of the last five lectures, which moved on from Shakespeare to Milton. They were evidently lively and confident, and the *Rifleman* newspaper reported a spectacular discussion of "the Sublime" in Lecture 16. Coleridge contrasted Milton's poetical conception of God's creation of the universe with Erasmus Darwin's astronomical one. In so doing Coleridge gave an impressive account of what is now the Big Bang theory, but objected to it – in one of his splendid asides – on *aesthetic* grounds. It was one of his earliest comments on evolution, a subject which would occupy much of his later thinking.

Erasmus Darwin had "imagined the creation of the universe to have taken place in a moment, by the explosion of a mass of matter in the womb or centre of space. In one and the same instant of time, suns and planets shot into Systems in every direction, and filled and spangled the illimitable void! [Coleridge] asserted this to be an intolerable degradation – referring, as it were, all the beauty and harmony of nature to something like the bursting of a *barrel of gunpowder*!"[183]

The lectures concluded with a number of such firework-displays on poetry, cosmology and the character of Satan, the last (No. 17) on 27 January 1812. "They ended with *éclat*," wrote Crabb Robinson on leaving Fleet Street, with satisfaction and some relief. "The room was crowded; and the lecture had several passages more than brilliant; they were luminous. And the light gave conscious pleasure to every person who knew that he could . . . see the glory."[184]

7

Phantom Purposes

1

Coleridge was elated with his success. This year, 1812 – the year that Napoleon invaded Russia – would surely be the year of his resurgence. Ideas for essays, books and even a play began to march about his head. The London firm of Gale and Curtis proposed to republish *The Friend* in book form. Three influential patrons – Sir George Beaumont, Sir Thomas Bernard of the Royal Institution, and the wealthy *littérateur* William Sotheby (with whom he had corresponded about poetry in the Keswick days) – suggested a new set of lectures to be held in May at Willis's Rooms, an ultra-fashionable Mayfair address. The Great Lecture Room there – used by the Society of Dilettantes – could hold an audience of 500 people. Perhaps also he would submit a drama to Drury Lane.

In his euphoria, Coleridge's lecture topics expanded to the horizon. Perhaps a complete tour of European literature – "Dante, Ariosto, *Don Quixote*, Calderón, Shakespeare, Milton, and Klopstock" – two lectures each; or maybe a grand historical sweep of moral subjects and the conditions of contemporary life – "the causes of domestic Happiness and Unhappiness – the influence of Christianity on Christendom independent of theological differences, & considered merely as part of the *History* of Mankind . . . on Education . . ."[1]

He wrote breezily to Mrs Coleridge, saying his literary plans would certainly please her. "They will enable me not only to pay off all Keswick Debts in a few months, but to remit you £200 a year regularly."[2] He also told the Morgans that they could now afford a more central and smarter address, which they quickly found just north of Oxford Street at No. 71 Berners Street. It was a fine, newly built brick house that they could rent for £60 a year, which he considered "very cheap, as houses go" for the district.[3] He would finally have his own suite of rooms, and space for his books and clothes which he now intended bringing down from Keswick, after a lapse of eighteen months. At last he would be settled in his new life, and ready to take on the world again.

But first, of course, he must undertake a rapid sortie to the north, to see his children, arrange his affairs and manuscripts (there were unused sheets of *The Friend* at Kendal), and receive some sort of explanation from Wordsworth. Speed was of the essence, and he told Morgan he planned merely to stay a fortnight, and would certainly be back in time to move into the new house in April, when he would supply £50 as his part of the deposit.[4]

On 10 February 1812, he bundled into the northern night mail coach from the City, scrawling off a last-minute letter of optimistic plans from the shop-counter of the Brent family business in Bishopsgate Street. He thought he could reimburse all his travel expenses with "a couple of Lectures" given en route at Liverpool. Further letters sped back to the Morgans from various coaching inns at Slough, Birmingham and Kendal, and his spirits were high.

He was pursued, he said, by fleas and fumigated them with his "Snuff Cannister". (He discovered the Liverpool Mail was nicknamed the "Lousy Liverpool".) A fellow passenger, a "*handy* Gentleman" heaped straw round his legs and unsuccessfully tried to pick his fob-watch.[5] He did his Devonshire voices, made appalling puns about his companions, and teased Charlotte in little footnotes. "I know you are fond of *Letters* in general, from A to Z, Charlotte, with the exception of three; but yet don't throw it into the fire, when you find it from S.T.C."[6] (Charlotte may not have noticed that it rhymed.)

Passing through Birmingham he observed the huge new factories from his carriage window, "a cluster of enormous Furnaces, with columns of flame instead of Smoke from their chimneys", and alongside the great slag-heaps of the coal mines with "pools and puddles of water smoking" between them.[7] This new infernal landscape, the product of wartime industry, fascinated him as a vision of England's future industrial might. He made notes on production and transport costs ("£1.7.0 for the double Cart-load, weighing 35 Cwt." by canal) but also had strange dreams, "Sleep-adventures" which involved travelling through an underground Hell of "Brimstone". (Forty years later these same infernal cityscapes at Birmingham and Preston would inspire Dickens's vision of Coketown in *Hard Times*.)

He soothed himself by talking knowledgeably through the night with a Dutch jeweller about the symbolism of precious stones, and before long the amiable Hollander was promising to make him a pair of seals in red cornelian, "gratis". Coleridge sketched out two designs: one a heraldic riddle based on Charlotte's name; the other his own initials STC entwined decoratively by CB and MM.[8]

By the time he reached Liverpool he was so travel-sore and flea-bitten that he postponed all thoughts of lecturing, and retired for several days to the country residence of his old friend Dr Peter Crompton, where he sampled another industrial product, the delicious thick ale from Crompton's "enormous Brewery in Liverpool". Dr Crompton, in turn, was soon promising to send half a hogshead for the housewarming at Berners Street. Coleridge thought it so fine that he would never need to taste another drop of hard spirits "in secula seculorum".[9]

But as he drew nearer to the Lakes, his mood sobered. He arrived in Kendal at midnight on 17 February, and the following morning called in to collect the unbound copies of *The Friend* for the new London edition, only to find his faithful printer Brown was mysteriously absent. It emerged that he had "absconded" to Scotland a fortnight previously, taking with him all Coleridge's remaining stamped paper worth £20 or £30, and the special typeface worth another £36.[10] Trying to dismiss this ill omen, Coleridge suddenly decided to collect his children instead, and hired a chaise for 5 a.m. on Wednesday, 19 February.

That morning he rode directly over Kirkstone Pass, scene of many heroic delivery-runs, down to the boys' school at Ambleside. The headmaster Mr Dawes called them out of class in the middle of first lesson. The unheralded arrival of their father, dramatically announcing that he had come to take them home for a surprise holiday, produced markedly different reactions in his two sons. The chubby, open-hearted little Derwent (now eleven years old) "came in dancing for Joy"; while Hartley (now rising sixteen and recognized as the cleverest boy in the school) was overcome with embarrassment and anxiety at the sight of his beaming father and the presentiment of family turmoil to come: "he turned pale & trembled all over – then after he had taken some cold water instantly asked me some questions about the connection of the Greek with the Latin . . ."[11]

Coleridge tried to respond tenderly to each in turn, petting Derwent on the drive home ("he can't help crying when he is scolded . . . he ain't such a genius as Hartley"). But when they rattled through Grasmere without stopping at the Wordsworths' new house, both boys were stunned into silence, as Mrs Coleridge later heard. "Poor Hartley sat in speechless astonishment as the Chaise passed the turning to the Vicarage where Wordsworth lives, but he dared not hazard one remark and Derwent fixed his eyes full of tears upon his father, who turned his head away to conceal his own emotions." When she tried to explain to the boys about the quarrel (typically, Coleridge had said nothing to them) Hartley turned "as white as lime".[12]

This set the tone for much of the visit: great bursts of family excitement and cheerful plans, repeatedly punctured by awkward truths and sad realities. Worst of all for the children was the slow realization that their father had not really come home at all, but was making plans for a new life in London far away. In the event Coleridge remained for six weeks, and the Morgans were kept in suspense about his return until mid-April. Coleridge stayed on partly because of the children, partly because he hoped until the very last minute for a reconciliation with Wordsworth and a meeting with Asra. If this had occurred it is not clear whether he would have abandoned London once again, even at so late a date.

After all the high-spirited letters on his journey, there was an ominous break in correspondence with the Morgans for a month. At last, on 24 March, they received a brief note, still dated from Keswick. "Nothing can justify my not writing to you; but in very truth I have been dreadfully bewildered – first of all, I was trifled with most egregiously, off and on, about the Liverpool Lectures – secondly, the Grasmere business has kept me in a fever of agitation – and will end in complete alienation – I have refused to go over, and Wordsworth has refused to apologize . . . and to omit less matters, lastly, Brown, the Printer of the *Friend* . . . has absconded."[13]

He still promised, "if everything else fail", to send a draft of £50; but the growing confusion in his feelings is evident. "I have been in such a state of fever and irritation about the Wordsworths, my reason deciding one way, and my heart pulling me the contrary

– scarcely, daring to set off without seeing them, especially Miss Hutchinson who has done nothing to offend me . . . I have suffered so much that I wish I had not left London."[14]

According to Coleridge, Greta Hall had taken his own side in the Wordsworth affair. Southey thought Montagu had acted with an "absolutely incredible" degree of folly, and that Wordsworth had been "blamable" in his indiscretion: "I do not wonder at Coleridge's resentment."[15] Both Mrs Coleridge and Mrs Southey had twice confronted Wordsworth and Dorothy over the matter, and Mrs Southey had so far "overcome her natural timidity" as to shout at Wordsworth: "it is *you* Sir! *you* – not the things said, true or false!"[16]

That at any rate is what he told the Morgans, but matters may have been less clear cut, especially among the women. In fact, Dorothy had tried secretly to effect a reconciliation, sending "innumerable" private letters and messages to Mrs Coleridge, urging that Coleridge should be encouraged "to write to her and not to leave the country without seeing them". But both men remained immovable on their points of honour. As Mrs Coleridge put it philosophically: "he would not go to *them* and *they* would not come to him".[17]

Curiously it was Asra who now took the hardest line against Coleridge, writing to her cousin John Monkhouse at the end of March: "he is offended with William, or fancies himself so – and expected William to make some advances to him which as he did not he was miserable the whole time he was in Keswick, & Mrs C. was right glad to get him off again, for she had no satisfaction in him – and would have given the world, I dare say, to have had him well again with William."[18] Yet Coleridge still thought Asra was his greatest supporter in the Grasmere household. As for Wordsworth himself, he merely observed that since Coleridge was lecturing and "wearing Powder" on his hair, it was "all pretence".[19] He still confidently expected that Coleridge would eventually appear at his door.

2

Another poet had also been awaiting Coleridge's arrival in the Lake District, but for different reasons. The young Percy Bysshe Shelley and his sixteen-year-old wife Harriet had rented a tiny cottage on the hill outside Keswick in December, anxious to discuss politics and metaphysics with the author of "The Ancient Mariner". The *Cumberland Packet* reported strange goings-on at Chestnut Cottage throughout the winter: extensive postal deliveries, the printing of political pamphlets, and dancing round a bonfire in the garden at night. What the newspaper did not know was that one of Mr Shelley's printings was a broadsheet ballad called "The Devil's Walk", designed to be distributed to unemployed workers in Dublin, and directly based on Coleridge's famous newspaper ballad of 1799, "The Devil's Thoughts".[20]

Shelley frequently visited Greta Hall, but found only Southey in residence, and fell asleep under the tea-table when Southey tried to convince him that his belief in atheism and revolutionary politics was really an adolescent form of Pantheism, from which he had once suffered himself. ("He is just what I was in 1794 . . . I have put him upon a course of Berkeley.") When Coleridge still did not appear, Shelley wrote to introduce himself to William Godwin instead, a shift in ideological direction that altered his whole life.

In the end they only missed each other by a fortnight. Shelley became known locally in Keswick as a radical agitator and his sudden departure was precipitated by a mysterious attack by patriotic "ruffians" one night at his door, which he repelled with drawn pistols. He hurried off with his pamphlets to carry on the struggle in Dublin, catching the boat from Whitehaven on 3 February. Coleridge ever after regretted this lost meeting, while Shelley's admiration for Coleridge's ballads – especially "Christabel" – invested the elder poet with legendary status.[21]

3

Coleridge did make one unexpected and wholly delightful discovery at Greta Hall: the growing brilliance of his third child, little Sara. It was she who had inherited the more academic side of the Coleridge character, and promised to be even cleverer than Hartley. At ten, she was astonishingly widely read, had pursued her Italian, and could even read French "and Latin". She was becoming extremely pretty, and yet her character had none of the self-consciousness or eccentricity that was increasingly evident in Hartley. "She is such a sweet-tempered, meek, blue-eyed Fairy, & so affectionate, trustworthy and really serviceable!"[22]

Coleridge was amazed by her clear thinking, her studious habits, and her linguistic sophistication. One evening reading together by the fire, the word "hostile" came up, and Coleridge casually asked her what exactly it meant. Sara answered without hesitation: "why! inimical: only that inimical is more often used for things and measures, and not, as hostile is, to persons and nations." This perfect dictionary response, a true presentiment of Sara's future scholarship, enchanted him.

Coleridge half-hoped to take her back to London with him "for 4 or 5 months" to oversee her education, but acknowledged that his wife was managing her exceptionally well, and that it would be rather too much to ask the Morgans.[23] Instead he urged that Charlotte should make a special bonnet for "little Sariola", as a mark of his favour. From now on there was a third Sara in his life, who would slowly become of increasing importance. He also began planning to set aside money to send Hartley and Derwent to university.[23] His pride in all his children shines out of these letters to the Morgans; each one is appreciated for his or her particular talents.

But this growing sense of his family life and responsibilities, at the very moment that he was deciding to settle permanently in London, suggests a tragic complication of feelings and divided loyalties. It seemed that he was fated to be a father *in absentia*. It was really the promise of successful London work (he talked of making £800 a year from lecturing) which eased his relations with Mrs Coleridge, together with renewed reassurances over the Wedgwood annuity and the life assurance policy. (The receipt for the 1812 payment was to be meticulously posted to her in May, while he also discovered that she had saved £100 in her own bank account opened at Keswick.)[24]

He told Morgan (discreetly in Latin) that any idea of resumed sexual relations filled him with "horror", but that "thank God! that is neither wished or desired". At the same time he praised his wife as "modest, prudent and the best of mothers", and said that in many ways he found her "more beautiful than when I first met her".[25] Mrs Coleridge for her part, despite the Wordsworth affair, found him "cheerful & good-natured & full of fair promises".

She had no pressing desire, now, to join him in London, and found contentment in the bustling, well-ordered household at Greta Hall with Southey and her sisters. She listened to his optimistic plans, as she later told Tom Poole, with detached but kindly scepticism. "He talked of our settling finally in London, that is, when he had gone on for a year or so giving me, and all his friends satisfaction as to the possibility of making a livelihood by writing so as to enable us to live in great credit there – I listened, I own, with incredulous ears, while he was building these 'airy castles' and calmly told him that I thought it was much better that I and the children should remain in the country until the Boys had finished their School-education and then, if he found himself in circumstances that would admit of it, would cheerfully take leave of our dear Keswick, and follow his amended fortunes . . ."

Meanwhile she approved of his living with the Morgans, was pleased about "the Lectures at Willis' rooms", but had no particular confidence that his literary work would ever amount to anything compared to Wordsworth's or Southey's. It was this lack of respect for his professional abilities, what Coleridge called painfully her inability to appreciate his "sensibilities", which made the marriage so intolerable to him.[26]

Yet the quarrel with Wordsworth, and the break with Asra so intricately enmeshed with it, brought out a curious loyalty in Mrs Coleridge. She may not have told Coleridge that she had seen Sara Hutchinson several times before his arrival at Greta Hall. On these occasions she had defended her husband with spirit. More than that, she had even criticized Asra for the way *she* had betrayed the man who had so obviously loved her. This was an extraordinary reproach to the woman that Mrs Coleridge might reasonably have regarded as her bitter rival in the affections of her husband. It emerged in a subsequent note that Asra sent to Wordsworth from Greta Hall sometime that winter, and throws unexpected light on both women.

"Mrs C. and I have many a battle", Asra wrote confidentially to Wordsworth, "but we do not quarrel – she wonders how I could ever love any one of whom I think so ill; and thinks he [Coleridge] ought to know what I *do* think of him. – Why, I say, every thing that I say to you *have I said to himself* – and all that I believe of him now I believed formerly (except that he should ever have behaved as he has done to you) [Wordsworth] . . . she is angry and thinks I speak resentfully . . . She is sure that we think far worse of him than ever she did, and is now on his *side quite*."[27]

Coleridge hung on for a last few days at Greta Hall, still hoping for some sign from Grasmere, but finally decided that he would return to London for Easter. The boys were dispatched back to Ambleside, he took an "affectionate" farewell from his wife, and rode over to Penrith to catch the mail coach south, promising regular letters and money from his lectures. But Wordsworth obviously controlled the winter elements in the Lake District, and he was not to be allowed to escape so easily.

Heavy snow fell on the eastern passes, and by Good Friday evening Coleridge found himself marooned alone in the inn at Penrith, with the roads closed by twelve-foot drifts.[28] He was stuck there for fifteen days. Only one solitary traveller got through on a horse from Carlisle, with "a most tremendous account of his adventures", having cut a single narrow "horse-path" through the snow which closed up behind him. Ironically, the one means of reaching London was to go back, in a hired post-chaise, via Keswick and Grasmere, to pick up the coach from Kendal. It was as if the very weather had conspired against Coleridge to force him back to Wordsworth's door.

Several letters also reached him from Wordsworth's friends, demanding that he should not leave without calling at Grasmere, including "a most impassioned one" from Catherine Clarkson. Mrs Clarkson had also written to Crabb Robinson, saying that there was "a complete hue & cry" after Coleridge, and that if he did not meet with Wordsworth he might as well "put a pistol to his brains".[29]

How Coleridge withstood this wintry siege is not known. He once wrote frantically to Morgan, "O would to Heaven! I were but once more at your fireside!", but added that he could not accept the humiliation of going back to Grasmere. It is just possible that he wrote secretly to Asra, asking her to join him at Penrith as in the old days, one last time. His Notebooks contain two entries which may date from this grim, lonely fortnight: one a tiny love-poem, the other a heavily deleted paragraph in Greek and German cipher.

The coded entry has been tentatively deciphered as follows. "I don't mean that you have no regard or friendship for me. I know and am grateful for the contrary. But I ere long suspected and now am convinced that it was her personal bondage of usableness . . . from me . . . wholly with any person . . . if with a marked repulsion . . . This had been always so – but at first I was far otherwise. Now I know this clearly – and even now feel myself less and less pained

– and dare promise myself that I shall become perfectly indifferent."[30] The poem is quite clear, a perfect lyric stanza, struck out with a single pen-stroke and not published until 1912, under the anonymous heading "Metrical Experiment". Its imagery goes back to the love-trysts of Gallow Hill:

> Once again, sweet Willow, wave thee!
> Why stays my Love?
> Bend and in yon streamlet – lave thee
> Why stays my Love?
> Oft have I at evening straying,
> Stood, thy Branches long surveying
> Graceful in the light Breeze playing, –
> Why stays my Love?[31]

The one thing Coleridge definitely did do was severely practical: he sent an urgent note to Mrs Coleridge, begging her to send a banker's draft for £50 to Morgan, so the house-purchase would be safe if he did not reach London in time. But that note, too, was lost in the bad weather.[32] Whether he finally escaped from Penrith on the mail, or was forced to take a chaise to Kendal first, is not recorded. But if he used the latter method, as is probable, Coleridge would have driven alone through the snow along the old road of his happiness under Helvellyn, over Dunmail Raise, by the boundary stone carved with their initials and passed within sight of Wordsworth's house at the crossroads to Ambleside. It was the last time he ever visited the Lake District, a bitter farewell.

4

The return to London, which he reached at 5 a.m. on 14 April, was like a return to life. He slept for ten hours at the Bull and Mouth Inn in the City, and then rushed over to the Morgans at Berners Street. The news that the £50 had miscarried was "a thunderbolt", but Morgan had found temporary funds, the house was safe, and all "uneasiness" dispelled by the traveller's return, though Morgan admitted he had suffered much "distress of Mind" on Coleridge's account.[33] Gale and Curtis advanced £50 on the unbound copies of *The Friend* he had managed to retrieve, and Coleridge handed this over to Morgan so the house was now secure.

The publishers were in "high Spirits" with their new author, and thought a second edition would soon be in demand. There was talk of his editing an encyclopaedia and rewriting his play *Osorio* for Drury Lane. His lectures were scheduled to begin on 12 May, and socially he was much in demand.

He dined with Sir George Beaumont and Lady Beaumont announced that she had booked 30 guineas' worth of lecture-tickets to distribute to their friends. He met up again with the painter Washington Allston, who had returned from Italy, and was now flourishing at the Royal Academy, where Dawe's bust of Coleridge was on prominent display. Coleridge felt his "Star" was at last firmly in the ascendant, and promised to set him "even with the World".[34]

A parcel of school-books was sent off to Hartley, Derwent and Sariola, and a cheerful letter to Mrs Coleridge saying he was "an altered man" and took no stimulants "of *any* kind" except for an after-dinner glass of something bravely described as "British White Wine", together, of course, with three or four glasses of port to mitigate its effects.[35]

Yet much of the social interest surrounding Coleridge this spring really concerned his relations with Wordsworth. There had been a good deal of gossiping, and the quarrel had suddenly become the talk of literary London. Coleridge was free with his confidences, and sometimes spoke as if his departure from the Lakes had liberated him from an entire cycle of addiction and dependency. Writing to the MP Richard Sharp (one of *The Friend*'s original subscribers) on 24 April, and confident of obtaining further patronage for the lectures, Coleridge unwisely entered into details of the quarrel, assuming Sharp's sympathy in the matter.

He described Wordsworth as his "bitterest Calumniator" whom he had previously cherished in his "Heart's Heart". He went on: "I gradually obtained conquest over my own Feelings and now dare call myself a freeman, which I did not dare do till I had been at Keswick, & satisfied myself that no possibility remained of my being deluded." He added that his health and activity had since been transformed, and that the Morgans declared that until the break "they had never seen me as *myself*".[36]

Such confidences might well have been understood in the Lambs' circle, but they were hostages to fortune in a wider world. Sharp was outraged. He refused to have anything to do with the lectures, talked abroad of Coleridge's accusations, and with inexplicable malice actually passed the letter on to Grasmere. It was a situation that could not endure. Indeed Wordsworth had already decided to act. Having failed to confront Coleridge privately at Keswick or Penrith, he at last determined on the much more dramatic and public step of pursuing him openly to London to seek a formal explanation. Three weeks before the lectures were due to begin, he arrived at Sir George Beaumont's in Grosvenor Square. On 27 April he was consulting with Charles Lamb, determined to have "the business sifted to the bottom" immediately.[37]

All their friends were now forced to take sides as if it were a marital divorce. Wordsworth was evidently very angry with the tales of Coleridge's "plentiful abuse", and was indignant when Lamb tried to defend his old friend with tactful explanations. "I do not know that I was ever more roused in my Life", he wrote to Mary Wordsworth, "and I feel the effects in my stomache at this moment."[38] When urged that he would upset Coleridge's lectures, he remarked bitterly: "One guinea the course upon the Drama. This is a most odious way of picking up money, and scattering about his own and his friend's thoughts."[39] Coleridge in turn was angry and dismayed when he heard the news. "Mr Wordsworth is in town; & at a time when I require the most perfect tranquillity of mind, I am plunged into the hot water of that bedeviled Cauldron, Explanation with alienated Friendship."[40]

5

Both men revealed a good deal of themselves in the series of confrontations and manoeuvres that followed. Wordsworth was restrained, self-confident and relentless in the pursuit of justice to his reputation. Coleridge was wildly emotional, self-dramatizing and desperate for some show of tender-heartedness. Ultimately Wordsworth believed the "business" could be settled; while Coleridge feared that the "magic" of friendship had been lost forever.

Wordsworth conducted the affair something like a military campaign, keeping well clear of the actual battleground. His first salvo from Grosvenor Square arrived at Berners Street in the shape of Charles Lamb, deputed as his emissary, on 1 May. Wordsworth would not meet privately with Coleridge, the most obvious thing to do in the circumstances. Instead, he proposed a formal confrontation between Basil Montagu and Coleridge in his presence, with Josiah Wedgwood as judicial arbiter. Wordsworth would then listen to both sides, and decide who was telling the truth.

Not unnaturally, Coleridge refused to attend such a court-martial. It was wholly unsuitable that Wedgwood, as his patron, should be involved. And besides, if Montagu declared to his face "that he did not say what I solemnly aver that he did", then Coleridge would be forced to challenge him to a duel.[41] Moreover there was the sensitive subject of Asra, which could only be discussed in private. Prior to any meeting, Coleridge wished "to transmit to Wordsworth a statement which I long ago began with the intention of sending it to Mrs Wordsworth's Sister – but desisted in consequence of understanding that she has already decided the matter against me." Would Wordsworth now read this letter, and then meet in private?

Lamb took back these remarks, which Coleridge clarified in a letter to Lamb on 2 May. The substance was passed on to Wordsworth as intended. It contained notable concessions. "I never felt as matter of serious Complaint, *what* was stated to have been said – (for this, tho' painfully aggravated, was yet substantially true) – but *by* WHOM it was said, and *to* whom, & *how & when*." It also urged the untimeliness of the whole affair, "when every Thought should be given to my Lectures". He did feel "cruelly & unkindly treated".[42]

Wordsworth immediately sensed dangerous waters. He withdrew the proposed confrontation with Montagu, but refused absolutely to read any document involving Sara Hutchinson, which would "degrade him" and which was an "unmanly" suggestion "to say the least of it".[43]

Coleridge then wrote a long letter directly to Wordsworth on 4 May, describing in detail the events of October 1811 when he first came to London with the Montagus, but making no reference to Asra. He denied that he had gossiped unnecessarily to Southey, or Sir George Beaumont about the quarrel (though he did not mention Sharp), and suggested that Mrs Clarkson was responsible for much of the public scandal. As to the famous powder in his hair, he pointed out rather pathetically that he was growing increasingly grey.

He ended "whatever be the result of this long delayed explanation, I have loved you & your's too long & too deeply to have it in my own power to cease to do so."[44]

However, Wordsworth simply refused to open this letter either. First Coleridge must send assurance that it contained "nothing but a naked statement of what he believes Montagu said to him", which he would only then read and pass on to Montagu "to see how their reports accord".[45] This arctic response seems to have hurt Coleridge very deeply, for it was, as he told Crabb Robinson, plainly "insulting or unfriendly". Lamb too was astonished by Wordsworth's coldness, and knowing how deeply Coleridge's feelings ran, he sorrowfully withdrew from all further negotiations. There matters rested for four days, with Coleridge's lectures now less than a week away. It was, he told Lamb, "grievously unseasonable . . . just as I had begun to feel the firm Ground under my feet".[46]

However, by stonewalling Wordsworth had manoeuvred himself into a corner. He had come to London specifically to settle "this vile business . . . the Coleridge matter", but he had made no progress, and he had glimpsed the troubled waters of Asra beginning to stir once again. The public gossip continued to mount.[47] Dorothy had written with further tales from Mrs Clarkson, and concluded that Coleridge was now incapable of telling the truth about anything and was determined to make a scandal. She now thought, rather bitterly, that Coleridge was "glad of a pretext to break with us, and to furnish himself with a ready excuse for all his failures in duty to himself and others".[48]

She had been shaken to receive instructions from Mrs Coleridge at Keswick to pack up three chests of Coleridge's books from their library at Grasmere (most of them German books for his lectures), and a formal request for permission to reprint Wordsworth's conclusion to the "Essay on Epitaphs" in the new edition of *The Friend*. Wordsworth did not grant this permission, but he saw that he had done nothing either to silence Coleridge or to appease him.

The possibilities of the whole affair now escalating further under its own momentum were not attractive. Wordsworth had recently applied to the Lord Lieutenant of Cumberland, asking to be considered for any convenient minor public office that lay at his Lordship's disposal, as a way of augmenting his literary income which was no longer enough to support his growing family.[49] As a candidate for such an appointment, he simply could not afford a scandal. His friendship with Coleridge, for so many years the great support and sustenance of his literary career, now looked more and more like a dangerous professional liability.

On 8 May, with Coleridge's lectures only four days away, Wordsworth renewed his campaign. He took the unexpected and perhaps slightly risky step of consulting Coleridge's friend Henry Crabb Robinson, a man whom he only knew through the Clarksons. Crabb Robinson proved a far shrewder plenipotentiary than Lamb. Flattered to be confided in by Wordsworth, and genuinely keen to effect a reconciliation, he revealed great talents as a diplomat, while secretly noting down every stage of the manoeuvres in his diary. He was fascinated to be so closely involved with "two *such men* as W. & C. . . . One I believe the greatest man now living in this Country. And the other a man of astonishing genius & talents, though not harmoniously blended as in his happier friend to form a great & good man."[50]

After talking for some time of poetry and politics (especially the war in Spain) to sound Robinson out, Wordsworth then spoke with great frankness about Coleridge. The one thing he denied was actually having "commissioned" Basil Montagu to pass on his views. For the rest he did not deny "having said he had no hopes of Coleridge"; or having conveyed the opinion that Coleridge was "rotting out his entrails by intemperance", though he doubted if he had used that exact expression. He did not object to meeting Coleridge, but would rather not see him alone. "He was fearful of those bursts of passion – or rather weakness – of which Coleridge is capable"; and hated it when Coleridge burst into tears "instead of defending himself". He detested Coleridge's drunkenness and opium-taking, yet still had the highest opinion of his gifts. "Coleridge's habits had, in fact, been of a kind which he, Wordsworth, could not have endured but for the high estimation he had formed of Coleridge." Wordsworth thought his powers of mind "to be greater than those of any man he ever knew. From such a man, under favourable influences everything might be looked for. His genius he thought to be great, but his talents greater still, and it is in the union of so much genius with so much talent, that Coleridge surpasses all the men Wordsworth ever knew."[51]

When Robinson asked tentatively if Wordsworth thought Coleridge might be jealous of him, Wordsworth "totally rejected the supposition", adding that "envy & jealousy of that kind were faults of which Coleridge was utterly free".[52] On the other hand, nothing was said of Asra.

Robinson was much struck by the decided and sensible way in which Wordsworth spoke, and by his extraordinary praise of Coleridge. Yet like Lamb he was surprised by Wordsworth's evident coolness. However, he agreed to walk round immediately to Berners Street, and to give Coleridge a carefully edited version of what Wordsworth had said, to ask for a written statement of what Coleridge had heard from Montagu, and to press for a reconciliation.

This he did, with some success. Coleridge agreed to draw up the statement, but asked in turn for a written reply from Wordsworth. What struck Robinson was the emotional difference between the two men. "Coleridge manifested certainly much more feeling than Wordsworth. He was agitated and affected, even to tears . . . then burst into strong expressions of his love for Wordsworth."[53] Robinson did not stay long – "I was apprehensive of saying too much" – but went round to Lamb's, continuing his shuttle diplomacy. Lamb still thought Wordsworth "cold", but Robinson said he preferred "healthful coolness" in negotiations to Coleridge's "heat of disease". Both agreed that Coleridge was "disturbed" by Wordsworth's presence in London, "and the effect on his lectures may be bad". The reconciliation must be speedy.[54]

Accordingly, on Sunday, 10 May, just two days before the lectures, Robinson called round "by appointment" at Berners Street, and collected Coleridge's written statement. It was evident that Coleridge had been upset the entire weekend, and when he tried to read the statement he burst into tears again. But the statement impressed Robinson as containing "the most indubitable internal evidence of truth". When he took it immediately back to Wordsworth it had its "due effect".

They had a further long conversation about Coleridge – "much was confidential" – and decided to draw up a written reply the following day, answering everything point by point. This document required all Crabb Robinson's legal skills to draft and re-draft, and took all the morning of Monday, 11 May, the very day before the lectures were due to begin. Wordsworth had "great difficulty" with it, as he had "to reconcile things very difficult to unite – the most exact truth and sincerity with the giving his friend the least possible pain".[55]

They finally arrived at the following formula. Wordsworth "most solemnly denied" the general charge of having commissioned Montagu to say anything against Coleridge on his behalf, and one by one turned aside the offensive phrases as inaccurately reported to him. "I also affirm as sacredly that though in some of the particulars enumerated by C. as having wounded his feelings there is something of the *form* of truth there is *absolutely nothing of the Spirit* in any of them." He freely acknowledged "an error in judgement" in having ever spoken to Montagu "upon so delicate a subject". He accepted Coleridge's version of events, not as necessarily true in itself, but "as an expression of his conviction" of what was said by Montagu (Robinson's skilful touch was evident here). He reiterated the "love and affection" which he still entertained for Coleridge, and which he trusted Coleridge still "entertains for me". Finally he hoped that no other "points" remained to be settled between them, but it there were, that "no farther steps may be taken till C. has closed the Lectures".[56]

It was an admirable document of its kind, and Crabb Robinson was convinced, correctly as it turned out, that Coleridge would accept it. It also made a convert of Crabb Robinson himself, who was deeply impressed by Wordsworth's behaviour under circumstances that were not unlike a cross-examination at the bar. "The conversation that accompanied the writing it was highly interesting and exhibited Wordsworth in a most honourable light. His integrity, his purity, his delicacy are alike eminent. How preferable is the *coolness* of such a man to the heat of Coleridge."[57] The document was delivered to Berners Street that afternoon, and Coleridge later said it was "perfectly satisfactory to him", though by then quite other and dramatic events had overtaken them all.

6

It was also, in the longer perspective, a deliberate evasion. There is a sense in which Coleridge was evidently seeking a far more fundamental confrontation with his old friend, and which Wordsworth was determined to avoid – and did so successfully. Crabb Robinson's back-and-forth diplomacy reduced to almost legalistic quibbles and concessions a current of feeling between the two poets, in which artistic debts and emotional claims of the most profound kind were censored and suppressed. Ten years later Coleridge would still speak of this break with Wordsworth, and the loss of Asra which it involved, as two of the "griping and grasping Sorrows" that darkened his whole life: "the former spread a wider gloom over the world around me, the latter left a darkness deeper within myself."[58]

At the time, writing directly to Wordsworth on the afternoon of 11 May, he tried to reaffirm their ancient allegiance in a burst of feeling quite different from anything that Wordsworth's careful sentences had expressed. "I declare before God Almighty that at no time even of my sorest affliction did even the *possibility* occur to me of ever doubting your word. I never ceased for a moment to have faith in you, to love & revere you: tho' I was unable to explain an unkindness, which seemed anomalous in your character."[59]

But privately Coleridge knew that Wordsworth, in some irretrievable way, had rejected him. He had closed down that dialogue of intense emotions which had animated their work and friendship, in sickness and in health, for some fifteen years. He would write later to Tom Poole with an expressive mixture of grief and anger: "a Reconciliation has taken place – but the *Feeling* which I had previous to that moment, when the ¾ths Calumny burst like a Thunder-storm from a blue Sky on my Soul – after 15 years of such religious, almost superstitious, Idolatry & Self-sacrifice – O no! no! that I fear, never can return. All outward actions, all inward Wishes, all Thoughts & Admirations, will be the same – *are* the same – but – aye there remains an immedicable *But*." It was a loss that "cut to the Heart-core of STC".

As Mrs Coleridge put it in her best, laconic manner: "I may venture to say, there will never be *that* between them which was in days of yore – but it has taught C. one useful lesson; that even his dearest & most indulgent friends . . . are *as* clear-sighted to his failings, & much *less* delicate in speaking of them, than his Wife . . ."[61]

For Wordsworth, one suspects, it was precisely the *feeling* that had become the problem. His "loss of hopes" in Coleridge, his knowledge of his opium addiction, his experience of endless prevarications and domestic impracticalities, his derelictions of duty and professional disasters, were all accepted now as an inevitable part of what he still considered as matchless gifts and potential "under favourable influences". But Coleridge's emotional turmoil, his insatiable claims on the whole Grasmere household through Asra, had become too much, too oppressive, too dangerous. As Crabb Robinson saw, with almost feline acuity, it was the emotional confrontation that Wordsworth flinched from, and indeed perhaps feared.

In rejecting Coleridge, Wordsworth was in his own way defending his own domestic life in the Lake District. He was saying goodbye to the claims of his youth. He was stabilizing his affairs, both financial and emotional, within a more conventional framework. During these weeks in London he was waiting upon Lord Lonsdale, and negotiating for the post as Distributor of Stamps for Cumberland that would assure his family income for the next decades.[62] He was also writing his wife Mary a series of passionate love-letters, which confirmed all his domestic loyalties to her, to their children, and to his extended household at Grasmere.

These letters are unique in his correspondence, an expression of marital fidelity and explicitly sexual happiness, which runs in close alternation with his detailed accounts of "this ugly affair of Coleridge".[63] They surprised and delighted Mary, who answered them in kind, while hoping the "unpleasant business of Coleridge" would soon be concluded. Something was evidently released in Wordsworth during this whole episode, even to the point of rapture. He wrote to Mary on 7 May: "My sweetest darling . . . I love thee so deeply and tenderly and constantly, and with such perfect satisfaction, delight & happiness to my soul, that I scarcely can bring my pen to write of anything else."[64]

On one occasion he found he had carried his "tender and overflowing expressions of Love" unwittingly on to the outside of the franked envelope, and had much trouble in making them illegible with blottings-out so they should not be read by strangers, but only the one person "that I absolutely pant to behold".[65]

In one of his most moving and voluptuous passages, written over the same weekend that he was drafting the reconciliation document to Coleridge, his thoughts were carried back to Gallow Hill exactly as Coleridge's had been in his last love-lyric to Asra. But what Wordsworth remembered was not Asra but Mary, his true wife. "Oh could I but see thee again . . . [as] thou wert when thou came down the lane to meet at Gallow Hill on my return with Dorothy from France. Never shall I forget thy rich & flourishing and genial mien & appearance. Nature had dressed thee out as if expressly I might receive thee to my arms in the full blow of health and happiness."[66]

This was a memory from the time of their courtship in 1802. But now Wordsworth also expressed a sense of a secured and completed domestic circle, which included Asra as well as his children. "O my Mary, what a heavenly thing is pure & ever growing Love; such do I feel for thee, and Dorothy and Sara and all our dear family. Write thou to me long and tenderly . . ."[67] But of course it no longer included Coleridge, who was cast out from that circle of tenderness, just as he had feared for so long.

The carefully negotiated peace-treaty with Coleridge had secured the new boundaries. Wordsworth was now willing enough to call upon him and attend his lectures. But public violence suddenly burst upon them all and swept private affairs aside. At 5 p.m. on Monday, 11 May 1812, just two hours after Coleridge had dispatched his note of acceptance to Wordsworth, the prime minister, Spencer Perceval, was shot dead in the lobby of the House of Commons.

7

The assassin was John Bellingham, a bankrupt businessman from Liverpool, who blamed the government's wartime policies for the widespread unemployment and civil unrest in the industrial cities of the North and Midlands. Coleridge had seen some of these conditions on his coach trip in February, and for months the newspapers had been full of reports of Luddite frame-breaking and rioting. Now the violence had come south.

No such political assassination had taken place in Britain since the time of the Civil War, and a general feeling of crisis quickly spread across the whole country. There was talk of mass demonstrations in the Midlands, of the radical MP Sir Francis Burdett leading a parliamentary coup in London, and a written threat against the Prince Regent's life received by *The Times*. Ballads celebrating Bellingham were openly on sale in the streets. There was a widely reported fear of "a general uprising in the manufacturing districts". The unrest was fuelled by general economic hardship: wartime taxes, inflation, high unemployment, appalling working conditions in the factories – as well as a feeling that the war had gone on too long, the government was corrupt, the monarchy unpopular, and the House of Commons increasingly unrepresentative. For the Romantic radicals of the 1790s – for men like Coleridge and Wordsworth – the Prime Minister's assassination was a watershed in their perception of public affairs. It no longer seemed possible to identify with the disillusion and violence of the popular cause.[68]

Yet their reactions were subtly different. Wordsworth stood back from events in shock and alarm; while Coleridge, all of his journalistic instincts aroused, hurried out into the streets to see for himself. Wordsworth wrote grimly to his wife: "the lower orders of the People in London cry out 'Burdett for ever' in the Pot houses, deeming him their champion . . . The country is no doubt in a most alarming situation; and if much firmness be not displayed by the Government confusion & havoc & murder will break out and spread terribly."[69] He later booked a place to witness Bellingham's execution from the tower of Westminster Abbey. (In the event it took place on 18 May outside Newgate Prison, and Wordsworth missed it.)

But when he hurried over to Berners Street at 8 o'clock on the morning of 12 May, he found that Coleridge had already left for the offices of the *Courier* in Fleet Street, offering to write whatever leader or obituary Stuart might require. His article appeared two days later, deploring "this atrocious assassination", praising Perceval as a statesman, and contrasting the military despotism in France with the constitutional government in England. He acknowledged "the distresses" of the people, but argued that this was part of "the perturbed state of the civilized world". Nonetheless, he concluded, "our country demands the voice of alarm and warning": a hint that reforms as well as repressive measures were required.[70]

Coleridge then postponed his lectures at Willis's Rooms, and set off to take his own soundings in the large public houses around Oxford Street. He was shaken by what he heard. "Nothing but exultation – Burdett's Health drank with a Clatter of Pots – & a Sentiment given to at least 50 men & women – 'May Burdett soon be the man to have Sway over us!' – These were the very words. 'This is but the beginning' – 'More of these damned Scoundrels must go the same way – & then poor people may live' – 'Every man might maintain his family decent & comfortable if the money were not picked out of our pockets by them damned Placemen' . . . 'They won't hear Burdett – No! he is a Christian man & speaks for the Poor' – etc. etc. – I do not think, I have altered a word."[71]

Coleridge was not able to publish such inflammatory reportage in the daily press, but he sent it verbatim to Southey, and urged him to use it in the *Quarterly*. He felt no one had appreciated the "true gigantic magnitude" of the event and its social implications. Nobody in power had recognized the forces that drove it: "I mean, the sinking down of Jacobinism below the middle & tolerably educated Classes into the Readers & all-swallowing Auditors in Taprooms etc. of the Statesman, Examiner, Cobbett etc."[72]

Coleridge reflected a good deal on this political sea-change coming over Britain, both frightened and fascinated by it. Later in the summer, when the initial panic had died down, he wrote to John Rickman at Westminster saying that *The Friend* (then just republished) had foreseen, but not clearly enough, these "momentous" issues. He now felt "perplexed & darkling & dissatisfied", seeing that something must be done to make the constitution more representative, but uncertain how this could be achieved without making the House of Lords "a Puppet-shew", and the Commons into a French-style National Convention. "The Subject is the Constitution of our Country & the Expediency? and (if expedient) the practicability? of an Improvement (for Reform is either a misnomer or a Lie to all our History) of the House of Commons."

He was struck by the weakness of the ministries and party factions within parliament; and outside it by "the rapid Increase both of unorganized and of self-organizing Power & Action throughout the Kingdom". This was a shrewd intuition of the age of reform clubs and trade unions (first legally recognized in 1825) which was dawning. All this made a "deep impression" on him as far as "the wish for some Improvement goes". But there was as yet no "grand *outline*" for change, no "true virile productive strong-Sense" in the government, and the landed and propertied MPs were "cowardly". He felt it was a hopeless business until "some fortunate Giant-mind starts up & revolutionizes all the present notions concerning the education of both Gentry & Middle Classes".[73]

It was to this idea of a revolutionized national education that Coleridge's later political thinking would steadily turn.[74] It was not democratic in the fullest sense, indeed it was in many ways essentially elitist, but it offered a way out of the *impasse* of reactionary Toryism, into which many of his contemporaries like Wordsworth and Southey were now to be forced. Their position suggested to him "the Image of the Irishman on the Bough with his face toward the Trunk sawing himself off".[75] What he feared most was not popular passion, but popular ignorance. As he put it in his Notebooks in May: "that thin & meagre Knowledge, which spreads over the people at large, in taking away their errors takes away too those feelings, those magnificent Truths implied in those errors or consequent from them which are the offspring of the human Heart, the god-like Idea, breathed into Man as Man".[76]

8

The political crisis had one most immediate effect on Coleridge's fortunes. There was a complete collapse of attendance at Willis's Rooms. When his postponed lectures opened on 19 May, the day after Bellingham's execution, the expected audience of 500 had dwindled to fifty. Though Lady Beaumont had distributed thirty tickets among her Mayfair friends, and the publishers John Murray and Gale and Curtis had made small group bookings, the sense of major literary occasion had dissipated, and was never recovered.

The *Morning Chronicle* optimistically advertised all six lectures of the first series up to 5 June under the rubric "The Mirror of Fashion". It noted the Beaumonts, Sir James Mackintosh, Samuel Rogers, William Sotheby, "Mr Wordsworth and other literary men" in attendance. But in fact the series was now entirely unfashionable. This was clearly indicated by the signal absence of Lord Byron, who was now the true "glass of fashion and mould of form", having taken the literary world by storm with the publication of the first two Cantos of *Childe Harold's Pilgrimage* in March. ("All the world is talking of it," said Coleridge in one of his most wonderfully rueful asides, ". . . but from what I hear, it is exactly on the plan that I myself had not only conceived six years ago, but have the whole Scheme drawn out in one of my old Memorandum Books.")[77]

The *Sun* newspaper recorded "an admirable display of profound research conveyed in an extraordinary proof of extemporaneous eloquence", but in reality Coleridge was quite disheartened and attempted nothing new. He fell back on a learned discussion of ancient Greek and classical French drama, developed point by point from Schlegel and Schelling. Crabb Robinson described them as "excellent and very German", but was evidently rather bored.[78] When the second series of six began on 9 June, the season was very late, fashionable London was departing for the country, and the newspapers stopped reporting them altogether.[79]

Far from securing his new aristocratic audience, Coleridge had barely covered his costs. He wrote wryly to Murray: "I dreamt, that a great Lord had made me a most splendid Promise; awoke, and found it as much a delusion, as if the great Lord had really made me a Promise."[80] He broke off his second series on 16 June, attempting a final flourish with his great set-piece lecture on *Hamlet*, but there were barely a score of people to hear him in the huge echoing lecture-room. Crabb Robinson (who had not attended) "felt degraded" to hear that "a great man" had been reduced to collecting 5/6d tickets at the door of Willis's Rooms.[81]

Wordsworth had decided, as a gesture of goodwill, to attend all the first series before leaving London on 6 June. He also attended, unusually for him, a number of smart literary salons, meeting Lord Byron, the recently knighted Sir Humphry and Lady Davy, the Scottish playwright Joanna Baillie, the poetess Mrs Barbauld, an unnamed duchess with "a native bosom so huge and tremendous" that it trembled over him "like two great hay-cocks", and the Princess Regent with her permanent expression of "hilarity".[82] For the first time in his life he was lionized, and felt clearly the position he had established. Crabb Robinson basked in the reflected glow of "the homage involuntarily paid him" on these occasions. "Everybody was anxious to get near him", and several young ladies were "ludicrously fidgety" to catch Wordsworth's attention.[83]

By contrast, Wordsworth felt that Coleridge's social stock had fallen low. He made no comment on the lectures, except to observe that he did not think "they will bring him much profit". He noted with something suspiciously like satisfaction that Coleridge was much criticized in smart circles. "He has a world of bitter enemies, and is deplorably unpopular. – Besides people of rank are very shabby for the most part, and will never pay their five shillings when they can avoid it . . . But you cannot form a notion to what degree Coleridge is disliked or despised not withstanding his great talents, his genius & vast attainments."

Wordsworth did not explain the cause of this hostility, but implied that the world now thought as he did, that Coleridge was a hopeless case, unreliable in all his dealings, with his daily actions "as little under his own power as at any period of his life". It was true that he now got up in the mornings "between 8 & 9 or earlier"; but he was still chaotic by any conventional standards. When the young Lord Thurlow had sent him a first volume of his poems, privately published and "superbly bound", Wordsworth had heard that Coleridge had not even bothered to reply.[84]

He himself felt at ease in society, except on one occasion when he gave his opinion that Sir Francis Burdett was indirectly responsible for the assassination, by inflammatory speeches about soldiers "murdering the people". To his surprise, all the young men in the room immediately turned on him "in a rude offensive manner".[85]

Wordsworth was, nonetheless, very curious to see Coleridge's new household with the Morgans, and especially the two Morgan women. Though he met Coleridge in company several times, as a public token of their reconciliation, and once walked with him before lunch as far as Hampstead, he continued to call round at Berners Street unannounced until he found the whole family at home after one of the lectures, and dined with them. He wrote to Mary that he liked the two women "much", and would describe them in more detail; while he referred to John as "that good Creature Morgan".

He went round again the morning before he left London on 8 June. "Mrs Morgan I think, I once described as a handsome woman, but she is not so. – She has a round face, dark eyes, an upturned or a pug nose, nevertheless as her complexion is good, her eye bright, and her countenance animated & good-natured and she has the appearance of being in redundant health, she is, what would be called, a desirable woman . . ."

He was similarly intrigued by Charlotte. "The other Sister has a smaller round face, an upturned nose also, and is thinner & more delicate in appearance, and of more still & gentle manners." It is odd that Wordsworth did not remark on Charlotte's physical likeness to the young Asra, which Charles Lamb thought so striking as to be uncanny.[86] But he did hint to Mary that the Morgan women were very much city people, the daughters of trade, with a certain brashness and vulgarity about them. If Charlotte was comparatively shy and quiet, Mary Morgan's "carriage" – by which he meant her dress as well as her physical deportment and manner – was what he called "unwary, luxuriant & joyous".

Wordsworth knew very well that he was looking at Coleridge's chosen substitute for the Grasmere household, and his reactions were guarded. He thought Coleridge in much better health at Berners Street, well looked after, and living "far more rationally than he did with us, so that he has changed for the better assuredly". He added, dryly: "I think his present situation & employments upon the whole quite eligible for him."[87]

With that Wordsworth left London, to go walking with his brother Christopher in Kent. All further thoughts of Coleridge were shortly after swept from his mind by the terrible news from Dorothy that his little daughter Catherine had unexpectedly died at Grasmere. At the very moment that he and Mary had been rejoicing in their family happiness and security, it was shaken by this death; and six months later the blow was to be repeated in the death of their little boy Tom. For Wordsworth the year 1812 was to be one of loss and bereavement, and the loss of Coleridge came to seem in retrospect part of a tragic pattern, and the end of the most hopeful part of his life.

As Dorothy later wrote of Coleridge in sombre, reflective mood: "God bless him. He little knows with what tenderness we have lately thought of him, nor how entirely we are softened to all sense of injury.'[88]

9

For Coleridge, the bustle and drama of spring 1812 gave way to a drear and directionless summer. Despite the comforts of Berners Street, he could settle to no clear plan. He wrote few letters – none at all to Keswick – and his Notebooks were almost silent. In the new political situation he felt discouraged with the idea of continuing *The Friend*, though he still worked intermittently on his play.

In August he wrote to Stuart offering a series of political essays on general themes: the disturbed state of parliament, the war with America, the feeling of "Disorganization" throughout the country, the political role of the Church, and the principle of toleration.[89] To John Murray he also offered a curious anthology, to be culled from his "Memorandum & common-place Books", of anecdotes and epigrams from German, Spanish and Italian authors "of which no translation exists", and to be entitled *Exotics Naturalized*.

But he felt ill and dispirited, and none of this was done. Opium-dosing increased, his digestion was bad, his chest painful, and his right leg swelled up with a kind of "Erypsypelatous Inflammation". He consulted a new physician, Dr Robert Gooch, who bluntly diagnosed all his symptoms as "evils produced by the use of narcotics". He prescribed mercury in the form of Corbyn's Blue Pills, nitric acid in water, and "a known & measured quantity of Stimulant, with an attempt to diminish the Opiate part of it little by little, if it were only a single Drop in two days". But Coleridge felt the sickness was in his heart, and the best part of the cure lay simply in talking to the doctor and trying to put him "in possession of the *whole* of my Case with all its symptoms, and all its known, probable and suspected Causes."[90]

He thought much of these "symptoms and causes". Inevitably, he was turning increasingly to Mary and Charlotte for sympathy, and perhaps something more. But beyond a certain point, here he felt obscurely rejected. Their very closeness as sisters, which he had once celebrated in his poem of 1807, now tantalized him with an inner circle of affection he could not enter. Ironically, in this too they seemed very like Mary Wordsworth and Asra. They were "beautiful, feminine, attractive, without affectation – add to this amusing and . . . of excellent Good Sense". Yet with all this they were not "permanently lovely or loveable", in the way that he had hoped.

He puzzled over this harsh verdict. "How can this be? They are loveless – if any trait of the Lover appear, it is to each other. To each other I have noticed a soft, soothing, caressing character. But to men, however intimate . . . they will *do* indeed everything that can be wished – but they will *look* nothing, *say* (attune) nothing." If this revealed something of the Brent sisters' closeness, it revealed even more of Coleridge's continuing, greedy hunger for feeling and tenderness – still cuckoo-like, still unappeased, still demanding nesting-rights within his companions' hearts. It was almost as if he expected the same conjugal treatment as John Morgan. Indeed he wanted so much – "the flush, the overflow, the rapture" – but who now could give him all this?[91]

Sometimes he still thought of Asra, but now he tried to tell himself bitterly that this was his own weakness. In September he came across a passage from Schiller's *Don Carlos* which he carefully copied down (editing and improving as he went) as a dramatization of what his feelings should be. If his life had been a play, then this is how his character should respond. "O! this terrible love has swept away all the early burgeoning of my spirit, never to return . . . I have been sunk in a long, heavy dream – that I loved! – Now I am awake! Let the past be forgotten. At last I see there is a greater, more desirable good than to possess you. – Here are your letters back. Destroy mine. Do not fear any more outbursts. It is past. A pure fire has burnt clean my spirit!"

But Coleridge could not sustain such noble renunciation. He listed all the places of their love as a litany of regret "Sockburn, Middleham, Gallow-Hill, Keswick, Grasmere!" For him, such memories could never be burnt away. He could *act* as if they could, "but to *feel*, to be it. O weak of heart, never! Asra, Asra . . ." Yet slowly he thought the intensity of his longing was fading into the past.[92]

He thought too of his own children, as well he might. Here the case was different. The very fact of their existence brought him hope, and altered the sense of his own identity. Whereas his life had once contained a single continuous Self, like a single advancing line, there was now a divided Self like two paths, separated by the past and the future. At certain moments he could be conscious of the two trajectories simultaneously, like the pagan god with two faces, "Janus, capable of both".

He valued "that *much-suggesting* Mood, with which we look back on our own youth with a feeling strictly analogous to that with which we regard our offspring: as if the line on each side of the central point representing the Present . . . were different only by an arbitrary relation like that of Right & Left." It was as if he moved forward over a great flat plain, and "by an arbitrary accident of my turning North or South", could see these two Selves travelling parallel in the past and in the future. He drew a little compass diagram in his Notebook, with a zero at the centre, and "Past Self, in Childhood Youth etc." fanned out to the left; and "Future Self in others, children, Sons etc." fanned out to the right.[93]

It was a conception similar to his poem "Hope and Time". This may have been first drafted at Stowey in 1807, but he seems to have worked on it throughout these years and it was not published until 1817. It is both an image of his own childhood in "ancient days", and of his own children in the future. It has the same mysterious movement across a symbolic landscape, "some Elfish Place", and the same mysterious division between two identities, past and future. But it can also be seen as a simple memory of Hartley and little Sara playing, and it is this which makes it so strange and compelling:

> Two winged Children run an endless Race –
> A Sister and a Brother!
> But HOPE outruns the other –
> Yet ever flies she with reverted Face,
> And looks and listens for the Boy behind;
> TIME is his Name – and he, alas! is blind,
> With regular Step o'er rough and smooth he passed,
> And knows not whether he is first or last.[94]

But the diagram in his Notebook of 1812 is not a poem. It is a retreat from a fully imagined world into one of pure symbolic abstraction. Abstraction seemed to soothe Coleridge at this time, like a navigator at sea in a storm quietly drawing course-bearings at his chart-table.

He drew another one on the back of a letter enquiring if he intended to lecture again at the Royal Institution. This diagram consisted of pairs of back-to-back triangles, and was headed "True Love Illustrated Geometrically". Its proposition was that the ideally matched couple were held together by their differences as much as their similarities: "i.e. Opposites & yet Correspondences". The long shared base-line of "Love's compound triangles" represented a common nature, the foundation of a relationship. But they were drawn together by the "opposite poles" of character which only met at the apex of the triangle. Perfect love was essentially "reciprocal". The man and the woman took "spiritual Possession" of each other, precisely through the qualities each lacked.

His triangles no longer had the old beloved Grasmere initials attached, as in earlier Notebooks; they were marked blankly A, B and C. When Coleridge put this geometry of human passion into explanatory notes, the images that came to him were equally impersonal and mechanical, though none the less vivid and sexual for that. "Thus the wards of a Lock are at once opposite and yet correspondent to the Turns of its Key – so the Cup and Ball, as in the moveable Bones of the Knee – thus too the sexes throughout all Nature." One exception struck him, from one of Blumenbach's learned botanical volumes he had read long ago in Göttingen: the bisexual earth-worm, which was "at once Male & Female". Yet even with the earth-worm, he surmised, "the species is continued in pairs, so each is Male & Female to the other, and not to itself".[95] So Coleridge continued to dwell on the mystery of love, even though it had slipped away from him in so many forms, and perhaps for that very reason.

In his withdrawn mood Coleridge had no communication with Keswick throughout the summer and autumn, hoping he would have better financial tidings before the year was out. Mrs Coleridge had learned of the "reconciliation" directly from Wordsworth, and was kept in mind of her husband by Hartley, who was growing up more and more like his father – deeply absorbed in his classical reading, maddening and procrastinatory in his habits, and quite astonishing in his talk. When the educational expert Dr Bell visited Greta Hall, he described Hartley as "a Genius by the manner of opening his Mouth".

Mrs Coleridge took a more down to earth view: perhaps Hartley would make his fortune in the Law. "He has the 'Gift of the Gab' – in no small degree, and, notwithstanding what he says of fears and tremblings, a great confidence in speaking. – He is a great favourite in the neighbourhood of his School, and perhaps a little spoilt by being often in the company of people of fashion, where he is not only permitted, but *expected* to talk." Like father, like son. She told Poole that she had now approached both Wordsworth and Southey about getting her sons into university, as she openly doubted Coleridge would ever be able to finance them. She was touched that Wordsworth showed "a most friendly regard for these Boys, and an ardent interest in their future well-doing".[96]

10

In fact Coleridge had roused himself, and planned a return to lecturing. By September he had proposed an immensely ambitious new course to Richard Saumarez, the director of the Surrey Institution in Blackfriars Road. He set out a programme which would look at the development of Romantic poetry within European culture as a whole. He would begin with the "Origination" of all the arts within civilization: "Dress . . . Dances, gymnastic Sports . . . Architecture, Eloquence, Music, Poetry, Statuary, Painting, Gardening". He would then continue with the impact of Greek mythology, religion and republican institutions on classical art forms, and contrast these with "the Establishment of Christendom" and the development of "Gothic, Celtic, or Moorish" cultures and the Romance languages and forms.[97] From this essentially "mixed" European inheritance he would derive the root meaning of the word "Romantic", and proceed to demonstrate "the true Origin of the Romantic Drama in Shakespeare".[98] The course would end with a detailed "philosophical analysis" of four Shakespeare plays: *Romeo and Juliet*, *Hamlet*, *Macbeth* and *Othello*.

This greatly expanded programme, with its new emphasis on the religious and cultural forces that had created Romanticism as a European movement, was something quite new in English criticism. It was inspired both by Coleridge's increasingly detailed annotations of Schlegel's lectures, and also by the kind of attentive audience he expected.

The Surrey Institution had been founded in 1808 on the site of a converted museum on the Blackfriars Road in Southwark, south of the Thames. The entrance to the building was colonnaded like a Greek temple, with life-size bronze statues of eminent scientists and literary men – Plato, Aristotle, Bacon, Locke and Newton – standing loftily between the Corinthian columns. It was designed as a secular temple to self-improvement, included a library, a laboratory and a reading room, and was financed largely by wealthy dissenters and Quaker businessmen.

Lectures were given by candlelight at seven o'clock in the evening, strictly after working hours. The south London audience were all voluntary subscribers to the Institution; eager, attentive, anxious to learn, they looked for instruction rather than entertainment. Crabb Robinson dubbed them "the Saints". Coleridge had to make special application for free seats for the Morgans, describing them as "members of my own Family".[99] It was not at all a glamorous venue like Willis's Rooms, and the proposed fee was a mere £50; but it was in many ways the kind of earnest audience he most needed.

The lectures were scheduled to begin on 3 November 1812. Coleridge made no secret of the fact that he was interpreting the latest developments in German cultural criticism, and openly carried his three volumes of Schlegel's *Vorlesungen* in their pink paper covers up to the lecture dais. (He later recalled to the Morgans that the Shakespeare volume was "more dirtied than the other two" from constant use.)[100]

He seems to have started each lecture with a section of Schlegel's argument, and then improvised along his own line of criticism, freely using the materials he knew so well from previous lectures. Crabb Robinson, still a faithful attendant at every lecture, noted the use of "Kantian theory", the "rhapsodic" digressions, and the religious dimension which Coleridge gave to the Romantic outlook. Sometimes he felt this verged on "pious – cant, I fear", designed for the evangelical element in the audience; and once, having drunk too much wine to fortify himself against the wilderness of the Blackfriars Road, he fell asleep.[101] But gradually he too was gripped by the lectures, and considered the last five of the series had wholly won over the audience.[102]

It is impossible to know most of what was actually said at the Surrey Institution this winter, for the simple reason that Coleridge decided that he would make virtually no notes. The only newspaper account which appeared, in the *Morning Chronicle*, gives a tantalizing glimpse of the first lecture opening with a firework display of verbal definitions. How could we know precisely what the word "Beauty" means, when every schoolboy knew how the simplest adjective might have "nine or ten meanings"? He took the Greek *liparos*, which Homer used to mean shining, or flashing or radiant. But, asked Coleridge in the candlelight, how many bright different things in nature this might apply to: "the moon reflected on a lake, a storm at sea, the teeth of a lion discovered through the foliage . . ."[103]

Coleridge later claimed that the Surrey Institution series "On Belles Lettres" was the most spontaneously improvised he had yet given: "I never once thought of the Lecture, till I had entered the Lecture Box."[104] This almost reckless willingness to perform without the safety-net of scripted preparation suggests a curious mixture of confidence and carelessness. If his emotional life lay temporarily in ruins, his intellectual identity struggled to rise into some larger, more commanding sphere. Like many brilliant public performers, he seems to have sought a rapport with his audience which replaced the reassurance and appreciation he could not find in his personal relations. More and more he invested himself in his public persona, and seized every chance – in the lecture hall, in the literary salon, and soon in the theatre – to assert himself in this self-dramatizing and often mesmeric way. To be the central, hypnotic figure in a circle of candlelight was to demonstrate that he was still alive.

Two of the fragmentary notes which have survived give a precise, focused snapshot of the way he worked. In Lecture 7, on the distinction between Classical and Romantic forms, Coleridge used a single sheet of prompt notes which are little more than a verbatim summary of Schlegel's first lecture. But they end with his own brilliantly compact conclusions, which he evidently used for free, spoken elaboration.

It would be difficult to define the complex aesthetic distinction more succinctly than in these few, carefully weighted and balanced terms. The classicism of the Ancients implied above all a sense of the Finite: "Grace, Elegance, Proportion, Fancy, Dignity, Majesty, whatever is capable of being definitely conveyed by defined Forms or Thoughts." By contrast Romanticism, and the spirit of the Modern age, implied a restless Expansion: "the infinite, & indefinite as the vehicle of the Infinite – hence more to the Passions, the obscure Hopes and Fears – the wandering through Infinite – grander moral Feelings – more august conception of man as man – the Future rather than the Present – Sublimity."[105] For Coleridge's audience the building they sat in beneath its Greek cupola represented the former, while the speaker in front of them weaving and gesticulating in the candlelight was a living embodiment of the latter.

In Lecture 8, on the organic nature of Romantic form, Coleridge again used a single sheet of prompt notes, this time based on Schlegel's twelfth lecture. But this time he took specific sentences or short paragraphs from the German text, translated them literally, and then developed them with his own wholly characteristic images and arguments.

Thus Schlegel wrote in a central passage: "The poetic spirit required to be limited, that it may move within its range with a becoming liberty, as has been felt by all nations on the first invention of metre; it must act according to laws derivable from its own essence, otherwise its strength will be evaporated in boundless vacuity."[106] This is typical of Schlegel: dry, logical and relentlessly abstract. The argument is philosophically so generalized that many of its characteristic terms (such as "essence" and "vacuity") retain very little meaning in English.

Coleridge brought it to life, in his prompt notes, as follows: "The Spirit of Poetry like all other living Powers, must of necessity circumscribe itself by Rules, were it only to unite Power with Beauty. It must embody in order to reveal itself; but a living body is of necessity an organized one – & what is organization, but the connection of Parts to a whole, so that each Part is at once End & Means! This is no discovery of criticism – it is a necessity of the human mind – & all nations have felt and obeyed it, in the invention of metre, & measured Sounds, as the vehicle & Involucrum of Poetry itself, a fellow-growth from the same Life, even as the Bark is to a living Tree."[107]

11

There may have been one other reason why Coleridge embarked on these lectures with such bravado. Just before they began, at the end of October, he received the astonishing and exciting news that his play *Osorio* had been accepted for a major production at the Theatre Royal, Drury Lane. The newly formed Theatre Committee, under the wealthy businessman and MP Samuel Whitbread, had admired it "exceedingly". The commercial manager Mr Samuel Arnold was "confident of its success".[108] At last he would make his way.

It was an extraordinary opportunity. The Drury Lane Theatre had been owned by Richard Brinsley Sheridan, the very man who had originally rejected *Osorio* in 1797. But it had burnt down in 1809 (thus bankrupting Sheridan, who sat by the blaze philosophically drinking a bottle of wine). The ambitious new management were launching their first season in a splendidly re-equipped theatre, with the latest in stage technology and lighting.

The market for new plays was extremely restricted and demanding. Only one other theatre, Covent Garden, was licensed for serious new works; all the rest could only show musicals, burlesques, operas or pantomimes. Few productions lasted more than a week, and no new verse tragedy had run for more than ten nights since 1777 (the feat achieved by Hannah More's *Percy*). When Godwin's best-selling novel *Faulkner* had been dramatized in 1807, Godwin had spent £800 on a house in expectation of certain success, and then lost the entire sum when the play immediately failed.[109]

The management's choice of *Osorio* was therefore a carefully judged gamble, balancing both literary prestige and commercial considerations. The play was set in Grenada at the time of the Spanish Inquisition, and dealt in passion, mystery and menacing violence. Historical dramas of this kind were popular, and the Committee were particularly taken with the potential of its *mis-en-scène*, since the Peninsular campaign had brought everything Spanish into vogue. Its author was widely known in London through his lecturing, and the text offered spectacular staging opportunities. Above all, with Coleridge on hand to adapt the text, the production could be mounted speedily, as it had to be ready for staging in January 1813, less than two months ahead.

Coleridge announced his coup on the evening after his first lecture on 3 November. Dizzy with excitement, he told Crabb Robinson and other assembled friends that he had "five or six" other ideas for plays ready for the London stage if the first proved a success. Robinson was amused to see Coleridge in such a "strange burst" of high spirits, and noted how he was quickly carried away into extravagant behaviour. At one point in the evening he asked to borrow a copy of Spinoza's *Ethics*, and surprised everyone by kissing Spinoza's picture on the title page, and announcing that Spinoza was "his gospel". But a few minutes later he was to be heard rapidly demonstrating that Spinoza's philosophy "was, after all, false". Robinson thought it an extraordinary display of his showmanship, and was even more surprised to observe that everyone seemed delighted with it, with one earnest cleric remarking afterwards that it demonstrated Coleridge's "comprehensive faith and love".[110]

The original version of the play, *Osorio*, had been written at Stowey in the spring of 1797, in the months before Wordsworth and Dorothy came to Alfoxden. The story concerns two brothers in love with the same woman, a distinctive Coleridgean theme. The drama was evidently still alive for Coleridge in 1812, and had the peculiar importance for him that it was a work written almost entirely independent of Wordsworth's influence, although short sections of it ("The Dungeon" and "The Foster Mother's Tale") had been published anonymously in the *Lyrical Ballads*.

Like most Romantic verse drama of this period it was an uneasy attempt to combine two genres that were not really compatible: popular costume melodrama with a modern form of Shakespearean tragedy. The first required continuous colourful, theatrical action on stage, with the rapid unfolding of a thriller plot. The second depended on the slow, stately, interior evolutions of dramatic verse soliloquy. The model for such a play, but crushing in its brilliance, was of course *Hamlet* (also set at a time of war in Scandinavia); and the most successful contemporary version of it was not British, but German, as in Schiller's *Wallenstein* (set during the Thirty Years' War) which Coleridge had translated himself so effectively in 1800.*

The melodrama of *Osorio* was provided by the theme of fraternal betrayal, and the passionate rivalry for the love of the same beautiful woman. Its plotting has all the tortuousness of the genre, and sounds wonderfully absurd in summary. But it sets up some strange echoes. The good brother Albert is returning from a long sea-voyage to claim his bride Maria. The beautiful Maria has been waiting faithfully in the royal palace of Grenada, repelling the advances of the evil brother Osorio. Albert is shipwrecked on the coast of Grenada, and the scheming Osorio sends a Moorish captain to murder him in secret. Osorio then presses on with his treacherous seduction of Maria, confidently assuming Albert is dead.

But of course Albert is not dead. He has been befriended by the Moor (and the Moor's wife, Alhadra) after showing sympathy for their cause as persecuted aliens in Spain. With the Moor's help, he returns in disguise to the court at Grenada to win back Maria and seek justice from his evil sibling. Albert proceeds by indirections and tricks. He adopts a disguise, avoids openly confronting either Osorio or Maria, and with psychological cunning slowly forces the one to admit his guilt and the other her true love.

In one crucial scene in Act III, Albert puts on "a sorcerer's robe"

---

* Many other British poets would make the attempt in Coleridge's lifetime – Wordsworth in *The Borderers* (1797), Byron in *Manfred* (1817) and *Sardanapalus* (1821), Shelley in *The Cenci* (1819), Keats in *Otho the Great* (1819) – but none of them reached the commercial stage. It says much about contemporary taste that the most successful of "literary" adaptations in the West End was Mary Shelley's *Frankenstein* in 1823. It is one of the enigmas of cultural history that it was the French Romantic poets – Hugo, Alfred de Vigny, Alfred de Musset – who succeeded in taking the popular stage by storm. (See for example Graham Robb's wonderfully melodramatic *Victor Hugo*, 1997.)

and pretends to conjure up a ghost (amidst burning incense and claps of thunder). The ghost carries the keepsake picture of Maria belonging to the "dead" brother (really Albert himself, though at times this is hard to remember). However, by Act V Albert is reunited with Maria; Osorio, driven half-mad with guilt, has begged for forgiveness ("Forgive me, Albert! – *Curse* me with forgiveness!"); and Alhadra has led a successful Moorish insurrection against corrupt Spanish rule.

Clearly at this level the action is as much *grand guignol* as melodrama. The speeches are too long; the central device of Albert's disguise is unconvincing; the subplot of Moorish persecution is confusing; and the stage business of ghosts, swords, poisoned goblets, seems close to pantomime. It was hardly surprising that Sheridan had rejected it as a farrago, wholly unsuitable for the stage at that date.

Yet Coleridge's 1797 version had really been a cabinet play designed for reading, "a sketch of a tragedy" with the external plot "half-told". As a piece of stagecraft he realized that "all is imperfect, and much obscure".[111] His conscious, artistic intention had been to use melodrama as a vehicle for a physiological study in tragic guilt. This was the Shakespearean dimension of the play, and it was a theme common to his ballads. His central interest lay in the character of Osorio, as revealed by his soliloquies. Osorio is a powerful, commanding man inwardly destroyed by guilt, but who refuses to recognize its moral force. He is guilty but not remorseful; agonized but not repentant. In the first version Coleridge felt he had not made this dramatically clear, or linked the inner tragic turmoil with the outward action. Other characters, notably the forceful Moorish woman Alhadra, who has some of the finest speeches in the play, inexplicably came to life while Osorio remained as colourless as his name.*

Coleridge's acute summary of this central weakness also curiously suggests its Romantic appeal. "The growth of Osorio's character is nowhere explained – and yet I had most clear and psychologically accurate ideas of the whole of it . . . A man, who from constitutional calmness of appetites, is seduced into pride and the love of power . . . and from thence, by the co-operation of envy, and a curiously

* Alhadra's dreamy landscape descriptions, and their connections with the writing of "Kubla Khan", are examined in *Early Visions*, pp. 162–3.

modified love for a beautiful female (which is nowhere developed in the play), into a most atrocious guilt. A man who is in truth a weak man, yet always duping himself into the belief that he has a soul of iron."[112] In 1797 Coleridge had so little hope of finding a theatrical solution that he left his only remaining copy of the manuscript (although four were in fact made) to gather dust in William Godwin's archives.[113]

Yet even in its first version, the play is oddly gripping in its broad conception. The neurotic love-triangle, the suggestions of necromancy, the atmosphere of gloomy menace, the whole notion of spiralling inward darkness (prisons, caves, chasms, guilt) is arresting. Now, after a lapse of some fifteen years, tastes had changed and these gothic elements obviously struck the Drury Lane Committee as having tremendous potential. (The much odder fact that during that same lapse of time it also seems to have become a gothic variation of several events in Coleridge's own life since his return from his sea voyage to Malta in 1806, is much harder to explain but adds greatly to its interest.)

What now transformed the play was the perceived demands of the Drury Lane audience. The whole piece was revamped with an eye to the kind of popular fashion that Byron's Eastern tales of illicit passion and inexplicable villainy had inspired. The actor-manager Samuel Arnold wanted a bold, well-carpentered action-drama, with plenty of opportunity for his lavish stage-sets and startling scenic effects. Far from seeking further psychological motives to Osorio's character – which had been Coleridge's instinct – he asked for cuts, dramatic simplifications and more external colour.

Character names became more explanatory – Osorio became Ordonio (suggesting force), Albert became Alvar (suggesting mystery), Maria became Dona Teresa (suggesting exotic romance). The play itself was re-titled and the first posters announced *Remorse: A Tragedy in Five Acts*, with a setting that promised bloodshed: "The reign of Philip II, just at the close of the civil wars against the Moors, and during the heat of the Persecution which raged against them."

There was a tremendous new emphasis on the melodramatic elements. Alvar's sorcery scene in Act III was to become a grand set piece, with full choir and orchestra rather than the humble "Celestina stop, or Clagget's Metallic Organ" suggested in the original. A "Cavern" scene in Act IV was to have a dreadful chasm disguised in a pool of moonlight, down which Ordonio's Moorish chieftain first imagines falling, and then actually falls (thrown by Ordonio). It was a classic "falling" nightmare come to life, with the peculiar overtones of one of Coleridge's own opium dreams.

> . . . My body bending forward, yea, o'erbalanced
> Almost beyond recoil, on the dim brink
> Of a huge chasm I stept. The shadowy moonshine
> Filling the void so counterfeited substance,
> That my foot hung aslant adown the edge . . .
> When a boy, my lord!
> I could have sat whole hours beside that chasm,
> Push'd in huge stones and heard them strike and rattle
> Against its horrid sides . . .[114]

In the final Act, the villainous Ordonio, rather than being swept off to prison, was to be stabbed to death on stage by Alhadra.

Coleridge conceded these lurid alterations without protest, and even with a kind of fascination at what popular taste apparently demanded of him. (The process was similar to a modern novelist watching his work adapted for Hollywood.) The brutal stabbing was the one contrivance that worried him, and was to be played on the first night without his permission. (He "absolutely had the Hiss half way out of my Lips" when he first saw it but then "retracted it", when he registered its stunning effect on the audience.) For the rest, he said tactfully that everything was improved, and that he earned the reputation of "*the Amenable Author*" in the green room, from his willingness to cut and rewrite up to the last moments.[115]

The plot changes were largely a matter of clarifying what always remained a slightly hectic story-line. A new opening scene in Act I laid in the back-story of fraternal rivalry for the audience, and announced the psychological theme:

> Remorse is as the heart in which it grows:
> If that be gentle, it drops balmy dews
> Of true repentance; but if proud and gloomy,
> It is a poison-tree, that pierced to the inmost
> Weeps only tears of poison![116]

A fuller, and highly emotional "recognition" scene between Alvar and Dona Teresa was placed at the beginning of Act V to prepare for the violent climax. But where Coleridge was allowed to tinker with the verse, he added images of solitude and grief, drawing directly on his experiences in London over the last two years. In Act IV, waiting outside the "iron Dungeon gate" where Alvar is imprisoned, Dona Teresa is given lines almost directly transposed from Coleridge's private Notebooks of 1811:

> The moon is high in heaven, and all is hush'd.
> Yet anxious listener! I have seem'd to hear
> A low dead thunder mutter through the night,
> As 'twere a giant angry in his sleep . . .[117]

To Ordonio, Coleridge gave a short, new Shakespearean soliloquy on death (the echo is from *Measure for Measure*) which became a favourite not only with the actors, but with the stage-hands. "It was pleasing to observe, during the Rehearsal all the Actors and Actresses and even the Mechanics on the stage clustering round while these lines were repeating, just as if it had been a favourite strain of music." Dona Teresa asks Ordonio where the body of his brother Alvar lies (assuming him to be dead). Ordonio replies with an image of the dark grave which really reveals his own dream-haunted darkness in life. The passage, though in blank verse, is indeed curiously musical and lilting, like a sinister lullaby, and again the autobiographical resonance was strong.

> *Teresa*: "Where lies the corse of my betrothéd husband?"
> *Ordonio*: "There, where Ordonio likewise fain would lie!
> In the sleep-compelling earth, in unpierce'd darkness!
> For while we live –
> An inward day that never, never sets,
> Glares round the soul, and mocks the closing eyelids!
> Over his rocky grave the fir-grove sighs
> A lulling ceaseless dirge! 'Tis well with him."[118]

12

Even as Coleridge was settling into this intensive work, he was painfully reminded of how much depended on its success. On 9 November Josiah Wedgwood wrote from Staffordshire, announcing in a dry and almost curt letter that his business losses were such that he would probably be forced to discontinue his half share of £75 in Coleridge's annuity, which he had been paying since 1798. Like many other British manufacturers, the high wartime taxes combined with the collapse of the home market, had left him running his Etruria potteries from an "annually diminishing" capital fund. While his brother Thomas Wedgwood's share of the annuity was secured by his will, Josiah now asked Coleridge to consider whether in these circumstances he was "bound in honour" to continue his own share. "I hope you will write to me without reserve on this subject."[119]

Coleridge was placed in an acute quandary by this letter. For a fortnight he gave his Surrey Institution lectures in a state of "nervous depression" and anxious indecision. Ever since 1804 he had been making the whole annuity over to Mrs Coleridge, thereby at least supplying his family with a secure basic income whatever the fluctuations of his own literary earnings. But the prospect of any other regular income was still remote. Both Wordsworth and Southey had relied on similar private annuities, though now in middle life their literary reputations had secured them better earnings. (Wordsworth's post as Distributor for Stamps for Westmorland and Cumberland brought in between £200 and £400 per annum; and Southey – working immensely hard – earned two or three times that from the *Quarterly*. Even Hazlitt had recently secured a permanent post at the *Morning Chronicle* for a salary of 200 guineas.)[120]

At the same time, Josiah's letter was obviously phrased in such a way as to allow Coleridge to plead the case of his family, and to beg for an extension of the full annuity at least for a year or so longer. He also suspected that news of the quarrel with Wordsworth, and the now widely circulated story of his "hopelessness" and opium addiction, had led Josiah to underestimate his professional efforts in lecturing and journalism, which was almost certainly true. Above all there was the Drury Lane production, which might persuade Josiah that he was still worth helping, or alternatively convince him that he could now fend for himself. How much should he reveal of all these circumstances, and how far should he beg Josiah to honour his original promise?

The temptation to write a passionate, pleading and somewhat disingenuous letter was very strong. No one could do this better than Coleridge. He had often taken advantage of rich friends – Daniel Stuart and William Sotheby had experienced his insistent touch. Yet he was not feckless about money – his handling of the annuity, as well as the insurance premium for his wife, was exemplary – and he could be generous, not to say quixotic on occasions, as later events proved. In this instance, his quixotic side triumphed.

On 1 December he wrote handsomely to Josiah, releasing him from all further responsibilities in the half share of the Wedgwood annuity. He praised him and his "reverend Brother's past Munificence", and made no mention of the fact that he had steadily made over all these payments to Mrs Coleridge. (Her share would now be reduced to £67, after wartime income tax.)

He was frank about both the difficulties and the potential of his own position, and tried to reassure Josiah that he had continued the annuity much longer than could have been expected. "Permit me to assure you, that had *The Friend* succeeded . . . or had my Lectures done more than merely pay my Board in Town, it was my intention to have resigned my claims on your Bounty – and I am sure, that I shall have your good wishes in my behalf, when I tell you that I have had a Play accepted at Drury Lane . . ."

He felt he was on a "not dishonourable road to competence", and would soon have "heart & spirits (still more necessary than time) to bring into shape the fruits of 20 years Study & observation". If he had been "cruelly" calumniated for his faults, he hoped only that Josiah would soon have reason to think better of him. He ended on what was, in every way, a high note: "I declare that to have an annuity settled on me of three times or thrice three times the amount, would not afford me such pleasure, as the restoration of your Esteem & Friendship – for your deeply obliged S. T. Coleridge."[121]

Josiah might have been forgiven for half-suspecting that Coleridge, having resigned the £75 with such a noble flourish, was mildly wondering if £225 might one happy day replace it. Josiah, however, made good his escape from his incorrigible client. In a prompt and measured reply, he thanked Coleridge, praised his genius and the "tender and deep feelings" of their former intimacy, but added that he could not hope that "we can again feel towards each other as we have done", as their pursuits and characters were now "so dissimilar". He wished him all success with his play. It was an honourable exchange, yet a sad one. Coleridge was left with the bitter knowledge that another of his oldest friends and supporters had stepped aside.[122]

13

All Coleridge's hopes were now centred on Drury Lane. While the weekly lectures continued on Tuesday nights, he began attending regular rehearsals at the Theatre Royal as Christmas rapidly approached. Despite the vaunted new technology the huge, empty auditorium was freezing cold and the actors wandered about in rugs and army greatcoats. There was much cutting and rewriting to be done, a Prologue and Epilogue to be composed, and a great need to soothe the hysterical outbursts of Miss Smith, the actress playing Dona Teresa – the romantic lead – who approached every dramatic incident, both on stage and off, as an occasion for tragic greatness. (The *Satirist* magazine would later remark that Miss Smith was "considerably unfit for the delivery of anything pretending to be humorous".)[123]

Coleridge began "labouring with much vexation & little success" to improve Miss Smith's part. But he was enchanted by the stage equipment which responded to his commands by conjuring forth (with much creaking and hissing) the glimmering likeness of a stormy seashore, an echoing cavern, mountains by moonlight, a dungeon, and a mystic firelit chamber of music and sorcery. He felt like Prospero, and found the emotional storms and crises of his thespians curiously familiar and reassuring. The "alterations & alterations" were sometimes tedious, but he found he could supply new lines quickly, "somewhat unlicked", and only the "bowel-griping Cold from the Stage Floor & Weariness from cutting Blocks with a Razor" would send him "packing home" to Berners Street.[124] He had told Mrs Coleridge the bad news about the annuity – "Poor woman! she is sadly out of heart" – but he promised that his play would save them yet.[125]

As the rehearsals continued through December, with the première now scheduled for 23 January, the managers grew steadily "more sanguine" of the play's success. Coleridge hardly dared hope for a more than ordinary run of eight or ten days, but even this might bring salvation. In sending out complimentary tickets to friends, he pointed out that at least their children might come and enjoy the pantomime which traditionally preceded it at that season.[126]

The plotting now had "simplicity and unity", and like the spokes in a turning wheel "every ray in the Tragedy converges to Ordonio".[127] He would like to have cut further descriptive passages, but Arnold would not let him do so. The actors were not quite how he had once imagined Kemble and Sarah Siddons playing the parts, but they could be enthusiastic and hardworking. Alexander Rae (playing Ordonio) was physically unimposing and lacked "depth" of voice, but he could be subtle in his interpretation of evil and malice. Robert Elliston (Alvar) relied on shouting, bombast and "self-Conceit", though he could be dazzling at moments of high drama. Miss Smith remained her usual tragic self. Oddly it was Mrs Glover (Alhadra), previously renowned for comedy, who brought the most varied life and energy to her part. What Coleridge always looked for in great acting was what he had once seen Dorothea Jordan achieve: to hold an entire audience so that "their very breath was suspended".[128]

Yet if no individual performance achieved this height, there was one piece of ensemble playing which did promise magically to transcend the limitations of melodrama. This was the sorcery scene in Act III, for which *Remorse* eventually became famous. The management concentrated its entire range of resources on preparing this episode, rightly identifying it as a theatrical climax. Coleridge skilfully recast the dialogue and stage directions to achieve the desired effect.

In the original version, the ghost – a "wandering shape" – produces a small picture of Albert's assassination hoping to startle Osorio into an admission of his guilt. Coleridge realized this device was "miserably undramatic" as a scene of magic. It merely confused the audience who cannot see the picture or fully understand the reactions of those on stage. "All, though in different ways, think or know it to be a trick."[129]

In *Remorse* the magic was to be made palpable and genuinely uncanny, and both Ordonio and Teresa were directed to play the scene in terror. A huge illuminated picture of Alvar's assassination was flown down through "ascending flames", a choir of monks appeared in a medieval chapel, and a chorus of boatmen floated across the stage. Special music was composed by the Irish singer Michael Kelly for the beautiful "Incantation" which was to accompany the summoning up of Alvar's ghost beneath the picture. Coleridge had based this dirge on the Latin Mass for the Dead. Far from masking the poetry, these special effects heightened its intensity, and threw a spell over the whole theatre. The "Incantation", originally written in 1797 but never previously published, was revealed as one of Coleridge's supreme pieces of verbal magic.

Hear, sweet Spirit, hear the spell,
Lest a blacker charm compel!
So small midnight breezes swell
With thy deep long-lingering knell.

And at evening evermore,
In a chapel on the shore,
Shall the chaunter, sad and saintly,
Yellow tapers burning faintly,
Doleful masses chaunt for thee,
Miserere Domine!

Hush! the cadence dies away
On the quiet moonlight sea:
The boatmen rest their oars and say,
Miserere Domine![130]

Michael Kelly long afterwards recalled its hypnotic effect in the darkened auditorium at Drury Lane when it was eventually staged. "The poetry of the incantation was highly animating . . . The chorus of the boatmen chaunting on the water under the convent walls, and the distant peal of the organ, accompanying the monks while singing within the convent chapel, seemed to overcome and soothe the audience; a thrilling sensation appeared to pervade the great mass of congregated humanity . . . and at the conclusion the applause was loud and protracted."[131] Here was an attempt to embody the "witchery" of Coleridge's poetry in a form of ritualized, orchestrated psycho-drama intended to hold a mass audience spellbound.

14

With stage effects such as these, the theatre was investing a great deal of money in the production. Throughout December Coleridge came under increasing pressure to attend rehearsals, cutting and reworking the script for the actors, while simultaneously continuing his Surrey Institution lectures. It was at this moment of maximum effort that he received a wholly unexpected and desperate summons to Grasmere. At the beginning of the month, the Wordsworths' second son, their adored little boy Tom, had suddenly died from measles at the age of six. Both Wordsworth and Mary were distraught, and Dorothy wrote urging Coleridge to come north for Christmas to console them.

Coleridge had genuinely loved little Tom, who was "nearest his heart" among Wordsworth's children. He recalled how the "affectionate little fellow" had often crept into his study at Allan Bank, during the memorable struggles with *The Friend*, sitting silently on a little stool at his side, gazing up at him and stroking his arm.[132] He was also haunted by the whole idea of the death of children, ever since the loss of his own baby Berkeley during his absence in Germany. Any childhood death reminded him of his own sons. It filled him with "the sense of uncertainty, the fear in enjoyment, the pale & deathly Gleam thrown over the countenances of the Living, whom we love . . ." Thinking of poor little Tom lying "in his Coffin", he had an awful, guilty vision of "Derwent lying beside him".[133] When the Morgans came in, they found him weeping uncontrollably over Dorothy's letter.

But what should he do, should he go north? (De Quincey, who had received the same summons, announced he was departing the following day.) Coleridge was presented with an acute dilemma. It was not merely that he was being asked to abandon his professional commitments in London at such a crucial moment (perhaps they had forgotten those). It was more the assumption that, once again, he was willing to take on the role of Wordsworth's unquestioning friend and supporter, as if nothing had happened between them. After a first quick, grief-struck note, sent care of De Quincey, he hesitated.

For three days he struggled with his conscience, and at last poured all his feelings into a long private letter to Wordsworth on

7 December. From the start it was full of passionate sympathies and unresolved contradictions. "Write? My Dearest Friend! O that it were in my power to be with you myself instead of my Letter. The Lectures I could give up; but the Rehearsal of my Play commences this week – & upon this depends my best Hopes of leaving Town after Christmas & living among you as long as I live."[134] This last wild suggestion was no doubt as startling to read at Grasmere as to write from Berners Street.

Coleridge believed that Wordsworth, in his own unspoken and unbending way, was putting forth an olive branch from his sorrows. Every instinct in Coleridge's expressive nature drove him to grasp it. To share their mourning at Grasmere would prove that nothing had really changed between them. But for Coleridge it had changed, irrevocably, and as he wrote the complication of his feelings overtook him. He could not pretend that they were merely discussing poor little Tom. He knew they were discussing the mourning for a friendship, as well as the mourning for a child. His letter became both a declaration of complete love (which still included Asra), and a declaration of complete loss.

> O dearest Friend! what comfort can I afford you? What comfort ought I not to afford, who have given you so much pain? Sympathy deep, of my whole being, & a necessity of my Being – that, so help me God at my last hour! has never been other than what it is, substantially! In Grief, and in joy, in the anguish of perplexity & in the fullness & overflow of Confidence, it has been ever what it is. – There is a sense of the word, Love, in which I never felt it but to you & one of your Household – I am distant from you some hundred miles, but glad I am that I am no longer distant in spirit, & have faith, that as it has happened *but once*, so it never can happen again. An awful Truth it seems to me, & prophetic of our future, as well as declarative of our present *real*, nature, that one mere Thought, one feeling of Suspicion or Jealousy or resentment can remove two human Beings farther from each other, than winds or seas can separate their Bodies.[135]

Dorothy read this letter with her "wonted affection". She felt that their sorrow had "sunk into him", and saw none of its painful ambiguities. She still confidently expected Coleridge's arrival after

Remorse had been produced. But Wordsworth remained silent, and did not respond directly, overwhelmed by the loss of Tom, "who was the hope, delight, and pride, of us all".[136] Domestic grief engulfed him, and to cope with Coleridge's wounded feelings among these accumulated family sorrows was beyond his emotional resources.

He grew thin, and Dorothy thought he looked ten years older. He could not bear the thought of remaining at the Grasmere Parsonage, so near the graveyard with its little tombs. He busied himself with finding a new house, two miles away at Rydal Mount, where they moved in May 1813, and grappled with his duties as Distributor of Stamps.[137] Like Dorothy, he still hoped that Coleridge would eventually reappear in the Lakes, and he continued to keep a fatherly eye on Hartley. For the rest, he sank himself in a renewed attempt to finish his long poem "The Excursion".

So Coleridge and the Wordsworths continued to drift apart in 1813, borne on the "winds and seas" of their separate struggles. Mary suffered from depression for many months. Asra became an ever more devoted guardian of the three remaining Wordsworth children, teaching and nursing them like a second mother. Dorothy continued to chronicle their domestic routines in longer and longer letters to Catherine Clarkson and other friends. Coleridge's name appeared less and less frequently in the Wordsworths' correspondence. Perhaps it was only Hartley who reminded them of what had been, and what might yet be.

15

The première of *Remorse* took place as planned on the night of Saturday, 23 January 1813. The Theatre Royal was packed, and the *Christian Monitor* noted the large number of well-dressed prostitutes doing business in the foyer, a sure sign of a fashionable occasion.[138] Coleridge and the Morgans slipped into a private box in the circle, and tried to keep well back in the shadows. But to their alarm, Coleridge was soon "discovered by the Pit", and he sat through the opening Acts in an agony of authorial doubts.

To his amazement, the play was greeted with "unexampled APPLAUSE" from all sections of the house. After the closing scene "they all turned their faces towards our Box, & gave a treble cheer of Claps". Back at Berners Street an "endless Rat a Tat Tat" of congratulatory visits began, which continued over the whole weekend. The same thing happened at the Surrey Institution. When he went down to give his last lecture the following Monday, he was greeted with "loud, long, & enthusiastic applause at my entrance, & ditto in yet fuller Chorus . . . for some minutes after I had retired".[139]

Crabb Robinson, who attended both the opening night with the Godwins and other friends, and the last lecture, reported the same impression of a popular triumph. He did not quite understand it, as he thought the play was full of "clumsy contrivance" and dramatic improbabilities. It had too much poetry and not enough action, and "owes its success rather to its faults than its beauties". It was extraordinary that such a "metaphysical" and psychological theme should have caught the public's imagination. "His two great characters are philosophers of Coleridge's own school, the one (Alvar) a sentimental moralist, the other (Ordonio) a sophisticated villain; both are dreamers." But that, paradoxically, seemed to be the great appeal of the play, which had caught something of the introspective, self-questioning mood of its audience. It was received "with great and almost unmixed applause, and was announced for repetition without any opposition".[140]

After the third night, Coleridge wrote a full account to his wife, boisterous with excitement, and triumphantly enclosing a draft for £100, which more than made up for the lost annuity. "In the course of a month I have no hesitation in promising you another £100 – & I hope likewise before Midsummer, if God grant me Life, to repay whatever you have expended for the Children." He was anxious to have Southey's reaction, but made no mention of Wordsworth.

He was scathing about the early press – the "infernal Lies" of *The Times* (who had claimed it lasted five hours), and the "dirty malice" of the *Morning Herald*. But he was amused and amazed at the stir he had caused. "One of the malignant Papers asserted, that I had collected all the *Saints* from Mile End Turnpike to Tyburn Bar."[141] If the piece did not run (and he was still doubtful), it would be from bad acting and "from the want of vulgar Pathos in the Play itself".[142]

He was now full of other theatrical schemes, including surely one of his wildest fancies, "a German Musical Play" based on the Genesis story of Adam and Eve in the Garden. Once again he felt the tide was turning back in his favour. "I must try to *imitate* W. Scott . . . in making Hay while the Sun shines."[143]

Over a dozen other reviews quickly appeared in newspapers and periodicals, and though many were unfavourable, fashionable talk about the play quickly spread, and the management booked it for a fortnight with a possible extension. By convention, dramatic authors were paid for the third, sixth and ninth nights of any production, and this guaranteed Coleridge at least £200. There remained the tantalizing chance of reaching a twentieth night, when traditionally the fee was then doubled. "That Coleridge should ever become a popular man," remarked Crabb Robinson wonderingly, "would once have been thought a very idle speculation."[144]

Almost every critic who reviewed the play – even the unfavourable ones – agreed that the sorcery scene from Act III was the dramatic high-point. Here stagecraft, music and poetry had combined to produce a piece of theatrical magic which was far beyond the conventions of Regency melodrama.

The 27-year-old Thomas Barnes (who within five years would become editor of *The Times*) contributed a long critique to the radical *Examiner*, a paper almost invariably hostile to Coleridge. He greeted the play with something close to astonishment. Mr Coleridge had "excelled" in a "very poor story, well-conducted"; he had transformed the "picturesque" elements of German drama with the skill of "a veteran dramatist". Barnes enthused: "we never saw more interest excited in a theatre than was expressed in the scorcery-scene in the third act. The altar flaming in the distance, the solemn invocation, the pealing music of the mystic song, altogether produced a combination so awful, as nearly to overpower reality, and make one half believe the enchantment which delighted our senses."[145]

By the middle of February *Remorse* had earned Coleridge £300, and the script had been published by the bookseller Pople in Chancery Lane at three shillings a copy.[146] A second edition appeared on 17 February, and a third in May. The theatre management told Coleridge that the play would make them profits of between eight and ten thousand pounds, the equivalent of a quarter of a million in modern currency.[147] It was adopted as part of their regular spring repertoire, playing at first three times a week, and then apparently weekly on Saturday nights from late February. It seems to have reached its twentieth performance early in May, when Crabb Robinson noted that Coleridge was now "certain" to earn £400.[148]

Remorse entered the provincial repertory, and was widely performed over the next two years in cities like Bristol, Birmingham and Manchester, though Coleridge received no royalties as performing rights were not established for half a century in England. Oddly, Coleridge never went back to see it after that first, rapturous night at Drury Lane. But he was proud of his offspring: "the *Remorse* has succeeded in spite of bad Scenes, execrable Acting, & Newspaper Calumny," he told Tom Poole. "I shall get more than all my literary Labors put together, nay, thrice as much, subtracting my heavy Losses in the *Watchman* & the *Friend* – £400: including the Copyright."[149] He was not displeased with its metaphysical reputation – he felt it had "purified" the stage. Mr Arnold had shown magnificently what stagecraft could add to "a Dramatic *Poem*"; and although "not fully developed", in the figures of Dona Teresa and Alhadra he had altered the insipid stereotype of the Romantic heroine. "I succeed for others as well as for myself."[150]

There was much truth in this. Leigh Hunt, who wrote regular dramatic criticism in the *Examiner*, later called *Remorse* "the only tragedy touched with real poetry for the last fifty years".[151] With Coleridge's success many new plays began to be submitted, money was invested, and within two years even Byron thought it worthwhile to serve on the Drury Lane Committee.

Southey was particularly impressed and generous about Coleridge's achievement, asking Murray to review the script for the *Quarterly*, and only regretting that it had not been staged in 1797. He thought Coleridge might have had a career in the theatre, "to the amendment of the existing stage and the permanent honour of English literature".[152] As it was, he was delighted about Coleridge's new popularity. "There is no man upon whom the applause of pit box and gallery would produce more effect. Better late than never, and the success is in a seasonable time for his family."[153]

16

Coleridge's sun appeared to be shining brightly in the spring of 1813. His finances were in order, his work was in demand, and he was comfortably established with the Morgans at Berners Street.

This was the moment to bring some of his many projects to fruition: a new play for Drury Lane, the publication of his lectures, maybe a second series of *The Friend*, even a new collection of his poetry. It was also a time when he could have visited his children at Keswick, and called upon the Wordsworths at Rydal Mount to express his sympathies in person. (Dorothy was still telling Mrs Clarkson that he was expected in March, now that his play had proved so successful.)[154]

But none of these things were done. If Coleridge was making hay, as he told his wife, there was no sign of a harvest. On the contrary, Coleridge almost dropped from view for the next six months, and the absence of letters or Notebook entries is one of the most inexplicable of his later career. Even the indefatigable Crabb Robinson rather lost touch. At the end of February he had noted that Coleridge seemed strangely unmoved by his theatrical triumph, a thing not to be expected from a man of "so highly nervous" a sensibility. When he called round at the Morgans, Coleridge was frequently "not at home (or rather not visible)".[155]

In March Mrs Clarkson corralled him into several fruitless missions to urge Coleridge, yet again, to go north to see Wordsworth. She had, she said, been receiving "very distressing letters from the Lakes", and could not understand his cruel inaction. Mrs Clarkson also bombarded Berners Street with notes taken round by her footman, and when Coleridge steadfastly refused to reply her curiosity became voracious. "I would give a great deal to know how he manages himself – and whether some one measures out to him the abominable drug," she admitted to Crabb Robinson, and urged him to investigate further. "Do go to Berners Street & fish out what you can for me."[156] But there were no further revelations, and finally on 2 May he noted blankly: "A call on Morgan. Coleridge, I see, will not go to the Lakes. Of course, I did not press the subject any further."[157]

On one rare occasion he recorded Coleridge discussing music and reciting Mignon's song, "Kennst du das Land" from Goethe's *Wilhelm Meister*, with tears in his eyes. Coleridge's exquisite translation of Mignon's song, a single stanza of dreamy longing for distant heartlands, seems almost the only thing he wrote during these lost months. It was perhaps intended as part of his "German musical" (there is evidence that he was in touch with Thomas Harris, the stage-manager of Covent Garden); or it may have been an oblique expression of some more private mood.

> Know'st thou the land where the pale citrons grow,
> The golden fruits in darkest foliage glow?
> Soft blows the wind that breathes from that blue sky!
> Still stands the myrtle and the laurel high!
> Know'st thou it well, that land, belovéd friend?
> Thither with thee, O, thither would I wend![158]

Various odd rumours spread about Coleridge's disappearance from circulation. Once the morning papers solved it by reporting that the author of the renowned tragedy *Remorse* had just committed suicide in Regent's Park. A "stout and well-dressed man" had been found hanging from a tree: he carried no personal papers by which he could be identified, "but his shirt was marked S. T. Coleridge at full length," and by this he had been identified. The gardener at Greta Hall read the same news item in Keswick, and nearly collapsed before – "ashen-faced" – he could gasp out the news to Southey. The explanation lay of course in the long and scattered history of Coleridge's lecture shirts, which had migrated widely between his lodgings and his laundry over the past five years. It was Morgan, not Coleridge, who sent a reassuring note to Keswick, though adding Coleridge's whimsical comment that he was probably the first man "to hear of a lost shirt in this way".[159]

Much of this suggests a kind of retreat into himself, a period of nervous reaction after the months of publicity, and a continuing process of mourning and depression over the break with Wordsworth. Now that success had come, he found himself temperamentally incapable of capitalizing on it. There were a few social fixtures, gallery visits, quiet suppers with friends like the Aders, and the occasion he dined with Madame De Staël, who afterwards delivered herself of the memorable verdict: – "*avec M. Coleridge, c'est tout à fait un monologue.*"[160] He also kept up with Allston, but the painter's young wife was ill, and these were sickbed visitations and nostalgic talks about Italy.

Perhaps his refreshed finances made him feel less guilty about spending money on his old indulgences, opium and brandy. There is no definite evidence that he ever sent the second instalment of his £400 to Keswick. Yet by September 1813 he was almost penniless again. Where had all the money gone, if not to his wife and children? Had Coleridge simply swilled it away, in a long sabbatical summer of literary dreams and therapeutic opiates?

It was certainly what Southey and the Wordsworths came to believe. Dorothy wrote that she expected no good of him, "especially as I hear from all quarters so much of his confident announcement of plans for this musical drama, that comedy, the other essay. Let him doubt, and his powers will revive. Till then they must sleep." Hartley's stock had also slipped in sympathy. The boy was "as odd as ever, and in the weak points of his character resembles his father very much; but he is not prone to sensual indulgence – quite the contrary – and has not one expensive habit." She now found Derwent "a much more interesting Boy".[161]

But there may be another explanation for Coleridge's mysterious eclipse. All that spring of 1813 a quite different crisis had been gathering pace at Berners Street. The first sign of it was a sudden illness that struck down John Morgan in March. He was "so dreadfully sick" that Coleridge hurried him off in a coach for a fortnight's convalescence at Bexhill. He dosed Morgan on "good roast Beef very well drest – boiled Slices of Plum Pudding, & an apple Pie", and marched him along the sea front. A rare glimpse of careful financial accounting also suggests that Coleridge paid for this whole trip, including the untoward luxury of a post-chaise. He also appeared anxious that Morgan should settle a pressing bill due on the Brent family business at 103 Bishopsgate by the end of the month.[162]

Coleridge worked hard to be cheerful and reassuring in holiday notes sent back to Mary and Charlotte. He emphasized Morgan's recovery, and teased them with the tale that he himself was growing a nautical beard of Ancient Mariner proportions. "I mean to shave infant-smooth the very last Stage, before we reach London."[163] They were safely back by 20 March, and spending "at least 5 evenings out of 7" quietly at home.[164]

Mrs Clarkson later confidently reported that this whole seaside trip was just another excuse for Coleridge to avoid seeing Wordsworth. But the anxiety over Morgan's health and affairs was genuine enough. Like Josiah Wedgwood, his business investments were in deep trouble because of wartime inflation, and they proceeded to collapse that summer with appalling rapidity. In May there were mounting bills; in June the whole Brent business was threatened by creditors; in August their bank foreclosed; and by October 1813 Morgan had lost all his invested capital and fled to Ireland to avoid arrest. The Berners Street house was let; the furniture was sold; and Mary and Charlotte moved into cheap lodgings at 19 London Street, Fitzroy Square. Quite suddenly Coleridge was shipwrecked again.[165]

Rumours of Morgan's losses had been reaching Keswick since July, and in August Dorothy reported bluntly that "the Morgans have *smashed*". She assumed that Coleridge, rudely awakened from his haze of opium and theatricals, would now come creeping home to Greta Hall. Worse still, he would probably have two destitute Morgan women in tow. Dorothy passed on Mrs Clarkson's latest illuminations to Asra. "Mary says that she doubts not Coleridge has given them to understand there was room enough a G. Hall; but Mrs C. has taken lodgings for them. Where will the poet's home be now? Dear Sara, it is altogether a melancholy business – coming with *them* and would not come to see his children! No plans laid for Hartley! I foresee nothing but Jealousies and discomfort. Happy we in being 15 miles off!"[166]

As usual, Mrs Clarkson's interesting speculations were acute but inaccurate. The poet revealed more worldly plans. He was going to save the Morgans by his own efforts. From the start of John Morgan's difficulties in the spring, it looks very much as if Coleridge had been channelling more and more of his theatrical earnings into helping his adopted household. Certainly they had been absorbed at an alarming rate, which nothing else can quite explain. By 25 September he was so short of funds that he pawned forty books, his watch and his beloved snuffbox for the paltry sum of £6. He had even dug out half a dozen of his books that he remembered leaving at the *Courier* offices, to make up the amount.[167]

He knew that much of this money should really have been sent as promised to Greta Hall. But his loyalty to the Morgans, for good or ill, prevailed. He knew this would be held against him as a dereliction of parental duty, particularly in the case of Hartley, although the expenses of university were still one year away. But he simply felt unable to abandon the Morgans, who had so recently saved him in his own terrible distress. Looking back at this desperate time he later wrote: "the successive Losses and increasing Distress of poor Morgan and his family while I was domesticated with them . . . scarcely left me the power of asking myself the Right or Wrong . . ."[168]

17

The story of Coleridge as financial knight errant, riding to the rescue of the Morgans, is one of the most unlikely of his whole career. Yet it emerges in an astonishingly punctual (if chaotic) series of business letters running unbroken from the beginning of October till the end of November 1813. The man who had been Sir Alexander Ball's First Secretary, and the editor who had launched *The Friend* against every obstacle, resurfaced at this moment of peril.

Coleridge first took advice in the City, assessed the business debts and main creditors, and began to negotiate loans, raising an initial promise of £100 on 15 October.[169] The rescue plan was remarkably sophisticated. They would save the retail silverware business in Bishopsgate, transfer the legal ownership to Charlotte Brent (thereby making it immune to bankruptcy proceedings against Morgan himself) and sell off the Brent trading company to raise capital against the remaining debts. To do this, a breathing-space had to be secured against the most pressing creditor, Lloyd's Bank, who were threatening to institute proceedings and make the whole family destitute.

After a day's reflection, Coleridge proposed to go to Bristol, where John Morgan had many family friends among the Unitarian merchants. Here he would raise further loans, and at the same time give a new series of lectures to provide further money. By this means he believed he could "preserve for Miss Brent the unembarrassed Business of Bishopsgate Street, with every favourable presumption of considerable Increase, as soon as it shall be rescued from Lloyd's Tyranny".[170]

So instead of creeping north, Coleridge was actually posting west. By 24 October he had set up his headquarters at the White Lion Inn, Bristol. From there he wrote briskly to Charlotte at Fitzroy Square. "I will not trouble you with the Detail of my operations, or of the difficulties I have met with . . . Suffice it, that I have no doubts of succeeding so far as to secure the B. St. Business for the nonce. – The proposed Scheme of Lecturing has met with such support, that I have resolved on it – and shall give the first at the White Lion, on Thursday Evening at 7 o'clock." He thought he could send a first instalment of money "within a week".[171]

Next he set up a series of meetings with a list of wealthy well-wishers – Mr Michael Castle, Mr William Hood, Mr Hart Davies and Mr Kiddle are mentioned – and two Bristol members of parliament. He also traded unashamedly on his own literary connections, calling on friends of Sir Humphry Davy, and even contacting local celebrities, including rather appropriately a man who had recently made a famous ascent from Clifton in a Montgolfier balloon.[172]

There was a sense in which Coleridge himself became airborne during these weeks at Bristol. The feeling of urgency, of knight-errantry, lifted him up over every obstacle. He dined, negotiated, drank and lectured on behalf of his " dear Loves" with extraordinary energy and buoyancy. The six lectures began as promised on Thursday, 28 October, and continued twice a week until 24 November, finally expanding to eight in all by popular demand. They were widely and enthusiastically reported in the local press. He launched straight into his most dramatic subjects – *Hamlet* and then *Macbeth* – and the *Bristol Gazette* noted that by the second lecture the candlelit upper room at the White Lion "overflowed".[173] *Felix Farley's Journal*, the most literary of the local papers, spoke of his "power of philosophical analysis", his "luminous and reflecting mind", and – rather acutely – of his "peculiar faculty" of expressing complex ideas in vivid and "appropriate imagery".[174] Subscriptions for the lectures were charged at a guinea for the course, or five shillings at the door, and went on "with a steady Breeze".[175]

He had sent for his old lecture notebooks and his copy of Schlegel, but when these did not arrive in time, he seems to have lectured quite comfortably from half-a-dozen headings jotted down on the back of a letter addressed to him at his inn.[176] Later he would walk into the room carrying the relevant volume of Joseph Rann's Oxford edition of Shakespeare (1794), a volume of Schlegel, and a single sheet of notes – and frequently look at none of them for the entire course of the lecture.[177] He was unusually full of sudden critical insights and innovations: Lady Macbeth proved herself a woman "in the very moment of dark and bloody imagination"; Hamlet's abstraction was like a man looking at "a waterfall"; Macbeth became a tyrant like Napoleon, "both indifferent to means".[178]

His old publisher Joseph Cottle was among the crowded audience, and was impressed by a sense of Coleridge's ease and mastery. They were not the "polished compositions", painstakingly written out and read, that the provincial lecture-goers still expected. They were "conversational", indulging in "harangues" and asides, treating his audience like friends, seemingly effortless so "he might have lectured continuously". Every so often came "racy and felicitous passages, indicating deep thought, and indicative of a man of genius". The attention of his listeners "never flagged, and his large dark eyes, and his countenance, in an excited state, glowing with intellect, predisposed his audience in his favour".[179]

The glow may also have been the result of relentless socializing. Every financial discussion involved a bibulous evening, and Coleridge was "seldom out of his bedroom" until eleven the next morning.[180] "Lectures are nothing, were they every day," he told Mary and Charlotte heroically, "it is dinnering, dinnering that is the Devil."[181]

But steadily he put the financial rescue-package together. "After frequent, & long Discussions however I have succeeded in convincing them that the BG St Bss may be saved, ought to be saved, & can only be saved by making some immediate satisfactory settlement with Lloyd."[182] The debt had now mounted to £290, and there were also the Morgans' household bills. Coleridge held himself responsible for all, and soon the money began, miraculously, to arrive in his letters. Money from his lectures came in banknotes, money from Bristol friends came in banker's drafts. There were delays, confusions, missed posts and postponed meetings (when he got up too late). There were agonized apologies for instalments missed – "that the £100 was not sent on Monday, was not my fault . . . I think, I can now command £80 more . . ."[183] There were confused promises: "but perhaps, I shall be able to raise £130 . . ."[184]

Sometimes it seemed nothing would actually materialize. But it did. The correspondence is tangled, often cut short by last minute dashes to the post and to lectures, and may have failed to mention several payments slipped in at the last moment. But on close inspection a skeleton account of Coleridge's fund-raising emerges. It is clear that at least six payments were definitely sent to the desperate Morgan women. On Sunday, 31 October, there was a bank note for £20; on Wednesday, 3 November a banker's draft for £100; on Sunday, 14 November another banknote for £10; on the following

Wednesday, 17 November a further £20; and on Friday, 19 November a second large draft for £100.[185] Finally on Saturday, 20 November came a promise to "settle Lloyd" – the balance was about £50 allowing for household bills – within four days.[186] This was evidently done, because the business was saved by December, and the Morgans were able to leave London. In total Coleridge had managed to raise through donations, and his own lecture fees, a sum not less than £250 – and probably as much as £300 – in less than six weeks: about twice his own annual income.

The strain, and the excitement, of these weeks swept over Coleridge. What he could not achieve for his own family, he was inspired to do for the Morgans, in one of those bursts of energy which took him back to his youth. For most of November he was living like a man possessed, giving a second set of lectures at Clifton, getting drunk every evening, scrawling intimate letters till dawn, and the next day looking forward "with Terror" to the expected public performance.[187] When he did not receive daily replies from Mary and Charlotte, he was "tormented" with doubts about their affection for him, writing desperately: "you never believed that I loved you & Morgan, as (God knows!) I have done".[188]

When they did write, expressing their gratitude, he was overcome by idealized visions of their life together in the future. Sailing on his midnight fantasies, he came perilously close to proposing a *ménage à trois* in secret lodgings at Clifton: "we all three might lodge and board, and have two bedrooms, and one sitting-room private to ourselves. I can feel & understand your Objections; but I am certain, that the getting *them* over would greatly smooth the way to Morgan's *comfortable* Return & Settlement."[189] That Coleridge was partly inspired by romantic feelings for Charlotte, as well as his genuine sense of indebtedness to John Morgan, is clear from his more drunken and less guarded letters.

A late-night missive on 17 November begins rapturously: "Well, my dear Loves! I have made a famous Lecture to a crowded Room – & all the better because . . . I had not prepared one single word or thought, till ten minutes before the Lecture commenced." He goes on with his knight-errant promise to look after them, and "accompany" them anywhere in England, "till I re-deliver the goods to the rightful owner, J. J. Morgan Esquire", and then begs for a letter from Charlotte personally.

This is followed by one of his teasing, suggestive, imaginings of Charlotte's prettily blushing refusals of such an advance. 'O la! no! Write to a man, tho' old enough to be my father –! – my neck-and-breast kerchief is downright scorched & iron-moulded with the intensity of my expansive Blush." Continuing the game, he traces the blush from the roots of Charlotte's "beautiful Hair" down to "a little beyond the lowermost end of her tiny pretty Bird's Neck". He tells Mary this is only his "sky-larking", but it is a flirtatious flight.[190]

Three days later, he is teasing Charlotte again for her bad spelling, but praises her for womanly "Understanding" and her lack of "Blue-stockingism". The implication is that for "Love and Friendship" the Morgan women are quite as valuable to him as the Grasmere woman once were. "You yourselves *cannot* write half as sweetly & heart-touchingly, as with *your* thoughts & feelings you would have done, if you had never heard of Grammar, Spelling etc. – O curse them – at least as far as Women are concerned. The longer I live, the more do I loathe in stomach, & deprecate in Judgement, all, *all* Bluestockingism." He urges Charlotte to have "confidence" in him, and promises to burn every letter from her the moment he has read it.[191] If Charlotte did respond to these overtures during November, then Coleridge kept his word, for no letters from her have survived.

Unwittingly, the two women were slipping into a difficult position. Coleridge was saving them financially, but also trapping them emotionally. They responded gratefully to the idea of joining him in the West Country, until Morgan returned from his Irish exile. But perhaps they did not realize the full extent of his secret dreams and demands on their affection. Even when he once suggested that they settle together in a "comfortable Dwelling" near Tom Poole's at Stowey, it is possible that they did not recognize his fantasy of recapturing the domestic happiness of 1797.[192] Or perhaps all three of them were simply whirled along by desperation and euphoria.

Certainly, the last few days at Bristol seemed like a triumph. Coleridge had been invited to stay at his old friend Josiah Wade's, in the luxurious house at 2 Queen's Square, and he was fêted at dinners and soirées. He was enchanted one evening when the businessman Michael Castle solemnly presented him with an expensive snuffbox during a game of whist. It seemed a symbol of acceptance, a sign that the local worthies recognized his achievements and celebrity. He reported the incident proudly to the Morgans.

Castle rose from the card table, and announced in the hearing of the assembled company: "'I have wished a Keep sake of yours – let us exchange Boxes – I assure you, I shall preserve yours as a Relic'". Coleridge gave up his ten pence tin box (a replacement for the one he had pawned), and received in return "one of the most elegant boxes of richest Tortoise shell mounted in Gold". When he turned it in the candlelight, it glowed like a piece of jet.[193] It was as if he had received a decoration from the city, a medal for services rendered.

Two days later he was on the night mail coach for London, determined to settle the last of the Morgans' affairs and sweep them back with him to some idyllic haven in the West Country. He now considered them, he told Wade, his family and his "Protégées". On the journey, he talked rapturously all night with two serving Officers from Malta and Sicily, of battles and courage and sticking to one's post. One of them had had half his jaw blown off by a blunderbuss, yet "conversed intelligibly" when confronted by Coleridge's conversational firepower.[194]

He was received like a hero at Fitzroy Square, and whatever doubts remained were silenced. Within a week he had Mary and Charlotte packed up, and had reduced his own worldly baggage to a small library of German lecture texts – Fichte, Schelling and Jean-Paul Richter – largely borrowed from Crabb Robinson. He explained to the startled Robinson that his sudden migration to the West was a matter of simple duty. "If the health & circumstances of two virtuous, pure-hearted, & kind-hearted Women, the Wife & the Sister of a Man, I call my Friend – & whom, in his Prosperity, I found a *Friend* – can constitute Duty."[195] No message was sent to Keswick or to Grasmere. Coleridge was driven with the impetuosity of a man eloping to a happier world. It was as if the Pantisocrat had come to life again and everything could be renewed.

18

Coleridge, Mary and Charlotte left London on Monday, 29 November 1813. They spent four days on the road, travelling by hired post-chaise, and stopping off at Reading, Chippenham and Bath. All three seem to have become ill on the journey, with Coleridge resorting more and more heavily to opium and brandy at each inn. Quite suddenly the atmosphere of romantic escapade began to dissipate.

Coleridge had found them secluded lodgings in the tiny hamlet of Ashley, near Box, some five miles east of Bath on a wooded hillside above the Great West Road. It was little more than an isolated cluster of stone cottages, straggling up a steep track with a farm and an ancient manor house at the top. Their cottage belonged to a grocer from Box, a Mrs Smith, who let rooms cheaply and discreetly without enquiring too closely about her tenants (though she was later to hear all about Coleridge's children). Southwards the rolling countryside stretched away towards the bare hills of the Marlborough Downs. Below them in the valley stood Box church, surrounded by graves. Twice a day the mail coach rattled through the fields of somnolent cattle towards London. It was beautiful but very remote, especially in winter.

Coleridge had planned to begin a new series of lectures at Bristol on Tuesday, 7 December, and to return to his "dear Loves" each weekend. But the whole plan collapsed before the first week was out. Instead of a rural idyll Coleridge found himself sunk in one of the loneliest and most desperate periods of his entire existence.[196] Exactly what went wrong is difficult to reconstruct from his correspondence which again becomes very broken. The *Bristol Gazette* simply reported that he had been "surprised and confined by sudden and severe illness at his arrival at Bath, six days before the promised commencement of his second course, 7 December 1813", and that new lectures would begin in January 1814. But in the event he was unable to undertake these either.[197]

In a confused note to Josiah Wade, written from Bath on 8 December, Coleridge hints at some sort of confrontation and crisis at Ashley within three days of their arrival. He had left the lodgings precipitously on the evening of Sunday, 5 December, in a rainstorm and with a "violent cold", and had missed the last scheduled stagecoach. He was obliged to walk with his bag of books the five miles into Bath, slipping and stumbling through "Mud or Mire, the whole way".[198]

Parts of this note are heavily inked out, but clearly refer to Mary and Charlotte. The surviving passage reads: ". . . I can only answer sorrowfully, – the passions & pride of Women, even of in most respects good & amiable Women: – passions that thwart all I do to serve them . . ."[199] It seems likely that "passions" were raised on both sides, and Coleridge was in a fury of opium and making outrageous demands. Months later, in one of an agonized series of confessions about his opium addiction, he spoke of his "excess of cruelty to Mary and Charlotte, when at Box, and both ill – (a vision of Hell to me when I think of it!) . . ."[200]

Having stumbled into Bath that Sunday night, he staggered to the first coaching inn, the Grey Hound, and crawled up to an attic bedroom. Here he lay prostrated for nearly a fortnight. He was suffering from the most acute opium overdose of his life. After those last weeks of heroic effort, the knight errant had utterly collapsed into a nightmare of hallucinations, sweating, agonizing muscular pains, and a burning fever that left him unable to sleep, eat or talk coherently. The landlady of the Grey Hound, Mrs May, was convinced that the battered traveller was dying. She called in a local doctor, as Coleridge was "too wild with suffering" to do anything for himself.

By sheer good luck this doctor recognized him and instantly identified his symptoms. It was Caleb Parry, the father of Coleridge's friends the Parry brothers whom he had known at Göttingen. Mrs May later told Coleridge that Dr Parry took charge of him with "parental kindness". He called several times a day, sat by his bedside for two or three hours at a time, and acted like a nurse (an unheard of thing for a doctor, observed Mrs May), sponging his face and talking him through the worst of his hallucinations. Dr Parry also noted that Coleridge, after his weeks of manic activity, was now severely "deprest in spirit", and needed company to draw him away from his own "Thoughts". He suspected suicidal tendencies, and indeed Coleridge was to suffer from these for several months, even more badly than he had on leaving Italy. It was to Parry, said Coleridge later, "under God's Mercy I owe that I am at present alive".[201]

In a way, Coleridge had been sinking towards this crisis ever since he left Grasmere in the autumn of 1810. The success of his lectures, and then his play in London, had postponed it; and his new household with the Morgans had sometimes promised that he might escape it altogether. But the contradictions in his life were still largely unresolved, or at least unaccepted. Guilt for his many failings – opium, Asra, his unhappy marriage, his abandoned children – had put him in a condition of perpetual flight from inner realities. He was destroying himself, destroying his capacity for work, destroying the love of all those around him.

Somehow he had to make a stand, to face up to the worst. Otherwise, one way or another, he would commit suicide. The dream of recreating the cottage life with Mary and Charlotte was really a last desperate fantasy attempt to go back to the Wordsworth household, to re-enter what now seemed a Paradise Lost, "before the Fall". But in reality, he had to make a different kind of accommodation with existence, if he was to survive at all.

Lying on his sweat-soaked bed in the Grey Hound Inn, Bath, as homeless now as he had ever been in his life, a man with a bag of old clothes and some borrowed books, addicted to opium, incapable of work, clutching a tortoiseshell snuffbox as the only proof that he had ever achieved anything, Coleridge looked into his own dark night of the soul. "O I have seen far, far deeper and clearer than I ever saw before the ground of pernicious errors! O I have seen, I have felt that the worst offences are those against our own souls! . . . Should I recover I will – no – no may God grant me power to struggle to become *not another* but a *better* man . . . O God save me – from myself."[202]

On 19 December he crawled out of bed, wrapped in a blanket, to write to Mary Morgan. The tone of his letter was utterly changed, fearful and contrite, with a looming sense of sufferings yet to come. "The Terrors of the Almighty have been around & against me – and tho' driven up and down for seven dreadful Days by restless Pain, like a Leopard in a Den, yet the anguish & remorse of Mind was worse than the pain of the whole Body. – O I have had a new world opened to me, in the infinity of my own Spirit! – Woe be to me, if this last Warning be not taken. – Amidst all my anguish you and Charlotte were present to me – & formed a part of it."[203]

19

It was this experience of December 1813 that inspired perhaps the darkest of all Coleridge's poems, "Human Life: On the Denial of Immortality". It opens with a vision of the utter spiritual bleakness to which he had now been reduced:

If dead, we cease to be; if total gloom
Swallow up life's brief flash for aye, we fare
As summer-gusts, of sudden birth and doom . . .

It is a Hamlet-like soliloquy of the "shadowy self", facing total extinction. The echoing, abstract language suggests a state of vacuous horror, on the very edge of personal collapse. Yet the poem is severely controlled (it takes the form of a double sonnet), and is driven forward by a series of relentless metaphysical speculations (rather in the style of the Jacobean poet Fulke Greville), which flinch at nothing.

Perhaps the self is "rootless" and "substanceless". Perhaps laughter and tears "mean but themselves". Perhaps the heart is filled with "hollow joy for hollow good". Perhaps Man faces a world without spiritual meaning or the possibility of redemption. "Why waste thy sighs, and thy lamenting voices . . . That such a thing as thou feel'st warm or cold?"

At a philosophical level, Coleridge was grappling with Schelling's notion of Nature as a vast "unconscious" force, an impersonal universe of busy fruitless "activity". Perhaps Man was never created by God, but is merely an evolutionary "accident" without divine "purpose" or future. All his efforts may mean nothing in the scheme of things.

O Man! Thou vessel purposeless, unmeant,
Yet drone-hive strange of phantom purposes!
Surplus of Nature's dread activity.
Which, as she gazed on some nigh-finished vase,
Retreating slow, with meditative pause,
She formed with restless hands unconsciously.
Blank accident! nothing's anomaly!

But at a personal level, this "Nothing" was the dark chasm that Coleridge now saw beneath him in "the Infinity" of his own spirit. All his efforts, all his suffering might be part of a meaningless, cosmic accident. The terrible, slow, booming poem ends in a kind of hopeless mutter, as if even Coleridge's wonderful gift with words had finally failed him. The very syllables close up upon themselves, and groan to a halt:

Be sad! be glad! be neither! seek, or shun!
Thou hast no reason why! Thou canst have none;
Thy being's being is contradiction.[204]

What life remained for him now in such a world?

8

True Confessions

1

But the world had not finished with Coleridge. Just before Christmas 1813, a carriage appeared at the Grey Hound Inn, and Coleridge was bundled off to 2 Queen's Square, Bristol and installed in a large guest-room. This time it was Josiah Wade who had come to his rescue, and Wade's personal physician, Dr Daniel, who began treating him for addiction and suicidal depression. A burly manservant was employed to sleep on a truckle bed in his room to restrain him from violence or secret opium-dosing. Once, when Coleridge "skulked out" at night to obtain laudanum, he came back begging to be sent to a lunatic asylum.[1] Razors, penknives and "every possible instrument of Suicide" had to be removed from his room, as he later recalled "with horror".[2]

Here Coleridge remained for the next nine months, until September 1814, fluctuating between the status of house-guest, medical patient and in the early weeks almost that of a prisoner under restraint. There were periods of remission – in April Coleridge managed to give a series of seven lectures on Milton and Cervantes – but his condition was far worse than he had ever experienced. He continually relapsed, and at times it seemed that he would never recover his mental balance.

He wrote to the Morgans, begging their forgiveness. Charlotte herself wrote back, and there was talk of his coming to convalesce at Ashley.[3] But Coleridge's physical and mental condition was too unstable, and even when John Morgan returned from Ireland in May 1814, there was no immediate plan for such a move. Morgan was grateful to Coleridge, but evidently wary of taking him back after everything that had happened in his absence.

Coleridge had tearful confrontations with his "faithful, *inexhaustibly patient* Friend" Wade, exclaiming "in agony" that he had destroyed himself and ruined his family. "Had I but a few hundred pounds, but £200, half to send to Mrs Coleridge, & half to place myself in a private madhouse, where I could procure nothing but what a Physician thought proper, & where a medical attendant could be constantly with me for two or three months (in less than that time Life or Death would be determined) then there might be Hope. Now there is none!"[4]

All this time Dr Daniel worked doggedly at reducing Coleridge's laudanum dose, teaspoonful by teaspoonful, week by week. Coleridge now admitted he had been in the habit of taking up to a pint each day, "besides great quantities of liquor". With many backslidings, this was gradually reduced to a minutely controlled dose of "four teaspoonfuls in the 24 hours".[5] It is doubtful if this low dose was regularly sustained at first, and Cottle recalled "from an undoubted source" that during 1814 Coleridge had been known to consume "in twenty-four hours, a whole quart of laudanum!" (two pints).[6]*

Modern knowledge of addiction would suggest that psycholog-

* Modern medical opinion holds that an addict may tolerate some 5 grams of morphine a day, before overdose and death; but it is difficult to establish the equivalent in the unregulated concentrations of nineteenth-century pharmacists' opium. Depending on its composition, a pint of laudanum might contain 3 grams of morphine, but Cottle claimed Coleridge had been consuming 2 pints per day (6 grams) at this time. (*Early Recollections*, 1837, 2, p. 169.) Opium was also measured in "grains", and "drops". One grain equals approximately 25 drops, or half a teaspoonful. A medical analgesic dose, used like aspirin, was one or two grains (a teaspoonful) every six hours. Coleridge claimed to have reduced his dose to this level (8 grains per day) under Dr Daniel in April 1814, but it is very doubtful if he sustained this for any length of time. Violent, uncontrolled fluctuations in dose-levels are characteristic of the unsupervised addict, depending on health, mood, social demands – and, of course, money. Coleridge's experience was probably like De Quincey's, who records that in 1816 his own dose sometimes rose as high as "8,000 drops" (320 grains) *per day*, and sometimes dropped as low as "160 drops" (6 grains). Such a regime, wrote De Quincey, "defeats the *steady* habit of exertion; but creates spasms of irregular exertion. It ruins the natural power of life; but it develops preternatural paroxyms of intermitting power." (De Quincey, *Confessions of an English Opium Eater*, 1822; see also his article "Coleridge and Opium-Eating", *Blackwood's Magazine*, January 1845.) Various assessments are given in Alethea Hayter (op. cit., 1968); Molly Lefebure, *Coleridge: A Bondage of Opium*, 1974; and Stephen Weissman, *Coleridge*, 1989, "Appendix on Opium". Until proper research began in the 1820s (notably by German chemists) the only contemporary study of the drug and its effects was Samuel Crumpe, *An Inquiry into the Nature and Use of Opium*, 1793. The supply of opium only began to be regulated with the foundation of the Pharmaceutical Society of Great Britain in 1841, and the first Pharmacy and Poisons Acts of 1868.

ically, a far more significant advance was made in April when Coleridge began writing a series of long, detailed, confessional letters to his friend publicly admitting that he had been an opium addict for well over a decade. He had acknowledged this before, in 1808, but never with such a degree of self-exposure.

Significantly, these letters did not go to his family, but to long-standing friends in Bristol. Coleridge wrote to John Prior Estlin, to his old publisher Joseph Cottle, to John Morgan, and even to Wade (though they were under the same roof). These confessions are strikingly similar in tone – bitterly self-accusing and humiliated, yet also shrewdly self-analytical and to some extent self-exculpating. They reveal a strong philosophical or religious dimension, based on the notion of the corrupted human will – Coleridge's version of original sin – which is so prominent in all his later writing. What he had explored so brilliantly in his *Hamlet* lectures – the idea of imaginative power destroyed by moral paralysis – was now brought to bear on his own case, and seen as part of a universal human condition. Opium of course was his own particular sin, but it arose out of the fallen condition of mankind. In this way he could acknowledge his own guilt, but also begin to accept it, and beg his friends likewise to accept the terrible truth about his fallen and divided nature.

A letter to John Morgan, written from Queen's Square on 14 May, is representative. Morgan knew as well as any friend, better even than the Wordsworths, the real state of Coleridge's addiction; and for this reason Coleridge's profound need to confess, to admit the worst, to beg for understanding, is revealed most starkly on its own terms. Of the many other letters and Notebook entries he had written about addiction – in Malta, at Coleorton, at Allan Bank, at Stowey – this stands as perhaps the most frank and the most terrible. But it was also, perhaps, the most courageous and healing.

> I know, it will be vain to attempt to persuade Mrs Morgan or Charlotte that a man, whose moral feelings, reason, understanding, and sense are perfectly sane and vigorous, may yet have been *mad* – And yet nothing is more true. By the long Habit of the accursed Poison my Volition (by which I mean the faculty *instrumental* to the Will, and by which alone the Will can realize itself – its Hands, Legs, & Feet, as it were) was

> completely deranged, at times frenzied, dissevered itself from the Will, & became an independent faculty: so that I was perpetually in the state, in which you may have seen paralytic Persons, who attempting to push a step forward in one direction are violently forced round to the opposite. I was sure that no ease, much less pleasure, would ensue: nay, was certain of an accumulation of pain. But tho' there was no prospect, no gleam of Light before, an indefinite indescribable Terror as with a scourge of ever restless, ever coiling and uncoiling Serpents, drove me on from behind.

Coleridge emphasized the moral as well as the physical state of his addiction. It had led him to neglect every family duty and "most barbarously" to mistreat his friends "by silence, absence, or breach of promise." He was unsparing now in the acknowledgement of his guilt.

> I used to think St James's Text, "He who offended in one point of the Law, offendeth in all", was very harsh; but my own sad experience has taught me its awful, dreadful Truth. – What crime is there scarcely which has not been included in or followed from the one guilt of taking opium? Not to speak of ingratitude to my maker for the wasted Talents; of ingratitude to so many friends who have loved me I know not why; of barbarous neglect of my family; excess of cruelty to Mary & Charlotte, when at Box, and both ill – (a vision of Hell to me when I think of it!) I have in this one dirty business of Laudanum a hundred times deceived, tricked, nay, actually & consciously LIED.[7]

In fact his physical symptoms had been more terrible than ever. Besides the "intolerable aching, weakness, & feverish restlessness" which filled his whole body, his knees swelled so painfully he could sometimes barely walk, and his bowels and stomach were twisted with the acute discomfort of constipation (dosing) and diarrhoea (withdrawal). In May he wrote to London for a brass "Clyster Machine" to be purchased at Everall and Wilson's of St James's Street, so that he could administer his own enemas, a process that had become a daily humiliation. All the time his nights were disturbed by the return of the nightmares which accompanied the withdrawal phase, and he sent to Dr Daniel a rewritten fragment of "the Pains of Sleep":

> My waking thoughts with scorn repell
> Loveless Lust, Revenge[ful] spell: –
> O why should Sleep be made *my* Hell.[8]

To both Morgan and Charles Lamb, he wrote that he could say "with little appearance of profaneness" that he had been "crucified, dead, and buried, descended into Hell, and am now, I humbly trust, rising again, tho' slowly and gradually". Lamb, though shocked by Coleridge's reports ("I think I never read anything more moving, more pathetic"), still had his own way of expressing sympathy, and wrote back a letter beginning characteristically, "Dear Resuscitate", and asking how that "frank-hearted circle, Morgan and his cos-lettuces" were coping with his promised resurrection.[9]

2

News of Coleridge's illness filtered back to Keswick, but was not received in quite the same spirit. When Joseph Cottle wrote to Southey in April, asking him to join in an annuity to help Coleridge back on his feet, he received a biting refusal. Unsparingly, Southey enumerated Coleridge's failings. He had wasted the Wedgwood annuity; he never wrote to his wife or children; he had abandoned himself to "most culpable habits of sloth and self-indulgence"; it was "a wonder" that he was still alive.[10] All Coleridge had to do was give up opium and his "frightful consumption of spirits", and start lecturing again. If he now wrote letters acknowledging the guilt of his habit, "he imputes it still to morbid bodily causes, whereas after every possible allowance is made for these, every person who has witnessed his habits, knows that for the greater – infinitely the greater part – inclination and indulgence are the motives." Coleridge suffered from "an insanity of that species which none but the Soul's physician can cure".[11]

When Cottle passed these views on to Coleridge (but without mentioning the annuity plan) the latter replied, "You have poured oil in the raw and festering Wound of an old friend's Conscience, Cottle! but it is oil of Vitriol!"[12] Again he pleaded that he had been "seduced into the ACCURSED Habit ignorantly"; and later sent a long letter on prayer and his renewed belief in the Trinity and the healing powers of Christ. It was this letter that recalled the pit of "total darkness" he had gazed down into, from the summit of Mount Etna in 1804.[13]

Coleridge also wrote to Cottle about the "Christian doctrine of the resurrection of the body", but this time with great earnestness. He thought it contained a profound spiritual truth, if not a literal one. He could not accept it in its "grosser form". But he supposed the body might be subjected to "a sublimating process, so as to be rendered compatible with spiritual association". He found this "an *exhilarating belief*, with many remote analogies in nature".[14] What he did not say was that he was also haunted by the opposite possibility, that his life was "a summer-gust": brief, turbulent and futile.

If Southey was ignorant of the physiology of Coleridge's addiction, and cruelly impatient of his struggles, his practical generosity towards Coleridge's children was admirable. More and more he took on the role of substitute father. He set about organizing a subscription to send Hartley to Merton College, Oxford, the following spring. During the course of 1814, he established an annual fund of some £90, drawing on the Beaumonts, Poole, Cottle and Basil Montagu. He even achieved the feat of obtaining money from Colonel James Coleridge at Ottery. The Colonel drily observed: "Southey seems to have behaved most kindly and generously whilst their *Mad* Father is at Bristol, or God knows where, living on the bounty of his friends . . . unless Opium or something removed him to another World. What a humbling lesson to all men is Samuel Coleridge."[15]

This rather seems to have been Coleridge's own view, as his health gradually improved in June. It is true that he grew weary of the pious exhortations of Cottle, who told him he was possessed not by opium but by the Devil ("God bless him! he is a well-meaning Creature; but a great Fool").[16] But he wrote formally to Wade to thank him for all his care. "Dear Sir, For I am unworthy to call any good man friend – much less you, whose hospitality and love I have abused; accept, however, my intreaties for your forgiveness, and for your prayers . . . After my death, I earnestly entreat, that a full and unqualified narration of my wretchedness, and of its guilty cause, may be made public, that at least some little good may be effected by the direful example. May God Almighty bless you, and have mercy on your still affectionate, and in his heart, grateful – S. T. Coleridge."[17]

In the event it was not Wade, but the pious Cottle who took him at his word, and dutifully published many of these confessional opium letters in his *Early Recollections* (1837), just three years after Coleridge's death, causing endless grief and embarrassment to the surviving family.

Coleridge was still being attended by his keeper (now tactfully his "Valet"), the strong-bodied Mr Haberfield, but Dr Daniel encouraged a careful return to social life in Bristol. On one memorable evening in mid-June, he took him out to dinner until 11.30 p.m. and toasted his recovery in "a jorum of Hollands & Water". Gin and good humour suddenly united the doctor and the patient after all their trials. "The Conversation was mantling like Champagne – & Laughter, as I have often observed, is the most potent Producer of Forgetfulness, of the whole Pharmacopeia, moral or medical."[18]

Coleridge held morning "Levées" in his bedroom, and began making little weekend trips to the Morgans at Ashley in late June and July. They were impressed by the carefully measured doses of laudanum he brought with him, and the old, teasing relations crept back into his thank-you letters. "My best Love to Mary & Charlotte . . . In Bristol they will have it, that Mary is handsomer than Charlotte – how provokingly obstinate!"[19]

3

Slowly Coleridge began to write again, first of all turning his hand to help his old friend Washington Allston. Allston's hopes had been disappointed at the Royal Academy in London, his young wife had died, and for much of the winter he too had been very ill at Clifton. With the peace of 1814 (Napoleon had abdicated to Elba in April) Bristol was in celebratory mood. Among the planned festivities was a grand retrospective exhibition of Allston's paintings at the Merchant Taylor's Hall. Accordingly, Coleridge agreed to puff these in a series of five articles published in *Felix Farley's Bristol Journal* through August and September.[20]

Much of what he wrote was actually a popularization of Kant's art criticism in the *Critique of Judgement* (1790), a surprising but significant journalistic use of German sources. Coleridge's aim was to distinguish an absolute notion of Beauty, as an aesthetic or generative principle universal in the arts, as distinct from what was loosely described as "Agreeable", "Grand" or "Sublime" by reviewers. He began with the image of "an old coach-wheel" lying covered with dirt in a yard, and ended with "the fundamental doctrines of colour, ideal form, and grouping" in Renaissance painting. If this was not quite what was expected in a provincial paper, it gave Allston's work a highly sophisticated context. It also gave Coleridge an opportunity to continue applying philosophical principles to artistic practice. The essays were entitled "On the Principles of Genial Criticism", not in the sense of "pleasing" but of "generative" power.[21]

But they were pleasing, especially in their autobiographical charm, with many memories of his and Allston's visits to the Roman art galleries in 1806. Together they had stood before a canvas showing "Diana and Her Nymphs" in a Swiss landscape, and "felt the breeze blowing out of it".[221]Together they had admired the "sportive wildness of the component figures" in Raphael's "Galatea", the famous fresco at the Villa Farnesi. And together they had discovered Raphael's principle of harmony, a monumental circular structure within the central group (the old coach wheel), geometrically controlled by a "multiplicity of rays and cords".

Coleridge used a striking scientific analogy to sum up the harmonious beauty of Raphael's composition, in one of his most original pieces of art criticism. He praised the "balance, the perfect reconciliation, effected between these two conflicting principles of the FREE LIFE, and of the confining FORM! How entirely is the stiffness that would have resulted from the obvious regularity of the latter, fused and (if I may hazard so bold a metaphor) almost *volatilized* by the interpretation and electrical flashes of the former."[23]

The chemical image was recalled from Davy's method of isolating primary elements with charges from a voltaic battery. It emphasized the dynamic, almost explosive, concept that Coleridge had of Beauty; or rather Beauty as an explosion of energy perfectly contained. Moreover he linked this dynamic aesthetic with the moral nature of mankind: happiness required that we had the individual sense of "free will" and "spontaneous action", balanced and reconciled with "regular forms" of duty and obligation.

In the circumstances, it was no coincidence that Coleridge chose

Allston's large canvas "The Dead Man Restored to Life by Touching the Bones of the Prophet Elisha" for his most detailed commentary. He tenderly described the cluster of figures surrounding "the reviving body" – the faithful Slave, the wife, the daughter, and "the exquisitely graceful girl who is bending downward, and whose hand nearly touches the thumb of the slave". They were subtly structured, so as to produce "what you had not suspected", a circular group. The perception of this stately, platonic, underlying form, "concealed by the action and passion" of the human participants, generated the sense of Beauty in a moment of revelation.[24]

Coleridge summed up his whole position in a formula that he was to use frequently in his later criticism: Beauty was the intuition of the one in the many. "Thus the Philosopher of the later Platonic, or Alexandrine, School named the triangle the first-born of beauty, it being the first and simplest symbol of *multeity in unity*."[25]

Despite the erudite, not to say recherché nature of these essays – they began with a long citation from Giordano Bruno, and ended with another from Plotinus – Coleridge did not forget that he was writing for a Bristol audience in the midst of victory celebrations. Among his more topical remarks was the observation that an Englishman might instinctively use the term "beautiful" to describe "a mass of cloud rich with the rays of the sunrise"; while a Frenchman was more likely to call "the flavour of a leg of mutton a *beautiful* taste". He was never above such popular chauvinism where the French were concerned.[26]

Besides visiting Allston's exhibition to make his notes, Coleridge was also well enough to share in the more patriotic festivities celebrating Napoleon's departure. He visited the triumphal arch erected in Corn Street, inspected the *flambaux* burning on the battlements of St Mary Redcliffe church (where he had been married all those years ago), and saw from afar the huge bonfire lit on Brandon Hill. The wealthier households hung out illuminated signs or "transparencies" from their upper windows, and Coleridge sat up half the night with Wade guarding "the abominable lamps" of their own creation, which constantly threatened to catch fire in the wind.

Now an expert in theatrical effects, he had designed the transparency himself, "a Vulture with the Head of Napoleon chained to a Rock", and a busty Britannia flourishing a pair of shears inscribed with Nelson's name.[27] The rhyming motto he attached was curiously prophetic of Napoleon's escape from Elba, and the Hundred Days leading to Waterloo the following June. "Britons, rejoice! and yet be wary too! – The Chain may break, the Clipt Wing sprout anew."

He sent fresh salmon, and a turtle, to the Morgans at Ashley for their victory feast, and made jokes about "old Blacky, alias Opium".[28] The amorous asides to Charlotte were also renewed. In one humorous fantasy he supposed himself "married to little Megrim" (his new pet-name meant "little Headache") and producing a famous son, "Brentus Coleridge", who would invent a steamship and discover the North West Passage, and so become "Baronet, Sir Brentus Coleridge, of Coleridge Hall & Hundred".[29] He did not speculate what Hartley would have made of this imaginary sibling.

4

Allston was deeply grateful for Coleridge's articles, the last of which ran on 24 September. He proposed in exchange to celebrate his friend's recovery with a grand, three-quarter-length oil painting of Coleridge, dramatically posed in the shadowy solemnity of the Merchant Taylor's Hall. The result is probably the finest portrait from life that Allston ever executed, and it now hangs in the National Portrait Gallery, London. It was completed in a series of studio sessions during August, with Coleridge dressed entirely in black except for a white silk cravat tied formally high under his chin (see frontispiece.)

At first sight, it is the conventional picture of a solemn, heavy, middle-aged professional man. He might be a banker, a tutor, a non-conformist clergyman (or just possibly an exiled revolutionary). But Allston has also captured something visionary, a disturbing other-worldly radiance, a sense of distance and disaster. It is as if Coleridge had disguised himself for the occasion, and beneath the respectable clothes stood someone quite different: the Ancient Mariner immobilized under the uneasy glow of a full moon.

The dark background is emphasized by the glimmering half-light from a tall gothic window behind his right shoulder, with the carved figure of a medieval knight standing sentinel in a niche. Coleridge's face glows out of the darkness, round and full. His hair is almost entirely white, his eyes large and abstracted, his full mouth closed and slightly downturned, with an expression suggesting both suffering and determination. In his left hand he carries what looks like a small book, but turns out to be his snuffbox, the precious one given him by his admirer Michael Castle.

Years before Coleridge had humorously mocked his portrait, also painted in Bristol (in 1796), by Peter Vandycke. It was "a mere carcass of a face, fat, flabby and expressive chiefly of inexpression". Now, nearly twenty years later, he mourned it, both for its weakness and what seemed to him its lifeless immobility. "Of my own portrait I am no judge – Allston is highly gratified with it . . . I am not mortified, though I own I should better like it to be otherwise . . . The face itself is a FEEBLE, unmanly face . . . The exceeding Weakness, Strengthlessness, in my face was ever painful to me." Yet Coleridge also saw that Allston had suggested something fleeting and magical, the power that he could still summon if he began to speak. "Whatever is impressive, is part fugitive, part *existent* only in the imagination of persons impressed strongly by my conversation."[30]

Allston himself thought the picture among his best, but some years later he reflected on the technical difficulties of rendering his subject. What he picked out was not the weakness or suffering in Coleridge's face, but the hidden energy and animation he had found impossible to capture. It led him into a rapturous flight of praise, a memory of Coleridge's undiminished fascination even at this most troubled time.

"So far as I can judge of my own production the likeness of Coleridge is a true one, but it is Coleridge in repose; and, though not unstirred by the perpetual ground-swell of his ever-working intellect, and shadowing forth something of the deep philosopher, it is not Coleridge in his highest mood, the poetic state, when the divine afflatus of the poet possessed him. When in that state, no face that I ever saw was like his; it seemed almost spirit made visible without the shadow of the physical upon it. Could I then have fixed it upon canvas! but it was beyond the reach of my art."[31] Long after Coleridge's death, Wordsworth saw it in Wade's drawing room and called it the "finest" image of his friend; adding with a certain irony that it was "the only likeness that ever gave him any pleasure".[32]

5

Coleridge was now set on returning to the Morgans at Ashley, and in mid August sent down a single box of books and clothes by the canal to Bath, containing all his worldly possessions. He still had some anxieties about his reception, writing to John Morgan; "God grant that with a quiet Conscience I could never be out of the sight of green Field, or out of company with you, Mary & Charlotte – tho' the two latter quarrel with me in a very inexplicable way." He did not expect "anything like praise, or sugar comfits" from them; but perhaps he would write out a few sheets "full of the soothing, handsome speeches" with exact rules and directions "for the time & place of administering them".[33]

He was also anxious about his slow return to health, wondering what permanent damage his appalling excess of opium might have caused. He suffered from a bout of erysipelas inflammation on his legs, and had Dr Daniel examine him for a catalogue of suspected complaints: stricture of the urethra, cirrhosis of the liver, kidney stone, gout, "angry Itching". He grew familiar with a huge tome on "Cutaneous Complaints". On some days he still felt "thoroughly *be-belzebubbed*".[34]

Nevertheless, his hypochondria had its limits. ("I tell Dr Daniel, that I have a schirrous Liver: & he laughs at me for my Information.") It was a good sign that his appetite was modestly returning – "I have dined out at York Place . . . Turbot, Lobster Sauce, Boiled Fowl, Turtle, Ham, a quarter of Lamb, Tatas & Cauliflower etc. – then Duck, green Peas, a gooseberry & a currant Pie, and a soft Pudding."[35] On other evenings he spoke wistfully of confining himself "rigorously to the Pint of Madeira prescribed".[36]

Coleridge was most anxious about what direction his work should now take. He was reading widely from Cervantes and Goethe, but several attempts to restart his lecturing on these subjects had been broken off during the summer. The strain was too much, and he would not lecture again for four years. What he wanted was work he could do quietly and steadily at Ashley. At the end of August, on a hint from Lamb, he wrote to the publisher John Murray at Albemarle Street, proposing a verse-translation of Goethe's *Faust*, to be prefaced with a short critical biography.

Murray was now the most fashionable and commercially successful publisher in London. The poetry of Byron, Scott and Rogers had made his fortune. Coleridge hoped that his own work might be re-launched among these glittering names, but he was very uncertain of his standing. Had he already been forgotten or dismissed in London? In writing, he was reduced to giving an awkward curriculum vitae. He reminded Murray of *Remorse* (recently re-staged at Bristol) and of *Wallenstein* (his Schiller translation of 1800), though not of "The Ancient Mariner". He admitted that his own work had never sold, but pointed out that Goethe's *Faust* was "characteristic of a new & peculiar sort of Thinking and Imagining" in Germany, and that he was uniquely qualified to translate it. Faust should be rendered "in wild *lyrical* metres"; and though it was "odious" to attempt a literary work from "any motive of *pecuniary* advantage" he was prepared to bring his "*Intellect* to the *Market*". Murray replied that the market was prepared to commission the work for £100.[37]

In fact Murray, with his shrewd appreciation of literary tastes and fashion, was keen to publish *Faust*. Byron admired it, and Crabb Robinson (having heard "Christabel" recited) had advised him that Coleridge was the man "most likely to execute the work adequately".[38] But he was discouraged by Coleridge's manner (both humble and high-handed), and puzzled by his further stipulation about terms. "1. That *on the* delivery of the last Mss sheet you remit a 100 guineas to Mrs Coleridge, or Mr Robert Southey, at a bill of five weeks. – 2. that I, or my Widow or Family, may any time after two years from the first publication have the privilege of reprinting it in any *collection* of all my poetical writings, or of my Works in general – which set off with a Life of me might perhaps be made profitable to my Widow."[39]

In reality, Coleridge was hoping for some general contract with Murray, and some way of guaranteeing a source of income for his family at Greta Hall. But to the shrewd publisher, the vague suggestion of posthumous publications and collected works had an ominous ring. He must also have wondered exactly what revelations Coleridge's "Life of me" might entail. When he hesitated, Coleridge wrote again on 12 September, now casting himself as Goethe's champion in England.

"I cannot persuade myself, that I can have offended you by my openness. I think 'Faust' a work of genius, of genuine and original Genius. The Scenes in the Cathedral and in the Prison must delight and affect all Readers not pre-determined to dislike. But the Scenes of Witchery and that astounding Witch-gallop up the Brocken will be denounced as *fantastic* and absurd. Fantastic they *are*, and were meant to be; but I need not tell you, how many will detect the supposed fault for one, who can enter into the philosophy of that imaginative Superstition, which justifies it." Not discounting these difficulties, Coleridge compared Goethe to Shakespeare, and described him as one of "the living Stars, that are now culminant on the German Parnassus".[40]

This second letter was a much more direct challenge to Murray to take the risk of publishing a controversial work. Coleridge's memories of his own trip to the Brocken in 1799 were mixed with his perennial fascination with "imaginative Superstition" and the poetic world of "witchery". But Murray was unmoved. When Coleridge added, with a touch of desperation, that he was also prepared to translate Cervantes or Boccaccio instead for "any moderate price", the exchange lapsed.[41]*

Though still without commissioned work, Coleridge moved back to Ashley in the second week of September 1814. His return to the countryside was to be as momentous as his departure from Bristol to Stowey almost twenty years before in the winter of 1796. His literary schemes – as then – were fluid, but a second great period of writing lay ahead. He had survived a time when he had struggled "against the immoral Wish to have died at the commencement of my Sufferings".[42] As he rode out, he greeted a large white sea-bird heading southwards for the Bristol Channel:

---

* The loss of Coleridge's version of *Faust*, which would surely have been spectacular, had a curiously suspending effect on Goethe's reputation in Victorian England. Shelley (who said that only Coleridge could do it justice) translated fragments of the drama in 1822 in Italy, which were published by Leigh Hunt in *The Liberal*; and Coleridge in turn said he admired these "very much" (see *Table Talk*, I, p. 574). But full translations did not appear until the late 1820s, by which time it was heavily bowdlerized. By 1833 even Coleridge claimed he had turned it down as "vulgar, licentious and most blasphemous". (*Table Talk*, I, p. 343) Gérard de Nerval translated it magnificently in France (1828), but no major poet attempted *Faust* in England until Louis MacNeice (1951). Instead there were somewhat guarded essays by Carlyle and Matthew Arnold, and a fine humorous biography by George Eliot's "husband", G. H. Lewes (1855).

Seaward, white-gleaming thro' the busy Scud
With arching Wings the Sea-mew o'er my head
Posts on, as bent on speed; now passaging
Edges the stiffer Breeze, now yielding drifts
Now floats upon the Air, and sends from far
A wildly wailing Note.[43]

He arrived at Ashley as the autumn rains began, and it seemed like the end of a long dry season. His Notebooks flooded slowly back into life. One evening he stood at the window for two hours, listening to the sounds of "a steady soaking Rain". When the sky cleared, he walked out and stood beneath a "full uncurtainment of sprinkled Stars and milky Stream and dark blue Interspaces . . . so deep was the silence of the Night, that the *Drip* from the Leaves of the Garden Trees *copied* a steady shower."[44]

6

As far as the literary world was concerned, Coleridge's retreat to Ashley in the autumn of 1814 marked the final disastrous collapse of a once-brilliant career. Among family, friends and professional colleagues, his opium addiction was an open secret. Nothing more was heard of him at Keswick, and very little at Bristol except through Joseph Cottle, who continued to urge repentance (prompting Coleridge to repeat philosophically, "sooner or later my Case will be published").[45] He had no plans to lecture, and no publisher either in Bristol or in London. The *Quarterly Review* ran a long, retrospective article (by his nephew John Taylor Coleridge) placing him high among "the Lake Poets" – one of the earliest uses of the term – but regretting his failure to publish any mature work, suffering "the fruits of his labour to perish", and accusing him of having dissipated his life "in alternations of desultory application, and nervous indolence".[46]

News of Coleridge's fate spread rapidly among the younger generation, who bewailed his loss to literature. Keats's friend, the young poet J. H. Reynolds, who had been corresponding with Wordsworth, recorded the tragedy. "Poor Coleridge! I understand he is out of his Mind! – or at least in that state of dejectedness that is akin to it. – Good God! What a genius is lost! What a mind is overthrown! Did you ever read his Poems of 'Love' and 'The Nightingale' in the *Lyrical Ballads* or his sublime translation of Schiller's Plays of *Wallenstein* & *Piccolomini*? – if not – Pray read them & you will see how delicately he can write & how strongly. It has been hinted that a Subscription will be started – I hope there will."[47]

From Greta Hall, Mrs Coleridge wrote in real despair to Tom Poole at Stowey. She recognized the "great kindness and solicitude" of Southey, Wordsworth and the Ottery Coleridges in providing for her children, but she was humiliated and terrified by the "unfortunate situation" in which Coleridge had abandoned her. The literary success of his friends – Southey's *Roderick* was running to a second edition, Wordsworth's great philosophic poem *The Excursion* was published – made his failure more public, and had now begun to affect Hartley and the other children as they grew conscious of their position in the world. "You will be shocked to hear that I never hear from C. I dare not dwell upon the painful consequences of his desertion but if in the Spring he does not exert himself to pay some of my debts here – I really do not know what will be the result. – The poor children, are miserable if their father is mentioned for fear they should hear anything like blame attached to it, but I believe I mentioned to you before their great sensibility on this unhappy subject."[48] But there was no mention of what Coleridge might have suffered.

In return, Coleridge maintained his perverse but self-protective silence for many months. In his darker moments, his guilt burst from him with all the knowledge of what worldly duty required, both for himself and for his family. He must write, he must earn, he must be responsible like Southey. But he could never give up the idea of some major *oeuvre* that, against all the odds, still lay within him. "O God! it is very easy to say, why does not Coleridge do this work & that work? – I declare to God, there is nothing I would not do consistent with my Conscience which was regular Labour for a regular Revenue – But to write such poetry or such philosophy as I would wish to write or not write at all, cannot be done amid distraction & anxiety for the day."[49] He jotted in his Notebook a "plaintive" verse, adapted from two lines of Phineas Fletcher, addressed to his Muse as a Shepherd's pipe that was slipping from his fingers:

Go, little Pipe! for ever I must leave thee,
        Ah vainly true!
Never ah never! must I more receive thee?
        Adieu! adieu!
Well, thou art gone! and what remains behind
        Soothing the soul to Hope?
        The moaning wind
Hide with sear leaves my Grave's undaisied Slope![50]

Yet this was not his dominant mood at Ashley, for now if ever his extraordinary powers of resilience were indeed flooding back to save him. Within two days of unpacking his solitary book chest, he wrote to his old stand-by Daniel Stuart in London proposing a whole range of political articles for the *Courier*, as a way of raising immediate money. Suggested topics for this *tour d'horizon* included France, America and Ireland. When the latter was accepted, he at once began a vigorous defence of the rights of the Protestant Orangemen against an upsurge of Catholic persecutions (which John Morgan witnessed during his flight to Ireland). These immediately began to appear in the paper, running as "Six Letters To Mr Justice Fletcher" from 20 September to 10 December. They were startling proof of Coleridge's ability to re-engage with public affairs on apparently so remote a topic, as well as his recovered industry. A manuscript copy made by Morgan, and later emended by Coleridge, ran to seventy-two pages of a quarto notebook.[51] For this he was paid the princely sum of £20.

During the autumn Coleridge also wrote several confidential letters to Stuart, describing his battle with addiction and the professional challenge that now confronted him. His tone was never hopeless, and often combative. "I am abused, & insolently reproved, as a man, with reference to my supposed private Habits, for *not publishing* . . . but I *could* rebut the charge, & not merely say but prove – that there is not a man in England, whose Thoughts, Images, Words, & Erudition have been published in larger quantities than *mine* – tho', I must admit, not *by* or *for* myself."[52]

He rejoiced in the "increased and increasing" reputation of Southey and Wordsworth, though he felt he was grievously misunderstood by them, and found it hard "to bear their neglect, and even detraction – *as if I had done nothing at all*". Terrible though his illness at Bristol had been, he felt he had survived and learned from it, "having escaped with my intellectual Powers, if less elastic, yet not less vigorous, and with ampler and far more solid materials to exert them on".[53]

He drew a tranquil, not to say bucolic, picture of his well-ordered regime with the Morgans. "I am now joint-tenant with Mr Morgan of a sweet little cottage at Ashley, half a mile from Box, on the Bath Road. I breakfast every morning before nine – work till one – & walk or read till 3 – thence till Tea time, chat or read some lounge-book – or correct what I have written – from 6 to 8, work again – from 8 to Bed time play whist, or the little mock-billiard, called Bagatelle, & then sup & go to bed."[54]

He was catching up with topical matters by reading a year's back-numbers of both the *Quarterly* and the *Edinburgh* reviews and making notes on them every day, admittedly a "painful & disgusting task", but one which he completed by November.[55] The opium-taking was also for the moment strictly controlled: one dose each day at four in the afternoon, which he held back till half-past six, if the "*pain proper* as distinguished from *haunting*" did not become too great.[56] Now he was trying to write without stimulants in that part of the day when his head was still clear.

This humdrum, convalescent existence freed his mind for greater things. His Notebooks and letters suggest a return to intense philosophical reading – Spinoza, Fichte, Schelling – and the problem of reconciling his renewed Christian faith with German idealism. This was his "most important Work", for which he kept his morning hours "sacred". Coleridge now conceived, or rather resurrected, the great philosophical book which would sum up the whole structure of his thought and experience. His working title was the *Logosophia*, and in one form or another it would haunt the remaining twenty years of his life.

In an early reference he described it as a study of "the communicative intelligence in nature and in man". Sometimes it was a "single large volume", at others a series of five or six linked "Treatises".[57] Usually it began with a purely secular work on logic, advanced through Kantian metaphysics and natural theology, and ended with an inspired poetic commentary on the Gospel of St John, which opens with the great declaration which gave Coleridge his master-theme: "In the Beginning was the Word."

The *Logosophia* ("Wisdom of the Word"), or *Opus Maximum* ("The Great Work") as it eventually became, was never to be completed in Coleridge's lifetime. But paradoxically it became one of his most fruitful failures, and his determination to confirm it as his ultimate literary goal, after the crushing experiences of 1814, salvaged his literary self-respect and saved him from a dwindling career in miscellaneous journalism. The fundamental structure it proposed – of a philosophical argument advancing from the secular to the sacred – underlies almost all his later work, and became central to Romantic doctrine and epistemology.

Whether interpreted through science, art, philosophy or theology, Coleridge believed that the world presented a dynamic unity, which was ultimately divine. In an unbroken progression, from rational perception ("Understanding") through artistic vision ("Imagination") to the highest forms of intuition ("Reason"), all human experience moved towards a transcendent meaning. For Coleridge, the challenge to articulate this faith in a single apocalyptic work was never met. But by seeing each of his future books as a necessary preface or prelude to the final achievement, he was able to continue productively.

It was, in a uniquely Coleridgean way, an art of prevarication. Many, like Hazlitt, would soon mock him for it. But it meant that, in a psychological pattern originated years before with the poetic fragment of "Kubla Khan", the unfinished work generated the finished with surprising and brilliant effect. So to Daniel Stuart he wrote of the *Logosophia* as ready for "printing at Bristol" that autumn. "The Title is: Christianity the one true Philosophy – or 5 Treatises on the Logos, or communicative Intelligence, Natural, Human, and Divine:– to which is prefixed a Prefactory Essay . . . illustrated by fragments of *Auto*-biography."

Beneath that grand, sheltering claim – his shield against futility and despair – it was the small "prefactory" idea of a literary autobiography that now sprang into life.[58] Tentatively, Coleridge began to dictate notes to Morgan. It would, of course, be merely a fragment and the dictation process had its old companionable charm. A dull phrase like "officious for equivalents" could enliven a whole morning's work. "This my Amanuensis wrote – 'Fishing for Elephants' – which as I at the time observed could hardly have occurred except at the commencement of the Deluge."[59]

7

As Coleridge's confidence and good humour returned, the regime at Ashley seemed a little restricted. Social visits spread out into the neighbourhood. A day was spent with the poet William Bowles, embowered in his country parsonage at Bremhill, a "sweet place" with church bells tolling which reminded Coleridge of his childhood. An expedition to see the famous private collection of pictures at Corsham House, seat of the MP for Wiltshire, produced an invitation to dine with the Marquis of Lansdowne at Bowood House. This in turn led to Coleridge being offered the run of the Bowood House library, where Priestley had once conducted his experiments in a special laboratory set up under Lord Lansdowne's patronage. The great house, with its splendid terraces and idyllic lake, spoke of aristocratic *douceur* and soothing recognition of intellectual genius. ("A servant begged to know whether I was *the* Mr Coleridge, *the* great Author.")[60]

They decided to move from Ashley to the market town of Calne, fifteen miles up the Great West Road, and conveniently situated just over the hill from Bowood House. Lying between Marlborough and Devizes, and close to the ancient stone-circle of Avebury, Calne epitomized the sleepy magic of Wiltshire life. Surrounded by large farms and rich estates, its traditional cattle market and local brewery (largely controlled by the Lansdowne family) had quietly flourished for centuries.

It was Coleridge's network of friendly doctors who had found these new lodgings at Calne. Through Dr Daniel, Coleridge had become intimate with Dr R. H. Brabant and his family at nearby Devizes, and frequently rode over with Morgan to spend the day there. It was Brabant in turn who recommended them to Dr George Page, a surgeon who lived in the centre of Calne in Church Street.[61] Dr Page was a man of some standing in the district, and after the Reform Act of 1832, he became an alderman and then mayor.[62]

In fact Dr Page owned two houses side by side in Church Street, part of an elegant little terrace of three-storey buildings running down the west side of the hill. His properties stood in a prime position, just opposite the parish church of St Mary's, with its fine colonnade of ancient yew trees. Page lived in the larger house, with its "offices, garden and stable", and rented out the smaller one with a little courtyard to Coleridge and Morgan.[63]*

Coleridge seemed to be moving instinctively back to his provincial roots, to a country town very like Ottery St Mary, where he had been born. Even the position of his lodgings was curiously reminiscent of his father's house, opposite St Mary's church in Ottery, with the churchyard where he had played as a child. Calne also had a river, the Marden, a tributary of the Avon, which ran under the wooden bridge at the bottom of Church Street where he walked each day to collect letters from the Catherine Wheel coaching inn. (The old Wheel Barometer, from which the inn took its name, is still mounted in the exterior wall.) All these things recalled his past.

Coleridge also established good relations with the Calne chemist, Mr Bishop, who supplied his opium. He found pleasant rambles along the banks of the Marden to the lake at Bowood, and up the hill to the Green (where Priestley had lived). Most spectacular of all, a mile outside the town on Oldbury Hill was one of the famous White Horses of Wiltshire, which had been cut into the chalk hillside in 1780. It hung there above the coaching road, permanently galloping eastwards towards London, its glittering eye formed from a small round pit filled with the broken glass of innumerable wine and brandy bottles. Local legend also supplied the tale of a naked highwayman, who was supposed to accost benighted travellers as they set out on the long journey from Calne across the Marlborough downs to the distant capital.[64]

Coleridge and the Morgans spent most of the early spring of 1815 quietly settling into the local society, continuing their visits to Lord Lansdowne at Bowood, Dr Brabant at Devizes, and Bowles at Bremhill (from whom they often borrowed a horse). With Dr Brabant, Coleridge was soon exchanging letters on local politics, German metaphysics and the comparative quality of Rapee and Maccabau snuff which they both enjoyed. Lord Lansdowne's beer, however, did not pass muster. "I am requested to ask, whether there is a public Brewer at Devizes, & whether we can be served from thence with good Table Beer? – Excuse this liberty – but Calne is a

* Coleridge kept this address secret for some time, and his exact place of residence has not been previously identified. It is perhaps coincidental that in the 1990s the area round Calne and Avebury became famous for its mysterious "crop-circles".

sepulchre in a Desart – & the Ale here from the Public Houses is either Syrup or Vinegar."[65]

A rare local excitement was provided by agitation against the Corn Law Bill. Post-war unemployment threatened many poor families with starvation, and the huge increases in the price of bread found Coleridge firmly on the side of the "pale-faced Consumers" against the government. Sending Brabant a copy of his Quantocks poem of 1798, "Fears in Solitude", the ghosts of his old political radicalism stirred uneasily. "You cannot conceive how this Corn Bill haunts me – and so it would you, if you had seen the pale faces and heard the conversation of the hundred poor Creatures, who came to sign the Petition." He calculated that the Bill would increase the old 8d loaf to 15 or 16d.[66]

Coleridge was moved to a quixotic gesture, identifying with the unemployed at Calne, and causing some satisfactory scandal among the squires. "So much for theological Metaphysics! – On Wednesday we had a public meeting in the market-place at Calne to petition Parliament against the Corn Bill. I drew it up for Mr Wait, and afterwards mounted on a Butcher's Table made a butcherly sort of Speech of an hour long to a very ragged but not butcherly audience: for by their pale faces few of them seemed to have had more than a very occasional acquaintance with Butcher's Meat." Coleridge's speech was a success – "Loud were the Huzzas!" – and he briefly toyed with a new career. "If it depended on the Inhabitants at large, I believe they would send me up to Parliament."[67] However, despite his personal intervention, the Corn Law was passed on 10 March 1815.

Though working on his collection of poems, and making desultory attempts to draft a Preface, Coleridge felt both unemployed and oddly exiled from the centre of things. Money was a growing anxiety, and through March he wrote a series of increasingly desperate letters to his old publisher Cottle. Would Cottle consider advancing £40 on all his poems, including those in "scattered" publications and those still in manuscript? He was already £25 in debt to the Morgans, even though he had pared his expenses to the bone, spending no more than £2.10s a week. "You will say, I ought to live for less – and doubtless, I might, if I were to alienate myself from all social affectations, and from all conversation with persons of the same education."

He had now heard of the subscription scheme which Southey had prevented. "But I would die, after my recent experience of the cruel and insolent Spirit of Calumny, rather than subject myself as a slave to a Club of Subscribers to my Poverty."[68] He would try anything to get the poems properly published: sell outright the copyright on *The Friend*, write a treatise on the Corn Laws, or even start a day school for twenty pupils at £15 a year each. "To this I am certain I could attend with strictest regularity; or indeed to anything mechanical. But Composition is no voluntary business: the very necessity of doing it robs me of the power of doing it. Had I been possessed of a tolerable Competence, I should have been a voluminous Writer – but I cannot, as is feigned of the Nightingale, sing with my Breast against a Thorn. – God bless you!"[69]

But Joseph Cottle had heard of this tune too often, and like so many others he had abandoned hope of Coleridge ever doing anything. He sent £5, and broke off the correspondence. "Knowing that whatever monies he received would, assuredly, be expended in opium, Compassion stayed my hand."[70]

Coleridge stubbornly persisted. He now turned to the proprietors of *Felix Farley's Journal*, Hood and Gutch, who had published his Allston Essays. He made the same proposal for an advance, promising a manuscript of 250 to 300 pages to be ready by mid-June. To his delight in April they agreed not only to provide £45 towards the work, but also to pay the next instalment of his life assurance premium of £27.5s.6d.[71]

With this secured, he took a deep breath and wrote a long letter to Lord Byron in London. He began with awkward solemnity – "anxiety makes us all ceremonious" but not without a certain wry humour. They were both labourers in the same poetical vineyard, "your Lordship's ampler Lot is on the sunny side, while mine has laid upon the North, my *growing* Vines gnawed down by Asses, and my richest and raciest clusters carried off and spoilt by the plundering Fox." But he was also businesslike, in a way that both appealed to Byron and flattered him.

Coleridge enumerated the works he had in hand – the poems, a new edition of *Remorse*, perhaps some translations – and explained both his débâcle with Longman of 1807 and the more recent difficulties with Murray. If Byron personally should think well of any "MSS volumes" he should send him, "as soon as they are fit for your perusal", would he recommend them to some respectable publisher in London? "Your weight in society and the splendour of your name would, I am convinced, (and so is Mr Bowles, who in truth suggested this application . . .) treble the amount of their offer . . ."[72]

He knew that he was widely attacked in the reviews. He had even been subject to "the Lash of your Lordship's Satire" in *English Bards and Scotch Reviewers* (a shrewd admission). Worst of all, he had been lumped together with Southey and Wordsworth as a Lake Poet, a very watery injustice. "The cataracts of anonymous criticism never fell on them, but I was wet thro' with the Spray . . ." But now he wished to publish and take a stand on his own account. He gave a first sketch of the *Biographia*, still describing it as "a general Preface" to his collected poems "on the Principles of philosophic and genial criticism relative to the Fine Arts in general; but especially to Poetry". It would now, however, include a "Particular Preface" to the "Ancient Mariner" and on "the employment of the Supernatural in Poetry" . . . All would be ready for the press "by the first week in June".[73]

It was an apt moment to contact Byron, who was now living at Piccadilly Terrace, married, and flushed with the succes of his *Corsair* (1814) and *Hebrew Melodies* (1815) – 10,000 copies sold in the first week – in high favour with Murray, and on friendly terms with Walter Scott. He replied immediately, saying it would be "a great pleasure" to comply with Coleridge's request, warmly praising his work – especially *Remorse* – and assuring him that indeed he was very far from forgotten.

With his gracious and timely touch, Byron lifted Coleridge's thoughts from "the sordid trade" to the eternal values of their art. "I trust you do not permit yourself to be depressed by the temporary partiality of what is called 'the public' for the favourites of the moment; all experience is against the permanency of such impressions. You must have lived to see many of these pass away, and will survive many more – I mean personally, for *poetically*, I would not insult you by a comparison."

In a charming postscript, he also laughed away the "Satire or lampoon". It was written when Byron was "very young and very angry" and he now regarded it as "pert, petulant, and shallow enough". He was sure that Coleridge was proceeding in "a career which could not but be successful", and he had the honour to be his "obliged and very obedient servant".[74] So Coleridge had secured a powerful ally, and the prospect of a triumphant return to London under such noble patronage subtly sustained him in the months ahead. Everything now turned on a simple question: buried away in his Wiltshire retreat, gone to ground beneath the sign of the White Horse, could he ever get the promised work done?

8

The writing of the *Biographia*, between April and September 1815, became the decisive creative struggle of Coleridge's later career. It is, in many ways, astonishing that he ever produced it at all. After the opium collapse of 1813–14, the possibility of sustained composition – maintained in the event, at an ever-increasing pace over six months – must have seemed very remote. The baroque involutions of its final structure, which have maddened scholars ever since,[75] are largely explained by the particular ways in which he found it possible to keep going.

In the first place, Coleridge continued his habit of dictating to John Morgan (as Asra had once acted as the amanuensis and midwife to *The Friend*). Coleridge talked the *Biographia* into life, and the pattern of an extended conversation (with its good days and bad, its moments of inspired intensity and its interludes of rambling and reflection) give the book both its companionable atmosphere and its sense of intermittence. In a Freudian sense, one may think of it as a "talking cure", an attempt to come to terms with his own achievements and failures, to re-edit his "literary life and opinions" (its final subtitle) into a retrospective form – part fact, part fiction, part theory – which had both meaning and justification.

Its extraordinary shifts in tone, from mournful apologia (very evident at the outset) through sprightly reminiscence and passionate philosophizing, to the steady, measured, brilliantly authoritative note of the critical sections, evidently reflect this. Nowhere is this extreme shift between the subjective and the objective voice more striking than in the metaphysical section (the last to be written, at a point of near-exhaustion) whose Olympian discourse hides a desperate resort to wholesale plagiarism from German sources, while at the same time making a generous and winning disclaimer of originality. In all this the *Biographia* has an acute psychological interest, and its shape-shifting and paradoxes, its intimacy and disguises, its frankness and its fraudulence, make up a genuine literary self-portrait. Anything less complicated, less fascinating and less maddening, would really not be Coleridge at all.

In the second place, Coleridge's concept of the book altered and expanded as he worked, virtually week by week. He began with the idea of the simple personal preface to his collected poems, the *Sibylline Leaves*. Then he moved on to an "Autobiographia" (his next working title), and then to a critical history of the Romantic Imagination from Shakespeare to Wordsworth. Finally, he wanted to write something like a complete history of modern philosophy from Locke to Kant. Elements of all these ideas crowd into the final version, though not exactly in that order, or with that logic.

In the third place, the form of publication did not reflect the original sequence of composition. The middle (philosophical) section of the book was written last, and the end of the book was filled out with extraneous materials when it finally came to be published, after tortuous complications and in two volumes, in July 1817. So the broad three-part structure that emerged – Autobiography in Chapters 1–4, Philosophy in Chapters 5–13, Criticism in Chapters 14–22 – was full of extreme oddities and digressions. Not the least of these was the superb and humorous account of life at Stowey and Bristol in the 1790s, which was placed in Chapter 10, and succinctly titled "A chapter of digression and anecdotes, as an interlude preceding that on the nature of the Imagination or plastic power – On pedantry and pedantic expressions– Advice to young authors respecting publication – Various anecdotes of the author's literary life, and the progress of his Opinion in religion and politics."[76]

No doubt, as with *The Friend*, the disordered internal structure of the book (with these many narrative loops, and unfulfilled promises, coming to an extraordinary climax in Chapter 13, "On the Imagination, or esemplastic power") was also partly the result of a failure of steady architectural control so characteristic of Coleridge's opium state. Yet disorder in the larger design also freed Coleridge at a local level. The genius of the *Biographia* lies in local passages, individual paragraphs and short sequences, chambers within the crazy edifice, of unsurpassed clarity and power. Many of these are defined by the use of extended metaphors and similes, and show Coleridge's essentially poetic mode of thought and explanation still ascendant within a prose argument. Similarly, much of the autobiographical material is told through carefully shaped, humorous anecdotes, which have the quality of poetic fables of his life and times, rather than a strict historical account of the period.

The one book that Coleridge never set out to write, strangely enough, was a Confession. His ambition is closer to a prose version of Wordsworth's *Prelude* ("the Growth of a Poet's Mind"), than to De Quincey's *Confessions of an English Opium Eater*. The fact that Coleridge had already disburdened himself of his most humiliating guilts in his Bristol letters may well have given him the initial confidence to create the public persona of the *Biographia*. He writes almost nothing of his addiction ("bodily pain and mismanaged sensibility"); little of his marriage (except in one painfully defensive footnote); and nothing at all of course of Asra. There is no mention even of his composition of "Kubla Khan".

Yet the appeal to his readers is still intimate. The *Biographia* opens with an epigraph from Goethe, which comes to haunt the whole text. "He wishes to knit anew his connections with his oldest friends, to continue those recently formed, and to win other friends among the rising generation for the remaining course of his life. He wishes to spare the young those circuitous paths, on which he himself had lost his way."[77] The idea of his book as a difficult journey, reflecting the chaos and disorientation of his own life, but from which "the rising generation" might learn the true path of the Imagination, is a dramatically effective key. It suggests Coleridge's dual role as narrator, both hapless victim and philosophic guide, both absurd and wise, which – with many ironies and self-mockeries – developed quite naturally as he dictated to Morgan.

He also repeats early in the first chapter the familiar idea of literary friendship. Remembering the impact of his first reading of Bowles's sonnet at the age of seventeen, he observed: "The great works of past ages seem to a young man things of another race, in respect to which his faculties must remain passive and submiss, even as to the stars and mountains. But the writings of a contemporary, perhaps not many years older than himself, surrounded by the same circumstances, and disciplined by the same manners, possess a *reality* for him, and inspire an actual friendship as of a man for a man."[78]

The first three chapters, written in April and early May, have a loose, apologetic, preliminary feel. "It has been my lot to have had my name introduced in conversation, and in print, more frequently than I find it easy to explain . . ."[79] They still read like the Preface to his Poems, as first conceived. They recount the various influences on his youthful work: of his headmaster Bowyer, of Bowles, and of Southey, and give a highly critical description of his own first publications. But with Chapter 4 and the arrival of Wordsworth, the *Biographia* bursts into life. Coleridge's language takes on a confident stride and a vivid metaphorical life which is as good as any prose he ever wrote.

> During the last year of my residence at Cambridge, I became acquainted with Mr Wordsworth's first publication entitled "Descriptive Sketches"; and seldom, if ever, was the emergence of an original poetic genius above the literary horizon more evidently announced. In the form, style, and manner of the whole poem, and in the structure of the particular lines and periods, there is a harshness and acerbity connected and combined with words and images all a-glow, which might recall those products of the vegetable world, where gorgeous blossoms rise out of the hard and thorny rind and shell, within which the rich fruit was elaborating. The language was not only peculiar and strong, but at times knotty and contorted, as by its own impatient strength . . .[80]

9

In fact Wordsworth had burst in upon Coleridge's tranquillity at Calne in May, just as he had burst into Chapter 4, and the two events were intimately related. Hitherto the greatest excitement had been a smallpox scare, when an infected traveller on the coach from Newbury (banished to a cowshed) had inadvertently had contact with Charlotte Brent. Coleridge wrote urgently to Dr Brabant at Devizes, asking for "any vaccine virus" and remembering his own vaccination in childhood at Ottery. He could not love her any more than a "younger Sister", and they were both "greatly alarmed" and anxious for her to be inoculated.

He rode over himself to Devizes to collect the vaccine, and on his return on 30 May found another unexpected messenger from the outside world awaiting him. Wordsworth had written a polite but somewhat peremptory letter, the first for many months. He had heard from Lady Beaumont that Coleridge intended to publish the "poem addressed to me after hearing *mine* to you" ("To William Wordsworth") in his forthcoming collection; and also that Coleridge had some "*comparative* censure" of supposedly "commonplace truths" in *The Excursion*. Would Coleridge do him the "kindness" of omitting the former, and explaining the latter. "Pray point out to me the most striking instances where I have failed, in producing poetic effect by an overfondness for this practice, or through inability to realize my wishes."[81] He signed off: "believe me my dear Coleridge in spite of your silence, Most affectionately yours W. Wordsworth."

Coleridge was pained by the thin tone of the letter, but touched by the reproach. Wordsworth was anxious about his literary reputation – *The Excursion* had received an infamous mauling by Jeffrey in the *Edinburgh Review*, beginning "This will never do" – and Coleridge's old instinct to defend his friend now began to shape the emerging *Biographia*. But first he immediately sent back a long reply, affirming his love and admiration for "an absent friend, to whom for the more substantial Third of a Life we have been habituated to look up". He did have criticisms, but also a "dread of giving pain, or exciting suspicions of alteration and Dyspathy". He copied out a long passage in praise of Wordsworth's *Prelude* from "To William Wordsworth" (though promising not to publish it), and then rose to a superb description of the sort of epic he had expected from Wordsworth. This touches on many points of the arguments of the *Biographia*, and is itself a sort of prose poem.

> In the very Pride of Confident Hope I looked forward to the Recluse, as the *first* and *only* true Philosophical Poem in existence . . . I supposed you first to have mediated the faculties of Man in the abstract . . . to have laid a solid and immovable foundation for the Edifice by removing the sandy Sophisms of Locke, and the Mechanic Dogmatists, and demonstrating that the Senses were living growths and developments of the Mind & Spirit . . . to have affirmed a Fall in some sense, as a fact, the possibility of which cannot be understood from the Nature of the Will, but the reality of which is attested by Experience & Conscience – Fallen men contemplated in the different ages of the World, and in the different states – Savage – Barbarous

> – Civilized – the lonely Cot, or Borderer's Wigwam – the Village – the Manufacturing Town – Sea-port – City – Universities – and not disguising the sore evils, under which the whole creation groans, to point out however a manifest Scheme of Redemption from this Slavery, of Reconciliation from this Enmity with Nature.

Above all, he had hoped that Wordsworth would promulgate a philosophy of "Life, and Intelligence" in place of that "philosophy of mechanism which in everything that is most worthy of the human Intellect strikes *Death*".[82]

Coleridge kept all personal bitterness out of this letter, as he would faithfully do in the *Biographia*. He invited Wordsworth to Calne, and signed off: "God bless you! – I am & never have been other than your affectionate S. T. Coleridge."

Yet in his Notebooks he confided his horror of what he saw as Wordsworth's growing professional self-obsession, his anxiety for reputation, and what he called in a lethally vivid phrase "the force of self-vorticity". "Were *intellect* only in question, STC would rather groan under his manifold sins & sorrows, all either contained in or symbolized by OPIUM, than cherish that self-concentration [of W.] which renders the dearest beings *means* to him, never really ends." He added miserably (but in the event quite wrongly): "I would almost wager my life, that if [W.] published [*The Prelude*], he would cancel all the passages relating to STC." But Coleridge would never live to know this.[83]

Until this time at the end of May, Coleridge was still referring to the *Biographia* as a "Preface" which would be finished, as planned with Gutch, in early June.[84] It was a single essay, with no chapter divisions, and ran to less than sixty pages. But now he was grappling directly once more with Wordsworth: the disappointment of *The Excursion*, the memories of the *Lyrical Ballads*, the challenge of Wordsworth's new *Poems* of 1815. So he launched into the materials that became Chapters 4 (and eventually 14 onwards), and began one of the most intensive periods of composition of his life.

For eight weeks throughout June and July 1815 he dictated to Morgan in four- or five-hour stints, both morning and evening, breaking off for nothing but an early supper. He rarely left the house at Church Street, except to walk in the meadows, or to visit a company of itinerant players who were acting in the little theatre at the top of the town. When their producer, a Mr Falkner, announced that he would mount a production of *Remorse*, and take it on to Devizes and Bristol, Coleridge had the satisfaction of becoming a provincial celebrity. He was proud of their efforts: "On my conscience, they appear to me to act just as well as those on the London stage; indeed, far beyond my expectation."[85]

In Chapter 4 a whole new structure to the *Biographia* begins to emerge. Coleridge announces that this is a study of the poetic revolution that Wordsworth and he created in the *Lyrical Ballads* in the Quantocks. He will show the literary tradition out of which they worked, and will demonstrate Wordsworth as the commanding poetic genius of the age, despite the weaknesses of his "critical remarks" (which Coleridge will correct).[86] It will show that the power "in which all Mr Wordsworth's writings is more or less predominant, and which constitutes the character of his mind", was that of Imagination. And by philosophical analysis, it will argue that "fancy and imagination were two distinct and widely different faculties, instead of being, according to the general belief, either two names with one meaning, or at furthest, the lower and higher degree of one and the same power".[87] This theory "would in its immediate effects furnish a torch of guidance to the philosophical critic; and ultimately to the poet himself".[88]

There are still apologetic asides – the book will be an "immethodical miscellany", and "metaphysics and psychology have long been my hobby-horse" – but the thrust is now surprisingly direct.[89] The subtitle to Chapter 4 clearly points the way ahead: "The Lyrical Ballads with the Preface – Mr Wordsworth's earlier Poems – On Fancy and Imagination – The investigation of the distinction important to the fine arts."[90] This material runs straight forward to Chapter 14 (no middle chapters existing on this plan), and continues the argument with perfect continuity: "During the first year that Mr Wordsworth and I were neighbours, our conversation turned frequently on the two cardinal points of poetry, the power of exciting the sympathy of the reader by a faithful adherence to the truth of nature, and the power of giving the interest of novelty by the modifying colours of imagination . . ."[91] There follows his account of the origins of the *Lyrical Ballads*, which includes Coleridge's most famous description of imagination at work on the reader's mind: "that willing suspension of disbelief for the moment which constitutes poetic faith".[92]

What is so striking about this new version of the *Biographia* is that it had changed from an autobiography to a book that is essentially a long dialogue with Wordsworth himself. Once more he had been magnetized or seduced by Wordsworth's presence, even at the distance of 300 miles and across the no-man's land of their quarrel. The *Biographia* had become passionate conversation, or collaboration, by other means. It can also be seen as one more re-enactment of the old power struggle between Coleridge and Wordsworth, the river breaking round the rock.

10

One other influence may have helped to inspire Coleridge's efforts. In mid-June the eighteen-year-old Hartley came to Calne from Oxford, to spend the whole of his first ever summer vacation with his father. The Morgans had formally extended the invitation, knowing that Coleridge felt guilty about being unable to support his son financially. They saw that far from being a distraction, Hartley's presence would reassure Coleridge and bring a sense of family unity to the household. While for Hartley, the example of his father so hard at work during the day, as well as providing "great service" with his undergraduate studies in the evenings, would bring a closer and more adult understanding.[93]

For the first time in his life, Hartley was a free agent to decide where he would go outside Greta Hall, and it is significant that he chose to stay with his father, especially as this was in direct opposition to his uncle Southey's wishes. Southey thought Hartley would easily be led astray: "his greatest danger arises . . . from his father".[94] Lamb, by contrast, thoroughly approved of the visit; it would form "a quintuple alliance" as he put it, between the Coleridges and the Morgans.[95]

In fact the summer visit was a great success, and Hartley remained until October.[96] Despite his odd manners and odder appearance (now sporting a scrawny black beard), Mary Morgan found him "extremely amiable".[97] No letters from Hartley survive, but years later he wrote a nostalgic essay on Calne – "a place I can never think of without a strong twitching of the eye" – recalling the jumbled and irregular houses, the chalky hills and streams, and "some wildish, half-common fields . . . with old remains of hawthorn bowers and clumps of shady trees, where I used to dream my mornings away right pleasantly."[98]

Hartley became very much part of the household. In late June they joined in the Calne celebrations for Wellington's final victory over Napoleon at Waterloo. He accompanied his father on several visits to Bremhill and Bowood House. Another highlight was the revival of *Remorse* at the Calne Assembly Rooms in mid-August. Hartley discovered a shared fascination with John Morgan. Both of them were entranced by theatricals and strolling players, and according to Mary they were "behind the scenes all the time and assisted in the music etc.".

It is even possible that Hartley had some influence on the writing of the *Biographia*. It was always addressed to the younger generation, and some of the running chapter heads – "Advice to young authors respecting publication" – "An affectionate exhortation to those who in early life feel themselves disposed to become authors" – could have had Hartley in mind. It is also easy to see how Coleridge might have used his clever, Oxford undergraduate son as an appreciative audience for his anecdotes and a sounding-board for his philosophical ideas.

Indeed Hartley's natural attraction to the labyrinth of Coleridge's thought was one of the things that Southey had most feared. "Hartley is able to comprehend the powers of his father's mind, and has for it all that veneration which is both natural and proper that he should feel . . . [But] Coleridge, totally regardless of all consequences, will lead him into all the depth and mazes of metaphysics . . ."[99] It is interesting that later in the summer, Coleridge complained that Hartley was squirrelling away many of his philosophical books in his bedroom.[100]

Hartley also greatly took to the Morgans, finding them more easygoing than the Wordsworths. "They were good, comfortable, unintellectual people, in whose company I always thought STC more than usually pleasant. And there were for a time strolling players, for whom, and indeed for all itinerants, I have a great liking." There is a hint of loneliness, of adolescent solitude and restlessness about these reminiscences; yet Hartley looked back on this long vacation as one of the "happiest of my life".[101]

With the help of Charlotte and Mary, Coleridge's study room became neat and highly organized. His German books were shelved, the manuscripts of his poems for *Sibylline Leaves* were disinterred and stacked ready for the printer, his Notebooks were sorted for reference and quotation. (It was probably at this time that the copy of "Kubla Khan" resurfaced, and the gloss to the "Ancient Mariner" was begun.) Contemplating the unaccustomed order of his surroundings, Coleridge wrote a miniature essay on the aesthetics and psychology of artists' studios.

He thought there were fundamentally two kinds: those that appeared totally chaotic except for the small concentrated area in which a book or a painting was being worked on (typically male); and those which were completely ordered and arranged throughout (typically female). These expressed not only gender, but creative psychology, the one with an active "concentrated" sense of the Beautiful, the other with a broader, passive "pleasure in Beauty, modified by the sense of Propriety".

On the one hand, "See an artist's Room, see a *littery* literary Man's Room! – all in disorder – much dirt, more Confusion – but here and there some exquisitely finished Form or combination of Forms." The owner of such a studio "annihilates for himself all non-Pertinent Objects". On the other hand, "a well-tuned and sensitive female mind must have the whole of the given Space *in keeping*". Such a mind could hardly endure "the rags, brushes & broken gallipots of an Allston, or the scattered Books, fluttering Pamphlets, & dusty Paper-wilderness of a Wordsworth".

This argument shadows forth the polar metaphysics of the *Biographia*, in which active and passive principles are "seminal" to the understanding of creativity. Coleridge, the great generator of domestic chaos, now modestly claimed that (with Southey) he embodied both. "I know but two individuals who combine both, viz. – the Lady-like *Wholeness* with creative delight in *particular forms* – & these are Mr Robert Southey, Poet Laureate etc. etc. etc. and Mr Sam. Tayl. Coleridge, whose whole Being has been unfortunately little more than a far-stretched Series of Et Ceteras. Calne, Wiltshire."[102]

11

This touch of his old ebullience was a sort of foam leaping from the great flood of his renewed dictation, as it found its path. In recounting the literary story of the *Lyrical Ballads*, Coleridge found the way forward by attacking Wordsworth's theories of poetry in order to praise the poetry itself. This method released many of his greatest formulations of the creative act, seen as a psychological process or unique functioning of mental and spiritual powers. In Chapter 14, drawing on the many earlier hints from his lectures and letters, he defined poetry in a vocabulary part metaphysical and part scientific. It was a complex act of energy and synthesis, unique to the human spirit. Coleridge's prose had never been more confident, or more inclusive.

> The poet, described in *ideal* perfection, brings the whole soul of man into activity . . . He diffuses a tone and spirit of unity, that blends and (as it were) *fuses*, each into each, by that synthetic and magical power, to which we have exclusively appropriated the name of imagination. This power, first put into action by the will and understanding, and retained under their irremissive, though gentle and unnoticed control reveals itself in the balance or reconciliation of opposite or discordant qualities: of sameness, with difference; or the general, with the concrete; the idea, with the image; the individual, with the representative; the sense of novelty and freshness, with old and familiar objects; a more than usual state of emotion, with more than usual order; judgement ever awake and steady self-possession, with enthusiasm and feeling profound and vehement . . ."[103]

Each of these polarities gives the reader pause for thought. The experiencing of poetry is opened up, or fanned out, for contemplation. Coleridge even produced one of his most wonderful asides to describe the nature of that pause in the reader's mind. "Like the motion of the serpent, which the Egyptians made the emblem of intellectual power; or like the path of sound through the air; at every step he pauses and half recedes, and from the retrogressive movement collects the force which again carries him onwards."[104]

Through the next eight chapters (15 to 22 as they became) he applies these observations in great detail to specific passages of poetry (a technique for which he invented the term "practical criticism"), running right through the history of English poetry, starting with Shakespeare and Milton, going on with the Metaphysical poets (with some highly original observations on Italian Renaissance poetry), and gradually returning to Wordsworth.

In Chapter 18, he traces the origins of metre to "that spontaneous effort which strives to hold in check the workings of passion", and compares its effect to "wine during animated conversation". In another fine aside, he remarks that an inappropriate, jingly metre has a peculiarly jarring impact, "like that of leaping in the dark from the last step of a stair-case, when we had prepared our muscles for a leap of three or four".[105]

While attacking Wordsworth's "insufficient" theories of language and metre, he triumphantly vindicates his poetic practice in the *Lyrical Ballads* and the *Poems in Two Volumes*. The poems always have "weight and sanity" of thought. They are "*fresh* and have the dew upon them". They have the "sinewy strength and originality of single lines and paragraphs". There is "perfect truth of nature in his images and descriptions". And throughout there is "a meditative pathos, a union of deep and subtle thought with sensibility; a sympathy with man as man".[106]

In distinguishing so magisterially between Wordsworth's "defects and beauties", Coleridge reasserted a critical and moral independence he had not really felt since the disaster of 1810. Once more he was engaged in a dialogue of equals. This released in him some of his finest and most beautiful flights of poetic appreciation. Praising that "perfect truth to nature" which was so central to Wordsworth's genius, he was now able to draw unencumbered upon their shared memories of the Lakes to evoke that sovereign power:

> Like a green field reflected in a calm and perfectly transparent lake, the image is distinguished from the reality only by its greater softness and lustre. Like the moisture of the polish on a pebble, genius neither distorts nor false-colours its objects; but on the contrary brings out many a vein and tint, which escapes the eye of common observation, thus raising to the rank of gems what had often been kicked away by the hurrying foot of the traveller on the dusty high road of custom.[107]

After some hundred pages, or forty thousand words of this limpid, well-argued and constantly surprising text, Coleridge turned back to his original distinction between Fancy and Imagination. Here he made his highest critical claim for his old friend, towards the end of Chapter 22.

> Last, and pre-eminently, I challenge for this poet the gift of IMAGINATION in the highest and strictest sense of the word. In the play of *Fancy*, Wordsworth, to my feelings, is not always graceful, and sometimes *recondite*. The *likeness* is occasionally too strange, or demands too particular a point of view, or is such as appears the creature of predetermined research, rather than spontaneous presentation . . . But in imaginative power, he stands nearest of all modern writers to Shakespeare and Milton; and yet in a kind perfectly unborrowed and his own. To employ his own words, which are at once an instance and an illustration, he does indeed to all thoughts and to all objects
>
> "... add the gleam,
> The light that never was on sea or land,
> The consecration, and the poet's dream."[108]

Wordsworth would never receive more intelligent, sustained or ambitious appreciation in his lifetime.

12

By the end of July 1815, Coleridge thought the *Biographia* was finished. He saw it now so clearly as a dialogue with Wordsworth that he even wanted the book and its companion volume *Sibylline Leaves* set up in a typeface exactly matching that of Wordsworth's two-volume *Poems* of 1815.[109] The volumes would answer the other, as in the old days of their intimacy.

He was satisfied that he had produced his best and most coherent work for over a decade, asserting at long last his independence as both critic and poet. Yet he was almost alarmed at what he had done. In a revealing letter to Dr Brabant of 29 July, he vaunted his achievement while admitting his fears of Wordsworth's reaction. Amazingly, he thought that Wordsworth, like some schoolmaster, like Bowyer himself, would be "displeased" as with an inadequate prep.

> My dear Sir, The necessity of extending, what I first intended as a preface, to an Autobiographia literaria, or Sketches of my literary Life & opinions, as far as Poetry and *poetical* Criticism is concerned, has confined me to my Study from 11 to 4, and from 6 to 10, since I last left you. – I have just finished it, having only the correction of the *Mss*. to go through. – I have given a full account (raisonné) of the Controversy concerning Wordsworth's Poems & Theory, in which my name has been so constantly included – I have no doubt, that Wordsworth will be displeased – but I have done my Duty to myself and to the Public . . .[110]

He was exhausted with the effort, and so was Morgan with the pressure of the overrun deadline (originally promised for June). However, he added that there was still "One long passage" of metaphysical disquisition, concerning the "generic differences between the faculties of Fancy and Imagination", which he had largely omitted from the text. He had "extended and elaborated" it purely for his own interest and was sending it to Brabant for his personal perusal. It dealt with the theory of Associationism, and laid "the foundation Stones of the Constructive or Dynamic Philosophy in opposition to the merely mechanical". It was, as it happened, the very theme – Locke and Hartley, versus Kant and Schelling (or Life versus Death) – that he had mentioned in his letter to Wordsworth back in May, as the proper subject for a philosophic epic.

Of course, it could form no part of the book, which was – surely, certainly, well virtually – finished. Indeed, Coleridge apologized for mentioning it at all. "I am running on as usual" and he would "like a Skater, strike a Stop with my Heel". He intended to relax, and was taking Hartley to dine with the Marquis of Lansdowne at Bowood. Could Mrs Brabant purchase him, Coleridge, a pair of best black silk stockings and some finest Rappee and Maccabba snuff, so he would be properly equipped for social life again?[111]

In early August Mary Morgan wrote proudly to the Lambs in London about their industry. "Your old friend Coleridge is very hard at work at the preface to a new Edition which he is just going to publish in the same form as Mr Wordsworth's – at first the preface was not to exceed five or six pages it has however grown into a work of great importance. I believe Morgan has already written nearly two hundred pages, the title of it is 'Autobiographia Literaria' to which are added 'Sybilline Leaves', a collection of Poems . . ."[112]

Mary Lamb pointedly forwarded this news to Sara Hutchinson. The Lambs now felt perfectly free to make joking mention of Coleridge's amorous susceptibilities, and how they had been transferred to Calne. Mary wrote to Charlotte herself that Asra was so like her, "that every time I see her I quarrel with her in my mind for not being you, Miss Brent".[113] While Charles, in one tipsy summer note to Mary Morgan ("I am not sober, that is I am not *over* sober") wrote teasingly: "Wordsworth is going to be Knighted. Miss Sar. Hutchinson is not like Miss B(rent). Miss (B) is a great deal prettier etc. than Miss (H)."[114]

13

The moment that Coleridge felt the *Biographia* was absolutely finished, he began to have second thoughts. Returning from Bowood he began to think again of the metaphysical "disquisition" he had innocently sent to Dr Brabant. There was also a great deal of personal material, concerning his own philosophic "Autobiographia" between 1797 and 1812, which he had suppressed in writing so concentratedly of Wordsworth.

Did the book have some sort of theoretical hole in its middle? Did his concept of the Imagination need a philosophic and spiritual grounding, as well as a critical one? And should he trace his own "circuitous" journey to these intuitive truths of the "Reason" as revealed by the German philosophers? As he would write: "The term, Philosophy, defines itself as an affectionate seeking after the truth; but Truth is the correlative of Being."[115]

By mid-August, Coleridge was again dictating hard to Morgan. The threat of an ever-expanding *Biographia* – the skate sliding on unstopped – caused astonishment but also growing alarm. Morgan wrote three anxious letters to Gutch's partner William Hood, trying to reassure him about the slipping deadline. On 10 August he actually sent the first fifty-seven pages of manuscript so the printing could begin (Chapters 1 to 4), adding as confidently as he could: "the rest (full 100 sides) is finished, and not finished – that is, there is a metaphysical part of about 5 or 6 sheets which must be revised or rather rewritten – this I trust will be done in a few days, and the next parcel (coming I think certainly next week) will contain the whole . . ."

Morgan felt his responsibilities, and tried to adopt a businesslike tone. He promised Hood that no days would be lost. "C. can not work without me – but you need no assurances from *me*. I am no dreamer, my *facts* are not *ideas* you know."[116] Further reassurances were posted out on 14 and 17 August. "Don't be afraid – you may go boldly on with the printing . . . depend upon my word: we *shall have soon done quite*. I am no poet no day-dreamer you know."[117] He recommended an engraving of Allston's Bristol portrait as a frontispiece.

In fact Coleridge did not "have done" for six weeks, the time of Hartley's return to Oxford. But during this second intense period of composition he expanded the "5 or 6 sheets" to another 45,000 words, virtually doubling the length of the *Biographia*. He almost seemed to begin the book again, on a note of intense, inward philosophical speculation. It is a new voice, setting out in a new direction. "There have been men in all ages, who have been impelled as by an instinct to propose their own nature as a problem, and who devote their attempts to its solution." This became the opening to the middle section, which was to run from Chapters 5 to 13, wonderfully transforming the book and also threatening to wreck it in the process.[118]

What Coleridge now set out to dictate was a detailed account of a philosophical and spiritual conversion. Over twenty years, he had gradually moved from the materialist views of the British empiricists (notably Locke and David Hartley), to the new "dynamic" German philosophy of Kant and Schelling. The essential change was from a reductive concept of the human mind as a tabula rasa, "a mirror or canvas" which passively registered physical experience. In place of this (or rather, subsuming it) was a transcendental idea of the mind, with its own mysterious and intuitive faculties, which actively shaped experience and had access to spiritual dimensions beyond rational "Understanding". It was, in effect, a philosophic conversion from a materialist to a religious view of the world.

Coleridge also wanted to use this "dynamic" view of the human mind to provide a genuinely philosophical basis for his central distinction between Fancy and Imagination.*

Hitherto, in the dialogue with Wordsworth, the argument had merely been presented as literary criticism. Now, with young men like his son in mind, he wanted to return to metaphysical first principles. If the mind was merely a mirror, then Fancy and Imagination were really the same thing, a form of passively "associating" ideas and images, not truly creative.[119] But if the mind was active and shaping, "esemplastic" as he called it, they were fundamentally different in their operation.[120] Fancy remained "mechanical", but Imagination was a genuine spiritual power of creativity. They were, in the language of the German *Naturphilosophie* 'polarities' of the consciousness.

Coleridge embarked on this immensely difficult territory with what was certainly a profound religious impulse. It can be ultimately related to his escape from spiritual despair in the crisis of his opium addiction. He *needed* to affirm that the human spirit was not mechanically determined (as the empiricists implied) and passive in the face of external reality or Nature. Man was not controlled by "phantom Purposes", and his Being was not "contradiction". Instead the creative powers of the human imagination were active and free. They expressed "the free-will, our only absolute *self*".[121] Nor were they merely "transcendental" in the technical Kantian sense, but also shared or reflected a divine power: they were transcendent powers reaching to infinity. The imagination, metaphysically considered, was a proof of the liberty of the human spirit. He was, in short, attempting a "sketch" of his long-dreamed *Logosophia*, a staircase from secular to divine epistemology.

In this new version, the *Biographia* became a hugely – and perhaps impossibly – ambitious book. It was now to include a compact

* Because Coleridge made the distinction famous in Romantic criticism, it is sometimes thought he invented it. On the contrary, it was a popular battle-ground among 18th century poets and philosophers, and can be found in Shaftesbury's *Characteristics* (1711), Johnson's *Dictionary* (1755), James Beattie's *Dissertations Moral and Critical* (1783), Maass's *Einbildungskraft* (1792), Kant's *Anthropologie* (1800), and not least in Wordsworth's Preface to his *Poems* (1815). Scholars have shown that Coleridge knew and annotated all these sources – most are mentioned by name in the *Biographia* – and his originality lay in the particular psychological and ultimately religious weight he gave to the terms.

history of Western philosophy in eight chapters, or little more than 100 pages. It would also involve, as part of his philosophical odyssey, an enormous expansion of his personal history, especially in the years between Stowey and Greta Hall. Indeed Chapter 10 – the chapter of "digressions and anecdotes" – became the longest, liveliest, and most openly tragi-comic in the whole book. It was here that he came closest to a public avowal of his opium addiction, and what it had cost him.

> By what I *have* effected, am I to be judged by my fellow men; what I *could* have done, is a question for my own conscience. On my own account I may perhaps have had a sufficient reason to lament my deficiency in self-control, and the neglect of concentrating my powers to the realization of some permanent work. But to verse rather than prose, if to either, belongs the voice of mourning for
>
> "Keen pangs of love awakening as a babe
> Turbulent, with an outcry in the heart;
> And fears self-will'd that shunned the eye of hope,
> And hope that scarce would know itself from fear;
> Sense of past youth, and manhood come in vain,
> And genius given and knowledge won in vain . . ."[122]

The citation was, of course, from his poem to Wordsworth; the one he had promised not to publish. But the *Biographia* in its new form was driving him to ever greater levels of self-exposure; and he remarked at this time that he was haunted by the "constant craving" to attend his own post-mortem: "if I could but be present while my Viscera were laid open!"[123]

14

The philosophical section of the book became the new Chapters 5 to 13. Coleridge now insisted that there must indeed be chapters, and dismissed the idea that the two volumes of prose and poetry had to be printed like Wordsworth's: "I care nothing, provided only the Volumes be a handsome Octavo, in clear Type . . . I think [his] too *open* and naked for a Book."[124]

What he dictated, at increasing speed, was a characteristic mixture of logic and digression. Chapters 5 to 8 contained a highly compact history and critique of Associationist philosophy ("traced from Aristotle to Hartley"), and an outright attack on the passive and mechanistic view of human creativity. Within the technical discussion, Coleridge constantly rose to passages of vivid and highly accessible popularization. Here is his attack on the determinism of the Associationists:

> The inventor of the watch, if this doctrine be true, did not in reality invent it; he only looked on, while the blind causes, the only true artists, were unfolding themselves. So it must have been too with my friend Allston, when he sketched his picture of the dead man revived by the bones of the prophet Elijah. So it must have been with Mr Southey and Lord Byron, when the one *fancied* himself composing his 'Roderick' and the other his 'Childe Harold'. The same must hold good of all systems of philosophy; of all arts, governments, wars by sea and land; in short, all things that ever have been or that ever will be produced . . . We only *fancy*, that we act from rational resolves, or prudent motives, or from impulses of anger, love, or generosity . . . The existence of an infinite spirit, of an intelligent and holy will, must, on this system be mere articulated motions of the air.[125]

We can still recognize this as an attack on the philosophy that became modern Behaviourism, and the neo-Darwinism of "the blind watchmaker".

In place of the mechanical psychology of Associationism, Coleridge begins to feel his way to a far more subtle picture of the creative mind at work. Here he writes with all the authority of a poet, and finds vivid ways to describe the actual process of sustained mental concentration, "the mind's self-experience in the act of thinking". One of the most memorable occurs in Chapter 7. Coleridge, by using his own observation from physics and botany, makes this whole experience peculiarly alive and accessible. The active–passive movements of the human mind (in the special case of composing poetry, but also in any act of particular concentration) reflects a dynamic "process" which can be seen all around us in nature.

> Let us consider what we do when we leap. We first resist the gravitating power by an act purely voluntary, and then by another act, voluntary in part, we yield to it in order to light on the spot, which we had previously proposed to ourselves. Now let a man watch his mind while he is composing; or, to take a still more common case, while he is trying to recollect a name; and he will find the process completely analogous. Most of my readers will have observed a small water-insect on the surface of rivulets, which throws a cinque-spotted shadow fringed with prismatic colours on the sunny bottom of the brook; and will have noticed, how the little animal *wins* its way up against the stream, by alternate pulses of active and passive motion, now resisting the current, and now yielding to it in order to gather strength and a momentary *fulcrum* for a further propulsion. This is no unapt emblem of the mind's self-experience in the act of thinking. There are evidently two powers at work, which relatively to each other are active and passive; and this is not possible without an intermediate faculty, which is at once both active and passive. (In philosophical language, we must denominate this intermediate faculty in all its degrees and determinations, the IMAGINATION . . .)[126]*

The psychology of this passage is remarkably modern. It seems to describe the actual process of creative inspiration, without resorting to the traditional idea of a Muse. Instead it proposes a model of the

---

* The image of the "waterboatman" insect is marvellously original, and seems to expand on a simile from the philosopher David Hume. In the *Treatise of Human Nature*, (1739–40) Book I, Section 4, Hume remarks on the intrinsic energy of the Imagination, which "is apt to continue, even when its object fails it, and like a galley put in motion by the oars, carries on its course without any new impulse." Coleridge's image was passed on in turn to W. B. Yeats, a master of the poetic "trance", who used it superbly in his poem "The Long-Legged Fly" from *Last Poems* (1939), which ends:

> There on that scaffolding reclines
> Michael Angelo.
> With no more sound than the mice make
> His hand moves to and fro.
> *Like a long-legged fly upon the stream*
> *His mind moves upon silence.*

engagement between the conscious forward drive of intellectual effort ("propulsion"), and the drifting backwards into unconscious materials ("yielding to the current"), constantly repeated in a natural diastolic movement like breathing or heartbeat. This is how creativity actually works: a mental (ultimately spiritual) rhythm which arises from the primary physical conditions of the natural world.

Clearly such a passage is really a poet's vision, as much as a philosopher's. It works at several levels of metaphor, besides the logical and explanatory one. A poem is itself a form of *leap*, of making language momentarily airborne. A poet is himself like the humble water-insect, casting those beautiful "shadows fringed with prismatic colours" (his poems) as he struggles up the stream of self-intuition, "the brook" of his inward thoughts. Even the five-pointed form of his vision, the "cinque-spotted" shadow like a star, has mystical implications and is curiously suggestive of Coleridge's concept of unity-in-multiplicity. (It also recalls the "image with a glory round its head", of his Malta poem "Constancy to an Ideal Object".) With such dense and radiant metaphoric episodes as these, Coleridge began to give *Biographia* its new dimension.

15

Coleridge had now shown that the "mechanistic" account of the human mind was inadequate. With Chapter 9, he introduced the counter-philosophy of Immanuel Kant, whose *Critique of Pure Reason* (1787) and *Critique of Judgment* (1790) "took possession of me as with a giant's hand. After fifteen years of familiarity with them, I still read these and all his other productions with undiminished delight and increasing admiration."[127] With Kant came his disciples Fichte and Schelling, especially the latter's *Naturphilosophie* and his key work *The System of Transcendental Idealism* (1800). With Schelling, "I first found a genial coincidence with much that I had toiled out for myself, and a powerful assistance in what I had yet to do."[128]

Behind these contemporary German philosophers, with their new view of a creative human mind shaping our perceptions of the universe, Coleridge also aligned an older tradition of Christian mystics who denied a purely passive, mechanistic view of the human spirit. These were the prophets of the Protestant revolution – George Fox, Jakob Boehme, and "the pious and fervid William Law" – who opposed the traditional Aristotelianism of the Church Fathers. Philosophically, this was a daring and unconventional connection to make. But Coleridge, never forgetting his personal struggles, bore witness to the spiritual life and hope with which they had animated his thought in the darkest days.

In a beautiful, introspective passage (the voice shifting its register towards the solemn intimacy of the King James Bible), he reverted to the imagery of the circuitous journey.

> The feeling of gratitude, which I cherish towards these men, has caused me to digress further than I had foreseen or proposed . . . For the writings of these mystics acted in no slight degree to prevent my mind from being imprisoned within the outline of any single dogmatic system. They contributed to keep alive the *heart* in the *head*; gave me an indistinct, yet stirring and working presentiment, that all the products of the mere *reflective* faculty partook of DEATH, and were as the rattling twigs and sprays in winter, into which a sap was yet to be propelled from some root to which I had not penetrated, if they were to afford my soul food or shelter. If they were too often a moving cloud of smoke to me by day, yet they were always a pillar of fire throughout the night, during my wanderings through the wilderness of doubt, and enabled me to skirt, without crossing, the sandy deserts of utter unbelief.[129]

Years later this image of the long, parched desert journey (the lonely caravan), would resurface in Coleridge's late poetry and prose; and Hazlitt would use it – with a kind of cruel salutation – to sum up Coleridge's whole life. For Coleridge it became perhaps the land-borne equivalent of the Mariner's ocean voyage.

16

In Chapter 9 Coleridge set out not merely his personal debts to the German philosophers, but the central position of their work in the argument of the expanded *Biographia*. (He even put a rhyming "burlesque on the Fichtean Egoismus" in a footnote.) He specifically denied philosophical originality, stating that his aim was only to interpret and explain the system to English readers, and to apply it in a new way to poetry. (In fact, neither Kant nor Schelling make any detailed study of imaginative literature, and always treat of Imagination – *Einbildungskraft* – in most abstract technical terms, as "reproductive, productive, and aesthetic").[130] "God forbid! that I should be suspected of a wish to enter into a rivalry with Schelling for the honours so unequivocally his right, not only as a great and original genius, but as the *founder* of the PHILOSOPHY OF NATURE, and as the most successful *improver* of the Dynamic System which, begun by Bruno, was re-introduced (in a more philosophical form, and freed from all impurities and visionary accompaniments) by Kant . . . To me it will be happiness and honour enough, should I succeed in rendering the system itself intelligible to my countrymen . . ."[131]

Nothing could appear more open than this, and no contemporary reader could mistake it. The *Biographia* was now being openly grounded in German philosophy, and the whole cast of its technical vocabulary – "objectivize", "potence", "polarity", "transcendental", "evolution of self-consciousness", "armed vision", "dynamic" – was specifically assembled from Coleridge's translations of German terminology. Moreover, modern scholars, hypersensitive to Coleridge's use of German sources, have pointed out that there is no single citation from Kant that is not given a full reference to the relevant work (often with page number); and that all the works that Coleridge used from Schelling are somewhere named in the text.[132] Coleridge's advance towards his own theory of Fancy and Imagination, via the German epistemology, would seem fully and (for its period) even meticulously documented.

But in reality it is not. At the heart of the philosophical discussion, the problem of plagiarism returns with a vengeance, and threatens to undermine Coleridge's authority. From Chapter 8 onwards all the technical areas of the text are packed with plagiarisms, in the exact sense of unacknowledged quotations, disguised summaries, silent borrowing and close verbal resemblances. At the end of Chapter 12 one can speak of a tight, almost impenetrable, "mosaic" of citations running continuously for a dozen pages.[133] Exactly as with

A. W. Schlegel in the later Shakespeare Lectures, Coleridge's work is transformed into a kind of secret dialogue with his unacknowledged German source.*

But what is much less clear, paradoxically, is what damage this does to the *Biographia* as a whole. If it weakens Coleridge's claims as a professional philosopher, it demonstrates his powers to dramatize and popularize the most intractable ideas, assembled from a fantastic range of (what were then) genuinely arcane sources. It also brings a new kind of tension into the autobiographical narrative, in a way that he may well have intended.

Coleridge's plagiarisms form a kind of psycho-drama within the heart of the *Biographia*. He himself deliberately brings up the subject in Chapter 9, and makes a series of most eloquent admissions and defences, laying himself astonishingly open to criticism.

> It would be a mere act of justice to myself, were I to warn my future readers, that an identity of thought, or even similarity of phrase will not be at all times a certain proof that the passage has been borrowed from Schelling, or that the conceptions were originally learnt from him. In this instance, as in the dramatic lectures of Schlegel to which I have before alluded, from the same motive of self-defence, against the charge of plagiarism, many of the most striking resemblances, indeed all the main and fundamental ideas, were born and matured in my mind before I had seen a single page of the German Philosopher . . . Whether a work is the offspring of a man's own spirit, and the product of original thinking, will be discovered by those who are its sole legitimate judges, by better tests than the mere reference to dates. For readers in general, let whatever shall be found in this or any future work of mine,

* This much was first identified in Sara Coleridge's 1847 edition of the *Biographia*, and has been meticulously clarified by the most modern edition (1983) which prints every possible parallel passage from German authors – Maass, Jacobi, Kant, and Schelling most notably – in its footnotes, frequently, and symbolically, threatening to overwhelm the main text with its sources. The editors even print a percentage summary of "Direct Unacknowledged Translations" compared to original materials: overall about 13% in the exclusively philosophical sections. However, taking Chapters 5 to 13 entire, a text of about 45,000 words, on the most rigorous showing only about 4,000 words are indisputable plagiarism. One wonders what Coleridge would have made of such literary mathematics. See *Biographia*, II, Appendix A.

> that resembles, or coincides with, the doctrines of my German predecessor, though contemporary, be wholly attributed to *him* . . . I regard truth as a divine ventriloquist: I care not from whose mouth the sounds are supposed to proceed, if only the words are audible and intelligible.[135]

Of course this does not exculpate Coleridge. But it wonderfully dramatizes his dilemma, and in a single winning phrase about truth – "the divine ventriloquist" – it appeals to a court beyond the bench of scholarship and statistical annotation. Plagiarism, in other words, becomes one of the most exciting narrative drives of the *Biographia*. Like his opium dependency, it threatens to wreck Coleridge entirely – he seems swept towards inevitable disaster. The question becomes whether or not he can break out of the vortex of scholarly theft and dissembling, and find his own voice again. So his autobiographical self-dramatization is fantastically intensified.

17

How far did Coleridge know what he was doing? Did he deliberately draw the reader conspiratorially into the process, leaving clues and begging for understanding? It seems possible. He had written earlier to Dr Brabant a striking account of the psychological progression of people secretly enslaved to some unnamed "vicious Habit", and the description applies equally to opium addiction and plagiarism. "This, I long ago observed, is the dire Curse of all habitual Immorality, that the impulses wax as the motives wane – like animals caught in the current of a Sea-vortex, (such as the Norwegian Maelstrohm) at first they rejoice in the pleasurable ease with which they are carried onward, with their consent yet without an effort of the will – as they swim, the servant gradually becomes the Tyrant, and finally they are sucked onward against their will . . ."[136]

Such water-images occur at crucial points throughout the *Biographia*, and metaphors of floating, flooding, flowing and sinking are used to dramatize much of Coleridge's spiritual and intellectual journey. Like the maelstrom, too, the pace of his plagiarisms increases with each chapter, tightening and thickening, as if he will never break free to give his own promised account of Fancy and Imagination.*

But with Chapter 10, the famous chapter of personal "digressions", Coleridge does break free of the vortex by returning to the more personal narrative. Having thrown down the invented term "Esemplastic" – from the Greek *eis en plattein*, "to shape into one" – as his preliminary definition of the imaginative power, he slides away from technical philosophy. He is soon back at Stowey. "I now devoted myself to poetry and to the study of ethics and psychology; and so profound was my admiration at this time of Hartley's Essay on Man, that I gave his name to my first born . . ."[137]

The story here meanders back, river-like, in time to 1797, before he had read Kant, or been to Germany, and was still a believer in Associationism. But the effect is gripping, because it transforms the philosophical argument back into a personal adventure of discovery. This was the material that the "dialogue" with Wordsworth had suppressed, and which the summer conversations with his Hartley had perhaps released.

The voice again becomes limpid and intimate, with the biblical and visionary note intensified. "I retired to a cottage in Somersetshire at the foot of Quantock, and devoted my thoughts and studies to the foundations of religion and morals. Here I found myself all afloat. Doubts rushed in; broke upon me '*from the fountains of the great deep*', and fell '*from the windows of heaven*'. The fontal truths of natural religion and the books of Revelation alike contributed to the flood; and it was long ere my ark touched on Ararat, and rested."[138]

The chapter runs freely on over the next decade, diversified with accounts of his journalistic adventures with the *Watchman* and *The Friend*, his trips to Germany and Italy, his lecturing and playwriting.

---

* Coleridge's water-images also connect with those of flight, as with the famous flock of starlings, "thickening, deepening, blackening", he had glimpsed from a coach window in November 1799. All these express problems of imaginative freedom balanced against artistic and moral control, and are linked with Coleridge's analysis of nightmares and visions. (See *Early Visions*, pp. 253–4.) Perhaps they could be described as his poetry of "psychological fluid-mechanics". It is no coincidence that Edgar Allan Poe, an alcoholic and great admirer of Coleridge's poetry and prose, used many such images as the key to his stories of entrapment, obsession and addiction, notably "The Maelstrom" in *Tales of the Grotesque and Arabesque*, (1840).

There is a strong political thread, with a defence of his attitude to Jacobinism and the French Revolution.

The "circuitous path" of this fine chapter is the widest and longest in the *Biographia*, and the term "esemplastic" does not reappear until the opening of Chapter 13. Yet the idea of the Imagination as the emerging power in Coleridge's life is kept constantly in play. It is most memorably dramatized in the comic account of the government agent, "Spy Nozy", who mistakes the Quantock poets discussing philosophy in the woods and coombes for political subversives planning a seaborne invasion of French Jacobins up the rivers of Somerset in 1797. "At first he fancied, that we were aware of our danger; for he often heard me talk of one *Spy Nozy*, which he was inclined to interpret of himself, and a remarkable feature belonging to him; but he was speedily convinced that it was the name of a man who made a book [Spinoza] and lived long ago."[139]

This lighthearted tale leads, with typical skill, to Coleridge's lyrical and moving description of the epic philosophic poem "The Brook", the real subject of their supposedly subversive ramblings. "Such a subject I conceived myself to have found in a stream, traced from its source in the hills among the yellow-red moss and conical glass-shaped tufts of bent, to the first break of fall, where its drops become audible, and it begins to form a channel . . . thence to the sheepfold . . . the lonely cottage . . . the hamlet . . . the market-town, the manufacturies, and the seaport."[140]

The water imagery here suggests, in context, a deep connection with the flowing thematic of the entire *Biographia* and its meandering journey. It also recalls the unwritten philosophic epic of Coleridge's May 1815 letter to Wordsworth, and perhaps signals the recovery of "Kubla Khan", that miniature epic of a "sacred river" originally written at this time. With these subtle connections and fluid echoes, Coleridge brought the *Biographia* back to life in his own familiar voice. But time was pressing relentlessly now, and he still had not reached his philosophic destination.

18

On 17 September, 1815, urged on by a frantic Morgan, he wrote directly to John Gutch about the cause of the slipped deadline. He apologized for his "accursed Letterophobia", and admitted he had been "constantly deluding" himself since August about being nearly finished with the book. On 10 August, when Morgan's "extreme anxiety and depression of Spirits" had led him to post off the first part of the manuscript, "the whole was written, excepting the philosophical Part which I at that time meant to comprize in a few Pages". But in the intervening weeks the expansion of this small section had radically changed the size, nature and general interest of the *Biographia*.

"This has now become not only a sizeable Proportion of the whole, not only the most interesting portion to a certain class, but with the exception of four or five Pages of which due warning is given, the most *entertaining* to the general Reader, from the variety both of information and of personal Anecdotes." He now thought the *Biographia* would prove more important than his collected poems, and was the "Pioneer to the great Work on the *Logos*, Divine and Human, on which I have set my Heart . . ."[141] He was now dashing to the conclusion, which he expected in less than a week.

He had left himself desperately little time. It is clear from Coleridge's letter to Gutch that he had only just finished Chapter 10 ("personal Anecdotes") by early September. But Coleridge still had to expound his term "esemplastic", and draw his own philosophic definition of Imagination and Fancy clear of Kant and Schelling. Without this his literary critique and appreciation of Wordsworth (Chapters 14 to 22) would have no epistemological foundation or "resting place", and the bridge between the two parts of the *Biographia* would be fatally incomplete.

It is evident from Chapter 11 (the"affectionate exhortation" to young authors, in which he mentions that money and necessity are "narcotics" rather than "stimulants" to a work of genius) that Coleridge was struggling and prevaricating.[142] The material was more intractable than anything he had previously attempted. The highly technical matter involved the Kantian notion of "intuitive forms" (time, space, causality) as subjective modes of human perception, in opposition to the unknowable reality of the "noumenal" world, things in themselves and in their essence. He had, as he put it, to distinguish between the temporary "I am" of the human Mind, and the eternal "It is" of Nature, and define the "intermediary" power of Imagination which reconciled them.[143]

Not only did this involve a philosophic account of Schelling's definition of the "subjective" and "objective" poles of reality, the "Polar Science".[144] But also – what was not in Schelling, but was vital to Coleridge's religious views – the demonstration of a personal Creator within this system of ultimate knowledge. Language, especially the language of a poet rooted in "passionate particulars", almost broke down into meaningless abstraction under this pressure. "We begin with the I KNOW MYSELF, in order to end with the absolute I AM. We proceed from the SELF, in order to lose and find all self in GOD."[145]

Coleridge had gone over this material again and again in the elusive style of his private Notebooks; but to present it for a general readership, to make it popular and accessible, was quite a different level of challenge. "Great indeed are the obstacles which an English metaphysician has to encounter," he dictated plaintively to Morgan. "Among his most respectable and intelligent judges, there will be many who have devoted their attention exclusively to the concerns and interests of human life, and who bring with them to the perusal of a philosophic system an habitual aversion to all speculation, the utility and application of which are not evident and immediate."[146]

It was now, in evident desperation, that he flung himself back into the vortex of Schelling's three main publications: the *Transcendental Idealism* (1800), the *Abhandlungen* (1796–7), and the collection *Philosophische Schriften* (1809). From these he assembled a condensed list of ten main propositions or "Theses" in his Notebooks, to sweep him through to the end of Chapter 12.[147] It was the failure to acknowledge this composite source which laid him open to the most serious charge of plagiarism in the *Biographia*. Working flat out (including now an evening stint from 6 to 10 p.m.) he dictated verbatim from these notes (adding his own commentaries) to John Morgan, and perhaps even to Hartley. He must have produced some 14,000 words in about four days.[148] He supplied no more than the ghost of a scholarly reference to Schelling's work, "on a like occasion".[149]

19

Composed under this extreme pressure of his deadline (which Morgan felt as much as he), Chapter 12 is nonetheless a formidable and unexpectedly poetic piece of work. He opened it, "a chapter of requests and premonitions", with a series of appeals to the reader. The material would be difficult, and the reader might want to skip directly to Chapter 13 and the final, promised definition of Imagination or the esemplastic power. He invoked the Pythagorean maxim, "until you understand a writer's ignorance, presume yourself ignorant of his understanding".[150] He argued that philosophic knowledge, as a technical discipline, was like a retreating range of hills and higher ascents, "hidden by mists and clouds", which the ordinary reader might never scale, though he could still see the natural beauty and fitness of its conclusions. "On *its* ridges the common sun is born and departs. From *them* the stars rise, and touching *them* they vanish."[151]

Drawing again on a water-image of haunting simplicity, he suggests that the philosopher and the poet are exceptional in their pursuit of knowledge. "But in all ages there have been a few, who measuring and sounding the rivers of the vale at the feet of their furthest inaccessible falls have learned, that the sources must be far higher and far inward . . ."[152] Yet intuitions and glimpses of these higher truths are accessible to all. Coleridge urges his reader to make what is in effect an existential leap of faith. The philosophic connection between Imagination and spiritual powers can be intuited poetically, without technical language, if only the reader will look into their own inner life, and respond to its mysterious potential. Here he turns back to his Notebooks of 1811, and the long, pensive "dialogues" with Jean-Paul Richter.

> They and they only can acquire the philosophic Imagination, the sacred-power of self-intuition, who within themselves can interpret and understand the symbol, that the wings of the air-sylph are forming within the skin of the caterpillar; those only, who feel in their own spirits the same instinct, which impels the chrysalis of the horned fly to leave room in its involcrum for antennae yet to come. They know and feel, that the *potential* works *in* them, even as the *actual* works on them! . . . They exist in all, and their first appearance discloses itself in the *moral* being.[153]

This combination of natural science and metaphysics is characteristic of Schelling's *Naturphilosophie*. Yet the fundamentally religious drive of the argument, its carefully unfolded imagery, its Platonic overtones, are wholly original and Coleridgean. They come from the rivers of the Quantocks and the Lake District, from the natural creatures of his poems and Notebooks, from the long solitary nights of his readings and reflections. All have a homely touch which is unmistakably his. These central passages, these gleams of the transcendent, in many ways embrace the entire argument of the chapter in a single poetic vision of an infinite universe accessible to man. Here, there can be no question of plagiarism.

At this point Coleridge almost seemed to halt, appending a long and splendidly irrelevant note on philosophic dictionaries. Its interest lies in the fact that he dated it "this morning (16th September 1815)". This was precisely three days before he despatched the completed manuscript to Gutch.[154] So, with his deadline now bearing down on him, Coleridge shut himself in his study with Morgan and dictated recklessly from his Schelling notes until the end of Chapter 12. The two general "Postulates" and ten "Theses" he produced now have little but technical interest. He never later acknowledged that they were plagiarized, but mournfully dismissed them as "unformed and immature . . . not fully thought out".[155] This much is certainly true, and they have never attracted serious philosophic commentary.

He hurried on to Chapter 13, "On the Imagination, or esemplastic power". For a few paragraphs he seemed to be embroiling himself more and more deeply with Schelling's problem of "constructing" nothing less than the entire universe on polar principles. This did not promise a rapid conclusion. "The transcendental philosopher says: grant me a nature having two contrary forces, the one of which tends to expand infinitely . . ."[156] No doubt Morgan, as he took down these ominous words, would gladly have reached for Occam's razor.

20

But it was Coleridge who made the cut. Abruptly, he found a startling way out of all his spiralling difficulties. He had just, he announced, received a "very judicious" letter from a friend, urging him to suspend his tortuous metaphysical chapters. Why not give a simple aphoristic description of his philosophical distinction between Fancy and Imagination, and leave the rest for a later book? This Coleridge had decided to do – in two paragraphs.

The letter – probably inspired by his exchanges with Dr Brabant

– was of course a pure fiction. Coleridge later said he wrote it himself with inspired desperation, "Without taking my pen off the paper except to dip it in the inkstand."[157] He inserted it boldly into the manuscript, with instructions to print in italics. It was also another invented voice and it bears an intriguing relation to his future Preface to "Kubla Khan".

Both are explanations of his failure to complete a literary work, which have the paradoxical effect of making the remaining "fragment" more fascinating and richly suggestive. In the letter the "friend" describes the experience of reading Coleridge's metaphysical arguments as like being "left alone, in one of our largest Gothic cathedrals in a gusty moonlight night of autumn. 'Now in glimmer, and now in gloom'; often in palpable darkness not without a chilly sensation of terror; then suddenly emerging into broad yet visionary lights with coloured shadows of fantastic shapes . . ."[158]

Coleridge, said the friend agreeably, had done "too much, and yet not enough". The argument was either so elliptical, or so compressed, that what remained was "like the fragments of the winding steps of an old ruined tower". The philosophical "disquisition" was valuable as history, but further "speculations on the esemplastic power would be utterly unintelligible". He would be like the celebrated idealist Bishop Berkeley, who announced an essay on "Tar-Water", beginning with Tar and ending with the Trinity . . . He concluded, pleasantly, that knowing Coleridge as he did, there was "a small portion of pig-nature" in his literary character, and that as far as actually finishing a book was concerned, he must be "pulled back from the boat in order to make him enter it". In all the circumstances, this was a peculiarly fitting marine analogy.[159]

So with this extravagant, provoking, and curiously humorous gesture (as if he were mocking himself from the shadows of his own creation), Coleridge completed, or escaped from, the *Biographia* at the end of September 1815. The manuscript was placed on the evening mail coach to Gutch in Bristol on Tuesday, 19 September, and Coleridge took in the *Sibylline Leaves* by hand the following Friday.[160]

21

Yet Coleridge left behind, at the end of Chapter 13, the most famous critical fragment of his career. It became in many ways the prose equivalent of "Kubla Khan". Its 199 words – clear, compact, Delphic – were destined to generate as much discussion, as much source-hunting, as much praise and controversy, as the poem. It summed up seven chapters of argument, and defined for the English-speaking world the Romantic concept of creativity. It did indeed distinguish between Fancy and Imagination. And more than that, it formed the vital bridge between the two halves of the *Biographia*, so bringing the philosophical principle to bear on the critical practice.

> The IMAGINATION then I consider either as primary or secondary. The primary IMAGINATION I hold to be the living Power and prime Agent of all human Perception, and as a repetition in the finite mind of the eternal act of creation in the infinite I AM. The secondary I consider as an echo of the former, co-existing with the conscious will, yet still as identical with the primary in the *kind* of its agency, and differing only in *degree*, and in the *mode* of its operation. It dissolves, diffuses, dissipates, in order to re-create; or where this process is rendered impossible, yet still at all events it struggles to idealize and to unify. It is essentially *vital*, even as all objects (*as* objects) are essentially fixed and dead.
>
> FANCY, on the contrary, has no other counters to play with, but fixities and definites. The Fancy is indeed no other than a mode of Memory emancipated from the order of time and space; and blended with, and modified by that empirical phenomenon of the will, which we express by the word CHOICE. But equally with the ordinary memory it must receive all its materials ready made from the law of association.[161]

That the concepts of Fancy and Imagination had such a long history, both in German and English philosophy, makes this precision and brevity all the more remarkable. Coleridge's memorable definition combines the quality of an algebraic formula and a witch's spell or incantation. It is simultaneously cold and logical, and hot and mystical. Elements of the English tradition of empirical psychology mingle with German concepts of polar energies, and purely scientific notions of chemical and electrical reactions. There is also a religious affirmation that Imagination is "a repetition in the finite mind of the eternal act of creation". If all this draws on the common intellectual currency of European discussion at the turn of the century, and the notion of some form of active–passive dialectic or polarity in the human mind, it also does something that no previous writer had achieved.

Coleridge made such ideas familiar, indeed famous, for the ordinary reader. Moreover he wrote about them as a practising poet, and he brought them to life as part of his own intellectual and spiritual journey. For him the escape from the passive world-view of Associationism was a necessary step on the path to spiritual redemption. "All the products of the mere reflective faculty partook of DEATH . . ." To be trapped in an empirical, materialist view of the world meant that his own fate was sealed (especially as an opium addict), without creative choice, moral will, or degrees of freedom. But to believe in an active, transforming world of the imagination, and to believe this was an unquenchable "power" and energy in Nature, part of man's divine inheritance, promised salvation. It is for this reason that Coleridge's theory of the Imagination goes far beyond traditional epistemology. It was a poet's view of how the world really was, and ultimately a religious affirmation of freedom and hope.*

What was most original in Coleridge's account of the Imagination, throughout the *Biographia*, was the vivid and personal way in which he described its workings in his own mind. To this extent, Coleridge did not write like a traditional philosopher at all, but closer to a modern existential viewpoint, in which the actual experience of moral

---

* The limits of scientific "materialism" and "determinism" still engage us in the largest possible way. After a long period of eclipse in the nineteenth century, apparently overwhelmed by the "hard" sciences of physics, chemistry and mathematics, Coleridge's view of a mysterious, dynamic universe of "powers" and energies, of "uncertainty principles" and continual "process" (which he shared with the German *Naturphilosophie*) is returning to confront us in new forms of speculative science. (See John Horgan, *The End of Science: Facing the Limits of Knowledge in the Twilight of the Scientific Age*, 1996.) Following a fine contemporary re-assessment of Kant and Schelling, Brian Magee writes: "After the two great revolutions of twentieth-century physical science – relativity theory and quantam physics – we know that matter cannot be, as had previously been believed by so many people, the ultimate constituent of the universe, because elementary particles consist of energy. We also have exceedingly powerful grounds for believing that the universe is not deterministic." (*Confessions of a Philosopher*, 1997, p. 355.)

choice and the creative act are invoked as formative events. The philosophical term "Fancy" in fact represents his rejection of the passive mind-set of Associationism, which is connected for him with submission, addiction and death, while "Imagination", the active and unifying power, is connected with joy and freedom. In the moment of creativity, the two become reconciled in the poet's mind, and animate him with images from the deeps of memory and longing.

This is, convincingly, the product of an original vision, not a borrowed philosophy, born of much thought and suffering and reflection. When he completed the original manuscript in September, Coleridge closed it with an oracular passage (in what became Chapter 24), which insisted on the religious basis of his vision, far beyond any such affirmation in Kant or Schelling. The Imagination was, fundamentally, the faculty that communicated with divine creative power in the universe. Through it, man could bear witness to knowledge beyond the limits of discursive Reason. The image that he chose, of the stars seen at night, linked back not only to the experience of the Mariner, but as far back as he could remember, to the star-gazing he had once shared with his father in the fields of childhood at Ottery St Mary. Now, as a father himself, he had tried to show

> that Religion passes out of the ken of Reason only where the eye of Reason has reached its own Horizon; and that Faith is then but its continuation: even as the Day softens away into the sweet Twilight, and Twilight, hushed and breathless, steals into the Darkness. It is Night, sacred Night! the upraised Eye views only the starry Heaven which manifests itself alone: and the outward Beholding is fixed on the sparks twinkling in the aweful depth, though Suns of other Worlds, only to preserve the Soul steady and collected in its pure *Act* of inward Adoration to the great I AM, and to the filial WORD that re-affirmeth it from Eternity to Eternity, whose choral Echo is the Universe.[162]

22

With both manuscripts finally off his hands by the September deadline, there was every prospect of speedy publication in the winter of 1815. Coleridge at last felt he had put together two books that, whatever their shortcomings, he could finally take pride in. With the Morgans' help, he had fought his way back from the utter despair of the previous year. In prose and in verse, he had achieved a poet's testament, a proof that his life was not quite worthless.

Briefly, he was swept by a quiet sense of happiness, of things coming back under control. He invited Gutch over to Calne, promising to "row him about" the beautiful lake at Bowood and conduct him around the paintings at Corsham, while they discussed publication details. He also asked Gutch to bring the symbolic tortoiseshell snuffbox, which he had left in Bristol until his work was done, and he had truly earned it back. Not forgetting Hartley, he discreetly negotiated £10 to send his son back to Oxford with some money in his pocket and a small share of his father's good fortune. Only when Hartley was gone was it borne in on him that he was penniless.[163]

On 7 October Coleridge wrote soberly to Daniel Stuart announcing the two volumes as the unexpected fruit of his long retreat at Calne – "all corrected & finished to the best of my power – For the last 4 months I have never worked less than six hours every day". Now at last he felt able to plan ahead again: a new play for Drury Lane, a new edition of *The Friend*, and of course the *Logosophia* "for which I have been collecting the materials for the last 15 years almost incessantly".

He claimed his health was good, "better than I have known it for the last 12 years". It was now only his finances which seemed incurable – "what can I do if I am to starve while working? . . . Would to God, I had been bred a Shoemaker!" At this stage in his career, he could not face a return to daily journalism, especially as he considered all the papers, including the *Courier*, "so entirely devoted to the Government". He had tried offering translations to Murray, "but all in vain". He could not expect any more money from Gutch, his advances already standing at £107.5s.6d. He must find new patrons, "otherwise, I must sink".[164]

Now at last he played his only trump card. In a fever of anxiety, he resumed his correspondence with Byron. Three long letters went out in October, outlining his publishing plans, and wildly promising a tragedy for Drury Lane by Christmas. Coleridge could not know that Byron's own affairs – gathering debts, a broken marriage, tempestuous scandals – were suddenly crowding round him that autumn. Yet miraculously the reply came, prompt and enthusiastic.

Byron would indeed recommend the new books in London, he would "negotiate with the Trade" and (as a representative of Drury Lane) he would anxiously await the play – "it is a field in which there are none living to contend against you and in which I would take pride and pleasure in seeing you compared with the dead. I say this *not* disinterestedly, but as a *Committeeman.*"

He added some stirring praise of "Christabel", extracts of which he had heard Walter Scott reciting from memory the previous spring. The poem was "the wildest and finest I ever heard in that kind of composition . . . I mention this, not for the sake of boring you with compliments, but as a prelude to the hope that this poem is or is to be in the volumes you are now about to publish. I do not know that even 'Love' or the 'Ancient Mariner' are so impressive – and to me there are few things in our tongue beyond these two productions."[165]

This was the kind of recognition from the younger generation (Byron was still only twenty-seven) that Coleridge had long dreamed of. When Byron engagingly admitted, in a second letter, that he thought he had unconsciously plagiarized from "Christabel" in his own poem "The Maid of Corinth" Coleridge was overcome with gratitude at this acknowledgement of his poetic influence. Greatly emboldened, he sent Byron a copy of the poem. (It is extraordinary that he only possessed two copies of "Christabel": the first made long ago by Asra in the Lakes, the second very recently by Charlotte at Calne. Coleridge sent Asra's and retained Charlotte's.)

Then he poured forth a long recital of his professional troubles into his Lordship's receptive ear. His poetic influence on others – on Wordsworth, on Scott – had indeed been unrecognized. The reviews had universally mocked him with failure to fulfil his literary promise. What he had published was described as "over elaborate, obscure, paradoxical, over subtle etc.". Ever since the *Lyrical Ballads* he had been "forced in bitterness of Soul" to turn off from the chosen path of serious work, "to earn the week's food by the week's

Labour for the Newspapers & the like". Since 1800, in fact, there had not been "any three months" that he could devote "exclusively" to the poetry and metaphysics that delighted him. Only his new publications might justify fifteen years of long pilgrimage through this desert.[166]

Needless to say, it was a highly partial account. (He made no mention, among other things, of the Wedgwood annuity; of Stuart's loans or Southey's support of his family; and no mention of opium.) But Byron, with his flamboyant sense of *noblesse oblige*, was touched and also intrigued. He could be suspected, in his charming way, of flattering Coleridge in their courtly correspondence. But he had a low opinion of Wordsworth – *The Excursion* was "rain upon rocks where it stands and stagnates" – and a genuine sense that Coleridge was the undiscovered genius of the partnership.[167]

There was no mistaking the excitement with which he immediately wrote to his old friend, the poet Tom Moore, on 28 October. To relaunch Coleridge would be a good deed in a naughty world. "By the way, if C[oleridge] – who is a man of wonderful talent, and in distress, and about to publish two vols. of Poesy and Biography, and who has been worse used by the critics than ever we were – will you, if he comes out, promise me to review him favourably in the *Edinburgh Review*? Praise him, I think you must, but you will also praise him *well*, – of all things the most difficult. It will be the making of him. This must be a secret between you and me, as Jeffrey might not like such a project; nor, indeed, might C[oleridge] himself like it. But I do think he only wants a pioneer and a sparkle or two to explode most gloriously."[168]

The game was now afoot. A week later Byron secretly sent the copy of "Christabel" to his publisher. Byron was confident of its value, and did not stand on ceremony, even with Murray: "in fact I have no authority to let it out of my hands. – I think most highly of it – & feel anxious that you should be the publisher – but if you are not – I do not despair of finding those that will."[169]

Coleridge did not learn immediately of these manoeuvres on his behalf. But the very fact of his resumed contact with Byron in the autumn of 1815 was immeasurably heartening. For the first time he had the sense that a long exile might be ending. His thoughts turned increasingly towards London. He pledged his "Honour & Existence" on completing a new tragedy by December ("if I live"), and then added a little discovery of his own. He recommended to his Lordship a young provincial actress, Miss Hudson from the Calne travelling company, who in his opinion performed Shakespeare better than any actress since the famous Dorothea Jordan. She would grace Drury Lane and its new programme admirably, provided that she had her teeth fixed by "the London Dentists", which would cost £10.[170]

23

Printing of the *Biographia* and *Sibylline Leaves* in two companion volumes began in Bristol promptly in October, under Gutch's supervision. Coleridge also wrote to Wade and Washington Allston with plans for a simultaneous American edition, which eventually appeared in New York in 1817.[171] But it soon became apparent that the printer, accustomed to newsprint, was slow and unfitted for such a demanding text (poetry, footnotes, Latin, Greek, glosses, epigraphs). Proofs arrived in more than fifteen separate signatures through the autumn and winter, and were still being dispatched to Calne the following February.

Of course the printer was not solely to blame. After all the effort and excitement, Coleridge had collapsed again into opium in November 1815, and he continued to be intermittently ill until the spring. On his forty-third birthday in October, he had written ominously to Allston: "in *all* but the Brain I am an *old* man! Such ravages do anxiety & mismanagement make."[172]

Secret notes began to fly off to a number of chemists in Calne and Devizes. "Mr Coleridge . . . requests, that there may be sent by the Bearer three ounces of Laudanum – (in the accompanying bottle – or whatever quantity it may hold) half an oz. of crude opium (if there be none purified) – & two ounces of the Tincture of Cardamum. As soon as the weather relaxes, Mr Coleridge will call . . . and settle his general account."[173] There were stormy scenes at Church Street (much alarming Charlotte and Mary), and drunken embarrassments at the houses of friends in Calne.

On one occasion in December, at the home of the Rev. William Money (with whom Coleridge had been corresponding about the doctrine of salvation) there was a scandal over a pile of brandy bottles found in the bedroom. Coleridge later explained patiently to his confidant Dr Brabant that these were merely bottles of medicine that he had sent a servant to collect from the "Calne Druggist", and had inadvertently left behind after his visit. There was no brandy among them – merely tinctures of rhubarb, cardamom, laudanum, "with a half-pint flat bottle of British Gin". He could not conceive why the Reverend William Money should be shocked.[174]

Throughout December and January 1816, work on the proofs progressed ever more slowly, and the tragedy for Byron at Drury Lane came to a complete halt. Morgan became depressed at the opportunities that were slipping through their fingers, when success had seemed within their grasp. Coleridge would disappear into his bedroom, leaving him pathetic little notes. "Tomorrow morning, I doubt not, I shall be of clear and collected Spirits; but to night I feel that I should do nothing to any purpose, but and excepting Thinking, Planning, and Resolving to resolve – & praying to be able to execute."[175] Morgan – still his "faithful, zealous, & disinterested Friend" – jotted sadly on the back of this missive a revised version of the opening stanza from the *Mariner*:

There is an ancient Mariner
And he stoppeth one of three
By thy grey beard and glittering eye
Now wherefore stopp'st thou me?

The old guilts and sense of moral paralysis came creeping back into Coleridge's Notebooks, with their brilliant touches of painful poetry. "Vain Prayer to Heaven (repentance with amendment or abandonment of the Vice) = huge mass of ignited Rock flung perpendicular upward to an immense Height by the volcano, still falling back."[176] Sometimes the old sense of futility returned. "We all look up to the Sky for comfort, but nothing appears there – nothing comforts, nothing answers us – & so we die."[177]

Mary and Charlotte, irritated and alarmed, grew less patient with his gloomy relapses and tearful retreats. They made him dream of escaping the household altogether, leaving Morgan as his literary executor. He entered a bitter note in his Latin and Greek code. "Calne: and if it please God, the last month of my being with the Morgans – for his Wife and his Wife's Sister exult so despotically in the scope of their Woman's domain."[178]

Later, more calmly, he thought of turning the whole experience into a novel, "Men and Women". Its theme would be ingratitude, and the failure of sympathy between the sexes. "That which I have to strive for now in the discipline of my own mind is independence of female Society." He thought Morgan would sympathize. "Mem. To write out the *Story*: that if I die, my friend M. may make use of it."[179] It may also have been prompted by the fact that Charlotte was now being invited out to dances by young men of her own age.[180] For the first time Coleridge, in his mid-forties, felt old as well as unloved. At Christmas time he wrote bleakly to Dr Brabant of looking back at "the years before I began to take the *Death* . . ." Brabant tactfully consoled him with a plump and seasonable pheasant.[181]

Yet even in these bitter, alienated months of relapse, he was visited by moments of transcendence, and hope for the work he had achieved. It was while slowly editing the proofs of *Sibylline Leaves* that he caught up a consoling remark of Jean-Paul's and turned it into one of his most haunting and magical formulations. "If a man could pass through Paradise in a Dream, & have a Flower presented to him as a pledge that his Soul had really been there, & found that Flower in his hand when he awoke – Aye! and what then?"[182] He never published it, but it came to seem like one version of his entire life, the whole of the *Biographia* in a single sentence.

24

Despite everything, the Calne household held together though the early months of 1816. Gradually Coleridge did more work on his proofs, and walked about on windy days under Oldbury Hill. "All things are, that though their substance dissolve into the Universal, yet their Figures or Shadows remain – like Rainbows on fast-sailing Clouds."[183] The White Horse, with its glittering eye of broken brandy bottles, still galloped towards London.

One of the most striking things he did was to finalize the beautiful prose gloss, or marginal commentary, to the "Mariner". For this he had invented another voice, standing outside his own creation, and so adding another frame or level of meaning as he looked back on it. (It was the device he used in his "metafictional" letter in the *Biographia*.) This time he adopted the voice of a learned antiquarian, a Christian commentator from the seventeenth century, who seeks to interpret the ballad like some mystical allegory of punishment and redemption.

It was as if the older, philosophical Coleridge was now writing about the younger Pantheist Coleridge of the Quantock days. He speaks of the "crime" of shooting the Albatross, followed by a supernatural "curse", a "horrible penance", and a final "expiation". This could be taken as a conventional Christian interpretation, with the older Coleridge's new emphasis on a Fall ("in some sense") followed by a religious Redemption. Yet Coleridge's commentator is clearly a mystic, who speaks out of a less orthodox, Gnostic tradition. "A Spirit had followed them; one of the invisible inhabitants of this planet, neither departed souls nor angels; concerning whom the learned Jew, Josephus, and the Platonic Constantinopolitan, Michael Psellus, may be consulted. They are very numerous, and there is no climate or element without one or more."[184]

He also recognizes a more ancient, pagan theme of "vengeance" in the ballad. He points out that the Mariner is subjected to a female supernatural power, the "Spectre Woman" Life-in-Death, who has no place in traditional theology. He suggests that Nature herself has become conscious of the offence that the Mariner has committed against her own laws of "hospitality". He draws attention to those moments of beautiful Nature imagery – "No twilight in the courts of the Sun" – which invest the natural world with elements of sacred, almost aristocratic power, far older than Christian cosmology.

The gloss became one of Coleridge's most remarkable pieces of "ventriloquism". One might almost catch, behind the stately seventeenth-century phrasing, a hint of Germanic accent and oracular inversion. The swift, bare stanzas of the poem are given a kind of rainbow shimmer of the transcendental about their edges. This effect was emphasized visually by marginal print-settings (very difficult even for a modern typesetter to achieve) that Coleridge insisted upon at the proof stage. So, the plain astronomical beauty of the Moon stanza from Part Four (the image partly inspired by the star-clock at Ottery) was now encircled by a halo or Brocken-spectre of retrospective and mystical commentary:

In his loneliness and fixedness, he yearneth towards the journeying Moon, and the stars that still sojourn, yet still move onward; and every where the blue sky belongs to them, and is their appointed rest, and their native country, and their own natural homes, which they enter unannounced, as lords that are certainly expected, yet there is silent joy at their arrival."

The moving Moon went up the sky.
And no where did abide:
Softly she was going up,
And a star or two beside –[185]

On the other hand the commentator also speaks with an autobiographical voice, a confessional voice that is recognizable from passages in the *Biographia*. It is impossible not to think of Coleridge's own life – his addiction, his restless exiles, his compulsive and spellbinding talk – when reading the final gloss on the penultimate stanzas of the ballad:

And ever and anon throughout his future life an agony constraineth him to travel from land to land; And to teach, by his own example, love and reverence to all things that God made and loveth.

Since then, at an uncertain hour,
That agony returns:
And till my ghastly tale is told,
This heart within me burns.

I pass, like night, from land to land;
I have strange power of speech;
That moment that his face I see,
To know the man that must hear me:
To him my tale I teach[186]

When the gloss was completed, and many fine adjustments made to the verse, Coleridge decided to place the "Mariner" at the opening of *Sibylline Leaves*. He also grouped several of the Asra poems in a section of "Love Poems"; and for the first time gathered a number of the Conversation Poems together (including "Frost at Midnight", "This Lime-Tree Bower", and "The Eolian Harp") under a heading "Meditative Poems in Blank Verse". In direct contradiction of its subject's wishes, he finally decided to print "To William Wordsworth" as well. It was, after fifteen long years, his declaration of poetic independence.

25

The corrected proofs accumulated with frustrating slowness at Bristol. At the end of January 1816, he sent one back to Gutch with the comment: "useless to pluck single thorns from a Thorn-bush. I groan *in spirit* under this whole Sheet; and but that every Hour is precious . . . I would cancel [it]."[187] Coleridge began to think more and more longingly of his return to London. If he did not seize the opportunity this spring, he felt he might never live to see another one. Opium was barely back under his control, and he confided to Dr Brabant that he was trying not to exceed "the smallest dose of Poison that will suffice to keep me tranquil and capable of literary labour".[188] He went on "pretty well" and was "decently industrious", but one more relapse might finish him.

He now had three works to present in London. Though he had abandoned the tragedy for Drury Lane, he had somehow managed to put together a lighter "verse Entertainment" to present to his Lordship. It was to be entitled *Zapolya* – a chivalric romance set in the imaginary mountains of "Illyria" – with several beautiful short songs to be set to music.

However, none of the works in hand – the play, the prose, the poems – would supply him with immediate money to finance his return. On 10 February he wrote gloomily to Gutch of the "*dead water*" of his finances.[189] He despaired of ever leaving Calne, and thought desperately of which old friends might still help him – William Sotheby, Sir Humphry Davy, Daniel Stuart.[190] But who had not given him up for lost?

Yet there were still homes for lost causes. Sotheby applied on his behalf to the Literary Fund in London, an august institution of anonymous philanthropists, whose statutes allowed them to help "men of genius in poverty and distress". Sotheby also spoke in confidence, and without Coleridge's knowledge, to Lord Byron.[191]

On St Valentine's Day, 14 February 1816, the Fund noted in its minutes: "The Case of Mr Coleridge, Author of various Poems and Dramatic Works of merit, was taken into consideration, and it was Resolved that Thirty Pounds be voted to the above Applicant . . ."[192] On the very same day, with splendid generosity, Byron despatched one of his heavily crested and franked envelopes containing a kindly letter and a £100 banknote.[193]

At Church Street, Coleridge was found by a breathless Charlotte – "You have had a letter franked by Lord Byron?" – sitting up in bed, silent and immobile, with the letters open before him, "completely lost . . . in thinking of the thing itself and the manner in which it was done".[194] Within little more than a month, Coleridge was galloping up to London, leaving the Morgans to tidy up the "chaos of loose manuscripts" in his study, after the plunging hoofs were gone.[195]

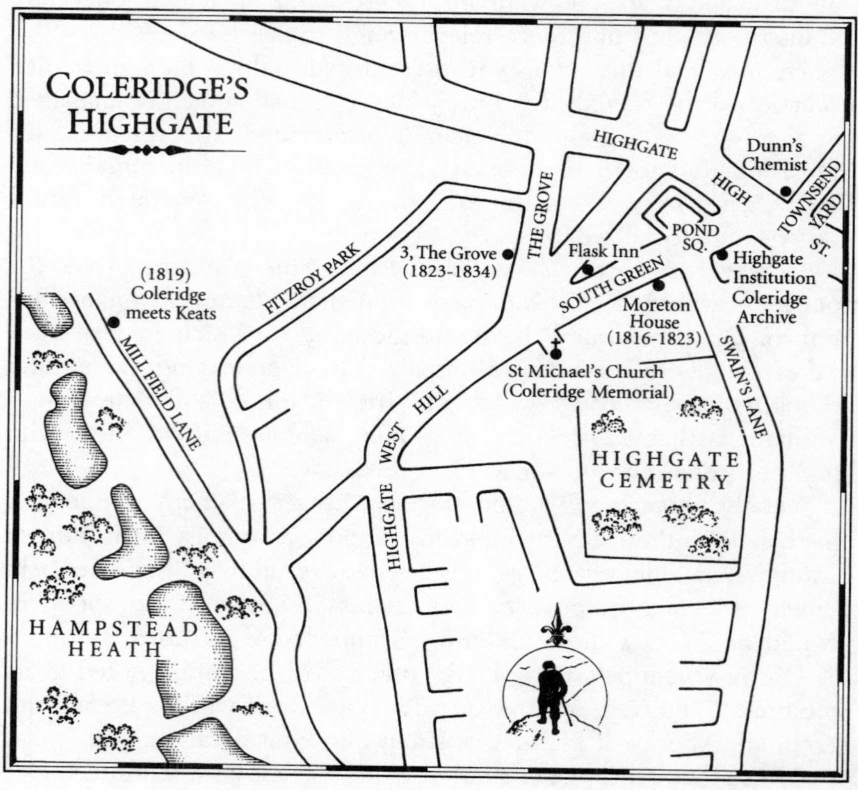

9

Climbing Highgate Hill

1

On 25 March 1816 Coleridge tumbled out of the night mail, ordered up the newspapers, and put himself to bed at the Gloucester Coffee House in Piccadilly. He had been absent from London for nearly two and a half years – as long as he had been away in the Mediterranean – and he awoke with the same sense of a strange city which had largely forgotten him. The news was of bread riots, unemployment and demands for parliamentary reform. When the *Edinburgh Review* eventually reported his return, it treated him like a premonition of Rip Van Winkle: "forth steps Mr Coleridge, like a giant refreshed from sleep . . . as if to redeem his character after so long a silence . . ."[1]

He had of course arranged nowhere to stay, but eventually found lodgings, with inspired economy of means, above the shop of an apothecary, Moore & James of 42 Norfolk Street, behind Covent Garden. Then he hurried off to make his ritual visit to the Lambs.

Charles, who had faithfully awaited Coleridge's "reappearing star", greeted this historic return with his usual mixture of affectionate concern and hilarity. "His health is tolerable at present, though beset with temptations . . . He has two volumes together at Bristol, both finished as far as the composition goes; the latter containing his fugitive Poems, the former his Literary Life. – Nature who conducts every creature by instinct to its best end, has skilfully directed C. to take up his abode at a Chemists Laboratory in Norfolk Street. She might as well have sent a Hulluo Librorum [Bookworm] for cure to the Vatican. – God kept him inviolate among the traps & pitfalls. He has done pretty well as yet."[2]

Actually Coleridge had fallen straight back into heavy opium-dosing, overcome with the stress and excitement, and within a week was in bed and summoning John Morgan from Calne to help him. For the first time his pains and breathlessness suggested symptoms of the chronic heart disease which would steadily undermine his health in these later years. "My heart, or some part about it, seems breaking, as if a weight were suspended from it that stretches it, such is the *bodily feeling*, as far as I can express it by words."[3]

Crabb Robinson, also hearing of the Prodigal's return, tracked him down at Lamb's on 6 April. He thought Coleridge had been drinking, but seemed "mystically eloquent"; while Morgan looked "very pale" and worried by his charge. "He attends Coleridge with his unexampled assiduity and kindness." He was impressed by reports of all Coleridge's work at Calne – "I am told he has written popularly and about himself" – but was alarmed that he was "printing without a publisher". He also noted that Hazlitt had been reviewing a translated volume of Schlegel's *Lectures* very knowledgeably in the *Examiner*, and foresaw the coming critical clash in the reviews which would cause a very different, but no less damaging, kind of heartache for Coleridge.[4]

The moment Morgan arrived at Norfolk Street he found Coleridge a new physician, Dr Joseph Adams, "an old acquaintance", who had some knowledge of addiction. The case was urgent, but obviously delicate. Accordingly, on 6 April Dr Adams wrote from his surgery in Hatton Garden to James Gillman, a newly elected member of the Royal College of Surgeons. Gillman had just set up his practice, and lived in a large family house on the southern slopes of Highgate, three miles north of London.

The letter was discreet but pointed.

> Dear Sir, a very learned, but in one respect an unfortunate gentleman, has applied to me on a singular occasion. He has for several years been in the habit of taking large quantities of opium. For some time past, he has been in vain endeavouring to break himself off. It is apprehended his friends are not firm enough, from a dread, lest he should suffer by suddenly leaving it off, though he is conscious of the contrary; and has proposed to me to submit himself to any regime, however severe. With this view, he wishes to fix himself in the house of some medical gentleman, who will have courage to refuse him any laudanum, and under whose assistance, should he be the worse for it, he may be relieved. As he is desirous of retirement, and a garden, I could think of no one so readily as yourself.

Dr Adams did not mention Coleridge's name, but added that he was "of great importance" as a literary man, and that his "communicative temper" made his society very interesting. Gillman replied non-committally, but agreed for an interview to be arranged one "evening" during the coming weekend.[5]

In the interval, Coleridge despatched "his excellent and faithful friend" Morgan to Byron's house in Piccadilly, with the manuscript of *Zapolya*. In an accompanying letter, he at last admitted the cause of all the delays at Calne. His Lordship would consider Coleridge "an inexplicable Being" unless he understood that for fifteen years he had been an addict – "I refer to the daily habit of taking enormous doses of Laudanum" – and had viewed life "thro' the magic glass of an opium-poisoned imagination". He was now about to embark on a cure, he hoped, with "a respectable surgeon and Naturalist" at Highgate. He added some details about *Zapolya*, now described as "a Christmas Tale" which might require some "re-plotting" for Drury Lane. Finally, he appended a learned note on Werwolves, which were currently interesting Byron. Coleridge of course knew all about them, and could refer his Lordship to a passage in Drayton's *The Man in the Moon* where we are advised to approach them "with hallowing charms". Perhaps addicts were similar creatures.[6]

How could Byron have resisted this introduction? He read *Zapolya* straight through that night, and urged Coleridge to rise from his lair the following morning. The invitation was all the more remarkable since Byron was, as it turned out, frantically busy: not only was he conducting a clandestine affair with Shelley's friend and future sister-in-law, Claire Clairmont; but he was preparing to leave England forever in less than a fortnight.

2

The single, momentous meeting between the two poets took place on 10 April 1816. Byron was at his most winning: he flattered, praised and joked, making remarks – not recorded – that Coleridge said were "enough to make one's hair bristle". He convinced Coleridge to do what he had put off for a decade, to publish "Christabel" in its unfinished state. He also somehow charmed out of him the story of "Kubla Khan" and got him to recite the poem in his drawing-room. When Coleridge dismissed it as "a psychological curiosity", Byron waved the objection aside and urged him to publish that too.[7]

Quite unknown to Coleridge, this recital was witnessed by another writer waiting in a next-door room – none other than Leigh Hunt. Hunt later recalled: "He recited his 'Kubla Khan' one morning to Lord Byron, in his Lordship's house in Piccadilly, when I happened to be in another room. I remember the other's coming away from him, highly struck with his poem, and saying how wonderfully he talked. This was the impression of everyone who heard him."[8]

The enchantment was mutual, for Coleridge in turn was dazzled by Byron, his wit, his physical beauty, and the extraordinary expressiveness of his features. "If you had seen Lord Byron," he later wrote, "you could scarcely disbelieve him – so beautiful a countenance I scarcely ever saw – his teeth so many stationary smiles – his eyes the open portals of the sun – things of light, and for light – and his forehead so ample, and yet so flexible, passing from marble smoothness into a hundred wreathes and lines and dimples correspondent to the feelings and sentiments he is uttering . . ."[9]

On Byron's recommendation, John Murray came round to arrange a publishing contract at Norfolk Street two days later on 12 April. He indicated his willingness to become Coleridge's general publisher. In the first instance he wished to publish a slim volume, sixty-four pages octavo, containing "Christabel", "Kubla Khan", and a third opium poem, "The Pains of Sleep", to be issued with Prefaces as swiftly as possible the following month. For this he initially offered £60 (with reversion of copyright). However, alterations to the contract showed that (again probably through Byron's influence) this was raised first to £70 and finally to £80.[10] Murray also introduced Coleridge to John Hookham Frere, a translator of the classics as well as a diplomat, who would later help him financially. Coleridge described this introduction as "among the most memorable Red Letter Days of my Literary Life".[11]

3

Coleridge took the local coach up from Tottenham Court to Highgate in the late afternoon of Friday, 12 April. To his delight he arrived outside the decorative iron railings of a substantial property, Moreton House, situated close to the parish church of St Michael's with its tall spire, and overlooking gardens and wooded slopes running southwards in the evening sun. (The grounds below eventually became Waterlow Park and the extended wilderness of Highgate Cemetery.)

To the west lay the rural undulations of Hampstead Heath, the lakes and the Vale of Health, and the beautiful Palladian mansion of Kenwood House, then still the property of Lord Mansfield. In front stood the clustered houses of Highgate village, grouped round a trim little green, Pond Square, embowered in oak and elm trees. A few shops ran down Highgate Hill to the tollgate, including bakers, butchers, two taverns and (rather conveniently) T. H. Dunn's the chemist. To the north lay open countryside.

When Coleridge was ushered in by a young laboratory assistant, James Gillman already had a visitor in his parlour, and was not in a hospitable mood. He was a tall, anxious, clever man, already overworked from a growing medical practice. At thirty-four, he had a household consisting of his wife Ann, two young sons James and Henry (the younger only two years old), and his wife's sister Lucy Harding. He had, he later recalled, "no intention of receiving an inmate into my house".

Dr Adams had already paid him a confidential visit, and they had discussed opium addiction and the danger and "frightful consequences" of attempting a detoxification regime. "I had heard of the failure of Mr Wilberforce's case, under an eminent physician at Bath, in addition to which, the doctor [Adams] gave me an account of several others within his own knowledge."

Gillman was primarily a physiologist, a disciple of the great surgeon John Hunter. His dissertation at the Royal College had been *On the Bite of a Rabid Animal* (1812). Yet unlike many physicians of the day he was something of an intellectual, fascinated by the new medical advances in France and Germany, and interested (as Coleridge quickly discovered) in the contemporary debate among leading London surgeons on Vitalism – the exact physiological nature of the life force in the human organism. Behind his shy and rather earnest professional exterior, lay a lively mind and, as it proved, an exceptionally kind and loyal heart.

Gillman had understood that Coleridge (probably incoherent, and possibly dangerous) would arrive escorted by Dr Adams. Instead "came Coleridge *himself* and alone", instantly genial and talkative, charming and old-fashioned in his manners, courteous to Ann, and giving the extraordinary impression that he had known Gillman all his life. James Gillman could never afterwards account for this effect, though he described it very well. "We met, indeed, for the first time, but as friends long since parted, and who had now the happiness to see each other again. Coleridge took his seat – his manner, his appearance, and above all his conversation were captivating. We listened with delight, and upon the first pause, when courtesy permitted, my [other] visitor withdrew, saying in a low voice, 'I see by your manners, an old friend has arrived . . .' "

Coleridge talked of his poetry, his travels and his medical history, and recited "some exquisite but desponding lines of his own" – the lines "To William Wordsworth" quoted at the end of Chapter 10 of the *Biographia*. The interview lasted about two hours, and Gillman was captivated. "I felt indeed almost spell-bound, without desire of release."

He thought the previous medical opinions of Coleridge's case were "unprofessional and cruel", and that a detoxification regime could be managed without danger or excessive suffering if it were supervised over several weeks. Coleridge asked to come to Highgate immediately, as a paying guest and in-patient; and within "a few minutes" what normally would have "cost many hours to arrange" was fixed. Coleridge left Moreton House with the agreement that he should move in with the Gillmans the following Monday.[12]

Both men immediately had second thoughts. Gillman felt "deeply interested", and rather flattered that someone "so highly gifted" should have sought him out, but he began to "reflect seriously on the duties imposed" and awaited the approaching day with "anxiety". Coleridge in turn wondered if James Gillman fully realized what he had undertaken. The following morning he wrote a long letter to Gillman from Norfolk Street, reviewing their arrangement with great candour. He had been convinced within "the first half hour" that in matters of intellect they would be "reciprocally serviceable to each other". But in the matter of opium, Gillman must beware. He would never *tell* a falsehood, but he was more than capable of *acting* a lie, "unless watched carefully". His need to procure the drug would drive him to "*Evasion*, and the cunning of a specific madness". Here Coleridge was humiliatingly frank, and showed great self-knowledge. "No sixty hours *have yet passed* without my having taken Laudanum – tho' for the last week comparatively trifling doses . . . For the first week I shall not, I *must not be permitted* to leave your House, unless I should walk out with you. – Delicately or indelicately this *must* be done: and both the Servant and the young Man must receive absolute commands from you on no account to fetch anything for me."

He also gave a penetrating sketch of his psychological state, when the drug was withdrawn. "The stimulus of Conversation suspends the terror that haunts my mind; but when I am alone, the horrors, I have suffered from Laudanum, the degeneration, the blighted Utility, almost overwhelm me."[13] If Gillman could effect a cure in these circumstances, and where so many others had failed, Coleridge would think of him, "with reverence". Meanwhile, he intended to work as hard as he could, and trusted there would be no objection to John Morgan, his "literary Counsellor and Amanuensis" coming up each day from 11.30 to 3.30 in the afternoon. "I have been for so many years accustomed to dictate while he writes that I now cannot compose without him."[14]

Coleridge moved into Moreton House, as agreed, on Monday 15 April 1816. Ever afterwards Gillman liked to say that Coleridge appeared at his door, "bringing in his hands the proof sheets of 'Christabel'". In fact the poem could not have been printed, even with Murray's great efficiency, for another week. But it was an understandable blur of memory and myth-making, of the kind that Coleridge himself would frequently encourage in his noble doctor in the years ahead.

Lamb wrote a lively and faintly provoking account of Coleridge's good fortune to Wordsworth (using the back of a weights and measures form from India House). Contrary to all the gloomy prognostications at Rydal Mount, Coleridge had risen from the dead again, and found powerful new supporters in London. "Coleridge is printing Xtabel by Lord Byron's recommendation to Murray, with what he calls a vision Kubla Khan – which said vision he repeats so enchantingly that it irradiates & brings Heaven & Elysian bowers into my parlour while he sings or says it . . ." He loved the poem, but like Crabb Robinson foresaw trouble ahead in the reviews. He feared it would be attacked as "nonsense" when put into clear light of print: "an owl that wont bear daylight". As to the Highgate arrangement, he also had his doubts. "He is at present under the medical care of a Mr Gillman (*Killman?*) a Highgate Apothecary, where he *plays at leaving off Laudanum.*"

But then Lamb's loyalty to Coleridge, especially when writing to Wordsworth, burst forth in a magnificent declaration of praise. "Coleridge is absent but 4 miles, & the neighbourhood of such a man is as exciting as the presence of 50 ordinary Persons. Tis enough to be within the whiff and wind of *his* genius, for us not to possess our souls in quiet . . . I think his essentials not touched, he is very bad, but then he wonderfully picks up another day, and his face when he repeats his verses hath its ancient glory, an Arch angel a little damaged."[15]

4

Coleridge's life changed radically and permanently in these first months of 1816 at Highgate, and the detoxification regime was not a game. As agreed, Gillman strictly controlled his opium doses and also severely restricted his social life. Dining out in London was discouraged, except in exceptional cases, as when Hookham Frere arranged an 8 o'clock supper party for Coleridge to meet the future Foreign Secretary, George Canning.[16]

Coleridge's early attempt to smuggle in laudanum, wrapped up in proofs from Murray, was quickly nipped in the bud. In late June he described to Morgan a typical evening of withdrawal, being overcome by "a sensation of indefinite *Fear*" which shook his whole frame. "I fought up against it and went to bed. I had a wretched night – and next morning the few drops, I now take, only increasing my irritability, about noon I called on G. for the performance of *his* part of our mutual engagement, & took enough and *barely* enough (for more, I am certain, would have been better) to break the commencing Cycle before the actual Craving came on. Today I am much better." So he struggled on, like all addicts, coping day by day.[17]

A few suitable visitors were entertained – Daniel Stuart came to dinner and arranged for some *Courier* articles – but other old roistering companions were evidently frowned upon. These included Lamb, who came in July expecting one of their bibulous soirées, and found Gillman virtually showing him the door. He was with Crabb Robinson in the parlour at Moreton House, getting Coleridge to hold forth about Goethe, when after barely half an hour, "Mr Gillman entered the room very much with the air of a man who meant we should understand him to mean: 'Gentlemen, it is time for you to go!' We took the hint . . ." Lamb, much piqued, said he would never call again; but Robinson admitted that he had never seen Coleridge look so well under his "sort of medical surveillance". He talked "sensibly but less eloquently and vehemently than usual". Secretly they both wondered if Coleridge's special magic could actually survive, after all, without opium.[18]

For the first time in three years Coleridge began to write regularly to his wife. There was no more immediate money from the Murray contract, as most of it had been absorbed by "poor Morgan's Necessities", but he promised to send any profits from *Zapolya* for Hartley and the other children.[19] Mrs Coleridge was not, however, disposed to be enthusiastic about Lord Byron and Murray. She wrote grumbling to Poole: "Oh! when will he ever give his friends anything but pain? he has been so unwise as to publish his fragments of 'Christabel' & 'Koula-Khan' [sic]. Murray is the publisher, and the price is 4s. 6d. – we were all sadly vexed when we read the advertisement of these things."[20]

If Coleridge sometimes felt a captive in these early months at Moreton House, he loved the "delicious" walks round Hampstead Heath and took much pleasure in the walled garden where many of his later poems sprouted. He had "four gaudy Flower-pots" that he tended especially, and likened the riot of plants to a vast poetic dictionary: "there is formed for common use a vast *garden* of Language – all the shewy, and all the odorous Words, and Clusters of Words, are brought together . . ."[21]

His friendship with the Gillmans was at first rather formal, shadowed by struggles over the opium regime, and with none of the chaotic intimacies of the Morgan household. Initially Gillman had to assert his medical authority, and Coleridge described him to Stuart as "a man of strong, fervid and agile Intellect", with "a master passion for Truth". Ann Gillman had a great "feminine Fineness of Character". But by September, when it was clear that his stay would be extended, they had become "my medical friend and his excellent wife, who has been a most affectionate and sisterly nurse to me".[22]

The friendship deepened when Coleridge, with his extraordinary intellectual adaptability, began to help Gillman with his own theoretical work, providing him with two chapters for *An Essay on Scrofula* which Gillman intended to submit for the Royal College of Surgeons' Jacksonian Prize in December 1816, as a follow-up to his work on hydrophobia.[23] This would soon draw both men even more closely together in a contribution to the Royal College's great debate on Vitalism, in a combined paper begun in the autumn, *A Theory of Life*.[24] In it Coleridge would sketch a metaphysical theory of evolution.

Coleridge's growing sense of security at Highgate emerged in the unparalleled harvest of literary work which was published over the next three years. At no other time in his life was Coleridge so consistent or productive in bringing finished work into print. His literary career had an extraordinary second-birth, and he became a national figure of great controversy. He was the subject of over forty-five major reviews, and numerous articles and parodies in the daily press. He was the target of an astonishingly bitter and sustained campaign by his old protégé, William Hazlitt, in the liberal press which almost fatally damaged his reputation but ended by making him famous among the younger generation. His name appeared regularly in the private correspondence of Byron, Shelley and Keats. And, in that peculiar tribute with which the English recognize their leading intellectual figures, he became the subject of satire and mockery, making an annual appearance in three comic novels by the young Thomas Love Peacock (a junior clerk under Charles Lamb in India House).

This transformation could never have taken place without the support of the Gillmans. (Indeed they could be considered the unacknowledged patron saints of the modern detox clinics for media celebrities making a come-back.) But their remarkable success was achieved at a certain, and perhaps incalculable, cost. Coleridge was never entirely weaned off the drug. There were to be relapses, periods of subterfuge dosing, and times of tense confrontation. (The alkaloid morphine had been isolated by French and German pharmacologists in 1804, but its addictive mechanism was still obscure.)[25]

If Coleridge became a more sober and better regulated citizen, he also rapidly became a much older-seeming man, reliant on his creature comforts, much cosseted by disciples, and gratefully adapting to the role of stately, shuffling sage. Something of what Byron

Hartley Coleridge aged ten. This picture of 1807 was used as the frontispiece to his *Poems*, published posthumously in 1851. Coleridge wrote, "What Queen Mary said, on the loss of our last stronghold in France – that if her heart were opened, Calais would be found written at the Core – I might say of my poor dear Hartley."
Letter, July 1829

Mary and William Wordsworth in silhouette, 1820

Two versions of Coleridge's "Asra": Sarah Hutchinson from Wordsworth's Silhouette book (*c.* 1820); and the figure of Ruth which he saw at Bolton Abbey in 1810, from 'The Marriage of Boas and Ruth' by Ciro Ferri

Robert Southey by Edward Nash, 1820

William Wordsworth by Benjamin Robert Haydon, 1818

Crabb Robinson, from a drawing by Masquerier, date unknown

William Hazlitt, by William Bewick, 1825

Above Nineteenth-century laudanum bottles

Right Frontispiece to the first illustrated edition of 'The Ancient Mariner', 1837

Percy Bysshe Shelley, by Amelia Curran, 1819

Thomas Love Peacock, by Roger Jean, 1805

John Keats, by Charles Armitage Brown, 1819

Lord Byron, by Richard Westall, 1813

James Gillman, surgeon. From a sketch by C. R. Leslie, 1816

Mrs Ann Gillman. From an oil painting by Maria Spilsbury

Coleridge's daughter Sara, aged about twenty-seven

Hartley Coleridge, aged about fifty

The Grove, Highgate

Aerial view of Highgate Village, St Michael's Church on the right, and The Grove at lower left. Compare with the Highgate map on p. 422

The Mariner's ship sails on. Engraving by Gustave Doré, 1877

Coleridge talks on. Cartoon by Max Beerbohm

would call that "wild originality" was certainly lost over the next few years. With one exception, no major work was published after 1819. His Notebooks, increasingly filled with intricate technical speculations on science and theology, lose much of their intimacy. But, at least until 1820, they are also far less painful and unhappy, apart from the occasional visitation of the ghosts and wolves of memory and loss. In December 1816, after a long metaphysical speculation on "the three Protoplasms, or primary Forms" of Gravity, Light and Water, he suddenly stopped short and wrote: "ASRA. Written as of yore. Christmas 1816. ASRA. Does the Past live with me alone? Coleridge."[26]

Privately, his friends questioned the retreat to Highgate. Morgan never reproached him directly, working away to conclude the tortuous negotiations with Gutch over the *Biographia* until they were completed in summer 1817. But others did, among them Dr Brabant who wrote an "angry" and "unkind" letter in September 1816, accusing Coleridge of having "hypocritically" abandoned his old friends from Calne to disappear into the comforts of Highgate. Coleridge gently defended himself. Gillman's restrictions were his only hope: "If I was to live, an absolute seclusion became necessary". Morgan's own financial "Circumstances" had become impossible, and after he had helped him with the "Christabel" money there was little more he could do. "O Brabant! Indeed, indeed, you ought not to have suspected my heart."[27]

Southey put his own enlightened interpretation of events in a malicious letter full of gossip to Wordsworth. Gillman had *not* at all been "bewitched" by Coleridge's tongue, but was "speculating upon him, and hoping to ride his reputation with notoriety and practice". He had deliberately got Coleridge "largely in debt to him", and if Coleridge attempted to leave "the Apothecary will arrest him". Gillman was sustaining Coleridge's "habits of opium", which were as bad as ever, and isolating him from his friends. Morgan had suffered most of all. "He has turned his back upon the Morgans – after all the unexampled sacrifices personal and pecuniary they have made for him – and this has manifestly cut Morgan to the heart."[28] But Southey misunderstood the solidity of the Gillmans' friendship. It was to be proved in a time of trial and adversity which gradually engulfed Coleridge as his return to London became public knowledge.

5

The "Christabel" volume was published on 25 May 1816. Initially the omens were set fair. Byron had trailed the poem in a long, admiring footnote to *The Siege of Corinth*, which Murray's advertisements proudly quoted, calling it "a work of wild and original genius". Then Hazlitt entered the lists, with a prominent article in the *Examiner*, on 2 June. It saluted Coleridge's return with a fierce attack on his "dishonesty" and laziness in publishing unfinished work. "The fault of Mr Coleridge is, that he comes to no conclusion . . . from an excess of capacity, he does little or nothing." But he seized on the essentially dream-like nature of the poem, and (alone among contemporary critics) identified the sexual confrontation hidden within it. Praise and condemnation were lethally balanced, in a high-handed and provoking style that became characteristic of everything he wrote about Coleridge over the next years.

> In parts of "Christabel" there is a great deal of beauty, both of thought, imagery, and versification; but the effect of the general story is dim, obscure, and visionary. It is more like a dream than a reality. The mind, in reading it, is spell-bound. The sorceress seems to act without power – Christabel to yield without resistance. The faculties are thrown into a state of metaphysical suspense and theoretical imbecility. The poet, like the witch in Spenser, is evidently "Busied about some wicked gin." But we do not foresee what he will make of it. There is something disgusting at the bottom of his subject, which is but ill glossed over by a veil of Della Cruscan sentiment and fine writing – like moon-beams playing on a charnel-house, or flowers strewed on a dead body.[29]

Then he added that the Conclusion to "Christabel" was "absolutely incomprehensible", and that "Kubla Khan" merely proved that "Mr Coleridge can write better *nonsense* verses than any man in England." "Kubla Khan" was not a poem, but a musical composition. Yet, "we could repeat these lines to ourselves not the less often for not knowing the meaning of them".[30]

Further long if mixed reviews appeared in the *Critical Review*, the *Eclectic Review*, the *Literary Panorama* and elsewhere during the summer. The poems were extensively quoted, parodies appeared (one by James Hogg) and some amused discussion of the circumstances of the opium "revery" in which "Kubla Khan" was composed. The *Eclectic* observed: "We could have informed Mr Coleridge of a reverend friend of ours, who actually wrote down two sermons on a passage in the Apocalypse, from the recollection of the spontaneous exercise of his faculties in sleep."[31]

However, no contemporary critic saw the larger possible significance of Coleridge's Preface to "Kubla Khan", although it eventually became one of the most celebrated, and disputed, accounts of poetic composition ever written. Like the letter from the fictional "friend" in the *Biographia*, it brilliantly suggests how a compressed fragment came to represent a much larger (and even more mysterious) act of creation.

After taking "an anodyne" (opium) at his lonely Exmoor farmhouse,

> The Author continued for about three hours in a profound sleep, at least of the external senses, during which time he has the most vivid confidence, that he could not have composed less than from two or three hundred lines . . . On awaking he appeared to himself to have a distinct recollection of the whole, and taking his pen, ink, and paper, instantly and eagerly wrote down the lines that are here preserved. At this moment he was unfortunately called out by a person on business from Porlock, and detained by him above an hour, and on his return to his room, found, to his no small surprise and mortification, that though he still retained some vague and dim recollection of the general purport of the vision, yet, with the exception of some eight or ten scattered lines and images, all the rest had passed away like the images on the surface of a stream into which a stone has been cast, but, alas! without the after restoration of the latter![32]

The account is teasingly circumstantial, particularly about the number of elapsed hours and missing lines involved, and with the famously mundane detail of the "person on business from Porlock". Yet the effect is to produce a much larger allegory of creativity and its fatal interruption. Here might be a model for the whole problem of fragmented or unfinished work in Coleridge's *oeuvre*. The striking water imagery of the broken "stream" of poetic concentration also clearly links it with the many similar parables of the imaginative process in the *Biographia*.

But who *was* the person from Porlock? Wordsworth himself, Mrs Coleridge, John Thelwall, even the publisher Cottle have all been suggested. Alternatively, he (or she) may simply have been a convenient fiction. But the symbolic identity is clear, and marvellously effective. At one level, the Porlock figure represents the humdrum world (the world of business, money, domestic affairs) breaking into the fine, solitary, detached world of artistic creation. It is, if one likes, the world of social duties bursting upon the supreme, lonely egotism of the Romantic poet. At a more subtle level, the figure may be a psychological personification of the inhibiting factors which haunted so much of Coleridge's unfinished poetry: "the faculty of reason as a censor of the imaginative faculty".[33] Like the "judicious friend" of the *Biographia*, he may be Coleridge's escape device.*

Equally, the mysterious impact of "Christabel" never reached the

---

* For the original circumstances of composition, see *Early Visions*, pp.162–8; and the discussion in *Selected Poems*, pp.336–7. This reading has been humorously explored in a poem by Stevie Smith, "Thoughts on the Person from Porlock":

> Coleridge received the Person from Porlock
> And ever after called him a curse,
> Then why did he hurry to let him in? –
> He could have hid in the house.
>
> It was not right of Coleridge, in fact it was wrong
> (But often we all do wrong)
> As the truth is I think he was already stuck
> With Kubla Khan.
>
> He was weeping and wailing: I am finished, finished,
> I shall never write another word of it;
> Then along comes the person from Porlock
> And takes the blame for it . . .
> (*Collected Poems of Stevie Smith*, Allen Lane, 1975)

The idea that poetry or visionary prose might be composed in sleep, dreams, or drug-induced "revery" became increasingly influential after the publication of "Kubla Khan", and reached an apogee in De Quincey's dream-sequences in *Suspira De Profundis* (1849). These were later imitated by Theophile Gautier, Baudelaire and Cocteau in France; and the "automatic writing" of the Surrealists. Coleridge's Preface appears to claim that poetry could be the direct product of the unconscious, without artistic intervention. Yet despite the lack of "any sensation or consciousness of effort" in such composition, Coleridge felt that the Imagination, the "esemplastic" or shaping power, must still be at work in the artist's mind if the result was not to be mere "phantasmagoria" or delirium. "A poem may in one sense be a dream, but it must be a waking dream." (*Literary Remains*, 1836, I. p.36.) For an alternative view of "unconscious processing" in "Kubla Khan", see the fascinating comparison with the supposed dream-discoveries of scientists, analysed by Lewis Wolpert: "Creativity" in *The Unnatural Nature of Science*, 1992.

public reviews either, but was registered privately by the younger poets. The earliest to respond were Byron and Shelley, when they came to read the poem aloud one stormy night at the Villa Diodati, Lake Geneva, on 18 July. It was the aspect of dangerous sexual mystery that fascinated them, as Dr William Polidori recorded in his diary. "Twelve o'clock really began to talk ghostly. Lord Byron repeated some verses of Coleridge's 'Christabel', of the witch's breast; when silence ensued, and Shelley suddenly shrieking and putting his hands to his head, ran out of the room with the candle." Shelley later told Mary that the poem had conjured a vision of a woman "who had eyes instead of nipples". From the discussions of sexuality and horror which followed (lamias, werewolves, night monsters) Mary Shelley began to write *Frankenstein*, and Polidori began his tale *The Vampyre*.[34] Byron himself never wavered in his high opinion of the "fine, wild" poem.

6

Coleridge and Murray must have been reasonably satisfied at the initial stir caused by so small a volume. After the first May edition of 500 copies, Murray quickly printed a second and a third in the course of the summer. (Murray later told Byron that he lost money on these, though in fact his financial outlay was comparatively small. At this period, for example, he was paying Southey £100 for a single article, and offering 1,000 guineas each for a book-length poem and a *History of the Peninsular War*.) In July he was still considering a contract for the *Biographia* and *Sibylline Leaves*, and Coleridge was cheerfully inviting him up "to sun and air yourself on Highgate Hill".[35]

Coleridge now felt confident enough to plunge back into public affairs and deliver his views on the political and moral state of post-war England. This was to be his first appearance in his new role as sage. He proposed to write his first *Lay Sermon* on what he saw, correctly, as the national crisis for the small publisher Gale and Fenner, without even agreeing a fee. He also proposed a monthly newsletter on German literature to the bookseller Thomas Boosey. In this he would expound the "new system" of Kant and Schelling, examining its impact not only on imaginative writing, but also on "Medicine, Chemistry, Magnetismus, and the Naturphilosophie".[36]

It would take up where the *Biographia* had left off. On 31 August he confidently told both Boosey and Murray that at last he was in the state of mind and health "to finish my Christabel".[37]

7

But in September "Christabel" was effectively destroyed by a single review. It came precisely from the poet whom Byron had specially enlisted to help Coleridge relaunch his career. In a long and immensely detailed article in the *Edinburgh Review*, Thomas Moore (writing anonymously) carefully pulled the whole publication to pieces, virtually line by line. The poems were a tissue of absurdities, exhibiting nothing but "incoherence", "extravagance" and "incongruity".

> Upon the whole, we look upon this publication as one of the most notable pieces of impertinence of which the press has lately been guilty . . . The thing now before us, is utterly destitute of value. It exhibits from beginning to end not a ray of genius; and we defy any man to point out a passage of poetical merit in any of the three pieces it contains . . . There is literally not one couplet which would be reckoned poetry, or even sense, were it found in the corner of a newspaper or upon the window of an inn.

As for Lord Byron's recommendation of a work of "wild and original genius", this had obviously been a mere "courtesy" from a brother poet, for in truth "Christabel" was simply "a mixture of raving and driv'ling". It was time for Coleridge to seek a place and a pension.[38]

Few other reviews of the period, except for the notorious attacks on Keats's "cockney" "Endymion" (1818), had such a damaging effect. For the next three years, all other reviews of Coleridge were almost universally hostile, and Hazlitt in particular felt free to lead the hounds. Murray, the shrewdest of all publishers when it came to business, sensed the way the tide had turned. He slowly withdrew his interest during the autumn. By the winter of 1816 Coleridge had become fatally entangled with the much lesser house of Gale and Fenner (partly owned by Thomas Curtis), which was to prove both dilatory and dishonest.

In retrospect, the unhappy chain of events was very clear to him.

"The Sale of the Christabel sadly disappointed Mr Murray. It was abused & ridiculed by the *Edinburgh Review*; & the *Quarterly* refused even to notice it . . . In this mood Mr Murray expressed himself in such words, as led me, nervous and imperfectly recovered as I was, to suppose that he had no pleasure in this connection – at least, that he would have nothing to do with what he called *my Metaphysics* – which were in truth my all. At this time and under this impression I was found out by that consummated Integrity of Scoundrelism, the REVEREND Mr Curtis."[39]

Another blow soon fell. Moore's attack in the *Edinburgh Review* was followed on 8 September by a long, jeering assault from Hazlitt in the *Examiner*. Hazlitt had seen the advertisement for Coleridge's *Lay Sermon*, and invented a new form of journalism for the occasion. What he wrote was a pre-emptive review, in which he excoriated the monograph before it was even published (in fact, had he known, before it was even *written*). He claimed that the advertisement alone, announcing Coleridge's "spiritual appearance for the next week", was sufficient grounds to "guess at the design" and ridicule the inevitable contents.

Like *The Friend* it would be "an endless Preface to an imaginary work", full of religious obscurantism and political apostasy advocating "despotism, superstition and oppression".[40] Coleridge had become a sophist and a charlatan. "Truth is to him a ceaseless round of contradictions: he lives in the belief of a perpetual lie, and in affecting to think what he pretends to say. His mind is in a constant state of flux and reflux: he is like the Sea-horse in the Ocean; he is the man in the Moon, the Wandering Jew . . . His mind has infinite activity, which only leads him into numberless chimeras . . . He belongs to all parties and is of service to none."[41]

The motive for this all-out attack, as the last phrase suggests, was ostensibly political. But beneath it were layers of personal animus, furies and disappointments with Coleridge, which probably had at their base Hazlitt's old sense of youthful idealism betrayed. "We lose our patience when we think of the powers he has wasted . . ." If Coleridge had had the single intellectual virtue of sincerity, "he would have been a great man; nor hardly, as it is, appears to us – 'Less than arch-angel ruined, and the excess/Of glory obscur'd.'" It was doubly bitter that this traduced the very words of praise that he must have heard from Lamb.[42]

Coleridge was profoundly shaken by this "brutal attack". Here was the young man he had befriended in the Stowey days, had helped at Keswick when Hazlitt was accused of beating a local girl, and had encouraged in his earliest journalistic writing at Southampton Buildings.[43] He did not see that political differences could justify such savagery. With these two articles, his professional confidence – so recently restored by Byron – began to ebb away, and other difficulties came crowding in.

Gutch had written from Bristol, unexpectedly announcing that the second volume of the *Biographia* was 150 pages short. If Coleridge did not provide new copy by Christmas, he threatened to publish it unfinished, "in the state in which it was placed in my hands", simply in order to recoup his costs. When Coleridge demurred, Gutch sent him an enormous bill of accumulated expenses: £284.18*s*.4*d*. for printing costs, and a further £107.5s.6d. representing the personal advances made by Hood in the spring of 1815.[44]

8

Now Coleridge could not even finish his *Lay Sermon*, let alone "Christabel". The Gillmans watched anxiously as he worked from nine till five and then began to sit up all night, "writing & erasing". He demanded more opium and made scenes. Finally, he dictated a chaotic text to Morgan, "not able even to look over the copy" before he sent it off.[45]

Coleridge had originally intended to address the political divisions of English society, not with a party tract about social legislation, but with an inspirational call to a return to spiritual values. "At the annunciation of *principles*, of *ideas*, the soul of man awakes, and starts up, as an exile in a far distant land at the unexpected sounds of his native language, when after long years of absence, and almost of oblivion, he is suddenly addressed in his own mother-tongue. He weeps for joy, and embraces the speaker as his brother."[46]

Yet *The Statesman's Manual* (as he now nervously renamed it), emerged as the most obscure and disorganized short work that Coleridge ever published. Even the rambling subtitle suggested that Hazlitt's attack had become a self-fulfilling prophesy. "The Bible The Best Guide To Political Skill And Foresight. A Lay Sermon Addressed To the Higher Classes of Society. With an Appendix

Containing Comments And Essays Connected With The Study Of The Inspired Writings." Its mixture of metaphysics and sentimental pieties, of conservative politics and calls to visionary brotherhood, suggest confusion and self-contradiction. At Grasmere, Dorothy observed grimly that it was "ten times more obscure than the darkest parts of *The Friend*".[47]

Yet *The Statesman's Manual* puts forward two ideas of great social and cultural significance. The first was his old idea, originally broached in his Royal Institution lectures, of the need for a public policy on "national education". This was by no means fulfilled when "the People at large" had merely been "taught to read and write". Education, "which consists in *educing* the faculties, and forming the habits" of the whole man, was the primary foundation of a liberal society. The privileged classes would have to undergo a revolution in their own ideas of power and status, if this was to be achieved. "I am greatly deceived, if one preliminary to an efficient education of the labouring classes be not . . . a thorough recasting of the moulds in which the minds of our Gentry, the characters of our future Landowners, Magistrates and Senators, are to receive their shape and fashion."[48]

The second idea was a development of the religious theme of the *Biographia*. In a secular age, the language and philosophy of science, and its extension into utilitarian politics, was putting a new and unparalleled pressure on the notion of the sacred. But without some concept of the sacred (enshrined for most Englishmen, "directly or indirectly", in the Bible), men in society would be reduced to mechanical objects, material statistics. Far worse than this, they would begin to think of themselves as such, having lost a traditional and literal-minded faith, and having no new language of spiritual assertion or value.

> A hunger-bitten and idea-less philosophy naturally produces a starveling and comfortless religion. It is among the miseries of the present age that it recognizes no medium between *Literal* and *Metaphorical*. Faith is either to be buried in the dead letter, or its names and honours usurped by a counterfeit product of the mechanical understanding, which in the blindness of self-complacency confounds SYMBOLS with ALLEGORIES.[49]

This distinction is not merely a linguistic one, but represents two radically opposed visions of reality. The one is, in effect, materialist; the other in some sense transcendental. Coleridge championed the symbolic interpretation of religious faith, in terms shorn of all Christian vocabulary, using a bardic language which is a curious anticipation of William Blake. "A Symbol is characterized by a translucence of the Eternal through and in the Temporal. It always partakes of the Reality which it renders intelligible; and while it enunciates the whole, abides itself as a living part in that Unity, of which it is the representative." In a long Appendix C, he also explored these ideas in psychological terms, looking at the way dreams and the unconscious also give hints of such a sacred realm of the human spirit, suggesting hidden truths and even "divinations" about our nature.[50]

Hazlitt returned to the attack in the *Edinburgh Review* for December and again in the *Examiner*. In column after column he tore into the political apostasy of "the mob-hating Mr Coleridge", and ridiculed his attempts to draw metaphysical meanings from the Bible. "So that after all the Bible is not the immediate word of God, except according to the German philosophy, and in 'something between a literal and a metaphorical sense'. Of all the cants that ever were canting in this canting world, this is the worst!"[51] He dwelt with lively sarcasm on Coleridge's suggestion that the French Revolution was prophesied in the Book of Isaiah, or that "popular philosophy" had been corrupted by "the circulating libraries and the periodical press".[52]

But what really infuriated Hazlitt was Coleridge's apparent refusal to engage directly with the political realities of the day. This was a time when the unemployed weavers of Manchester were starting on their Blanket March to London; when the Green Bag Committee was investigating revolutionary sedition; and when Habeas Corpus was about to be suspended in March 1817. The true lay preachers were journalists like William Cobbett or William Hone, or cartoonists like Cruikshank, who risked imprisonment with every line or sketch they published. "Our Lay-preacher, in order to qualify himself for the office of a guide to the blind, has not, of course, once thought of looking about for matters of fact, but very wisely draws a metaphysical bandage over his eyes, sits quietly down where he was, takes his nap, and talks in his sleep . . ."[53]

9

At Highgate Coleridge felt reduced "into compleat outward nothingness" in September. He broke out into terrible sweating whenever he heard "the Post Man's Knock", bringing news of reviews, or debts, or dead lines.[54] He told Brabant that he secretly "longed for Death with an intensity that I have never seen exprest but in the Book of Job". It was as if the worst times at Bristol were about to return. But now James Gillman made another decisive intervention in Coleridge's "case". With inspired judgement, and the medical authority that only he exerted, he insisted that Coleridge should take a holiday. He should leave his desk immediately, and go off to contemplate the sea.

By 20 September Coleridge and the Gillman family were installed in a charming, rambling cottage backing on to Christchurch Bay in Hampshire. Here Coleridge remained – walking, boating, swimming and riding – until November, when he was greatly recovered with his opium doses back under control.

These long, annual autumn holidays were to become a new and permanent feature in Coleridge's later life, always taken on the coast in Hampshire, Sussex or Kent. It is not too much to say that they transformed his physical condition, and they were one of Gillman's most simple effective treatments for his addiction. They broke the cycles of stress and depression connected with his work, and rekindled some of the youthful energy and happiness he had known on his native shores of North Somerset and Devon. He made many new friends on these visits, and much of his later poetry was written or begun by the sea.

But more than this, they made Coleridge feel less like Gillman's patient and more like a valued member of his family. They brought him very close to Ann Gillman over the years, and turned him into an unofficial uncle to her children, James and Henry. All this brought back the playful, affectionate, mischievous side of Coleridge's personality, so much of which had been lost or hidden in the dark years after 1810.

This is apparent in the delighted letters he wrote from the little cottage at Mudeford. In one to Gillman's young medical assistant John Williams (already designated as "Wiz", the laboratory wizard), he exulted in his new seaside kingdom. The parlour glass door gave directly on to a beach garden, "abounding in Sea-rushes, with some potatoes that make most virtuous *efforts* to lift their dwarf heads above the ground". There was a fine old mulberry tree with a seat, and then a kind of lapping, inland sea where they besported themselves alternately as botanists, paddlers, and sailors. "Up to this Garden comes a sort of sea-Lake, which at High-Tide is (to my eyes) very interesting – with a Sea-Ditch, 2 or 3 yards wide, which is filled every Tide, and a Boat in which Mr Gillman and I can row & paddle."

The bathing machines were three-quarters of a mile away along the beach at Christchurch, but Coleridge was already plunging in with the children "from under a rock". He was attempting to conquer Mrs Gillman's "Thalosso-phobia" – sea-terror – in this respect. ("NB This is to remind you of your Greek.") Best of all was little Henry Gillman's excitement, which Coleridge touchingly shared in a way that reminded him of baby Hartley. He was "the dancing sunspot of the Family", and was crowned with many extravagant nicknames: "Hen-Pen, alias, learned Pundit, alias, infant Conchologist, alias, Child of the Sun . . . alias, mischievous Doggie, alias, Fish of all Waters . . ." Like Hartley, he slept in Coleridge's room, protected from all night terrors (and perhaps, in his own way, protecting Coleridge). He was a "kissable Vagabond, and Comfort of his Mother's Heart", and sent his love to "dear Wiz". When he was bathed for the first time, he "called the Froth of the Sea, *Beer*".[55]

The childlike pleasures of Mudeford did Coleridge much good, and steadied his thoughts. "As to Hazlitt," he announced, "I shall take no notice of him or his libels."[56] Encouraged by Gillman, he wrote firmly to Rest Fenner about debts and deadlines – "I *dare* not send off what dissatisfies my own judgement" – and insisted that his opium addiction should be accepted as a medical condition, and not used to undermine his professional standing by gossip or "calumnies".

Gillman's calm support, and even his clinical vocabulary, is evident in these assertions to his demanding publisher. There was now a "total absence of all concealment" about his addiction, which had after all begun "*unwittingly*" in the dread physical necessity "of taking antispasmodic drugs". His case was far from unique, and he should be treated accordingly. "For instance, who has dared blacken Mr Wilberforce's good name on this account? Yet he has been for years under the same necessity. Talk with any eminent druggist or medical practitioner, especially at the West End of the town, concerning the frequency of this calamity among men and women of eminence." It was true that he could not be relied on to compose and deliver copy with the regularity and "facility" of a man like Robert Southey. "But *I am not Southey* – and according as it is given to each, each must act."[57]

With this renewed self-confidence, Coleridge prepared to return to Highgate for Christmas. He also brought with him the first sketch of the paper that would occupy him and Gillman throughout 1817, perhaps inspired by their botanizing on the sandbanks of Christchurch Bay. This was to become *A Theory of Life*, a foray into the contemporary debate on Vitalism.

Coleridge, with his extraordinary feel for theoretical developments, was intending to apply German *Naturphilosophie* to the conflicting theories of the British anatomists like John Hunter (1728–93), Astley Cooper (1768–1841) and John Abernethy (1764–1831). The text of the *Theory of Life* would open, dramatically, in front of Hunter's bust in the Royal College, with the daring claim that his largely practical and anatomical approach to the life-principle had not allowed him to "unfold and organize" sufficiently "distinct, clear" conceptions of its true meaning.[58]

For Coleridge, this meaning had to be a universal law of development, working through some larger evolutionary force. He sent ahead to Gillman (already returned to Highgate) a Delphic outline of the way in which they would explore the subject in the spring. "I propose to begin at once with Life; but with Life in its very first manifestations – demonstrating that there is no other possible definition of Life but *Individuality* . . . in the fluxions or nascent forms of Individuality it will be absolutely necessary to shew the analogy between organic growth, and self-repetition, and a more universal form whether it be called Magnetism or Polarity."[59] Typically, these weighty matters were concluded with little Henry's affectionate greetings to "Papa & Mr Wiz".

10

Throughout the spring of 1817, Coleridge buckled to the task of dealing with his new publishers, Rest Fenner and the Reverend Mr Curtis, and extracting himself from the claims of John Gutch. The negotiations were tortuous, and increasingly ill-humoured. By May, Gutch was writing to Fenner that had he been aware of all the difficulties in reaching a settlement, he would have put the entire manuscript of Coleridge's work "behind the fire".[60]

The upshot was that by June Curtis had secured for Rest Fenner the complete copywright in all Coleridge's work – poetry, prose and drama – for a very modest outlay. He settled Gutch's printing bill of £284.18s.4d. but waived all responsibility for William Hood's advances and also left Coleridge to pay carriage expenses of £28, and to return the £50 Murray had advanced on *Zapolya*.[61] He made no separate payment for either of the *Lay Sermons*, and secured Coleridge's agreement to write a general Introduction to a part-work *Encyclopaedia*. The contract, not finally signed until 18 August 1817, included the future reissue of *The Friend* in three volumes, as well as the two-volume *Biographia* (with added materials), and *Sibylline Leaves* (both published in July). For this huge body of work, in effect everything that Coleridge had produced (except the "Christabel" volume), Curtis advanced a total sum of £300, of which £255 was not made available until January 1818.[62] It was, for a minor publishing house known mainly for small editions of religious works, a triumph to have secured an author like Coleridge so cheaply and so completely.

To Stuart, Coleridge wrote sadly that he felt "bullied" by his new publishers, and was "angry" at his own weakness in agreeing to various stipulations.[63] John Murray was now completely alienated, and the powerful guns of the *Quarterly Review* (which he also published) joined the batteries trained on Coleridge's forthcoming publications. When Southey himself suggested to "the Grand Murray" that he review Coleridge's *Biographia* in the *Quarterly*, "and under that text make a direct personal attack upon Jeffrey and Hazlitt", even this indirect offer of support to Coleridge was turned down.[64]

So Coleridge continued to advance into the public arena almost uniquely exposed to criticism, undefended from either party-political wing, unsupported by any influential journal of the day, and now bound hand and foot to a second-rate publisher whose main aim was (as it quickly emerged) to shore up its own crumbling finances.

11

But there was no going back, no retreat. In March 1817 Coleridge published his second *Lay Sermon*, "addressed to the Higher and Middle Classes on the Existing Distresses and Discontents". It was better organized, but no less rhapsodical than the first, urging in biblical language and imagery the Christian duties of the governing class towards the governed. It opened with another text from Isaiah, "Blessed are ye that sow beside all waters".[65] It was an extraordinary appeal to appear in the year of the Pentridge Revolution, when working-class leaders were being tried and hung for sedition.[66]

Yet Coleridge offered little comfort to the Tory establishment. He bitterly attacked the economic selfishness and laissez-faire attitudes that were tearing Britain apart. The rich landlords and manufacturers were coming to regard society simply as a wealth-creating machine: they were "Christian Mammonists" hardened by "the Spirit of Trade".[67] These attacks contained some of his most powerful passages, as biting as any political journalism Coleridge had written since 1800.

> We shall perhaps be told too, that the very Evils of this System, even the periodical *crash* itself, are to be regarded but as so much superfluous steam ejected by the Escape Pipes and Safety Valves of a self-regulating Machine: and lastly, that in a free and trading country *all things find their level* . . . But persons are not *Things* – but Man does not find his level. Neither in Body nor in Soul does the Man find his level! After hard and calamitous season, during which the thousand Wheels of some vast manufactory had remained silent as a frozen water-fall, be it that plenty has returned and that Trade has once more become brisk and stirring: go, ask the overseer, and question the parish doctor, whether the workman's health and temperance . . . have found *their* level again![68]

He particularly singled out the sufferings of child-workers, as the ultimate victims of economic callousness and cruelty. They were exploited, sick and "ill-fed", ill-clothed". He had watched them on hot summer afternoons at Calne, "each with its little shoulders up to its ears, and its chest pinched inward" with the memory of perpetual cold from the "unfuelled winters" they endured. "But as with the Body, so or still worse with the Mind."[69]

Coleridge urged the need for social change and social policies. "Our manufacturers must consent to regulations; our gentry must concern themselves in the *education* as well as the *instruction* of their natural clients and dependents . . ."[70] These passages, radical in their implications, did find some welcome response in surprising places. The working-class publisher William Hone quoted them extensively in the April edition of *Hone's Reformist Register*, as "good seed" that he had found "unexpectedly". Again in July, he praised Coleridge for "the homage which his pen has honestly paid to the best feelings of our nature".[71]

But the final position of the second *Lay Sermon*, with its attacks on Cobbett and other democratic reformers, was also seen as conservative. Coleridge expected to be assaulted from all sides. He sent an inscribed copy to Southey, with an anxious annotation in Latin. "My fate has drawn me unwilling and unforeseeing into these tempests, so that I am allowed neither to keep silent nor to speak as befits a philosopher. The butcher who hacked my first *Lay Sermon* to pieces with such malign ignorance in the *Edin. Rev.* is that wretch Hazlitt, no man but a monster. As regards his work, I beg you to help me, who was once your Coleridge (*olim tuum Coleridgium*) . . ."[72]

Southey praised the work in private, but did nothing. Another copy inscribed to Wordsworth remained uncut and unread.[73] Hazlitt simply ignored it, saving his fire for the *Biographia*. Crabb Robinson, who was again visiting Coleridge at Highgate, managed to place a short, judicious appreciation in the *Critical Review*, but betrayed some nervousness at Coleridge's "intemperance of expression" on matters of "party politics and polemical divinity". It is not clear if he thought the tract too radical, or too conservative: possibly both at the same time.[74]

12

What in fact was Coleridge's political position in the turmoil of these post-war years? It was, in reality, a very isolated one, and his retirement to Highgate and medical regime had removed him from the immediate pressure of events. One of the problems of the *Lay*

Sermons was a confusion about his style and readership: he moved uneasily between topical journalism, political philosophy and religious exhortation. Whom was he addressing? He could identify with neither the government nor any opposition faction, and as Hazlitt pointed out he belonged to no party. The radicals, loosely grouped round Hunt's *Examiner*, had hoped the poet and journalist of the *Watchman* days would re-emerge in all his fiery splendour. But the older Coleridge, while clearly distinct from the establishment figures that Wordsworth and Southey had become, no longer showed democratic enthusiasm. Instead he wrote provokingly of social "Duties", universal "Education", and the "human Soul".

In private he could speak very bitterly of the "Jeffries, Cobbetts, Hunts, Hazlitts and Co." whom he believed would provoke a new period of Tory repression, "the suspension of Freedom of all kind". In his worst moments he thought of them as "vipers" and "Liberticides".[75] He was also nervous of the new movement for parliamentary reform, which he thought at first would reawaken a French spirit of Jacobinism. For the younger generation all this was, of course, "apostasy".

Yet Coleridge still recognized the urgent need for social change in England, and for political action to direct it. He thought society was increasingly polarized between rich and poor, an "Anti-magnet of social Disorganization" as he called it in a vivid metaphor, with the labouring classes as the "positive Pole" demanding change, and the landowners and merchantry as the "negative Pole" inhibiting it.[76] He thought the Clergy, a class he would later expand to include all teachers, writers and intellectuals, were criminally asleep – "Sleeping with their eyes half-open!"[77]

The experience of the *Lay Sermons* gradually disenchanted him with the idea of any further direct, political engagement as a writer. That had to be left to younger men. What he eventually found instead was a way of addressing the younger men themselves, the elite, "the *Few* in all ages", whom he believed would shape the national destiny.[78]

There were signs that this audience was already coming into existence. One of the most interesting responses to the *Lay Sermons* appeared in March 1817 not as a review, but as a novel, *Melincourt*. Thomas Love Peacock, Shelley's close friend, then aged thirty-two, already saw Coleridge emerging as one of the representative intellectual figures of the new age. He was, to be sure, a figure to be satirized, but also one to be reckoned with. Peacock's first, tentative, broadly comic sketch had appeared as Mr Panscope, the indefatigable polymath ("who had run through the whole circle of sciences, and understood them all equally well") in *Headlong Hall* (1816).[79]

Now Coleridge, as Mr Mystic, was given an entire chapter in *Melincourt*, which recounts a chaotic visit to Mr Mystic's shadowy abode, Cimmerian Lodge, situated on a small prominence on "the Island of Pure Intelligence" (an obvious reference to Highgate). On their arrival, the visitors are immediately engulfed in an impenetrable and metaphysical fog. This is described in a parody of lines from "The Ancient Mariner": "the fog was here, the fog was there, the fog was all around".[80] Mr Mystic, quoting directly from the first *Lay Sermon*, then observes that he can easily find his way about with his eyes closed, since "Experience was a Cyclops, with his eye in the back of his head".[81] He leads them safely through the "darkness Visible" with the aid of a "synthetical torch", which sheds around it rays of "transcendental illumination". They end up with an exceptionally good dinner.

This light-hearted caricature of Coleridge leaves a mixed impression of eccentricity, humbug and genuine power. It is his first appearance as the sage of Highgate, a figure to be made famous by Thomas Carlyle. But the fictional form suggests the early crystallization of a myth which was to make Coleridge steadily larger than life, larger than criticism. Slowly he would become aware of this himself.

Other groups began to form round Coleridge this spring. His idea for a German newsletter led to the formation of "the Friends of German Literature", whose first guest was the German poet Ludwig Tieck whom Coleridge had last seen in Rome. Their reunion took place in early June at the house of J. H. Green, splendidly situated in Lincoln's Inn Fields. Green, a wealthy young surgeon in his mid-twenties, was a friend of Gillman's and also, as it would turn out, Keats's supervisor at Guy's Hospital. Green had philosophical interests and a ranging mind that moved far beyond his expertise as an eye-surgeon. He would eventually become President of the Royal College of Surgeons.

Tieck and Green, with Crabb Robinson, made an expedition to

Highgate of the sort that would become famous over the next decade. First they all took a brisk drive in Gillman's gig to Caen Wood, then embarked on a contemplative amble through the "delicious Groves and Alley" along the top of Hampstead Heath, and lingered under the "grand Cathedral Aisle of giant Lime-trees" above the lake (where Pope had composed his verse *Epistles*). Then indeed back to Moreton House for a good dinner. All the while Coleridge was talking and speculating.[82] This was an actual visit to Cimmerian Lodge.

13

The *Biographia* and the *Sibylline Leaves* were now scheduled for July 1817. Curtis had put much pressure on Coleridge to fill out the second of the prose volumes with miscellaneous materials, without any regard to its unity. His manipulative manner was further revealed when he offered to increase the general contract to £500, if Coleridge would take over the overall editorship of the part-work *Encyclopaedia*. This sounded generous, until he revealed the stipulation that Coleridge would have to abandon Highgate and go to live close to the publisher's offices in Camberwell, where he would be in effect Curtis's employee.

Haunted by his debts, Coleridge entertained the plan for some weeks, though he saw the way he would be trapped and harassed. For a moment he even considered fleeing England altogether, and going to live in solitary lodgings in Berlin where, he told Tieck, he might study animal magnetism.[83] Once again, the kindly Gillman intervened in these wild flights, and insisted that he must remain at Highgate, free to write at his own pace, expanding his circle of friends, and continuing his medical treatment.[84]

Gillman also invited Hartley to spend his third university vacation with his father, free of expenses, to bring him company and some measure of paternal solace. It was a happy visit, Coleridge finding his son "very much improved" by Oxford, though still eccentric in his manners, and not very "systematic in his studies and in the employment of his Time". Perhaps there was too much wild talk and fondness for drinking in the evening, a symptom of Hartley's curious, childlike, unappeasable loneliness. But he struck up a surprising friendship with Coleridge's sophisticated nephews, Henry and John, who were now in London. They were "very good and affectionate" towards Hartley, and to Coleridge it was a great comfort "to see the chasm of the first generation healing up in the second".[85]

Hartley also knitted up another old friendship, when Tom Poole came up from Stowey and met Coleridge and his son after a lapse of nearly a decade. Many fond memories were rekindled, and Coleridge asked Poole if Hartley might visit him in the West Country: "he is very desirous to visit the place of his Infancy, poor fellow!" Poole, who was still contributing to Hartley's university fees, extended the invitation in a touching and heartfelt letter, which showed great understanding of both son and father. "I will introduce him to all your acquaintance, and, among the most interesting, to every Brook, Hill and Dale, and all which they furnish; not forgetting my own devious Paths, nor the Orchard and *the now* classic old Apple tree bent *earthward*."[86]

Hartley indeed was destined, perhaps doomed, to relive this idyllic childhood from which he never entirely escaped. Widely known as the poet's son in Stowey, he tried to pay court to the local girls under the moonlight. But they recognized his melancholy and strangeness, emphasised by his dark undergraduate's beard, and behind his back they called him "the Black Dwarf".[87]

Poole continued to correspond confidentially with Mrs Coleridge about the children and their father. He had no doubts at all about the value and good sense of the Highgate arrangement, and had none of Southey's scornful suspicions. "I think no circumstances should induce you to leave your *present residence*," he wrote to Coleridge in his old, avuncular manner. "You are happy in your friends near you. Mr Gillman is an invaluable treasure. He gives you *himself*; and I respect, I had almost said revere, him for it, and for the feelings which prompt the conduct. Remember me to him with great kindness . . ."[88]

The Rest Fenner contract enabled Coleridge to make some satisfactory financial offerings. From the first £25 of his advance, he bought Hartley new boots and clothes at Highgate and gave him pocket money to the tune of £18.[89] The next £50, paid in October, was all given to Mrs Coleridge through a banker's draft drawn directly on the publisher. From the remaining £225 due in January 1818, he authorized his wife to buy Derwent "a proper *fit out*" of new clothes, and promised to start a fund to send him to Cambridge in three years' time.

His remaining worry was his daughter, whom he longed to see – "Would to God! I could but hit on a possibility of seeing my dear Sara." But there was as yet no money for her travel, or proper accommodation at Moreton House. She remained continually in his mind. He sent his "love to all" at Greta Hall, and promised he was working hard for them.[90]

14

The reviews of Coleridge's new books began to appear in the autumn of 1817. They were as bad as he feared, or rather worse. Hazlitt immediately set about the *Biographia* in an enormous, 10,000-word assault in the August issue of the *Edinburgh Review*, calling it a "garrulous" production from "the maggots of his brain". Hazlitt concentrated his fire on what he regarded as Coleridge's well-established weaknesses: obscurity of style, shifts of political opinion, "maudlin egotism", "garrulous" reminiscences, and above all the passion for metaphysics which "have been a dead weight on the wings of his imagination".[91]

Hazlitt simply did not engage with the great strengths of the *Biographia*. The story of the philosophical pilgrimage was a "long-winding metaphysical march". The emerging theory of the Imagination was "unintelligible". The superb critical dialogue with Wordsworth was "not very remarkable either for clearness or candour". The memorable psychological accounts of how a poet's mind works, and how poetry is actually composed (with all its arresting imagery) were "mawkish spleen in fulsome eulogies of his own virtues".

It was the most unrelenting of Hazlitt's attacks, giving no quarter, and returning again and again to the charge of intellectual charlatanism and political apostasy. His old mentor was now "a disappointed demagogue" who kept up, in vain, "that pleasurable poetic fervour which has been the cordial and the bane of his existence". "Till he can do something better, we would rather hear no more of him."[92]

This funeral bouquet was closely followed in October by a majestic damnation from *Blackwood's Magazine*, written under the pseudonym of "Christopher North". Its author was another old friend from Keswick days, the minor poet John Wilson, who would soon be elected to the appropriate position of Professor of Moral Philosophy at Edinburgh. "We cannot see in what the state of literature would have been different, had [Coleridge] been cut off in childhood, or had he never been born . . ." Professor Wilson mounted a general attack on what he deemed to be the "miserable arrogance" of the "original members of the Lake School", and the "Quackery" of Coleridge's "pretended account of the Metaphysical Systems of Kant, of which he knows less than nothing".[93] He wrote "in the cause of Morality and Religion".[94]

Other long reviews – in the *British Critic*, the *Literary Gazette*, the *Monthly Review* – were tepid ("on the whole, an entertaining performance"). They were somewhat kinder to the accumulated poetry of *Sibylline Leaves*, though it is extraordinary to see "The Ancient Mariner" still denounced as a farrago of German "horrors", from which many passages were too terrible to quote.[95] But there was growing appreciation of the group that became the Conversation Poems ("very pleasing in thought and . . . very powerful in realizing those visions of retirement"). Too much, however, was vitiated by Mr Coleridge's "cold metaphysical abstractions". Alone among the poems, it was the ballad "Love", inspired long ago by Asra, which received almost universal praise.[96]

On the evidence of his letters, Coleridge was now largely resigned to this reception in the public press, except when Professor Wilson accused him, as a finer point of literary criticism, of betraying his family at Greta Hall. "A man who abandons his wife and children is undoubtedly both a wicked and pernicious member of society . . ." He considered suing *Blackwood's* in the courts, but was finally persuaded by Crabb Robinson and Gillman that though it was an "atrocious Calumny", it was beneath notice.[97]

It was again the young writers, in their work and private letters, who represented the real response to Coleridge, rather than the professional critics. Shelley and Mary had repeatedly read the "Christabel" volume in Switzerland, and when they settled at Great Marlow in the summer of 1817 they read the *Biographia*, discussing it with Peacock, who was in the process of creating Mr Flosky, the Germanic metaphysician of *Nightmare Abbey*. Significantly, Mr Flosky with his "inspired gaze" and "his eye in a fine frenzy rolling" is made the "dearest friend" of the Shelley-figure in the novel, Scythrop Glowry, with his mystical "passion for reforming the world".[98]

When Shelley dined at Leigh Hunt's in Hampstead, his future friend Horace Smith observed him across the table, radiating a Coleridgean mystique. "My companion, who . . . talked much and eagerly, seemed to me a psychological curiosity, infinitely more curious than Coleridge's Kubla Khan, to which strange vision he made reference."[99] Shelley agreed with Hazlitt about Coleridge's politics, and would satirize him accordingly in his poem "Peter Bell the Third" (1819). But unlike Hazlitt, he could easily separate this from Coleridge's poetic vision (a thing he could never manage with Wordsworth).

After he had gone to Italy in 1818, Shelley constantly quoted the "Mariner" (parts of which he seemed to have known by heart) and its form partly inspired his political ballad, "The Mask of Anarchy" (1819). Shelley's great essay, *The Defence of Poetry* (1821), written as a dialogue with Peacock, reflects many of the ideas and images of the *Biographia*, particularly on the mysterious nature of the Imagination, its fluid form, and its transient existence "like a fading coal". Coleridge became for him a partly mythic figure, when he looked back on his memories of London, precisely perhaps because he had never met him in the flesh, but saw him so well in his writings:

> You will see Coleridge – he who sits obscure
> In the exceeding lustre and the pure
> Intense irradiation of a mind,
> Which, with its own internal lightning blind,
> Flags wearily through darkness and despair –
> A cloud-encircled meteor of the air,
> A hooded eagle among blinking owls.[100]

This mixture of inner power and external weakness, of brightness and blindness combined, is part of what Coleridge came to represent. To be called an "eagle" by Shelley, even if a hooded one, was no small compliment. When Mary returned to London after his death in 1822, she was anxious to meet Coleridge personally, regarding him in some strange way as the spiritual link with her drowned husband. It was the disasters and aberrations of Coleridge's life which authenticated him and linked him to the Shelleys.*

John Keats was also reading Coleridge at his lodgings in Well Walk, Hampstead, and discussing him with the Hunt circle. He too initially took Hazlitt's line on the politics. "I would not for 40 shillings be Coleridge's *Lays* in your way," he joked to Benjamin Bailey.[101] But he was fascinated by the *Sibylline Leaves* which were to have a direct influence on his mature poetry in 1819, and when he began to read the *Biographia* in December 1817 his whole intellectual being was engaged. He was drawn in especially by Coleridge's account of Shakespeare's "protean" imaginative power and the idea of poetry demanding "a willing suspension of disbelief" (Chapter 4).

He had also evidently read Coleridge's extended similes of the imaginative process (like the water insect in Chapter 7) with great appreciation. Characteristically he found them more powerfully suggestive in themselves than the critical theory expounded from them. "Coleridge, for instance, would let go by a fine isolated verisimilitude caught from the Penatralium of mystery, from being incapable of remaining content with half knowledge."[102]

Already far away in Italy, Lord Byron was also reading Coleridge. The *Biographia* reached him in Venice in autumn 1817, and greatly irritated him both by its "metaphysics" and by what he saw as an ungentlemanly attack (in Chapter 23) on *Bertram*, the gothic melodrama that had finally been produced in place of *Zapolya* at Drury Lane. "He is a shabby fellow, and I wash my hands of him," he complained to Murray.[103] In verse he mocked Coleridge for being "drunk" on visions, and flying blind with ideas."

---

* Shortly after his death, when Shelley's reputation was still almost universally reviled in England except among extreme radicals, Coleridge expressed a characteristically warm and avuncular opinion. "Shelley was a man of great power as a poet, and could he only have had some notion of order, could you only have given him some plane whereon to stand, and look down upon his own mind, he would have succeeded. There are flashes of the true spirit to be met with in his work . . . He went to Keswick on purpose to see me and unfortunately fell in with Southey instead . . . Southey had no understanding or toleration of such principles as Shelley's. I should have laughed at his Atheism. I could have sympathized with him and shown him that I had once been in the same state myself, and I could have guided him through it. I have often bitterly regretted in my heart of hearts that I never did meet with Shelley." (*Table Talk*, I. p. 574.)

And Coleridge, too, has lately taken wing,
But like a hawk encumber'd with his hood,–
Explaining metaphysics to the nation–
I wish he would explain his Explanation.

But privately he too recognized Coleridge's strange power and was perhaps more influenced by his work than he would consciously admit. He never went back on his admiration for "Christabel" – "I won't have you sneer at *Christabel*," he corrected Murray, "it is a fine wild poem"; and he frequently quoted it in his letters, referring to Coleridge as a genuinely prophetic writer, a "vates".[104]

He was intrigued by Coleridge's remarks on the effect of reciting poetry aloud (as he had done with "Kubla Khan" at Piccadilly). Coleridge had written that recitation threw a spell over the audience, quite different from the effect of reading it on the page. "For this is really a species of Animal Magnetism, in which the enkindling Reciter, by perpetual comment of looks and tones, lends his own will and apprehensive faculty to his Auditors. They *live* for the time within the dilated sphere of his intellectual Being."[105] Both Byron and Coleridge were conscious of this hypnotic power, and proud of it.

Most intriguing of all, it is possible that Coleridge gave Byron the subject, or rather the persona, of his last great poem, *Don Juan*, not begun until 1818. In Chapter 23 of the *Biographia*, he suggested that such a poem would draw, like "Christabel", on the "mysteries", on the polar attraction between good and evil, on "the dark groundwork of our nature". Coleridge even summoned up the inner voice of Don Juan, in a kind of Byronic monologue. "To possess such a power of captivating and enchanting the affections of the other sex! to be capable of inspiring in a charming and even a virtuous woman, a love so deep, and so entirely to *me*! that even my worst vices, (if I *were* vicious) even my cruelty and perfidy, (if I *were* cruel and perfidious) could not eradicate the passion!"[106]

And what of Wordsworth at Rydal Mount? He never wrote a word to Coleridge on the subject. In June he remarked to a friend, R. P. Gillies: "I have not read Mr Coleridge's 'Biographia', having contented myself with skimming parts of it . . . Indeed I am heartily sick of even the best criticism . . ."[107] But he *had* read it closely, because he later confided to Crabb Robinson that he had taken "no pleasure" in the volume, especially in the parts that concerned himself. "The praise is extravagant and the censure inconsiderate." Of the *Sibylline Leaves*, of the "Mariner" with its new gloss, of "Christabel", of "Kubla Khan" and its extraordinary Preface, he said nothing at all.[108]

15

In September 1817 the Gillmans again spirited Coleridge away to the seaside, this time to lodgings on the promenade at Littlehampton, in Sussex. Here he remained until the end of November, working hard on the Introduction to the *Encyclopaedia Metropolitana*, for which Rest Fenner ("my malignant Taskmaster") was pressing him. But he made time for regular morning and evening patrols along the sandy shingle. He often walked long after dusk, until his old friend the moon rose over the sea, and had various poetical encounters on the windy front.

Once a tall man came crunching over the pebbles towards him, reciting Homer aloud to a small boy at his side. Coleridge was intrigued, and immediately introduced himself with a flourish. "Sir, yours is a face I *should* know; I am Samuel Taylor Coleridge." It turned out to be Henry Francis Cary, the first great English translator of Dante, whose version of the *Divina Commedia* had been published in an obscure private edition in 1814. His son Henry (the small boy then aged 13) remembered how this first meeting effortlessly extended into a dinner party the same evening, and Coleridge went off bearing a copy of Cary's *Inferno* to peruse.

Both father and son were amazed the following morning when Coleridge reappeared on the beach, miraculously able to recite long passages from the translation by heart, and what was more, recalling the parallel sections of the Italian original.[109] Coleridge then wrote to Cary, praising the accuracy and the "learned Simplicity" of the blank verse – "the most varied and harmonious to my ear of any since Milton" – and subsequently arranged for it to be reissued in a popular edition by Keats's publisher, Taylor and Hessey, the following year. This became the standard version for Victorian readers over the next fifty years. Cary became a devotee of the *Biographia*, and circulated copies among his friends.[110]

It was this meeting that also sparked off Coleridge's sonnet – the first for more than a decade – "Fancy in Nubibus, or The Poet in the Clouds". It opens with a dreamy evocation of his seaside walks, "Just after Sunset or by moon light skies", his eye travelling out across the shifting waters with their "flow of Gold", and then upwards "From Mount to Mount, through Cloudland" above the English Channel. Then, in a transposition to be used years later by Matthew Arnold in "Dover Beach", the English sea becomes the Greek Aegean. The poet, "listening to the Tide, with closed sight", changes from Coleridge to Homer, whose outward blindness becomes a surging image of inner, imaginative vision:

> . . . that blind Bard, who on the Chian Strand,
> By the deep sounds inform'd with inward Light,
> Beheld the Iliad and the Odyssee
> Rise to the swelling of the voiceful Sea![111]

Ann Gillman was particularly delighted with this new poem, which Coleridge described as "a first Resumption" of what he called his "rhyming Idleness" at Littlehampton, and a proof of his health. He added a touching comment that recalls his early theories of the sonnet, as essentially a single "lonely thought". It has the character of a Sonnet – that it is like something that we let escape from us – a Sigh, for instance."[112]

16

On his return to Highgate in November, Coleridge found the reputation of the *Biographia* was spreading, and the attack in *Blackwood's* had rallied old friends and new ones to his side. Joseph Green rode up from Lincoln's Inn Fields, and gave him a standing invitation to dinner whenever he could manage.[113] A young lawyer, Charles Augustus Tulk, began to correspond enthusiastically about the *Naturphilosophie* in the *Biographia* and pressed Coleridge to expound his metaphysics further.

Tulk was also a Littlehampton acquaintance, having first met Coleridge on a wet and unpromising afternoon in the Public Reading Room, when they exchanged newspapers. "If I had met a friend & a Brother in the Desart of Arabia," exclaimed Coleridge afterwards, "I could scarcely have been more delighted."[114] Tulk turned out to be the heir to a large fortune, who owned Marble Hill House in Twickenham and was also a founder member of the Swedenborg Society (1810).

His father had known William Blake and Flaxman, as members of the New Jerusalem Church. Young Tulk, then in his thirties, had a lively interest in poetry, music, design and social reform, all inspired by the unworldly and philanthropic creed of Swedenborg; and was also a hospitable family man. He was later to be an independent MP, and founding proprietor of the new London University.

He was puzzled but gratified to receive an enormous, sixteen-page letter on Coleridge's "Dynamic Philosophy" – from Heraclitus to Schelling, via Magnetism and symbolic Geometry – a "slight sketch" of what had been omitted from the *Biographia*. There were two fundamental points of contact between their views, wrote Coleridge in his most winning manner: first, that all matter consisted in "the interpretation of opposite energies"; and second, that there was "no matter without Spirit".

The letter, of a metaphysical complexity that would have driven Hazlitt mad, also shows Coleridge beginning consciously to adopt his new Highgate role of mentor and sage. "I teach," he informed Tulk, "a real existence of a Spiritual World without a material. – But this belongs to a higher science – and requires something of a Pythagorean Discipline."[115]

Among other admirers of an unorthodox kind was Hyman Hurwitz, the gifted director of the private Hebrew Academy for Jews at Highgate. Hurwitz was a poet and Hebrew scholar, a distinguished man of Coleridge's age, whose race and culture had isolated him from the intellectual life of London. Coleridge, who never forgot the anti-Semitism he had witnessed in Germany in 1799,[116] responded warmly to Hurwitz's approaches and quickly found common ground in biblical scholarship, linguistics and learned discussions of religious symbolism.

The friendship with Hurwitz grew steadily over the next decade, and led Coleridge to visit several synagogues both in London and later Ramsgate, where he formed unusually close contacts with other Jewish scholars. In 1820 he and Hurwitz collaborated on a public poem, on the death of George III; and in 1828 Coleridge was instrumental in obtaining for Hurwitz the first professorship in Hebrew at London University. Hurwitz quoted Coleridge's work in his lectures, and Coleridge always argued for the integral role of the Jewish intellectual in the national culture. His later letters suggest a particular delight in Jewish humour, with its irony and self-mockery. "I happen," he wrote in the very last year of his life, "to be a favourite among the Descendants of Abraham . . . I therefore intend to be at the Synagogue on Friday."[117]

17

All this time Coleridge was working on his Introduction to the *Encyclopaedia*, which was finally rushed into print by Rest Fenner in January 1818. They had designed it to compete commercially with the fifth edition of the *Encyclopaedia Britannica* (twenty volumes, 1817). Frustrated with Coleridge's demands for more time and more revisions, they cut and edited the text themselves and did not allow him to see the proofs. He had planned it as a "Preliminary Treatise on Method", a grand tour of the intellectual horizon of knowledge, to rival Bacon's *Novum Organum*. It encompassed both arts and sciences in a single exemplary schema, unified by the notion of the moral function of all human knowledge in society.

"The first pre-conception, or master-thought, on which our plan rests, is the *moral origin and tendency* of all true science; in other words, our great objects are to exhibit the Arts and Sciences in their philosophical harmony; to teach Philosophy in union with Morals; and to sustain Morality by Revealed Religion."[118] This was in direct opposition to the Benthamite or utilitarian concept of knowledge as an empirical gathering of value-free data.

In fact Coleridge's conception was quite different from that of his publishers. For him it was not really a conventional encyclopaedia at all, but a kind of general university course which would teach the reader "intellectual Method" in every sphere. Its final aim was cultural in the largest sense, and had "national application". It aimed at "the *education of the mind*, first in the man and the citizen, and then, inclusively in the State itself".[119]

Coleridge saw it as a political statement in the widest sense. It promoted the liberal ideal of the "diffusion of knowledge" as the essential channel of social progress. But it insisted that knowledge involved moral judgements, and the sense of historical continuity.

Knowledge produced the "historic sense" which evaluated all social advance and political revolutions against the past. In this it opposed the writers of the European Enlightenment (who had invented the very idea of the encyclopaedia) and demonstrated that the concept of "universal Reason" in human affairs was dangerously insufficient.

> Without advocating the exploded doctrine of *perfectibility*, we cannot but regard all that is human in human nature, and all that in nature is above herself, as together working toward that far deeper and more permanent revolution in the moral world, of which the recent changes in the political world may be regarded as the pioneering whirlwind and storm. But woe to that revolution which is not guided by the historic sense; by the pure and unsophisticated knowledge of the past: and to convey this methodically, so as to aid the progress of the future, has been already announced as the distinguishing claim of the *Encyclopaedia Metropolitana*.[120]*

Coleridge never got the chance to clarify these ideas further in a popular format. Rest Fenner abandoned the entire *Encyclopaedia* the following year, having published only five part-volumes out of twenty-eight. The whole project was, Coleridge thought, "a Humbug".[121]

Yet the first volume, dominated by his 10,000-word essay, had a larger print-run than any other work published in his lifetime. His proposed arrangements of the material, with their structured hier-

* This is close to the philosophy of historicism, and the theory of recurring "Epochs", advocated by Giambattista Vico (1668–1744) whom Coleridge had read in Italy. (See *Coleridge in Italy*, by Edoardo Zuccato, 1996, pp. 138–44.) Isaiah Berlin described the imaginative leap across time and customs which Vico advocated. "Unless we are able to escape from the ideological prisons of class or nation or doctrine, we shall not be able to avoid seeing alien institutions or customs as either too strange to make any sense to us; or as tissues of error, lying inventions of unscrupulous priests. The doors which, according to Vico, myth and fable and language open to us will remain romantic delusions." (*The Crooked Timber of Humanity*, 1992, p. 86.) The same power of imaginative identification, (or indeed "suspension of disbelief") was seen as central to Coleridge's approach to historical truth by the philosopher J. S. Mill, in a key passage from his essays *On Bentham and Coleridge* (1840). "By Bentham, beyond all others, men have been led to ask themselves, in regard to any ancient or received opinion, Is it true? And by Coleridge, What is the meaning of it? The one took his stand *outside* the received opinion, and surveyed it as an entire stranger to it; the other looked at it from within, and endeavoured to see it with the eyes of a believer in it . . ." For an illuminating discussion, see Charles De Paolo, *Coleridge: Historian of Ideas*, 1992.

archy and historical framework (as opposed to mere alphabetical ordering) were eventually recognized as an epoch in the genre. Many years later his commercial rival, the *Encyclopaedia Britannica*, made amends with this fine compliment from the fifteenth edition of 1974, in its article on the history of encylopaedias: Coleridge's Introduction "was the most notable contribution to the philosophy of encyclopaedia-making since Bacon".

18

The Christmas season was sociable, with several dinner parties in town. Hartley came down from Oxford, and there were two meetings with Wordsworth which went off as well as could be expected. Though he had journeyed from Rydal Mount to London, Wordsworth was not prepared to go as far as Highgate, still fearing some emotional outburst.[122] But he consented to meet Coleridge in company, first at a supper party at Tom Monkhouse's house in Queen Anne Street, and later at an unusually subdued dinner given by Lamb.

Their mutual friends observed the reunion with interest, especially as Sara Hutchinson was with Wordsworth's party. It was the first time Coleridge and Asra had met for nearly seven years, and he took along Hartley for support. The Monkhouse evening was rather awkward, according to Crabb Robinson. "I was for the first time in my life not pleased with Wordsworth, and Coleridge appeared to advantage in his presence. Coleridge spoke of painting in that style of mysticism which is now his habit of feeling. Wordsworth met this with dry, unfeeling contradiction."

There was a particularly awkward moment when Coleridge was praising the "divinity" of Raphael's Madonnas, and Wordsworth interjected that "the subject of a mother and child" was not "a field for high intellect", an oblique suggestion that Coleridge was no authority on parental affections. He asked if Coleridge would have discerned such "beauties", had he not known that Raphael was the painter. "When Coleridge said that was an unkind question, Wordsworth made no apology." Both Lamb and Crabb Robinson thought Wordsworth harsh in his manner and "substantially wrong" in his argument.[123]

At Lamb's soirée, there was a kind of stand-off. Wordsworth sat gravely at one end of the table, talking *tête-à-tête* with the literary lawyer Sergeant Talfourd; while Coleridge sprawled genially at the other end, surrounded by "the larger body" of the guests. The ladies, no doubt sensing a "polarity of forces", gathered quietly round Mary Lamb in a corner. Crabb Robinson observed one moment of exemplary comedy, when both of the poets could be heard quoting verses to their listeners. Moving surreptitiously between the two groups, Robinson found Coleridge quoting Wordsworth's poetry by heart; and Wordsworth quoting "– *not* Coleridge's, but his own". It needed no comment.[124]

As for Asra, she carefully avoided any moment of intimacy, and was rather caught off-guard when Coleridge openly called her "my dear" and asked for an address where he could write to her privately.

Once she had safely escaped to the country in January, she wrote to Monkhouse with some wry praise of Coleridge's Highgate reformation – "indeed he has exhibited many wonders lately". She could not forebear to ask, in turn, if *he* had said anything about *her*: "pray have you any conversation with him? And did he enquire after 'my dear' or his other friends?"[125] But Coleridge was silent, even in his Notebooks.

These meetings convinced him of what he already knew in his heart, that his old life was over, and what future he had lay in London. He wrote a kindly letter to the Morgans, setting out his plans, and wishing them a Happy New Year for 1818 – "if the word 'happy' did not sound like Arabic Diabolic for 'wretched' from *my* mouth – However, there is that within, thank God! Which is at Peace – So may God bless you and your sincere and faithful Friend, S. T. Coleridge."[126]

Another pair of eyes had watched the Wordsworths and Sara Hutchinson in London this December. John Keats had called on them in Mortimer Street, and the very day after the awkward Monkhouse evening with Raphael's Madonna, he had joined Wordsworth and Lamb for the "Immortal Dinner" at the painter Benjamin Robert Haydon's studio at Lisson Grove. (This was the famous dinner party when Lamb got wonderfully drunk and insulted Wordsworth's foolish superior from the Stamp Office – "Do let me have another look at that gentleman's organs.")

Keats was very proud to be admitted into Wordsworth's London circle. He thought his poetry "one of the three superior things in the modern world" (the others being Haydon's painting and Hazlitt's "depth of Taste").[127] Wordsworth was "a great Poet if not a Philosopher". Yet he also found him stiff and self-important, dressing up in a high collar, knee breeches and silk stockings; and expecting deference from everyone, especially from the women. Keats was amazed when he tried to put a question, and Mrs Wordsworth pulled his arm with the hasty aside, "Mr Wordsworth is never interrupted." He thought that wherever Wordsworth went in London he left a personal impression of "egotism, Vanity and bigotry".[128] He found Sara Hutchinson "enchanting", but from her manner at first thought she was Wordsworth's daughter.[129]

19

Among the "many wonders" that Asra had remarked on was Coleridge's return to lecturing in 1818. His old patrons at the Philosophical Society, in Fleur de Luce Court, invited him to give a new series on European literature to begin in the New Year. These were his first lectures since Bristol, four years previously, and marked a growing sense of his return to the heart of a national debate about culture and education. What Coleridge offered was in effect a pioneering course in comparative literature: a lifting of the English intellectual horizon after years of wartime insularity. The course was also conceived in direct competition to Hazlitt, who was simultaneously lecturing at the Surrey Institution on "The English Poets".

Coleridge planned to cover the literary developments of the Dark Ages, medieval Europe and the Renaissance in a broad perspective; then focus on Dante, Cervantes, Rabelais and Shakespeare; and finally make a selection of his favourite special topics – the role of education, the psychology of the supernatural, and the philosophic appreciation of the fine arts. After the financial disappointments of the Rest Fenner contract, Coleridge hoped the lectures would be profitable, and advance his plan "to lay by £200, little by little, in the course of the next year" exclusively for sending Derwent to Cambridge.[130] He sent out invitations to his nephews and many old friends, the Godwins, the Lambs, the Morgans, John Payne Collier and several newspaper editors, including John Thelwall at *The Champion*. Crabb Robinson faithfully attended, and he and J. H. Green took notes.

Coleridge's fourteen lectures began on 27 January 1818, and continued regularly each Tuesday and Friday evening at 8.15 p.m. "precisely", until 13 March. With Hazlitt lecturing (at 7 p.m.) just a few minutes walk away down Fleet Street, at the Surrey Institution in Blackfriars, Coleridge was particularly anxious about his audience. He wrote to several newspapers asking for free advertising and, if possible, friendly notices – and most responded, including the *Courier*, the *Morning Chronicle*, the *New Times*, and even the radical *Champion* where Thelwall wrote a leader saying that few men in England were better qualified to talk about European literature.[131]

He also openly raised the question of his indebtedness to A. W. Schlegel, vigorously defending his position, and warning editors that both Hazlitt and even Wordsworth had denied his originality. (Hazlitt had done so in the *Edinburgh Review*, February 1816, while reviewing a translation of Schlegel's *Lectures on Dramatic Literature*; Wordsworth in his "Essay Supplementary to the Preface" of his 1815 *Poems*.) Writing to William Mudford at the *Courier*, he was particularly reproachful about Wordsworth's slight. "Mr Wordsworth for whose fame I had felt and fought with an ardour that amounted to absolute Self Oblivion, and to which I owe mainly the rancour of the Edinburgh clan . . . has affirmed *in print* that a German Critic *first* taught us to think correctly concerning Shakespeare."[132]

His nerves, as in the days of the Royal Institution, produced a sudden physical collapse on the eve of the first lecture. He had a heavy head-cold and "hoarseness" so bad he could barely speak. Gillman forbade him to leave Moreton House, with an oblique reference to his opium treatment. "With such a cold on you it would be dangerous – under the influence of the medicine, madness. Excuse plain speaking from yours faithfully, J. Gillman."[133] Gillman also wrote officially to the organizers, as Coleridge's physician.

But Gillman's grasp of Coleridge's psychology was growing ever more acute. This "peremptory Veto", on medical grounds actually convinced Coleridge that he could fulfil the engagement by an act of willpower alone. Though the first lecture lacked animation and Coleridge's voice was, according to Robinson, rendered "scarcely audible" by his "exceeding bad cold", he carried it off successfully. (Coleridge called it "a battle between the croaks and squeaks".) For the rest of the series he never faltered.

Fleur de Luce Court was continuously full, with "a large and respectable audience – generally of very superior looking persons", as Robinson put it. The subscription was better than any other lectures he had given. Unlike Hazlitt's, it was a largely middle-aged audience now, with distinguished figures like Sir James Mackintosh and Mrs Barbauld. But there were several younger men from the City and university. Among these was Thomas Allsop, a young businessman, who was to become one of Coleridge's most intimate confidants; and a young don from Cambridge, Julius Hare. Coleridge's nephews, William Hart and John Taylor Coleridge, also came.

Surprising reports were posted back to Ottery St Mary. His brother George marvelled at these "excellent" accounts, and wondered "what sort of a Balance sheet he is likely to make of it". He suspected that fame was "coming rather too late to fill his pockets", but was gratified to hear that his disreputable brother ("Poor Fellow!") was now behaving "in a manner more consentaneous with reason and commonsense". He surmised that sound "Theology" had done the trick, where all else had failed.[134]

Coleridge's lectures have been described as "the first English attempt at a comparative history of literature in the modern sense".[135] What is remarkable about them is their entirely new emphasis on the influence on English poetry of the Italian Romance writers, especially through translation and imitation. Thus Coleridge linked Boccaccio and Petrarch to Chaucer and Spenser; and Dante to Milton and John Donne. In some of his lecture notes which have survived, he insisted that his object "in adverting to the Italian Poets, is not so much for their own sakes . . . but for the elucidation of the merits of our Countrymen, as to what extent we must consider them as fortunate Imitators of their Italian Predecessors, and in which points they have the higher claims of original genius".[136]

Coleridge was responding to the interests of the younger generation of writers who, with the publication of Leigh Hunt's *The Story of Rimini* (1816), based on Dante's account of the lovers Paolo and Francesca di Rimini, were turning back to Italian models. There was growing interest in such tales of southern passion and an elaborate, highly visual style of poetic narration. It was no coincidence that Keats began his tale from Boccaccio, "Isabella, or the Pot of Basil" in April 1818. Coleridge spoke of "the wild and imaginative character" of Boccaccio's "happy art of narration", his elaborate mythology and "incongruous paganisms", and his astonishing "licentiousness".[137]

Coleridge's tenth lecture, on 27 February, was largely given up to a comparison of particular images in Dante and Milton, and to praise of Cary's translation of the *Commedia*. He had already convinced the publishers Taylor and Hessey to bring out the new, three-volume pocket version of the translation, and he urged Cary to have some copies of the book ready by that date, even perhaps on sale after the lecture.[138]

Cary's son wrote later: "the effect of his commendation was no other than might have been expected. The work, which had been published four years, but had remained in utter obscurity, was at once eagerly sought after. About a thousand copies of the first edition, that remained on hand, were immediately disposed of; in less than three months a new edition was called for. The *Edinburgh* and *Quarterly Reviews* re-echoed the praises that had been sounded by Coleridge, and henceforth the claims of the translator of Dante to literary distinction were universally admitted."[139] One of the eager purchasers was Keats, who carried the pocket edition in his knapsack on a three-month walking tour of Scotland that summer, the only book he took with him.

20

All the time that Coleridge was lecturing in Fleur de Luce Court, Hazlitt was lecturing in Blackfriars, and soon their rivalry became open. The two courses converged as Hazlitt began to speak of contemporary poets. Nothing could have been more contrasted than their styles. Hazlitt was perfectly in tune with his young audience: clever, witty, iconoclastic, brilliantly incorporating well-prepared passages from his critical journalism, and fearlessly mocking the great names of the day like Byron and Wordsworth in the very act of praising them. He was also responsive to his listeners, so that when in one lecture he spoke too dismissively of Chatterton, and found afterwards that Keats was disappointed, he thoughtfully corrected his views in the next lecture.[140]

Coleridge by contrast was his usual, rambling, magnificent, highly metaphysical self, appearing to speak without proper notes, circling through his subjects, and suddenly producing great passages and long philosophical perspectives of dazzling power and suggestion.

Crabb Robinson shuttled doggedly between the two, sometimes keeping a carriage waiting to whisk him from one lecture hall to the other, and frequently reduced to utter confusion by the contrasts in style and approach. Coleridge was slow, repetitious, but full of "splendid irregularities throughout". Hazlitt was "bitter, sprightly, and full of personal allusions"; and sometimes "almost obscene".[141] It struck him as wholly characteristic that while Hazlitt's lectures were collected and carefully published (by Taylor and Hessey) by the end of the year, Coleridge's went as usual totally unrecorded, except for a few scattered notes made by friends like J. H. Green.

On one particular evening, 24 February, Crabb Robinson found to his alarm that he had first completely lost his temper at Hazlitt's lecture, standing up and "hissing" at contemptuous remarks about Wordsworth; and then, having walked out, leaped into his coach, and dashed over to Coleridge's lecture, he found himself virtually lulled to exhausted slumber by the "obscurity and metaphysics" of Coleridge's learned analysis of "the great writers of wit and humour" from Rabelais to Sterne.[142] He may have missed the wonderful aside that "Swift was the Soul of Rabelais dwelling in a dry place".[143]

It was Hazlitt who finally acknowledged the historic confrontation. In March he dedicated the final part of his last lecture "On the Living Poets" to Coleridge himself. Hazlitt was wholly conscious of the ironies of the situation. The brilliant protégé at the height of his critical power and fashion, was now facing down his old, embattled master and mentor. With his sure, sardonic touch, he presented it as a Roman tragedy worthy of Shakespeare.

"It remains that I should say a few words of Mr Coleridge; and there is no one who has a better right to say what he thinks of him than I have. 'Is there here any dear friend of Caesar? To him I say, that Brutus's love to Caesar was no less than his.' But no matter . . ." Like Brutus, the great republican, he would stab his erstwhile poetical master out of love for the greater good, a political good.

Hazlitt pushed in the blade, dramatically and repeatedly. All Coleridge's journalism, from the *Watchman* to *The Friend*, was "dreary trash". His plays, apart from a few poetical passages, were "drawling sentiment and metaphysical jargon". He had "no genuine dramatic talent". His *Biographia* was not worth mentioning, since Hazlitt had already destroyed it elsewhere. Of his poetry, there was one fine early sonnet to Schiller which gave an idea of Coleridge's "youthful enthusiasm"; and there was the Jacobin polemic against the government of 1799, "Fire, Famine and Slaughter", which Coleridge had republished in *Sibylline Leaves* with a long "Apologetic Preface". This indeed showed "strong political feeling", though – as Hazlitt added with a conspiratorial grin at his audience – "it might seem insidious if *I* were to praise it".

What remained? Well – "Christabel" and "The Ancient Mariner". As for the "Mariner", it was Coleridge's most remarkable performance" and the only thing from his entire *oeuvre* that gave "an adequate idea of his great natural powers". Yet it was Germanic in manner, and seemed to conceive of poetry "as a drunken dream, reckless, careless and headless, of past, present and to come". As for "Christabel", there was indeed one memorable passage as it seemed to Hazlitt, about the quarrel between two men who had been "friends in youth". Here Hazlitt, for the first time and with great feeling, quoted Coleridge to his young listeners:

> Alas! they had been friends in youth,
> But whispering tongues can poison truth;
> And constancy lives in realms above;
> And life is thorny; and youth is vain;
> And to be wroth with one we love,
> Doth work like madness in the brain:
> And thus it chanced, as I divine,
> With Roland and Sir Leoline.

Hazlitt did not need to substitute the names. At this point he paused to survey the literary reputation he had laid waste for his breathless audience. Then abruptly, and wholly unexpectedly, he delivered a panegyric straight from the heart. It was the most dramatic and the most personal moment in his whole lecture series.

> But I may say of him here, that he is the only person I ever knew who answered to the idea of a man of genius. He is the only person from whom I ever learnt anything. There is only one thing he could learn from me in return, but *that* he has not. He was the first poet I ever knew. His genius at that time had angelic wings, and fed on manna. He talked on for ever; and you wished him to talk on for ever. His thoughts did not

> seem to come with labour and effort; but as if borne on the gusts of genius, and as if the wings of his imagination lifted him from off his feet. His voice rolled on the ear like the pealing organ, and its sound alone was the music of thought. His mind was clothed with wings; and raised on them, he lifted philosophy to heaven. In his descriptions, you then saw the progress of human happiness and liberty in bright and never-ending succession, like the steps of Jacob's ladder, with airy shapes ascending and descending, and with the voice of God at the top of the ladder . . .

This was, almost literally, an apotheosis: Coleridge as the "*un*damaged Archangel", divinely inspired, the only true "genius" of English Romanticism. Nothing Hazlitt had said of Wordsworth, "the most original poet now living", had approached this degree of personal intensity. It is impossible to know what inflexions of "sprightly" irony Hazlitt gave to his valedictory lecture that night. One can, however, guess at the "one thing" that Coleridge could have learned from Hazlitt: loyalty to his youthful radical beliefs. But he referred to Coleridge's *talk*, not his writing; and he used the past tense, as a form of funeral oration. Hazlitt intended to bury Coleridge, by praising him. In his closing phrases, he covered Coleridge's genius with a kind of rhetorical shroud, in a final dismissal. Up there, in Fleur de Luce Court, Hazlitt implied, there was nothing to be heard, just the voice of a ghost. "And shall I, who heard him then, listen to him now? Not I! . . . That spell is broke; that time is gone for ever; that voice is heard no more: but still the recollection comes rushing by with thoughts of long-past years, and rings in my ears with never-dying sound."

Hazlitt closed this brilliant and deadly performance with a few more lines of verse. They were not from Coleridge, but from Wordsworth's "Immortality Ode": "What though the radiance which was once so bright/ Be now forever taken from my sight . . ."[144]*

---

* The enigma of Hazlitt's sustained animosity towards Coleridge, rooted in both personal and ideological disappointment with a hero-figure, is broached in *Early Visions*, pp.178–80. But it must also be remembered that Hazlitt (a fine and aggressive fives-player) always wrote best when on the offensive. "I crawl about the Fives-Court like a cripple till I get the racket in my hand, when I start up as if I was possessed by a devil." ("A Farewell to Essay-Writing", 1828.) Other admired figures like Edmund Burke, Byron and Shelley, also received such

footnote continued overleaf

21

In his Notebooks that spring, Coleridge scribbled down a few lines of verse on his old Quantock friend the nightingale, who he now found had faithfully followed him to the woods of Hampstead Heath. This nightingale's situation, as he imagined it, was curiously like his own as a lecturer. The bird sat on the slim branch of an ash tree above a waterfall, half hidden in the leaves that "Shook in the Gale and glittered in the Spray", singing its heart out. But the roar of the waterfall made its song inaudible to any listener. Only the nightingale itself could tell that it was singing.

The lines were quickly sketched out, not finding their metre until the last couplet. But in a tell-tale shift in gender – from she to he – Coleridge became the bird.

> . . . I saw a Nightingale.
> And by the heaving plumage of her Throat
> And busy Bill that seemed to cut the Air,
> I saw he sang –
> And sure he heard not his own Song
> Or did but inly hear –
> With such a loud confuséd sound
> The Cataract spread wide around.[145]

22

Yet Coleridge's retired life at Highgate did not isolate him from the cataract of public affairs, however much Hazlitt wished to confine him to a posthumous existence. Throughout spring 1818 he had been corresponding with C. A. Tulk on Swedenborgian matters,

---

footnote continued

brilliant and sustained bastinadoes. (See his revealing essay, "On the Pleasures of Hating", 1826.) Lamb said Hazlitt's articles on Coleridge were "like saluting a man: 'Sir, you are the greatest man I ever saw,' and then pulling him by the nose." While Keats observed cheerfully: "Hazlitt is your only good damner, and if ever I am damned – damn me, if I shouldn't like to him to damn me." Moreover nothing could be finer, or in its own way more tender, than Hazlitt's unforgettable evocation of young Coleridge and Wordsworth in "My First Acquaintance with Poets", 1823. (See the shrewd discussion, in terms of a war of intellectual styles, by Tom Paulin: "Coleridge the Aeronaut", in *The Day-Star of Liberty*, 1998.)

and at the end of April this led unexpectedly to his last and most direct intervention in political controversy since the *Watchman* days over twenty years before. They had been exchanging apparently remote and hermetic concepts of the "two great Laws" of identity and polarity, which produced the human soul. "The two great Ends (& inclusively, the processes) of Nature would be – Individualization, or apparent detachment from Nature = Progressive Organization and Spirit, or the re-union with Nature as the apex of Individualization – the birth of the *Soul*, the Ego or conscious Self, into the Spirit."[146]

These ideas also produced reflections on the unconscious self, in a long twelve-point note on the "Language of Dreams". Coleridge suggested that there was a universal dream symbolism, which like poetic symbolism was common to all peoples. "It is a (Night) language of Images and Sensations, the various dialects of which are far less different from each other, than the various (Day) Languages of Nations. Proved even by the Dream Books of different Countries and ages."[147] Such symbolism might be grounded on analogy ("deep water = Death"), or "seemingly arbitrary" ("the signification of Colours") or "frequently ironical" ("Dung = Gold etc"). The Soul was in this sense a combination of the conscious and the unconscious self: "the Unity of Day and Night – Query: Are there two Consciences, the earthly and the Spiritual?"[148]

Encouraged by the sweep and poetical mysticism of these speculations, Tulk carried up to Highgate in February one of the very rare copies of William Blake's *Songs of Innocence and Experience: Shewing the Two Contrary States of the Human Soul* (1795). At this time the ageing Blake was living in great poverty and almost total obscurity, with his wife Catherine, in two cramped rooms in Fountain Court, The Strand. A few young artists like Samuel Palmer, and a scattering of Swedenborgians like Tulk, were his only supporters. Tulk clearly hoped that the mystical doctrine of "Opposites" underlying the *Songs*, and the startling originality of their symbolism, would appeal to Coleridge. Blake's notions of childhood, of the soul driven from Innocence to Experience, might also strike some deep chord in the author of "Christabel".

Initially Coleridge was impressed but somewhat quizzical, writing not to Tulk but to Cary on 6 February, "I have this morning been reading a strange publication – viz. Poems with very wild and interesting pictures, as the swathing, etched (I suppose) but it is said – printed and painted by the Author, W. Blake. He is a man of Genius – and I apprehend, a Swedenborgian – certainly, a mystic *emphatically*. You perhaps smile at *my* calling another Poet, a *Mystic*; but verily I am in the very mire of common-place common-sense compared with Mr Blake, apo- or rather ana-calyptic Poet, and Painter!"[149]

A week later he wrote appreciatively to Tulk himself, returning Blake's "poesies, metrical and graphic, with thanks", and providing a detailed appreciation of the work. He thought Blake extraordinary, "a man capable of such faults + such beauties". His faults were "despotism in symbols"; his beauties "such as only a Master in his art could produce". Coleridge then listed the poems he had particularly liked, including "The Tiger", "London", "The Sick Rose", "The Lamb" and "The Divine Image".

What particularly struck him was Blake's radical understanding of child-exploitation. He marked with a double-sign of emphasis "The Little Black Boy", with its reflection on the slave trade; and remarked on one of the earliest references in print to child prostitution, "The Little Vagabond". Coleridge commented: "I would have had it omitted – not for the want of innocence in the poem, but from the too probable want of it in many readers." He thought there was much to shock pious readers in Blake's vision of childhood (though he was not shocked himself), and he imagined one of "the modern *Saints* (whose whole being is a Lie)" reading a poem like "The Little Vagabond" with "the whites of his Eyes upraised at the *audacity* of this poem!"[150]

23

At this point the whole subject of child-exploitation suddenly presented itself in the most urgent and practical form. On 21 February, Coleridge (while still lecturing) wrote again to Tulk "with much grief" at the news that Sir Robert Peel and his son the Irish Secretary had prematurely introduced into the Commons a Bill to regulate the labouring hours of "the poor Children in the Cotton Factories". He felt that "without due preparation of the public mind" it would almost certainly be thrown out by the Lords. Such a rejection might set back reform for a decade, at a time when the labouring classes were ignored by Lord Liverpool's dilatory government. "The Friends of outraged Nature" should intervene before the second or third reading of the Bill.[151]

As the Bill passed its first reading in the Commons at the end of April and the crisis approached, Coleridge determined on direct intervention. With Gillman's anxious blessing, he left Highgate and moved his base of operations to Westminster, where he could work once again like a professional journalist. He stayed with a medical friend of Green's, the surgeon T. J. Pettigrew, who had a house next to the Spring Gardens coffee-house.[152] His plan was to write a polemical pamphlet in support of the Bill, to be printed (at Tulk's expense) and circulated directly to members of both Houses. In the event he wrote three, two of which have survived.[153]

Coleridge co-opted Crabb Robinson to provide "legal information" and comb "that pithy little manual, yclept, the Statutes of Great Britain" for constitutional arguments, and an analysis of the First Factory Act, passed in 1802.[154] He sent bulletins to J. H. Green, noting on Thursday, noon, 30 April: "I am writing as hard as I can put pen to paper, at the Spring Garden Coffee House in defence of the Bill for regulating the labour of the Children in Cotton Factories – and cannot hope to finish it in time to return to Highgate before night . . . For it must be done now or not at all."[155] Four days later, on Monday, 3 May, he was still at his post in Spring Gardens writing and correcting.

In practical terms the Bill was the most primitive form of social legislation, simply prohibiting child labour under nine years old, and limiting working hours to less than twelve in twenty-four. But in constitutional terms it was a watershed, setting an historic precedent for government interference in privately owned industry. The Peel family fortune was based on Lancashire cotton mills, and many industrialists regarded both men as traitors, opposing the measure with great bitterness.

Coleridge had already argued the practical case for state intervention in such cases. But his grounds depended ultimately on the very notions of society and the human soul that he had been discussing as philosophical principles with Tulk. The questions he put to Crabb Robinson clearly show the connection in his mind. "Can you furnish us with any other instances, in which the Legislature has directly, or by immediate consequence, interfered with what is ironically called *Free Labour*? (i.e. DARED to prohibit Soul-murder and Infanticide on the part of the Rich, and Self-slaughter on that of the Poor)."[156]

To Mudford at the *Courier* he described the condition of the poor cotton factory children as "an abomination, which has weighed on my feelings from earliest manhood, I have been indeed an eye-witness of the direful effects." The rich manufacturers were blindly justifying such treatment through the "so-called" science of political economy, which allowed them to manage human beings in terms of profit and accountancy, as pure abstractions, "like Geometry". This was a profoundly false philosophy. "It is a science which begins with *abstractions*, in order to exclude whatever is not subject to a technical calculation: in the face of all experience, it assumes these as the *whole* of human nature – and then on an impossible hypothesis builds up the most inhuman edifice, a Temple of Tescalipoca!"[157] Tezcatlipoca was the Aztec god, whose throne was built of human skulls.

Coleridge's campaigning journalism was as lively as anything in the *Watchman*, and far more concentrated than anything in the *Lay Sermons*. First came a polemic letter signed "Plato", in the *Courier*, which mixes a Blakean radicalism with biting Swiftian irony. It purported to be from one of Peel's conservative opponents, terrified of reform.

> This legislation in cases of mere humanity is pregnant with fatal dangers to our most glorious Constitution. A renovated spirit of Luddism will affect these very children, whose present love and veneration for the machines, by which they are enabled to support their aged parents, can only be exceeded by the love and respect they bear towards their indulgent masters. But how fearfully will the scene be changed! Give them but the notion that they are under the protection of the laws, and instead of quietly piercing the yarn, and of cleaning the machinery during dinner, their little hearts will be beating high for radical reform, annual Parliaments, and universal suffrage . . . Let us then hear no more useless defences of Sir Robert Peel's Bill.[158]

Next came his pamphlet, *Remarks on Objections to Peel's Bill*. Here the style is direct and passionate, on broad humanitarian grounds. "But *free* Labour! – in what sense, not utterly sophistical, can the labour of children, exhorted from the wants of their parents, 'their poverty, but not their will, consenting', be called *free*? . . . Has it or has it not been proved, that the common result of the present system of labour in the Cotton Factories is disease, of the most painful and wasting kinds, and too often a premature death? This, we repeat, *has* been *fully* proved." Coleridge also made a historic connection with Clarkson's and Wilberforce's great campaign against the slave trade. Abolition was the "glorious precedent" that should be followed.[159]

Finally, came the pamphlet, *The Grounds of Peel's Bill Vindicated*. This was largely a briefing-paper, clarifying and summarizing the medical evidence concerning conditions in the cotton factories, much of it hidden away in a Commons Select Committee Report of 1816, which Coleridge and Robinson had disinterred from Hansard and other sources. It is not literary, but it is impressive in its detail, covering specifics of shop-floor temperatures (up to 85 degrees), air-pollution, and recorded diseases among labouring children ("debility, rickets, scrofula, mesenteric obstruction"). It is notable for the "eminent medical authorities" it cites, including several doctors that Coleridge knew personally (Dr Carlisle, Dr Tuthill) and the great surgeon from Guy's Hospital who had encouraged Keats, Astley Cooper.[160]

The immediate political outcome was much as Coleridge feared. The Bill was passed by the Commons on 30 April 1818, but then blocked by the Lords. Robert Peel (the son) resigned, exhausted by his efforts, but was to return in 1822 as one of the great reforming Home Secretaries. A weakened version of the Bill was eventually passed by both Houses in 1819, but the principle of government intervention was established, and led to a great sequence of Factory Acts and select committees in the early Victorian period.[161] It also established the increasing power of journalism, public petition and expert evidence to influence parliament, and this was to be crucial in the years leading up to the Great Reform Bill of 1832.

Coleridge felt he had played some small part in this movement (as with the slave trade agitation), with his "inefficient yet not feeble Efforts in behalf of the poor little white slaves in the Cotton Factories", as they seemed to him in retrospect. The experience left him with increasing doubts about Tory social policy, asking himself in February 1819: "But are we not better than other Nations of Christendom? Yes – perhaps – I don't know – I dare not affirm it. Better than the French, certainly! . . . But Sweden, Norway, Germany, the *Tyrol*? – No."[162]

24

For a moment in May 1818 it looked very much as if Coleridge might return to the world of politics and public controversy. It was a time of increasing social turmoil. Demand for reform would rise to the bitter climax of "Orator" Hunt's great public meetings and the Peterloo Massacre the following year. Leigh Hunt's editorials in the *Examiner*, Hazlitt's lectures and reviews, even Keats's letters, were full of this sense of imminent crisis. As Keats wrote: "This is no contest between Whig and Tory – but between right and wrong. There is scarcely a grain of party spirit now in England. – Right and Wrong considered by each man abstractedly is the fashion."[163]*

But in the event this was to be the last time that Coleridge stepped directly into the political arena. From now on, all his remaining efforts would be concentrated on work that looked beyond the controversies of the day. He was exhausted by his pamphlet-writing, and for much of May and June he was "ill", very likely from an opium relapse. When Thomas Phillips asked to include him in a series of celebrity portraits, Coleridge refused to let the painter come to Highgate. "I should have substituted a wretched pathognomy for a physiognomy."[164]

He arranged to spend a week away by the sea with J. H. Green, proposing as their relaxation a step-by-step analysis of Schelling. The philosophers quartered themselves at Green's mother's house, a large and comfortable establishment amidst extensive gardens near Maldon in Essex. A number of fragmentary philosophical papers and "Dialogues" arose from these discussions, most notably a symposium on "The Sciences and Theology". The three voices of Coleridge, Green and Gillman are recorded in this paper, with several exchanges that bear on the *Theory of Life*.[165]

Nothing could be further from topical politics. Coleridge was now questioning the validity of Schelling's system of "Polarity" as

---

* Andrew Motion, *Keats*, 1997, is especially valuable on this growing awareness among writers.

put forward in the *Naturphilosophie*, and trying to establish if there could be an alternative philosophical system which was "the common ground of all Sciences in all classes".[166] He likened this to the astronomer Herschel's speculation, that while the sun provided the gravitational centre to the solar system, the solar system itself might depend on a gravitational centre elsewhere in the galaxy.[167]

Coleridge thought everything would depend on the definition of life itself, and whether this was susceptible to an adequate scientific description, or could only be defined in theological terms. His speculations eventually conclude that all life-sciences describe "Mechanisms" and "Structures", but not the grounds of life itself. "You see clearly that Life is not a result of *structure* generally – or a watch would be alive." Instead one must assume a primary act of "Creation", and a continual process of "transition" by which creative "power" is diversified through the physical universe. Coleridge would eventually trace this up the whole scale of evolution, a process of "Individuation" which became the central subject of his *Theory of Life*. The result is not quite "Evolution" as Lamark or Darwin understood it, but a Platonized version of Schelling: "the *power* which discloses itself from within as a principle of *unity* in the *many*".[168]

Coleridge was happy at Maldon, working amidst "a perfect Blaze of Roses", and potting up local plants to bring back to the garden at Highgate. The house was surrounded by flowering beanfields, and from a wooded hill above them there was a view of the open sea that reminded him of Stowey and Alfoxden. The local cottagers seemed comfortably off, and there was no talk of political disaffection, but "an abundance of Cream". The only drawbacks were a plague of gnats, and a shortage of snuff. He wrote reassuringly to Ann Gillman, that for all the delights of the Green household, he felt nothing could now replace Highgate: "I feel more and more that I can be well off nowhere away from you and Gillman . . . again & again & again God bless you, my most dear Friends."[169]

When Coleridge returned in July, all thoughts of further political activity had dissipated. He determined to concentrate on completing his revisions of *The Friend*, and had a vague idea for "a novel or romance" which would dramatize his new theories of the "constructive Philosophy". Perhaps it would be something like Novalis's *Heinrich von Ofterdingen*, but the problem of "form" perplexed him.

In discussing this with Green, he imagined a philosophic "dialogue" in the framework of a walking-tour. It would start in a library with introductory "lessons"; then move to a cavern by the seashore for "theosophical" conversations; then stride up over the moors for "Travel-Talk"; linger by the lakes for "Ethics"; and finally climb to the mountain tops for "Religion".[170]

It reflected his own life at Highgate. Rather than moving downstream from the hills to city, he was moving back up into the hills and high visionary places. He was moving from the topical to the eternal. He would rise above the ephemeral attacks of the world. "Little does that man know me, who supposes that the Hunts, Hazlitts, Jeffreys, etc. have ever inflicted one serious pang," he assured Green.

For the first time too, he spoke of the idea that Green "and one or two others" who would survive him might carry on his work. They might edit his papers, protect his "calumniated" reputation, and prevent others "pillaging" his ideas with impunity.[171] Clearly some tacit agreement was reached at Maldon, and from now on Green began to consider himself both as a future executor and possibly as a collaborator on a philosophic *summa*, the long-projected *Opus Maximum*. He also attended to more worldly matters, and took over the annual payments of Coleridge's life assurance policy.

Charles Lamb sent his own form of greetings up to Highgate. The first two-volume collection of his prose and verse *Works* (1818) was dedicated to Coleridge in an affectionate Preface, recalling their friendship going back to schooldays. "The world has given you many a shrewd nip and gird since that time, but either my eyes are grown dimmer, or my old friend is the *same* who stood before me three and twenty years ago, his hair a little confessing the hand of time, but still shrouding the same capacious brain – his heart not altered, scarcely where it 'alteration finds'."[172]

25

The revised edition of *The Friend*, in three handsome volumes, finally appeared in November 1818. It was now dedicated to "Mr and Mrs Gillman of Highgate", and made no mention at all of the circumstances in which it was originally composed at Allan Bank. "I owe in great measure the power of having written at all to your medical skill," he wrote to Gillman in the dedication; adding that Mrs Gillman had provided "almost a mother's watchful and unwearied solicitudes".[173]

Coleridge cut other links with the past by removing Wordsworth's sonnets and his "Essay on Epitaphs", and rewriting the opening essays. He cut his own poems, and the travel-letters from Germany (which had reappeared at the end of the *Biographia*), but kept the "literary amusements interspersed" including a beautifully polished and moving version of Sir Alexander Ball's biography.

The problem of revising his past, in a political sense, also haunted the early part of the work. How would he deal with the revolutionary years of the 1790s? He left in his essay on Pantisocracy, "Enthusiasm for an Ideal World", virtually untouched. But he added a skilfully softened version of his political lectures at Bristol, in the heady days of 1795, from his pamphlet *Conciones ad Populum* (1795). Coleridge tried to show the continuity of his position by adding new references to the recent cotton children campaign and suppressing older ones attacking oppressive government and defending certain English Jacobins transported to Australia in 1794. (In an explanatory note to Morgan, he added: "Written by Southey. I never saw these men.")[174] It must all have seemed a long time ago.

The single biggest addition, now a substantial treatise of some two hundred pages in volume 3, was his "Essay on the Principles of Method". It was adapted from his ill-starred Introduction to the *Encyclopaedia*. He came to consider this, rightly, as one of his outstanding pieces of later prose.[175] Coleridge begins with a deceptively simple question: "What is it that first strikes us, and strikes us at once, in a man of education? And which, among educated men, so instantly distinguishes the man of superior mind, that (as was observed with eminent propriety of the late Edmund Burke) 'we cannot stand under the same archway during a shower of rain, *without finding him out*?'."[176]

The obvious answer, that it is breadth of knowledge, encyclopaedic capacity, "a mere repository or banqueting-room" of information, is soon dismissed.[177]Instead, Coleridge develops a highly sophisticated concept of "intellectual Method". This is the "germinal power" of ordering and relatings facts and ideas through "progressive transition", and the grasp of the underlying principles and laws which generate them.[178] "Method, therefore, becomes natural to the mind which has been accustomed to contemplate not *things* only, or for their sake alone, but likewise and chiefly the *relations* of things."[179] Considering the closeness of this terminology to his scientific speculations in *A Theory of Life*, one can glimpse here a fascinating parallel (or unified) theory of the physical "evolution" of biological forms, and the cultural "evolution" of mental powers.

This concept is brilliantly ramified through a short history of the European arts and sciences, as only Coleridge could manage. The illustrations he chose were a conscious and dazzling display of his own polymathic virtuosity, but were also intended to appeal to the broadest possible range of readers. He began with Shakespeare, "our myriad-minded Bard", and laid out his central argument in a fine piece of literary criticism. He took two speeches – one by Mistress Quickly from *Henry IV Part I*, the other by Hamlet – and contrasted their logical structures and linking images. Mistress Quickly's was dominated by "mere events and images"; Hamlet's, on the other hand, was dominated by "meditative excess" and obsessive "digressions and enlargements". "If overlooking the different value of the *matter* in each, we considered the *form* alone, we should find both *immethodical*; Hamlet from the excess, Mrs Quickly from the want, of reflection and generalization; and that Method, therefore, must result from the due mean or balance between our passive impressions and the mind's own reaction to the same."[180]

Coleridge then launched into an extraordinary *tour d'horizon* of intellectual endeavour. The idealism of Plato and the empiricism of Aristotle, are followed by the scientific method of Linnaeus and Sir Humphry Davy. A crucial distinction is established between the mere "classification" of observations (as in contemporary botany) and the discovery of scientific "laws" which unify and explain them (as in contemporary chemistry).[181]

Coleridge moved on next to Galileo, Kepler and Bacon, Here he argues that a scientific law is universal, in the same sense that a Platonic Idea is eternal.[182] Both are expressions of that true method, in either science or art, which expresses an "originating" impulse in the human intellect. "Hence too, it will not surprise us, that Plato so often calls ideas LIVING LAWS, in which the mind has its whole true being and permanence; or that Bacon, vice versa, names the laws of nature, *ideas*; and represents what we have, in a former part of this disquisition, called *facts of science* and *central phenomena*, as signatures, impressions, and symbols of ideas."[183]

By this stage the argument, as in sections of the *Biographia*, is in danger of slipping away into abstraction. But Coleridge leaves one memorably vivid demonstration of his notion of the way underlying "law" supports (literally in this case) the theory of "progressive transition". He ingeniously reverts to his opening image of the "man of superior mind" standing under an archway.

In this case the arch was the brass model of a bridge, actually constructed by George Atwood FRS, a distinguished mathematician at the Royal Observatory. "Mr Atwood's arch" was intended to prove "the compound action of simple wedges". It was constructed of polished brass sections; mounted on "a skeleton arch of wood". The brass sections were slotted into shape, but not otherwise attached to each other. When the wooden scaffolding was removed, the brass arch stood perfectly firm. Thus the self-supporting properties of the wedges were apparently proved.

But Coleridge neatly reversed this conclusion. What was proved was "the property of the arch". For the wooden skeleton came first, and "presumed the figure". The brass wedges would hold up in no other shape, except as an arch. Even when the skeleton of the arch was removed, the physical "law" of the arch, the "idea" of the arch remained. It was that, ultimately, that sustained the visible brass construction. "The whole is of necessity prior to its parts; nor can we conceive a more apt illustration of the scientific principles we have already laid down."[184]

Coleridge's idea of the truly "educated mind" depended on an analogous principle. It was the Platonic arch of "Method", not the brass wedges of knowledge, that structured and defined human intelligence. He rose finally to a prophetic passage that would echo down to the Victorian educationalists, to men like Matthew Arnold and Newman. "Alas! how many examples are now present to our memory, of young men the most anxiously and expensively be-schoolmastered, be-tutored, be-lectured, any thing but *educated*; who have received arms and ammunition, instead of skill, strength and courage; varnished rather than polished; perilously over-civilized, and most pitiably uncultivated! And all from inattention to the method dictated by nature herself, to the simple truth, that as the forms in all organized existence, so must all true and living knowledge proceed from within; that it may be trained, supported, fed, excited, but can never be infused or impressed."[185]

Coleridge believed that *The Friend* had no impact at all. Yet gradually some of his ideas drifted down, like blown seeds, upon fertile ground. In 1822, Julius Hare, now a newly appointed tutor at Trinity College, Cambridge, began to spread news of *The Friend* to a circle of young undergraduates. These included John Sterling, who became one of the founder members of the Cambridge Apostles.[186] Sterling later came to visit Coleridge at Highgate, bringing with him the young philosopher J. S. Mill. Both were deeply dissatisfied with what they saw as the "mechanistic" nature of contemporary Benthamite philosophy, and Mill greeted *The Friend* as the first step in the foundation of a Coleridgean movement quite distinct from "all Tory and Royalist writers".[187]*

A year later, the young John Ruskin was writing in his diary that *The Friend* "gives one a higher notion of [Coleridge] than even his poetry".[188] In 1842, F. D. Maurice, the inspiration of the Christian Socialists, also referred specifically to *The Friend* in his Preface to *The Kingdom of Christ*, adopting Coleridge as the posthumous prophet of their movement towards a spiritual renewal in Victorian society. Maurice did not believe that Coleridge's philosophy was "complete and satisfactory"; or ever painted a clear path to social reform. Yet "the power it has exerted" was by the 1840s an historical fact: "he shows us what we have to seek for".

The mystery was how to account for Coleridge's subtle but pervasive influence on a whole climate of opinion: "to explain how a book, which is said to be utterly impractical, has wrought a change in men's minds upon the most practical subjects; how a book, which is said to have no sympathy with the moving spirit of this age, should have affected the most thoughtful of our young men . . ."[189]

---

* Looking back after nearly twenty years, J. S. Mill saw the creation of an intelligentsia very much as Coleridge had hoped: ". . . The peculiarity of the Germano-Coleridgean school is, that they saw beyond the immediate controversy, to the fundamental principles involved in all such controversies. They were the first (except a solitary thinker here and there) who inquired with any comprehensiveness or depth, into the inductive laws of the existence and growth of human society . . . They were the first who pursued, philosophically and in the spirit of Baconian investigation . . . not a piece of party advocacy, but a philosophy of society . . . a contribution, the largest made by any class of thinkers, towards the philosophy of human culture." "On Coleridge", *London Review*, March 1840.

26

Coleridge's pervasive presence now filtered, like some wondrous philosophic protoplasm, into the third of Peacock's satirical novels, *Nightmare Abbey* (1818). He bubbles into life as Mr Ferdinando Flosky, the interminable and inimitable transcendental talker. It was certainly fame to be given such a position among contemporary figures and fashionables. Mr Flosky holds centre stage with the misanthropic poet Mr Cypress (Lord Byron), with the revolutionary idealist Scythrop Glowry (Shelley), with the modish novel-reader Mr Listless, and the full-lipped, hazel-eyed romantic heroine Marionetta Celestina O'Carroll.

Peacock caricatured the Highgate Coleridge with a curiously affectionate mixture of respect and ridicule. He mocked, but he celebrated Flosky's genius. For Flosky, eighteenth-century rationalism had been proved abortive.[190] "Mystery is the very key-stone of all that is beautiful in poetry, all that is sacred in faith, and all that is recondite in transcendental psychology. I am writing a ballad which is all mystery; it is 'such stuff as dreams are made of,' and is, indeed, stuff made of a dream; for, last night I fell asleep as usual over my book, and had a vision of pure reason. I composed five hundred lines in my sleep . . . and am making a ballad of my dream and it shall be called Bottom's Dream, because it has no bottom."[191]

In fact Peacock, like Shelley, had become a great admirer of both "The Ancient Mariner" and "Christabel". Mr Flosky's dramatic role is really as a foil to Scythrop's dreams of pure, rational, social progress. In pictorial terms, it is the image of Flosky in his crepuscular study, receiving his young and enthusiastic disciples behind closed shutters and Delphic curtains, which is Peacock's imaginative triumph and greatest tribute to Coleridge.

Mr Flosky "had ceased to be visible in the morning", but is discovered in the throes of composition by the breathless Marionetta. "He was sitting at his table by the light of a solitary candle, with a pen in one hand, and a muffiner in the other, with which he occasionally sprinkled salt on the wick to make it burn blue. He sat with 'his eyes in a fine frenzy rolling', and turned his inspired gaze on Marionetta as if she had been the ghastly ladie of a magical vision; then placed his hand before his eyes, with an appearance of manifest pain – shook his head – withdrew his hand – rubbed his eyes, like a waking man – and said, in a tone of ruefulness most jeremitaylorically pathetic, 'To what am I to attribute this very unexpected pleasure, my dear Miss O'Carroll?'"

Flosky answers all Marionetta's questions with incomprehensible metaphysics, including a short dissertation on Fancy and Imagination ("seven hundred pages of promise to elucidate"). He finally concludes with disarming candour: "if any person living could make report of having obtained any information on any subject from Ferdinando Flosky, my transcendental reputation would be ruined forever." The divine Marionetta retires in disarray, determined to declare her love for Scythrop Glowry.[192]

27

At Highgate Coleridge was also visited this winter by a mysterious and beautiful young woman. She arrived in the form of a portrait, brought up for his inspection by the young American painter C. R. Leslie. Her name, on the canvas, was simply "The Highland Girl". A slim, pensive figure in a dark dress, she sat beneath a solitary tree on a wild moorland, holding a tiny basket of flowers in her lap. Her exquisite, rather melancholy face with huge downcast eyes was surrounded by soft ringlets of dark brown hair. Coleridge was entranced: "the most beautiful Fancy-figure, I ever saw", he exclaimed.[193] Leslie then asked if, perhaps, she reminded Coleridge of anyone? After some hesitation, Coleridge at last said wistfully that he had never seen any such woman, but he might have imagined "that little Sara Coleridge would have grown into such a Lass".

It was indeed his daughter, whom he had last seen when he left Keswick in 1812. The mystification surrounding the painting was later explained by Mrs Coleridge. William Collins had been commissioned to do a picture of the eighteen-year-old Sara at Keswick by Sir George Beamont, but "in the character of Wordsworth's 'Highland Girl'", for showing at the Royal Academy. Mrs Coleridge thought her husband might be offended by having his daughter used as an illustration to a Wordsworth poem. (Wordsworth had thought "she might do for a Sylph".) Leslie had been chosen as the emissary for the delicate presentation, as "good Mr Collins" did not understand "the extreme eccentricity of Coleridge's character" in such a matter.

Coleridge was overwhelmed, and later wrote to Collins himself: "your exquisite picture of Sara Coleridge . . . has quite haunted my eye ever since."[194] The painting formed a new bond between father and daughter, and Coleridge was increasingly anxious that she should be brought to London. Sara too was "very uneasy about not seeing her father". Her love of books knew no bounds, and she had just finished reading *Don Quixote* in the original Spanish. Mrs Coleridge held out the promise of bringing her south the following year, for a "re-introduction" to her father. As for the picture, it was given to Coleridge after the Academy exhibition and hung over his desk at Highgate for the remaining years of his life.[195] It came to symbolize Hope, and the future which the third Sara and her generation helped to give him so fully.

28

By the spring of 1819 more and more visitors were being drawn up the hill to Highgate. Over Coleridge's last decade it would gradually become a place of pilgrimage.* Under Gillman's assiduous care, Coleridge's intellectual reputation was altering just as his physical health was stabilizing. The wild figure whom the Wordsworths and the Morgans had known, was being replaced (in part at least) by a sedate and genial sage who looked much older than a man in his late forties.

Two Highgate portraits of this period, one by Thomas Phillips, and another by C. R. Leslie, show the physical change. (*see Illustrations.*) An enigmatic inward smile animates Phillips's avuncular subject, the silver hair grown long again, the symbolic snuffbox held between first and second finger with a gesture of easy sociability. A growing heaviness of the jowl proclaims the comforts of Ann

* The pilgrims, some more pious than others, would include among many celebrities, Thomas Carlyle, Edward Irving (preacher), Charles Mathews (comic actor), Gabriel Rossetti (poet), John Sterling (writer), John Stuart Mill (philosopher), Philarete Chasles (French historian), Charles Cowden Clarke (critic and biographer of Keats), James Fenimore Cooper (American novelist), Ralph Waldo Emerson (American writer and sage), John Frere (Cambridge Apostle), Sir William Hamilton Rowan (Irish astronomer), Julius Hare (Cambridge Apostle and preacher), Thomas Hood (poet), and Harriet Martineau (educationalist). Their accounts, ranging from the enchanted to the exacerbated, are collected in a splendid echo-chamber of memoirs, *Coleridge the Talker*, edited by Richard W. Armour and Raymond F. Howes, 1940.

Gillman's cuisine. Already Coleridge has the brooding weight and gravitas of a man of sixty.

In Leslie's penetrating study (a drawing of the head and shoulders alone), this impression is even sharper, the body hunched beneath the fleshy neck, dragging him towards earth. The large eyes alone seem to recall his youth, still raised upwards towards some visionary horizon. There is, too, a certain self-consciousness in the pose, as if Coleridge had at last become aware of the gaze of posterity. He looks beyond the immediate viewer, but knows he holds his attention anyway.

Imperceptibly, Coleridge was growing into his own legend. The original inner group of disciples – Tulk, Cary, Thomas Allsop, Hookham Frere and the increasingly indispensable J. H. Green – were still his confidants, drawn by his philosophical speculations as much as by his poetry. But already his public reputation was becoming something larger and more magnetic. The young Thomas Carlyle did not reach Highgate until 1824 (and was strangely disconcerted when he did so), but in those five years possibilities presented by Mr Flosky had enlarged and solidified into a palpable myth:

> Coleridge sat on the brow of Highgate Hill, in those years, looking down on London and its smoke-tumult, like a sage escaped from the inanity of life's battle; attracting towards him the thoughts of innumerable brave souls still engaged there. His express contributions to poetry, philosophy, or any specific province of human literature or enlightenment, had been small and sadly intermittent; but he had, especially among young enquiring men, a higher than literary, a kind of prophetic or magician character. He was thought to hold, he alone in England, the key of German and other Transcendentalisms . . . The practical intellects of the world did not much heed him, or carelessly reckoned him a metaphysical dreamer: but to the rising spirits of the young generation he had this dusky sublime character; and sat there as a kind of *Magus*, girt in mystery and enigma; his Dodona oak-grove (Mr Gillman's house at Highgate) whispering strange things, uncertain whether oracles or jargon.[196]

To all appearances, the sage was at last secure on his leafy hilltop.

10

Magic Children

1

He determined on one last descent into the smoke-tumult below. Wearied by the unbroken sequence of publications since 1816, and confident of the profits now accruing with Rest Fenner – he put them at over £1,000 – Coleridge indulged the idea of his swan-song on the public platform.

He proposed a double series of lectures "On Shakespeare" and "On the History of Philosophy". The series was accepted by the committee of the "Crown and Anchor" at Seven Dials, off the Strand. This was one of the biggest and most popular venues in London, with a long tradition of public meetings and events, and in the 1790s had been associated with radical and controversial causes. Fourteen weekly lectures were booked, to run between 14 December 1818 and 29 March 1819.[1]

When Hookham Frere discovered this, he privately commissioned a shorthand writer to cover the Philosophical series at heavy expense. ("I was astonished to learn thro' Mr Gillman from the Scribe himself, at *how* heavy an expense!" mused Coleridge.)[2]

From henceforth, he told Thomas Allsop, after the ill success of his literary toils – "and Toils they have been, tho' not undelightful Toils" – he hoped to be free from "the anxieties of the To Day" to complete the *Opus Maximum* contemplated for twenty years and now destined for posterity.[3] To have continued his public appearances, begun more than a decade ago at the Royal Institution in 1808, "would have turned my Lecture into an Auctioneer's Pulpit, and with Hammer suspended over me have cried out, Going! Going! Going! – Three Pound three only! – Gentlemen of the Dissecting Rooms – A curious Case! A rare Subject – rather fat indeed – but remarkable as a fine specimen of a broken Heart – etc. etc."[4]

The sense of premature ageing, which came to him frequently

now, was a complicated thing. He wrote a hopeful entry at the beginning of his lecture notes. "Trees in winter neither dead nor inactive – nor, tho' the sap may not flow, are they sapless – but they are forming new radicles underground for an additional supply for Spring & Summer – not merely to supply the same as last year, but more – to be progressive."[5] He also rejoiced that Hartley was again with him, having gained a respectable second-class degree at Oxford, and with some hopes of obtaining a Fellowship in the spring.

2

There was no weariness in his preparations for the Philosophical Lectures, which filled 123 pages of a brown leather-bound notebook, and covered the entire history of Western philosophy. From Plato and Aristotle in Lectures 1 to 5, he advanced to the medieval Christian Schoolmen (with some interesting asides on the "despised" contribution of Jewish philosophers) in Lectures 6 to 9; then through the Reformation and Enlightenment in Lectures 10 to 12; and concluded with a highly compressed account of Kant and Schelling in Lectures 13 to 14. He even supplied a printed outline. He told Green that this overview would lead directly to his work on the *Opus Maximum*.

Coleridge's final aim was to make philosophy a living subject for his listeners, of immediate relevance to their lives. "What, and *for* what am I made? What *can* I, and what *ought* I to, make of myself? And in what relations do I stand to the world and to my fellow men? . . ."[6] He used biographical details to bring his subjects alive, and constantly sought contemporary analogies. Thus in Lecture 6, while apparently submerged in the remote "dead low water" of the Greek Sceptics, he read with great emotion his own poem of 1814, "On the Denial of Immortality":

> If dead we cease to be; if total gloom
> Swallow up life's brief flash for aye, we fare
> As summer gusts, of sudden birth and doom . . .

He too had "at one time felt within himself" the black terror of such a philosophy.[7]

In a similar way he related the conditions of medieval vassalage to the contemporary struggle over the West Indian slave trade, and the cotton children in British factories. "True notion of Slavery – Hopelessness".[8] And when speaking of Descartes's mind–body dualism, he related it to the contemporary debate over John Hunter's theories of Vitalism.[9]

He had lost none of his ability to illuminate intellectual arguments with the reflections of a poet. Speaking of Erasmus and the transition between the Reformation and the Enlightenment, he summed up the complex exchange of ideas in a sudden, musical analogy. "If we listen to a symphony of Cimarosa, the present strain still seems not only to recall, but almost to *renew*, some past movement, and yet present the same! Each present movement bringing back, as it were, and embodying the spirit of some melody that had gone before, anticipates and seems sometimes trying to overtake something that is to come . . . The events and characters of one age, like the strains in music, recall those of another."[10]

Coleridge wanted these lectures "to be permanently useful to Auditors of both Sexes", and he intended much more than an academic history of philosophy.[11] He presented ideas as living "powers", which evolved in a continuous chain-reaction in the human mind: "a living movement in the progress of human philosophy".[12] Central to the course was the notion that the three powers of Science, Magic and Religion had battled for supremacy in the development of European thought since the Greeks.

Here Coleridge raised an issue that still haunts modern thinkers in connection with the Holocaust. How can a period of great humanist achievement coincide with a time of barbarism and persecution? How can the mind simultaneously countenance enlightenment and savagery? The illustration he used was the co-existence of science and witch-hunting in the seventeenth century, when tremendous advances in "experimental physics" coincided with widespread and totally irrational fears of the powers of witches.

> How ought it to humble us when we reflect that it was not in the Dark Ages, that it was not in countries struggling only out of barbarism, but in the very morning, in the brightness of reviving letters, in the age of a Kepler and a Galileo, when every department of human intellect was felt and supported in greatest splendour, – it was then that the dreadful contagion

> of witchcraft and persecution of witches raged, not in one country but passed like a postillion through all Europe, till it died in North America among the Puritans of New England . . . I mention this as a proof that it is not by learning merely, no, nor even by the knowledge of experimental physics, that the most disgraceful enthusiasm can at all times be prevented. The sole prevention, in reality, is the recurrence to the highest philosophy – know thyself: study thy own nature, but above all do no evil under the impression that you are serving God thereby.[13]

Coleridge suggested that the history of all philosophy was really that of "the same mind in different modes or at different periods of growth".[14] This led to the master-thesis of the course, that the Aristotelian and the Platonic approaches represented a permanent polarity in the human intellect. Once again Coleridge put this with historic clarity and immediacy.

> The difference between Aristotle and Plato is that which will remain as long as we are men and there is any difference between man and man in point of opinion. Plato, with Pythagoras before him, had conceived that the phenomenon or outward appearance, all that we call thing or matter, is but as it were a language by which the invisible (that which is not the object of our senses) communicates its existence to our finite beings . . . Aristotle, on the contrary, affirmed that all our knowledge had begun in experience, had begun through the senses, and that from the senses only we could take our notions of reality . . . It was the first way in which, plainly and distinctly, two opposite systems were placed before the mind of the world.[15]*

---

* Coleridge (perhaps thinking of Goethe) would later sum this up in a famous formula. "Every man is born an Aristotelian, or a Platonist . . . They are the two classes of men, besides which it is next to impossible to conceive a third." (July 1830, *Table Talk*, II, pp.111–12.) Charles Lamb was so delighted with this suggestion that he parodied it in a brilliant *Elia* essay, "Two Classes of Men", those who borrowed books or money and those who lent them; while F. D. Maurice added that "all little children were Platonists", but sadly "grew up" to be Aristotelians. Later Matthew Arnold used the idea to divide the world between enlightened Hellenists and barbarian Philistines (*Culture and Anarchy*, 1869, which owes much else to Coleridge's idea of education); and later still W. S. Gilbert sang that "every boy and every gal,/ That's born

3

From mid-March both *The Times* and the *Courier* were dramatically announcing in headline type that "MR COLERIDGE WILL DELIVER HIS LAST ADDRESS AS A PUBLIC LECTURER" on the 29th of the month. To his Notebooks Coleridge confided: "O pray Heaven, that it may indeed be the Last", and added in Latin: "May this not be an omen of another death to follow: as for the first, it will be enough if only after death there is peace."[16]

The Crown and Anchor was crowded with Highgate friends, as well as the young men of the city like Allsop, Abernethy's medical students from Guy's Hospital, and painters from the Academy. He summarized the course, and brought back his theme to "the two great domains" of Plato and Aristotle.[17] But then he climbed towards the horizon, to the meeting-place of philosophy and religion, and the paramount need for self-knowledge.

He had praised the new spirit of science, and argued that it was not incompatible with the higher Reason of religion. But he urged his listeners to reject the philosophy of materialism, the reductive and mechanistic thinking that had arisen in France, "with the loss of the life and the spirit of Nature".[18] The great spirits of Europe (he named the Italian Cosimo de' Medici, the Dutchman Erasmus, the German Luther, the Englishman Sir Philip Sidney) had always "delighted in the study of human nature", had "loved metaphysics" and instinctively turned to philosophy. "We are peculiarly called upon to this study. Are we, in the unceasing change of all sublunary things, to imagine that the soul . . . is alone in the world, and without a sympathizing feeling throughout Nature? If self-knowledge prevent this unmeaning blank, is it not a delightful, desirable object?"[19]

The great aim of philosophy, he repeated, was the largeness and generosity of mind that came from self-knowledge. To what particular faith it might bring a man, was not the question. It was the

into the world alive" was either "a little Liberal,/ Or else a little Conservative!" (*Iolanthe*, 1882.) This declension of a seminal concept through several generations, including its shift between serious and comic applications, is a characteristic example of Coleridge's subtle, bifurcating bequest of ideas to posterity. The tradition has been cleverly explored by David Newsome in *Two Classes of Men: Platonism and English Romantic Thought*, 1974. Modern neurological theory now seems to find the same division between the left and right hemispheres of the brain.

rejection of the "little unthinking contemptible self" that mattered, the independent awareness of a greater life. "To have genius is to live in the universal."[20] Coleridge took his bow on a smiling, gentle, English note. Let his listeners go away and read the author who brought philosophy and poetry into "delightful harmony" and reconciled "all the powers of our nature" – William Shakespeare.[21]

4

In the exhausted aftermath of these lectures, while wandering over Hampstead Heath in the first days of spring, Coleridge wrote one of his late sonnets, "To Nature". It dwells half-humorously and half-anxiously on that "life and spirit of Nature" he had been attempting to champion for his listeners in his final address. Perhaps he would be "mocked" for his beliefs (as Hazlitt had mocked him). Perhaps in the emotion of the moment his closing lecture had veered back to the Pantheism of his early philosophy of the Stowey days. If so, with a poignant impulse and a kind of defiance, he accepted this in the privacy of the poem:

> It may indeed be phantasy, when I
> Essay to draw from all created things
> Deep, heartfelt, inward joy that closely clings;
> And trace in leaves and flowers that round me lie
> Lessons of love and earnest piety.
> So let it be; and if the wide world rings
> In mock of this belief, it brings
> Not fear, nor grief, nor vain perplexity.
> So will I build my altar in the fields,
> And the blue sky my fretted dome shall be,
> And the sweet fragrance that the wild flower yields
> Shall be the incense I will yield to Thee,
> Thee only God! and thou shalt not despise
> Even me, the priest of this poor sacrifice.[22]

Coleridge had not thought of himself as Nature's "priest" for twenty years. But now, as age closed prematurely around him, the need for religious affirmation and comfort increasingly filled his innermost thoughts.

5

But so too did the needs of the younger generation. This spring he wrote a long letter of advice to Allsop on the question of marriage. How far should love overcome "prudential" motives? Many memories of his own unhappy marriage shadowed his thoughtful reply – above all to avoid "the wretchedness of having your heart *starved* by selfishness and frost-bitten by moral frigidity!" There was much emphasis on the duties and sympathies of a prospective wife.[23] But a young man must not mistake "the sexual impulse" for enduring love – "what are called Love-matches are so proverbially unhappy". He remarked that his own daughter, Sara, with "her Beauty, winning manners, and attractive gentleness", was sure to have many young men "*fall in Love* (as the striplings phrase it)" with her in mere "intoxication of mind".[24]

Yet true love was the goal of marriage and was achievable, and again and again Coleridge urged both parties to look into themselves and ask, "do I *really* love?" His final advice, born of experience, was both tender and curiously down-to-earth. "We must not expect Angels . . . If the one pouts, the other must kiss, & both make it up."[25]*

Many young people would come to Coleridge for this kind of advice at Highgate, not least the members of Gillman's own growing family. There formed around him a circle of substitute sons, many of whom he could counsel better than his own. Yet he tried hard with Hartley and Derwent too. University plans and reading lists

---

* Coleridge continued to philosophize about love until the end of his life. In a Notebook of 1829, he can be found speculating on the way each gender contains elements of the opposite sex, in a way very close to Carl Jung's theory of Animus and Anima (see *Man and his Symbols*, 1964). "In the best and greatest of men, most eminently . . . there is a feminine ingredient. – There is the *Woman* in the Man – though not *perhaps* the Man in the Woman – Adam *therefore* loved Eve – and it is the Feminine in us even now, that makes every Adam love his Eve, and crave for an Eve. – Why, I have inserted the dubious 'perhaps' – why, it should be less accordant with truth to say, that in every good Woman there is the man as an Under-song, than to say that in every true and manly Man there is a translucent Under-tint of the Woman – would furnish matter for a very interesting little Essay on sexual Psychology." (See Heather Jackson, "Coleridge's Women", in *Studies in Romanticism*, No.32, 1993.) The whole subject of dissolving sexual identities (and once again, Wordsworth's fear of those Coleridgean "monsters") is explored with sensational gusto ("his dream poems are an alchemic bath of swirling Dionysian liquidity") by Camille Paglia, "The Daemon and Lesbian Vampire: Coleridge", in *Sexual Personae*, 1991.

went out to Derwent, from his "loving father". When in April Coleridge learned that Hartley had been elected a Probationary Fellow of Oriel College, Oxford, he was overflowing in his praise.

The news delighted him more than any family event since leaving Keswick. He was bursting with "Fatherly Pride", wrote round to his friends, and unblushingly circulated the examiners' opinion that Hartley was palpably superior to all other candidates, with a "display of original Talent, and self-formed Views". Any anxiety about Hartley's increasing drinking and eccentricity were temporarily swept away. His absentee fatherhood had, in the end it seemed, been justified.

At Ambleside Hartley's old schoolmaster, Mr Dawes, declared a public holiday and there were cheering and huzzas for Coleridge's son. The child of "Frost at Midnight" had proved their finest alumnus. Hartley himself would never forget this time of triumph, or how for one moment he had lived out his father's poetic prophecy. He hurried back from a holiday in the Isle of Wight to celebrate at Highgate.

6

Another gifted young man crossed Coleridge's path in April 1819. John Keats was back from his Scottish tour reading Dante, and was beginning to write "Hyperion". He was also deeply depressed from the terrible experience of nursing his brother Tom, who had died from tuberculosis at Well Walk, Hampstead, the previous December. Keats was himself suffering from the first symptoms of the disease – a persistent sore throat and cough – and was profoundly uncertain of his future or the direction of his poetry. "My passions are all asleep," he wrote at the end of March. "Neither Poetry, nor Ambition, nor Love have any alertness of countenance as they pass by me: they seem rather like three figures on a Greek vase . . ."[26]

In this dreamy, suspended state of mind, Keats took a lonely Sunday afternoon walk across the Heath on 11 April, pulling on an old coat and scarf to protect his throat, crossing over Parliament Hill and cutting across Highgate Ponds till he reached Millfield Lane where it begins to climb towards Highgate Village. This, as it happened, was Coleridge's "favourite Walk",[27] and down the hill by happy chance came the familiar white-haired figure deep in conversation with J. H. Green. Coleridge did not recognize Keats, but Green, having taught him at Guy's Hospital, did so, and kindly made the introductions.

What Coleridge remembered was not the meeting but the parting. "A loose, slack, not well-dressed youth met Mr Green and myself in a lane near Highgate. Green knew him, and spoke. It was Keats. He was introduced to me, and staid a minute or so. After he had left us a little way, he came back and said: 'Let me carry away the memory, Coleridge, of having pressed your hand!' – 'There is death in that hand,' I said to Green when Keats was gone; yet this was, I believe, before the consumption showed itself distinctly."[28]

What Keats remembered was Coleridge's talk. Coleridge's "minute or so" obviously lasted more like an hour, which Keats recalled with great relish and obvious amusement. He described the miniature lecture, in a famous letter to his brother George in America, just four days after.

> In the lane that winds by the side of Lord Mansfield's park I met Mr Green our Demonstrator at Guy's in conversation with Coleridge. – I joined them, after enquiring by a look whether it would be agreeable. – I walked with him at his alderman-after dinner pace for near two miles I suppose. In these two miles he broached a thousand things. – let me see if I can give you a list. – Nightingales, Poetry – on Poetical sensation – Metaphysics – Different genera and species of Dreams – Nightmare – a dream accompanied by a sense of Touch – single and double Touch – A dream related – First and Second Consciousness – the difference explained between Will and Volition – so many metaphysicians from a want of smoking the second Consciousness – Monsters – the Kraken – Mermaids – Southey believes in them – Southey's belief too much diluted – A Ghost Story – Good morning. – I heard his voice as he came towards me – I heard it as he moved away – I heard it all the interval – if it may be called so. He was civil enough to ask me to call on him at Highgate. Goodnight![29]

Keats never took up that invitation to visit Highgate (though he wrote a comic verse about Coleridge's hypnotic drone in his ear). But perhaps it was because he was too busy. The impact of meeting Coleridge, as with young Hazlitt long ago in the spring of 1798, seems to have galvanized him into life. A few nights later he had an experience curiously resembling Coleridge's with "Kubla Khan". He took opium (for his throat) while reading a book, the description of the lovers Paolo and Francesca, from Dante's *Inferno*. He fell asleep and had an extraordinary dream. "The dream was one of the most delightful enjoyments I ever had in my life – I floated about the whirling atmosphere, as it is described, with a beautiful figure to whose lips mine were joined as it seemed for an age . . ."[30]

The first result was a haunting sonnet, his first for months, "A Dream", which ended: "Pale were the lips I kiss'd and fair the form/ I floated with about that melancholy storm."[31]

Almost immediately after, he composed "La Belle Dame sans Merci", which appears four pages later in his letter to George, dated 21 April. This was his vision of the mysterious "knight-at-arms", wandering about the bleak heathland, "alone and palely loitering". Its ballad form and demon-lover theme are also clearly influenced by Coleridge's poem "Love" which he had read in *Sibylline Leaves*: the tale of the "bold and lovely Knight" who is "crazed" and driven to death by a "beautiful" Fiend:

> There came and looked him in the face
> An angel beautiful and bright;
> And that he knew it was a Fiend,
> This miserable Knight![32]

In May and June Keats went on to write his great odes, which have many half-conscious echoes of Coleridge's Stowey poems. Indeed both poets, in curious synchronicity, were listening to the nightingales around Hampstead Heath. Coleridge ironically complained that they were as numerous and "incessant with song" as frogs that May, and combined with indigestion to keep him awake. "Ah! (I groaned forth a few nights ago, when qualmy and twitchy from the effects of an Aperient) Ah! Philomel! Ill do thy strains accord with those of Calomel!"[33] But Keats sat out under a tree, and composed his "Ode to a Nightingale".

7

Did Coleridge really feel "death" in Keats's hand in 1819? Or was this an example of Highgate myth-making? Years later he told exactly the same story about another young man, Adam Steinmetz, who died from consumption in August 1832. "After he had shaken hands with me on leaving us, I have turned round with a tear on my cheek, and whispered to Mrs Gillman – Alas! there is *Death* in that dear hand!"[34] In fact the two reminiscences date from exactly the same time, August 1832. So the Keats' story seems retrospectively inspired by Steinmetz's death, rather than an act of prophesy at the time.

Yet Coleridge was extraordinarily responsive to gifted young people, and his preternatural sensitivity to Keats's state may have been perfectly genuine. Two years earlier, long before Steinmetz's illness, he told another version of the same story to Hookham Frere in December 1830.

> Poor Keats, I saw him once. Mr Green . . . and I were walking out in these parts, and we were overtaken by a young man of very striking countenance whom Mr Green recognized and shook hands with, mentioning my name; I wish Mr Green had introduced me, for I did not know who it was. He passed on, but in a few moments sprung back and said, "Mr Coleridge, allow me the honour of shaking your hand." I was struck by the energy of his manner, and gave him my hand. He passed on and we stood looking after him, when Mr Green said, "Do you know who that is? That is Keats, the poet." "Heavens," I said, "when I shook him by the hand there was death!" That was about two years before he died.

Frere himself doubted this account, and quizzed Coleridge more closely: "But *what* was it?" – expecting the old man to evade the question. But Coleridge surprisingly insisted. What he felt was not necessarily the physical consumption, the disease itself, but a psychic impression of Keats's anxiety about himself and his threatened future.

> I cannot describe it. There was a heat and dampness in the hand. To say that his death was caused by the Review is absurd, but at the same time it is impossible adequately to

> conceive the effect which it must have had on his mind. It is all very well for those who have a place in the world and are independent to talk of these things, they can bear such a blow, so can those who have a strong religious principle. But all men are not born Philosophers, and all men have not those advantages of birth and education. Poor Keats had not, and it is impossible as I say to conceive the effect which such a Review must have had upon him, knowing as he did that he had his own way to make in the world by his own exertions, and conscious of the genius within him.[35]

Coleridge's sympathy evidently reflects his own experience of devastating criticism from *Blackwood's* and the *Edinburgh Review*. Coleridge also told Frere that he had read two sonnets of Keats's, and "a poem with a classical name" – "Hyperion." So he may have been strangely struck by the lines at the end of the opening verse stanza, "When this warm scribe my hand is in the grave".[36]

He thought increasingly of Keats in his final years, and one of the many young men who visited him from Cambridge remembered him reading aloud, "with keen delight", the whole of "St Agnes Eve" one winter evening at Highgate. The listener was Tennyson's friend, Arthur Hallam.[37] When in 1829 the Paris publisher Galignani produced a pirated anthology of three English poets, Coleridge was moved to discover that his work had been chosen alongside that of Keats and Shelley.[38] He had become one of the young English poets again, and Keats had paid the long-delayed visit to Highgate after all.

8

Coleridge had now been settled at Moreton House for three years, a period of stability at one address longer than any time since his departure from Greta Hall in 1803. His sense that his life was coming under control, that his family flourished, that he was surrounded by friends and a growing circle of admirers, seemed assured. But he was now destined to receive a series of bitter shocks that once again shook him to the foundations.

They began in the summer of 1819. Economic conditions throughout England had continued their post-war decline, and the hardships of the factory workers (which he had written about so eloquently) now spread inexorably to small business owners and retailers. More and more bankruptcies were declared, and two of these touched him closely. In April, *Blackwood's Magazine*, which had started carrying monthly listings of business failures, announced that the publisher Rest Fenner was among them. Initially Coleridge was not much alarmed, and saw it as an opportunity to open negotiations with a more sympathetic house, Taylor and Hessey, the publisher of Cary and Keats.[39] But he was desperately concerned when, in May, his old friend and erstwhile amanuensis John Morgan also went bankrupt for the second time.

Morgan suffered a dangerous stroke, and Coleridge hurried down to their house in Camberwell. He was frightened by Morgan's state, which was partly paralysed, but tried to convince everyone that it would improve. Then, quite unexpectedly, something Mary Morgan said – some reproach or reference to the opium scenes at Ashley and Bath – plunged him back into a series of nightmare memories about his own chaotic past.

His Notebooks record two profoundly unsettling dreams. The first was the haunting memory of his struggles with Wordsworth over Asra, and the terrible Saturday at Coleorton in 1807, when he had believed he had seen them in bed together, "Wordsworth and SH, mammia pulcherrima aperta" (in Greek transcription), Asra with her most beautiful breasts displayed.[40] But the second dream, on the following night, released an even more terrifying series of guilts and regrets.

He believed the Morgans had come to hate him, were murderously jealous of his life at Highgate, and would destroy him with revelations about his behaviour under opium. "I have this morning had a fearful dream in which I saw Mrs Morgan, threatening to publish all my letters to them, shewing how grateful I felt myself – and to abuse these over-flying feelings of Gratitude to give confirmation to their scandalous Lies. – Then poor J. J. Morgan himself, frightfully distorted with Palsy, attempting with shaking and tottering limbs to assassinate me, first with a pen knife and then with a Razor."[41]

The odd congruity of the two dreams suggests that Coleridge's night-fears of scandal and revenge included revelations of his sexual feelings for Charlotte, which the Morgans had countenanced, and which his letters of that troubled time had indeed exposed. The past had not been laid to rest, even at Highgate.

Morgan declined towards a tragically premature death. When in November he had a second, more severe stroke, depriving him of speech and movement in his right side, Mary Morgan's first instinct was to rush up to Highgate in a carriage to see Coleridge. He at once returned with her to Camberwell, organized doctors, and remained by Morgan's bedside with her and Charlotte for several days. He wrote bulletins to their friends, trying to be optimistic, "eager to *hope*", while realizing there was in reality no possibility of recovery.[42]

He spoke warmly of his "honoured Friend", and praised the selflessness and practical energy of the man to whom he owed so much. "Whatever Mr Morgan undertook to do, he always did it as if his Life was in it – tho' for the advantage of others: because he believed *that* was what has been ever dearer to him than Life . . ."[43] After John Morgan's death that winter, Mary and Charlotte continued to visit Coleridge, and several times asked for financial help which he always somehow managed to supply even as late as 1829. In that year he received an advance of £30 on a new edition of his poems, and immediately sent them £20 of it, a typical gesture of his gratitude.

Yet these night-hauntings also suggested a submerged world of guilts, fears and frustrated longings, that never entirely left him at Highgate. If the outward man appeared more solid, more tranquil, more genial than ever before – the familiar white-haired figure, so kindly and so talkative, ensconced in his Highgate study or perambulating over the margins of Hampstead Heath – the inner man remained anxious, unstable, self-questioning, even at times furtive and childlike. It found expression not only in his dreams, but also in a renewed recourse to illicit opium-taking, and the sudden welling-up of his late poetry, so much of it concerned with themes of self-doubt, depression or incipient despair.

Now in his old age – or what he felt as such, recording on his forty-eighth birthday in October 1820, "in *Life*, if not in years I am, alas! nearer to 68" – any incident or setback could throw him back upon this second, trembling, inner self.[44] He would describe it, with great feeling and psychological acuity, in letters to a few chosen intimates, all of them from the younger generation, like Thomas Allsop, whom he felt understood him and appreciated him better than his contemporaries. He would also find Ann Gillman becoming his greatest confidante, and the last really close emotional attachment of his life. It would be to her that much of his late poetry was directed.

Being Coleridge, he also philosophized about it, pushing through a characteristic form of psychological self-analysis towards some kind of religious consolation. In the midst of a complex series of "Chemico-Philosophical" notes made with Green, touching on the dialectical constructions of the German *Naturphilosophien* and ideas of biological evolution, he suddenly broke off to examine his own spiritual state.[45]

He began, as in much of the poetry, with a recognition of bleakness and a stretching inner wasteland. "In Youth, our Happiness is Hope: in Age, The Recollection of the Hopes of Youth. What else can there be? For the substantial Mind, for the I, what else can there be? Pleasure? Fruition? . . . It is the *Death* of the I – a neutral Product results that may exist for another, but no longer for itself – a Coke or Slag."

From this bleak truth, that sense of alienation from the young productive self which is such a common experience of age, Coleridge sought a philosophy of reclamation and redemption through rediscovering the self in others. His terms are highly compressed and Kantian; the subject must be rediscovered in the object, but the moral or human meaning is simple and even traditional. We can redeem the self in age by loving the other, whether it is a domestic pet, a human friend or God himself in the sacramental. "To make the Object one with us, we must become one with the Object – ergo, *an* Object. Ergo the object must be itself a Subject – partially, a favourite dog – principally, a friend; wholly, *God* – the *Friend*. God is Love – i.e. an Object that is absolutely Subject – (God is a Spirit) but a Subject that for ever condescends to become *Object* for those that meet Him subjectively – Eucharist."[46] Such meditations would feed into his poetry and find public expression in his last important book, the *Aids to Reflection*.

9

While he worked away with Green, he was consoled with other fruits, the first crop of cherries and strawberries from Mrs Green's garden at St Lawrence.[47] But the world continued to press in upon

Coleridge. By July 1819 it had become clear that the Rest Fenner bankruptcy would affect him disastrously. There had been irregularities in the accounting of his book-sales, large royalties had been due but not paid, and all his copyrights had fallen into the control of Fenner's creditors. Both the *Biographia* and the *Sibylline Leaves* had, unknown to him, effectively sold out – a cause for great satisfaction, except that none of the earnings had ever been made over to him. Five hundred copies of the *Friend* (out of the edition of 750) were also held against Fenner's debts, with the prospect of being pulped. No royalties had been paid on the *Lay Sermons* or *Zapolya*, and Fenner's last financial life-raft, the part-work *Encyclopaedia* which had been largely sold on the strength of Coleridge's Introduction, had sunk without trace.[48]

The full implications of all this did not emerge until the autumn of 1819. But it was, in financial terms, the greatest professional blow of Coleridge's life. With the exception of Murray's "Christabel" volume, Coleridge had lost the earnings and copyright on everything he had published since his return to London in 1816. Fenner's bankruptcy put this beyond any hope of legal redress.

The final position at the end of 1819 was that Coleridge had used all his small reserves from the Crown and Anchor lectures (intended for Derwent) to buy back his copyrights. He had also lost royalties initially calculated at £1,000, but finally thought to be nearer £1,200. All he effectively retained was the right to republish his poems if a new publisher could ever be found; and of this there was no immediate prospect. All the years of accumulated work he had counted on to fund his children, and support himself at Highgate, had come to nothing.[49]

When he wrote to his friends of this bitter news, he tried to be philosophical and even light-hearted. "You have perhaps heard, that my Publisher is a bankrupt", he told Allsop, "and his Bankruptcy has disclosed a scene of fraud on the part of the *Reverend* Thomas Curtis (nb. *by virtue of a shilling licence*) and of infatuation on the part of Fenner . . . Well! I am now *sole proprietor* . . . This is rather hard – but perhaps my Comet may some time or other have its perihelion of popularity and then the *Tail*, you know, whisks round to the other end and for 0000I, low and behold, I0000."[50] But this was little short of bravado.

The Gillmans, who were themselves implicated in the disaster, immediately recognized the depth of the crisis, both in its practical implications and its effect on Coleridge's self-belief. They responded in the simplest and kindest way possible. They swept Coleridge off for another long holiday by the sea.

10

This time they went to Ramsgate, an expanding new resort on the north Kent coast. Originally a fishing village under the chalk cliffs of the North Foreland, it had flourished during the war, and sprouted new terraces with patriotic names – Nelson, Wellington, Albion. Its harbour and pier were rebuilt, bathing-machines were introduced, and a visit by George IV and his mistress in 1821 was commemorated by a Theban obelisk which became known locally as "the Royal Toothpick". Already the place was fashionable – the Prime Minister Lord Liverpool had a villa there – but still relatively inexpensive. It could be reached in a few hours, either by the mail coach through Rochester, or by a new steamer service that plied from St Katherine's Docks in the City, and down through the Thames estuary without having to wait upon the tides.

They found lodgings at the very top of the East Cliff, in the newly completed Wellington Crescent (1818), commanding from its charming ironwork balconies a superb view of the North Sea and Goodwin Sands (where ships were regularly wrecked). A crooked flight of ancient fishermen's steps, Kent Place, led down to the beach and harbour. Here they remained until the end of August, with Gillman commuting back in the mid-week to look after his practice. The arrangement worked so well that the visit to Ramsgate, at various addresses on the East Cliff, and with various combinations of friends, became an annual fixture for the rest of his life.

A new intimacy and confidence grew between Coleridge and Ann Gillman. The first lines of "The Garden of Boccaccio" (later dedicated to her) appeared in his Notebooks, set off by the sight of a "Child collecting shells and pebbles on the Sea shore". The child's "fresh shout of Delight and Admiration" with each new shape, carried proudly to its mother and then carelessly flung back on to the sand, was a type of "our first discoveries both in Science and Philosophy".[51]

At Ramsgate, Coleridge found that he could himself revert to the condition of a child on the beach. Each morning he set out alone to a secret cave he had found a mile and a quarter away along the East Cliff. This was at Dumpton Gap (a supposed lair of eighteenth-century smugglers), reached by a sunken lane cut steeply down through the chalk rocks to the shore-line. "Exactly a hundred of my Strides from the end of the Lane there is a good roomy arched Cavern, with an Oven or cupboard in it where one's clothes may be put free from the sand." Here he stripped off and had "a glorious tumble in the waves".[52]

His anxieties slipped away with his clothes, and his memories went back to other shores: the plunges from the sunlit rocks at Malta, the freezing swims when he was visiting Asra near Scarborough, the schoolboy bathing in the New River, the childhood paddles in the river Otter near the Pixies Parlour Cave. Only when he dressed again, and made his way back through "the deep crumbly Sands" beneath the East Cliff, did he feel the "wearisome Travail" of the walk home, his dragging legs reminding him that he was no longer young.*

The feeling would prompt his beautiful poem "Youth and Age", completed at Ramsgate two years later:

> When I was young? – Ah, woful When!
> Ah! for the change 'twixt Now and Then!
> This breathing house not built with hands,
> This body that does me grievous wrong,
> O'er aery cliffs and glittering sands,
> How lightly then it flashed along: –
> Like those trim skiffs, unknown of yore,
> On winding lakes and rivers wide,
> That ask no aid of sail or oar,
> That fear no spite of wind or tide!
> Nought cared this body for wind or weather
> When Youth and I lived in't together.[53]

---

* One such cavern still exists at Dumpton Gap, exactly as Coleridge describes, the white chalk walls stained pantomime green with seaweed, like a decorated gothic niche for a baroque Triton. When I hunched there, one freezing afternoon in late spring, exactly ten years after crawling into Coleridge's childhood cave at Ottery (see *Early Visions*, p. 12) I knew that one version of Coleridge's story certainly ended here – the child and the old man perfectly reconciled in a Platonic cave of visions and memories. But then the cold North Sea flooded in, with its thousand inflexions and crying seagulls, and drove us on to a different conclusion. (See Leon Edel, "Narratives", in *Writing Lives: Principia Biographica*, 1984.)

11

Coleridge pursued negotiations with several publishers – *Blackwood's Magazine*, John Murray, Taylor and Hessey – which went on into the autumn, but without result. By the time he was back at Highgate, his friends had taken stock of his financial situation and, one by one, they discreetly came to his aid. Not all the details of their generosity are known; some did not emerge until after Coleridge's death and others may never be known. The Gillmans simply waived their lodging charges, and there is no evidence that they were ever resumed in full. Thomas Allsop sent a gift of £100 in October, which reduced Coleridge to tears. "Why should I be ashamed to say this –? For such tears and such only will be shed at the threshold of the Gate, within which all tears will be wiped away."[54]

Green quietly confirmed that he would continue to pay Coleridge's annual life assurance premium. John Hookam Frere took over the fund to send Derwent to Cambridge in 1820, as Coleridge had promised, contributing at least £300.[55] Daniel Stuart, his old editor, began the custom of sending Coleridge each summer £20 or £30 to pay for his Ramsgate holiday, and this arrangement never lapsed. It is likely that Charles Aders, and C. A. Tulk, both wealthy men, also quietly helped him with birthday or Christmas gifts.

So Coleridge never achieved the professional independence strived for and dreamed of for a lifetime, but finally snatched from him by the Rest Fenner disaster of 1819. There would also be further financial crises in connection with his children, especially Hartley; and he never forgot that at Greta Hall he was looked on as a father who had never managed to provide properly for his family. When in August 1821 Thomas De Quincey quite unexpectedly applied for the return of the £300 donated at Bristol in 1807, Coleridge replied with a long and grim recital of his financial disasters since 1816, and refused him.

But in so doing, he also revealed the astonishing generosity of the Gillmans. "I declare solemnly, that I must have wanted the necessities of Life, but for the almost unprecedented friendship of Mr and Mrs Gillman, under whose roof I live. Tho' the nominal sum, which I am engaged to contribute towards the expenses of the House, is barely adequate to the first-cost of my actual maintenance – and tho' medicine, & medical attendance are not put down at all – yet so many sums have been paid by Mr G. on my account – that at this moment I stand indebted to him for £500 . . ." There is every reason to believe this sum simply mounted over the remaining years.

But Coleridge in turn gave something to the Gillmans and their household that was equally valued, if less tangible. His presence certainly boosted Gillman's medical reputation throughout North London, and Coleridge began to make humorous references to this.[56] But he also became an irreplaceable family confidanté and advisor, trusted and greatly liked by the Gillman boys as they grew up, and bringing an emotional warmth to Ann Gillman's life that her busy husband did not always have time to provide. By 1824 Ann Gillman could write confidentially to Coleridge, after a brief misunderstanding, "indeed I feel for you as *formerly*, and know not how to bear up against the fear, even, of losing you".[57]

12

In October 1819 *Blackwood's Magazine*, which had carried the devastating attack on the *Biographia* three years previously, recanted in the handsomest manner possible. The youngest member of their editorial board, the 25-year-old J. G. Lockhart – the future son-in-law and biographer of Walter Scott – wrote a 7,000-word essay of brilliant appreciation, expressing the judgement of the new generation in the broadest terms. "The reading public of England (speaking largely) have not understood Mr Coleridge's poems as they should have done." No English poet "since the age of Elizabeth" had used language with such a delicate sense of beauty and "with so much exquisite subtlety of metaphysical perception".

Lockhart analysed the "Ancient Mariner" at length, and also praised "Christabel": "he is the prince of superstitious Poets". He remarked too on the "wonderful translation, or rather improvement of the *Wallenstein*". He characterized all his work as "poetry of the senses *strung* to the imagination", a fine image of Coleridge's stretching and tuning of the ballad line. What Coleridge evoked best was "a romantic and spiritual movement of wonder".

Lockhart made no mention of the prose, and turned some gentle asides about "indolence". He also shrewdly questioned Coleridge's presentation of himself as a poet of pure and instinctive inspiration, rather than as a master craftsman of refinement and revision. "In many respects Mr Coleridge seems too anxious to enjoy the advantages of an inspired writer, and to produce his poetry at once in its perfect form, like the palaces which spring out of the desert in complete splendour at a single rubbing of the lamp in the Arabian Tale."

But the article championed Coleridge as a poet virtually without reservation, and clearly prophesied what Victorian readers would draw from him. "In his mixture of all the awful and all the gentle graces of conception, in his sway of wild, solitary, dreamy phantasies, in his music of words and magic of numbers, we think he stands absolutely alone among all the poets of the most poetical age."[58]

Coleridge never forgot this fanfare, which heralded a new era of critical assessment. He tangled with *Blackwood's* subsequently, when articles and letters of his own were mischievously mishandled, and was shocked when Lockhart – still very much the young Turk – involved another critic in a duel with pistols in 1821. Yet Lockhart remained one of his earliest acknowledged champions. They eventually met and became friends at Ramsgate, and Coleridge sent teasing letters and poems to Lockhart's young wife. He played out his role as the poet of "Kubla Khan", ending one poetic fragment: "*Meant* to have been finished, but *somebody* came *in*, or some*thing fell* out – & tomorrow – alas! Tomorrow!"[59]

13

Coleridge might have been poised on an Indian summer of writing in 1820. But this was delayed for another two years – and perhaps forever – by an altogether different kind of collapse, far closer to home and far closer to his heart. As he told Thomas Allsop, "a heavy, a very heavy Affliction came upon me, with all the aggravations of surprise – sudden as a Peal of Thunder from a cloudless Sky."[60]

One of the great benefits of Coleridge's life at Highgate was the growing sense of closeness to his sons, and the feeling that he was at last helping to launch their careers. Hartley visited every vacation from Oriel, and joined in his philosophic work. Coleridge had suggested he compose a dissertation on Greek mythology, and father and son exchanged learned disquisitions on the subject. Hartley intended to publish a prose translation of Aeschylus, and "begin with Prometheus, which will serve as a sort of text, for some observations on the sacerdotal religion of Greece, and on the sources and spirit of mythology." This he planned to submit for the Oxford Prize Essay in the autumn of 1820. All this was music to his father's ears.[61]

Derwent was now preparing for Cambridge, and in April 1820 it was agreed that he too should join his father at Highgate. He was rapturously excited at the prospect. The sense of family optimism even caught up Mrs Coleridge, who had written cheerfully to Tom Poole that winter of both boys. Hartley was "most sanguine in his hopes of success in tutorship" at Oriel; and thought "his fellowship and exertions" would help Derwent both intellectually and financially. As for Derwent, Poole should see "the flush of hope & joy" that spread over his face at the idea of seeing his father again. "C. will be quite overpowered, and the boy too, I conjecture, at their meeting." Derwent was now nineteen and had not seen Coleridge for eight years. Hartley was twenty-three, "some days older than his father was on the day of our marriage. I think H. is as eccentric as his father *to the full*." Mrs Coleridge added wistfully, "May he be happier!"[62]

The April vacation was a great success, and the Gillmans paid for all the young men's expenses. Derwent was awarded an Exhibition at St John's College, Cambridge. Father and sons ambled round Highgate, an instantly recognizable threesome: Coleridge stately, smiling, white-haired; Hartley small and darting, with his strange black "turkish" beard and mercurial laughter; Derwent plump and good-natured, with the round, innocent Coleridge face, happy to listen and enjoy whatever company he was in. They were tenderly introduced to Coleridge's friends: Allsop, Hookham Frere, and a new neighbour, the comic actor Charles Mathews.

Coleridge was immensely proud of his two sons, delighted with their "affectionate attachment" to each other, and their "boyish high spirits with manly independence of intellect". He loved the lively contrast of their characters ("for no two can be more distinct") and the way they bounced off each other in conversation. They were like two footballers passing a ball, who "shoot & play" across a common ground. He only wished the seventeen-year -old Sara could complete the group – "the cup of paternal Joy would be full to the Brim". Ann Gillman was particularly struck by the "rapture" with which the two brothers talked of their sister.[63]

Gillman was still a little anxious at Hartley's evident eccentricity of appearance and manner: unreliable at mealtimes and sometimes inclined to drink too much wine. But this did not prevent him keeping open house for the boys. In May, Robert Burton, a double first and like Hartley a junior fellow (at Exeter College), came to stay. Young ladies from Highgate – Miss Chisholm, Miss Kelley (an actress relation of the Mathews') – were invited to tea. The Coleridge cousins, William Hart Coleridge, and John Taylor Coleridge, dropped in.[64] Coleridge senior (he began to feel like that) basked in a benign glow of paterfamilial satisfaction.

In this happy mood, Coleridge planned a light work of summer fiction. It would draw on the French romances of D'Urfé and the German "Faery Work" of Tieck. The title alone inspired him, as he told Allsop: "The Weather-Bound Travellers: or, Histories, Lays, Legends, Incidents, Anecdotes and Remarks contributed during a detention in one of the Hebrides". He mused: "in whatever laid firm hold of us in early Life there lurks an interest and a charm for our maturest years . . ." Perhaps his philosophy could finally be expressed in fairy tales, legends and children's stories. His anthology would create an enchanted solitude, and he imagined his reader "by the parlour Fireside of a rustic Inn, with the Fire & the Candle for his only Companions". He would "remove the *childish*, yet leave the *childlike* untouched".[65]

14

All this was shattered at the end of June 1820. News arrived at Highgate that Hartley Coleridge was not to have his Fellowship renewed, and that Edward Copleston, the Provost of Oriel, was dismissing him for drunkenness, irregular behaviour, and keeping low company. This was the "peal of Thunder" which burst upon Coleridge, and whose rumblings were really to continue for the remainder of his life.

It was not mere academic failure. Coleridge could have coped with this, better than most fathers, given his own experience at Cambridge. It was the social stigma of "intemperance", so chillingly close to his own reputation for opium addiction. But far worse than either of these, it was the cause of an ever-deepening emotional rift between a father and his favourite son. Both of them tried very hard to heal it, but within two years it was permanent, and the tragic consequences continued until Hartley's own premature death in 1849. It also had its effects on Derwent (though he remained devoted to his increasingly wayward elder brother), and the happy family circle of spring 1820 was never re-established. It became what Coleridge was to call in 1822 one of "the four grasping and griping Sorrows" of his entire life.

The events unfolded with a kind of fatality. The original news was not broken by Hartley himself, but came in a sombre letter from John Taylor Coleridge (who maintained his Oxford connections after beginning his career as a distinguished lawyer on the Western Circuit). He wrote confidentially to Gillman on 29 June 1820. "The charges against [Hartley] are very painful ones to repeat . . . they are 'sottishness, a love of low company, and generally inattention to college rules. Coupled with this I am informed . . . that he has contracted an attachment for a young person, the daughter I think of an architect . . . It is a case of a most afflicting nature; what to advise in it I really do not know."

It then emerged that Hartley had completely disappeared. When Derwent was despatched by Coleridge to Oxford, there were wild rumours that he had gone to Liverpool looking for a ship to America. It immediately struck Coleridge that poor Hartley was doomed to live out his own early misadventures at Cambridge. His agonized letters – sent posting after Derwent – are full of this foreboding. "I have this moment received your heart-wringing intelligence . . . the same Dread struck at once on Mr G's mind and on mine – that [Hartley] is wandering on some wild scheme, in no dissimilar mood or chaos of thoughts and feelings to that which possessed his unhappy father at an earlier age during the month that ended in the Army-freak – & that he may even be scheming to take passage from Liverpool to America."[66]

Initially, Coleridge expressed very little blame towards his son's conduct, and instinctively took Hartley's part against the Oriel dons. What weakness he did suspect, he immediately transferred to his own shortcomings as a father. "Woe is me! – the Root of all Hartley's faults is Self-willedness – this was the Sin of his nature, and this has been fostered by culpable indulgence, at least, non-interference on my part . . ."[67] Yet here already was a curious paternal blindness, for it was obvious to all outsiders (such as the

Gillmans) that Hartley's downfall was the result precisely of a *lack* of self-will – expressed by his drinking, his unreliable social behaviour, and his intellectual oddity. It was these traits that he had inherited from his father's character. Coleridge always found this difficult to accept, most of all, perhaps, because it suggested an almost biblical guilt: that the sins of the father, especially in the matter of addiction, should be visited on the son.

What caused Coleridge the most pain was Hartley's refusal to turn immediately to his father for help in such a crisis. He had not even dared to write from Oxford. This humiliated him far more than the academic scandal. The note is repeated pathetically again and again to Derwent: "So surely if Hartley knew or believed that I love him & linger after him as I do & ever have done, he would have come to me . . . Oh! if he knew how much I feel *with* him as well as how much I suffer for him, he could not so forget that he has a most affectionate Friend as well as Father in – S. T. Coleridge."[68]

Derwent himself later recalled he had "never seen any human being, before or since, so deeply afflicted".[69] Ann Gillman told Allsop that Coleridge "was convulsed with agony, though at first he was calm".[70] She took him out for walks on the Heath, and Gillman stood by at night to wake him when he began screaming in his dreams. Coleridge only screamed in the first hours of sleep; after that he only wept, so that when he woke at dawn his pillow was soaking with tears.[71]

His reaction was so extreme that it is clear that he was reliving his own experiences through Hartley. At night he had become again the lost and rejected child. "While I am awake & retain my reasoning powers, the pang is gnawing but I am – except for a fitful moment or two – tranquil. It is the howling Wilderness of Sleep that I dread."[72] This feeling would both propel, and hinder, everything he tried to do for his son subsequently.

In fact Hartley had not gone to Liverpool (or to his mother at Greta Hall), but had gone to ground with friends in Oxford. Derwent found him and persuaded him to return to Highgate by mid-July. He would not remain with his father, but agreed to stay with mutual friends in London, and continue with his Prometheus project. Ironically, the friends who took him in were the Montagus, now living in Bedford Square, and no doubt anxious to succeed better than they had done in the comparable situation of 1810.

Coleridge spent the rest of the year trying to get Hartley reinstated, using every diplomatic channel in his power, and doing much painful soul-searching in the process. He subjected Hartley to a well-meaning, but over-intense and probably humiliating interrogation, forcing him to give not one, but three, written statements of "all his transactions" at Oriel. He also wrote to individual Fellows at the college, and compiled a complete dossier of character witnesses.[73] The ostensible aim of all this was to prepare for a grand personal confrontation with the Provost, Edward Copleston, in October and to seek justice and reinstatement for his son.

All the time the college authorities offered an urbane, Oxford solution. Hartley Coleridge could simply resign, the matter would be smoothed over, and a compensation of £300 would be tendered. Most fathers would have settled for this, and it seems to have been what Hartley secretly wanted.

15

Oxford was not generally renowned for its temperance, or even its scholarship at this period – though reforms were in the wind. Hartley's previous college, Merton, was celebrated for its laxities. But Oriel was a special case: its tone was tea-drinking and austere, its Fellows' Common Room spartan and intellectually formidable, and its membership included John Keble and J. H. Newman (future founders of the Oxford Movement) and Thomas Arnold, soon to become the charismatic headmaster of Rugby school. Hartley had fallen among saints, and they were unsparing in their righteousness.

As Coleridge discovered, it was Keble who had outlined the original charges against Hartley: "habits of such continued irregularity, & frequent sottishness, with all their degrading accompaniments of low company". It was the Dean, Richard Whately, who had advised Hartley to emigrate to Canada, and to seek forgiveness from the "All-Seeing Judge". It was a third Fellow, Edward Hawkins, who informed Hartley that his continued fellowship would be "an indulgence [not] at all consistent with the spirit of our Foundation".[74] All these letters found their way into Coleridge's dossier, together with the bitter intelligence that Southey and Wordsworth had been appraised of the disaster before he had.

Hartley's own statements of "all his transactions" to his father were tortuously detailed: a curious mixture of disarming frankness and agonized dissembling. Indeed they recalled Coleridge's own letters to his elder brother George after his flight from Cambridge nearly thirty years before. He denied absolutely an amorous intrigue with Mary Harris (the architect's daughter), though much later he admitted to Derwent he was passionately in love though (again like his father with Mary Evans) unrequitedly so. He admitted being drunk on at least three occasions, and once alarming his lodging-house keeper that he would set the rooms on fire with his candle. But he was never "frequently drunk".[75]

In the Common Room he claimed that he "measured my expressions by the strictest standards"; though again he afterwards admitted to Derwent that he considered his superiors tyrannical "Bigots", and at least once was induced "to vent my chagrin in certain impotent, but I dare not say forgotten, threats" concerning the overdue reformation of the college system.[76] He agreed he had shown "no little eccentricity", but omitted to mention that one Fellow claimed to have found him lying "dead drunk in the streets".[77] He informed his father that he had given him "a plain statement of *facts*, which may prevent you committing yourself by defending me on untenable points".[78]

Coleridge surveyed the evidence and committed himself absolutely to defending his son. In October he drafted a long letter of point by point refutation, which Hartley copied out and sent to the Provost.[79] He then fixed an interview with Copleston at Oxford for Sunday, 15 October, and sat down to compose his own letter of personal appeal. It caused him immense difficulties, and the extended fragments of at least four drafts have survived, although the final document has disappeared forever in the Oriel archives.

Coleridge had no clear strategy, but his general approach was to appeal to Dr Copleston's better feelings and ask him to take a broad and generous view of the case. He began by emphasizing his immense personal pride in Hartley's original appointment at Oriel, and his respect for the college. His feeling was, that "whatever I am, my Hartley is a Fellow of Oriel! It was & had so long been the prayer of my Heart to see my Sons in that profession, for which I was myself best fitted both by my studies and my inclinations . . ." He added that the terrible news had, by "a cruel kindness" been withheld from him by his friends for several weeks.

Here, for a moment, the poet in him rose up. The news "burst upon me at once and irrevocably like a Squall from a Fogbank in which the secure Mariner had been fancying images of shore and Coastland, all calm and not a sail in reef". But then he crossed this passage out, as too obvious a reference to his own most famous poem.[80]

Next he turned to the question of Hartley's general character. Here he decided to pull rank and drop names, which at Oxford was perhaps a risk worth taking. He cited Sir George and Lady Beaumont, William Wordsworth and Robert Southey (Poet Laureate) as people who had known Hartley intimately from childhood and thought highly of his talents. He also touchingly added Tom Poole, who was now a local magistrate. Sir Walter Scott and the poet Samuel Rogers were also somehow introduced as character witnesses.[81]

Then he gave his own assessment of Hartley. Here was a young man of great gifts but admitted eccentricity, who would "never be the man of the world" that his brother Derwent would become. He moved from "whirling activity" to sudden fits of abstraction. He loved paradox and fantastical talk, but he was essentially honest and almost childlike in manner, of "unregarding Openness". His indulgence in drink was a sort of absentmindedness. He took drink "in the eagerness of conversation", he seized whatever was set before him, "utterly unconscious of what he was doing". This was a trait he had displayed since childhood.

Hartley was certainly not a solitary drinker, nor was he an alcoholic. At Highgate he had left off wine and spirits at table, on his father's advice, without a moment' hesitation. (There was of course table beer, and one glass of wine during dinner, and perhaps one more after it . . . but this showed "more self-command than an entire rejection at all times".) The charge that he had formed "a *habit* of intemperance" was cruel and utterly untrue.[82]

All these explanations have the shadow of Coleridge's own experience of addiction barely concealed behind them. Yet there can be little doubt that Coleridge essentially believed them at the time. Or at least, he suspended disbelief. Yet thus far, Coleridge's letter was one that any father might have written in similar circumstances: loyal, anxious, to some degree self-deluding.

But then he did something unique. He conjured up for the donnish, dusty, bachelor Copleston, a vision of Hartley as the Magic Child. Hartley was the fruit of all his hopes – and of his best poetry. This was the highest risk strategy of all, a naked appeal to the Provost's emotions. It is all the more extraordinary when one recalls (what is easy to forget), that Hartley was now a young man of twenty-four. But for Coleridge he was still, in some essential sense, a boy and even a baby.

Hartley, wrote Coleridge, had always been a free spirit, a creature of the natural world. "From his earliest childhood he had an absence of any contra-distinguished Self, any conscious 'I'." His intellectual brilliance arose from an unselfconscious natural joy, and it was that youthful spirit which the college should foster. "Never can I read De la Motte Fouqué's beautiful Faery Tale . . . of Undina, the Winter-Fay, before she had a Soul, beloved by all whether they would or no, & as indifferent to all, herself included, as a blossom whirling in a May-gale, without having Hartley recalled to me, as he appeared from infancy to his boyhood – never, without reflecting on the prophesy, written by me long before I had either thought or prospect of settling in Cumberland, addressed to him then but a few months old in my Poem, entitled Frost at Midnight –

> Dear Babe! that slumber'st cradled at my side,
> Whose gentle Breathings heard in this deep Calm
> Fill up the interspersed vacancies
> And momentary intervals of Thought –
> My Babe so beautiful! . . ."[83]

It is doubtful if the Provost of Oriel had ever received an appeal like this in the course of his long career.

On Friday, 13 October 1820 Coleridge set off in the Oxford mail to plead for his son in person. Fearing the worst, Gillman insisted that Allsop accompany him. "Of this journey to Oxford," Allsop wrote much later, "I have very painful recollections; perhaps the most painful recollection (one excepted) connected with the memory of Coleridge."[84]

Copleston received him graciously, "talked in a very smooth strain" of Hartley's great talents and acquirements, and did not give an inch. The possibility that Hartley might continue as a non-residential Fellow was held out as a diplomatic offering; but was rejected three days later at the college meeting. Copleston suggested that they meet again in London at the end of the month, but at this second conference, additional evidence of drunkenness was produced and the appeal was closed. Copleston's final gesture was to offer Hartley the compensation of £300 from college funds, but this was unofficial. The verdict of dismissal from Oriel was confirmed. Crushed and humiliated, Coleridge refused the money on his son's behalf. A year later Hartley secretly accepted it, through the intermediary of John Taylor Coleridge.[85]

16

Even now, Coleridge would not accept the accusations against his son. Hartley swore to him on the Bible that they were false.[86] Coleridge insisted that Hartley should write individually to each of the friends who had financed him at Oxford – the Beaumonts, Tom Poole, and Edward Coleridge – enclosing copies of the dossier in his defence which he had compiled. He also wrote to the warden of his old college, Merton.[87]

With many misgivings, Coleridge then allowed Hartley to settle with the Montagus, and spend the next year trying his hand at journalism. He placed a few small pieces with the *London Magazine* (probably through Lamb's influence), and continued to write poetry; but he was not productive. He frequently disappeared from Bedford Square to spend days with London friends, other journalists or young lawyers, who loved his company and joined him in heavy drinking. He would turn up unannounced at Highgate, throwing Ann Gillman's domestic arrangements into chaos.

Gillman exerted the best influence he could, and Coleridge wrote a long description of finding him and Hartley one evening in the garden, gravely discussing the problem of Hamlet and why everyone identified with him and his intense self-consciousness. Coleridge threw in the suggestion that Hamlet was like a young man flying in a balloon, for whom the world seemed to move around him, disconnected and uncontrolled.[88] Privately he was sick with worry, "with great depression of Spirits, loss of Appetite . . . and a harassing pain in my left knee".[89]

His own work, though continuing with Green on the *Opus Maximum*, was desultory during these months. He abandoned his

"Faery Work" anthology, and began to assemble a dry book on grammar and logic.[90] One of the few cheering events of the winter was an *Elia* essay by Lamb, entitled "Christ's Hospital Five-and-Thirty Years Ago'. In it Lamb drew the touching and famous picture of Coleridge as "the inspired Charity-boy" holding forth on neo-Platonic philosophy in the school cloisters.[91] Lamb recalled how much he had been isolated in London, cut off from parents and friends "far in the west" at Ottery. Coleridge did not forget this as he struggled with his own son.

He remained endlessly indulgent towards "poor Hartley's" irregular life and "procrastination" with work. "Indolence it is not," he told Allsop hopefully, "for he is busy enough in his own way, & rapidly bringing together materials for this future credit, as a man of letters & a poet; but shrinking from all things connected with painful associations, and of that morbid temperament, which I too well understand, that renders what would be motives for men in general, narcotics for him in exact proportion to their strength."[92]

He still held out great hopes for the "Prometheus" poem. By the spring of 1821 he had supplied Hartley with "a small volume almost . . . containing all the materials and comments on the full import of this most pregnant and sublime Mythos". Sometimes he even wanted to write it for Hartley, but reassured Derwent that he restrained his paternal interference. He had "simply brought together such Stuff, as the Poet must have sought for in Books, & therefore could not subtract an atom from his Poetic Originality. I know, that in work of this kind a man must wait for genial hours and cannot *sit* down to it mechanically." Yet he saw the plan becoming too "large and circular", and feared Hartley's enthusiasm for the subject had cooled.[93]

Still he closed his eyes to his son's drinking. But Hartley had become thin and ill, his eyes inflamed in "a woeful condition". When he tottered into Highgate one day in May, the Gillmans simply put him to bed.[94] On the night of 11 June, a pitiful small cart of books, papers and old clothes arrived at the door of Moreton House. The Montagus had thrown Hartley out of Bedford Square, and refused to have anything more to do with him. Again, it was as if the events of 1810 were repeating themselves. It emerged that for several weeks Ann Gillman had been writing to Mrs Montagu, begging her not to execute this threat. Her greatest fear was the effect it would have on Coleridge's health.[95] But of course the Gillmans took him in, along with Derwent, who had just come down from Cambridge for the summer vacation.

Once again, everyone rallied round Hartley. His relations with Derwent were especially close (they communicated through endless bad puns), and the Gillmans paid his bills and showed "parental kindness".[96] Once Hartley had recovered, Coleridge agreed that he could share lodgings with an old school-friend, Robert Jameson, at Gray's Inn Square near Fleet Street, and continue trying his hand at poetry and journalism. Coleridge also seems to have arranged a book contract with Taylor and Hessey.

Hartley's letters to Derwent show he was capable of writing a fine, whimsical prose, rather in the manner of Lamb. He also began to compose the tender, melancholy sonnets on which his literary reputation would eventually rest. Now, if ever, Hartley had a chance to make his own career in London; and this arrangement held together – despite drinking bouts and disappearances – for the next year. He told Derwent he was reasonably happy, but desperate at his inability to attract women: he felt his diminutive size and eccentricity would always prevent him from being taken seriously, and negated the prestige of his name.[97] Nor could he maintain the essential discipline of a freelance writer; to find his own writing routine, and deliver work to a deadline. In the event it took Hartley ten years to complete his first book.

Coleridge was exhausted with coping with Hartley. In July 1821 he told Tom Poole that he longed to "fly to the Sea Shore at Porlock & Lynmouth, making a good Halt at dear ever fondly remembered Stowey".[98] Yet other young people increasingly turned to him for support and advice. Allsop's sister consulted with him about a marriage proposal. ("You must have a *Soul*-mate as well as a House- or Yoke-mate!")[99] Gillman's sons sought help with their schoolwork. Gillman's laboratory assistants, John Watson and Charles Stutfield, came to him about their future careers. They all became what he called his "substitute children", and their numbers would increase as his own sons grew away from him.

It was not easy being a prophet in his own family. When his brother George came up to London that summer, Coleridge was astonished and hurt that he refused to visit him in Highgate, despite invitations and long conciliatory letters.[100] George took fright at Hartley's situation, seeing the recurrence of his young brother's life of "mismanagement", and terrified at being involved once more. George died in 1828, without ever having seen Coleridge again. Coleridge told George's own son that, nevertheless, he had loved George as "Father and Brother in one".[101]

17

All the strains of these disastrous years had another insidious effect. They were driving Coleridge back towards secret opium-taking, outside Gillman's regime. He eventually established a compliant and sympathetic supplier in the chemist at the top of Highgate Hill, T. H. Dunn. From 1821 there are Notebook entries of various disguised medicaments infused with "Tinct. of Opium", including fennel water, nitric ether, and a rather delicious-sounding "syrup of Marshmallow".[102]

By 1824 he had a regular account at Dunn's shop, then situated ten doors down from the present chemists, on the corner with Townshend Yard. While the shop front (now an estate agents) opened directly on to the busy thoroughfare of Highgate Hill, there was a discreet side-door on to the yard with its own bell-pull and gas-lamp. This is where Coleridge came to collect his supplies, perhaps after dark, partly hidden from inquisitive eyes. There can be no doubt that this was, initially, without Gillman's knowledge. His first surviving note to Dunn dates from May 1824, but clearly refers to a well-established account dating back some time, on which a large sum is long overdue. Coleridge had not been able to pay "without imprudent exposures", but promised to pay the "£25 Account" within seven days, and marks his note "Destroy this instantly".[103]

Dunn's young assistant, Seymour Porter, the teenage son of the Independent Minister of Highgate, left a long and sympathetic account of these transactions, after he had retired.[104] Coleridge always called in at the "Back Shop", and brought his own flat half-pint bottle to be filled at the laboratory table rather than at the front counter. A certain "talk, gossip, buzz" grew up about these visits. "So the old gentleman comes still for his dose!" "What does such a good-looking old fellow want with so much physic!" "Can't Gillman give him all the medicine he wants without sending him to you?"

Porter always defended his distinguished old client – "I liked the very sight of him" – and it seems a certain conspiracy grew up between them. "Mr Dunn, too, was very deaf; so that he could not hear Mr Coleridge's soft & mellifluous speech unless circumstances allowed this to become unnaturally strong." And of course Coleridge soon cast his spell over young Porter, who on his afternoons off used to track Coleridge down "in the green lane nearly parallel to the West Hill as it descended from Highgate to Kentish Town . . . a favourite resort of Mr Coleridge's". Whether "reading or making notes", Coleridge always broke off to talk to the apothecary's assistant and "gratify him with a few minutes' dissertation" on some totally unexpected subject.

Porter also left an interesting account of Mr Coleridge's consumption and expenses. "In those days the ordinary retail price of good laudanum, the 'Tinct. Opii' of the Pharmacopeia, was eight pence an ounce; but Dunn had undertaken to supply Mr Coleridge for five pence, that is, to fill his bottle for five shillings. The money was tendered usually in the form of a £5 note; & if this had not been handed in at the usual time, a few words were said . . . Of course Mr Dunn gained little by such a sale . . . the entire affair, indeed, was one of honourable neighbourliness rather than of trade." Porter reckoned that Coleridge was dosing himself with "a wine-glass" a day, and replenishing his bottle about once every five days. (This would have amounted to an annual cost of some £18 or £20, but no doubt Porter's retrospective accounting was rather kindly – double the sum seems nearer the figure.)

18

Yet there was no collapse, and if Coleridge could not work, he remained busy. He was corresponding with Tulk about Swedenborgian matters, and at the same time lending support to the governors of the Highgate Free Grammar School in a dispute with the government Charity Commission.[105] When in October he went with the Gillmans to Ramsgate, he found them slightly better sited lodgings at 7 Wellington Crescent, on the "good" end of the East Cliff, and encouraged Ann to take up sea-bathing for her own health, "a Sea-nymph in Amphitrite's Train" as he put it.

He discovered for himself the pleasures of the new bathing

machines, which could be wheeled into surf (they were built rather like gypsy caravans) so as to provide a sort of mobile diving-board from the wooden steps at the seaward end. "It was glorious! I watched each time from the top-step for a high Wave coming, and then with my utmost power of projection *shot* myself off into it, for all the world like a Congreve Rocket into a Whale."[106] It was with these marine explosions that he celebrated his forty-ninth birthday.

They brought him back refreshed to Highgate, but by the end of the year the *Logic* textbook was still "interrupted", and a valuable invitation to lecture on Shakespeare in Dublin had been rejected as "out of the Question". There was still no advance of the *Opus Maximum*.[107] Steadily his life was turning back on itself, eddying, slowing down, dissipating like foam on the pebbles. Or it was going out again to join "the swelling of the voiceful sea".[108]

19

Now Coleridge's thoughts turned continually on all his children, whoever they were, whoever they might be. His dearest, Hartley, showed some signs of settling into his career, and in February 1822 published a learned article in the *London Magazine*, "On the Poetical Use of Heathen Mythology", a subject to delight his father. He made perceptive reference to the work of Keats and Shelley, and showed that he had now read Shelley's *Prometheus Unbound* (1820). But he also realized that his own epic poem on the subject had been anticipated, and he secretly and miserably abandoned it. The fragments show that Hartley's Prometheus reflected his creator's temperament: he capitulates to Jupiter, gives way to the seductions of Ocean, and merges with the great blind forces of Nature.[109]

Now it was Derwent who was causing Coleridge anxiety, becoming secretary of clubs and societies at Cambridge, making mocking references to religion, and neglecting his mathematical studies. Coleridge feared "accursed Coxcombry" and stern letters of advice flew out; though in fact Derwent was just being his easy sociable self.[110]

Coleridge found a much surer touch in encouraging Gillman's assistant John Watson (who soon became another youthful disciple), and writing yet more marital advice to Thomas Allsop, whose love-life seems to have been star-crossed. Coleridge confided to Ann Gillman that Allsop was "more than a Son to me". He was relieved to hear he had finally fallen in love "*at first sight*", which had now become "an article of my philosophic Creed' in matters of the heart. "Only remember," he told Allsop tenderly, "that what is dear to you, becomes dear to me."[111]

20

Coleridge felt all the accumulated experiences of these years, now spiritual as much as purely intellectual, should be put to work while there was still time. On 25 February 1822 he placed a formal advertisement in the *Courier*, offering to hold a weekly seminar or tutorial for young men between nineteen and twenty-five, "for the purpose of assisting them in the formation of their minds, and the regulation of their studies".[112]

His aim was to attract the highest calibre of pupils, in a sort of postgraduate seminar. He did not want academics, but those who would have some impact on the outside world: ideally men intending to go into the Church, the law, or parliament. He told Daniel Stuart that sessions would be held between midday and four o'clock, at Green's fine reception room in Lincoln's Inn Fields. The first two hours would consist of a lecture or dictation, drawn from the various branches of the *Logic* and *Opus Maximum*; the second two of "conversation, questions, discussions etc." on general subjects of the day. Philosophy would be applied to life.

Coleridge felt he would be extending and formalizing the talks he was already holding with young friends like Allsop, Watson and Stutfield.[113] The courses would run for two years, and payment would be voluntary. These classes, although interrupted in the summer of 1822, do seem to have run regularly thereafter until Coleridge's health declined in 1827. In the year after Coleridge's death, an anonymous member published two long extracts from his class notes in *Fraser's Magazine*, "beautiful fragments . . . taken down from his own lips". One, "On Life", reflects his scientific work with Gillman and Green; the other "The Science and System of Logic", reflects an early phase of the *Opus Maximum*.[114] They seem to have been memorable occasions.

Coleridge also began to think in terms of publishing an inspirational work for young men, a sort of spiritual guidebook for those setting out in life. Turning back to the seventeenth-century divine,

Archbishop Leighton, whose sermons and meditations he had first discovered, he now revealed, in his own crisis years of 1813–14, he proposed "an interesting Pocket Volume" to John Murray. He did not feel capable of writing a wholly original book, but suggested it take the form of a selection from Leighton's works, with a critical and biographical commentary.[115] Initially it was to be little more than an anthology – "The Beauties of Archbishop Leighton".

As a worthy volume of Christian apologetics for earnest youth, it sounded like the least promising of all Coleridge's late projects. But working on it over the next three years, he transformed it into one of the most idiosyncratic and influential productions, which found an astonishing range of readers, from the philosopher J. S. Mill to the sublime poet of the Victorian nonsense-world, Lewis Carroll.[116]*

21

These plans advanced so slowly because of his own sons. Throughout 1822 Hartley's drinking and chaotic life became more and more evident. Coleridge wrote to his wife that he was at his wit's end to know how to handle Hartley, loving him so much and feeling so responsible for him. He blamed himself "for the extreme delicacy with which I speak to him of his follies, and my terror of giving him pain".[117]

He felt the London journalism was doomed, and in May he wrote a long and desperate letter to John Dawes, Hartley's old headmaster at Ambleside, begging him to offer Hartley a place as an assistant teacher. "Whatever else is to be done or prevented, London he must not live in – the number of young men who will seek his company to be *amused*, his own want of pride, & the opportunity of living or imagining rather that he can live from hand

* There are few stranger examples of Coleridge's liberating influence whispering down the years than Charles Dodgson. As a young man, troubled by scientific attacks on the Bible, he drew profound comfort from Coleridge's prose work. Influenced by "Christabel", he also plucked up courage to write his only overt account of his suppressed sexual obsession with young girls, in a virtually forgotten ballad-poem, "Stolen Waters" (1862). He was then free to write *Alice's Adventures in Wonderland* (1865), in which the proud and eccentric old Caterpillar, ensconced on his high mushroom with his hookah pipe (of opium?), may seem faintly familiar. (See Morton N. Cohen, *Lewis Carroll*, 1995.)

to mouth by writing for Magazines etc. – these are Ruin for him."

His assessment of his son was much sharper since the Oriel débâcle. He praised Hartley's natural innocence, and his good temper "in the management & instruction of Children". These exceeded those of any young man he had ever known. But he also filled his wine-glass "too often", and he could be "as selfish as a Beast". Since the days at Calne, Coleridge had consistently tried to improve him by "admonition, persuasion, intreaty, warning". Yet he knew that he had failed, and failed in that very point in which Hartley was most like himself. Like his father, he lacked moral willpower. This was an agonizing admission, couched in painful contradictions.

"But let it be, that I am rightly reproached for my negligence in withstanding and taming his Self-will – is this the main Root of the Evil? I could almost say – Would to God, it were! For then I should have more Hope. But alas! it is the absence of a Self, it is the want or torpor of a Will, that is the mortal Sickness of Hartley's Being, and has been, for good & for evil, his character – his moral *idiocy* – from his earliest Childhood."

He apologized to Dawes for having written with a father's "wounded Spirit", and indeed it was a strange letter of recommendation to a future employer. But the wise old headmaster knew both father and son well, and the teaching position was held open. It took Coleridge a further six months to persuade Hartley to leave London, and in the end it was Gillman who carried the day.[118]

At the end of June Derwent came down from Cambridge with a fever, which rapidly developed into typhus. For six weeks Coleridge and the Gillmans nursed him night and day, in a tiny top room hired next door to Moreton House.[119] Several times he was thought to be dying, and news came that seven other undergraduates at St John's had been fatally struck down by the epidemic. It was a terrible summer.

From the wild time at Henley Pest House in 1794 (when he had heroically nursed a fellow-dragoon with smallpox), Coleridge had proved himself fearless and dedicated at a sickbed, and he did not fail his son now.[120] Night after night, he kept vigil in Derwent's bedroom, sponging his face and making him drink water. Sitting by the bedside he made desultory entries in his Notebook by candlelight, "harassed with Hartley's idiocies" and tortured by the idea of losing his second son. "Tuesday July 1822 – 23rd day of Derwent's Fever!

– God be merciful to me. – Turned a poor (very large & beautiful) Moth out of the Window in a hard Shower of Rain to save it from the Flames!"[121]

It seemed to him that both sons were now in mortal danger. He wrote to Hartley urging him to give up the "experiment of trying to maintain yourself by writing for the Press". He begged him to assert himself in an adult way, and accept the schoolmastership. "To Mr Dawes exclusively you must look and apply yourself. – God bless you! While you live, I will do what I can – what and whether I can, must in the main depend on yourself not on your affectionate father."[122]

Surely one practical thing that Hartley could do, was to come to Highgate and help care for his beloved brother. Hartley did so, for some days, but his vagaries antagonized the Gillmans and the tension between father and son became unbearable. One July afternoon, when Derwent's fever "trembled in the scales whether he should live or die", Coleridge and Hartley hurried into London on some errands together.[123] What then occurred remained frozen in Coleridge's mind for the rest of his life.

Hartley suddenly said he had a debt to pay, borrowed some money from his father, and arranged to meet him again at six o'clock at a shop in York Street. Coleridge called after him, as he later told Allsop, "Hartley! – Six!" Hartley turned back for a moment, and Coleridge had a terrible premonition, "And tho' he was not three yards from me, I only saw the colour of his face thro' my Tears!" Then Hartley's small figure disappeared into the busy crowd. Hartley had run away forever.

Coleridge and his son never met face to face again. By October 1822 only Hartley's publisher, Taylor and Hessey, knew where he was ("safe in his friend Mr Jameson's care") in London; and by November Hartley had appeared unannounced at Ambleside where John Dawes took him in. Meanwhile Derwent had recovered, and Gillman despatched the exhausted Coleridge to Ramsgate once more.

From there he wrote to Gillman, still griefstruck and confused, but trying to see his way ahead. "I am still too much under the cloud of past Misgivings, too much of the Stun & Stupor from the recent Peals and Thunder crash still remains, to permit me to anticipate, other than by wishes & prayers, what the effect of your unweariable Kindness may be on poor Hartley's Mind and Conduct.

I pray fervently . . . that on my own mind and spring of action it will be proved not to have been wasted. I do inwardly believe, that I shall yet do something to thank you, my dear Gillman, in the way in which you would wish to be thanked – by doing myself honour."[124]

Broken images of this terrible loss gradually took the form of a poem, restlessly drafted over many scattered sheets. It is bleakly entitled "The Pang More Sharp Than All: An Allegory". To Copleston, Coleridge had referred to his son as "a blossom whirling in a May-gale", a picture of delight that went back to the happiest days at Greta Hall. Now that blossom had blown away: "Like a loose blossom on a gusty night/ He flitted from me . . ."

The opening stanza (it has various forms) mourns the experience of paternal loss.

> He too has flitted from his secret nest,
> Hope's last and dearest child without a name! –
> Has flitted from me, like a warmthless flame,
> That makes false promise of a place of rest
> To the tired Pilgrim's still-believing mind; –
> Or like some Elfin Knight in kingly court,
> Who having won all guerdons in his sport,
> Glides out of view, and whither none can find!

Coleridge explores these images in four further verses, using the Spenserian stanza (with its archaisms) which are characteristic of his later poetry. ("Guerdons" are rewards, or prizes.) Initially they read as if he were holding emotion at arms' length, using the formal "Allegory" to suppress intense personal feelings. But as with Hamlet, "suppression leads to overflow". The poem rises to a stanza of great symbolic power and pathos, in which Hartley the "Magic Child" is finally seen to be something within Coleridge himself, some irreducible element of his own imagination, which is still present and alive, though "languishing" and unfulfilled.

> Ah! he is gone, and yet will not depart! –
> Is with me still, yet I from him exiled!
> For still there lives within my secret heart
> The magic image of the Magic Child,

Which there he made up-grow by his strong art,
As in that crystal orb – wise Merlin's feat, –
The wonderous "World of Glass", wherein inisled
All long'd-for things their beings did repeat; –
And there he left it, like a Sylph beguiled,
To live and yearn and languish incomplete![125]

22

Glide, Rich Streams, Away!

1

At fifty, prematurely aged but still praeternaturally alive, Coleridge entered a last autumnal period of stock-taking, self-examination and sombre looking back at the "circuitous paths" of his life. Where once he might have written to his son, he now wrote to his "substitute son" Thomas Allsop, in a series of highly emotional and confessional letters. They show the syntactical flood and self-exposure of late-night opium-taking. For the first time since his youthful letters to Tom Poole and John Thelwall written at Stowey in 1797, a quarter of a century before, he described the lack of control in his life, the outpourings of "sensibility" (which he compared to Garrick's acting), and the "species of Histrionism" which had always driven his friendships. He thought that this had produced his "Eloquence", his famous unstoppable talk. But sometimes it was not a genuine means of self-expression, but a way of disguising his own feelings from himself. Paradoxically, his talk was – in psychological terms – a form of flight and self-escape.

These self-observations were acute, and gave rise to a memorable Dante-esque image of Purgatorial circles or Piranesi-like labyrinths. "My eloquence was most commonly excited by the desire of running away and hiding myself from my personal and inward feelings, and not for expression of them . . . I fled in a circle still overtaken by the Feelings, from which I was evermore fleeing, with my back turned toward them . . ." Here Coleridge's "Feelings", with their personalized capital letter, are given very much the role of pursuing "Furies".[1]

He returned to the subject after a long series of walks by the beach. He looked back at a pattern of emotional disasters that, as it seemed to him at this bleak time, had shaped much of his life.

He told Allsop that in his past life he counted "four griping and grasping Sorrows, each of which seemed to have my very heart in his hands, compressing or wringing".

The first was his alienation from Mrs Coleridge, in the early years at Greta Hall, when "the Vision of a Happy Home sunk for ever", and he came to realize that he would never achieve domestic happiness at least "under the name of Husband". The second was his quarrel with Wordsworth in 1810–11. He still evidently felt the bitterness of this, an "idolatrous Fancy" which had filled "the fifteen bright and ripe years, the strong summer of my Life", and then burst "like a Bubble".

The third was the loss of Asra, though she is not specifically named. "What the former (Wordsworth) was to Friendship, the latter was to a yet more intimate Bond – the former spread a wider gloom over the world around me, the latter left a darkness within myself . . . a Self emptied."

The fourth and last sorrow began with Hartley's loss of Oriel, and the slow revelation of the deceptions and moral weakness of his son. They spread out to the gloomy feeling that he himself had failed as a father, "with the sad conviction that neither of my children thought of or felt towards me as a FATHER, or attributed any thing done for them, to me". These were painful, profoundly undermining revelations.[2]

Yet in a sense they were not new. They had already been faced in his Notebooks, and they had been imaginatively described in his poetry. For this is the dark, autobiographical stratum of pain which glimmers through the "Dejection" ode (1802), "To William Wordsworth" (1807), "Constancy to an Ideal Object" (1805), "Limbo" (1811) and "The Pang More Sharp Than All". What was new was Coleridge's capacity to expose them to a young friend like Allsop. Perhaps it meant that they were no longer paralysing, no longer capable of reducing him to real despair. By admitting them, he was in his own way coming to terms with them. Or perhaps it meant that he was growing old.

To James Gillman, in the calmer letters he wrote at midday, he spoke of the inspiriting fragrance of pine on the sea-breezes, his conquest of snuff, and the prayers he made for Hartley. He was pleased when Lord Liverpool recognized him as he emerged like a

Triton, with streaming white locks, from the Ramsgate bathing machine. The Prime Minister accompanied the amphibious poet arm in arm along the East Pier.[3]

2

But if one sorrow never released Coleridge from its grip, it was surely the fate of his eldest son. Hartley was like his own spirit, a little ghost of himself, his lost youth as a poet, wandering in the hills unappeased. He never wrote to his father, and Coleridge was doomed only to hear of him indirectly through family letters, vague rumours, or heartless literary gossip. By Christmas 1822, Hartley appeared to be settled at Ambleside, though Coleridge was angry that neither Wordsworth in his grand establishment at Rydal Mount, nor Southey in his full occupation of Greta Hall, would consider giving Hartley houseroom during the holidays. Southey had written crisply to Wordsworth: "I think you had better write to Mr Gillman . . . and remind him, which he seems to have forgotten, that Mrs C. has no establishment in which Hartley can be received."[4] Hartley eventually rented a room at the little Red Lion Inn in Grasmere, and told Derwent that he considered Greta Hall "a House of Bondage".[5]

His schoolmastering continued with some success for the next five years, though he always had trouble maintaining discipline among the younger boys. When John Dawes retired, Hartley became co-partner in a larger teaching establishment at Ambleside, and this venture continued until 1827. But his private life remained solitary and increasingly melancholic: he did not find the wife he hoped for among the farmers' daughters of the Lake District (as De Quincey had done), and he sought solace in his drinking and his exquisite sonnet-writing, many of them written late at night and addressed to imaginary lovers or girls he had glimpsed on their summer tours. Once he called in at Rydal Mount and "vexed" Dorothy by talking "about suicide in a lax way – said he could not find it prohibited in scripture". He talked too "in a wild way about destiny, signifying that a man's actions are not in his own power".[6]

3

In as far as he worked at all, Coleridge spent the next two years on preparing his anthology from Leighton, which was eventually published as *Aids to Reflection* in 1825. But the leisurely round at Highgate did bring other forms of domestic happiness, new family ties, and satisfactory moments of professional recognition. He dined out with an increasingly wide circle of wealthy friends – the Greens, the Tulks, the Aders, the Wranghams – and the reputation of his weekly classes spread among the universities, especially Cambridge.

Among the flow of young visitors to his parlour at Highgate was his nephew Henry Nelson Coleridge. A tall, florid, intense youth, he was even more in awe of his uncle since the famous weekend at Richmond in 1811. In his last year at Eton, Henry had published a long and ecstatic article in the school magazine, "On Coleridge's Poetry". He described his uncle, with due solemnity, as "the greatest Genius, in every respect, of the present day"; and concluded that together with Wordsworth, Coleridge had revolutionized "the poetry, the philosophy and the criticism" of English literature over the last thirty years.[7] He added that no one should miss the chance of hearing his "extraordinary" conversation, or his sudden magical recitations of his own verse.

As with many schoolboy articles, this reflected what was already being said in the more advanced sections of the popular press. Even the *Examiner* had forgotten most of its political quarrels with Coleridge, and Leigh Hunt himself evoked Coleridge as the poet who now spoke most directly to the aspirations of young readers everywhere, of whatever social standing or political persuasion. "Every lover of books, scholar or not, who knows what it is to have his quarto open against a loaf at his tea, to carry his duo-decimo about in his pocket, to read along country roads or even in streets and to scrawl his favourite author with notes . . . ought to be in possession of Coleridge's poems . . ."

What had once been dismissed by Hazlitt in the same paper as the musical "nonsense" of "Kubla Khan", was now hailed as the peculiar signature tune of Coleridge's genius. "'Kubla Khan' is a voice and a vision, an everlasting tune in our mouths, a dream fit for Cambuscan and all his poets, a dance of pictures such as Giotto or Cimabue, revived and re-inspired, would have made for a Storie of Old Tartarie, a piece of the invisible world made visible by a sun at midnight and sliding before our eyes. 'Beware, beware,/ His flashing eyes, his floating hair!/ Weave a circle round him thrice . . .' "[8]

4

It was now, at last, a propitious time for Coleridge to meet his daughter. After much bustle and preparation at Greta Hall, and an extended coach-journey south, a flustered Mrs Coleridge presented the nineteen-year-old Sara to her father at Highgate in January 1823. She also showed her off to the Beaumonts, and various relations, so it became Sara's coming-out season in London. She was a striking success. Sara dazzled everyone by her sylph-like beauty – "the little sylph of Ullswater" – and astonished them with her bookishness.

She delighted Coleridge by shyly presenting him with a copy of her first publication. It was a work of alarming scholarship, translated in three volumes from the Latin of Martin Dobrizhoffer, describing the "Equestrian People of Paraguay", and issued by Murray. Charles Lamb wondered admiringly how the beauteous and frail-looking Sara had "*Dobrizhoffered* it all out . . . thro' that rugged Paraguay mine".[9]

Coleridge found her "a sweet and delightful Girl", but he was much restrained by his wife's presence. He took every opportunity to peer into Sara's book, and retreat to his bedroom. The day was saved by handsome Henry Coleridge, who made a dashing walk across the Heath in a rainstorm to greet them, arriving soaked and glamorous on the Highgate doorstep (much as his uncle used to do in the old days at Grasmere). Henry was excessively charming to his provincial aunt, and quietly amusing to his clever cousin. A flurry of operas, exhibitions and dinner parties followed with the other young Coleridges.

Henry had fallen beneath a double spell at Highgate. He began making notes of his uncle's conversation, and these would grow into an entire volume of *Table Talk*, eventually published in 1835. The earliest entries from 1823 remind one of Keats's experience of Coleridge's "thousand subjects", from philosophical topics to excruciating puns. Henry noted talk of Shakespeare's *Othello* and *Hamlet* – the House of Commons – Plato – Byron – ghost stories – the Book of Genesis – and the tale of a tinker's boy calling at Moreton House asking for "any old poets" (it turned out that he meant "any old pots"), Coleridge's Delphic humour including the observation that "Snuff was the final cause of the human nose".[10]

But this enchantment was accompanied by another, "the "sufficiently tempting" lips of that "lovely creature" Sara. Within a few days Henry had fallen deeply in love, and he soon suspected that his passion was returned. How far the unworldly glow of his uncle's reputation had lit up his daughter's "perfectly proportioned figure" is not clear. But unlike so many Coleridgean affairs of the heart, this one was destined to be genuine, requited and enduring. By March, when Sara and her mother left to visit the Ottery Coleridges, Henry was certain of her affections. They exchanged a secret and solemn vow of engagement, and Henry recorded quietly in his diary that Sara had given him two ringlets of her hair. On their last morning together, Sara made the heart-stopping gesture of taking a coral necklace warm from her neck and placing it in Henry's hands.[11]

The literary lovers were not to be united for another six years, but from now on Henry's sense of himself as Coleridge's disciple and future son-in-law never wavered. In 1825 he would even go abroad to the West Indies, and write his own book about his travels, to prove his worth and the enduring nature of his commitment. (He disguised his romance with Sara as a folktale.) Coleridge himself took some time to realize what passions had been started under his own roof. "You will wonder at my simplicity", he remarked to Ann Gillman in 1826. She, of course, had long been *au courant*.[12]

His only regret was that he had not been let into the secret earlier. He worried whether first cousins could respectably marry, and that he had "no fortune" to leave them as a dowry. "As a friend, I was ready to give them my best advice . . . but as a Father, I had only my Prayers and my Blessings to give." Like all fathers, too, he felt that no man, not even Henry, was really quite worthy of his daughter. But his soul shrank from "the thought of my only Daughter – & *such* a daughter – condemned to a miserable Heart-wasting".[13] In return, Coleridge was given the most faithful editors and defenders of his work in the next generation.*

In many ways Sara was more like her father, and understood him far better, than either of his sons. When she later embarked on his massive and disorderly collection of papers, she wrote that she was rediscovering him in her own heart. "I feel the most complete sympathy with my father in his account of his literary difficulties. Whatever subject I commence, I feel discontent unless I could pursue it in every direction to the farthest bounds of thought, and then, when some scheme is to be executed, my energies are paralysed with the very notion of the indefinite vastness which I long to fill. This was the reason my father wrote by snatches. He could not bear to complete incompletely, which everybody else does."[15]

5

Coleridge found himself increasingly lionized among his old friends in London. In April 1823, John Monkhouse gave a splendid dinner party which Crabb Robinson and Lamb attended, with a few other luminaries. Lamb recorded the occasion in his best style. "I dined in Parnassus, with Wordsworth, Coleridge, Rogers, and Tom Moore – half the poetry of England constellated and clustered in Gloucester Place! It was a delightful evening. Coleridge was in his finest vein of talk, had all the talk, and let 'em talk as evilly as they do of the envy of the Poets, I am sure not one there but was content

---

* With lifelong dedication, Sara Coleridge re-edited the two volumes of the *Biographia* (1847); three volumes of *Essays on his Own Times* (1850); and (with Derwent) a revised edition of *The Poems* (1852), completed on her own deathbed. What this cost her is hinted at in a late poem, "To My Father", which opens: "Father, no amaranths e'er shall wreathe my brow, / Enough that round thy grave they flourish now . . .", an echo that will become poignantly clear in a moment. (See Bradford Keyes Mudge, *Sara Coleridge, A Victorian Daughter*, 1989.) Henry Nelson Coleridge edited four volumes of the *Literary Remains* (1836–9); and the *Table Talk* (1835) before his own premature death in 1843. The latter, despite some fine entries, is too respectful and desultory to form a living portrait. Leslie Stephen reflected: "a Life of Coleridge may still be put together by some judicious writer, who should take Boswell rather than the 'Acta Sanctorum' for his model, which would be as interesting as the great "Confessions"; which should in turn remind us of Augustine, of Montaigne, and of Rousseau, and sometimes, too, of the inimitable Pepys; . . . which should show the blending of many elements of a most complex character and most opulent intellect; and defy the skill of a psychologist to define." (*Hours in a Library*, 3, 1888.)

to be nothing but a listener. The Muses were dumb, while Apollo lectured on his and their fine Art."[16]

Crabb Robinson noted that "the five wandering bards" got on splendidly round the table, and that now Coleridge "chiefly talked to" Wordsworth, and was not inhibited by Sara Hutchinson's presence. He had not seen him in "such excellent health and spirits" for years. Lamb whispered that Coleridge "ought not to have a wife or children; he should have a sort of *diocesan* care of the world, no parish duty". Later, in his cups, he said that he wanted to take Coleridge and Asra away on a little trip together to the seaside, but he was sure Gillman would not allow it. "I have a malicious knack of cutting of apron strings."[17]

6

In the autumn, still working on the *Aids to Reflection*, Coleridge was back in Ramsgate, and completed his poem "Youth and Age". As if to hold time back, he carefully dated the manuscript in his Notebook, "Wednesday Morning, 10 o'clock, 10 Sept. 1823".[18] He recorded how the "air" of the poem had come to him like a sudden gift, which recalled a walk thirty years before over the Quantocks. On that occasion he had stopped to listen to a skylark, and a bumblebee had unexpectedly "whizzed' close by his ear, "at once sharp and burry, right over the Summit of Quantock, at earliest Dawn". That was how the tune of the poem had come to him now.

Skilfully he fitted the image of the bee, of the steamboats effortlessly plying in the Thames estuary, and of his own clumsy steps and white hair in old age, together into a kind of halting dance movement or minuet. Some of his rejected phrases are as moving as the final ones: his body was "This snail-like House, not built with hands"; and the bee tune was originally tried out as, "Hope's a Breeze that robs the Blossoms/ Fancy feeds on . . ."[19] The dance plays poignantly, and with great psychological acuity, with the idea of age as a form of charade, dressing-up, or grotesque fancy-dress:

> O Youth! For years so many and sweet,
> 'Tis known, that Thou and I were one,
> I'll think it but a fond conceit –
> It cannot be that Thou art gone!

Thy vesper bell has not yet toll'd: –
And thou wert aye a masker bold!
What strange disguise hast now put on,
To make believe, that thou art gone?
I see these locks in silvery slips,
This drooping gait, this altered size:
But Spring-tide blossoms on thy lips,
And tears take sunshine from thine eyes!
Life is but thought: so think I will
That Youth and I are housemates still.[20]

On his fifty-first birthday, he noted: "Were I free to do so, I feel as if I could compose the third part of Christabel; or the Song of her Desolation."[21]

7

John Murray rejected a first version of the *Aids to Reflection* manuscript, but it was immediately taken on by Taylor and Hessey. They did not press him for a deadline, but encouraged him to expand his own Commentaries on Archbishop Leighton.[22] The effect was immediately apparent when, after a delightful "Swimlet Bath", he wrote what was to become for Victorian readers one of the crucial "Aphorisms" concerning intellectual doubt and religious truth.

Leighton had written: "Men that know nothing in sciences, have no doubts . . . Never be afraid to doubt, if only you have the disposition to believe, and doubt in order that you may end in believing the Truth." Coleridge interpreted this as follows. "He, who begins by loving Christianity better than the Truth, will proceed by loving his own Sect or Church better than Christianity, and end in loving himself better than all."[23] J. S. Mill would later cite this as central to his notion of liberalism, adding his own aphorism to Coleridge's. "Imputations of horrid consequence ought not to bias the judgement of any person capable of independent thought."[24]

This accumulating structure of short, linked commentaries (to which the reader was invited to add his own, in a kind of intellectual chain-letter) became the highly unusual form of the *Aids to Reflection*. It was one more variation of the Coleridgean idea of the "friendly" conversation: an exchange that passed continually back and forth between Leighton, Coleridge and his reader.

His central concern now was the validity of religious belief within the context of early nineteenth-century scientific thought. He believed passionately that the two could co-exist. Coleridge wanted his readers to reject the scepticism of the Enlightenment. But he urged that calm and serious reflection on man's place in nature led logically to a belief in the divine which was wholly compatible with scientific rationalism. It included it, but necessarily moved beyond it. His full title – *Aids to Reflection in the Formation of a Manly Character on the Several Grounds of Prudence, Morality, and Religion* – was representative of this position.

The word "Manly" struck a deliberate chord. It would be easy to link this with the later Victorian developments of "muscular" Christianity, with its emphasis on revivalism, philanthropy, robust ethical simplicities and virtuous cold baths. But this was hardly Coleridge's style. He emerged from this sportive sea bathing with a wholly different emphasis. For him a "manly" outlook was absolutely opposed to "the pugnacious dogmatism of *partial* Reflection". To be manly was to be fully aware of the mysteries of the human condition, to avoid intellectual cowardice and spiritual blindness, to look on all things with "a patient, manly, and impartial perusal".[25]

He arranged the anthology in three parts, rather like *The Friend*, but without "Amusements" interposed. These were: one, "Prudential Aphorisms"; two, "Moral and Religious Aphorisms"; and three, "Aphorisms on Spiritual Religion". Despite the forbidding titles, it was far from being a pious handbook, and contained little discussion of strictly theological issues or any defence of Trinitarian Christianity. Instead there was a good deal of scientific reference, arising from his work with Green and Gillman; and a prolonged examination of the distinction between animal instincts, "rational" understanding, and the higher or "intuitive" reason which culminated in religious faith.

Aphorism 36 from the "Moral" section deals beautifully with Coleridge's favoured theme of "the Ascent of Powers" in nature. It grapples prophetically with the idea of evolution, understood as a spiritual force of expanding moral consciousness. "And who that hath watched their ways with an understanding heart, could, as the vision evolving, still advanced towards him, contemplate the filial and loyal Bee; the home-building, wedded, and divorceless Swallow; and above all the manifoldly intelligent Ant tribes, with their Commonwealths and Confederacies . . . and not to say himself, Behold the shadow of approaching Humanity, the Sun rising from behind, in the kindling Morn of Creation? Thus all lower Natures find their highest Good in semblances and seekings of that which is higher and better. All things strive to ascend, and ascend in their striving. And shall man alone stoop?"[26]

A parallel entry, Aphorism 9 of the final "Spiritual" section, begins with the notion of "wonder" as central to all philosophical thought, and continues with an examination of instinct in dogs and the dawning of moral values in the natural kingdom. Why will a dog defend, and even avenge, its master? "Here the Adaptive power co-exists with a purpose apparently *voluntary*, and the action seems neither predetermined by the organization of the Animal, nor in any direct reference to his own preservation, or to the continuance of his race. It is united with an imposing semblance of Gratitude, Fidelity, and disinterested Love. We not only *value* the faithful Brute: we attribute *worth* to him."[27]*

The poet and the enthusiast of *Naturphilosophie* are both evident in these entries, driven by the uplifting rhetoric of Coleridge's late style of benign sermonizing. A highly original book was emerging, whose open speculative manner – the sage at his most genial and relaxed – would have great and unexpected appeal.

8

While Coleridge was away at Ramsgate during the autumn of 1823 James Gillman moved house to No. 3 the Grove, in Highgate. It was a fine three-storey brick Georgian residence, set back from

* The idea that biological "selfishness" and relentless competition are the driving mechanism of evolutionary "ascent", can be traced from Bernard Mandeville's poem *The Fable of the Bees* (1714) through Darwin to Richard Dawkins' *The Selfish Gene* (1976). Coleridge belongs to an alternative intellectual tradition which observes the same phenomena in terms of an emerging "altruism", which may be traced from the German Naturphilosophien to Peter Kropotkin's *Mutual Aid: A Factor in Evolution* (1888) to Matt Ridley's *The Origins of Virtue*, 1996. But Coleridge's evolutionary thinking is always fundamentally religious, and he held what many scientist would currently dismiss as the "teleological heresy": that evolution has a purpose beyond survival and adaptation. To the end he mocked the "Boa Constrictor of Materialism" (to J. H. Green, May 1828, *Letters*, VI, p. 737).

a gravelled alley of chestnut trees on the eastern flank of Hampstead Heath. The move indicated that his medical practice was flourishing, and that the ménage with Coleridge was secure. Gillman gave him the finest upper room, a large attic bedroom, to which he later added an extension looking westwards across the Heath to Caen Wood. Reached by a fine oak staircase, this became his final home, an airy retreat fitted out with a long wall of bookshelves and decorated with portraits of his family and friends, the picture of Sara having pride of place. On his working table he kept pots of plants, especially a myrtle which he had described in a poem as the symbol of love lost and found.[28]

When he had moved to Greta Hall, so long ago in 1800, he had been delighted to discover that the building once housed an astronomical observatory, and he described himself gazing from the roof as "S. T. Coleridge Esq., Gentleman-poet and philosopher-in a-mist".[29] Now again, when he stood at his high west-facing window, he had the same feeling of transcendence. He often called the Gillmans' sons up to the window, "if he found some uncommon glory in the evening sky".[30] In the spring of 1824, he was elected to one of the small band of Fellowships at the Royal Society of Literature, with an annuity of 100 guineas. He gave his inaugural lecture on the Prometheus myth.

9

Nonetheless, the move provoked a number of stressful incidents. Ann Gillman came up to say goodnight to Coleridge one evening, and on leaving fell down the stairs and broke her right arm.[31] Gillman cut himself while performing an anatomical dissection.[32] Coleridge began drawing more heavily on the medical supplies of T. H. Dunn, and in March 1824 settled a large opium bill with the postscript: "I entreat you, be careful not to have any note delivered to me unless I am alone and passing your door."[33]

Somehow this alternative supply was now discovered, for unusually Coleridge spent a week away with Thomas Allsop and his young wife and sister, until entreated to return by Mrs Gillman. With her customary acuteness, Ann Gillman may have glimpsed Coleridge about to fly to a new nest. But she called him back with heartfelt feeling: "G. loves you so much, I am sure if things are well arranged matters may be adjusted. And I feel confident that the happiness, perhaps well doing, of all *three* is concerned, so do not let us two suffer pride or temper to interfere in such a serious affair where there exists so much love."[34]

From later remarks of Dunn's assistant, Seymour Porter, it seems that Ann Gillman went round to remonstrate personally with the obliging Highgate chemist.[35] But the enquiry was allowed to drop, and it is clear that, from 1824 onwards, Gillman adopted a policy of deliberately allowing Coleridge a small illicit supply of opium, to be surreptitiously added to the prescribed medical dose. This was an extremely acute method of dealing with the psychology of Coleridge's addiction. It allowed him the guilty release of obtaining his own secret supply – an almost unconquerable instinct in the confirmed addict – while in practice restricting the overall dose within reasonable bounds.

Certainly Seymour Porter remained much in favour. When in July 1824 he stood watching Byron's funeral cortège passing slowly up Highgate Hill, on the long journey from Missolonghi to Nottinghamshire, he found Coleridge standing beside him at the chemist's door. Porter never forgot the spontaneous funeral oration that Coleridge suddenly poured forth in the middle of the pavement. It was "a strain of marvellous eloquence", lasting not less than a quarter of an hour, starting with "Byron's unhappy youth" and going on with great generosity over his whole career up to his climactic death in Greece. Porter was moved by Coleridge's sense of Byron's greatness, and his view that the "satanic" reputation was ephemeral. "Byron's literary merits would seem continually to rise, while his personal errors, if not denied, or altogether forgotten, would be little noticed, & would be treated with ever softening gentleness."[36]

10

Coleridge's popularity in Highgate, now the well-known, white-haired, shuffling sage, spread through the neighbourhood. He was followed by squalls of small boys, and greeted by distinguished matrons. He cultivated a certain eccentricity. When he was caught pulling down branches of blossoms from a neighbour's garden (an escapade he had favoured as a schoolboy at Christ's Hospital), he made friends for life with the outraged proprietor, Mrs Chisholm, by sending her an apology in verse, entitled "The Reproof and Reply".

The bleak garden of "Limbo" here reappears as a verdant, North London Eden where he wanders like a child, innocently stealing forbidden fruit:

> Thus, long-accustomed on the twy-fork'd hill,
> To pluck both flower and floweret at my will;
> The garden's maze, like No-man's-land, I tread,
> Nor common law, nor statute in my head;
> For my own proper smell, sight, fancy, feeling,
> With autocratic hand at once repealing
> Five Acts of Parliament 'gainst private stealing . . .[37]

11

One summer evening, when Gillman was prostrated by a fever, Coleridge deputized for him as an emergency physician, panting down Highgate Hill to soothe a distraught mother whose new-born baby had suddenly died. He poured out his sympathies to the woman, and secretly wished he could become a faith-healer. "I felt a vehement impulse to try Zoo-magnetism, i.e. to try my hand at resurrection. I felt or fancied a power in me to concentre my will that I have never felt or fancied before."[38]

He reported back to Gillman, and then sat up writing a learned letter to Tulk about the possibilities of Magnetism revealed in the latest research papers: "A Berlin Physician discovered a power in himself to fling long sparks from his fingers by pure Force of his Will . . ."[39]

12

When the young Thomas Carlyle made his first pilgrimage to Highgate in June 1824, his initial impression was of a great "curiosity", with an extraordinary and somewhat alarming physical presence. "Figure a fat, flabby, incurvated personage, at once short, rotund, and relaxed, with a watery mouth, a snuffy nose, a pair of strange, brown, timid, yet earnest looking eyes, a high tapering brow, and a great bush of grey hair; and you have some faint idea of Coleridge. He is a kind good soul, full of religion and affection and poetry and animal magnetism. His cardinal sin is that he wants *will*. He has no resolution."

They walked up and down the garden together, Carlyle rather impatient with Coleridge's shuffling gait and drifting conversation. "He wanders like a man sailing on many currents." But they parted "very good friends", and Carlyle sent him a book.[40] It was this figure of "great and useless genius", whom Carlyle finally transformed some twenty-seven years later into the "Magus" sage of Highgate. Like Hazlitt, he could not escape writing about him, and the more irritably and brilliantly he pricked and punctured Coleridge (with his "logical swim-bladders, transcendental life-preservers, and other precautionary and vehiculatory gear") the more Coleridge's caricature seems to balloon and sway overhead, smiling and moon-like above Carlyle's pages.[41] When Carlyle moved to London, his whole career as social prophet and champion of German literature became an echo of Coleridge's, and he ended as "the Sage of Chelsea".

Another more grateful visitor was Gabriel Rossetti, who had just arrived penniless in London, forced to flee after taking part in an uprising in Naples, friendless and barely able to speak English. Coleridge received him as "a gentleman, a scholar, and a man of talents", and wrote a long letter of recommendation to Cary. "He is a poet who has been driven into exile for the high morale of his writings." Rossetti gradually established himself, and seven years later was appointed Professor of Italian at the newly founded King's College, London.[42]

13

Throughout the autumn at Ramsgate, Coleridge was correcting and adding unstoppably to the proofs of the *Aids to Reflection*. He wrote long letters to Gillman, assuring him how much his and Ann's friendship had come to mean to him. He also described, with intense feeling, the wreck of an East Indiaman which ran aground in a storm at the harbour mouth, in the very sight of safety.[43]

He watched in an agony of suspense as the "poor sailors" tried to leap from the bowsprit on to the huge granite blocks of the harbour wall. The next day his friend, Mr Philpot the bathing-machinist, accounted it "a *good* Wreck" with an explanation that much struck Coleridge. Surveying the piles of coffee bags, brandy barrels, wine casks and telescopes washing up in the surf, Mr Philpot defined the wreck as "a *diffusion* of Property . . . a providential *multiplication* of Properties . . . It is a loss to the Underwriters . . . but it is a *great thing* for the Poor Folks and for our town of Ramsgate".[44] Coleridge mused on the symbolism of this, and reflected how a drama that began as "a deep Tragedy" could end as an instructive "Entertainment".[45]

14

The *Aids to Reflection* was now due to be published in May 1825. There was considerable tension at No. 3 The Grove, which spread from Coleridge to the Gillmans. Ann was restless, with "a care-worn countenance", affectionately but anxiously worrying at him, as he reported to Allsop. "Mrs G.'s restless and *interrogatory* anxieties . . . put the whole working Hive of my Thoughts in a Whirl and a Buzz . . . Are you going on? – what are you doing now? – is this for the Book? Etc. etc., precisely as if I were Henry at his Lesson."[46]

Another note sped out to T. H. Dunn, Chemist: "I must interest your patience for another ten days. The last sheet of my work is going to the Press – and be assured that for every week since Autumn I will consider the sum as out of interest."[47]

William Hazlitt, with inspired foresight, chose exactly this moment to publish his brilliant and damaging portrait of "Mr Coleridge" in *The Spirit of the Age*. The note struck was the familiar one of elegiac satire: "If Mr Coleridge had not been the most impressive talker of his age, he would probably have been the finest writer . . ." Hazlitt ran through the cruel critique of Coleridge's career which he had fixed a decade before, but now brought it to a crushing conclusion in which opium is for the first time explicitly mentioned. "Alas! 'Frailty, thy name is *Genius*!'"

Little had changed in Hazlitt's line of attack, although he himself was much changed, and deeply embittered by the personal disappointments of his own life and unhappy love affairs. He had separated from his wife, and published his *Liber Amoris*, the tale of unrequited passion for a teasing, teenage servant girl, two years previously.

But one concession was now made. Coleridge had sounded the political retreat for his fellow Lake Poets, Wordsworth and Southey, "by the help of casuistry and a musical voice", until they settled in the safe fortress of the Establishment. But he himself had remained, at the last, independent. "They are safely inclosed there. Mr Coleridge did not enter with them; pitching his tent upon the barren waste without, and having no abiding place nor city of refuge!"

Coleridge could perhaps laugh at this from his garden watchtower at Highgate. Yet one phrase still touched him painfully, probing an old wound, the failure to complete "Christabel" and so much other poetry. He was one of those, according to Hazlitt, who should have gathered "fruits and flowers, immortal fruits and amaranthine flowers", but had been swept away by "the pelting of the pitiless storm".[48]

15

On 21 February 1825 Coleridge wrote a thoughtful letter to Ann Gillman, his "dear Friend", on the subject of work and old age. Highly compressed and poetical, it begins by exploring one of his most curious natural images, that of a spider. "Have you ever noticed the Vault or snug little Apartment which the Spider spins and weaves for itself, by spiral threads round and round, and sometimes with strait lines, so that its Lurking-parlour or withdrawing-room is an oblong square? . . . As we advance in years, the World, that *spidery* Witch, spins its threads narrower and narrower, still closing in on us, till at last it shuts us up without four walls, walls of flues and films, windowless – and well if there be sky-lights, and a small opening left for the Light from above."[49]

Perhaps there was something in that spider that Coleridge saw in himself: an image of self-revulsion that he found in his own attic retreat. But he then summoned up a series of other creatures, all to be found outside in the Highgate garden, which he unexpectedly gathered round him in the most beautiful and poignant of his late sonnets. It was "Work Without Hope":

All Nature seems at work. Slugs leave their lair;
The Bees are stirring – Birds are on the wing –
And Winter slumbering in the open air,
Wears on his smiling face a dream of Spring!
And I, the while, the sole unbusy Thing,
Nor honey make, nor pair, nor build, nor sing.

Coleridge's vision of himself as the "sole unbusy thing" at Highgate – a touching echo of the "sole unquiet thing" long ago at Stowey in "Frost at Midnight" – has an infinite irony. In the second part of the sonnet, the octet, Coleridge introduced the phrase from Hazlitt:

Yet well I ken the banks, where Amaranths blow,
Have traced the fount whence streams of Nectar flow.
Bloom, o ye Amaranths! bloom for whom ye may –
For me ye bloom not! Glide, rich streams! away!
With lips unbrightened, wreathless brow, I stroll:
And would you learn the spells that drowse my soul?
Work without Hope draws nectar in a sieve,
And Hope without an object cannot live.[50]

Amaranths are the immortal flowers which, in Greek mythology, bloom in paradise for successful poets and artists. The poem is rich with associations going right back to "Kubla Khan", and the paradise flower he dreamed of at Calne. Yet for all its sense of grief and loss and exclusion, and even the references to opium ("the spells that drowse my soul"), it somehow magically remains a poem of springtime, a poem of renewal in a garden. Having completed the sonnet, Coleridge wrote several more lines of verse which became "The World that Spidery Witch". This too ends on a note of suspended Hope: "But cease the prelude and resume the lay."[51]

16

The *Aids to Reflection* received almost no immediate notices, except for a long and perplexed analysis in the *British Critic* for 1826. But the book slowly gathered a wide and influential readership.

In 1829 it was published in America, with a long introductory essay by James Marsh, the president of the University of Vermont. In 1831 a second English edition was called for, and it began to be read in Cambridge.

Coleridge's attack on the "vaunted Mechanico-corpuscular Philosophy" still holds many surprises. In an extraordinary passage, inspired by Green's work at the Royal College of Surgeons, he described a human body on the dissecting slab, and a detached eyeball. "Behold it, handle it . . . Tendon, Ligament, Membrane, Blood-vessel, Gland, Humors; its Nerves of Sense, of Sensation, and of Motion . . ." He then asked why such language was inadequate to define the true nature of the living eye, or its symbolic meaning as a faculty of vision.

> Alas! all these names, like that of the Organ itself, are so many Anachronisms, figures of Speech, to express what has been: as when the Guide points with his finger to a Heap of Stones, and tells the Traveller, "That is Babylon, or Persepolis". – Is this cold Jelly "the Light of the Body"? Is this the Micranthropos in the marvellous Microcosm? Is this what you mean when you well define the Eye as the Telescope and the Mirror of the Soul, and Seat and Agent of an almost magical power?[52]

The old language of eighteenth-century materialism was restricted to the human senses, what was fixed and solid to perception. But the new language of "dynamic science" had returned to the notion of energy, force fields, invisible powers and constant transformation. "It is to the coarseness of our Senses . . . that the *visible* Object appears the same even for a moment . . . But the particles that constitute the size, the visibility of an organic structure are in perpetual flux."[53] The new science had shown that the human body itself was no more fixed or permanent, from moment to moment, than the sound of a voice, than "pulses of air".

> As the column of blue smoke from a cottage chimney in the breathless Summer Noon, or the steadfast-seeming Cloud on the edge-point of a Hill in the driving air-current, which momently condensed and recomposed is the common phantom of a thousand successors; – such is the flesh, which our *bodily*

eyes transmit to us; which our *Palates* taste; which our Hands touch.[54]

The new science in effect demanded a return to spiritual perceptions, a "recalling of the drowsed soul from the dreams and phantom world of sensuality to *actual* Reality".[55] Without this realization of the validity of the religious vision, renewed by science, the spiritual world would dwindle to "mere Metaphors, Figures of Speech, Oriental Hyperboles!"[56]

17

John Sterling's reaction to this kind of oracular writing gives some clue to its impact. Sterling was then twenty years old, and promising to be one of the great intellectual lights of his generation at Cambridge. In his first enthusiasm, he wrote to a friend in November 1829: "I scarcely hold fast by anything but Shakespeare, Milton, and Coleridge and have nothing to say to any one but to read the 'Aids to Reflection on the formation of a *Manly* Character' – a book the more necessary now to us all because except in England I do not see that there is a chance of any *men* being produced any where."[57]

When he came down to visit Coleridge at Highgate in 1828, sometimes accompanied by J. S. Mill, his impressions took on yet more apocalyptic tones. Coleridge looked "as if he belonged not so much to this, or to any other age, as to history". They talked of everything, from landscape gardening to Pantheism to the missionary preaching of Edward Irving. But what remained with Sterling was something more unsettling, the sense of a man who had been through some great personal and historical storm.

> It is painful to observe in Coleridge, that, with all the kindness and glorious far-seeing intelligence of his eye, there is a glare in it, a light half earthly, half morbid. It is the glittering eye of the *Ancient Mariner*. His cheek too shows a flush of over-excitement, the red of a storm-cloud at sunset. When he dies, another, and one of the greatest of their race, will join the few Immortals, the ill understood and ill requited, who have walked the earth.[58]

Two years after Coleridge's death, Sterling told Julius Hare: "To Coleridge I owe *education*. He taught me to believe that an empirical philosophy is none, that Faith is the highest Reason, that all criticism, whether of literature, laws, or manners, is blind without the power of discerning the organic unity of the object."[59]*

18

The *Aids to Reflection* was Coleridge's last major publication. In his final years at Highgate he continued to work with Green on the *Opus Maximum*, and fill his Notebooks with science and philosophy. The sense of his retreating into himself, of talking an increasingly private language, half mystical and half poetic, is strong. "The Will of the Chaos – its dark disactualizing, clinging Self-Contrariety suspended, and forced asunder to become actual as opposites – Light and Gravity. Yes! This supplies the link that was missing. Now the Life of the living Thing opens on me – what it is – and its necessary union with *Mass* – The clinging wrestle, the old war-embrace of Light and Gravity renewed . . . These are but Glimmer – the Sky-blink . . . And now the *living* Soul – what was the Life of the Adam? This is still below the Horizon for me."[61]

Yet little of his old humour was lost. In 1826 he wrote that he had "difficulty in making my own thoughts sufficiently distinct and clear to communicate them, connectedly and consecutively, in writing. They are mature enough to climb up & chirp on the edge of their Birth-nest; but not fledged enough to fly away, tho' it were but to perch on the next branch."[62]

He accepted the changes that wracked and bent his body, and weakened his heart, confident that the spirit still burned strongly within. "For in this bleak World of Mutabilities, & where what is not changed, is chilled, and in this winter-time of my own Being,

---

* Sterling's own subsequent career was full of disappointments, and he died prematurely at the age of thirty-eight, the obscure curate of Herstmonceux, an allegory of Victorian promise unfulfilled. Hence Carlyle chose to write his *Life* (1851) and connect it to his view of Coleridge. In his last months, Sterling said that his own disillusion now included Coleridge, a man whom he now saw – for "all the imagery of Nature about him at his command" – as self-contradictory: a man who could not bear to live "without admiration and notoriety".[60] (See Bibliography, John Beer.)

I resemble a Bottle of Brandy in Spitzbergen – a Dram of alcoholic Fire in the centre of a Cake of Ice."[63]

Writing to Stuart in 1827, Coleridge added a postscript: "Excuse paper – I did not observe I had taken a sheet on which Mr Green had drawn the digestive system of an Oyster."[64] Green became Professor of Anatomy at the Royal College of Surgeons in 1825, and was elected to the first Chair of Surgery at King's College London, in 1831.

19

The life of friends, family, and visitors continued vigorously around him. Gillman arranged that Coleridge's callers at Highgate should be organized into regular Thursday evening soirées. On a typical day they would include "Merchant, Manufacturer, Physician, Member of Parliament & keen politician, chemist, Clergymen, *poetic* Ladies, Painters, Musical Men, Barristers & Political Economist", to each of whom Coleridge would talk "in his own way".[65]

He maintained a huge correspondence, notable among which are a series of letters on "the Ascent of Powers" to his nephew Edward Coleridge, then a master at Eton;[66] and a further dissertation on the role of education to Gillman's eldest son, James. These were familiar, but nevertheless delightful, saws. "And what is a liberal Education? That which *draws* forth and trains up the germ of free-agency in the Individual . . . For believe me, my dear young Friend! It is no musty old Saw but a Maxim of Life, a medicinal Herb from the Garden of Experience that grows amid Sage, Thyme and Heart's Ease, (– This word reminds me of an Ode to Punning which I wrote at School, when I was your age –) that He alone is *free* & entitled to the name of a Gentleman, who knows himself and walks in the light of his own consciousness."[67]

Old friends – Lamb, Crabb Robinson, the Aders, the Montagus (now back in favour) – visited him constantly. "Leigh Hunt stepped in sometimes, and Coleridge took him into the garden, and talked to him of some favourite flower as an emblem and miniature of the Universe."[68]

20

There was a new vogue for annual magazines, and rival editors of the *Bijou* and the *Amulet*, competed for Coleridge's poems, encouraging him to write several fresh ones and finish old. In 1827 he completed "The Garden of Boccaccio" for Ann Gillman, first sketched out on the beach at Ramsgate five years before. It describes a familiar relapse into one of his opium-induced depressions: "when life seems emptied of all genial powers". Then it rises to a rare evocation of the remembered landscapes of "star-bright Italy", inspired by an illustrated edition of Boccaccio's *Tales* which Ann had brought him, to "soothe by silence what words cannot heal". It was less the Italy that Coleridge had known himself, but more a kind of tranquil, tapestried Byzantium:

> O Florence! with the Tuscan fields and hills
> And famous Arno, fed with all their rills;
> Thou brightest star of star-bright Italy!
> Rich, ornate, populous, – all treasures thine,
> The golden corn, the olive, and the vine . . ."[69]

He also wrote, or completed, a last full-length ballad, "Alice Du Clos".

Coleridge set no great store by these verses. In March 1828 he wrote to Lady Beaumont that he could never "resume Poetry". But in the very act of denying it, he gave one of his most moving and suggestive descriptions of inspiration at work. "Is the power extinct? No! No! As in a still Summer Noon, when the lulled Air at irregular intervals wakes up with a startled *Hush-st*, that seems to re-demand the silence which it breaks, or heaves a long profound Sigh in its Sleep, and an Aeolian Harp has been left in the chink of the not quite shut Casement – even so – how often! – scarce a week of my Life shuffles by, that does not at some moment feel the spur of the old genial impulse – even so do there fall on my inward Ear swells, and broken snatches of sweet Melody, reminding me that I still have within me which is both Harp and Breeze."[70]

21

There was a final reconciliation with Wordsworth, which took the form of a six-week tour to Germany, and down the Rhine into Holland, in the summer of 1828. They were accompanied by Dora Wordsworth, and played out the parts of two eccentric English gentlemen revisiting the scenes of their youth. Each complained vigorously of the other's habits. Wordsworth was parsimonious and taciturn and got up too early in the mornings; Coleridge was garrulous and disorganized and constantly criticized the bad German wine and appalling medieval plumbing. But they rubbed along easily enough.

A satirical English clergyman, Julian Young, observed them at a house-party near Bonn. Coleridge shuffled round distractedly in "well-worn slippers, much trodden down at heel", clutching a ponderous tome to his side, "musing and muttering to himself". Wordsworth paced imperiously across the room, holding an alpenstock in one hand, and "a sprig of apple-blossom overgrown with lichen" in the other. They were then joined by Schlegel, who coquettishly adjusted a "brown scratch wig" in the mirror, and made provoking remarks about Scott and Byron. Finally Coleridge could stand this no longer, and caught the eye of his old friend. "Ah," said he, "Byron is a meteor. Wordsworth there (pointing to him) is a fixed star."[71]

As a result of this tour Coleridge wrote a minor comic masterpiece, "The Delinquent Travellers" in rollicking, wittily rhymed verse which made fun of the whole modern vogue for tourism.

> Keep moving! Steam, or Gas, or Stage,
> Hold, cabin, steerage, hencoop's cage –
> Tour, Journey, Voyage, Lounge, Ride, Walk,
> Skim, Sketch, Excursion, Travel-talk –
> For move you must! 'Tis now the rage,
> The law and fashion of the Age.

It concludes with a vision, not unrelated to the "Ancient Mariner", of another great voyage south. But now Coleridge imagined himself near his magical Ramsgate cavern, "beneath the cliffs of Dumpton Bay", captured by a party of "smock-clad smugglers" and finally setting out on a last search for Pantisocracy across the ocean – all the way to Australia:

> . . . Receive me, Lads! I'll go with you
> Hunt the black swan and kangaroo,
> And that New Holland we'll presume
> Old England with some elbow-room.
> Across the mountains we will roam,
> And each man make himself a home:
> Or, if old habits ne'er forsaking,
> Like clock-work of the Devil's making,
> Ourselves inveterate rogues should be,
> We'll have a virtuous progeny;
> And on the dunghill of our vices
> Raise human pine-apples and spices.[72]

22

Coleridge could still enjoy a romp nearer to home. One evening Lockhart and several other friends took him out to a bachelor dinner party in the City, where after many rounds of claret and punch, the literary guests began throwing crockery through the window. Coleridge benignly observed these proceedings, until a large silver fork was placed in his hand, and a wine-glass balanced on a punch-tumbler was set up as a suitable target at the other end of the long dining-table.

Lockhart never forgot "the roseate face of Coleridge, lit up with animation, his large grey eyes beaming, his white hair floating, and his whole frame, as it were, radiating with intense interest, as he poised the fork in his hand, and launched it at the fragile object".[73]

23

But from 1829, Coleridge was more and more frequently ill, suffering from progressive heart disease, and much confined to his bedroom. From afar he blessed the marriage of Henry and Sara, which took place in Keswick, and then formally received the new family when they came to settle (with Mrs Coleridge), at a prudent distance across the Heath in Hampstead. Henry continued his assiduous walks across the Heath, helping to organize a completely new edition of Coleridge's *Poetical Works*, much enlarged and corrected. It was issued by Pickering, whom Coleridge referred to darkly as "my poetical publisher, Mr Pickle-Herring".[74] Henry also took down his uncle's Table Talk almost daily, while the completion of the *Opus Maximum* was officially confided to Green.*

24

In December 1829 Coleridge published his last work, a monograph *On the Constitution of the Church and State*. He proposed a Platonic "Idea" of both institutions, which distinguished them from their temporal shortcomings. He then argued for a political balance between the forces of "Progress" and "Permanence" – partly inspired by the urgent public debate surrounding the Great Reform Bill, over which he was greatly divided. The little volume also contained his influential concept of "the Clerisy". He appealed for the formation of an intelligentsia in England, which would include writers, artists and scientists, as well as actual clergymen and teachers.[75] In a characteristic way, he saw this ideal body as a force for "reconciliation", permanently committed to "National Education" and the free flow of liberal ideas in society. Beneath the tangle of topical arguments, his impressive idea of a continuous cultural "evolution" still holds its ground.

---

* The unfinished *Opus Maximum* has still not been published, but will eventually appear as Volume 15 of the great Bollingen *Collected Coleridge*. (See Bibliography.) The faithful Green, much taken up with his later duties for the Royal College of Surgeons, attempted to incorporate some of Coleridge's ideas in his Hunterian Lectures; and in his *Spiritual Philosophy: Founded on the Teaching of the late Samuel Taylor Coleridge*, published after his own death, in 1865. A strikingly affectionate and protective account of his old friend appears in a manuscript essay, "Introduction to the Philosophical Remains of S. T. Coleridge", preserved by Derwent. "How often during the last years of his life have I found him languid, listless, with 'drooping gait' and heavy eye . . . till some question arose that roused his dormant intellectual powers, his bodily ails were then forgotten, his infirmities thrown off, the mind lived for itself, and . . . the fascinated auditor could not choose but hear!" (*Shorter Works*, II, p. 1526.)

25

Coleridge was preparing for death, but he did it in his own way. In May 1830 he collapsed in his bedroom, and the crash of his falling body brought the Gillmans hurrying up the stairs. Seeing him unconscious on the floor, they assumed that all was finally over. But Coleridge was merely practising for his resurrection, and to their astonishment and relief soon burst back to life. He gave a wonderful, mocking account of his experience to William Blackwood.

> All my faculties returned entire, and in the first instance exactly as from ordinary sleep. Indeed, before I had opened my eyes, I merely found that my medical friends and Mrs Gillman were flustering over me: my first words were, "What a mystery we are! What a problem is presented in the strange contrast between the imperishability of our thoughts and the perishable fugacious nature of our consciousness . . ."

He was then gratified by Gillman, hearing the familiar unstoppable eloquence once more in full flood, exclaiming with unconscious humour, "Thank God! . . . there is nothing of apoplexy in this seizure."[76]

26

Coleridge wrote his own epitaph, and discussed the design of his tombstone with the greatest interest. He wavered long over a tender, voluptuous Muse figure; and then a broken harp; but finally decided that an old man under an ancient "yew tree" was more suitable.[77] He wrote two last poems, one on the subject of meeting his younger self, "Phantom or Fact", who gazes down at him with a "weary, wandering, disavowing look!"

The other, "Love's Apparition and Evanishment", is a subtle, lyrical interweaving of his traditional themes of Love and Hope. Like many of his late poems it is set in the garden at Highgate, where the old poet sits musing on a bank of scented camomile grass. But it recalls many earlier images, from "Limbo" to "Kubla Khan". It opens with the idea of the long, desert journey that so much of his life had been, in search of the shining oasis of inspiration:

Like a lone Arab, old and blind,
Some caravan had left behind,
Who sits beside a ruin'd well
Where the shy sand-asps bask and swell;
And now he hangs his aged head aslant,
And listens for a human sound – in vain!
And now the aid which Heaven alone can grant,
Upturns his eyeless face from Heaven to gain . . .[78]

It ends with the visitation of "Love, a sylph in bridal train"; perhaps the last retreating glimpse of Asra.*

27

For all his self-doubts, Coleridge had some confidence that his work would now endure. Many of his family affairs were also settled. Mrs Coleridge was peacefully domesticated with Henry and Sara at Downshire Hill, Hampstead. If husband and wife were not exactly reunited, they were largely reconciled. In 1832 Mrs Coleridge wrote to Tom Poole with some pride that Coleridge had "talked incessantly for full five hours" at his granddaughter's christening.[79]

Derwent had emerged from his period of Oxford high-life and fashionable atheism, married happily, and settled as vicar of Helston in Cornwall. Later, he would live out part of his father's legacy as an educator, becoming the principal of St Mark's College in Chelsea, and a founding figure in the movement for working men's colleges. His son, Ernest, edited the great Oxford edition of Coleridge's poetry (1912).

---

* Coleridge's epitaph can now be found gravely incised on a memorial flagstone in the nave of St Michael's Church, Highgate, where it is regularly walked over by numerous schoolchildren, a circumstance which would have surely pleased him. It ends with two of the most wonderfully ambiguous lines he ever wrote:

"Mercy for praise – to be forgiven for fame
He asked, and hoped, through Christ. Do thou the same!"

But in a letter of 1833 he also put on his Devonshire yokel voice to bid farewell, and wrote this alternative version:

"In truth, he's no beauty!' – cried Moll, Poll and Tab,
But all of them owned – He'd the gift of the Gab."

28

The figure who still haunted Coleridge was Hartley, a reproachful ghost of his own lost youth. The schoolmastering had failed, a second attempt at journalism in Leeds had been abandoned, and from 1829 he was again adrift in the Lake District, living mainly with a kindly family of farmers outside Grasmere. He had faithfully promised to attend his beloved sister's wedding at Keswick. "I will be present at the celebration – if I walk all night, and all night again." But in the event he never appeared, missing the last chance he would ever have to gather with his family in their old northern haunts.

Just before this last exile, he wrote one of his most tranquil, terrible letters to his mother. "My Brother gets a Wife – well – my Sister is to have a Husband – well – I remain alone, bare and barren and blasted, ill-omen'd and unsightly as Wordsworth's melancholy thorn on the bleak hill-top. So hath it been ordain'd, and it is well."[80]

Coleridge sent him a £50 bequest he had been left by Lady Beaumont, but he heard nothing directly from his son in all these years. In 1833 he was surprised by the gift of Hartley's first and only book of *Poems*, which he found was dedicated to himself. The opening sonnet called back, with exquisite pathos, the child he had loved and nursed at Stowey, and celebrated all those years ago in "Frost at Midnight":

> Father, and Bard revered! to whom I owe,
> Whate'er it be, my little art of numbers,
> Thou, in thy night-watch o'er my cradled slumbers,
> Didst meditate the verse that lives to show,
> (And long shall live, when all alike are low)
> Thy prayer how ardent, and thy hope how strong,
> That I should learn of Nature's self the song,
> The lore which none but Nature's pupils know.
>
> The prayer was heard: I "wander'd like a breeze",
> By mountain brooks and solitary meres,
> And gather'd there the shapes and phantasies
> Which, mixt with passions of my sadder years,
> Compose this book. If good therein there be,
> That good, my sire, I dedicate to thee.[81]

This was the last greeting that Hartley sent his father, and it was in its own way also an epitaph.

29

Coleridge never stopped his pursuit of knowledge and its mysteries. His last important expedition from Highgate was to a conference of the British Association for the Advancement of Science, at Cambridge in the summer of 1833. He was accompanied by Gillman and Green, and showed them round the college scenes of his undergraduate triumphs and disasters. He met Sir Humphry Davy's pupil Michael Faraday; he discussed the evolutionary implications of new discoveries in geology published by Charles Lyell; and he went to contemplate Titian's "Venus" at the Fitzwilliam Museum. "That glorious picture of the Venus – so perfectly beautiful and perfectly innocent – as if Beauty and Innocence could not be dissociated."[82]

30

By the spring of 1834 he was very ill, his heart was failing, his breathing difficult. Gillman's final and miraculously intelligent handling of the opium problem was to administer laudanum by hypodermic injection (still a very rare procedure) and increase the dose until it performed its original function: as a pure analgesic. In his will, Coleridge left "small, plain gold mourning rings" to those who had been closest to his heart: Charles Lamb, Tom Poole, Josiah Wade and Sara Hutchinson. Green and Gillman were made his executors, his estate was left to his wife, a trust was set up for Hartley.

On 5 July 1834 he made a last, painful walk across his room with a stick, to gaze out at "the glorious landscape" of Hampstead Heath from his window. It seemed to hover below him like the magic world, "the sunny spot of greenery", that he had spent a lifetime finding and losing and finding again. He said he felt joy and thankfulness at this "apparent Dawn of Convalescence".[83]

On 10 July, Henry made a final entry in the *Table Talk*. But what he recorded was actually something his uncle had already written in a letter, several years before. Perhaps it was what Coleridge now repeated to him. Or perhaps it was what Coleridge's legend was meant to say afterwards. Who could tell what point Coleridge had reached in his wonderful story, whether he was still voyaging outwards, or already coming back?

> I am dying, but without expectation of a speedy release. Is it not strange that very recently by-gone images, and scenes of early life, have stolen into my mind, like breezes blown from the spice-islands of Youth and Hope – those twin realities of this phantom world! I do not add Love – for what is Love but Youth and Hope embracing, and so seen as *one*? I say *realities*; for reality is a thing of degrees, from the Iliad to a dream . . .'[84]

At 6.30 a.m. on 25 July 1834 he slipped into the dark. He was talking almost up to the end. As he closed those extraordinary eyes, he told Green that his mind was clear and "quite unclouded". Then he added with growing interest, "I could even be witty . . ."[85]

12

Afterword

So he sets sail again, expecting to die but half-hoping to be re-born. There is much to be said about those who remained behind (for example that Lamb died the same year, and Asra the following one, and Wordsworth lived to climb Helvellyn at the age of seventy). But there is a particular kind of silence which falls after a life like Coleridge's and perhaps it should be observed.

It is an expectant and companionable silence, I think; the silence before the questions begin, and the reckonings are made. It is like the silence in a concert hall when a symphony has just been played. The music has ended, but it hasn't in any conceivable way finished. Coleridge's life continues in one's head, and mixes with the sounds of one's own existence, and starts up again somewhere else in other hands with a different interpretation.

This is the peculiar music of biography, haunting and uniquely *life-like* for a moment, but always incomplete and unsatisfactory and sending out many echoes into the future. I think this is particularly true of Coleridge's unfinished voyage, with its black storms and glittering sunlit spells, forever chasing each other over the horizon. Perhaps Goethe had this in mind when he said that one proof of genius was posthumous productivity. Once you have heard Coleridge (as I suggested at the opening of *Early Visions*) there is no stopping his sound, his voice, his ideas, his poetry, his pains, his puns.

Charles Lamb, his great and faithful friend, wrote this: "When I heard of the death of Coleridge, it was without grief. It seemed to me he had long been on the confines of the next world, that he had a hunger for Eternity. I grieved that I could not grieve! But since I feel how great a part he was of me, his great and dear Spirit haunts me. I cannot think a thought, I cannot make a criticism of men and books, without an ineffectual turning and reference to him.

He was the proof and touchstone of all my cogitations. . . . Never saw I his likeness, nor probably can the world see it again."

After fifteen years in Coleridge's extraordinary presence, I know that feeling.

Bibliography and References

Bibliography

As in my first volume *Early Visions*, 1989, sources for this Life of Coleridge will be found in the Reference Notes that follow, with major materials listed under "Abbreviations". The emphasis falls increasingly on the great Bollingen Series of the *Collected Coleridge*, a superb work of collective twentieth-century scholarship, which will eventually conclude with complete editions of the poetry and the elusive "Opus Maximum", as well as the remaining Notebooks.

My own special edition of the poetry, *Coleridge: Selected Poems*, 1996, was conceived very much as a third companion volume to *Early Visions* and *Darker Reflections*. My ideal biography-reader – what Coleridge called the "great Mogul diamonds" – would constantly turn aside to read and re-read the poetry. In this edition, I have attached prefaces and extensive commentaries to a hundred and one of Coleridge's poems intending to add a whole other "voice" or perspective to my biography. I believe passionately that one of the main purposes of a literary Life is to renew the appreciation of – no, the *love* of – a neglected body of literary Work, and make it alive for a new generation. My first and last loyalty has been to Coleridge the poet, in all his amazing manifestations. So much of his writing was poetry by other means.

Suggestions (sometimes *provocations*) for further study and exploration are contained *passim* in my footnotes, with a particular attempt to show how Coleridge's fantastic range of ideas and intuitions rippled out through the nineteenth century, across many disciplines in both arts and sciences, and are still breaking on the shores of the twenty-first. As in *Early Visions*, I give below not a standard bibliography but a carefully chosen pharmacology of Coleridgean *stimulants*, to carry the reader onwards.

BIBLIOGRAPHY

M.H. Abrams, *The Mirror and the Lamp: Romantic Theory and the Critical Tradition*, Oxford, 1953.

Patricia Adair, *The Waking Dream: A Study of Coleridge's Poetry*, London, 1967.

Rosemary Ashton, *The Life of Samuel Taylor Coleridge: A Critical Biography*, Blackwells, 1996.

Isaiah Berlin, "The Apotheosis of the Romantic Will", in *The Crooked Timber of Humanity: Chapters in the History of Ideas*, Vintage, New York, 1992.

Martin Booth, *Opium: A History*, Simon and Schuster, 1996.

Marilyn Butler, *Romantics, Rebels and Reactionaries*, Oxford, 1981.

John Beer, *Romantic Influences: Contemporary, Victorian, Modern*, Macmillan, 1993.

Thomas De Quincey, *Confessions of an English Opium Eater*, 1822, edited by Alethea Hayter, Penguin, 1971.

Stephen Gill, *William Wordsworth: A Life*, Oxford, 1989.

Alethea Hayter, *Opium and the Romantic Imagination*, Faber, 1968.

John Horgan, *The End of Science: Facing the Limits of Knowledge in the Twilight of the Scientific Age*, Little Brown, 1997.

Ted Hughes, "The Snake in the Oak", in *Winter Pollen: Occasional Prose*, Faber, 1994.

Molly Lefebure, *The Bondage of Love: A Life of Mrs Samuel Taylor Coleridge*, Gollancz, 1986.

Trevor H. Levere, *Poetry Realized in Nature: Samuel Taylor Coleridge and Early Nineteenth-Century Science*, Cambridge, 1981.

Brian Magee, *Confessions of a Philosopher*, Weidenfeld & Nicolson, 1997.

John Stuart Mill, *On Bentham and Coleridge*, 1840; edited by F.R. Leavis, London, 1969.

David Newsome, *Two Classes of Men: Platonism and English Romantic Thought*, John Murray, 1974.

Morton D. Paley, *Coleridge's Later Poetry, Oxford*, 1996.

Roy Porter and Mikulas Teich (editors), *Drugs and Narcotics in History*, Cambridge, 1995.

Camille Paglia, "The Daemon as Lesbian Vampire: Coleridge", in *Sexual Personae*, Yale University Press, 1990.

Leslie Stephen, "Coleridge", in *Hours in a Library*, vol 3, 1888.

Lewis Wolpert, "Creativity" in *The Unnatural Nature of Science*, Faber, 1992.

Virginia Woolf, "The Man at the Gate" and "Sara Coleridge", in *The Death of the Moth and Other Essays*, Hogarth Press, 1942.

References

ABBREVIATIONS USED IN REFERENCE NOTES

(1) Works by Coleridge

Letters – *Collected Letters of Samuel Taylor Coleridge*, 6 vols, edited by E.L. Griggs, Oxford, 1956–71.

Notebooks – *The Notebooks of Samuel Taylor Coleridge*, 4 double vols, (Texts and Notes), 1794–1826, edited by Kathleen Coburn and (vol. 4) Merten Christensen, Bollingen Series, Princeton University Press and Routledge, 1957–90.

S.P. – *Coleridge: Selected Poems*, edited by Richard Holmes, HarperCollins, 1996.

P.W. – *Coleridge: Poetical Works*, edited by E. H. Coleridge, Oxford, 1912, 1980.

Complete Poetical Works – *The Complete Poetical Works of Samuel Taylor Coleridge*, edited by E.H. Coleridge, 2 vols (I, Poems; 2, Drama and Fragments), Oxford, 1912, 1975.

Biographia – *Biographia Literaria*, 2 vols, edited by James Engell and W. Jackson Bate, Bollingen Series, Princeton University Press and Routledge, 1983.

Friend – *The Friend*, 2 vols, edited by Barbara E. Rooke, Bollingen Series, Princeton University Press and Routledge, 1969.

Literary Lectures – *Lectures 1808–1819: On Literature*, 2 vols, edited by R.A. Foakes, Bollingen Series, Princeton University Press and Routledge, 1987.

Philosophical Lectures – *The Philosophical Lectures of Samuel Taylor Coleridge*, edited by Kathleen Coburn, London, 1949.

Shakespearean Criticism – *Shakespearean Criticism*, 2 vols, edited by T.M. Raysor, Dent, 1960.

Essays – *Essays on his Times*, 3 vols, edited by D.V. Erdman, Bollingen Series, Princeton University Press and Routledge, 1978.

Lay Sermons – *Lay Sermons*, edited by R.J. White, Bollingen Series, Princeton University Press and Routledge, 1972.

Aids – *Aids to Reflection*, edited by John Beer, Bollingen Series, Princeton University Press and Routledge, 1993.

Church and State – *On the Constitution of the Church and State*, 2 vols, edited by E.E. Bostetter, H.J. Jackson, and J.R. de Jackson, Bollingen Series, Princeton University Press and Routledge, 1995.

Table Talk – *The Table Talk of Samuel Taylor Coleridge*, 2 vols, edited by Carl. R. Woodring, Bollingen Series, Princeton University Press and Routledge, 1990.

Talker – *Coleridge The Talker*, edited by R.W. Armour and R.F. Howes, New York, 1940.

(2) Manuscript sources

Dove Cottage – Manuscripts relating to the Wordsworth-Coleridge circle, including John Morgan and Thomas Clarkson, held by the Wordsworth Trust, Dove Cottage, Grasmere, Cumbria.

British Library – Manuscripts held at the British Library, Euston Road, London: including Coleridge's published Notebooks (1794–1826) Adds. Mss. 47, 496–47,527; and largely unpublished (1827–1834), Adds, Mss. 47,527–47,545; Tom Poole's papers, Adds Mss 35,343–5; Daniel Stuart's papers, Adds Mss 34,046; Sir Alexander Ball's papers, 37,268; Nelson's papers, 34,932; and Captain Pasley's adventurous Life, Adds. Mss. 41,766.

Royal Institution – Manuscripts relating to the Davy–Coleridge circle, held by the Royal Institution of Great Britain, Albemarle Street, London.

Highgate Institution – Coleridgeana, documents and illustrations held at the Coleridge Archive, Highgate Literary and Scientific Institution, South Green, Highgate, London.

(3) Secondary Sources

Allston – The Life and Letters of *Washington Allston*, by J.B. Flagg, 1892.

Chambers – *Samuel Taylor Coleridge: A Biographical Study*, by E.K. Chambers, Oxford, 1938.

Cottle – *Early Recollections, chiefly relating to the late Samuel Taylor Coleridge*, 2 vols, by Joseph Cottle, 1837.

De Quincey – *Thomas De Quincey*, edited by Bonamy Dobrée, London, 1965.

Devonshire – *The Story of a Devonshire House*, by Lord Coleridge, 1905.

Gillman – *The Life of Samuel Taylor Coleridge*, by James Gillman MD, 1838.

Hartley – *The Poems of Hartley Coleridge; prefaced with a Memoir of his Life by his Brother*, edited by Derwent Coleridge, 1851.

Hazlitt – *William Hazlitt: Selected Writings*, edited by Ronald Blythe, Penguin Classics, 1987.

Heritage – *Coleridge: The Critical Heritage*, edited by J.R. de J. Jackson, Routledge, 1970.

Hutchinson – *The Letters of Sara Hutchinson (Asra): 1800 to 1835*, edited by Kathleen Coburn, 1954.

Keats – *Letters of John Keats*, edited by Robert Gittings, Oxford, 1970.

Lamb – *The Letters of Charles and Mary Lamb*, 3 vols, edited by Edwin J. Marrs Jnr, Cornell University Press, 1975.

Minnow – *A Minnow Among Tritons: Mrs S.T. Coleridge's Letters to Tom Poole*, edited by Stephen Potter, 1934.

Moorman – *William Wordsworth: A Biography*, 2 vols, by Mary Moorman, Oxford, 1965.

Poole – *Thomas Poole and his Friends*, 2 vols, by Mrs Henry Sandford, 1888.

Robinson, *Books* – *Henry Crabb Robinson: On Books and their Writers*, edited by Edith J. Morley, London, 1938.

Robinson, *Letters* – *The Correspondence of Henry Crabb Robinson with the Wordsworth Circle*, 2 vols, edited by Edith J. Morley, Oxford, 1927.

Robinson, *Selections* – *Blake, Coleridge, Wordsworth, Lamb: Selections from the Remains of Henry Crabb Robinson, edited by Edith J. Morley*, London, 1922.

Southey – *New Letters of Robert Southey*, 2 vols, edited by Kenneth Curry, New York, 1965.

Sultana – *Samuel Taylor Coleridge in Malta and Italy*, by Donald Sultana, New York, 1969.

Wordsworth, *Middle Years* – *The Letters of William and Dorothy Wordsworth: The Middle Years, 1806–1820*, 2 vols., edited by E. de Selincourt, Oxford, 1937; vol I. revised by Mary Moorman, 1969.

Wordsworth, *Love Letters* – *The Love Letters of William and Mary Wordsworth*, edited by Beth Darlington, Chatto, 1982.

Reference Notes

Chapter 1: Adrift in the Mediterranean

1 *Notebooks*, II, 1993.
2 *Prelude* (1805), Book VI, lines 249–56.
3 *Notebooks*, II, 2018.
4 Ibid, 1993.
5 Ibid, 1996.
6 Ibid, 1993N.
7 Ibid, 2026.
8 Ibid, 2016.
9 Ibid, 2005.
10 Ibid, 1997.
11 Ibid, 2004.
12 Ibid, 2001.
13 *Letters*, III, p. 1123.
14 *Notebooks*, II, 2024.
15 *Letters*, II, p. 1127.
16 *Notebooks*, II, 1993.
17 Ibid, 2014.
18 Ibid, 2014.
19 Ibid, 1998.
20 Ibid, 1999.
21 Ibid, 2012.
22 *S.P.*, p. 60; *P.W.*, p. 405.
23 *Notebooks*, II, 2012.
24 Ibid, 1998.
25 Ibid, 2000.
26 *S.P.*, p. 185; *P.W.*, p. 393.
27 *Letters*, II, p. 1128.
28 Ibid, p. 1127.
29 Ibid, p. 1127.
30 *Notebooks*, II, 2026.
31 Ibid, 2026.
32 Ibid, 1993n.
33 *Letters*, II, p. 1129.
34 *Notebooks*, II, 2044.
35 Ibid, 2050.
36 *Letters*, II, p. 1133.
37 *Notebooks*, II, 2045.
38 Ibid, 2045.
39 *Letters*, II, p. 113–5.
40 *Notebooks*, II, 2036.
41 Ibid, 2050.
42 Ibid, 2051.
43 Ibid, 2060.
44 Ibid, 2070.
45 Ibid, 2064.
46 Ibid, 2055.
47 Ibid, 2063.
48 Ibid, 2071.
49 Ibid, 2084.
50 Ibid, 2085.
51 Ibid, 2085.
52 Ibid, 2091.
53 Ibid, 2091.
54 Ibid, 2090.
55 Ibid, 2086.
56 Ibid, 2099.
57 *Letters*, II, p. 1139.
58 *Friend*, II, p. 253.
59 *Notebooks*, II, 2101.
60 *Friend*, II, pp. 250–3.
61 Ibid, p. 252.
62 Sultana, pp. 165–77.
63 *Letters*, II, p. 1140–1
64 *Notebooks*, II, 2118.
65 *Letters*, II, p. 1143.
66 *Notebooks*, II, 2153.
67 Ibid, 2140.
68 *Letters*, II, p. 1148.
69 *Notebooks*, II, 2144.
70 Ibid, 2174.
71 Ibid, 2171.
72 Ibid, 2171–6N.

73 *Letters*, III, p. 482.
74 *Notebooks*, II, 2172.
75 Ibid, 2176 (my translation).
76 Ibid, 2256.
77 Ibid, 2189.
78 Ibid, 2184.
79 Ibid, 2192.
80 Ibid, 2196.
81 Ibid, 2245.
82 Ibid, 2235.
83 Ibid, 2238.
84 Ibid, 2209 (probably deleted by Mrs Gillman).
85 Ibid, 2356.
86 Ibid, 2207.
87 Sartori, Index to Opera Singers.
88 *Notebooks*, II, 3404.
89 Ibid, 3404.
90 Ibid, 2237.
91 *Prelude* (1805), Book X, lines 941–1039.
92 *Syracuse: Art, History, Landscape*, Co. Grafa (Italy), 1985, p. 39.
93 *Notebooks*, II, 2202, 2217.
94 *S.P.*, p. 244; *P.W.*, p. 394.
95 *Notebooks*, II, 2261.
96 *Notebooks*, II, Notes, p. 411.
97 *Letters*, II, p. 1151.
98 Ibid, p. 1152.
99 Ibid, p. 1155–6.
100 Ibid, p. 1157.
101 *Notebooks*, II, 2268.
102 *Letters*, II, p. 1158–9.
103 Ibid, p. 1159.
104 Ibid, p. 1159.
105 *Notebooks*, II, 2284.
106 Ibid, 2293.
107 Ibid, 2279.
108 *Letters*. II, p. 1157.
109 Sultana, pp. 27–71.
110 *Letters*, II, p. 1163.
111 Ibid, p. 1165.
112 Ibid, p. 1169.
113 *Notebooks*, II, Notes, mainly 15, 21, 22, 18.
114 *Notebooks*, II, 2368.
115 Ibid, 2373.
116 Ibid, 2372.
117 Ibid, 2387.
118 Ibid, 2399.
119 Ibid, 2398, 2495.
120 Ibid, 2549.
121 Ibid, 2398.
122 Ibid, 2444.
123 Ibid, 2453.
124 Ibid, 2546.
125 Ibid, 2420.
126 *The Early Letters of William and Dorothy Wordsworth*, edited by E. de Selincourt, Oxford, 1935, p. 438.
127 *Letters*, II, p. 1170.
128 Wordsworth, *Early Letters*, op. cit, p. 448.
129 *Notebooks*, II, 2527.
130 Ibid, 2517.
131 Wordsworth, *Early Letters*, op. cit. p. 453.
132 *Notebooks*, II, 2536.
133 Ibid, 2556.
134 Ibid, 2557.
135 Ibid, 2541.
136 Ibid, 2564.
137 *Letters*, II, p. 1168.
138 Ibid, p. 1168.
139 Sultana, p. 336.
140 *Notebooks*, II, 2583.
141 Ibid, 2609.
142 Ibid, 2600.
143 *S.P.*, p. 242; *P.W.*, p. 396.
144 Ibid, p. 243; Ibid, p. 396–7.
145 *Notebooks*, II, 2606.
146 Ibid, 2610.
147 Ibid, 2614.
148 Chambers, p. 186.
149 *Notebooks*, II, 2606.
150 Sultana, p. 272–4.
151 Dove Cottage Mss, Decatur.
152 *Letters*, II, p. 1169.
153 *Notebooks*, II, 2628.
154 Wordsworth, *Early Letters*, op. cit., pp. 510–12.
155 *Notebooks*, II, 2638.
156 *Letters*, II, p. 1171.
157 Dove Cottage Mss, Ball.
158 *Notebooks*, II, 2670–1.
159 Ibid, 2672.
160 *Friend*, II, p. 365.

161 British Library, Add Mss 37, 268. f. 90–92.
162 Wordsworth, *Early Letters*, op. cit., p. 560.
163 *Notebooks*, II, 2828.
164 Sultana, p. 385.
165 *Notebooks*, II, 2791.
166 *Talker*, pp. 433–4.
167 Allston, p. 5.
168 *Notebooks*, II, 2832.
169 Ibid, 2815.
170 Ibid, 2794N.
171 Ibid, 2817.
172 *Letters*, III, p. 351.
173 *Talker*, p. 109.
174 *Biographia*, II, pp. 116–8 and note.
175 Sultana, p. 394.
176 *Notebooks*, II, 2829.
177 Ibid, 2833.
178 Sultana, p. 392.
179 *Notebooks*, II, 2843.
180 *Philosophical Lectures*, pp. 193–4 (January 1819); Edoardo Zuccato, *Coleridge in Italy*, Cork University Press, 1996, pp. 93–5.
181 *Notebooks*, II, 2860.
182 Ibid, 2860.
183 Chambers, p. 190.
184 *Letters*, II, p. 1173.
185 *Biographia*, I, p. 216 and note.
186 Sultana, p. 394.
187 *Notebooks*, II, 2861.
188 Ibid, 2861.
189 *P.W.*, p. 498 and *Notebooks*, II, 2865.
190 *Letters*, IV, p. 569.
191 *Letters*, II, p. 1176.
192 *S.P.*, p. 192; *P.W.*, p. 456.
193 *Letters*, II, p. 1177.

Chapter 2: The Sense of Home

1 *Letters*, II, p. 1176.
2 Notebooks, II, 3322.
3 Ibid, 2233.
4 Ibid, 2868.
5 Ibid, 2880; see *S.P.*, p. 88 for published version.
6 *Letters*, II, pp. 1186–7.
7 *Letters*, II, p. 1182.
8 Ibid, p. 1178.
9 Ibid, p. 1178.
10 *S.P.*, p. 22; *P.W.*, pp. 402–3.
11 Wordsworth, *Middle Years*, I, pp. 78–9.
12 Lamb, II, p. 240.
13 *Letters*, II, p. 1181.
14 Ibid, p. 1188.
15 Ibid, p. 1191.
16 *Letters*, III, p. 8.
17 *Letters*, II, p. 1187.
18 Ibid, p. 1189.
19 Ibid, p. 1192.
20 Ibid, p. 1197.
21 *Notebooks*, II, 2893.
22 Wordsworth, *Middle Years*, I, pp. 86–7.
23 *Notebooks*, II, 2938.
24 Wordsworth, *Middle Years*, I, p. 78.
25 Ibid, p. 110.
26 *Letters*, II, p. 1199.
27 Ibid, p. 1200.
28 Southey, I, pp. 44–9.
29 *Notebooks*, II, 2935.
30 *Letters*, II, p. 1203.
31 *Notebooks*, II, 2934, 2937.
32 *Shorter Works*, I, p. 185.
33 Ibid, p. 179.
34 *Letters*, III, p. 6.
35 Hartley, p. xxxi.
36 *Letters*, II, p. 1205.
37 J.B. Frith, *Highways and Byways in Leicestershire*, 1926, pp. 150–2.
38 Wordsworth, *Middle Years*, I, p. 98, p. 110.
39 *Letters*, III, p. 1.
40 Wordsworth, *Middle Years*, I, p. 110.
41 Ibid, p. 110.
42 Ibid, p. 124.
43 Ibid, p. 121.
44 *Notebooks*, II, 2984.
45 Ibid, 2975.
46 Ibid, 3148.
47 Ibid, 3328.
48 Ibid, 3148.
49 *Notebooks*, II, 2975, Notes.
50 *Notebooks*, IV, 4537.

51 *S.P.*, pp. 60–1; *P.W.*, pp. 406–7 text contains alternatives and suppressed versions.
52 Ibid, pp. 61–2; Ibid, p. 406.
53 Moorman, 2, p. 95.
54 Wordsworth, *Middle Years*, I, p. 150.
55 *Notebooks*, II, 2998.
56 *S.P.*, p. 187.
57 *S.P.*, p. 246; *P.W.*, p. 498.
58 *Notebooks*, II, 2997.
59 *S.P.*, p. 188; *P.W.*, p. 498.
60 Ibid, p. 249; *Notebooks*, II, 2991
61 *Notebooks*, II, 2998.
62 Ibid., 2988.
63 *Letters*, III, p. 5.
64 Wordsworth, *Middle Years*, I, p. 138.
65 *Letters*, III, pp. 24–5.
66 Ibid, p. 14.
67 Ibid, p. 7.
68 Ibid, p. 7.
69 Ibid, pp. 8–9n.
70 Wordsworth, *Middle Years*, I, pp. 176, 184.
71 *Letters*, III, pp. 9–11.
72 Hartley, pp. xxxiv–v.
73 *Letters*, III, p. 12.
74 Ibid, p. 22.
75 Ibid, p. 18.
76 *Notebooks*, II, 3041N.
77 Ibid, p. 3048 and Notes.
78 *Letters*, III, p. 22.
79 *Notebooks*, II, 3064.
80 Ibid, 3072.
81 Ibid, 3100.
82 Ibid, 3078.
83 Ibid, 3078.
84 Poole, II, p. 184.
85 *Letters*, III, p. 20.
86 *Friend*, II, p. 118.
87 *Letters*, III, p. 25.
88 Poole, II. p. 185.
89 Letters, III, p. 21.
90 Ibid, p. 19.
91 Ibid, p. 9n; p. 102n.
92 Ibid, p. 25.
93 *Notebooks*, II, 3024.
94 De Quincey, p. 122.
95 Ibid, pp. 122–3.
96 Ibid, pp. 121–2.
97 Ibid, p. 47.
98 Grevel Lindop, *A Life of Thomas De Quincey*, Dent, 1981, p. 145.
99 *Notebooks*, II, 3108.
100 *Letters*, III, p. 23.
101 Poole, II, p. 190.
102 *Letters*, III, p. 26.
103 *Notebooks*, II, 3128.
104 Ibid, 3164.
105 Ibid, 3161.
106 Ibid, 3094; Poole, II, p. 200.
107 Poole, II, p. 195.
108 *S.P.*, p. 245; *P.W.*, p. 486.
109 Ibid, p. 190; Ibid, p. 409.
110 *Notebooks*, II, 3107.
111 Ibid, 3107.
112 Ibid, 3137.
113 Ibid, 3151.
114 Ibid, 3159.

Chapter 3: The Lecture Shirt

1 Poole, II, p. 193.
2 *Notebooks*, II, 3148.
3 *Letters*, III, p. 30.
4 Ibid, p. 38.
5 *Notebooks*, II, 3182.
6 *Letters*, III, p. 29.
7 British Library, Add. Mss 47,523.
8 *Notebooks*, II, 3246; *Literary Lectures*, I, p. 66.
9 Poole, II, p. 203.
10 Lindop, op. cit., p. 137, 147.
11 *Letters*, III, p. 34n.
12 Lindop, op. cit., p. 146.
13 *Letters*, III, p. 33, p. 73.
14 *Letters*, III, p. 37.
15 Dove Cottage Mss, (Morgan 6 July 1808).
16 *Letters*, III, pp. 37–8.
17 Ibid, p. 46.
18 Ibid, p. 36.
19 *S.P.*, p. 204; *P.W.*, p. 411.
20 *Notebooks*, II, 3146.
21 Wordsworth, *Middle Years*, I, p. 183.
22 Ibid, p. 188.

23 Davy's Laboratory Notebook, quoted in David Knight, *Humphry Davy: Science and Power*, Oxford, 1992, p. 66.
24 Royal Institution Minutes, 1808.
25 *Literary Lectures*, I, pp. 36–7.
26 *Letters*, III, p. 51.
27 De Quincey, p. 131.
28 Royal Institution Archives, 1808.
29 *Literary Lectures*, I, p. 16.
30 Ibid, pp. lvi–lx.
31 *Letters*, III, p. 52.
32 Ibid, p. 73.
33 Ibid, p. 60.
34 Ibid, p. 51.
35 Lamb, III, p. 274
36 Royal Institution Archive, Davy.
37 *Literary Lectures*, I, p. 147.
38 *Letters*, III, p. 61.
39 Ibid, p. 73.
40 Ibid, 47.
41 Ibid, p. 67.
42 Ibid, p. 66.
43 Ibid, p. 73.
44 Ibid, p. 68.
45 Ibid, p. 76.
46 Ibid, p. 75.
47 Wordsworth, *Middle Years*, I, p. 196.
48 Moorman, II, p. 118.
49 Moorman, II, p. 118N.
50 Wordsworth, *Middle Years*, I, p. 238.
51 *Literary Lectures*, I, p. 65.
52 Ibid, pp. 67–8.
53 Ibid, pp. 81–2.
54 Wordsworth, *Middle Years*, I, p. 208.
55 Ibid, p. 207.
56 Ibid, p. 230.
57 Ibid, p. 209; Moorman, II, p. 126.
58 *Literary Lectures*, I, p. 82.
59 Ibid, p. 118.
60 Ibid, p. 145.
61 *Literary Lectures*, I, p. xlvi.
62 Ibid, p. 149.
63 Ibid, p. 143.
64 Ibid, pp. 114–5.
65 Ibid, pp. 131–2.
66 Ibid, pp. 134–5.
67 *Letters*, III, pp. 96–7.
68 *Literary Lectures*, I, p. 99.
69 Ibid, p. 102.
70 Ibid, p. 105.
71 Ibid, pp. 106–8.
72 Ibid, p. 103.
73 *Letters*, III, p. 98.
74 Ibid, p. 101.
75 Ibid, p. 98.
76 Ibid, pp. 107–8.
77 Ibid, pp, 108–9.
78 Ibid, p. 86, see *Early Visions*, Chapter 3.
79 Ibid, p. 85N.
80 *Notebooks*, III, 3304.
81 Ibid, 3325.
82 Ibid, 3314.
83 *S.P.*, p. 247; *P.W.*, p. 412.
84 *Notebooks*, III, 3320.
85 Ibid, 3342.
86 Ibid, 3303, 3343, 3347.
87 *Letters*, III, p. 111.
88 Ibid, p. 111N.
89 *Literary Lectures*, I, pp. 144–5.
90 Ibid, p. 122.
91 Royal Institution Archives; *Letters*, III, pp. 117–8.
92 *Letters*, III, p. 104.
93 *Notebooks*, III, 3304.
94 *Letters*, III, p. 116.
95 Ibid, pp. 110–11.
96 Wordsworth, *Middle Years*, I, p. 245.
97 Ibid, p. 240.
98 Ibid, p. 244.
99 *Letters*, III, pp. 78, 117.
100 Lamb, III, pp. 289, 284.
101 Wordsworth, *Middle Years*, I, p. 256.
102 Letters, III, pp. 148–9; *Shorter Works*, p. 227.
103 *Shorter Works*, I, p. 233.
104 *Letters*, III, p. 179.
105 Deirdre Coleman, 'Jeffrey and Coleridge', in *The Wordsworth Circle*, XVIII (1987).
106 *Letters*, III, pp. 124–5.
107 Ibid, p. 97.

108 Dove Cottage Mss, Morgan.
109 *Letters*, III, pp. 141–2.
110 Ibid, p. 174.
111 'The Twelve-Step Treatment', Institute for Drug Dependency, London.
112 *Notebooks*, III, 3356.

Chapter 4: The Friend in Need

1 Dove Cottage Mss, Clarkson.
2 *Notebooks*, III, 3349.
3 Ibid, 3355.
4 Ibid, 3352.
5 Ibid, 3353.
6 Friend, II, p. 9.
7 Wordsworth, *Middle Years*, I, p. 270.
8 *Letters*, III, p. 120n.
9 *Notebooks*, III, 3370.
10 Letters, III, pp. 120–1.
11 Ibid, p. 122.
12 Wordsworth, *Middle Years*, I, p. 282.
13 Sara Coleridge (daughter), *Memoir and Letters of Sara Coleridge*, edited by Edith Coleridge, 2 vols, 1873, I, pp. 17–20.
14 *Letters*, III, p. 121.
15 Sara Coleridge (daughter), *Memoir*, op. cit., pp. 17–20.
16 *P.W.*, p. 500; *Notebooks*, III, 3379.
17 *Notebooks*, III, 3376.
18 Ibid, 3386.
19 Ibid, 3383.
20 Ibid, 3386.
21 Ibid, 3388.
22 Ibid, 3403; *S.P.*, p. 220; *P.W.*, pp. 484–5.
23 *Letters*, III, pp. 130–1.
24 Lamb, II, pp. 287–8.
25 Dove Cottage Mss, Morgan.
26 *Letters*, III, p. 143.
27 Ibid, p. 144.
28 *Friend*, II, pp. 16–17.
29 Ibid, p. 18.
30 *Letters*, III, p. 135.
31 Ibid, pp. 125–6.
32 Ibid, p. 150.
33 Wordsworth, *Middle Years*, I, pp. 276–7.
34 *Notebooks*, III, 3407.
35 Wordsworth, *Middle Years*, I, pp. 282–3.
36 *Letters*, III, p. 140.
37 Ibid, p. 140.
38 Ibid, p. 141n.
39 E.V. Lucas, *Charles Lamb and the Lloyds*, 1898, pp. 241–2.
40 *Letters*, III, p. 160.
41 Ibid, p. 169.
42 Ibid, p. 175.
43 Ibid, p. 173.
44 Ibid, p. 176.
45 Ibid, p. 177.
46 Ibid, p. 178.
47 *Friend*, I, p. xiv.
48 *Letters*, III, p. 179.
49 Ibid, p. 180.
50 Ibid, pp. 181, 184.
51 Wordsworth, *Middle Years*, I, p. 293.
52 *Letters*, III, p. 183.
53 *Friend*, I, p. lxxi and note.
54 Wordsworth, *Middle Years*, I, p. 325.
55 Ibid, p. 310.
56 *Letters*, III, p. 193.
57 Ibid, p. 204.
58 Ibid, p. 204n.
59 Wordsworth, *Middle Years*, I, p. 356.
60 Ibid, p. 332–6.
61 Ibid, pp. 350.
62 Ibid, pp. 352–3.
63 *Letters*, III, p. 211.
64 *Friend*, I, p. 277.
65 Ibid, p. 73.
66 *Friend*, II, pp. 116–7.
67 Ibid, pp. 120–1.
68 Lamb, III, p. 26.
69 *Friend*, II, p. 141.
70 Ibid, p. 142.
71 Ibid, pp. 146–7; see *Early Visions*, Chapter 5.
72 Ibid, p. 147.
73 *Letters*, III, pp. 226–7.
74 Ibid, p. 233N.

75 *Friend*, I, p. lxiv, note.
76 *Letters*, III, pp. 253–4.
77 Moorman II p. 144.
78 *Friend*, I, p. ix, note.
79 Ibid, p. lix.
80 *Friend*, II, p. 150.
81 *Letters*, III, pp. 253–4.
82 Ibid, p. 254.
83 *Friend*, II, pp. 495–9.
84 Ibid, pp. 151–2.
85 Ibid, p. 494.
86 Ibid, p. 189.
87 Ibid, p. 187.
88 *S.P.*, pp. 206–7; *P.W.*, p. 413.
89 Wordsworth, *Middle Years*, I, p. 391.
90 Ibid, pp. 374–5.
91 Deirdre Coleman, *Coleridge and 'The Friend'*, Oxford, 1981, p. 41.
92 *Notebooks*, III, 3483–4.
93 Ibid, 3539.
94 Ibid, 3562.
95 Ibid, 3430.
96 Ibid, 3547.
97 Ibid, 3498.
98 Ibid, 3555.
99 *Letters*, III, p. 262.
100 Ibid, p. 261.
101 *Friend*, I, p. xciv, note.
102 *Friend*, II, p. 253.
103 Ibid, p. 252.
104 Wordsworth, *Middle Years*, I, p. 382.
105 *Notebooks*, 3593.
106 Ibid, p. 3593.
107 *Letters*, III, pp. 270n, 284; *Friend*, I, p. lxx, note.
108 *Friend*, II, p. 283.
109 Ibid, p. 282.
110 *Letters*, III, p. 271.
111 *Friend*, II, p. 501.
112 *Friend*, I, p. lxvi.
113 *Letters*, III, pp. 271–2.
114 *Essays*, II, pp. 37–100.
115 Moorman, II, p. 172.
116 Wordsworth, *Middle Years*, I, p. 397.
117 *Notebooks*, III, 3705.
118 *Letters*, III, p. 273.
119 Wordsworth, *Middle Years*, I, pp. 389–91.
120 *Friend*, II, pp. 285–7.
121 Ibid, p. 298.
122 Ibid, p. 291.
123 For a superb study of men under fire in the Napoleonic period, see 'Waterloo', in *The Face of Battle* by John Keegan, Pimlico, 1991.
124 *Friend*, II, p. 293.
125 *Dictionary of National Biography*, Nelson.
126 *Friend*, II, p. 305; Coleman, op. cit., p. 172.
127 *Letters*, III, p. 280.
128 Ibid, p. 281.
129 Wordsworth, *Middle Years*, I, p. 391.
130 *Notebooks*, III, 3692.
131 *Friend*, II, p. 365.
132 *Notebooks*, III, 3708.
133 Wordsworth, *Middle Years*, I, p. 398.
134 *Letters*, III, p. 287.
135 Ibid, pp. 285–6.
136 Wordsworth, *Middle Years*, I, pp. 398–9
137 Ibid, pp. 399–400.
138 *S.P.*, p. 192; *P.W.*, p. 456.

Chapter 5: In the Dark Chamber

1 Dove Cottage Mss, Morgan.
2 Wordsworth, *Middle Years*, I, pp. 407–8.
3 Minnow, p. 11.
4 Minnow, p. 14.
5 Notebooks, III, 3748.
6 Ibid, 3720; see *Early Visions*, p. 289 and note.
7 *Letters*, III, p. 375; *Shorter Works*, I, pp. 260–9.
8 *Letters*, III, p. 290.
9 Ibid, p. 284.
10 Minnow, pp. 12–14.
11 Southey, I, p. 537.
12 *Notebooks*, III, 3796.
13 *Notebooks*, II, 2531.
14 *Notebooks*, III, 3795.
15 Ibid, 3826.

16 Ibid, 3912.
17 Ibid, 3874.
18 Ibid, 3831.
19 Southey, I, p. 537.
20 *Notebooks*, III, 3731.
21 Ibid, 3762.
22 Ibid, 3824.
23 Ibid, 3763.
24 Ibid, 3784.
25 Ibid, 3818.
26 Ibid, 3835.
27 Ibid, 3878
28 Ibid, 4510.
29 Ibid, 3743.
30 Ibid, 3825.
31 Ibid, 3881.
32 Ibid, 3911.
33 Ibid, 3911.
35 Ibid, 3925.
36 *S.P.*, p. 91; *P.W.* p. 198.
37 *Notebooks*, III, 3915.
38 Ibid, 3925.
39 Ibid, 3911.
40 Ibid, 3911.
41 Ibid, 3959.
42 Ibid, 3913.
43 *Letters*, III, pp. 290–1N.
44 Ibid, pp. 291–3.
45 Ibid, p. 294.
46 *Notebooks*, III, 3952, 3970.
47 Ibid, 3995n; Moorman, II, pp. 191–4.
48 *Notebooks*, III, 3983.
49 Southey, I, p. 537.
50 Robinson, *Books*, p. 77.
51 Wordsworth, *Middle Years*, I, pp. 488–9.
52 *Notebooks*, III, 3989, 3995.
53 *Letters*, III, p. 400.
54 *Notebooks*, III, 3991.
55 Ibid, 3997.
56 *Letters*, III, p. 382.
57 Ibid, p. 376.
58 Robinson, *Books*, p. 75.
59 Ibid, p. 77.
60 *Notebooks*, III, 3999; see *Early Visions*, p. 330.
61 Ibid, 4001.
62 *Letters*, III, p. 399.
63 *Notebooks*, III, 4000.
64 *Letters*, III, p. 399.
65 Ibid, p. 298.
66 Wordsworth, *Middle Years*, I, p. 489.
67 *Letters*, III, p. 298n.
68 *Notebooks*, III, 4002.
69 Ibid, 3996.
70 Ibid, 4005.
71 Ibid, 4006.
72 Ibid, 4006.
73 Ibid, 3996.
74 Ibid, 4005.
75 Ibid, 4006.
76 Ibid, 4006.
77 *S.P.*, p. 212; *P.W.*, p. 416; see also *Notebooks*, III, 4106.
78 *Notebooks*, III, 4013; *Letters*, III, p. 399.

Chapter 6: Hamlet in Fleet Street

1 *Letters*, III, p. 301.
2 *Notebooks*, III, 4019.
3 *Letters*, III, p. 399.
4 Lamb, III, pp. 61–2.
5 Southey, I, p. 548.
6 Robinson, *Books*, p. 17.
7 Ibid, pp. 16–17, 30–34.
8 *Notebooks*, III, 4016.
9 Ibid, 4017.
10 Robinson, *Selections*, pp. 33–4.
11 Ibid, pp. 36–40.
12 Ibid, p. 35.
13 Essays, I, p. cxliv.
14 Ibid, p. cxlvi.
15 Roy and Dorothy Porter, *Patient's Progress*, 1989, p. 57 and 88.
16 *Letters*, III, p. 301.
17 Ibid, p. 301.
18 *Notebooks*, III, 4046.
19 *Letters*, III, p. 323.
20 Southey, II, pp. 3–4.
21 Ibid, p. 8.
22 Letters, III, p. 302.
23 Ibid, p. 304–5.
24 Ibid, p. 305.
25 Robinson, *Selections*, p. 38.
26 Wordsworth *Love Letters*, see below.

27 *Letters*, III, p. 309.
28 Ibid, p. 323.
29 Wordsworth, *Middle Years*, I, p. 490.
30 *Notebooks*, III, 4052.
31 Ibid, 4055.
32 P.W., pp. 16–17.
33 *Notebooks*, III, 4094.
34 Ibid, 4092.
35 Ibid, 4093.
36 Ibid, 4106; *S.P.*, p. 211; *P.W.*, p. 419.
37 Ibid, 4102.
38 Ibid, 4106.
39 *Letters*, III, p. 311.
40 Ibid, p. 310.
41 Richard Holmes, *Shelley: The Pursuit*, 1974, HarperCollins, 1994 Chapter 2.
42 *Essays*, II, p. 121.
43 Ibid, pp. 198–9.
44 Ibid, pp. 140–1.
45 Robinson, *Books*, p. 32.
46 Robinson, *Letters*, I, p. 66.
47 William Hazlitt, *The Spirit of the Age*, 1825.
48 Wordsworth, *Middle Years*, I, p. 495.
49 *Letters*, III, p. 319.
50 Ibid, p. 333.
51 Minnow, p. 14.
52 *Letters*, III, p. 327.
53 Ibid, p. 325.
54 *Letters*, IV, p. 797.
55 *Essays*, II, pp. 213, 314.
56 *Essays*, I, p. clxv.
57 *Letters*, III, p. 334.
58 *Essays*, II, p. 186.
59 Robinson, *Books*, pp. 34–5.
60 Ibid, p. 37.
61 *Essays*, II, pp. 220–35.
62 *Letters*, III, p. 334 and note.
63 Robinson, *Books*, p. 37.
64 *Essays*, II, p. 247n.
65 Ibid, p. 247n.
66 Hutchinson, *Letters*, pp. 26–37.
67 *Talker*, p. 153.
68 *Table Talk*, 1835.
69 *Talker*, pp. 154–8.
70 Ibid, pp. 158–60.
71 Ibid, pp. 154, 160.
72 *Notebooks*, III, 4070.
73 Ibid, 4081n.
74 Ibid, 4069.
75 Ibid, 4072.
76 *Notebooks*, III, 4073–4; *S.P.*, p. 214; *P.W.*, pp. 429–31.
77 *Notebooks*, III, 3684.
78 Ibid, 4076.
79 Jean-Paul Richter, *Geist*, 1801, no. 386.
80 Ibid, no. 4.
81 *Notebooks*, III, 4088.
82 *Geist*, no. 4; *Notebooks*, III, 4088n.
83 *Notebooks*, III, 4088.
84 Ibid, 4061.
85 Ibid, 4086n.
86 Ibid, 4087n.
87 *Letters*, III, p. 340n.
88 Lamb, 'On the Genius and Character of Hogarth', 1811.
89 *Notebooks*, III, 4096.
90 *S.P.*, pp. 258–9.
91 Robinson, *Books*, p. 41.
92 *Letters*, III, p. 336.
93 *Essays*, II, p. 318.
94 Ibid, p. 306.
95 *Talker*, pp. 167–8.
96 Ibid, p. 43.
97 Ibid, p. 47.
98 Ibid, pp. 47–8.
99 Ibid, p. 49.
100 *Letters*, III, pp. 137–8.
101 Ibid, p. 338.
102 Ibid, p. 338.
103 Ibid, pp. 338–9.
104 Ibid, p. 337.
105 Ibid, p. 377.
106 Ibid, p. 377.
107 Lamb, III, p. 74.
108 Southey, II, p. 68.
109 *Letters*, III, p. 369.
110 *Letters*, III, p. 363–4.
111 Ibid, p. 349.
112 Ibid, p. 342.
113 *Literary Lectures*, I, p. 179.
114 Southey, II, p. 12.
115 *Letters*, III, p. 343.

116 Ibid, p. 346.
117 Ibid, p. 348n.
118 Ibid, p. 347.
119 *Literary Lectures*, I, p. 195.
120 Ibid, pp. 190, 196.
121 Ibid, p. 203.
122 Ibid, p. 209.
123 Ibid, p. 209.
124 Ibid, p. 212.
125 Robinson, *Books*, p. 52.
126 Ibid, p. 52.
127 *Literary Lectures*, I, p. 221.
128 Ibid, p. 222.
129 Ibid, p. 222.
130 Ibid, p. 223.
131 Ibid, p. 224.
132 Ibid, p. 225.
133 Ibid, p. 257.
134 Ibid, p. 259.
135 Ibid, pp. 232–3.
136 Ibid, p. 316.
137 Ibid, p. 307.
138 Ibid, p. 308.
139 Ibid, p. 293.
140 Ibid, p. 295.
141 Ibid, p. 287.
142 Ibid, p. 291.
143 Ibid, p. 304.
144 Ibid, p. 327.
145 Ibid, p. 283.
146 Robinson, *Books*, p. 54.
147 *Literary Lectures*, I, p. 333.
148 Robinson, *Books*, p. 55.
149 Byron, *Letters and Journals*, 12 vols, edited by Leslie A. Marchand, Murray, 1973–94, II, pp. 140, 147.
150 *Letters*, III, p. 352.
151 *Literary Lectures*, I, p. 409.
152 *Letters*, III, p. 359.
153 *Literary Lectures*, pp. 113--8.
154 *Letters*, III, p. 360.
155 *Literary Lectures*, I, p. 345.
156 Ibid, p. 345.
157 Ibid, pp. 353–4.
158 Ibid, p. 354.
159 Robinson, *Books*, p. 63.
160 *Literary Lectures*, I, p. 358.
161 *Shakespearean Criticism*, I, p. 197.
162 see *Early Visions*, pp. 325–7.
163 *Notebooks*, II, 2444.
164 *Literary Lectures*, pp. 364–5.
165 Ibid, p. 367.
166 see *Early Visions*, pp. 231–2; 334–5.
167 Robinson, *Books*, p. 57.
168 My reconstruction uses an amalgam of texts, notes, and reports from *Literary Lectures*, I, Lecture No. 12; and *Shakespearean Criticism*, I, 'Hamlet'.
169 *Lectures of Schlegel on Dramatic Art and Literature*, translated by John Black, London, 1815, II, pp. 194–6.
170 *Hamlet*, Signet Classics.
171 *Literary Lectures*, p. 386.
172 *Shakespearean Criticism*, I, p. 23.
173 Ibid, p. 30.
174 Ibid, p. 20.
175 *Literary Lectures*, I, p. 387.
176 *Shakespearean Criticism*, I, p. 36.
177 *Literary Lectures*, I, pp. 386, 388.
178 *Shakespearean Criticism*, I, p. 26.
179 Ibid, p. 35.
180 Ibid, p. 34.
181 *Literary Lectures*, I, p. 391.
182 *Table Talk*, II, p. 61 (June 1827).
183 *Literary Lectures*, I, p. 401.
184 Ibid, p. 407.

Chapter 7: Phantom Purposes

1 *Letters*, III, pp. 364, 366.
2 Ibid, p. 365.
3 Ibid, p. 366.
4 Ibid, p. 377.
5 Ibid, pp. 367–9.
6 Ibid, p. 367.
7 Ibid, p. 371.
8 Ibid, p. 372.
9 Ibid, p. 370.
10 Ibid, p. 380.
11 Ibid, p. 375.
12 Minnow, p. 16.
13 *Letters*, III, p. 380.
14 Ibid, p. 380.
15 Ibid, p. 383n.
16 Ibid,p. 383.

17 Minnow, p. 16.
18 Hutchinson, pp. 45–6.
19 *Letters*, III, p. 376.
20 see *Early Visions*, pp. 106–7.
21 Ibid, pp. 94–116.
22 *Letters*, III, p. 375.
23 Wordsworth, *Middle Years*, II, p. 496.
24 *Letters*, III, p. 385.
25 *Letters*, III, p. 377.
26 Minnow, pp. 16–17.
27 Molly Lefubure *The Bondage of Love: A Life of Mrs S. T. Coleridge*, Gollancz, 1986, p. 202.
28 *Letters*, III, p. 381.
29 Robinson, *Letters*, I, p. 68; *Letters*, III, p. 382n.
30 *Notebooks*, III, 4148n.
31 Ibid, p. 4149; S.P., p. 253; P.W., pp. 514–5.
32 *Letters*, III p. 383.
33 Ibid, p. 384.
34 Ibid, p. 388.
35 Ibid, p. 385.
36 Ibid, p. 389.
37 Wordsworth, *Love Letters*, p. 109.
38 Ibid, p. 124.
39 Ibid, p. 125.
40 *Letters*, III, p. 403.
41 Ibid, p. 395.
42 Ibid, p. 394.
43 Ibid, pp. 395–6n, 398n.
44 Ibid, p. 402.
45 Ibid, p. 397n.
46 Ibid, p. 394.
47 Wordsworth, *Middle Years*, II, p. 498.
48 Ibid, p. 496.
49 Ibid, p. 486.
50 Robinson, *Letters*, p. 70.
51 Robinson, *Books*, pp. 73–7.
52 Wordsworth, *Love Letters*, p. 136.
53 Robinson, *Books*, p. 77.
54 Ibid, p. 78.
55 Ibid, p. 79.
56 Wordsworth, *Love Letters*, pp. 139–40.
57 Robinson, *Books*, p. 80.
58 *Letters*, V, pp. 249–50.
59 *Letters*, III, p. 407.
60 Ibid, pp. 437–8.
61 Minnow, p. 16.
62 Wordsworth, *Love Letters*, p. 215.
63 Ibid, p. 148.
64 Ibid, p. 134.
65 Ibid, p. 157.
66 Ibid, p. 142.
67 Ibid, p. 142.
68 Ibid, p. 143; see *Early Visions*, p. 138.
69 Wordsworth, *Love Letters*, p. 148.
70 *Essays*, II, pp. 347–8.
71 *Letters*, III, p. 410.
72 Ibid, p. 410.
73 *Letters*, pp. 413–4.
74 *Church and State*, 1829.
75 *Letters*, III, p. 414.
76 *Notebooks*, III, 4154.
77 *Letters*, III, p. 387.
78 Robinson, *Books*, pp. 87–8.
79 *Literary Lectures*, I, p. 475.
80 *Letters*, III, p. 387.
81 Robinson, *Books*, pp. 87–8.
82 Wordsworth, *Love Letters*, pp. 210–15.
83 Robinson, *Books*, p. 83.
84 Wordsworth, *Love Letters*, p. 163.
85 Robinson, *Books*, p. 83.
86 *Lamb*, III, p. 160.
87 Wordsworth, *Love Letters*, pp. 242–3.
88 Wordsworth, *Middle Years*, II, p. 557.
89 *Letters*, III, p. 416.
90 Ibid, p. 415.
91 *Notebooks*, III, 4172.
92 Ibid, 4164.
93 Ibid, 4168.
94 *S.P.*, p. 210; *P.W.*, pp. 419–20 as 'Time, Real and Imaginary'.
95 *Shorter Works*, I, pp. 285–7.
96 Minnow, p. 18.
97 *Letters*, III, pp. 418–19.
98 Ibid, p. 419.
99 Ibid, p. 420.
100 Ibid, p. 446.
101 Robinson, *Books*, p. 113.
102 Ibid, pp. 117–8.

103 *Literary Lectures*, I, p. 488.
104 *Letters*, III, p. 430.
105 *Literary Lectures*, I, pp. 492–3.
106 *Lectures of Schlegel*, translated John Black, op. cit., second edition, London, 1840, II, p. 97.
107 *Literary Lectures*, I, p. 494.
108 Robinson, *Books*, p. 112.
109 R. M. Fletcher, *English Romantic Drama 1795–1843*, New York, 1966, pp. 70–2.
110 Robinson, *Books*, p. 112.
111 *Complete Poetical Works*, II, p. 1114.
112 Ibid, p. 1114.
113 Ibid, p. 518.
114 Ibid, pp. 859–60.
115 *Letters*, III, p. 428.
116 *Complete Poetical Works*, II, p. 820.
117 Ibid, p. 867.
118 Ibid, p. 856.
119 *Letters*, III, p. 420n.
120 Moormon, II, p. 246; Lamb, III, p. 86.
121 *Letters*, III, p. 421.
122 Ibid, pp. 421–2n.
123 Heritage, p. 130.
124 *Letters*, III, p. 428.
125 Ibid, p. 426.
126 Ibid, p. 429.
127 Ibid, p. 434.
128 Ibid, pp. 436–7; *Shorter Works*, I, p. 290.
129 *Complete Poetical Works*, II, p. 555n.
130 *S.P.*, p. 254; *P.W.*, p. 420; *Complete Poetical Works*, II, p. 849.
131 Heritage, p. 138.
132 *Letters*, III, p. 424.
133 Ibid, p. 424–5.
134 Ibid, p. 423.
135 Ibid, p. 424.
136 Wordsworth, *Middle Years*, II, p. 526.
137 Moorman, II, p. 228–9.
138 Heritage, p. 145.
139 *Letters*, III, p. 430–1.
140 Robinson, *Books*, p. 117.
141 *Letters*, III, p. 430.
142 Ibid, p. 431.
143 Ibid, p. 431.
144 Ibid, p. 430; Robinson, *Books*, p. 118.
145 Heritage, p. 132.
146 *Letters*, III, p. 438.
147 Ibid, p. 437.
148 Robinson, *Books*, p. 128.
149 *Letters*, III, pp. 436–7.
150 Ibid, p. 431.
151 Leigh Hunt, *Dramatic Criticism 1808–1831*, edited by L. H. Houtchens, 1950, p. 103.
152 Southey, II, p. 49.
153 Ibid, p. 43.
154 Robinson, *Letters*, p. 75.
155 Robinson, *Books*, p. 119.
156 Robinson, *Letters*, p. 73.
157 Robinson, *Books*, pp. 119–28.
158 *P.W.*, p. 311.
159 Southey, II, p. 49.
160 Chambers, p. 259.
161 Wordsworth, *Middle Years*, II, p. 557.
162 *Letters*, III, pp. 439–40.
163 Ibid, p. 440.
164 Ibid, p. 441.
165 Ibid, p. 442.
166 Wordsworth, *Middle Years*, II, p. 565.
167 *Letters*, III, pp. 442n, 455.
168 Ibid, p. 442n.
169 Ibid, p. 442.
170 Ibid p. 442.
171 Ibid, p. 443.
172 Ibid, p. 444.
173 *Literary Lectures*, I, p. 533.
174 Ibid, p. 512.
175 *Letters*, III, p. 446.
176 *Literary Lectures*, I, p. 509.
177 Ibid, p. 525.
178 Ibid, pp. 532, 544–5.
179 Ibid, p. 597.
180 *Letters*, III, p. 450.
181 Ibid, p. 455.
182 Ibid, p. 445.
183 Ibid, pp. 450–1.
184 Ibid, p. 452.

185 Ibid, pp. 452–7.
186 Ibid, p. 458.
187 Ibid, p. 453.
188 Ibid, p. 452.
189 Ibid, p. 454.
190 Ibid, p. 457.
191 Ibid p. 458.
192 Ibid p. 460.
193 Ibid, p. 460.
194 Ibid, p. 461.
195 Ibid p. 461.
196 Ibid, p. 462.
197 Ibid, p. 464n.
198 Ibid p. 462.
199 Ibid, p. 462.
200 Ibid, p. 490.
201 Ibid, p. 464.
202 Ibid p. 463.
203 Ibid, p. 463.
204 *S.P.*, p. 213; *P.W.*, pp. 425–6.

Chapter 8: True Confessions

1 *Letters*, III, p. 490.
2 Ibid, p. 491.
3 Ibid, pp. 464–5.
4 Ibid, p. 477.
5 Ibid, p. 490.
6 Cottle, II, p. 169.
7 *Letters*, III, pp. 489–90.
8 Ibid, p. 495.
9 Lamb, III, pp. 101–2.
10 Southey, II, p. 94.
11 Ibid, p. 97.
12 *Letters*, III, p. 476.
13 Ibid, p. 482.
14 Ibid, p. 485.
15 Devonshire, pp. 214–5.
16 *Letters*, III, p. 502.
17 Ibid, p. 511.
18 Ibid, p. 506.
19 Ibid, p. 510.
20 Ibid, p. 520.
21 Allston, p. 75.
22 *Shorter Works*, I, p. 373.
23 Ibid, p. 373.
24 Ibid, p. 369.
25 Ibid, p. 373.
26 *Letters*, IV, pp. 564–5.
27 Ibid, pp. 513–4.
28 *Letters*, III, pp. 513–4.
29 Ibid, p. 518.
30 *Letters*, VI, p. 1030.
31 Allston, p. 104.
32 Allston, p. 107.
33 *Letters*, VI, pp. 1030–1.
34 *Letters*, III, p. 509.
35 Ibid, p. 519.
36 Ibid, p. 506.
37 Ibid, p. 521–5.
38 Robinson, *Books*, p. 448.
39 *Letters*, III, p. 525.
40 Ibid, p. 528.
41 Ibid, p. 528–9.
42 Ibid, p. 529.
43 *Notebooks*, III, 4194; *S.P.*, p. 248.
44 Ibid, 4220.
45 *Letters*, III, p. 529.
46 Heritage, p. 188.
47 *Letters from Lambeth*, edited by Joanna Richardson, Royal Society of Literature, 1981, p. 132.
48 Minnow, p. 32.
49 *Letters*, III, p. 544.
50 *Notebooks*, III, 4234; *S.P.*, p. 252; *P.W.*, p. 513.
51 Berg Collection, NYPL; *Essays*, II, p. 373n.
52 *Letters*, III, p. 532.
53 Ibid, p. 530.
54 Ibid, p. 533.
55 Ibid, p. 543.
56 *Notebooks*, III, 4235.
57 *Letters*, III, p. 533n.
58 Ibid, p. 533.
59 *Notebooks*, III, 4239.
60 *Letters*, III, p. 536.
61 Ibid, p. 542.
62 *A History of the Borough Town of Calne*, by A.E.W. Marsh, 1903, p. 100.
63 Wiltshire County Record Office, *Calne Survey Book* (1828) and *Street Property Guide Map:* house sites no. 614 and no. 615.
64 Marsh, op. cit., p. 284.
65 *Letters*, IV, pp. 549–50.
66 Ibid, pp. 549, 553.
67 Ibid, p. 549.

68 Ibid, p. 547.
69 Ibid, p. 552.
70 Cottle, II, p. 183.
71 *Letters*, IV, p. 551.
72 Ibid, p. 561.
73 Ibid, pp. 559–63.
74 Byron, *Letters & Journals*, op. cit., pp. 285–6; *Letters*, IV, p. 563n.
75 see Catherine Wallace, *The Design of the Biographia Literaria*, Allen and Unwin, 1983; Kathleen Wheeler, *Sources, Processes and Methods in Coleridge's Biographia Literaria*, Cambridge, 1980; and Rosemary Ashton, *The Life of Samuel Taylor Coleridge: A Critical Biography*, Blackwell, 1996: all invaluable sources for my account.
76 *Biographia*, I, p. 168.
77 Ibid, p. 3.
78 Ibid, p. 12.
79 Ibid, p. 5.
80 Ibid, p. 77.
81 Wordsworth, *Middle Years*, II, pp. 669–70.
82 *Letters*, IV, pp. 574–5.
83 *Notebooks*, III, 4243.
84 *Letters*, IV, p. 576.
85 Ibid, p. 577.
86 *Biographia*, I, p. 70.
87 Ibid, p. 82.
88 Ibid, p. 85.
89 Ibid, p. 85.
90 Ibid, p. 69. For an account of the *Lyrical Ballads*, see *Early Visions*, pp. 186–96.
91 *Biographia*, II, p. 5.
92 Ibid, p. 6.
93 Lamb, III, p. 192.
94 *Selections from the Letters of Robert Southey*, 4 vols, edited by John Warter, 1856, II, pp. 408–9.
95 Lamb, III, p. 187.
96 *Letters*, IV, p. 551n.
97 Lamb, III, p. 192.
98 Hartley, Appendix B, p. cxcviii.
99 *Selections from the Letters of Southey*, op. cit., II, pp. 408–9.
100 *Letters*, IV, p. 596; *Notebooks*, III, 4260.
101 Hartley, Appendix B, 'Calne'.
102 *Notebooks*, III, 4249.
103 *Biographia*, II, pp. 15–17.
104 Ibid, p. 14.
105 Ibid, pp. 64, 66.
106 Ibid, pp. 144–50.
107 Ibid, pp. 148–9.
108 Ibid, p. 151.
109 *Letters*, IV, p. 585.
110 Ibid, p. 579.
111 Ibid, pp. 579–80.
112 *Lamb*, III, p. 192.
113 Ibid, p. 160.
114 Ibid, p. 162.
115 *Biographia*, I, p. 142.
116 Ibid, II, p. 283.
117 Ibid, p. 285.
118 Ibid, I, p. 65.
119 Ibid, p. 82.
120 Ibid, p. 168.
121 Ibid, p. 114.
122 Ibid, p. 151.
123 *Letters*, IV, p. 578.
124 Ibid, p. 585.
125 *Biographia*, I, pp. 119–20.
126 Ibid, pp. 124–5.
127 Ibid, p. 153.
128 Ibid, p. 160.
129 Ibid, p. 152.
130 Ibid, p. lxxxv.
131 Ibid, pp. 161–4.
132 Ibid, pp. cxxi, cxxv.
133 Thomas McFarland, *Coleridge and the Pantheist Tradition*, Oxford, 1969.
134 *Biographia*, II, p. 254.
135 *Biographia*, I, pp. 161–4.
136 *Letters*, IV, p. 553.
137 *Biographia*, I, p. 187.
138 Ibid, p. 200.
139 Ibid, p. 194.
140 Ibid, p. 196; quoted in full in *Early Visions*, pp. 161–2.
141 *Letters*, IV, pp. 585–6.
142 *Biographia*, I, p. 224.
143 Ibid, pp. 272–5.
144 Ibid, pp. 272–83.

145 Ibid, p. 283.
146 Ibid, p. 290.
147 *Notebooks*, III, 4265.
148 *Biographia*, I, p. 238n.
149 Ibid, p. 244.
150 Ibid, p. 232.
151 Ibid, p. 239.
152 Ibid, p. 239.
153 Ibid, pp. 241–2.
154 Ibid, pp. 237–8 and note.
155 *Table Talk*, II, p. 293.
156 *Biographia*, I, p. 297.
157 *Letters*, IV, p. 728.
158 *Biographia*, I, p. 303.
159 Ibid, pp. 303–4.
160 *Letters*, IV, p. 588.
161 *Biographia*, I, pp. 304–5.
162 *Biographia*, II, pp. 247–8; for the stars of childhood see *Early Visions*, pp. 18–19.
163 *Letters*, IV, pp. 551n, 587.
164 Ibid, p. 592.
165 Byron, *Letters and Journals*, op. cit., IV, pp. 318–9/
166 *Letters*, IV, pp. 603–5.
167 Byron, *Letters and Journals*, op. cit., IV, p. 324.
168 Ibid, p. 324.
169 Ibid, p. 331.
170 *Letters*, IV, p. 606.
171 Ibid, p. 607n.
172 Ibid, p. 609.
173 Ibid, p. 615.
174 Ibid, p. 613.
175 Ibid, p. 611.
176 *Notebooks*, III, 4278.
177 Ibid, 4294.
178 Ibid, 4269.
179 Ibid, 4272.
180 *Letters*, IV, p. 617.
181 Ibid, p. 615.
182 *Notebooks*, III, 4287.
183 Ibid, 4306.
184 *S.P.*, p. 85; *P.W.*, p. 191.
185 Printed with gloss compact on verse; *S.P.*, p. 85 ; *P.W.*, p. 197.
186 S.P., *p. 99;* P.W., *p. 208.*
187 *Letters*, IV, p. 619.
188 Ibid, p. 612.
189 Ibid, p. 622.
190 Ibid, p. 618–9.
191 Ibid, p. 622n.
192 The Royal Literary Fund Archive, London. The Fund received its Royal title in 1818, and continues its noble work for distressed authors to this day. *Letters*, IV, p. 621n.
193 *Letters*, IV, p. 622n.
194 Ibid, pp. 622–3.
195 Ibid, p. 624.

Chapter 9: Climbing Highgate Hill

1 Heritage, p. 277.
2 Lamb, III, pp. 210–11.
3 Letters, IV, p. 625n.
4 Robinson, *Books*, p. 182.
5 *Letters*, IV, pp. 628–9 and Note. Gillman, p. 272.
6 Ibid.
7 Preface to 'Kubla Khan', *S.P.*, p. 229.
8 *Talker*, p. 269.
9 *Letters*, IV, p. 641.
10 Ibid, p. 634.
11 Ibid, pp. 662, 681.
12 Gillman, pp. 271–3.
13 *Letters*, IV, p. 630.
14 Ibid, p. 630.
15 Lamb, III, p. 215.
16 *Letters*, IV, p. 630.
17 *Letters*, VI, pp. 1041–2.
18 Robinson, *Books*, p. 185.
19 *Letters*, IV, p. 634n.
20 Minnow, p. 48.
21 *Notebooks*, III, 4313.
22 *Letters*, IV, p . 669.
23 *Shorter Works*, I, p. 454ff.
24 *Letters*, IV, p. 690.
25 *The Greatest Benefit to Mankind: A Medical History of Humanity*, by Roy Porter, HarperCollins, 1997, p. 334.
26 *Notebooks*, III, 4319–20.
27 *Letters*, IV, pp. 672–3.
28 Southey, II, pp. 155–6.
29 Heritage, p. 207.
30 Ibid, pp. 208–9.

31 Ibid, p. 212.
32 *S.P.*, p. 229; *P.W.*, p. 296.
33 'Kubla Khan and the Art of Thingifying', by Katherine Wheeler in *Romanticism: A Critical Reader*, edited by Duncan Wu, Blackwell, 1995.
34 Holmes, *Shelley*, op. cit., pp. 328–31.
35 *Letters*, IV, pp. 649, 652–3.
36 Ibid, p. 666.
37 Ibid, p. 663.
38 Heritage, pp. 234–5.
39 *Letters*, V, p. 437.
40 Heritage, p. 250.
41 Ibid, pp. 249–50.
42 Ibid, p. 252.
43 *Letters*, IV, pp. 669–70.
44 Ibid, p. 658.
45 Ibid, pp. 672–3.
46 *Lay Sermons*, p. 24.
47 Wordsworth, *Middle Years*, II, p. 780.
48 *Lay Sermons*, pp. 40–2.
49 Ibid, p. 30.
50 Ibid, pp. 30, 81.
51 Heritage, p. 255.
52 Ibid, pp. 257–9.
53 Ibid, p. 263.
54 *Letters*, IV, p. 673.
55 Ibid, pp. 682–4.
56 Ibid, p. 685.
57 Ibid, p. 678.
58 *Shorter Works*, I, p. 486. The full title is: 'Hints Towards the Formation of a More Comprehensive Theory of Life', and it was first published posthumously, edited by Seth B. Watson, London, 1848. For an animated account of the Vitalist controversy see Hermione De Almeida, 'Polarity and Coleridge', in *Romantic Medicine and John Keats*, Oxford, 1991.
59 *Letters*, IV, p. 690.
60 *Biographia*, II, p. 296.
61 *Letters*, IV, p. 659, 704N.
62 *Biographia*, II, pp. 298–9.
63 *Letters*, IV, p. 711.
64 Southey, II, p. 176.
65 *Lay Sermons*, p. 139.
66 *Early Visions*, pp. 384–6.
67 *Lay Sermons*, pp. 189–91.
68 Ibid, pp. 203–7.
69 Ibid, p. 207.
70 Ibid, pp. 228–9.
71 Ibid, p. xl.
72 Ibid, p. 243.
73 Ibid, p. 240.
74 Heritage. pp. 289–94.
75 *Letters*, IV, pp. 714, 718.
76 Ibid, p. 711.
77 Ibid, p. 711.
78 Ibid, p. 714.
79 Thomas Love Peacock, *Headlong Hall*, 1816, Chapter 3. See *The Complete Novels of T.L. Peacock*, 2 vols, edited by David Garnett, 1963, I, p. 21. There is a fine discussion in *Peacock Displayed: A Satirist in his Context*, by Marilyn Butler, Routledge, 1979.
80 Peacock, *Melincourt*, 1817, Chapter 31. See *Complete Novels*, op. cit., I, p. 277.
81 Ibid, p. 277.
82 *Letters*, IV, p. 739.
83 Ibid, p. 751.
84 Ibid, p. 755.
85 Ibid, p. 755.
86 Poole, II, p. 257.
87 Ibid, p. 258.
88 Ibid, p. 257.
89 Letters, IV, pp. 766–7.
90 Ibid, pp. 766–7.
91 Heritage, p. 320.
92 Ibid, pp. 298–322.
93 Ibid, pp. 330, 348.
94 Ibid, p. 350.
95 Ibid, p. 405.
96 Ibid, pp. 405–8.
97 *Letters*, IV, p. 786.
98 Peacock, *Complete Novels*, op. cit., I, p. 394.
99 Holmes, *Shelley*, op. cit., p. 360.

100 'Letter to Maria Gisborne', 1820, lines 202–08.
101 Keats, *Letters* (28 October 1817), p. 31.
102 Ibid, p. 43, (27 December 1817).
103 Byron, *Letters and Journals*, op. cit., V, p. 267.
104 Byron, 'Dedication' (September 1818), to *Don Juan*, Canto 1, lines 21–4. *Letters and Journals*, op. cit., V, p. 267. Quoted in 'Detached Thoughts', October 1821, op. cit., IX, p. 24; "Tell me if I have not as good a right to the character of 'Vates' in both senses of the word [divinely inspired bard or prophet–poet] . . . as Coleridge." op. cit., VII, p. 84, (April 1820).
105 *Biographia*, II, pp. 239–40.
106 Ibid, p. 216.
107 Wordsworth, *Middle Years*, II, p. 791.
108 Robinson, *Books*, p. 213.
109 *Talker*, pp. 125–6.
110 *Letters*, IV, p. 780–1, p. 832.
111 *Letters*, IV, p. 780; S.P., p. 23; *P.W.*, p. 435.
112 *Letters*, IV, p. 779.
113 Ibid, p. 783.
114 Ibid, p. 775.
115 Ibid, pp. 767–76; Richard Lines, 'Charles Augustus Tulk: Swedenborgian Extraordinary', 1997 in *Arcana*, vol III, No. 4, Swedenborg Association, Charleston, USA, 1997.
116 *Early Visions*, p. 219.
117 *Letters*, IV, p. 784 and *Letters*, VI, p. 943.
118 *Shorter Works*, I, p. 674.
119 Ibid, p. 683.
120 Ibid, p. 685.
121 *Letters*, IV, p. 801.
122 Robinson, *Books*, p. 213.
123 Ibid, pp. 214–5.
124 Ibid, p. 216.
125 Hutchinson, p. 122.
126 *Letters*, IV, p. 796.
127 Keats, *Letters*, p. 49 (21 January 1818).
128 Ibid, p. 69 (21 February 1818).
129 Ibid, p 47 (5 January 1818).
130 *Letters*, IV, p. 799.
131 *Literary Lectures*, II, p. 28.
132 Ibid, p. 839.
133 Ibid, p. 819.
134 Devonshire, p. 273.
135 Zuccato, op. cit, p. 109.
136 *Notebooks*, III, 4388.
137 Ibid, 4388.
138 *Letters*, IV, p. 824.
139 *Memoir of the Reverand H. F. Cary*, 2 vols, by Henry Cary, 1847, II, p. 28.
140 Hazlitt, *Lectures on the English Poets*, 1817, No. 7, 'On Burns', edited by C. D. Maclean, 1967, pp. 123.
141 Robinson, *Books*, pp. 218, 219.
142 Ibid, p. 220.
143 *Table Talk*, II, p. 109.
144 Hazlitt, *Lectures on the English Poets*, 1817, No. 8, 'On the Living Poets', op. cit., pp. 165–8.
145 *Notebooks*, III, 4365.
146 *Letters*, IV, p. 807.
147 *Notebooks*, III, 4409.
148 Ibid, 4409.
149 *Letters*, IV, pp. 833–4.
150 Ibid, pp. 836–7.
151 Ibid, p. 842.
152 Ibid, p. 865.
153 Ibid, p. 857N.
154 Ibid, p. 855.
155 Ibid, p. 853.
156 Ibid, p. 854.
157 Ibid, p. 856.
158 *Essays*, II, p. 488.
159 *Shorter Works*, I, pp. 719, 723.
160 Ibid, pp. 731–8.
161 J.L. and B. Hammond, *The Town Labourer*, 1917, revised edition 1978, Chapter 8.
162 *Notebooks*, III, 4482.
163 Keats, *Letters*, p. 313 (18 September 1819).
164 *Letters*, IV, pp. 866–7.

165 *Shorter Works*, I, pp. 758–61.
166 Ibid, p. 760.
167 Ibid, p. 761.
168 Ibid, pp. 510–12. For a further exploration see 'Coleridge's "A Light in Sound": Science, Metascience and Poetic Imagination', in *The Correspondent Breeze* by M. H. Abrams, Norton NY, 1984; and Trevor Levere (see Bibliography).
169 *Letters*, IV, pp. 867–9
170 Ibid, p. 870. For Novalis, Friedrich von Hardenberg (1772–1801), see Penelope Fitzgerald's wonderful novel *The Blue Flower*, Flamingo, 1996.
171 Ibid, p. 870.
172 Charles Lamb, 'Dedication' to *Collected Works*, 2 vols, London, 1818.
173 *Friend*, I, p. 4.
174 Ibid, pp. 332, 334N; *Early Visions*, pp. 105–6.
175 *Letters*, IV, p. 925.
176 *Friend*, I, p. 448.
177 Ibid, p. 473.
178 Ibid, pp. 457, 473, 476.
179 Ibid, p. 451.
180 Ibid, pp. 450–3.
181 Ibid, p. 466.
182 Ibid, p. 492.
183 Ibid, p. 495.
184 Ibid, pp. 496–7.
185 Ibid, p. 500.
186 For an affectionate account of Sterling, Hare, Maurice and their circle of 'Coleridgeans', see J. S. Mill, 'A Crisis in My Mental History', in *Autobiography*, 1873.
187 J. S. Mill, *On Bentham and Coleridge*, edited by F. R. Leavis, 1950, pp. 129–30.
188 *Friend*, I, p. cv.
189 Ibid, p. ciii; F. D. Maurice, *The Kingdom of Christ*, 1842, 'Dedication' to Derwent Coleridge.
190 Butler, *Peacock Displayed*, op. cit., p. 109.
191 Peacock, *Nightmare Abbey*, 1818, Chapter 8; *Complete Novels*, op. cit., I, pp. 395–6.
192 Ibid, p. 397.
193 *Letters*, IV, p. 878.
194 Ibid, p. 891.
195 Minnow, pp. 67, 75.
196 Thomas Carlyle, *The Life of John Sterling*, 1851. *Talker*, p. 113.

Chapter 10: Magic Children

1 *Letters*, IV, p. 881N; *Philosophical Lectures*, pp. 66–69.
2 *Letters*, IV, p. 917.
3 Ibid, p. 889.
4 Ibid, p. 882.
5 *Notebooks*, III, 4468.
6 *Philosophical Lectures*, 'Prospectus', p. 67.
7 Ibid, p. 211.
8 Ibid, p. 285.
9 Ibid, pp. 355–60; see Chapter 9, reference 58 (above).
10 Ibid, pp. 305–6.
11 *Letters*, IV, p. 890.
12 *Philosophical Lectures*, p. 185.
13 Ibid, p. 320.
14 Ibid. p. 263.
15 Ibid. p. 186–8.
16 *Notebooks*, III, 4504.
17 *Philosophical Lectures*, p. 398.
18 Ibid, p. 394.
19 Ibid, p. 394.
20 Ibid, p. 179.
21 Ibid, pp. 394–5.
22 *S.P.*, p. 24; *P.W.*, p. 429.
23 *Letters*, IV, pp. 905–6.
24 Ibid, p. 909.
25 Ibid, p. 908.
26 Keats, *Letters*, p. 228 (19 March 1819).
27 *Letters*, IV, p. 940.
28 *Table Talk*, II, pp. 186–7.
29 Keats, *Letters*, p. 237 (15 April 1819).
30 Ibid, p. 239.
31 Ibid, pp. 239–40. 'A Dream', after reading Dante's 'Episode of Paolo and Francesca', in *John Keats: The*

Complete Poems, edited by John Barnard, Penguin, 1973, p. 333.
32 *S.P.*, p. 124; *P.W.*, p. 333.
33 *Letters*, IV, p. 942.
34 *Letters*, VI, p. 322.
35 *Table Talk*, I, pp. 325–6N.
36 'The Fall of Hyperion: A Dream', 1819, Canto 1, line 18, *John Keats: The Complete Poems*, op, cit., p. 435.
37 *Table Talk*, II, p. 313.
38 *S.P.*, p. xxxiii.
39 *Letters*, IV, p. 938.
40 *Notebooks*, IV, 4537.
41 Ibid, 4537.
42 *Letters*, IV, p. 977.
43 Ibid, p. 977.
44 *Notebooks*, IV, 4606.
45 Ibid, 4550, 4604.
46 Ibid, 4632.
47 Ibid, 4547.
48 *Letters*, IV, p. 947N.
49 Ibid, p. 947N.
50 Ibid, pp. 953–4.
51 *Notebooks*, IV, 4608, 4623.
52 *Letters*, IV, p. 946.
53 *S.P.*, p. 215; *P.W.* pp. 439–40.
54 *Letters*, p. 956.
55 Ibid, p. 940.
56 Ibid, p. 940.
57 *Letters*, V, p. 346N.
58 Heritage, pp. 436–51.
59 *Letters*, VI, p. 946.
60 *Letters*, V, p. 79.
61 *Shorter Works*, II, p. 1252.
62 Minnow, pp. 81–4.
63 *Letters*, V, pp. 38–9.
64 Ibid, pp. 45–6.
65 Ibid, p. 36.
66 Ibid, p. 68.
67 Ibid, p. 80.
68 Ibid, pp. 83, 85.
69 Hartley, p. lxxv.
70 *Letters*, V, p. 80.
71 Ibid, p. 83.
72 Ibid, p. 80.
73 Ibid, p. 69.
74 Ibid, p. 64.
75 Ibid, p. 63.
76 Ibid, p. 71.
77 Ibid, p. 77.
78 Ibid, p. 70.
79 Ibid, pp. 103–6.
80 Ibid, p. 108.
81 Ibid, p. 110.
82 Ibid, pp. 114–5.
83 Ibid, pp. 110–11.
84 Ibid, p. 117N.
85 Ibid, p. 76.
86 Ibid, p. 251.
87 Ibid, pp. 120–23.
88 *Notebooks*, IV, 4714.
89 *Letters*, V, p. 119.
90 *Notebooks*, IV, 4771. Published posthumously as *Logic*, edited by J. R. de J. Jackson, Bollinger Series, Princeton University Press and Routledge, 1981.
91 *Early Visions*, p. 27.
92 *Letters*, V, p. 119.
93 Ibid, p. 143.
94 Ibid, pp. 149–50.
95 Ibid, p. 149N.
96 Hartley, p. xci; Letters, V, p. 148.
97 Hartley, p.lxxxiv.
98 *Letters*, V, p. 160
99 Ibid, p. 153.
100 Ibid, p. 145–8.
101 *Letters*, VI, p. 720.
102 *Notebooks*, IV, 4788, 4789.
103 *Letters*, V, p. 362.
104 'Notes Respecting the Late S. T. Coleridge by Seymour Porter', published in 'Samuel Taylor Coleridge and Opium', by E. L. Griggs, *Huntingdon Library Quarterly*, 1954.
105 *Letters*, V, pp. 171–3N.
106 Ibid, p. 185.
107 Ibid, p. 189.
108 *S.P.*, p. 23; *P.W.* p. 435.
109 Nigel Leask, *The Politics of Imagination in Coleridge's Thought*, 1988, pp. 147, 201.
110 *Letters*, V, p. 192.
111 Ibid, p. 201–3.
112 Ibid, p. 203N.

113 Ibid, p. 204.
114 *Shorter Works* II, pp. 1008–32.
115 *Letters*, V, p. 200.
116 Morton N. Cohen, *Lewis Carroll*, 1995, pp. 223–6; and *passim* Chapter 4 and 11.
117 *Letters*, V, p. 209.
118 Ibid, pp. 231–3.
119 Ibid, p. 240–1.
120 *Early Visions*, p. 54–5.
121 *Notebooks*, IV, 4903, 4905.
122 *Letters*, V, p. 245.
123 Ibid, p. 251.
124 Ibid, pp. 254–5.
125 *S.P.*, pp. 208–9; *P.W.*, pp. 457–8.

Chapter 11: Glide, Rich Streams, Away!

1 *Letters*, V, p. 239.
2 Ibid, p. 249–51.
3 Ibid, p. 257.
4 Southey, II, p. 257.
5 Hartley Coleridge, *Letters*, edited by E. L. Griggs, 1941, p. 32.
6 Lefebure, *The Bondage of Love*, op. cit., p. 240.
7 Heritage, pp. 468–9.
8 Ibid, p. 475.
9 Bradford Keyes Mudge, *Sara Coleridge: A Victorian Daughter*, 1989, p. 26.
10 *Table Talk*, I, pp. 25–39.
11 Mudge, op. cit., p. 30.
12 *Letters*, VI, p. 589.
13 Ibid, pp. 590–91.
14 Leslie Stephen, *Hours in a Library*, III, 1888.
15 Mudge, op. cit., p. 99.
16 *The Letters of Charles Lamb*, 3 vols, edited by E.V. Lucas, 1935, II, p. 376–7.
17 Robinson, *Books*, p. 289–90; *The Letters of Charles Lamb*, Lucas, op. cit., II, p. 468.
18 *Notebooks*, IV, 4993, 4996.
19 Ibid, 4994.
20 *S.P.*, pp. 215–6; *P.W.*, pp. 440–1.
21 *Notebooks*, IV, 5032.
22 *Letters*, V, pp. 290–1.
23 *Notebooks*, IV, 5026; *Aids*, pp. 106–7.
24 Mill *On Bentham and Coleridge*, op. cit., p. 113.
25 *Aids*, p. 241.
26 Ibid, pp. 117–8.
27 Ibid, p. 248.
28 Highgate Institution Archive, numerous drawings of Coleridge's study and back garden. Described in *Coleridge at Highgate*, Lucy Watson, 1925.
29 *Early Visions*, p. 277.
30 Lucy Watson, op. cit., p. 52.
31 *Letters*, V, p. 317.
32 Ibid, p. 317.
33 Ibid, p. 342.
34 Ibid, p. 346N.
35 'Notes . . . by Seymour Porter', op. cit., *Huntingdon Library Quarterly*, 1954.
36 *Letters*, V, p. 207N.
37 *P.W.*, pp. 442–3.
38 *Letters*, V, p. 350.
39 Ibid, p. 352.
40 *Talker*, pp. 111–2.
41 Carlyle, *Life of Sterling*, op. cit., pp. 46–54.
42 *Letters*, V, pp. 403–4.
43 Ibid, p. 398.
44 Ibid, p. 401.
45 Ibid, p. 402.
46 Ibid, p. 411.
47 Ibid, p. 414.
48 Hazlitt, p. 244.
49 *Letters*, V, p. 414; *S.P.*, p. 258.
50 *S.P.*, p. 25; *P.W.*, p. 447.
51 *Letters*, V, pp. 414–6; *S.P.*, pp. 258–9; Complete Poetical Works, II, pp. 1110–11.
52 *Aids*, pp. 396–7.
53 Ibid, p. 397.
54 Ibid, pp. 397–8.
55 Ibid, p. 407.
56 Ibid, p. 407.
57 *Romantic Influences: Contemporary, Victorian, Modern* by John Beer, Macmillan, 1993, p. 152.

58 *Talker*, pp. 344–5.
59 Beer, op. cit., p. 152.
60 Ibid, p. 153.
61 *Notebooks*, IV, 5249.
62 *Letters*, VI, p. 532.
63 Ibid.
64 Ibid, p. 673.
65 Ibid, p. 592.
66 Ibid, pp. 593–601.
67 Ibid, p. 629.
68 *Talker*, p. 223.
69 *S.P.*, p. 219; *P.W.*, p. 48.
70 *Letters*, VI, p. 73 and Note.
71 *Talker*, p. 383.
72 *S.P.*, pp. 290–2; *P.W.*, pp. 443–7.
73 Chambers, pp. 307–8.
74 *Letters*, VI, pp. 700, 976.
75 *Church and State*, p. 46.
77 *Letters*, VI, pp. 968–9.
78 *S.P.*, p. 221; *P.W.*, pp. 488–9.
79 Minnow, p. 165.
80 Hartley Coleridge, *Letters*, op. cit., pp. 99–101.
81 Hartley, 'Dedication to his Father', p. 2.
82 *Table Talk*, I, p. 397.
83 *Letters*, VI, p. 986.
84 *Table Talk*, II, p. 296.
85 *Letters*, VI, p. 992.

Acknowledgements

For the use of copyright materials and kind permission to consult and refer to manuscripts and archives, my most grateful acknowledgments are due to the British Library, London; the Bodleian Library, Oxford; the Royal Library, Valetta, Malta; the Museo Archelogo, Syracuse, Sicily; the New York Public Library; the University of Toronto Library, Canada; the Royal Institution of Great Britain, London; the Royal College of Surgeons, London; the Wordsworth Trust, Cumbria; The Wiltshire County Record Office; the National Trust, Stowey; The Civic Society, Calne, Wiltshire; the Highgate Literary and Scientific Institution; the London Library; Lord Coleridge of Ottery St Mary; Mrs Joan M. Coleridge of West Sussex; Oxford University Press for permission to quote from the *Collected Letters of Samuel Taylor Coleridge* edited by E.L. Griggs, and the *Letters of William and Dorothy Wordsworth* edited by Mary Moorman; Routledge for permission to quote from the *Notebooks of Samuel Taylor Coleridge* edited by Kathleen Coburn; and James MacGibbon and Allen Lane for permission to quote from *The Collected Poems of Stevie Smith*.

Mr warmest personal thanks are due to Professor John Beer at Cambridge; Professor Heather Jackson at Toronto; Dr Jon Cook at East Anglia; Professor John Henry of the National Poisons Unit, London; William St Clair at All Souls; Professor George Steiner who has never let me forget that Coleridge was a European; Robert Silvers at the *New York Review of Books*; Professor Peter Day at the Royal Institution; and Alan Judd at the Pied Bull. My gratitude also to Richard Lines of the Swedenborg Society; Sir John Baynes, descendent of Danial Stuart; Roger Fenby of the BBC World Service; Tim Dee and Simon Callow who helped me explore "The Unknown Coleridge" for BBC Radio. Ion Trewin helped me start the long journey, Peter Janson-Smith kept me constantly afloat, and

Stuart Proffitt supported me through to the end with his passionate conviction. I am grateful to Douglas Matthews for the Index, and John Gilkes for the maps. I have been lucky to find a matchless working editor in Arabella Pike, a great enthusiast in Michael Fishwick, and a shrewd and comradely advisor in David Godwin (with Sebastian Godwin's computer cavalry to hand). I have had a candle lit in Kent, and a rose flowering in Norfolk. Indeed without Rose Tremain there would be no book.

Index

About the Author

Richard Holmes's first book, *Shelley: The Pursuit*, won the Somerset Maugham Prize in 1974. Among his other books are *Coleridge: Early Visions, 1772-1804*, which won the 1989 Whitbread Book of the Year Prize. *Dr. Johnson & Mr. Savage*, which won the 1993 James Tait Black Prize, and *Footsteps: Adventures of a Romantic Biographer*. A fellow of the British Academy, he was awarded an OBE in 1992.

S0-BAJ-004

OUT
NEW YORK 19

POSTS OF SCIENCE

A JOURNEY TO THE WORKSHOPS OF OUR LEADING MEN OF RESEARCH

BY BERNARD JAFFE

SIMON AND SCHUSTER

Science that blinks its eyes incessantly
With a new light that fades and leaves them aching.

EDWIN ARLINGTON ROBINSON
in *Matthias at the Door*

We stand today on a bright oasis of knowledge in an illimitable desert of the unknown.

LORD SALISBURY

From time to time we seem to reach a stage in which the horizon of discovery is also its boundary.

W. F. G. SWANN

CONTENTS

ILLUSTRATIONS

PLATES

ILLUSTRATIONS IN TEXT

INTRODUCTION

PURPOSE, PLAN AND PILGRIMAGE

How this book was written

THIRTY-SIX THOUSAND scientific journals, one-third of them in English, have been trying to keep pace with the bewildering march of science, belching forth tens of thousands of papers on every scientific topic imaginable. During the last few years in particular this breathless advance has been perplexing. New discoveries have crowded upon each other with ever increasing unmannerliness. Scientists themselves have been unable to keep abreast of this prodigious progress. The lot of the lay person, of course, is even more pathetic. He finds himself in a maze of quasi-scientific beliefs, Sunday supplement panaceas, anhydrous academic treatises, and plain facts hidden in the forbidding vestments of highly technical jargon.

Could this shapeless, tangled mass of information be gathered together within the covers of one book? Could it be set down in simple language which would give the average reader some idea of the tremendous activity going on behind the doors of the laboratories of science? Are there definite authoritative answers to such questions as: Has science learned enough about the laws of heredity to furnish hope for a planned and controlled human society? What outstanding conquests have been made in the realm of the physical diseases such as pneumonia, infantile paralysis, the common cold, and hardening of the arteries? Has science found the cause, an early diagnostic test or a cure for cancer? What of the mental diseases? Are we still where we were a hundred years ago, or are the insanities yielding to the remorseless drive of the men in white? Is sterilization the only way out of the menace of dementia praecox and schizophrenia?

Can glandular extracts reverse the sex of an individual? Could Japan hope to increase the stature of her fighting forces by injections of glandular extracts or did this news trickle out of some twentieth-century alchemical workshop? Have physics and chemistry approached any nearer the solution of the problem of the nature of matter or have they both lost themselves in metaphysics and waves of probability? What are cosmic rays, and why the unremitting battle to find out their nature? With what philosophical implications was this new type of radiation entwined? Was science getting anywhere in its attempt to find laws which would enable meteorologists to forecast weather months in advance? What was this talk of new island universes, new models of an exploding, bursting, rushing, expanding and contracting universe? In short what had already been accomplished and what were the outstanding problems still left for science to solve?

The temptation to write such a book finally overcame my meager scientific equipment. I had therefore to lay out a carefully planned procedure. First I was to follow through an intensive reading program which would make it possible for me to decide upon the most important fields of research and also to pick out the men who had done the most crucial work in each field. This reading project was to be reinforced by conversations with numerous scientific men whom I knew in New York. For various reasons such as the intrinsic difficulty of the subject, the lack of general interest and the paucity of scientific experimentation I abandoned such fields as relativity, geology and psychology and finally selected the topics which comprise the contents of this book.

The task of selecting the most eminent men in each field whom I could visit and around whose researches each story could be told was a much more difficult one. As one distinguished scientist told me, " You cannot easily pick out a single man in any field and build the whole story around him. It might have been possible in the early days of research but today, when a new field is opened up, a whole flock of frenzied men quickly descend upon it and scores of these scientists must be considered." However, the situation was not quite so hopeless in certain cases. For example, Thomas Hunt Morgan was easily the most outstanding figure in the field of genetics not only in America but throughout the world. Likewise, George E. Hale knew more than any other living man about the sun, and the startling work of Edwin P. Hubble who was probing the farthest outposts of extra-galactic space placed him at the very center of the important developments relating to new structures of the universe. In a few cases, where the choice was not so clearly defined, decisions were made after considering such factors as the number of years of research through which the men had lived and their positions as pioneers in the lines of investigation. (The average age of the men named in the table of contents is about 64 years.)

Having listed the men I wanted to see, I mapped out an itinerary — a wide circle around the United States which would bring me to about fifty of the most important research laboratories in the country. In September, 1932, I started from New York on a scientific pilgrimage to the firesteps and outposts of the present battlefronts of science in America. I was armed with little more than an impertinent belief that eminent men busy in scientific workshops might stop for a while to tell me what they were doing and hoping so that the general public might catch a glimpse of the many new discoveries.

Several pictures stand out more clearly than others. The Cancer Research Laboratory of the University of Pennsylvania where, under the leadership of Dr. Ellice McDonald, young biochemists, physicists, bacteriologists, radiation experts and biophysicists are groping in a stygian darkness to find the cause of cancer; The Laboratory for Endocrine Research of Johns Hopkins University where John Jacob Abel, in white skull cap and long white laboratory coat, still wrestles, after more than a half century of labor, with insulin and other products of the ductless glands — glands of destiny as they have been called; The Department of Biochemistry of the School of Hygiene and

Public Health of Johns Hopkins University where Elmer V. McCollum, risen from ploughboy on a Kansas farm to leadership in a new nutrition, directs a corps of workers in further problems in this field; a private residence in Washington, D. C., where Leland Ossian Howard, 78-year-old warrior against the insect hosts, still cooks up plans to beat man's most menacing rivals; St. Elizabeth's Hospital outside Washington where William A. White supervises a city of the mentally afflicted while he watches for even the dimmest light that may banish the blackness of that world of the insane; The Bureau of Physical Anthropology of the United States National Museum where Aleš Hrdlička, erstwhile immigrant boy from Bohemia, sits measuring a bundle of ancient bones dug out of the rocks of China; The Steward Observatory of the University of Arizona where a strange hybrid of astronomer, engineer and tree-ring expert, Andrew E. Douglass, is making Tucson the center of some fascinating investigations linking the weather of the distant past with long-range weather forecasting of today.

From the desert country of Arizona where numerous sanitariums for the tubercular stand as stark evidences of the failure of science to win a complete victory over the white scourge, I went on to the coast. When I reached Pasadena I headed straight for Thomas Hunt Morgan, director of the Kerckhoff Laboratories of the California Institute of Technology. I had already met Dr. Morgan the previous summer at Woods Hole. At that time he was patient enough to listen to my plans and offer advice. Morgan took me into the inner sancta of his famous laboratory. For more than two weeks I hovered around the place. I watched many of the men and women at their multifarious researches — rearing flies, etherizing them, counting them, drawing pictures of new mutants, preparing their diets, subjecting these insects to all sorts of strange experiences, and constructing new gene maps. I was fascinated — there is no other spot quite like this one in the whole world. The layman has not the remotest idea of what this fly nursery is like. I attended the evening seminars, spent hours on end browsing through the thousands of abstracts on genetics which Morgan had collected in this perhaps the most complete genetics library on earth. There were moments when I wished I could leave my own life groove and throw myself completely into this new one.

Other equally magical places in and near Pasadena drew me. On the outskirts of the city rises Mt. Wilson. At its top is the famous observatory from which had come news of world-wide interest. News of nebulae and galaxies rushing away from our planet with ever increasing speeds, news of island universes and their trillions of stars, news of new cunning devices which were reaching nature in its most distant outposts. I was eager to see this modern citadel of the heavens and talk to the men who were working there. I wanted, if possible, with my own eyes to catch a glimpse of the new universes they were discovering. Dr. Walter S. Adams, the eminent director of this observatory, gave me permission to visit it. I spoke then to Edwin P. Hubble who was at the forefront of the new developments in astronomy. He was at the time at the foot of the mountain working over some of the sky photographs and spectrum prints that had been taken with the huge telescopes. Walter Baade, the astronomer, was getting ready to ascend the mountain that afternoon. Baade volunteered to take me and show me around.

We reached the summit of Mt. Wilson at dusk. I was escorted through the observatory building which housed the 100-inch telescope. We climbed to near the top of it where Adriaan van Maanen, dressed in almost polar costume, was observing the stars. He stopped his work for only a moment to exchange greetings and to let me peer through the eyepiece. Every second counted with these men at the big telescope, and I was assured I could have more time at the 60-inch. A number of visitors had gathered to get a peek at star clusters through this smaller giant. At its eyepiece was a young lady, a movie actress who had come from Berlin to Hollywood. The language barrier which arose with the introduction of the talkies had been too much for her, and she was getting ready to return home. But she must first see this famous telescope. For a few minutes she kept her eyes to the tube and then as she made way for me I could hear a familiar phrase, somewhat distorted by a pure Aryan accent: *Aw nerts.* There was really nothing to see, she added. She had been gazing at a star cluster hundreds of thousands of light years away, at a nebula perhaps already cold yet still visible by the light which had left that distant universe before mankind had even learned to walk upright.

There were still other luminaries to be seen in this modern Alexandria, Robert A. Millikan and George Ellery Hale among them. More than its sunshine held me in California. Hale's name had been familiar to me for years. I knew him as the great man of the mountain who had brought the sun down to our terrestrial laboratories. I knew him as the vigorous organizer of astrophysical research, the man behind the erection of many an important solar observatory. I knew also, however, that he was not strong, that a life of continuous research and organization work had almost broken him. I was afraid I would not be able to see him, for he had been forced to cut down his visitors to a minimum. Morgan, however, arranged for an interview, and Dr. Hale saw me in the library of his own solar observatory on the outskirts of Pasadena. A meeting with this man, the very spirit of scientific research, is one of the unforgettable incidents of my trip.

More interviews, more visits, more notes, more abstracts. The number of scientific papers that I had collected was increasing at an alarming rate. I did not send them home to await my return for I wanted to read them in my leisure hours between visits to the various centers of research. I had carefully hidden them away in my luggage. As they kept piling up, more and more of my personal belongings were mailed home — camera, shirts, socks, even underwear. By the time I reached New York I had hardly anything but abstracts in my luggage.

Millikan, who could jump quite dexterously out of some intricate problem in science into a full-dress suit for a political rally, was busy campaigning for Herbert Hoover. I spoke rather briefly with the Nobel laureate who had made of electrons and protons and cosmic ray research a living, throbbing thing even for the man in the street. He turned me over to some of his young associates for more information. Just a few months before, perhaps the most important discovery in physics of the last generation had been made by one of these men, Dr. Carl D. Anderson. Millikan had set him on the track which ended in the discovery of the positron, the third fundamental building stone of the material universe. I was quite fortunate therefore in hearing from Anderson the details of this tremendously important discovery which had just been announced.

Months before, while I was trying to choose the outstanding workers in the many fields of scientific research, I had been puzzled for a while as to what selection to make in the realm of cancer investigation. Many were engaged in this difficult undertaking, some had added a fact here and there, some had done conspicuous work in cancer surgery and cancer radiation therapy, but none had devoted a whole lifetime and made contributions in this field comparable to those of Maud Slye of the University of Chicago. Stories had reached me from time to time of an " American Curie " who was searching for the cause, an early diagnostic test and an effective treatment of this disease. They were tales of a relentless hunt, an all-absorbing passion, an heroic life-struggle in a world of — mice.

I called on Professor Slye in her laboratory at 5836 Drexel Avenue. Before me thousands of visitors from all parts of the world had been led through this building. Men of science had come from Europe and Asia to watch this woman at work. Maud Slye, of medium height, with deep-set eyes and gray bobbed hair, conducted me through the three-story building which housed ten thousand mice. These animals had been bred by Maud Slye in her efforts to solve the age-old problem of cancer in human beings. We talked for hours. In her eyes was the fire of a modern crusader. At times she spoke with deep emotion as when she referred to the plight of thousands of impoverished human cancer cases. There was no haven, not a single sanitarium in which they could live out the rest of their harassed lives in comfort. No convalescent home or hospital for incurables would admit them. My mind went back to a scene in a train speeding from Tucson to Los Angeles. Across the aisle from me was a tall, bony cattleman from the southwest, hardly more than a skeleton of a man. He was on his way to San Francisco where a new cancer clinic had just opened. He had spent almost the last of his money at medical centers, cancer clinics, radiation specialists, and surgeons but the wild growth of cancer could not be stopped, for the diagnosis had come too late. He asked me about the Coffey-Humber cancer clinic in San Francisco. And although I knew that the American Medical Association had outlawed it, I could not destroy his last hope. There was no other place for him to go.

There were many other men who held me before I ended my trip. For months I had been subjected to all kinds of experiences and had met all manner of research men. Now on my return I tried to summarize my varied impressions. I had met among research workers in science, men of broad vision as well as petty men obsessed by their own often inconsequential pieces of research. There were among them many to whom victory wreaths held no allurement and others who could not work happily except with the glare of publicity shining upon them. Among the disciples of science were many who refused to stoop to the pettiness of squabbles over priority of discovery as well as some who did not hesitate to poach on the property of their colleagues and whose own self-aggrandizement was the mainspring of their efforts. In trying to fathom the forces by which science had attracted the majority of its devotees it seemed to me that Julian Huxley has probed them as deeply as anyone. " The man of science," he writes, " devotes himself to research for precisely the same reason that the poet devotes himself to the arduous business of writing poetry, the explorer to the dangers and hardships of unknown lands, the mystic to the time-consuming rigors of the devotional life, or the mother to the never ending service of her child." In short the forces that throw men into research are the same as those that are operative in other activities.

It had been planned that the leaders in each field of science whom I had met were to correct those portions of the manuscript dealing with their own work. This would, of course, insure a greater measure of authenticity for the book. This plan was carried through with but one exception. The chapter on Physical Disease reached Baltimore the day on which Dr. William H. Welch died in his eighty-fourth year. Dr. Fielding H. Garrison, the eminent historian of the Institute of the History of Medicine of The Johns Hopkins University, and a close friend of Welch, was kind enough to edit the historical material of this chapter and Dr. Coleman B. Rabin of Mt. Sinai Hospital, the clinical data. Without the aid of Garrison, Morgan, Millikan, Compton, Slye, Abel, Howard, Hale, Hubble, Tolman, Hrdlička, Meyer, McCollum, Douglass, Abbot and many others this book could not have been written.

This personal checking of the material in the book unconsciously revealed some interesting sidelights. Several of the chapters came back to me with personal notes tragically blue-pencilled. In general there was objection to any attempt at glorification of their own personalities or overestimation of their achievements. Personal vanity, however, was by no means lacking in some. One man erased every reference to rivals in his field on the ground that they were "unimportant." Another made such voluminous additions to his own life and work that only an obituary would be obliged to print them. In spite of all the care with which the manuscript was checked, errors may have escaped detection and for all these the responsibility is my own.

The most significant impression I got was the change in the type of research gradually emerging in this country. The United States has kept pace with and even forged ahead of her European contemporaries in the fields of invention and applied science. American men of science have shown extraordinary ingenuity in building new tools with which to apply the fruits of abstract science. The harnessing of the steam and internal combustion engines, the invention of the telegraph, telephone and airplane, and the developments in the fields of radio communication and television are but a few of the outstanding contributions which typify America's utilization of discoveries in theoretical science.

Yet in the realm of pure science — the search for truth with no thought of practical application or pecuniary returns — the United States until recently had lagged behind the leading European nations. We look in vain through our annals for a Darwin whose scientific genius gathered the tomes of data in the realm of biology and shaped them into a theory of evolution which revolutionized man's ideas about his place in nature. We search without success among our leading universities for an Einstein who introduced into modern science as wide-sweeping a synthesis of natural phenomena as did Newton in his *Principia.* We cannot find an American counterpart of James Clerk Maxwell who, with uncanny insight, enunciated the electromagnetic theory of light and prophetically predicted the discovery of wireless waves. We have given to the world no equal of Pasteur who introduced the germ theory of disease, or of Arrhenius who created the theory of ionization, J. J. Thomson of England and Ernest Rutherford of New Zealand who gave us a novel conception of the structure of matter, Max Planck, the German, who gave birth to a new conception of quanta or atoms of energy, Niels Bohr, the Dane who, taking the bricks fashioned by Thomson, Rutherford, Einstein and Planck, builded a structure to explain the mysteries of the spectra of the elements which, though somewhat outmoded today, was nevertheless the starting point of a vigorous onslaught on this fundamental problem — all of these men are products of the soil of Europe. We have no Minkowski to change our deep-seated notions of time and space. We cannot point with pride or even scorn to an American Freud who startled mankind with a dynamic conception of the workings of the mind — one of the greatest contribution in this still semi-scientific field since the dawn of reason. Our De Broglies, Heisenbergs, Schroedingers and Diracs have either not yet been born or have failed to emerge to creative manhood.

We can point, of course, to the twelve Americans who have received the Nobel Prize, the greatest honor possible in science. Leaving out of account Karl Landsteiner who received his life molding and training on the other side, Thomas Hunt Morgan and Harold C. Urey two of the most recent recipients, we find a curious picture. Manual dexterity rather than broad theory is the dominant note. Michelson's great achievement was the creation of the interferometer, a piece of apparatus difficult of construction yet simple in principle, with which he was able to pursue epochal experiments in more accurate determinations of the speed of light, in the absence of ether drift and in star diameters. Theodore Richards' brilliant work was the experimental determination of the atomic weights of a large number of elements to a degree of accuracy never before attained — a bit of research demanding unusual technique but hardly more than ordinary theoretical cerebration. Alexis Carrel's contribution was an ingenious and unerring technique for sewing blood vessels, making it possible to perform blood transfusions safely and to transplant arteries, veins and organs. Millikan's genius consisted in devising delicate apparatus — " machine shops in vacuum tubes " — which he employed to find crucial experimental evidence of the validity of theoretical conclusions born in the minds of Europeans. His work on the photoelectric effect which culminated in the first complete and direct determination of Planck's constant h, and his classic determination of the mass of the electron are brilliant examples of remarkable technique; as products of the world of theoretical science they are but secondary exhibits. Arthur H. Compton showed that X-rays were material bullets of light which upon striking material particles lost some of their energy and changed to rays of longer wave length — a scintillating piece of experimentation which is a tribute to his skill as a manipulator of the material tools of the scientist.

Irving Langmuir, keen theorist though he is, has done his outstanding work on the mechanism of chemical reactions which take place on the surfaces of extremely thin films of metals. Without his genius for devising apparatus so delicate that he could detect the presence of a single atom of cesium in 35 cu. ft. of space (equivalent to finding one solitary fly in a hollow sphere of the diameter of the earth), his results would never have been attained.

To explain the supremacy of America in applied science is fairly easy. America was a new country. Huge natural resources were here to be tapped. Vast prairies and fertile fields smiled graciously on the pioneers. Immense forests stood ready to be stripped. Mountains of gold were here to be dug. Enormous deposits of coal and bursting reservoirs of petroleum needed but to be struck to give forth a steady flood of power. A virgin country stood waiting to be peopled and exploited. Long distances, high mountains, rushing rivers, and wide lakes had to be crossed. The mind, the hand, and the energy of the people were occupied for more than two hundred years with the practical problem of subduing a country and gaining dominion over it. There was a cry for labor-saving devices. The inventive genius and the technological skill of Americans were stimulated to a fever heat. A new royalty sprang up among this restless people dazzled by great possibilities of conquest. Coal barons, steel magnates, captains of industry vied with one another in applying the products of science to the building of a new country.

There was no time or thought for pure theory when every value of science was expressed in terms of service and function. Theoretical speculation and contemplative philosophy were engulfed in the rush to subdue a land overflowing with material resources. In such an atmosphere as this the pragmatic philosophy of William James was born, and the guiding star of " learning by doing " rose under the leadership of John Dewey. These forces, reflecting an industrial revolution, made it very difficult to breed and sustain men who could be happy in the pursuit of science for science's sake. Less than ten years ago, when a fund of twenty million dollars was sought to raise the United States on the scale of scientific accomplishment, "there ran through the appeals for subscription," wrote Charles Beard in *The Rise of American Civilization*, "the obtruding note that in the end even the most remote and abstract search for truth would pay dividends to business enterprise."

But things have changed and are still changing, altering the shape of things as they are, giving new forms to things that are to come. The frontier days of the country are gone. Science now offers the excitement of new frontiers of discovery. Education at the same time is penetrating deeper and wider into the masses. Leisure will be more common and no American Copernicus will any longer have to take holy orders to find time for study. Our centers of learning are slowly changing their philosophy. Further emancipation from the load of teaching and the treadmill of class routine is giving our university teachers more time and clearer heads for contemplation and experimentation. Philosophy may still return after fleeing from the ogre of the frontier days and the machine age. Pure research is being subsidized as never before. It may be that our Keplers may never again have to sell horoscopes to keep alive.

Perhaps this fresh spirit has already brought us beyond the threshold of a new burst of scientific accomplishment. We may already be witnessing a Golden Age in American science. We can point to Morgan's *Theory of the Gene*, the greatest single theoretical conception we have as yet produced with the exception of the monumental contributions to thermodynamics of Josiah Willard Gibbs, who died in 1903. We may point also to the theoretical work of Richard C. Tolman who, in interpreting the observational data furnished by Hubble and Humason, has constructed new cosmogonies so compelling that Einstein himself has been forced to give up his own static model of the universe in favor of the non-static picture of the American. Gilbert N. Lewis of the University of California and William D. Harkins of the University of Chicago have made important contributions to the theoretical conception of the atom's structure. Other younger and brilliant men like Carl D. Anderson, Harold C. Urey, Ernest O. Lawrence, and Linus Pauling are moving swiftly to the front of scientific thinkers. "Today," said De Broglie recently, "scientific publications from the United States are awaited with an impatience and curiosity in France inspired by those of no other country." Our young men, losing themselves in the pleasures of research in pure science and perhaps even in preoccupation with metaphysics, will yet cut new roads for fresh scientific advances. The march has only just begun.

PART ONE

CHAPTER ONE

GENETICS

THE FRUIT FLY, DROSOPHILA, BECOMES THE BIOLOGICAL CINDERELLA

The classic researches of the school of Thomas Hunt Morgan

SCIENTIFIC DISCOVERY has been compared to the fitting together of the pieces of a huge jig-saw puzzle. New theories in science do not mean that the old pieces have to be discarded, but rather that the newly discovered bits of information can frequently be added within the old. The final picture appears then as a composite of the old and the new. The new mosaic is more complete, somewhat different, and more clearly comprehended. So has it been with our conception of heredity. Within the last few years new fragments have been brought to light which have altered our ideas about this perplexing problem.

There have been many attempts to find the laws of inheritance; to discover in what arithmetical order, if any, hemophilia, eye color, albinism, and the characteristic Hapsburg lip were transmitted from generation to generation. There have been many theories to explain the appearance of new species of living things such as the one-toed horse, the Ancon breed of short-legged sheep, and the Lombardy poplar. Darwin, after spending a lifetime on the problem, admitted that " our ignorance of the laws of heredity and the origin of new species is profound," and he died without finding an answer satisfactory even to himself.

Up to the opening of the twentieth century it was generally accepted that environment alone was the cause of those slow changes in organisms which eventually resulted in definitely new species. But this explanation was not altogether convincing. For centuries the Chinese had bound the tender feet of female children to make them small. Yet today when with the rise of nationalism in China this custom has been officially abolished, the feet of infants left free to grow are still the normal-sized feet of the race that existed before the custom was introduced thousands of years ago. Man-made environment had evidently had no effect on the transmission of this new characteristic, small feet, to coming generations. Is there, then, another process at work to explain the appearance of new characteristics which are inheritable?

By chance, as frequently happens in the haphazard advance of science, a Dutch biologist, Hugo de Vries, came across a new type of evening primrose growing wild in a field near Amsterdam. This was eighteen years after the death of Darwin, when the appearance of new types of living things was still only partially explained. The whole story was still an enigma. De Vries, in an effort to find whether the new type of plant was really a new species, that is, would breed true, planted fifty thousand of its seeds. Before long he found that this variation did breed true, and he was further rewarded by the appearance of several entirely new types of the same plant, such as dwarf primroses that gave rise only to dwarf offspring. This evidently was incontestable proof that one species could suddenly give rise to another which could maintain itself. *Mutation* was the name De Vries gave to this process whereby a new character spontaneously appeared from a pure ancestral stock and bred true. A few cases of this sort of sudden appearance of a new character or variation had previously been vaguely reported, but De Vries actually showed the process at work and emphasized its importance.

Here was a key to further research — to breed living things and watch for mutations. For the first time science had at its disposal a tool which could place evolution and heredity upon the experimental table. In 1909 Thomas Hunt Morgan, then forty-three, took hold of this key. He felt that it was more significant than most biologists suspected. "Mutation," Morgan was convinced, "plays a role in the evolution of living forms, and the old speculative method of treating evolution as a problem of pre-history is ready to fade." He had no patience with those who cried out *Ignorabimus* — "We shall not know."

Science often does not have to wait for natural phenomena to take place before it can study them. It prides itself upon its ability to set the stage for controlled experimentation, thus saving time and effort. Investigations concerning the many problems connected with evolution could now be brought into the laboratory. The evening primrose did not satisfy Morgan. He wanted a short-lived organism and one that could be easily bred in the laboratory under changing conditions. He tried the mouse, the rat, the pigeon, and even undertook some painstaking experiments on the intricate life cycle of a plant louse, until one day he heard of another insect which W. E. Castle of Harvard had been using in connection with certain investigations in inbreeding.

Drosophila melanogaster, the vinegar fly, is a tiny organism about a quarter of an inch long, the type commonly seen feeding on decaying fruits. In one day its eggs change to slender white larvae which after two or three days more change into pupae, and five days later emerge as winged adult flies. Completing its life cycle from egg to fly in about ten days, this insect supplies as many as thirty generations a year, an enormous advantage compared to the relative slowness of the usual laboratory animals. Drosophila was an ideal organism — easily bred, fertile, amenable to laboratory conditions, adapted to careful microscopic analysis, and with a life span which may reach ninety days. Thousands could be handled in a few milk bottles, while the cost of feeding and keeping them healthy was negligible. Morgan obtained a few of these flies, scarcely suspecting that within a few years this Cinderella of the biological kitchen was to become, in the queenly robes of genetics, the most famous experimental organism in the world.

During the fall and winter of that first year, 1909, Morgan subjected his flies to all sorts of abnormal conditions, hoping that this treatment would produce new species or mutants. He exposed eggs, larvae, pupae, and adult flies to such drastic changes as unusually high and low temperatures, he immersed them in acid and alkali solutions, fed them on strange and varied diets, and even tortured them with radio-activity. But nothing of striking scientific interest resulted. Then one day in April, 1910, " in a pedigreed culture of Drosophila which had been running for nearly a year through a considerable number of generations, a male appeared with white eyes." This was an exciting development; the eyes of the normal wild fruit fly are red. Morgan's colleagues came in to look at it under a hand lens. Here was a sharply defined mutant which could be used in experiments in heredity. Morgan planned to cross this precious white-eyed fly to the red-eyed species, just as Gregor Mendel fifty years before him had crossed a yellow edible pea to a green one in the garden of his monastery in Brünn.

Mendel had entered the church to find time for reflection and experimentation. He continued his interest in the problem of heredity. A considerable amount of empirical knowledge in this field had accumulated as a result of the work of practical breeders. This knowledge indicated that like did not always beget like, rather it only *tended* to beget like. Thus the crossing of two black animals did not always result in dark-haired offspring. As far back as 1669 Becher, creator of the phlogiston theory, knew this and had written: " When a black cock-pigeon and a white hen-pigeon unite, the young birds of the first generation are usually some of them entirely black and others entirely white. Examples of the same kind can also be seen in the case of humans. If, for instance, a Spaniard who is markedly brunette marries a woman with a very fair skin, we find that the offspring of the first generation are fair like the mother, but should these children marry among their like, then they will have grandchildren with dark skin, like that of the grandfather. Sometimes we can even see the same thing in the third generation." Mendel wondered if any mathematical laws could be discovered which governed the inheritance of characters. It was of course more than a mathematical question, for it perhaps involved an answer to the enigma of the origin of new species. He set himself the task of making a statistical study of the inheritance of one pair of contrasting characters at a time.

In the year Morgan was born, Mendel published the results of seven years of his plant-breeding experiments. He found that when he crossed the tall strain of a pea with a dwarf strain of the same species, all of the progeny of the first generation were tall. When the members of this first tall generation, called F_1, were self-fertilized, they gave birth to three times as many tall plants as dwarf, instead of producing tall offspring only. This Mendelian ratio of three to one held good only when a single character was involved. It was an average result when large numbers of plants were used. Since the dwarf variety had apparently disappeared in the first generation of offspring, but reappeared in the next, he called this dwarf character *recessive*, while the tall character was called *dominant* (Law of Dominance). He also found that the dwarf progeny of the second generation, called F_2, when self-fertilized, bred true, giving all dwarf offspring. When the tall progeny of F_2 were self-fertilized the result was different. Only one-third of the tall plants of this F_2 bred true, that is, gave tall progeny. The other two-thirds behaved like the first tall F_1, giving three tall and one dwarf plant. (See Fig. 1 on the next page.)

None of the offspring was intermediate in size, nor did one character merge with another. Mendel had discovered not only the Laws of Dominance and Single Unit Characters, but also the fundamental Law of Segregation: "The units (individual characters) contributed by each parent separate in an exact ratio in the germ cells of the offspring without having had any influence on each other." The black and white characters, the tall and dwarf, do not interfere with each other but carry on as individual characters or units. For thirty-five years Mendel's work lay hidden in the pages of the *Transactions of the Brünn Society for the Study of Natural Science.* In 1900 three men working independently came across the paper, and a great deal of statistical investigation and experimentation was started to

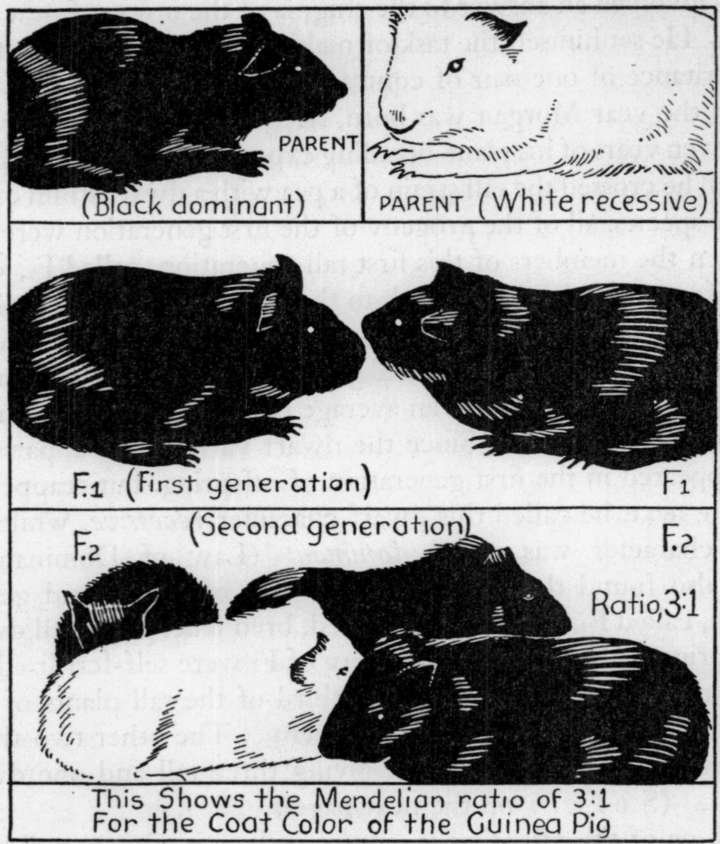
PARENT
(Black dominant)
PARENT (White recessive)
F.1 (First generation)
F1
(Second generation)
F.2
F.2
Ratio, 3:1
This Shows the Mendelian ratio of 3:1
For the Coat Color of the Guinea Pig

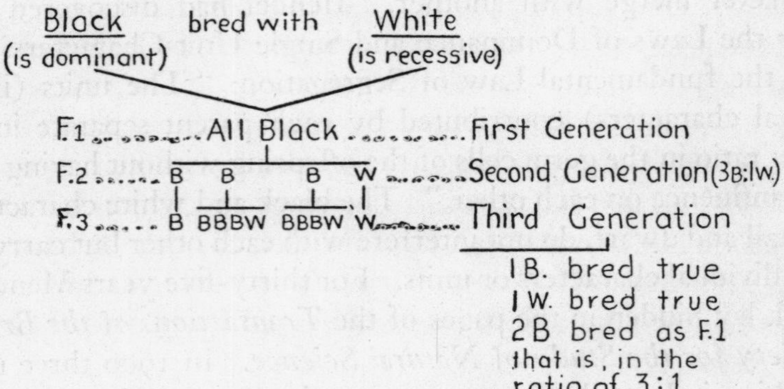
Black (is dominant)
bred with
White (is recessive)
F.1 .... All Black .... First Generation
F.2 .... B B B W .... Second Generation (3B:1W.)
F.3 .... B BBBW BBBW W .... Third Generation
1B. bred true
1W. bred true
2B bred as F.1
that is, in the
ratio of 3:1

FIG. 1

test the validity of Mendel's findings. William Bateson of Cambridge took up the cudgels for Mendel. Inheritance of the shape of comb and the color of plumage in fowls, the coat color of guinea pigs, the eye color of man, the color of horses, the waltzing habit of mice, and similar unit characters were reported by various observers. The conclusions of the genial abbot of Brünn seemed confirmed.

But Mendel's deductions were by no means universally accepted. Karl Pearson, who had founded a school of biometry, which concerns itself with the application of the statistical study of biological phenomena, stood out as the arch-opponent of Mendel's law. As late as the end of 1908 Pearson shouted, " There is no definite proof of Mendelism applying to any living form at present," and in rebuttal he offered the figures from his crossbreeding experiments. Morgan himself was skeptical of " this sort of Mendelian ritual which explains the extraordinary facts of inheritance." Was Mendel really right? Morgan wondered. Perhaps his flies could help settle the problem. Drosophila was to be drafted for an answer.

Morgan mated the white-eyed male fly (the mutant he had discovered early in 1910) to a virgin red-eyed female in a half-pint milk bottle containing some banana. He plugged the bottle with cotton. The union was a prolific one, for nine days later out of that bottle came a swarm of flies which after careful etherization and examination under a lens showed 1237 red-eyed offspring (F_1). That was as expected, for red eye was a dominant character. Some of these 1237 hybrids were then inbred, and in another ten days the second generation (F_2) appeared. Every one of these four thousand odd offspring was as carefully guarded and scrutinized as so many diamonds. What did Morgan find? 2459 red-eyed females, 1011 red-eyed males, and 782 white-eyed males. Mendel's law which called for a ratio of three red-eyed to one white-eyed fly had worked out approximately.

The white-eyed Drosophila was not the only mutant that Morgan had detected. In March of the same year he had noticed the appearance of a fly with a definitely different wing which he called *speck*. Even before this, in January, he had picked out among the thousands of flies he was rearing one with a much darker trident pattern on its thorax than the normal fly. This mutant was named *with* to distinguish it from another, designated *without*, in which the pigmentation was so faint that all traces of the trident pattern had disappeared. Morgan kept breeding more and more of these flies; his desk and shelves became overcrowded with milk bottles and vials of all shapes. There seemed to be more activity in his multiplying colony of insects than in a three-ring circus. Mutants continued to turn up spontaneously. In May he had discovered a fly with an *olive* body instead of the usual brown, as well as another mutant which differed in that the marginal vein of its wing was *beaded*. Before the month of June had passed another mutant with a small *rudimentary* wing was identified, together with a new variety of Drosophila with *pink* eyes. August saw the emergence of both a *miniature*-wing mutant and a *truncated*-wing variety, October a *black* fly, November a fly with vermilion eyes, one with a *balloon*-shaped wing, and another with a very deep black pigmented thorax, *superwith*. The last month of that eventful year brought to light a fly with hardly any wings at all, the *vestigial*-wing mutant.

Morgan now had fifteen different mutants of Drosophila. Every one of the new types bred true. Rearing these mutants, inbreeding and crossbreeding them, and watching for the appearance of new ones involved a tremendous quantity of work. In addition to playing nurse to a host of flies, he had other duties. There was teaching to be done in the graduate school at Columbia University. Just at this time, moreover, a professor who gave a course in zoology was absent, and Morgan had to take his place.

In that class was Calvin Blackman Bridges, a shaggy-haired boy from Schuyler's Falls, New York, who was interested in all of science in a general way. Morgan opened up to this lad the comparatively new and fascinating world of genetics. The

Thomas Hunt Morgan

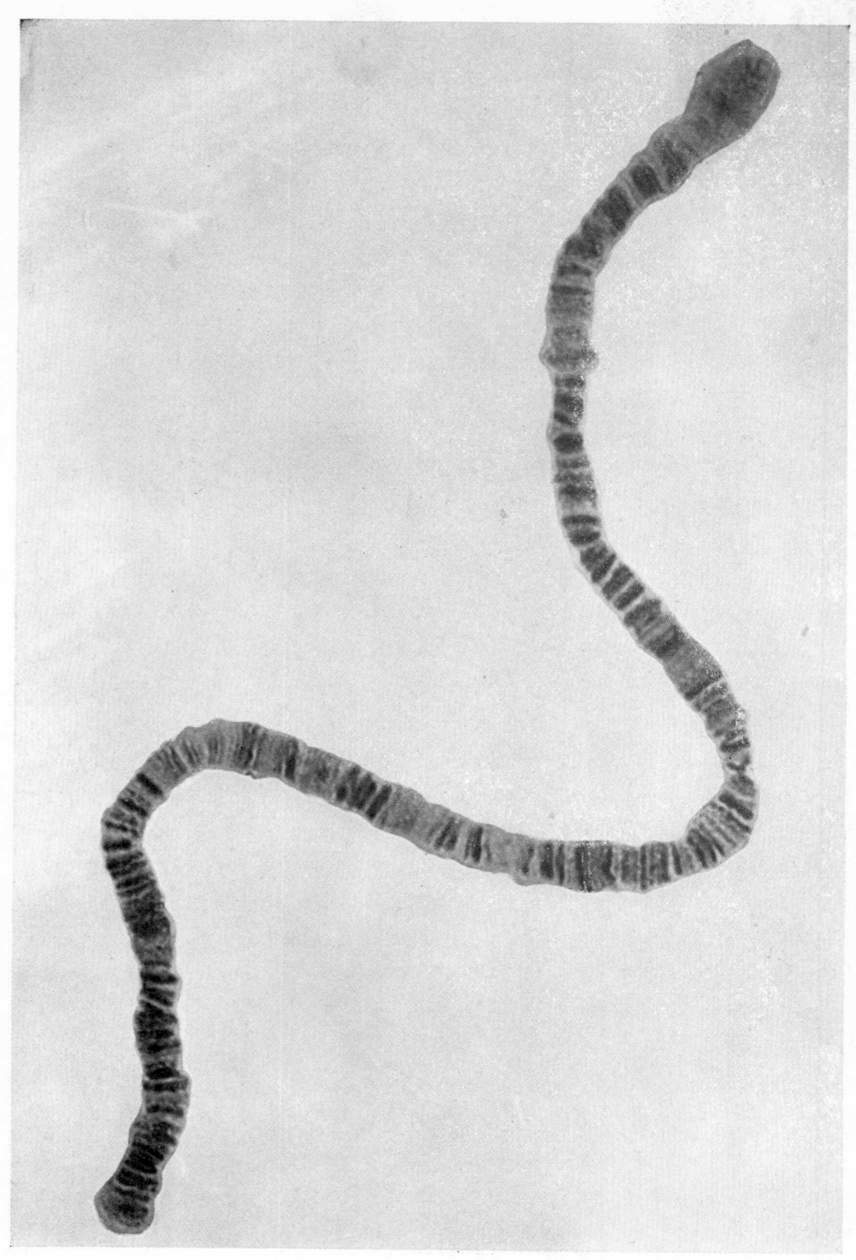

Portrait of a salivary gland chromosome of the fruit fly taken for the first time by T. S. Painter of the University of Texas late in 1934. We may be looking here at the actual genes.

(*Courtesy*, Journal of Heredity)

professor's private talks with his students between and after classes provided an opportunity for Bridges to visit his office. Bridges suggested someone might be needed to help with those innumerable flies breeding prolifically in the miscellaneous collection of fruit jars, milk bottles, and assorted laboratory glassware. Morgan admitted his need for help, but assured him he did not intend taking on an inexperienced novice. But day after day Bridges came back, until one morning he picked up a jar and noticed one fly with a vermilion eye color instead of the usual red. At once Morgan etherized all the flies in that jar, sprinkled them on a sorting plate, and went searching for the mutant among the hundreds of insects. Finding it under the hand lens, he was amazed. " Your eyes are so keen, you might be of help to me," he told Bridges, and added, " If you want to feed these flies and take good care of them and wash the bottles and prepare their food, you may start right now."

Hardly had 1911 begun, when a single male fly with a *yellow* wing was discovered in a batch from a typical stock characterized by gray wing color. This was found by Miss Edith M. Wallace, one of Morgan's research assistants. Then Morgan came across another fly with an *abnormal* abdomen, and on November 16 of that year Bridges, who by this time was permitted to make fly counts, distinguished a new mutant which he called *blistered*. He added two more mutants with wings (*jaunty* and *curved*) quite different from the normal, soon after Morgan had announced the appearance of a fly with a *bifid* wing and Miss Mildred Hoge had thrilled the laboratory with a mutant showing *reduplicated* legs.

The fly squad on Columbia heights was now well under way, and new recruits had to be added to catch up with the work. " Mutations," said Morgan, " have appeared in such rapid succession that my time has been almost entirely consumed in producing pure strains of the new forms which can be utilized later for a thorough study of the inheritance of the new types." The mutating speed of Drosophila completely eclipsed the snail-like pace of the evening primrose. Three times in both February and March of 1912 new mutants were added. Miss Elizabeth Rawls found that certain females from a wild stock were giving birth to only half as many males as was expected. These mutants contained a very harmful characteristic which prevented the normal development and birth of some of their offspring. It affected only some, since it is a recessive character, called *lethal*. All yellow-colored mice carry a similar lethal factor, and many embryos which die *in utero* have been found in such pregnant mice. Because they possess this lethal factor, yellow mice are rare.

The Drosophila workers had been gaining momentum, and before the year ended twenty-five new mutants had been discovered, making a total of forty. In less than three years Morgan's original wild-stock Drosophila had produced more new varieties than science had ever dreamed could actually be so quickly produced in nature. The gates of discovery, it seemed, had been thrown wide open. Mutation must undoubtedly be a factor in the origin of new types. With this wealth of easily controlled and variegated mutants, Morgan made ready to elevate genetics to the rank of an exact mathematical science.

All through these busy days another problem had puzzled him. In the crossing in 1910 of one of his first fly mutants, a white-eyed female with a red-eyed male, Morgan had noticed that in the second generation *not a single white-eyed female* appeared although both white-eyed and red-eyed males were born. The failure of white-eyed female offspring to appear could not be explained, since as a rule male and female progeny are born in almost equal numbers. " Nature is sometimes as oracular as the priestess of Delphi," mused Morgan. In seeking the solution to one problem he had stumbled upon another puzzle. Evidently this character, white eye, was transmitted to only one of the sexes, just as in humans hemophilia is transmitted by the female only. Such characters are said to be sex-linked in the sense that they tend to associate themselves with only one of the two sexes. Other characters, such as rudimentary wing and yellow wing, were also proved by appropriate breeding experiments to be sex-linked.

Morgan noticed another strange phenomenon in connection with these sex-linked characters. If, for example, a white-eyed female also possessed a yellow wing and this fly was crossed with a red-eyed, gray-winged fly, the white-eyed progeny that appeared always had yellow wings and not gray wings. Yet according to Mendel's Law of Independent Assortment of Unit Characters, such characters are inherited as units and separate independently during crossbreeding. It looked here as though certain characters were not only sex-linked but also tended to appear together.

Morgan now offered an ingenious theory for this adherence or linkage of certain characters in crossbreeding experiments. He explained that all of these sex-linked characters were inherited together as a rule because they were carried together as a unit or block in the nucleus of the original cell. This tendency of certain characters to appear together in groups Morgan called *linkage*. Sex linkage was not the only kind of linkage he observed. In 1911 he found that black body and vestigial wing were linked together, but not coupled with any sex-linked characters; that is, they could be transmitted to both male and female, and always together. Black body could also appear with curved wing, balloon wing, or speck wing, but never with a sex-linked character such as yellow wing. The sex-linked group was called Linkage Group No. 1. Another group, called Linkage Group No. 2, contained black body, vestigial wing, and other characters. Two years later it was discovered that pink-eyed flies were never seen with either yellow or vestigial wings, nor ebony-bodied flies with white eyes; while pink-eyed flies having ebony bodies had been bred and found fertile. Ebony body and pink eye seemed to be linked to each other, but not to the other two linkage groups. Hence this was a third Linkage Group.

By the summer of 1914 the many mutant characters that had been discovered and accurately studied for hereditary relations seemed to fall into three distinct groups. There was a large group which were all sex-linked, such as white eye and bifid wing. Another still larger group had numerous characters located on many organs of the body, such as vestigial wing and black body, which were not sex-linked at all, but were all linked to one another. Finally there was another equally large group of bodily characters which were neither sex-linked nor linked with those in the second group, yet were joined to each other. Morgan theorized that since there were three groups of characters, there must be three separate bodies in the germ cell, each responsible for a whole series of characters linked to one another but not linked to other characters found in the other two cell bodies. Morgan thus added another law to those of Mendel, for the corpulent cleric of Brünn never even dreamed of such a linkage phenomenon.

But what evidence had Morgan besides the results of his crossbreeding experiments? He had the testimony of high-powered microscopes. One hundred and fifty years after the discovery of the male germ cell in 1677, it was found to contain an even smaller body called the nucleus. By 1885 the fact that this nucleus of the germ cell was the " vehicle of heredity " had been independently and almost simultaneously announced by at least three eminent biologists. Later the nucleus, too, was found to contain still smaller bodies, which Waldeyer in 1888 named the *chromosomes* because they stained more easily than the rest of the cell. Thus by means of the microscope the hieroglyphics of the germ cell had been gradually deciphered.

It had also been shown that the number of chromosomes in the germ cells of different organisms varied greatly. Morgan, who had spent almost a quarter of a century in the study of the cell, looked carefully into the nucleus of the cells of Drosophila. It was known that it contained four distinct chromosomes, three large ones and one very small one which appeared as a mere dot. Miss Nettie Stevens, a former student of Morgan's at Bryn Mawr, had found them in 1907. The three large chromosomes could account for the three linkage groups of characters. And all the new mutant factors which popped up from time to time in his laboratory fitted into this mystic three. Morgan's theory of linkage seemed established.

But what of that tiny chromosome — the *m* chromosome, as E. B. Wilson, dean of American cell investigators, had called it? It was an enigma until one day in 1914 Hermann Muller, working for his doctorate under Morgan, came across a new fly with a *bent* wing. The usual routine for a new mutant was followed in an attempt to find its linkage group. After an elaborate series of selected breeding experiments, the new character refused to associate itself with any of those in the three demonstrated linkage groups of chromosomes. The obvious conclusion was drawn. It belonged to that small fourth chromosome which all this while had been floating apparently uselessly in the nucleus, waiting for a mutant character with which to be associated. What for a moment appeared as an obstacle to the acceptance of the validity of the linkage theory was converted into additional evidence of its plausibility. From now on it was called the *fourth* and no longer the *m* chromosome.

Once again the laboratory at Columbia was thrilled; the fly hunters redoubled their efforts in the hope of finding new mutants with characters that might be linked to the bent wing of the fourth chromosome. Again Morgan and his squad set their eyes to the eyepieces of their microscopes. Morgan recalled the words of his friend Bateson: " Treasure your exceptions. Keep them always uncovered and in sight." He did. He searched through the thousands of flies until his head ached, looking for other mutants which might strengthen his conclusion. Before long such mutants actually appeared. Miss Hoge was the first (1914) to set her eye upon an *eyeless* fly, and Bridges five years later found a fly with bristles absent from its thorax which he called the *shaven* mutant. This was linked to bent wing as well as to Miss Hoge's eyeless mutant, but not to a single other character from any of the three large chromosome groups. The evidence was most impressive. Even more amazing was the fact that the number of mutants found for each of the four groups was closely proportional to the size of the chromosome. Thus very few mutants were discovered for this dot chromosome, while more than a hundred different characters were found for each of the other three chromosomes.

Not only was Morgan a great master but Fate, too, was kind to him. He was fortunate in having gathered under his wing a

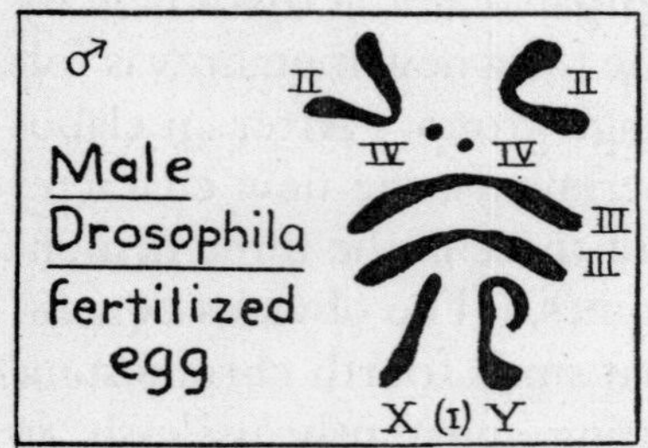

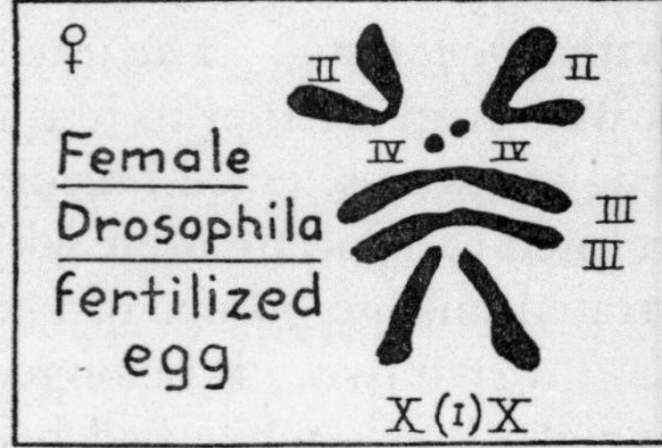

FIG. 2

I, II, III and IV are the four chromosomes representing the four Linkage Groups, as seen under the microscope. Note the X and Y chromosomes of the male egg.

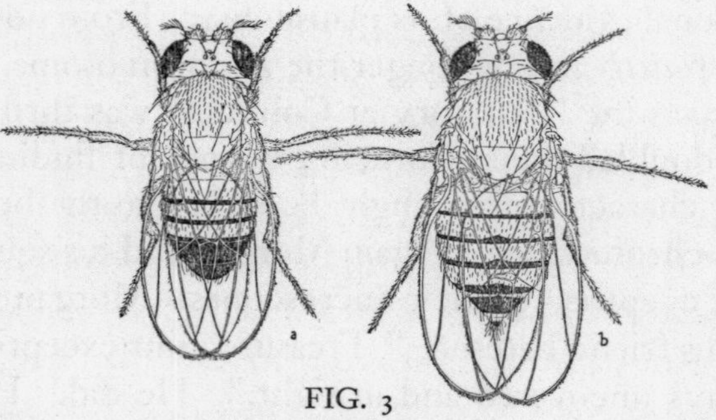

FIG. 3

Male (a) and female (b) vinegar flies (Drosophila melanogaster). Note that the male fruit fly is somewhat smaller than the female. (Courtesy T. H. Morgan)

trio of workers in genetics whose equal it would be difficult to find in any branch of scientific investigation. There were Bridges, Muller, and the brilliant biologist Alfred Henry Sturtevant, who more than once stepped in and helped to cross a treacherous chasm. Sturtevant, brought up on a farm in Alabama, became interested in genetics at a very early age. His father and brother bred race horses, and the boy made a beautiful study of the genealogy of a line of these animals. He showed this *Study of the Pedigrees of Blooded Trotters* to Morgan, who thought so highly of the work that he helped the author, who was still an undergraduate, to publish it. Later Morgan set him to work on a more careful study of sex-linked factors in Drosophila, which in 1912, when Sturtevant was only twenty-one, resulted in his enunciation of a very fruitful theory.

It had been believed by some biologists that each chromosome contained still smaller units, *genes*, each of which represented a particular character. For example, the characters white eye, yellow wing, and rudimentary wing were thought of as existing in the first chromosome. Likewise black body and vestigial wing were believed to be present in the second chromosome. It was not unnatural to look at the chromosome in this way. In fact De Vries and others had this notion, but could find no experimental evidence in support of the idea. The word *gene* was derived from a Greek word meaning race and was equivalent to *gen,* the word which Johannsen had introduced. Johannsen, a Danish physiologist, had come to Columbia University in 1909 to lecture about his now classic work on the inheritance within pure lines of beans, and Morgan then used the word *gene* to represent each unit character or " factor," as the English called it, such as red eye, bent wing, black body, and forked bristles.

The exact position of these genes in the chromosomes was of course not known, but they were believed to be arranged in a straight line in each chromosome thread. Sturtevant now postulated for the first time that the genes, instead of being present in the chromosome in any haphazard positions, were present in a linear arrangement, one gene below another. The idea of a necklace of genetic beads, each in a fixed position and threaded on a transparent ribbon, was more than a colorful picture. It formed the basis of another theory which actually located the relative position of each gene in each chromosome.

This was only the beginning of the " modern fairy tale," as one writer has called the conception of the four groups and their genes. There were more hurdles ahead. Hardly had Morgan jumped one when another and more formidable obstacle appeared. The white-eye factor and the yellow-wing factor, believed to be linked in the sex chromosome, were found to have separated from each other in a very small percentage of cases. For instance, when a red-eyed, gray-winged female was mated with a white-eyed, yellow-winged male, one out of every hundred flies in the second generation had red eyes and yellow wings, or white eyes and gray wings. Obviously something was wrong — something more than linkage must be involved — otherwise there would never be born two new kinds of flies having white eyes with gray wings or red eyes and yellow wings. Perhaps his critics were right, after all, and the theory of linkage was at best only a poor substitute for one of nature's still hidden laws.

Again Morgan went after an explanation for this apparent exception. Once more his search ended at the eyepiece of a microscope focused on the germ cell of the banana or vinegar fly. It had been shown that just before the female egg cell and the male sperm of an organism were ready for fertilization, both of these cells, called the gametes or marrying cells, go through a unique and peculiar process of separation known as a *reduction-division.* Each cell of most organisms contains two full sets of chromosomes. The germ cells of Drosophila, for example, contain eight chromosomes or two full sets of four chromosomes each. Before fertilization the members of each pair of chromosomes in each cell come together, twist around each other and then separate, one member of each pair going to one end of the cell, the other member to the other end. After the process is complete there are two rows of four chromosomes facing each other. Soon after, this cell divides into two cells, each of which, still unfertilized, contains four chromosomes. This is the reduction-division process. Without this reduction-division the number of chromosomes would multiply *ad infinitum* when the egg and sperm unite. (The eight chromosomes of the egg would be added to the eight chromosomes of the sperm to make a new cell of sixteen chromosomes, etc., etc.) When a mature sperm now burrows its head into a mature ovum, leaving its tail outside, the nuclei of the sperm and ovum fuse, and once more the fertilized egg contains eight or two sets of four chromosomes, one set from the father and one set from the mother. The new organism therefore begins life with a set of characters from each parent.

Preceding this reduction-division process, strange things might happen, for, as we know, the two sets of chromosomes of the immature egg and sperm lie side by side twisting around each other just before fertilization. Morgan believed that during this twisting process they might be so intertwined that on separating part of one chromosome would separate with part of the other member of the set, resulting in a new chromosome made up of sections of both. Janssen, a Catholic priest of Lou-

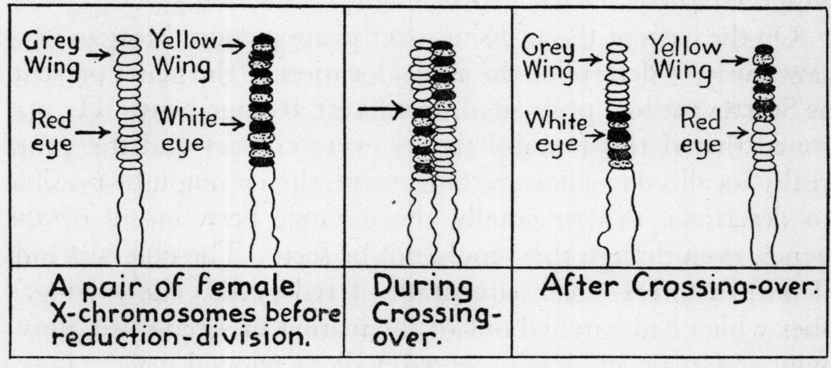

FIG. 4

vain, without knowing anything about linkage had vaguely hinted at this before. This " chromosomal embrace " was responsible for new combinations of characters and, according to Morgan, for the break in the usual linkage groups, since sometimes the two members of the same (homologous) chromosomes, although usually similar in almost all respects, might differ in a few. It explained the one and one-half per cent of flies with yellow wings and red eyes or red eyes and yellow wings as due to an interchange or *crossing-over* between the two original sex or X-chromosomes of the female, as shown in the above diagram.

Actual photographic evidence from microscopical investigations has since confirmed this amazing process of crossing-over, and the quantitative data from breeding experiments makes it extremely unlikely that Morgan's explanation of the exceptions noted is incorrect. (In 1906 Bateson and his pupil Punnett had accidentally come across this phenomenon among the flowers of the sweet pea, and had attempted to explain this as the result of certain unexplained " repulsions.")

No case of human linkage is definitely known. If it were really true, as some wrongly believe, that blond hair and blue eyes are linked in the chromosomes of man, then crossing-over could be offered as an explanation for the fair-haired boy with brown eyes. And H. H. Newman has remarked that if red hair and a certain well known disposition were linked, as is popularly supposed, then " crossing-over might be a saving grace."

On the basis of this crossing-over phenomenon, Morgan now saw a way to determine the actual location of the genes present, as Sturtevant had postulated, in a linear arrangement. He reasoned that if this fanciful theory were correct and the genes really localized in a linear arrangement, then it might be possible to determine experimentally the distance between all of the genes, even though they could not be seen. The clue was hidden in that very small percentage of red-eyed, yellow-winged flies which had hatched out of the mating of a red-eyed, gray-winged female and a white-eyed, yellow-winged male. These apparent exceptions had been explained by the crossing-over phenomenon which took place while homologous chromosomes were twisting around each other prior to a final separation. Where would the breaks in the chromosomal thread be more apt to occur? Morgan asked himself. Obviously the distance between genes would determine the frequency of their separation during crossing-over phenomena. " During crossing over," he said, " it is those genes that are farthest apart that become separated more freely, since there is between them a longer distance in any part of which the chromosome may break." Hence if certain factors rarely become separated by crossing-over, then these genes must be very close together, while on the other hand if certain other factors are easily separated during crossing-over, then they must be far apart in the chromosome.

No time was wasted in following up this idea. Sturtevant reduced the number of cross-overs to percentages and thus laid the basis for an orderly comparison of the gene distances. Gradually everybody in the laboratory joined in the adventure of mapping the unexplored lands of the chromosomes of Drosophila. There began one of the most exacting and amazing pieces of research in the history of biology. Tens of thousands of elaborate and carefully controlled cross-over experiments, involving millions of flies and scores of different mutants of the fruit fly, had to be skillfully executed, and the numerical results tabulated and analyzed. Numerous obstacles had to be overcome. In the cold nights of winter many of the fly cultures failed to start on time. To prevent this delay, Bridges built special incubators for these tiny insects which were to bring man closer to solving the riddle of inheritance. Never was such a huge colony of insects so zealously guarded. Thousands of glass containers had to be used, and so their size and shape were standardized. Before long every other detail in this colossal task of creating a fly map was cunningly worked out, and the architecture of the chromosome began to emerge.

When the first numerical results came in, Morgan began to apply his theory. Crossing-over, he reasoned, between yellow wing and white eye occurs in 1.5% of cases, and we find 5.4% of crossing-over between bifid wing and white eye. This would indicate that the gene of bifid wing is farther away from the gene of white eye than is yellow wing. Now if bifid wing is on the opposite side of white eye in relation to yellow wing, then it would be expected to give with yellow wing a crossing-over value of 6.9%. If, on the other hand, bifid wing is on the same side as yellow wing it should give a crossing-over value of 3.9% with yellow wing, as shown in Fig. 5. The number 6.9 was the one actually determined, so Morgan placed bifid wing below white in the chromosome map — a map which had to be magnified forty thousand times to make it fairly visible. By similar experiments and reasoning the location of scores of other unit characters or genes were located on the chromosome map.

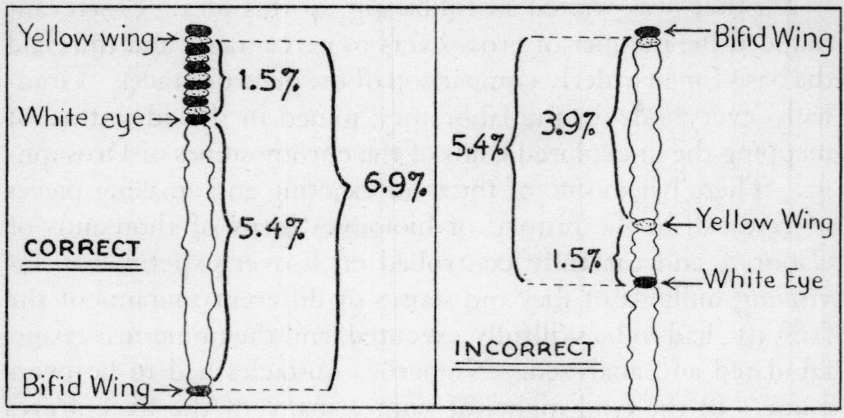

FIG. 5

This gene map of Drosophila, shown on the next page, may be likened in importance to the Table of Atomic Numbers of the chemical elements. " It is doubtful, if in any book there may be found four straight lines that mean so much." The map and its spacings had to be repeatedly corrected. The appearance of new mutants, the data from fresh crossing-over experiments, the discovery of temporarily unexplained and seemingly anomalous results all demanded frequent revamping of these chromosome blueprints. The inevitable changes evoked fierce criticism, and added fuel to the fire of those who would destroy this monstrous theory of heredity. Morgan was never seriously perturbed by this opposition; he never lost faith in the plausibility of the theory of the gene. Now and then, when the doubters shouted too loudly, he spoke out to defend the tireless work of his school. " It has been said," he reminded them, " that the changes made from time to time in the genetic map of the Drosophila chromosomes discredit the method by which the localization is determined. It might as well be said that the method by which the atomic weights in chemistry were gradually improved discredited the procedure of the chemist."

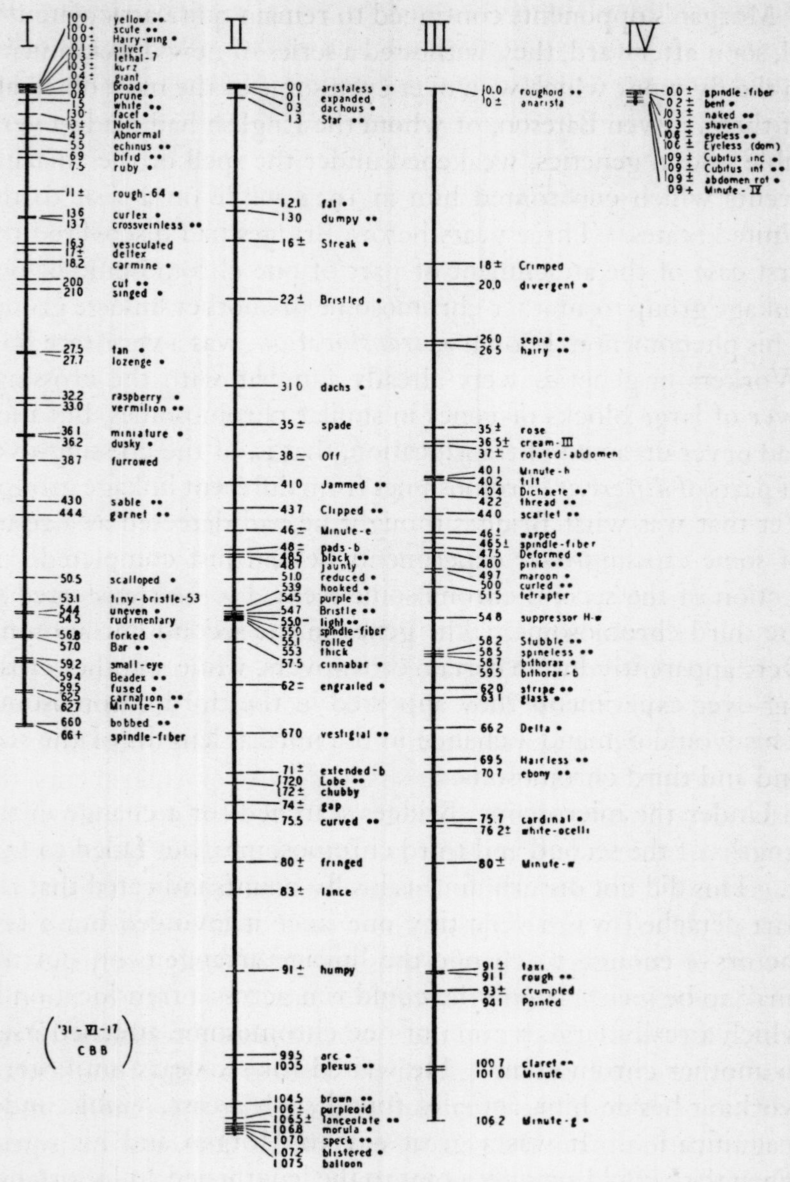

FIG. 6

Chromosome map or chart of the location (loci) of the genes of the four chromosomes of Drosophila. (After Bridges)

Morgan's opponents continued to remain quite articulate until, soon afterward, they witnessed a series of new developments in the fly work which won over even some of the most obstinate of them. Even Bateson, of whom the English had made a veritable god in genetics, weakened under the spell of the amazing events which confronted him in 1922 while on a visit to the United States. Three years before Bridges had discovered the first case of the attachment of part of one chromosome of one linkage group to another chromosome of another linkage group. This phenomenon, known as *translocation,* was a very rare one. Workers in genetics were already familiar with the crossing-over of large blocks of genes in similar chromosomes, but they had never dreamed of translocation, that is, of the crossing-over of parts of *different* chromosomes from different linkage groups. Yet that was what Bridges thought he had detected as a result of some crossing-over experiments he had just completed. A section of the second chromosome seemed to be transferred to the third chromosome. The genes in the second chromosome were apparently lost in certain cross-overs, while in other crossing-over experiments they appeared in the third chromosome. This would demand a change in the normal lengths of the second and third chromosomes.

Under the microscope, Bridges searched for a change in the lengths of the second and third chromosomes, but failed to find it. This did not disturb him, as his fly counts indicated that the part detached was a very tiny one since it involved but a few factors — enough to change the linkage arrangement, but too small to be seen. If only he could run across a translocation in which a really large section of one chromosome attached itself to another chromosome! He waited for six years until Stern, working beside him, actually found such a case, visible under magnification. It was a great day to Morgan and his squad, when they could actually point to the lengthened and shortened chromosomes predicted by the figures of their genetic experiments. The phenomenon had occurred spontaneously, and there was no doubt about the evidence.

Equally startling proof had in the meantime come from another direction. In May, 1922, appeared a paper from Morgan's laboratory which was to add further luster to its name. It was written by Lillian V. Morgan, whom the scientist had married

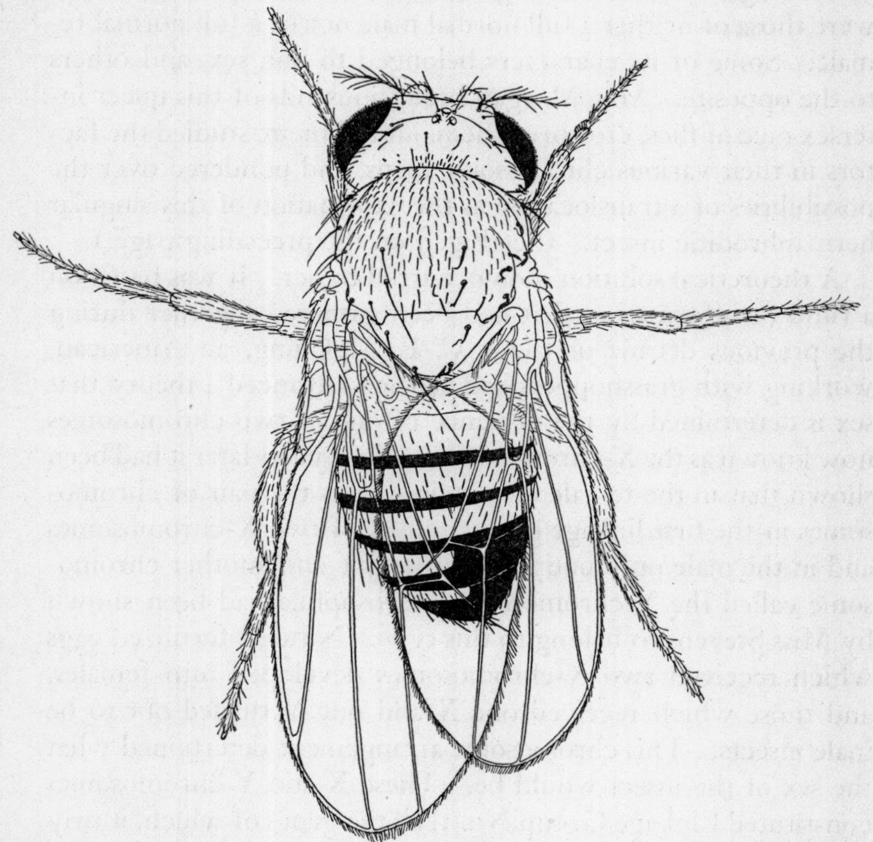

FIG. 7. A GYNANDROMORPH (HERMAPHRODITE) OF DROSOPHILA
The right side shows the organs of a male throughout except for its genitalia which are female. (Courtesy T. H. Morgan)

eighteen years before while she was his student at Bryn Mawr. Mrs. Morgan had left the laboratory to raise a son and three daughters. Thirteen years later, when the discoveries from her husband's laboratory began to crowd one another with overwhelming rapidity, she came back to assist the small band wrestling with Drosophila. Working independently Mrs. Morgan had discovered a female fly with male characters. That mosaic fly was baffling. On one side of the body there was a complete reversal of certain recessive sex-linked characters. Its head, thorax, legs, color, eyes, wings, balancers, and shape of abdomen were those of neither a full normal male nor of a full normal female. Some of its characters belonged to one sex, and others to the opposite. Mrs. Morgan bred thousands of this queer intersex race of flies, crossbred them, inbred them, studied the factors in their various chromosome maps, and pondered over the possibilities of a translocation as the explanation of this singular hermaphroditic insect. (See Fig. 7 on the preceding page.)

A theoretical solution soon occurred to her. It was based on a fund of information that had been gathered together during the previous decade or two. C. E. McClung, an American, working with grasshoppers had in 1901 advanced a theory that sex is determined by the presence of one or two chromosomes now known as the X-chromosomes. Four years later it had been shown that in the female of certain insects the pair of chromosomes in the first linkage group consist of two X-chromosomes and in the male only one X-chromosome and another chromosome called the Y-chromosome. Drosophila had been shown by Miss Stevens to belong to this type. Now all fertilized eggs which received two X-chromosomes developed into females, and those which received one X and one Y turned out to be male insects. This chromosome arrangement determined what the sex of the insect would be. These X and Y chromosomes constituted Linkage Group No. 1, all the genes of which, it may be recalled, are inherited usually as a whole.

With this knowledge of the X-Y mechanism of sex determination, Morgan had been enabled to trace those characters which were sex-linked. The crucial discovery of a difference in the pairs of sex chromosomes carried by the male and female made it a fairly simple matter to explain also such sex-linked characters in man as color blindness, night blindness, and hemophilia. This last abnormality is characterized by the failure of blood to clot, so that even a slight cut often results in death due to excessive bleeding. Hemophilia was studied in such famous bleeders as the Czarevitch Alexis of Russia and the Prince of the Asturias, son of the former Spanish king. "Bleeders" are almost always males. The mother carries hemophilia, which she transmits to her son. A male child gets his single X-chromosome exclusively from his mother, and the X-chromosome of the son

FIG. 8

Illustration to show the genetic explanation of the transmission of hemophilia. (**X′** represents the chromosome carrying hemophilia.)

goes only to his daughters. Since this process is continued from generation to generation, therefore if a bleeder male marries a normal female, a carrier female results, and from the union of a normal male with a carrier female, a bleeder male is born.

Mrs. Morgan reasoned that the two X-chromosomes of the female fly might pass together into one ovum if accidentally united at their tips by failure of the two halves to separate at reduction-division. This would produce a fertilized egg containing the sex chromosomes of both male and female. If this were actually what had occurred, the microscope should show the evidence. Carefully she sectioned a selected female egg, and actually found the two chromosomes joined like a V end to end. The cytological picture fitted beautifully with her genetic deductions. The male-female fly possessed the sex chromosomes of both male and female, hence the characteristics of both sexes. This brilliant piece of work was not Mrs. Morgan's last, for to this day she continues to contribute valuable discoveries in this field.

Other chromosomal abnormalities were revealed. For example, a broken fragment of one chromosome was found attached to two normal chromosomes of the same linkage group (*duplication*), causing this individual to carry certain genes in triplicate. Such an oddity, unless the extra piece was extremely small, brought death to the fly. Bridges also deduced from genetic results that certain sections of some chromosomes disappeared altogether, lost in the chromosome shuffle. He showed that when this *deficiency* was considerable, it, too, proved fatal to the insect. Mrs. Morgan, in 1925, was the first to find cellular evidence for this phenomenon — she actually saw a sex chromosome with a large part missing. Then from breeding experiments she furnished sufficient data to account for this abnormally small chromosome.

The new testimony was overwhelmingly in favor of the gene theory. Until then Bateson had looked askance at the Drosophila work, which he considered interesting, to be sure, but "pernicious" because it went beyond the evidence. When in 1922 he visited Morgan and under his beetling gray eyebrows watched the Drosophila workshop in full swing, the cellular data they showed him worked wonders. However uncongenial the evidence was to his trend of thought, he had to admit the fruit fly was unbiased. Overcome with excitement, he wrote back to his wife in England: "I can see no escape from capitulation on the main point. The chromosomes must be in some way connected with our transferable characters." And he added, "We must try to get a cytologist for our work." Until then his genetic conclusions had been drawn wholly from statistical data. He had not made use of the evidence of cytology; that is, the microscopic investigation of the cell.

Bateson's published conversion made a tremendous stir all over the world. "We have turned," he admitted, "still another bend in the track and behind the egg and sperm cells we see the chromosomes. For the doubts — which I trust may be pardoned in one who has never seen the marvels of cytology — cannot, as regards the main thesis of the Drosophila workers, be any longer maintained. The arguments of Morgan and his colleagues, and especially the demonstration of Bridges, must allay all skepticism as to the direct association of particular chromosomes with particular features of the mature germ cell." The response was instant. From all over Europe came requests for cultures of Drosophila mutants. England and Japan soon had Drosophila workers, young geneticists from Germany came to study with the fly squad in New York, then returned home to carry on the work. Norway, Sweden, Portugal, China, Hungary and France became interested in the genetics of the fruit fly. Russia received ample fly supplies, kept in constant touch with the American school, and her Drosophila workers rapidly increased in numbers. By 1935 the Soviet Republic ranked second in the number of researchers busy with Drosophila. The United States led with 45%, Russia followed closely with 37% and Germany, although third, accounted for only 7% of the total number of research men engaged in the problems connected with the hereditary makeup of the famous fly. Russia has sent us some of its most brilliant workers, including Theoditius Dobzhansky of the University of Leningrad.

The Drosophila work was not the only convincing evidence that made Morgan's theory the outstanding biological principle since Darwin's contribution. About the time the first Drosophila flies were being bred at Columbia University, R. A. Emerson, son of a long line of farmers including the Adams family, was teaching horticulture at the University of Nebraska. He had spent some time on the genetics of beans, which he had found extremely difficult to unravel. In an effort to supply his students with an organism from which they could more easily learn the laws of Mendel, he turned to corn. He crossed white rice pop corn with sweet corn, and distributed a bushel of the interpollinated grain to his classes to check the Mendelian ratios. When the laboratory results came in, he was surprised to find that the expected three-to-one ratio did not materialize. He wanted to know the reason for this. He soon found the answer but from that day to the present he never left the field of corn genetics.

In 1914 he had discovered the first mutant in corn, *blotched leaf*. Then he came to Cornell, where he developed a group of workers in genetics now spread over the country, and initiated a remarkable organization for co-operative work. Once a year he and his pupils meet at Cornell, the clearing house of corn genetics in America, to exchange notes and unpublished data. The voluminous work of linkage, cross-over, and chromosome mapping is discussed, and the mass of problems which would overwhelm any single worker is parceled out for research.

The corn work, starting independently of Morgan's, took fresh impetus from the publication of the first important Drosophila papers. Emerson and his fledglings watched the Morgan group for leads and tagged along, feeling that the complete genetic architecture of their botanical Drosophila might prove a weighty ally. They had to tag along for various reasons, not the least the fact that the fruit fly would produce thirty generations before the corn plant completed one. But they had one great advantage over the fly workers. The chromosomes in corn cells are more easily studied under the microscope, and this cytological simplicity made their mapping less difficult. Corn (*zea mays*) has ten chromosome pairs, which are all shaped differently.

Certain markers present on some of the chromosomes, such as a knob, a constriction, a nonstainable area, a satellite, and a spindle fiber attachment, have helped in the mapping of the genes. Most of this delicate cyto-genetic work has been done by Miss Barbara McClintock, one of the most skilful and persevering of the young genetic workers in America. Already more than two

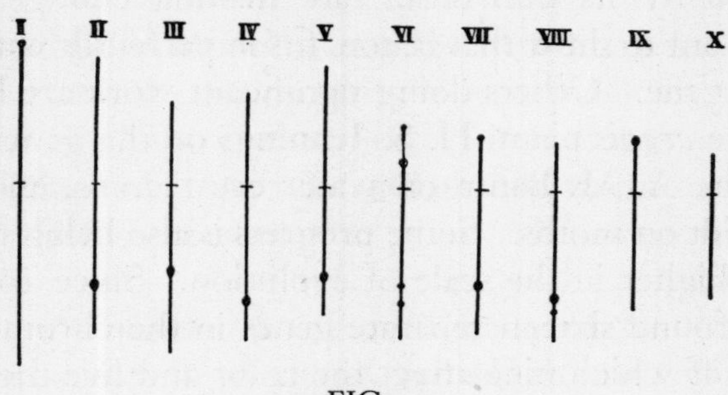

FIG. 9
The ten chromosomes of corn (*zea mays*).
(Courtesy R. A. Emerson)

hundred mutants have been reported. More than a hundred genes influencing color, leaves, anthers, pollen sterility, disease resistance, carbohydrate metabolism, plumule, silks, number of kernel rows, root development, and sex abnormalities have proved the existence of ten and only ten linkage groups. This *zea mays* chart well merits a place beside the genetic map of Drosophila.

The inheritance of several different organisms is engaging other workers. For example, the jimson weed, a species of plant from which the drug belladonna is obtained, has been the subject of interesting investigations, especially by Blakeslee at the Cold Spring Harbor Station for Experimental Evolution of the Carnegie Institution of Washington. *Polyploidy*, or the increase in the normal number of chromosomes of an organism, is particularly observable in the jimson weed. Tetrapoids, for example, contain double the number of chromosomes of the fertilized egg, due, it is believed, to the failure of the cell to divide when the chromosomes divide. The offspring of such a cell continue to have this double number of chromosomes, offering for study many interesting and complex problems of heredity.

The evening primrose made famous by the pioneer observations of De Vries still presents baffling abnormalities of inheritance. A few geneticists, including George H. Shull at Princeton, and Ralph E. Cleland, who have stubbornly refused to be discouraged by its difficulties, are making enough headway with this plant to show that it, too, fits in perfectly with the theory of the gene. Others doing significant work are E. B. Babcock on the *crepis* plant, H. S. Jennings on the genetics of the paramecium, A. M. Banta on water crustaceans, and Richard Goldschmidt on moths. Some progress is also being made with organisms higher in the scale of evolution. Since 1911 W. E. Castle has found sixteen separate genes in the chromosomes of the rabbit, of which nine affect the color and five the structure of its coat. Their actual location in any particular chromosome is still unknown. Sewell Wright has worked with the twenty-one pairs of chromosomes of the guinea pig. In this famous experimental animal black coat, dark eyes, and short hair have been shown to be dominant over white coat, pink eyes, and long hair. Oscar Riddle is using pigeons, Charles R. Stockard has chosen the dog, others are handling the mouse, the rat, and the cat, while C. B. Davenport is studying the genetics of man. Horse genetics, which had already demonstrated that bay color is dominant over black, is being extensively studied on the Kellogg Farm of the University of California. This institution has recently received an endowment of $600,000 for a forty-year program of research on the horse.

The study of the genetics of man offers the most complicated picture and at the same time the most alluring hopes. We are a relatively long-lived species, our cells have forty-eight chromosomes, and aside from the field of fiction and dubious speculation, very little has been accomplished in positive human genetics, largely due to the tremendous difficulty of converting *homo sapiens* into a laboratory guinea pig or Drosophila melanogaster. In no other field of science has so much rubbish been published about the potentialities of eugenics. At best, it is still a pseudo-science, and its most optimistic champions might justly be classified with the phrenologists and astrologers of bygone ages.

The tantalizing possibilities of creative and controlled evolution were dramatically brought before the world in 1926 by the startling announcement made by one of the early workers in Morgan's laboratory to a distinguished audience at the Sixth

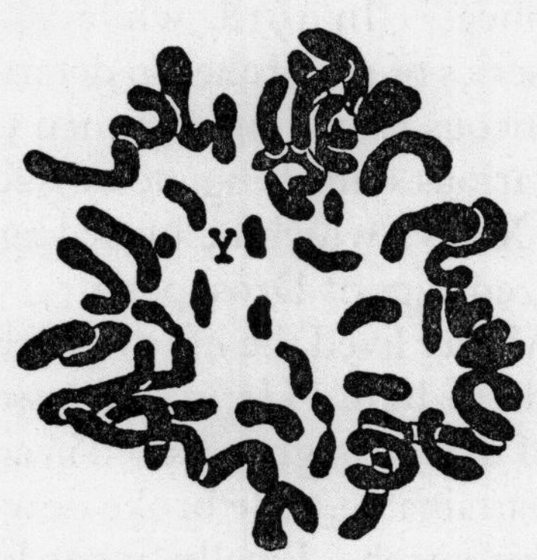

FIG. 10. THE CHROMOSOMES OF MAN

The X-chromosome may be distinguished at the upper left-hand corner of the letter "Y" which has been inserted. The Y-chromosome is the small round body to the left and just below the X-chromosome. The cell of a woman would have a second X-chromosome instead of the Y-chromosome. (After T. S. Painter)

International Congress of Genetics in Berlin. Again the fruit fly was the experimental organism used. Hermann Joseph Muller reported the results of several years of experimentation with the germ plasm of Drosophila. Muller had been interested in genetics ever since he was a small boy. His father took him when he was seven to the American Museum of Natural History in New York. Here he saw a display of the evolution of the modern horse which haunted him from that day on. His father had explained how the four-toed *Eohippus borealis*, the dawn horse which had lived in the Bad Lands of Wyoming forty-five million years ago, had gradually evolved into a three-toed *Mesohippus*, then to a two-toed *Merychippus*, later to the small clumsy one-toed *Pliohippus* — ancestor of the modern horse.

Perhaps, thought Muller, a knowledge of the mechanism of inheritance would enable mankind to cut down this tremendous time scale needed for evolution. "It was basically," he said recently, "because of my belief in the future artificially controlled biological evolution of the human species that I started studying genetics by myself in the summer of 1908. This possible eventual application has been the mainspring of my interest in genetics ever since." In 1918, while at the University of Texas, he began a series of researches to determine first, the normal rate of spontaneous mutation, and then the speed of mutation induced by various outside agencies, such as heat and the newly introduced X-rays which he hurled against the chromosomes of the fertilized eggs of Drosophila.

For eight years Muller lived the life of a recluse. Hours, days, seasons, meant little to him. He was obsessed by an idea and sustained by a belief that he might succeed in achieving what was then considered unattainable. He broke down from overwork, but later renewed his search. Finally, when he had checked the mass of data he had collected and was sure of his results, he made his epochal announcement. He had jolted the genes in the chromosomes of Drosophila, had broken them apart and rearranged them, he had increased the mutation rate one hundred and fifty times; he had artificially speeded up the evolutionary process. He had actually transmuted species and created new ones! He had accomplished this by exposing flies to the action of ordinary X-rays. The X-rays had a strange effect on the germ plasm of Drosophila. Muller had, with the aid of this radiation from an X-ray tube, stolen into that holy of holies, the germ plasm, and tampered with it. Controlled mutation was a fact! We were no longer at the mercy of the slowness of nature. Some maintained that a critical period in human history had arrived. Man could here and now take a hand in creative evolution by creating new species of living organisms and replacing natural selection by human selection.

Muller had placed his finger on the spring controlling inheritance; overnight, at the age of thirty-six, he became world famous. Hearing of this monumental achievement, Morgan was proud of this man Muller who had cut his scientific eye teeth under him at Columbia in 1911. At about the same time L. J. Stadler of the University of Missouri published a paper on the speeding up of mutation in the barley plant, while T. H. Goodspeed of the University of California had done the same with the tobacco plant. They had both been beaten by a few weeks in the announcement of results which though similar were by no means as clear-cut or significant, for Muller had used large numbers and accurate controls. But that is one of the gambles in the adventure of scientific research, one of the disappointments of success in the laboratory.

Others set their feet on the path Muller had opened. It led to a virgin field of great wealth and promise. The male Drosophila, the virgin and the pregnant female, and the fertilized egg were all forced to undergo this new ray treatment. Drosophila was subjected to other cunning devices and techniques. Ultraviolet light, rapid sound waves, radio-activity, high temperatures, drying, ageing, rapid whirling of germ cells, and other methods were used to produce translocations, deletions, and new mutants in all sorts of organisms. One Russian investigator X-rayed the germ cells of Drosophila and produced mutations in the first generation. Then he bombarded the offspring with these radiations and reversed the changes, causing the third generation of flies to become normal again, thus indicating that perhaps mutations were reversible. An American research worker experimented with X-rays to produce new species of jimson weed. This plant mutated into a form which yielded a higher percentage of belladonna. The General Electric Company used X-rays on seeds and produced flowering of grapefruit in six weeks, whereas the normal period of the flowering of this tree is about six years. They also succeeded in changing the color of the sorghum plant, and in altering the sex ratio in the hemp plant.

Others subjected the tips of tomato plants to radium and X-ray bombardment, and obtained a new tomato which refused to crossbreed with the ordinary variety. In Moscow, genetic workers exposed seeds in closed bottles for twenty days to a temperature of 131° F., and found new mutants with chromosomes which were badly damaged. These may be but the beginning of similar accomplishments in higher organisms. It is, however, risky to forecast the future of this line of attack, for scientific advance in this field is unpredictable.

As we survey the quarter of a century which has elapsed since that lucky moment in 1909 when Morgan turned to the problem of inheritance, we find the new genetics applied in many branches of scientific advance. In laboratories spread over the civilized world, geneticists have proclaimed the truth of the theory of the gene. The gene is a definite, conclusively proven entity whose existence is as accurately established as that of the atom, the electron, and the virus units of medicine, which " although unseen are nevertheless by no means unreal." They are no longer to be ranked with the theoretical " gemmules " of Darwin, the " plastidules " of Haeckel, the " micellae " of Nägeli or the " pangenes " of De Vries. These were the names for the hypothetical forerunners of the experimentally proved genes. The genes are submicroscopic bodies, perhaps of the nature of a very complex organic molecule of protein composition, each gene being chemically different from every other. These genes are the beads strung by nature on the nebulous threads of the chromosomes, which seal the fate of all life, including that of mankind. If the Fates are spinning our destinies, it is gene-filled chromosomes that they spin.

Morgan, in moments of relaxation when the buzz of Drosophila has set his mind to pondering ultimate sizes and shapes of the genes, has tried to picture them. He sees a definite structural unit with perhaps slight differences of form and about the size of a large protein molecule. The fourth chromosome of Drosophila contains about 35 genes and is about 7 μ in length (1 μ = 1. micron = .001 mm.). Some idea of the actual size of a gene may be obtained by imagining a hen's egg raised to the size of the earth, and a gene increased in volume on the same scale. The individual gene would then, says J. B. S. Haldane, the eminent geneticist of Cambridge, be large enough to place on a table, while the electron would just be visible to the naked eye. The gene seems to act like an organic compound in resisting change, responding to radiation and other physical and chemical changes. It does not easily decompose, but when it does it breaks suddenly. Genes are not contaminated by their closeness to other genes. Each gene is a definite substance, so that, in general, if it is changed or displaced, a definite character of the individual undergoes a simultaneous change. But we must not forget Morgan's warning: " The idea that for each character there is a specific gene was never a cardinal doctrine of genetics. *That each character is the product of all the genes is more nearly correct.*" For example, at least fifty genes work together to produce the red color of Drosophila eyes. The presence of one particular gene will not result in red eye unless forty-nine other genes are present. Hundreds are needed to produce a normal straight wing. Just how these genes work together is not as yet understood.

The genes have thus far never actually been seen. Many have worked for years to produce ocular proof of the existence of these genes. Among these men was John Belling, a former science teacher in England and later cytologist for the Carnegie Institution, who spent twenty years improving the microscope and developing new staining and fixing methods in the attempt to get clear photographs of the genes in the chromosome. Failing with Drosophila, this pale, bent, eccentric genius turned to the twenty-four-chromosomed tiger lily of California. He cut open its anthers, pressed the mother cells of the pollen on a clean slide, quickly fixed the smear in chrom-acetic formalin mordanted in iron alum, and after twenty-four hours stained the cell for three hours in brazilin color. Then he took photographs under a high-powered microscope. Belling, who died only recently, thought he saw individual dots in each chromosome, and counted 2200 of these " genes " in one of the chromosomes of the lily. When Belling was told that his photographs had not convinced the critical Morgan, his only comment was, " It takes five years for a great scientist to believe."

The structural details of the chromosome were still pretty much a matter of conjecture until the publication of a paper on December 22, 1933, on *A New Method for the Study of Chromosome Rearrangements and the Plotting of Chromosome Maps.* It appeared in *Science* and described the work of Theophilus S. Painter of the University of Texas. It was a brilliant piece of research which Morgan regards as one of the classics of genetics. For the first time, undeniable evidence was furnished of a definite chromosomal structure which made the Drosophila map a stereometric reality. (See Fig. 11 on the next page.)

Until now practically all of the work on Drosophila had been done with the chromosomes of the egg cells. For some time, however, it had been known that the chromosomes of the salivary gland cells of the mature Drosophila larvae were about seventy times larger than the chromosomes of the egg cells of this insect. Painter worked out a technique for bringing out some of the details of their structure by staining them with an aceto-carmine dye. As a result of this treatment he succeeded in identifying about a thousand bands or rings on these giant chromosomes. As soon as Painter had opened the pages of this new and extremely exciting chapter, Bridges joined the investigation for further refinement of technique and fuller and more salient details. He stretched the chromosomes of the salivary gland cells of Drosophila until they were more than 150 times longer than those of the egg cells. Under the outside wrappings of the chromosomes he made out almost three times as many segments as Painter had photographed: 537 bands in the X-chromosome, 1032 in the second, 1047 in the third and 34 in the fourth chromosome. He was also able to make out greater detail in these banded affairs. He considers the bands as representing the edges of solid discs that run clear through the chromosomes, the spaces between the discs representing the homes of the individual genes. The old idea of beads on a string has been replaced by the conception of sixteen slender strands twisted to form a cable.

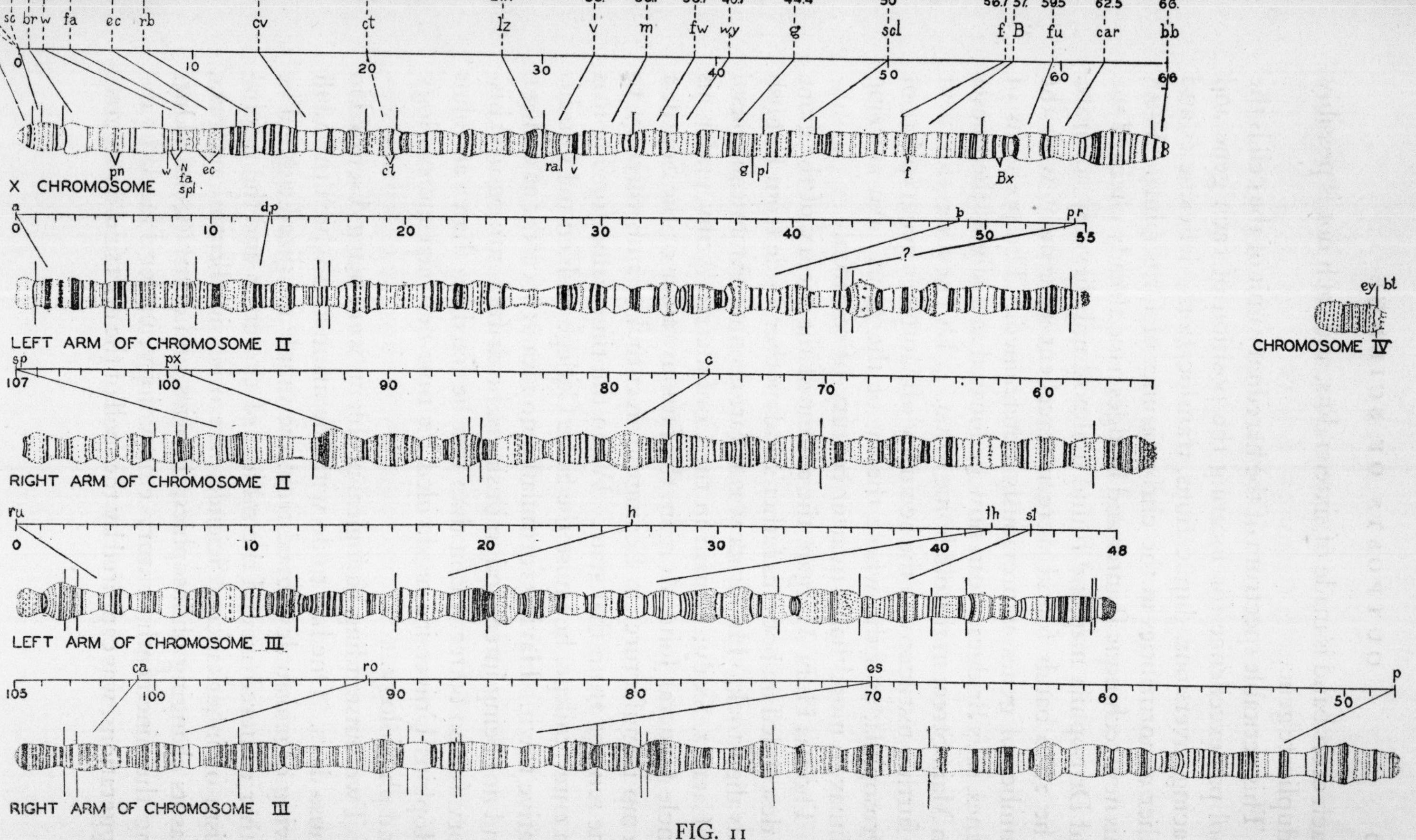

FIG. 11

This drawing made by T. S. Painter in December, 1934 shows the typical accordion-like structure of the four chromosomes of Drosophila melanogaster and indicates the positions of all the gene loci then known. Note the relatively small Chromosome IV with its relatively small number of genes. This fourth chromosome from the *germ cell* of Drosophila would appear as a dot on the same scale. This reference map was made from the salivary chromosomes. Bridges has pointed out certain landmarks in these maps such as the *turnip*, the *Chinese lantern*, and the *ballet skirt* which are used to locate the positions of certain genes. (From the *Journal of Heredity*)

Each cross band is made of sixteen dots, and each dot is possibly a duplicate gene.

This veritable spectrum of the hereditary unit of the cell is the tool par excellence for locating the position of each gene and tracing inversions, duplications, translocations, deficiencies and other abnormalities in the chromosomes of Drosophila. With this new technique Painter and Bridges have already checked the old Drosophila map and found it almost unbelievably accurate. The 2650 bands found were in excellent agreement with the number of genes as previously determined. The positions of genes, says Bridges, " can now be located as easily as the houses on Main Street in the old home town." This new development is further testimony to the accuracy of Morgan's geographers of Drosophila, and the whole theory of the gene. An amazing climax to more than a quarter century of research!

Thomas Hunt Morgan, the author of the theory of the gene, is descended on both his father's and mother's side from English Cavalier stock. His father was at various times American consul at Catania, Sicily; captain in the Confederate Army under his uncle General John Morgan, the famous raider of the South; a hemp manufacturer in Lexington, Kentucky; and secretary to the senator from that state. When the time came for Thomas to enter college, he chose the State College of Kentucky in his native town. Having formulated no idea of a career at college, and not being interested in business, he drifted into natural history for no better reason than that he liked it. Later at Johns Hopkins University he divided his time between morphology and physiology.

Two outstanding biological problems were being discussed in those days. One had to do with the manner in which the adult living organism developed from the simple fertilized egg. The other centered around the subject of evolution and the mechanism of inheritance. Science, like other intellectual pursuits, has its changing philosophies, theories, and even vogues. During the nineteenth century embryology, under Haeckel's exaggerations, was captured by the spell of the doctrine " ontogeny repeats phylogeny"; that is, the life history of the development of an individual repeats the race history of the species. The numerous studies of the forms of the developing embryos of different species seemed to point to the truth of this hypothesis, for the developing embryo of a pig, for example, seemed to pass through various stages indicating features of lower organisms such as reptiles and fishes.

Morgan was brought up on this nineteenth-century point of view and at the beginning he, too, was completely absorbed in this study. But this idea, although in general true, was very narrowing. The student became interested in descriptive biology rather than in the explanation of the mechanism of the development of organisms. This conception, too, often lost itself in a maze of philosophical implications. Morgan began to feel that experimental embryology in the light of this doctrine was running after false gods and was leading to metaphysical subtleties. He was no mystic and the flavored food of the ontogenists was no sustenance to him.

At this time a school of biologists known as the *vitalists* was teaching that any attempt to explain or understand the mechanism of development from purely scientific laws would prove sterile, for, they maintained, such life processes were under the control of creative forces outside the knowledge of science. When, however, there arose a school which looked for a strictly chemico-physical explanation of the development of the embryo, the bent of Morgan's mind took kindly to the new "developmental mechanics." An experiment of the anatomist Wilhelm Roux had impressed him deeply. Roux had succeeded in killing one of the first two cells of the developing egg of a frog, and had shown how instead of dying, this half embryo had actually developed into part of a frog. Man had actually changed the predestined course of the development of an egg not only by physical but by chemical changes as well. Jacques Loeb, Morgan's one-time colleague at Bryn Mawr, also startled the scientific world with the first complete demonstration of the artificial fertilization (parthenogenesis) of the eggs of a sea urchin by chemical and other mechanical agents. He and other members of the school of *mechanists* pointed to all sorts of alluring possibilities of changing the course of life. The older school of *vitalists* fought back. The classic struggle was renewed with greater vigor. Physico-chemical changes, the vitalists insisted, could not explain altogether the marvelous development of the fertilized egg to the fully adult organism. The vitalists accepted the physical and chemical changes which took place, for example, when the sperm entered the ovum during fertilization. They insisted, however, that behind and beyond these relatively inconsequential changes were forces that guided the process and brought it to a successful and purposeful completion. The mechanists, on the other hand, believed that every phenomenon of nature was the result of physical and chemical changes completely divorced from any mystic or vitalistic force which controlled it. They were ready to believe that eventually perhaps every one of the complex biological phenomena would be duplicated by scientists in the laboratory.

In 1895, five years after receiving his doctor's degree for a piece of research on the embryology and phylogeny of " sea spiders," Morgan went first to Germany and then to the famous zoological station at Naples, where in a room next to his own worked Hans Driesch. The long battle between the mechanists and the vitalists was still waging. The shouts of the mechanists, certain that all of life could be explained by the ordinary laws of physics and chemistry, were becoming louder. The vitalists held their ground against the new phalanx of younger zoologists. Hans Driesch the philosopher joined the vitalists. " One day entelechy (an agent which according to the vitalists directs and regulates all life to a purposive end) appeared to him as a dream. From that time he believed, very soon he ceased to work." Morgan, however, fought for neither side. Vitalism, and the terms invoked by it such as entelechy, *élan vital*, holism were but words to him, for just as he insisted more than once that *ex cathedra* statements are not arguments, so also did he believe that any appeal to mysticism is outside of science. At the same time he declared that mechanism in its present state is still frankly a naïve philosophy. But this admission, he wrote in the preface to his *Scientific Basis of Evolution* in 1932, " may not altogether be a drawback, if progress along scientific lines is looked upon as more worth while than a stultification of the whole field of investigation by arbitrary metaphysical subtleties." And while not an extremist, he is a severe judge of scientific claims.

Morgan does not hesitate to tell us that we are visionaries when we pretend to solve the ultimate problems of nature. He himself has come perilously close to solving one, not with intricate apparatus, but with skilled hands, an imaginative mind, broad and deeply planted in the literature of science, and his persistence in probing phenomena which seem to offer solutions to large problems. Morgan's contributions have brought us nearer to the solution of more than one important riddle.

He has supplemented and clarified the theory of evolution. Darwin stressed the mechanism of evolution resulting from slight variations produced by changes in environment, variations eventually inherited and sifted out during nature's great drama of the struggle for existence. Harmful changes were nipped, but changes advantageous to the survival of the species were allowed to develop. Unfortunately, Darwin knew nothing of Mendel's work, although they were contemporaries, nor had the name of Darwin ever passed the lips of the obscure monk. Today we know that natural selection while a matter of inexorable logic is not the creative force in evolution, although it may explain in part the absence of many of nature's trials — species which have died out because they could not adapt themselves to their merciless environment. We no longer harp so much on natural selection and the struggle for existence, since Morgan has demonstrated the creative part played by mutation. Today, from the great body of new knowledge still in flux it seems fair to conclude that the many different species of increasing complexity have resulted from the interaction of some sort of selective process upon the raw material furnished by mutation. The mechanism of heredity must be at the basis of any theory of evolution that pretends to be scientific. At any rate, Morgan believes that we can rest our case for the acceptance of the mutation theory on the same experimental scientific procedure that has led to the great advances of chemistry and physics. "And it may be," says Hogben, "that when the history of the evolutionary hypothesis is written two centuries hence the name of Thomas Hunt Morgan will be mentioned in its pages more often than that of Charles Darwin."

The new genetics has already been of practical help in the breeding of better animal stock — cattle that give better beef, cows that supply more milk, and hens that lay triple the number of eggs that were formerly laid. In plant breeding, too, more valuable plants from the extremely important rustless, cold-enduring and even grasshopper-resistant wheats and a new type of tobacco leaf genetically constructed for cigar manufacturers, to the lowly non-odoriferous cabbage, have been produced for the first time. The old empirical methods of plant breeders like Luther Burbank have been placed on a more accurate and easily controlled basis. Attempts have even been made to alter the sex ratio of cattle so that larger numbers of females might be born than males. Koltsov and Schroder at the Moscow Institute of Animal Breeding have reported success in separating the sex chromosomes of the rabbit in such a manner as to increase the number of female rabbits born. The results of experimental work of this sort are quickly disseminated among the livestock breeders of Soviet Russia.

The theory of the gene has pointed the way toward the solution of even more vital problems — social problems involving marriage, idiocy, feeblemindedness, and a number of the insanities. We know already that various characters in humans such as eye color, hair color, blood grouping, albinism, the appearance of extra digits (polydactyly), short and crooked little fingers or toes (brachydactylia), and lobster claw, that is, the absence of all digits except sometimes the thumb and little finger, are inherited according to the Mendelian laws. We know much more, of course, about the hereditary factors in plants and animals. On the basis that nature uses the same mechanism on all living things, medical science has already begun to attack such serious and possibly hereditary diseases as cancer, tuberculosis, and diabetes insipidus. The award of the Nobel prize in physiology and medicine to Morgan in 1933 was a recognition of the significance of this modern theory of heredity for physiology as well as the part which genetics is destined to play in the future of medicine. Perhaps in years to come the proper study of the ills of mankind will be the study of the genetics of Drosophila. On the other hand, the control of heredity in humans may prove so complex that science may never succeed in putting it under its control. And even if this were possible for a while, " It is still a question," says Morgan, " whether in the human race it will ever be possible to get entirely free from the undesirable recessive genes which may crop up faster than those now present are being eliminated."

Bolder spirits, however, are even dreaming of isolating those crucially important genes for use in the creation of new forms of life, even as the chemist has used the atoms to synthesize new compounds and new alloys. Already, Morgan told a congress of geneticists in 1932, there is afoot a decided effort to approach the problem of the isolation and purification of these gene substances by methods partly genetic, partly embryological, partly physical and chemical. Men are talking of finding chemicals that will dissolve out some genes and not others, destroy some genes and leave others untouched, and of learning the secret of focusing radiation on specific parts of the chromosomes where mutations are desirable. But the impossibility of producing philosophers such as Plato dreamed of for his Republic will not hinder geneticists from trying to achieve other lesser miracles.

At the reception given in his honor on his joining the California Institute of Technology in 1928, Morgan remarked, " Of course I expected to go to California when I died, but the call to come to the Institute arrived a few years earlier, and I took advantage of the opportunity to see what my future life would be like." If the present is a faithful picture of the future, Morgan will be surrounded by many more than five hundred mutants of that famous fly which may yet show us its ways and make us wise. He will be the guardian of thousands of living specimens of Drosophila which men have been able to see for the first time — flies with all shapes and colors of eyes, wings, thorax, legs, bristles, sex mosaics. Thousands of bottles in air-conditioned rooms, millions of flies living (since the more expensive banana diet was abandoned) on a mixture of yellow cornmeal, molasses, water, agar, and yeast, and making public their private lives. A little group of men and women watching and plodding, counting bristle for bristle and hair for hair, waiting for favorable mutants, hoping for new openings, trusting to luck and spinning hypotheses, probing into the ever present and still unsolved problem of the cytoplasm or medium in which the genes live, trying to discover the reason for the mutation process. That is the spirit of the quiet, cloistered William G. Kerckhoff Laboratory of the California Institute of Technology where Morgan holds sparkling seminars watched by the whole scientific world.

Perhaps some day, as has already been proposed, the name of Morgan will be lifted on the wings of the insect Pegasus to immortality like those of Faraday, Ohm, and Volta, in the unit *morgan*, the space between genes on the Drosophila map having a cross-over value of one per cent.

CHAPTER TWO

ANTHROPOLOGY

HOW DIGGING INTO MAN'S PREHISTORY HAS RATTLED MANY BONES OF CONTENTION

With emphasis on the work and opinions of Aleš Hrdlička

Few books in the history of the world created a greater stir than Charles Darwin's *Origin of Species.* The small edition of 1250 copies was sold on the day of issue, November 24, 1859. Previously most men had believed that "There never are any new species; there are just as many species now as there were forms created by the Infinite Being in the beginning." Even the great botanist Linnaeus, son of a pastor, taught the constancy of species stocked a mere five or six thousand years ago during the biblical creation. As a young man, Darwin himself accepted this notion on faith, but with years of study he had piled up enough facts to strike a death blow to this myth of the immutability of life forms.

Centuries before Darwin there were thinkers who doubted the simultaneous creation of all species. They vaguely conceived an orderly development from one species of organism to another, hinting that life on earth might involve a continuous progression from more lowly to higher forms. But the tested knowledge which they could muster to confirm this belief was meager. Even the eminence of Anaximander, Empedocles and Aristotle could not bring the world to take their idea seriously. But by the end of the eighteenth century a body of evidence had accumulated. Georges Cuvier, a Frenchman, had opened up a new field of investigation which found surprising resemblances in the anatomy of many different living things. Comparative anatomy proved to be the entering wedge of the champions of organic evolution.

Paleontology, the study of fossil forms of life, was also well under way. Digging into the rocks scientists unearthed bony, mineralized and petrified remains or imprints of extinct plants and animals, which seemed to supply the missing links to the unbroken chain in the evolution of organisms now living. In addition to all this Lamarck, who had left first theology and then the army for zoology, had proclaimed the appearance of new species as the result of the inheritance of new characteristics acquired from environmental influences. Finally in the hands of Alfred R. Wallace, a young English architect, and four French zoologists all this newer knowledge and theory was shaped and ready for Darwin's epochal synthesis.

The *Origin of Species* challenged the ages-old belief in the special creation of each species. The battle between the special creationists and the believers in organic evolution was a long and bitter one. Even today it cannot be said that the last skirmish has been fought. Out from the mountains of ignorance still come bigots to attack it from time to time. Tennessee dangled a law " forbidding the teaching that man has descended from a lower order of animal," and the schoolteacher John Thomas Scopes was prosecuted, found guilty, and fined for this crime only a decade ago. Tennessee still retains its anti-evolution law but the well-informed and unprejudiced world accepts organic evolution as an established doctrine, even though the complete mechanism of the evolutionary process still remains a matter of opinion. " Evolution cannot be proved, but like wisdom, it is justified of its children," wrote the late Sir J. Arthur Thomson in answer to an invitation to come to America to defend Scopes.

So long as Darwin and other biologists debated the evolution of a frog from a fish, or the modern camel from a lower form of extinct animal no larger than a cat, or the modern horse from a tiny woodland Eohippus, the arguments were loud and sharp but fought within the ropes of a scientific arena. But in 1871 when Darwin hurled another bombshell, the *Descent of Man*, the floodgates of bigotry and fanaticism were opened wide, and the world was deluged in controversy. Had his two books been published a few centuries earlier, there is no question that the block would have been red-drenched with the blood of heretics and the gallows gorged with the corpses of nonbelievers. *De Orbium Celestium Revolutionibus* of Copernicus, which dethroned the earth as the center of the universe and turned men's eyes to the sun, caused less of a furor.

Man, declared Darwin, could not be excluded from the doctrine of evolution. "We must acknowledge," he said, "that man, with all his noble qualities and godlike intellect still bears in his bodily frame the indelible stamp of his lowly origin." He was not the first to announce this. The ancient Greeks had classified man with the animals. Lamarck, in the year Darwin was born, was bold enough to teach that man had evolved from an ape. But Darwin was more dangerous. He had mustered weighty arguments from scattered scientific laboratories, and had welded them into a mighty battering ram which broke into the citadel of the problem of man's origin. Man and the chimpanzee, he claimed, were co-descendants of a common anthropoid which had its habitat in Africa. What a shock that was! Even level-headed scientists accustomed to dispassionate weighing of evidence and steeled in the discipline of suspended judgment, rushed out with denunciations worthy of romancers. They refused to believe that "somewhere in their family tree there squats an ape."

Sickly and unwilling to hurt, Darwin himself took no active part in the verbal hurricane, although he stood in the center of the storm. One American visitor to England wrote home: "I saw Darwin receive an honorary degree today. There were two stuffed monkeys — one with a music box inside — suspended from the galleries by cords and dangled over Darwin's head." Thomas Henry Huxley, however, fought like his gorilla ancestor for Darwin's words. Facing his arch-opponent, Bishop Wilberforce, who begged to know whether it was through his grandfather or grandmother that he claimed descent from a monkey, Huxley made a memorable reply. "I have certainly said," he shouted, "that a man has no reason to be ashamed to have an ape for his forefather. If there were an ancestor whom I should feel shame in recalling, it would rather be a man of restless and versatile intellect who plunges into such questions with which he has no acquaintance, only to obscure them by aimless rhetoric and skilled appeals to prejudice."

More than half a century has passed since Darwin joined the immortals. In these fifty years science has advanced with ever increasing momentum. A vast store of facts has been accumulated to explain a galaxy of hypotheses concerning the origin of man. The science of comparative anatomy, the study of biochemistry, researches in blood grouping, developments in immunology, and other fields of scientific investigation have thrown a flood of light upon the justice of Darwin's choice of the ape as man's closest kin. For surely the deep-seated similarities between man and the anthropoid apes which are consistently being disclosed must be more than coincidences. Organ for organ and function for function the ape is closest to man. The leading English anatomist and student of physical anthropology, Sir Arthur Keith, maintains, for example, that man shares ninety-eight anatomical characteristics with the chimpanzee, eighty-seven with the gorilla, and eighty-four with the gibbon — more than with any other animals.

There is other evidence also. Of all the animals, only the anthropoids can be inoculated with syphilis. Hans Friedenthal showed that the blood of man could be safely transfused into the blood stream of the chimpanzee, while a similar procedure would clot the life stream of other animals and kill them. C. H. F. Nuttall of Cambridge University has shown that many biochemical reactions of the blood of man point to his relation to other primates. The chimpanzee alone with man suffers from gout, for he, too, is unable to change uric acid into allantoin.

For seven months the development of the human and ape embryos run near parallel. The human foetus is at one time in its development completely covered with hair arranged in the same manner as on the ape. Then marked changes begin to be noticed and the human loses most of this hair. The legs of all new-born infants are curved like those of tree-dwelling apes, and move more freely than later in childhood. The chest of the human child at birth is barrel-like as that of the climbing ape, but changes its shape when the child is ready for walking. Men, like apes, have their right arms and one leg longer than the other.

Man's brain, which marks his high estate, is closest in structure, blood supply, and chemical composition of its nerve cells to that of the ape, and next to human beings the ape is the most intelligent of creatures. Robert M. Yerkes at Yale has shown striking similarities in the emotional and intellectual activities of the chimpanzee and man. " The chimpanzee," he says, " thinks in a manner comparable to man. He can solve easy problems requiring logical deduction. His memory is longer than that of the average human." Yerkes has watched the ape reach with pointed sticks to get food from long hollow tubes. He has seen him fasten two sticks together to enable him to rake in food placed outside his cage. He has photographed him building a stairway with boxes to reach food hanging from the ceiling. Recently W. K. Kellogg and his wife played nurse to both their infant son and a young chimpanzee of seven and a half months, borrowed from the Anthropoid Experiment Station of Yale University. For almost a year both were reared under the same conditions as sons, companions, and playmates. For a while the little ape learned faster than the boy. He could even beat the child in pointing out a bow-wow in a picture book. But soon the human rival outstripped his primate companion.

There are, however, several sharp structural differences between modern man and the ape. Man does not exhibit prehensile hands and feet adapted for tree life. Man walks erect. Beetling brows, underslung jaw, and apish teeth are not present in man. His nose has a prominent bridge and tip. Comparative anatomy was at a loss to explain these wide differences in structure. Perhaps, if man actually had developed from some simian ancestor, this evidence hidden away as fossils in the rocks could be unearthed, just as paleontology had supplied evolutionists with the fossils of plants and lower animals.

The enormous antiquity of man had already been suggested.

Tournal in 1829, gazing upon stone implements he had excavated from caves and grottos beside fossil bones of animals long extinct, proclaimed, "Geology would reveal to man the antiquity of his race." Cuvier howled him down — these stones were of Roman origin, he insisted; "All the evidence leads us to believe that the human species did not exist where the fossil bones were found." Boucher de Perthes, controller of customs at Abbeville, continued to dig up such stones, and above the jeers of his colleagues contended, "They prove the existence of man as surely as a whole Louvre would have done." Darwin recognized the contributions of this Frenchman, but the French Institute would not listen, and at his death, the writings of Boucher de Perthes were sold for waste paper. Science in this field was still a "cemetery of hypotheses." What was needed was the evidence of the spade digging into deep rock strata and bringing up the fossil bones of missing biological links that would connect ape to man.

In the year Darwin died, there passed through Ellis Island a lad of twelve whom his father had brought from Bohemia to try his luck in the New World. From high-class cabinet making, Maximilian Hrdlička turned to the cigar trade in the lower East Side of New York City, and his son Aleš helped in the stripping of tobacco leaves. The bewildered lad went to evening school, and further developed his English by listening to sermons; he had been intended for the Church before leaving the Jesuit teachers in his native town of Humpolec. At eighteen he was confronted with the problem of planning a future. He thought of entering a business school, came down with typhoid, and developed pneumonia and pleurisy. The doctor who attended him, an ex-rabbi, suggested a career in medicine. As there was at the time a schism in medicine, he matriculated both at the New York Eclectic Medical College and the New York Homeopathic College, also taking courses at Bellevue and the College of Physicians and Surgeons.

After hardly a year of private practice, Hrdlička in 1894 accepted a research interneship at the State Lunatic Asylum at

Middletown, New York, where eleven hundred patients offered a wealth of material for research. Here for the first time he was drawn into the study of physical anthropology — the measurement of mankind. All through his schooling he had never even heard of the new science of anthropology or of human paleontology. In Paris the Société d'Anthropologie had with great difficulty been established in the same year that the *Origin of Species* appeared. The French considered this group a potential danger. Government officials were sent to attend its meetings, and its founder was made responsible for any serious controversies which might arise. This first organization of anthropologists was soon followed by similar societies in England and other countries, and before long, serious efforts were made to search for the fossil bones of prehistoric man. Fossil man was to be the final evidence to test the theory of the evolution of man.

While Hrdlička was attending his first medical school, Eugène Dubois, junior member of the staff of anatomy at the University of Amsterdam, was turning down an offer which would have led to a professorship. Like Hrdlička, he wanted an opportunity for research. He had heard stories of the discovery of several bones of ancient man: *La Naulette Jaw* in a Belgian cave, the *Sipka Jaw* fragment in Moravia, the *Banoles Jaw* in northeastern Spain, two mineralized *Spy Skeletons* in a terrace in front of a cave on a steep wooded mountainside in Belgium, and the *Malarnaud Jaw* from an ancient clay in France. He had made up his mind to search for buried bones way out in the East Indies, which he believed the home of ancient man. His colleagues were dumbfounded. Anthropology could hardly then as yet be dignified by the name of science, yet here was a young fellow of great promise running away to some god-forsaken hell-hole to waste his time digging for bones that might never exist in a place where early man might never have set foot. But men inspired by ideas of research do strange things and dream queer dreams. To meet expenses Dubois joined the army, and went as health officer to Sumatra and Java.

Not long after, his friends heard from him. A miracle had

happened. "It was near Trinil," he wrote, "in the left bank of the Solo River that I came in August, 1891, upon a place rich in fossil bones, and found the bones and teeth of a great manlike mammal whom I have named *Pithecanthropus erectus*, considering it a link connecting together apes and man." Dubois was a thorough student of anatomy. Those fragments of a lower jaw, three teeth, thighbone, and skullcap picked out of the gravel belonged neither to a true ape nor to a true man. They belonged to one creature that linked ape to man, declared the Hollander. He exhibited his find before an International Zoological Congress in Leyden. What a hullaballoo it raised! Plaster casts and bronze replicas of the precious fragments were made. The great anatomist Rudolph Virchow refused to accept the conclusion of Dubois. "There exists no pro-anthropos, there exists no ape-man, the intermediate link remains a ghost," he insisted. The bones belonged either to an ape or a giant gibbon, in his opinion. Others maintained the fragments came from a misshapen idiot, for to them the skull and thighbone showed evidences of pathological features. Ernst Haeckel of Jena, in 1879, had indeed prophesied the discovery of the remains of an ape-man, which he named Pithecanthropus. But surely these bones were not of this hypothetical ancestor of modern man. The evidence was too slim.

The discussion aroused by the finding of the Java bones emphasized not only the poverty of human paleontology, but also the urgent need for a more thorough knowledge of the normal man and his normal variants with which further fossil discoveries might be compared. Living men differ markedly in height, shape of head, facial parts, size of brain, and other features. It was necessary to know more of these normal and abnormal variations if new finds were to be properly evaluated in the effort to bridge the gap between modern man and his progenitors. The essence of anthropology is comparison. Hrdlička felt this keenly. When an offer came to become associate in anthropology at the New York State Pathological Institute created by the Commission in Lunacy for research in abnormal humanity, he accepted promptly. To prepare himself for this new work he went to Europe, visited museums, penal institutions, asylums, universities, and even morgues, everywhere taking body measurements. In Paris he studied under Manouvrier, who showed him a bronze cast of the skull of the Pithecanthropus. He told him of the other bones of that find lent him by Dubois, who had almost lost these famous fossils one day while carrying them in a satchel. Hrdlička marveled at the rare luck of this man who had brought to light bones more controversial than the relics of any saint or sinner.

Influenced by the Lombrosian conception of the criminal as constituting a degenerate type of humanity, Hrdlička spent several years in studies among the insane, the epileptic, the feeble-minded, idiots, imbeciles, and prostitutes, all of whom were at the time classified together as " degenerates." But the tens of thousands of measurements he took made him realize the crying need for a study of normal human variants with which the abnormals could be compared. When the pathological institute collapsed, Hrdlička accepted a call from the American Museum of Natural History to join an expedition into Mexico to study the Indian. It fitted in perfectly with his plans. He had failed to find the indispensable standards for the normal man and woman. " Perhaps here," thought Hrdlička, " among the primitive people, I might find something like normal humanity." He did find it, but the racial differences proved greater than he had expected. The standards obtained on the Indian could not be used for the studies on the whites.

Then in 1903 Hrdlička was called to Washington to organize a division of physical anthropology at the United States National Museum and the Smithsonian Institution. Not far away, in the East Room of the White House, paleontology and ethnology had their beginnings in the United States just before the eighteenth century came to a close. Here Thomas Jefferson who, it was said, could calculate an eclipse, survey an estate, plan an edifice, break a horse, tie an artery, and play a violin, had also written the first paper in American paleontology on the *Discovery of*

Certain Bones of a Quadruped in Virginia, and published the first scientific notes on the Indians and their languages. In the gallery of the National Museum was a kitchen table, a chair, an inkstand, and a dust-covered collection of skulls and bones. This was the modest beginning of the great division planned by Hrdlička. Especial attention from the first was to be given to man's antiquity. Hrdlička, of course, was thousands of miles away from the generally accepted cradle-land of early man. But he could at least watch the scene of an awakening interest in the digging for prehistoric bones, and try to interpret rightly the findings in this bristling field of research.

He did not have long to wait. From northern Croatia, near Zagreb, came news of the unearthing after five years of digging of parts of twenty skeletons from deposits in an ancient rock shelter, where some teeth of an extinct rhinoceros had accidentally been picked up. The thousands of chipped stones, the bones of extinct animals, and the shape of the skulls, all pointed to the great antiquity of the men, women, and children who had left these remains. But the discovery of this *Krapina Man* raised no furor; the fossils were obviously of a type of man not very far removed from the modern. The specter of an ape did not obtrude itself. Two years later, in 1907, an eighty-foot quarry near the village of Mauer, six miles from Heidelberg, surrendered the massive lower jaw of an adult male buried there for perhaps a hundred thousand years. The fossil had been dug up by a laborer who had been told to watch out for all strange specimens. The shovel had struck and cut the jaw in two, and four crowns of its teeth had been lost. The owner of the sand pit was called. The massiveness of the jaw was so unusual that he telephoned to an anthropologist of the University of Heidelberg, who " once he got hold of the specimen would not leave it out of his hands." Cleaned up in his laboratory, the much mineralized yellowish red jaw, spotted with black, looked both human and like that of a great ape. Again a storm broke out over the identity of this *Homo Heidelbergensis*. And while Hrdlička studied replicas of the jaw and declared it human, others cried ape, man-ape, and ape-man, until a fresh item of news from the far-flung graves of ancient man turned their attention to another bone of contention.

Not long after, during archaeological excavations in a limestone rock shelter at Le Moustier, France, O. Hauser stumbled over the almost complete skeleton of a sixteen-year-old boy. It was found lying on its right side in an accumulation of debris, the face turned down and a pillow of stones placed under the head. The body had apparently been deliberately buried five feet below the floor of the cave. Very much excited, Hauser had his find carefully guarded. "Further excavations were stopped until the autumn, when surrounded by a company of anthropologists the skeleton was finally extracted with expert eyes looking on to bear witness to its authenticity and antiquity." This unusual skeleton made a great impression, and the Kaiser paid Hauser one hundred twenty-five thousand marks so that he might present it to the Berlin Museum.

Three Catholic priests, engaged in archaeological excavations in several rock shelters in the little village of La Chapelle-aux-Saints in France, made the next find of a being who toiled and fought long before the Noachian flood. They carefully gathered up the rust-colored remnants of bones and brought them to Professor Marcellin Boule in Paris. Some of these fossil bones were very large, and might have been hung in churches as evidence of the existence of biblical giants or of an Adamite who from the length of the bones was calculated to be a hundred twenty-three feet and nine inches tall. But science had made sufficient strides to label these largest bones those of extinct mammoths. From the rest, Boule picked out an almost complete skull, with lower jaw intact, twenty-one vertebrae, twenty ribs, and a number of hand and feet bones, all of which belonged to one ancient man.

The earth apparently had made up her mind to give up more of her hidden secrets, for shortly after, while Hrdlička was visiting the museums and anthropological laboratories of Europe and the Near East, several skeletons of great antiquity were dug out of a shallow rock shelter near Bugue, France. For ten long, barren years Q. Peyrony had explored this cave. When finally human bones appeared Boule and Breuil and other authorities in the world of prehistory were called to witness the removal of almost complete skeletons which had apparently been laid out for burial scores of millenniums before. Then the *Man of Jersey* came to light out of an old cave on the Island of Jersey in the English Channel. Although nothing more than thirteen teeth were actually found, it was shown that their structure and the many thousands of accompanying stone implements pointed undeniably to an ancient origin. Even this partial set of stony teeth set tongues wagging. Were they lowers or uppers, milk or permanent, male or female, monkey, ape, man-ape, or manlike? Students of comparative anatomy went to tooth collections for verification.

Once again Hrdlička sailed for Europe to see all those bones and sites from which they came, and to obtain replicas for his collections at Washington. Photographs and verbal accounts were not sufficient basis for decisions in such vital matters. Hardly had he returned when the report of an even more provocative discovery was made, a find which involved almost a hundred leaders of prehistory and human paleontology in a bitterly waged battle. Charles Dawson as a lad of twelve had begun to collect fossils, and his interest in geology and paleontology did not wane while he studied law and became a barrister at Lewes, England. One day he attended court at the Manor of Barkham near Piltdown, not thirty miles from the study at Doorn where Darwin had made the question of man's origin a flaming sword. Dawson noticed that the road leading to the courthouse was being repaired with brown flint. Strange, he thought, that they should be using flint which had to be carted from five miles away, when they could have bought better and cheaper material for road building near by. The barrister knew every foot of that section, which he had thoroughly studied and where he had already discovered natural gas. All during the trial Dawson's mind kept slipping back to that road and the flint.

Aleš Hrdlička

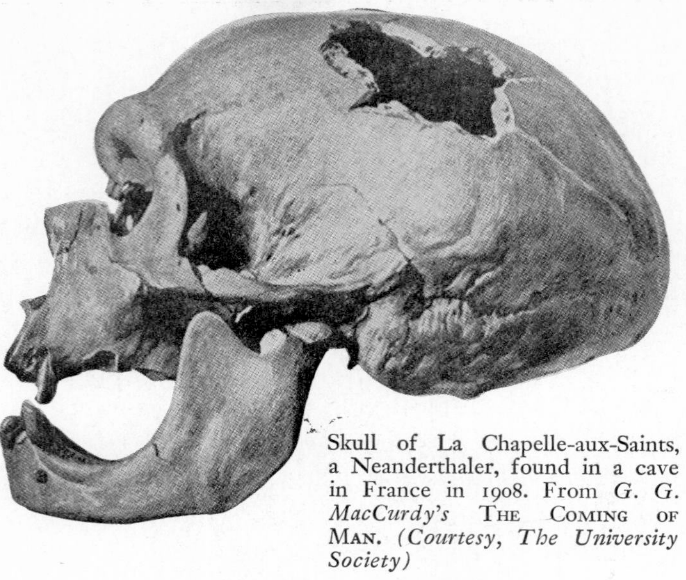

Skull of La Chapelle-aux-Saints, a Neanderthaler, found in a cave in France in 1908. From *G. G. MacCurdy's* THE COMING OF MAN. *(Courtesy, The University Society)*

The *Pithecanthropus* skull, side view. (After Dubois, 1924.) *(Courtesy, The Smithsonian Institution)*

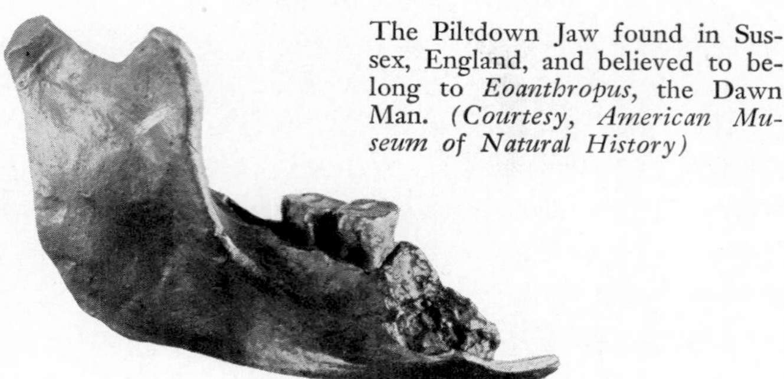

The Piltdown Jaw found in Sussex, England, and believed to belong to *Eoanthropus,* the Dawn Man. *(Courtesy, American Museum of Natural History)*

During the court recess he spoke to the workmen and was told they were using flint because there happened to be a pile of it on the spot. He had never examined this accumulation of flint, but cautioned the men to watch out for any man-shaped tools and fossil bones.

Several years passed before Dawson had occasion to revisit this spot. He saw laborers throwing stones at a petrified cocoanut they had picked up from the gravel of a river long since dried up. That cocoanut to Dawson looked like something more than a cocoanut. After a careful scraping and cleaning, there emerged what appeared to be a fossil fragment of an unusually thick braincase of ancient man. Reluctant to trust his own judgment, he brought it to Sir Arthur Smith Woodward, one of the leading paleontologists of Europe. To Woodward it resembled the braincase of some hitherto unknown species of prehistoric man. Perhaps there were other fragments of this creature buried away in the same spot. They " decided to employ labor and to make a systematic search among the spoil heaps and gravel." They sifted loads of the materials themselves, and were rewarded by a piece of a highly mineralized lower jaw seeming to belong to the same individual whose braincase had already been discovered.

At a meeting of the Geological Society of London in December, 1912, Woodward described his discovery and christened the new creature *Eoanthropus*, the Dawn Man, on the ground that here was probably the first genus of man to emerge from the tangle of apes which preceded him. He maintained that the jaw was apish and the skull human. His announcement was met with vigorous opposition. Boule said the jaw was that of a real ape and that the skull did not belong to the same creature. Most of the German anthropologists were positive all these Piltdown bones belonged to an ape. Into the maelstrom of three different theories, arguments, and counter-arguments leaped an ex-New York dentist, Dr. James L. Williams, who had come to live in England twenty-five years before. Williams, with the help of Sir Arthur Keith, examined a molar found by Woodward two miles away from the original discovery, and announced that this very ancient tooth was human and that it might have belonged to the Dawn Man — that Eoanthropus was indeed a man, not a missing link, half man, half ape. Woodward had insisted that while the skull, that of a woman, was completely human, the jaw was almost precisely that of an ape, pointing out that the jaw lacked the inside ridge to which the muscles controlling the tongue of a talking man are attached. Williams was made a fellow of the Royal Anthropological Institute of Great Britain, and returned to New York in 1915 to resume the practice of dentistry.

During the controversy anthropologists were busy reconstructing the skull of Eoanthropus from the bone fragments. Some went so far as to mold the whole creature, adding even such obviously hypothetical features as the hair, lips, eyes, and tip of the nose, for which there were no bones to leave clues. Boule objected. "Our duty," said the French anthropologist, "is to protest. For such attempts, however agreeable they may appear in certain respects, are of a nature to throw discredit on a science which is still having so much difficulty in getting official recognition." And he added, "These attempts may serve as pleasurable pastimes to men of science; they ought never to go outside of their laboratory." Ernest A. Hooton of Harvard is even more severe, for he reminds us that "you can with equal facility model on such a skull the features of a chimpanzee or the lineaments of a philosopher."

Then out of Africa came a strange tale. Hans Reck of the University of Berlin had come to a desert in East Africa not to search for human bones, but to subject a cross-section of this area to geological examination. In this desolate spot an old ravine had cut open a series of deposits laid down on the bottom of ancient lakes. A negro helper pointed out a shining piece of white bone protruding from one of the layers of rock. Reck sweated to cut the bone out of the solid rock, and found it to be part of the skeleton of an ancient man who, he believed, had perhaps been buried tightly wrapped in hides, for his arms were pressed close to his body and his knees drawn up. Just as the World War broke out, Reck brought his find back with him. To all the diggings of eminent anthropologists and all the drawings of comparative anatomists this discovery added further proof that modern man had kinship with the beasts of the jungle. For a decade, the guns of the Somme and the other shambles drowned the outcries over Reck's *Oldoway Man*.

In 1921 the anthropological scene shifted back again to Africa where another "tantalizing epic of man's prehistory" was staged. A Swiss miner was working with his black boy in a huge crevice filled with lead and zinc ores in the Broken Hill Mine of northern Rhodesia, thirty-nine hundred feet above sea level. They were several feet below the surface of hard limestone rock. "We were hand-picking," the miner later told Hrdlička who made a special trip to the locality, "in a pocket where there was much lead ore. After some of the strokes of the pick some of the stuff fell off and there was a skull looking at me. It was very strange and with some of the matter adhering to it looked so unlike an ordinary human skull that I thought it was a big gorilla." A heated discussion ensued among the miners who crowded around for a good look. Like professionals they debated whether it was man or ape, and the discussion lasted far into the night. Perhaps it had been lying in that rock for all the thousands of years which geologists figured it had taken to fill the cavity.

The miner brought his find to the attention of the overseer, who photographed the discoverer holding the weird skull against the place where it had lain. Overcome by a feverish excitement, they began searching for more of such treasure. "Next day we looked for the lower jaw which was missing, but nothing was found." Then the mining captain joined the exploration and in the afternoon of the same day picked up portions of another skull with its teeth in good condition. He jotted in his notebook that it looked very much like the skull and teeth of a lion. A petrified human leg bone was also found.

Popular interest in the progenitors of man ran high as a result of all these finds. Explorers coming back to civilization told of seeing anthropoid apes that walked like men in the forests. Sunday newspaper supplements, magazine articles, pseudoscientific lecturers, motion pictures, plays, and novels filled the public with a strange conception of man's origin. The world was becoming ape-minded. People spoke sententiously of missing links and our forefathers the apes. Those better informed cited cases of children born with tails, cleft palates, hare-lips, and bodies covered completely with thick hair. They argued that man and the ape were close kin, for children were known occasionally to run on all fours like apes. Also in some men the remnants of a twitching muscle for moving the skin of the scalp as well as the ears still function, as in the chimpanzee. They pointed out the similarity of the drawing of the human lips in anger to the snarl of the cornered gorilla.

Women, too, were becoming actively engaged in anthropological explorations. From the Rock of Gibraltar came word of the discovery of the skull of a ten-year-old child securely enclosed in solid rock beneath a stone shelter. Miss Dorothy A. Garrod was the leader of the British expedition that dug out this ancient fossil. She had been led to this spot as the result of several interesting finds there. The first was that of a human skull dug out seventy-five years ago and subsequently lost. Many years later, in 1917, numerous stone implements of great antiquity found near the Devil's Tower of Gibraltar indicated the habitation of early man in this vicinity. Miss Garrod decided to reinvestigate the possibilities of this locale. She started in November, 1925. "Towards the end of May, 1926," she wrote home, "I was obliged to put a heavy charge of blasting gelatine into the rock which blocked the terrace in front of the cave. The explosion opened a large number of cracks in the surrounding limestone. On June 11 a big lump of travertine was removed. On examining the face of the travertine left in place I noticed a thin edge of bone." The heat was oppressive, but Miss Garrod continued digging until she had minutely examined the deposit surrounding the bone. She found nothing, and at the end of the week "was obliged to close down the dig on account of the heat." Returning to the strenuous task three months later, she was rewarded with a human lower jaw, right maxilla, and temporal bones, all of which evidently belonged to the same child.

Strange that the world had as yet heard nothing of fossils of prehistoric man from the biblical cradle of mankind. But in the spring of 1925 the Cave of the Robbers near the shore of Galilee yielded parts of the skull of a young adult — dark red bones dug out of the interior of some natural limestone by the picks and spades of the British School of Archaeology. Then the American School of Prehistoric Research, organized by George MacCurdy of Yale, joined the British for further exploration first in Iraq and later in Palestine. To date a dozen other human skeletons have been added from Mt. Carmel, the Cave of the Kids near Athlit, and other sections of Palestine. Most of these finds embedded in huge blocks of solid rock weighing three tons were either chiselled out of their stony matrix by Theodore McCown, or shipped to London where, under the direction of Sir Arthur Keith and with the aid of delicate dental drills, the skulls and bones were extricated. Keith has called the type of man represented by these fossils *Paleanthropus Palestinus*, a modern term perhaps equivalent to the biblical Adam and Eve and their early descendants.

And while from a breccia-filled cave near Rome came the report of the first important ancient human fossil found in Italy, strange news flashed for the third time out of Africa, from the very spot where Reck had bumped into the Oldoway Man just before the outbreak of the World War. For nearly two decades science had neglected this important site. To L. S. B. Leakey, born in Africa and educated at Cambridge, it was imperative to survey and dig deeper in this region. He finally succeeded in raising funds for an expedition to this desolate place. Working without pay himself, he began operations in the same ravine surveyed by Reck. After finding stone tools and animal fossils of great antiquity, he went to Munich to ask Reck to join him in further explorations. In 1933, in a dried-up ancient lake about two hundred miles from the Oldoway site, Leakey found part of a lower jaw bone. He sent the jaw bone to England where, on the basis of an X-ray examination which clearly indicated certain features in the roots of its teeth, it was declared to be the fragment of a new genus of man — *Homo Kanamensis*, found in Kanam — almost as old as Pithecanthropus if the telltale animal bones and stone tools found with it could be trusted, yet close in structure to the modern black man living in northeast Africa today.

The hunt for the trail of the ancestors of modern man kept gaining velocity. Hrdlička had made further trips to Europe and other parts of the world to examine both the original sites and the actual skeletal remains of man's progenitors. And then suddenly the anthropological scene shifted. Not a single word had come out of China to help unravel the mystery of man's birthplace, despite the fact that a few men had scraped the earth of China. In 1903 some dragon's teeth were picked up in a Peking drugstore, and as one of them seemed to belong to some prehistoric human, further investigation was urged. Eighteen years later J. Gunnar Andersson, directing a geological survey for China, secured funds from the late Ivar Kreuger, the match king, to undertake a search in a cave at Chou Kou Tien, about thirty-five miles from Peking, where the natives said were piles of fossil bones. The Swedish geologist actually found many bones, but not human ones. Several years later O. Zdansky picked up two teeth and announced his discovery in a carefully worded statement: "I decline absolutely to venture any far-reaching conclusion regarding the extremely meager material discovered here, and which, I think, cannot be more closely identified than as Homo sapiens. It is interesting but not of epoch-making importance."

So said this perhaps overcautious scientist. At the Peking Union Medical College a young professor of anatomy, Davidson Black, thought differently. He had come to China from Canada in the hope of finding prehuman fossils. After a careful examination of the teeth Zdansky had found, Black was convinced they belonged not to modern man, but to some creature very close to human. Believing other fragments of the being to whom these teeth had belonged might be embedded in the rock near by, he obtained a two-year grant from the Rockefeller Foundation to undertake a thorough survey of the neighborhood. A lone lower molar was his first find. On the basis of its structure, Black announced to the Geological Society of China that he had discovered a tooth of a new genus of man, *Sinanthropus Pekinensis.* Meager evidence for such a daring announcement, it was thought. And while students of prehistory argued, Black went back to his digging for stouter testimony.

The following year he unearthed parts of two lower jaws and fragments of a braincase which he insisted belonged to the same species of man that had left behind the tooth. This was followed in 1929 by an important find made by a young Chinese student of anthropology, W. C. Pei. He had come across a fossil bone in a block of hard yellow travertine. Four months of cutting finally exposed an almost complete braincase with the facial part of the skull missing. Black wrote to Hrdlička, who was waiting in Washington for news: "This is just a hasty chit to let you know that Pei discovered an uncrushed and almost complete adult Sinanthropus skull in the Chou Kou Tien deposit. . . . We need the leg, arm and foot bones now to complete the picture, but if our luck holds as it has so far we should get them next year." Within the next three years other bones of at least ten different skeletons were added, so that by 1934 the high arched front portion of the skull, the advanced development of the speech area of the braincase, the shape of the wrist bones, and the appearance of a piece of a collar bone all pointed to the definitely humanoid character of this China Man of Peking. Stone tools, bone ornaments, fossil animals, and fragments of charred bones also bore testimony to the antiquity of Sinanthropus.

This discovery, instead of clearing the air, made the fog thicker. Some declared the Peking man was similar to Pithecanthropus — the "ape-man" of Java. G. Elliot Smith regarded it as the nearest common ancestor of man. Hrdlička and Dubois consider it close to the Neanderthal man. Black told an International Congress in Washington in 1933 that the Peking man was not the direct ancestor of modern man, perhaps only an uncle. " He was in a blind evolutionary alley, an offshoot from the main stem that died out." Some even doubted it was human, and the old verbal battle was renewed.

Throughout all this Hrdlička continued to evaluate the mass of reports and the museum of bones. He had seen with his own eyes the fossil bones of all of the dozens of skeletal remains found up and down the stream of prehistory except the most recent ones of Peking, Africa, and Palestine. He had made measurements of every conceivable nature. Craniometers, calipers, goniometers, and other anthropological instruments were brought into play to wring the last secret bit of information out of every one of those mute bones. The teeth of man, normal and abnormal, were compared with those of the fossil men and of apes both living and extinct. He consulted personally the anthropologists, geologists, and miners who had made the various finds, and visited, in some cases repeatedly, almost every site of the original discoveries.

After all this Hrdlička frankly admits that notwithstanding the great advances that have been made, the science of anthropology is still young — we are still like babes in this field. Important gaps and many uncertainties make the past of man too hazy to be as yet read clearly. Although the essential outline appears to have been brought out from the hieroglyphics of human paleontology, embryology, physiology, and comparative anatomy, the shadows of time still hide most of the truth.

Although sufficient evidence is still lacking, Hrdlička offers a provisional theory concerning the origin of man in the evolutionary process. Man, he says, evolved not from a monkey nor even from an anthropoid ape, but from forms that must have been nearer to him than any of these, and which we call human precursors. The ancestors of these precursors were naturally among the highest primates though probably not among any of the genera or families thus far discovered. From these human precursors modern man gradually developed within approximately five hundred thousand or one million years.

Every evolutionary tree from the first drawn by Haeckel in 1871 to those of today shows man as an offshoot of a parent stem — the primate stem. The apes are also offshoots of this stem. Men and the anthropoid apes (chimpanzee, gorilla, orang, and gibbon) are terminal twigs of this same ancient stem. Other offshoots from the parent stem are the many monkey branches. The evolutionary trees differ, however, in the order of appearance of these various offshoots and also in the way in which some died off and others continued to produce other twigs. Four important and different evolutionary trees have been drawn by four eminent men of science. The differences between them may be seen from the diagrams on the next page.

With respect to missing links — that is, creatures which were part ape and part man and which, as transitional types, gradually evolved into real man — Hrdlička emphatically disagrees with Haeckel's picture. Pithecanthropus according to Haeckel was an ape-man, a forerunner of modern man. Hrdlička, however, dismisses the claims of the Java skull as belonging to man. The most that appears justifiable is to regard Pithecanthropus as a high primate of as yet uncertain ancestry and no known progeny, although far advanced in a humanoid direction.

But what of the hundreds of other human bones which have been unearthed? With the probable exception of the Heidelberg Jaw, they may be attributed, says Hrdlička, to the genus of *Neanderthal Man.* (*Homo Neanderthalensis* had been named after Neander Gorge situated in West Germany. Here in 1856 in a limestone cave a human skullcap and other bones had been found.) Even though they have been discovered in such widely separated geographical areas as France, Italy, Belgium, Germany, Croatia, and Palestine, Hrdlička classifies them all as Neanderthalers for many reasons. They all come from the latter part of the glacial period. The men to whom the bones belonged all made and used implements of similar type. They all

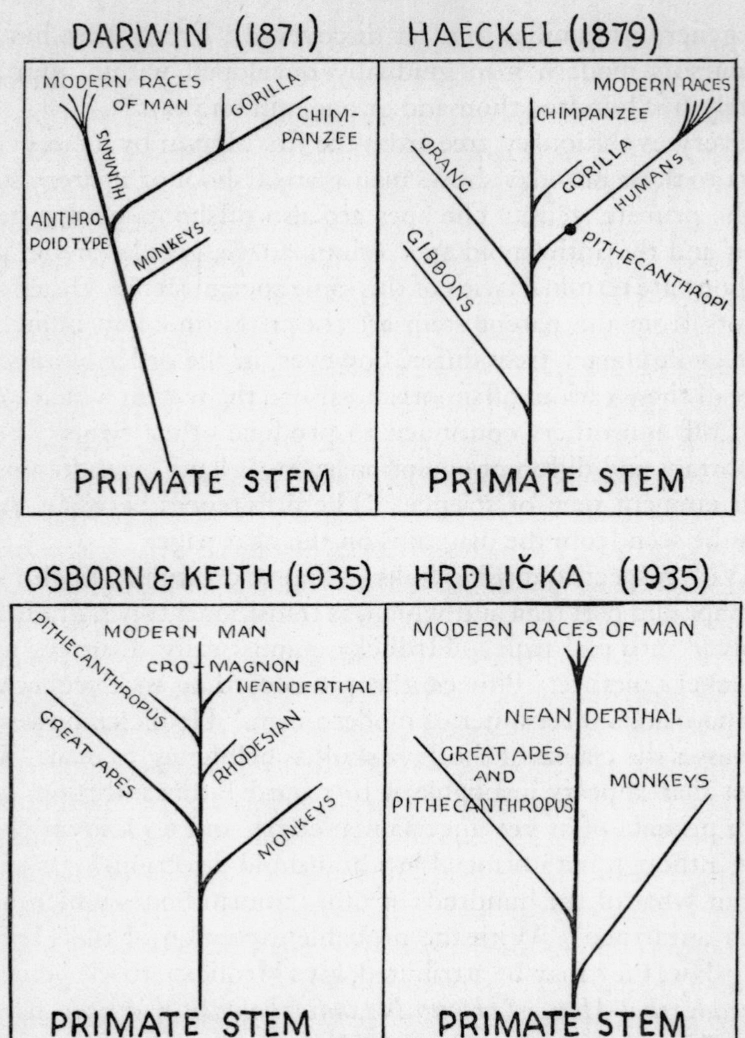

FIG. 12. Four evolutionary trees of man.

lived in open sites or in shallow rock shelters during warmer times, or in caves during the colder periods, and they used fire. They are all associated with the same groups of animals, such as the woolly rhinoceros, the cave bear, and species of elephant, lion, and hyena, all of which no longer exist.

They all exhibit the same primitive physique. The Neanderthal man was short to submedium in height — about five feet four inches. He was thickset, had a stout neck, large thorax, and short limbs with broad rather than long feet and large hands. The face was relatively large. The nose was broad and flat, the mouth large, the jaw heavy, and the chin receding. His teeth were larger than those of man today. His most outstanding features were the large, heavy, prominent ridges around the skull cavities in which the eyes are buried, and his low, receding forehead — mark of a real old lowbrow. His brain, although large, in some cases was poorly developed in those areas associated with thought. His head and shoulders were somewhat bent forward, and it is doubtful if he walked perfectly erect, although he walked on his feet, and may have shuffled a little.

It is this creature, the last representatives of which must have strolled through Eden some thirty thousand years ago, who, in more or less attenuation, still lives today in such people as the Australian aborigines. Until the last phase of the Pleistocene (glacial) period Europe was inhabited by beetle-browed, slouching Neanderthal man. Then amid the exigencies of climate, Neanderthal man became transformed by a slow evolutionary process into modern man, who made his first appearance a very short time ago. This is Hrdlička's belief, and he points out many skulls such as the Gibraltar, Galilee, and Cro-Magnon as representing transitional forms which finally evolved into the modern *homo sapiens*. Here he stands clearly and firmly apart from most other eminent authorities, who still maintain the older view that Neanderthal man was one branch of the primate stem which ended suddenly and was completely extinguished. Then, according to this same view, there came at the same time a new and superior type — the *Cro-Magnon Man*. He represented another branch from the primate stem and appeared about twenty-five thousand years ago during the glacial period. Cro-Magnon man, they believe, is the direct ancestor of modern man.

The first skeletal remains of Cro-Magnon Man were discovered in 1868 in a rock shelter of Cro-Magnon in the village of Les Eyzies in France. Other fossils of this genus indicate that he was taller than Neanderthal man, stood erect, had a more modern-shaped head with a higher forehead, a pointed chin, and no beetling brow. Associated with him were implements and ornaments of a distinctly higher culture. He left pictures of animals on the walls of caves — etchings of reindeer, mammoth, bear, stag, and horse, as well as a clay model of a bison. MacCurdy, in opposition to Hrdlička who believes Cro-Magnon man simply a more highly developed Neanderthaler, says, "The Cro-Magnon race was a new race which completely supplanted the archaic Neanderthal race." Keith agrees, "Neanderthal man apparently suddenly disappeared and was replaced with Cro-Magnon man of the same type as now occupies Europe." Boule of France echoes these statements, while M. C. Benedict goes further with "Neanderthal is a throwback in the line of evolution, and this retrograde sport had no successors." Henry Fairfield Osborn, formerly President of the American Museum of Natural History and dean of American paleontologists, tells us that "Neanderthal is an instance of arrested and perhaps partly retrogressive development." It is known that not all evolution is upward; at times a process of degeneration produces a less complex from a more complex species. Parasites, in general, exhibit this retrogressive development, often losing not only limbs and wings for which they have no further use but sight and even digestive systems as well. Thus the hookworm, having found a reliable host in the intestines of man, has sacrificed its digestive organs almost completely, and the tick now parasitic on the sheep is today a wingless fly.

In the face of such stout opposition, Hrdlička cannot bring himself to believe that twenty-five thousand years ago Cro-Magnon man from some unknown somewhere suddenly invaded Europe, destroying and then replacing Neanderthal. This would imply, Hrdlička hinted during the Huxley Medal address which he delivered in London in 1926, that Europe was invaded during the height of the last glacial invasion, since no Cro-Magnon fossils have been found in earlier rocks. But, he reminded his audience, the movements of men have always tended toward a place in the sun and away from the cold rather than toward the cold. In other words, if the coming of Cro-Magnon man was an invasion, he would not have come from warm Asia to cold Europe. Hrdlička brings other weighty arguments to support his dissenting opinion. There have been discovered no Cro-Magnon fossils or artifacts outside of the home of Neanderthal man, nor any remains of the ancestors of Cro-Magnon. If he existed at the same time as Neanderthal man and in the same territory, says Hrdlička, it is impossible to understand why with his greater intelligence he did not destroy Neanderthaler sooner, or why he did not mix, or above all, why he left no culture and other remains of his existence in the region from which he is supposed to have come as an invader.

On the other hand, he continues, the Neanderthal man is now known from his fossils to show wider variations in his make-up than was formerly supposed — variations which approach more and more the modern aborigines of both Australia and Africa and even some people of modern Europe. The only alternative, concludes Hrdlička, is the evolution of the Neanderthaler into modern man, rather than his disappearance — Cro-Magnon man was really a Neanderthaler.

When did that branch from the primate stem emerge to give us the first of man's precursors, and when did the oldest of the Neanderthalers originally appear? These are questions which have not yet been answered to complete satisfaction. We are dealing here in periods of hundreds of thousands of years and the error of even the best judgment must be large. Still we have some information which helps to fix these shadowy dates. Geologists and paleontologists have transformed the crust of the earth into an immense tome whose stony chapters are the layers of rock. Some of its pages have already been cut, but for the most part it is a difficult volume from which to learn definite facts. Many of the leaves are still partly blank, some torn, crumpled, burned, some doubtless still missing altogether. In this misty book, prehistory has been divided into the following geologic ages:

The Archeozoic Age began some 1500 million years ago.
The Protozoic Age began some 1000 million years ago.
The Paleozoic Age began some 500 million years ago.
The Mesozoic Age began some 150 million years ago.
The Cenozoic Age began some 60 million years ago.

The last, Cenozoic or Tertiary Age, is further conveniently divided into five epochs, as follows:

The Eocene
The Oligocene
The Miocene
The Pliocene
The Pleistocene, or Ice Age, in which Neanderthal man appeared some thirty thousand years ago.

It has been estimated that it takes about nine hundred years for a sedimentary rock one foot thick to be deposited. On this basis the bottom layer of stratified rock fifty feet deep must have been deposited about 45,000 years ago. From the thickness of sedimentary rocks, the saltiness of lakes, the percentage of radioactive elements in deposits, the thickness of deposits left by dried-up lakes, the cutting through of gorges and canyons like the Grand Canyon of Arizona, truly an "abyss of time cutting across the ages," and from various other ingenious clues, men of science have estimated the age of the present hard crust of the earth to be between two and ten billions of years. They have also been able to approximate the time when certain rock formations made their appearance. Paleontologists have shown that in the most ancient of these periods, the Archeozoic, only the simplest forms of life were extant. The first forms of living matter were too soft to leave any traces. In Protozoic layers, marine invertebrates first left evidence of their existence; Paleozoic time furnishes us with the mineralized remains of fish and forest life. Reptiles and plants with seed in pod first flourished in Mesozoic time, while the age of mammals was ushered in during the Cenozoic Age which began some sixty million years ago.

This record is a monument to the ingenuity of man in bringing some order out of the chaos of life and time. Never have Archeozoic rocks furnished fossils of fish, nor have mammalian traces been found in Paleozoic rocks. The rocks and their stony prisoners follow a regular course and in spite of the numerous upheavals of the earth's crust and the weathering process of ages which scrambled the layers completely out of place, the entombed evidence indicates forcibly that the order which man has deduced is not simply a clever tale based on accidents.

During the Eocene epoch foxy-faced lemurs ranging in size from mice to dogs, tailed monkeys, and the big-eyed little tarsoid, the first arboreal hand-feeding ape ancestor, were rampant. The Oligocene witnessed the antics of the anthropoids, while during Pliocene days some form of human precursors must have muttered their wants. Finally, the Ice Age or Pleistocene period was the period intimately associated with the early history of man. During this Ice Age there occurred several glacial advances and retreats. The world is even now slowly emerging from the last advance. It was during this last glaciation period, which ended about thirty thousand years ago, that Neanderthal man existed.

How did the first humans emerge from the common primate stem? How did Neanderthal man spring from his human precursors? How did modern man develop from the earlier Neanderthal or later Cro-Magnon? The mechanism of this change is still shrouded in mystery. But if we are to follow the same reasoning for the human species as for other organisms, certain hypotheses present themselves for consideration. Thomas Huxley maintained that if evolution could produce the structural gap which separates the monkey from the gorilla, it could also bridge the chasm between the gorilla and man. But how? Bolk says man evolved from an apelike ancestor as the result of a change in the development of the embryo. For some time the embryos of both man and ape resemble each other. Then certain further developments take place in the ape embryo which do not occur in the human embryo. The skin becomes pigmented, the jaw longer, and the body covered with thick hair. This hypothesis is known as the *theory of foetalization.*

A newer and more fascinating explanation is offered by Morgan's theory of the gene as applied to the appearance of new types or mutants. It contributes two facts to the problem. First, it has been established that a gene may suffer a change at any stage of the development of an organism. Then this change may alter its final stage of development, and the organism may breed true as a new species. Hornless cattle, tailless cats, waltzing mice, hairless dogs, albino goldfish, and the Ancon sheep — a type having short and crooked legs — have all appeared as such mutants and bred true. In the case of the Ancon sheep, this sport appeared first in Massachusetts in 1791. It was bred because the short crooked legs prevented it from jumping fences, and thus the animal could more easily be kept in pasture. This stock died out, to reappear a hundred years later, far off in Norway, again as a mutant from normal parents.

Perhaps a manlike hand and a manlike foot first appeared as mutants; perhaps even the structure of the brain mutated to give speech and better reasoning powers. Both Keith and Charles R. Stockard have expressed the opinion that a mutation may have modified the balance of the glands of man's precursors, changing not only their appearance but their mental fiber. There is some evidence to lend plausibility to this theory. It has been found that when the pituitary gland, located near the base of the brain, is unusually large or overactive it produces an abnormally large amount of a certain secretion or hormone. This results in a disturbance known as *acromegaly*, characterized by an unusually rapid growth of the body, especially of such organs as the hands, feet, lower jaw, lips, tongue, and nose. The normal person is gradually transformed into a hideous caricature of himself, an acromegalic, whose heavy features, protruding lower jaw, beetling brow, and gorilla-like proportions resemble the features of an ape. Other glands control other bodily changes. It has also been experimentally shown that a difference in the thyroxin output of the thyroid gland will produce round-headed and long-headed animals, the latter resulting from an abundance of thyroxin.

When we consider the question of the location of the cradle of man, we are again met with uncertainties. Hrdlička is inclined to place it to the west rather than the east, in Europe or Africa rather than in Asia. Keith thinks man first emerged in some country farther to the east than Palestine, perhaps on or near the Persian Plateau. G. E. Smith and Woodward accept the view expressed by Darwin in the *Descent of Man* that Africa was man's original home. Another scientist, on the basis of an analysis of climatic factors, places it near Turkestan not far from the biblical Garden of Eden. A Russian geneticist traces the centers of the origin of various grains, concluding that Afghanistan where, he believes, wheat was first cultivated, and North Africa, where oats were first grown by man, were probably human cradles. Osborn disagrees with Darwin that man originated in "some warm forest-clad land," but holds rather for some plateau like that of central Asia.

Or perhaps, says Osborn, the Garden of Eden was widely scattered, and different species of early man originated at various centers. This theory of the parallel evolution of several different species of man in different parts of the world, leading to the present four races of mankind, was elaborated by Osborn. He theorized by analogy from what happened in the case of other animals, such as the horse, which apparently went through similar evolutionary changes simultaneously at widely separated regions of the earth and gave rise to different species of horses. It is not easy to understand how such a process could have taken place. But Osborn infers that different stems from the same branch may have inherited some "latent" characteristic, presumably certain genes present in their common ancestor. This combination of genes exerted its influence on the later stages of the evolutionary process so that the progeny of the different stems as they appeared in different lands went through a similar evolutionary development.

A number of eminent anthropologists have of late been disposed to consider seriously this doctrine of independent evolution as applied to the present races of man. Keith, early in 1935, pointed out that newly discovered evidence seems to bear testimony to its plausibility. For example, fragmentary bones of *Homo Soloensis*, intermediate between Pithecanthropus and the most primitive known living Australian aborigines, together with some of his tools and weapons were found in 1931 by Dr. Oppenoorth in a terrace of the Solo River not ten miles from the site in Java where Pithecanthropus roamed possibly a million years ago. In Australia, too, have been unearthed two fossil skulls of *Wadjak Man*, a creature who Dubois, its discoverer, believes was of a higher order than his Pithecanthropus. After inspecting this evidence Keith wrote, "It is hard to resist the notion that in the course of about one million years the descendants of the ape-browed Pithecanthropus had been converted into the aborigines of the continent of Australia."

Coincident with this development, they believe, a similar evolutionary process was going on in Africa leading from the Rhodesian man, oldest discovered human fossil from Africa, through intermediate types of man which finally culminated in the parent of the modern negro race of Africa. They cite various discoveries reported by Leakey in Kenya Colony and Tanganyika Territory in eastern Africa since 1931. In addition to a mandible of *Homo Kanamensis*, Leakey found fossil bones of extinct animals of the Pleistocene period together with stone implements and fragmentary skulls of the *Kanjera Man* — another intermediate type. To Keith and Leakey these skulls already show negro specialization and are believed to be higher forms of the Rhodesian man which gradually changed to the modern negro of Africa.

Coincident also with these two parallel evolutionary processes another race was being born in Asia. Some of the members of the Mongolian race which still occupies eastern Asia are believed to be the issue of a human being represented by the Peking Man of China. They even go as far with this theory as to infer that Eoanthropus of England may by a similar process have been the ancestor of the modern white man or Caucasian of Europe. In fact Osborn, who at first regarded these baffling bones now resting in the British Museum at South Kensington as those of an ape-man, recently recanted and now believes that they indicate that " we are descended from an early man, not an ape man. He walked erect, thought as man, and probably spoke as man."

In other words, all the modern races of man are descended from human precursors and not from ape-men, by a process of parallel evolution which went on in several widely separated regions. Hrdlička cannot agree that the evidence at present available justifies such a doctrine that the modern races of mankind issued from an extremely remote common ancestor perhaps in mid-pliocene time, three million years ago — an ancestor with certain latent evolutionary tendencies which led to a parallel evolutionary process in widely scattered portions of the globe. For one thing the actual sites and geological age of the rocks in which the Leakey finds were made have been questioned by Percy Boswell of the Imperial College of Science who made a careful study of the claims in 1935. Mountains of earth will have to be moved and many bones broken before this question can be finally answered. Another two or three hundred years of systematic and zealous digging and above all, exceptional luck, thinks Hrdlička, may see the solution of the problem.

Throughout the whole drama of man's search for his birthplace in the Old World, sporadic reports of human bones contemporary with the oldest found abroad appeared in the New World. Florida, Texas, New Mexico, Nevada, Nebraska, and Mexico, as well as the Argentine, have been the scenes of discoveries of artifacts and human skeletal remains which seemed to date back to glacial times. But their great antiquity on critical inquiry has been generally disproved. The bulk of this iconoclastic work has been done by Hrdlička, who traveled widely to the sites involved in both Americas.

Here, too, are differences of opinion. John C. Merriam, President of the Carnegie Institution of Washington, declared in 1933, " Early representatives of man may have been present in America and we are not justified in eliminating the possibility that a considerable part of the history of man as a tool-making animal may have a record in America." This, of course, is rather indefinite. A few others insist that the Indian represents a different genus of man who could trace his ancestry back to fossils yet to be unearthed on the American continents. How else could man have appeared here with oceans on all sides? Hrdlička has given an answer. The northern tip of Alaska is separated from the northeastern tip of Asia by the Bering Straits, not fifty miles wide, and this is divided in halves by the Diomede Islands. On a clear day one can see the hills of the coast of Asia from the mainland of Alaska. A land bridge may have connected the two continents at one time, for the topography of this area changes rapidly, but man did not really need this, since travel by water is so much easier. Asia must have been the original home of our natives. For the last eight years Hrdlička made a survey of the Yukon, Bering Sea, and the coasts of Alaska from Point Barrow to Kodiak Island, making observations among the natives and digging for bones and artifacts. He also visited many parts of eastern Asia and found living remnants there of the same stock. The American Indian, in Hrdlička's opinion, was originally of a branch of the Mongolian stock, an emigrant from northern Asia within the period of the new (polished) stone age (from 12,000 to 3000 B.C.). Hrdlička found the Eskimo a blood relation of the American Indian, and in 1934 Gates of Kings College, London, made blood tests on some Indians of British Columbia and found a close relationship to tribes on the islands off the Siberian coast. While all pure blood American Indians belong to blood group O, the Mongolians of Asia and the Japanese have blood of type B.

In the National Museum at Washington is a monument to the interest in physical anthropology of this immigrant boy from Bohemia. It is an imposing collection of the remains of prehistoric as well as of later humanity. It contains approximately sixteen thousand skulls arranged in boxes especially built to protect them against dust and weather changes; tens of thousands of other bones which surgeons, dentists, lawyers, as well as students of anthropology come to study every year; a unique collection of brains, human and animal; and casts of full-blooded American Indians and Eskimos made largely by Hrdlička himself over a period of forty years — invaluable study materials which will be left to posterity.

More than once Hrdlička has crossed lances with fanatics and pseudoscientists. The field in which he works is crowded with them. To Hrdlička, the purity of the Aryan " race " and the supremacy of the Nordics are infantile myths. There is still diversity of opinion as to the meaning of the number of human races extant today. While he labels the White, the Yellow-Brown, and the Black as the three basic races of man, Hrdlička emphasizes that there are people living today at every stage of racial differentiation, comparable to the varieties of domesticated animals. Scientifically speaking, the idea of a superior race is preposterous. So thoroughly diluted has the Nordic race become that even in Scandinavia not even half are pure Nordic. Besides, Aryan is a linguistic and not a racial term, and from the point of view of language the Hindus, too, are Aryans. The blonds of the north are in truth Africans bleached by a process of environmental depigmentation.

Hrdlička has exposed the iniquitous stupidity of the alleged superiority of highbrows over lowbrows. When he had completed a long series of measurements of American Indians, Eskimos, full-blooded negroes, Old Americans (descended on both sides from Americans of at least three generations), members of the National Academy of Sciences, the poor whites living in the mountains of Tennessee (one of the most backward groups educationally and otherwise), and immigrants of fourteen different nationalities passing through Ellis Island, he analyzed the records and wrote his report. " The data permit but one possible conclusion, which is that the lowness or height of the forehead does not express or have any relation to, in normal human beings, the kind of brain it helps to harbor." His measurements also showed conclusively that the height of the forehead taken in relation to body structure placed the D. A. R.'s at the tail end of four groups which included the full-blooded American negro, the Eskimo, and the American Indian. The height of the brow is a racial character, although wide individual variations exist, and is due merely to the higher or lower insertion of the hair.

No subject, says Hrdlička, has occupied the attention of man more than the future of the individual after death, but the amount of thought devoted to the terrestrial future of man has been astonishingly small. If you ask him what of the future, he tells you that man is still plastic in body and mind, and that the drama of change in the human race is by no means ended. Civilized man will be taller, his head will be somewhat broader and larger but balder and the features more delicate, the skull and facial bones thinner, and his physiognomy more lively and expressive. His teeth will be smaller and fewer, with the wisdom teeth missing altogether. The body will tend to slenderness in youth, the breasts will be smaller but the pelvic parts will remain unchanged. Hands and feet will be narrower, the fingers more slender, and the fifth toe will disappear. The lower limbs will be longer and the arms shorter. A livelier metabolism will make his pulse and respiration more rapid, and his body temperature will be higher. He will possess a more highly developed brain, and if self-destruction does not put an end to him, our remote descendant will probably live longer and better than we do today.

However, Hrdlička is not a blind optimist. He sees no easy way onward and no promise of eventual equality of races. Social problems will still be knotty ones, and the intellectual gulf between the front and back ranks of a people will probably increase rather than decrease. And his last words are, "Mental derangements will be more frequent." Not such a pretty picture, after all, for our bald, almost toothless, four-toed remote posterity.

CHAPTER THREE

PHYSICAL DISEASE

MEDICAL RESEARCH IS STRAINING TO LENGTHEN LIFE'S TETHER

Written around the life and work of the late William H. Welch

It is not improbable that Eoanthropus, the dawn man, disappeared from the face of the earth as the result of some tremendous ill to which the flesh of man was then heir, just as the great Mayan civilization of South America succumbed within much more recent times to the invisible virus of yellow fever. Man's struggle to maintain himself against a cruel environment, glacial invasions, earth cataclysms, scarcity of food, and animal enemies may have been as naught compared with those bodily degenerations and deadly plagues which take the breath of life from animate things. Destruction rode triumphantly on the wings of the Black Death which, during the Middle Ages, took tens of millions of human lives in Europe alone. The Great Fire of London in 1666 fortunately relieved England of the hordes of rats which carried this bubonic plague. Destruction also came in the form of smallpox pandemics, one of which alone in 1770 wiped out three million lives in the East Indies. Cholera, malaria, typhoid, influenza, syphilis, dysentery, and a score of other diseases took frightful toll.

Diseases swooped down with merciless fury not only among semi-civilized peoples, but even where man had advanced to a culture never before attained. Men who had invented steam engines and railroads and harnessed electricity were still powerless against these forces that piled up millions of corpses before they tired of destruction and rested to await new generations of victims. If we are to take stock in the gloomy prophecy of Charles Davenport, the geneticist, the threat of extinction still faces mankind. He visions the sudden appearance, from some existing and relatively harmless organism, of a most virulent mutant virus which may sweep us away before we have time to combat it.

Man's struggle for health has been a long and dramatic one. Hippocrates, Galen, Vesalius, Harvey, Paré, Morgagni, Hunter, and others labored to clear a path upon which mankind could set its feet toward the banishment of disease. Superstition, ignorance, tradition, and blind fumbling were among the many obstacles of the task. By the middle of the nineteenth century medicine as an art had gone far, but as a science its growth was still unbelievably slow. Empirical knowledge had accumulated; laboratory data from scientific experimentation were still meager. Then suddenly, as if by divine edict, a new method of investigation was discovered, and the progress of medicine rushed along at such a dizzy pace that within six decades it passed more milestones than during the previous sixty centuries.

William Henry Welch, late dean of American medicine, lived through the stirring period of these great triumphs. He had chosen this profession because by tradition at least he was destined for a medical career. His great-grandfather, descended from Irish folk who had come over in 1650, as well as his grandfather had been country doctors; his father and four uncles were practicing medicine. After graduating from Yale, Welch matriculated at the College of Physicians and Surgeons, one of the very few of the seventy-two medical colleges of the country which maintained a real standard of excellence.

In 1870, medical education in the United States consisted primarily of an indoctrination. It was didactic rather than experimental. The lectures were uninspiring, uninteresting, and almost wholly descriptive. Medical students discussed surgical operations they had never witnessed, and described symptoms of diseases they had never treated. "They taught us medicine," said one eminent physician, "as you teach boys to swim, by throwing them into the water." The first physiological laboratory was opened by Harvard in 1871. Not until that late date did the catalogue of the leading American medical school even mention the microscope. It is almost impossible to believe that this important tool had already been available for two hundred years; that, almost a century before, Morgagni at Padua had published his classic *Seats and Causes of Disease,* which laid the foundations of the relations between symptoms of diseases and diseased organs; that the anatomist Bichat, dead at thirty-one, had already introduced the study of tissue pathology; and that Rudolf Virchow had just written his *Cellular Pathology.*

Virchow had introduced a new idea. The microscope had shown him the diseased as well as the normal cells of the body and had indicated their relationship. This led him to write that " the healthy body is a cell state in which every cell is a citizen, and disease is a conflict of citizens brought about by the action of external forces." This began an era of the study of disease based upon microscopic investigations of the cells of tissues and organs suspected of being the seat of the disease. Thousands of slides showing millions of cells of every part of the body, diseased and normal, were carefully scrutinized by young medical students as a preparation for later medical practice. These means of investigation and diagnosis were considered the touchstones of successful medical knowledge and practice. Yet medical students in America were given no opportunity to acquire even the rudiments of this new method of the microscopic study of disease. The microscopic study of cells, tissues, and organs was not included in his professional education. His only contact with the laboratory was the study of the anatomy of dead men which until the seventeenth century had been forbidden by both state and church.

The blind acceptance of dogma, handed down by professors in dull textbooks, was irksome to Welch. In contrast to this deadening exposure to medical lore, even smelly cadavers in the dissecting den were interesting, so he turned to pathology — the study of the diseases of body tissues. As there was no opportunity at home for post-graduate work in medicine, Welch set sail for Europe in 1876. Medical science on the continent was miles ahead of American medicine. Europe was in the throes of a great medical revolution.

America was almost oblivious to this stirring period through which medicine was passing. Pasteur, son of a tanner, had been led by a strange approach to the most tremendous discovery in the whole history of medicine. From a commercial research on the cause of fermentation in beet sugar, followed by another investigation into the imminent collapse of the silkworm industry in France, Pasteur discovered that microscopic organisms played the leading role in infection. Preventive medicine was ushered in by this germ theory of infectious diseases.

The idea was not altogether a new one. Centuries before, Athanasius Kircher had said that the plague was due to some minute living organism in the body of its victim. A Veronese physician of the sixteenth century had declared that disease is caused by minute seeds or germs in the patient. Plenciz in 1762 dared to theorize that *every* disease was caused by a separate organism which could be grown outside the body. Bacteria, to be sure, had been seen in the blood of diseased animals, but their connection with disease, while suspected by some, had not been definitely proved.

Then came Pasteur to establish his germ theory of disease upon the firm foundation of accurate scientific experiments. Blessed with imagination and sustained by a tenacity and courage which kept him working even when half paralyzed, Pasteur showed that the blood and tissues of diseased animals contained specific bacteria from which those of healthy organisms were free. He demonstrated further that the injection of even as little as a drop of highly diluted blood containing these microscopic cells into the blood of healthy subjects produced all the symptoms of the disease. And he proved conclusively that from the tissues and organs thus rendered sick he could again isolate the identical bacteria. Europe was in a ferment over these discoveries, but surgeons and physicians in America scarcely took notice. Our doctors still spoke of strange *miasmas* or vapors that rose from the earth and spread disease.

Welch, as a student in New York, had heard faint rumblings

of the new developments in Europe. He set himself the task of breaking the powerful grip of sterile and outmoded medical practices in this country. He went first to Germany, to the Strassburg laboratory of the great authorities on anatomy and histology (the study of the cell). His next stop was Leipzig, where he worked under Karl Ludwig, the foremost physiologist of his day. When ready to leave, Welch mentioned that he was going to the man who dominated German medicine. Ludwig asked: " Why do you go to Virchow? He is a greatly overestimated man. Go to Cohnheim." Those words were a great shock to the American, but Ludwig explained that the cellular pathology of Virchow was becoming barren, for this " old intellectual tyrant " had refused to see the tremendous importance of the discoveries of Pasteur. Welch changed his plans and took the train for Breslau.

Here, in Cohnheim's laboratory, he found a wild enthusiasm for the new medical tool introduced by Pasteur. Cohnheim considered this " the greatest discovery in the field of microorganisms." With the fresh blood of Pasteur's genius, he was giving new life to Virchow's cellular pathology. Here Welch watched that zealous man Ehrlich up to his wrists in dyes, which he dreamed might give him the magic chemicals to kill the bacteria that caused several infectious diseases such as syphilis. Here, too, he saw the developing of new staining methods to make bacteria more easily visible under the microscope. With all of these inspired workers, Welch, the first American student to come here, formed a lifelong friendship. Here, too, he met Ivan Petrovich Pavlov who later became world famous for his classic studies of conditioned reflexes. Taken into their inner circle, Welch climbed mountains and tramped with them through the Black Forest. Picnics, operas, museum visits, were the occasions for lively discussions about the new world of medicine which was being born. The inspiration of those Breslau days never left Welch, who had even then made up his mind to put an end to America's isolation from the foreign medical centers of research.

It was during this time that Welch met Koch, a new luminary

in the medical sky. While resident physician in the insane asylum at Hanover, financial troubles had made this young man despondent. He had almost given up medicine, when a microscope, presented by his wife as a birthday gift, started him on the glorious road of scientific adventure. Koch, following up the work of his French contemporary, made Pasteur's foundation more secure and fertile by introducing the *solid* culture medium for rearing colonies of bacteria. Just then he was continuing the work on anthrax, a disease of cattle. Using a liquid from a rabbit's eye as culture medium, he had placed the blood of anthrax victims on a glass slide which was kept warm. He saw the rod-like bacteria of anthrax develop into threads, spores, and then back again into rods in his new culture medium. He came to Cohnheim to demonstrate for the first time the life history of this anthrax bacillus. " I shall never forget," Welch wrote, " his coming through the room with Cohnheim." " There is a great man," said Cohnheim later, " of whom we shall hear much in the future." The work of Koch marked a new turning point in medical progress.

Then Welch went to Prague to watch Klebs struggling with the causative agent of diphtheria: to Vienna, where Stricker refused to see him because he came from the laboratory of the heretical Cohnheim. Before returning to America, Welch spent three weeks in Paris listening to lectures on the nature of cells, and made a trip to London to listen spellbound in Kings College to Lister, son of a Quaker wine merchant, who had introduced antiseptic surgery a whole decade before Pasteur's work had been verified.

" I returned from Germany thrilled with enthusiasm at the dawn of a new era, and with some training and capacity to use the master key forged by pathology and bacteriology which was to transform the face of modern medicine." The twenty-eight-year-old medico was offered the professorship of pathological anatomy by Bellevue and, at the same time, a lectureship at the College of Physicians and Surgeons. Since the latter institution had no private research laboratory, where he could carry on the work he had seen in Europe, Welch, in 1878, joined the Bellevue Medical College, which had provided two small rooms for his primitive laboratory. Economic difficulties forced him to undertake at the same time a little private practice, and to become a " quiz master " — a sort of free-lance medical preceptor who drilled the weaker medical students for their examinations. But at the height of his popularity, he abandoned this lucrative enterprise when he realized the dangers to medical education of this cramming practice.

Besides, momentous events were taking place in the new field of bacteriology, and he needed more time for research. Albert Neisser, whom Welch had met in Cohnheim's laboratory, was announcing his discovery of that frail germ which causes blindness in children, the coccus of gonorrhea. Eberth had isolated the typhoid bacillus, Laveran had found the parasite of malaria, Loeffler had described the bacillus of glanders, and Pasteur had just drawn the first picture of the streptococcus which he thought was responsible for puerperal fever. This was the disease which had taken frightful toll among thousands of mothers, especially in lying-in hospitals. In 1773 an epidemic of puerperal fever raged in European maternity hospitals for almost three years. In Lombardy, in that year, not a woman lived after bearing a child in a hospital. It was only as late as 1843 that our own Oliver Wendell Holmes insisted for the first time that puerperal fever was contagious, that it was carried from maternity patient to maternity patient by doctors and nurses who took no precautions to prevent its spread. Holmes read a paper before the Boston Society for Medical Improvement but his audience was either completely indifferent to his warning or openly hostile. His paper was not even published. Three years later, Ludwig Ignaz Semmelweis introduced the practice in European lying-in hospitals of doctors washing their hands in basins of chlorine water to protect their patients from the contagion of puerperal fever. Today, in spite of all precautions, we still lose seven thousand mothers annually in the United States from this disease.

In 1882 Koch electrified the world with the announcement that he had found the causative agent of tuberculosis. An Associated Press dispatch had brought this news to America in advance of its publication in the medical journals. Koch had grown the tubercle bacillus on a culture medium of solidified blood serum. When spots of large colonies of bacteria appeared in the culture, he injected some of it into an animal, which contracted tuberculosis. He found the bacillus of tuberculosis in the diseased animal. He isolated the organism from the injected victim and grew it in a pure culture. The bacteria that grew into large colonies in the culture medium were the same as those which were found in the diseased animal. This completed the proof that the tubercle bacillus was the cause of tuberculosis and opened up the possibility of prevention of the White Plague. Welch first heard the news from Professor Austin Flint who, on reading the newspaper account, jumped into a cab, tore down Fifth Avenue, and rushed right into his bedroom, waving the newspaper and crying, " Welch, I knew it, I knew it! " But Austin Flint was considered an old fogey, and the rest of the American medical world received the news with a great deal of skepticism. At this time, the leading surgical textbook in the United States was " chary " of antiseptics and bacteriology and their " alleged " success.

" New discoveries were being announced like corn popping in a pan." Klebs trapped the bacillus of diphtheria. Fehleisen found the cause of erysipelas, an acute disease associated with inflammation of the skin. Koch, risking his life in Egypt and India at the very height of a deadly epidemic, exposed the bacillus of Asiatic cholera, a deadly disease of filth. Nicolaier, from the pus of mice and rabbits, unmasked the bacillus of tetanus. Fraenkel showed the presence of a spherical shaped bacterium or coccus in pneumonia patients. Chamberland, in the newly opened Pasteur Institute in Paris, was introducing his porcelain filter as an additional weapon against the microbes. This is an unglazed porcelain cup or plate containing very tiny holes through which liquids can be forced while even the smallest bacteria are held back. But America was still apathetic.

About this time President Gilman, of the Johns Hopkins Medical School, was looking for a man to fill the chair of pathology. He wrote to Cohnheim. "Why do you come to the Germans," came back the answer, "there is a young American, Welch, competent to take that professorship." And Welch, the most active exponent of the new medicine which was flowering in Europe, was the unanimous choice. To gather more of the new knowledge and to gain further inspiration from the masters, he again sailed for Europe. The sixty-three-year-old Pasteur, then at the height of his powers, made a tremendous impression upon Welch. He dropped his test tubes and took the American around his laboratory, speaking about the new world of *immunology* which he had accidentally opened up. Four years before he had stumbled upon the important scientific principle that the body under certain conditions can produce substances called *antibodies* which attack germs or neutralize their poisons. These antibodies are found in the blood of an immune animal. A culture of chicken cholera with which he had been working had been weakened by age. When injected into a hen, instead of killing the animal it produced only a mild form of the disease. More than that, the hen could then withstand the injection of fresh virulent cultures of chicken cholera. Thus after being subjected to a mild attack of the disease, the animal was rendered *immune* (from the Latin *im-munis*, not a slave) from later attacks of this microbe. Medical men refused to believe this although the phenomenon of immunity had been known for centuries. Pasteur faced the skeptics with a dramatic experiment in 1881. Anthrax was playing havoc with France's cattle. He picked twenty-five healthy sheep and injected into their blood a vaccine made of anthrax bacteria weakened by heat. A few weeks later, he passed virulent anthrax germs into the blood streams of these vaccinated sheep, as well as into twenty-five healthy unvaccinated animals. "The twenty-five unvaccinated sheep will all perish," predicted Pasteur, "and the vaccinated sheep will survive." His prophecy came true. His vaccine was effective. The science of immunology was born.

Still the skeptics argued. Vaccination might be effective with cattle, but what of the infectious diseases of man? The answer came while Welch, after leaving Pasteur, was still traveling on the continent. Joseph Meister, a nine-year-old boy, had been brought from Alsace to Pasteur's laboratory in Paris. He had been severely bitten by a mad dog and was doomed to a horrible death. Since there was nothing to lose, Pasteur decided to inject the boy with the virus of rabies sucked from the foam of a mad dog and weakened by partial drying. For three weeks, watching the dying boy, he almost collapsed from worry, blaming himself for not having first tried the experiment on himself, as he had planned. Then the seemingly impossible happened, and the boy was saved. At last the whole world believed. From Russia were sent victims horribly mutilated by wolves, and from New York were brought several boys bitten by mad dogs. All were given the vaccine, and the miracle was repeated.

Welch had by this time arrived at the Berlin laboratory of Koch, the master technician of bacteriology. They spoke about the discovery of the tubercle bacillus, which Koch showed him under the microscope. And while the German taught Welch his steam sterilization technique and many other strange tricks of the new science, they often mentioned the great Frenchman who held the center of the world's glaring limelight. Koch could not hide his contempt for Pasteur, whom he regarded as a bungling scientist, for had not Pasteur once believed that earthworms carried anthrax, and had not he, Koch, disproved his theory. Even behind the antagonisms of great scientists, Welch saw the bitterness of the Franco-Prussian War.

Among the foreign students present in Koch's laboratory at this time was T. M. Prudden, whom Welch had recommended for the chair of pathology at the College of Physicians and Surgeons when he himself had accepted the Bellevue post. The climax of the four-weeks course given by Koch was a study of

William Henry Welch

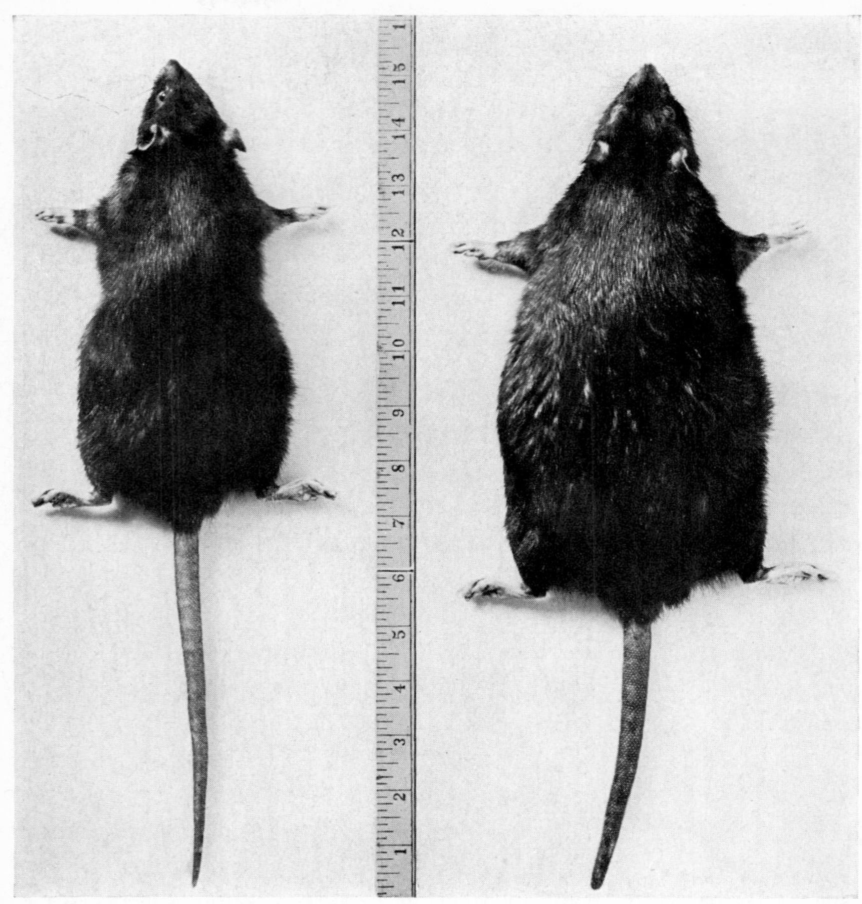

At the right is shown a gigantic rat, obtained for the first time by Herbert M. Evans of the University of California. This huge rat, as large as a guinea pig, was produced by injecting the young rat over a period of many months with the water extract of a chemical (hormone) found by Evans in the pituitary glands of oxen. (Note the relative size of a normal rat shown at the left.) This same growth-producing hormone of the pituitary has also been used with some degree of success on underdeveloped children. *(Courtesy, Herbert M. Evans)*

the bacillus of Asiatic cholera, which had just broken out in Europe. The men were half afraid of this germ. They handled it with extra care, especially after Koch had cautioned them about its virulence. He warned his students not to take this particular microbe out of his laboratory, although he permitted them to take back cultures of several other microbic diseases. It was altogether too dangerous; a few of these deadly bacteria might start a frightful epidemic of cholera. Next morning Prudden and Welch walked into each other on the bridge across the River Spree. They were two minds with but one thought — how safely to get rid of the tubes of cholera culture they had secretly planned to bring back to the United States. Each had independently purchased sulfuric acid and had poured it over the cholera cultures. Then, with one mighty fling, both threw their tubes into the river, praying they might have successfully destroyed the death-dealing microbes.

In September, 1885, Welch was back again in Baltimore. He was now convinced that " the higher purposes of medical education could be attained only by the establishment of well equipped laboratories." Waiting for the new buildings of the Johns Hopkins Medical School to be completed, he set up his laboratory on the top floor of the biological department. Here he followed the path of the European pioneers. And while Bruce was discovering the coccus of Malta fever, Weichselbaum exposing the meningococcus, and Robert Louis Stevenson entering the newly opened Trudeau Clinic for tuberculosis treatment, Welch was completing his *Modes of Infection.* This textbook was to be the guide to the new medicine for his students at Hopkins. Welch, the American Aesculapius, by publishing the revolutionary methods of combating infectious diseases, was to uproot archaic ideas still bred in the bone of American medicine, and start the new generation of physicians on the scientific road of preventive and experimental medicine.

At Johns Hopkins medicine was not only taught but studied. Here among the group of eminent medical teachers and experimenters, the great Osler captivated with his culture, wit, and skill. The stage was set for radical changes in medical education, and Welch was the leading actor. The tide of students was turned from the European medical centers to Baltimore, where he helped to build up an institution which became the model for other medical schools throughout the country. To be sure, Welch had not created the current which, beginning in Paris and Berlin, had spread to America and was washing the shores of medicine, purging it of its sterility. But he did give it force and direction in this country. " Under him," wrote Flexner, " medicine in the United States was raised from a beneficent art to an expanding science."

To his laboratory came Walter Reed and James Carroll with the advice from Washington " not to waste their time on pathology and bacteriology but to devote their attention to practical things." But under the spell of Welch, they found themselves on a dangerous road whose end might be destruction. Jesse Lazear, a member of Osler's staff, was also among that little band of men that gambled with death in Cuba. They were searching for the method of transmission of yellow fever. On September 13, 1900, several days after he had watched a mosquito take its fill of his blood, Lazear died. But the medical adventurers had proved the stegomyia mosquito to be the carrier of yellow fever, and laid the foundation for its subsequent eradication.

Others came to Welch both for work and inspiration. Two of his students made brilliant contributions to the knowledge of the cause and conquest of malaria, a disease which in India alone was taking a yearly toll of nearly a million and a half souls. This was the pestilence that had helped destroy Greece, and over which Ronald Ross, a British army doctor with no specialized training in biological research, was to triumph. The late Theobald Smith, America's greatest bacteriologist, reading every word Welch published on bacteriology, pathological anatomy, and experimental pathology, came to Baltimore to find consolation whenever he felt troubled in his work. From Johns Hopkins came a stream of medical men armed with new tools, new methods, and a new spirit, who were to spike the guns of Death in unexpected places.

Preventive medicine was swiftly becoming more and more of a science. Bacteriology and immunology had opened up a new world to the physician. One by one, diseases of hitherto unknown origin and hopeless outcome yielded to a host of research workers. Diphtheria, tetanus, bubonic plague, typhoid, dysentery (the " summer complaint " of infancy), scarlet fever, syphilis, were all brought into the circle of preventable diseases. Antitoxins, vaccines, serums, blood tests, and general sanitation were new words which spelled the banishment of some of man's most ancient, most persistent, and most rapacious enemies.

It is in the nature of science to reach out into new and unexplored territory after the old has been conquered. With all the advance of preventive medicine, science dare not become enamored of its victories and lull humanity into a sense of security. There remains a world of the unknown to be penetrated. Even the frontiers which separate us from the dark continent of the infectious diseases the causes of which are known are still vulnerable. Tuberculosis, for example, in spite of our half century of knowledge of its cause and despite its drop from first to seventh place in mortality tables (from 250 out of 100,000 population in 1892 to about 60 out of 100,000), is still the leading cause of death of people in this country between the ages of 15 and 40. It is still a national problem especially among negroes and women between 16 and 25.

Except in small measure, the fall of the death rate of this disease was not due to medicine. Tuberculosis is primarily a disease of poverty. From the " lung blocks " of the East Side of New York City came thousands of its victims. The more fortunate of us, almost daily exposed to the tubercle bacillus, fight it off. Natural selection has played and is playing no small part in lowering the death rate of tuberculosis. Certain inherited constitutions are known to be more susceptible to this disease than others. For example, among the American Indians tuberculosis is about seven times as common as among other Americans.

The death rate has been lowered and the number of cures increased in several other ways. It has been found that in the treatment of this disease, rest, fresh air, selected food, surgery, light therapy and proper climate are of greatest importance in the order given. The old idea was to give the patient all the food, especially milk, he could take and to encourage exercise. Today we depend upon rest and upon a moderate amount of food of excellent quality. The therapeutic powers of the sun, especially in the treatment of bone, joint and gland tuberculosis (not lung TB), has also been recognized. Since 1903 Dr. Rollier, a Swiss, has directed a famous sanitarium on the slopes of the Swiss Alps where his young patients romp through the snow in the sunlight with nothing but boots and loincloths to protect them. Another method of treatment which has been used for years in Europe and which is gradually being re-introduced in this country where it was first discovered, is therapeutic pneumothorax. Air is injected into the pleural cavity and usually one lung is made to collapse to give it a chance to rest and fight off the infection, while the other lung carries on the work of getting air. In some cases both lungs are partially collapsed. Today it may be safely claimed that a very large proportion of tuberculosis in its incipient and moderately advanced stages can be cured or arrested. Even in far advanced cases nearly half of them are arrested or cured.

The tubercle bacillus had many years ago been found to be tough and coated with a waxy covering which resists the action of chemicals. About ten years ago the National Tuberculosis Association launched a drive for the further study of the chemistry of the tubercle bacillus in the hope of learning its composition and finding chemicals with which to attack it directly. Very recently it was reported that at the Henry Phipps Institute of Philadelphia a protein, in chemically pure form, had been isolated from the tubercle bacillus. This chemical seems to be the destructive agent of this bacteria. But thus far no chemical has been discovered or synthesized which can search out the tubercle bacilli in the body and destroy them without injuring the host.

Within the last few years, however, three vaccines have been prepared which it is claimed can protect mankind from the ravages of tuberculosis. The first of these is made from tubercle bacilli weakened by growth on bile-soaked potatoes. For thirteen years the late Alfred Calmette and Dr. Guérin of the Pasteur Institute used it on anthropoid apes in French Guinea and on newborn calves, before daring to administer it orally to a three-year-old infant in July, 1921. Since then more than a million infants of tubercular parentage have been vaccinated, chiefly in France, with the B.C.G. (Bacillus Calmette-Guérin) preparation. All the available data gathered from France, Indo-China, Madagascar, Germany, Belgium, Roumania and New York City (which has already vaccinated about a thousand babies from tuberculous families) seem to indicate to many that B.C.G. has already lowered the death rate of tuberculosis. But this conclusion has not been accepted by all. Veterinarians even doubt the efficacy of B.C.G. against cattle tuberculosis. S. A. Petroff, director of the Trudeau tuberculosis clinic at Saranac, N. Y., is strongly opposed to its use, for he fears that this weakened tubercle bacillus may suddenly become virulent and play havoc.

And while the merits and dangers of B.C.G. vaccination are being discussed, two other methods of immunization against tuberculosis are being tried out. Dr. Stephen Maher of Philadelphia uses a substance he has prepared from colonies of cocci and diplococci, bacteria which, he reports, have been produced by the tubercle bacilli raised on his special medium containing glycerine and milk. Maher, who for twenty-five years has battled tuberculosis, read a paper in 1933 before a medical gathering on *The Progeny of the Tubercle Bacilli.* He claimed that these cocci and diplococci are produced by the tubercle bacilli and have the power of destroying their parents. He has already tried his preparation on animals, and further experiments are under way to prepare for tests of the efficacy of his vaccine on humans.

The third method of immunizing against tuberculosis is already being tried with humans. In Colorado, two healthy lifers, with the promise of executive clemency from the governor of that State, offered themselves as human guinea pigs for inoculation with virulent tubercle bacilli. A new vaccine was then tried on them. This vaccine was developed by H. J. Corper of the National Jewish Hospital at Denver over a period of fifteen years and had already been tried on animals. The first injections in humans were given in April, 1934, and seven months later the two men showed no signs of tuberculous infection. The experiment is being continued, and, if it proves promising, larger numbers and more adequate controls will be used. In the meantime, medicine remains skeptical. A convention of the National Tuberculosis Association at Saranac in 1935 went on record that as yet, in spite of the apparent effectiveness of B.C.G. vaccination, no artificial method of immunization has been discovered. Men are still groping for an effective weapon against this ancient and stubborn "weed of sluggish growth" which flourishes in every organ of the body, especially the lungs.

Mankind is still struggling against a number of other infectious diseases caused not by bacteria but by the so-called viruses or filter passers, so small that they can squeeze through the finest of filters, so tiny that even the ultramicroscope will not reveal their presence. Oddly enough, the first great scourge to be arrested by blundering medicine belonged to this group of virus diseases. For centuries it had been known that milkmaids and farmhands who caught the cowpox were never attacked by smallpox. Then someone — no one knows who — reasoned that perhaps if the sores of the relatively innocuous cowpox were rubbed into a scar in a healthy individual, it might save him from the dreaded smallpox which, in the eighteenth century alone, struck down sixty million people in Europe. In Turkey, it was the practice of old women to inject matter from smallpox sores into young children whom they had pricked with a needle. This procedure was based on no scientific experimentation. It was purely empirical and the custom was continued because it did save the children from the pock or death. In China, powdered pock scales were blown into the nose. In India, children were wrapped in clothes worn by smallpox victims. African slave owners inoculated their slaves with the smallpox to prolong their usefulness. The negroes of Nubia had practiced this preventive method against smallpox from time immemorial. In 1721 Zabdiel Boylston of Boston *inoculated* his only son against smallpox, and was almost killed by a mob for doing it. In 1789 Edward Jenner, an English physician, *vaccinated* (from *vacca*, a cow) his eighteen-months-old son by placing part of a cowpox postule in some needle pricks which he had made in the child's arm, and raised a furor. The Royal Society refused to print his first report on vaccination. A Society of Anti-Vaccinationists was organized and functions to this day. But vaccination against smallpox gradually spread over the world. A year after two millions of her subjects had died of smallpox Catherine, Empress of Russia, had herself and many of her subjects vaccinated. Among the first to get this treatment were Napoleon's soldiers, the entire family of Thomas Jefferson, and various royal children. A queer conquest before the age of the test tube, the microscope, and the knowledge of immunology. Even today, when the whole world can be made immune to smallpox, we have not yet isolated the virus of this disease.

Influenza may be another of the virus diseases. It still ravages whole populations in recurring epidemics. During the World War millions died of it. During the 1918 pandemic tens of thousands melted away before this strange destroyer. As a result of it, the Metropolitan Life Insurance Company of America alone paid out twenty-eight million dollars in death benefits! The fight against influenza has been long and discouraging. Starting with the possibility that a bacillus discovered in 1889 by Pfeiffer rather than a virus might be the cause, thousands of experiments were carried out to prove this theory. But the Pfeiffer germ has been found in the throats of healthy individuals, and is not always present in those suffering from influenza. Monkeys as well as men were inoculated with Pfeiffer's bacillus, but the results of these years of investigation remained inconclusive. The possibility of a filterable virus was also considered. At the Rockefeller Institute for Medical Research experiments were performed on rabbits and monkeys. When the filtered nasal washings of influenza sufferers were injected into the nose, throat, eyes, blood, or under the skin of the animals, nothing seemed to happen, but when these washings were sent into the trachea so that they ran down into the lungs, symptoms of the " flu " followed. The filtered sputum of influenza patients was even fed to healthy individuals. Twelve Japanese in 1912 were the first human guinea pigs to undergo this test, and thousands of others have offered themselves for such risky experiments. But again the results were not always consistent. Some contracted the disease, others did not. After almost twenty years of investigation, the Rockefeller Institute was still at work on this problem when in 1934 the news came that the virus cause of influenza had been found by research workers of the National Institute for Medical Research in London. The following year another important discovery was made there. An animal susceptible to human influenza had been found. It was the ferret, which after being inoculated directly into its respiratory tract with the virus from the throat of an infected person came down with the disease, and in its blood was present an antibody which could protect a mouse against this disease. They then prepared what appears to be an effective anti-influenza serum for animals. This work has been confirmed in other laboratories such as the Rockefeller Institute and the Yale Medical School. We may in fact be on the threshold now of an effective method of immunization against human influenza. This, if true, will mark a new conquest in the history of medicine. In the meantime, the doctor still waits on nature to save his patient. The next pandemic, however, will find a corps of experts in this field who will perhaps be ready to save most influenza patients and prevent its spread.

Less deadly in its direct attack, but none the less dangerous, is the common cold which still plagues most of us. M. J. Rosenau, one of the most assiduous workers in this field, says, " Could the sum total of suffering, inconveniences, sequelae, and economic loss resulting from common colds be obtained, it would at once promote these infections from the trivial into the rank of the serious diseases." A bad cold may really be the "flu" and lead to pneumonia. It is likely that many colds are mild cases of influenza. Running noses, headaches, and watery eyes must be seriously reckoned with. It is believed by some that the common cold and the common sore throat are responsible for many cases of nephritis or Bright's disease (inflammation of the kidneys). After a generation of research by some of the ablest investigators both here and abroad, what can we say of their results? Very little. The common cold still baffles. The present status of the problem was succinctly summed up in the answer that one of the leaders in this investigation gave to the question, "What do you do when your body aches, and you feel weak and feverish and feel a bad cold coming on"? "I go home, take a laxative, get into bed, eat lightly, and stay there until I get well." It is indeed difficult to find a problem more complex than the cause of the common cold.

Two lines of investigation are still being followed in the attempt to solve some of the problems connected with the nature and prevention or cure of the common cold. Some are studying the nature of the bacterial world in the upper respiratory tract, while others are attacking the cold on the assumption that it is caused by a filterable virus. The three most ambitious investigations are being carried on by a commission of the Columbia University Medical School which has functioned for more than a decade, by a number of men connected with Harvard's Medical School, and by men working under the John J. Abel Fund for Research on the Common Cold at Johns Hopkins University. The Harvard group have completed four expeditions since 1927 headed chiefly by Wilson G. Smillie. They made a study of the common cold among isolated groups living at St. Johns in the Virgin Islands, at a Labrador trading post, at the little village of Happy Hallow in Alabama, and at Spitzbergen, the most northern permanent settlement in the world. The miners at Spitzbergen, it was found, seldom catch cold even though they are subjected daily to rapid and severe changes of temperature. But soon after the supply ship comes in from the outside world, colds break out. The consensus of opinion to-day is that the common cold is caused by a virus. It is a virus, not simply a draught or sudden chill, which is the cause. It is furthermore believed that a person with a cold is infectious for about three days.

Alphonse R. Dochez of the Columbia University Medical School Commission believes that further investigation as to the part played both by bacteria and by virus should be undertaken. He is of the opinion that some filterable virus prepares the soil for the bacteria. " In swine influenza," he told the American Medical Association in the summer of 1933, " there exists a virus which by itself produces only the mildest of disease; if administered together with a culture of certain bacteria it gives rise to contagious swine influenza." The culture of the influenza bacteria alone, even in large doses, produces no ill effect. The virus must also be present. This may also be true for the common cold. The conquest of the common cold, according to Dochez, lies in the development of some vaccine which will act against the virus rather than against the bacteria. Vaccines against the common cold are on the market and have been used both by private practitioners and by medical staffs of large corporations in the effort to cut down loss of general efficiency due to colds. The value of these vaccines is highly problematical. They may be as effective as the string around a toad's neck, which was long supposed to cure a cold. The healing vaccine which will stave off the cold, prevent influenza, and banish pneumonia is still to be discovered. In the meantime, millions of dollars are being made on hundreds of patent medicines which have been concocted against colds and coughs.

The common cold is often followed by some form of pneumonia, one of mankind's severest scourges. It occurs chiefly in temperate climates during the winter and early spring, and attacks us mostly in infancy and old age. The human race does not even enjoy temporary immunity after an attack of most types of this disease. In fact, we can be hardly out of one attack of pneumonia when another attack may lay us low. Some believe that almost any organism that becomes active in the lungs may produce pneumonia. The most frequent organisms however found in the lungs of pneumonia patients are the different types of pneumococci bacteria. Pneumonia is spread by secretions of the nose and throat but it seems certain that other predisposing factors play a part in its incidence, such as general debility and hereditary susceptibility.

In 1913, after a classic series of experiments, members of the Rockefeller Institute divided pneumonia into four types depending upon the presence in the patient of four groups of pneumococci having different immunological traits, that is, reacting differently towards blood serums. Rapid methods of pneumonia-type determinations were then developed. With years of the most painstaking investigations an anti-pneumococcus serum has been made available against pneumonia of Type I. This serum is obtained from the blood of a horse which has been injected intravenously with a pneumococcus grown on broth and then killed with formalin or heat. This Type I serum, if given during the first four days of illness, is said to be fairly effective. Unfortunately Type I is neither the most common type nor the most fatal. For Type II another serum has been developed but it is frankly of doubtful potency. For Type III where the fatality is highest and for Group IV where the subtypes are numerous and difficult to identify (Group IV activates at least thirty different types of pneumonia), science at present offers very little in the way of preventive vaccines or protective serums. The Rockefeller Institute, The United States Public Health Service, and numerous other research organizations are still hard at work on this problem. Several hopeful lines of attack are being pursued. Lloyd D. Felton of Harvard, who has made important contributions in pneumonia serums, has been trying out a new vaccine made of chemically treated pneumococci on himself, on hundreds of C.C.C. men, and on other volunteers, in the hope of establishing the efficacy of this new preventive against all types of pneumonia. It is still in the experimental stage. The Mellon Institute and the Mercy Hospital of Pittsburgh are fighting pneumonia in mice with oral administrations of quinine derivatives. They are ready to try this new method of treatment on humans. Yandell Henderson of the Yale Medical School has encouraged the administration of carbon dioxide and oxygen mixtures to patients after major surgical operations and near drownings which often result in pneumonia. He believes this is an effective treatment against all secondary pneumonia. In the meantime, pneumonia still kills by the tens of thousands each year in the United States.

Yellow fever — what martyrdom and what scientific skill have been expended in its eradication! We know already how it is transmitted by the mosquito, and with care and money we can banish it both from Africa and South America, as we have driven it from North America. The specific cause, however, remains a mystery. Chief among the great microbe hunters who fought yellow jack was Hideyo Noguchi, who came here in 1899 from the mountains of northern Japan. Through the jungles of Ecuador and Peru, through Yucatan and Brazil, Noguchi hunted out the victims of this fever. In spite of a left hand crippled in infancy, with marvelous skill he developed a special medium in which to cultivate the causative organism of yellow fever found in the blood of its victims. He worked like one possessed, sleeping on a mat before his laboratory table for a few hours, then awakening to resume his work. One day he believed he had tracked down the cause of yellow fever. He thought the culprit was one of those deadly spiral bacteria of the leptospira type. Noguchi called it *Leptospira icteroides*. He got mosquitoes to carry the spiral bacterium to guinea pigs, and then obtained the same spirilli from the livers and kidneys of his animals. He claimed to have obtained this organism from the blood of human sufferers. Others tried his technique, but failed to obtain his results. Noguchi, convinced that he was right, called them inexperienced schoolboys.

Then Adrian Stokes and his associates went out, in 1927, to West Africa where an epidemic was raging. They repeated the work of the wily little Japanese, but failed to get his results. They tried another theory, that of Manson who in 1914 said yellow fever might be caused by a filterable virus. Their first results seemed to indicate that the causative agent of yellow fever was a filter passer. Stokes died of the fever, and Noguchi, reading his report, hurried to Africa to test his findings. Noguchi was weak and worn out from work and diabetes. He knew the dangers that lurked on the Gold Coast, but refused to listen to Flexner and other friends. " I am not afraid," he told them. " I just want to finish this piece of work. I have been put into the world to do it." His end came in Accra, struck down at fifty-one by this same fever the cause of which still remains a riddle.

But the failure to isolate the causative agent of yellow fever has not prevented research workers from attempting to find a liquid potent enough to protect one from the bite of the stegomyia mosquito. The isolation of a filterable virus is not essential to the development of a protective serum. In 1927 Stokes found that *macacus rhesus*, the sacred monkey of India, could be infected with yellow fever virus. But the infected animal refused to return a serum effective enough to combat the disease. Three years later Max Theiler of Harvard succeeded in transmitting yellow fever to the mouse, an experiment which had been tried before but without success. The Harvard worker used an ingenious technique. While he was injecting the yellow fever virus, he also injected some irritating substance into the brain, and the white mouse came down with a typical case of yellow fever. Here was another and smaller experimental animal on whom yellow fever serum work could be carried out.

At the Rockefeller Institute in New York, the virulent virus of yellow fever from a human patient was first passed through two hundred white mice. Thus weakened, the virus was then mixed with the blood serum of people who had recovered from an attack, and then injected into a mouse by the Theiler technique. The mouse was actually immunized against fresh virulent yellow fever. Then they took the next step. They called for volunteers. The first human vaccination was performed on May 13, 1931, and protected the man. After trying the serum on a number of other laboratory workers and finding it safe, they tested it in 1932 on a group of fifteen criminals who, with pardons as rewards, offered themselves for experiment. In every case the new serum was found effective.

Soon after, a dried mixture was made of this serum and, embedded in ice, was rushed to the Rockefeller medical men fighting yellow fever in Africa. Several Rockefeller workers had already succumbed to the deadly bite of the stegomyia. However, after the new serum was used not a single one of more than sixty members of the African commission vaccinated with the new serum was attacked by the fever. It seems to be a perfect protective agent although it is not effective when given after the onset of the disease. Missionaries, explorers, and business men traveling through yellow fever areas are also being immunized by this method. However, there is difficulty in spreading this protective serum because large supplies of yellow fever blood serum from survivors of this malady are at present not available.

One attack of yellow fever seems to insure almost lasting immunity. This was shown by injecting the virus of yellow fever into the blood of one of the original volunteers of the Reed drama in Cuba. After more than thirty years since his yellow fever attack he was found to be immune. The virus of yellow fever was then tested on various groups which had never been exposed to yellow fever. Whole groups of Canadians were found to be immune. The negro, it was found, is much more resistant to this disease than is the white man. This investigation indicated that millions were undoubtedly immune. But other millions had to be protected. Already a start in this direction has been made in Africa. In time the use of the yellow fever serum will be extended to protect not only the white man, but thousands of African carriers of a mild form of yellow fever, as well as the huge reservoir of the East which also remains a menace to the West. We may be at the threshold of the day when yellow fever, consigned to the limbo of forgotten diseases, will no longer enter the ports of the world in recurring waves to snatch millions of victims.

Of all the modern diseases which steal swiftly and without warning into the homes of poor and rich alike, none is more terrifying than poliomyelitis, commonly known as polio or infantile paralysis. It strikes principally in changeable climates and concentrates its attack on children. Adults, however, are not immune. Franklin D. Roosevelt, for example, became its victim when he was in the prime of life. Sir Walter Scott, on the other hand, was singled out in infancy. If it does not kill outright, it leaves its victims permanently paralyzed and deformed, for it attacks the cells of the spinal cord which controls the motions of muscles, and these cells cannot be regenerated. Fortunately, however, the mind is spared from the assaults of this virus. How it suddenly appears in epidemic form and how it spreads are still not understood. Direct contact does not seem necessary for its transmission for rarely do we find two members of the same household attacked at the same time. There is the possibility that it is spread by mild carriers of the disease just as in the cases of typhoid and diphtheria.

Chief among those who have wrestled with poliomyelitis stands the former director of the Rockefeller Institute for Medical Research in New York, Simon Flexner, one of Welch's first assistants, who has struggled for a quarter of a century to immunize mankind against this crippling virus. The disease is known to have existed at least four thousand years ago, as is evidenced by typical paralytic deformities found in bones of Egyptian mummies, but its infectious and communicable nature was not established until an epidemic in Stockholm in 1889.

During a pandemic of polio twenty years later, Landsteiner, the Rockefeller research man who recently earned the Nobel Prize for his work on blood grouping, succeeded in transmitting the disease to macacus monkeys — the only animal thus far known to be capable of contracting this illness. He injected into the animal emulsions of the spinal cord from children stricken with the disease, and found that the monkey reacted as humans do. Flexner repeated the experiment, and then developed a method of transmitting the disease from monkey to monkey, thus making the further study of this illness a laboratory possibility. Flexner and Noguchi worked together in 1913 and were hot on the trail of the causative organism, but in spite of their masterly work they failed to isolate the agent. Today, men of science classify it among the virus diseases.

Flexner has recently written that " the evidence is strong that the virus of infantile paralysis is normally confined to the human host, and passes from individual to individual in the secretions of the nose and throat." The virus travels to the brain and spinal cord by way of the nerves of smell located in the membrane of the nose. Flexner calls it a " smelling " infection, and finds that by severing the olfactory nerves of a monkey, the animal will not contract the disease. This has been confirmed. In the case of monkeys it had been noticed that one attack of polio seemed to protect them from further attacks. Hence the possibility of the presence of chemical substances produced in the body to fight the virus. As far back as 1910, Flexner suggested the protective use of the blood serum of a convalescent patient, injected into the muscle tissues. During the 1931 epidemic in the eastern part of the United States, more than 140 quarts of human convalescent serum were collected and used. Interesting results were obtained by the Harvard Polio Commission, as well as by other groups, but no definite conclusions could be announced and not too much confidence could be placed in this method. If the blood serum of a healthy parent or of a convalescent person is injected into the patient before the actual onset of paralysis or during its very early stages, it seems, in some cases, to arrest the spread of the disease. But unfortunately, early diagnosis of this infection is not clean cut (the incubation period is believed by some to be 14 days), and many a child is overcome before the doctor reports with his serum.

A number of other serums have been tried. Rosenau used on thirteen hundred patients an antistreptococcus serum obtained from the horse. Two other serums developed in 1934 are being used on large numbers of children. One was prepared by John A. Kolmer of Temple University Medical School of Philadelphia and consists of the virus of polio obtained from the spinal cords of infected monkeys. The virus is devitalized by treatment with a chemical, sodium ricinoleate, obtained from the castor bean. One monkey can supply enough vaccine to immunize fifty children. Before testing its effectiveness on children, Kolmer tried it on himself, and his two sons. The vaccine is injected under the skin and if administered at least six weeks before exposure it is said to protect against infantile paralysis.

The other vaccine was prepared by Maurice Brodie of New York City. It, too, is obtained from the spinal cord of a rhesus monkey which has been inoculated with the virus of the disease. The virus is killed with formalin and not merely weakened as is Kolmer's. Dr. Brodie, two of his women assistants, and seventy-two-year-old William H. Park director of the New York City Research Laboratories, who has further developed this vaccine, inoculated themselves with the vaccine before using it on children. After this " purely routine matter " as Park called it, weekly shipments of the Brodie-Park vaccine were sent by plane to a stricken area in California where about seven hundred children were inoculated in 1935 as a protective measure. Thousands of children in New York City were also inoculated with it that same year. Not a single one of the inoculated children, it was reported, came down with polio, and Park believes this vaccine to be 85 per cent effective, giving an active immunity for at least five months.

Such reports are hopeful but the end of the road has by no means been reached. These vaccines are only protective vaccines. They are powerless to save if injected after the onset of the disease. The inoculation of the whole population with this vaccine were it proved effective would be a colossal job and a needless one since it has been estimated that only one child in a thousand is susceptible to the virus of polio. What is needed is a sure susceptibility test like the Schick test for diphtheria. Besides, it will take years to gauge the effectiveness of the new serums. In the meantime W. Lloyd Aycock who, as head of the Harvard Polio Commission, has wrestled with infantile paralysis for seventeen years maintains that control and prevention of this dread illness is very far away. He considers vaccination hazardous and, on the ground that polio is of an hereditary basis, believes that some other method of attack must be found.

There is still, however, one definite hope in this dismal story of failure. One attack of this virus means life protection, and the epidemics of the last decades have become less virulent. The 1916 epidemic in this country killed 21 out of 100,000 population, the 1931 epidemic took only 8 out of the same number, the 1933 visitation destroyed less than one out of 100,000 of our population and the 1935 epidemic was even milder. And today medical science confronts the next outbreak with less trepidation.

Other viruses continue to attack man. When the first epidemic of *encephalitis lethargica* (incorrectly called sleeping sickness) reached this country in 1918, it struck a people tired out from the horrors of war and the ravages of influenza. It raised its head suddenly and brought consternation and misery. Inflammation of the central nervous system produced symptoms of fever, headache, stiffness of the neck and back, restlessness, convulsions in children, and usually drowsiness. Tens of thousands of cases were reported. The attack was long and virulent enough to set our medical researchers to work on this perplexing problem. As usual, an effort was made to find an animal suitable for laboratory experimentation. In 1919, the Mount Sinai Hospital in New York City issued a bulletin announcing that they had given the disease to monkeys by injecting them with emulsified brain tissues of men killed by the disease. Even the washings of the nose of sufferers would communicate the illness to the monkey. Others worked with rabbits. But no germ could be isolated, and all the data seemed to indicate that here, too, a virus was responsible.

In the meantime, the epidemic had passed and human sufferers of the disease were no longer available. The work shifted to other sections where here and there the virus found its way into man. In 1923, another epidemic broke out. Approximately one thousand cases were reported in New York, of which three hundred forty-nine resulted in death. Ten years later on July 31, 1933, the first case of what turned out to be one of our most severe epidemics of encephalitis appeared in St. Louis. By September of the same year, it had killed ninety-eight out of six hundred and thirty-five patients. There were a number of strange variations in this 1933 attack. It came in high summer rather than in winter. It attacked the middle-aged and old rather than the young. The United States Public Health Service rushed its research men to the area. Congress appropriated twenty-five thousand dollars for a campaign to learn more about encephalitis. The etiology was still an enigma. Some believed it due to a poison, elaborated in the gastrointestinal tract, which attacks the central nervous system. The possibility of an insect carrier was not overlooked. Research workers of the United States Public Health Service permitted mosquitoes which had been observed sucking the blood of encephalitis patients to bite them also. Nothing happened. Then ten short-term convicts from a Mississippi jail volunteered for an extension of this test. They risked the tortures of brain inflammation for an early freedom, and left the laboratories a few weeks later well men, for the mosquito again was proved innocent of carrying this disease. The National Institute of Health and the Rockefeller Institute working with mice (recently found to be susceptible to the sickness) reported at the close of 1933 that encephalitis patients develop immune bodies in their blood which when injected in mice protected them. They then prepared a serum which when injected under the skin of the mouse's abdomen gives the animal immunity for at least five weeks. Will this protective serum which, as yet, has not been tried on man save us from the horrors of another such epidemic? Only another epidemic will give the answer. We still dread encephalitis, against which medicine has not as yet found an effective weapon.

The World War brought forth other agents of destruction besides those fashioned by man out of steel and chemicals. Typhus fever raged in Serbia, Poland, Russia, and elsewhere. Thousands died and millions prayed to be saved from its ravages. Typhus had accompanied armies before. As *jail fever*, it had also spread in prisons. This malady had appeared at Granada in the days of Columbus, and as *el tarbadiglo*, the red cloak, it had played havoc with a defenceless people. During the four years preceding 1923, seven million cases of typhus had been reported in Russia alone. A third of the doctors caring for these victims in Siberia contracted the disease and died. The mortality rate is as high as sixty per cent during epidemics. Typhus is a disease of filth and poverty. Its onset is sudden, its duration short. Charles Nicolle showed that the carriers of this " ancient death " are the body louse and the flea which transmit it from man to man with the help probably of the rat. In 1898 Nathan E. Brill discovered among a number of immigrants in New York City what he thought was a hitherto unrecognized disease. It was named *Brill's disease* until it was realized that the sickness was really typhus which its victims had brought over from Europe.

In addition to this European type of typhus there is another variety — the New World typhus. The rat is definitely known to be a carrier of this type of typhus. The virus was found in the brains of rats, and it remained a question whether it was carried to man by the bite of a flea which had sucked the blood of such infected rats. Rolla E. Dyer undertook to study the method of transmission of the American variety of typhus. Dyer is a clergyman's son who, after practising medicine for a while, joined that small, brave band at the United States Public Health Service in Washington which was fighting new diseases. Before many weeks had passed Dyer, like Goldberger, and several other medical investigators of the Service before him, contracted typhus fever. While still convalescent, he called for some body lice which he knew thrived on human blood. He placed them in a pill box, strapped them to his leg below the knee where he had inflicted an open wound, and nursed them with his fresh blood for weeks. Then the typhus-infected lice were permitted to bite healthy monkeys. The monkeys contracted the disease.

Dyer has been working with a vaccine which he hopes will protect men from the bite of the cootie. He mashed typhus-infected fleas in a salt solution, added carbolic acid to weaken the causative agent, and then injected it into guinea pigs, half of which developed an immunity within a few months. When he has improved his preparation, he intends trying it on himself before calling for other human volunteers. In the meantime, Hans Zinsser of Harvard is working on the same problem in cooperation with the United States Public Health Service and the Mexican government. The type of typhus which appears both in the southeastern part of the United States and in Mexico is less virulent than the European type. Zinsser employed a different technique, using the typhus organism obtained from rats weakened by X-ray treatment. This was injected into a horse, and the horse serum then tried on guinea pigs. Some hopeful results have been obtained, but Zinsser reported in 1933 that his work was " only a beginning and much remains to be done " to immunize mankind against one of its deadliest enemies.

The causative agent of typhus is still unknown. In the closing days of 1933, word reached America that the Metchnikoff Institute of Moscow had succeeded, after thirty-five years of continuous work, in cultivating the typhus germ. This report has not been confirmed, and a filterable virus is still generally assumed to be the cause of typhus. The presence of Rickettsia bodies in typhus victims has not yet been explained. These little bodies, unlike bacteria in that they cannot be cultivated, were first discovered by Ricketts in 1910 in the intestinal tract of lice fed on typhus-infected blood. Their nature is still a matter of conjecture. Fresh from college, Howard T. Ricketts had gone out to the Bitter Root Valley of Montana to study Rocky Mountain Spotted Fever. Sheep herders and hunters had been its commonest victims. Using the monkey as his test animal, he found that this disease was carried by the common wood or dog tick.

In the bodies of the wood tick he found the same Rickettsia bodies which he had seen in typhus-infected lice. After preparing a serum which could effectively protect man against Rocky Mountain Spotted Fever, Ricketts continued his researches on typhus. In 1910 another epidemic of typhus broke out in Mexico and Ricketts went there to help, only to succumb to it.

In that chamber of horrors which is human disease, leprosy is no mild denizen. Mankind has feared it more than death. In India three million lepers are slowly decaying to a wretched doom. Twenty thousand of these unfortunates live death every day within the borders of American territory, chiefly in the Philippines. There are about a thousand lepers in the United States proper of whom 350 are being cared for by the National Leper Home at Carville, La. Our treatment of these afflicted has changed completely. In Babylonia they were driven into the deserts to die. In Europe the leper was considered legally dead, and the Christian Church conducted the burial service over him while he was still alive. Within much more recent times efforts have been made to control the disease by injecting into the bodies of its unfortunates all sorts of chemicals including such dyes as methylene blue and eosin. Many years ago it was discovered that chaulmoogra oil and its derivatives injected into the muscles could arrest the development of the disease and at least hold it in check. This was an empirical discovery, and the cause of the disease is still not firmly established.

Leprosy is believed to be very infectious, but the method of its transmission is still unknown. Almost a hundred years ago Danielsson, a Norwegian, gave evidence of the supreme and not uncommon heroism of medical researchers. He inoculated himself with the tissue, blood and pus of lepers, yet did not develop the disease. There is still much controversy over the cause of human leprosy. The possibility of a virus cause has not been eliminated. Several workers at the laboratories of the Leonard Wood Memorial for the Eradication of Leprosy claim to have isolated a leprosy germ reported by Hansen in 1872 and to have grown it in monkeys and chickens. Ernest L. Walker, professor of tropical medicine at the University of California, went to Honolulu to test a different theory. He found rats carrying a disease, rat leprosy, similar to human leprosy. The causative agent of rat leprosy seems to enter the animal through its nose or skin. He believes that the same method of infection might be true for humans.

Rabies is about where Pasteur left it half a century ago. An efficient vaccine cures the patient, but the virus, although Noguchi claimed to have cultivated it in 1913, still remains hidden. The rabies vaccine is an attenuated vaccine. The diagnosis of this malady is sure and quick, thanks to the discovery by Negri in 1903 of tiny bodies called Negri bodies. These are found present within the nerve cells of the spinal cord and the saliva of victims of rabies. Their nature is still unknown.

At the present time measles, whooping cough, scarlet fever and diphtheria are among the most common diseases of childhood. According to the general opinion of bacteriologists the first two should be grouped with the virus diseases. Ruth Tunnicliff of Chicago, however, believes measles is caused by a streptococcus bacterium. In 1927 she introduced a goat serum of questionable protective value against this rarely fatal disease. William H. Park has used a serum of convalescents, first introduced in 1918. At one time Park obtained striking success with the convalescent serum of a group of students who came down with measles during an epidemic in a southern university. He obtained enough serum to test the efficacy of this method on more than two thousand children. At present work is going along in this field with the aid of monkeys whom the Rockefeller workers discovered could be given the disease. The invaluable guinea pig is also employed. One attack almost invariably leads to a permanent immunity.

Whooping cough is a disease chiefly of children, and while not frequently fatal caused the death of 6000 children in 1932 out of 300,000 cases reported in this country. One apparently promising method of protection against it has been worked out within the last few years. A vaccine developed by Louis W. Sauer is made from a type of bacteria commonly found present during whooping cough, although the cause of whooping cough may be a virus. The bacilli are cultured in human blood and then killed with phenol. The vaccine is injected into the child over a period of several weeks as a prophylactic against the disease. While recognizing that these injections have no harmful effects, the Journal of the American Medical Association went on record in March, 1934, as follows: "Although Sauer's work appears promising, the Council on Pharmacy and Chemistry does not feel justified at this time in recognizing the use of *pertussis* (whooping cough) vaccine of any sort of therapeutic prophylaxis until more convincing evidence becomes available." In spite of this, Sauer's vaccine is being used by hundreds of physicians, and this method of protection is gradually spreading. Perhaps within the next few years this or some other vaccine will have definitely established its value as a protective agent against whooping cough.

For many years scarlet fever, which for centuries had occurred in epidemic form and took heavy human toll, was considered a virus disease. Later, a streptococcus was suspected as the causative agent and a hunt was started to track it down. In 1923 Dr. George F. Dick and his wife, also a physician, carried out what turned out to be crucial experiments in this field. From the abscess on the finger of a nurse suffering from scarlet fever they prepared a culture of streptococci. The throats of human volunteers were then swabbed with this germ. Out of the five volunteers one developed the disease and another contracted a sore throat. The throats of five other people were then swabbed with the filtrate of the same cultures. None were the worse for this treatment, indicating that a virus was not responsible for the onset of the disease since the virus would have been present in the filtrate of this scarlet fever culture. Eleven days later, this second group was then swabbed with the streptococcus culture and one of them developed scarlet fever. The disease was certainly not of virus origin.

The Dicks then made another important advance. They

proved the presence in the blood of scarlet fever patients of a poison or toxin produced by the streptococcus responsible for this disease. They prepared a toxin-antitoxin to lower the severity of the disease and check its ravages. Then still another step was taken. They developed a vaccine which, when injected early enough, gave the person an immunity against scarlet. While this immunity is only of short duration, it is effective and widely used by nurses and for children in hospitals. The mortality from this disease has been consistently and steadily decreasing. The success of the Dicks after twenty years of work was due partly to the fact that they used human subjects rather than animals in their research. For this great achievement, the Cameron Prize of the University of Edinburgh was awarded them in 1933. At the present time there are three main centers in this country where both the serum and the toxoid may be quickly obtained.

The story of the almost complete eradication of diphtheria is well known. Soon after Pasteur's epochal discoveries, the Klebs-Loeffler bacillus was shown to be the cause of this disease. Then the discovery that this bacillus produced poisons or toxins which could be separated, led to further animal experimentation. It was found by Behring that this poison when injected into the guinea pig in larger and larger doses produced antibodies or antitoxins in their bodies. The blood serum of these animals containing these antibodies could protect other animals from the germ of diphtheria. The value of these facts was at once recognized. Horses were injected with the toxin of diphtheria. They contracted a mild case of diphtheria and produced large quantities of the antitoxin of diphtheria in their blood serum. This blood serum was tried on animals and then children and it worked a miracle. Dr. Biggs was in Europe at the time of these demonstrations (1894) and he cabled back to William H. Park in New York: "Start the horses. Antitoxin great success." Toxin-antitoxin treatment was then given to children to build up a permanent immunity against the disease. Then the Schick test was developed. This is to determine whether a child is immune or not to diphtheria. In this test, developed by Bela Schick, now pediatrician at Mt. Sinai Hospital in New York City, a tiny amount of weakened diphtheria toxin is injected under the skin of the forearm. If the area around the point of injection becomes inflamed it indicates that the child is likely to get the disease if exposed to the germ. In the case of the child who has been naturally or artificially immunized against diphtheria, no such inflammation results. Recently a new toxin-antitoxin substitute has been introduced called the diptheria toxoid. This contains the toxin weakened by formaldehyde, and contains no serum proteins. Today no child need die of diphtheria. Its complete eradication is now a matter of vigilance only.

Many diseases caused by bacteria such as diphtheria and typhoid are now under control. The virus diseases are still among the most difficult ones to conquer. At least fifteen diseases of man belong apparently to the filterable virus class. The mosaic disease of tobacco plants (the first virus disease to be identified), foot-and-mouth disease of cattle, and more than forty other ailments of plants and animals have been laid at the door of the virus, the nature of which still remains a mystery. Various theories have been advanced to explain the virus. Some believe these organisms are bacteria so small that even the finest filter cannot hold them back. Others consider them toxins, since they cannot be cultivated. Life in the making — missing links, floating in some nebulous world between the living and the inanimate — affords another explanation. But out of the complexity of the problem has already emerged some apparent advance in the solution.

A British medical officer, F. W. Twort, reported a curious phenomenon he had observed while preparing vaccines during the World War. A colony of bacteria spontaneously underwent a sort of degeneration. Twort stained the culture and found a mass of debris instead of clearly shaped bacteria. More surprising was the fact that this mangled colony, after being filtered, yielded a fluid which could cause a similar degeneration in a fresh colony of the same bacteria. He suggested that a particular virus present in the bacteria was responsible for the degeneration of the bacteria, for when the fluid was added to other types of bacteria, the phenomenon could not be repeated.

Two years later Felix d'Herelle, a French Canadian working at the Pasteur Institute in Paris, came across a similar phenomenon. A squadron of cavalry had been struck by an epidemic of dysentery. D'Herelle had prepared cultures of the Shiga bacillus of this malady and passed them through fine porcelain filters. He accidentally added some of this filtrate to a fresh colony of the bacillus of dysentery and found that the Shiga bacillus was actually destroyed by that filtrate. A case of the destroyer being wiped out by one of its own products, or something which grew on it. He named this unknown entity *bacteriophage* (bacterium devourer), popularly known as *phage*. He reported that on the addition of a drop of this liquid to a colony of Shiga bacilli, the germs first grew faster, then imbibed water, swelled, burst, and finally disappeared completely. This was hailed as a revolutionary discovery — as epoch-making as that of Pasteur. It opened up a prospect for mankind's complete annihilation of all infectious diseases. Phage became as popular as microbe, inspiring Sinclair Lewis to write *Arrowsmith*. The discovery sent thousands of bacteriologists searching for phage in the intestinal tract of men, in pus, urine, sewers, aquarium waters, cesspools, soil, and polluted water of streams, and ended in the isolation of more than fifty types of phage, each specific for its own particular disease. This agent has been used with varying success against cholera, dysentery, blood poisoning, boils, and skin eruptions. It is a new ally to the white corpuscles. D'Herelle pictured the rise and fall of epidemics as the struggle between the bacteria and their phages. His accidental find started a controversy comparable to that which followed Elie Metchnikoff's discovery of the function of the white blood corpuscles or phagocytes — a controversy which still rages in bacteriological and immunological laboratories.

But the full chapter of this discovery is still to be written, even though the first sentence has already been penned. Twort later said that phage was either an animate or inanimate catalyst, that is, a substance whose mere presence produced changes although the catalyst itself was not permanently effected. Phage is destroyed by heat, chemicals, and ultraviolet light. D'Herelle pictured it as a mutant of its bacterial parent. Philip Hadley of the University of Michigan reinvestigated the whole problem. He actually succeeded in obtaining the filterable or virus *stage* of the microbes of cholera, typhoid, dysentery, and diphtheria by growing them on special media furnished with different chemicals and foods.

Then came Arthur Isaac Kendall, an admirer of Hadley. He was an eminent bacteriologist whom Welch had recommended for more than one difficult investigation. He had a hunch he could reverse the process — convert the filterable virus of influenza into a visible form which could be grown under control and possibly made to produce a potent serum against itself. To Kendall it seemed that phage was nothing else but the invisible form of the visible microbe which it attacked. In other words, certain bacteria had the power of changing into an invisible organism — small enough to pass through a filter. Kendall reasoned that perhaps the food upon which the organism lived might be responsible for this change in size. He knew that germs feed upon proteins in the body, whereas the common medium upon which they are grown outside the body contains only peptones, the split fragments of these more complex proteins. Therefore, he attempted to grow these filter passers on a new special medium, his K medium.

The K medium was prepared from the small intestine of man, dog, pig, or rabbit. Non-proteins were removed with alcohol, benzol dissolved out the fat, a salt solution was added to the dried extract, and then it was sterilized in a steam bath. On January 2, 1931, Kendall put eight rabbits under observation. Then he called for 10 cc. of the blood of an influenza patient lying in a Chicago hospital. This he injected into the rabbits who thereupon promptly developed the disease. Then he took the blood of both the human and rabbit influenza patients and planted them separately on the K medium and incubated them for ten days at 30° C. The medium became cloudy, but nothing appeared under the microscope. Kendall kept transferring the blood to fresh K-culture media. Then on March 10 he injected a few drops of the cloudy yet bacterially invisible culture into the ear vein of three healthy rabbits. The next day the rabbits were sneezing paroxysmally. They had the " flu."

Kendall then planted the cloudy material which had produced influenza on a mixture of protein and peptone agar. Colonies of micro-organisms appeared in this mixed diet, and under the microscope he saw hundreds of diplococci. These bacteria were returned to the pure protein diet, whereupon they disappeared from sight. Attempts to transmit the flu when the causative organism was in the visible stage failed. Kendall repeated this study with the virus of yellow fever and polio, the streptococcus of scarlet fever, the bacillus of typhoid, and the staphylococcus of boils. In every case invisible agents changed to visible micro-organisms when grown on the mixture of protein and peptone agar. They changed back again to the invisible form when placed on his K medium.

Most bacteriologists refused to believe the change of virus to bacteria had been accomplished. They pointed to the conflict of reports from the far-flung bacteriological laboratories of the world. They mentioned the possibilities of poor technique and even contamination. In the meantime, Kendall " attends to his knitting " and refuses to be disturbed while others are peering into newly developed microscopes and messing with new media to confirm or confuse him. What is important is that men have been stirred to a new attack upon seemingly insoluble problems in contagious disease.

The new sciences of bacteriology and immunology have lowered infant and child mortality considerably, thus increasing the individual's expectation of life about twenty-five years. At the time of Welch's birth, fifteen per cent of all infants died before they were a year old. Today only six per cent die before the age of one. At the time of Queen Elizabeth the average span of the life of man was only about twenty years. When Welch was born his expectation of life was about thirty-five years. This was the normal life-span of an infant born at that time. Today a boy born into the same environment may hope to reach an age of fifty-nine. Out of each hundred people alive today, 35 will be alive at the age of 72, 13 at the age of 82 and only 1.3 men (and 1.9 women) at 92.

Yet this glowing picture of advance has another side, which shows with pungent strength that man's struggle against death is still far from victorious. In 1850, a man who survived to the age of thirty-five years might have hoped to live almost another twenty-five years. Today, after eighty-five years of medical advance, the expectation of the thirty-five-year-old man is still hardly twenty-five years. The efforts to prolong life have resulted simply in a diminution of the chances of premature death due particularly to the infectious diseases of infancy and childhood. The diseases of middle and old age such as heart disease, high blood pressure and their concomitants — cerebral hemorrhage, apoplexy and nephritis — still strike in a concentrated fire and prevent men from going beyond that sixty-year limit.

Raymond Pearl of Johns Hopkins University, after an elaborate study of the families of very old people, came to the conclusion very recently that "longevity would appear to be biologically a rather fundamental attribute of the organism." While he found such factors as even temper, no excessive exercise, and proper food contributing ones to old age, heredity was undoubtedly the controlling factor. It bore out the belief of many that certain genetic constitutions are more easily attacked by tuberculosis, pneumonia, cancer, and even smallpox than others subjected to similar conditions. "The best you can do," said Welch, "to live to a ripe old age is to pick your ancestors carefully." "The work of certain genes is essential for vigorous adult life," adds H. S. Jennings. "If such a gene pair is defective, the individual may develop to adult life, but is weak and short lived." Life's tether varies in length in each species; long and short life seem to follow a true Mendelian ratio. What we inherit is a certain bodily constitution which runs down at a definite pace, if we do not abuse it too much.

But science does not allow the bogy of heredity to halt its attempt to control human illness. For environment also plays a part by influencing the rate at which our patrimony will be spent. "Either poor heredity or poor handling can ruin a machine or an organism. If the materials are worthless, if the individual starts with thoroughly poor genes, the method of treatment and the environment can do little." But something has been done even in those cases where the hereditary equipment is poor. Science has begun to reckon with the maladies of middle and old age. These virgin fields are, of course, more forbidding and less hopeful, for it is a question whether man can ever surmount those hereditary constitutional weaknesses which cut short his life.

The cruelest captain of Death today is no longer a disease of infection. It is heart disease. Three million Americans suffer from cardiac ailments. In 1934 about 320,000 (six times the number of Americans killed in the World War) died of heart failure in the United States. And this number is increasing. The three next greatest human killers are cancer (135,000), nephritis (110,000), and cerebral hemorrhage (90,000) none of which is of an infectious nature. Infants and children spared from the germs of communicable diseases add to the hosts of victims, for we have more people living today in middle and old age than ever before.

Today we know more about the various heart diseases than we did fifty years ago. The electro-cardiographic machine, capable of measuring a current as small as a millionth of a volt, gives a picture of the action of the heart muscles which is of great value in diagnosis. Infrared or "black light" photography penetrates below the skin and shows up congestion of blood vessels which is the earliest manifestation of heart attacks. Heart abnormalities are recognized sooner, and various remedies can be called into play early enough to avert serious trouble. We know more of the relation of certain infectious diseases, such as pneumonia and syphilis, and others like kidney trouble and rheumatism, to the incidence and course of heart failures. Ninety-five per cent of cardiac diseases in children below sixteen is due to rheumatism. Rheumatic fever is a disease of young people which attacks the heart. It is accompanied by acute pains in the joints.

Even in heart trouble due to valvular derangements, something can be done. We can cut down life's throttle with a proper regimen of rest and diet which can accomplish wonders. Physiological or indirect surgery has been successfully tried to slow down the action of the heart. In 1933 at the Peter Bent Brigham Hospital in Boston an entirely new method of treatment was tried by Drs. H. L. Blumgart and D. D. Berlin on a heart disease sufferer. The thyroid gland was removed to eliminate the supply of thyroxin poured by this gland into the blood. Thyroxin stimulates the heart to greater action. Numerous other patients have been similarly treated since that day. A less radical operation has been introduced by Drs. J. A. Lyon and E. Horgan of Washington, D. C. Instead of removing the thyroid gland in such cases they cut some of the nerves and blood vessels leading to the gland and in this way reduce the blood supply. They have reported a number of cases which have been relieved by this treatment from the pain and danger of angina pectoris and congestive heart failure. Some even believe that further advances in direct heart surgery will be made, for they feel that the heart can tolerate more surgery than most of us suspect. The proper use of the life-saving drug, digitalis, has been skillfully worked out, and is helping thousands. Forty-six large heart centers are operating in the United States. In New York City alone there are fifty cardiac clinics. A movement has been started to establish an international organization for the study of heart disease. "It is not too much to hope," says W. D. Stroud, "that during the next twenty-five years as big strides can be made in the prevention and relief of heart disease as have been made in the attack on tuberculosis."

Death from heart disease is often caused by the hardening of the arteries of the heart. Attacks of angina pectoris are due to insufficient blood flow through the coronary arteries of the heart which are narrowed by this hardening of the arteries or arteriosclerosis, as it is also called. These arteries may be completely clogged by a blood clot which may cause death by stopping the natural flow of blood to the heart muscle. Amyl nitrite is used to facilitate blood circulation and relieve the terrific pain of angina pectoris, but this treatment does not cure the hardening of the arteries. This is due to the deposition of lime in the blood vessels. We do not know what hastens this deposition of lime. Tobacco, coffee, protein diet, and alcohol play little if any part in the development of this malady. Some even believe that worry and the stress and strain of life are not fundamental factors in its appearance. Arteriosclerosis of the main blood vessels occurs in all kinds of animals. It also seems to run in families. The condition of high blood pressure or hypertension is generally regarded as part of the aging process of the body, against which little can be done.

One of the research men of the Mayo clinic has reported a test that he has discovered for a nerve sensitiveness that he believes may be the cause of high blood pressure. This test, if reliable, may possibly warn subjects to take such precautions against the condition as proper dieting early in life. In 1935 Dr. Felix Bernstein of Columbia University reported a very hopeful discovery. In trying to determine the physiological rather than the chronological age of a person — that is, whether he was younger or older in physical health than his real age would warrant, he came upon a relationship between the hardening of the lens of the person's eye and the hardening of his entire arterial system. He then devised an apparatus to measure the hardening of the eye lens and worked out a mathematical formula which enabled him to predict, years in advance, the probable life span of that individual on the basis, of course, of normal death due to the aging process of the body. The scheme was tried on 2500 people in middle and old age and his predictions were almost uncannily accurate. They died when his figures said they would.

Arthritis, or chronic rheumatism, is another ailment of middle and old age. Its cause is another medical mystery, although theories to explain it are legion. Almost every type of bacteria has been found in the blood of sufferers from this malady, and every one of these germs, with streptococcus as the favorite, has been charged with causing this painful topic of conversation. The filterable virus, too, has been accused. Dozens of vaccines and salts of various metals have been prepared, and from the flood of fluid injected into rheumatics, some degree of success has been claimed. But against this mass of shadowy cures the bulk of the medical world stands unconvinced. In the meantime, other clues are being followed up. Two investigators at Georgetown University found in the fingernails of arthritis victims a deficiency of cystine, a sulphur-containing organic compound. By the injection of cystine into the blood stream, fingernails return to normal and arthritis abates. These results, however, have not been confirmed.

The ailments of middle and old age have by no means been put under control. This century may yet give birth to a new Pasteur of these diseases. If he cannot change man's heritage, the new deliverer may at least assuage the pains of senescence. Victories in the fields of vitamin deficiency, glandular malfunctionings and pernicious anemia give hope for such a triumph. Hardly more than a decade ago pernicious anemia was one of those illnesses against which medicine had no weapon. It was a disease which prevented the formation of sufficient numbers of mature, healthy red blood corpuscles in the body. Today pernicious anemia is treated quickly and successfully; it is no longer something to be dreaded. Three men collaborated in its conquest and in 1933 shared the Nobel prize in medicine for this achievement. Dr. George R. Minot, suffering from diabetes, depended upon insulin (which had only just been announced), and upon a rigid diet. He was accustomed to weighing out his food, and became interested in the diets of others, especially anemia patients. He came across the work of Dr. George H. Whipple of the University of Rochester who was experimenting with dogs in an effort to learn how the body builds up the hemoglobin of the red blood corpuscles. Whipple had found that liver diets helped his anemic dogs by stimulating an increase in their supply of hemoglobin. Why would not that work with humans? thought Minot, and he tried to answer the question by prescribing quantities of liver to his patients in 1924. They improved. Then William P. Murphy, Minot's colleague at the Harvard Medical School, joined in the problem which now resolved itself into getting concentrated liver extracts. His patients had to eat half a pound of liver daily, and consuming pounds of liver every week was not very pleasant. And while liver, formerly the poor man's steak which had been thrown to cats and dogs, skyrocketed in price, Murphy went to work on liver concentrates. Recently, Murphy announced that he has finally obtained an extract which when injected between the muscle tissues in very small amounts only once a month increases the red blood corpuscles miraculously. And finally, in September, 1935, the active principle of this liver extract was isolated in pure form by H. D. Dakin and R. West of New York City. Few would have dreamed ten years ago that within such a comparatively short time pernicious anemia would be practically under complete control.

Arthritis, diseases of the heart, defective nutrition, glandular and blood disturbances, and allergic maladies such as asthma and hay fever are attracting more and more biochemists and biophysicists. When a foreign protein body gets into the system, the body often reacts by producing a rash, hives, fever, or a paroxysm of sneezing or in some other way. This condition of bodily hypersensitivity is known as allergy. Among the most common forms of allergy is hay fever, so called because prior to 1831 it was believed that hay was responsible. Later the pollen of certain grasses was found to be the cause. Today we know that the most common cause of hay fever is the pollen of the long and low ragweed and, in the case of rose fever, the pollens of timothy and orchard grass are the offenders. Science is bending every effort to save millions of sufferers from the debilitating sneezes and other inconveniences of allergic disturbances. Some progress has already been made. The patient is first subjected to a series of tests to determine what particular food protein or pollen protein is causing the trouble. Then specially prepared glycerine and salt solutions of these substances are injected under the skin over a period of several weeks prior to the expected onset of the disturbance. The theory is that the body gradually builds up a resistance against the intruder until it finally becomes desensitized. Protection lasts only a short time and the pollen antigen must usually be injected annually. This method of therapy is still the most effective for some victims although tens of thousands of hay-fever sufferers still remain outside the pale of this method of prophylaxis. These must either travel to places like the White Mountains of New Hampshire where the offending proteins are absent, or must continue to sneeze and lachrymate until science has made a sure victory in this field. Why desensitization will work with some and not with others is not understood.

Hand in hand with the development of bacteriology, immunology is still arming against the battalions of bodily disabilities. After almost half a century of investigations on the composition and mode of action of antibodies, antitoxins, and antigens which nature and man have prepared to fight bacterial and protein invasions, very little is known. The chemical composition of these antibodies which are produced in the body and remain, in some cases, for years, is still unknown. We do not even know how they act. Science is still working with highly complex serums and impure solutions of unknown chemical constitution. The goal of science is the ultimate analysis and subsequent synthesis of the pure chemicals which will search out the invaders and destroy or neutralize them. J. S. Sumner and S. F. Howell of Cornell University, who in 1926 isolated an enzyme, urease, in the pure form for the first time, reported nine years later the isolation of a chemical compound from white beans which they consider to be the same as one of the many immune bodies found in the blood.

The 1934 prize of the American Association for the Advancement of Science was awarded to Reuben L. Kahn of the University of Michigan for his researches on *Tissue Reactions in Immunity*. Kahn, who is the inventor of a new syphilis test which resembles the Wassermann test, believes that the blood with its antibodies is not the most powerful of the shock troops which protect against disease. Experiments on rabbits have convinced him that the protective action of such tissues as the skin, peritoneum and muscles are even greater. He regards what is generally looked upon as hypersensitiveness of the skin as actually a defence activity. This may open up a new technique in immunology. These results are still in the experimental stage and it may be that decades will pass before important results along these lines can be definitely announced.

William Henry Welch died in 1934, more than three score years after he had taken the Hippocratic vow. He had lived long enough to watch and, in no small measure, to direct that white-clad cavalcade which, with aseptic technique, surgical anesthesia (America's greatest single contribution to medicine) and the new tool of the X-ray, has cleaned up the shambles of the operating room, reduced the horrifying mortality of infancy and childhood, and is now wrestling with those demons which still defy man to pass beyond his allotted span of years. Few men have made a greater success of the art of living and of serving humanity. Few have faced ugly facts with more directness. Almost half a century ago, when a wave of sanitary reform was sweeping Baltimore, Welch was not afraid to declare: " I do not for a moment suppose that this is the only agency in elevating the condition of the poor. The roots of these evils lie far beneath the surface. It may be that they are inseparable from existing conditions of society and that nothing short of a social revolution can wholly remove them." He realized that much sickness is fundamentally the result of poverty and economic instability.

Welch's eightieth birthday in 1930 was the occasion of one of the most spontaneous outbursts of homage ever paid to a living man. Eminent men gathered all over the world and, linked by radio, paid tribute to the inspiration of this kindly scientist. Welch took occasion to remind the world: " It is my inclination, even at four score years, to look forward rather than backward, and to avoid a feeling of self-complacency through the rehearsal of past triumphs. All along the line so much more remains to be done than has been accomplished. How wide is the gap between what is achieved and what might be realized! "

One of Welch's many students has summed up the life of this bachelor as follows, " I love most to think of him as the quiet, gentle teacher, who has taught us the grace and charm of the pupil's adoration of the master, the sanctity of a life in science, and the beauty of a love for one's fellow man."

CHAPTER FOUR

CANCER

MAN STRUGGLES WITH THE ANARCHY OF THE CELL

With special attention to the epochal work of Maud Slye

IF YOU FIND a disease of fat and it moves hither and thither under your fingers, it is a fatty tumor. Treat it with the knife." This was written five thousand years ago in the *Ebers Papyrus*, one of the oldest medical documents known. The advice is still good.

In the United States the death certificate of one out of every ten men who die after the age of thirty-five bears the diagnosis of cancer. The situation with regard to women is even more serious — cancer claims one out of every five. Three hundred people die of this disease every day in this country, and the figures are growing worse with the years. In the fifty leading American cities cancer deaths have increased from 70 to 125 per 100,000 of population during the last twenty years. Science must admit that with all the great advances in her laboratories, in the study of cancer the fundamental problems of the causes, early diagnosis, and cure still remain obscure.

The literature of medicine has been examined and re-examined innumerable times in the hope of finding a clue to the etiology of those growths which start no one knows why, spread no one knows how, and grow remorselessly until they invade other tissues and kill by obstructing some vital organ or by paving the way for some fatal infection. The data available from clinical records are so confusing that the more one studies them the more one becomes befuddled. The cause of cancer has been attributed to bacteria, viruses, food preservatives, chronic constipation, cosmic rays, overweight, vitamin deficiency, a long and capacious stomach, the presence of minute amounts of radium in the body, worry, sour lymph, eating of tomatoes and walnuts, altered metabolism due to the decline of the sex organs, glandular disturbances, toxins produced in the intestinal tract or at other foci of infection, lack of exercise, sunburn, acid blood, alkaline blood, the concentration of mineral salts in the blood, smoking clay pipes, the use of mineral oil as an internal lubricant, and milk stagnation in the mother's breast. Chronic irritation has been associated with the incidence of cancer for many hundreds of years. Long before inquiring young scientists massaged the ears of rabbits and noticed that the treatment promoted tumor growth, this belief had been current. In China, for example, where men shave their heads with dull razors, cancer of the scalp is common; in India where some of the natives carry little stoves under their robes close to the stomach, cancer of the skin at the point of contact is not infrequent; in South Asia among the millions of betel-nut chewers, cancer of the mouth goes with scarlet mouth and spittle, and among the Hindus cancer of the penis is quite common, although very rare among Jews and Mohammedans who, unlike the Hindus, practice circumcision. Yet cancer of the little toe has hardly ever been recorded, in spite of the fact that few parts of the body are subject to such continuous friction as the foot.

The complete conquest of cancer is still to be written. Mankind may have to wait generations, and millions of victims will continue to die of the anarchy of cellular growth before science can point to achievements in this field comparable to its triumphs in the realm of the infectious diseases. Until now medicine stood confronted with the problem of exploring a subterranean tunnel shut off from the sky, without even a sputtering candle to guide it through the darkness. Today there is some light coming from at least one spot on the wide front of the cancer battle line. It is the light kindled by a woman who twenty-five years ago consecrated her life to the solution of the cancer problem, so solemnly that after a quarter century of herculean effort she still has not given up the struggle.

Although she has discovered no magic radium, Maud Slye has

frequently been called "The American Curie." This does not describe her, for the object of her search is not a single element, perhaps to be struck upon partly by chance. Instead, it is the complicated objective of the nature, the cause, and the prevention of the most obscure disease known to man.

Maud Slye entered the University of Chicago as a freshman in 1895, and secured the position of undersecretary to President Harper. By working in his office when she was at leisure from classes, she financed unaided three years of undergraduate study. But this extremely heavy work proved too much for her physical strength, and in the spring of 1898 she broke down and was obliged to leave Chicago. Upon medical advice she went to Woods Hole, where she continued her studies. In the autumn of that year she entered Brown University. While there she was offered a position as teacher of psychology in the Rhode Island State Normal School. Her work took her into the field of psychiatry, she became interested in problems of human heredity, and definitely decided to embark on an extensive undertaking in the field of human heredity.

Those were the days following the rediscovery of Mendel's laws, when echoes of the bitter controversy between geneticists and biometricians still sounded. These echoes reached Miss Slye and drew her into the camp of geneticists. She went back to Chicago where Professor Charles Otis Whitman, the outstanding American biologist of his day and founder of the laboratory at Woods Hole, was head of the department of biology. Whitman secured for her a small fellowship which barely paid for her room and board. In return, she was to act as assistant in his research work.

With the idea of continuing her early interest in psychic heredity, she purchased a pair of Japanese dancing mice. This strain exhibited a peculiar waltzing motion which was attributed to some nervous disturbance. From Abby Lathrop, fancier of Granby, Massachusetts, she obtained some albino mice and set to work crossing them, in an effort to determine the various factors which determined the inheritance of this nervous abnormality. Her own laboratory was a corner of the basement greenhouse of the zoology department.

When her stock had increased to more than a hundred mice, she was given a room on the third floor of the building. Her animals kept breeding prolifically and the work mounted. With no assistant to relieve her, she spent eighteen hours and more in the laboratory daily, working with her mice, scrubbing and sterilizing cages, tables, and apparatus. She had been financing the experiment almost entirely herself, until one day Dr. John Watson, the good behaviorist, then head of the work in comparative psychology, dropped in to see her laboratory. He wondered where she had procured the money to feed that growing colony, and when he heard her story invited her to help herself to all the milk and bread she needed for her mice, from his refrigerator. That was the first solid support she received, and it stays in her memory.

One day in the spring of 1910, Miss Slye noticed that one of her mice had developed an abnormal growth. It was a spontaneously formed breast cancer. She had been hearing and reading about some interesting cancer research of two men, one in the middle west and the other at the Harvard Medical School. Leo Loeb, a young pathologist, now of Washington University, while making a study of the endemic occurrence of cancer, had gone to the Chicago stockyards and found that a large number of the slaughtered animals had suffered from cancer of the eye. More interesting, he had discovered upon investigation that this disease attacked especially cattle from a certain ranch in Wyoming. It looked very much like either an epidemic of infectious cancer among that Wyoming stock, or a strain of animals with hereditary cancer.

Five years later Loeb came across what looked like an endemic occurrence of cancer of the thyroid in three rats living in adjacent cages. This seemed to point to heredity rather than infection as the predominating factor, and he made the suggestion that perhaps breeding experiments with rats and mice might give the answer to the cause of cancer in animals. This was the first suggestion of such an approach. Three years later, in 1907, Loeb made a thorough investigation of the breeding establishment of Miss Lathrop, and found the occurrence of cancer in her animals to be greater in certain of her inbred strains. Then for the first time he announced that cancer in animals was probably due to some hereditary predisposition. In that same year Ernest E. Tyzzer, pathologist of the Harvard Medical School, published a paper on the inheritance of cancers in mice, pointing out the high frequency of lung tumors in this animal. He, too, thought heredity an important factor in the incidence of mouse cancer. Medical literature also contained some vague references to the occurrence of cancer in human families. Broca, for instance, in 1866 reported on the famous cancerous family of Madame Z. Of its twenty-six members reaching the age of thirty, sixteen, including mother, children, and grandchildren, died of breast, liver, and uterine cancer.

Near the close of 1908, the Royal Society of Medicine in England held a conference to discuss the question of inheritability of disease. During the course of the discussion its president remarked, "Cancer is very generally regarded as a typical example of hereditary disease, but strong reasons have been adduced to show that this belief is not based on such sure grounds as was supposed." Dr. E. F. Bashford, basing his reply on some work done by the Imperial Cancer Research Laboratory on the breeding of mice for cancer study, disagreed. "Cancer of the breast so common in the human female," he told that gathering of eminent medical men, "is also common in the mouse and dog, but practically unknown in the cow, which, however, suffers quite frequently from primary growths of the liver and the adrenal gland. These tendencies are so constant that it is difficult to escape the conclusion that they depend on innate characters which are hereditarily transmissable." But his words fell upon deaf ears.

Thus far no elaborate program of carefully controlled breeding experiments had been carried through for the purpose of establishing the inheritability or non-inheritability of cancer. Recognizing the importance of such an investigation, Maud Slye determined to study the genetics of spontaneous cancer in mice, following the exact technique used by geneticists in researches on the inheritance of characters such as the coat color of mice. She was not going to start with any preconceived theory, or attempt to interfere with the spontaneous cancers of her mice. Instead, she would try to find out by appropriate breeding experiments what happens when large numbers of cancerous and noncancerous mice are crossed. She realized that it meant a lifetime of work. Her conclusions must be based on thousands of matings, for Karl Pearson and other biometricians were fighting Mendelism and genetics with the cry of " Pedigrees, more pedigrees."

Through the same summer that Morgan at Columbia was breeding his Drosophila for further mutants, Maud Slye bred her much slower growing and infinitely hungrier mice for spontaneous cancer. Other growths cropped up, and she wrote: " When I had the first litter of babies from a cancerous mother, I took them in my hand and showed them to the department head, saying, ' Here is the material to determine whether or not cancer is inherited.' He answered, ' That was all settled long ago — it is not inherited.' " Superb example of the open-mindedness of science, and the inspiration of some teachers in high places.

She appealed to Dr. Ludvig Hektoen, head of the department of pathology at the University, asking him whether the question had been settled; to which he replied, " So far from being settled, there is not even anyone who has the material to settle it, unless you have." " And," said Maud Slye, " once more my heart started to beat regularly." Dr. Hektoen thought it distinctly worth while to carry such a project through. But she had come for more than permission to go ahead. She needed funds. Until now she had often gone hungry herself to feed her mice. But she needed substantial financial assistance to rear thousands of animals. Hektoen promised to try to help, and while those hungry mice, which every four days consumed their own weight of whole cow's milk, fresh wheat bread (crispy toast for the dancers), timothy hay and mixed bird seed, kept eating and breeding and dying, Maud Slye waited. Then Otho S. A. Sprague died, leaving millions of dollars for medical research. The Otho Sprague Memorial Institute was founded and Maud Slye was made a staff member, with the eminent pathologist, H. Gideon Wells, as director of the Institute. For the first time she received a salary and a laboratory large enough to work in comfort. "Until then," she remarked years later, "I hung on by my teeth."

The primitive little mouse-breeding place was moved to an old two-story building on the edge of the University campus. Miss Harriet Holmes, a trained pathologist and a woman of means and culture who felt the need of sustained intellectual work, offered her services free. She was placed in charge of the preparation of all the tissue slides for microscopic examination — a position she fills to this day. Wells agreed to collaborate with Miss Slye in all microscopic analyses so that no professional question could be raised concerning the accuracy of her diagnoses. Her mice, splendidly cared for, were strong, prolific, superb. She kept adding cages row upon row until they reached the ceiling. Later larger quarters were found in a three-story house at 5825 Drexel Avenue, which today is tenanted by more than ten thousand living mice. In the basement is the equipment for cleaning and sterilizing the cages. On the first floor are housed the offspring of cancerous mice. On the second floor is the hospital where all mice showing cancers are immediately transferred for constant watching. On the top floor are the cancer-free stocks of mice; and in the building of the pathology department of the University is a huge museum of tissue slides and autopsied mice, every one of which has passed through her hands. All these mice are descendants of that handful of forbears bought twenty-five years ago.

Out of this singular kingdom of mice have come Maud Slye's

epoch-making results. On May 5, 1913, before the American Society for Cancer Research, she read her first paper on *The Incidence and Inheritability of Spontaneous Cancer in Mice.* In this paper she showed how in the first three years of her work she had performed autopsies on five thousand mice who had died in her laboratory, two hundred ninety-eight of which showed cancer. Every one was carefully examined once a week for nodules. When anything new happened to a mouse, it was inscribed on the metal door of its cage, checked, and entered into a permanent record book. As soon after death as possible the mouse was removed, given a number, autopsied, and its tissues were examined under the microscope. These findings were checked by both Wells and Miss Holmes, and a complete history covering date of birth, matings, troubles, and cause of death, as well as the pedigree of the animal, was entered in the record.

At this medical meeting Miss Slye exhibited Chart No. 1. It told the strange story of female mouse No. 1274, which had been mated to an unnumbered male. From their marriage came a litter of six. Of this litter, male No. 2849 and his brother No. 3053 had died of mammary gland cancer. Another brother was living and appeared free of cancer. A sister No. 4363 had succumbed to a lung cancer, another had developed cancer of the mammary gland but was still alive, while a third sister was as yet noncancerous. Here was an exact scientific description of a pedigreed cancerous family of mice. The results pointed to heredity rather than contagion as the cause of the large number of cancerous individuals in this family. "I have eliminated contagion," Maud Slye wrote in this report, "as a factor in the transmission of cancer as follows: cancerous and noncancerous mice were kept in the same cage. When a cancerous mouse died, nontumorous mice were given the soiled cage with all the debris soiled by the dead mouse. Yet noncancerous mice mated with noncancerous mice in these cages produced noncancerous offspring." She also pointed out that a daughter frequently developed cancer before the mother did and months after they had been separated.

This was a telling blow to the theory of the infectivity of cancer — a theory hundreds of years old and still persisting. While Maud Slye was a little girl in St. Paul, Scheinlein had announced that he had isolated a bacillus from breast cancer (this was the heyday of bacteriological investigation), and with it had claimed to have produced cancer of the breast in dogs. In 1909 Erwin F. Smith isolated from crowngall, a growth on plants, a specific bacterium (*bacillus tumefaciens*) which he claimed could produce cancer in plants. Since then plenty of germs have been reported in cancer tissues, but in every case they were found to be only secondary invaders which were not responsible for the tumorous growths. Even today the theory of the microbic cause of cancer is by no means dead. In March, 1933, this hydra-headed monster appeared once again. From the laboratories of the United States Health Service, Drs. T. J. Glover and J. L. Engle announced that they had produced a typical cancer in one adult female guinea pig by injecting it with a culture of bacteria isolated from the tissues of human breast cancer. But the evidence, which no laboratory has been able to confirm, was far from conclusive.

In the meantime, Maud Slye made frequent reports of the progress of her work before meetings of the American Society for Cancer Research and other medical societies. She showed that the belief that cancer was the result of some toxin acting on the body as a whole, and especially on certain tissues, was entirely erroneous. She cited case after case of cancerous mice carrying tumors twice the size of their normal bodies and yet living on until some hemorrhage brought death. Had the cancer been caused by a toxin, the mouse could never have survived that tremendous growth so long as it did. She showed that while mice were delicate and easily susceptible to the toxin elaborated during typhoid, yet a mouse with cancer stretching from neck to tail, so large, in fact, that it could hardly move, continued to live. A cancer toxin would have killed it much earlier. Her data showed, also, that cancer did not interfere with normal reproduction unless the tumorous growth was present in the reproductive organs or in some organ vital to life. She had records of thousands of mice born of mothers suffering from cancer at the time of conception. Cancerous mothers often had as many as eight healthy litters, each of twelve and even sixteen young, all of which were well nourished by the parent. The life span of these children was normal, and they in turn gave birth to large healthy litters. On the other hand, it was impossible, she said, to derive families of mice from mothers suffering from the various different diseases which infect mice.

Other interesting results came out of her laboratory. The theory of cancer as a diet-deficiency disease was shown to be untenable. For decades she raised tens of thousands of mice on the same standard diet with never a change. All her mice were given the same solid food, the same filtered sterile water in sterile dishes. Her mice carrying tumors were among the most vigorous, not the undernourished. "They were not the victims of any abuses common in the human species," added Miss Slye.

The results of this huge genetic experiment kept piling up. It looked very much as though Maud Slye were going to nail the inheritability of mouse cancer on a rampart so high and so impregnable that even those who hated to think this deadly disease might be of chromosomal origin would have to admit it. Then came what appeared to be balm in Gilead to those who were reluctant to accept the implications of the Chicago laboratory. Over in Denmark Johannes Fibiger, a pathologist of the University of Copenhagen, had been working thirteen years on the problem of tuberculosis among laboratory animals. During a series of postmortem examinations of tubercular rats, he found three had suffered from stomach cancers. Fibiger knew enough about cancer to realize that he had come across a singular phenomenon. Rats rarely suffered from tumors of the stomach.

Fibiger made a visit to the dealer who had been supplying him with these rats, and on questioning found that those sent to his laboratory had all come from a sugar refinery. Was there any-

Maud Slye

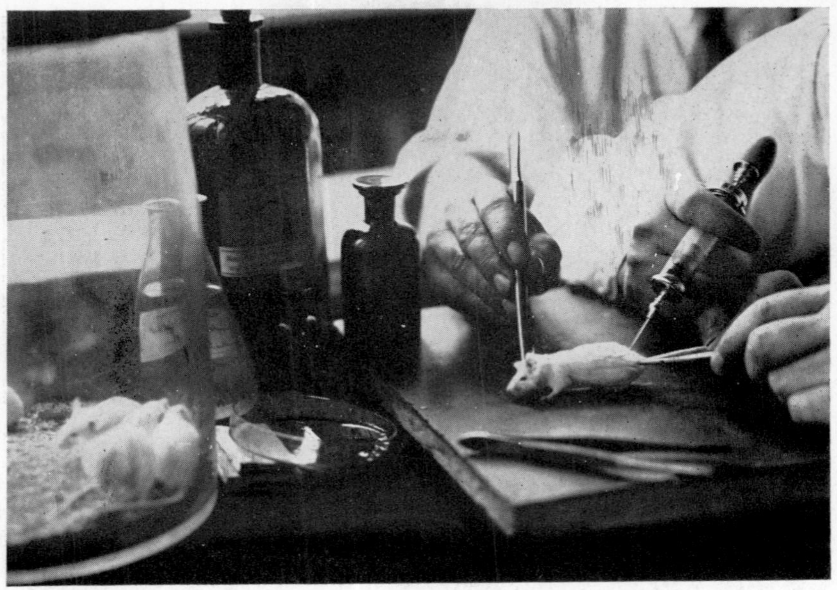

Inoculating a mouse with a chemical to produce an artificial cancerous growth. *(Keystone View Co.)*

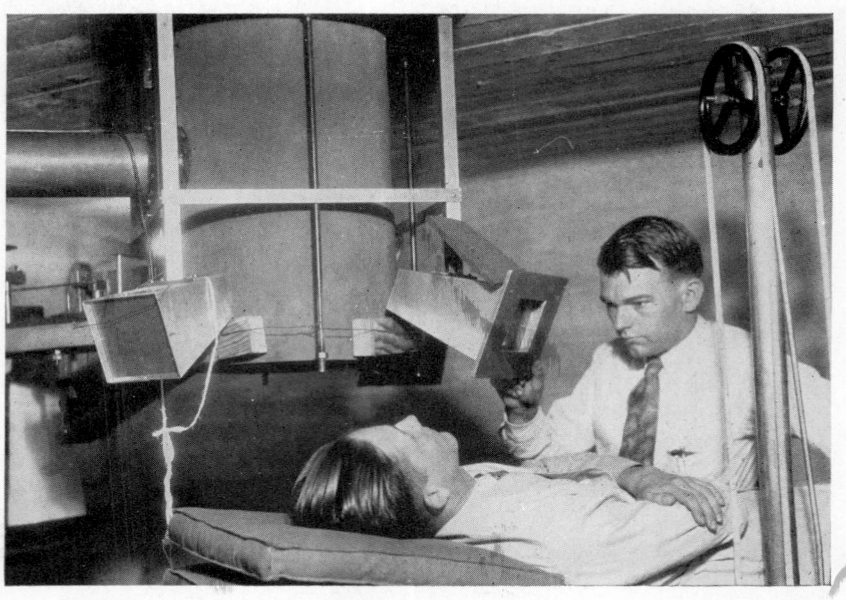

Professor C. C. Lauritsen of the California Institute of Technology using his million-volt X-ray tube in the treatment of cancer. *(Acme)*

thing peculiar about this refinery which could account for the unusually large percentage of stomach-cancerous mice from this spot? He investigated the place and found nothing unusual except a high infestation with cockroaches, which formed a fairly large part of the diet of its rats. Could he find some connection between roaches, rats, and cancer? Cancer as a disease of filth had been spoken about for years, and vermin were said to be responsible for the so-called "cancer houses," private homes from which emerged many a human cancer victim of the same family.

Fibiger planned a controlled experiment. He collected thousands of the refinery roaches and fed them to rats from another breeding establishment. The rats enjoyed this strange treatment, and for three years — that was the normal life span of his rodents — Fibiger remained skeptical. Then they died, and one by one he opened them up. To his astonishment, he found many stomach cancers. Fibiger made a careful microscopic study of the growths. He discovered that in every case they had formed around a parasitic worm, the same worm to which the roach had been host before it was fed to the rat. The larva of the worm coiled up in the muscles of the rat, later developing into an adult worm in the animal's stomach. Around this the tumorous growth had appeared. Fibiger had actually for the first time produced artificial cancer in a laboratory animal.

Fibiger's work seemed to give the lie to the claim of the inheritability of cancer. This Dane could produce a cancer almost at will. His epoch-making achievement, recognized by the award of the Nobel prize a year before his death in 1927, was the beginning of a wide program of investigation on the artificial production of cancer by other methods and in other laboratory animals. Fibiger could produce his worm cancer in rats, but failed with other animals. An important investigation along this line was that made by Frederick Bullock, Maynie R. Curtis, and Wilhelmina Dunning, working in the Institute of Cancer Research of Columbia University. They succeeded, following the technique of the Dane, in producing liver cancer in rats by feeding them with the larvae of the common tapeworm (*Taenia*) derived from a group of twenty-seven cats maintained for this purpose. The rats were fed Taenia larvae from the infested cats. Malignant tumors developed in the livers of some of the rats. Between 1920 and 1933 more than twenty-five thousand rats were infested with the parasitic tapeworm and these, together with an equal number of uninfested rats of the same strains, were autopsied.

The conclusions of the Columbia investigators contained the following statement: "While Taenia eggs were effective in producing the disease and the associated malignant tumors, *the rats showed marked strain and family differences.* This observation is in line with the observations of Slye for the occurrence of spontaneous tumors in mice." In fact, some of the rats developed cancer of other organs, such as the mammary gland, instead of liver tumors, showing no connection between the irritation and infection and the incidence of cancer. "They seemed to develop in due time the cancer to which they were predisposed," commented Miss Slye. "These cancers were produced only in susceptible members of susceptible strains of susceptible rats." Nonsusceptible rats, even though infested like the others, did not develop cancer. Hereditary predisposition and irritation were both needed to produce cancer, not only in her own mice but also in the rats of these and other experimenters.

These were not the only temporarily disconcerting setbacks to the recognition of Maud Slye's work. Dr. P. Potts in 1775 had called attention to the frequent occurrence of cancer of the scrotum among chimney sweeps, and thought it might be in some way connected with soot. Coal tar and paraffin shale workers were also known to be subject to warts, which often became cancerous. Two Japanese, a century and a half later, decided to test out the relation of tar and cancer. Yamagiwa and Ichikawa used rabbits. At regular intervals they painted the ears of their rabbits with tar and actually witnessed the appearance of tumorous growths at the points of irritation. Then these tumors were transplanted by other scientists to normal rabbits, and the grafts took. This was a startling piece of scientific news. Here was another form of experimental cancer in animals which could be studied under controlled laboratory conditions.

The optimists saw the dawn of a new era in cancer control. Research men crowded into this promising field; tar cancer experimentation began running full blast in many laboratories. It was found that tar cancer could be produced in mice rather easily, but only with great difficulty in rats. Other anomalies were discovered. English investigators obtained from coal tar various chemicals, such as 1:2 benzpyrene, 1:2 benzanthracene, and 5:6 cyclopentene, which they could synthesize and which proved to be as effective as coal tar.

But the problem, after all, was not so simple. It is now more than ten years since the first tar cancer appeared under the tar stain in that Japanese laboratory. The investigation is still far from having solved anything fundamental. It only served to confirm the two facts that Maud Slye had been telling the world for years; namely, that irritation — tar, other chemical or mechanical irritation — was one necessary factor in cancer incidence. The other factor, as Slye showed by similar treatment on her mice, was a hereditary predisposition which supplied the soil upon which such a stimulus could give rise to tumorous growths. Many mice, even though subjected to irritation, did not develop the growths.

From the Imperial Cancer Research Laboratory of England spread another ripple presaging, some thought, a mighty tidal wave which would engulf Maud Slye and her mice and the whole pernicious theory of cancer inheritance. William Gye, pathologist, and William Barnard, microscopist, had been following up a clue first discovered by a research pathologist of the Rockefeller Institute in New York. Francis Peyton Rous had found a tumor projecting sharply from the right breast of a barred Plymouth Rock hen. In an effort to find out the nature of this growth, Rous had anesthetized the fowl with ether and removed nearly the whole of the tumor. Bits of it were immediately inoculated into the left breast of the same hen, as well as into its abdomen. Two other hens from the same setting of eggs were likewise inoculated with bits of the growth. Thirty-five days later (November 5, 1909), the original tumorous hen died of cancer of the peritoneal cavity, and even more astounding, one of the other inoculated hens developed a large tumor. This was the first recorded bird tumor that had proved transplantable to other hens. Arthur Hanau twenty years before had transplanted rat tumors, and ended his career by committing suicide because of the neglect he had suffered from his brother scientists. Rous cancer of fowls or Rous Tumor No. 1 became a classic experimental tool. The growths are always virulent tumors, minute portions of which are often carried by the blood stream to the lungs and other tissues where they form secondary growths, or *metastases*. Cancers are thus spread from one part of the body to other parts.

Rous had shaken the medical laboratories of the world by obtaining from his chicken tumors a solution which could pass through the finest filters and yet lose none of its virulence. The filtrate showed no organism under the most powerful microscope, yet could produce tumors in fowls. It could be frozen in dry ice and thawed out more than half a hundred times and still prove active. Apparently it behaved as a catalyst. He could even plunge a needle into this tumorous mass, stick it at once into the breast muscle of another chicken, and obtain a tumor on the same spot. Alexis Carrel, the wizard of tissue culture, studied these growths and considered them true cancers.

Gye and Barnard undertook a further investigation of Rous Tumor No. 1. They split the alleged cancer-producing agent into two portions. One seemed to be a chemical, and the other a true virus which could definitely produce cancer (in fowls only) and could be cultivated. Neither of the two constituents of the potent filtrate could alone produce a cancer, but together they seemed to be able to initiate a tumorous growth. Gye claimed the chemical portion could also be obtained from a human cancer, while the virus portion could be isolated from other sources, such as mouse cancer 37/S (discovered at the Imperial Cancer Research Laboratories), Jensen's rat cancer, and even from human breast cancer. Several fellow workers in their own laboratory actually inoculated each other with this virus to test their theory. But they did not contract true cancers. Many years have passed since Gye and Barnard made their original claims. Workers in other cancer laboratories have attempted to repeat the work, but thus far all have failed. Harvard brought Gye over here and gave him every opportunity to repeat his work. But he got nothing more. The world of pathology refuses to credit their conclusions. The generally accepted explanation of their alleged artificial cancers is that either they were dealing with growths other than cancers, or that their technique was at fault. Maud Slye's theory of the hereditability of cancer is still safe from this attack, also.

The years rolled by. Years of patient, almost superhuman effort. Maud Slye worked like one possessed. She gave her mice every care and attention. None of her thousands of animals had ever been swept away by bacterial epidemics such as mouse typhoid or mouse pneumonia, which always threaten large colonies of mice. Every cage was thoroughly scrubbed and sterilized with steam. The outside and floor of each cage were covered with clean Manila paper changed weekly. The nest inside each home contained a bedding of hay and paper excelsior, all kept scrupulously clean. It was a colossal, never-ending job. More autopsies, more microscopic examinations, more material for her museum until this stock, intensively studied for so many years, had yielded practically every type and location of cancerous growth known in human pathology. More papers, more meetings, more obstructions, until Maud Slye grew gray and older and more tired-looking.

One night as she lay asleep in her room she was awakened by a terrific blizzard. She thought of the boy " nightman " in the basement of her laboratory who might have forgotten to shut the windows of the mouse sanctuary. Rushing through the storm to the laboratory, she found everything safe. But that fear forever haunted her — some of her precious strains might have been lost. She moved to other quarters across the street from the laboratory where she could watch it more closely, and penned:

At night my laboratory stands
Sheltered in dark, all its wide work of day
Silenced for rest. On both its sides
Flanked by still space, it looms alone,
The sky above it and the dark around.
Oh, all my heart is there!
I watch it standing in the night
And silent dark . . .

And the quest is still on. Many facts have been definitely established by Maud Slye as the result of more than a hundred thousand autopsies she has performed on mice put through the genetic ropes in her laboratory. First, nonsusceptibility to mouse cancer acts as a Mendelian *dominant;* susceptibility to tumorous growths as a *recessive* character. The presence of one gene seems to mean the difference between cancer-susceptibility and nonsusceptibility. Or as Miss Slye has worded it in her last report of 1933, "Cancer involves a complexity which differs in only one gene from the complexity involved in insusceptibility." At this late date, few would dare quarrel with this statement, although some, like Loeb, the pioneer in cancer heredity, hold to a difference in several genes. Felix Bernstein, one of the most eminent of European mathematical statisticians, who as one of the victims of Nazi terror is now teaching at Columbia University, subjected the data from Loeb's breeding experiments to his own statistical method of analysis, and found they agreed with Slye's conclusion. This surprised Loeb, for he had thought his results contradicted the work of the Chicago investigator. In 1933 Bernstein made a preliminary analysis of the figures from Maud Slye's laboratory and confirmed it once more, while the results of N. Dobrovolsiia-Zavadskaia, who repeated some of the work of Miss Slye at the University of Paris, indicated the same fact. This great contribution of Maud Slye can no longer be denied by fair-minded men.

The second clear fact which has emerged from her work is that in addition to this internal factor of inheritance, the external factor of irritation must be present to produce cancer, in most cases. "The inheritance of cancer susceptibility alone is probably not always sufficient to insure the occurrence of malignancy," says Miss Slye. "An external factor acting with internal factors upon a susceptible soil is probably the cause of cancer." Chronic irritation in a mouse of a pure noncancerous parentage will produce no cancer. Chronic irritation of a mouse susceptible to cancer according to its known pedigree will produce cancer. A mouse free from irritation, even though it comes of a cancerous background, has in many cases not developed a neoplasm. "In a family of mice with a high frequency of cancer of the skin it is possible to prevent the occurrence of cancer by preventing chronic skin inflammation. This has been done in my laboratory. In a family with a high incidence of cancer at the base of crooked and overgrown teeth, it is possible to prevent such cancers by keeping the teeth cut short and thus preventing overgrown crooked teeth with consequent pressure on the soft tissues."

Maud Slye's work seems to indicate another fact; namely, that cancer inheritance in mice is even restricted to definite locations, such as the breast, uterus, or thymus. That is, certain mouse families will develop cancer only of the breast, others only of the knee, still others only of the mouth. Thus if a mouse of a breast-cancer-susceptible family is struck on the face, thigh, feet, knee, hip, tail, back, mouth, or leg, and a lesion occurs, it will heal normally and cancer will not develop at any of these places; but the animal might develop cancer of the breast if struck at that spot. Miss Slye cites some classic examples from her voluminous files safely tucked away in a steel safe. "Mouse 7618, a member of a strain carrying cancers of various organs, was struck on the face by a cage door and developed a cancer at the site of injury. . . . Mouse 3117 of a family showing mammary gland cancer, was almost killed by his brothers in his cage. He was picked up on the field of battle and placed in the cancer hospital. All the wounds healed except those on the rump and mammary gland, both of which developed cancers." Miss Slye has produced strains of mice which never show but one type and one location of a neoplasm or tumor. Among her records is the statement: "The members of a strain derived from female 8619 and male 8751 with cancer of the liver showed eleven liver tumors out of twenty-four individuals. This is very noteworthy, because outside of this laboratory there have been only two spontaneous liver tumors in mice reported in all the literature." Again, of the first nineteen thousand autopsies and among the hundreds of abnormal growths, Miss Slye found only twenty-eight cases of tumors of the testicles and seminal vesicles. "Twenty-seven of them occurred in a family of a single strain and its hybrid derivatives." Her latest work, now nearly ready for publication, indicates that in addition to the susceptibility factor there is also a factor which determines on what organ of the body cancers will arise.

What is the nature of cancer? Maud Slye is inclined to think with most eminent pathologists that cancer is an abnormal method of cell growth. It seems to be an uncontrollable regeneration which fails to stop because of the absence of some normal factor in the cell. The division of the cell seems to be set off by some spark, and cells in the region of irritation appear unable to check this rapid division. This multiplication of cells gets out of hand and a cancer results.

Cancer apparently depends also upon certain elements which control the growth of an individual. The miserable little mouse down with other diseases cannot develop cancer though she live through the cancer age and come from a susceptible strain, because in the weakened condition she has not enough strength to support such growths. The more vigorous the susceptible mouse is, the more apt is it to develop a cancer. In addition, cancerous growths often appear at the time when the body is growing rapidly. In 1927 Miss Slye reported that many hundreds of breast cancers under constant observation in her stocks were known to have arisen synchronously with beginning pregnancy. It is most interesting to note then, that concurrently with general bodily growth and the growth of an accessory blood system and blood supply and the breast tissues and their secretions, there is also a stimulus for the beginning of breast cancer in breast-cancer-susceptible females. However, when the embryo starts developing it takes precedence over all other growths, and as a result tumor growth is arrested.

Evidently the metabolism or functioning of the cell holds the key to the riddle of the anarchy of cancer growth, just as it does of normal growth. To discover this secret, Otto Warburg of the Kaiser Wilhelm Institute of Biology in Berlin started in 1924 an amazing series of experiments on the metabolism of normal and wild cells. He cut thin slices from human and mouse tumors (both spontaneous and transplanted cancers), and quickly placed them in an apparatus, ingeniously devised by him, to study their reactions with sugar. He found that the normal cell burns or oxidizes this sugar with oxygen that it is able to obtain. A minute amount of gas is liberated during the process; this volume of gas can be measured. The cancer cell, on the other hand, cannot, for some unknown reason, get enough oxygen to oxidize the sugar and so it attacks the sugar in a different way and thus produces the energy it needs. It breaks it down into simpler compounds, just as yeast breaks sugar down into carbon dioxide gas and alcohol.

Warburg's conclusion, after six years of first-class work which helped win for him the Nobel Prize, was as follows: "Interference with the respiration in the normal growing cell is from the standpoint of the physiology of metabolism the cause of tumors." For reasons we do not as yet understand, certain unfortunate cells are being suffocated for lack of oxygen. As a rule such cells die. Some, however, struggling for life, find another way to get energy. But in so doing, they keep multiplying without end, and a cancer results which finally brings death to the whole organism. This is no theory, but a comprehensive summary of all the data at present available. Warburg's experiments have been an important contribution to the cancer problem. Thus far, however, no application in the diagnosis, cure, or prevention of cancer appears even likely from the conclusion arrived at by the German investigator. For we have no way of controlling the normal absorption and utilization of oxygen of the cancer cell.

Mice and men. Miss Slye has been interested in cancers of both. Her work has centered around the problem of cancer prevention rather than of the cure. In mice, she has actually succeeded in eliminating cancers by persistently mating through successive generations pure noncancer strains with hybrid susceptible cancer carriers. After several generations she obtained cancer-free progeny. Somewhere in that elaborate crossbreeding process, the cancer factor had been wiped out. She had worked similar miracles before. By such controlled breeding, she had got rid of albinism and the dancing habit of Japanese waltzing mice. "If I wish to produce any kind of mouse," says Miss Slye, "I can do it. I can make him to order. I have produced cancer in mice and then bred it out."

What have mice cancers to do with those growths that afflict and decimate the human animal? Mice cancers, Miss Slye believes, are almost identical with those of men in types, organs involved, and clinical course. The development of a tumor at six months is an early cancer age in mice, approximately the equivalent of thirty years, an early age, in man. The percentage of tumors which have arisen in her mice is about ten per cent, almost the same as in the human species. Cancer localization, which has been proved in mice, is believed by many to be true also of human cancer. Dr. Charles H. Mayo, the eminent American surgeon, cites the case of "a brother and sisters who were patients in our hospital at the same time with cancer of the ascending colon. The mother and one sister in the same family had suffered from cancer in the same exact spot of the colon." Sibley observed cancer of the *left* breast in a mother and all of her five daughters, and Paget reported cancers of the uterus in a mother, her daughter, and her granddaughter. And many are familiar with the clinical record of the Bonaparte family — Napoleon, his mother, sister, and brother all died of a stomach cancer. " Similar tissues," explains Miss Slye, " derived in the course of evolution from the same ancestry must respond in the same way to the same type of irritation."

Men cannot be locked in cages and mated like mice or guinea pigs. Since our knowledge of human genetics is so limited, Maud Slye has been obliged to jump from the conclusions of her mice experiments to implications regarding cancer in men. At the Mohonk conference which met in 1926 to consider the problems of cancer, Miss Slye, who was invited to attend though not to read a paper, took occasion to introduce her program. No cure being known, she announced her belief in the control and prevention of human cancer upon the basis of the knowledge she had built up in the genetics of mouse cancer. Men frowned and even attacked her. Dr. Charles J. Hastings of Toronto insisted that " the public must be assured that cancer is not hereditary."

Maud Slye felt that this opposition was unwarranted. Her picture, after all, was not so dismal. She had emphasized time and time again that susceptibility to cancer was not a dominant character, but a recessive. " This," she said, " is most encouraging, for it means that large numbers of individuals are by inheritance exempt from the probability of cancer."

Furthermore, Miss Slye had told the medical world repeatedly, there was another factor besides cancer susceptibility which played an important part in cancer incidence; namely, the factor of irritation. Her very first report in 1913 had emphasized this fact. " Hereditary strains determine whether or not a given irritating cause shall produce cancer." A person might come of a cancer-susceptible family, but if the element of irritation were not present, that individual would never develop tumors. This removed the fatalistic attitude that members of cancerous families must develop cancers. The exact defining of the type of irritation that leads to each type of cancer, Miss

Slye believes, gives us our greatest hope for preventing cancer until such time as we find a method of eliminating the disease completely. Unfortunately, we do not yet understand all the various kinds of irritation that induce cancerous growths. Where there has been cancer in a family, however, especial care should be taken to avoid all types of chronic irritation, such as unhealed wounds, slight chronic burns such as might be caused by foods that are too hot, jagged teeth, lacerations from child-bearing; all of these should be immediately cleared up. This is the reason Miss Slye feels the public should be informed of the facts of mouse cancer and warned of the possibility of their validity for human cancer.

The American Society for the Control of Cancer, in a printed program for public information, once mentioned the relation of heredity to cancer in humans as follows: " Cancer itself is not hereditary, although a certain predisposition or susceptibility to cancer is apparently transmissible through inheritance. This does not signify that because one's parents or other members of the family have suffered from cancer, cancer will necessarily appear in other persons of the same or succeeding generations." Five years later this same organization issued a statement which admitted: " Members of certain families are more likely to have the disease. The relation of heredity to cancer, however, is not sufficiently understood at present to warrant any statement which may be of real practical value." The following year, the *Journal of the American Medical Association* commented editorially on the results of an extensive investigation of human cancer in Norway. The Norwegian Medical Society followed up the case and family histories of six thousand cancer patients over a period of twenty-three years, and found heredity as well as other factors to be the cause of human cancer. They also found localization of cancer hereditary. " The report from Norway," said the *Journal of the American Medical Association* (May 7, 1932), " seems to strengthen the view that the role of heredity must be the same in human cancer as in animal cancer, even if it cannot be seen so clearly because of the difficulties inherent in observing genetic phenomena in human biology."

It was during the very year that Maud Slye detected the first case of cancer in mice that Karl Pearson in England was calling for statistical data. "What we want at the present time is to get a wave of inquiry as to family histories started in the medical profession. If only one medical man in ten once in his life constructed two such pedigrees, we should have, in the course of a generation, all the material necessary to answer the question of the inheritance of the constitutional tendency to certain diseases." Twenty-five years had passed, and still the world was deaf to this counsel. At a meeting of the American College of Physicians at New Orleans, Maud Slye explained the results of her mice experiments, hinted at their implications for mankind, and pleaded for a universal program of collecting data based on case histories and more autopsies. Medicine had fumbled blindly long enough. It was high time to get some definite statistical data. She asked for the creation of a central bureau for cancer statistics in Chicago, and offered her services to take care of such records. If we should establish permanent records of examination of each living individual and permanent recorded examination findings of all dead, declared Miss Slye, in three generations we should have valuable scientific data. These data would undoubtedly include matings of double cancerous parentage, matings of double noncancerous parentage, matings of noncancerous with hybrid carriers, and matings of cancer with hybrid carriers. Such data would furnish an exact test for the human species.

A more general inclination on the part of the public to allow human autopsies would mean the gathering of information which would give mankind the most powerful tool ever fashioned for the prevention of cancer. By the right selective methods it might then prove possible to eliminate cancer, as Maud Slye has consistently and completely eliminated it from hundreds of families of mice in her laboratory. For the first time in the history of the study of cancer, the way for the elimination of cancer would then be open. Miss Slye knew the usual argument against human autopsies. But she was not afraid to remind those who spoke of the sanctity of the dead that we are infinitely more unmindful and even cruel to the living. And she agreed with Ewing, renowned pathologist, that " it would be a wise decision for members of such families which seem to be especially susceptible to cancer not to intermarry, or if they do, to take unusual precautions against the disease."

The assembled physicians at New Orleans voted unanimously to study her plan for a bureau of human cancer statistics, and appointed a committee to report. Then C. C. Little, sometime president of the University of Michigan, attacked Miss Slye's findings, and although this same organization recommended her for the Nobel Prize in medicine, the project fell into silence and decay. Maud Slye went back to her mice, and no Nobel Prize came to her, although the gold medal of the Radiological Society had been awarded to her at the same time that it was awarded to Madame Curie. She had more to fight than the secret of a genetic and etiological problem.

In the meantime medicine had come to realize that its greatest hope for the prevention of cancer deaths lay in prompt diagnosis. If the disease could only be detected in its early curable stage! But thus far no general diagnostic test has been discovered, in spite of the ingenuity and reckless experimentation of many men. A survey of the hundreds of diagnostic methods which have been claimed for the early detection of cancerous growths presents a somber picture. Every new discovery is quickly seized upon and tried out. Some are extremely simple. Schiller of Vienna paints the tissue with a water solution of iodine, claiming that normal tissue stains almost black, while cancerous tissue stains pink or remains white. Hans Fuchs of Berlin announced that the blood serum of a cancer patient, when mixed with the blood serum of a noncancerous patient and kept warm for several days, changes the amount of nonprotein nitrogen of the mixture. He uses this serum reaction as a test for the early diagnosis of cancer. A member of the staff of the Mayo Clinic suggested that the nucleolus of the cancer cell is always larger than that of the normal cell. Another investigator found that a certain chemical from the pituitary gland is always present in tumors of the sex organs, and uses this for an early diagnosis of this type of cancer. Some report a specific urine analysis which indicates a cancerous condition. Another contributor to the *American Journal of Cancer* contends that a higher condition of acidity of the blood indicates cancer. R. Dodge of Yale suggests an electrical exploration, based on the electrical properties of normal and cancerous growths, might determine the borders of a suspected cancer. The more active the growth of the cell, the more electrical energy it will exhibit, and with sensitive tubes capable of recording one hundred-millionth of a volt, the diagnosis could be made quite a delicate one. Alexander Gurwitch of Leningrad made the discovery more than a decade ago that all living, growing cells give off certain radiations (called mitogenetic rays). The tip of the nose, the end of the nails, the tip of a root, all give off different rays of different wave length, which can be measured by delicate instruments. A German scientist reported later that the blood of cancerous people emits rays different from those given off by the blood of noncancerous persons. During the last four years several men have been using another diagnostic test devised by B. Gruskin of Temple University. The test may be applied even in early cases of cancer. It consists of injecting under the skin of the person to be tested substances obtained from the embryonic cells of calves. Within about ten minutes a slight area of inflammation appears around the point of injection. If the area is circular, the person is noncancerous. If a cancerous growth is present in any part of the body, however, spokelike projections protrude from the circumference of the area.

The principles underlying the majority of these tests are scientific, but not a single one of them has proved to be of universal application. We have no certain diagnostic test of cancer today, with the exception of those which deal with cancers already well under way, or those which are far from dangerous, such as skin cancer. And as proof that we are still ignorant of the early signs of cancer, Dr. Charles H. Mayo made the statement that "as great a proportion of doctors as of laymen come to us with cancer."

But if we have not a bell that rings a warning of the early start of this treacherous cell multiplication (pain is never a symptom of early cancer), we have nevertheless three modern tools which have saved thousands of men and women from premature death. The knife, radium, and radiation from X-ray tubes are still the only cures for cancer. The knife of Hippocrates, who gave us the name Cancer from the Latin word meaning crab, may have been a sharp one, and the skill of Leonides of Alexandria one to marvel at, yet today the surgeon equipped with modern aids can go deeper and probe vital spots more successfully than ever before.

One of the first applications of Madame Curie's discovery of radium was its use in the treatment of cancer. The element radium gives off powerful, penetrating rays which destroy some cancerous tissues, or at least arrest their further growth. Radium finds its greatest practical use in this field. Bellevue Hospital and the Memorial Hospital of New York City each have about five grams, and the Cancer Institute of Buffalo eight grams of this, the most precious of the chemical elements.

The X-ray machine produces a somewhat different type of radiation from that spontaneously emitted by the element radium. The use of the X-ray for cancer treatment began soon after its discovery by Roentgen in 1895. Forty years of improvement have changed the small, crude X-ray tube into mighty guns. These giant machines shoot filtered rays which pass flesh and bones to the depths of the body. Larger and more powerful tubes are still being built. The General Electric Company recently constructed an 800,000-volt X-ray tube for the Mercy Hospital of Chicago. This new engine is a two-sectional cathode tube, fourteen feet long, with a four-inch tungsten target cooled by circulating twenty gallons of water around it each minute. It is doing the work of fifteen hundred grams of radium worth seventy-five million dollars. Through a porthole in the ceiling of a lead-sheathed room, the operator aims the cathode stream at the cancer spot, watching the patient through a lead glass window. X-ray machines built to break down the atom are also being used to break down cancer cells. The Kellogg Radiation Laboratory of the California Institute of Technology has a still more powerful tube built with funds donated by W. K. Kellogg, the breakfast food king. This 1,200,000-volt X-ray tube is helping to penetrate the secrets of the subatomic world, and is also being used to save cancer patients from death.

"Cancer is still the greatest of all the natural hazards in the adventure of living," wrote Ewing about ten years ago. Since that time radium treatment, X-ray diagnosis and treatment, and especially the skillful use of the knife have done something to keep down the death rate from cancer. Earlier and more accurate diagnoses and prompt treatment are actually curing large numbers of cancers which a decade ago would have been fatal. In the metropolitan area of New York City alone eighty-two cancer clinics are in operation. The medical profession regards as cured those cancer cases which five years after treatment show no evidences of the disease. On this basis, medical men gathered at Chicago in 1933 reported 24,448 men and women who had been cured of serious cancer for five years, and now survive to add their voices to the cry of physicians that some cancers are curable. "Deaths from cancer of the skin, mouth, and cervix," declared Dr. Joseph C. Bloodgood of Johns Hopkins, "are largely due to ignorance. Continued medical and dental supervision will wipe them out," and save three thousand victims every year in this country alone. The outlook of the cancer patient is in many respects greatly improved, and the cure of at least fifty per cent of certain types of cancer cases lies in early diagnosis. Even for tumors of the brain and the spinal cord, advances in surgery have cut down the mortality at least forty per cent. Physicians have issued the general warning: "When a new symptom of pain, discharge, bleeding, lump, ulcer, indigestion, or loss of weight presents itself and persists, you should at once seek the advice of your physician."

From the statistics of the American Society for the Control of Cancer, together with the report of the Cured Cancer Clinics of Massachusetts (1932), the following table has been prepared to indicate a definite trend.

Organ affected		Percentage of all cancer deaths	Percentage cured in *early* cases	Percentage of *all* (both early and late) cases cured
Stomach		35	24	4
Unspecified		23	—	—
Rectum		15	65	23
Genitals		13	40	20
Breast		9	65	30
Mouth	Lip	3	88	50
	Tongue		30	5
Skin		2	96	65

The hopelessness of many cancer cases and the helplessness of medicine, coupled with the avarice, craving for publicity, or serious obsessions of men, have drawn an army of practitioners into the sphere of cancer cures. The field is a vast one, a meadow strewn with the corpses of cancer victims who tried them all, an acre of quack medicos and charlatans who have heaped up fortunes upon the misfortunes of their fellow men. Alleged cancer cures are many. Organized medicine, especially the American Medical Association and the American Association for Cancer Research, have been fighting quackery vigorously. The government has instituted court action against scores of cancer quacks. Science is trying to stamp out those traffickers in fake cancer cures who are seeking profit at the expense of cancer sufferers. But the battle is by no means won — witness California with its many pseudo-scientific cancer clinics, fattening on the misery of such men.

Most of the old remedies for cancer are gone with the ignorant past — application to the tumorous growth of live toads, the juice of garlic, a poultice of Turkish figs, an infusion of the dark, spongy contents of birch-tree cancer, licorice powder, salt herring bones, dried puppies, rusty water from a blacksmith's shop, crow's feet, and the wooden shells used by Benjamin Franklin to treat his sister's cancer. Today we have remedies from other quacks, men trained in our medical and engineering schools; men more dangerous because they have the scientific background of specialists, men who can mouth medical terms and handle complicated machinery, men to whom patients mentally unbalanced by fear and suffering give themselves as new victims to these worshippers of Mammon.

In spite of the opposition of the American Medical Association and the *American Journal of Cancer*, in spite of a highly unfavorable report of a commission appointed by the Kellogg Foundation to investigate their method, Walter B. Coffey and John D. Humber are operating a hospital in California for the treatment of cancer. Nailing their banner to the mast of cancer as a disease of the whole human system, they are using injections of extracts from the suprarenal glands of sheep to save patients many of whom are in the last stages of the disease. This treatment was patented in July, 1930 (Patent No. 1,771,976), and as soon as the news reached the public, thousands of sufferers made the long trek to California.

Other cures have been tried. The chemical attack is still booming. Intravenous injections of all kinds of solutions — colloidal gold, copper, platinum, sulfur-selenium, and arsenic among them — black cobra and other snake venoms, serums made from live cancer cells or killed cancer growths, all manner of bacterial antitoxins and glandular extracts are still being used with an appalling recklessness. Even "heavy" water has been tried. This orgy of injections recalls the palmy days of alchemy, when everything conceivable, fair and foul, was mixed to make the magic potion which would ward off old age and bring eternal life.

Of the numerous metallic injection methods which have been tried, that in which colloidal lead salts are used is one of the oldest and at the same time one that medicine still considers well worth trying. About fifteen years ago Dr. Blair Bell, an eminent Liverpool surgeon, introduced the method of injecting lead salts into the tumorous mass. The treatment, which is extremely dangerous even when given by specialists, is used only on patients who have been declared hopelessly incurable. It has alleviated the condition in about twenty per cent of those so treated. A number of hospitals, however, have abandoned its use because its toxic effects are too severe.

Cancer is still being fought with many weapons and on many fronts. The Rockefeller Institute for Medical Research is deep in the study of the metabolism of the cell, and James B. Murphy has already reported the extraction of various constituents from animal tissues which seem to have inhibiting effects upon tumorous growths. At Johns Hopkins human cancer cells have been kept alive and growing outside the body for three years by George O. Gey, and this will no doubt enable scientists to study the process of cancerous growth more easily. In London, J. W. Cook and his associates succeeded in preparing from the bile acid of the body another chemical called methyl cholanthrene which in mice produced cancerous growths. This chemical is closely allied to cholesterol found in all living cells, to the female sex hormone, and also to vitamin D. All of these different chemical substances belong to what the chemist calls the sterol group. It has been suggested that cholesterol which ordinarily stimulates normal, healthy growth might, in the presence of some still unknown ferment, stimulate some pathologic growth such as cancer. This possibility is at the present time being thoroughly investigated in many laboratories. The Crocker Institute of Columbia University is still busy with the genetics of cancerous animals and with transplanted tumors. At the Cancer Research Laboratory of the University of Pennsylvania Medical School, Ellice McDonald, its director, is steering a group of young scientists trying desperately from various angles to converge on the final attack and solution of the problem, which according to Dr. Henry Sigerist is not altogether a question of money and ingenious tools, but " to a certain extent a philosophical problem." Many states including fourteen in the South have adopted five-year programs of cancer research.

Maud Slye, too, is still at work. Her routine of a generation has not stopped for a day. She still lives across the street from her laboratory in Chicago. No zealot ever led a more strenuous life, dedicated to a single purpose, to rid mankind of the curse of the wild growth of the cell. In moments of relaxation she has cooled the fire within her with the writing of poetry. No verse expresses the soul of a research worker in science better than:

So many paths that lead!
'Twas not for me to go the happy road
Of flower-decked bride, and mother whose rich arms
Clasped all her babies; and of grandam set
Beside her late life's fire, who sees her brood
Of second generation gather round her knees
To be beguiled with tales.
O rosy firelight glow across her aged heart!
'Twas not for me to go that road of peace,
My head against your breast when evening came.

So many paths that lure!
I was not set upon the way that flames
With glory and acclaim, and accolades that ring
Deep in a sanctioned heart;
Or heard the bells peal out
In rioting, to sound the people's praise,
Or take the guerdon of a triumph won.
Oh golden glory of a trumpet's call!
'Twas not for me to go the victor's way,
A laurel on my brow when night closed in.

So many roads that go!
My feet were set upon the service path,
Whose glory of the day is toil,
Whose peace at nightfall is the peace of dreams

That reach beyond the stars!
Whose golden trumpet call
Is to the service of a higher toil.
O accolade of work folded away
And finished! It was for me to know the lonely feet,
The weary hands — but Oh the peace within my heart!

Today Miss Slye's laboratory is spurred by the momentum of greater certainty and newer accomplishments. It is only on the threshold of genetic possibilities and the interrelations of heredity and environment in the causation of cancer. And yet Maud Slye's position is such that even after twenty-five years of devoted service to truth, the professional existence of this scientist is still precarious.

CHAPTER FIVE

GLANDS

LOOKING AT PERSONALITY THROUGH CHEMICAL CRYSTALS

An account of the tremendous activity started by John Jacob Abel

IN 1474 a common barnyard cock in Basle laid an egg. Its terrified owner immediately notified the authorities. The cock was at once tried for witchcraft and sentenced to be burnt to death. In 1923, four and a half centuries later, F. A. E. Crew of the University of Edinburgh reported the equally fantastic case of a female fowl which had laid eggs, then later produced sperm like a male. This announcement, however, produced no unusual flutter. Some of the mystery of sex abnormalities in fowl, cattle, and even man has been removed during the last half century by the new science of endocrinology (*endo*, within; *krino*, separate), or the study of the internal secretions of the ductless glands. Begun in a welter of fraud, quasi-science, and careless credulity, and in its early stages sharply reminiscent of the balmy days of the search for the elixir of life, this new branch of scientific research still suffers from exaggerated claims. The story of the rise of endocrinology is a study in human frailty and the struggle between honest scientific investigation and flamboyant pseudo-science.

John Jacob Abel has lived through almost the whole of this history. He was the first to extract a pure product of the ductless glands, and he has worked continuously in the field for fifty years. Through his pioneer influence, America has taken a leading role in this tremendously important branch of science. American students had gone to Europe to study bacteriology, but the world later came to us to learn about the functioning of certain glands such as the thyroid, pituitary, adrenal, and pancreas, which pass their products directly into the blood stream without the use of ducts.

Abel was born near Cleveland of immigrant parents from Württemberg. He had no scientific forbears among either his paternal or maternal families in the Rhine Valley of the Palatinate. He grew up as an average child, and left college in his junior year to become principal of a small high school at La Porte, Indiana, where part of his job was to teach Latin, physics, and chemistry. The following year he became superintendent of schools of La Porte, and three years later returned to the University of Michigan, where at twenty-six he received a degree. In the meantime, he had been thinking of the possibilities of the application of medicine to criminal law, and had made up his mind to study both. At Johns Hopkins where he had matriculated for post-graduate work, he came under the spell of Newell Martin, the great physiologist, and research in physiological chemistry became his passion.

Like Welch, Abel wanted to spread out, and like Welch he sailed for Europe to spend seven *Wanderjahre* in the great centers of scientific learning and research. The most eminent teachers of Europe brought him the newer knowledge of science. Clinical medicine, surgery, pathology, neurology, ophthalmology, biochemistry — all were absorbed with equal appetite. In 1888 he was awarded an M.D. at Strassburg.

Abel became aware of the great events taking place in medicine. Bacteriology thrilled him, of course, but this was not the only startling growth of the time. Men were slowly returning to the dictum of Paracelsus that the animal body is a huge and complicated chemical workshop. "In the human being," said this Martin Luther of medicine, "there is present an invisible pharmacy and an invisible physician who produces, prescribes, dispenses and administers suitable remedies as occasion demands. Had not God created them, then, notwithstanding all the efforts of our physicians, not a single creature of the earth would remain alive." Paracelsus, the firebrand of Switzerland, had steered chemistry away from the vain attempt to make the philosopher's stone that would transmute the baser metals into gold, and from the equally false search for the elixir of life that would delay the encroachments of old age. He had pointed out to chemistry the road that led towards its application to medicine.

Abel felt that the words of Paracelsus, clothed in the new language of modern mechanistic science, were true. He believed that a sound knowledge of the physics and chemistry of the various body fluids, tissues, and organs would help to illuminate their function, and that this information would add a potent tool to the armamentarium of the physician at the bedside. Abel, the modern Paracelsus, dreamed of developing the old iatro-chemistry of herbs, extracts and chemical salts into the new physiological chemistry of tissues and organs for the relief of mankind.

It was while Abel was walking the wards of Vienna to obtain a sound basis for practical medicine that the world was stirred and entertained by some strange experiments performed in Paris by Brown-Séquard. This man was a queer mixture of eminent scientist and dreamy romanticist. Born on an island off the coast of Africa, of a French mother and an American sea captain, he had a colorful career, struggling from poetry and play writing to the practice of medicine. He came to New York a failure, married a niece of Daniel Webster, became professor of neuropathology at Harvard, and later occupant of the chair of physiology at the Collège de France. At seventy-two he found himself aging rapidly, and in the effort to rejuvenate himself attempted to prove his theory that secretions of the sex glands mobilize the energy of the body and neutralize the changes which come with advancing years.

On May 31, 1889, Brown-Séquard reported to the Society of Biologists in Paris that he had injected under his own skin by means of a hypodermic needle crude water extracts of the secretions of the testes of a dog. This treatment, he explained, had warded off the effect of old age, made him feel vastly more lively, changed the white of his cheeks to the flush of youth, and had improved his memory. He was no longer lethargic and had no further use of cathartics, he added. This episode has been called a triumph of psychological or suggestive therapy. Accurate and controlled experiments during the last few years on both old rats and senile men have shown that it could have been nothing else. But Brown-Séquard had started something. A whole cult of gland therapeutists and rejuvenation charlatans sprang up overnight. They were armed to the teeth with the "evidence" of this distinguished professor who occupied the chair left vacant by the death of Claude Bernard, the greatest physiologist of France — the man who had coined the term *internal secretions.*

This craze for rejuvenation by replacing sex glands reached its height thirty years later in the widely advertised experiments and claims of Serge Voronoff in Vienna and Eugen Steinach in Paris. Said Voronoff, after elaborate preliminary experiments with castrated rams, goats, bulls, and horses: "In 1913 I discovered a stock of spare parts for the human machine in the bodies of the higher species of monkeys. Between 1920 and 1928 I did one thousand human grafts. My first two patients were an engineer and a priest. Both had lost their sex glands from tuberculosis at twenty-one and twenty-seven. . . . On November 16, 1920, I used an ape for grafting a man of seventy-four who was in the most characteristic type of precocious senility, and found it successful. . . . On June 10, 1924, I grafted the ovary from a female chimpanzee to a woman of sixty-four. . . . My method assures the survival of the transplanted gland for several years. . . . By grafting sex glands on lambs, we have succeeded in developing super-rams. Why not try creating a race of supermen? The first mother who would entrust me with her child for this purpose might perhaps stimulate a new chapter in the history of humanity." Newspapers gave wide publicity to these reports, some believed tales of monkey children born of parents who had taken the monkey-gland treatment. Cartoons satirized the stories, rumors spread of men murdered to furnish surgeons with their healthy glands. Gertrude Atherton shocked many with her novel, *Black Oxen*, which told the story of a woman who, getting on in years and losing her old vitality, subjected herself to gland therapy. One distinguished scientist summed up the majority of scientific opinion with the remark, "If the transplant be from goat or monkey, the surgeon is the monkey; the patient is the goat."

When Abel returned to America he was called to the University of Michigan to become the first incumbent of a chair of pharmacology in America to devote full time to teaching and research in this particular field. Later, at the opening of the School of Medicine of Johns Hopkins in 1893, he came there as professor of pharmacology and temporary head of the department of physiological chemistry to join the Big Four — Welch, Osler, Kelly, and Halsted. Like the great Wöhler, whose researches leading to the synthesis of urea he vividly remembered, Abel began a study of urine, and was the first to separate carbamic acid from the human body. While investigating the chemical nature of the pigment in the skin of the negro, he read of an interesting experiment that Oliver and Schäfer had reported in England. They had found that a water extract of the adrenal gland, when injected into the veins of an animal, raised its blood pressure. The news that two Polish scientists had independently obtained the same results followed soon after. Abel accepted mankind's mandate to science, and set to work to isolate the pure form of the substance responsible for this action.

The adrenal glands (or suprarenal capsules) from which the blood-raising substance had been obtained are two small structures, yellowish in color and shaped like a cocked hat, perched on top of each kidney. These glands, which in the adult human weigh about four grams each, were first described in 1563 by the Italian anatomist Bartolommeo Eustacchi. They were known to receive great quantities of blood, but their function was a mystery. To obtain large quantities with which to work, Abel chose the adrenals of sheep. He scraped the fresh glands, dried them at 60°C., ground them up, and dissolved out all the fatty material with ether. A grayish white powder was left, of which the water solution showed great power to raise the blood pressure of the test animal, a morphine-anesthetized dog.

A carefully worked-out procedure was then followed in the attempt to isolate the active substance or principle free from all impurities. In 1897 Abel, assisted by Albert C. Crawford, obtained the pure or nearly pure product in the form of an active sulfate of a monobenzoyl derivative. This powder was the first derivative of the active principle of a ductless gland ever to be obtained by man. On May 6 of that year Abel announced this achievement at a meeting of the Association of American Physicians. The substance which he had isolated, however, was not the blood-raising constituent, but a derivative of it. The glory of obtaining the pure base was snatched from his hands by a Japanese chemist. While Abel was still endeavoring to improve his process of extraction and purification, he was visited one day in the fall of 1900 by Jokichi Takamine, who wanted to learn his process and see his final product. " He inquired particularly whether I did not think it possible that my salts could be prepared by a simpler process than mine. I told him that I was quite of his opinion that the process could no doubt be improved and simplified." Takamine listened attentively, and after remarking that " he loved to plant a seed and see it grow in the technical field," returned to his private laboratory in Clifton, New Jersey. Within a short time, by a slight change in Abel's procedure, Takamine obtained burrlike clusters of minute crystals of the base, which he patented under the name of *adrenalin* and placed on the market. This compound, known to the chemist as dihydroxymethylaminoethylolbenzene, $C_6H_3CHOH.CH_2NH.$-$CH_3(OH)_2$, was synthesized five years later by Stolz in the laboratory of a dye factory, thus marking the successful culmination of the combined labors of physiologists, pharmacologists, and biochemists.

Abel was urged by some friends to fight Takamine's claim to priority of discovery, but he refused. He could have been made rich at this time when all sorts of spurious glandular extracts flooded the market, but he opposed the private exploitation of scientific discoveries. He was sufficiently rewarded, he said, when in 1911 the United States Pharmacopeia officially accepted his name *epinephrin* (Greek, "upon the kidney") for the blood-raising constituent of the adrenal gland. What was of far greater importance was the fact that science and medicine now had in pure form a life-saving drug which could keep feeble hearts pumping and save the lives of thousands during critical emergencies of shock and collapse, when it is injected directly into the heart muscle. By constricting the blood vessels, the drug checks local hemorrhages of nose, ear, throat, and other organs, arrests acute hemorrhages, and checks paroxysms in bronchial asthma.

The function of adrenalin or epinephrin in the body has been studied by many investigators. In 1910 Walter B. Cannon found that the adrenal glands increased their output of adrenalin when the body was subjected to strong emotional disturbances. Adrenalin is of extraordinary potency. One millionth of a gram of it will raise the blood pressure of an adult ten millimeters. Its entry into the blood stream in even extremely minute amounts acts as a chemical SOS, mobilizing every organ to meet an emergency. Adrenalin is the compound of the hero and the coward; when present in large amounts it stimulates man or beast to fight. Here was scientific reason, some thought, for the custom of ancient warriors who ate kidneys to increase their fighting strength. This emergency theory of Cannon, generally accepted today, was tested on a cat. He drew some blood from the animal while it was quiet and undisturbed, and showed that it had no effect on the contractions of the muscle of a segment of a rabbit's intestine which had been removed for this experiment. (Many organs continue to function for some time after their removal from the living animal.) Then he brought in a barking dog, the cat was frightened and angered, and while it was in this condition of extreme emotion, Cannon again drew some blood and repeated the test. The effect on the contraction of the muscle was very marked. Adrenalin had been poured into the blood stream soon after the dog entered. Cannon also showed the inhibiting action of adrenalin on the muscular movements of the stomach and intestines of a living cat. He fed a cat with a meal rendered visible to X-ray by admixture with bismuth salts and watched the rhythmical movements of its alimentary canal. When the scrappy dog was again brought in, the movements of the cat's stomach were inhibited. He produced similar effects in the cat by the injection of a solution containing only one part of adrenalin in 200 million parts of water.

While Abel was occupied with his studies on adrenalin, the discovery of a second internal secretion was announced. It resulted from the attempts of physiologists to unravel the mechanism by which pancreatic juice was poured into the stomach to aid in digestion. Among the many who had worked on this problem was Pavlov, the veteran Russian scientist who has since won world-wide fame through his experiments with dogs on conditioned reflexes. Like everyone else, Pavlov believed that the secretion of pancreatic juice was caused by some nervous mechanism of a complexity too baffling to be understood. At this time William Bayliss was working in the physiology laboratory of the University of London. Ernest L. Starling had joined him in 1899, and together they tackled the problem. After carefully cutting the nerves leading to the pancreas, they were surprised to find that juice was still secreted. Evidently the nervous mechanism was not the controlling factor. "It must be a chemical reflex," Starling told Bayliss.

Now to test this theory. Through the open door of the laboratory on January 16, 1902, Bayliss could be seen holding a flask in one hand, and with the other introducing an extract into the blood of an anesthetized bitch whose small intestine had been tied off from the pancreas. The injected liquid was a clear acid extract of the small intestine of another dog. Starling was on his haunches, his eye on the level of a glass tube which had been inserted through an incision in its body into the pancreatic duct. This tube projected out from the animal's body so that he could watch any flow of fluid from that organ into the tube. The intestinal extract went in, the blood pressure fell, a pause; and then drop, drop, drop from the glass tube. " The moment when the first drop of pancreatic juice was sent into the glass tube by the injection of this intestinal extract must have been the most dramatic in their scientific careers," reported one who had watched the experiment.

Part of the mechanism of pancreatic pouring was indeed a chemical one. The cells lining the beginning of the small intestine produced a chemical which entered the blood without a duct. The chemical was carried to the pancreas by the blood and excited it to supply pancreatic juice to the food canal. This *hormone*, or " chemical messenger," as Starling first called it, belonged to the same group of vital chemical compounds as adrenalin. W. B. Hardy coined the word hormone from the Greek " I excite," or " I stir up." This word has been generally accepted to embrace any substance normally produced in the cell of some part of the body and carried by the blood to distant parts that it affects for the good of the organism as a whole. This is Starling's definition. Hormones were now added to the other mechanisms of the body, such as the nervous system and the blood, which coordinate the multitudinous activities of the living organism.

Potent extracts of the new hormone, named *secretin*, were prepared from the mucous membrane of the upper intestinal tract, and further experiments conducted. Bayliss became the special target of the anti-vivisectionists. The magazine *Life* shot a bitter broadside against him and published a picture of the dog which had suffered at his hands. He was harassed by lovers of animals and obstructors of medical progress; he sued a prominent lady anti-vivisectionist for libel, was awarded substantial damages, which he turned over to charity, and his work went on. The new hormone has not as yet been obtained in pure form, although the isolation of almost pure crystals was reported in 1933.

Twelve years of hard work were to pass before another of these essential hormones was extracted. During this time Abel was busied with the two active principles of that most poisonous of mushrooms, the *Amanita phalloides*, and finally succeeded in obtaining them in a high degree of purity from this " destroying angel." His laboratory resembled the filth pharmacies of seventeenth-century Germany where these *Dreck Apotheken* sold urine, excrement, hearts of animals, saliva of fasting men, lice, perspiration, and other sundries of ancient and forbidding vintage. No plant or animal substance was too vile, poisonous, or ill-smelling for Abel's research. He studied the odoriferous substances of the secretions of the common skunk. He found them to be none other than the evil-smelling sulphur compounds known as mercaptans that had long before been synthesized by organic chemists. The skunk is a very clever chemist, for it manufactures along with the very volatile mercaptans another substance which prevents the malodorous mercaptans from evaporating too rapidly after the skunk has sprayed his enemy. European manufacturers extract this substance from the skunk and add it to their perfumes to prevent them from evaporating too rapidly.

While investigating the convulsant effects of certain dyes on the tropical toad *Bufo agua*, Abel isolated from the milky secretion of the two large collections of skin glands situated on each side of the neck of the toad both the same epinephrin which he had obtained from the adrenals of cattle, and another powerful heart stimulant belonging to the digitalis group. *Bufagin* ($C_{18}H_{24}O_4$) was the name he gave to this new crystalline substance which for fifty years had eluded the efforts of chemists. Thus the old belief found in Shakespeare's *As You Like It* of the " precious jewel " found in the toad's head was not all fantasy. The Chinese had for centuries used powdered toad skins in a form called *senso* in the treatment of heart disease, just as digitalis is used today.

Answering the appeal of surgeons at Johns Hopkins for a good hypodermic purgative that could be used after serious abdominal operations, Abel began a study of various dye stuffs, some of which were known to have a purgative action. With

John Jacob Abel

Jack Earl, the world's tallest man, height 8 feet, 6 inches, age 20 years, is shown with some of his friends. His tremendous growth is the result of an overactive pituitary gland. *(Photos: Underwood & Underwood)*

This Lion-Faced Man, illustrates an abnormal hairiness due to the failure of the hair which covered him when he was an embryo to disappear. A somewhat similar condition of hairiness is due to abnormal glandular activity.

his co-worker L. G. Rowntree, he was led to another important discovery. In tracing the paths of dye secretions from the body, they found that bright red non-toxic phenolsulphonephthalein after injection under the skin or in a vein was excreted solely and almost completely by the kidney. This discovery has since been widely used as a test of the functioning of the normal or diseased kidney, because of its simplicity and freedom from complications. When injected into a healthy person, from 60 to 80 per cent of this dye can be recovered within two hours after injection into the blood. When, however, the kidneys are diseased, there is a great reduction in the amount of dye excreted.

While Abel was thus busy, a new hormone, *thyroxin*, was announced on Christmas Day, 1914, by E. C. Kendall. This young man had stolen a march on foreign scientists working feverishly in the same field. Hardly a pinch of this crystal is present in the human body at any one time, and yet it stands between life and death, normal mentality and idiocy. The search for this potent elixir had been a long adventure strewn with strange attempts and discarded theories. Kendall, starting in 1910 in the Pathological Laboratory of St. Luke's Hospital in New York, had reached the goal on the shoulders of hundreds of other investigators. One hundred and fifty years ago, an English physician described a trio of symptoms — protruding eyeballs, palpitating heart, and swelling of the neck — which seemed to be associated with enlargement of the purplish thyroid gland, situated around the larynx and windpipe. The average weight of the thyroid of an adult man is about one ounce, and it can be seen with a mirror. The ailment responsible for these symptoms was known in Germany as Basedow's and in England as Grave's disease. In 1850 another Englishman, studying large numbers of cretins in Salzburg, found associated with this pitiful condition a badly diseased thyroid, or the total absence of this gland. Cretins had been known for centuries. The village of Bozil had 190 of them out of a population of only 1472. They were misshapen humans, fat of belly, stary of eye, helpless and hopeless, vegetating in spite of all the attempts of medicine to help them, and usually died before they were ten years old. In 1858 animal experimentation was attempted in an effort to find the exact relation between these conditions and the functioning of the thyroid. When the thyroid of an animal was completely removed the animal died. This gland was evidently essential to life, according to the findings of this experiment.

Perhaps other vital organs besides the thyroid had been accidentally removed at the same time. Other experiments had to be tried. The thyroids of monkeys were therefore very carefully removed. It was found that instead of dying the monkeys developed symptoms similar to those of humans with diseased thyroids. For the first time science had experimentally produced *myxedema*, the disease appearing much later in life than cretinism and resulting from thyroid deficiency, characterized by thickening and drying of the skin, falling hair, low body temperature, low metabolism, and diminished sex function. A similar operation was performed on a human by a Swiss surgeon, and again myxedema resulted. To make up for the loss of the gland, the patient was given portions and extracts of the thyroids of sheep. He seemed to improve for a time but later died probably because of the impurity of the extract. The rather indefinite results, however, induced further trials with humans. One physician in England administered glycerine extracts of thyroid glands to a woman patient suffering from myxedema. The woman was saved from an early death, and before she died in 1919 at the age of seventy-four, she had consumed over a period of twenty-eight years the thyroid glands of eight hundred and seventy sheep.

Still this was all empirical. No one knew how the cures were being effected. The next important development was the extraction by Baumann of an impure iodine compound from his thyroid extract. This was a major step forward, for he had shown the presence of iodine in the potent principle of the thyroid. The discovery of the presence of iodine in the potent extracts of the thyroid recalls the strange use of seaweed centuries ago as a cure for goiter. Sticks of seaweed (now known to contain iodine) were collected by the coast inhabitants of South America, dried and carried across the pampas to the highlands where these " goiter sticks " were used in the treatment of goiter. Also for more than a century certain spring waters of Colombia, South America, were recognized and used against this sickness. These springs have since been found to be rich in iodides.

But Baumann's extract was still very crude. Then followed a scramble to obtain the hormone in the pure state. Years passed. It was known that the elusive hormone increased the metabolic activity of the body. This fact was used as a test of the potency of thyroid extracts. But this property allowed researchers to test the purity of their extracts only roughly. A more delicate test was needed. Then in 1912 J. F. Gudernatsch discovered that tadpoles fed on extremely minute amounts of thyroid extract metamorphosed into adult frogs very rapidly; so rapidly, in fact, that he could get from tiny tadpoles frogs no larger than flies. Since the first effect of metamorphosis was shortening of the tail of the tadpole, and since the rapidity of change depended upon the amount of thyroid principle employed, this change could be accurately used as a test of the purity of thyroid extracts.

Kendall, using all of these experimental techniques, finally forced thyroxin to capitulate. From three tons of the fresh glands of cattle he obtained thirty-five grams of the pure compound. The composition of thyroxin was at first inaccurately reported by Kendall, but its true formula was later determined. In 1927 C. R. Harington and Barger synthesized it as crystals of colorless needles, $C_{15}H_{11}O_4NI_4$, containing 65 per cent of iodine. Synthetic thyroxin was subjected to every physiological test on myxedema patients, and found to be identical in every way with the thyroxin obtained from sheep or man. Another triumph of synthetic chemistry!

The discovery of the function of the thyroid gland, namely, to control the metabolism of the body, and the isolation of thyroxin brought cretinism, myxedema, simple and exophthalmic goiter into the field of therapeutic medicine. Thyroxin placed many cretins on the road to normality. This new iodine-containing hormone speeded up the human engine in the case of myxedema patients, changing them from sluggish, weary beings into individuals with a renewed zest for life. Patients suffering from overactive thyroids (exophthalmic goiter) which kept pouring into their blood stream too much thyroxin, thus enormously increasing their metabolic rate, were cured by removal of the gland, in whole or in part. This lowering of the thyroxin supply slowed down their heart action, rendered them less nervous, less excitable, and their eyes returned to normal. Simple goiter, a condition increasing the size of the neck due to enlargement of the thyroid — giving the swanlike throats of Rossetti's painted ladies — has been enormously diminished by the statutory inclusion of salts containing iodine to foodstuffs and water in localities where there is a deficiency of this element in the food and water. Thyroid treatment has also been tried for the relief of sufferers from acute angina pectoris and congestive heart failure. Drs. H. L. Blumgart and D. D. Berlin of Boston have removed the thyroids of a score of such patients with hopeful results. The lowering of thyroxin supply slowed down the cardiac action, and this throttling of the human engine decreased the strain on the heart.

Then came Banting with *insulin*, and the pulse of the whole world was quickened by as spectacular an achievement as that of Pasteur or the Curies. Millions of diabetics saw another Messiah, in the raiment of the research worker, raising the dead to life again. *Diabetes mellitus*, first described two thousand years ago as " a melting of the flesh which flowed away in the urine," was associated with the pancreas two hundred and fifty years ago by a German investigator who chanced upon the discovery while working on problems of digestion. Almost two centuries passed until Langerhans, a young research worker, found in the pancreas a collection of cells which differed from the rest of the gland. They were named after their discoverer the *islets of Langerhans* and their function remained long unknown. In 1889 animal experimentation was successfully resorted to in this field. Minkowski removed the pancreas of dogs, which soon developed symptoms similar to those of human diabetes. Some of the urine of the dogs was left overnight on the laboratory table and evaporated, leaving a white solid. A curious assistant tasted it and found it sweet. Minkowski was told about this and, so the story goes, the presence of sugar in the urine of dogs deprived of their pancreas was first established. Others ascribe this discovery to Naunyn, the eminent Strassburg professor of medicine and Minkowski's chief, who watched flies collect on the urine of dogs from which the pancreas had been removed, and in an effort to find what attracted the insects tasted the fluid and found it to be sugary.

During these years, autopsies on diabetics disclosed that the islets of Langerhans were the part of the pancreas most seriously diseased in diabetic patients, and it was inferred that when healthy they elaborated some chemical which prevented the sugar sickness. The usual thing happened. Extracts of the gland were prepared in dozens of different ways and tried on animals and even men. But diabetes kept taking its deadly toll. Advances in chemistry, in the meantime, had placed in the hands of investigators a rapid and accurate method for determining minute amounts of sugar in the blood, where it appears before it is found in the urine. This enabled them to test the potency of their pancreatic extracts. When the research was in full swing, a young Canadian surgeon fresh from a wound at Cambrai came back to the University of Toronto from which he had been graduated some years before. Frederick Grant Banting was the scientist who was to make the great discovery.

Banting got the notion that he was going after a cure for diabetes. He had stumbled over a fresh clue. On the night of October 30, 1920, he was preparing a lecture, and read something that Moses Baron had reported in a medical journal to the effect that the tying up of the pancreatic ducts led to the death of the cells which produced a chemical named trypsin. It was this trypsin which destroyed the excess of the active principle of the islets of Langerhans, and this accounted to a great extent for the failure of many of the early experimenters to get successful results with their pancreatic extracts. Previous to Banting the ducts were not cut off and hence the trypsin destroyed the insulin which had accumulated in the pancreas. Banting reasoned that before the pancreas is removed, the duct leading to it should be tied to prevent trypsin from destroying the cells which produced the active principle (insulin) which prevented diabetes. At two in the morning, he jotted down three sentences in his notebook: "Tie off pancreatic ducts of dogs. Wait 6–8 weeks for degeneration. Remove the residue and extract." He came to the late Professor J. R. Macleod, an authority on the pathology and physiology of diabetes. Banting told him his story — he wanted laboratory facilities, an assistant for eight weeks, and ten dogs on which to experiment. His wish was granted.

Banting prepared an extract of the pancreas of dogs whose pancreatic ducts had been tied, and on the morning of July 27, 1921, shot the filtered liquid into the jugular vein of one of his dogs which he had rendered diabetic by removing his pancreas. Charles H. Best, a twenty-one-year-old medical student, had been assigned by Macleod to do the blood sugar analyses. When the cry of " the blood sugar is down " reached across that hot laboratory, Banting knew he had saved a dog from a diabetic death. Six months later a still purer pancreatic extract was tried for the first time on a human being, a young lad of fourteen lying in the Toronto General Hospital in the coma that meant diabetic death. The magic juice brought him back from the brink of the grave. Today a million living insulin takers bear testimony to this miracle of medicine and chemistry.

The function of insulin is not fully understood. The starch in our foods is changed to glucose (sugar) in the intestines, the sugar is taken up by the blood and carried to the liver, where it is converted into glycogen and stored there as such. This glycogen is supplied to the muscles of the body and reconverted into sugar. When a muscle is in use, some of its sugar is broken down and energy is released. This breaking-down process consists in the chemical union of the sugar with oxygen supplied by the blood from the lungs. The insulin merely acts as the spark which sets off this chemical reaction by which the sugar is decomposed.

Without insulin the sugar cannot be properly utilized, accumulates, and gradually passes off in the urine. The diabetic patient whose pancreas cannot produce any or enough insulin loses this very necessary source of energy. By injecting this missing insulin into the patient we relieve the condition, but do not cure it. Diabetics are doomed to insulin therapy until medicine can find a way to prevent the sickening or atrophy of the pancreas.

Banting had completed a dramatic piece of research. He was awarded the Nobel Prize, a life annuity of seventy-five hundred dollars from the Canadian Parliament, and was elevated to knighthood. Several other men had come very close to beating the Canadian in this adventure. Gley in 1906 had left a sealed note with the Société de Biologie telling of a pancreatic extract he had prepared which diminished the symptoms of diabetes in his test dogs. He failed to continue those promising results. In 1908 Zuelzer, with an alcoholic extract of the pancreas of calves, had treated six diabetic patients, only to drop his work when they contracted fever, showed weakness, nervousness, great hunger, and mental lapses. He had unknowingly given his patients too much of a good thing, causing them to exhibit the symptoms of hyperinsulinism. Said Macleod years later, "Had Zuelzer tried it more carefully on animals first, insulin might have been available in 1908." Again in 1911 E. L. Scott, working in a Chicago laboratory, actually tied the pancreatic ducts of dogs, and when success was almost in his hands, failed to interpret some of his findings and dropped the investigation. Then there was John R. Murlin of the University of Rochester, who rendered the urine of a pancreatomized dog sugar-free for six continuous hours, only to drop his hypodermic for a gun to go overseas. It was the old story so often repeated in the gamble of science. Priestley, discoverer of oxygen, had attributed his success to chance — chance which, to be sure, favored the mind prepared with the proper tools at the most opportune moment.

From Baltimore, Abel had followed breathlessly the drama of insulin. He knew personally most of the early investigators from Langerhans down to those of our day. Then at the invitation of A. A. Noyes, director of the Gates Chemical Laboratory of the California Institute of Technology, and with a grant from the Carnegie Foundation, he entered the adventure. He set himself the task of obtaining the pure principle or hormone of the potent extract that the Toronto pioneer was using. With such a chemical, any diabetic sufferer could exorcise from his breath that acetone odor which spelled doom. He leaned heavily on a group of younger men, including E. M. K. Geiling, who were working with him through the blackness of the pancreatic-extract mess. He accepted the suggestions of younger men with the remark that he was " an older soldier, not a better one." He never could forgive one professor who had cut short the work of a promising student in his laboratory, hot on the trail of the cure of diabetes, with a curt, " There is nothing in it." After finding a clue, Abel returned to Baltimore and held grimly to the task of inducing the still unknown hormone to free itself entirely from its unwanted contaminants and to obey the call of its own molecules to arrange themselves in a pure race of crystals. Finally one afternoon in November, 1925, four-tenths of a gram of insulin crystals appeared on the sides and bottom of his flask. They were tested on rabbits and found to be pure. By micro-analysis its chemical composition was found to be $C_{45}H_{69}O_{14}N_{11}S.3H_2O$ — a complex protein. Abel had added another chapter to the conquest of diabetes. Today any quantity of pure insulin can be obtained from the pancreas of cows, bulls, and steers. The fish islets of cod and pollock also contain this hormone.

But he was not ready to lay down his beaker and stirring rod. Insulin was a mean deliverer; it had to be injected under the skin. Unstable towards many body fluids, it could not be effectively taken by mouth, as the ferments of the digestive tract split it into pieces and rendered it innocuous. Abel wanted to save diabetics from the dreaded prick of the needle. How much more pleasant it would be to be able to take insulin by mouth. Perhaps the whole of the insulin molecule was not needed for its life-saving effects. If he could break it apart into fragments, discover the architecture of this complex compound, he might be able to find one potent portion resistant to the juices of the alimentary canal.

Not a moment was lost. Even when he sustained a broken leg in a street accident, within two days he was back at his crystals, on crutches, his leg in a cast. Planning the attack across a bridge table in his old laboratory while experimental monkeys screeched on the floor above, Abel in white coat and skull cap sips his afternoon tea, Hans Jensen and E. A. Evans, Jr., his assistants, review for the old master a few of the cleavage products which they have obtained in splitting the insulin protein compound. A number of amino acids — lysine, cystine, histidine, argenine, leucine, tryosine, phenylalanine, and glutamic acid — as well as proline, all already known to chemistry have so far been obtained, and they probably constitute the whole of the insulin molecule, whose tentative structural formula has been taken as:

```
      O
     //
    C – NH2
    |              HO
    CH2            |
    |              C = O
    CH2            |
    |              |
    CH – NH2       |
    |              |
    C = O          |
     \             |
      NH  –  CH  –  CH2 – S – S –
```

(Note: *The structural formula of a chemical compound gives much more information than the simple formula. The former tells the chemist how its atoms are arranged and thus gives a clue towards its synthesis.*)

But none of these single fragments have been found to be effective in relieving diabetes. They are trying to combine a few of them in the hope of obtaining an active compound which will not be destroyed by the juices of the alimentary canal and which will save diabetics by oral administration. There are dozens of theories and thousands of isomers and derivatives to take into account. Many laboratories — Toronto, London, Washington, Columbia University, Heidelberg, and Amsterdam — are busily engaged in this piece of research. They are all still in a jungle, Abel admits, but the insulin molecule must surrender, and let us hope that he will be the first to enter the citadel. He has been laboring more than ten years on the problem, while other men have been engaged in the study of other hormones.

One of that countless number of diabetics whose lives were saved by insulin was a country surgeon in the San Joaquin Valley of the West. His son, Herbert McLean Evans, obtained his M.D. at Johns Hopkins in 1908, and had gone in for research. Evans' father had frowned upon his early determination to take up scientific research as a career, but when the miracle of insulin saved his life, he agreed with Herbert that " this monkey business was all right." Evans had spoken of the possibilities of specialization to his teacher, Jacques Loeb, who had counseled him: " Don't be a classified scientist. Step out into new fields, and don't be afraid to impinge on other fields." Evans took the advice and jumped from one research to another. The boundaries of science were fast falling; men were poaching on each other's territories with reckless abandon, and it was difficult to remain pent up in one's own chosen field. Evans started as anatomist, became interested in embryology, grew tired of cutting up tissues, and wanting to see each step in the body drama, was caught up in the snare of the dynamics of biological research, including gland work.

Even as Banting was slaying dogs to save men, Evans was achieving a startling discovery in this field with another mysterious gland, *hypophysis cerebri*, commonly called the *pituitary*. This is a bit of an organ safely housed in a small pocket of bone attached to the base of the brain. Both Galen and Vesalius knew of this gland and thought it supplied the body with spit (in Latin, *sputus*). It is one of the most inaccessible glands in the living body. For many years, there appeared to be some connection between body growth and the functioning of this gland. In 1783 John Hunter had bargained with an undertaker for the body of an Irish giant of eight feet, four inches — Charles O'Brien, who had died at the age of twenty-two. The physician finally bought the body for twenty-five hundred dollars, and found a pituitary almost as large as a hen's egg. That of a normal adult man weighs hardly more than half a gram. A century later, *acromegaly*, an enlargement of the hands, feet, nose, lips, and jaw, was declared to be due to a tumor of the pituitary. The pituitary glands of dwarfs, some of them only eighteen inches high, all showed relatively small development or partial atrophy.

In the attempt to find whether the pituitary elaborated a hormone which controlled growth, Evans prepared water extracts of the pituitary glands of oxen obtained from slaughter and packing houses. In 1920 he first unsuccessfully tried oral administration of large masses of the pituitary, and then turned to injection of his extracts in baby rats. Within a few months he obtained giant rats; not just fat ones, but giants with overgrowth of bones, heart, liver, lung, kidneys, alimentary tract, and other organs. When Evans stopped the injections soon after the weaning of the rat, the growth stopped immediately. When he injected his extract into rats dwarfed by removal of their pituitaries, the beasts regained their normal size. Hogben in England later used a similar extract on a large aquatic salamander, and got a rapid metamorphosis.

If this miracle could be achieved with rats, why could it not be repeated with man? Were not the compositions and physiological actions of hormones identical regardless of the kind of animal from which they had been obtained? Was not insulin from sheep identical with insulin extracted from man, cow, pig, or even pollack or codfish? When Evans had prepared a purer and more potent extract, this experiment was actually tried on a girl, J. M., nine years old. Dr. William Engelbach of New York City treated this child, whose physical development had been dormant for almost four years, and in 1931 was able to announce a growth of 2.7 inches obtained over a period of about eight months. Other physicians followed this treatment and many striking successes were reported. One undersized boy of fifteen gained eight and a half inches in twenty-one months.

Some saw visions of a not far distant day when midgets, giants, and dwarfs would go the way of the *Brontosaurus* and the armored dinosaur, themselves the victims of faulty glands, into oblivion. Perhaps the mushroom which Alice in Wonderland had found, one side of which will make you grow taller and the other side will make you grow shorter, was in reality the pituitary extract of Evans in California. Some pictured a race of giants springing up at the prick of a hypodermic. What would such men of very small stature as Croesus, King of Lydia, and Attila, the Hun, not have given to be changed to giants or even to men of normal size? But Evans himself did not break out in wild romancing. "It is said," he remarked, "that the Mikado wished to add to the stature of the Japanese soldiers. The growth-promoting hormone should be able to do it, but even the Mikado could not pay the price that it would cost at present. It may take a decade to determine its formula and even longer to synthesize it from coal tar as the raw material. We are but the faint beginners of the work." To date, the hormone, called by some *phyone*, has not yet been obtained pure from its extracts.

Several years before Evans' investigation of the growth-stimulating hormone of the pituitary, Harvey Cushing, famous surgeon of the Harvard Medical School, had removed parts of the pituitaries of two hundred dogs, and had reported other changes besides arrest of growth. His dogs become obese, sluggish, and their sex organs shrank. Evans had found that his extract, while enabling the animal to resume growth, was powerless to restimulate the sex function of his rats. Mating in female rats deprived of their pituitary did not result in discharge of ova, but if the gland was removed less than one hour before coitus, ova were discharged. Perhaps the pituitary was the seat of a second hormone — one which stimulated the production of ova. A number of investigators undertook this research. A technique for handling the problem was available, worked out in 1917 by Charles R. Stockard and G. N. Papanicolaou, his student. They had found that smears made from the vagina of the guinea pig taken at various times showed under the microscope a differentiation in the kind of cells present. In animals the period of sexual activity, or oestrus, coincides with the discharge of ova. When their guinea pig was in oestrus, the cells consisted of clearly defined types and stained a bright red with the dye eosin. When it was not in heat, the cells were different. Hence, by examining vaginal smears taken at different times, the sexual activity of the animal could easily be determined. In 1922 Evans and Long worked out by means of this technique the regular clocklike cycle of the rat. It was found to be four days as compared with the guinea pig's oestral cycle of seventeen days and the human cycle of about thirty.

The following year Philip E. Smith, working in Evans' laboratory at Berkeley, California, illuminated the whole field by devising a very skillful technique including the use of a dissecting microscope which enabled him with comparative ease to reach and remove the pituitary of the rat through incision in the throat. Deterioration of the sex function always followed removal of the pituitary. Then he also conclusively proved that it was something in the pituitary which had powers of sex stimulation by implanting under the skin of a rat from which the pituitary had been removed the same gland obtained from another rat. This transplant led to repair of the sex damage and even to precocious sex functioning. Grafting the entire gland was not altogether necessary because injections of extracts of the gland produced the same effect.

Philip E. Smith, now professor of anatomy at the College of Physicians and Surgeons in New York, was fortunate in using the rat in his transplantation experiments, for the guinea pig, rabbit, cat, and dog do not respond to this treatment. But he was also very unlucky. Four months before he could announce the results of his work, B. Zondek and S. Aschheim in Germany published a report of their pituitary implants in immature young animals. They had also succeeded for the first time in obtaining fairly potent extracts of the sex-stimulating hormone of the pituitary. *Prolan* was the name they gave to their extract. The honor of discovering the sex-stimulating hormone of the pituitary was thus snatched from the American, as the result of prior publication by the Europeans.

Furthermore, in the course of these investigations Zondek found that injections of the urine of pregnant women had the same effect on mice as did his pituitary extract. This led Aschheim and Zondek to the discovery of the first reliable human pregnancy test. This test, much modified and improved since 1928, consists of injecting urine of the woman being tested under the skin of a non-mated female mouse or rabbit. About forty-eight hours later the animal is killed, and its sex organs upon examination show certain definite cellular changes. This method, which is 99 per cent accurate, will determine human pregnancy as early as the third week after conception. It has proved a great boon to thousands of women concerned about their condition. (An even quicker and cheaper method has also been introduced. The Japanese bitterling has an externally visible ovipositor. When a few cubic centimeters of the urine of a pregnant woman is introduced into the bowl in which this little fish is swimming about, its ovipositor increases in length tenfold until it becomes almost one inch long. This change takes about 24 hours, and after a few weeks the fish can be used over again for another test.)

Hard on the heels of prolan came the announcement of the discovery of a third hormone of the pituitary. Oscar Riddle of Cold Spring fed a pituitary extract to pigeons, and found that their ability to secrete crop-milk was appreciably enhanced. This milk-producing hormone, which Riddle named *prolactin*, produced milk in the mammary glands of other animals, including the males. Even a tomcat gave milk after being injected with this hormone. Recently Riddle reported that his prolactin may be a mixture of two hormones with somewhat different physiological effects. It stimulates the mother instinct. A hen two days after being injected with this hormone started to cluck and the next day it began to incubate and nest. A full-grown unmated female rat after being injected with the extract, instead of devouring two helpless pigeon squabs placed in its cage tenderly nursed them. Perhaps some day, it has been suggested, mother-love will be bought at the corner drugstore at so many pennies a bottle. A fourth hormone in the pituitary was reported in 1933 by a French investigator, who claims thyroid stimulation as one of its effects.

In the meantime, in the biochemical laboratory of the University of St. Louis Medical School, Edward A. Doisy read Zondek's original report, which gave him a new lead in his hunt for the hormone of the ovary gland. He had already worked with the follicular liquid of pig's ovaries with some success. To check the potency of his extract he made use of the vaginal smear method developed by Edgar Allen, who had made a brilliant study of the sex cycle of another animal, the mouse. From lying-in hospitals, Doisy collected thousands of gallons of urine of pregnant women. By devising new condensers and novel set-ups of distillation apparatus, he was able to handle as much as fifty gallons of urine at a time. For six years he worked with all sorts of solvents on the problem of separating a hormone from this fluid, until he obtained an extremely potent substance present in urine only to the extent of one part in four million. On August 23, 1929, Doisy announced his isolation of the pure hormone of the female sex organ. Two of the most skillful biochemists of Europe, Adolf Butenandt of Göttingen and E. Laqueur, had been beaten in the quest by but a few months. *Theelin* (from the Greek word *theelus* meaning female) was the name chosen for the new hormone by its discoverer. Its composition was found to be $C_{18}H_{22}O_2$. Other investigators later found theelin in the ovaries of monkey, horse, sheep, cow, pig, fowl, and fish, and in their feces. Several other female sex hormones have been found by various workers. Among these is *progestin* which is elaborated by the corpus luteum, the yellowish liquid formed from the mature (Graafian) follicles of the ovary after rupture and discharge of their ova. Progestin, which was prepared in pure form, inhibits the growth of ovarian follicles and prepares the uterus for the reception and nourishment of the developing embryo. Butenandt who determined the formula of this new hormone in 1935 also reported a theelin duplicate in palm nuts. Theelin has been used with some apparent measure of success in the treatment of hemophilia, and thickening of the vagina of children, in the alleviation of abnormal menstrual conditions, in the temporary adjustment of severe menopause symptoms, in the prevention of periodic migraine, and senile affections, in cases of functional sterility, delayed puberty, infantilism and frigidity.

After this dramatic American scoop, a renewed attack was launched on the hormone of the male sex gland. A group of University of Chicago workers under the direction of F. C. Koch and the guidance of the Committee for Research on Problems of Sex had been busy on this research since 1923. Lemuel C. McGee, one of these workers, succeeded in obtaining an extract from fresh finely chopped bull testes tissue, which proved effective in a test, based on a fact known for centuries. The removal of the testes of a cock changed it into a bird with flesh more tender than that of the normal male. The castrated fowl, called a capon, was different from the cock in other respects, also. The operation had psychic effects. The courageous, combative rooster changed to a timid, peaceful, maternal animal. It seldom crowed, and in some cases even took care of chicks like a hen. Another very noticeable change took place on the head furnishings. The comb and wattles became less developed, and the bright, exuberant, ornamental feathering of the male less colorful.

McGee injected his extract into a capon in April, 1927. Its small comb became large and upright. Its wattles, too, grew larger. His extract contained the male hormone which was responsible for the growth of these male characters. Then Koch and his wife began purifying this extract in the hope of obtaining the pure crystal principle. As test animals they used capons from which every vestige of the sex glands were surgically removed. And while other members of the same laboratory were trying out both the guinea pig and the rat as possible test animals, word came from Europe in 1932 that a pure male hormone had been isolated in crystal form. This time Adolf Butenandt, who had previously lost out to Doisy in the isolation of the female sex hormone, was the victor. He had obtained the hormone from the kidney fluids of men rather than from their sex gland. Its formula was given as $C_{19}H_{30}O_2$, not very different from that of theelin. In fact, Butenandt theorized that it could be made from the female hormone. Late in 1934 L. Ruzicka of the Zurich Technical High School synthesized it from cholesterol obtained from the grease of sheep's wool.

This male hormone, named *androsterone*, is not the hormone of the testes. The testicular hormone, called *testosterone*, was first obtained in the pure crystal form by E. Laqueur of Amsterdam, Holland, in June, 1935. He isolated it from the testes of bulls, in which it is present in extremely minute quantities. It is the same substance obtained from the male sex gland of boar, goat, man and, strangely enough, the male blossoms of the pussy willow. This second male hormone has the same chemical formula as androsterone but its chemical structure is somewhat different. In September, 1935, Ruzicka reported the synthesis of this hormone also.

For the first time science had the two pure male sex hormones to evaluate the claims of the school of rejuvenation through sex-gland operations. Steinach replaced his famous monkey-gland technique which required surgical operation by theelin or androsterone injections, but thus far there is no indication that they are of any great value in restoring vigor to the old. Says Stockard: "Steinach and Voronoff were misled into the belief that degeneration of the sex gland is itself responsible for the aging process. This is based on error. It is a symptom and not a cause. The ox, the castrated horse, and the capon do not age either faster or slower than their normal prototypes, the bull, the stallion, and rooster." In the meanwhile, Voronoff, after performing twenty-six hundred monkey-gland operations, left for Persia to find a new clue to the secret of longevity. Senile and otherwise foolish people still pursue him dreaming of the restored vigor of youth.

The isolation of theelin, testosterone, and androsterone has enabled science to fathom a little deeper the many problems of sex which have bothered men for centuries. It explained the results of the research of A. A. Berthold who in 1849, varying similar experiments of almost a century before, removed the testes of cocks and reimplanted them under the skin elsewhere on the body. No castration effects were noticeable, because the testes continued to pour into the blood stream the hormone responsible for male characteristics. A similar explanation can now be advanced to explain the experiments of another investigator who in 1900 grafted ovaries in all sorts of unusual places on the body, and still obtained sex stimulation in animals. Goodale's curious experiments of 1916 are also clearer today. When he transplanted the ovary of a hen into a capon, the castrated male bird turned female with complete feminization of plumage and head furnishings, and even behavior. The hormone of the ovary entered the blood of the castrated male and changed it into a female.

Frank R. Lillie, later president of the National Academy of Sciences, also made a capital discovery at this time, not knowing that six years before two Austrians had already done the same work. It involved an explanation of *free martins.* Cattle sometimes produce twins, one of which is a male, while the other, a female, shows characteristics of both sexes. The latter, called a free martin, is sterile and has deformed genitalia. Lillie studied a large number of free martins obtained from slaughter houses. He found that the blood systems of these twins, instead of being separately connected to the parent, were in direct communication with each other before birth. The hormone of the male testes entered the blood stream of the undeveloped female, causing bodily changes characteristic of its male twin. A few years later Sand in Copenhagen produced a gynandromorph or sex-mosaic by giving a cock an ovarian implant, following which he plucked the feathers on one side of the bird. The new feathers, under the influence of the female hormone elaborated by the transplanted ovary, were female. At the University of Chicago Mary Juhn in 1930 injected male brown leghorns with the sex hormone of women and the birds put on female plumage.

These discoveries shed light on the changes that boys underwent after being castrated to fit them as guards in Turkish harems or as soprano singers in the Sistine Chapel at Rome (as late as 1878). The wan, hairless, flabby, corpulent, weak-memoried eunuchs are as different from a virile man as the gelded horse and the docile ox from the wild stallion and the wild bull. The study of the sex hormones has also thrown a penetrating light into such sex abnormalities as that reported by Karl Menninger. This psychiatrist wrote: "A soldier after the war had sleeping sickness. After his illness, his beard ceased to grow, his voice became high pitched, his breasts enlarged until they had to be amputated, he gave up masculine in favor of feminine pursuits and interests, so that when I saw him he was sitting in a bed in a ward in a hospital, contentedly knitting." In this particular case, illness had resulted in a glandular disturbance of the sex organs. Hermaphroditism, common among most plants and many forms of animals, very infrequently but none the less actually occurs in man. A typical case is that of a full-breasted person with feminine form and behavior, and male sex organs. These partly male, partly female humans present strong evidence of the power of the sex hormones to change personalities.

The explanation of sex based on glandular factors was not the only one advanced. The gene theory of sex was also well established. The bubbling kettle of hormone research boiled over and almost engulfed the theory of sex determination based on the gene or XY chromosome mechanism first demonstrated by T. H. Morgan's school of geneticists. They had piled up convincing evidence of its plausibility, especially in the case of Drosophila. Now the data gathered by endocrinologists seemed to point to the fact that the secretions of the internal glands, especially those of sex, were the controlling factors in sex development. There had been theories galore to explain why certain organisms were male and others female. Aristotle thought that the male supplied the form of species, and that if the male seed was not vigorous we got an imperfect organism, or female. For centuries many believed that the contents of the right testicle produced the male while that of the left produced a female; that when an old male mated with a young female, a female was always born; that the age of the father, the diet of the mother, the temperature at the time of conception, and even the wind direction were determining factors. As late as 1933, one scientist attempted to prove that an excess of alkaline substances such as sodium bicarbonate produced male progeny, while an excess of acid compounds like lactic acid found in sour milk stimulated the birth of females.

Today science, while still very far from one universally accepted theory of sex determination, has taken the position that both the nature of the chromosomes and the functioning of the various glands of the body are the chief determining factors. Morgan, who believes that many if not all of the genes are sex-determining in the same way that many if not all affect the development of each character, has said: " There is a double relation in sex-determination. Normally the presence of certain genes determines sex, but under unusual conditions its power may be partially overcome and even a reversal of sex may take place. Temperature, light, hormones, or ' age ' may cause the reversal." Many examples of sex reversals have been cited to uphold this position. In cold weather, the gypsy moth produces more females. The worm *guibea protanduca* is male in autumn and winter, female in the spring, and neuter in the summer. A starved male salamander may turn into a female. Nansen, the explorer, reported the deep-water bagfish remains male when small but changes to female when a foot long. The starfish *asterina gibbosa* may be male, female, or both, according to age and circumstances. Certain old female fish develop testes and function as males.

The subject is extremely complicated. There is still another explanation. Lillie believes that each cell produced by the union of an ovum and a sperm is potentially hermaphroditic, and that glandular disturbances, environment, or other conditions might cause one sex to become stronger than the other. He also maintains that the sex of these cells and the sex in the body structure are two different things. Aside from the theoretical importance of this topic, it has possible practical implications. Breeders of cattle and other animals are tremendously interested in the sex of the young which are born. Cows are more valuable to them than bulls, and hens more wanted than roosters. Attempts have been made to control the sex of animals on the basis of the scientific facts available, and already some measure of success has been reported. Workers in the Indiana University Zoological Laboratory announced in July, 1934, that by injecting theelin into the air-spaces of the large ends of eggs, the sex ratio of nine hundred chicks was changed from a 50 : 50 to a 35.22 male : 64.78 female percentage. From Moscow at the same time came the news that artificial sex control had been achieved with rabbits. A different method was employed. The Russian experimenter, N. K. Koltsov, used a technique which electrically separated those sperm cells of the male rabbit whose chromosomes showed characteristics which would lead to the birth of females. He then injected them into female rabbits who were thus artificially made pregnant. Of the first two hundred trials made one hundred and eight came out as planned, that is, produced female rabbits. The others proved inconclusive either because of failure to produce young or because of the production of fewer females than expected. The method, says the Russian, is applicable to cattle and probably also to man. Jennings in 1932 summed up the problem of sex determination as follows: "Many of the effects of the gene in development are produced through the action of the hormones they manufacture. *What hormone is present depends again on what set of genes was present in the beginning.*"

While Evans, Zondek, Riddle, and others were investigating the extracts of the front or anterior lobe of the pituitary, Abel attacked the rear or posterior lobe of this strategic gland. As early as 1917 he had already invaded this sanctum. Five years later he obtained an extract which produced a sharp and sustained rise in arterial blood pressure, and seemed to function as one of the regulators of the body metabolism. It appeared to have other functions. This extract (the pure principle is still un-isolated) is so powerful that a dilution of one part in fifteen billions is sufficient to produce maximum contractions of the uterus of a pig. Its clinical uses for stimulating the contractions of labor, to induce labor during the last three weeks of pregnancy, or to control hemorrhage during delivery are still considered too dangerous by obstetricians.

Other workers entered this field of the posterior pituitary. Oliver Kamm announced that the extract reported by Abel could be separated into two portions named *pitressin* and *pitocin*. These extracts contained the blood-raising principle and the uterine stimulant respectively. To date in various laboratories, altogether twenty-two different extracts of hormones have been squeezed out of the posterior lobe of the pituitary. Abel resists the coinage of new names for these alleged posterior pituitary hormones, for his researches have led him to the belief in a *unitary theory* of several of these posterior pituitary principles. He believes this gland secretes one mother molecule or master hormone which splits up and produces other smaller entities, such as pitressin and pitocin, having varying physiological properties. In the body itself each of these components plays its own role without being detached from the master molecule. In spite of the mass of reports being published in this field, Abel still clings to his unitary theory, although it may well be that this may some day be added to his "cupboard of mistakes." And even this would not ruffle Abel.

Philip E. Smith showed that removal of the pituitary led to underdevelopment of the sex organs, impairment of the thyroid, and interference with the secretion of the adrenals. Evans found a relation between the pituitary and the body's use of sugar. He produced a true diabetic dog by feeding it extracts of this gland. It has also been demonstrated that pituitary extracts produced the symptoms of an overactive thyroid. Removal of the sex glands apparently changes the hormones of the pituitary. The omnipotence of the pituitary has led some to call it the master gland of the body, which controls the balance between all the others.

Research men were busy with other glands besides the pituitary which produced more than one hormone. The adrenal glands, seat of the adrenalin extracted by Abel, gave up another chemical messenger which if thwarted on its errand of life, left dangerous consequences. In 1855 Addison, senior physician to Guy's Hospital in London, described a number of cases of a peculiar disease which often ended in death. The outstanding symptoms were weakness of the nervous, muscular, and circulatory systems. Heart action became feeble, and a bronzing of the skin accompanied a general breakdown of the body. Addison associated with this disease, now known by his name, lesions of the adrenal glands which he had found during the post-mortems. With the rise of endocrinology, glandular treatment was resorted to in the attempt to cure or at least arrest this fatal malady. Extracts of the adrenals were prepared and tried, but they proved powerless against the skin discoloration which presaged an early doom.

The dramatic achievement of Banting had brought another physiologist into the field of hormone research. Frank A. Hartman had taught at the University of Toronto and remembered Banting leaving for overseas service years before he became famous. When the insulin discovery was announced, Hartman was teaching at the University of Buffalo. He immediately picked up the trail of the adrenal workers, and set to work to isolate some potent principle from the outer layer or cortex of the adrenal gland. It was this portion of the organ which seemed to be most intimately connected with Addison's disease. From the Armour Packing Company of Chicago and the Hygrade

Packing Company of Buffalo, Hartman received the fresh adrenal glands of cows. He was able to work with more than a hundred pounds of these glands per week. The cortex was separated from the inner portion of the adrenal gland, ground in a meat chopper, treated with various solvents, adrenalin, its other hormone, was removed by washing, and finally, with the aid of his son, a medical student at the time, Hartman obtained a highly concentrated extract. By subcutaneous injections of this substance he was able to prolong the lives of twenty-one cats, from each of which both adrenals had been surgically removed in two stages. Instead of dying, the animals remained in perfect health so long as they were given the adrenal cortex extract. These cats played, ran, fought, ate canned salmon and beef, even went into heat, mated, and some of them became pregnant.

In October, 1927, Hartman announced the production of *cortin,* a potent extract of the hormone produced in the cortex of the adrenal gland. The absence of this substance led to Addison's disease in man. Could his extract actually save the lives of victims of this malady? The whole medical world waited. The National Research Council and the Carnegie Foundation made grants to Hartman to continue his work. On July 8, 1930, the test was made on a twenty-four-year-old man close to death from Addison's disease. Injections of cortin kept him alive and improved his condition. Withdrawal of the extract or reduction of the dosage brought immediate relapses. The man's life was prolonged for some time, but the disease was already too far advanced and he died later at the Buffalo General Hospital. Hartman, now at Ohio State University, and others worked untiringly to obtain purer and more effective extracts. W. W. Swingle and J. J. Pfiffner of Princeton University prepared extracts which were also successfully tried on men. On animals, their preparation seemed to act as a brain tonic. They gave sheep and goats the jitters with all sorts of psychological tricks, then cured them of this nervousness by injections of their adrenal cortex extracts. Early in 1934 the isolation of pure cortin in the form of crystals was reported for the first time by E. C. Kendall of thyroxin fame. Whether this compound whose formula has been given as $C_{20}H_{30}O_5$ is the pure principle is still unsettled. Pure cortin will be a new boon to medicine, a chemical compound which can almost bring the dead back to life, for even the extracts used are already saving many lives from Addison's disease. Cortin is also being used successfully against glaucoma. This condition of hardening of the eyeball is a common cause of blindness among aging people.

The Banting exploit had another repercussion. When the Canadian had saved the lives of dogs and was ready to apply his extract to men, James B. Collip, a graduate of Toronto University, was set to work to improve the method of making large batches of insulin extract. When that job was over, he got to work on two pairs of glands, the parathyroids. These had been discovered in 1855 as four brown bean-shaped and pea-sized bits of tissue situated in pairs on the sides of the thyroid gland. Their function had remained a mystery. Later, however, it was found that when they were diseased or removed, tetany resulted, that is, muscular twitchings of hands, feet, face, and even windpipe, took place, which often ended in death. W. G. MacCallum of Johns Hopkins found that removal of the parathyroids led not only to those symptoms of tetany mentioned, but also to a lowered calcium content of the blood. He succeeded in actually alleviating tetany by ample doses of calcium salts. Collip noticed that tetany resulted also from long-continued and heavy forced breathing. J. B. S. Haldane, in an effort to test this observation, experimented on himself. Not only did he verify Collip's report by getting tetany after forced breathing but he also found that he suffered no ill effects if heavy breathing was preceded by the consumption of large quantities of ammonium chloride salt.

The calcium method of treating tetany was not the only one used. As usual, gland therapy was also tried. Its partial success led Collip and others to attempt the preparation of an extract against tetany from cattle parathyroids. Collip obtained an extract, *parathormone*, which proved effective when used on dogs whose parathyroids had been surgically removed. He was, however, not the first to obtain a potent extract. Adolf M. Hanson, a practising physician of Faribault, Minnesota, had reported a similar extract in a little-known journal, and later proved priority. The patent received for this product he assigned to the Smithsonian Institution. And while the search for the pure hormone of this gland is still under way, its extracts are being used to treat not only cases of tetany but also adolescents suffering from a deficiency of calcium which, according to some, results in a variety of disorders from misbehavior to slowness of growth and bone deformities. Overactive parathyroids cause softening of the bones. This can be treated by gland surgery. Harvey B. Stone of Baltimore told the American College of Surgeons late in 1934 that he and his associates had succeeded for the first time in transplanting parathyroid tissue from one human being to another. The graft, which is usually absorbed or thrown off, continued to grow in the armpit of the patient where it was grafted and in due time corrected the patients tetany. The success of the method depended to a great extent on the new technique of growing the tissue outside the body for some time in the serum of the person on whom the graft was to be made to accustom the glandular tissue to its new environment. Stone also succeeded in transplanting bits of thyroid tissue and his successes give hope for future advances in this field of gland therapy by gland transplantation. Instead of the patient being doomed to continuous medication with hormones he will be given a new healthy gland which will function normally.

The mystery of still another gland is gradually being solved. In 1855 a little memoir appeared on the thymus, but the author had no notion of its function. Some believed it to be a vestigial organ which had outlived its usefulness. It sometimes enlarged and choked off the life of a child by closing its windpipe. This thymus gland is a soft pinkish mass located above the heart, which grows from about a quarter of an ounce at birth to a full ounce at puberty, then gradually shrinks, leaving but a tiny remnant. Until very recently not even an inkling of the function of this " baffling badge on our hearts " had been found. Gudernatsch had fed bits of thymus to tadpoles, which grew to enormous sizes without ever changing to frogs. Riddle had given extracts of ox thymus to pigeons with defective thymus, and reported a remarkable effect. Thymus-defective pigeons had been laying yolks instead of complete eggs, but when given the extract they laid normal eggs.

In 1934 Leonard G. Rowntree, who had worked with Abel many years before, obtained some thymus extract. He fed it to rats and obtained most curious results. Each succeeding generation of thymus-fed rats developed faster growth rates and greater sexual precocity. Fourth- and fifth-generation rats erupted their teeth in less than twenty-four hours, as compared to the eight days required by the normal animal. The eyes of the young opened in two instead of fourteen days; their fur covering was completed with the same speed. Within less than three days after birth they were weaned, and within another three could swim. The thymus extract rushed them into parenthood at an alarming speed. A tenth-generation rat had a litter of eight within forty-three days, while a normal animal required from eighty to one hundred and twenty days. Translated into human terms, " girls and boys might become sexually mature at the age of eight or ten if they, their parents, grandparents and great-grandparents had been treated with thymus extracts." The implications of this discovery were obvious. This " precocity " hormone might revolutionize the entire livestock industry. In the future cattle might be raised in a fraction of the time now required, with a corresponding decrease in cost. The Federal Bureau of Animal Husbandry as well as other laboratories have already begun further investigations along this line. Thymus extracts have already actually been tried for both mental and physical stimulation of backward children, and some are hopeful of successful results. These are strange dreams, but science has turned more than one dream into a reality. One quivers at the possibilities of the pure crystalline thymus hormone now being sought in various laboratories.

The last of the organs of the body to be probed thus far is the pineal gland (from Latin, *pinea*, pine-cone). This cone-shaped tissue hidden in the brain still holds tenaciously to the secret of its function. The extreme difficulty of removing this little organ has not frightened away some of the bolder spirits in the endocrine field. Water extracts of this pineal gland have already done fantastic things. With it the normal rate of division of the paramecium was increased. By means of this extract, the transformation rate of tadpoles into frogs has been speeded up by other investigators. The development of chicks and rats, too, has apparently been accelerated. Dr. Henry H. Goddard tried it on retarded children in the hope of hastening their development. Thus far the data collected have been contradictory and difficult of analysis. Descartes thought the pineal the seat of the soul; some investigators wonder if it is really a gland which can pour out a specific hormone. Perhaps a yet unborn Abel will find the key to unlock the riddle.

The adrenals, thyroid, parathyroids, pancreas, pituitary, sex glands, thymus, and pineal are thus far the generally accepted ductless glands, that is, glands which pour their hormones directly into the blood stream without the aid of ducts. In a larger sense, however, all juices that get into the blood stream may be regarded as hormones — " letters sent through the blood to instruct certain organs to do certain things for the body's well-being." After fifty years of research, science can point with pride to pure epinephrin, thyroxin, insulin, theelin, androsterone, and cortin, and to many other hormones in the form of extracts. The more water that has been drawn from this apparently limitless well, the deeper has it become. Almost monthly, new extracts of hormones with unexplainable potency are being announced from all over the world. *Entonen* from cattle liver, which relieves heart failure; *cortisupren* and *interrenin* from the adrenal cortex; *centronervin* from the brain, which increases the ability of frogs to catch flies; *intermedin*, from the anterior pituitary, which controls animal pigmentation or coloring, and seems to have a beneficial effect on one form of diabetes; *aquamedin* from the same gland which regulates the water supply of the body; *hippurin* and *equiline*, two sex hormones slightly different in composition from theelin and obtained from the kidney secretion of pregnant mares; *emmenin*, which has physiological effects similar to the growth-promoting hormone of the pituitary, was obtained by Collip from the placenta of animals; *inhibin*, a second male hormone which inhibits the growth of the pituitary; *hebin* from sheep pituitary which produces phenomenal growth of the head furnishings of fowl; *trephones*, juices expressed from the embryonic hearts of chicks, necessary for growth; *relaxin*, obtained by Hisaw and Fevold from the corpus luteum of the sow, which relaxes the pelvic ligaments of the guinea pig; *yakriton*, a new hormone of the liver which according to its Japanese discoverer neutralizes various poisons; *neurohumor*, secretions of nerve centers, which help relay messages; *corticin* from the adrenal gland, which speeds up bodily functions; *cortilactin* from the same gland, which is necessary for production of milk in rats; *desension* from corpus luteum, and *sympathin* from nerve muscles, which like epinephrin quickens the heartbeat, are but a few of the gland extracts reported within the last few years. One Chicago investigator reported an anterior pituitary hormone extract with which he claimed to have cured human baldness, but unfortunately he alone seemed able to effect the miracle.

Even the plant world has its hormones. Went, a botanist of the University of Utrecht, discovered in plants a growth-stimulating substance resembling hormones. Workers in T. H. Morgan's laboratory found this hormone, auxin, in yeast, fungi, and bacteria as well as in molds, and have successfully tested their synthesized product on young oat sprouts, which, as a result, grew faster.

In addition to the large diversity of hormones elaborated in the body, there seems to be an interrelation between many of them, making the path to their understanding a veritable labyrinth. The numerous byways and side paths often obscure the main road. Adrenalin seems to inhibit the action of insulin. Sugar metabolism appears to be under control also of the thyroid and adrenals. Cortin acts as a brake on thyroxin; theelin affects the action of the testicular hormone. The pineal hormone seems to act as a neutralizer of the thymus hormone. The removal of the thyroid affects the hormone production of the ovaries. The growth hormone of the pituitary seems to be necessary as a stimulus for cortin. The thyroid stimulates the thymus gland's secretion. Hoskins has shown that sexual abnormality is often related to a tumor of the adrenal cortex. " Not a few cases are on record of handsome well-built young girls who undergo change in sex, exhibiting symptoms of virilism — excessive growth of hair, atrophy of breasts, change of form to that of a boy." Some were treated for removal of the tumors of the adrenal cortex and returned to femininehood. Even the vitamins are involved, for cortin helps the body to utilize vitamins B and C.

The discovery of the intricate reciprocal action of the various ductless glands, the finding of some hormones which incite to action and others which inhibit or act as brakes, has led scientists to compare the endocrines to " a system of weights and pulleys, in stable equilibrium, in which removal of any one weight causes the whole system to hang awry." Collip has advanced the theory that every hormone has its anti-hormone, and, citing evidence of anti-growth and anti-maturity hormones, makes the statement that glandular disturbances in general may be regarded as primarily a lack of balance between its hormones and anti-hormones. According to this theory diabetes may result either from an insufficient insulin production or from too much of the anti-insulin hormone.

The study of the endocrines has introduced a new medicine and a new psychiatry which are still in their infancy. In the field of psychiatry Stockard has produced some evidence to show the relation between glands and personality. Working with dogs at the Cornell University Experimental Morphology Farm he has shown that pronounced personalities are often hereditary, but that in all cases they are associated with peculiar reactions of the glands of internal secretion. He found a glandular complex responsible for a paralytic condition in some races of his dogs. And he has produced types of dogs which practically parallel in growth and form certain human freaks whose abnormalities have been traced to glandular disturbances. It has also been shown that the nervous system acts on the sex glands. A bird from whose nest the eggs had been removed as fast as she laid them produced as many eggs in forty days as she might normally have laid in five years. Some are convinced that the applied physiology of the future will discover ways of modifying personality by means of hormones. Abel does not talk of making robots with temperaments according to specifications — kind, even-tempered, able men instead of mean, irascible, stupid ones — but he is pegging along wherever there is light, hoping to make the biological control of life a more certain achievement.

The older Abel gets the more his work piles up. Today, retired from the chair of pharmacology at Johns Hopkins that he held for nearly forty years, he may still be found working as the head of the new Laboratory for Endocrine Research. Work on hormones and allied chemicals of the body remains the breath of his nostrils and the blood in his veins. More humble and awed at the complexity of life's mechanism than ever before, this slender man continues to tend the tree of knowledge, fertilizing, watering, and pruning it even though its most precious fruits may never be gathered by him.

Abel's glorious enthusiasm for research attracted to him a host of brilliant students, now spread throughout the world. He has always been a thrilling and thoroughly unconscious catalyst. His spirit is far greater even than his most brilliant scientific discoveries. He described his own teacher Ludwig as "a man whose desires are drawn towards knowledge in every form, and who is therefore absorbed in the pleasures of the soul — one who is not covetous or mean, or a boaster or a coward — he has no secret corner of meanness and is a searcher after and lover of the truth in all things." That tribute, first written by Socrates for his ideal philosopher, also fits John Jacob Abel.

CHAPTER SIX

MENTAL DISEASES

HOW MAN STILL GROPES IN THIS, THE DEVIL'S OWN DOMAIN

With some attention to the psychobiological approach of Adolf Meyer

EVERYWHERE, skin deep below our boasted science, we are brought up short by mystery impalpable, and by adamantine gates of transcendental forces and incomprehensible laws." This was Charles Kingsley's reaction to the panorama of the onward march of science, an advance which only *seemed* to demolish every obstacle in its path. He was thinking of man's efforts to banish not only all the multitudinous sicknesses of the body but also the countless tortures of the mind. Millions of souls with their minds in ruins — one out of every twenty-two destined for mental hospitals — is the dark picture which still confronts science as its outstanding challenge to redeem mankind from illness.

Throughout the ages four furies pursued those frames from which the mind had gone awry. Superstition, nourished on a demonological conception of insanity, burned, harassed, and beat those frames to exorcise the devils playing havoc with their thoughts and behaviors. Skulls were trepanned to allow egress of demons, bats, snakes, crows, vultures, and other animals housed within the sacred precincts of what would otherwise have been rational men. And when the devil was too firmly intrenched and would not leave, thousands of unfortunates, as late as the beginning of the eighteenth century, were burned amidst heinous cries of " witch."

Fear, strengthened by ignorance, threw these mind derelicts into gray, somber, grim prisons, into stinking poorhouses worse than hell, into wet barns, sheds, and caves, into dungeons un-

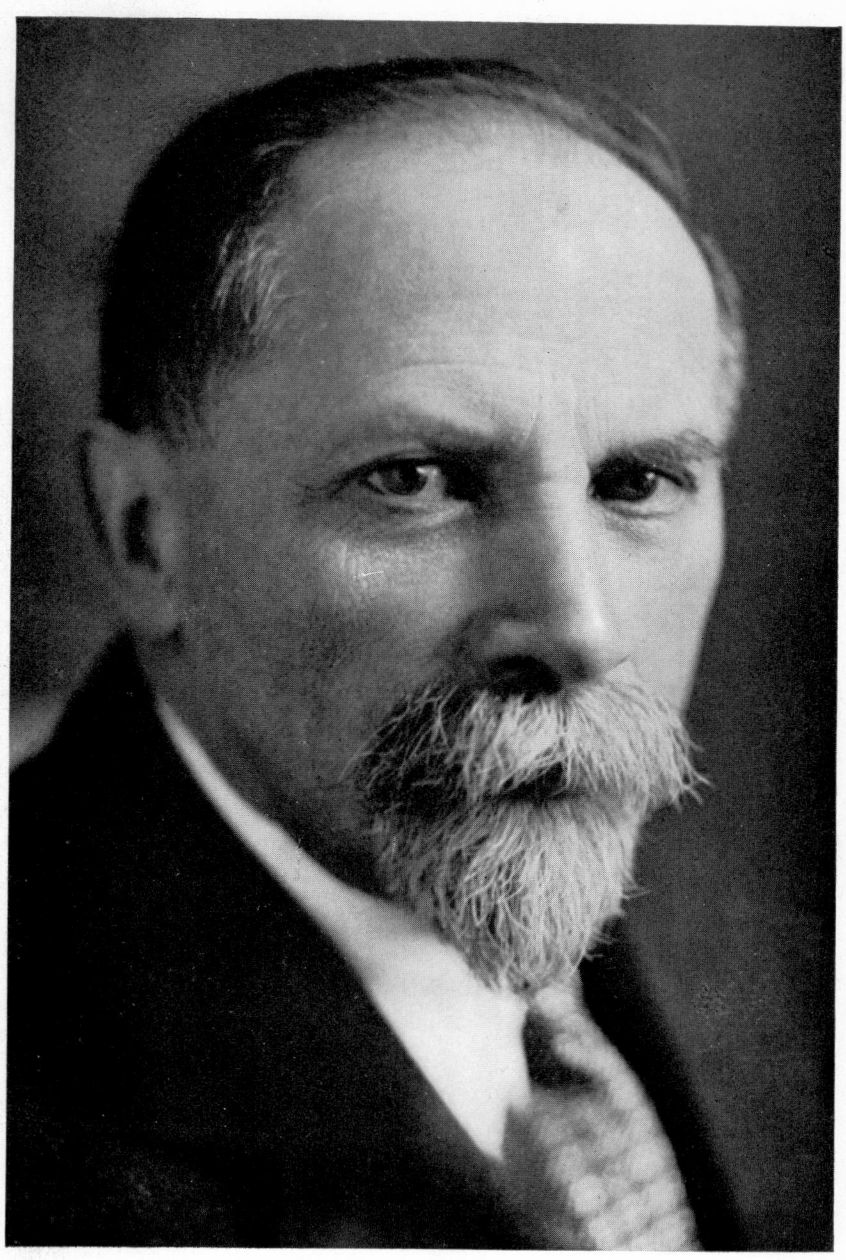

Adolf Meyer

Sigmund Freud

fit for cattle, where death was most merciful when it came quickly.

Brutality, under the cloak of necessity, tortured these " wild beasts " by methods worse than those of the Inquisition, strapped them into choking straightjackets, shackled them to tranquilizing chairs, crucified them on the bed saddle — a steel cross strapped to the bed — and pinned them down in restraining sheets of canvas. To frighten the insane into submission when they became difficult to manage they were placed in wells where the water rose slowly until it reached their mouths, ice-cold water was poured down their sleeves to the aching armpits, or they were whirled on rapidly rotating wheels until they lost consciousness. Keepers threatened their wards with death, and often beat them into insensibility. The same treatment was meted out to the poor and the rich. Wallowing in their own excrement, they fell victim to every passing epidemic.

Pseudo-science, glorying in its primitive method of therapeutics, blood-let its patients consistently until they were shadows; starved and purged them with cathartics; doped them with sedatives, narcotics, drugs, and other chemicals. Every institution for the insane had its own potent medical formulas for the various types of madness. Tartar emetic ointment, for instance, was used in some places to maintain a steady chronic irritation on the back of the neck as a pacifying measure. In this country Dr. Benjamin Rush introduced a method of treatment which was not discontinued until 1817. He blistered the skin of the chest by rubbing it with horsehair. This formed large abscesses from which came large quantities of pus. This " laudable pus " was thought, in those days, to have curative powers in all kinds of bodily disturbances. And when by the grace of chance or nature's oracular method of saving the doomed, some of these insane pulled through and returned to a semblance of normality, medicine exaggerated its victories and justified its horrible methods. But here in truth science was beaten, an impertinent trespasser in a strange realm.

Then in the century which followed the French Revolution

three independently conceived movements emerged to insure the rights of the insane. Twice Philippe Pinel, newly appointed physician at the Hôpital Bicêtre in Paris, implored the friends of Robespierre to break the shackles of the insane. One of Pinel's friends had lost his mind, wandered into the woods and been devoured by wolves. That picture never left Pinel. He kept up the appeal. Then one day the minister of prisons relented and visited the shambles. When his eyes met the scene at Bicêtre he turned to Pinel. " In truth, you must be out of your wits yourself. Is it these brutes you would unchain? " But Pinel finally had his way, and a new deal dawned for the insane. Their fetters were loosened, they were given sunlight, better food, cleaner housing, and kindlier treatment. Pinel told France he was dealing not with mad criminals but with people mentally ill.

At about the same time, William Tuke in England started a retreat for these unfortunates. This Quaker set a new model for the care of the mentally afflicted. And here in America, Dorothea Lynde Dix, who after a bitter childhood became a teacher, saw an insane man chained for years in an unheated stone vault on a farm, and dedicated her life to the new humanitarianism. In 1841, when she was thirty-nine, Miss Dix was attacked by tuberculosis, but before her death she had seen the establishment of thirty-two State asylums for the mentally afflicted.

But the new philosophy of mental disease did not revolutionize man's inhumanity to man overnight. Cruelty and barbarism still prevailed. The economic specter rose to halt the movement of reform, and many a life was blasted by miserliness which sacrificed human beings to dollars and cents. Before 1850 most of the insane in the United States were housed in prisons or almshouses. Poormasters boasted of how cheaply they could keep their wards alive. Similar conditions prevailed in Europe. When William A. White, now director of St. Elizabeth's Hospital in Washington, one of the largest and most advanced of such institutions in the world today, visited Europe twenty-five years ago he saw: " One ward occupied by some forty men, every one of them stark naked and strapped to his bed. There was only one bed that was not occupied by a patient, and that was occupied by a giant of an attendant who was asleep. He jumped up as I came in and walked through the ward with me, and I remember those naked men cursing and spitting at us as we went by." To this day some insane asylums, even in civilized countries, reek with primitive ideas and methods. But most of the old lunatic asylums are now things of the past, gone with the rack and other instruments of torture. London's Bedlam, open till 1777, and the Lunatics' Tower of Vienna, closed in 1853, where caged insane were exhibited to sightseers who paid for admission, have been banished forever. Lunatic asylums have been changed to hospitals in more than name.

The conception of insanity as a disease of the mind was not altogether a new one. The Greeks had considered it a disease because during high fevers accompanying some illnesses they had often noticed manifestations which were similar to those of the madman. The Arabs treated their mentally afflicted with soothing stories and soft music, in the hope of clearing up the confused mind. Here and there physicians, less learned in medical books, perhaps, but more sympathetic of heart, treated the insane not with drugs but with words. Finally science, fearful at first to encroach upon a field which had been left to philosophers and clerics, ventured to peer into this forbidding realm. Some of the more adventurous of its devotees even began to explore its strange territory.

The first map they used was the brain, seat of reason and intelligence. Brain injuries, tumors, and inflammation had already given surgery some data; autopsy findings and animal experimentation had supplied further information, and various abnormalities of body and mind had been more or less definitely associated with certain brain lesions and other physiological and pathological conditions. Various regions of the brain had been established as the seats of taste, smell, vision, and so on, and this localization of brain function was verified in part by the definite brain deteriorations which accompany senility. With the rise of brain anatomy and physiology, mental aberrations came to be more positively considered diseases of the brain. The microscope, aided by improved staining techniques, was brought into active play. Before long the era of " brain mythology," as some dubbed it, was proclaimed the key which was to open the door of mental diseases.

Science entered the field of mental disturbances principally through the death house. A cry went up for more and more brains — dead ones, to be sure, but at least brains of mental cases as well as those of superior individuals. Anthropometric societies sprang up among intellectuals who pledged themselves to bequeath their gray matter for scientific investigation. Such a group as the Brain Association of Cornell University still operates. G. Stanley Hall, Osler, Laura Bridgman, the deaf-mute, and others willed their brains.

Every insane asylum that would boast of modernity took on a brain pathologist, and the section-cutting machine and microscope became their potent tools. Hardly a day passed without the appearance of a paper linking some obscure brain condition with some mental affliction. This alliance with the cell biology ushered in by Virchow was blessed with reams of writing, but hardly a line of fundamental discovery. The poverty of results was balanced by the optimism of the brain investigators. They had the faith of children that some day, somehow, they would bring forth a miracle. But out of the welter of brain sectionings came the realization that in most diseases of the mind, the affected brain, even when placed under the most powerful microscopes, could not be clearly distinguished from that of a normal person.

This attack has by no means been given up. Henri Langier, director of psychological research at the Center of Medical Prophylaxis in Paris, still believes that the problem of the biological functioning of the human brain is the central problem of psychiatry and the prevention of nervous diseases. A gigantic program is under way there collaborating a group of studies of the human brain. A similar and even more elaborate series of researches is being carried on at the Institute of Psychiatric Research in Munich aided by the Rockefeller Foundation. And at the Kaiser Wilhelm Institute for Brain Research in the village of Buch-Berlin, two hundred different fields of the brain have been mapped out. Clinical material for this work is drawn from mental patients who die in Berlin's largest insane asylum.

Chemistry, too, came to the aid of researchers in this field. The march of this fertile science gave brain investigators a new tool. Biochemistry with its surer and clearer technique was invoked to solve the riddle of mind sickness. The brain was subjected to every chemical attack conceivable. The blood, urine, tissues, and nerve fibers were analyzed in thousands of cases. From time to time fantastic reports were published. Some found large quantities of a chemical known as indican in the urine of people suffering from melancholia. Neurotic individuals who were oversensitive and diffident were found to possess less calcium, more sugar, and less hemoglobin than well-poised, self-confident, sociable people. Another worker reported the presence of another chemical (choline) in the cerebro-spinal fluids of the insane. Still another found that in the brain of one mental case, the amount and distribution of phosphorus showed no marked change, the neutral sulphur was greatly diminished, while the inorganic and protein sulphur content was slightly higher than normal. Not a single element or chemical compound in the normal brain and blood was omitted in this comparative analysis of the normal and abnormal. "Chemists never wearied of fishing in distilled water for the chemical causes of mental disease," and hardly a substance, declared an eminent American psychiatrist, was not made the beast of burden of the great puzzle.

But the brain and the blood were not the only parts of the body suspected of hiding the cause of the insanities. In 1811 a Paris physician found the intestines and gall bladder of several maniacs to be badly diseased. He straightway attributed mental disturbances to the stomach and the bowels. One hundred years later Dr. Henry Andrew Cotton, director of the State Hospital at Trenton, New Jersey, undertook some investigations of his own, and came to the conclusion that most cases of insanity were due to toxins elaborated in decaying teeth, bad tonsils, infected sinuses, diseased intestinal tracts, and other centers of infection. The poisons spread to the brain, where they set up tissue changes which led to behavior abnormalities. When these poisons were permitted to bathe the brain too long, the brain deteriorated completely and no recovery was possible. At this time it was quite fashionable to ascribe insanity to focal infection, for the first two decades of the twentieth century witnessed wholesale tooth extractions, colonic irrigations, tonsilectomies and appendectomies as cure-alls for many a perplexing ailment.

Cotton gave every one of his hundreds of patients thorough medical examinations. Every tooth, tonsil, and appendix that was found diseased was removed. Every suspicious sinus was drained, every colon was irrigated and medicated to keep its poisons from reaching the central nervous system. He was frankly enthusiastic. In every discharge from his hospital and in every improvement of his patients, he saw a vindication of his great theory. Cotton died in 1933, but not before he had claimed a doubling of the recovery rate for his institution, and the possibility of preventing at least fifty per cent of potential insane cases from ever reaching a mental hospital. Other mental clinics followed suit. A generation has passed since Cotton's new attack was launched, and the public has been more careful of its teeth and tonsils. Yet the theory of focal infection, though it still has some adherents, is outmoded today, for it has proved no panacea in the treatment of the insane. Witness the new and larger buildings being erected to overcome the serious crowding conditions in asylums, and to house the mentally afflicted who are increasing at the rate of ten thousand a year in the United States alone. New admissions in 1929 were 72,000. Of a total of 736,000 hospital beds, half were occupied by victims of nervous and mental diseases.

With the rise of bacteriology, another method of attack was tried upon this stubborn fortress. The etiology of other diseases had been traced to bacterial infections. Perhaps they were also the cause of the diseases of the mind. The brain was searched for micro-organisms which might be interfering with the normal functioning of this master organ. In 1902, a French scientist claimed to have found the neurococcus present during epileptic attacks, and insisted that he could produce convulsions and even death in rabbits with it. Another investigator announced the same year that he had injected a serum made from bacteria which reduced the number of epileptic attacks. But these claims were clouded in uncertainties.

In one form of mental disease, however, there seemed to be strong indications of some connection with a bacterial infection. Ten per cent of all new admissions to insane asylums were general paretics. Their Wassermann blood tests were often positive and their spinal fluid was always positive. Their histories showed venereal infection of some ten or more years' standing. Syphilis and paresis seemed linked. Often they had fared well socially for more than twenty years after infection, until suddenly a strange change came over them. Their memory began to fail, they became contrary, irritable, suspicious, and suffered from illusions. Frequently, like Ivan the Terrible of Russia who was undoubtedly a paretic, they were drawn to acts of violence. The deterioration of the mind was progressive. Half of the victims died within a year after reaching the hospital; few survived as long as five years after commitment.

A diagnosis of paresis was a verdict of a sure and ugly death. There were few exceptions and no method of treatment. Syphilis was shown to be the *sine qua non* of paresis. But no one knew just how the connection existed. Salvarsan, the magic chemical weapon which Ehrlich had forged in his laboratory, brought healing to some syphilitics, but never to paretics. These were doomed. Some talked about sexual excesses, sunstroke, religious excitement, and the stress of life. Emil Kraepelin taught the equation, Syphilis + Alcohol = Paresis, but nothing had really been proved. Then with the discovery by Schaudinn of the pale spirochete bacterium which showed its spiral form in every syphilitic, began the search for this organism in the brains of paretics. Perhaps it was this microscopic invader which was sending its host to a paretic death. And while thousands of paretics died of emaciation, with bed sores exuding daily pints of pus from the back of their heads to their heels, only one persistent man searched unrelentingly for the spirochete in paretics.

Hideyo Noguchi, who knew more about spirochetes than anyone else alive, had carefully examined one night a lot of two hundred slides of paretic brain material stained for spirochetes. In the early morning he had detected what he thought were spiral organisms in seven slides. He would not trust his eyes and rushed to the home of Simon Flexner for confirmation. This discovery proved a landmark in the study of paresis. The organism responsible for syphilis sometimes reached the brain and, lodging there, changed its victim into a paretic.

These facts accounted for a phenomenon that a Viennese physician, Julius Wagner-Jauregg, noticed while treating soldiers during the Italian Campaign of the World War. Syphilitics, after getting over an attack of malaria, showed a milder form of the " social disease." Paretics, on recovering from some infectious disease, had long been known occasionally to improve considerably. Wagner-Jauregg reasoned that the spirochete, which could not endure high temperatures, might have been killed off by fever, thus reducing the virulence of the disease. Perhaps this was the explanation of the occasional cure of feverish paretics from whose chests laudable pus had been forced. The infection which produced the pus brought on the fever.

Wagner-Jauregg was almost sixty at the time. He had seen an army of paretics die in asylums. He was going to test out a hunch. Surely there was nothing to lose. Into the veins of two men crazed by the spirochete of syphilis, he injected two cubic centimeters of the blood of a shell-shocked malarial patient. Then he waited for the fever to burn out those bacteria. It was frankly a dangerous experiment. His patients might succumb to malaria. The fever rose and almost burned out their lives. But they recovered from the malarial attack, their memories returned, they became less irritable, and with frequent doses of salvarsan the symptoms of paresis never reappeared.

This epochal achievement which found a cure for one form of insanity, in those cases where the disease was not too far advanced, earned the Viennese psychiatrist the Nobel Prize in 1927. While his discovery constitutes the only clear-cut conquest of science in the field of mental diseases, it gives hope that other forms of mental derangements may likewise be traced to some definite cause. When in 1922 William A. White heard of these startling results, he undertook similar treatments in his own hospital, where among five thousand inmates a goodly number were paretics. On December 10, 1922, the hundredth anniversary of the discovery of paresis as a medical entity, the first patient in America was inoculated with the germ of malaria to cure paresis. The patient was subjected to sixteen attacks of fever, the temperature ranging from 103.7° to 104.4° Fahrenheit. He made a complete recovery, a splendid social readjustment, and is still at work. Since then more than five hundred patients have undergone the same treatment, with wholly satisfactory results. Before the malarial treatment, out of 214 successive paretic admissions to St. Elizabeth's, 137 died during the first year, and only five remained alive after five years. After the fever treatment had been introduced, out of 192 selected cases at the hospital, all but eighteen were still alive after five years.

The fever attack on paresis has become a standard practice in mental hospitals. In many venereal clinics, especially in large cities, this treatment is given even before symptoms of paresis develop. Improvements have been made in the general method. Danger of death during malarial inoculation has led others to try rat-bite fever, relapsing fever, or typhoid vaccine, to bring on the high temperature. Recently at the State Hospital of Columbia, South Carolina, where mosquitos were bred for malarial investigations, a very delicate operation on the malarial carrier was successfully performed. With the aid of a dissecting microscope the insect's salivary glands, in which the parasite of malaria lives, were removed. A preparation made from these glands was then used instead of the mosquito's bite to bring on the fever. This method diminished the dangers of malarial infections.

High fever has been produced in other ways. C. A. Neymann, a psychiatrist, used the electric metal blanket for more easily controlled high body temperatures. At the Cook County Psychiatric Hospital in Chicago he straps his paretics in these blankets, through which he sends an electric current. A rectal thermometer automatically records the patient's temperature, which is maintained at 105.8° F. for two and a half hours, on a self-recording machine watched by the attending nurse. Many are now using the new Fever Machine (Inductotherm) developed by the General Electric Company. Its invention came about in a curious way. The Schenectady research workers were trying to discover whether very short radio waves could be used against our insect enemies such as the boll weevil. Not having any boll weevils in the laboratory they experimented on the common fruit fly, and found that Drosophila could be burned to death when placed in a ten-million-cycle electrostatic field. It was later accidentally discovered that the blood temperature of research workers near short-wave radio transmitters was slightly raised. It then occurred to the director of the laboratory that this phenomenon could be used to produce controlled body temperatures at will without danger to paretics, for example. These were the starting points in the development of the new Fever Machine. Between the condenser plates of this electrical machine which generates an alternating current of 12 million cycles per second, the patient reclines while a strong electrostatic field is produced. His body acts as an electrical conductor and the resistance offered to the current gradually raises the temperature of the whole body. Heat is generated within the body tissues.

The brain has been the target of still another flank attack, captained by a man who has always been independent, fearless, and a champion of heterodox theories, Wilder D. Bancroft. This veteran colloid chemist of Cornell University, aided by a young pharmaceutical chemist, decided to work on anesthesia and nervous diseases. Examining the literature of the subject, they came across Claude Bernard's theory of anesthesia. The great French physiologist believed that an anesthetic dissolved the jellylike chemicals or colloids of the sensory nerves of the brain, producing a deep sleep, and that when the effect wore off, the reversibility of the change brought the patient back to the waking state. Now Bancroft made a guess — the best he could — from all the available facts, which, to be sure, were not entirely adequate.

Bancroft reasoned that mental disease was a state of haze or a fog of unreality, produced at the center of consciousness because the brain plasma had been rendered too thin or too thick by certain chemical changes. Hence all that was necessary was to send to the brain through the blood stream chemicals which were known to be thickeners (coagulators of protein) or thinners (dispersers of coagulation). We lie awake and are excited, Bancroft said, when the proteins in the brain become thick or coagulate. We become stuporous or go to sleep when the proteins in the brain dissolve. Hence, claimed the sage of Cornell, sodium rhodanate which, like bromides, dissolves proteins, ought to calm excited patients, while sodium amytal, a coagulating agent like morphine, ought to bring stuporous patients back to a semblance of normal activity. It was a pretty theory, Bancroft was not afraid to admit. But he reminded us: " If a man like Faraday is pleased if he guessed right once out of ten times, most of us can rejoice if we make one successful guess in a hundred. If one really believes that, there is not much danger of clinging unfairly to any working hypothesis."

Bancroft first tested his theory on rabbits. Later he obtained the cooperation of two physicians who used the two drugs on forty-six hospital patients suffering from various mental disorders. At the conclusion of their investigation, they reported that they had actually found two distinct classes of insanity. One type is made better by sodium amytal and worse by sodium rhodanate, while the other is made worse by sodium amytal and better by sodium rhodanate.

At various times Bancroft appeared before the National Academy of Sciences to elaborate upon his theory, and to plead for the assistance of organized medicine and psychiatry for further trials. But the medical world almost to a man has ostracized him. The medical society of his own county repudiated his findings. The United States Public Health Service tried his treatment on twenty cases at Fort Leavenworth in 1932, and obtained negative results. Bancroft is an eminent colloid chemist, they agree, but what does he know about medicine or mental diseases? His chemistry of insanity might better be termed the insanity of chemistry, and with this they dismiss his attempts to find a cure for lunacy. But " Big Banty doesn't mind being in the minority. He would probably be unhappy if everybody agreed with him." He has not given up the fight.

He points to other facts, uncovered before he entered the field, to show that his theory is not so wild, after all. In the early days of the making of Ethyl gasoline, workmen breathing tetraethyl-lead often manifested violent mental symptoms, which gradually abated. This chemical reacts with the fatty substances in the brain (lipoids) and produces a temporary insanity. A St. Paul physician, treating high blood pressure with sulphocyanates, found side effects such as weakness, dizziness, disorientation, hallucinations of sight and hearing, ideas of persecution and mania. In 1918 Arthur S. Loevenhart, professor of pharmacology at the University of Wisconsin, working with sodium cyanide as a respiratory stimulant, noticed a peculiar reaction in several insane patients in a state of stupor. For example: A man aged 21 had not spoken for months since admission to the hospital. Immediately following injection of sodium cyanide he talked freely and gave a history which was later verified. This condition of mental lucidity did not last long. When the effects of the injection wore off, the patient returned to his former uncommunicative state.

Ten years later Loevenhart, still at work on this problem, became a pioneer in another novel method of treatment. Insane patients were made to inhale a mixture of carbon dioxide and oxygen. After several minutes of this inhalation, the patient would relax. His face became animated and flushed. His respiration was deeper and more rapid. Finally he began to talk, he started to answer questions and behaved in a fairly normal manner for a period of twenty-five to thirty minutes. Thereafter retrograde changes began. The patient sank into his stuporous or *catatonic* state, showing the same posture, the same facial grimace, and apparently the same mental state. In fact, in some cases the lapse to the original state was so remarkably sudden, that a sentence begun was left unfinished.

Chauncey D. Leake, a pupil of Loevenhart, repeated this procedure at the University of California, using a mixture of 30 per cent carbon dioxide and 70 per cent oxygen, and obtained the same results. Another investigator varied the treatment. Before inhalation he talked to the patient half an hour each day for three consecutive weeks, using friendly, reassuring, and encouraging expressions. Then a malaria-like fever was produced in the patient by intravenous injections of a streptococcus vaccine. He obtained results similar to those of the Wisconsin investigator. He reported one patient stupor-free for four hours after a complete silence of seven years. A forty-one-year-old schoolteacher was brought back to the world of reality for eighteen months, after being in a catatonic state for seven. Later, however, she returned to her state of mental confusion.

Walter Freeman, while biochemist at St. Elizabeth's Hospital, subjected catatonic patients to high oxygen pressures in a compression chamber. Under a pressure of about six atmospheres the patient often became hilarious, talked a little, and wrote replies to questions. When the pressure was reduced the effects wore off. This, coupled with his demonstration of a brain deficiency of iron, the oxygen-carrying constituent of the blood, has led Freeman to announce that one kind of mental disease may tentatively be explained from the biochemical standpoint upon deficiency in oxidative processes in the cerebral cortex. Eventually, he maintains, it may prove to be a deficiency disease just as definitely characteristic and almost as effectively handled as rickets. Working on the theory that the insane use less oxygen than the normal, J. M. Looney of Boston in 1934 treated schizophrenics with two drugs which are known to speed up oxidation. These chemicals (trinitrophenol and dinitro-orthocresol) have thus far been found ineffectual in curing the insane. (Their use in reducing diets is a dangerous practice. A number of deaths have been reported.) This theory of Freeman's resembles Warburg's explanation of the cause of cancer as due to failure of the cancer cell to obtain sufficient oxygen.

At the Ontario Hospital dozens of insane have been treated with solutions of another chemical, manganese chloride, and favorable improvements have been reported. A member of the faculty of the University of Wisconsin has been using sodium amytal since 1930, and in many cases has succeeded in breaking through the mental fog. " We are using," he wrote, " psychotherapy and other methods during the lucid intervals to produce recoveries and we have had excellent results." The success of all of these methods, maintains Bancroft, are evidences of the validity of his theory, for sodium amytal and carbon dioxide are thickening agents, and the stuporous state is due to a thinning of the brain colloids. Yet the new day of a cure for insanity has by no means dawned. No successful general method of treatment has yet been uncovered by this chemical approach, although isolated instances of apparently permanent cures have been reported.

Research men have been driven into other channels of investigation. The most recent attempt to explain and treat mental disorders from the viewpoint of abnormal physiology is with the data and tools of glandular investigations (endocrinology). As far back as 1881 Kraepelin had fought insanity by introducing extracts of every possible gland of thyroid, testes, ovaries, and so on, but unfortunately without effect. When later, however, cretins, hopeless humans disabled in both body and mind, responded miraculously to treatment with the iodine compound thyroxin produced in the thyroid gland, and this glandular therapy had actually succeeded in salvaging those who for centuries had been considered doomed souls, visions of a new day for all the mentally disabled loomed on a blurred horizon.

Hoskins and Sleeper, working at the Evans Memorial Hospital in Boston on an elaborate cooperative effort to try to establish normal standards of glandular activity, made a metabolic and glandular study of scores of insane suffering from the worst form of mental aberration — dementia praecox. In September, 1931, they reported on one hundred thirty cases of dementia praecox. They found eighteen suffering from thyroid deficiency — slightly more than the average percentage among all hospital cases. Of these, sixteen received treatment. Mental improvement followed in fourteen, five of whom became well enough to be dismissed. The State Hospital at Elgin, Illinois, in 1934 reported treating one hundred seventy-two cases of supposedly incurable dementia praecox with glandular extracts, in addition to psychiatric routine, with the result that twenty-seven per cent were well enough to be sent home.

There seems to be no question that endocrine deficiencies as well as glandular overactivity cause serious personality changes and vivid mind dislocations. Stockard found an unfavorable glandular complex responsible for a paralytic condition in certain races of his dogs. Another investigator reported that sixty per cent of dementia praecox cases showed symptoms of liver affection. Puberty, pregnancy, and the menopause, periods of tremendous glandular and other physiological changes, are known to be the most common periods of mental disturbances. Something wrong in the glandular balance has been found in many mental cases. Glandular therapy with fragments of glands, gland extracts, and even pure chemical hormones, has been tried on cases by the tens of thousands. Here and there improvements and recoveries have been reported. Theelin used during the menopause has sometimes been found of help in acute cases of melancholia. Cortin administered in cases of nervous exhaustion is said to have done marvels. The removal of tumors from the pancreas, the parathyroids, and the pituitary glands has relieved a certain number of cases of clouding consciousness. One experimenter claims improvement of dementia praecox with liver extracts, on the theory that insanity of this type is analogous to pernicious anemia. Yet no specific glandular therapy has been found effective for any class of mental disease, with the exception of cretinism, notwithstanding statements to the contrary by over-enthusiastic workers. Only isolated cures have been reported, but here one must allow for the long arm of coincidence. Our knowledge of the ductless glands is so immature that endocrinology, the medical fledgling, can do no more at present than fumble with a highly complex machine. A little brook here and there has been dragged, while the great ocean of mind disorders remains uncharted and unprobed. Glandular treatment at the present time is only a vision. No miracles have been wrought here which even begin to approach the successful attack on the infectious diseases.

The many attempts thus far described to explain the cause of and find therapeutic weapons for the diseases of the mind have all been based on the principle that mental diseases are produced by definite physical and chemical changes in the body structure. " Mind cannot become diseased, all real disease is physical." Followers of this materialistic conception, faced with the paucity of facts concerning brain lesions or cellular changes in the cortex, or chemical changes in the blood, fell back on a new argument. These invisible changes, they said, are molecular or ionic, and our various techniques are still too crude to detect these differences. They spoke of colloidal changes which cannot be detected, and mentioned electric potentials which could not be measured. W. Spielmeyer, one of the most eminent workers in this field, finds sufficient circulatory disturbances to produce severe mental disorders without producing *recognizable* changes in the brain tissue. The physico-chemical picture of mental disease inherited from the nineteenth century was evidently encountering difficulties.

William McDougall, physiological psychologist of Oxford, was not alone when he expressed his belief that " mind has a nature and a structure and functions of its own which cannot be adequately described in terms of the brain and its processes." He hinted at conflicts of instincts and emotions as probable causes of mental disturbances. The microscope and the test tube were powerless where a good dose of philosophizing might help. It seemed like a return to those good old days when Kant declared that the diseases of the mind were topics for philosophers and not physicians. In fact, in 1894 the clergy of Germany endeavored to force mind diseases away from medical men and into the hands of moral and religious advisers.

For a while this change of front did not disturb the large body of scientists. There was no harm in armchair discussions of the interrelations of mind and behavior. Then the appearance of Sigmund Freud startled the medical world "like a pistol shot in a church." Freud rebelled against the mechanistic interpretation of the mental diseases. He asked for medicine a greater degree of freedom, insisting that in the treatment of disease it was justifiable to act on hypotheses which lacked full or even any scientific validity. To Freud chemical analysis, microscopic studies, glandular excursions, were mere side shows in a great dynamic interplay of mind and emotions which underlay mental sicknesses. Breaking with traditional psychology, he painted a picture which brought a flush to the prude and terror to the romanticist.

We must seek the origin, said Freud, for the neuroses and those psychic disturbances where no organic cause could be detected, in the functional interplay of two great forces. Consciousness was one, and the other was the force of the unconscious which though invisible was nevertheless of tremendous influence on illness and well-being. In fact, the shadow world of the unconscious was even more important than the conscious realm. Furthermore, he believed, man was controlled by the primordial will to pleasure called the libido. Of the various instincts which strive for gratification, the sexual drive was the most potent. It started not at puberty, but immediately after birth. (Ferenczi, one of his Hungarian disciples, insisted it was already present in intra-uterine life.) The babe suckling at its mother's breast and the infant sucking its thumb were giving free play to sex gratification. When, especially in later life, social mores, barriers to love, economic situations or accidents prevented the gratification of this sexual instinct, a battle began.

Freud taught that the mental abnormalities known as the psychoneuroses developed when the person lost its capacity to control or deal with the libido. The mind then sank below the conscious world — "the well-ordered parlor of the personality," and buried itself in the unconscious — "the cellar of the caveman," where, still powerful, it struggled on for expression. Gradually, however, it sank deeper and deeper till the individual completely gave up the struggle with his environment, seeking total freedom in the world of the unconscious. The tie with reality was broken and a typical case for the asylum emerged.

The sexual drive was not, to be sure, the whole story. In fact, the sex picture was sometimes absent altogether. Other forms of the will to pleasure operated. Ambitions frustrated by an inadequate constitution or lack of inherent ability would be crushed by the outside world, but not in the invisible subconscious realm. The individual broke completely with his outside world and lived his own more satisfying life in a state of grandiosity. A new Napoleon, a brighter Disraeli, a richer steel magnate, a handsomer heiress, took the field in some institution where they were allowed to have full sway. The unconscious wish-life took control over the conscious self. Such a psychological knockout was at once a capitulation and a victory. The individual capitulated to the cruel environment, but at the same time triumphed in his own subconscious world. This shrinking from reality was the explanation of certain psychoses such as that which is known as the Napoleonic complex — a complex of the man who believes himself a superman with ability to achieve his ambition to dominate all others in his field.

Freud was a man to watch carefully. He was preaching a dangerously revolutionary doctrine. His sweeping and audacious theory was packed with dynamite. What proof did this physician from Vienna offer? Plenty. In 1881 Joseph Breuer, a Viennese physician, was called upon to treat Miss Anne O., a twenty-one-year-old girl who had developed a paralysis of the right arm. Her vision had become blurred, she found difficulty in swallowing, and exhibited other strange symptoms of abnormality. A thorough medical examination uncovered no organic lesions — the girl had apparently suffered no physical injury. It was a medical mystery. Breuer had been trained in hypnosis at Charcot's clinic in Paris. Here hysteria, the most widely prevalent of the psychoneuroses, long believed to be a manifestation of the devil, or the traveling of the womb (*hyster* in Greek) from its natural moorings to various parts of the body, had been shown to be a disease of suggestion which could be cured by suggestion during the trance or hypnotic state. This was the first great contribution to psychiatry.

Breuer tried suggestive therapy. He hypnotized the girl. Breuer questioned her. From her unconscious self came a strange tale of staying up late one night while nursing her invalid father. She had become tired and sleepy. She fell asleep, her arm resting over the back of the chair. She suddenly awoke, her arm was numb. She *thought* herself paralyzed. And now in her waking state she *was* paralyzed. Breuer brought her back from hypnosis. He repeated that story to her, told her she really was not paralyzed at all. She repeated the story to him over and over again, and gradually the symptoms of paralysis disappeared. The girl was cured.

A man suddenly became a fanatical atheist. He stopped work, acted queerly, halted people on the street to preach hatred of God, attacked clergymen, claimed his wife had been immaculately conceived. He was finally taken to a psychopathic ward. A physical examination gave no clue to the cause of his insanity. When he was made to talk freely and his domestic history examined, it was learned he had heard that his wife had run away with the minister. He believed it. But when he was persuaded that the news was false and that his wife had really gone to visit her mother, he recovered in part at least.

During the early days of the World War, while Freud was

still developing his theory of mental dislocations, queer tales trickled across the firing lines of men brought to hospitals with minds all distorted. Shell shock, they called it. Men who had never been near the front lines, men who had been spared the horrors of bayonet fighting and shrapnel explosions, went to pieces, developed facial and limb paralysis, tremor, speechlessness, deafness, hallucinations, and other abnormalities. Surgical operations were performed on the affected parts and thousands of sound limbs were thrown into slop pails, until it was remembered that Charcot had successfully treated hysterical paralysis with suggestion. Freud's theory of anxiety neuroses which led to an escape from uncomfortable situations was invoked. Many soldiers to escape the dangers of battle wished they were paralyzed and kept thinking and brooding until gradually and unconsciously they became paralyzed. Mind had brought on a real physical ailment. The men were taken to quiet retreats. They were impressed with the idea that they were never to be returned to the front. Gradually their paralysis left them, their normal vision returned, they became sane. Free from the terrors of war, some of them came up from below the surface of consciousness and once again took their places in a real life where the conscious mind was in control. But many, too deeply buried in their peaceful, dangerless, painless, stressless, well-guarded life of the unconscious could never pull themselves up out of the pit. Freud's theory of anxiety neuroses was thus handsomely yet gruesomely vindicated. Fear was proved to be as damaging as a blow to the brain. The strife between self-preservation and the hostile environment was clearly responsible for certain mental disorders.

Freud not only explained the dynamics of mental aberrations, but he also introduced a fresh system of therapeutics which he called *psychoanalysis*. There was really nothing new in the idea, Freud admitted to a Vienna audience in 1904. His strange system of healing was but an intricate building up of a complex system of communication between patient and analyst, which had been an old remedy of medicine. With the psychological tools and trappings of the new knowledge of psychiatry, the older methods were given renewed life. Different twists were given to those sympathetic talks between doctor and patient, to the purging of the soul practised at the temple of Aesculapius, to the suggestive therapy of hysteria, and to the other methods practiced by the many cults of drugless healing. Mental diseases belonged to the psyche, and a mental prophylaxis, a scientific probing of the mental congestion, a clearing of the intellectual jam, brought the patient back to mental health.

Freud threw overboard the method of hypnosis which Charcot, a neuro-biologist, had revived. He also gradually discarded Breuer's *catharsis* or mental purging carried out during the hypnotic state of the patient. He started the analysis of free association, encouraging his patient to talk freely of anything he cared to mention. Bit by bit he drew him out, cleverly he led him into the secret corners of his soul, guided him to those nooks in the unconscious ego which he had kept secluded too long. Gradually the mental insult or shock was uncovered, and as this pent-up knowledge overflowed, it freed the mind of a mess of poison which was dispossessing reason. When the unconscious world refused to open itself, Freud watched for slips of the tongue and pen and for other inadvertent false steps. With these as sign posts, he led the patient back to his inner self, and elicited the wished-to-be-forgotten truths.

Not every doctor could be an analyst, Freud cautioned. Only those who could effect *transference* from patient to himself would succeed. " The patient," said Freud, " will make the communication only under the conditions of a special effective relationship to the physician." When the hidden conflict between the libido and the ego was made clear, the patient was shown the fallacy of taking the apparent conflict too seriously, or was given a method of overcoming it. If this worked, the patient recovered and made the proper adjustment. Freud agreed his method was an imperfect weapon of investigation and healing, but for lack of any other effective treatment it was worth trying.

In America not a word was heard of this new theory until it appeared in the *Journal of Abnormal Psychology* in 1906. Three years later G. Stanley Hall invited Freud to come to Clark University in Massachusetts to lecture on his newly introduced method of psychoanalysis. The public began to hear about it. The layman was fascinated or repelled. The sex garment appealed to many — it led the way for the " repeal of reticence " on sex talk, as Agnes Repplier expressed it. People picked up some of the terminology. They began to speak of adolescents, undersexed and oversexed adults, of repressions, abreactions, inhibitions, Freudian analysis, catharsis, libido, and the sublimation of animal impulses into social movements. Psyching parties became common. Wealthy neurotics made pilgrimages to Vienna to make it a city of psychoanalytic clinics. Psychiatric quackery became rampant.

The medical world on the whole offered great resistance to the spread of psychoanalysis. Medicine had eagerly accepted the rational psychology of Wundt, Janet, McDougall, and James, but Freud, the false Messiah, was trespassing on their territory. Some likened his theory to phrenology, and considered it outside the bounds of scientific investigation. When at the 1914 meeting of the American Medico-Psychological Association (now the American Psychiatric Association) a paper was discussed by Brill who had undertaken to become Freud's interpreter to America, one of the medical men present pounded the table, shouting that the psychoanalysts " savored themselves of mental disease." But William A. White, who had just launched the *Psychoanalytic Review*, came to its defense as a mighty new tool of investigation in a field sterile of results. White went further and recommended Sigmund Freud to the Nobel Committee for the Nobel Prize in medicine. Today Freud is retired from his position as lecturer at the University and has been rendered by a surgical operation incapable of addressing an audience. But through his writings he still reaches a very wide audience all over the world. Several years ago hundreds of men who were convinced that his contributions are cardinal in the history of medicine met in most of the great cities of the globe to honor him on the occasion of his seventy-fifth birthday. Only in Vienna, his own city, was no recognition made of his greatness.

"The diseases of the mind," said Cicero, "are more numerous than those of the body." The ancients recognized this, yet for convenience divided all mental ailments into two classes. The individual was either melancholic or manic. In mania, said Aurelius, the head was disordered; in melancholia, the stomach. This classification, in more or less modified form, lasted until the nineteenth century. Then many began to make more careful studies of the mentally sick, watching their histories, listening to the language of lunacy, and daily recognizing new groups of symptoms. Descriptive psychiatry became the dominant form of investigation in this field, and reached its highest peak about fifty years ago in the work of Emil Kraepelin, a pioneer in experimental psychology of which Wundt, his teacher, was the father. From a mass of classic case histories he drew a new classification of the insanities, which included as its two most important groups the manic-depressive and the dementia praecox. The latter is now commonly termed schizophrenia.

Manic-depressive insanity is a psychosis of adults. It begins with nervousness, restlessness, and emotional irritability, and ends in such morbid states that incarceration becomes necessary. The afflicted often becomes suicidal or homicidal. Schizophrenia, the most frequent form of insanity, usually begins at puberty or even earlier. The child becomes queer, shy, dreary, seclusive, different, and a cleavage of the mind develops insidiously. An internal break in the harmony of the personality occurs; the individual becomes, in fact, a split personality. The adult grows even more sensitive and suspicious and less capable of making concessions. The outer world is gradually renounced, and the victim drifts into a realm of fantasy, delusion, and hallucination. Charles MacFie Campbell, professor of psychiatry at the Harvard Medical School, cites a typical case: Agnes B., a twenty-year-old girl whose mother had died of insanity, had been a satisfactory office worker. A promising love affair had been broken off because of religious differences; she had made a minor error in her office, and was worried and upset when corrected. Emotional turmoil grew worse, she became very restless, and began to talk incoherently. The patient said that she talked with God and "the end of the world was coming and we all have got to see things as they are." She heard strange voices and imagined all sorts of queer objects around her.

Various forms of schizophrenia have been classified. The *catatonic* variety finds the victim plunged in a deep despondency followed by sudden irrational excitement. He may refuse to talk (mutism), and to comply with any request (negativism). He may adopt and maintain certain fixed and peculiar positions such as keeping one arm outstretched for hours at a time. These periods of depression and excitation vary both in length and in suddenness of change. The *paranoiac* is recognized by fixed and systematized delusions. The patient appears perfectly normal except on certain topics. Reason seems preserved but sidetracked, as in this typical case: A childless Russian woman is being tortured every night in her sleep by operations removing children from her body, and she believes that her husband cooperates to get children for scientific experimentation. Otherwise she is apparently quite normal.

The new Kraepelinian classification set thousands observing, recataloguing, reclassifying. Ernst Kretschmer, in *Body Structure and Character*, declared that certain bodily structures were intimately related to certain definite personalities. It was an old idea sometimes expressed in some such form as the virtuous and the devil must have a pointed nose and the comic must have a fat one. Kretschmer divided people into two types. The *asthenic* — the lean, long, flat-chested, long-nosed person if struck down by a mental disease — was associated with the schizophrenics, and the *pyknic* — medium height, round, deep-vault-chested individual who became insane — was of the manic-depressive type. Other classifications have been suggested, but thus far they mean nothing. The broad clinical pictures are blurred, one-word diagnoses are unscientific, and disease entities are constantly being changed. It is held by some that many of the inhabitants of the schizophrenic territory, the frontiers of which are not at all well marked, are not permanent residents but transients who move from one type of insanity into another. Science still hopefully prays for the birth of a new Linnaeus who will accurately classify the insanities, just as Carl Linnaeus brought order in the field of biology.

Brain pathology, biochemical investigations, endocrinology, metabolic studies, psychoanalysis, all together have hardly scratched the surface of this deep mine of the unknown. To some its solution is utopian, for they believe it lies outside the bounds of science. They point to heredity, and with the rise of genetics, that pointing finger becomes more ominous. Below the statue of Mendel at Brünn are the figures of a youth and a maiden, nude and kneeling, with joined hands, symbol of the far-reaching importance of his laws. But what facts and opinions does science offer us here? Experimental genetic work with man in this field is practically impossible. " If man were self-fertilized," said Jennings, " wise men would produce wise children, fools would produce fools, and society and its problems would be simple." Animal investigation is out of the question, for as far as we know man alone is heir to such dementing sicknesses. (Pavlov, at eighty-five, recently turned to the application of the information gained by him from his study of conditioned reflexes in dogs to the problem of human insanity. He feels that he will be able to produce in his dogs the various types of mental aberration that afflict mankind, and then will attempt to find ways to avoid, arrest or eradicate them in humans.) With the meager knowledge of classification of these diseases, and with the vagueness of genetic histories, even the most painstaking and objective statistical conclusions must rest upon extremely loose foundations. On the one hand, E. Ruedin, an assiduous worker in the statistical study of the hereditary transmission of mental diseases, tells us that if a single parent is afflicted with manic-depressive insanity, thirty-three per cent of the children turn out to be manic-depressives and an equal number suffer other mental diseases. If both parents are afflicted with this disturbance, sixty-three per cent of their children are cursed with the same illness, and the remainder are otherwise mentally abnormal. Not quite as terrifying a picture is drawn for the schizophrenics.

On the other hand, there are many who will not accept these figures on the ground that no dogmatic statements such as these statistics would evoke are scientific in the face of the complexity of the problem of the interrelation of heredity and environment. They declared that fully fifty per cent of these diseases can be prevented by the proper control of the social, economic, and religious environment, through guidance of behavior and emotions during childhood and adolescence, as well as later. They point to the figures of the National Committee for Mental Hygiene (1934) that 30–40 per cent of the yearly admittances of mental patients are annually discharged from hospitals as recovered or improved. They cite the record of the Federal Bureau of Census showing thirty-eight thousand patients discharged as cured or improved from State mental hospitals in the United States during 1930 — a number equivalent to half the new admissions and readmissions. These figures of discharged mental patients, higher than those of 1922, lead William A. White to remark that "the things which have been happening in the past forty years are the beginning stages of what may be perhaps the most significant thing that has ever happened to man in the course of his life on earth."

Dismissing both the extravagant belief of Watson that "we do not inherit our character, temperament and special abilities; they are forced upon us by our parents," and the pronunciamento of E. A. Wiggam that the environment plays no part, and that we can never escape the effects of heredity, science is drawing closer to the conviction that with the mental diseases as with such physical characteristics as sex and stature, T. H. Morgan's opinion is the most trustworthy. Morgan says: "The gene acts as a differential turning the balance in a given direction affecting certain characters more conspicuously than others. Let us not forget that the environment may also act as a differential, intensifying or diminishing as the case may be the action of the genes."

The evidence from the studies of H. H. Newman of the University of Chicago on *identical twins reared apart* points to the same conclusion, that both heredity and environment play a part in development. Identical twins come from the same fertilized egg and have an identical set of genes. Hence their hereditary equipment is the same, and any differences they may exhibit must be due to environmental forces. Identical twins agree in eye color, hair, skin, stature, shape, arrangement of teeth, footprints, handprints, and even fingerprints and freckles. Even in mannerisms and abnormalities they are alike. An authenticated case has been cited of identical twins called before the principal of a school for making the same mistake in a mathematics examination. It turned out that they were in different rooms at the time. Another case is that of a well-known scientific investigator who, thinking his identical twin brother was in the room with him, once addressed his own naked form reflected in a mirror.

Over a period of about ten years, Newman gathered together the records of twenty sets of identical twins reared apart for many years, and found that environment may thwart or even destroy genetic possibilities. Hereditary differences, he concluded, are twice as responsible for differences in the physical and mental characters studied as are the actual environmental differences. This conclusion was based, of course, on a very small number of cases. It is, however, generally believed that heredity plays a more important part in the development of an individual than does environment. Opinions differ as to the exact ratio of importance. A study was recently made of ninety pairs of twins one or both of whom had suffered from some form of insanity. It was found that of the twenty-three identical twins included in this group there were sixteen pairs both members of which were victims of the same type of mental abnormality, and only seven pairs of which only one member was afflicted. On the other hand, of the sixty-seven twins who were not identical twins, there were only eleven instances of insanity in both members of the twins, whereas fifty-six pairs of twins showed insanity in only one member of each of these pairs. Lange, a German investigator, made a study of crime and delinquency among thirteen pairs of identical twins and seventeen pairs of ordinary twins. He found that ten pairs out of the thirteen identical twins had similar records, whereas there was no agreement in the crime and delinquency records of fifteen out of the seventeen ordinary twins.

Neurotics are both born and made, and it is wise not to be too alarmed at the implications of genetics. Defective genes, those material demons of evil, do not live in a fixed *sanctum sanctorum.* White-eyed flies have been crossed with eyeless flies, and produced offspring with perfect eyes. Even the child of parents both of whom are mentally defective need not choose his asylum and wait for the breakdown. Genetics holds out hope — insanity is not inevitable. If mental abnormality is due to a single gene, the defective genes of the child inherited from both parents may be so arranged in the chromosome threads that they do not lie side by side, and the child will not inherit this defect.

● = defective gene in the chromosome thread

0 = normal gene in the chromosome thread

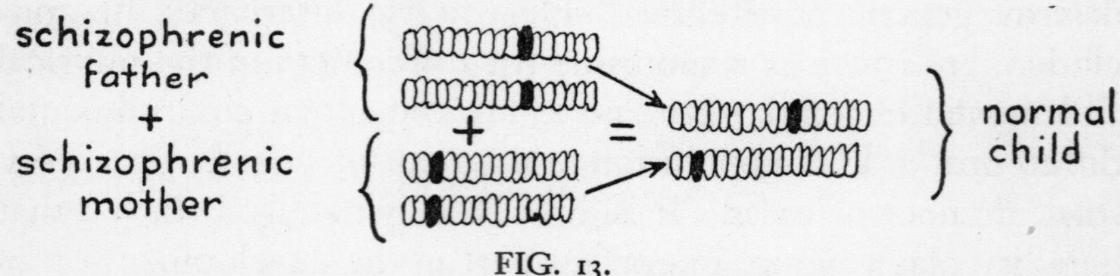

FIG. 13.
A normal child may be born to schizophrenic parents.

For the character of a pair of genes coming from each parent to show itself, both genes having the same function must lie side by side. Even if they are present but do not lie side by side, the character is not inherited, although it may appear in future generations.

These facts and opinions have divided men interested in the future of mankind into two opposing camps. There are those who see the feebleminded, the epileptics, those who suffer from Huntington's chorea (a disease of middle life characterized by tremors, speech disturbances and mental deterioration) and other mental diseases which are apparently hereditarily transmitted, outstripping with larger families the mentally sound. This menace of reckless propagation they would destroy by strict laws of sterilization. Said Ray Lyman Wilbur, at one time president of the American Medical Association, to a gathering of psychiatrists in Washington: "Human beings do not deal with our defectives, our insane, in the same way as do animals. No doubt foolish dogs are born, but unless they happen to get into the hands of foolish ladies, they soon succumb." Nazi Germany in 1934, in the name of race purity, issued a decree ordering the sterilization of its 200,000 feebleminded, 60,000 epileptics, 50,000 schizophrenics, 20,000 manic-depressives, and another 47,000 defectives including "hereditary" alcoholics and the hereditary deaf, decisions to be made by Hereditary Hygiene Courts. More than fifty-six thousand sterilization operations were performed there within one year of the issuance of the decree.

Soon after this German act was passed, a Committee on Sterilization in Great Britain recommended the legalization of the *voluntary* sterilization of both mental (and physical) defectives whose abnormalities were known to be of hereditary nature. This was intended "to remove the dead weight of social inefficiency and individual misery entailed by the existence of more than 300,000 mental defectives in Britain." It opposed, however, any such general, unscientific, and drastic decree as that of Hitler which might very conveniently be used as a powerful weapon against undesirable citizens. They wondered how many Jews, Marxists, and pacifists in Germany had suddenly been found to be mental or physical defectives — fit subjects for compulsory and probably brutal sterilization.

Eugenic sterilization laws are on the statute books of twenty-seven states in our own country but they are seldom enforced. New York passed such a law in 1912, but it was declared unconstitutional. Oklahoma sterilizes the hereditarily insane as well as its three-time convicts. California, home of the overzealous Human Betterment Foundation which would sterilize fifteen million Americans, accounts for two-thirds of all the eugenic sterilization in the United States. During the last thirty years, more than four thousand insane and two thousand feebleminded persons were sterilized by this state. It uses the painless technique of tying the ducts from the testes or ovaries without modifying the internal secretions of the gonads or otherwise interfering with the sex life of the individual. Such individuals, however, can no longer become fathers or mothers.

The other camp numbers a larger army of men and women who oppose sterilization on the ground that science knows too little about mental diseases. Who can say, they insist, what will be incurable tomorrow? They point to Mozart, Pascal, Mohammed, Schiller, Paganini, as great men who were epileptic. They single out Kepler, both of whose parents were clearly mentally diseased, and they tell us that Francis Bacon's mother was insane. And some are willing to pay the price of mental disease for the world's geniuses. Convinced that the partition between sanity and insanity is indeed a thin one, and that very often genius and insanity are not so far apart, they would not sacrifice one single genius for relief from the burden of tens of thousands of mentally diseased persons. This is also the tenor of the report of the committee appointed by ex-President Hoover to study social trends in America. In this report a difference is made between those insanities whose strict inheritability is still a matter of opinion and those clear cases of feeblemindedness which appear of undeniable hereditary nature. "More immediately urgent," advised this committee, in 1932, "is the need of preventing individuals with undesired inheritable traits from having offspring. Such a policy could be enforced in the more marked cases of feeblemindedness of which there are less than a hundred thousand in institutions, but for the large numbers outside of institutions variously estimated in the millions who is to decide? *It is not at all certain that low grades of mentality are carried by heredity. So with the other objectionable type, the insane, it is not known that the factors producing them are inherited.*"

The attack of science upon the burning questions of mental disease is a most confused one. The objectives are fairly clear, but the army of recruits are largely novices, eager yet bewildered for lack of effective training. They are battling in little-known terrain. Many of their guns are spiked by old ideas. Their ranks are hopelessly divided. Scientific demagogues and fanatics have brought disorder into their camps. Their lines bend and break with each passing psychiatric fashion. There is no one commander-in-chief whom all would follow without questioning.

However, the most outstanding psychiatrist in America is Adolf Meyer. To the many attempts to meet the challenge of the insanities, Meyer offers a program known as *psychobiology*. This system of psychobiology is a middle-of-the-road philosophy which in a common-sense way tries to integrate the valuable features of the numerous approaches to the understanding and treatment of the mental diseases. It recognizes no boundaries between the physical, biological, and psychological sciences. It refuses to emphasize a contrast between mind and body, but considers mind (mentation) to be a function of the body. It tries to overcome this sanctioned split in the consideration of man. It treats body and mind as structure and function to be studied as closely as possible, just as we study any other experiment of nature. It grants anything to be a fact that can in turn become a factor in the determination of the course of life of the person.

Meyer's psychobiology involves a thorough study of each individual from the day of conception through infancy, childhood, adolescence, maturity, and the aging period. "For the short-lived rats we have life records, but for human beings what have we?" he asked. The essence of every fact concerning the physical changes as well as the behavior and emotional acts of the individual must be determined in order to form a picture of the whole personality. This life history of the person is recorded on what he calls the life chart; the result is a record of a smooth or broken life history of each of the main organs and functions, and in addition, a record of the main events of the life of " the individual as a whole." This life chart, scrupulously kept and showing every possible important physical and mental incident in the life of the individual, was Meyer's map which aided him in the early treatment to prevent or postpone mental breakdowns, as well as in the diagnosis of mental disturbances. " We need not think," he wrote, " that nothing but the unusual or the abnormal is worth our attention, as little as I should consider bankruptcy as the most interesting event in economics." The tendency in the past was to study the mental case only after or perhaps just before the person had reached the condition when commitment was imperative. Meyer's plan was to study the individual right through life so that perhaps early symptoms of the coming abnormality might appear and be corrected.

This practice of recording the mental and physical life history of the patient had been followed, to some extent, by many physicians for decades. Meyer, however, emphasized the importance of this procedure, and through his influence, this life chart has become a generally accepted tool of the psychiatrist of today. Meyer, moreover, opposed the practice of damning the mental patient at the outset with a name that anticipated a definite mental course of events. He was influenced by the many cases which he himself had treated, and especially by that of his mother. She had fallen into a serious state of melancholia from which after three years she recovered against the expectations of other psychiatrists.

Psychobiology with Meyer was a progressive development. To him, the son of a Zwinglian minister and nephew of a medical practitioner, the problem of the nature of man, of mind, of body, and of their integration had interested him from early days. He read much of philosophy, studied Hebrew, planned for a while to specialize in Semitics, but then turned to medicine. In 1890 he obtained a license to practice in Switzerland. Two years later, when the University of Zurich granted him the medical degree for his study of the brains of reptiles, he had already made up his mind to follow psychiatry as his life work.

Landing in the United States at twenty-six with the promise of a possible appointment under G. Stanley Hall, who was pioneering in the field of child psychology, he received instead an appointment as fellow in the newly opened University of Chicago. A few months later the lure of a mine of brain material brought him to the pathological laboratory of the Illinois Eastern Hospital for the Insane at Kankakee. Here he was drawn into the maelstrom of microscopic brain investigations, but most of his time was devoted to the study of the patient as an individual. In 1902 he became director of the Pathological (Psychiatric) Institute of New York on Ward's Island, and used this opportunity to spread his new conception of personality studies of the insane to the staffs of all the state hospitals.

With respect to the Freudian conception of the mental diseases, psychobiology again takes a common-sense position. Three years before Freud's first communication of his thesis was published in this country, Alexander Peyer, one of Meyer's teachers in Zurich, had also dealt with sex frustrations as causes of psychoneuroses. Consequently Meyer already had a basis for a clear understanding of the revolutionary conceptions of the Viennese doctor. While he has always considered Freud's contribution stimulating in the history of psychiatry, and given due credit to much of his teachings, he has nevertheless insisted on remaining on the relatively accessible ground of the conscious in preference to the unconscious.

When Henry Phipps, the philanthropist, asked William Welch what he considered the greatest need of the Johns Hopkins Medical School, the answer was "a psychiatric clinic." And Adolf Meyer was called to become professor of psychiatry and director of the Henry Phipps Psychiatric Clinic which was formally opened in 1913. It was deemed best by the trustees to make the admissions voluntary, and to limit them to those willing and able to cooperate for purposes of observation, diagnosis, and treatment. No distinction is made between sane and insane patients. The clinic is intended for the better care of patients, especially in the earlier and often curable stage, under conditions similar to those of a general hospital. The goal is that of treating each case as an individual and then trying to adjust him to a place in society without any one-sided adherence to any narrowing school. The sick in mind are given quiet surroundings, the sort of physical or mental work which will keep them busy (occupational therapy), and when overexcited are quieted by submersion in lukewarm water (hydrotherapy) rather than by the use of drugs, as was the former common practice. Many patients are cured to such an extent after some time that they can carry on a normal life even outside the four walls of the clinic.

Here at Johns Hopkins, Meyer introduced his lectures on psychobiology — a course for medical students which was to instill in the young physicians a new outlook on mental diseases — an understanding of the mental patient as a normal individual whose mind had been twisted, instead of as a creature produced by a diseased brain or a poisoned body which was to be drugged or chained. From Baltimore he sent out a school of psychiatrists, new recruits for public health who are forging ahead in the path he cleared. His students heard Meyer declare: "I should quit being a physician and a teacher if I felt compelled to doubt the dependability of my natural observation and understanding of your mind and those of my patients as good enough to draw practical conclusions from such knowledge. There is no need of making an esoteric puzzle of the mental functioning of 'the other.' If solipsistic philosophy, that is, the assumption that one can know only one's own mind, were true, one might as well retire into absolute solitude."

And he has equally encouraged the physico-chemical attack. "In both brain and focal infection pursuits and in endocrinological claims, I am ready to grant whatever can be gathered and used quasi-experimentally provided all the facts are included." He is certain that the last word in these fields has by no means been said.

In the matter of the prevention of mental diseases, Meyer again is not to be found among any particular dogmatic group. He realizes that there are but poorly known and poorly controllable factors of destiny in the form of heredity over which preventive measures have little if any effect. Nevertheless, he believes that the healthy resources of each individual can be effectively used to offset harmful hereditary traits by proper guidance and control. More than thirty years ago he said that heredity is spread into immature minds as a doctrine of fatalism, so that even high school pupils excuse themselves in some such way as "I can't help this. It is hereditary in the family." Part of this may be sadly true. But it is the duty of trained teachers of pedagogy and psychiatry, he maintains, to distinguish what is to be accepted as inevitable from what is open to modification. We have faith in gymnastics for the correction of physical defects. Let us devise more efficient gymnastics for the mental processes.

It was Meyer who urged *mental hygiene* as the line of progress and reform to correct the horrors of Clifford Beers' experiences in insane asylums, public and private. Beers, a graduate of Yale (1897), had the misfortune to suffer three years of mental disorder. He was first haunted by a fear of epilepsy which afflicted his brother, and in an attempt to commit suicide, failed and lost his mind. He was shuttled from one asylum to another, where he suffered the worst kind of brutality. At one time he was confined to a padded cell for days in freezing weather. At another he was kept in a straightjacket for three hundred hours at a stretch. After three years, however, he was judged sane and released.

Beers came to Wilbur L. Cross, his teacher of English at Yale and later Governor of Connecticut, to show him a book he had written. Cross advised him to cut out that portion of the manuscript which contained his project for reforming the brutal treatment of the insane. "If you do that you will have a book comparable to De Quincey's *Confessions of an English Opium Eater.*" Beers disagreed, and went to Adolf Meyer, who read his *A Mind That Found Itself*, and advised him to publish the book.

Instead of starting old-fashioned legislative inquiries, Beers organized in New Haven on May 6, 1908, the first Mental Hygiene Society in the world. In the following year, under the leadership of Beers, the National Committee for Mental Hygiene was founded, to become the standard of similar organizations in twenty-five countries of the world. Through them remarkable improvements have been made in the physical care of the insane, in upholding the rights of the mentally afflicted, and in removing among laymen false impressions regarding insanity. The mental hygiene movement has fought pseudoscientific beliefs, has fostered early treatment and prevention, has led to the opening of six hundred psychiatric clinics in the United States, has attempted to remove the stigma of mental disorders, and has encouraged the study of psychiatry among large numbers of medical men — a study, which until recently, was sadly neglected. The Rockefeller Institute, opened in 1903, the School of Hygiene of Johns Hopkins which started in 1919, and the National Research Council up to 1931 had no representatives of psychiatry on their staffs when they were organized. Today, however, psychiatry is being taught at twenty-two Grade A medical colleges.

Mental hygiene as a philosophy of prevention, says Meyer, is an ideal and a guiding principle working wherever possible with the assets of life before their differentiation into the normal and the pathological. And while today, after a generation of effort, the word is still larger than the performance, we may hope to witness interesting results in the generations that are to come. Data on the effectiveness of the mental hygiene program are difficult to evaluate. While Meyer is not blind to the exaggerated claims of mental hygienists and to the limitations of their movement, nevertheless he has no patience with those obstructionists whose attitude of fatalistic indifference is their excuse for ignorance and inaction.

Birth control and eugenics as solutions of the mental disease problems are dangerous tools, thinks Meyer. Imbeciles and those whose mental afflictions are definitely known to be of hereditary nature should not be allowed to have children. In the present stage of development eugenics has no right to attempt a stronger negative policy than this. If it does so, it runs the risk of depriving the race of individuals such as geniuses and law-abiding, industrious citizens of low mentality who would be a benefit to it. Then he asks, What is the duty of those who have become parents but with hereditary taints? "Train yourselves and your children," he answers, "to look upon physicians and hospitals as constructive rather than corrective agencies. If I felt that I had to conceal the fact that my mother had two attacks of melancholia, I should thereby corroborate the false efforts at concealment of many others." There is no stigma attached to the insanities, and many mental disturbances may be cured or at least alleviated.

The natural history of the mind is as yet only imperfectly understood. The study of the mental diseases has been left far behind in the onward march of science, and today Meyer says, "We are very much in the beginning with the outstanding problems still to be solved in this field." And in such a complicated world Adolf Meyer believes with Voltaire, "It is part of a man to have preferences but no exclusions," especially when this mortal is exploring in the devil's own domain.

CHAPTER SEVEN

VITAMINS

NEW HUNGERS OF SATIETY

With particular reference to the life and work of Elmer V. McCollum

FOR HUNDREDS OF YEARS it was believed that the personality of an individual depended to a great extent on what he ate. "Tell me," said Brillat-Savarin, "what you eat and I will tell you what you are." It has been pointed out that Napoleon, Bismarck, and Boies Penrose were prodigious eaters who ruled with blood and iron. In just what way the composition of the fifty tons of food consumed by the average person in a lifetime was related to the health and even to the personality of the eater was not known.

Science has learned a few facts about this interesting relationship. For example, sterile worker honey bees, fed during infancy on the royal jelly diet of the queen, develop full maternal powers as well as the other characteristics of the ruler of the hive. Deprived of this special food, they are doomed to the sexless slave life of the worker bee. By partially starving flour beetles while in their larval or grub stage, scientists have appreciably modified the sex ratio of this insect. Even among higher organisms an alteration in diet results in important physiological changes. The fox, for example, when fed on a special diet has been made to grow a thick fur with a black sheen instead of a rusty-colored coat.

Very recently Professor Henry C. Sherman of Columbia University expressed the opinion of the most optimistic workers in this field when he said, after an extended series of experiments with rats, that by proper diet man could be made taller and stronger, and furthermore, that the quality of the life processes may be improved and the *average length of life may be signifi-*

cantly extended at least ten years. Just how has science arrived at these remarkable conclusions?

In 1897, a disease called beri-beri, known in the East as *kak-ke* for nearly two thousand years, was ravaging the population of the Dutch East Indies. Beri-beri was a peculiar disease. In its victims the nerves of motion and sensation were gravely affected. General weakness, mental depression, dropsy, and anemia accompanied a creeping paralysis, which usually originated in the legs and spread upward till it reached the heart and ended in death. The Dutch government appointed a committee to study the cause of beri-beri and to seek a cure.

Among the men sent to fight the disease was Christian Eijkman. These were the halcyon days of that vigorous newcomer bacteriology, and Eijkman, as might have been expected, began searching for a causative germ. Scientists might still be hunting for the microbe had not this Dutch doctor followed through a chance observation. A number of hens around his laboratory had developed paralysis which looked very much like that of beri-beri. This did not surprise Eijkman. Animals were subject to human diseases, and these hens had caught beri-beri from human patients. Yet while he hunted for the bacterial cause, he watched the hens more closely. How did they contract this sickness?

Eijkman noticed that those hens which were allowed to run around in the sun and scrape up their meals from garden and dunghill never came down with polyneuritis (beri-beri in fowl). The chickens which had sickened had been fed indoors on the remains of rice given to the inmates of the prisons of Java. He made an investigation of prison food. The only unusual feature he found was that the rice, the chief item of food given to the prisoners, had in some cases been milled with modern machinery to remove its outer yellowish cover. This process prevented spoilage of the rice, and incidentally turned out a white polished product. The polishings were discarded as unfit to eat. It occurred to Eijkman to compare the incidence of beri-beri in the various prisons with the kind of rice fed to their inmates. He discovered some striking facts. One hundred and fifty thousand prisoners had been fed almost exclusively on white rice. One out of every 39 of these men had developed beri-beri. Of the 35,000 who had been fed on partially milled rice, one out of 400 came down with the nerve ailment; while of the 100,000 prisoners who had received rations of unpolished rice, only one out of 10,725 had ever suffered the ravages of this disease. The incidence of beri-beri among the polished-rice eaters was almost three hundred times as great as among the unpolished-rice eaters.

The next step was clear. Eijkman fed a group of chickens exclusively on white rice. They all developed polyneuritis and died. He fed another group of fowl unpolished rice. Not a single one of them contracted the disease. Then he gathered up the polishings from rice and fed them to other polyneuritic chickens, and in a short time the birds recovered. He had accurately traced the cause of polyneuritis to a faulty diet. For the first time in history, he had produced a food deficiency disease experimentally, and had actually cured it. It was a fine piece of work and resulted in some immediate remedial measures. Eijkman was later recalled to Holland to a professorship at the University of Utrecht.

In his interpretation of the results, however, Eijkman had really erred. True, he had advised the eating of the whole rice grain, but he could not interpret the results. He did not know why the outer covering of the rice was essential to health. His work was not considered significant at the time and the controversy over the cause of beri-beri did not subside. Besides, his was a more or less obscure piece of research of which most of the world heard little. Millions continued to succumb to this paralyzing disease. During the Russo-Japanese War fully one-sixth of the Japanese forces, fed principally on rice, were put out of active service by this malady. All over the world rice-eating peoples kept paying heavy toll to beri-beri.

Thirteen years after Eijkman's pioneer experiments, Casimir Funk, a young investigator from Warsaw who secured a fellowship at the Lister Institute in London, unearthed the classic investigation of the Holland professor. Reasoning that rice polishings contained some chemical constituent essential to health, Funk attempted to extract this life-giving compound, using pigeons as test animals. After innumerable solutions, precipitations and filtrations, he obtained from one pound of rice polishings less than one-fiftieth of an ounce of a white powder. A few milligrams of his product when fed to pigeons gravely ill with polyneuritis, strengthened their legs, straightened out their drooping necks, and transformed them again to normal birds.

Since it was essential to life (*vita*) and contained the amino group of chemical elements, Funk christened this anti-beri-beri compound *vitamine*. Funk was entirely mistaken in his belief that he had isolated the pure vitamine. The name he had chosen was a misnomer, since the true compound does not contain the amino group. Yet such are the quirks of scientific glory that his term persisted, although slightly abbreviated in 1920 by the dropping of the "e." Funk was prophetic when he made the suggestion that in time other diseases would be traced to deficiencies of vitamins — certain essential chemicals present in foodstuffs in extremely small amounts.

At that time science was busily engaged in measuring the calorific value of all sorts of foods and estimating the fuel requirements of man, woman, child, and beast, not only asleep but also at work or play, but no attention was paid to the chemical composition of the diet. Respiration calorimeters, bomb calorimeters, chair, bed, and portable calorimeters were invented and brought into action in elaborate and often fantastic attempts to evaluate the advantages of meat, vegetable, nut, and mixed diets. In the meantime chemistry had advanced far enough to place in the hands of investigators the purified chemical components of many foods. The idea occurred to a number of research workers to feed test animals on chemically pure components of foodstuffs, and in this way attempt to arrive at an ideal diet for each species. The living organism was, after all, something more than an iron furnace stoked with coal or oil to produce so many calories of heat. It seemed reasonable to suppose that perhaps only certain components of foods were essential to physiological well-being regardless of their calorific values. Was it not possible that an animal fed to satiety on certain foods might yet starve to death?

Already in 1881, Lunin, working at Basle, Switzerland, had tried this method with six mice. When fed on a milk diet they thrived, but when he substituted for the milk a mixture of the purified components of whole milk, that is, milk protein (casein), milk fat, milk sugar (lactose), the various mineral salts found in milk, and water, the animals died within a month. Lunin concluded, " Substances other than casein, fat, milk sugar, salts, and water are indispensable to health."

A decade later Lunin's teacher asked: " Are there really other substances in milk besides fats, proteins, and carbohydrates necessary to the vital process? Had Lunin used a faulty technique? " And he added, " It would be useful to continue these researches." Pekelharing at the University of Utrecht accepted the suggestion in 1905. When he found that his own white mice fed exclusively on the purified casein and other constituents of milk refused to grow, and died young, he declared emphatically, " There is a still unknown substance in milk which even in very small quantities is of paramount importance to nourishment." There seemed no other conclusion to be drawn from his painstaking experiments. In the following year Frederick G. Hopkins, of the University of London, ignorant of the work of Lunin, Pekelharing, and even Eijkman, took two batches of eight young male rats each, and fed one group on purified casein, starch, cane sugar, lard, and mineral salts. The rats ate greedily but refused to grow. The other batch received the same diet plus 3 cc. (about a small teaspoonful) of fresh milk daily. These rats grew normally. Then he took away the milk from the second group and gave it to the rats that had refused to grow. At once they continued to grow as normal rats. The second group, now deprived of milk, began to lose weight. (See next page.)

When his curves showed the remarkable growth effect of even small doses of raw milk, Hopkins, in 1912, reiterated the statement that "No animal can live upon a mixture of pure proteins, fats, and carbohydrates, and even when the necessary inorganic material is carefully supplied, the animal still cannot flourish." For this piece of research Hopkins shared the 1929 Nobel award in medicine with Eijkman, the Dutch scientist who had to wait thirty-two years for this recognition.

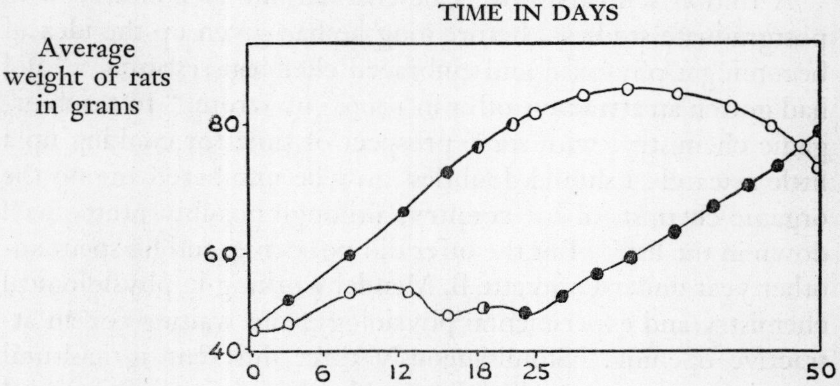

TIME IN DAYS

Average weight of rats in grams

80

60

40

0 6 12 18 25 50

FIG. 14. HOPKINS' GRAPH

Lower curve: First group kept on a diet with no milk as far as the 18th day. *Upper curve:* Second group took in addition 3 cc. milk daily. On the 18th day the milk was taken away from the second set and added to the first.

In June of the same year that Hopkins started on his classic study, Elmer Verner McCollum had just completed some work in organic chemistry at Yale. It was now ten years since he had reluctantly left the Kansas cornfields to go to the city for an education. Of Scotch-Irish descent, McCollum liked the soil immensely. Without the urging of his mother, he might have become a successful farmer fighting the heavy rains, the hot winds and the droughts of the Kansas prairies, the blistering sun that burned the corn crops year after year, the insect pests, and the fluctuating prices of farm products with all the skill he later showed in scientific research. For reading and schooling there was small opportunity. He learned to count by throwing three ears of corn to each pig in a pen. In those early years he was sickly, shy, and a rather dull pupil, because of chronic fatigue. Loathing grammar and arithmetic, he never passed the examinations for entrance to high school, but was permitted to enter on probation. At school McCollum gradually lost his self-consciousness and did well in his studies. He earned his way through school by lighting the gas lamps in the streets of Lawrence, carrying the morning newspapers, and acting as assistant in the chemical laboratory.

A tuition scholarship at Yale enabled him to continue with postgraduate studies. Before long he had given up the idea of becoming a physician and embraced chemical research. "If I had gotten an attractive offer in 1906," he wrote, "to teach organic chemistry, with some prospect of time for cooking up a little research, I should doubtless now be numbered among the organic chemists of the country, although possibly pretty well down in the list." But the offer did not come, and he spent another year under Lafayette B. Mendel working in physiological chemistry and experimental physiology, and waiting for an attractive opening. Simultaneously three different agricultural experiment stations called him. Mendel, a rare inspirational teacher and a sound counsellor of men, set McCollum on the road to the University of Wisconsin where at its Agricultural Experiment Station a unique experiment in animal nutrition was getting under way.

It was still the old question. Did it make any difference what the food was, provided its chemical composition and energy values were the same? Stephen M. Babcock planned an experiment to test the various theories then in vogue. He himself felt that calorific value was not the whole story. "Why not feed 'em coal or hot water?" he would ask. Besides, it was more than an academic question. Farmers around the University were constantly asking embarrassing questions about the *kind* of feed to give their cattle. On May 1, 1907, the experiment was started, and Edwin B. Hart was put in charge.

Four groups of young heifers were fed different rations. One received wheat, another corn, a third oats, and the last group was given a mixture of all three. By careful chemical analysis and accurate weighings, it was made certain that all animals received similar chemicals capable of supplying equivalent amounts of energy. All the sixteen animals were given all the salt they demanded, and were exercised in outside enclosures free from vegetation. The intake of these heifers was not the only mixture subjected to accurate testing. The feces and urine of the beasts were also quantitatively determined, and it was the largest part of McCollum's first job after reaching Madison to analyze the contents of the pails brought in from the experimental field.

Every morning the men would meet to talk over the progress of their work. Of course McCollum was interested, but somehow he looked askance at this attack on a problem that to him demanded a more easily controlled procedure. It was a well worth-while investigation, and probably would yield interesting results, but it did not reach the heart of the great problem of nutrition. "Research men who were using small animals, on the other hand, were on the right track," thought McCollum. He was going to try Hopkins' technique with one important change. Nothing was to enter into the diet of his animals which could not be identified as a pure chemical whose composition was accurately known. Instead of corn, a complex substance of indefinite composition, he was going to use starch $C_6H_{10}O_5$, and similarly for milk he would substitute chemically purified milk protein (casein), chemically pure milk sugar, or lactose, and so forth.

A few months after arriving in Wisconsin, he started a rat colony for his experiments. The director of the Station was a believer in the Malthusian theory, and looked unsympathetically on McCollum's plan "to save the world from a shortage of food." The dean of the school was also opposed to this new attack on the problem. No State money was to go to feed rats. Cattle — that was another story. Farmers had to feed them, and it was important to know the best and most economical ration. But Babcock came into McCollum's laboratory, perched himself on a high stool, surveyed the plan of the young man with that one good eye of his, and was for it. So McCollum kept on. He knew rats. As a boy on the farm at Redfield where he was born, he had caught hundreds of them in a special trap he had devised with his brother. They are excellent experimental animals, with a life span of three years. Their pregnancy period is three weeks, the female produces her first litter at three months; at fourteen months she has usually had six litters. It would not be very expensive to handle a large colony.

While Babcock's heifers were frolicking, and Hart and McCollum were doing the innumerable analyses, McCollum found time even with his teaching program to work with his rat colony. This was housed in his office in cages built by himself out of empty boxes in which chemicals had been shipped. He could work hard. His farm training made eighteen hours of research seem a picnic. He was thorough, a good interpreter of events, a good theorizer, and knew how to husband his strength carefully. Ambition took hold of him at the start, and he was confident enough to believe he was on the right road. He regarded those experiments at Yale undertaken to determine the relative efficiency of flesh eaters and meat abstainers as superficial. The device of determining men's endurance by means of arm-stretching and knee-bending tests to prove that flesh abstainers showed from three to six times the endurance of the others was to him not a very deep inquiry into so fundamental a problem. Even the experiments of Russell H. Chittenden, the grand old man of physiological chemistry in whose classes he had sat while at Yale, were not to his liking. Feeding professors, students, soldiers, and other volunteers on diets poor in proteins to find if there were any deterioration in well-being would never solve ultimate problems of human nutrition. McCollum was dealing with accurately controlled experiments, not with pseudo-scientific sideshows. The live rat in its cage was his unfailing test tube; his foods were pure chemicals, and his results could be accurately described and repeated by any student. That was his program from which he refused to swerve.

In 1911, while McCollum was busy with his rats, Research Bulletin No. 17 of the Wisconsin Agricultural Experiment Station appeared, giving the final results of the heifer experiment.

It was a strange announcement. Every animal had received the same quantities of starch, sugar, protein, salt, and mineral matter as well as water, and yet they had reacted very differently. Only the corn-fed heifers grew sleek and vigorous and gave birth to healthy young. The wheat-fed cattle were weak, fuzzy-haired, sluggish, and never carried their calves to birth alive. The oat-fed animals as well as the heifers fed on a mixture of wheat, corn, and oats, were not normal. Some of their young were born prematurely, and were sickly or died within a short time. Evidently the source of the food components *did* make a tremendous difference, but this did not explain why corn maintained the animals whereas oats did not. At this time McCollum had not heard of Eijkman, nor had Funk yet discovered that elusive vitamin. The answer to the puzzle of animal nutrition seemed to be still as far off as ever.

McCollum was giving his rats the right amount of inorganic calcium phosphate, pure edestin from hemp seed, and pure zein from maize (two proteins), wheat starch and corn starch, milk sugar, cane sugar, and glucose, and enough fats to complete their energy requirements. Yet the weight curves showed they could not maintain themselves normally, and they died prematurely. At first he thought something was lacking to make the diet palatable. " Palatability of the ration is important to the diet," he wrote at that time. That was a mistake, but he did not know it; and so he added appetizing flavors to prevent failure of appetite, and kept changing the combination of the various components of his diets. Many continued to die but some of the rats actually gained weight and lived at least until they were ready to be chloroformed. McCollum believed that he had actually carried out the first successful growth experiments with nothing but *highly purified foodstuffs.*

In the meantime, Thomas B. Osborne, of the Connecticut Agricultural Experiment Station, and Lafayette B. Mendel had been working on the relative nutritive value and physiological importance of the different pure proteins. Different proteins contain different amino acids. They were trying to determine which amino acids had to be present in the proteins used as foods — experiments which ended in a classic contribution. They, too, had been using some highly purified foodstuffs for their white rats, but failed to get McCollum's rising growth curves. When, however, they added to their rat diet "protein-free milk," a yellow powder obtained by removing the fat and casein and then evaporating the milk to dryness, they secured growth. Mendel attributed the growth of his rats to the nice adjustment of inorganic materials in his "protein-free milk." This was another mistake.

The paper of Osborne and Mendel appeared in 1911. McCollum studied it carefully. That "protein-free milk" bothered him. It was not altogether protein-free. It contained 0.7% of nitrogen, and might presumably contain in minute amounts other substances which could account for the normal growth of the rats. This paper gave his work fresh impetus, and with the help of Miss Marguerite Davis who took care of the rat colony, McCollum continued to search for a pathway through this dietary maze. The following year he was getting more perplexing results. Rats fed on his standard diet to which some butter fat had been added grew normally; rats which received lard instead of the butter fat were far below normal. The growth curves showed this singular phenomenon quite clearly. Just then, in spite of the care of Miss Davis, the rat colony was carried off by an epidemic, and further experiments were held up for a year, and then resumed.

In 1914 the *Journal of Biological Chemistry* published a paper from McCollum's laboratory which opened up a new era in nutritional investigations. This paper entitled *Isolation of the Substance in Butter Fat which Exerts a Stimulating Influence on Growth* contained a curve which cleared up a number of errors, and led to the discovery of a vitamin. For eighty days Rat No. 141 grew on a ration of pure casein, starch, lactose, agar agar, salt mixture, and lard. Then a sharp decline in weight set in. An extract of butter was added to the diet in a very small amount. A definite increase in weight promptly resulted. The rat gained

Elmer Verner McCollum

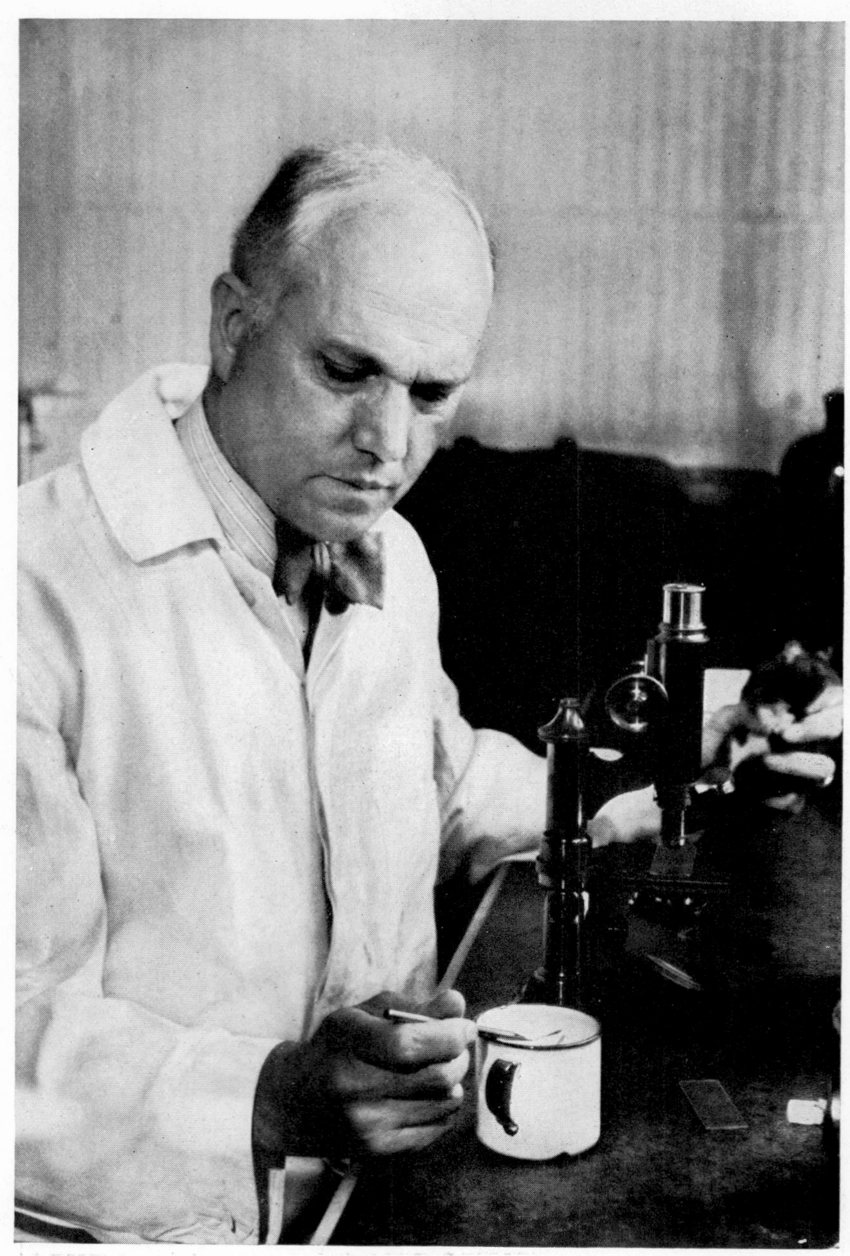

HERBERT McLEAN EVANS

fifty grams in the next thirty-five days. McCollum then used the extract of egg yolk instead of butter, and the curve kept moving upward. When, however, the extract of olive oil was substituted, growth stopped. McCollum drew his conclusion.

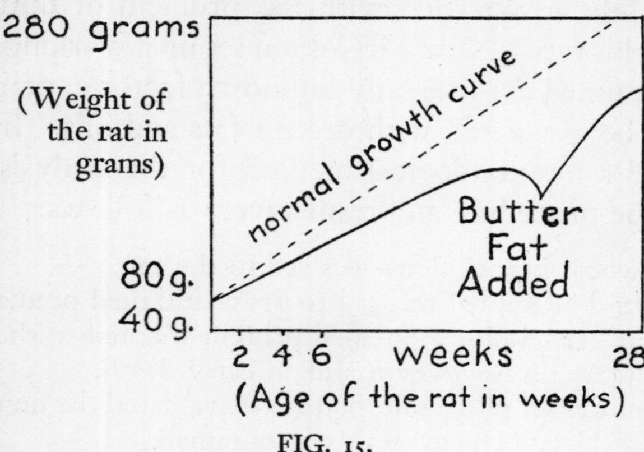

FIG. 15.

Graph showing the effect of butter fat in a diet.

Fats and oils, differing slightly in chemical composition, were of different growth-promoting potency, because associated with their ether extracts was some "*yet unidentified dietary factor — fat-soluble* (*vitamin*) *A*." (This use of an algebraic term to designate a vitamin gained wide acceptance.) McCollum had identified that " accessory food factor " which Pekelharing and Hopkins had suspected to be present in milk.

Mendel repeated the experiments and confirmed the results of McCollum. But Mendel could not understand why his own " protein-free milk " gave the rising growth curves. Furthermore, he was unable to decide whether the deficiency of the purely artificial diet he used before he could get a rising growth curve was to be " attributed to improper proportions of its constituents or to the lack of some essential element." McCollum, too, was puzzled. His butter-fat and egg-yolk extracts worked with some diets, but not with others. Funk bobbed up and insisted that the potent factor in McCollum's butter fat was his own anti-beri-beri vitamin. It seemed one great comedy of errors.

McCollum went back to his rats. The heifer experiment was over and he had more time. Frequent colds, sore throat, bronchial infection, constant headaches and toothaches, and never-ending work ran his own weight down to a hundred twenty-two pounds while he wrestled with the problem of putting more weight on his rats. Now McCollum set up a working hypothesis. He assumed that the only unknown factor contained in his diet must be associated with certain fats and oils. In 1914 he introduced a new biological method for the analysis of foodstuffs. The procedure and results were as follows:

1. The wheat kernel alone was fed to the rat.
   Result: The animal refused to grow and died prematurely.
2. Wheat kernel plus a purified protein was fed to the rat.
   Result: Again no growth and an early death.
3. Wheat kernel plus a salt mixture constituted the new ration.
   Result: Very little growth was obtained.
4. Wheat kernel plus butter-fat extract was now fed to the rat.
   Result: The magic butter fat *refused* to add weight to the animal.

This indicated a second dietary factor absent in wheat and necessary for growth. McCollum carried through a second series of experiments:

1. Wheat, a purified protein, and salt constituted the new diet of the rat.
   Result: Good growth for a time, but the animal had either no young at all, or small litters which died very early.
2. Wheat, a purified protein, and butter fat were now used.
   Result: No growth could be obtained and the rat's life was short.
3. Wheat, salt, and butter fat were given to a new batch of rats.
   Result: The animals showed a fair growth, but gave few young, and died prematurely.
4. Wheat, protein, salt, and butter fat were now tried.
   Result: Good growth, normal litters, and a healthy life span for his animal.

These results indicated that wheat was deficient in salts, vitamin A, and some protein. It seemed also to point to the need in an adequate diet of proteins, carbohydrate, salts, and vitamin A. With this hypothesis, McCollum continued his biological analysis of cereal grains, selecting rice in his next experiments. More months of labor. He obtained growth with the use of unpolished rice, but polished rice could not be supplemented with salts, butter fat (vitamin A), and a purified protein to induce growth in his animals.

McCollum now made a change. Milk sugar or lactose was added as a fourth supplement to the protein, butter fat, and salt. Again his rats grew normally. That was a fortunate trial. Evidently besides that potent substance in butter fat, another unknown factor distributed in lactose (and soluble in water) was also needed. Then followed a painstaking effort to determine the purity of the milk sugar he was using. He found it was not pure, after all. There was something in the water from which the sugar had been crystallized that could actually cure polyneuritis in pigeons just as rice polishings could. This he had proved to his own satisfaction. This new factor he called water-soluble B since, unlike vitamin A, it was soluble in water but not in fat. Vitamin B was altogether different from the potent substance in butter fat. It was identical with Funk's vitamin which cured beri-beri.

McCollum's anouncement of the discovery of " water-soluble vitamin B," the antineuritic vitamin which prevented polyneuritis, cleared up a number of difficulties. Both fat-soluble vitamin A and water-soluble vitamin B were necessary for normal growth. That was why his rats would not grow when given butter fat but no lactose or milk sugar. His milk sugar had contained vitamin B as an impurity. That was also why Osborne and Mendel had obtained growth with their " protein-free milk," which contained vitamin B. That was why Hopkins, too, was able to show a rising growth curve when his rats were given very small portions of whole milk. The vitamin problem was now clear-cut. There were certain chemicals which in infinitesimal quantities were necessary for well-being. McCollum had identified two of them. Perhaps there were more.

The whole vitamin question was thrown open for general discussion and research. With McCollum's improved technique, there was great promise for further discoveries in this field. It was an extremely important problem. A Japanese scientist in 1904 had studied among children of his own country four hundred cases of xerophthalmia, an eye disease which he believed due to faulty nutrition. Since the days of Hippocrates it had been successfully treated by adding chicken liver and eel fat to the diet. Nine years after the work of the Japanese investigator, Osborne and Mendel had noticed a similar disease among their test animals, which they had cured by adding butter fat to their rations. McCollum, for the first time in history, produced this eye disease experimentally by omitting foods containing vitamin A, and then cured his animals by adding vitamin-A-rich foods. H. Gideon Wells, in Europe at the time with the American Red Cross, had found thousands of Roumanian children, undernourished as a result of the war, suffering from this disease. He cabled for a supply of cod-liver oil, known to be rich in vitamin A, and cured them. Denmark which had been selling its butter to blockaded Germany during the World War and eating cocoanut oil instead, found its children developing xerophthalmia. When butter was restored to the diet the situation was relieved. Xerophthalmia is not the only injury which results from a lack of vitamin A. Night blindness, formerly common among badly nourished Russian peasants who lessened their already feeble resistance by living during Lent on a vegetable diet, was also cured by means of cod-liver oil. Absence of this food factor damages the tear, salivary, digestive, and reproductive glands, and *seems*, according to some investigators, to lower the resistance of the organism to other kinds of infections, such as colds and tuberculosis.

McCollum was only thirty-seven when the papers that came out of his laboratory on the hill at Madison made a great impression. Johns Hopkins University called him to become Professor of Biochemistry, and again Mendel counseled him to make the change. He was really ready for it. Matters were getting strained at Wisconsin. There was a great deal of jealousy, not too much tact, and a working at cross purposes. In 1917 the entry of the United States into the World War brought McCollum to Washington, where he helped to shape a new program for feeding troops and guiding the food habits of the people at home.

Soon after coming to Johns Hopkins, McCollum had noticed and reported that many of his rats fed on artificial diets developed beaded ribs and collapsed thoraxes. He showed some of these rats to the Professor of Pediatrics at Hopkins who confirmed his suspicion that they were true cases of rickets. McCollum's laboratory and the pediatric department of the university undertook a cooperative investigation to study the matter further. Shipley and Park made the microscopic analyses. McCollum tried various diets. His No. 3143, standard now in many of the world's laboratories, produced a typical rickety rat.

Meanwhile E. Mellanby of the pharmacology department of the University of Sheffield, England, had been working on the same problem and had found that some of his animals developed soft bones and rickety legs when fed on a vitamin-A-free diet. Rickets, he said, was another deficiency disease due to a lack of vitamin A. Mellanby claimed he could cure rickets in his puppies by proper diet. Now rickets was and still is an important problem of mankind. It had been recognized in England since 1600 as " wrikken," meaning bent or twisted. China and India today are rampant with rickets. Even in highly developed countries from fifty to ninety-six per cent of the children develop the disease in various degrees of severity. Aside from leaving many of them bowlegged, a lack of deposition of calcium salts in their chest bones exposes the victims to respiratory infections which often prove fatal. Often, faulty nutrition of the mother during the prenatal life and the early nursing period of the child so debilitates her young that later a proper dietary regimen fails to save the child from the ill effects of rickets.

But Mellanby was wrong about the cause of the disease. It was not due to a lack of vitamin A. With the aid of a former pupil, Miss Nina Simmonds, who had taken the place of Miss Davis in the summer of 1915, McCollum proved conclusively that butter fat containing vitamin A was valueless as a preventive of rickets, while cod-liver oil, which also contained this vitamin, was a most potent antirachitic factor. To determine whether cod-liver oil contained some other vitamin, it was necessary to remove its vitamin-A content. The clue to this separation was supplied by Hopkins, who had already discovered that vitamin A could be easily oxidized and its potency thus destroyed. McCollum passed oxygen gas for about fourteen hours through cod-liver oil heated to the boiling point of water, and then tested the oil on xerophthalmic rats. They refused to respond, showing that the vitamin A had been destroyed. The oxidized cod-liver oil was then fed to rachitic rats, which were cured. Thus cod-liver oil was shown to contain also an antirachitic vitamin which McCollum, in August, 1922, named " fat-soluble vitamin D."

On December 8 of the same year came the announcement of the discovery of still another vitamin. Its identification came about in a curious way. Seven years before, while making the differentiation between vitamins A and B, McCollum had allowed this discovery to slip through his fingers. He had been at a loss to explain why all of his rats " failed to repeat reproduction at normal intervals. This failure," he wrote in 1915, " is certainly the result of some factor other than the character of the mineral content, and must remain unexplained for the present." Neither McCollum, busily engaged in other pressing problems, nor anybody else followed through this interesting observation. Even the failure of the heifers to give birth to live calves in the famous Wisconsin experiment did not stimulate further investigation.

At Berkeley, Herbert Evans was studying the sex cycle of the rat in connection with hormone investigations. Evans was neither an agricultural chemist nor a biochemist. He was an anatomist and physiologist interested in factors that affected the rat's sex cycle. Among these factors he included diet. He fed his rats on various diets rich in both vitamins A and B. (Vitamin

D was still unknown at this time.) To the surprise of Evans and his assistant, Miss Katherine S. Bishop, the animals would exhibit normal sex cycles, mate, and conceive, but could not go through a normal pregnancy. Death of the developing embryo invariably occurred. No live progeny was born. Neither vitamin A nor B could prevent this strange intra-uterine death.

Then began a search for foods which might contain some element essential to normal development of the embryo. Fresh leaves of lettuce seemed to contain it, for when added to the diet sterility was prevented. The wheat germ was also potent. Even in infinitesimal amounts, Evans found, the rich golden oil extracted from it meant all the difference between barrenness and fecundity. When Evans was positive that absence of this hitherto unrecognized dietary factor led to sterility in male rats and to destruction of the developing embryo in females, he felt justified in announcing the discovery of vitamin X, later changed to vitamin E by Barnett Sure, who the following year independently confirmed the results of the Berkeley investigator.

Evans, with a splendid technique cleverly guarded by controls, uncovered some interesting facts in connection with this new vitamin. He reared mother rats on a strict ration lacking all traces of vitamin E, and then induced fertility by administering minute doses of highly concentrated vitamin E extracts. He found that he could cure female rats of the threat of dead embryos by giving them vitamin E extracts as late as the fifth day of pregnancy. Evans killed normal young female rats and fed their pancreas, spleen, or muscle tissues to sterile mother rats who later bore normal litters. "Therefore," he concluded, "normal young female rats begin life with initial fertility, their tissues containing vitamin E conveyed to them in intra-uterine life by their mothers." However, the supply of vitamin E must be continued in their diet, otherwise a deficiency results which causes sterility. Some of his rats were given an overabundance of his magic yellow wheat-germ oil, but this excess vitamin E had no effect on the size or the frequency of their litters.

The application of this discovery to human life occurred to

Evans and many others. They thought of the thousands of women who, though otherwise normal, lose children again and again before birth. Though Evans has made no claims for the vitamin E potency in humans, Dr. P. Vogt-Möller of the County Hospital at Odense, Denmark, tried vitamin-E therapy on a group of cows known to be chronic aborters, and obtained favorable results. Then on July 25, 1931, he reported to the English medical journal, *Lancet*, the results of his next step. Case No. 1 was that of a twenty-four-year-old woman who after four miscarriages was given Evan's wheat oil orally. Her next pregnancy followed a normal course and a healthy baby was born. Case No. 2 was that of a twenty-nine-year-old woman who after the birth of her first child miscarried four times in succession. This woman was given about two tablespoons of wheat oil each week, and responded as successfully as the first case. Others, too, believe that vitamin E is necessary for the human, but the medical world still awaits more conclusive testimony. Evans, himself, in 1935, cautioned medical men against "the indiscriminate use of vitamin E in attempting to cure human sterility which is most frequently due to other causes." Henry C. Sherman of Columbia University had found evidence that a lack of vitamin A also impairs the reproductive functions, and Evans was aware of at least four other naturally occurring substances possessing vitamin E activity. Vitamin E is, therefore, not *the* fertility vitamin but one of several chemicals which are necessary for normal reproduction.

The first disease of man recognized as definitely a disease of malnutrition was scurvy. Its victims came to Hippocrates with pains in their legs and suffering from gangrene of the gums. He did not know how to treat them. Thousands among the Crusaders succumbed, not to the swords of the Saracens, but to a slow illness bringing fatigue, sallow complexion, loss of weight and appetite, and nervousness. Destruction of the capillaries brought on hemorrhages. Bleeding gums, brittle bones, swelling knees, ankles, and joints, and general exhaustion often ended in convulsions, delirium, and death. Scurvy was also known as the "sailor's calamity," for it took frightful toll among those who went down to the sea in ships on long voyages. Here and there individuals had solved the scurvy problem in their own way. As early as 1535 Cartier had used the extract of pine needles to prevent this disease among his crew. Captain Cook, too, sailed the seas for three years without losing a man from this illness, by feeding his sailors sweetwort and sauerkraut in addition to the usual ration of salted meat. In 1750 John Colbatch recommended lemon and orange juice in the treatment of scurvy, and almost half a century later the British Admiralty ordered rations of lime juice on all its ships.

Finally, ten years after Eijkman pointed the way to the secret death hunger of beri-beri, A. Holst and Fröhlich began working with guinea pigs to uncover the specific cause of scurvy. They had chosen the right experimental animal, for neither the rat, cat, dog, nor the bird develops this disease. They restricted guinea pigs to a diet of bread and cereal, and the animals developed scurvy. Then they added various fruits and vegetables. Five years' work beginning in 1907 showed a preventive factor was present in large amounts in lemons, oranges, cabbage leaves, and germinating seedlings. Dry seeds or dry cereals, strangely enough, did not contain the protective substance. Commander Richard Byrd made use of this discovery when he went to Antarctica in 1928. He took along dry beans which could be germinated in the event that his men contracted scurvy.

Holst obtained potent extracts of the scurvy-preventing substance, which he described as a water-soluble chemical present in certain foods and capable of curing scurvy in animals. This was just before McCollum had discovered vitamins A and B, and science was not altogether ready to accept scurvy as a vitamin deficiency disease. Some believed scurvy was due to too high an acidity in the food, or to some form of poisoning similar to ptomaine. Steffansson, the explorer, thought the excess of salt in salted meats was responsible. Others pointed to Captain Scott's experience near the South Pole in 1902, when some of his men came down with scurvy in spite of their ample supply of limes. However, in 1918 scurvy was experimentally proved for the first time to be due to a special vitamin deficiency when a guinea pig was fed on a diet complete in all the dietary requirements including all the then-known vitamins except the foods containing the vitamin which prevented scurvy. The animal was then cured by the administration of a potent extract of the protective factor. This extract contained vitamin C, which was now definitely added to McCollum's list.

Soon another vitamin was to be added. Of all the workers in the field of food deficiency diseases, none was more fearless than Dr. Joseph Goldberger. He had to deal with a disease which attacked human beings, but no animal so far as he knew. For him the only test animal available in the battle against this scourge was man himself. For fifteen years, as a member of the United States Public Health Service, he had fought and in the battles had contracted not only typhus but yellow and dengue fever as well. In 1914, this immigrant boy, son of a grocer in New York's East Side, was assigned to fight pellagra. This was a devastating illness known for at least two centuries. At that time it had been playing havoc in the South, and the government was implored to stamp it out. Children and adults in the poor sections of the South were suffering from soreness and a burning inflammation of the tongue and mouth; from eruptions, blackening, thickening, and cracking of the skin, especially on the back of the hands, feet, and forearms; from indigestion, diarrhea, dizziness, and nervous disorders which all too often ended in the burial service.

The medical world was inclined to believe that pellagra was due to some bacterial agent. It seemed to be contagious — it was epidemic in jails, orphan asylums, and the poorer sections of the corn country. Goldberger was skeptical, even though the Thompson-McFadden Pellagra Commission had just reported it to be an infectious disease carried by a blood-sucking insect. The startling achievement of the Reed Yellow Fever Commission which found an insect the carrier of yellow fever, and the dramatic discovery of Ronald Ross who proved that malaria was transmitted by a mosquito, had a psychologic effect, but Goldberger, nevertheless, had his own ideas about the probable cause of the " hard times disease " of the South.

Goldberger paid a visit to the State Hospital of South Carolina. Not a nurse, doctor, or attendant had come down with pellagra in this institution, although many of its inmates had succumbed to the disease. After experimenting here with diets, he went on to Georgia. At the State Sanitarium there he found many pellagra sufferers among its insane, and again he tried changes in the diet. Then he investigated several orphanages in Mississippi, and found that most of their pellagra victims were children between the ages of six and twelve who were receiving very little milk in their daily food. His ideas about pellagra were now pretty clear. He went to the governor of Mississippi and asked for human volunteers. Twelve convicts from the Rankin Prison Farm where pellagra had never attacked were selected. If they survived the experiment, they were to be freed.

All of these long-termers were fed on white flour, white rice, cornmeal, pork fat, and cane syrup. If they cared to, they could gorge themselves within the limits of this menu. But they were to eat nothing else — Goldberger made sure of this. After several weeks of this strict regimen, one of that dozen began to complain of pains, a sore tongue, and sores and cracks at the corners of his mouth. More weeks went by until at the end of the six months' experiment one of the prisoners showed the rash of pellagra on his body. Five more of Goldberger's group came down with pellagra. Not a single case of this disease appeared among the hundreds in the Prison Farm who were not subjected to the special diet of the investigator from Washington. The volunteers were then given the proper diet including milk, meat, vegetables, and fruits, which are now known to contain the vitamin which prevents pellagra. They quickly recovered and won their freedom. Goldberger was certain he had produced experimental pellagra in humans, but others still insisted the disease was caused by some bacterial invasion.

There was but one step left, and Goldberger did not flinch

from taking it. On April 25, 1916, he injected into his own veins the blood of a woman suffering from an acute case of pellagra. But that was not enough. The following day he swallowed the intestinal discharge of another victim. Then he and his wife ate the powdered skin rash of still another sufferer from this disease. For weeks Goldberger waited for pellagra to seize hold of him. But it did not attack him — pellagra was not of bacterial infection. In 1929 cancer of the kidneys cut short his life. Goldberger's name, however, was not lost, for the American Society of Biochemists changed P-P (pellagra-preventive) vitamin to vitamin G, in memory of this hero of medical science.

Years before, when McCollum had opened up this new realm, thousands of other scientists rushed in. More and more researchers — medical, physiological, chemical, agricultural — kept turning out an ever increasing number of papers in this field. Although in 1911 only forty-seven appeared, by 1930 there were more than fifteen hundred articles on vitamin research to be abstracted. Rats, dogs, pigeons, guinea pigs, and even roaches were sacrificed by the thousands. All sorts of new discoveries were made showing the relations of the various vitamins to each other, to hormones, to general metabolism, to susceptibility to infectious diseases, to vitamin complexes, to general bodily health and longevity. A committee appointed by the League of Nations adopted international standards for vitamin potencies, and distributed vitamin extracts gratis to dozens of laboratories engaged in new vitamin research. The whole world was abuzz with vitamin work.

Food industries became tremendously interested. Advertisements were filled with exaggerated and untested claims of vitamin potency. Every can, box, or other container of food bore a compelling announcement of vitamin contents that warded off heaven knows how many insidious diseases. Overnight the public became vitamin-conscious. The baby in its crib and the child at the dinner table were dosed with foods rich in vitamins. At first the public bowed down to the vitamin gods which lived only in fresh foods — they were wary of canned, vitaminless foodstuffs. The large companies engaged in the sale of foods quickly opened laboratories and employed chemists or subsidized university research laboratories to undertake studies of the comparative vitamin potencies of fresh and canned goods. Where the cooked or canned foods were found to be poor or altogether deficient in the various vitamins, chemists found means of enriching them with the necessary accessory factors. An amazing amount of work was done in Sherman's laboratory at Columbia University in quantitative studies of the vitamin contents of all kinds of edibles, as well as in the development of methods of controlling the vitamin contents during preserving and processing. In the great vitamin campaign, appeals were even made to patriotism. The English hailed the " unrivaled medical value of the cod-liver oils found in Scotland and Newfoundland," while Norway called the attention of the world to the fact that Norwegian fish were superior, " possessing twice the anti-rachitic potency of Newfoundland oil." Here was a perfect example of economic nationalism.

" Sciosophy," a word coined to denote the pseudo-scientific dicta found in the industrial advertising of vitaminized foods, held the consumer in a strong grip. The public was fooled and cheated. The Drug and Food Administration in this country spent thousands of dollars to run down the more flagrant of the violators. Then the public began to wonder how the human race had survived through the long centuries without this essential knowledge. Some recalled the words of George Sarton, " Unfortunately most men are incapable of grasping an idea unless they exaggerate it to the exclusion of all others." Slowly this vitamin mania passed when the profit motive behind it became increasingly evident. People soon realized that the average diet was rich in the essential vitamins, and that mankind had infinitely more to fear from a malnutrition problem brought on by a crazy social structure that allowed lands of plenty to witness millions in hunger, especially in times of economic depression. Dr. James S. McLester, President of the American Medical Association, speaking before a convention of medical men in

June, 1935, said, "Something like twenty million American people are living near or below the threshold of nutritive safety." Scurvy, pellagra, and even xerophthalmia and similar eye diseases which are common in the Orient have become rather widespread in this country during the last few years. Even in the boom days of 1929, a decade after Goldberger traced the cause of pellagra, as many as seven thousand people died of this disease in the South alone. Japan still offers a sacrifice of seventeen thousand humans every year to beri-beri.

Recently, another insidious danger lurking in this diet ballyhoo was reported. Several research workers, including American, Scandinavian, and German investigators, found that the taking in of very large quantities of cod-liver-oil concentrates and viosterol appeared to produce harmful results not only in their experimental animals but also in humans. This was especially true with children below two years of age who apparently developed heart lesions largely resembling those which appear after infections such as scarlet fever. Some even pointed to the ominous rise of heart troubles among New York City school children as evidence of this widespread practice of dosing babies with vitamin concentrates. Notwithstanding the fact, however, that the *British Medical Journal* as early as 1928 warned of this danger editorially, and that the Cornell University researchers suggested " the wisdom of a careful reconsideration of the use of large intakes of cod-liver oil concentrates," most medical men dismiss the claim as completely unfounded.

In the meantime, in the centers of research in pure science and of course in the laboratories of pharmaceutical and food corporations, a hotly contested race had begun to isolate the chemically pure compounds which were the real vitamins. Previously only food extracts containing the vitamin had been used. The preparation of the vitamins in pure form stood as a thrilling challenge to the genius of organic chemists. For twenty years not a single one could be obtained in pure crystalline form, even though many of the cleverest workers in the world of chemistry had tried.

There had been so many premature announcements of the isolation of pure vitamins that when, within the space of a few weeks toward the close of 1931, four different laboratories reported the isolation of pure crystalline vitamin D, it was realized how keen was the rivalry and how rapid the pace set by the workers in London, Göttingen, Holland, and Evansville, Illinois. The road to success had been a tortuous one, in which chance had played a leading role. More than once several men had actually brushed past a solution. In 1908 one investigator confined eight puppies in a dark room and they developed rickets, while unconfined dogs fed on the same diet did not. Another research worker in 1912 again showed that young dogs deprived of light developed rickets. Harry Steenbock, who had helped McCollum at Wisconsin, observed a goat add lime to its bones while playing for weeks in the sun, although it had lost calcium on the same diet of straw and grains when confined indoors in a metabolism cage. He did not follow up that observation, for the reason that his hogs did not seem to react in the same way. Six years later K. Huldschinsky, a Berlin pediatrician, scanning the ricket situation in sunny lands and cloudy countries, in summer and in winter, noticed a queer situation. Rickets was less prevalent during the sunshiny seasons and in sunny regions. Rickets was rampant among the infants of the top caste Hindus kept indoors because of the custom of purdah, which kept them screened from the public gaze. Yet among the much more poorly nourished children of the Hindu laborers who brought their families to the fields while they worked under the hot sun, twisted bones were almost absent. Perhaps light was the effective agent against this disease, thought Huldschinsky, and he actually cured rickets in many children of post-war Germany by exposing them to the rays of a quartz mercury vapor lamp.

Then another scientist working at the Lister Institute in London was led, as the result of several experiments, to the conclusion that the anti-rachitic substance in cod-liver oil was the same produced inanimately by light. Toward the end of 1922, her paper appeared telling of the curing of rachitic rats fed on the liver of rats exposed to the radiation from a quartz mercury vapor lamp. She did not, however, follow through this interesting observation. The following year three modern priests of the sun independently, and almost simultaneously, discovered the physiological power of light and produced an amazing synthesis. Alfred F. Hess, late pediatrician of New York, Goldblatt of the Lister Institute of London, and Steenbock of Madison, all turned ultraviolet light upon foodstuffs poor in vitamin D, and changed them into nutrients rich in this sunray chemical.

Steenbock, aided by Black, used a very simple method. They raised rats in a dark room on a ricket-producing diet worked out by McCollum. The animals developed the disease. Steenbock then allowed light to shine on the hog millet and other components of the diet, and fed the irradiated food to the rats still imprisoned in a dark room. The animals recovered from the rickets. Steenbock tried his process on other foods of human consumption which lacked vitamin D and found the method effective. Then Steenbock, to protect the public from the exploitation of greedy and irresponsible business interests patented his process of increasing the vitamin D content of food by irradiation. This act, he felt, would enable him to control its general use by a large public. Besides he was in a dairy state, he explained, " and there was a fight on between the oleomargarine interests and the dairy interests. I realized that the dairy industry should be supported. Since butter is not very high in vitamin-D content, I saw the possibility of making a product high in vitamin D " which could be sold at a reasonable price and increase the demand of this dairy product. Steenbock turned over his United States Patent No. 1,680,818, for which he had applied on June 20, 1924, to the University of Wisconsin to be administered by the Wisconsin Alumni Research Foundation. Royalties paid by numerous food companies employing the Steenbock method of food irradiation provide funds for further research at the university. In spite of these and other similar arrangements by other research men, criticism has been heard against the patenting of the fruits of research of pure science, which belong to all humanity.

Light had evidently produced a powerful synthesis. Steenbock suspected cholesterol, found in all living cells, as the chemical compound upon which irradiation had produced the miracle. But when it was later found that pure cholesterol when irradiated failed to cure rickets in animals, Steenbock left this research problem and turned to the study of the cause and cure of anemia in rats. But others did not turn away so readily. In 1926 three laboratories in England, Germany, and the United States discovered almost simultaneously that ergosterol was the compound that light could convert into vitamin D and that this was the light sensitive chemical which was present as an impurity in cholesterol. It had been known for some years that ergosterol was present in many plant and animal tissues in quantities of less than one per cent. For a long time it had been an obscure chemical curiosity found in yeast, blood, the skin and in ergot (a fungus of various grasses from which it derived its name). Ergosterol is not a fat as was first suspected, but belongs to a group of organic compounds named sterols which have been called " the root of the tree of life whose branches are vitamins, hormones, and enzymes." (An enzyme is a complex chemical compound [such as zymase] produced by a living organism [such as the yeast cell] and capable of producing a chemical change [such as the fermentation of sugar].)

Now chemists had a definite chemical with which to work. On November 23, 1931, the first news of success came in an Associated Press dispatch from Berlin. Adolf Windaus of Göttingen, a Nobel Prize winner in chemistry, had obtained crystalline vitamin D by irradiating ergosterol and extracting the vitamin. The first vitamin in pure form had at last been obtained! Windaus found that if he irradiated ergosterol completely, the product was inactive, but if treated with certain wave lengths of ultraviolet light (only down to 2900 Ångström) it offered a crystalline substance " three-billionths of a gram of which is sufficient to relieve rickets yet one five-thousandths of a gram is poisonous." Within a month the National Institute for Medical Research in London also announced crystalline vitamin D under the name of *calciferol*, likewise obtained from irradiated ergosterol; and Charles E. Bills, a former student of McCollum, told chemists at New Orleans that he had synthesized the same vitamin by treating ergosterol not with light, but with nitric oxide gas. His product was not pure, but his announcement was important because, though still unconfirmed, it represented the first synthesis of a vitamin without the use of radiation.

Windaus believes that his vitamin D consists of two chemical forms (isomers) of ergosterol. The chemical formula of ergosterol is known. It is $C_{27}H_{41}OH$. Men are at present doggedly working to unravel the structural formula of this vitamin.

Hardly had Windaus announced the isolation of pure vitamin D, when Charles G. King, working with another young chemist, W. A. Waugh, at the University of Pittsburgh, flashed the news that they had obtained vitamin C in pure crystalline form. This was a really startling announcement, for they had just nosed out a number of other laboratories in a hotly contested race. King had started on this research back in 1925. Since lemons were known to be rich in anti-scorbutic properties, many eminent chemists had attempted to extract the elusive vitamin C from this fruit, only to drop the difficult work. But from the juice of dozens of crates of lemons provided by the California Fruit Growers Exchange, King tried every trick of the chemist's trade to extract the pure chemical. Each operation was carefully controlled. All the water he used was triply distilled. Suspecting that vitamin C was attacked by oxygen, he excluded air from every operation and worked with his lemon juice extracts under nitrogen. To check the potency of his extracts, he used the guinea pig as the test animal. As smaller and smaller doses protected their animals from scurvy, he knew that he was getting closer to the pure vitamin. Hundreds of guinea pigs struggled against the extract-filled glass pipettes which were thrust down their throats to make sure they were getting their vitamin C. On April 4, 1932, after seven years of continuous work, King finally isolated fifty milligrams from one liter of lemon juice, and identified the pure crystals of vitamin C. Before scientists gathered at a meeting of the American Society of Biological Chemistry at Philadelphia, King described his method and exhibited some of the crystals. McCollum, who was in the audience, rose to give King his scientific blessing for having made a great scoop for American chemistry.

King found the chemical formula of his vitamin C to be $C_6H_8O_6$. Like vitamin D, this compound also contains only three elements — carbon, hydrogen, and oxygen. Strangely enough, identical crystals known as hexuronic acid (or ascorbic acid) had actually been discovered, and their chemical properties studied by Albert Szent-Györgyi, a Hungarian chemist, five years before. E. C. Kendall, discoverer of thyroxin, had also handled vitamin C before King. He had obtained it from the adrenal glands of cattle, but thought he was dealing with a new hormone. Neither of these men recognized any relation between their crystals and the vitamin problem.

It was King, however, who extracted this white, odorless, water-soluble, crystalline substance from lemon juice and for the first time showed it to be vitamin C. It is sold today (as *cebione*) for oral administration in 0.01 gram tablets said to be equivalent to the vitamin C content of 30 cc (a small wine glass) of fresh orange juice. Paul Karrer of Zurich, after a series of brilliant chemical analyses, determined the probable structural formula of this compound and soon after an English chemist claimed its synthesis.

The isolation of another vitamin was soon announced. This time it was vitamin A, on which Steenbock had worked for fifteen years. He found that his rats could get along on carrots, squash, yellow corn, butter, egg yolk, and sweet potatoes, all of which were tinted yellow, but that when they were fed on white corn or any other white foodstuffs, they failed to maintain themselves. He formed a provisional hypothesis that the yellow pigment present in foods was the missing vitamin A. But his theory encountered serious obstacles. Testing cod-liver oil, he found no correlation between its color and its vitamin A potency. For a while Steenbock wavered, but when he learned that pork liver, containing no yellow pigment at all, possessed a high vitamin A potency, he dropped this research and went back to his work with vitamin D.

Other investigators took up the yellow pigment clue to the nature of vitamin A. This yellow color was found to be due to a complex organic compound discovered a century before and named *carotene*. Consisting of but two elements, hydrogen and carbon, its formula is $C_{40}H_{56}$. By 1928 two Swiss biochemists, by means of animal experimentation, established the fact that there was a relationship between carotene present in yellow foods and vitamin-A potency. In the meantime J. C. Drummond, a London biochemist, split carotene into two fractions. Then, he thought, since vitamin D had been conquered by means of light, perhaps vitamin A would respond to the same treatment. He tried the experiment and it proved successful. Again light or irradiation solved a riddle. Carotene, when subjected to light of certain wave lengths, was changed to an extremely potent substance which Drummond extracted as pure vitamin A. This was soon confirmed. Carotene *was* the chemical which changed into vitamin A when irradiated and is therefore known as pro-vitamin A.

The simple formula of vitamin A is $C_{20}H_{29}OH$. Its structural formula is still to be completely worked out. The vitamin is a heavy thick oil which has been found in the blood, the liver, spleen, suprarenal glands and several other organs. These organs obtain carotene from the food taken in by the body. This carotene, it is believed, is quickly changed by means of some enzyme into the true vitamin A and stored as such.

Pure vitamin B, too, seems to have capitulated to man's relentless attack. After a plethora of claims starting from that of Funk's original announcement in 1911, Windaus, conqueror of the sunshine vitamin, prepared in 1932 a seemingly pure crystal both from yeast and rice bran. Then in the opening month of 1935 the isolation of pure crystalline vitamin B from rice polishings was reported by Robert R. Williams, chemical director of the Bell Telephone Laboratories and research associate at Columbia University. Williams had started on this quest while he was working among beri-beri victims in the Philippine Islands. At the end of a quarter century of research he had finally succeeded in obtaining appreciable quantities of the anti-beri-beri vitamin even though it was present to the extent of only one ounce in six tons of the rice polishings. Williams also determined the structural formula of this compound whose composition is $C_{12}H_{16}N_4OS$.

In August of the same year in which the isolation of vitamin B was announced, vitamin E was also obtained in pure crystalline form for the first time. It was thirteen years after the publication of the discovery of this vitamin that Herbert McLean Evans, now director of the Institute of Experimental Biology of the University of California, reported this achievement. The isolation of pure vitamin E will enable men to carry on more easily controlled experiments designed to shed more light on the intricate processes of animal reproduction. Pure vitamin E will also enable research workers to continue some interesting experiments dealing with a suspected relationship between this vitamin and cancerous growths. In 1934, a Canadian investigator found that mice fed on a diet very rich in vitamin E proved much more resistant to tar cancer than other mice who received normal doses of vitamin E. Another research man working at the University of Illinois reported that chicks fed on a diet from which vitamin E was absent showed certain unrestricted cellular growths similar to cancer.

Vitamin G still remains to be isolated in the pure form. Its chemistry is still very far from solved. Originally vitamins B and G were thought to be one, until Goldberger and other workers at the United States Public Health Service in 1926 showed the existence of two vitamins in water-soluble vitamin B. Today what is known as vitamin G is thought by some to consist of two chemicals both necessary to each other to prevent pellagra.

There is a difference of opinion as to whether a lack of vitamin G is really responsible for pellagra. One investigator writes: " Lack of iron rather than lack of vitamin G may be the cause of pellagra. A diet of molasses and corn, on which most of the poor of the South live, is lacking in iron as well as in vitamin G, and pellagra-preventive foods all contain iron." Another investigator, on the other hand, explains the apparent inconsistencies of the Goldberger theory in this way. It has been found that foods apparently rich in vitamin G are not very effective in curing pellagra. He believes that the poor showing of vitamin-G foods in curing pellagra may be interpreted to mean either that what is known as vitamin G in foods is not the anti-pellagra vitamin, or that when vitamin-G foods are fed to pellagra sufferers, they have little effect due to the vital changes which have taken place in the pellagra victims — changes which cannot be reversed by vitamin treatment. Animal experimentation with dogs which are subject to canine black tongue disease, an ailment similar to human pellagra, is being tried to settle the question.

The work of isolating the vitamins in pure form is a triumph of modern chemistry. Even though some of the structural formulas of these essentials of life are not yet positively known, the next few years will undoubtedly see this tremendously difficult job completed. The synthesis of all of the vitamins in the laboratory will be the next step, and it is quite certain that even this will soon be accomplished.

The story of vitamin research is a tale not only of pure chemistry but of applied science as well. Irradiated ergosterol in oil (viosterol) has become a standard diet of millions of children. Millions of people are now eating bread impregnated with vitamin D under the direction of the Wisconsin Foundation and the Pediatric Research Foundation of Toronto. Tons of yeast, dry milk, oats, biscuits, and other foods to which vitamin D has been added, are being yearly consumed all over the world. Cows are being fed on irradiated yeast and milk to increase the vitamin content of their milk. A number of dairies are pasteurizing milk by a specially controlled electrical heating in order to preserve all of its vitamin-C content. Vitamins A and D are being added to oleomargarine to equalize its vitamin content with that of pure butter. Pro-vitamin A has even been added to cough drops and cough syrups to prevent or shorten colds. The claims of these manufacturers, however, have by no means been definitely established. A great deal of clinical research on the vitamin-A needs of the human organism is now in progress.

For years special diets have been prescribed by physicians for many ailments such as asthma, rheumatism, epilepsy and other nervous diseases, migraine, heart troubles, colds, sinus, gout, and even senility. Such dietetic therapy received fresh impetus with the vitamin publicity. Special vitamin dosing now began to be experimentally tried against various sicknesses. For example, vitamin C was tried to correct pyorrhea, certain types of hemorrhages and even hemophilia. The same vitamin was also administered in an attempt to cure rheumatic fever and tuberculosis in guinea pigs with the hope that, if successful, it might be tried out on humans. The antineuritic vitamin (vitamin B) is even now being tried out in the fight against the mental diseases in the Elgin State Hospital at Elgin, Illinois.

Dentistry, too, has felt the repercussions of the vitamin explosion. Tooth troubles until very recently had been a matter almost wholly of therapy. Today this has become a problem of prevention and control. Oral hygienists and dentists in conventions assembled have for years flaunted their banner: " A clean tooth never decays." Some see that flag now in tatters, and dieticians in the near future replacing dentists. It all began at the close of the World War when Mrs. May Mellanby of Sheffield noticed a large number of rough, pigmented, and irregularly arrayed teeth among the puppies that her husband had been feeding on rachitic diets. It needed no remarkable scientific mind to see that diet might control bone formation and calcium-

TABLE OF

Vitamin	Discovery of its Presence	Vitamin-Rich Foods	Protects Against	Some of its Properties	Pure Vitamin Obtained
A	McCollum 1912–14	Cod liver oil, Halibut liver oil, Butter, Milk, Egg yolk, Cheese, Carrot, Lettuce, Tomato, Liver, Oysters, Spinach, Watercress	Xerophthalmia (an eye disease), Nightblindness, Retarded growth, Injury to epithelial tissues, Low resistance to infections (?)	*Fat-Soluble;* Loses potency on exposure to air; not destroyed at temperature of cooking	From Carotene ($C_{40}H_{56}$) in 1932 by J. C. Drummond [$C_{40}H_{56}+2H_2O \rightarrow 2C_{20}H_{29}OH$]
B	McCollum 1915–16	Yeast, Rice, Egg yolk, Pea, Wheat germ and Wheat bran, Oats, Corn, Orange juice, Tomato, Watercress	Beriberi, Injury to nerve tissues and digestive processes, Loss of weight, vigor, and appetite, Neuritis (?)	*Water-Soluble;* Fairly heat-stable, destroyed at 120° C.	From rice polishings in Jan., 1935 by R. R. Williams
C	Holst 1912	Orange juice, Lemon juice, Cabbage, Celery, Lettuce, Lime, Tomato, Onion, Rhubarb, Spinach, Germinating seeds	Scurvy, Injury to endothelial cells, Loosening and decay of teeth, Loss of weight, Swelling joints, Loss of bodily resistance	*Water-Soluble;* Sensitive to heat; Easily oxidized; reducing agent; Melts at 189° C.	From lemon juice by C. G. King and W. A. Waugh April 4, 1932 (Identical with Hexuronic Acid)
D	McCollum 1922	Cod and other fish liver oils, Egg yolk, Salmon, Foods irradiated with ultraviolet light, Caviar	Rickets, General muscular weakness, Faulty Ca–P metabolism, Dental caries, Rheumatism (?)	*Fat-Soluble;* Stable to heat and oxidation; Melts 114.5° C.	From Ergosterol by irradiation by Windaus on Nov. 23, 1931
E	Evans 1922	Wheat germ oil, Lettuce, Watercress, Spinach, Cereals, Cottonseed oil, Soy bean, Yellow corn, Commercial olive oil	Sterility in male rats, Resorption of the foetus in female rats	*Fat-Soluble;* Heat-stable; withstands oxidation; Melts at 158° C.	From wheat oil by H. McLean Evans (and O. H. and G. A. Emerson) in Aug., 1935
G	Goldberger 1916	Yeast, Egg, Liver, Kidney, Spleen, Milk, Lean meat, Spinach, Salmon, Turnip, Potato	Pellagra, General debility, Gastro-intestinal disturbances	*Water-Soluble;* Stable to the heat of cooking	

THE VITAMINS

Simple Formula	Structural Formula Obtained
$C_{20}H_{29}OH$	H_3C CH_3 C CH_3 CH_3 H_2C C – CH = CH – C = CH – CH = CH – C = CH – CH_2OH H_2C C – CH_3 (provisional) CH_2 after P. Karrer
$C_{12}H_{16}N_4OS$	CH_3 N = C – NH_2 C = C – CH_2CH_2OH HC C — N Cl C – S N – C – C_2H_5 H after R. R. Williams
$C_6H_8O_6$	O CH_2OH · CH · COH = CH · COH · COOH after P. Karrer
$C_{27}H_{41}OH$	H_2 H_2 C C HC H CH_2 C C C $C_{11}H_{23}$ H H HC C C CH_2 (provisional) HC C CH C H CH OH H after A. Windaus
$C_{29}H_{50}O_2$	

phosphorus metabolism, which meant the difference between healthy, well-formed teeth and teeth that decayed.

Mellanby conducted experiments first on some puppies, which seemed to be immune to dental decay, and then on a group of children most of whom had badly formed and carious teeth. By increasing their intake of irradiated ergosterol (vitamin D) and cutting down on their cereals, it was found that among the children dental decay was distinctly checked, and the spread of tooth cavities already present was diminished. Another group was given a diet very poor in vitamin D and rich in cereals, and dental caries increased. Other laboratories — Columbia University, the University of Michigan Dental School, and West China Union University at Chengtu — reported confirmatory data. McCollum's laboratory also took up the problem. With the help of Dr. Henry Klein, working on a grant from a dental association, a series of elaborate experiments was conducted with different diets. The test animals employed belonged to groups of inbred rats having high genetic uniformity.

The final report of this investigation contained the following revolutionary conclusion: " The quality of the saliva is the important thing in determining whether teeth will decay. The saliva acts as a buffer against the acid which breaks down the teeth enamel. The quality of the saliva is determined by the chemical composition of the blood (which is in turn dependent upon the foods consumed)." *Foods rich in calcium, phosphorus, and vitamin D will prevent teeth decay.* This discovery may save millions from false teeth. It may have already doomed the old dentistry to a quick death, and as in the Eskimo language, the dictionaries of civilized man will no longer contain the word " toothache." On the other hand, many are skeptical of the interpretation of animal experiments, and take refuge in this uncertainty. T. P. Hyatt, clinical professor of preventive dentistry at New York University, still clings tenaciously to the old adage about the clean tooth never decaying. L. M. S. Miner, dean of Harvard's Dental School, believes that the vitamin theory so far as it applies to dentistry is still very much a theory.

He points out the close relationship between the teeth of parents and children. " Often," he declares, " the pattern, size, shape, arrangement, and even definite predisposition to caries and other ailments are repeated from generation to generation," irrespective of wide differences in diets. Both inheritance and diet are undoubtedly the important factors in tooth decay.

Further interesting news has come from McCollum's laboratory in Baltimore. In 1931 McCollum and Elsa R. Orent found that when the last trace of the metal manganese was removed from an otherwise balanced diet, female rats lost their maternal instincts. Out of a group of fifty-nine rats, only one of the mothers built a nest, collected her young, hovered over them, and even suckled them. The others refused, so all their litters died of neglect soon after birth. Yet, when as little as 0.005 per cent of manganese was added to the diet, the mothers returned to their natural careers. (McCollum is studying the relation between manganese in the diet and the hormone, prolactin, which seems to produce the same effects.) Male rats deprived of manganese became sterile, because their sperm lost the ability to move about. And while scientists discussed the possibility that manganese was necessary for the proper functioning of a sex-stimulating hormone formed in the anterior pituitary gland, mankind began to look to its manganese.

The effects of depriving animals of another metal, magnesium, generally found with manganese in foods was also tried. Others had performed the experiment before, but obtained no startling results because it was a very difficult matter to rid food of all its magnesium. In McCollum's laboratory, however, after three years of work, magnesium was finally completely separated from manganese, and a diet prepared which contained less than two parts per million of magnesium. This was fed to a group of rats which gradually became red, grouchy, and extremely excitable. Selecting a spot in the side screening, they pace back and forth to it from the center of the cage. They snap as they wheel about in their pacing, until suddenly they sink their teeth into the wall of the cage and cling to it. Finally the animals go into convulsions and die. It is a new form of tetany. Some believe that magnesium bears the same relation to the adrenal gland as does iodine to the thyroid and calcium to the parathyroids — in any case, as McCollum has observed, it seems to sweeten one's disposition.

The causes of food-deficiency diseases are thus seen to be more than merely the lack of certain vitamins. McCollum lists thirty-seven chemicals which must be present in a complete diet. Aside from the need of carbohydrates (such as glucose), fats, water, linolenic acid, and proteins (or rather eighteen of the twenty-two amino acids known such as cystine, tryptophane, lysine, and histidine), the animal body requires calcium, phosphorus, magnesium, manganese, chlorine, iodine, iron, sodium, potassium, copper (which together with iron is necessary for the formation of hemoglobin), and sulphur, in varying amounts, together with the six vitamins now definitely known. Therefore there may be at least as many as thirty-seven food deficiency diseases. These may be further increased in number by the study of other elements, such as nickel, cobalt, fluorine, zinc, aluminum, and boron, now going on in various laboratories. Moreover, McCollum believed that other vitamins — " ministers of metabolic change " — might still be discovered. In April, 1935, this prediction apparently came true when the University of Copenhagen released the news that one of its research workers, H. Dam, had obtained evidence of the existence of another vitamin from hog liver, hemp seed, kale, and tomatoes. Concentrates of this vitamin when fed to chickens seemed to stop hemorrhages. The vitamin was named vitamin K and it is being tried at present as a cure for hemophilia. While it seems to be an essential food factor for chickens, it may not be, however, a new vitamin.

The facts uncovered by the modern science of nutrition leave the layman bewildered, and he has rightly asked for a way out of the waters of food deficiency diseases which threaten to engulf him. McCollum cautions us not to " leave apes or faddists guide us in our diet." He advises us, " Eat what you want after you have eaten what you should." And what *should* we eat?

Milk, leafy vegetables, fruit, and eggs, with meats in moderation — these are the protective foods. And to the diets of infants, children, expectant and nursing mothers, McCollum would add cod-liver oil and vitamin D, since none of the usual foods contain enough of this vitamin. "All the information available," says McCollum, "seems to warrant the conclusion that we may attribute in great measure the incidence of malnutrition among children of pre-school ages, the faulty bone growth, bad teeth, and faulty posture, to inadequacies in our diet, and to perverted appetites which result from pampering and the development of a preference for sweet foods." The United States is the largest per capita consumer of sugar in the world.

McCollum is too broad a scientist to have a polyphemic or single eye for the possibilities of nutrition. Food may not completely change a fool to a philosopher, or lengthen life or postpone old age to any considerable extent, as some have declared.

While McCollum refuses to magnify these scientific claims, science, he insists, has made a great contribution here. To those who dismiss the experimental data obtained from animals as of little or no significance as a criterion of the nutritive needs of man, McCollum answers that such data when correlated with human experience and numerous experiments on humans, such as he performed in 1919 on two hundred thirty-six negro children, enable us to establish human requirements with more than a fair degree of accuracy. His own work has helped to change the diets of millions of people. The old idea was to fill the belly with as much food as possible regardless of its composition. The new idea is to supply the body only with the essential factors necessary for healthy growth. One hundred years ago the Association for the Improvement of the Condition of the Poor fed their unfortunates on a diet of Indian meal, hominy, beans, peas, salt pork, and dried fish. Today the Bureau of Home Economics of the United States Department of Agriculture advises for minimum relief equally inexpensive meals comprising one pint of milk, one vegetable or fruit, bread, and cereals daily, with the addition of cod-liver oil for those under the age of two.

The work of McCollum and his laboratory has also convinced mankind that in more ways than one, "*La mort entre par la bouche*."

CHAPTER EIGHT

INSECTS

WILL THE INSECT'S INSTINCTS OUTLIVE MAN'S INTELLECT?

With special appreciation of the work of Leland O. Howard who for sixty years led the fight against our insect enemies

It is recorded that Count Dejean, aide-de-camp to Napoleon I and amateur collector of insects, delayed a battle charge in order to catch a rare bug. An insane act for a valiant soldier, it was thought in those times, but today the world has come to realize that the insect world presents a far more ominous menace to the survival of man than even man himself.

When we survey the field of entomology we are brought up sharply by the tremendous change in our attitude toward the insect realm — a change hardly less than a revolution, and not much older than a generation. Until very recently the entomologist was regarded as but a bug collector, a harmless perverted sort of individual who wasted his time in the trivial, often ludicrous pursuit of butterflies and wasps, armed with nothing but a net and an aloofness which defied rational understanding. Only one hundred years ago the Oxford Encyclopedia accurately described the situation in these words: " There is not perhaps any branch of natural history the study of which has been so generally regarded with indifference and contempt. The insect hunter is not infrequently treated with ridicule and his pursuit branded as frivolous."

Today, entomology attracts more followers than any other branch of zoology. Its army is a formidable and respected one. Its men trained in general zoology, insect physiology, chemistry, and agriculture are stationed at strategic points all over the globe to match wits with an enemy which is as powerful as it is numerous. Equipped with new weapons and large appropriations, they are aiming a never-ending and deadly barrage against their oldest yet newest foe. The greatest ecologic problem confronting mankind today is to learn enough about insects so that we will have complete control over them.

The insect world is a queer study in the evolution of life. Already sporting on our planet two hundred million years before the appearance of man, insect species struggled against devastating odds, multiplied and mutated, and, in spite of the apparent absence of brain and reason, survived cataclysm after cataclysm. Fossils tell us that many species perished. Flying cockroaches no longer torment us, and dragon flies with a wing spread of two and a half feet are found only in museums. Yet there are still alive more species of insects than of all the other forms of life put together, not excluding plants. More than five hundred thousand different varieties of flies, lice, beetles, ants, wasps, locusts, gnats, and other species of flying and creeping things have been collected and named. Five-sixths of all the species of animals alive belong to the insect realm.

It is not difficult to explain the survival of this Lilliputian host. In no other branch of lowly life do we find anything to surpass the marvelous behavior of these organisms. Fabre, the insect Homer, the Peckhams, Williston, Maeterlinck, V. L. Kellogg, W. M. Wheeler, and many others have described the uncanny instincts, tropisms, apparent emotions and even memories, the almost unbelievable social organization of many species. Although we have not as yet been able to explain the insect mind, we know it operates with unerring precision. Close scrutiny of the social system of the honey bee suggested to Robert Bridges that:

Bees were fully endowed with Reason and only lost it
By ordering so their life as to dispense with it,
Whereby it pined away and perish'd of disuse.

Their multifold adaptations have made many of the insects the aristocrats among living things. For as Sutherland has put

Leland Ossian Howard

Blotting out the light of the sun and taking a whole day to pass over a given point, this swarm of locusts passed over Gilgil, Kenya Colony, East Africa, on July 15, 1931. *(Acme)*

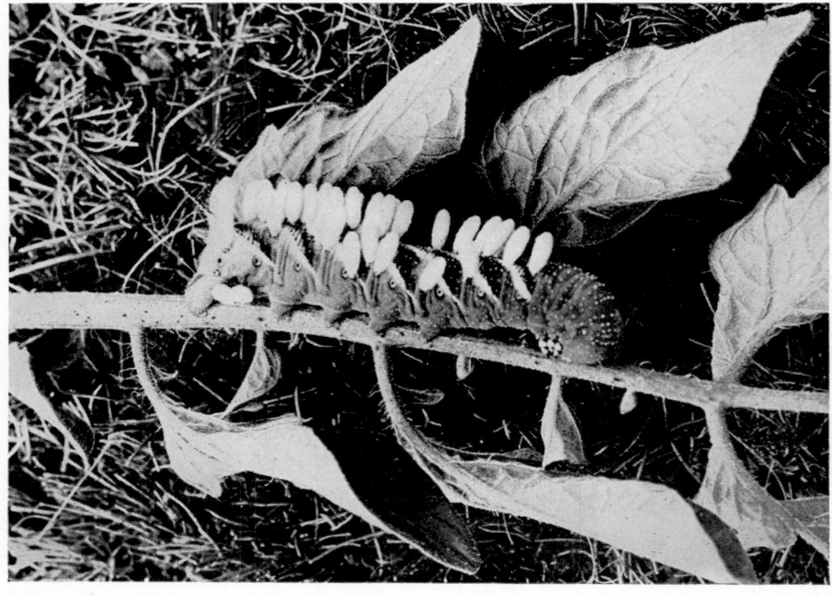

One insect destroys another. The parasite, *Sarcophagus Kellyi*, attaches itself to the tomato worm and lives upon it until it completely destroys the worm. *(Underwood & Underwood)*

it, " Man is but a creature of the last twenty minutes or so compared with the cockroach that hides behind the kitchen sink, but who can point his antennae to the coal in the hod and say, ' When that was being made my family was already well established.' " Chitin skeletons unattacked by acids or alkalis, digestive systems which can effectively assimilate anything from pepper and mustard plasters to mummies and Jefferson's *Manual on the Constitution,* springy legs enabling them to jump distances which would make it possible for man in comparison to his own weight to reach the moon in a few hops, structural and color specifications in walking sticks and measuring worms which closely resemble the twigs and foliage on which they live, smoke screen apparatus which goes into action when the bombardier beetle is in danger, reproductive powers which would enable one plant louse to produce enough progeny in one season to outweigh the earth's human population fivefold, heat-resisting powers which make it possible for larval midges to live in pools at 120° F., polyembryony, or the development of thousands of adult insects from one solitary egg — these are but a few of the reasons why insects still hold dominion on our earth.

It is outside the province of science to find a purpose for the existence of so many tens of thousands of insect species. But economic man can give various reasons. Various caterpillars constitute part of the diet of primitive peoples. Grasshoppers are used as food in the Philippine Islands and other places. Some of the Indians in the mountains of California cook and eat the big caterpillars of the Pandora moth. The manna which fed the Children of Israel was honey-dew secreted by a scale insect. The honey bee still furnishes mankind with sweet food and beeswax. The silkworm in its final stage, consuming its own weight of mulberry leaves each day, gives us a thread with which to weave silky garments. The cochineal bug of Mexico supplied man with a red dye until he learned to make it in inanimate flasks. The scales of *Carteria lacca* of India furnish us with shellac. Bumblebees with tongues long enough to reach down for the nectar pollenize the red clover crop. (When the bumblebee started on the road to extinction in the United States, queen bees were imported from Russia in 1934 to save the clover crop.) Many other insects are necessary for plant pollination. Numberless insects devour troublesome weeds, keep changing the soil, act as scavengers of dead and putrefying matter, supply food for useful birds and other animals. Drosophila, the fruit fly, has turned out to be man's most valuable organism for the study of heredity and evolution. Since 1930 sterile blowfly maggots have been reared by the Bureau of Entomology of the United States by the millions, for man has learned to exploit the peculiar eating tastes of these insects. During the World War these maggots had been found feeding upon the gangrenous tissues of wounded soldiers left for days unattended in no man's land. Instead of succumbing to the fatal affects of gangrene these men were found to recover rather quickly. Other infected men who were not visited by these maggots suffered amputations or died of their infected wounds. By producing the healing chemical, allantoin, by feeding upon dead tissue and by destroying bacteria, blowfly maggots cleared up stubborn infections and saved hundreds of lives. After the war, medical men used the maggot allies against gangrene, tuberculosis of the hip, other almost incurable bone infections and osteomyelitis (an inflammation of the bones common among children). The maggots are placed in boxes which are strapped to the infected tissues and the maggots do their work painlessly and effectively. A strange treatment indeed in these days of constant dread of the insect world!

Yet in surveying the bug world (bug originally meant the realm of ghosts and other terrifying apparitions) with its stingers, its poisoners, its bloodsuckers, its annoyers, its crop destroyers, its disease carriers, its killers, and its cannibalism, we are utterly confounded in any attempt to find purposive reasons for their existence. Or perhaps the Creator set these queer organisms on earth to test the ingenuity of man in understanding and triumphing over them. "They are a hard problem for religionists," says Julian Huxley, and, it might be added, an even greater one for scientists.

Joel was not the first to witness the destructive powers of God's strangest creatures: " For a nation has come up upon my land, strong, and without number. . . . He hath laid my vine waste, and barked my fig tree. . . . The field is wasted." Neither was the prophet of Israel the last of the great lamenters over their depredations. Recurring swarms of ravenous insects so thick that they blotted out the sun have plagued mankind through the centuries.

It was not until Leland O. Howard entered the fight that a man appeared who really fought our insect enemies with the weapons of a new science. This eminent American entomologist is Beelzebub's arch-antagonist. And if the insect world is ever to cease harassing and menacing mankind, it will be Howard and his army who will destroy it until the wickedest of its creatures shall be known only as fossils. Yet had Howard listened to the counsel of his relatives and friends, had he followed the advice of his elders and failed to see beyond the narrow attitude then current toward entomology, the world might have gained another lawyer, physician, or teacher of natural history, and the insect realm would have been spared its greatest threat to survival. After graduating from Cornell University, Howard took a year of postgraduate work, matriculated at the College of Physicians and Surgeons, then suddenly threw in his lot with his boyhood hobby, the study of insects, by accepting an offer as office assistant in the Entomology Service in Washington.

At the beginning, the words of his old grandmother rang in his ears. " Leland is a nice boy," she had remarked upon hearing his decision to become an entomologist, " but I do wish that he had not chosen such a trifling business." Doubts assailed him. Perhaps, after all, she might be right. What future was there for a young man whose only specialty was a knowledge of insects! It was all right when he was ten years younger to have spent his leisure trading insects with other boys and attending meetings of the Ithaca Natural History Society which he had helped organize. But surely entomology was no career for an ambitious young man! But Howard's absorbing interest in insects was greater than any promise of fame or fortune.

On the second floor of the Department of Agriculture Building Howard found the Entomology Service. He walked in unannounced. The headquarters consisted of two small rooms. In a corner of the one he entered worked Theodore Pergande, who had left his home in Silesia because his parents wanted him to study philology even though he preferred insects. Howard was to learn much from this classical scholar to whom insect habits were more thrilling than word derivations. But the moving spirit of that office was Charles Valentine Riley. He was a sensitive, controversial, poetic-looking young man whom Howard remembered from years back when he had come to Cornell to deliver a few lectures on insects. The picture of this sombrero-hatted entomologist, sketching with both hands at once, even more beautifully than the elder Agassiz could do, was not easily forgotten.

Riley had just succeeded T. Glover, who in 1854 had been appointed to the Bureau of Agriculture of the United States Patent Office. This was the first Federal appointment of an entomologist. One of Glover's duties was "to collect information on insects" and now, though old, decrepit, and almost blind, he was still kept on the payroll. Riley was much more than a mere collector of data. At twenty-one he had left a farm near Chicago to become entomologist editor of the *Prairie Farmer*. Four years later he was appointed entomologist of the State of Missouri. His annual reports even reached and aroused the admiration of Darwin. Before long, Riley found himself chief of the Entomology Service of the Federal Government. For thirteen years Howard worked under Riley.

During these years a number of pressing problems had to be met. A little midge was wreaking havoc on the clover seed crop all over the eastern part of the country. Evolution had played a peculiar prank by teaching this tiny insect to lay its eggs in the flower head of red clover. When the larvae hatched, they immediately set to work devouring the contents of the seed pod.

There was no depending upon birds, moles, shrews, or other animals to check their depredations. There was no use attacking the mischievous creature with traps or poison baits. Some other method had to be invoked.

Howard studied the life history of the insect. He learned the time of its transformations almost to the hour. Then he did some figuring. Three crops of clover were being cut annually. Howard calculated that if the time of cutting the first crop were advanced ten days in the spring, the completion of the midge's life cycle would be prevented, and the other two crops would be saved from the marauders. Howard published his findings under the name of his chief. The farmers of America followed his advice and the midge was doomed. This marked the first case in the United States where crop practice had been altered to get rid of a dangerous insect devourer. Howard at the age of twenty-two had done a neat job.

Other crop practices were also changed to meet the dangers from other insect pests. When, for example, the Hessian fly (so named because it first reached our shores in the straw bedding brought over for the Hessian troops during the American Revolution) threatened our wheat crop, Illinois and other states directed its farmers to plant wheat only between certain dates. This would eliminate the hordes of Hessian flies; the eggs would not hatch because when they reached this stage of their life cycle, the wheat plant upon which they fed would not be ready for them.

The insect armies in the meantime were advancing on numerous other fronts into man's territory. More than once Howard had to miss those weekly whist games at the White House with President Hayes' son in order to rush to the scene of activity of another insect enemy. In the vicinity of New Orleans he investigated a pest that was attacking sugar cane. Then an outbreak of the army worm brought him hotfoot to Illinois where he found an extraordinary scene. "Over many acres there was hardly a stem that did not bear one or more of these voracious caterpillars. Nothing could be done except to stop the march of the enemy by ditching." In Georgia he stared helplessly at the destruction caused by rice insects. And as he sat writing entomological definitions for the *Century Dictionary* and "inflicting new atrocities on the English language," he was rudely disturbed by the Mormon louse. This gnatlike insect, also known as the chinch bug, had been doing sixty million dollars' worth of damage to corn, wheat, and oat crops for several years. Entomologists tracked down the secret habits of this glistening white-winged louse, and finally showed the farmers how to get rid of this native pest temporarily by burning all the wild bunch grass along the roadsides, in which the insect made its winter quarters.

In 1888 Riley pointed the way to a new strategy. The orange and lemon groves of California were suffering from the cottony cushion scale. This insect sank its tink beak through the bark of fruit trees and sucked the sap until the tree was too weak to bear fruit. As the killer tapped the life blood of its host, it squeezed out of the pores of its back a waxy substance which congealed over its eggs and thus protected them. Spraying would not dislodge the eggs, and until now man had been at the mercy of this pest. Riley looked over the dreadful situation. Surely there must be some way to ëradicate this terror. Man's cunning must be a match against the million-year-old instincts of this quarter-inch scale insect! Riley had all the makings of a great scientist. He was curious, ingenious, courageous — qualities he proved in coping with this problem.

Why was this scale insect such a terrible destroyer in California while it was relatively innocuous in its other home in Australia? Perhaps, thought Riley, it was kept in check by some parasite or predacious insect which had not found its way to the New World. Then he got the notion to search for parasites and predators of this insect and liberate them in the California groves. He was going to set one insect against another. It was not just a crazy theory. He was not the first to get this idea, nor the first to put it to a test. Beetles had been used on rose bushes to eat the lice of this plant. Asa Fitch of New York, who in 1853 became the first official State entomologist in this country, had suggested this line of attack in connection with possible European parasites of the American wheat midge, but his advice was never acted upon. Riley, himself, in 1873 made the first definite experiment toward biological control when he sent an American predatory mite, *tyroglophus phylloxerae*, to fight the phylloxera which had cost the vineyards of France two billion dollars. Years before Bellanghi in Italy had declared that " entomological parasitism has a future." Would Riley make this prophecy come true?

Riley wrote to a friend in Adelaide, and within a short time received a box full of diptera parasites which had been devouring the Australian fluted scale. Bug was pitted against bug in the groves of California, but the scale insects emerged the victors. Riley planned to make a trip to Australia himself to hunt for more effective enemies. But he had got into trouble with government officials. He had been charged with playing politics. Ignoring his superiors he had gone direct to friends in both Houses for appropriations for his department. He was also accused of spending too much time on vacations abroad. Congress passed a bill forbidding foreign travel by employees of the Department of Agriculture, and Riley, who, of course, was affected by this measure was worried. His insomnia now kept him awake nights longer than ever. He would pay his barber to allow him to make up for lost rest in the barber's chair, where he found he could fall asleep rather easily. Finally he found a way to get one of his men to Australia. A World Exposition was to be held at Melbourne. He was going to send someone ostensibly to represent his department, but actually to hunt for insect predators and parasites.

Albert Koebele, a German immigrant whom he had met at a meeting of the Brooklyn Entomological Society, was selected. Koebele was the entomologist who had reared and liberated those parasites which had originally been sent over from Australia. In December, 1888, came a new parasite — twenty-eight adult ladybirds from Koebele. These were little black beetles with red spots, which had been found feasting on the scale insect of Australia. *Vedalia cardinalis* was its pretty name. It is itself completely free of insect enemies. The female lays three hundred eggs, and in five months a single ladybird may become the ancestor of seventy-five billion little ladybirds. Vedalia has two generations while its prey is going through but one. It is active both in the larval and adult stage of life. Daniel W. Coquillett, who had come to Southern California because of tuberculosis, was entrusted with the job of rearing these insects. He raised thousands in a tent constructed over an orange tree infested with the scales, and then released them in one of the most badly infested groves of the West, as well as in hundreds of other orchards. The predatory insects went at their work with a vengeance, and in a few years the scale was so reduced in numbers that today it causes no appreciable commercial damage.

Riley had initiated the most spectacular experiment in the history of insect control. Biological control of an insect pest with the aid of its natural enemies imported from foreign lands had proved its worth. Man now had a new weapon to fight his insect adversaries. Vedalia was sent to New Zealand, Portugal, South Africa, Egypt, Hawaii, Italy, Syria, France, Uruguay, and wherever the cottony cushion scale reared its head. Vedalia has not completely exterminated the scale. In fact, it is supposed that parasites and predators never do this, because when the host insect becomes scarce the predators, not having enough to feed upon, leave their impoverished feeding grounds. The strategic retreat of the parasites enables some of the insects to survive and the pest thus escapes complete destruction. California still breeds the ladybird for possible outbreaks. And while another bitter battle raged between Riley, some of the State officials of California, and the head of the American Commission in Melbourne over the credit for the successful experiment, the State Fruit Growers Association of California presented Koebele with a gold watch and chain and a set of diamond earrings for his wife, and some Germans began referring to the international exchange of natural enemies of injurious insects as the *Koebele method*, which Howard thought " was hardly fair to Riley."

While the shroud for the scale pest was being made ready in California, and Howard, for the honor of zoology, was writing the last word, *zyxomma*, in the English dictionary, another insect terror appeared in New England. The gypsy moth had been brought over from Europe by Leopold Trouvelot, a French astronomer employed at the Harvard observatory. He wanted to try mating them with silkworms in the hope of breeding a hybrid race of silkworms which would resist *pébrine*, a disease that was threatening the silk industry of France. One day during a gale, a box containing the eggs of the insect blew out of the window of his home in Medford, Mass. Trouvelot tried hard to retrieve the eggs — he realized the danger. On hands and knees, the astronomer searched with a magnifying glass among the grass and shrubs. But some of the eggs remained unaccounted for, and Trouvelot lost no time in notifying the proper Massachusetts officials of this accidental gypsy moth invasion.

The State of Massachusetts slept while the gypsy moth, so named because the buff color of the male resembled the shade of a gypsy's face, kept gathering its resources. Then twenty years later, in 1889, there descended upon Medford a swarm of gypsy moths which recalled the days of Egypt's plagues. Pharaoh probably never saw anything worse than did that wide-eyed populace of the little New England town. The streets were covered with caterpillars nearly three inches long, their sooty backs marked with yellow and a double line of blue spots followed by a double row of red spots. They were all over — in food, clothes, houses. No single nook or corner escaped them or their carcasses, from which rose a stench to add to the general discomfort. " The work of fire could not have been more thorough or alarming. The hungry caterpillars swarmed everywhere. They invaded houses and made homes uninhabitable. Pines and other conifers were killed outright, while shade trees and orchards were swept bare of foliage. . . . The pattering of their excremental pellets sounded like rain."

A meeting was quickly called. Something had to be done or the gypsy moth would take complete possession of the town. The moth was declared public enemy number one, and large appropriations were voted to meet the invader. It was not an easy fight. They were handpicked, crushed, sprayed with Paris green, trapped under burlap bag bands wrapped around the trunks of trees. When the caterpillars devoured the Paris green with impunity, the townsmen changed to more effective poisons. More squads of men were enlisted in the struggle. The insect's eggs are deposited in masses, each containing about five hundred, in the trunks of trees, crevices of houses, fences, and stone walls, where they winter, and it was a difficult matter to locate these nests.

For more than ten years the fight went on against the eggs, the larvae, the pupae, the silk-winged male moth which flies, and the nearly white-winged female which cannot fly because of its weight. Then in 1901 when the gypsy moth was getting the worst of the struggle Massachusetts stopped its appropriations and gave the enemy a breathing spell. The brown-tail moth, smuggled in from Holland on some rose bushes, joined the insect enemies. Four years later the gypsy moth was as strong as ever. Again New England was up in arms. The embattled farmers and city folk renewed hostilities, and Kirkland, superintendent of the fight, called upon Howard for help. The pest had by this time gained footholds in Maine, New Hampshire, and Rhode Island. There was imminent danger of further spread. The leaves of fruit, shade, and woodland trees, especially the apple, white oak, red oak, willow, and elm, were being devoured and the trees left to die. The invaders also fed on the foliage of shrubs, vines, bushes, flowers, grass, and field crops.

Could parasites of the gypsy moth be found to set against the invader? To search for them in the United States would probably be futile. In the first place the gypsy moth was a foreigner and its natural enemies had evidently not followed her across the ocean as baggage. Besides, various American predators had already been recruited and proved ineffective. Howard, however, placed his hopes on possible European destroyers. It is true, to be sure, that Howard had at first doubted the efficacy of Riley's plan to import the natural enemies of the scale pest of California on the ground that the Australian continent was in a different life-zone from that of California. But the conquest achieved by Vedalia changed their opinion. Howard believed that the gypsy moth must have its enemies in Europe and he made up his mind to confront the devilish pest with weapons from its own kingdom. The only doubt in his mind was whether the imported parasites and predators could survive the changed environment and be happy and prolific in New England.

In the summer of 1905 he sailed for Europe to consult a number of eminent entomologists. Among them was Filippo Silvestri of Naples who came to Howard's aid by sending his assistant to Sardinia to collect 1250 pupae and 2000 larvae of the gypsy moth lousy with its parasites. While these were being shipped to Boston, Howard went north to the woodlands around Milan, Vienna, Budapest, Dresden, Zurich, and Paris in search of more parasites. The French peasants explained his interest in bugs on the ground that "every millionth caterpillar has a diamond in its head, and that this was a somewhat laborious American way of accumulating a fortune." Other shipments of parasites reached Massachusetts to help stem the rising tide of the gypsy moth. The moth and its parasites were nourished and bred in specially constructed cages until Howard returned from abroad.

Then they selected an old orchard badly infested with the moth and built a large netted wire framework over three of its trees. Within this guarded enclosure the moth and its parasites were liberated, and the two entomologists watched the battle of the insect enemies as no commander ever watched a regiment of crack troops in action. It was a good performance. The parasites were more than holding their own, but the gypsy moth could not be stamped out so quickly. Congress appropriated funds and Massachusetts added ten thousand dollars for the importation of more foreign parasites. Three years later bug hunters in Japan sent over *Anatatus disparis*. This clever little wasp was a great ally. It would search out the gypsy moth's eggs, pierce them with murderous stings, and lay its own eggs in the cavities. When the eggs of the wasp hatched, their larvae proceeded to consume those of the gypsy moth.

The following year another insect, *Schedius kuvanae Howard*, came from Japan to fight as a new recruit for the American farmer. Fortunately the single fly which survived the long trip happened to be a female which reproduced parthenogenetically (without the aid of the male), and its offspring were established. The gypsy moth was now getting some real competition. Hardly had it recovered from the surprises of these two Japanese invasions, when it came face to face with another imported enemy. In the summer of 1911 W. F. Fiske came across *Limnerium disparidis*, a Russian parasite lost in the forests of Gioia Tauro in Sicily. It hangs suspended from a twig or leaf by a long silken thread which often breaks, the cocoons falling to the ground. Fiske offered the forest guards and children of the neighborhood one *centissimo* for every cocoon they would bring him. They thought him crazy, but a penny from a lunatic was still a penny, and the hunt went on for days until thousands were picked. After a cholera epidemic, uncertain boat sailings, overwise and overcautious consuls and customs officials, and the grim insect reaper, Fiske succeeded in getting some of his charges alive to the Melrose Highlands laboratory. This parasite, too, was firmly established throughout New England.

For eight years beginning with the World War foreign work was abandoned, and the gypsy moth profited by the great human holocaust. But in 1922 the insect battle was resumed with fury with the aid of more Japanese mercenaries and additional European shock troops. The pupae of these insect warriors were packed in wooden boxes, sent by airplane to Paris, then by fast rail to Cherbourg and placed in the cold-storage room of the first westbound steamer. These flies usually arrived at the Melrose Highlands insectory in July. They were supplied with loaf sugar as food, and placed in special cages. During the mating period the insects were constantly watched, and as soon as they were observed in coition, they were removed in glass tubes while still together. The fertilized females were then placed in the colonization cages and liberated together with the males in the infested areas.

The fight was a bitter one. Forty-seven different enemies of the gypsy moth were gathered from every corner of the globe. Fifteen of them, including a brilliantly colored beetle, *Calosoma sycophanta,* which preyed upon larvae and pupae, the tachinid *Compsilura concinnata Meig,* and others with equally formidable names, were successfully established and did valiant work. A barrier zone twenty-five miles wide east of the Adirondacks and extending all the way from the Canadian border down to Long Island Sound was established. Strict quarantine laws were enforced. New and strange methods were introduced to locate infestations. The sex organs of virgin female gypsy moths were removed and gathered together. Their odor was used to attract the male in heaps. Slowly but surely they were being drawn into an ever narrowing circle. In the fall, scouts hunted their egg clusters and wiped them out with creosote. In the spring crews sprayed them with lead arsenate through mile-long hoses. Today, after a half century of war, the gypsy moth is practically snuffed out. Though new and small infestations crop up from time to time, the battle seems won — the greatest battle of man against an insect pest by the method of biological control. More than a hundred million foreign troops were engaged in this supreme struggle to save New England.

Other insect pests appeared. The Entomology Service's counter-attack against them was weakened by the simultaneous appearance of these new invaders at widely separated fronts. While some insect enemy drew the fire of Washington at one point, another battalion suddenly appeared thousands of miles away to confound their human opponents. This was the situation in the summer of 1894 when Howard was appointed chief to succeed Riley, who had resigned in a fit of temper. Howard was enjoying this life of entomologist. The insect scrap fascinated him. Now as commander-in-chief, no day was without the lure of a great adventure. "Every morning at my desk," he wrote, "I have faced the possibility of finding a report that would affect the destiny of a whole people."

Indeed, hardly had he assumed his new duties when the mail brought a letter from a druggist of Corpus Christi, Texas, which heralded another great war. The writer complained of a tiny weevil which had attacked and almost destroyed the whole of his cotton crop. With the letter came a vial containing some of the marauders. Howard examined them. These gray quarter-inch insects were members of the tribe known as the Mexican cotton boll weevil, which had first been described and named by a Swedish entomologist half a century before. They had a shady reputation. They had been known to attack the wild cotton in Mexico, and between 1856 and 1862 did such great damage that cotton planting in that region had to be completely abandoned.

Howard was seriously alarmed. The cotton fields of Texas would offer perfect feeding grounds for this unwelcome newcomer. He rushed south immediately, and what he saw was enough to keep him awake nights. The insect had apparently been brought over the Rio Grande into Texas in cotton to be ginned around Brownsville. It had already punctured the bolls of cotton, laid its eggs, and the larvae were established in and feeding on the buds and bolls. Quick action was imperative, for the insect was spreading rapidly. Texas cotton was a delicacy, and the weevil gorged itself to the doleful tune of this negro folk song:

The boll weevil says to the farmer, "What makes yo' neck so red?"
"Tryin' to beat you devils: it's a wonder I ain't dead;
For you're takin' my home, Babe, just a-takin' my home!"

Howard persuaded Governor Charles A. Culberson of Texas to initiate legislation which would create a cotton-free zone fifty miles wide along the Texas border, to keep out the insect and check its spread. Culberson realized the little weevil was far more dangerous than any army of Mexican bandits, but the Texas legislature from sheer ignorance or stupid economy was on the side of the insect and turned down his bill. In 1899 a state entomologist was appointed, and Texas thought it had done its duty. They could not see the years of plague ahead of them, the ruination of business, bank failures, suicides of planters and bankers, migration of the unemployed negroes to the North, the immense sums spent annually to stem the tide, and the mountains of calcium and lead arsenicals to be sprayed from machine and airplane. Never was a country more shamelessly turned over to an invader than by this band of near-sighted lawmakers.

Faced with an extremely serious situation, Howard begged the farmers to change their methods. "In regions where other crops can be grown," he appealed to them, "it will be well to practice rotation of crops and not grow cotton two seasons in succession upon the same land." He also counseled them to plant an early maturing variety of cotton, force the crop, and collect the harvest in time to destroy the cotton stalks before the end of October. This would hold the boll weevil down. Farmers refused to take his advice. They clamored for quicker and more dramatic help from Washington. They had heard of Vedalia and the cottony cushion scale of the California citrus groves, and they wanted Howard to give them a host of predators and parasites of the boll weevil. "The success of Vedalia," wrote Howard, "blinded people and actually retarded the general progress of insect control in some places." He was helpless. The cotton boll weevil was either so vigilant or so disgusting that no parasite could be found boarding with this host.

The cotton boll weevil today is still the greatest menace of the southland. It is hardier than ever before. When it first arrived in the United States the frost took terrible toll, but today, either by mutation or selection, the weevil endures the cold winters of even the northern limits of the cotton belt. A repetition of Vedalia or Schedius seems very remote. Most entomologists believe that if the cotton of the South is to be freed of boll weevil, it will have to be done by crop rotation or with " Let Us Spray " on the banners and lips of the planters.

Chinch bug, cottony cushion scale, Hessian fly, gypsy moth, wooly root louse, hop aphis, sugar beet leaf hopper, grapevine flea beetle, Argentine ant, cotton boll weevil — those were only a few of the denizens of Beelzebub's realm. Many more came to afflict our farmers, and Howard was called upon to help fight one after another. When in 1893 he was shown some pears from Virginia covered with curious spots, " He jumped from his chair in excitement on recognition of the fact that the San José scale was at last in the East." This pernicious insect, brought east in some infected stock by nursery dealers, spread with lightning speed. Canada, Austria-Hungary, and Germany passed decrees prohibiting the admission of American fruits. When a shipment of American pears was refused at Hamburg and the American ambassador objected, he was handed a document by the foreign minister in Berlin. It was Howard's own official bulletin on the destructiveness of the San José scale. Lime-sulfur sprays and parasites have kept this orchard pest in check, although occasionally it stages a temporary yet vigorous come-back.

The codling moth was another uninvited immigrant whose chrysalis landed on our shores, even before the year of our independence, hidden away in the cracks of apple barrels and boxes. It had much its own way with our apple crops. When, however, it began to attack walnuts, S. E. Flanders of California reared *Trichogramma minutum* and matched them against the codling moth. This predatory insect used an ancient and effective method of attack. It laid its eggs in those of the codling moth, exterminating countless millions of them. When the government saw the power of this predator it bred them in huge numbers and sold orchardists *Trichogramma minutum* at a thousand dollars per million, or a hundred for a nickel.

In 1909 another unwelcome stowaway sneaked in via a cargo of broom corn from Hungary, and hid for a time in an old warehouse in Everett, Massachusetts. Some of its eggs hatched, and the yellowish moths which finally emerged found a cornland with boundless stores of food. The larvae of the ingrate basked in the sunshine of this haven of refuge. Breathing the pure air of the land of freedom and opportunity to all the hungry and oppressed insects of the world, it wasted no time in getting down to the business of its existence. It found a rich cornstalk and started tunneling its way down to the bottom and then up to the top again, eating all the while. This went on for from six to eight weeks until the insect had reached full size. In the meantime, others of its hungry kin have joined it in its dietary spree, and often fifty of them will convert the same stalk into a hollow lifeless tube. Man's method of raising his huge corn crop just suits the corn borer. The farmer could not contrive a better way to raise and shelter them. Man did more, he prepared a winter home for them. He cut his cornstalks high, and during the seven long winter months the corn borer lived in the stalk close to the ground, until the first warm breeze of spring woke it to resume its feeding.

The corn borer spread like wildfire. The East was on its knees praying for a deliverer. Farmers spending their last penny on a corn crop found the insect merciless. The West trembled at the possibility of its invasion. Congress appropriated ten million dollars in 1922 to check this new enemy within our gates. Howard's men issued bulletins and harangued the farmers for their negligence and stupidity. They advised them to cut their cornstalks low or burn them to the ground before the corn borer got a chance to find winter lodgings in them. That was the way Europe had successfully fought this pest, they were reminded. The U. S. Department also set up strict quarantine stations and every ear of corn that crossed the deadline had to be carefully examined. Parasites of the mothlike creature were brought over from Europe and Asia to check it. The corn borer has by no means been exterminated, due in great measure to the carelessness of the farmer.

There was no end to these alien invasions. From Japan, hidden in the roots of some iris bulbs, there arrived in 1916 a mischievous beetle whose grub ate lawns, golf-course grass, ornamental plants and shrubs around Philadelphia. When it grew to insecthood the adult beetle, an excellent flyer capable of a seven-mile sustained flight, turned from lawn and garden to orchards, tantalizing all of New England and many points west. It multiplied with terrifying rapidity. Between July 3 and 5, 1927, Howard received six hundred frantic letters for advice. In one peach orchard, merely by shaking the trees enough of these beetles were collected in an hour to fill ten sixteen-gallon tubs. And the next morning a similar treatment produced an equal volume of this Japanese peril from the same trees. Entomologists tried spraying the orchards with poisons, but the cunning coleoptera refused to eat the leaves so treated. So the bug hunters joined hands with chemists and botanists. About five hundred plant extracts were prepared and mixed with various pleasant oils and poisonous compounds. They worked wonders, but they could not accomplish the miracle of complete annihilation.

Predators and parasites of the beetle were hunted in the Orient. C. P. Clausen fought his way through the woodlands of Japan, Korea, and Manchuria, and sent back a curious little fly, *Centeter cinerea,* the female of which had developed the uncanny technique of depositing one of its eggs in the thorax of the beetle. As soon as the larva is born it begins feeding upon the inside of its host. When the executioner emerges as a full grown fly, it makes its exit from a hollow shell which was once the body of a voracious Japanese beetle. Four other enemies, including a wasplike creature discovered in the leaves of a noxious weed in Japan, have been established in the East to fight the beetle. In 1934 Dr. R. W. Glaser, of the Rockefeller Institute for Experimental Research near Princeton, raised *nematoda,* parasitical worms of microscopic size, to help in the fight. This nematode deposits its eggs in beetle larvae, an attack even more destructive than one upon the adult. The eggs when hatched destroy the immature beetle. Other methods have been introduced. Lands have been flooded to destroy the grub, farmers have delayed the planting of their corn so that the ears silk after the flight of the beetle, quarantine stations have been established in New England, New York, New Jersey, Delaware, Pennsylvania, Maryland, and Virginia to prevent its spread. Throughout the year, a thousand government men fight it with traps, insecticides, and parasites, at an annual expense of nearly a million dollars. But the brilliant green and coppery half-inch beetle from Japan is still unvanquished.

Nearly forty years after the spectacular success of Vedalia, California witnessed another striking victory against an insect pest. Since 1910 the citrophilus mealybug (*Pseudococcus gahani*) had been running amok among the rich citrus groves of that state. Fumigating, spraying, and waterwashing trees could not check it. Ladybirds were brought in to help the orchardists. Citrophilus soon formed an alliance with a species of ant which liked the sticky substance the mealybug was feeding it, and the ants in turn attacked the ladybirds. The University of California was called upon to save the situation. It staked all on imported parasites of the mealybug, and sent Harold Compere to search for them. C. P. Clausen and several other entomologists had previously combed China, Japan, Formosa, the Philippine Islands, and Indo-China without success.

Compere was luckier. On the first day of his inspection in Sydney, Australia, he picked a parasite off an oleander leaf in the city's Botanic Garden. It was *Coccophagus gurneyi*, which was holding the mealybug in check in Australia. His find was a female. A few weeks later, a male was captured. The pair were confined in a vial for a few minutes. Mating promptly occurred, and the fertilized female was carefully placed in a special jar and provided with new food.

Compere's luck did not end here. He managed to bring another murderous parasite, *Tetracnemus pretiosus* Timberlake, to the Citrus Experiment Station of the University of California. Harry Scott Smith, a paid collaborator of the Bureau of Entomology at Washington and one of the captains of the army of California entomologists, cared for these precious specimens and watched them handle a mealybug pest. When about to lay its eggs, the female cautiously approaches its unsuspecting host. It makes a quick, short, preliminary examination by delicately feeling the mealybug with the ends of its antennae. Instinct has taught her how to find the vulnerable spot even as her ancestors thousands of generations back had learned to identify it. Now, like an executioner, she stands defiantly on that spot selected for the insertion of her eggs. The end of her abdomen is flexed downward and forward as she brings its apex in contact with her victim. For several seconds she drills away until the mealybug's skin has been pierced. Then as the pointed tip of the ovipositor penetrates the skin she lowers her abdomen and with one mighty thrust forces the needle-like ovipositor its full length into the body of the mealybug. This process of inserting her eggs is such a serious business that the tiny wasplike creature will not be disturbed and will persist in its efforts unless forcibly removed. The bug is now doomed, for four days later those eggs which have been forced into the body of the mealybug hatch, and the larvae later proceed to consume the live mealybug. Nothing but a grayish, mummified body is left. The work of Coccophagus is swift and deadily.

Forty millions of these parasites from fourteen insectaries were put into the field annually at a cost of two dollars and fifty cents per thousand. This method was many times cheaper than fighting with poisons. In 1930 Smith wrote to Howard, "C. G. is a wonder. It looks now as though the citrophilus mealybug is doomed. Many groves have been completely cleaned up and the dead carcasses with exit holes are found by the million in the trees. I think we are about to witness another very successful case of biological control." Three years later the report was even more complete. "The citrophilus mealybug is *now under perfect control, in fact it is actually hard to find one in the citrus groves where formerly it was very destructive.* The saving to the citrus growers is in excess of a million dollars a year."

Out of every dollar spent by Americans on food and clothing, ten cents goes as tribute to those insect pirates whose tastes are rich and appetites Gargantuan. This loss is staggering when we realize that it is fifteen times greater than the country's fire loss and larger even than our cost of education. With an appropriation of about three million dollars during each of the last few years, Howard tried to save some of the two billions in annual crop losses in this country, as well as part of the colossal damage done by insects to stored foods, fodder, fibers, hides, clothing, and wood.

Howard has not looked upon the whole of the insect world as his enemy. It has, of course, some friendly members. Thirty-five years ago he thought he could call upon the insect kingdom to assist him in establishing a household industry in the hope of raising the subsistence level of the share-croppers of the South. He went to Europe and studied the silk industries of France and Italy. In the dream of establishing sericulture in America, he purchased a reel and brought over two expert reelers to teach the art of manufacturing silk. This project, however, proved a failure. Silk manufacturers could import raw (reeled) silk so cheaply that even if they were given a warehouse full of cocoons gratis, they could not afford to use them. And Congress refused to place a tariff on so-called " raw " silk.

Howard has been a leader not only in economic entomology but in medical entomology as well. That taste for medicine which led him to matriculate at a medical school never left him. When in 1880 Riley, who had resigned from the Bureau, was recalled on the election of President Garfield, Howard thought that his position was precarious and that he might be scrapped together with others to make room for political friends. His thoughts went back to medicine and he tried to study it again. Years later he wrote, " The work was hard, I contracted malaria and I married, and the combination of the two things was too much for the medical studies, so they stopped long before I got my medical degree."

But his interest in medicine continued. He saw the insect world not only as a danger to the food supply of man, but also as a direct threat to his bodily health. The Mesopotamians had sensed this thousands of years before when they carved gnats on their charms dedicated to Norgal, god of disease. The very year that Howard joined the Entomology Service Sir Patrick Manson discovered that an insect was the carrier of a minute filarial worm which was parasitic in the human body, and caused filariasis. Other organisms like the tapeworm, the hookworm, and trichina were known to bedevil man after working their way inside of us. For the first time Manson proved that an insect — the female mosquito, *Culex fatigans* — transferred the larvae of the filarial worm from man to man. The mosquito imbibed the minute embryo of the worm from the blood of one victim, gave it board and lodgings in its own body until it reached full development, and then dropped it in some water. A person drinking this water became another victim of filariasis.

Manson's finger pointing to that mosquito was the first scientific warning that other insects might be transmitters of disease. The medical world at first paid little attention to this interesting phenomenon. Even Howard could not see very clearly the implications of Manson's discovery. In fact, when in 1882 A. F. A. King of George Washington University spoke in Washington on the mosquito as a possible carrier of malaria, Howard was not at all impressed. When a few years later he developed a mild case of malaria, he got into bed, shut the windows of his room to keep out the dangerous miasma or bad air which his doctor told him came in from the Potomac flatlands, took plenty of quinine, and " got well but never suspected the Anopheles mosquito " as the carrier of the " chills and fever " disease.

Twenty centuries before, Varro, a Roman, had written, " See if there be any swampy land near, for certain tiny animals, invisible to the eye, breed there, and being carried through the air, may reach the inside of the body, causing diseases hard to cure." In 1897 Major Ronald Ross by a series of dramatic experiments proved that the female Anopheles mosquito of marshes was the carrier of malaria. This insect, loaded with one-celled animals called plasmodia in its salivary glands, punctured the skin of its victim with its pointed proboscis and injected this parasite into the blood. Each parasite entered a red blood cell and produced spores which elaborated poisons and caused a fever. Quinine killed the parasite. This clear-cut proof earned Ross, who was " more interested in mathematics and poetry than in entomology " (so he told Howard) the Nobel Prize in medicine, and started a bitter quarrel between the controversial Englishman and " that damned pirate," as Ross called Grassi, the Italian who made claim to priority of this discovery.

Even before Ross' historic announcement, Howard had already made the first biological study of Anopheles and other mosquitos. And when Reed, Lazear, and Carroll, appointed by the Surgeon-General of the United States to study yellow fever in Cuba, made ready to sail for the infected area they came to consult with Howard. The head of the Entomology Service showed them his collection of mosquitos, pointing out especially that infamous malarial Anopheles, and *Culex fasciata*, that silent, wary, town mosquito of the tropics. It was this latter, a beautiful insect with banded legs, also called the day mosquito, the house mosquito, and Stegomyia mosquito, which Dr. Carlos Finlay of Havana for eighteen years had accused as the purveyor of yellow fever. Howard described the life history of Culex as clearly as it was then known, explained that the female had a decided preference for human blood which it needed to develop its eggs, and showed the medical commissioners how to catch and kill it.

Reed kept Howard in touch with the progress of his experiments. Howard would meet friends at the Cosmos Club in Washington to discuss the work in detail. When Reed, with the help of human volunteers, finally and definitely proved *Culex fasciata* guilty of spreading yellow jack, Howard was overjoyed. On January 13, 1901, Reed wrote to him: "The mosquito theory for the propagation of yellow fever is no longer a theory but a well established fact. Isn't it enough to make a fellow happy? Anopheles and Culex are a gray old pair! What havoc they have wrought to our species during the last three centuries. *But with Howard and kerosene we are going to knock them out.*" It was Howard who as early as 1892 had popularized the method of destroying mosquitoes by pouring kerosene over their swampy breeding places — a procedure he had practised even as a boy.

Even before the conquest of malaria and yellow fever, many had learned to have respect for insects as possible carriers of disease. For example, Howard regarded the house fly as more than a domestic pest. He considered it a possible transmitter of pathogenic bacteria from polluted food and human and animal excrement. He suspected it might be a positive menace particularly to the health of children. In 1894 he determined to make a thorough study of this insect. He searched through the insect collections in Washington for specimens of flies. He found thousands of strange rare beetles from Brazil, fleas and gnats from Japan, moths from every corner of the globe. But of the domestic house fly or even the common cockroach there were none.

Howard started on a collecting expedition. He trapped flies in Washington; Azusa, California, or wherever he happened to be. The aid of hundreds of friends was enlisted. Some of the flies were marked, released, and then caught in the effort to trace their itineraries. During the hot summer of 1897, Howard bred flies in fresh cow dung, human excrement, and horse manure, and studied their life cycle. Down on his hands and knees, he counted the eggs laid by a single fly. He calculated the speed of their multiplication and estimated that a single female house fly might have 6,000,000,000,000 descendants in a few months.

When he discovered that out of 23,087 flies captured in dining rooms in various parts of the country, 98.9% belonged to the common species, *Musca domestica*, he launched a campaign against this insect enemy which soon reached every housewife and schoolchild in America. Dr. S. J. Crumbine, then a physician in Kansas, coined the slogan "Swat the Fly," and fly-killing contests became one of the most popular of the nation's pastimes. Howard issued bulletins with instructions for combatting the fly with screens, fly paper, chloride of lime, kerosene, and spe-

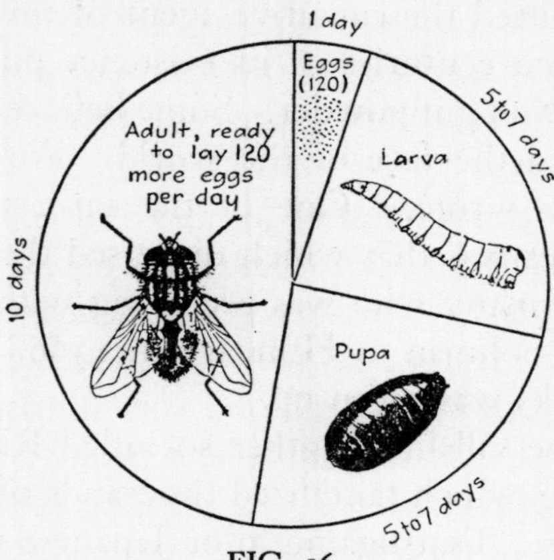

FIG. 16
Life cycle of the common house fly.

cial receptacles for manure. Newspapers, magazines, schools, and the church took up the fight. Howard led the fight into new quarters. At the Christmas 1908 meeting of the American Association for the Advancement of Science, he called the house fly the typhoid fly. Medical men objected because there were other carriers of this disease, but Howard stuck to his guns. The nasty name he had given persisted, and the swatting crusade never ended until every single fly became the personal enemy of every good citizen. In 1911 he published *The House Fly — Disease Carrier*, and spread the crusade to other countries.

In the years that followed men of science tracked down other insect disease carriers. Cleland in Australia caught *Stegomyia fasciata*, the culprit which transmitted dengue fever. Sir David Bruce, bringing his bride on an expedition to find the carrier of sleeping sickness in Africa, trapped the deadly tsetse fly by means of a dummy horse set up as a decoy. African sleeping sickness has depopulated vast fertile lands in that continent. In India, too, insect-borne diseases are responsible for more than a million and a half deaths each year. Both the body and the head louse of man were also caught red-handed. *Pediculus vestimenti* and *Pediculus capitis* were the organisms responsible for typhus. Both of these human parasites (who themselves succumb to typhus) transmitted the causative agent of this scourge which during the fifteen centuries of its existence piled up more destruction than even gunpowder. Some believe that typhus has actually changed the face of the world. For example, Hans Zinsser recently wrote, "One of the earliest really decisive typhus epidemics was that which dispersed the army of Maximilian II of Germany who was preparing with 80,000 men to face the Sultan Soliman in Hungary in 1566. The campaign against the Turks was given up."

Insects are the villains in other so-called Rickettsia diseases like trench fever which tantalized thousands of soldiers during the World War. Tsutsugamushi or Japanese valley fever also belongs to this category. This disease is conveyed to man by the bite of a harvest mite which picks it up from rats and mice, the natural reservoirs of this disease. Its American cousin, Rocky Mountain spotted fever, is spread by the common dog, rabbit or wood tick which often bite sheep herders and inoculate them with the disease. Kala azar, bubonic plague, and half a hundred more diseases of men and animals were all traceable either directly or indirectly to such agents. Insects have recently been the cause of another horror. In 1934 a little red fly deposited a parasite in the blood of forty-five thousand Indians in Mexico; tumors developed in their heads and they became blind.

For more than two score years Howard took part in the struggle between man and insect. Much was accomplished by the importation of insect parasites. The law, too, was called upon to keep out insect enemies. California passed the first quarantine law against insect pests in 1881 which provided for rigid inspection of imports which might harbor insect enemies.

A few years later by the passage of the Hatch Act numerous State Agricultural Experiment Stations were established throughout the country. Many states and even cities appointed entomologists to aid in the struggle. In 1889 the Association of Economic Entomologists, the first of its kind in the world, was founded by Riley and Howard. On August 12, 1912, Charles L. Marlatt, now Chief of the United States Bureau of Entomology, persuaded the government after thirteen years of propagandizing and in spite of the narrow attitude of importers, amateur horticulturists, and owners of private gardens, to pass a Federal Plant Quarantine Act. "We cannot have a reciprocity treaty on injurious insects," Marlatt had insisted, even as Howard over in Europe was inducing France, Belgium, and Holland to tighten down on their inspection service on outgoing goods. Sentinels were stationed at all ports and other strategic points to prevent insect invasions. Insects were stopped in the most unexpected places — in a bouquet of flowers on the Graf Zeppelin, in toys wrapped in rice straw in Japan and consigned to a chain of retail stores in New York.

Yet there was much left undone. Some were inclined to agree with a Canadian journalist who in 1930 had written, "I am afraid that the bug fight cannot be given the pride, pomp, and circumstance of human war. We could not march to it with flags flying and bands playing. And I am afraid that there would be no chance for the frenzied profiteering that is so stimulating to patriotism. I am afraid that the outlook is dark and that the insects will win." Howard, however, was not so pessimistic. He is neither an alarmist nor a romanticist. That same year, as retiring president of the American Association for the Advancement of Science, Howard, the first economic entomologist to be so honored, emphasized in no mild terms the great menace of the insect world which he felt sure could be destroyed by government cooperation. As the recognized world leader in his field, his words made a tremendous effect. Larger appropriations were voted by local, state, and the Federal government to fight insect invaders. Quicker action was taken against major pests.

For example, on April 6, 1929, larvae of the Mediterranean fruit fly, *Ceratitis capitata* Wild, were discovered in Florida grapefruit near the close of the citrus season. Seventeen years before when this same fly made its appearance in Hawaii, Howard had warned our farmers that " in the absence of quarantine its establishment in this country sooner or later is a certainty." At once the National Guard of Florida was called out to enforce the quarantine laws. Fruit from infested or immediately adjacent groves was completely destroyed, other fruit was carefully sterilized by the growers by heat treatment. Nineteen days after its appearance, the United States House of Representatives, with only a ten minute discussion, passed a joint resolution appropriating $4,250,000 to exterminate the Mediterranean fruit fly. It was the most dramatic instance of the extermination of a major pest within recent years.

New recruits were won for the field of entomology. All agricultural colleges and several other universities started to train fresh battalions of bug hunters. Students resumed the much needed study of the biology, the physiology and chemistry of flies, beetles, lice and other insect foes of mankind. New synthetic insecticides were prepared. Amyl salicylate mixed with deadly tartar emetic was discovered to be an attractant for the horn worm. Nicotine tannate was found effective against the codling moth. The effect of lead and arsenic taken into the bodies of insects through spraying mixtures was investigated. The respiration, metabolism, sugar and hydrogen-ion content of the blood of both normal and water-submerged insects were made the subjects of extended researches. The reactions of moths and flies to insect stomach poisons were also studied. Blowflies were placed in specially constructed olfactometers to test their reactions to various smells which might attract and help trap them. Even the diet of the common cockroach became a matter of grave concern to some entomologists. W. B. Hermes, chief entomologist of the College of Agriculture of the University of California, recently devised an ingenious method to attract certain pests in vineyards. He used a blue light which he found most effective in drawing the grape leaf-hopper to wires which electrocuted them. The blue light that he employed had the advantage that it did not attract other insects.

For the first time in history the children of the insect kingdom are being subjected to the scalpel, the test tube, and the metabolism chamber. It has at last been realized that if we are to fight them effectively, we must know them thoroughly. Entomology is no longer the exclusive plaything of eccentrics. It is now a science attracting some of the best brains of our younger research workers, who have come to realize that momentous discoveries are yet to be made in this boundless field. The chief outposts of this battle of science are located in the United States. At Albany, Georgia; Arlington, Massachusetts; Fort Valley, Georgia; Melrose Highlands, Massachusetts; Moorestown and Riverton, New Jersey; Riverside, California; Tallulah, Louisiana; Takoma Park, Maryland; Yakima, Washington, and other entomological centers, many of the unsolved problems are being tackled.

In these laboratories are being studied the brown-tail moth, pea, bean, cotton, and alfalfa weevils, Mediterranean fruit fly, scale insects, bark beetle, codling moth, turnip and alfalfa aphid, oriental fruit moth, pecan-nut borer, tobacco moth, army worms, cutworms, sugar-cane borer, black scale, cankerworm, oriental tip moth, termites, the angoumois grain moth — the worst destroyer found in granaries — and the ancient yet ever-present locusts and grasshoppers. The farmers of our West have never forgotten the years of the locusts that Rolvaag so vividly described in *Giants in the Earth*. For more than once their somewhat less voracious cousins came from their inaccessible hiding places in black swarms to cover the Great Plains and Mississippi Valley like a creeping carpet devouring and stripping every green thing in its path. The hoppers of the last few years seem to be mutating to a form more akin to the Rocky Mountain locust which harassed the Mormon pioneers of Utah. Chemical warfare with poison gas and molasses-sweetened bran mash loaded with sodium arsenate, rather than prayer, fasting, and the miracle of sea-gull alliance, is the weapon used against them today. In Minnesota alone a " minute man " organization of fifty thousand farmers wages war against them constantly, waiting for the new science to bring deliverance from this most destructive scourge of the West.

In this great entomological revolution Howard has been an inspiring leader. As a member of almost every important entomological society of the world, and as American representative at many agricultural and entomological congresses all over the earth, he has built up an international comradeship in this battle against the insect realm. He has raised economic entomology to the status of a science. In 1927, after a half-century of government service, he resigned as chief but was permitted at his own request to remain with the service for another four years as Principal Entomologist of the United States Department of Agriculture. Then on June 30, 1931, having reached his seventy-fourth birthday, he finally severed his official connections with the government service. Howard has always had to live closely. His salary, like that of other government employees in similar positions was a meager one. Soon after his retirement, fortunately, he received five thousand dollars as the Capper Award for outstanding work in agricultural progress. This gift enabled him to visit his friends working in the entomological laboratories of Honolulu, Kobe, Shanghai, Hongkong, Manila, and other parts of the world. The insect realm still held him. In Paris he attended the hundredth anniversary of the founding of the Entomological Society of France. Still a spirited fighter against the damaging hordes, he sent back to America reports and specimens of new insect allies and enemies.

Then his sight began to fail, and he came back to Washington to undergo an operation on cataract of both eyes. But Howard's humor was still with him. A few days before the operation he wrote to *Science:* " During the last few weeks my eyes have become very dim and I can no longer read. I have been interesting myself by watching my eye-spots — those fragile things that float before one's eyes, apparently in space. I have recognized three species, two plainly and the third rather dimly. Other biologists who have misused their eyes as I have may amuse themselves by classifying their eye-spots. The entomologist should have no trouble. The bacteriologist will have difficulty for lack of culture media, but I can't imagine that the chemist or the mathematician can use this method for passing the time away."

Such is the spirit of a great scientist who near the age of eighty still gives counsel to younger men in their battle against a common enemy. He cannot agree with Julian Huxley that " there is no danger from insects because they are tied down by instinct." Rather would he accept the prophecy of Harlow Shapley, once a zoologist and now an eminent astronomer, who visualizes a termite or some other insect crawling out of the skull of the last man on earth to muse, " Alas, the creature did not understand the business of survival."

There is the spirit of a great teacher who near the age of eighty still gives counsel to young men in their battle against a common enemy. He cannot agree with Julian Huxley that "the grim danger is an insect" because so much directed towards unities. Rather should he anticipate the prophecy of Huxley, simply being a zoologist, and to see an ironical circumstance when centuries hence a reptile or some other insect crawling upon the bed of the last man on earth to mark "Alas, the creature did not understand the business of survival."

PART TWO

CHAPTER NINE

MATTER

IS THE SOLID STUFF OF MATTER BUT A WAVE OF PROBABILITY?

Stressing the contributions of Robert A. Millikan and his laboratory

WHAT IS MATTER? That is a question man has asked for more than three thousand years. The long attempt to unravel the mystery of matter reveals at once a triumph of modern science and a confession of failure to solve fundamental problems.

Many centuries ago Kanada, the Hindu " atom eater," had conceived all matter to be in perpetual motion and discontinuous, that is, made up of small particles. In 500 B.C. at Abdera in Greece, Leucippus established a school where he taught that everything was composed of tiny particles of " changeless stuff " separated by space, through which they traveled. A century later one of his disciples, Democritus, developed this idea, writing that matter consisted of an infinite number of small invisible particles moving in empty space. He called these particles *atoms*, derived from a Greek word meaning indivisible. Matter exhibited different properties, he said, because it could be built out of different kinds of these atoms or " primal forms." Why is water a liquid, and iron a hard solid? asked Democritus. " Because," he answered, " the atoms of water are smooth and round and can glide over each other, while the atoms of iron are rough and hard." An all-embracing system of Atomism was thus constructed. Color was explained as being due to the different shapes of the different atoms. Sourness was produced by angular atoms. Atomism even invaded the realm of the spirit. The body of man, argued the Atomists, was composed of large, sluggish atoms, whereas his mind was built of small, mobile ones, and his soul of fine, smooth, round particles similar to those of fire. Even sight and hearing were considered atomic in nature. The Romans, too, were taught this strange conception by Lucretius in his poem *De Rerum Natura*, which described the entire universe in terms of atoms.

For centuries this conception of matter as composed of atoms was accepted, and even the great figures of the world of science believed in it, in one form or another. Isaac Newton, one of the greatest luminaries in the scientific heaven, wrote, "It seems probable to me that God in the beginning formed matter in solid, massy, hard, impenetrable, movable particles . . . so very hard as never to wear or break to pieces; no ordinary power being able to divide what God himself made One in the first creation."

In the meantime a vigorous pseudo-science, alchemy, was engaging the energies of honest men and rogues. In the effort to find the elixir of life (which would prolong life indefinitely) in the dirt and dross of centuries, men had stumbled upon new elements, such as antimony, arsenic, bismuth, and phosphorus, and hitherto unknown chemical compounds. In the attempt to reach the second of the two alluring goals of alchemy, the transmutation of metals, alchemy gave birth to a far more healthy child, chemistry. A few more centuries passed. Chemistry finally came of age with Priestley, the English dissenting minister who tore oxygen out of its compounds; Cavendish, the millionaire misanthrope of London who discovered pure hydrogen; Scheele, the Swedish apothecary who gave chlorine to the world, and Lavoisier, the French aristocrat whose head fell under the guillotine of the French Revolution after he had ushered in another revolution with the first accurate explanation of the process of burning.

The dawn of the nineteenth century saw John Dalton, an English Quaker schoolmaster, pondering over the old question of the nature of matter, until a new atomic theory was revealed to him. Not waiting for experimental verification, he drew pictures of his atoms. Each was represented by a sphere. He assumed that the atoms of the different elements were different since the elements were unlike. Then in order to differentiate between them he represented them as follows:

Hydrogen,	Gold,	Carbon,
Oxygen,	Silver,	Phosphorus,
Nitrogen,	Mercury,	Sulfur.

Like the ancient philosophers, Dalton could not really see the particles he pictured. Yet his atoms were only remotely akin to the atoms of antiquity. To the English chemist, they were definite, concrete particles of matter, even though the most delicate instrument invented by man could not render them visible to the human eye. For the largest atom is still a hundred times smaller than the tiniest particle that the ultramicroscope can reveal. It is about one one-hundred-millionth of an inch in diameter. A million million million atoms of hydrogen weigh hardly a single gram. Ten million generations of men placing five atoms each second on the face of a postage stamp continuously from cradle to grave would barely manage to cover the bit of paper. And yet Dalton spoke and worked with atoms as if they were tangible. These atoms, he claimed, were indivisible — even in the most violent chemical change the atom remained intact. The building stones of this Manchester philosopher and scientist were not the atoms of the ancients, which were thought to be infinite in number and infinitely various in form. To Dalton, there were only as many different atoms as there were elements, and the atoms of the *same* element were all alike, but differed from those of other elements.

Dalton's atoms started a heated discussion. The little circles of the Quaker were abominations to many who would accept nothing they could not actually see and handle in the laboratory. They would have none of this fantastic dream. It might be good enough for schoolboys who had to be amused while studying chemistry, or for natural philosophers who never entered the scientist's laboratory where the delicate balance and the glowing crucible told the truth. It was true that such eminent philosophers as Spinoza, Leibnitz, and Descartes had propounded similar ideas. But who listened seriously to speculative philosophy? Fifteen hundred years before Lactantius had laughed at the idea of atoms. "Who has seen, felt, or even heard of these atoms?" he jeered. And now once more men were sneering. How absurd! Was science to be fettered once again by such scholasticism? What was this but confounded pictorial jugglery? Could any serious-minded scientist accept a theory as baseless as the four elements of Aristotle that had chained men's minds for twenty centuries?

Davy, the most eminent chemist of his day in England, was hostile. He could not see "how any man of sense or science would be taken up with such a tissue of absurdities." As recently as twenty-five years ago, Wilhelm Ostwald, a Nobel Prize winner in chemistry who did not hesitate to champion the unorthodox theories of chemical dreamers, wanted to throw the whole atomic theory overboard. Ernst Mach of Vienna fought the hypothetical pellets of Dalton until his death in 1916. But gradually the scientific world accepted Dalton's Theory, and held tenaciously to the idea that all matter was composed of indivisible atoms. The theory was considered indispensable to chemistry, even though it might be remote from reality.

Then in 1897 one of the greatest revolutions in physical science shook the world. The bubble of the atom as the ultimate unit of matter was pricked by a great master who stood at the head of a brilliant group of disciples gathered in the Cavendish Laboratory of Experimental Physics in Cambridge, England. A year before he had entered Cambridge, Joseph John Thomson had heard of a peculiar glass tube constructed by his countryman, William Crookes. By means of a vacuum pump Crookes drew almost all the air out of this tube so that only an infinitesimal fraction remained in the sealed glass container. With the aid of an induction coil he discharged a high voltage current of electricity through this highly evacuated tube. Then Crookes observed a ghostly fluorescence issuing from the negative pole, or cathode, of the tube. What could account for this strange light? And was it really light he beheld? Light, as every responsible professor had taught, could neither be weighed nor was it material. Yet these *cathode rays* could be bent with the aid of a strong electromagnet held near the globe, showing properties of matter rather than of light. Crookes was flabbergasted. Light, and yet unmistakably matter! How to reconcile the two irreconcilables? For want of a better term, he called these cathode rays a *fourth state of matter*, for it was neither gas, liquid, nor solid. He ventured another name — *radiant matter*. That was the best he could do, and the mystery remained.

Thomson set to work to learn more about this " borderland where Matter and Force seemed to merge into one another." He constructed new big-bellied cathode tubes, and worked his vacuum pumps until the air inside was twenty million times thinner than the air he breathed. He wondered at the undeniable bending of that beam of light by a magnet. The stream of light was deflected as if it were made up of so many iron filings attracted by a lodestone. He began to understand why Crookes had been puzzled almost to madness. Thomson varied the conditions of the experiments. Years passed. His data kept piling up, and as the facts and figures mounted, his mind soared high.

In the meantime Michael Faraday, the eminent physicist, had studied the phenomenon of the passage of electricity through salt solutions, and was led to suspect *atoms* of electricity. His laws of electrolysis so strongly hinted at discrete particles of electricity that Ferdinand von Helmholtz in 1881 was bold enough to declare that " electricity is divided into definite elementary portions which behave like *atoms* of electricity." That same year Thomson, at twenty-five, had computed the mass of an electric charge. This was done by weighing a small pithball both before and after it was electrified and finding to his surprise that there was an increase in mass after electrification. This difference in mass was due to the electric charge on the pithball.

He was thus the first to determine the mass of an electric charge which until then was not suspected of having any mass at all. Later he examined theoretically the phenomenon of a moving electric discharge, and found that more work was required to give a definite speed to an electrically charged sphere than to the same sphere uncharged. These astonishing results indicated to him that an electric charge possessed *inertia*, the distinguishing characteristic of all matter.

Finally one Friday evening, on the 30th of April, 1897, J. J. Thomson announced to the Royal Society his epoch-making conclusion based on several years of work. " Cathode rays," he declared, " are particles of negative electricity." A stream of cathode rays is made up of *electrons*, or corpuscles, as he had at first called them, torn away from the atoms of the gas in the cathode tube by the electrical discharge. These electrons were part of the atom and were alike no matter where they originated. All atoms contained them. Thomson denied the ultimate reality of the indivisible atom. There was something simpler in the atom — the electron. Another sacred cow of science had been slaughtered.

To convince reputable scientists of the actual existence of his chemico-physical monstrosity — a disembodied atom of electricity — Thomson attempted to calculate its mass. No man ever set himself a more difficult task. He measured the amount of bending which the cathode stream of electrons suffered in the presence of magnets of known strengths. Through ingenious experimental arrangements and calculations, he arrived at a number. The electron was about eighteen hundred times lighter than a single atom of hydrogen, lightest of all the chemical elements.

The world was not altogether convinced by Thomson's experiments. True, the latter part of the nineteenth century was bewildering in its great scientific discoveries. Men had witnessed such vast miracles that they were afraid to deny the validity of Thomson's conclusion. But still they doubted. After all, they whispered, it was only a " calculation," another bit of scientific abracadabra. Thomson himself was not satisfied. He called in his research students and the whole subject of the reality of the electron was discussed. Finally he turned to C. T. R. — that was the way he addressed Charles Thomson Rees Wilson. Wilson had been working on a " dust counter " in connection with the phenomenon of cloud formation, a piece of research which had come to this farmer boy while he was vacationing on the cloudy Scottish hilltop of Ben Nevis. " Morning after morning I saw the sun rise above a sea of clouds. The beauty of what I saw made me fall in love with clouds and I made up my mind to make experiments to learn more about them."

Thomson spoke to Wilson. " Can you photograph the elusive electron? " C. T. R. had been working on ingenious devices for cornering nature in its most inaccessible aspects. There was nothing left to do but attempt it, even though it came perilously near to being the work of a magician. Dust counting had taught Wilson a great deal. He had noticed that particles of dust acted as nuclei around which moisture condensed as tiny droplets when the air was suddenly cooled by expansion. Dust particles in the air were themselves too small to be photographed, but when surrounded by droplets of water they became easily visible. Perhaps, thought Wilson, an electrical particle would act in the same way as a dust speck. He tried the experiment. He passed electrons through moist air in a sealed box called a cloud chamber, and then suddenly dropped the piston of the box, expanding and chilling the air in it. After innumerable trials, he finally saw water vapor condensing into tiny droplets around Thomson's negatively charged particles of electricity.

And now to prove the objective reality of electrons by capturing these moving particles long enough to imprint them on a photographic plate. Wilson worked for years on a supercamera to trap a single electron, and obtained his first rough photographs in 1911. A tangled skein of threads representing the paths of single electrons after expulsion from their atoms appeared on the plate. These *fog tracks* of electrons were faint, to be sure, but they were there. He had imprisoned (surrounded by water droplets) single electrons picked off atoms and moving dizzily through space. He had arrested their flight and taken their pictures. Here was as incontestable proof of the existence of electrons as a furrow of ruin is evidence of a cyclone's passing.

The invention of the Wilson cloud chamber with its manifold improvements that enabled science to obtain pictures of speeding particles has been without doubt the most valuable, if not the altogether indispensable ally of man in his attack upon the nature of matter. Without it nearly all of the spectacular raids on the citadel of the atom would have failed. Today it is as much a standard piece of apparatus in those outposts of science where the atom is being besieged as is the telescope in astronomy or the microscope in biology. Sixteen years after Wilson had obtained his first cloud chamber photographs of electrons, he was honored with the Nobel Prize for this vital contribution.

With the aid of this apparatus, J. J. Thomson and Harold A. Wilson set out to determine more definitely the mass of a single electron. One might as well have attempted to capture a mote in a sunbeam and weigh it on a grocer's scale. Yet they did it in a fashion. But the final unequivocal achievement belongs to one who here in America had been watching the wonders of the Cavendish School and decided to try the impossible.

In the science laboratory of the University of Chicago worked Robert Andrews Millikan, a man of about C. T. R.'s age. On his father's side he was descended from Scotch-English farmers who had come here during the Scotch-Irish migrations to buy land from the Indians and till the stubborn rocky soil of the Berkshire Hills around Pittsfield. The family name Millikan originally meant " milked the cows." With the opening of the Erie Canal in 1825 the Millikans moved westward in covered wagons, taking their sheep, their cattle and horses, together with an intense evangelistic religion. On the " Western Reserve " around Freedom, Ohio, they settled, and here Millikan's father was born, to become the Reverend Silas Franklin Millikan, Congregational minister. On the maternal side, Robert Millikan's descent could be traced to English ancestors of the Puritan type who had settled at Salem, Massachusetts. His mother, Mary Jane Andrews, came of seafaring folk from Taunton, Massachusetts.

His parents never dreamed of a career in science for Robert, the second of six children. The boy's entry into the life of a scientist was a pure accident. If he had any aptitude or leaning in that direction, he did not know it until he was in his twenty-second year, and he was twenty-five before he decided to try to get the training which would permit him to become a physicist some day. He had had just a touch of physics in his high school course in Iowa, " but just the worst touch that could be imagined," he said. " It was given by a man who spent his summer vacation locating water with a witch hazel divining rod." At Oberlin College, which his grandmother's family had helped to establish while Christianizing the Mississippi Valley, Robert immersed himself in the classics.

His teacher of Greek, who was in charge of appointments, asked him to take a class in elementary physics where a vacancy had occurred. " I told him," said Millikan, who was then only a junior, " that I knew nothing about physics. He, an enthusiastic classicist, replied that it did not make any difference; if I had enough head to pass his courses in Greek, that was all that was necessary. ' All right,' said I, ' if you can stand it so can I, for I need the money.' " That summer he went back to his father's home in Wichita, Kansas, and boned up on Avery's *Physics* to prepare for what was to turn out to be three years of teaching at Oberlin.

Science took hold of Millikan with steel fingers, and he determined on a career in physics. He studied under Michael Pupin, who later lent him money to go to Göttingen where Nernst, another great master, taught physics. From here he was suddenly recalled by Michelson, who offered him an assistantship in physics at the University of Chicago. Not having enough money to get home, Millikan went to London, persuaded the

Atlantic Transport Company to advance his passage, and reached the University of Chicago in 1896 to become not only a teacher but also a maker of science.

From the very beginning of his work, Millikan realized that "science walks on two feet, namely, theory and experiment. Sometimes it is one foot which is put forward first," he wrote, "sometimes the other, but continuous progress is made only by the use of both." J. J. Thomson had just advanced a startling theory of the constitution of matter and had introduced the electron as a new entity. What was urgently needed was a crucial experiment to test the exactness of this new conception. "It is the business of science," Millikan believed, "to doubt, and it always does so long as there is any room left for uncertainty." If he could devise a method, a foolproof method, to determine accurately the nature and charge of the electron, he could strengthen the new theory and once more send science forward. To a great extent, science is, after all, a matter of measurement of fundamental units.

Millikan was a master workman. First he tried the method of the Cavendish researchers, but was not satisfied. Then he developed a new technique. He constructed a new piece of apparatus consisting of two brass plates a foot in diameter placed about five-eighths of an inch apart. In the center of the upper plate he bored a hole the diameter of the point of a fine needle, and illuminated the space between the plates with a powerful beam of light. The brass plates were connected to the positive and negative terminals of a battery which could supply ten thousand volts. Here he was lucky, for he had chosen the right field strength. Had he tried any other, he would have failed. By means of an ordinary commercial atomizer, Millikan sprayed oil into the air above the upper plate. These drops of oil were less than one ten-thousandth of an inch in diameter. He was certain that eventually one single drop of this fine spray would find its way through the tiny hole to the space between the plates. To prevent convection currents in that area, he arranged for a suitable thermostatic control. For hours at a time Millikan sat watching the space through the eyepiece of a powerful microscope. Much of his laboratory work was done at night, sometimes while he was still in full dress after a late social engagement.

Suddenly one day against the dark background of his field of vision he noticed a single neutral droplet of oil fall gently through space like a glowing four-pointed star. Millikan repeated the experiment and observed the similar behavior of each drop of oil that stole its way through the pinhole. It took fully half a minute to make that fall of a fraction of an inch. Reversing the polarity of the plates did not affect its motion. Now he had to act quickly. He was going to strip an electron from an atom of this neutral oil droplet. Radium, the magic metal that had set the Curies on the road to scientific glory, could do this. He held a small tube of radium salts so that its rays might strike the oil drop. Immediately something happened. The droplet slowed down in its fall. It had evidently lost some of its mass as a lighter object falls more slowly in air than a heavier one. " When this occurred," Millikan knew, " the droplet was no longer electrically neutral; it had lost some of its electrons." This procedure was repeated with numerous other oil droplets exposed to radium. The velocity of the falling oil droplets varied, showing that one or more electrons were being removed. " It was easy to see," wrote Millikan, " that the slowest speed was the result of the loss of one electron."

He noticed, moreover, that the neutral droplet, before electrification, always traveled at a definite rate of speed. When electrified, however, there was a change in speed with which the droplets fell. There was a certain minimum speed imparted by the electric field of his apparatus that would be suddenly doubled or tripled. " This proved conclusively that the smallest invisible load which I was able to remove from the droplet," reasoned Millikan, " was actually one electron and furthermore that *all electrons consist of exactly* the same quantity of negative electricity."

He repeated the experiment with drops of mercury and even of glycerine. These were heavier than the oil droplets but the same incontrovertible result was obtained. " He who has seen this experiment," Millikan ventured to announce, " has literally *seen* the electron. It is a new experimental fact that this generation for the first time has seen but which anyone who wills may henceforth see." By means of his electrical balance thousands of times more sensitive than the most accurate mechanical scale, Millikan had apparently isolated and determined the charge of a single electron. His value agreed closely with that obtained by Thomson; namely, eighteen hundred and thirty-five times lighter than the atom of hydrogen. So exact was Millikan's determination that today, after hundreds of independent measurements by as many workers all over the world, his original figure, with but a very slight change, has stood the test of accuracy. In 1929 Sir Arthur Eddington obtained a slightly higher theoretical value for *e*, the mass of the electron. Some took this as a setback to Millikan. The Englishman immediately wrote to the American: " I want at the earliest moment to dissociate myself from such a silly attitude. My theory would never have got going if I had not had a nearly correct value of *e* to start from." In fact according to the most reliable measurements thus far made Millikan's value is more nearly correct than is Eddington's correction of it. Millikan's original determination, one of the classics of physical science, helped to gain for him the Nobel Prize in 1923. F. Ehrenhaft of Vienna, working with tinier drops, reported charges smaller than the electron, but his subelectrons proved to be nonexistant.

The electron was the smallest unit in every atom. It was the unit of negative electricity. So much was definitely established. But what else composed the structure of the atom? This question was even more difficult to answer. J. J. Thomson maintained that there must be in the neutral atom of all elements some positive electricity to counteract the negative electron. In 1904 he proposed the theory that the neutral atom consisted of negative electrons imbedded in a jelly-like sphere of uniform distribution of an equal amount of positive electricity.

But how was one to prove the presence of positively charged

particles in all matter? That was the problem that Ernest Rutherford, one of Thomson's students who had come from New Zealand to Cambridge, set himself to investigate. It was difficult enough to isolate, photograph, and determine the mass of an electron. The positive part of the atom was even more resistant to investigation. But the imaginative mind of Rutherford soon hit upon a thoroughly original and ingenious method of attack. If he was to discover the nature of the interior of the atom, he must use projectiles small enough to enter it. Yet his bullets must be powerful enough to disrupt the most stable thing in the universe. The mightiest battering ram ever used by man would be puny in comparison to the weapon he must use. He had such a bullet — the alpha particle. He had trapped it in thin glass tubes as it was given off by radium, and had identified it as the heart of the helium atom — a helium atom which had lost two electrons and had become positively charged. He himself had christened it in 1902 the *alpha particle*. This alpha particle was spontaneously ejected from radium during its natural disintegration at the stupendous velocity of twelve thousand miles per second, a speed which would bring it to the sun, ninety-three million miles away, in a little more than two hours. It moved three hundred times faster than a meteor. The mass of this tiny particle was almost eight thousand times greater than that of an electron. It possessed the greatest individual energy of any particle then known to science — seven million electron volts.

Rutherford in 1909 proceeded to fire alpha particles against films of gold so thin that three hundred thousand placed one over another would make a pile only an inch thick. The alpha bullets passed right through the metals. But one alpha particle out of every twenty thousand or so fired was found to have been deflected at right angles to the line of firing. This scattering was a clue to Rutherford, and once again science was ready to move forward. Thomson's " positive-jelly model " of the atom would not do. The deflection of the alpha particles told Rutherford that they had evidently encountered something very hard in the atom. Because of the rareness of these scattering effects, he reasoned that the *positive part of the atom was not evenly distributed throughout the whole atom but must be concentrated at a point in the center or nucleus of the atom,* otherwise deflections would have occurred more often. As far as electrons were concerned they should have practically no effect upon the helium bullet because of the extreme relative lightness of the electron. "An electron," he said, "would have little more effect on an alpha particle than a fly would on a rifle bullet." The large deflections must be due to alpha particles passing very close to the positive center. This was Rutherford's guess in 1911; and according to Eddington, it was the greatest change in our conception of matter since Democritus.

Rutherford wanted clearer evidence for his *nuclear theory* of the atom which postulated the concentration of the positive part of the atom in its center. This time he planned to shoot alpha particles through nitrogen gas rather than against thin sheets of metals. Fog tracks of the alpha particles shooting through nitrogen gas ought to show up as perfectly straight lines, since the electrons of the nitrogen atom would have no effect on the alpha particle. If, however, he argued, the center of the nitrogen atom consisted of a hard positively charged nucleus, then occasionally an alpha particle deflected by this nucleus should appear as a broken line among the fog tracks on his photographic plates.

For years Rutherford followed this technique with no convincing results. The World War broke out, and the Cavendish Laboratory ceased to be the busy hive of research students fighting a battle against the atomic world. Almost overnight the men scattered to enter government service. Rutherford, however, found time to continue his experiments. While he was hot on the trail of a solution, four bloody years were passing. At one time, he had to disappoint a committee of scientists working on a method for detecting enemy submarines. He explained that he was going to be delayed because he was at the moment completely taken up with experiments which seemed to indicate that the nitrogen atom was splitting into two parts. "If this is true," he told the startled committee which included Millikan, "its ulti-

Robert Andrews Millikan

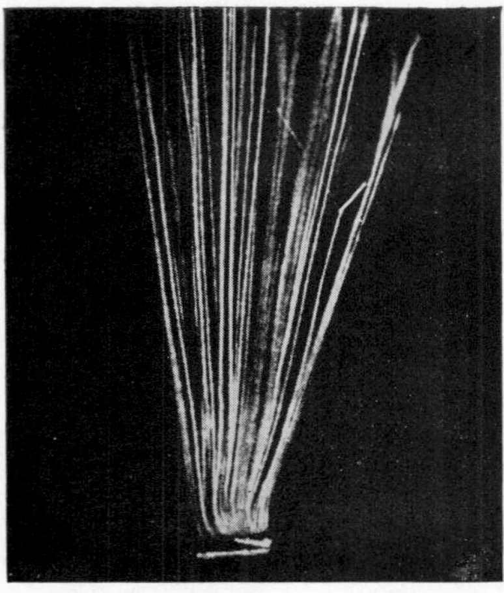

Fog tracks of alpha particles crashing through nitrogen. One of the tracks has split into a fork. Two new elements, oxygen and hydrogen, were formed. *(Courtesy, William D. Harkins)*

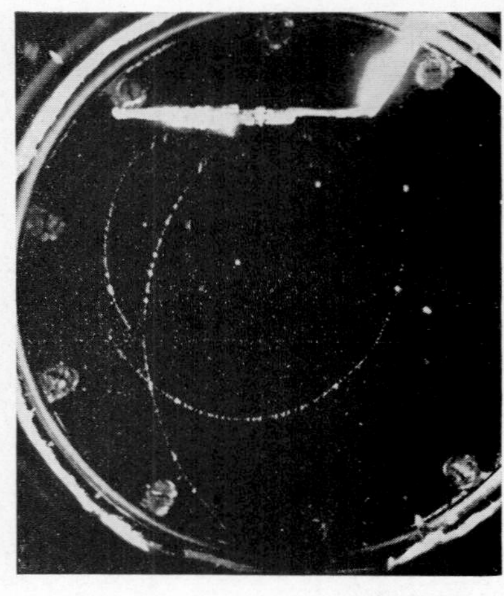

Photograph showing the fog track of a *positron* emerging from radionitrogen, artificially produced by Carl D. Anderson. *(Courtesy, Carl D. Anderson)*

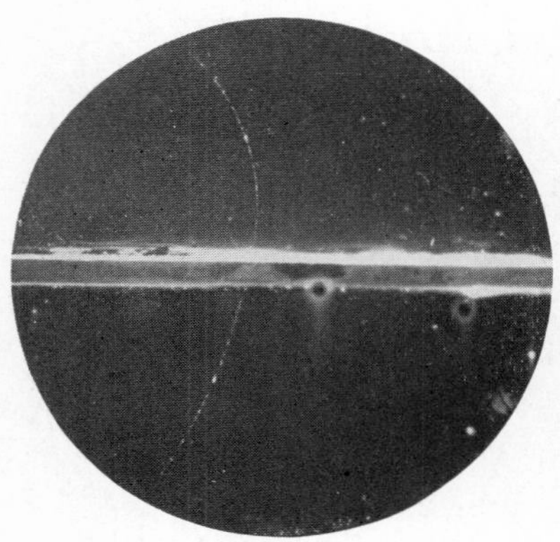

The discovery plate of the positron. Below the center, a positron strikes a lead plate, 6 mm. thick, passes through it and emerges much weakened as shown by the greater sharpness of its curve. Photograph taken Aug. 2, 1932 by Carl D. Anderson.

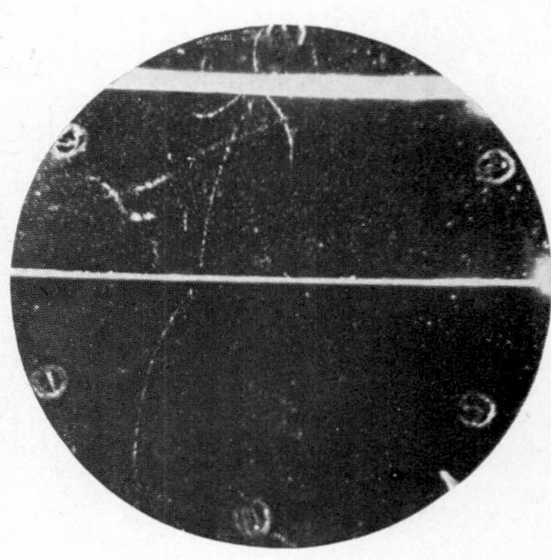

A positron produced by gamma rays. A positron was ejected from a 2 mm. lead plate shown at the top. It then passed through an aluminum plate, 0.5 mm. thick, with a consequent loss in energy as shown by the greater sharpness of the lower curve.

(Courtesy, Carl D. Anderson)

mate importance is far greater than that of the war." And this New Zealander did not forget that he was making this statement while the nations were still fighting to make the world safe for democracy.

The war ended, Rutherford succeeded Thomson as head of the Cavendish Laboratory, and in June, 1919, celebrated his return by announcing some startling conclusions. Thousands of the fog tracks he had photographed showed his alpha rays ploughing through millions of nitrogen atoms in straight lines. But there were a few alpha particles which seemed suddenly to have been thrown off their course as they crashed into something hard. The particles must have struck something extremely heavy and stable enough to turn these mighty bombs off their straight paths. Or, perhaps, the positively charged alpha particles ejected from his radioactive substance (thorium C) had approached close enough to some massive nucleus similarly charged to be repelled and deflected at an angle in some cases close to 180°. There must be, he had become convinced, something very solid in the center of the atom to twist the flight of this microscopic projectile with an energy four hundred million times greater than that of a rifle bullet at the moment of its discharge.

What was this heavy central core of the atom of nitrogen? Rutherford suspected positively charged hydrogen atoms, for he found them ejected from nitrogen during the bombardment experiments. He called in James Chadwick, a young assistant, and together they continued to hurl bombs at the atoms of other elements. They tried three metals, sodium, boron, and aluminum, and then the nonmetals phosphorus and fluorine. In every case they obtained undeniable evidence of the ejection of positively charged hydrogen atoms. *The positively charged atom of hydrogen*, lightest of all the elements, *must be present in the nucleus of all atoms*. There was no other possible conclusion. They had taken stupendous pains to keep errors out of their experiments.

Rutherford had here discovered another building block of

every atom, the counterpart of the negative electron. This positively charged atom of hydrogen was like the electron in certain respects. It could be deflected by powerful magnets, and obeyed the same laws of electrical attraction and repulsion. The great difference between them lay in their different masses. The positive particle in the nucleus was 1835 times heavier than the electron. A few months later, at a meeting of the British Association for the Advancement of Science, Rutherford christened the new arrival *proton*, just as twenty-three years before Thomson had announced the discovery of the electron. The proton was the ordinary hydrogen atom minus its single electron.

Rutherford now presented a new picture of the structure of matter. Matter was composed of atoms — Dalton's atoms still stood — but they were no longer indivisible. Each atom, as first suggested by Nagaoka in 1904, resembled the solar system. It had a massive nucleus of positive electricity or protons around which at a relatively large distance revolved tiny planetary electrons. Each electron was but a pinhead in the atomic cathedral. *All matter was made up of nothing but electrons and protons.*

How many protons were present in each atom? This was another crucial question which cried out for an answer. Rutherford had already calculated from his projectile experiments that the greater the atomic weight of the element bombarded, (the weight of its atom when compared with the weight of an atom of hydrogen, lightest of the chemical elements) the greater was the positive charge in its nucleus. He ventured a prophetic guess. "*The charge in the nucleus of every element ought to be proportional to the atomic weight of the element.*" Could this guess stand the test of experiment? In 1912 he had turned this problem over to Henry G. J. Moseley, one of his most brilliant students. Moseley started the attack at once. "His powers of continuous work were extraordinary, and he showed a predilection for turning night into day. It was not unusual for an early arrival at the laboratory to meet Moseley leaving after about fifteen hours of continuous and solitary work through the night." He sent electrical discharges through X-ray tubes containing different metals. These metals, when struck by a stream of electrons, gave off their own characteristic X-rays. He worked with such breathless activity that within six months he had examined the X-ray spectra of thirty-eight elements. He found that different elements gave rise to X-rays of different wave lengths. Setting all his figures on graph paper, he discovered that the elements actually arranged themselves on a straight line in the exact order of their atomic weights. What could this mean? Moseley heard the weak whisper of nature telling another of her secrets. It told the story: " There is in the atom a fundamental quantity which increases by regular steps as we pass from each element to the next. This quantity can only be the charge on the central positive nucleus." In 1912, at the age of twenty-six, Moseley had discovered the *Law of Atomic Numbers.* He prepared a new table of the chemical elements more fundamental than that of Dmitri Mendeléeff, the Russian who in 1869 had given the world the *Periodic Table of the Elements.* The atomic number of an element represented its numerical position in the list of all the 92 chemical elements. The first element in Moseley's table was hydrogen with an atomic number of one; uranium with an atomic number of 92 was the last element. For the first time, a scientific limit was set to the number of the building blocks of the universe. Three years later Moseley, a volunteer in the British Army, was on his way to the front at Gallipoli. Within a few months a Turkish bullet had pierced his brain at Suvla Bay.

The picture of matter was now a little clearer. It was composed of atoms consisting of electrons outside the nucleus, while the nucleus, in turn, contained protons as well as electrons. There were always more protons than electrons in the nucleus. The number of protons in excess of the number of electrons in the nucleus corresponded with the number of electrons outside the nucleus, and was the same as the *atomic number* of the atom. This made the atom electrically neutral. Thus, according to Moseley's Table, the atomic number of aluminum is thirteen. Outside the nucleus are thirteen planetary electrons.

Within are twenty-seven protons (27 is also the *atomic weight* of aluminum) and fourteen electrons. Hence there is an *excess* of thirteen protons in the nucleus.

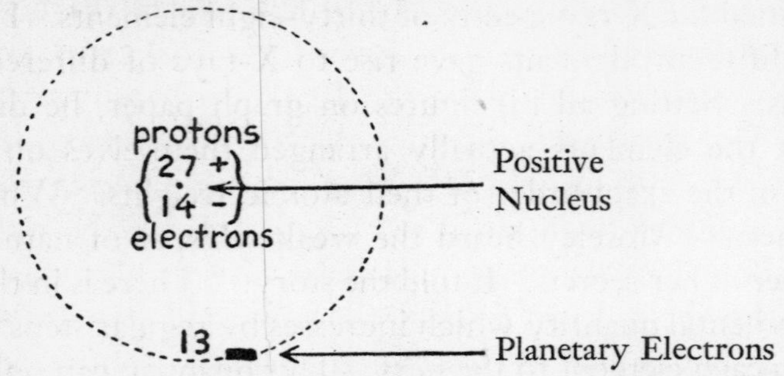

FIG. 17. MOSELEY'S PICTURE OF THE ATOM OF ALUMINUM

But this conception of the atom still left much to be desired. It lacked a consistent explanation of the peculiar spectra or bright lines given off by gaseous elements when heated to incandescence. Even before the discovery of the electron, Hendrik A. Lorentz of Amsterdam had come to the conclusion that these spectrum lines were due to the motion of electrified particles revolving inside the atoms of matter. Stationary electrons were inconceivable. He boldly predicted an effect which was later found by his countryman, Pieter Zeeman, in 1896. Zeeman showed that when incandescent gases were placed in powerful magnetic fields their spectrum lines were split up, indicating that the light was due to some electrical phenomenon which could be affected by a magnet. Seventeen years later the same effect was produced by using electrical instead of magnetic fields. Still another puzzle was this: If electronic motion was the cause of spectrum light, then Rutherford's atom ought to radiate this light *continuously* since the electrons were moving around all the time. The electrons, moreover, would gradually lose velocity because of the pull of the positively charged nucleus. The electrons would be attracted by and fall into the nucleus unless their stupendous speed around the center were maintained in some way to counteract the powerful pull of the atom's kernel. What the spectroscope had revealed, scientists could not explain by all the known laws of classical electrodynamics. Here was a mighty impasse.

"There are times in the growth of human thought," said W. F. G. Swann, "when nature having led man to the hope that he may understand her glories, turns for a time capricious and mockingly challenges his powers to harmonize her mysteries by revealing new treasures." Among those who accepted the challenge was a young Dane, Niels Bohr, working first at Copenhagen, then under Rutherford at Manchester. In the summer of 1913 Bohr bravely abandoned classical dynamics which failed to explain the spectral lines of elements, and seized hold of a new key — Max Planck's conception of *energy quanta,* one of the most revolutionary theories in the history of science. It had been announced on December 14, 1900. Planck insisted energy was granular. It was emitted not in a continuous flow, but in tiny, finite bundles called quanta, the mass of which depended upon the wave length. Bohr pictured the outer electrons of the atom as revolving in circular orbits around the nucleus unless disturbed by some outside force such as cathode rays, X-rays, or even heat. When thus disturbed, electrons would jump from one orbit to another closer to the nucleus. The transfer to each different orbit represented a distinct spectrum line. Every jump was accompanied by a characteristic light. "For each atom," he wrote, "there exists a number of definite states of motion called stationary states, in which the atom can exist without radiating energy. Only when the atom is disturbed and passes from one state to another can it radiate light."

Dr. E. E. Free has drawn a beautiful analogy to explain Bohr's theory of spectrum lines and planetary electrons. "Imagine a series of race tracks one inside the other. Imagine these tracks are separated by high board fences. Put a race horse in the outermost track and instruct him to run around it until, when he happens to feel like it, he is to jump the inside fence into the next track, run around it for a while, and then jump the next fence, and so on until he reaches the innermost track of all. If then, you watch this procedure from the field outside the outermost fence, you will not see the horse at all so long as he is running in a single track. The fences hide him. But whenever he jumps from one track into the next, you will see him for an instant as he goes over."

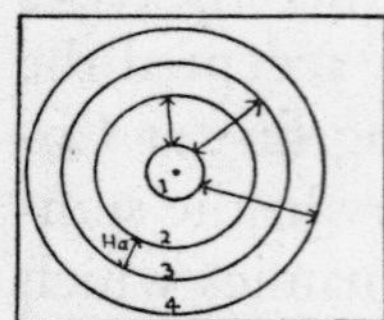

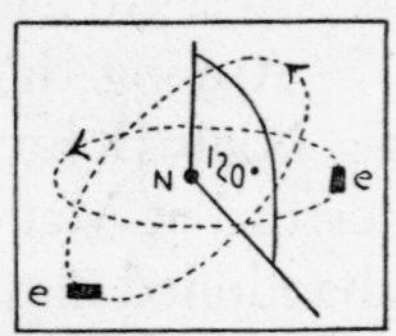

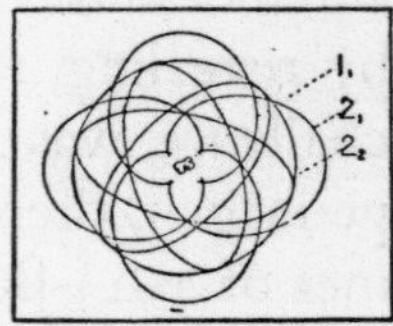

FIG. 18. THE *HYDROGEN ATOM*, THE *HELIUM ATOM* AND THE *NEON ATOM*

(according to Bohr, and magnified about 200,000,000 times.)

The *red Hα* line of the spectrum of hydrogen is due to the jump of an electron from orbit 3 to orbit 2. The *blue* line of the hydrogen spectrum is due to the electron's jump from orbit 4 to orbit 2, etc.

Using this method of attack, Bohr explained the complex spectrum of hydrogen, and attempted to locate the orbits of other elements. Arnold Sommerfeld of Munich verified some of his conclusions, and worked out the elliptical orbits of several more complex atoms as well as the distances between these orbits. Thomson, Rutherford, Moseley, and Bohr had each added to our conception of the structure of the atom. But the edifice was by no means complete. Further clarification of its structure followed. In 1916 Gilbert N. Lewis of the University of California, a brilliant theorist and experimenter, published a paper setting forth a new structure of the atom particularly with reference to the position of its planetary electrons. Around the nucleus, he said, were hypothetical cubical shells containing varying numbers of electrons occupying fixed positions. Fig. 19 on page 337 represents the atoms of lithium, neon, and chlorine. Three years later Irving Langmuir of the General Electric Company elaborated and extended this theory by introducing his *concentric shell theory* of the arrangement of the electrons outside the nucleus. He wanted a picture of the atom which would explain chemical activity. Moseley's Table of Atomic Numbers was his starting point. Helium (atomic number 2) and neon (atomic number 10) were stable elements which refused to combine with other elements. In these atoms the electrons outside the nuclei must therefore represent stable groups which rendered their atoms incapable of chemical activity. Langmuir

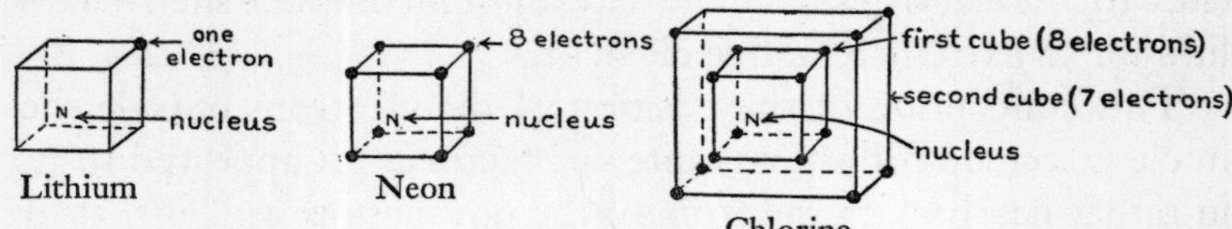

FIG. 19. ATOMS OF LITHIUM, NEON AND CHLORINE
(according to G. N. Lewis.)

pictured helium as containing a nucleus of fixed protons and cementing electrons, and two additional electrons revolving in a shell outside the central core. The distances between the shells were made to agree with the various orbits that Bohr had postulated. All atoms, said Langmuir, have a great tendency to complete the outermost shell. The first shell is complete with two electrons; the second shell with eight electrons. This tendency to form stable groups explains the chemical activity of the element. Hydrogen is very active because, since its shell contains but one electron, it is incomplete and needs another electron to form a stable group of two, as in helium.

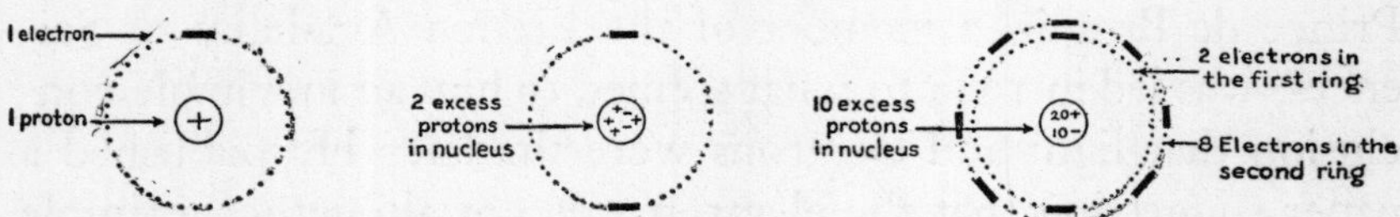

FIG. 20. THE *HYDROGEN ATOM*, THE *HELIUM ATOM* AND THE *NEON ATOM*
(according to Langmuir.)

Neon, with ten electrons outside its nucleus, represents another stable configuration having two electrons in its first shell and eight more in a second larger shell concentric with the first. All the elements with atomic numbers between 2 and 10 are therefore active to an extent depending upon the completeness of their second shells. For example, lithium, atomic number 3, possesses only one single electron in its second shell. Hence in its eagerness to complete the outside shell, it will readily give away this third electron to another element, and thus have left but two electrons in the first shell — a stable group. This tendency to lose electrons from the outermost incomplete shell makes lithium an extremely active element.

This conception of the position of the electrons outside the nucleus seemed for a time quite satisfactory. It appeared to fit in rather neatly with the atom of the physicist as well as that of the chemist. For a little more than ten years Planck's quantum principle as applied to the extranuclear structure of the atom rendered noteworthy service. But both the brilliant formulations of the Copenhagen School led by Bohr, and the Lewis-Langmuir picture of the atom developed in America, contained dark spots that no amount of experimentation could illuminate. Not only was it too artificial, but the experimental facts connected with the intensities of the spectrum lines of the elements, for example, proved an immovable objection to the complete acceptance of these theories.

From the field of light had already come rumblings of a violent upheaval in the definitions of science. Light seemed to be of a dual nature, exhibiting at one time the properties of a wave and at another the characteristics of a particle. Louis Victor, Prince de Broglie, a member of the French Academy of Sciences, was led in 1924 to what seemed to him an inevitable conclusion that light and electrons were similar. He published a paper suggesting that the electron was not altogether a simple particle of electricity. The electron, he thought, was composed of, possessed, or perhaps was attended by a group of waves similar to those of light which guided its path. If De Broglie's electron was of the nature of light, it ought to exhibit the peculiar characteristics of waves; namely, interference and diffraction. For two years after his hypothesis had been advanced, no direct evidence of its validity could be mustered. In 1927 two Americans, Clinton J. Davisson and Lester H. Germer of the Bell Telephone Company of New York, furnished the proof. They shot a narrow stream of electrons against a nickel crystal, and found that they were striking the crystal and being reflected in the same way as rays of light. " Our experiments," they concluded, " establish the wave nature of moving electrons with the same certainty as the wave nature of X-rays has been established." Albert Einstein, the most profound scientific thinker since Newton, could not refrain from exclaiming, " We stand here before a new property of matter for which the strictly causal theories hitherto in vogue are unable to account."

A few months later G. P. Thomson, son of J. J. Thomson, confirmed the wave properties of the electron in a different way. He shot electrons against metals and passed the reflected electrons through a tiny hole. When these struck a photographic plate, rings similar to the interference rings produced by light were registered indicating wave properties for the electrons. He then told the Royal Society of England that there was no such thing as the very simple material electron that his father had described thirty years before. " Rather one may picture the free electron," declared the younger Thomson, " as something like a gossamer spider floating through the air at the center of a number of radiating filaments which control its flight as the air wafts them about, or as they are caught by solid objects." Arthur Dempster of Chicago soon after showed that the proton, too, possessed wave properties. In 1929 Prince Louis de Broglie was honored with the Nobel Prize for his work, which culminated in the theory that the stuff of matter has wave properties like light.

In the meantime there had begun an orgy of speculation in the field of the physical sciences. Mathematical specialists entered the arena with a new attack. Physical and mathematical theories of the structure of the atom came " crowding on each other's heels with an increasing unmannerliness." In the forefront of these hypotheses stood that of Erwin Schroedinger, an Austrian. Advancing along the lines of De Broglie's concept of a material electron associated with a train of waves, Schroedinger abandoned altogether the material electron. " If the waves work so well, why a material electron at all? " he asked. He introduced a new mathematical treatment of the phenomena connected with electrons and waves known as Wave Mechanics. From intrinsically mathematical and somewhat metaphysical reasonings he concluded that an atom is a region permeated by waves. " A single atom," he wrote, " expands out into infinite space but with less density." The mathematical equations of his theory predicted the periods, intervals, and intensities of many spectrum lines which accurately confirmed the work of De Broglie. His *wave mechanics* seemed to predict even some facts connected with spectrum lines that were not predicted by the treatment of Bohr.

At the same time an equally profound and suggestive idea was being evolved by a theoretical physicist, Werner Heisenberg of Munich. He considered it impossible to determine with scientific accuracy not only the velocity of an electron within the atom but even the precise position of an electron at a given instant. With one bold stroke, this boy of twenty-three supplemented the established conceptions of the electronic orbits of Bohr, his teacher, with another conception. Heisenberg expressed the structure and composition of the atom, as well as other concepts of physical science, by mathematical formulas directly connected with the frequencies and intensities of the spectrum lines — phenomena which could be observed and actually measured. This departure was, of course, laudable, but his efforts to include in his scheme of the atomic world all the known facts of physics and chemistry resulted in the formation of a system, the *New Quantum* or *Matrix Mechanics,* which bothered even men accustomed to the twists and spirals of serpentine theoretical physics. Schroedinger, himself, whose own theories resembled those of Heisenberg, told his friends he had been " discouraged if not repelled by its difficult methods of transcendental algebra."

In the summer of 1927 Heisenberg published a paper in which he enunciated what is known as the *Principle of Indeterminacy.*

He postulated that " a particle may have a completely definite position or it may have a completely determined velocity, but it cannot in any sense have both." To some this signaled the collapse of the whole conception of electrons. The clearly defined electron which Robert Millikan, its measurer, had called " neither an uncertainty nor an hypothesis but a new experimental fact which anyone who wills may see " was to them now nothing but a ghost completely swamped under the waves of the newest cult of young theorists. Nothing was left of it, they declared, but its mirage in the form of waves in the ether — a mysterious something as vaporous as the " elixir of life." But they had misinterpreted the contribution of Heisenberg, and their " dummy electron " is still a very real thing.

Born, Pauli, Jordan, Brillouin, Dirac, and Gamow, playing with the mathematical formulas of Schroedinger and Heisenberg, constructed a highly complex system which seemed to account beautifully for the spectrum lines which had baffled both the physicist and the chemist for decades. And it is really remarkable that the wild speculations of the last ten years actually produced some astonishing results. Through abstruse calculations, for example, Heisenberg succeeded in explaining the complex spectrum of helium. Then from analogy with the behavior of the helium atom, it was predicted after a study of the spectrum of hydrogen that hydrogen gas under normal conditions ought to consist of two different forms of the same element. This prediction was later actually verified experimentally by the discovery of ortho- and para-hydrogen, two forms of ordinary hydrogen — an epochal contribution to chemistry from the field of wave mechanics. Other remarkable prophecies also came true. Both Schroedinger and Heisenberg later won the Nobel Prize for their contributions.

Bohr's working model of the atom was thus ten years ago found to be only partially satisfactory. " The picture of the atom was thrown out of focus by the newer discoveries, and the old conception lost the sharpness and definiteness of its original outline." But the atom, the electron, and the proton were still invaluable to scientists as building blocks of the universe. Some have imagined that they would be scrapped altogether. In fact, Bohr, a Nobel laureate, at one time insisted that we " forget our atomic models." But these concepts continued in use. Bohr's orbits were retained as the places of greatest probability for the positions of the electrons outside the nucleus of the atom. Said Millikan: " Nine-tenths of revolutionary discoveries are just as revolutionary as was the discovery of the seven-year-old boy who came home from school one day altogether disgusted, saying that for a week his teacher had been telling him that 3 and 4 made 7, and he had just got it well learned when she told him that 5 and 2 made 7. So it is with our discoveries in science. We do indeed discover new relations but for the most part the old ones remain." To him Heisenberg, De Broglie, and Schroedinger do not replace Thomson, Rutherford, and Bohr; they merely supplement them.

In spite of the bold raids of the young theoretical physicists, the nature of the atom outside its nucleus was cleared up to some extent and activity in this field slowed down. But the center of the atom remained a dark secret. All that was definitely known was that it contained protons and electrons. The nucleus was still a bundle of uncertainties which science was striving to resolve into some sort of acceptable model. Something of the composition of the nucleus of certain elements was already known. This information came from a study of the spontaneous disintegration of radium and other radioactive elements such as thorium, polonium, uranium, and ionium. These elements break down through no outside influence into simpler elements by a mechanism not completely understood. Soon after the Curies' discovery of radium, Rutherford and Soddy had found that the spontaneous and continuous breaking down of radium resulted in the emission of three types of rays and particles. Radium ejected alpha particles (ionized helium atoms), beta particles (electrons), and gamma rays (similar to X-rays). For radioactive elements, at least, it was believed that the nucleus contained electrons, protons, and electrified helium. (The gamma rays given off were energy rays rather than matter). Was this true for other elements as well?

Science was ready to take another step forward in the realm of theory. In a room close to Millikan's laboratory at the University of Chicago, William D. Harkins in the winter of 1914–15 attempted to find some characteristic of the atomic nucleus already observed which would serve as a basis of a new classification. The characteristic chosen was that of atomic stability. Since stability of the atom meant stability of the nucleus, this involved a study of nuclear stability. Harkins assumed that the abundance of an element was related to the stability of its atoms, and in general that the most abundant elements represented the most stable atoms. In 1915 he published a theory of the structure of the atom's nucleus based upon the idea that the nuclei of all elements are compounds of hydrogen and helium. The theory predicted a general difference of stability between the atoms of those elements having even atomic numbers and those possessing odd atomic numbers. Atoms having even atomic numbers were more stable than those of odd atomic numbers, and hence more abundant in nature. Two years later Harkins confirmed this prediction by showing that (1) elements of even atomic number were seventy times more numerous on earth than all those of odd atomic number; (2) all of the five still undiscovered elements were of odd atomic number; (3) all of the seven most abundant elements found in meteorites, were of even atomic number.

Harkins' hydrogen-helium theory also assumed that the heavier elements were built from lighter elements by a step-by-step process in which hydrogen and helium groups were gradually added. Back in 1904 Millikan had wondered whether such a building-up process really existed, " whether or not there is any natural process which does among the atoms what the life process does among the molecules; i.e., which takes the simpler forms and builds them up again into more complex ones." So far as radioactive elements were concerned, Harkins' theory was acceptable for they gave off both electrons and helium. The disintegration of radium, for example, takes place in the following stages:

RADIUM	→ RADON	→ RADIUM A	→ RADIUM B	→ POLONIUM	→ LEAD
at. wt. 226 loses one charged helium atom of at. wt. 4 and changes to	at. wt. 222 loses one charged helium atom of at. wt. 4 and changes to	at. wt. 218 loses one charged helium atom of at. wt. 4 and changes to	at. wt. 214 loses electrons and one charged atom of helium and changes to	at. wt. 210 loses one charged helium atom of at. wt. 4 and changes to	at. wt. 206 which is the end product of radium disintegration

But would it hold for other atoms? To be sure, Rutherford had already shown that nitrogen (at. no. 7) as well as all of the other odd atomic elements (5, 9, 11, 13, 15) which he had bombarded liberated hydrogen but, as far as he knew, no helium, whereas not a single even atomic-numbered element could be disrupted. Harkins decided to repeat Rutherford's experiments. A Japanese student working under Rutherford, had just developed an improved Wilson cloud chamber apparatus equipped with elaborate photographic devices. This machine allowed expansions of the chamber to be repeated very rapidly so that large numbers of photographs could be taken quickly on moving picture principles. In addition, the fog tracks were photographed synchronously from two points at right angles to each other, so that the complete film could be analyzed into a stereoscopic picture of three dimensions.

Harkins modified the Schimizu-Wilson apparatus to suit his procedure, and in 1921 began taking fog-track pictures of helium nuclei (alpha particles) from thorium shooting through nitrogen and other gases. Thousands of photographs were taken showing tens of thousands of fog tracks among billions of atoms. Occasionally one of the lines was deflected indicating that the alpha particle had approached or struck the nucleus of a nitrogen atom. An even rarer phenomenon also happened. One of the pictures showed among the broken fog tracks something entirely new — a double deflection with one line of the fork about ten times thinner than the other usual deflected line. To Harkins this solitary picture, one bull's eye from among a hundred thousand shots (good marksmanship in the sub-atomic world), indicated that Rutherford's interpretation of the ejection of an electrified hydrogen particle from the nitrogen nucleus was an incomplete story. There was more behind this atomic disintegration than even he had seen. In this destruction of an atomic world Harkins saw as well the synthesis of a new one. Not only was hydrogen (thin line) ejected but another element oxygen (thick line) was in this case formed. He interpreted the picture as showing the union of the helium nucleus (alpha particle) with the nitrogen nucleus to form an atom of the new element fluorine. This fluorine at once disintegrated to form an electrified hydrogen particle and an atom of oxygen. In other words, oxygen had been synthesized, or built up from nitrogen and helium. Harkins represented this result of seven years of intense work graphically and in equation form as follows:

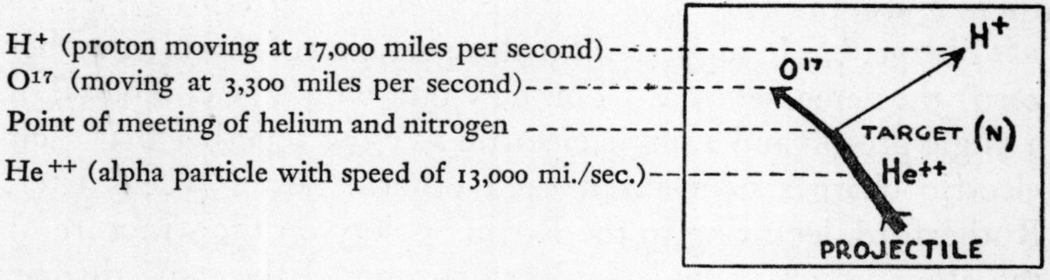

helium	+	nitrogen	⟶	fluorine	⟶	hydrogen	+	oxygen
He^{++}	+	N	⟶	F	⟶	H^{+}	+	O
mass 4	+	mass 14	⟶	mass 18	⟶	mass 1	+	mass 17

The oxygen which was formed was an atom containing seventeen protons in its nucleus. Its atomic weight was 17 instead of 16, the accepted atomic weight of the only kind of oxygen atom known at the time. In 1931, however, this new form or *isotope* of oxygen of atomic weight 17 was discovered, thus confirming what until then was only a possibility.

But the world of science was not convinced. True, Harkins' interpretation of the building up of both oxygen and fluorine out of nitrogen and helium was plausible enough. But it seemed too simple an explanation, and a mere handful of photographs was not sufficient evidence to destroy the atomic universe. There were many paradoxes in Harkins' picture of a nucleus composed of nothing but helium and hydrogen nuclei, and electrons. One of the greatest difficulties was to account for the way in which negatively charged and positively charged units of electricity could exist side by side in the nucleus without neutralizing each other. In other words, what prevented the negative electron and the positive proton from falling into each other since they were so closely packed in the tiny nucleus? Harkins realized the anomaly. Speculations were no longer unfashionable in twentieth-century science, and he was audacious enough to advance a seemingly preposterous theory of the existence of another entirely new unit in the nucleus. On April 12, 1920, he had written to the *Journal of the American Chemical Society* that in addition to the protons and alpha particles in the nuclei of atoms there is also present "*a second less abundant group with a zero net charge.*" He suggested for this particle (of atomic number zero) the name *neutron.* This new unit would be composed of a single proton and a single electron so close together that their electric charges neutralized each other. Seven weeks later, Rutherford, lecturing to the Royal Society on the structure of the atom's nucleus, independently proposed the same theory. "It seems very likely that one electron can *possibly bind one hydrogen nucleus* to form an atom of mass one with no nuclear charge." Such an atomic structure (*neutral doublet,* he called it) seems by no means impossible. Such a particle would have very novel properties. It should be able to move freely through matter since it possessed no electric charge.

For twelve years the experimental foot of science was powerless to move along this new path indicated by two of the world's greatest physicists. It stirred now and then, but seemed paralyzed by the complexity of the road. The mathematical treatment of the atom's structure permitted the use of the new entity, but it was regarded merely as "an attractive speculation." Har-

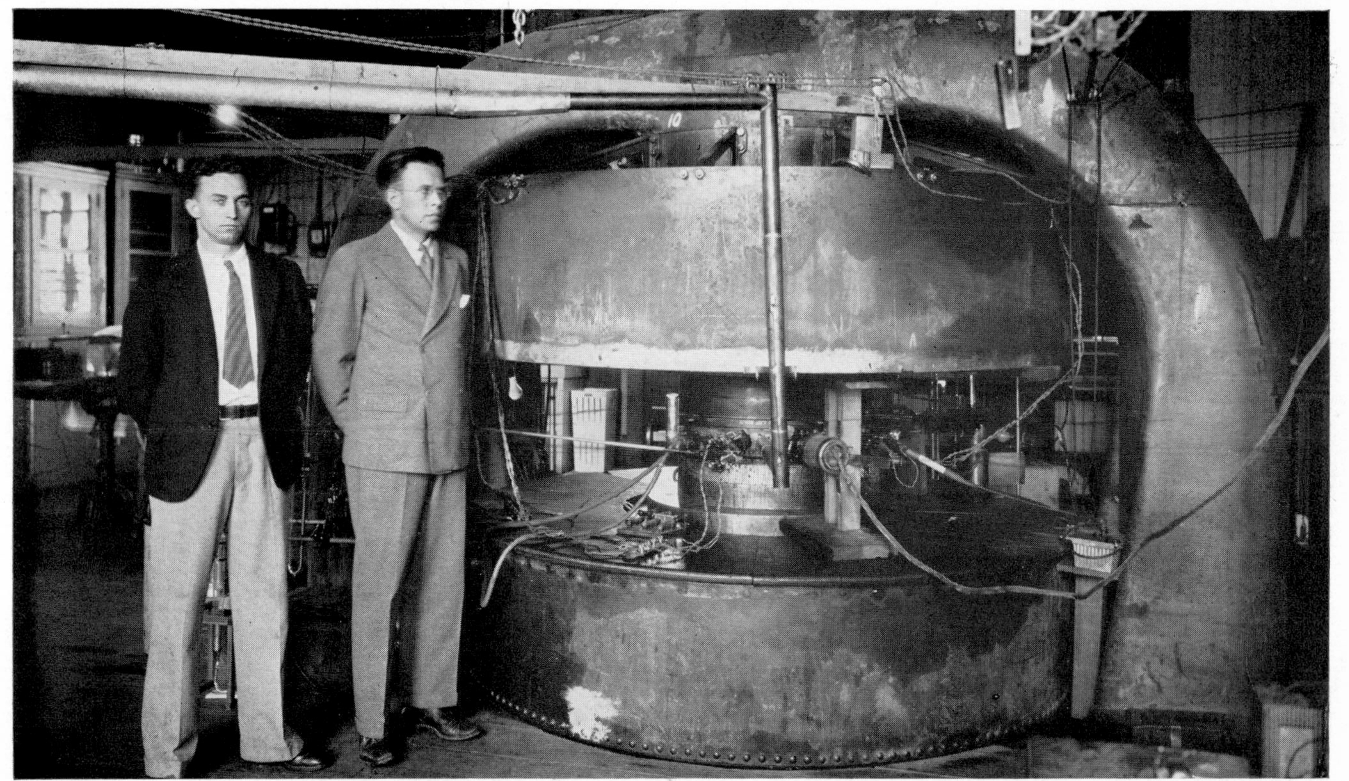

View of the *cyclotron*, the apparatus which accelerates subatomic projectiles to speeds equivalent to more than five million volts. This machine was developed by Dr. E. O. Lawrence, shown at the right, and his associate, Dr. M. S. Livingston, (left). *(Courtesy, E. O. Lawrence)*

The huge electrostatic machine of Van de Graaff in action. Voltages as high as seven million volts have been attained with this new artillery of the subatomic world. Note the operators in the protective enclosure. *(World Wide Photos)*

kins in 1928 felt certain it would be discovered. "That neutrons have not been discovered is not a valid argument that they are non-existent, since they would have no known ordinary properties except mass." Finally one wintry day in February 1932, experimental science made a healthy stride forward, and the neutron was discovered in Rutherford's laboratory by the same James Chadwick who had helped the now Baron Rutherford of Nelson more than a decade before.

This discovery was completed in a fortnight, a record for such an important achievement. The neutron was found in a peculiar way, indicating again the winding, devious path that research often takes to reach a goal. It had actually but unknowingly been obtained by two Germans, Walther Bothe and H. Becker, physicists at the University of Giessen, more than two years before Chadwick's announcement. Bothe was bombarding beryllium, an element isolated for the first time by Wöhler in 1828 and found to be lighter even than aluminum. In fifty years its price had fallen from $50,000 a pound to its present price of about $80 a pound. It was being used at the present time in small quantities in the manufacture of special steel alloy springs. Bothe's bombarding projectile was ionized helium from polonium which semed to yield carbon nuclei of mass 13 together with what he thought were extremely penetrating rays of some kind, several times more powerful even than gamma rays given off by radioactive substances. Over in the Radium Institute of the University of Paris two other scientists were performing the same experiment. Irene Curie, a tall, shy, serious-looking woman of thirty-four who had inherited also the Slavic features of her mother, was walking in the footsteps of the immortal Marie Curie. She had married Jean-Frédéric Joliot whom she had met in the laboratory even as Marie had met Pierre Curie, and together they were working side by side on the problem of atomic structure. Like Bothe, they obtained carbon and the "penetrating radiation" that the German had reported. What could this strange "radiation" with energies equivalent to 14 million electron volts be? They found that it

" passed through lead more easily than through hydrogen compounds such as paraffin, water and cellophane." This was very strange, for even X-rays and radium rays could not penetrate such thicknesses of lead. They wondered and kept working. They tried using sodium, magnesium, and then aluminum instead of beryllium as the targets for the helium bullets. In each case they obtained what appeared to be the same very penetrating radiation. They were frankly puzzled. The second generation of Curies upon whom the mantle of the first had fallen made another startling discovery that this " penetrating radiation," when allowed to strike ordinary hydrogen compounds, emitted swift electrified hydrogen particles of extremely high energy. They also presented evidence that they thought proved that this radiation could impart kinetic energies to the nuclei of hydrogen, helium, and carbon atoms. But such a transfer of momentum from radiation to matter violated the law of the conservation of energy.

In the meantime, Chadwick, using some old radium tubes presented to him by the Kelly Hospital of Baltimore, Maryland, found similarly that when his helium bullets struck not only beryllium but boron, carbon, lithium and argon, something of great penetrating power was knocked out of the nuclei of his targets. He pointed out that these results when interpreted as radiation were difficult to reconcile with the current conception of units of radiant energy of such high frequency or penetrating power. To account for the high energy of the unknown something which was thrown out of the targets and to save the law of the conservation of energy, Chadwick postulated that the new " rays " were really not rays at all but must be made of particles of the mass of protons but, unlike protons, they were not electrically charged. In other words, they consisted of the neutrons that Rutherford and Harkins had predicted twelve years before. Since these neutrons were electrically dead, the impregnable electric walls of the atom could not repel them, and hence they had such terrific penetrating power, two and a half inches of lead being capable of stopping only half of them. What had really happened in Bothe's original experiment could be expressed by the following equation:

beryllium	+	helium ions	$\longrightarrow$	carbon	+	neutron
Be	+	He^{++}	$\longrightarrow$	C	+	neutron
mass 9	+	*mass 4*	$\longrightarrow$	*mass 12*	+	*mass 1*

(Note that all weights are accounted for in this equation of a nuclear change.)

And so in the early part of 1932 a new arrival made its appearance as a result of actual experimentation. The announcement of this discovery made a tremendous stir. Millikan without hesitation declared that "Chadwick is one of the finest experimental physicists at work today and his interpretation should be given the greatest weight." Rutherford and Harkins were overjoyed. Their prediction had come true. Feverish activity followed to learn more about this new member of the family of fundamental entities. Lauritsen, in Millikan's laboratory at the California Institute of Technology, shot alpha rays from his million-volt tube at beryllium, and obtained larger concentrations of neutrons. Many other laboratories reported confirmations of Chadwick's classic discovery. Pegram and Dunning of Columbia University slowed down a stream of neutrons by passing them through paraffin, and Rabi, their colleague, calculated from their experimental data that the diameter of the neutron was even less than the diameter of the nucleus of the hydrogen atom, thus giving experimental proof to Harkins' estimation of the volume of the neutron which he gave as something in the neighborhood of one millionth of a millionth of the volume of the hydrogen atom. Its mass is still in doubt, some believing it is heavier and others lighter than the atom of hydrogen. The detection of the neutron is an indirect one, since, because of its electrical neutrality, it cannot produce ionization in its passage through matter. However, it sometimes collides with the nucleus of an atom and the nucleus recoils. This recoiling nucleus spends its energy of motion in stripping electrons from other atoms near it, that is, ionizing them. These ions are then detected either by their fog tracks, by the scintillations they produce when they strike a fluorescent screen, or by an electrical device called a Geiger tube.

This tube consists of an ionization chamber, a counting device, and an intensifier which makes audible the formation of ions.

Architects of the atom's nucleus now had another brick to work with and started building new structures of these mysterious cores. Harkins calculated that practically every atomic nucleus contained an *even* number of neutrons. Ninety-four per cent of all the atoms present in the earth's crust contained an even number of neutrons and an even number of extra protons in their nuclei. No independent electrons occur in the nucleus. Another three per cent contained in their nuclei an even number of neutrons and an odd number of extra protons. Only 0.008 per cent of all the atoms had an odd number of neutrons and an odd number of extra protons. Radioactive elements which are among the heaviest elements are very unstable because they have too many neutrons, some of which explode. This theory has been accepted by many physicists, including Heisenberg.

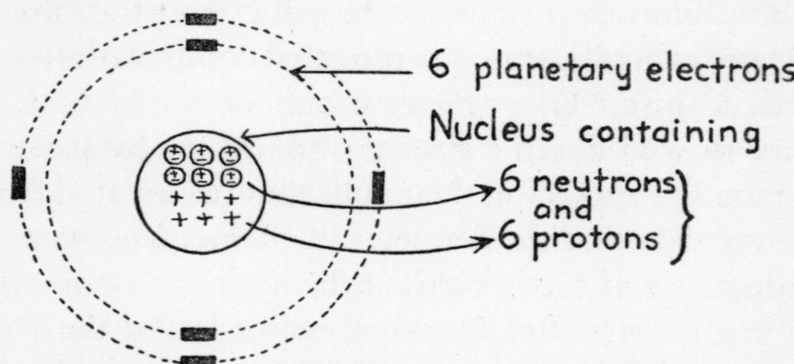

FIG. 21. HARKINS' PICTURE OF THE ATOM OF CARBON

George M. Gamow, Russian mathematical physicist who in 1935 came to George Washington University as visiting professor, pictured the nucleus as containing various energy levels. According to him, electrified helium groups all occupied the same energy level, and neutrons were on different energy levels the lowest of which was also occupied by protons. When any of these particles changed from high to low energy levels, energy in the form of gamma rays was emitted just as in the Bohr atom, light was emitted when electrons jumped from one orbit to another closer to the nucleus. This was his picture of radioactivity. Another scientist of the U. S. S. R. placed the neutrons in the outer zone of the nucleus and hydrogen and helium groups in its inner zone.

Thus far the nuclei of atoms were shown to contain not only protons and neutrons but, in the case of the heavier elements, helium hearts as well. This was true for all the elements except the lightest element hydrogen which was known to contain but one proton in its nucleus and nothing else. The neutron was not the last nuclear unit to be discovered. Rutherford, in 1920, in predicting the finding of the neutron also mentioned the possible existence of another unit in the nuclei of some elements. He suggested the possible existence of a form of hydrogen containing not one but two protons in its nucleus, a form of hydrogen of double the weight of ordinary hydrogen. This new double-proton unit might be present in other nuclei besides hydrogen. This double weight hydrogen would be an isotope of hydrogen of atomic weight one. *Isotopes* are varieties of the same chemical element having the same atomic number but differing chiefly in weight. An isotope never exists alone. It is always mixed with the other isotopes of the same element. Isotopes have been known since 1913, when Aston, working under J. J. Thomson, had discovered two different species of the element neon, one with an atomic weight of 20 and another of 22. Since then, two hundred and forty-seven isotopes have been discovered among seventy-nine different elements, including tin, which has eleven isotopes. The atomic weights of all isotopes are whole numbers, while the accepted atomic weights of the elements which have isotopes are usually not whole numbers, but represent the average weight of all the isotopes which compose them. Soddy, who in 1913 had coined the word isotope, speaking of the tremendous effort that had been put into the accurate determinations of atomic weights even to a fourth decimal place, declared that with the discovery of isotopes, "something surely akin to, if not transcending, tragedy undertook the life work of that distinguished galaxy of nineteenth-century chemists" who for years had labored to obtain accurate atomic weights.

Harkins, who in 1919 was the first to separate experimentally the isotopes of an element (the chlorine isotopes from ordinary chlorine gas), attempted to do the same with hydrogen, but failed. Fred Allison of Alabama, using his newly devised magneto-optic method for determining minute traces of elements, recognized two types of hydrogen, but this work could not be confirmed. Then three weeks before the announcement of the discovery of the neutron, the isotope of hydrogen with an atomic weight of two instead of one was prepared by Harold C. Urey in his laboratory at Columbia University. It is commonly known as *heavy hydrogen*. Urey, who had studied under Bohr, had suspected its presence as the result of his analysis of the spectrum of hydrogen. In the fall of 1931 F. G. Brickwedde of the United States Bureau of Standards evaporated a quantity of liquid hydrogen and sealed the last few remaining drops in a glass tube which he sent to Urey for examination. The Columbia scientist passed an electric discharge through the tube, scrutinized its spectrum lines, and announced the presence of the heavy isotope of hydrogen, which he named *deuterium* from the Greek word meaning second. Hardly had scientists caught their breath over deuterium when another isotope of hydrogen was announced — from the Cavendish Laboratory this time. Rutherford found signs of it in the spring of 1934, then Chadwick obtained minute amounts of it and finally research men at Princeton University confirmed its existence and worked out a method of obtaining appreciable quantities of triple weight hydrogen or *tritium* as it was called. Deuterium occurs in ordinary hydrogen to the extent of about one part in 4000, tritium is much rarer — ten billion parts of common hydrogen contain but one part of this heaviest of the three isotopes of hydrogen.

Rutherford called deuterium " one of the most important discoveries of the century." He was thinking of its significance in unraveling the mystery of the atom's structure. Urey was awarded the Nobel Prize for this contribution. Scientists and the public in general hailed the advent of deuterium as a great accomplishment for other reasons. If the hydrogen of ordinary water is replaced by heavy hydrogen or deuterium, heavy water is obtained with properties somewhat different from those of ordinary water. Aside from small disagreements in freezing and boiling points, its physiological effects seemed quite different from those of ordinary water. Heavy water (deuterium oxide) appears to stop the growth of seedlings, tadpoles die prematurely in it, and mice who drink it act queerly. When it is realized that the human body contains almost seventy per cent of water, the physiological importance of heavy water substituted in the body could easily be exaggerated. Some spoke of senility and old age being the result of the accumulation of heavy water in the body, because of its higher temperature of evaporation. Others mentioned the limitless possibilities of new compounds, since hydrogen occurs in three hundred thousand organic compounds alone. Besides, with the three isotopes of hydrogen and the three isotopes of oxygen, as many as eighteen different kinds of water may be formed, each of which would have different properties.

Here in the space of less than a month were revealed two new particles, parts of atom nuclei which might shed fresh light on the nature of the intranuclear world. The neutron and deuterium hearts were two brand-new projectiles ready to be brought up with the artillery that was once more to lay siege to the atomic world. The neutron especially was an ideal bullet. For its infinitesimal size it was so tremendously heavy that, according to Harkins, a lady's thimble tightly packed with them would weigh a million tons. What was needed to enter the secret citadel of the nucleus of the atom were high-speed particles even more powerful than the alpha particles of radium disintegration.

Everywhere researchers close to the problem recognized this need. A friendly yet spirited race had already begun in many laboratories of the world to build mighty armaments — new atomic siege guns which could hurl thunderbolts of staggering power to shatter — not mighty empires of men — but the tiny atomic nucleus into fragments that could be picked up and studied. High potential drops were to send every kind of sub-microscopic bullet available crashing into the sub-atomic defenses. Electrons, protons, alpha particles, neutrons, and deuterons (electrified deuterium atoms) have been used as projectiles against the atom's nucleus.

Fritz Lange and Arno Brasch of the Berlin General Electric Company put their hopes in the momentary flashes of electricity available during severe natural electric storms. Working since 1927 between two mountain peaks in northern Italy, they have snatched electrical energy from the sky by means of instruments hung from heavily insulated hemp ropes strung from summit to summit across the valley. Sparks of lightning fifty-five feet across have been passed for split seconds through a new type of oil-immersed X-ray tube built of alternate rings of pasteboard, rubber, and aluminum. In this way they have speeded up electrons to such velocities as to tear holes in brass plates an inch thick. In spite of the death of an assistant from one of these fitful flashes of perhaps sixteen million volts, the work still goes on, and they hope some day to harness this terrific weapon to disrupt atoms.

At the same time in Washington, D. C., in the laboratory of the Department of Terrestrial Magnetism of the Carnegie Institute, Merle A. Tuve worked out another method for obtaining high voltages. With the help of a modified Tesla coil and huge condensers made of glass plates four feet square, he and his assistants converted an alternating current of low voltage to one of much greater voltage. Both the primary coil and their modified X-ray tube surrounded by fine wire turns of the secondary coil were immersed under fifty pounds pressure in a tank full of oil eight feet deep to aid insulation. Intermittent excitation produced momentary voltages as high as five million volts. Tuve, guarded by thick plates of lead and the biological research of his wife who is studying the effects of these extremely penetrating radiations on rats, is driving electrons almost to their speed limit in the effort to batter down the innermost *sanctum sanctorum* of the atom.

Two other young Americans and their colleagues have, within more recent years, been building atomic artillery on somewhat new principles. Robert van de Graaff, an Alabaman, while a Rhodes scholar at Oxford got the notion that perhaps a return to simple principles might help solve the perplexing problem of high voltages. He gave up the idea of using transformers to increase voltage. In 600 B.C., Thales, the Greek philosopher of Miletus, knew about frictional electricity produced by rubbing amber with wool. Why not try to build up a high potential by gathering large quantities of static electricity from a friction machine such as first produced by Otto von Guericke in 1671? The idea was a simple one. Strange that no one had thought of this novel method or got down to the business of actually building a test model. Karl T. Compton, head of the Department of Physics of Princeton University, where Van de Graaff later served as a National Research fellow, talked it over with the young man and helped him construct the first working model. At the expense of about ninety dollars a direct current generator which gave as much as a million and a half volts was constructed out of a motor, tin cans, sealing wax, and silk ribbon. When Compton became president of the Massachusetts Institute of Technology, Van de Graaff followed him, and a huge machine was constructed there on the same principle. This Big Bertha consists of two units, each weighing sixteen tons, and mounted on wheeled trucks. A highly polished aluminum shell one quarter of an inch thick and fifteen feet in diameter is mounted on the top of a twenty-five-by-six-foot insulating cylinder. Inside this hollow cylinder is an endless, rapidly moving silk belt that sprays static electricity which collects on the surface of the sphere. In November, 1933, the two units, housed in an airship hangar at Round Hill outside of New Bedford, Massachusetts, were put through a dress rehearsal. Each was gorged with static electricity of opposite charge, and then a mighty flash was unleashed between the two spheres forty feet apart. Snakelike tongues of violet and pink flames announced seven-million-volt sparks, powerful enough to speed subatomic projectiles with tremendous velocities. A special five-section X-ray tube forty feet long and one foot in diameter (the largest in the world) is being constructed of layers of paper impregnated with shellac which, it is hoped, will be able to withstand the colossal energy of the seven-million-volt spark made to pass through it between the spheres. Inside the tube, provided with a series of metal shields, will be the projectiles to be fired at the heart of atoms, where colossal binding energies keep it intact. Even before this huge electrical Niagara was harnessed to attack the atom, plans were being discussed for the building on the same principle of an even more efficient electrostatic machine capable of supplying at least ten million volts and possibly even much more. This new machine, which will be smaller in dimensions, will be built in a steel tank evacuated of air in order to prevent loss of electricity.

Ernest Orlando Lawrence (at one time spelled Lauritsen) is another ordnance builder who at the University of California is gathering his forces against the nucleus of the atom. Like Merle Tuve, his boyhood playmate, Lawrence is of pure Norwegian ancestry. Both became interested in science through wireless experimentation; while Tuve went in for electrical engineering, Lawrence, overcoming first a hankering for medicine, threw in his lot with the physics of the atom and radiation. Late one evening in the spring of 1929 he came quite accidentally across a paper by an obscure German research man. This researcher had managed to impart to electrified potassium atoms in a vacuum tube, energies equal to twice the energy of the initial voltage he used. A small voltage could thus give high velocities to projectiles if the voltage could be applied repeatedly to the bullets at just the right time. This idea of multiple acceleration of atomic projectiles has been likened by Karl T. Compton to " a child in a swing. By properly synchronizing the pushes, the child may be made to swing very high even though each individual push would lift him only a short distance."

Lawrence, who according to his teacher, F. W. G. Swann, " had always shown an unusual fertility of mind and had more than his share of ideas," picked up and nourished this seed. He had been casting around to sidestep the difficulties of sustained or intermittent high voltage necessary for effective attacks on the kernel of the atom. He was searching for a technique which would require no high-tension currents of electricity and no elaborate vacuum-tube equipment, and yet be able to get immense speed with his projectiles. Now he thought he had a valuable clue.

Lawrence planned to whirl an electrical bullet in a circle by bending it under the influence of a powerful electromagnet. As it passed around half the circumference of a highly evacuated brass tank shaped like a covered frying pan, he was going to give the particle repeated electrical kicks which would gradually send it racing in ever-widening circles with greater and still greater speeds, until it reached the edge of the evacuated tube where it would emerge from a slit and hurtle into a collecting chamber. Here it could be harnessed as a mighty projectile against the nucleus of any atom. He was going to adjust the magnetic field so that the particle would get back just as the initial alternating current changed direction and at the exact moment when it was ready for another kick. The particle was to be speeded on its way by oscillating electricity of high frequency. Said Lawrence: "High frequency oscillations applied to plate electrodes produce an oscillating electrical field. As a result, during a one-half cycle the electric field accelerates ions into the interior of one of the electrodes, where they are bent around on circular paths by the magnetic field and eventually emerge again into the region between the electrodes." He gets the same effect, therefore, by applying five thousand volts one thousand times as by applying five million volts at once.

With the help of M. Stanley Livingston, a graduate student of Lawrence, the idea was worked out and an eleven-inch tank constructed. By February, 1932, their merry-go-round device was speeding protons obtained by ionizing hydrogen gas with energies equivalent to 1,200,000 volts, obtained by the use of an initial current of only four thousand volts. With a larger magnet, they were sure they could reach voltages only dreamed of before. A huge magnet casting had been lying idle in California since the World War. It had been built by the Federal Telegraph Company for shipment to the Chinese Government to be used for radio transmission, but had never crossed the Pacific. Lawrence asked for this magnet, and the eighty-five-ton monster was gladly presented to him for research work. In 1932 it was set up and wired with eight tons of copper in the newly established Radiation Laboratory of the University of California, of which Lawrence was made director.

Lawrence and his energetic group of very young assistants lost no time in trying the whirligig atom-gun encased in the frying pan placed between the poles of this Gargantuan electromagnet. They used every available projectile which they hurled against numerous elements in the hope of breaking into their nuclei and disrupting them. Protons, helium nuclei and neutrons were hurled with shattering effect. The nuclei of the newly discovered heavy hydrogen atom were also used as projectiles. Lawrence, at the suggestion of G. N. Lewis, called these bullets *deutons* against the objection of Rutherford who preferred *diplons* because, he thought, " deutons were sure to be confused with neutrons, especially if the speaker has a cold." Later by agreement of scientists here and in England the nucleus of heavy hydrogen was named *deuteron*. This atom core consists of two protons and one electron bound firmly together.

Lawrence split deuteron into one proton and one neutron and in this way increased his supply of neutrons a thousand fold. He shot deuterons against lithium and obtained helium, and effected many other similar transmutations. All this time he was gradually increasing the velocities of his projectiles until near the close of 1935 some of them were moving with speeds equivalent to five million electron volts. Yet he had by no means reached the limit of capacity of his magnet. His novel gun had a diameter of eleven inches, and the south pole of his magnet rising flat topped from the floor as high as a stove, had a diameter of forty-five inches. He therefore planned to increase the diameter of his gun from eleven to forty inches, with the expectation of increasing his voltage from five to perhaps thirty million electron volts. With such a tremendous power, Lawrence and his group may yet startle the world by forcing the surrender of even more impregnable and strategic posts than have so far been yielded by the atom's nucleus.

Other generals are in the field. Keesom at Leyden in Holland, following the path opened up by his master, H. Kammerlingh Onnes, is trying to realize the dream of wrenching atoms apart with his new fourteen-ton electromagnet immersed in liquid helium at a temperature of minus 272.29° C., just a few tenths of a degree above the lowest theoretically possible cold. Onnes in 1911 had sent a current through a ring of lead cooled to the temperature of liquid helium. When he broke the circuit, he found that the electricity kept flowing through the lead for some time — long enough to carry it from Leyden to London by air for demonstration. He called this phenomenon, *super-conductivity*. He had slowed down electrons in the atoms of lead by freezing them at extremely low temperatures. Under these same conditions Keesom hopes that the dance of the atom will be slowed down to an almost immeasurable walk so that it may give up its ghost more easily and expose itself to the gaze of every tyro. The " drops of doom " of liquid helium in which the phenomenon of super-conductivity can be invoked may yet yield the secret of the nucleus of the atom, which means the secret of matter.

Peter Kapitza, a brilliant Russian, is employing a different strategy. He is trying to rip the atom apart by subjecting it to tremendously powerful momentary currents strong enough, he hopes, to overcome the terrific magnetic forces (estimated as 7 million gauss) which hold it intact. More than ten years ago he came to Rutherford with his idea, and was given laboratory facilities to test his theory. Later he was made director of the Mond Laboratory of the University of Cambridge. This laboratory was built for Kapitza at a cost of $75,000 with the aid of the Rockefellers as an adjunct of the Cavendish Laboratory.

Here, still undaunted, he struggled with huge electromagnets, an electric alternator giving 20,000 ampere current, ingenious and elaborate systems of switches, and specially designed cables that carry great surges of magnetic pulls through coils which would melt if the surges were of longer duration than a hundredth of a second. The shock produced when the circuit is closed for a fraction of a second resembles a small earthquake, but the jar reaches the other end of the laboratory eighty feet away, where the delicate measurements are being taken, only after the experiment is over. Kapitza pitted all the knowledge of science and all the skill of man against the atom, whose symbol, a dragon, is carved over the entrance to his laboratory. In spite of the great danger of the experiment, it has not been abandoned.

In April, 1935, Kapitza went back to Russia to attend some scientific conference. The Soviet government refused to allow him to return to England. He was told he was needed in his own country which had appointed him Director of the Institute of Physical Research of the Leningrad Academy of Sciences. Here they had equipped a new laboratory with a forty-ton magnet and other devices that Kapitza might use to resume his researches in the nature of the atom's nucleus. The claim of the Russian Soviet government to its right to hold its own scientists in its own laboratories raised a storm of protest among scientists both in England and in other countries. However, it never reached the point of an international crisis, and Kapitza is still in Russia.

In his heart, Rutherford believes that atom-smashing should be more easily accomplished through bombardment than magnetic pulls, yet he continues to encourage Kapitza, for in science the unexpected often does the trick. Perhaps when Kapitza has added to his method the Leyden technique of cooling the atom to extremely low temperatures, we may yet hear startling news from him. Perhaps. And if not, there is enough of drama, gamble, and risk in the attempt to satisfy such men even in failure. Scientific research is a great adventure, and winning is not the only reason for playing the game.

Millikan, too, at the California Institute of Technology, is still immersed in the problem of the nature of matter and radiation. He has gathered around him in Pasadena a group of young men who under his inspiring leadership are tackling some of the most difficult problems in this most complex field. Here in the Kellogg Radiation Laboratory, C. C. Lauritsen, a Dane, who gave up a promising career as a sculptor to design electrical equipment and join the men arrayed against the atom, sits in the center of a great concrete block while he controls a million-volt X-ray tube. Deutons, protons, neutrons, and electrons are being speeded up into powerful bullets for atom smashing. Here, too, Carl D. Anderson, a young man who had wandered into physics and taken his doctorate under Millikan, photographed an unexpected curved fog track which turned out to be the face of another newcomer from the atom's nucleus — a strange wanderer that rocked the scientific world.

In the spring of 1930 Millikan, searching for a way to determine the energy of cosmic rays, a highly penetrating form of radiation which he believed was intimately connected with the building up of the atoms of matter, set Anderson at work on a machine which might succeed in bending these rays by means of strong magnetic forces. Others had tried and failed. Between the poles of the powerful magnet capable of producing a magnetic field of 24,000 gauss, a vertical Wilson cloud chamber 15 cm. in diameter and 2 cm. deep (the first of its kind) was placed. Photographs were taken through a hole in the pole piece of the magnet along the lines of force, thus capable of revealing a particle reflected by the magnetic field as an arc of a circle. On moving-picture film, thousands of photographs were taken of the effect of cosmic rays striking atoms of gas in the cloud chamber.

On the afternoon of August 2, 1932, one film, exposed and developed by Anderson, showed a picture of a blasted atom with a curved track which had never before been observed. "He at once realized its importance," wrote Millikan, "and spent the whole night trying to see if there were not some way of looking at it from what was already known about atomic nuclei." The direction of this curve, strangely enough, was opposite to that which might be formed by a negative electron and hence indicated that it was positively charged. Its ability to pass through a lead plate 6 mm. thick indicated a tremendous power of penetration possessed by no electron known. The length of the path of its fog track was ten times greater than the path of a proton of this curvature, proving that it could not be the positively charged proton. It seemed in fact to belong to a particle of positive charge, yet of mass equal only to that of a negative electron. It seemed to belong to a new particle — a positive electron.

Anderson repeated his experiments obtaining a multitude of new photographs, confirmed his result and in March, 1933, published an elaborate paper on *The Positron*, the name with which Anderson had christened the new arrival from the sub-atomic world. The name *oreston* had been suggested because Orestes, brother of Elektra, came to an early and tragic end even as his positron is quickly annihilated when it encounters an electron (or negatron) and changes into radiation (a photon). This discovery illustrated another case where an experimental fact followed a theoretical prediction, although Anderson's discovery had, in fact, been made without the guidance of this theory. The positron had been predicted two years before its discovery by a young English theoretical physicist, P. A. M. Dirac, later a Nobel laureate. Few, however, had dared emphasize the " mathematical hole " or " anti-electron " of Dirac before Anderson's achievement.

In the same month of Anderson's discovery of the positron, this same particle was obtained by Patrick Blackett at the Cavendish Laboratory, by Skobelzyn at Leningrad and also by the young Joliots in Paris. The French team had obtained their positrons by using gamma rays from radioactive elements instead of cosmic rays. The existence of the positive electron or proton was thus conclusively established.

After further study, Anderson declared in May, 1933, " It

looks as though it is a general property of electromagnetic radiation to give rise to positrons when the radiation penetrates matter." Positrons, however, are not released from atoms if the radiation is of an energy of less than one and one-half million electron volts. Millikan considered this discovery " fundamental, for it forced us to relinquish the beautifully simple conception we had heretofore been content with — a universe built up of but two primordial elements, positive and negative unit charges." Millikan now pictured a new architecture of the nucleus of the atom. It contained only neutrons, electrons, and positrons. The proton was no longer fundamental since it was really a combination of the neutron which gave it mass, and a positron which supplied the positive charge.

The positron soon appeared in another way. With it came a new type of radioactivity — an *artificial radioactivity*, a discovery which may yet prove a major contribution in the history of science. The announcement was made on January 15, 1934. Fate had waited for the Joliots to open up another room in that mansion of radioactivity first uncovered to the world by the Curies. When radium, recklessly throwing away electrons and alpha particles until it changed by stages into lead, was first described as an element that spontaneously disintegrated forming different elements, the first authentic case of transmutation, the change of one element into another, was actually found. Over this sort of transmutation, man had no control. He was like an astronomer witnessing the galaxies in the heavens spinning their mysterious tales. No control was possible. But this discovery gave man hope that perhaps some day he would find the mechanism of this transmutation and bring it within his own sphere of influence. More than two decades passed after the discovery of radium until Rutherford, chief of the atom smashers, actually succeeded in breaking nitrogen into hydrogen. A great ferment arose and physicists everywhere strove to develop the method. All kinds of claims issued from various laboratories announcing the great goal — the change of mercury into gold. But none of them were verified. Another decade, and Harkins submitted photographic proof not only of the breaking down of a heavier element into a lighter one (nitrogen into hydrogen) but an even more unexpected feat, the building up of oxygen from the lighter element nitrogen. Still the skeptics sneered. In every reported case of a transmutation, the means used, the alpha particle, had been itself obtained by the breaking down of a naturally radioactive element.

Men still hoped for a transmutation which could be effected by means of a simple tool not fashioned from spontaneously generating elements. The day of triumph came on April 28, 1932, a few weeks after the discovery of the neutron. The achievement had been accomplished in the Cavendish Laboratory where two of Rutherford's young lieutenants, J. D. Cockroft and E. T. S. Walton, had tried a new procedure. Instead of alpha particles they had used protons stepped up to a velocity of 7000 miles per second — equivalent to a voltage of 600,000. They had aimed these projectiles at lithium fluoride crystals and obtained visual flashes of helium atoms striking a special zinc screen placed in the right position to receive them. For the first time in history a method of transmuting elements by other than radioactive means had been accomplished. It was a marvelous announcement.

Li	+	H^+	⟶	2 He
mass 7	+	mass 1	⟶	2 (mass 4)

" The rubicon of artificial transmutation by means of man-made weapons which the human mind had so lightly vaulted over in imagination from the dawn of civilization was crossed," declared Soddy. Rutherford recognized the importance of this research. " We know now at any rate that we are on the right path," he announced. Lawrence and Livingston verified the results with their whirligig gun, and by using larger energies obtained a larger number of atomic disintegrations, as well as other similar transmutations. While in Millikan's laboratory, Lauritsen with his 1,200,000-volt tube with much larger currents carried them even much farther.

Not only had this new kind of transmutation been achieved but another new phenomenon had been observed. The Joliots produced a new form of radioactivity—radioactivity in non-radioactive elements. How did they do it? They bombarded boron with alpha particles from polonium (discovered by Marie Curie) and produced a neutron and a form of radioactive nitrogen which continued to disintegrate after the bombardment was stopped. Half of this radioactive nitrogen changed within fifteen minutes into an inactive form of nitrogen and a positron. The Joliots explained the phenomenon as a capture of the electrified helium particle forming a radioactive nitrogen nucleus and a neutron. The radioactive nitrogen nucleus then disintegrated, forming a stable nucleus of carbon and emitting a positron.

First step	Boron	+	helium $^{++}$	⟶	radioactive nitrogen	+	neutron
	mass 10	+	*mass 4*	⟶	*mass 13*	+	*mass 1*
Second step	radioactive nitrogen			⟶	non-radioactive carbon	+	positron
	mass 13			⟶	*mass 13*		

The experiment was repeated by the Joliots with other elements such as magnesium and aluminum, and similar results were obtained. Millikan's laboratory, using protons and deuterons instead of alpha particles in Lauritsen's 1,200,000-volt tube obtained positrons and artificial radioactivity more penetrating than the natural. Later, Lawrence and Livingston and the Cavendish workers added their verification with the data of more than forty other elements which they succeeded in rendering radioactive. One of the most interesting results of these experiments of Lawrence is his production of radioactive sodium whose half life is fifteen hours. This was obtained by bombarding sodium with deuterons shot with energies of 1¾ million electron volts. The explanation of this change according to J. R. Oppenheimer, a colleague of Lawrence, is based on the theory that the deuteron may be a combination of neutron and proton. As the deuteron approaches the nucleus of the atom at which it has been hurled, it is broken up. The strong electric field around the atom's nucleus stops the proton, but the neutron proceeds on and enters the nucleus producing a radioactive atom, thus:

Na^{23}	+	H^2	⟶	Na^{24}	+	H^+
non-radioactive sodium	+	deuteron	⟶	radioactive sodium	+	proton

This radioactive sodium produces gamma rays with energies of 5½ million electron volts, almost three times as penetrating as the gamma rays formed during the natural disintegration of radium. Already the use of radioactive sodium for producing this new type of gamma rays is being tried out in cancer therapy as a substitute for both X-rays and radium. The half lifetime of radium is 1700 years, that of radioactive sodium is only fifteen minutes. This is an advantage in cancer therapy. Besides, radiosodium gives only gamma rays, whereas radium gives other products which must be filtered out. The amount of radio-sodium obtained by Lawrence after his giant sling-shot machine has been in continuous operation for ten hours is still barely visible under a microscope. He hopes in time to increase his yield and be able to supply cancer hospitals as well as research laboratories with this and others of the more than fifty elements which can be rendered artificially radioactive.

New and sensational developments were being reported so rapidly that research workers were left almost helpless in the effort to study in detail the ground already won. On June 4, 1934, the world of science was again shaken up. At a meeting of the Academy dei Lincei at Rome, experimental science stirred once more in the direction heralded years before. On February 6, 1932, the last of the ninety-two chemical elements (alabamine) was named, and one of the most significant searches in physical science was considered at an end. Soddy, reading the news, bemoaned the fact. "The chemist cannot but feel, like Alexander, that something of the zest of life has departed, for the discovery of new elements, like the discovery of new worlds, has always been a powerful incentive." Sir James Jeans, however, assured the world that heavier elements were present in the stars, and Sir Arthur Eddington calculated that the existence of a hundred thirty-six elements was theoretically possible. The announcement from Rome told of the synthesis of a new element, No. 93, by a well-known young Italian physicist, Enrico Fermi. The new element was similar to manganese, fitted into its proper place in Moseley's Table of Atomic Numbers, and was radioactive, half of it disintegrating spontaneously within about thirteen minutes, thus accounting for its absence on earth. Fermi was among the scientists who had been completely absorbed in the new developments of atomic research of the last few years. While bombarding uranium, element 92, with neutrons, he found that the neutron insinuated itself in the nucleus of uranium and built up a heavier element, No. 93. He made a chemical test to convince himself that his interpretation was correct. After the uranium had been bombarded, he added a manganese salt to its solution and obtained a cloudy precipitate. The precipitate was a salt of element 93 and was radioactive. For some time the world of science regarded this achievement with a great deal of skepticism until two scientists in a Berlin laboratory apparently confirmed Fermi's findings.

Uranium	+	neutron	⟶	element 93
mass 92	+	*mass 1*	⟶	*mass 93*

Here was another proof of the building-up theory of Harkins.

Almost forty years have passed since the bubble of the indivisible Daltonian atom was first burst. Some of the fragments of that explosion — electrons, protons, alpha particles, neutrons, deuterons, and positrons — lie about us for examination. Other fragments, such as a light-weight neutron of mass equal to that of an electron and provisionally labelled *neutrino*, a double-weight neutron of mass 2, the deuteron-counterpart of helium christened *alphina* but so far unreported, a negative proton, and probably others as yet not even imagined, may be picked up among the debris of atom smashing in the years to come. The fact that these particles have not been found has not prevented theoretical physicists from employing them in explaining not only the nucleus but the universe as a whole. In fact, Einstein, in his most recent attempt in July, 1935, to unify all the phenomena of both stars and atoms in one all-embracing system, made use in his mathematical equations of the neutrino and still another new, very queer, and undiscovered particle — an electrical atom which weighs nothing.

Until all the parts of the intricate machinery of its nucleus can be located and put together, the real structure of the atom will remain unknown. Physical science may be lost in the nucleus for many more decades before it can find a way out. But the search is a vigorous one, and will continue a thrilling business, for "as yet," Millikan assures us, "it seems to show no signs of approaching senility."

CHAPTER TEN

RADIATION

ARE COSMIC RAYS THE BIRTH CRIES OF NEW ELEMENTS?

Dealing with the pioneer work of Millikan and the fruitful investigations of Arthur H. Compton

THE NATURE OF MATTER still eludes science. The new twentieth-century entities — electron, proton, neutron, positron — are just as mystifying in their fundamental meanings as the old conception of the atom was. They have brought science face to face with another monster which has tantalized it for centuries, a monster with which men must grapple to a finish, for it may be holding Matter captive. The long path which men of science have followed in the chase of the will-of-the-wisp called Matter has led them to another ghost, RADIATION. If we conquer Radiation, we may yet understand Matter.

Centuries back men had stumbled across several important facts regarding light. Alhazar, an Arabian astronomer and mathematician who lived in Spain during the eleventh century, studied the phenomenon of reflection of light from polished mirrors and lenses, and also drew attention to the bending of sunlight as it struck the earth's atmosphere. Roger Bacon, too, wrote about this phenomenon of *refraction,* that is, the bending of a beam of light as it passes from one medium into another of different density. But it was left to a Dutchman, Willebrord Snell, to discover the law of refraction of light in 1621. Half a century later, Newton's genius touched light and made it shimmer in vari-colored splendor. In an effort to understand the cause of the color fringe connected with telescopic lenses, he passed a thin beam of sunlight through a round hole in the window shutter of a darkened room and placed a glass prism in its path. The sunlight was split into its spectrum of various colors which he reunited with the aid of another glass prism. Newton thus demonstrated the composite nature of ordinary light, although some sided with the poet Goethe who opposed this spectrum theory as "an artificial hypothesis which must disappear before exact observations and acute reasoning."

A few years later, in 1675, Olaus Roemer, a young Danish astronomer, timing the lag in the reappearance of a satellite in Jupiter's shadow, found a lapse of sixteen minutes and thirty-six seconds. Reasoning that the speed of light was the cause of this lag, he calculated the velocity of light to be about 180,000 miles per second. Until then it was thought that light traveled from one point to another instantaneously.

Newton, an atomist at heart, believed that light was composed of small particles or corpuscles. His corpuscular theory, however, was poorly suited to elucidate certain phenomena such as refraction and interference. Unable to explain why glass should both reflect and refract light, Newton wrote to a friend in 1675, "I was so persecuted with discussions arising from my publication of the theory of light that I blamed my own imprudence for parting with so substantial a blessing as my quiet to run after a shadow."

Three years later Christian Huyghens, stirred by the great controversy over Newton's hypothesis, came forward with the first well-rounded theory of the nature of light as a wave motion. The science of the seventeenth century already knew that sound was due to a vibration of some material thing, such as a piece of metal or the gases in the atmosphere. The vibrations set up by a resounding bell, for example, traveled outward in all directions like ripples of water into which a pebble had been dropped. Strike a bell in a vacuum, and with no air to transmit the vibrations, no sound is audible. So it is with light, Huyghens told the French Academy of Science in Paris. Luminous bodies such as an incandescent bulb or the sun set up vibrations which travel as waves until they strike the eye. But it was not quite so simple as that, Huyghens knew. Light could travel through a vacuum where nothing material was present to carry his hypothetical waves. Then what carried the light? To answer this tantalizing question the Dutch astronomer and mathematician, who came very close to choosing the law as a career, did what pseudo-scientists before him had done and what pure scientists after him have continued to do. He coined a new word, the *ether*, to explain his wave or *undulatory theory of light*.

The ether was some mysterious entity which filled all space; it was present in solid matter as well as in a perfect vacuum. It was the vibrations set up in this jelly-like ether which transmitted light even in a vacuum. Ether, subject of the verb "to undulate," was invoked on numerous other occasions where it offered a plausible way out of some scientific morass. This ghost of the world of physics remains today, old and tottering, a monument to the limitations of science, and a challenge to some who, like Dayton C. Miller of Cleveland, are still trying to prove the existence of this something, which thus far has been only a convenient word.

Huyghens' wave theory of light was a pretty one. It climbed obstacle after obstacle with ease. The dispersion of sunlight by means of a prism could be explained. Sunlight consisted of a number of different kinds of light of different colors. They all traveled with the same velocity, but had different wave lengths; that is, the distances between two adjacent crests or troughs of

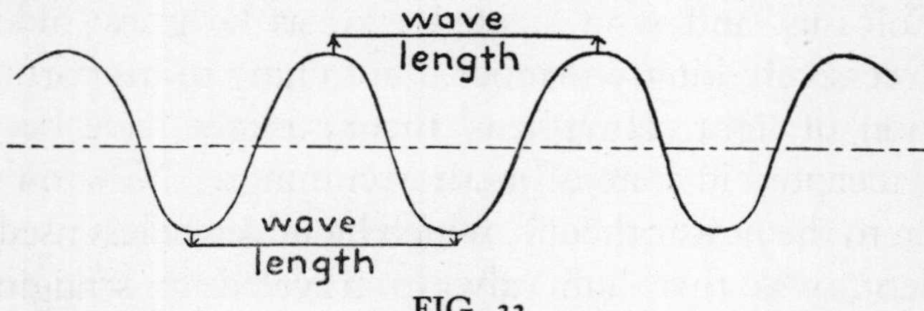

FIG. 22

their waves varied. Some were shorter than others. As a beam of this composite sunlight struck a glass prism the sunlight split up into its various colors or *solar spectrum*. This splitting of sunlight into its colors is called dispersion of light and is due to the phenomenon of *refraction* or the bending of light as it passes from one medium (such as air) into another medium (such as glass) of different density. The amount of bending of light during refraction varies with the wave length of the light. The shorter the wave length the greater the refraction. Red light, with the longest wave length of visible light, is hence bent the least, and violet light, with the shortest wave length of visible light, is bent most. The difference in the speed of light in different media coupled with the unequal bending of light of various wave lengths produces the solar spectrum. As the composite light reached glass, there took place an obstacle race, so to speak, and this difference in wave length resulted in unequal *refraction* (bending of light as it passes into a different medium) which produced a separation of the various colors.

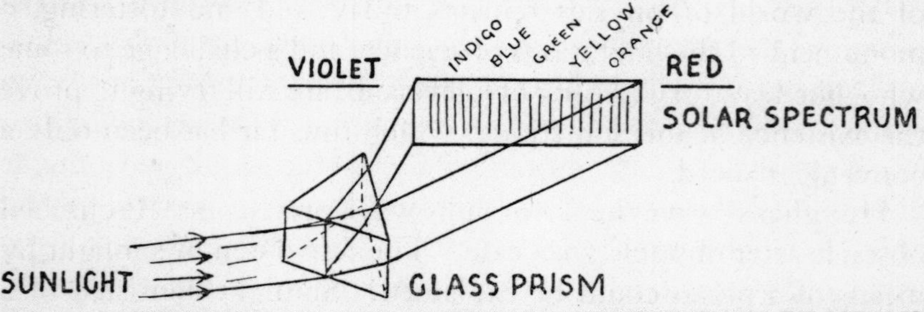

FIG. 23. DISPERSION OF SUNLIGHT INTO ITS SPECTRUM BY MEANS OF A GLASS PRISM

Had Newton, who bestrode the scientific world of his day like a Colossus, and who "ruled . . . as he grew older in a rather excessively kingly manner," not clung to his corpuscular conception of light, Huyghens' theory might have been universally accepted in spite of its shortcomings. Newton's chief objection to the newer theory, which he nevertheless used when convenient, was that light always traveled in straight lines rather than in curved lines; it did not curve around corners and show the phenomenon of interference as did wave-borne corpuscular sound. For nearly a century and a half Newton's corpuscles of light held the field. Then at the opening of the nineteenth century a simple experiment and a brilliant interpretation brought Huyghens' wave theory back to life. The resurrection came through the hand and mind of one of England's great geniuses of the nineteenth century. Thomas Young was a prodigy at two, an accomplished linguist at a very early age, and later a musician, writer, mathematician, physician, archaeologist, dabbler in hieroglyphics — a field in which he made outstanding contributions — artist, philosopher, and man of the world.

In May, 1801, this true polyhistor, before the Royal Society in London, made two very small holes close together in a screen and allowed light of one color from a distant source to pass through them and illuminate a second screen placed in its path. On this second screen the patches of light overlapped and produced fine bands, alternately light and dark. Young, careful to invoke the authority of Newton wherever he could, showed that the corpuscular theory could not, however, explain this darkening. The wave theory, on the other hand, offered a simple explanation of this light interference. Just as the crest of a wave in the sea might meet the trough of another wave and neutralize its effect, or the condensations set up by one sound wave might meet the rarefactions of another and result in silence, so the crest of a light wave might meet the trough of another light wave and neutralize it, producing blackness or the absence of light. This phenomenon had first been observed by Francis Grimaldi, an Italian Jesuit, who found that the shadow of a thin wire cast by a light coming through a narrow slit gave dark bands bordered by colored stripes. This experiment had been performed while Newton was still a student at Cambridge but the discovery was not considered important and the experiment was not even repeated.

Fifteen years after Young's classic experiment, a young French bridge builder, Auguste Jean Fresnel, helped place the wave theory of light on a more exact basis by a clever explanation of the baffling phenomenon of polarization. This phenomenon had first been described by a Danish doctor, Bartilonus, at about the time when Newton was splitting light into its spectrum. Bartilonus had obtained some peculiar crystals of a rock from Iceland, called Iceland spar. When two of these crystals were placed with their axes parallel to each other, light passed through both. If, however, the second crystal was turned through an angle of 90°, it could not be penetrated by the light which had passed through the first. The beam after passing through the first crystal was said to be polarized. Neither the

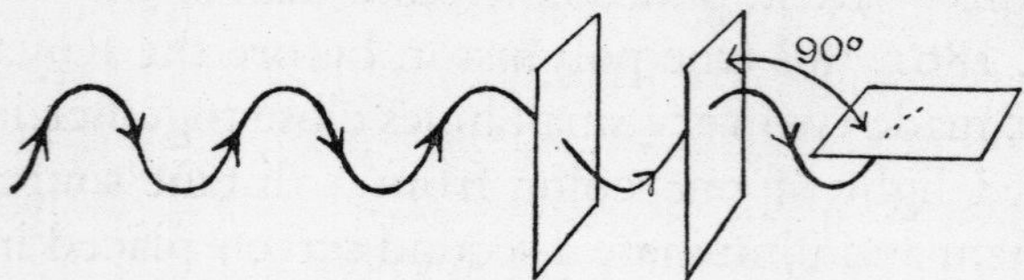

FIG. 24. POLARIZATION OF LIGHT

Dane nor Huyghens nor later Young could understand this behavior. In 1805 Stephen Malus, a mathematician, viewing reflected sunlight from the Luxembourg Palace through this same crystal, rediscovered the phenomenon and named it *polarization of light*. He, too, was at a loss for an explanation. Fresnel investigated the problem and advanced the theory that waves of light were transverse, that is, the motion of parts of the wave is transverse or *across* the line or direction of the movement of the wave. (Sound waves, on the other hand, are longitudinal.) Its parts move back and forth in the *same* line or direction that the wave itself is moving. Hence light could pass through an Iceland spar crystal in but one direction and would be stopped by the second crystal turned through an angle of 90°. The corpuscular theory, on the other hand, offered no plausible explanation for this strange polarization. Soon after the first quarter of the nineteenth century had passed, the wave theory of light was firmly intrenched. Newton was long dead and the smoke of the old battles had settled, so that men were now ready to state definitely that light was a wave motion in a hypothetical ether.

Measurements had shown that the wave length of red light was one twenty-five-thousandth of an inch and that of the violet about one fifty-thousandth. It was but natural for scientists to inquire whether there were any other waves beyond this range of visible light. Were there any other ether waves outside these limits of human vision? Apparently the answer should be "yes." There must be a wider range. It had been known for some time that a thermometer placed in sunlight becomes warm. In the year that Young was announcing the results of his interference experiments, Sir William Herschel, famous discoverer of the planet Uranus, was investigating the heating effects of the colors composing sunlight by placing thermometers in different parts of the spectrum. He found that the red end raised the mercury in the thermometer the highest, while violet had the least heating effect. He took the next logical step. He placed thermometers in the region beyond the red end of the spectrum, the so-called invisible infrared region, and found that even greater heating power was exhibited. It was known, of course, that the red of the spectrum could be reflected from polished surfaces and also refracted just as sunlight. If the infrared section was composed of invisible ether waves, they, too, should be capable of reflection and refraction. Herschel tried the experiment. It worked. A Scotch physicist later polarized and refracted these infrared waves, and a French scientist also showed interference in this region of the ether waves. The invisible heat waves in the area beyond the red were there, unseen by the human eye but measurable by thermometers and more delicate instruments such as thermocouples. Herschel, for the first time, had widened the range of ether waves. By 1912 this infrared region had been extended to a distance four hundred times greater than the wave length of red light, the longest visible ether wave.

Herschel also probed the region beyond the violet end of the spectrum of light, the so-called ultraviolet region. Here the heat-producing powers decreased the farther away he moved his thermometers. This he had anticipated. Silver salts were known to change color in the presence of sunlight. In effecting this change, the red end of the spectrum seemed to be least potent, while the violet light was the most powerful. Scheele, the Swedish apothecary, had discovered this fact. Perhaps the region beyond the visible spectrum would exhibit photographic effects. In 1802 the experiment was tried by Wollaston, who wrote, "I have myself observed, and the same remark has been made by Mr. Ritter, that there are invisible rays of another kind that are more refracted than the violet." Young then showed that the chemical power of the ultraviolet region was due to ether waves since the rays beyond the violet end of the spectrum could be reflected, refracted and polarized just as visible light could. Although objects are invisible to the human eye in ultraviolet light, yet it is now known that many insects can see in this ultraviolet region. Practical application of ultraviolet light to photography soon followed. With suitable films objects in a dark room were photographed in ultraviolet light, and by 1928 ultraviolet photography was using ultraviolet light of wave length thirty times shorter than visible violet light. Similarly, infrared rays given off by hot objects have been used with special films to take pictures. Recently G. E. K. Mees of the Eastman Kodak Company, using a newly invented film containing a dye, zenocyanine, photographed a hot (but not a glowing) flatiron in a perfectly dark room by the heat or infrared rays given off by the iron.

The spectrum was spreading out from both ends of visible light. Was there a limit to this spread? Light and heat were two aspects of the same natural phenomenon, a wave motion in a luminiferous ether. Light and heat had been found related. Could any other phenomenon be joined to this light and heat radiation? One of the deeply rooted convictions of men of science has been the simplicity of nature with its interrelation of seemingly disconnected phenomena. Here was a field where this philosophical concept might be put to a rigid test. It was but natural that Michael Faraday, the greatest English experimentalist of his time, should have been attracted to this problem. As early as 1822 he was busy searching for connecting links in the chain of natural phenomena. He firmly believed that "the various forms under which the forces of matter are made manifest have one common origin." Among the fields in which he worked were those of light, magnetism, and electricity. Polarized light puzzled him. He suspected some connection between this and both magnetism and electricity. He examined a beam of polarized light between the poles of a powerful electromagnet. To his delight he found that the light had actually been twisted around when the electromagnet was excited; when the circuit was broken, the light returned to its original position. Then he tried a charged coil of wire instead of the magnet, and obtained the same interesting result. From these experiments, " the jewels in his casket," Faraday drew the obvious conclusion that light must have magnetic as well as electrical properties. He had evidently found some link that seemed to join light to both magnetism and electricity. In 1846, this erstwhile bookbinder's apprentice predicted that some day light and electromagnetic vibrations in the ether would be found related. He, himself, could not explain it. Faraday was a brilliant experimenter but a poor mathematician. The discovery of the relationship he was bold enough to predict needed the touch of a great interpreter blessed with a keen knowledge of mathematics.

Faraday was fortunate. He had unearthed a mine of data which awaited some prospector to dig out the nuggets of gold. James Clerk Maxwell soon appeared. He was an experimenter of no mean worth, but as a mathematical theorist he had few peers. There must be some explanation of the peculiar behavior of polarized light and its magnetic and electrical properties, thought Maxwell. He took the data of his countryman and subjected them to careful analysis. Out of the mathematical equations which he scribbled on sheets of paper appeared constants and other symbols which seemed to show an undeniable connection between light and electricity. In his equations was a constant whose value corresponded with that of the speed of light, namely, 186,000 miles per second. It must be more than a coincidence, said Maxwell. Faraday's hint at an interrelation between light and electromagnetic vibrations, " one of the most singular speculations that ever emanated from a scientific man," seemed to take shape and crystallize. Out of this investigation grew a conviction that electromagnetic disturbances occur in the form of waves in the ether similar to those of light. In other words, Maxwell in 1863 came to the conclusion that just as light is a manifestation of a wave disturbance in the ether, so electrical disturbances from a spark, for example, are also manifested in the form of ether waves — invisible, to be sure, but nevertheless as existent as those that produce light and heat or photographic effects, and moving with the same speed of 186,000 miles per second.

In 1879 the genius that was Maxwell died at forty-eight. Seven years later experimental verification of his hypothesis was announced by a young physicist working at Carlsruhe. Heinrich Hertz had built two short flat coils of insulated wire each broken so as to leave a small air gap. One of these coils he connected to a Leyden jar to produce a spark across the gap. Suddenly an amazing thing happened. Just as a spark was jumping across the air gap of the first coil connected with the source of current, another spark appeared at the gap of the second coil, placed several feet away and in no way connected with any electrical source. The phenomenon in the first coil had been communicated to the second through the ether. The velocity of the disturbance that had crossed over from coil to coil was exactly that of the speed of light.

Hertz died a few years later of blood poisoning at the age of thirty-seven. But he had established beyond all doubt that electromagnetic vibrations could be produced which differed from light only in their wave lengths. Hertz had reflected and refracted these electromagnetic rays with the aid of mirrors, and later they were shown to exhibit both dispersion and interference. These Hertzian waves were found to range in wave length from a fraction of a foot to more than twenty miles. They are commonly known as radio waves. Their extremely wide range was millions of times broader than that of visible light and thousands of times wider than both the ultraviolet and infrared regions of the spectrum.

Known radiation now included visible light, heat, and Hertzian or radio waves, the last of tremendous practical importance

Arthur Holly Compton

The million-volt atom-smashing X-ray tube of the Kellogg Radiation Laboratory of the California Institute of Technology. *(Science Service)*

A shower of 15 positrons and 10 electrons emanating from a single point in the central lead bar of the photograph. This shower was the result of a cosmic ray of 3 billion electron-volt energy colliding with the nucleus of a lead atom. *(Courtesy, Carl D. Anderson)*

in the invention and development of wireless communication. The gap between the shortest of the electromagnetic waves that Hertz had discovered and the longest of the infrared or heat waves was slowly filled by advances from both ends. By 1923 radio waves as short as the longest heat waves were obtained and measured. These different forms of energy were really one. The same laws of optics were applicable to all of them. Visible light was but a very small manifestation of a far greater phenomenon, that of radiation. From one end of the spectrum radiation had now spread into a realm where wave lengths were measured in miles. What of the other end where they were being measured in terms of fractions of a centimeter? Was there anything smaller than the ultraviolet waves which affected silver salts? Could further consolidation and correlation be found?

The first inkling of an answer came scarcely ten years after the discovery of radio waves. In Wurtzburg, William Roentgen, working in a dark room with a Crookes tube covered with black paper, observed one day a curious phenomenon. While an electrical discharge was passing through the Crookes tube, a cardboard screen coated with barium platinocyanide, lying on a table several feet away, gave out a strange glow. At first he suspected cathode rays, but since they could not pass through the glass of the tube, he abandoned that explanation. Then he reasoned it must be some other ray powerful enough to penetrate not only the thickness of the glass tube but several feet of air as well. He tested the penetrating power of this radiation by producing the rays in front of several objects of varying hardness, including a hand behind which he had placed a sensitized photographic plate. To his astonishment he found that the rays passed through solid objects with varying ease depending upon the thickness and hardness of the opaque barriers, and left dim patterns on the photographic plates. He had actually taken photographs of a hand which showed up the bones as darker than the surrounding flesh. He had, so to speak, taken pictures through a solid. (Years before, Crookes, working with the glass tube of his invention, had complained to the manufacturers of a number of fogged photographic plates which he had found in his work-room, receiving the apologies of the film makers, who, like Crookes, little dreamed that here were the first X-ray pictures ever taken.)

Amazing! was the verdict of the Berlin Physical Society on that evening of December 24, 1895, when Roentgen announced the discovery of X-rays. Hardly had the news of the discovery of X-rays been heralded, when Roentgen, for a moment, regretted that he had shown the picture of that skeleton hand. The whole world became obsessed by these Roentgen rays. Some feared them and spoke of similar rays that might bring death and destruction to whole cities and armies by remote control. Others complained of the banishment of all privacy, for here was an agency that could take pictures right through clothes! A bill was actually introduced into the legislature of New Jersey forbidding the use of X-rays in opera glasses on the ground that public modesty would be endangered. A London firm advertised X-ray-proof underwear. It took a little time for this hysteria to subside.

Science, in the meantime, was busy trying to learn more about these new rays. Were they of the same nature of light but of much smaller wave length and hence of greater penetrating power? Could they be reflected and refracted? Was their velocity that of light? Sixteen years after the discovery came the first definite answer. Max von Laue of the University of Zurich succeeded in diffracting X-rays by means of crystals. Soon after, William Bragg measured the wave length of this new radiation by reflecting X-rays at crystal faces, and found it to be even shorter than the wave length of the ultraviolet light and several thousand times less than that of visible light. About 1925 the refraction of X-rays was also accomplished. X-rays were of the nature of ether waves, part of the ether spectrum which included visible light, heat, ultraviolet light, and radio waves. Once again the range of ether waves, or as it is also called, the *electromagnetic spectrum*, had been extended, and a new tool of research, the X-ray, was forged for science.

But the limit of radiation in the direction of smaller and smaller wave lengths had by no means been reached. Nature had another secret which was about to be exposed. Close on the heels of the discovery of X-rays, occurred an accident of great importance in the dark room of the modest laboratory of Henri Antoine Becquerel. Henri Poincaré had suggested to Becquerel that he search for some connection between the newly discovered X-rays and the phenomenon of *phosphorescence.* Phos-

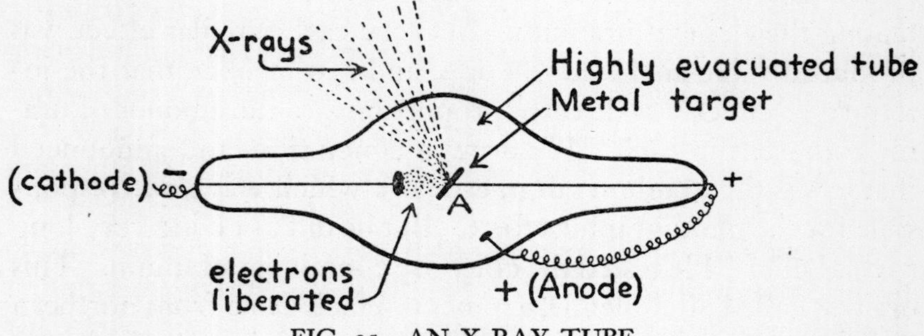

FIG. 25. AN X-RAY TUBE

An electric current is sent through the evacuated tube shown in the drawing. This causes electrons to be ejected from the cathode (−). The electrons strike a metal target which is the anode (+) or anticathode. This excites the atoms of the metal to throw off X-rays which are penetrating enough to pass through the glass walls of the tube.

phorescent substances after exposure to sunlight are found to be luminous in the dark. An explanation for this unusual behavior had been sought by both Becquerel's father and grandfather without success. Perhaps these substances gave off X-rays, thought this third-generation Becquerel, and he went searching for them. Among the ores that he tested he had luckily included uranium. Quite by accident he placed this ore upon a fresh photographic plate enclosed in a light-tight envelope lying on a table in his dark room.

One morning he happened to examine this plate and found that it had been changed under the very spot on which the ore had rested. It was not the sort of accident to reach the front pages of the newspapers, as the discovery of X-rays had done. Yet its results were tremendously important. From this chance observation came a train of events which culminated in the triumphant work of Pierre and Marie Curie. Becquerel could not explain what had happened. He deliberately and very carefully repeated the conditions, but this time he placed between the uranium ore and the photographic plate an aluminum medallion stamped with a head. Without visible light he again obtained a photographic effect — a faint picture of the medallion was imprinted on the plate.

Becquerel then repeated the experiment with other ores containing the element uranium. In every case a similar effect was produced. He analyzed the ores, and saw at once that the intensity of effect was directly proportional to the amount of uranium present in each. He drew a conclusion, and announced that it was the uranium salt in each ore which was *alone* responsible for the photographic effect. But he did not cling very long to this belief. He tested the chief ore containing uranium. This ore was called pitchblende, a mineral which came from northern Bohemia. It was a queer rock. Instead of giving an effect proportional to the amount of uranium present, it proved to have far greater power than its uranium content could account for. Becquerel now made the simplest inference. " There must be," he said, " another element with power to affect a photographic plate many times greater than uranium itself." Marie Sklodowska Curie, a Polish immigrant student at the Sorbonne, was called in to look for this element. And in Paris, in a workshop that closely resembled the laboratories of the ancient " gold cooks," Marie and Pierre, her husband, unearthed radium.

Radium was a strange element. It glowed in the dark, gave off heat continuously, and even acted at a distance. Shortly after its discovery, Rutherford and Soddy found that radium exhibited these properties because it was continuously disintegrating. During the breaking-down process (radioactivity) it emitted electrified helium atoms, electrons (beta rays), and rays much more penetrating even than X-rays which were named by Villard *gamma rays.* Radiation tests were at once applied to this new ray and although the difficulties of proof were almost insurmountable, Villard soon showed that these gamma rays could be reflected and refracted and traveled with the speed of light. In 1914 Rutherford and Andrade measured their wave length by crystal method and found it to be even smaller than that of X-rays, hence of greater penetrating power.

The spectrum of radiation had again been extended, and it looked very much as if the limit had been reached. It was difficult to conceive of ether waves shorter than 1/500,000,000th of an inch and more penetrating than gamma rays. Such rays were one hundred times more penetrating than the beta rays of radium. They could actually pass through two inches of solid lead. The twentieth century had just dawned, and radioactivity had the scientific world in a frenzy. Here was a brand-new tool and a new phenomenon which challenged investigations. Wherever a trace of radioactive materials could be obtained, all kinds of studies were carried out. Among the new facts that were soon learned was that the presence of a radioactive substance — even the minutest trace of it — rendered the air around it a better conductor of electricity, because it stripped electrons from atoms of the gases of the atmosphere and thus ionized the air.

One of the first instruments devised to detect the presence of radioactive materials or ionized air was the Wulff *electroscope*. This very delicate instrument consisted of two fine quartz fibres held in loose contact in a sealed container. These fibres were charged with the same kind of electricity. The two fibres now containing like charges of electricity repelled each other since like charges repel each other, and were bent in the form of a bow and string. Now if the electroscope was brought near a radioactive material or near ionized air, the molecules of gas between the two fibres would become a conductor and the charge would leak away from the quartz, causing a collapse of the fibres. The rapidity of collapse would measure roughly the amount of radioactive material or the number of air ions present.

In 1900 H. Geitel reported that for no reason he could ascribe the air in an electroscope gradually became more ionized even though tests seemed to indicate the absence of radioactive materials. The following year Elster, in attempting to find a cause for this, discovered a condition of increased ionization in caves and house cellars as shown by the behavior of his electroscope. Unable to detect radioactive materials in the air, he *assumed* their presence in the walls of these caves and cellars. Many tried to find the reason for the presence of this ionization. On the last day of 1902 H. L. Cooke, a Canadian working in Rutherford's laboratory in Toronto, read a paper before the American Physical Society in which he described his efforts to track the cause by surrounding his electroscope with a screen of lead 5 cm. thick to shut out radioactive effects. He found that the fibres of his electroscope continued to collapse but he noticed that the rate of discharge of his electroscope was actually *cut down* about thirty per cent. The lead screen had evidently shut out some phenomenon which was responsible for the electroscope's rapid discharge. A wall of water fourteen times thicker than the lead had the same effect of protecting the electroscope from a rapid loss of electricity. Strangely enough, however, a five-ton screen of lead around his instrument proved no greater protection against the discharge of the electroscope than the wall of water.

Some external radiation, apparently coming from all directions, seemed to be responsible for the slow discharge of the electroscope. Cooke and Rutherford attributed this radiation to something which emanated from the earth's surface and was present in the atmosphere. Then Theodore Wulff, a priest, carried an electroscope in 1909 to the top of the Eiffel Tower and reported an " additional source of the rays in the higher portions of the atmosphere." A further clue to the mystery of the rays was found soon afterward when from Freiburg, Switzerland, came the news that the physicist Albert Gockel, backed by the Swiss Aero Club, rose to a height of about three miles in a balloon equipped with an electroscope similar to the one used by Wulff. Gockel reported that while the ionization in the electroscope decreased at first, indicating presumably that the radiation emanated from the earth's surface, yet it decreased less rapidly rather than more rapidly as he reached higher altitudes. He concluded that " there presumably was an increase of this strange radiation with altitude." He had, however, no idea that it might come from some source beyond the atmosphere of the earth. Four years before this balloon ascension, O. W. Richardson had written from Trinity College to *Nature* suggesting that this radiation was of extra-terrestrial origin, perhaps of solar influence, but this conclusion was based on what he thought was a change in leakage with a change of day and night — an incorrect observation. Gockel's aerial adventure, however, gave the first experimental data that could be interpreted as placing the origin of the new radiation outside the earth, and really marked the beginning of active work in this field. " His discovery illustrates," said Soddy, " the scientist's obsession for pursuing the most trivial and infinitesimal effects."

During the next three years, Victor F. Hess of Vienna and Werner Kolhoerster of Potsdam, first independently, and then jointly, by similar balloon ascensions placed Gockel's observation upon a more rigid quantitative basis. They found the loss of electric charge at 5.6 miles above the earth to be at least seven times as great as it was at its surface, indicating, as Hess wrote, that " a radiation of very high penetrating power enters our atmosphere from above." This radiation was evidently capable of passing through the walls of the electroscope and causing a leakage of electric charge. They calculated the penetrating power of these rays and found it to be even greater than that of gamma rays of radium. For the next seven years no further scientific data came from Gockel, Hess, or Kolhoerster. The World War had swallowed them up, and the problems of the source and nature of these mysterious rays were temporarily forgotten. The spread of the electromagnetic spectrum was halted.

But it was only a temporary halt. While Hess became director of the Research Laboratory of the United States Radium Corporation of New York, and Kolhoerster was measuring the rays both above and below the glaciers of the Jungfrau, a more brilliant and indefatigable worker entered the lists. Millikan, fresh from his triumphs in the fields of matter and radiation, had just answered the call to the California Institute of Technology in the fall of 1921. Together with one of his graduate students, Ira Sprague Bowen, he constructed a new self-recording electroscope containing two quartz fibres, carrying a photographic film, and with the necessary driving mechanism to obtain a continuous record of the divergence of the two fibres, as well as the temperature and pressure of the atmosphere. The whole device weighed but seven ounces. In the spring of the following year they went to Kelly Field near San Antonio and attached four of these electroscopes to specially designed United States Army sounding balloons. Each electroscope was carried aloft by two balloons inflated with hydrogen. When one balloon burst, the other carried the apparatus safely down to earth with a note asking that it be turned over to the proper authorities. Of the four electroscopes sent up that March and April, three were returned with perfect records. The results of these tests, which carried the electroscopes into the stratosphere (the upper region of the atmosphere) to an altitude of nearly ten miles, were, after some doubt, interpreted as corroborating in general the findings of the European investigators. The total discharge of the electroscopes, however, was found to be only about one-fourth of that computed by Hess and Kolhoerster.

Up to this time the penetrating power of the rays had never been directly measured, so it was difficult to interpret these findings. Rays of low energy, for example, suitably distributed throughout the atmosphere might show any desired distribution of intensity with height. Rays, however, of external origin in order to be felt near the earth's surface would have to have a penetrating power sufficient to pass through more than 30 feet of water which is the equivalent in absorbing power of the earth's atmosphere. It was imperative that direct measurements of their power of penetration be undertaken. The following summer, therefore, Millikan with his customary vigor and care continued to search out the secret of these rays. To measure directly their power of penetration, he carried three hundred pounds of lead and a tank of pure water to the summit of Pike's Peak. This adventure convinced him of the necessity of an accurate determination of the zero point of his electroscope — the reading when all external radiation including gamma rays of radioactive material and the new rays had been shut off. Muir Lake, situated 11,800 feet above sea level, was a deep body of water fed by melting snow from high mountains near Mt. Whitney, California. Its waters, formed from snow uncontaminated by the minerals of the earth, was only one-hundredth as radioactive as ordinary tap water in Pasadena. On its surface Millikan found that only 13.3 ions per second were formed in his sealed electroscope by the penetrating radiation. Then he dropped his instrument to a depth of sixty feet below the water — a depth which he figured could never be penetrated by even the strongest rays imaginable. Here his electroscope registered only 3.6 ions per second. Now to check these data. Three hundred miles away lay Arrowhead Lake, another snow-fed body of water 5,100 feet above the earth's surface. With the help of G. H. Cameron he lugged instruments up the mountain and made further measurements. He obtained a similar curve, but each reading in Arrowhead was the same as the reading six feet farther down in the Muir waters. In other words, the radiation at the surface of Muir Lake was more intense than at the surface of Arrowhead Lake. This difference of six feet is equivalent to a layer of air 6700 feet deep — exactly the difference in altitude between the two lakes.

These experiments indicated that the rays came from beyond the earth's atmosphere. If they had originated in the air blanket around our planet they should have been at least just as intense and just as penetrating at the lower level of Arrowhead Lake as at the surface of Muir Lake. The layer of atmosphere 6700 feet deep which separated the two levels of the lakes had evidently absorbed a certain amount of the penetrating power of the rays and hence accounted for the smaller penetrating power of the rays at Arrowhead Lake. Furthermore, calculations of the absorption of the penetrating rays by the 6700 feet of atmosphere indicated that they had tremendous penetrating power, great enough to come from outside the earth's atmosphere. The results of these experiments justified the use of *cosmic rays* for "the most descriptive and appropriate name yet suggested for that portion of the penetrating rays which comes in from above." In spite of Millikan's acceptance of this term, popular writers insisted on calling them Millikan rays, much to his chagrin and to the resentment of several Germans who made unjustifiable charges of his deliberate encouragement of the use of "M rays." In 1930, at the suggestion of some of his foreign friends, Millikan issued the following statement, "I have never, directly or indirectly, by implication or suggestion used or authorized any other name (than cosmic rays), and I know of no designation which is as appropriate." Yet in spite of this, a textbook in physics written by two members of the faculty of the University of Chicago contained as late as 1932 the statement that "cosmic rays are being called Millikan rays in honor of Robert Millikan who recently discovered them."

In 1926 Millikan was struggling up the high Andes in Bolivia to test whether here, where he could get completely out of sight of the Milky Way, the intensity of the rays would be reduced. When he found no difference in intensity he concluded that the cosmic rays came from beyond the Milky Way. The following two summers he lowered electroscopes fifteen times as sensitive as any he had used before beneath the waters of Lake Gem in California. An external radiation continued to affect the charged electroscopes until they reached a depth of 280 feet when no further discharge could be detected. This showed that the external radiation he was measuring was powerful enough to pass through a layer of water 280 feet deep. Cosmic rays had evidently passed through the thickness not only of the entire atmosphere of the earth but in addition through a wall of water 280 feet deep — the equivalent of *twenty-five feet of solid lead*.

Here apparently was a new type of radiation which could penetrate a wall of solid lead at least a hundred times thicker than the barrier sufficient to stop X-rays, and even fifty times thicker than any wall that could hold back the hardest or most penetrating of the gamma rays. Cosmic rays, therefore, appeared to Millikan to be of the nature of gamma rays, but of even shorter wave length. They belonged to the extreme lower end of the electromagnetic spectrum which once again had been spread out to a length hitherto never even dreamed of. But what could be responsible for such a highly penetrating radiation coming from outside the atmosphere of the earth? Infrared rays were known to be caused by the actively moving molecules of hot bodies; visible and ultraviolet light were caused by electronic motions; X-rays by the stoppage of a stream of fast moving electrons by metallic targets; and gamma rays by the spontaneous nuclear disintegration of radioactive elements. What phenomenon gave rise to these *durchdringende Strahlungen?*

Possible explanations of the birth of cosmic rays soon appeared. They were based upon an equation first definitely and completely worked out by Albert Einstein in 1905. Holding a belief that God is clever but not dishonest, Einstein, while employed as examiner of patents in Berne, Switzerland, made a bold attack upon the problem of the interrelation of light and matter. In his now justly famous paper, this international Jew of twenty-five took Thomson's concept of the electron, combined it with the revolutionary facts of quanta or bundles of energy disclosed by Max Planck, and wrote a mass-energy conversion equation as part of his special theory of relativity. Einstein said that matter could be converted into energy, and conversely also that energy could be converted into matter. Energy (E) measured in ergs (one erg is the work done by one gram falling through a distance of 0.001 centimeter) was equivalent to mass (m) multiplied by the square of the velocity of light (a constant, *c*, measured in centimeters and equal to 186,000 miles per second). This equation may be written as: $E = mc^2$. A year before the publication of this epochal equation, a Viennese, Friedrich Hasenöhrl, who was killed during the World War in 1915, imagined a hypothetical experiment that led him to this same equation but he did nothing further with it. Einstein, too, worked with nothing but pencil and mathematical symbols, and had no experimental evidence for the truth of this equation, but at the moment, as at numerous other times, " felt certain he was right without knowing the reason." He was sure that mass could be converted into energy and, vice versa, that energy such as light was similar to mass.

Sir Isaac Newton more than two hundred years before had asked in Query 30 of *Optiks*, " Are not gross Bodies and Light convertible into one another? " And now Einstein had answered that question in the affirmative. A certain amount of evidence now at hand seems to indicate the truth of Einstein's statement. Four years before his paper appeared, Peter N. Lebedev at Moscow and Nichols and Hull at Dartmouth had already shown experimentally that light exerted pressure hence it possessed a property of mass. Einstein said furthermore that since light possessed mass, it would act as matter and therefore bend when the light from a distant star passed the sun. The sun being a very massive body ought naturally to attract the lighter body. This was in accordance with Newton's Law of Gravitation which stated that every body in the universe attracts every other body with a force that is directly proportional to the product of their masses. This prediction of Einstein's was fulfilled in 1919 when members of eclipse expeditions both at Prinkipo Island and at Sobral in Brazil measured the bending of the light from a distant star as it passed close to the sun, and found it to agree with Einstein's equation. Radioactivity furnished further proof. One ounce of uranium, it was estimated, disintegrated into 0.8653 ounces of lead and 0.1345 ounces of helium, giving off tremendous amounts of energy equivalent according to Einstein's equation to the extra 0.0002 ounces of matter which apparently disappeared (1.000 ounce uranium — 0.8653 ounces lead — 0.1345 ounces helium = 0.0002 ounces matter or its equivalent of energy). Einstein's equation gave one gram of matter equal to 900,000,000,000,000,000,000 or 9×10^{20} ergs of energy, or 120,000,000,000 horse power. This energy could raise one million tons of rock to the top of a mountain six miles high. According to this equation, too, a piece of coal the size of a pea if completely converted into energy could drive a liner across the ocean. This principle of the conversion of mass into energy also explained the mechanism of the maintenance of the sun's heat. Perhaps in the sun's interior, helium and other heavier elements are being built up out of hydrogen and the mass that is partially annihilated is converted into heat. " A pound of heat is enough to melt thirty million tons of rock," it has been estimated. On this basis the sun in radiating energy loses about four million tons of mass each second, about five pounds of which falls upon our earth and makes life possible on this planet. It has also been estimated that at this rate of heat loss it will take the solar furnace about fifteen million million years to radiate itself away.

Developments in the study of isotopes leading to more accurate measurements of atomic weights also supplied fresh evidence of the probable validity of Einstein's equation. Prout, in 1815, had theorized that all the chemical elements were complexes of hydrogen atoms. If that were true, it followed that atomic weights should all be whole numbers on the basis of the atomic weight of hydrogen as 1 or standard. But the atomic weights of many elements were far from being integers. Prout's theory fell into oblivion. In 1860 Marignac revived it but declared that " the weight of each group might not be the sum of the weights of the primordial atoms composing it." His reasoning, however, was not convincing and was also soon forgotten. It was believed that the helium nucleus was composed of four hydrogen nuclei. Its weight, therefore, ought to be four times that of the hydrogen nucleus. It was found, however, that it was actually somewhat less. This puzzled scientists for many years. In 1914 Rutherford introduced a new conception. He said that the atomic weight of helium, for example, believed to be made up of four hydrogen nuclei, was less than the sum of the weights of the four hydrogen atoms because of the fact that in the nuclei of normal atoms the *packing* of the electrons and protons caused a loss of mass which was converted into its equivalent of energy. This "packing effect," which Harkins announced the following year independently of Rutherford, was the percentage decrease in weight of a heavier element built up from a lighter one.

Then followed some exciting experiments at the Cavendish Laboratory initiated by Thomson and carried to epoch-making results by F. W. Aston, a Nobel laureate, who built and developed *mass spectrographs* of greater and greater precision, so that the atomic weights of dozens of isotopes were determined to a high degree of precision. The packing effect of more than thirty elements was found and the loss of weight suffered by these elements (on the assumption that they were built from lighter ones) agreed beautifully with the figures obtained from the Einstein equation.

In 1928 Millikan came out with a theory of the birth or origin of the cosmic rays based upon the energy-matter conversion theory. "That the Einstein equation and the figures of Aston are working so well in the nuclear results makes it at least natural to apply it to the cosmic ray," he wrote. Cosmic rays, said Millikan, were produced during the building up of the heavier elements, such as helium, oxygen, silicon, iron, and uranium, from the union of hydrogen nuclei. He believed this union was sudden and instantaneous. These instantaneous transformations were accompanied by a *partial annihilation* of matter resulting in the release of cosmic rays having energies high enough to account for the extreme hardness or penetration of these cosmic rays. Thus when 4 grams of helium are built up from 4.0032 (4 x 1.0008) grams of hydrogen, there is a loss of 0.0032 grams of matter, which according to the Einstein equation is equivalent to the liberation of twenty-eight million electron volts (an electron volt is the energy acquired by one electron falling through a potential difference of 1 volt). With the use of the fundamental quantum relation of Planck $\left(\frac{\text{amount of energy in a quantum}}{\text{frequency of the radiation}} = h = 6.5 \times 10^{-27}\right)$,

Einstein's equation, and the mass spectrograph figures of Aston, Millikan determined the wave length of the particular cosmic rays supposedly produced by the birth of helium from hydrogen as being equal to 6×10^{-10} cm. This figure happened to coincide with the actual wave length of the least penetrating of the cosmic rays known to Millikan.

With Millikan's explanation of the nature of the cosmic rays, the range of electromagnetic spectrum was again extended. The largest waves in this spectrum are the radio waves which may reach a length of twenty miles. The shortest are the newly discovered cosmic rays. Between these two limits are the various other types of radiation which are shown in the idealized diagram which follows on page 394.

During his cosmic ray measurements Millikan had found at least three groups of penetrating cosmic radiation and probably four. The first, corresponding to energies of twenty-eight million electron volts was attributed to helium building. The second group had a penetrating power not inconsistent with the energy of about one hundred sixteen million electron volts — that required by Einstein's equation for the birth of oxygen out of hydrogen. The third was consistent with the energy of two hundred million electron volts required for the building up of silicon; and the fourth, indicating energies as high as half a billion electron volts, was taken to be the cradle cry of iron. Millikan's theory was a fantastic one, and he did not hesitate to state, "I am not unaware of the difficulties of finding an altogether satisfactory picture of how these events take place, but the twentieth century does not wait on suitable mechanical models."

While this theory was becoming common talk in many of the great laboratories of the world, and men did not stop discussing this poetic conception of the origin of cosmic rays from the birth cries of heavier atoms in interstellar space, Sir James Jeans, brilliant mathematical astronomer of England, came forward with another singular hypothesis. He found it hard to believe in the sudden, instantaneous hammering together of hundreds of electrons and protons in the extreme cold of interstellar space, pro-

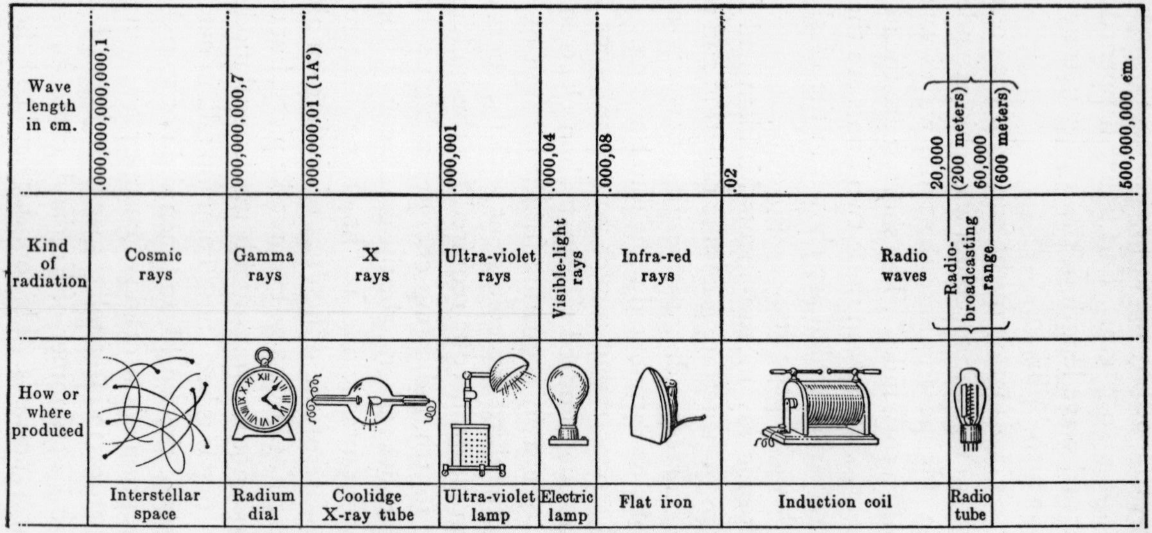

Wave length in cm.	.000,000,000,000,1	.000,000,000,7	.000,000,01 (1A°)	.000,001	.000,04	.000,08	.02	20,000 (200 meters) 60,000 (600 meters)	500,000,000 cm.
Kind of radiation	Cosmic rays	Gamma rays	X rays	Ultra-violet rays	Visible-light rays	Infra-red rays	Radio waves	Radio-broadcasting range	
How or where produced	Interstellar space	Radium dial	Coolidge X-ray tube	Ultra-violet lamp	Electric lamp	Flat iron	Induction coil	Radio tube	

FIG. 26. THE COMPLETE ELECTROMAGNETIC SPECTRUM

Both the wave length and the source of each type of ray are noted.
(from the author's *New World of Chemistry*)

ducing heavier elements and accompanied by the catastrophic emission of cosmic radiation, the most abundant form of radiation in the universe. That the hydrogen which was thus consumed was continuously being replaced by the change of the energy of the stars into new hydrogen atoms, as first suggested by W. D. MacMillan, a former colleague of Millikan, was also difficult for him to accept. " There can be no creation of matter. The fabric of the universe withers, crumbles and dissolves with age. . . . The road ends only in death and annihilation," said Jeans. He suggested the reverse process, and what to him was a far simpler and more plausible theory, based on the knowledge of the energies and lifetimes of stars and the rest of the universe. Cosmic rays, according to the Englishman, were the result of the *complete annihilation of matter*, both in the extremely thin and frigid regions of interstellar space, and in the interior of stars where extremely high temperatures and pressures destroy atoms. Millikan has interpreted Jeans' conception in a way characteristic of his strikingly vivid power of expression. " In the interior of heavy atoms, occasionally a negative electron gets tired of life at the pace it has lived in the electronic world, and desires to end it all and commit suicide; but being paired by nature in electron fate with a proton, he has to arrange a suicide pact with his mate, and so the two jump into each other's arms in the nucleus and two electric lives are snuffed out at once; but not without the letting loose of a terrific death yell, for the total mass of the two must be transformed into a powerful ether pulse which by being absorbed in the surrounding matter is supposed to keep up the mad hot pace in the interiors of the suns."

When Millikan advanced his cosmic ray synthesis theory, there was no shred of experimental evidence to show that energy was actually liberated in terrestrial furnaces when a heavier element was built out of a lighter one. But on April 28, 1932, the long hoped for experiment was announced. Cockroft and Walton, working under Rutherford, stepped up proton projectiles to a velocity equivalent to a voltage of several hundred thousand electron volts, and hurled them at lithium fluoride crystals. Out of that impact came alpha particles with energies equivalent to many times the energy of the protons which were fired. The young Englishmen explained the results of this startling experiment in the following way. Lithium atoms were hit by protons forming two particles of helium, each with an atomic weight of approximately 4. The actual weight of the lithium atom used was 7.0019, that of the proton was 1.00775, and that of the ejected helium atom was 4.0022. The difference between the sum of the masses of the lithium atoms and the protons and the weight of the two helium atoms ejected was equal to 0.00525. This lost mass had been converted into $0.00525 \times 9 \times 10^{20}$ ergs of energy, equivalent to several million electron volts. Mass had been converted into energy as helium, a heavier element, was built up from hydrogen, a lighter one.

Lithium	+	Hydrogen	⟶	2 Helium	+	Energy
7.0019 g.	+	1.00775 g.	⟶	2(4.0022) g.	+	0.00525 g. $\times$ 9×10^{20} ergs
8.00965 grams			⟶	8.0044 grams	+	16,000,000 electron volts

It looked very much as if they were dealing here with an action in which the ionized hydrogen projectile merely pulled a trigger, releasing a huge store of energy held guardedly in the nucleus of the lithium atom. The world of physics was stunned. Here was direct evidence of energy released during the atom-building process. For more than a century physicists had been kneeling to the old, narrow Law of the Conservation of Energy which declared that energy could neither be created nor destroyed. Science had worshiped this law as one of the few remaining gods which iconoclastic physics had not as yet demolished. Einstein's mass-energy equation — an extended form of this energy principle — had, of course, prophesied its death. Here was energy which had been directly obtained by the partial annihilation of matter. The process was very much like that assumed by Millikan in his interpretation of the least energetic component of the cosmic rays.

In an effort to test the validity of this interpretation of Cockroft and Walton's results — the first direct transmutation of an element without the aid of naturally radioactive material — Aston built a larger mass spectrograph and re-weighed the atom of hydrogen and other elements and made several important corrections. Kenneth T. Bainbridge of the Bartol Research Foundation also built a mass spectrograph weighing two tons and capable of weighing, photographically, of course, a difference in weight as small as one trillionth of a trillionth of a gram. A. J. Dempster of the University of Chicago built an even more delicate spectrograph. With these, protons, deuterons, and other isotopes have been weighed with such a high degree of accuracy that it has been possible to compare the infinitesimal losses and gains of weight during nuclear reactions and to compare them with the gains and losses of energy which took place at the same time. The results obtained by this method have verified rather roughly Cockroft's transformation of mass into energy. Efforts were also made to see whether the other part of the Einstein equation could be verified, that is, whether energy could really be converted into mass. But here, absolute conclusions could not be drawn. "The change of energy to mass reported by recent experimenters must still be viewed with caution," was Bainbridge's opinion in 1934.

Cockroft and Walton's was not the last of the matter-to-energy conversion experiments. Immediately after their work, other examples of such a change were reported. E. O. Lawrence bombarded lithium fluoride with deuterons and obtained alpha particles propelled by energies far greater than had been employed, indicating, once more, a loss of mass with a consequent increase in energy. Harkins fired neutrons at nitrogen and obtained boron and helium atoms of energy greater than had been employed. Light hydrogen atoms were bombarded with protons, and deuterons of greater penetrating power were produced. Lauritsen, in Millikan's laboratory, obtained even more startling results. He bombarded beryllium with protons fired by his million-volt tube and obtained gamma rays with energy equivalent to six million electron volts (two and a half times more penetrating than the gamma rays given off spontaneously by thorium C). When, in May, 1935, he succeeded in obtaining gamma rays of *sixteen million electron volts* energy by bombarding lithium with protons, Millikan reported, " We are now doing in our laboratories the same sort of thing which I have been assuming to be taking place in the birth of cosmic rays in interstellar space."

But while theoretical physicists argued over annihilation and building-up processes, there were some who were still very skeptical about the nature of these cosmic rays. True, Jeans and W. F. G. Swann, after doubting for a while the actual existence of this type of radiation, finally accepted Millikan's conception of cosmic rays as being composed of radiations of extremely small wave lengths. But disturbing data were being collected in the search for the source and nature of cosmic rays which pointed to a rival theory. There appeared to be evidence that this radiation was made up of swiftly moving material particles rather than of rays. In taking measurements of the concentration of cosmic rays, observers reported a change at different latitudes. They seemed to find a higher concentration near the magnetic poles and a lower one near the earth's magnetic equator. In 1927 J. Clay, Dutch physicist of Amsterdam, made several trips between Holland and Java, and reported that his cosmic-ray detectors showed the lowest concentration of this mysterious radiation near the earth's equator. This clustering of cosmic rays around the earth's magnetic poles was interpreted for the first time by Kolhoerster as pointing to the presence of electrons or other charged particles rather than to radiation.

Further observations were required to learn the true nature of cosmic rays. On May 29, 1931, Auguste Piccard, a Swiss physicist of the University of Brussels, locked himself up with an assistant, Charles Kipfer, in a sealed gondola dangling a hundred feet from a balloon, for the purpose of rising into the stratosphere. This was the first stratosphere ascension in a sealed chamber ever attempted with the object of studying the puzzling nature of cosmic rays. Risking his life, Piccard rose to a height of ten miles, where he saw a frigid, windless, cloudless sky ten times as dark as when looked at from the ground, but not dark enough to make the stars visible in daylight. The temperature of the gondola had risen much higher than he had expected, and he licked drops of water from the inner walls of his seven-foot aluminum prison to assuage his thirst. As he drifted far out from his starting point he was given up for dead. But the tall, thin, poetic-looking scientist came down on a glacier in the Alps to tell the world that his instruments seemed to indicate that the cosmic rays emanated from somewhere in the stratosphere. His observations as to the nature of the rays were practically worthless. The mystery was still dark, but Auguste Piccard, former pupil of Einstein at Zurich, had shown the way to a new method of exploring the upper regions of the atmosphere — a method which was soon followed by many other scientific explorers.

More than twenty years had now passed since a new cosmic radiation had been suspected; but the true nature of this radiation was still hardly more than a conjecture. No crucial evidence had as yet been presented to prove definitely that cosmic radiation was either of a particle or a wave nature. Millikan and his assistants, Bowen and H. Victor Neher, were redoubling their efforts. Piccard had made a second record leap into the stratosphere, disappointing D'Annunzio who had begged in vain to be taken aloft and dropped overboard as ballast if necessary, so that he might give his life for science rather than " die shamefully between two sheets." Erich Regener of Stuttgart was sending sounding balloons to record heights of more than nineteen and a half miles, while his assistant, who was the leader of an Andes Expedition, was measuring cosmic rays on a peak twenty thousand feet high in South America. Kolhoerster was reporting cosmic rays which had penetrated far into the Stassfurt salt mines to a depth equivalent to half a mile of water, and was also chopping cosmic-ray stations in the glacial ice of the Jungfrau. T. C. Poulter of Richard Byrd's Antarctic expedition was collecting cosmic-ray data in the lonely vigils of Little America. Axel Corlin of Lund Observatory in Sweden was searching for the rays in an iron mine in the mountains near Kiruna. Three intrepid Russian scientists had climbed into the stratosphere in a sealed gondola to a record height of nearly thirteen miles; soon after they had sent their last radio message to the ground, "We have studied the cosmic rays," they were dashed to death when their balloon collapsed. And in the meantime another scientist had entered the lists against the secret of cosmic radiation.

Arthur Holly Compton of the University of Chicago was a newcomer in this arena but not in the general field of radiation, where he had already determined the index of refraction of X-rays and their reflection from crystals. Compton was a skilled experimenter and a brilliant theorist who had won the Nobel Prize in 1927 for his contributions in the field of radiation. Brought up in the college town of Wooster, Ohio, Compton at a very early age had shown unusual interest and ability in applied science. Both his father, a professor of philosophy at Wooster College, and his mother, of German birth and Mennonite ancestry, encouraged the boy as they watched him photograph stars and build gliders and airplanes. At ten he had written a paper on the difference between the three-toed and five-toed fossil elephants and even offered a theory to explain it. At college he invented a patented gyroscopic device for airplane control and developed an ambition to become a mechanical engineer. His brother Karl, five years his senior, steered him away from engineering to pure research by interesting him in advanced mathematics and physics. At Princeton University, emulating Karl, he received in 1916 the degree of Doctor of Philosophy in physics *summa cum laude*. Up to that time the Compton brothers and Henry Norris Russell were the only students to achieve this high honor. A year's work in the Pittsburgh laboratory of the Westinghouse Electric Company, where he was engaged in the development of electric light lamps, was followed by another year's research in the Cavendish Laboratory under Thomson and Rutherford, which led him to make fundamental discoveries in the field of light.

Compton's entrance in 1931 into cosmic-ray research was intimately connected with his study of the nature of the aurora, that brilliant display of Northern Lights in the heavens in northern latitudes which seemed to be caused, according to Birkeland and Dauvillier, by electrons shot out from the sun and reflected by the earth's magnetism to the upper stratosphere. They were concentrated near the poles since the earth's magnetism is greatest there. Perhaps cosmic rays, too, could be explained by a similar phenomenon, thought Compton. Besides, the solution of the nature of cosmic rays might contain the clue to the structure of the nucleus of the atom. Millikan, his former colleague at Chicago, had made of this problem a living, throbbing adventure. Compton could not help being drawn into it. During that first year he made some preliminary measurements of cosmic rays from the summits of the Rockies and the Alps. Then in 1932 with funds supplied by the Carnegie Corporation of New York he organized an elaborate world-wide cooperative enterprise for the collection of cosmic-ray data.

If rays were coming into every corner of the earth from interstellar space, if they differed in intensity with latitude and altitude, if they were radiations or material particles or both, a mountain of data had first to be collected by scientists stationed in the far-flung laboratories of the globe. Millikan, to be sure, was doing great things, and a group of European investigators had by no means let the problem cool down. But Compton was impatient, and wanted thousands of measurements to bring the mystery into clear focus for an accurate analysis. Like the great emperors of old he divided the earth into several regions. Then he obtained the cooperation of eight associated expeditions within these eight zones of cosmic-ray research. D. la Cour of the Danish Meteorological Survey was to make measurements in Greenland and Denmark. J. M. Benade, physicist of Forman Christian College in Lahore, India, was to trail the rays in India, Ceylon, Java, and Thibet. S. M. Naude of the University of Cape Town was to make observations in South Africa. Bruno Rossi of the University of Padua was to hunt in Eritrea. P. G.

Ledig of the Carnegie Magnetic Observatory was to trap them all the way from Huancayo, Peru, around the Cape of Good Hope and back to the United States. E. O. Wollan of the University of Chicago was to take his electroscopes to Spitzbergen and Switzerland. R. D. Bennett of the Massachusetts Institute of Technology and Alan Carpe of the American Telephone and Telegraph Company's laboratory were to scale Alaskan peaks to trap the rays. Arthur Compton himself, accompanied by his wife and fourteen-year-old son, set out in March, 1932, on a trip around the world to make cosmic-ray measurements. Mt. Mauna Kea in Hawaii watched him set up his measuring instruments. Mt. Cook in New Zealand gazed upon strange electroscopes for the first time. Mt. Kosciusko in Australia was invaded by this cosmic-ray hunter; the silence of Mt. Chico in Panama was broken by the Chicago scientist; Mexico City, El Misti in Peru, Switzerland, and Canada's arctic north were also included in his itinerary, which covered fifty thousand miles before he brought his data back to the United States.

Every member of that cooperative enterprise was equipped with a new, carefully calibrated electroscope invented by Compton. It consisted, as had the preceding sensitive electroscope devised independently by Millikan, of a hollow steel sphere in which argon had been introduced under a pressure of thirty atmospheres. Cosmic rays cannot be measured directly, but their effects can be observed. The rays entering the sphere strike the argon gas and electrify some of its atoms. This ionization produces a very feeble current which is amplified by appropriate electric circuits or photographed on strips of motion picture film. The intensity of the current or the number of tracks varies with the intensity of the cosmic radiation present. The whole ionization chamber is shielded from local impurities by two hundred pounds of lead carried in the form of small grains. Geiger counters similar to those used by other cosmic-ray researchers were also extensively used to help determine the concentration of cosmic rays.

Upon his return, Compton collected and sorted out a mass of

data obtained by sixty observers spread over the earth at points extending from 46° south to 78° north of the equator. From these observations, confusing and apparently contradictory in some cases, Compton drew the following apparent conclusions: (1) The intensity of cosmic radiation *increased with altitude* wherever measurements were taken. This was in fair agreement with the findings of his predecessors, and led him to declare that cosmic rays come probably from interstellar space and are surely of extra-terrestrial origin. (2) The abundance of the rays varies with latitude in accordance with the earlier observations of Clay. There was as much as a twenty per cent difference in concentration of the rays between the earth's equator where they were fewest, and its north magnetic pole, where they occurred in greatest numbers. Compton had made these measurements himself. Even as Millikan was getting his own results in his supervised high altitude airplane flights near Cormorant Lake, Manitoba, the Chicago scientist was making further observations three hundred miles away around the barren lands of Churchill, nearest settlement to the earth's north magnetic pole. (3) Cosmic radiation is about 1.5 per cent stronger by day than by night, in general agreement with similar observations made by Millikan, and later by Hess over a period of three years of continuous observation in the Tyrol mountains.

The final conclusion that Compton drew from all these observations was that the incoming *cosmic rays consist mainly of charged particles* though a very small portion of them seemed to consist of photons or radiation. Millikan's cosmic-ray studies, on the other hand, had led him to reverse the emphasis. At least so far as sea-level ionization was concerned, Millikan concluded that *most of it was due directly or indirectly to incoming photons,* while probably not more than a sixth of it could be due to charged particles. Both agreed that the cosmic rays came from interstellar space beyond the Milky Way.

Just as the year 1932 was closing, there gathered at Atlantic City members of the American Association for the Advancement of Science to listen to the latest messages from the cosmic ray fronts. Men had participated in high adventure to get new information. Alan Carpe and Theodore Koven had carried cosmic-ray apparatus to Muldrow Glacier, thirteen thousand feet up Mt. McKinley in Alaska, only to die in the dangerous exploit. With new and more delicate electroscopes others, too, had hunted cosmic rays wherever the chance of finding significant data challenged. At this meeting Millikan and Compton were the chief speakers and the two Nobel laureates presented the results of their observations. The report made front page news the following morning for the general public was eager to hear more about these mysterious cosmic rays. The *New York Times* included in its description of the meeting how " in an atmosphere surchanged with drama in which the human element was by no means lacking, the two protagonists presented their views with the vehemence and fervor of those theoretical debates of bygone days."

A week later the *Nation,* more informed on elections, proletarians, and revolutions than on electrons, protons, and radiations, reported " there was more heat than light in the argument which revolved around stupendous deductions from highly dubious data," and in its cosmic wisdom added that " the heat of the discussion was generated entirely by that age-old disturber of the peace, the *odium theologicum.*" Nothing could have been further from the truth. The discussion was purely a scientific difference of opinion concerning various interpretations that might be drawn from incomplete data. The battle over the nature of the cosmic rays was no historic repetition of Galileo's struggle against the geocentric universe of the Church or of the Huxley-Wilberforce conflict concerning man's place in the organic world of nature.

Millikan like Newton, Faraday, Maxwell, Kelvin, Rayleigh, Pasteur, Pupin, and many other eminent scientists has a virile faith. He is an active member of the Congregational Church, and he holds that the creation of cosmic rays is proof that " the Creator is still on the job."

Compton, too, was brought up in a strictly religious environment. His mother always began the day with prayer and her son's graduation address was a defence and a plea for more parochial colleges. Compton has said that "science is the glimpse of God's purpose in nature, and the very existence of the amazing world of the atom and radiation points to a purposeful creation, to the idea that there is a God and an intelligent purpose back of everything."

But one question was on the lips of many. How could two men, each of the highest scientific training and achievement, each equipped with the most ingenious devices that the laboratory could fashion, make a similar series of observations and reach such different conclusions? Thomas Huxley long ago had framed the answer, "There is but one right and the possibilities of wrong are infinite." The great enigma of the cosmic rays is locked up in the whole problem of the nature of radiation, which according to Einstein still remains one of the most difficult riddles for science to decipher. The riddle of the nature of light led to some extent to the differences of interpretation of the cosmic rays by Millikan and Compton. Is light of a wave or of a particle nature? The undulatory or wave theory of radiation remained intrenched for a century. In 1888 it received a rude jolt. Hallwachs and Hertz found that a beam of light falling on a negatively charged body produced a rapid loss of the charge, while a nonelectrified body gradually became positively charged in the presence of light. No explanation could be offered for this unexpected behavior until two years after the discovery of the electron. J. J. Thomson showed that the emission of negatively charged particles or electrons from the surface of metals was the cause of this phenomenon. Electrons, being negatively charged particles of electricity, when given off by a metal leave it positively charged. Why this emission of electrons should take place in the presence of light could not be explained. Philippe Lenard, student of Hertz, measured the *velocity* of the ejected electrons and proved that it did not depend upon the *intensity* or brightness of the light although the *number* of emitted electrons did so depend. Several years later

Ladenburg showed that blue light (of lower wave length) threw out electrons with somewhat more energy than did red light (of larger wave length), in other words, he demonstrated that the velocity of the ejected electrons depended upon the wave length of the light which struck the metal.

To Millikan this " seemed the most amazing contradiction ever revealed in the history of physics." For how could light, if it consisted of ether waves, release electrons from the atoms of metals with an energy independent of its intensity but dependent upon its wave length. Einstein tried to interpret this phenomenon known as the *photo-electric effect* by assuming that light was of the nature of particles, that is, consisted of Planck's concentrated bundles of energy called *photons* travelling with the speed of light. (The term photon is used only with reference to radiation and never with reference to electrical or other units of matter.) The light wave, said Einstein, travels as a discrete entity or photon and the amount of energy of each photon is proportional to its wave length. A distinct characteristic of particles is their ability to impart energy and motion to targets which they strike. As each photon struck the metal it gave up its energy to one of the electrons outside the nucleus of its atom and dislodged the electron from the metal. He proposed an equation for the photo-electric effect, as follows:

$1/2\ m\ v^2$	=	$h\ v$,	—	p
{energy with which electron escapes}	=	Planck's energy constant	—	{work necessary to get electron out of the metal}

Millikan, using first light of different intensities and then of different wave lengths in a " machine shop in a vacuum " which he had devised, succeeded in 1914 after ten years of work in completing the first rigorous and complete experimental proof of this equation which incidentally furnished the first direct determination of Planck's " h."

Compton, too, shed some further light on the perplexing interrelation of matter and radiation. He went a step further than Einstein. When a photon hits an electron, he said, the meeting ought to resemble the impact of two billiard balls, for the photon bullet exhibited particle properties, such as momentum. An X-ray, for example, shot against the atoms of a gas should give up some of its energy to the particle with which it collided, thus lowering its own energy and consequently increasing its wave length (the longer the wave length the less energy the radiation possessed). The second effect should be the pushing of the struck target in the direction in which the X-ray was travelling — the X-ray itself recoiling at the same time. The first effect, that is, the lengthening of the wave length of the radiation used, had almost been observed by Barkla in 1918. He had shot X-rays of known wave length against graphite crystals and found that the reflected X-rays were more easily absorbed than the incident waves. It was this experiment that had given young Compton the clue which resulted in his discovery of what is now known as the *Compton effect.*

To establish the truth of the change in wave length, Compton built an extremely delicate piece of apparatus, so delicate in fact that it could measure the one ten-millionth of the energy exerted by a mosquito climbing one inch of screen. He shot X-rays of known wave length against a gas and obtained two lines, one representing the primary X-ray used, and the other the changed X-ray of longer wave length after collision with atoms of the gas — photographic proof of the Compton effect. After this amazing evidence Compton, still working in the Ryerson Laboratory of the University of Chicago to which he had been called by Michelson in 1923, made some calculations to prove the second of his contentions, namely that the X-ray after striking its target would recoil or jump back at some definite angle. Then C. T. R. Wilson brought his cloud chamber apparatus into play to get photographic data of this recoil action, and obtained cloud track pictures showing exactly the angles which Compton had predicted on the basis of his theory of photons or bullets of radiation. Compton gave an excellent picture to illustrate the thrilling implications of this discovery. "There was once a sailor on a vessel in New York harbor," he wrote, " who dived overboard and splashed in the water. The resulting wave, after finding its way out of the harbor, reached the harbor at Liverpool. Here another sailor was swimming beside his ship. When the wave reached him he was surprised to find himself knocked by the wave up to the deck. Impossible, you say? " Well, that is exactly what happens when radiation travelling thousands of miles through the " ether " exerts its full energy when it strikes a target. It is only then that it loses energy and increases in wave length. And, added Compton, " There is now no need to imagine an ether such as was necessary to propagate waves, for the inertia of these particles will carry them with undiminished speed to the remotest part of the universe without any such conducting medium and without loss of energy." For this classic piece of work which solved in a way the riddle which had existed since the discovery of the photo-electric effect, Compton and Wilson in 1927 were jointly awarded the Nobel Prize in physics.

From Millikan's laboratory, soon after, came further data which seemed to show a close interrelation between matter and radiation. Anderson, in the effort to bend cosmic rays by means of a strong magnetic field and in this way to determine their energy equivalents, had discovered a graceful curve on one of the hundreds of pictures he had taken in his Wilson cloud chamber apparatus. He and Millikan made a careful study of this picture and found that this curve was the fog track of neither an electron, a proton, nor an ionized helium particle. Its direction and length showed it to be a unit of electricity of positive charge and of mass equal to that of the negative electron. This new particle which had never been observed before was named the *positron* (see List of Illustrations).

Other equally interesting pictures were later obtained. One showed a shower of 15 positrons and 10 electrons emanating from a single point in the central lead bar of the photograph. Anderson and Millikan interpreted this picture as the result of a cosmic ray, after plunging with enormous energy (3 billion electron volts) through the lead plate, colliding head on with the nucleus of an atom, and being absorbed by it. As the result of this act, both free positive and free negative electrons were thrown out of the nucleus. Whether these electrified particles of matter are all knocked out of the nucleus or are created by the cosmic ray as a result of the nuclear encounter is still unsettled. In either case, here was evidence that electromagnetic radiation had disrupted the heart of an atom. Dirac is inclined to believe that such pictures indicate the change of radiation into electrified particles outside the nucleus. In other words, here is evidence according to the Englishman of electron pairs of matter created out of energy — further evidence of the validity of the mass-energy relation postulated by Einstein.

The dual nature of both radiation and matter, in addition to the fairly well established fact of their interchangeability, are the chief products of the new revolutionary physics of the twentieth century. With these discoveries science turned an unexpected corner and found itself in need of new moorings. For the first time two conflicting yet necessary theories have been accepted in polite scientific society, although as William Bragg has expressed it, " we still find it difficult to understand how these two theories can both be true." This difficulty may turn out to be the explanation of the disagreement about the nature of cosmic rays. Some have suggested that matter is waves going round in *circles* and that radiation is waves travelling in *straight lines*. The cosmic ray may not be a single phenomenon; both Millikan and Compton may be right because they may be measuring and talking about different portions of a complex phenomenon. In addition to this confusion, science does not always know exactly whether it is measuring radiations or high speed electrons with velocities approaching that of light and with colossal penetrating power, since little is known about such high speed particles. When an electrified particle acquires a velocity close to that of light, our limited knowledge prevents us from always distinguishing it from a photon or light wave. By associating the motion of such an electron with the propagation of a wave, and relating the energy and momentum of this particle with the frequency and velocity of the wave, a definite wave length for the electron can be calculated, and thus it can be treated as radiation.

At present Millikan believes: "Probably as much as 85 per cent of the cosmic rays *that are found at sea level* enter the atmosphere from beyond the Milky Way as pure photons or radiation produced by the *partial* annihilation of matter when heavier elements are built up from lighter ones. These photons are of the same nature as gamma rays but have much greater penetrating power. A smaller portion of the cosmic rays observed at sea level in equatorial regions are secondary rays produced within the earth's atmosphere by collision of incoming electrons with air atoms." In addition, another very small number of cosmic rays with energies as high as 10 billion electron volts have been observed by their latitude and longitude effects, and for these rays there seems to be no origin except the result of a *complete* annihilation of whole atoms of helium, oxygen, carbon, and other elements. According to the Einstein equation, the carbon atom when annihilated ought to give off a total energy equivalent to 12 billion electron volts, while oxygen, under the same conditions, ought to furnish 16 billion electron volts. Millikan indeed points out that in the present state of our knowledge there is no source of energies of several billion of electron volts in sight save in the theory of the *complete* annihilation of whole atoms as heavy as the atoms of carbon or oxygen (Jeans' theory). Millikan, however, adds "That such a complete annihilation of the whole of an atom can take place all at once will be doubted by many physicists and astronomers; and I am far from asserting it does. Nevertheless, it is true that there is no other tenable source of energy in sight which would explain the extreme cosmic ray energies that we actually observe. One can take this merely as evidence of the depth of our ignorance of the origin of these cosmic rays or he can take it as evidence that such annihilation processes actually take place."

Compton agrees with Millikan as to the place of origin of these cosmic rays but differs as to their nature. Today Compton

must develop a method of allowing the effective bombardment of the islands." At the present time we cannot pick the lock that holds this enormous reservoir of energy out of our grasp. It may be that " we are in the position of the first savage who made water boil over a fire with the steam engine lying a million years ahead of him." Or perhaps the achievements already reported lend weight to the hope that some young demiurge like Cockroft or Lawrence may find the solution within our own days. Cosmic rays may prove to be the long searched for key.

Perhaps the greatest implication which has come from discoveries in the realm of cosmic rays is the thought that they are the birth cries of new elements being born either out of simpler ones, as Millikan maintains, or out of radiation itself (as has been suggested on the basis of the discovery of the positron), giving to groping mankind evidence of a continuous creation to offset the gloomy picture of ultimate annihilation by the heat death of the universe. This conception may give man his greatest hope of immortality and purpose in a chaotic cosmos.

Three other theories of the origin of cosmic rays have very recently been suggested. Fritz Zwicky and Walter Baade of the California Institute of Technology say that cosmic rays may result from the cataclysmic changes which take place during the appearance of very rare super novae or exploding stars. E. A. Milne, distinguished English mathematician, on the other hand, advances the novel idea that cosmic rays are particles accelerated to a speed near that of light by the gravitational pull of the rest of the universe. And Abbé Georges Lemaître, eminent mathematician, physicist, and cosmologist, holds that cosmic rays are the wandering fragments of some huge super-radioactive atom which eons ago, perhaps during the biblical creation, exploded in space. " Cosmic rays," he says, " are a glance left for man of the primordial fireworks of the formation of a star from an atom coming from free space that marked the beginning of the expanding universe, ten billion or so years ago." Among all the numerous theories advanced to explain the origin of cosmic rays which we know today to be composed of both photons and electrical particles, this flight of the imagination of the cleric of Louvain seems to Einstein, as to many others, " the most beautiful, pleasant, and satisfying interpretation." The origin of the cosmic rays is one of the fundamental problems of science, and involves the origin of the universe. And until science has found the Rosetta stone of the origin of cosmic rays, it may well cling to this picture worthy of the philosophers of those days when science was little else than metaphysics.

CHAPTER ELEVEN

ASTROPHYSICS

HOW MAN IS BRINGING THE SUN DOWN TO EARTH

Centered upon the life and researches of George Ellery Hale

THE SUN, that great sphere of glowing matter " just off our bow," holds our planet with bonds far stronger than the toughest steel. And man, gazing at it with reverence for centuries, has recently come to realize that within this celestial crucible may lie hidden the clues to many of the mysteries he has determined to solve. Here temperatures which range from 6000° C. on the gaseous surface to perhaps 40,000,000° C. at its liquid core, and pressures which dwarf our puny terrestrial conquests, set the stage for phenomena that may yet clear up some of the most perplexing riddles on earth.

But how to bring that glaring star furnace with a diameter of 864,000 miles and a volume more than a million times that of the earth into our laboratories here below? It seemed a feat never to be attained. Auguste Comte felt certain of this when he wrote, " There are some things of which the human race must forever remain in ignorance; for example, the chemical composition of the sun and the other heavenly bodies." This eminent philosopher did not realize at that time, as many since have been convinced, that prophecy in science is a risky pastime.

Hardly two hundred years passed between that classic experiment of Newton's when with the aid of a glass prism he split sunlight into its spectrum to the equally historic day when Gustav Kirchhoff fetched the sun into his laboratory, and began to probe for its components. A number of important discoveries had preceded the work of this German physicist. In 1802, William Hyde Wollaston of the Royal Society of London, abandoning medicine for applied physics and chemistry, studied the spectrum not only of the sun but of electric sparks as well as luminous gases and vapors. Using a slit through which light was permitted to pass, he found that flames of *different gases and vapors* gave definite, thin lines of brightly colored light (*bright line spectra*) instead of the continuous bands of overlapping colors (*continuous spectrum*) observed when *incandescent solids* such as calcium or carbon were the sources of light. Furthermore, different luminous gases gave different lines; and these were specific for each gas. No two elements gave the same lines. Sodium vapor, for example, gave a yellow line, and potassium a violet line. Here was the beginning of spectrum analysis by means of which gaseous elements and compounds could be identified. A dozen years later a Bavarian optician, Joseph von Fraunhofer, ignorant of the researches of his English contemporary, rediscovered another phenomenon first noticed by Wollaston. Fraunhofer found hundreds of dark lines in the spectrum of sunlight. He drew a map of the solar spectrum and was able to locate upon it as many as three hundred and twenty-four different dark lines. The most conspicuous of these lines or groups of lines he indicated by the letters A, B, C, D, E, F, G, and H, a system of notation still used, together with the more recent and more accurate method of designation by wave lengths.

Here was a tremendously important find, but Fraunhofer was at a loss for an explanation. He felt, it is true, that these dark lines were in some way related to the nature of light but failed to find a reason for their presence. Forty years of effort passed until Stokes, an Englishman, hit upon a clue to the eventual understanding of the dark lines of the Bavarian eyeglass-fitter. He found that when sunlight was made to pass through the vapor of a salt containing sodium, two strong black lines appeared in the light that passed through the sodium vapor. These dark lines were always in the same place and coincided exactly with the positions of the two yellow lines which characterize the bright line spectrum of sodium. In other words, it appeared that sodium vapor had absorbed from the solar spectrum only those colors which it emitted itself and hence left dark lines where the yellow lines would normally appear. For the first time Fraunhofer's dark lines were explicable. Whatever vapors lay between the sun and the observer absorbed their own colored lines and left dark lines.

Then in 1859, Kirchhoff the physicist, working with Robert Bunsen the chemist, devised an instrument called the *spectroscope* for the detecting of elements by their spectrum lines. The light under investigation was passed through a narrow slit. This beam of light which passed through the slit was then made parallel by a lens before it reached a prism which dispersed it into its various colors. The image of the spectrum was sharply defined on a scale in the spectroscope. All of its lines could be located perfectly upon this scale on which were marked the various wave lengths corresponding to the different colors. With the aid of this instrument which Bunsen used to detect elements in his chemical analyses, Kirchhoff examined the spectrum of sunlight passing through various vapors, confirmed the above observations, and discovered a general law. "*A glowing gas*," he said in 1859, "*absorbs from the rays of a hot light source those rays which it itself sends forth.*" Iron, for example, when heated to a vaporous state and placed between an observer and sunlight gives a spectrum containing hundreds of dark lines. Sunlight contains among many other colored lines, the lines of the spectrum of iron since iron vapor is present in the glowing sun. The black lines seen by the observer on earth represent the absorption by iron vapor of its own colored lines.

The implications of this announcement were understood at once by many. Here at last was a key to the composition of the glowing vapors which surrounded the sun. The heavens and the earth had met in that laboratory in Heidelberg. Helmholtz was so excited with the possibilities that he said, "It has excited the admiration and stimulated the fancy of men as hardly any other discovery has done, because it has permitted an insight into worlds that seemed forever veiled to us." He was thinking of the composition of our sun and the myriads of others that dot the vault of heaven. Comte's prophecy was indeed proved wrong. Those dark bands in the sun's spectrum were due to metallic and other vapors through which the light from the boiling sun had to pass on its way down to earth. If the line spectra of a terrestrial element was known, the presence of that element in the sun could also be determined. Only the din raised by the simultaneous announcement of the theory of organic evolution "distracted attention from the newly formed probability of a far more comprehensive scheme of inorganic evolution" opened up by this classic discovery.

Kirchhoff set himself the task of learning the number and location of these dark bands. Iron, calcium, magnesium, barium, copper, strontium, zinc, sodium, nickel, chromium, cadmium, manganese, and several other metals were vaporized in an electric arc and their bright lines studied. The dark lines in the solar spectrum were black fingerprints that told as clear a tale as the bright ones, and even more. By comparing the position of the dark or absorption lines in the solar spectrum, he could pick out those same dark lines which exactly coincided with the bright line spectra of these elements. Kirchhoff was finally able to tell the world that these metals were present in the gaseous envelope of the sun with as much assurance as Bunsen could identify the metals in a terrestrial alloy. The science of celestial chemistry and physics was uttering its cradle cry.

Other scientists took up this alluring work. One by one more elements were found in the sun and stars which were also present on earth. As recently as 1934 the element phosphorus was added to those already found present in the sun. Not a single element was discovered in the stars which was not identified in our sphere. Science now had undeniable proof of the oneness of the material basis of the universe. Men, all life, inanimate matter, the stuff of which the sun, the earth, the stars, and, as we now know, the island universes in the still more remote depths of space, all are fashioned from the same chemical elements.

In 1868 another stirring discovery was announced. Two men independently and almost simultaneously observed a new phenomenon. Pierre Jules César Janssen, son of a French musician, while watching a total solar eclipse at Guntoor in Hindustan, and two months later Norman Lockyer, a clerk in the British War Office, using the spectroscope in his private observatory in England, saw several bright lines in the spectrum of a solar conflagration. One of these, as Lockyer was the first to point out, corresponded with no bright line belonging to any element yet discovered on earth. That was strange news. Was it possible that the sun held hidden in its atmosphere some element which was altogether foreign to man's planet? So, for a time, it seemed. Helium, they called that element (from a Greek word meaning the sun) dug out of a spectrum of light ninety-three million miles away. Twenty-seven years later, however, this new gaseous element was run down on earth by William Ramsay, who discovered it spectroscopically in the mineral cleveite and in mixtures of various terrestrial gases. Since then a total of sixty chemical elements have been identified in the sun, and not a single one of them is a total stranger on earth.

That year 1868 was doubly important in the realm of solar research. In the city of Chicago a son was born to Mary Scranton Browne Hale and William Ellery Hale. This boy, the third of five children of whom the first two had died in infancy, was brought up in comfort. George Ellery Hale might quite naturally have been expected to take over in due time the great hydraulic elevator company built up by his father and become another successful captain of industry.

But Hale's life turned out to be an all too rare phenomenon in a country like ours where the commercial spirit, the profit motive, the pragmatic philosophy, and the none too generous adoration of the pure scientist color the prevailing atmosphere in which most of us live. The elder Hale was partly responsible for his son's career. When at a very early age the boy showed an unusual interest in the microscopic life of rotifers and other infusoria in ponds and ditches, his father bought him a better and more powerful microscope as a reward for a careful study of these organisms. When his curiosity spread to the fossils buried in the limestone rocks that filled the breakwaters of Lake

Michigan and to rock collections in general, the father encouraged him again and nourished this interest. When the lad became enthralled with chemical and physical experiments he was helped in the building of a shop and laboratory in his bedroom. And finally when astronomy captivated him until, impatient to make more rapid progress, it almost engulfed him, he was cautioned by his parents to go a little more slowly and not try "to do things yesterday." His father, son of a New England Congregational minister, was not blinded by the glory of the business world. To him scholarship and reverence for research in pure science were at least equally worth striving for. He did not warp the child's mind.

When Hale was sixteen his father had already financed the building of his first telescope which he set up on his house top. Soon afterward George Hale had definitely chosen the study of the stars as his life work. The observation, listing, and mapping of stars were of course important enough, but "what I wanted," wrote Hale, "was a connected series of experiments leading step by step to the further development of that new branch of science, astrophysics. This was the study of celestial bodies which the spectroscope and the spectrograph had made possible." Lockyer's two books, *Studies in Spectrum Analysis* and *Contributions to Solar Physics*, and Young's book, *The Sun*, held the model of research which he determined to follow. With a simple spectroscope of his own construction, Hale began flame and spark spectrum observations and then turned to the solar spectrum.

Henry A. Rowland, the genius of Johns Hopkins University's department of physics, had invented a ruling machine for making very fine gratings on glass. He took a piece of glass and scratched very fine lines on it with this ruling machine. So delicate was his method that he was able to make as many as twenty thousand uniformly spaced and parallel lines on a single inch of either glass or metal. These extremely fine lines made a grating which acted much more effectively than a glass prism in splitting and spreading ordinary sunlight into its components.

These gratings, the best in the world, enabled science to obtain extremely high dispersions of the solar spectrum for close study. With it Rowland set to work on his classic mapping of the solar spectrum, and with it Hale, too, turned to the unraveling of some of the riddles of the sun.

Science accepted at that time the belief that the sun was surrounded by various layers of nearly transparent gases. Its so-called innermost surface was a very luminous layer called the *photosphere*, of which the light was white, and which would give a continuous spectrum but for a second thin layer surrounding it. This second layer contained luminous vapors of many of the heavier elements which by absorbing some of the colors of the photosphere gave the Fraunhofer dark lines to the observer on earth. This was called the *reversing layer*. The sun was guarded by still a third barrier about eight thousand miles deep — a layer of rarefied gas called the *chromosphere*, composed of vapors of the lighter elements like hydrogen, helium, and calcium, which were capable of floating not only in the atmosphere of the sun but even on its sunbeams. The soft, silvery *corona*, apparently made up of some very rarefied gaseous elements which reflected and scattered sunlight, was the outermost layer of all, stretching out for millions of miles. Both the composition and thickness of these layers were still matters of conjecture.

At Princeton University at the time, Charles A. Young, blessed with eyes extremely sensitive to wave lengths even outside those of the violet and red, after giving up an ambition to become a missionary, had pushed ahead in the field of solar spectroscopy. He was the leader of those American astronomers who after the startling work of Janssen and Lockyer had turned to the spectroscopy of the heavens. Hale met Young in his observatory and was given the opportunity to gaze upon a phenomenon he had never before witnessed and which he was destined to help clarify in the years to come. It was the mystery of solar prominences that definitely decided his career.

On the limb or circumference of the sun Hale saw huge

flamelike areas of light which in some instances, leaping at speeds close to two hundred and fifty miles a second, spread to heights of four hundred thousand miles or half the diameter of the sun. How were they formed? What supplied the fuel for these terrific fires? What effect had they on the earth? These and other similar questions had not yet been answered to the satisfaction of science. "This fiery crucible," thought Hale, "may afford the means of performing experiments and observing phenomena beyond the scope of terrestrial laboratories," where temperatures and pressures approaching those that prevailed in the sun could not be attained. This problem suited his scheme of research, for he could bring into operation the methods of both the physicist and chemist. Here was a subject for a lifetime of investigation.

Solar prominences had been reported by various observers ever since Vassenius in 1733 mentioned some that he had observed while watching an eclipse. One of the clearest of these earlier descriptions was made by Francis Baily, an English stockbroker and amateur astronomer, who on July 8, 1842, was watching at the eyepiece of a telescope mounted on the top floor of the University of Pavia. He was waiting for the moment of a scheduled total solar eclipse. Just as the last rays of the sun were cut off by the oncoming moon, he witnessed a spectacular sight. Baily reported, "The most remarkable circumstance attending the phenomenon was the appearance of three large protuberances apparently emanating from the circumference of the moon. They had the appearance of mountains of prodigious elevation; their color was red tinged with lilac and purple." When the first ray of light after total eclipse was admitted from the sun, they vanished.

Baily and many others attributed the source of these protuberances to the moon, around which they appeared to form against the fainter background of the corona. But from a careful study of the phenomenon made during the solar eclipse of 1860, it was definitely established that these tremendous tongues of luminosity issued not from the moon but from the surface of the sun. They had been drawn and photographed during a number of total solar eclipses but this was not enough, for their outlines were not clear and they could not be studied in detail.

If science was to learn more of these gigantic outbursts of glowing gas, obviously it could not depend upon those rare occasions of one minute or so during the year when total solar eclipses could give fairly clear momentary flashes. No one could hope to be able to watch this phenomenon for more than a single hour of his life, even were it possible for him to witness every total solar eclipse. Some method had to be devised which would enable scientists to observe, delineate, and analyze these solar conflagrations at all times and not merely during those few seconds when the whole face of the sun was completely hidden behind the cold moon.

That blinding glare of the solar furnace had to be overcome to allow men to see the prominences in full sunlight. The problem of " running the flames to earth," as Lockyer had expressed it, had perplexed Hale even while he was pursuing his studies at the Massachusetts Institute of Technology. It had already been partially solved by Janssen during the solar eclipse of 1868. While watching through his spectroscope for the spectrum lines in a prominence at the moment of total eclipse, he noticed that certain lines in the spectrum were so very bright that they might be visible even on any clear day in spite of the glare of the sun. He was so much struck by this idea that he exclaimed, " *Je verrai ces lignes-là en dehors des eclipses.*" And the next morning he actually saw the lines of a single solar prominence and thus showed the way to other investigators. Janssen determined visually the form of a prominence by placing the slit of his spectroscope on various parts of the solar flame. He knew that it was a prominence because of its characteristic bright lines. By moving the slit of his spectroscope he was able to build up an outline of the whole prominence. It resembled a tongue of flame and evidently consisted chiefly of hydrogen since the bright spectrum lines of hydrogen were present.

Later, Huggins, by widening the slit, was able to see an entire solar prominence as if through a window. And Young still later attempted to photograph a prominence in this way, but the image he obtained was so diffuse that he abandoned the use of photography in his study of the prominences. Hale, however, continued to search for an efficient and comprehensive solution of this problem. His goal was a clear photograph of the entire solar circumference with its prominences taken in full daylight. The year before his graduation he hit upon a solution. It was while sitting in the front end of a trolley car rattling through downtown Chicago dreaming of his work that the idea suddenly came to him. He did not know that a similar thought had independently occurred before to several other men who, however, had never converted it into a successfully working apparatus.

The idea was a rather simple one. Said Hale, " Cut a slit one one-hundredth of an inch wide in a piece of cardboard and hold it between the eye and an electric light bulb. Only a small part of the glowing filament can be seen. Oscillate the slit and the whole filament becomes visible. What is needed is some device between the oscillating slit and the eye which will cut off all the light except that due to one element." The principle of his new machine which he called the *spectroheliograph* involves the use of a spectroscope with a fixed second slit through which a single line of calcium or hydrogen (the most abundant elements found in the prominences) is admitted to a photographic plate. The whole spectroscope is moved by a motor so that the first slit crosses the image of the sun. The result is the image of a prominence made in the single bright light of one wave length (monochromatic light) which enables the building up on the photographic plate of countless adjoining images of a narrow spectrum line picked out of the glare of dozens of other elements burning in the sun.

The construction of the apparatus embodying the idea, however, was not so simple as the principle itself. It was not at first an easy matter to " take the sun to bits " in the rays of a single gas, which meant getting a single spectrum line of this gas di-

George Ellery Hale

An active solar prominence, 140,000 miles high photographed at Mt. Wilson Observatory on July 9, 1917 by the K light of calcium. The white disk represents the relative size of the earth. *(Courtesy, G. E. Hale)*

rectly behind the slit and keeping it there exactly in place during the entire time that the spectroscope was moving across the image of the sun while trying to get all of the prominences. Many obstacles had to be overcome. The heat of the sun, for example, distorted the glass mirror of the first apparatus and changed the outline of a prominence into a shapeless, indistinct mass. Stellar photography, in some of its phases, was still a crude affair. Harvard University astronomers were the first to use, in 1850, light-sensitive plates for photographing heavenly bodies. With the introduction of the spectroscope, plates sensitive to various colors had to be developed. When Hale began work on his spectroheliograph, photographic processes had improved greatly, but plates sensitive to the red light of hydrogen were extremely poor. He tried unsuccessfully to render his plates sufficiently sensitive to this color by treating them with the dyes cyanine and alizarine blue. It was not until the twentieth century that plates very sensitive to the red of hydrogen became available.

Hale had now graduated from the Massachusetts Institute of Technology and went back to the Kenwood Observatory near Chicago which he had built with his father's financial aid. With the help of an expert instrument maker, he went to work again on his spectroheliograph. Rowland supplied one of his gratings containing 14,438 lines to the inch, assuring a high solar spectrum dispersion. Martha and William, Hale's younger sister and brother, helped him in those early days to make the first preliminary trials. On May 7, 1891, the first successful photograph of the form of a solar prominence was taken in broad daylight with a simple spectroheliograph. A prominence on the sun's limb appeared clear and well formed.

Hale was overjoyed when the plates were developed. He showed them to his critical friends Young and Rowland. There was no question about the success of his new machine and method. At twenty-three Hale had completed an epochal piece of work. This successful adventure marked the beginning of a fresh attack on solar physics. He was invited by Sir William

Huggins, then President of the British Association for the Advancement of Science, to show his solar photographs at one of its meetings. Among those present at this gathering was Henri Alexandre Deslandres, director of the Astrophysical Observatory at Meudon, just outside of Paris. The French scientist quickly returned home to continue his own researches along the same lines. Within a few months he had repeated and confirmed the achievement of the American. The doors were now wide open; the sun had capitulated by showing its prominences. Science was now ready to photograph not only its profile but the full face of the sun.

After later succeeding with his spectroheliograph in getting on a single photograph all the prominences on the solar rim present at that time, Hale now attempted the monochromatic photography of the entire face or disk of the sun. He had no doubt of the existence there of similar solar blazes. There was no reason why these eruptions or prominences which kept constantly changing should occur only on the rim. These glowing gases were certainly present all over the surface of the sun. It was a much more difficult problem, of course, to get all the prominences on its surface since the spectroheliograph would have to pick out and build up an image of the disk from a few bright lines in that dazzling sea of flame. He succeeded, however, in finding many solar prominences on the sun's surface with the aid of the brightest hydrogen spectrum line.

Hale wanted to learn still more of the nature of the surface of the sun. Knowing the brighter areas of the disk to contain chiefly glowing calcium vapor, he proceeded to photograph the sun using the same principle but this time employed the monochromatic light of the bright violet K or calcium line of its spectrum rather than the red light of hydrogen. On January 12, 1892, the true state of the deep solar surface was revealed. Hale obtained the first photograph of the upper solar surface showing hydrogen prominences and also forms of the brighter calcium areas which lie lower down and nearer to the first layer of the sun's glowing envelope. These calcium clouds were found to be of greater area than had been supposed, appearing sometimes as large bright irregular zones extending clear across the disk. Hale called all these areas *flocculi*. For this work he was honored, when he was only twenty-five years old, with the Janssen medal of the Paris Academy of Sciences which subsequently elected him one of its twelve Foreign Associates.

These photographs also indicated certain black spots known as sunspots which in point of size were relatively insignificant. Around these sunspots there was a massive clustering of calcium vapor which appeared as cumulous clouds. Was there any connection between these flocculi and sunspots? The nature of sunspots had intrigued men since the Chinese had noticed some very large ones with the naked eye in 301 A.D. Galileo, thirteen centuries later, had observed and made numerous drawings of these areas which seemed to freckle the face of the sun. When he first saw them by projecting the solar image on a smooth white surface with the mirrors of his telescope, he refused to accept the general belief of an immaculate and immutable sun, and wrote to a friend, " I suspect this new discovery will be the signal for the funeral of the pseudo-philosophy of immutability of the heavens." He watched the motion and the change of size of these sunspots across the face of the great rotating sphere but could not satisfactorily explain them. Some believed them to be solid opaque objects revolving around the sun near its surface and blotting out the brightness of the sun wherever they happened to be. Others pictured them as made up of great volumes of smoke issuing from tremendous solar volcanoes. Clouds in the solar atmosphere offered another explanation, while to some they were clearly the summits of colossal mountains uncovered and then submerged from time to time by the ebb and flow of gigantic rivers of fiery molten metals and rocks. And it is almost unbelievable to read that Sir William Herschel, one of the world's greatest astronomers, saw them as the cold, opaque body of the sun visible through breaks in the solar atmosphere. Believing the sun to be a cold sphere like our earth, but hidden behind hot gases, he wrote, " I think myself authorized, upon *astronomical principles*, to propose the sun as an inhabitable world."

Hale, too, wondered what these sunspots really were. It seemed a problem, almost outside the ken of science. Yet he agreed with Karl Pearson who laid down the dictum, "Wherever there is the slightest possibility of the human mind to know, there is a legitimate problem of science." Perhaps his improved spectroheliograph might help to find the answer. With the aid of Ferdinand Ellerman, who had joined him in 1892, Hale made thousands of photographs with his spectroheliograph at the Yerkes Observatory of which he was director. These brought out many hitherto unknown details, and finally, at Mt. Wilson, Hale found that the dark hydrogen flocculi often exhibit a definite vortex or whirlpool structure centered in sunspots. Vortex theories of sunspots had been advanced before. Samuel P. Langley in 1873 had drawn pictures of sunspots which seemed to show an inflow of vapor, and he asked, "Are they ragged apertures — the craters as it were of eruptions whence metallic vapors are *being forced up?*" And now Hale obtained actual photographic evidence of high level hydrogen vortices *flowing downward* into these spots. Also by using different lines in which to photograph the disk of the sun, he was able to make out the structure of the hydrogen flocculi around sunspots at different levels above the lowest layer of the sun's envelope. "Thus," explained Hale, "we were able to sound the solar atmosphere through all its depth." He used the spectroheliograph as a ladder through space.

On June 3, 1908, the late Charles E. St. John, who had just joined Hale at Mt. Wilson, made a series of photographs showing a large hydrogen flocculus, which for days had hung on the edge of one of these whirlpool structures in the very act of suddenly flowing into a large spot at a velocity of about four thousand miles per minute. (In comparison, devastating terrestrial tornadoes move at a speed of about two miles per minute.)

Two weeks later, Hale announced that sunspots were regions where "clearly defined whirls point to the existence of cyclonic storms or vortices." For the first time science had been supplied with convincing evidence that sunspots, often larger than the whole earth itself, were the centers of gigantic whirls caused by solar tornadoes. Confirmation of this conclusion soon came from other centers of solar research. Here was another great achievement of this master astrophysicist. What was the complete cause or nature of these solar tornadoes? That was the next question which presented itself.

Before long, through pure deductive reasoning Hale reached the conclusion that sunspots were regions containing colossal magnetic fields. It was a bold theory as no magnetic phenomena had ever been detected outside the earth. But two decades of watching the face of the sun had made it appear at least plausible. Hale outlined this idea in his first paper on *Solar Vortices*, and explained his reasoning more fully in a paper *On the Probable Existence of Magnetic Fields in Sunspots* which he published on October 7, 1908. " In 1876 Rowland discovered that an electrically charged ebonite disk when set in rapid rotation produced a strong magnetic field capable of deflecting a magnetic needle. Hence it occurred to me that if a preponderance of charged particles could be supposed to exist in the rapidly revolving gas of a solar vortex, a magnetic field analagous to that observed by Rowland in the laboratory should be the result." The suggestion by J. J. Thomson, who in 1897 discovered the electron, that the sun might be emitting copious masses of these negatively charged particles as well as ionized gases strengthened his theory.

The method of finding proof for his theory was clear in Hale's mind. He planned to bring the sunspot into his laboratory and examine it with the tools of the experimental physicist. His method harked back to the days when Michael Faraday, searching for the answer to the problem of the nature of light, had examined light in a magnetic field. In 1845, he found that a magnetic field produced a rotation of the plane of polarization of light. This angle of rotation increased with an increase in the strength of the magnet he employed. For almost twenty years Faraday had kept at this problem, and the last experiment set down in his notebook before he died showed that he was still taken up with the examination of the spectrum lines of sodium and lithium vapors between the poles of a magnet.

Faraday died without discovering anything further to clarify the problem. Thirty-four years later Pieter Zeeman of Leyden, using a much more powerful magnet and spectroscope on the two yellow spectral lines of sodium, found that under the magnetic influence the lines widened and were split up into three or more thinner lines. As the strength of the magnet was increased, the distances between the split components grew wider and the light from the two outer components was turned in opposite directions. This magnetic effect on light, now known as the *Zeeman effect*, was a major discovery which helped to strengthen science in its belief that light was of the nature of electromagnetic vibration.

In 1905 the idea had occurred to Hale that he might be able to determine any magnetic condition in or around sunspots by analyzing the widened or split spectrum lines emitted by these regions. The basis of this new line of investigation had actually been laid before but the attack had never been launched. Four years before the Zeeman effect was observed Young had recorded spectrum lines which, although single in other parts of the sun's disk, were double in certain sunspots. But Young had misinterpreted his findings. Instead of ascribing these doublets to possible magnetic fields in sunspots, he thought they were caused by a reversal of certain lines produced by the absorption of a cooler gas above them.

Hale already had considerable terrestrial data with which to compare whatever information he could bring down from sunspots. In 1902, the year he was elected to the National Academy of Sciences, he had made a careful study of the spectrum lines of iron under normal conditions as well as in liquids and in air under high pressures. Later he passed electric sparks between two iron rods supported between the poles of powerful magnets and recorded the various distortions caused by the magnet, similar to those found by Zeeman. The positions, widths, and relative brightness of the various iron lines and their split components were accurately photographed with the best spectrographs at the disposal of science at that time. Would these Zeeman effects coincide line for line with the spectra of sunspots? Were sunspots really areas of magnetic forces?

Now to test his theory. At the top of a mountain just beyond the offices of the solar observatory in Pasadena, California, Hale could see a great tower telescope he had built for solar research. That was where the test was to be made. Up the narrow, winding nine-mile trail of the precipitous face of Mt. Wilson reaching to a height of six thousand feet in the Sierra Madre Range, Hale carried the instruments which he hoped would unravel the mystery of the nature of sunspots. He had come to Pasadena in 1903 to look for a site for a solar observatory. On the summit of Mt. Wilson he had visioned the great observatory he was dreaming to build, so that he might build to dream. And now within that citadel which had become a reality through his efforts and a grant of the Carnegie Institution of Washington, Hale, its director, sat down again to dig for information in the troubled surface of the sun.

For years he tried to obtain evidence of the magnetic condition associated with sunspots. Perhaps it was a question of larger and more sensitive apparatus. Hale built them. From the three-and-a-half-foot spectroscope originally constructed for his early work on spots and prominences to larger ones equipped with powerful Rowland gratings he kept developing his tools of research. His newest outfit was a sixty-foot tower telescope pointing straight to the sun, with mirrors sending the sun's image directly downward. Below its base, dug into the solid rock of the mountain, was a dry well in which was housed a spectrograph thirty feet long. It was a beautiful and powerful device, much better suited for his present purpose than any that he had built before, and as accurate as human ingenuity could then fashion. The driving clock of the coelostat at the top of the tower brought the image of a sunspot upon a slit only three-thousandths of an inch wide and held it there perfectly. At the bottom of the well, a Rowland grating, diamond-scratched with about fourteen thousand lines to the inch, decomposed the light and spread it out into thousands of lines in a spectrum longer than any other then available. The grating was so delicately constructed that the slightest heat would distort it. Hence he used a fan to cool the mirrors which reflected the sunlight, and the cold, dark depth of the well protected the spectrograph from other external heat. Plates sensitized with newly developed chemicals were now available to photograph the red end of the spectrum where the Zeeman effect is most easily detected. Everything in that spectrographic den was painted black. The whole arrangement was a marvel of workmanship. Would this tower telescope and its underground spectrograph give Hale his answer?

Opportunely, just as Hale reached the tower, a large sunspot stood out on the face of the sun as if to tempt him. A few exposures were made at once and there was keen disappointment when they proved negative. The next morning he took a few more pictures with higher dispersion and on June 25, 1908, he gazed for the first time upon the evidence for which the scientific world had been waiting. The iron lines in the sunspot spectrum were split into doublets, triplets, quadruplets, and even more components. The characteristics of the widened lines and their polarization phenomena all agreed line for line, width for width, and angle for angle with the data he had obtained in his laboratory at the foot of the mountain. This data was just what might have been expected for iron if an intense magnetic field were present in sunspot areas where this iron was known to exist (see List of Illustrations).

Hale was thrilled but did not rush headlong into print. He hated sensationalism of any kind, especially in science. "We mean," he announced, "to do all we can to discourage sensationalism, the evils of which have been only too apparent in recent astronomical literature." He was alluding to the pseudoscientific reports of human life on Mars and other such exaggerations.

Hale sent these first photographs to Zeeman. This Hollander was in a better position to evaluate them than any other research worker alive. It was Zeeman's prophetic words uttered more than ten years before that had pointed to the possibility of such an achievement. At that time Zeeman had written, "Further inquiry must also decide as to how far the strong magnetic forces existing, according to some, at the surface of the sun may change its spectrum." Within a few weeks after Zeeman had received Hale's letter, he replied in a letter published in *Nature*. "I can say at once," he reported, "that I have come to the conclusion that Professor Hale has given what appears to be decisive evidence that sunspots are strong magnetic fields."

This classic piece of research settled once and for all the question as to the magnetic nature of sunspots. Sunspots were whirlpools — centers of electromagnetic disturbances, and areas of heat more intense than the dazzling heat of a tungsten filament at its melting point of 3400° C., but much cooler than the rest of the solar surface whose average temperature is about 6000° C. Hale calculated the intensity of the magnetic field of large sunspots and found it to be as high as three thousand gausses as compared with half a gauss which is the strength of the earth's magnetic field. He further pictured sunspots as vortices in which gases were expanding and consequently cooling.

Another discovery made by Hale was that sunspots always occurred in pairs, each member of a pair whirling in a direction opposite to that of the other member. It was known, of course, that the numbers of sunspots which appeared on the sun's surface changed in a definite time cycle. Hale was able to show furthermore that "during the 11.1 years between one epoch of minimum sunspots and the next, all the pairs of sunspots in the northern hemisphere of the sun where they start at high altitudes will have their south poles to the west of their north poles. At the same time the opposite arrangement prevails in the southern hemisphere of the sun. When the succeeding sunspot period sets in, the polarities are reversed in both hemispheres of the sun. Hence the complete sunspot period," said

Hale, "is 22.2 years rather than the heretofore accepted 11.1 year cycle." This reversal of polarity has actually occurred at every sunspot minimum since that time. The reason for this reversal has not completely been explained.

The scientific world was electrified. The achievement was hailed as the opening of a new era in solar research. H. F. Newall, Director of the Solar Physics Observatory of Cambridge, England, said: "An important discovery is often followed by a period of apparent stagnation. But in the case before us, the advance has been rapid and continuous. It is scarcely possible to use restrained language in expressing admiration for the superb mass of observational material systematically gathered and discussed by Hale and his associates."

When Hale discovered the evidence of the presence of magnetic fields in sunspots he had just turned forty. He had already been responsible for an impressive collection of experimental data. During twenty years of research in pure science he had prayed as Huxley had done for "unclouded eyes and freedom from haste, for a quiet and relentless anger against all pretense and all pretentious work and all work left slack and unfinished, for a restlessness whereby he might neither sleep nor accept praise till his observed results equalled his calculated results, or in pious glee discovered and assaulted his error."

But Hale is more than the secluded scientific hermit dwelling in the pure air of some stellar ivory tower. He is far more than a genius in the laboratory. He is a builder of great observatories, a tireless initiator of worldwide cooperative undertakings, and a great leader with a supreme gift for imbuing his associates with his own tremendous enthusiasm for scientific research. He is a rare combination of the intense researcher in pure science and the capable executive. When in 1892 he saw the need for a common meeting ground for physicists and astronomers scattered throughout the earth, he planned an international journal of astrophysics. He made personal visits to all the brightest luminaries in the field. His enthusiasm and personality enlisted the ardent cooperation of those men who became associate editors or contributors to the *Astrophysical Journal.* For more than forty years this publication, established under Hale's editorship, has furthered the development of the physics and chemistry of the heavens.

Hale had determined to make solar research one of the most active fields in science. In 1903 before the National Academy of Sciences he urged the calling of a conference of experts for the purpose of establishing an International Union for Cooperation in Solar Research. He argued that science had not really caught up with the new discoveries in physics and chemistry which were waiting to be applied to the study of celestial bodies, and that solar observers were not adequately equipped with the newest tools of research. A conference of world leaders met the following year at the St. Louis Exposition, and of that brilliant galaxy of astronomers and physicists Hale was chosen chairman. The conference resulted in a permanent international organization of astrophysicists.

Hale was also the driving force behind the erection of the world's largest telescopes. Besides the 40-inch refracting telescope of the Yerkes Observatory on Lake Geneva, sixty miles from Chicago, and the 60-inch reflecting telescope of the Mt. Wilson Observatory, Hale was responsible for the 100-inch reflecting telescope — the world's largest astronomical eye in operation today. This last project had its birth in 1906. In that year John D. Hooker, Los Angeles business man in the role of potentate interested in astronomy, announced his readiness to undertake the cost of all the optical parts of a 100-inch telescope even as Charles T. Yerkes, the Chicago millionaire traction magnate had made possible the Yerkes Observatory. Hooker wanted Southern California to become the home of the largest observatory in the world. His gift did not cover the cost of mounting or housing the huge disk. Half a million dollars was needed to make that dream come true. Hale went after Andrew Carnegie. It was no easy matter to convince the wily little Scotsman that this was really sound philanthropy. Was the telescope actually necessary? Would it be so much better than existing instruments? Why all this scrambling for bigger and bigger fingers to reach the skies? Was there not a limit to the efficacy of Gargantuan telescopes? Was it advisable to spend more millions when the 60-inch telescope on Mt. Wilson had not as yet been taxed to its fullest powers? Hale answered that the contemplated 100-inch concave mirror would be able to collect three times as much light as the 60-inch glass. It would be able to concentrate this light into an image so sharp that the gain in brightness would be fully utilized. A hundred-inch telescope would push the frontiers of our celestial knowledge to farther and ever more distant spaces.

Carnegie capitulated. By a gift of ten million dollars he doubled the endowment of the Carnegie Institution of Washington which he had established in 1902. This made possible the completion of the Hooker 100-inch telescope and continued an era of stellar research at Mt. Wilson unequaled in history. Stimulated by the spirit of Hale, a new attack upon sunspots was launched by W. S. Adams, F. H. Seares, A. H. Joy and many others — a siege which is still in progress for many of the strategic outposts of this stubborn battlefield have by no means surrendered.

Efforts are also being concentrated here on the many problems connected with the elucidation of the nature of other stars in the heavens besides the sun. The surface temperatures, diameters and masses of many stars have already been determined in new and ingenious ways. For example, stellar temperatures are obtained by means of very delicate thermocouples containing wires of bismuth and bismuth alloys one-thousandth of an inch thick which can register electrical currents set up by the heat of a star falling on them as feeble as one-twenty-billionth of one ampere. This tiny current may, in turn, indicate a temperature rise as small as one-half of a millionth of one degree Fahrenheit. Other instruments containing delicate photoelectric cells and vacuum tube amplifiers are even more sensitive for measuring stellar temperatures. When attached to the 100-inch telescope of Mt. Wilson they could make out the heat of a candle shining in New York if there were no intervening air to absorb the light. Among the leaders in this field of stellar temperature measurement are Edison Pettit and Seth B. Nicholson of the staff of Mt. Wilson and Joel Stebbins of the University of Wisconsin. While much data has already been collected in this field it still remains one of the most pressing problems of astrophysics for an accurate knowledge of the temperatures of stars gives a great deal of information as to their nature, age, composition, size, and distance from us.

Various methods have been used to determine the diameters of stars and thus learn something about their sizes. With the invention of the *interferometer* by Albert Abraham Michelson a new era was opened up in this branch of research. Hale had first met this man in 1888 at a meeting in Cleveland where he sat listening breathlessly to his description of the interferometer, the new instrument which this scientist from Annapolis had invented for the purpose of measuring the speed of light. Hale had later watched him at his spinning mirror flashing lights from Mt. Wilson to Mt. San Antonio twenty miles away whence a fixed mirror reflected the lights back enabling him to make the most accurate measurements of the speed of light ever obtained.

Hale invited Michelson to Mt. Wilson, having in mind a broad plan of a study of stellar evolution. It was with Michelson's interferometer that the diameter of a star was first measured directly. The star was Betelgeuse, situated in the Giant's Shoulder of the constellation Orion, and this spot glowing with a red light turned out to be a tremendous giant of a star with a diameter of 215 million million miles as compared with that of the sun which is even less than a mere million miles. So large is this star that it could hold twenty-seven million of our own suns. It is a sphere almost large enough to hold within itself the entire orbit of Mars as it circles our sun. It was indeed an amazing announcement. Later the volumes of many other stars were also determined.

The masses, too, of many stars have been estimated. Knowing the volume of the sun, its distance from the earth and the pull of gravity we can calculate the mass of the sun from Newton's Universal Law of Gravitation. In a somewhat similar way the masses of many double or binary stars have been calculated. Binary stars were first observed by an Italian Jesuit in 1650. They are very common in the firmament and consist of two stars revolving around each other at a relatively small distance. From a knowledge of the orbits of these stars, their periods of revolution and their distance apart it is possible to estimate the masses of the glowing balls of these binaries. Walter S. Adams, present director of Mt. Wilson Observatory, did some history-making work in this field. The dog star Sirius has a faint little companion star circling it. Adams determined the mass of this faint body and obtained a result which was amazing. He found that while its diameter was only about one nineteenth that of the sun, yet its mass was so great that its density or weight per unit volume was four hundred times that of gold and thousands of times greater than that of water whose density is one. (The density of the earth is about 5.5, and that of the sun 1.4.) A tea cup filled with the matter of Sirius would weigh several tons on earth. Such tremendously dense matter had never been obtained on earth. The density of Sirius (and similar stars) has been explained on the basis that it is composed of atoms whose planetary electrons have been thrown off by the extremely high temperature of the star. This resulted in a body composed of atomic nuclei, probably of closely packed neutrons. On the other hand, many other stars have been found to be so thin that the air we breathe is very dense in comparison.

As a result of such measurements and estimates, science has divided the billions of stars into a number of types, and in the attempt to form some conception of the evolution of stars has pictured the life cycle of a star somewhat as follows. In early infancy the star is gigantic in volume. Unlike the animate world, stars in their embryonic form are tremendously larger than in their fully matured state. These *giant stars* are composed of very rarefied gases. Betelgeuse is such a star. Its density is two hundred times less than that of our atmosphere. It shines with a red hue and its surface temperature is comparatively low, about 2500° C. As these diffuse babies grow up their gases condense, they become hotter and smaller. We have now the white or bluish-white stars. Such a star is Rigel on the foot of Orion. It is an extremely bright star, thirteen thousand times brighter than our sun, and its surface temperature is as high as 30,000° C. These hottest stars have been called death stars because their radiation would destroy life on earth if it were not for the layer of ozone above our atmosphere which screens us from their rays.

Billions of years elapse and the star may pass beyond its maturity and start on its downward course of life. It becomes still smaller and cools off. It is now a yellow star in middle age whose surface temperature is about 6000° C. Such a star is our sun, a declining star which has already passed its greatest glory. More billions of years pass and the star is now a *dwarf star* extremely tiny and dense, glowing with a red light with a temperature of perhaps 2000° C. Finally may come senility, dimness, coldness, and death.

This is a very beautiful picture of the life history of stars. But it is an idealized picture with many inconsistencies. For example, some of the stars in binaries are born dwarfs rather than giants. It will take hundreds of years of watching the skies to give us much clearer and truer concepts of this perplexing phenomenon of stellar birth, existence and death.

In 1914, when the shot at Sarajevo set the world ablaze and stopped most of the work in pure science abroad, Hale redoubled his efforts to keep astrophysical research going at top speed here in America. In the solitude of his mountain retreat he also pondered over the dangers of that bloody international strife. He could see the United States being drawn into its whirlpool. Germany with marvelous skill was drafting her scientific genius upon which she depended for a speedy victory. England, on the other hand, was in the meantime losing some of her great scientists in the trenches. Many of her scientists, to be sure, were aiding the government in a multiplicity of ways, but she had not as yet taken complete steps to organize a government department of scientific research. This mistake of England was not to be repeated in America.

Hale tried to arouse the National Academy of Sciences into action of this kind. There was some opposition at first chiefly from those men of science who believed that " scientific genius cannot be organized. True research," they contended, " is the function only of creative imagination. No amount of organization or special stimulation or support of research can produce more or better science than the scientific genius will produce anyway." Finally, however, on April 16, 1916, the Academy voted to offer its services in the interest of national preparedness. President Wilson accepted the offer and an organizing committee was chosen headed by Hale. This committee recommended " that there be formed a National Research Council to bring into cooperation all agencies that will promote the national security and welfare." This was a year before America entered the World War. Soon afterwards Hale organized subcommittees. A. A. Noyes was put in charge of research in nitric acid and other important chemicals used in warfare. Millikan was set to work on problems of physics. Michelson was developing a new range finder for guns. Simon Flexner headed a group on preventive medicine. John J. Abel was called from Johns Hopkins to supervise research on toxicity of canned foods; the crime of the Spanish American War was not to be repeated. Hale himself accompanied William H. Welch, president of the Academy, on a trip to Europe to interview the men engaged in similar work among the Allies. They found J. J. Thomson, Ernest Rutherford, William Bragg, Ernest Starling, and other famous English scientists busy not with electrons, protons, ions, and hormones but with the applications of scientific discovery and method to modern warfare. In France they met Painlevé, Perrin and scores of others immersed in everything but pure science. The Duc de Broglie was absorbed with naval problems, and Count de la Baume Pluvinel showed them his newly invented device for removing shrapnel from the bodies of wounded soldiers.

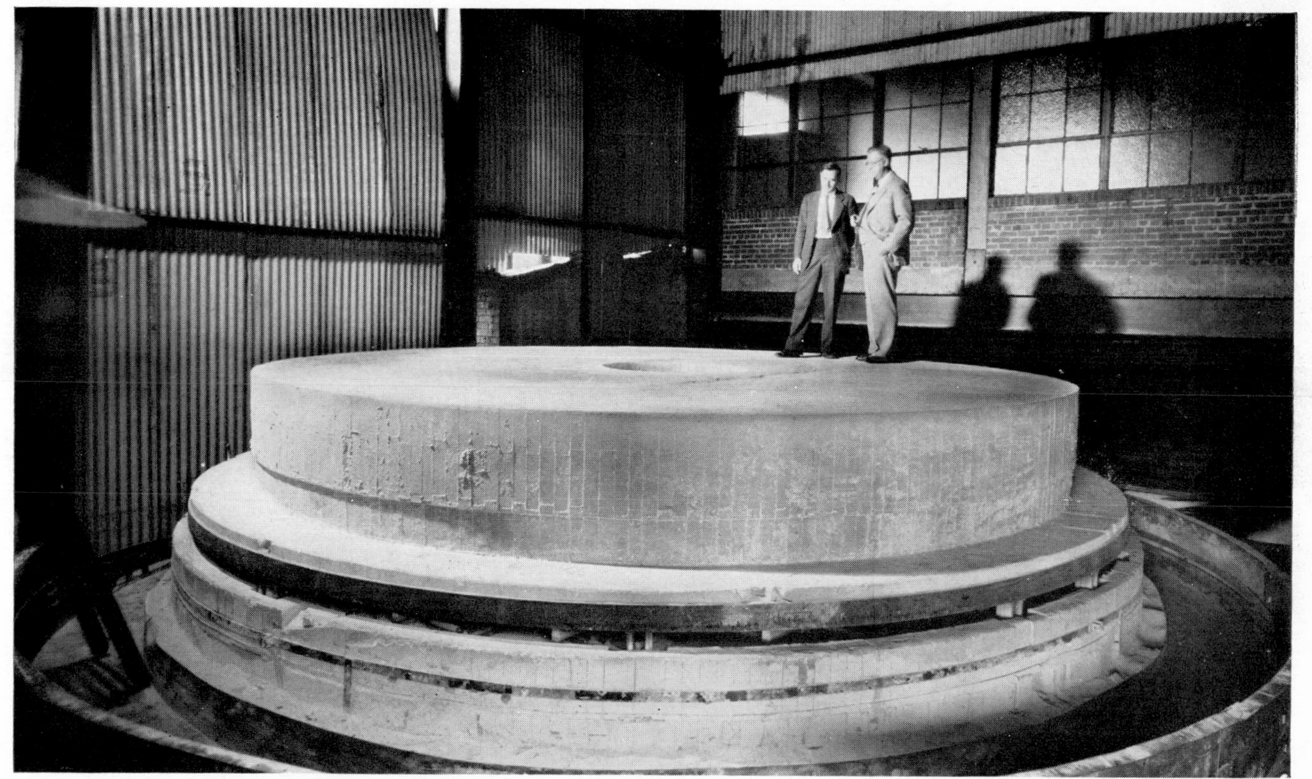

The first of two huge glass mirror disks cast by the Corning Glass Works of New York for the new 200-inch telescope to be erected on the top of Palomar Peak in California.

Photograph of a pair of sunspots taken at Mt. Wilson Observatory.
(Courtesy, G. E. Hale)

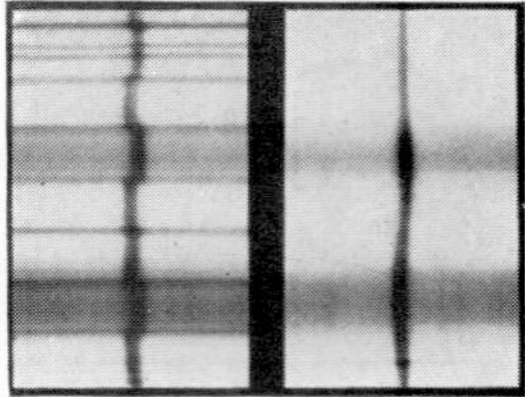

Widening and splitting of a spectrum line of iron by the magnetic field of the sunspot in which the iron was present.

All through the war Hale remained in Washington directing the National Research Council. When the Armistice was declared he wanted to save this newly created branch of the National Academy for peacetime work, and finally prevailed upon the President of the United States to issue an executive order, on May 11, 1918, perpetuating it for the purpose of stimulating research in the mathematical, physical, and biological sciences. That same year he went as chairman of an American delegation to assist in London and Paris in organizing the International Research Council, embracing at first members of only twelve countries. Most of the bitter feelings aroused and nourished during the war gradually dissolved, so that today forty countries are represented among its members. In his international work, Hale still finds reasons to be reminded, however, that chauvinism and other human frailties are often more powerful than the relentless search for truth.

Between the upper millstone of laboratory work and the nether one of innumerable organization details and delicate financial quests, Hale was gradually being crushed. The stress of work, his boyhood eagerness to get big things done as soon as possible, and his anxiety to justify by scientific discovery some of the expensive projects he had undertaken brought his nerves almost to the breaking point for the third time.

In 1921 Hale had to leave Mt. Wilson and get away to drive out of his head all thoughts of immediate work. It was a terrific struggle. No one who has not experienced being caught in the stream of scientific research to be suddenly shunted off in a side eddy and left there to stagnate could feel his misery at that moment. He thought he might later come back, but finally, in the hope that complete relief from the responsibilities of the Mt. Wilson Observatory might enable him to avoid another breakdown, he resigned its directorship and was succeeded by Walter S. Adams, member of the famous Adams family of New England, and a brilliant contributor in the field of stellar research.

As his health improved Hale resumed scientific investigations. On the outskirts of Pasadena facing the northern boundary of the grounds of the famous Huntington Library, a research organization in the humanities for which Hale was largely responsible, he erected a new solar laboratory. It was built outside his home as a branch of the Mt. Wilson Observatory. Here he decided to work quietly by himself, even as his illustrious predecessor Tycho Brahe, the Danish astronomer, had built himself *Uraniborg* (Castle of Heaven) on a little island between Denmark and Sweden, where for more than twenty years he carried on researches. Night work was out of the question for Hale. He had his observatory equipped with a vertical coelostat telescope, spectroheliograph, and a new seventy-five-foot spectrograph carefully housed in a seventy-five foot well. Here in his most modern observatory he has worked alone watching the sun that still held him spellbound, developing the spectrohelioscope and digging again into the question asked back in 1891, " Is the sun, too, a magnet like the earth? And if it is, why? "

Hale and his associates had already found evidence that the sun really was a huge magnet with its magnetic north and south poles close to its poles of rotation. It was like the earth in this respect. But because of the high temperature of the sun, he reasoned that this magnetism was not like that of the earth, since a glowing object such as a red hot steel bar could not be permanently magnetized. His researches now led him to the belief that the cause of the sun's magnetism might be its axial rotation. This was quite different from that of the earth, which being a solid, had every part of its surface making one complete rotation in the same period of twenty-four hours. The sun, on the other hand, was not a solid. It is probably somewhat liquid at its core and gaseous outside of this central area. Hence one part of its surface could move faster than another part. Not all of its surface took the same time to make one complete rotation around its axis. The surface near the sun's poles rotated once every thirty-one days while areas on the sun's equator moved at the rate of one complete rotation every twenty-five days. It might be this uneven movement causing friction that is the cause of its magnetism. But Hale is still far from satisfied with this theory, and he is still at work on this problem.

Evershed, a young Englishman who down in faraway India, at Kodaikanal Observatory, was among the first to obtain illuminating results in research on solar prominences, had remarked, " We have seen thousands of prominences but we cannot say, 'This caused it and thus it began, developed and ended.' " That was a legitimate complaint, and Hale wanted to answer it. This would necessitate the watching of solar phenomena every minute of the twenty-four hour day, and this in turn meant observatories in all parts of the globe. At any particular observatory the sun may not be visible when an important prominence begins to form. Cooperation is necessary. The sun must never be allowed to set on all spectroheliographs at once. " Suppose," said Hale, " the observer at Greenwich notices the beginning of an eruption not long before sunset. In the United States the sun stands high and the phenomenon may be followed by one or more spectrohelioscopes between Boston and Pasadena." (The spectrohelioscope was a modification of his spectroheliograph, which Hale invented in 1924 to enable scientists to observe the solar atmosphere directly and continuously instead of photographically.) A chain of spectrohelioscopes stationed around the world would solve the problem.

Accordingly a score of coelostat telescopes and spectrohelioscopes were constructed after his design and mounted at stations in Apia, Samoa; Watherhoo, Australia; Nanking, China; Kodaikanal, South India; Huancayo, Peru; Greenwich and Cambridge, England; Florence, Italy; Beirut, Syria; Athens, Greece; Zurich, Switzerland; and Cambridge, Poughkeepsie, Philadelphia, Columbus, Williams Bay, Chicago, Vermillion, Los Angeles and Pasadena. Here well trained men will never close their eyes while the sun sheds light into their telescopes. Perhaps this undertaking will bring us closer to a complete understanding of such still unsolved problems as the cause and nature of solar spots, prominences, magnetism, heat and composition, as well as their relation to auroras, terrestrial magnetism and the fading of radio signals.

Hale also expressed the hope that " the time will come when the striking phenomena which occur in the sun will be recorded with a suitable moving-picture machine attachment for more careful study." Three years later this hope was fulfilled when R. M. Petrie and R. R. McMath, amateur astronomers working in 1934 at the Observatory of the University of Michigan, obtained the first successful results with their *spectroheliocinematograph.* The spectroheliograph attached to a telescope and operating on moving-picture principles caught a great explosion on the sun which occurred on June 19, 1934. Their completed films showed a prominence as a dark, wedge-shaped cloud twenty-five thousand miles long shoot out of the sun's chromosphere at the speed of fifteen hundred miles a minute, and after fifteen minutes disappear, leaving a long dark streamer which seemed to be sucked back into the sunspot near which the bomb exploded.

This fine beginning had been made by two amateur astronomers. This was not an isolated instance in the history of astronomy. Hale knew it, and one of his absorbing interests has been the encouragement of amateur astronomers. He knew that from the ranks of amateur astronomers have come many major discoveries. He feels certain that there are others ready to join Herschel, the music teacher; Tycho Brahe, the law student; Schwabe, the Dessau pharmacist; E. E. Barnard, the Nashville photographer who made a classic study of the Milky Way and discovered the fifth satellite of Jupiter; S. W. Burnham, the Chicago court stenographer who reported more than six hundred double stars with a six-inch telescope mounted in his back yard; Lewis M. Rutherfurd, the New York lawyer who proved that the position of stars could be determined more accurately on photographic plates than by the eye; Huggins, the self taught amateur of Upper Tulsa Hill; and Lord Rosse; all of whom took up astronomy for pure love of the subject and made lasting contributions in this field.

Today, in the evening of his life after a half century of devotion to pure science, with his health impaired but his faculties still as alert as ever, Hale has not turned to the scientific mysticism which had ensnared other eminent scientists. He will have none of it, for he feels it upsets the real notion of the meaning of science and thus blocks the road to scientific advance. Instead he is still occupied with reaching out farther into limitless space with new instruments. Eight centuries ago the Arab, El Karakat, built a great astronomical observatory at Cairo, and after years of watching the heavens exclaimed, " How minute are our instruments in comparison with the celestial universe! " That plaint has echoed down the centuries and man's efforts to build mightier telescopes have not relaxed. The two-and-a-quarter-inch lens of Galileo's telescope has already been expanded to the 100-inch disk of the Mt. Wilson Observatory. The telescope of the Italian had increased the light-gathering area of the astronomer's eye eightyfold and exposed half a million stars instead of a mere six thousand. The 100-inch mirror increased the light-gathering area to about two hundred thousand times that of the naked eye and made possible the photography of billions of more stars. But man is still partially blind to the heavens. He is still hampered by insufficient light, which larger telescopes might be able to remedy.

Like Goethe, Hale cried for " more light." He looked into the possibilities of more powerful telescopes. His lifetime of experience convinced him that in spite of certain limitations, such as the changing density of the atmosphere which interfered with the sharpness of stellar images, still larger instruments would be practical. He felt it was safe to advance by a single stupendous leap to a 200-inch telescope — a colossal instrument which would penetrate fully three times deeper into the seemingly limitless space around us and open for investigation an unexplored sphere of about thirty times the volume of that hitherto sounded. One hundred million new nebulae, to say the least, should be brought into the range of astronomers for the first time, allowing for the testing of perplexing theories. Hale set to work on some of the construction problems. Light from the heavens was to fall on a 200-inch concave (paraboloidal) mirror. All the light collected by this concave mirror would then be concentrated by reflecting it to a point about fifty-five feet away at the other end of a huge tube. At this point observations could be made by an astronomer, or a smaller convex mirror could throw this light back through a hole in the 200-inch disk to the eyepiece or to a photographic plate. The moving parts of this celestial eye would weigh hundreds of tons, but this did not disturb Hale, who realized that " from an engineering standpoint our telescopes are small in comparison with modern battleships and bridges."

Hale discussed this project in *Scribner's,* and soon after, the International Education Board made a grant to the California Institute of Technology for the construction of the 200-inch mirror, mounting, buildings, and all the equipment of a new and complete astrophysical observatory. Hale was chosen chairman of the observatory council in charge of the great project, and the work is now well under way. In 1934, after three years of only partially successful experimenting with quartz mirrors by the General Electric Company, the council commissioned the Corning Glass Works of New York to pour a 20-ton pyrex pancake twenty inches thick and nearly seventeen feet in diameter from which the new mirror would eventually be ground. (The mirror for the 100-inch telescope at Mt. Wilson had been poured in a French glass factory in the Forest of St. Gobain which was later destroyed during the World War by enemy artillery.)

After testing various new devices of casting and annealing, a 200-inch disk of glass was poured late in 1934, and after an annealing period of almost a year it was shipped to the optical and astrophysical shops of the California Institute of Technology. Here the work of grinding and polishing down the immense piece of glass to an accuracy of one-millionth of an inch has already started. When this is completed it will receive a one-one-hundredth-thousandth of an inch film of pure aluminum as the reflecting surface. The 100-inch and most other mirrors were coated with a layer of silver. Aluminum has two advantages over silver. It does not tarnish as easily and reflects light of even smaller wave length thus enabling astronomers to extend their vision of stellar radiation in the region of wave lengths smaller than that of violet light.

On the table top of Palomar Peak, 6136 feet high and forty-five miles northeast of San Diego, will eventually soar (probably in 1940) the largest astronomical observatory in the world, housing the new 200-inch reflector telescope. This tremendous achievement will stand as a monument to the vision and efforts of one scientist. It would be a fitting tribute to George Ellery Hale to dedicate this magnificent modern temple of the stars to this great " man of the mountain."

CHAPTER TWELVE

WEATHER

LONG-RANGE FORECASTING—IS IT A CHIMERA?

An account of the researches of Charles G. Abbot and Andrew E. Douglass

TO MOST PEOPLE, including scientists, long-range weather forecasting still belongs in the category of ancient astrology and medieval alchemy — to be counted among the innumerable fads and follies which have blurred the pages of the history of science since the Babylonians and Chaldeans turned their versatile minds to prognostication.

To be sure, weather almanacs are still sold by the tens of thousands throughout the world. These almanacs are the heritage of the centuries when men predicted weather years in advance by means of dubious mathematical data derived from planetary and other celestial motions. They are a curious hangover from the days when quacks and charlatans, with a sprinkling of men of science, were deluded by coincidences of certain natural phenomena which seemed to point to exact formulas of weather prediction. Even the great biologist Lamarck believed firmly in the control of weather conditions by the movements of the moon. For ten years beginning with the opening of the last century, he issued annual volumes of predictions based on this idea. And when Patrick Murphy prophesied twelve months in advance that January 20, 1838, would witness " probably the lowest degree of winter temperature," and it actually turned out to be the coldest day in generations, weather prediction by almanacs jumped into the full glare of publicity. *Murphy's Winter* prophecy netted this Englishman thousands of dollars in the mad scramble to buy his magic almanacs. Even level-headed men found themselves believing in this weather formula. They recalled that throughout the centuries more than one scientific theory or formula had been laughed off the stage, to return soon after to the company of respectable science. Was this another case?

The search for some accurate means of learning the nature of the weather to come continued. With the twentieth century came a completely novel attack upon this problem of finding some scientific formula with which to predict weather months in advance. Three researches in widely separated sections of this country appeared. The first of these was begun by Charles Greeley Abbot in his early years at the Smithsonian Institution of Washington, D. C. Abbot was descended from Yorkshire folk who came over from England in 1642. His father, already sixty when the boy was born, owned a large farm in Wilton, New Hampshire, which he hoped his sons might take over when he was no longer able to care for it himself. Charles Abbot was not altogether studious, but neither was he enamored of the monotony of the farm. After completing all courses of study available in the neighborhood school he was sent to Andover. In 1890 while on his first trip to Boston with some of his friends who had come to take college entrance examinations, Charles Greeley Abbot also took the examinations for Boston Tech. He had not really planned to take them, but entered them as a lark. When he learned that he had passed without conditions, his sister, a schoolteacher, lent him funds in addition to those obtained by his parents from the sale of some Western land, and Charles was launched on a college career.

As a boy, Abbot had been fond of mechanical pursuits. His first preference was naturally for mechanical engineering. But since his best friends took the chemical engineering course, Abbot did the same, until at the recommendation of Professor Arthur A. Noyes he changed over to the course in physics, in which he showed unusual ability. Two years later, while engaged in a piece of research in the basement of the college, he was interrupted by an unexpected visitor. There in high hat and frock coat stood the eminent secretary of the Smithsonian Institution, Samuel Pierpont Langley. Langley was the man who was getting plenty of unwanted publicity for his attempt to make a heavier-than-air flying machine. Abbot had been recommended by the college authorities to Langley, who had now come to look him over before deciding whether to ask him to be assistant at the Smithsonian Astrophysical Observatory. The interview was satisfactory, and a few days later Abbot received a telegram to report to Washington at once.

When Abbot reached the office of the Smithsonian Institution, Langley had already left for Europe on some scientific mission. The newcomer soon after found himself acting in charge of the Astrophysical Laboratory. This was in 1895. Langley himself in 1881 at a station on Mt. Whitney had started mapping the spectrum of the invisible infrared portion of the sun's radiation. He had started these classic experiments for the determination of the heating effects of the solar spectrum beyond the red, using an instrument of his own invention. This device, which he called the *bolometer*, was an accurate measurer of radiant energy rather than merely an indicator of heat. The heart of this instrument is a thin blackened thread of platinum which on being exposed to the sun absorbs heat and produces tiny electrical currents proportional to the amount of heat falling upon it. These electrical currents may indicate changes of temperature as small as one-millionth of one degree. By exploring the various parts of the infrared region of the solar spectrum with the bolometer, Langley was able within the last five years of the nineteenth century to map 740 different areas of heat or absorption lines. These were recorded photographically.

As early as 1884, Langley had expressed his reason for his intense interest in solar radiation measurements. "If the observation," he wrote, "of the amount of heat the sun sends the earth is among the most difficult in astronomical physics, it may also be termed the fundamental problem of meteorology or the science of the weather." Nearly all the phenomena of the weather would become predictable if we knew both the original quantity and kind of this heat; how it affects the constituents of the atmosphere on its passage earthward; how much of it reaches the soil; how, through the aid of the atmosphere which acts as a blanket it controls the surface temperature of the earth, and how, in diminished quantities, it is finally returned to outer space. Langley regarded observations of the sun as the key to the secret of long-range weather forecasting. At the same time, he realized the extreme difficulty of determining the amount of the sun's radiation as it left its source and before it was absorbed, dissipated, and otherwise attacked and changed especially by the atmosphere on its way down. For it reached the earth as a sort of skimmed radiation hardly recognizable from its appearance when it started on its obstacle race of ninety-three million miles.

Yet Langley did attempt to determine the total amount of solar heat just before it entered the earth's atmosphere usually termed the *solar constant* of radiation. This was to include not only what he had already done in the case of the infrared but also the rest of the solar radiation. As long ago as 1838, Pouillet, a French scientist, had estimated this figure and found it to be equal to 1.7633 calories per square centimeter per minute. This meant that a layer of water one centimeter deep, exposed just above the earth's atmosphere and directly under the sun, absorbing all its radiation yet giving out none in exchange, would warm up at the rate of 1.7633° C. each minute. Pouillet's figure needed checking, for since his time great strides had been made in our knowledge of the many kinds of radiation given off by the sun, absorption effects of the atmosphere, and in the development of more delicate measuring instruments. Langley first made a careful study of the effect of various atmospheres on many solar rays of differing wave lengths. From measurements made both at a valley station and from an observatory 12,000 feet up Mt. Whitney, California, he made new determinations of the solar constant. He found it to be equal to approximately two calories per square centimeter per minute, a figure which for twenty years was accepted as the most accurate yet obtained. It was almost twice the value of the French pioneer's.

Abbot, in 1902, continued this elaborate series of solar radiation measurements, and obtained different results from those of Langley, whose figure was too high. In addition, the following year, while making observations at Washington, Abbot obtained data which apparently showed a sudden fall in the solar radiation of about ten per cent below the usual figures. This low solar output seemed to continue for a long while. He might have dismissed this observation as an unusual occurrence due to some unusual condition of the earth's atmosphere which had interfered with our proper heat reception. In fact, he was on the point of doing so. But fortunately, on reconsideration, he set to work to compare the observed temperatures of eighty-nine weather stations distributed over the north temperate zone with the mean temperatures of these same stations for many previous years. What astonished him was that the reports seemed to confirm the drop in solar heat which he had found in Washington, for these stations indicated an average fall in temperature of 2° C. The temperatures continued low during the remainder of the year. Could this have been merely a coincidence? Exceptions to normal phenomena are often most valuable. Abbot talked the matter over with Langley. They had both vaguely suspected such a coincidence before, and now they were sure it was significant. In June, 1904, they announced this apparent evidence that the sun was a variable star — that its radiation was subject to important variations. This was interesting enough, but the scientific world was even more surprised to read that the Smithsonian workers were bold enough to suggest that changes in terrestrial temperatures, hence the weather on earth, were definitely related to this variability in solar radiation.

Had Abbot actually discovered something which would usher in a new era in weather forecasting? Had he really stumbled over a formula which would clearly indicate how the sun was pulling the many strings which controlled weather? Were accurate determinations of the variations in the daily radiation of the sun which bathed the earth all that was necessary? Would meteorologists be able now for the first time to give to the farmer and to the power and fuel magnates of the world, who measured fractions of inches of rainfall and fractions of temperature drops in millions of dollars, a trustworthy long-range weather forecast?

Abbot was too solemn a scientist to get hastily excited and raise high hopes. He was, however, tremendously aroused. This hitherto undiscovered phenomenon spurred him on to more than thirty years of further efforts to find the secret of long-range weather forecasting. He made no optimistic promises. Langley, too, was very cautious. " While we are far," he wrote, " from looking forward to foretelling by such means the remoter changes of weather which affect the harvests, still it is hardly too much to say that *we appear to begin to move in that direction*."

Abbot and his associates set to work to get further data. In 1910 he invented the silver disk pyrheliometer for more accurate daily measurements of the solar constant. This was a highly improved form of a crude device first used by Pouillet. Abbot's instrument consisted of a thermometer inserted into a hole in a silver disk, the surface of which was blackened to absorb all of the solar heat. This silver disk pyrheliometer was pointed directly toward the sun, and for one hundred seconds the solar beam was permitted to enter its tube and fall at right angles on the disk. The rise of temperature during the exposure of the disk to the sun, plus the average fall of temperature in the two intervals before and after it, gave the corrected heat effect. With this device, Abbot made daily solar measurements in Washington. George E. Hale's invitation to come to Mt. Wilson to make further measurements found Abbot soon after on the mountain top getting closer to the sun's heat. Langley had died in 1906, and Abbot, now director of the Smithsonian Institution, redoubled his efforts.

Abbot soon realized that he ought to check his data with observations made at a second station in the clear rare atmosphere of some peak widely separated from Mt. Wilson. Mexico was at that time out of the question for revolutions were disrupting that country. In 1911 he packed up and went to faraway Algeria to assure himself that the supposedly solar variations he was getting at Mt. Wilson were not due to local atmospheric disturbances. Thirty boxes of his instruments arrived at Bassour, a station was set up, and through occasional terrific wind storms, heavy rains, and the annoyance of scorpions and centipedes, Abbot, assisted by Anders Angström of Upsala, Sweden, trailed the sun for ten cruel months. They would have stayed longer, but in Alaska, Mt. Katmai awoke from its long sleep and with one terrific eruption threw up enough volcanic ash to make the sky extremely hazy for many months even over Algeria, more than half way around the world. Nevertheless, the Algerian results seemed to confirm those of Mt. Wilson as indicating the variability of the sun's heat.

By 1913, Abbot had made enough measurements to issue a statement confirming his belief in the correlation between solar heat variation and terrestrial weather; that is, that as the sun's radiation decreased, the earth's temperature fell. It was met with much criticism. The strongest argument against the validity of his data was the doubtful nature of the role played by the atmosphere in absorbing part of the sun's radiation. It was contended by some that he had so underestimated the atmospheric absorption that the true solar constant was twice as high as he had reported. This matter had to be cleared up. In the following year, his colleague at Omaha, Nebraska, raised automatic recording pyrheliometers in sounding balloons almost to the top of the atmosphere. The records of the instruments retrieved after these high flights confirmed the accuracy of Abbot's value of the solar constant, and pointed definitely to the conclusion that the atmospheric absorption of radiation was measured with substantial accuracy from mountain peaks. Abbot, of course, realized that volcanic and other dust in the atmosphere interfered with the transmission of the sun's radiation by lowering the amount of this radiation that got through to the earth. This factor was therefore of some importance in determining the weather on earth. Abbot's work was recognized in 1915 by his election to the National Academy of Sciences. In the following year he was named the Rumford medalist of the American Academy of Arts and Sciences.

Ten years had now passed since Abbot had first noticed that strange apparent relation between the variation of the sun's radiation and earth temperatures. Nothing startling had as yet been proved to the satisfaction of meteorologists. Weather prediction in the United States had not advanced by any radical steps since the Federal Meteorological Service was organized in 1870 as part of the United States Signal Corps. The purpose of this Service was to issue storm warnings on the Great Lakes and the long fringe of the country's seacoast. It is true that the Chief Signal Officer, nicknamed "Old Probabilities," had changed his daily "probabilities" first to weather "indications" and finally in 1889 to weather "forecasts," but the methods of predicting day-by-day weather were substantially the same.

The official daily forecasts are still based on an analysis of various weather factors such as air pressure, temperature range, wind velocity and direction, sky condition, and the amount of rain or snowfall. Three hundred regular observation stations and 1700 other volunteer weather stations distributed throughout the United States, Alaska, and the West Indies report by radio or telegraph every morning and evening to the Weather Bureau in Washington. These data are then placed upon a map of the United States. (The first daily weather chart was issued as early as 1820 in Europe.) Regions of high atmospheric pressure, or "highs," are areas where the air is cool and dry and hence heavy, since dry, cool air is heavier than moist, warm air. The weather here will be clear and cool. Winds are found normally to rotate clockwise about high pressure centers and the wind movements are outward from the center of these *highs*. Regions of low atmospheric pressure or "lows" show different conditions. Here the air is warm, contains considerable moisture, and is hence lighter than normal air, since water vapor is lighter than air. As this lighter air moves upward it is cooled by expansion and this cooling results in the condensation of its moisture into rain.

This region is, therefore, usually warm, and cloudy if not rainy. Here winds normally rotate counterclockwise and the wind movements are inward toward the centers of these *lows*.

These regions of *highs* and *lows* are charted on the maps. When maps of several successive days are examined it is found that these *highs* and *lows* move eastward across the country at a fairly definite speed (about six hundred miles a day). Higher speeds govern in winter than in summer. They also follow more or less definite paths. Hence it is a rather simple matter to fore-

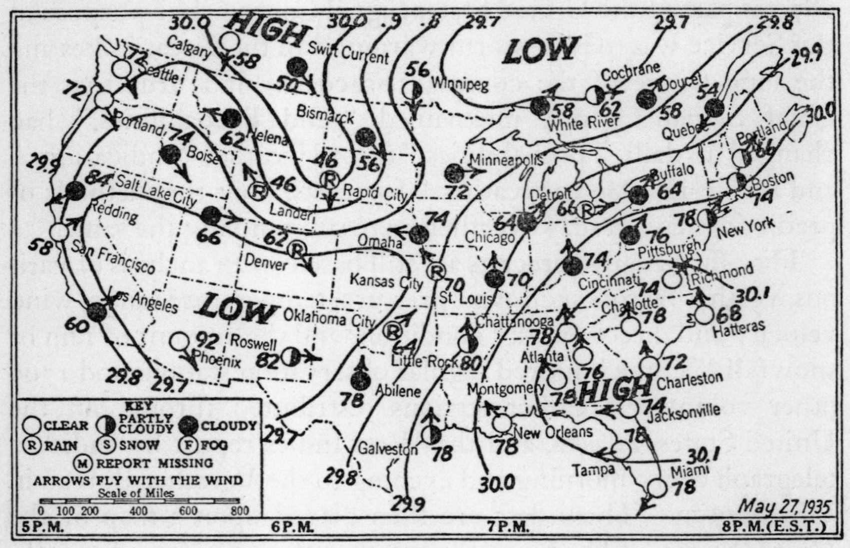

FIG. 27

A daily weather map showing regions of *highs* and *lows* as well as other factors which help to predict weather.

tell whether any particular region will be one of low or high pressure the following day or two. It has been found that *highs* that follow a *low* usually indicate clearing weather. *Lows* that follow a *high* usually indicate unsettled weather. Unless unexpected changes of the various weather factors take place, the weather man can therefore predict with a high degree of accuracy the weather of the next thirty-six hours. Forecasts are made at Chicago, New Orleans, Denver, San Francisco, and Washington.

Charles Greeley Abbot

Andrew Ellicott Douglass

This is the method used for day-by-day weather forecasting. But the world was still waiting, hoping for the day when long-range weather forecasting would be more than wild guesses bolstered up by almanacs, goosebones, the weather acumen of the groundhog, the position of the horns of the new moon, the thickness of the furs of animals and the feathers of birds, and by all manner of beliefs such as that attributed to the Chaldeans that "when it thunders on the day of the moon's disappearance crops will prosper." Abbot still had faith that he was on the right track. But he was apparently in rather thin company.

Then out of the Argentine came trickling the news of experiments and data that were to strengthen the findings of Abbot. The news first reached the notice of Abbot in 1917 in the form of a letter. "I enclose herewith," read the note, "a copy of a paper in which are given the results of a comparison of Dr. Abbot's solar measurements with temperature and pressure in various parts of the world." Abbot was accustomed to receiving all sorts of queer schemes for solving many of the most difficult scientific problems by people whose lack of scientific sense was more than counterbalanced by a profuse imagination. But this paper was evidently the work of a careful observer. It consisted of a masterly examination of the effects of short period variations of solar radiation on the earth's atmospheric temperatures and pressures, and Abbot was so impressed with its value that he recommended its immediate publication "with all its figures and graphs" by the Smithsonian Institution.

The author of this paper which seemed to establish an undeniable relationship between solar radiation variations and temperature and pressure conditions throughout the world was Henry Helm Clayton, then director of the forecasting department of the Argentine Meteorological Office. At the time when he sent his first paper to the Smithsonian Institution, Clayton was already fifty-six years old. He was a veteran meteorologist, connected with weather work ever since he was seventeen, when a severe attack of peritonitis had sent him into the Tennessee mountains in search of health. For four years the invalid occupied himself with weather observations, making the first systematic study of the rainfall of this region. His father, a physician, was mayor of Murfreesboro, Tennessee. Henry Clayton's schooling had been largely in the usual literary and classical studies, with no science except a few months' instruction in elementary physics and physiology taught without any laboratory work or illustrative material. But cherishing the hope of bringing the possibility of long-range weather forecasting nearer to man, he had undertaken a thorough program of reading the literature of weather and astronomy.

At twenty-three, Clayton had published an article in the *American Meteorological Journal* which led to his appointment as student assistant at the astronomical observatory of the University of Michigan. Then for fifteen years he was connected with the Blue Hill Meteorological Observatory of Harvard College at Hyde Park, Massachusetts, where he carried on an extended study of clouds and their relation to the general circulation of the upper atmosphere. He invented a box kite for raising meteorological instruments to high altitudes, joined an international undertaking which conducted investigations of the air in the trade wind region of the North Atlantic in 1905, won with Oscar Erbslöh, the international balloon race in 1907, and three years later found himself in Buenos Aires instructing members of the Argentine Meteorological Office in methods of exploring the atmosphere for weather data. In 1915 he had come across Abbot's work on solar variation, and found a definite relationship between the reported solar heat variations and those in the temperatures and pressures of many different areas. World weather, and the sun's variability of radiation output as observed by Abbot, were definitely linked, he was certain.

When Abbot received Clayton's communication, he was busy with other matters besides the sun. The United States had already been drawn into the World War, and his skill had been drafted for various scientific investigations relating to the conduct of the war, such as the matter of improving searchlights to be used against enemy aircraft. Abbot was an expert on mirrors and lenses. The same ingenuity which enabled him to invent and improve scientific instruments in his struggle against the secrets of the sun helped him in developing the photometer method of studying a searchlight beam and in designing new mirrors for it of greater effectiveness. But as he worked on these more immediate problems, his mind kept reverting to the many plans he had been hatching for testing out his theory of the relation of solar radiation variation to changing weather. He was dreaming of establishing solar radiation stations for this purpose on several continents, so that he could check the data of one station with those of the others. Even before the Armistice was signed he managed to establish a solar constant observatory. This was at Calama, in the nitrate desert of northern Chile, which, because of the constant clarity of its atmosphere, has proved to be the most favorable region in the world for these exacting observations.

Clayton's work had fascinated Abbot, and he hoped to initiate a cooperative venture with him. In July, 1918, Abbot joined with Clayton in an effort to test out their theories. The Argentine Government was easily persuaded to join in the undertaking. The work of gathering new data was begun in that mountainous outpost of clear and untroubled skies. It was decided that the observers at desolate Calama, 7500 feet above the desert, were to telegraph their daily solar constant determinations to Buenos Aires the morning after they had made their observations at Calama. This was no easy matter. Rapid yet very accurate calculations had to be made to get this daily data to Argentina in time to make the experiment valid. To enable the observer to collect more data within a short interval of time, Abbot devised a much quicker method for observing and computing the solar constant. This involved the use of a new instrument, the *pyranometer*, which he invented for the purpose of making measurements of the brightness of the sky near the sun. The new method, introduced in 1919, was many times faster than the older one, and enabled two trained observers with brain, eye, and hand working in perfect coordination, to make hundreds of observations and complete numerous complicated computations of five solar constant measurements in about five hours instead of two days — still a very slow process.

The results of this undertaking as interpreted by Abbot and Clayton added further proof that the variability of the sun's radiation was real, and that small though it was, it had a definite influence on the weather of the earth. The Argentine Government accepted their findings and continued for several years to furnish official long-range forecasts of temperature and rainfall prepared each Wednesday and covering the week beginning with the following Thursday.

The work of Abbot and Clayton, however, was not generally accepted. The opposition, and it was a formidable one, declared that they failed to see how the weather could be affected to any pronounced degree by minor solar heat variations. "Is it rational to believe," asked Herbert H. Kimball, veteran solar radiation investigator of the United States Meteorological Service, "that major weather changes are caused and explainable by alleged periodic changes of less than one per cent in the intensity of radiation? It is as if one were in a hall, illuminated by a hundred lamps. If one or two of these lamps would be put out, the illumination would not be changed to notice it at all." And William J. Humphreys, physicist of the United States Weather Bureau, insisted that "of the many factors of climatic control, all those of extra-terrestrial or cosmical origin either are demonstrably small or unproved, and apparently unnecessary to assume in accounting for known climatic changes."

These were but a few of the broadsides fired by men occupying positions of authority in the meteorological world. But Abbot stuck to his guns. He was, frankly, by no means firmly convinced himself, but he might be right, after all. His answer came back to the point. "A variation of one half of one per cent in solar radiation *seems* to produce noticeable changes in weather. Changes of cloudiness may accompany changes of solar radiation and thus multiply the effects. Solar changes alter ultraviolet rays, hence may change the density of the earth's blanket of ozone. This ozone is present about forty miles above the earth's surface, and is a powerful absorber of outgoing terrestrial radiation. The temperature of the atmosphere would respond to this interference. The pressures are then disturbed. Profound meteorological effects are thus in turn produced. Such, it *may be*, is the complex train of events by which the variability of the sun's radiation affects our weather."

The work of collecting data did not stop for a moment. John A. Roebling, son of the great suspension bridge builder, became interested. When the smoke of some newly opened copper mines interfered with the observations at the Calama Observatory, Roebling supplied the means which enabled Abbot in 1920 to remove the station to a nearby peak, Mt. Montezuma. The new site was no paradise, either. Rising nine thousand feet above the Atacama Desert where the absence of rain made any form of animal or vegetable life impossible, it was one of the most barren spots on earth. The Smithsonian observers had to go twelve miles to the nearest railway to get their water and other supplies. Of the numerous outposts of science, few were more desolate. Between watching the sun and making their calculations, the hours of loneliness were fought off with books, games, and the radio. Later, again with Roebling's help, another citadel was raised on Mt. Harqua Hala, three thousand feet above an Arizona desert fringed with thirty-foot cactuses.

Clayton, too, was collecting more data. He made a survey of all the world weather figures available. He showed that the permanent centers of action in our atmosphere, about which the winds revolve, shift by hundreds or even thousands of miles as the solar radiation rises and falls. These tremendous shifts alter the direction of the winds at many stations, and thereby alter the temperatures and pressures. Then he went on to say, "There is as yet no absolute proof that weather changes would not occur without changes in solar radiation, but my own researches have led me to the belief that without these solar changes there would result a *balanced system of atmospheric changes* such that the same conditions would return year after year at the same time of day and at the same time of the year, while the irregular changes known as weather result chiefly, if not entirely, from the irregular changes of solar variation." This was fifteen years ago. He still holds the same opinion today after years of further research.

In 1923, shortly after returning to the United States to cooperate more closely with the Smithsonian Institution, Clayton published *World Weather*. In this book he offered evidence to show that solar radiation changes intimately affect weather. His figures indicated that an increase in the solar constant, that is, an increase in the intensity of the radiation from the sun, lowers the pressure in the tropics, probably as a result of the absorption of the sun's heat by the water vapor of the upper air. Similar changes in intensity of the high and low pressure areas of the atmosphere are brought about by changes in the solar radiation and increase the general circulation of the atmosphere. Knowing the changes of solar radiation, Clayton could thus foretell the changes in both direction and intensity of large masses of cold and warm air. This information could then be used to forecast weather long in advance, since these changes took place over long periods of time following the changes in the solar constants.

It was now about time, Abbot and Clayton thought, to attempt some severe test of the validity of their new findings. Several conferences were held with Roebling. It was decided to support a research bureau to be conducted for two years by Clayton with the object of testing the correlation between daily solar variations and local weather conditions in some part of the United States. Clayton moved into a room of the Historical Society of Canton, Massachusetts, and started operations at once. Beginning with October 15, 1923, he received daily telegrams from the Smithsonian Institution giving the observed solar constant. Every afternoon he would then calculate how many degrees above or below normal the average maximum temperature of New York City would be, and daily dispatched to the Smithsonian his predictions for the next three, four, five, and even twenty-seven days. These predictions were based on

Clayton's conclusions derived from solar constant and weather correlations, and published in his *World Weather*.

This bold experiment went on for two whole years. An exact mathematical analysis of Clayton's predictions and the actual weather conditions which prevailed during these two years was then made. The twenty-seven-day-in-advance forecasts were found to be of no value. But the forecasts for three, four, and five days to come during the two summer months of 1925 showed an actual prevision, according to the following chart which had been drawn up.

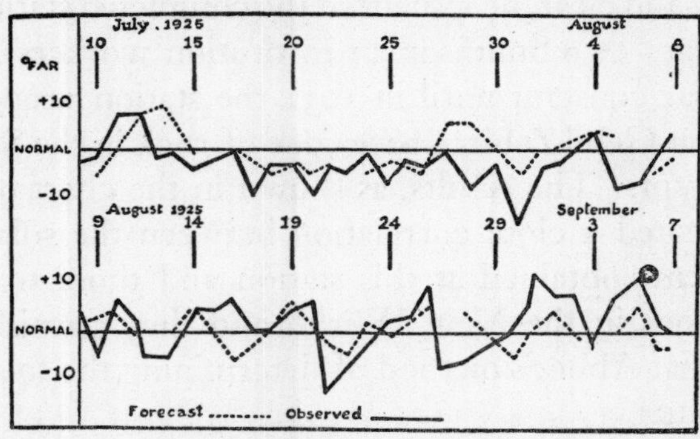

FIG. 28

Chart shows the temperatures at New York as they were forecast (dotted lines) five days in advance and the actual temperatures registered on the corresponding days (black line).

For simplification, the normal temperature is indicated by a straight horizontal line. The " breaks " in the forecasting line indicate Sundays, when no predictions were made by Clayton.

(Courtesy, Henry H. Clayton)

These results were promising, to say the least, even though they were far from being representative of prevision for months, seasons, or years in advance. Abbot knew that the road that led to accurate long-range weather forecasting was still a long one. First, it was necessary to have more data to prove conclusively that their solar constant measurements were the same when taken in widely separated parts of the world. Besides, more solar stations were required, since no one place affords good observing weather continuously for determining solar variation. He continued to dream of a network of solar observatories throughout the world. The National Geographic Society was persuaded to make a grant of $55,000 for the establishment of an observatory in the eastern hemisphere. Abbot left in search of a site which might add crucial evidence of the possibility of long-range weather forecasting. He stopped at Algiers, went on to Port Said, Cairo, Delhi, and Baluchistan. Many sites were turned down until he found himself 5200 feet up Mt. Brukkaros in southwest Africa, seven miles from the Hottentot village of Berseba. There in a barren crater a mile in the sky, where the air was dry and clear, he visualized the completed station. Later, for five years, two Smithsonian Institution workers lived there for the solar constant until in 1932 the station was dismantled and set up at Gebil Zebir, a bare cone of rock in the Sinai Peninsula of Egypt. The results, as shown in the chart on the next page, indicated a close correlation between the solar constant measurements obtained at this station and those made at two other stations in the New World, and they furnished strong evidence that Abbot's method of determining the solar constant was accurate.

In the meantime Clayton started a novel business of his own — a commercial service in long-range weather forecasting. In answer to criticism aimed at such a bold undertaking, he wrote: "No one can feel more strongly than I do the great difficulties of correctly interpreting the complex physical processes of the atmosphere; but working hypotheses are as necessary to an investigator as is the compass to a navigator. I regard my interpretation of the observed phenomena as a working hypothesis to be modified or abandoned for better interpretations, as facts accumulate." For the last ten years Clayton has been furnishing each of his clients, at fifty dollars annually, with temperature forecasts made a few days in advance, with probable dates of general rain or snow, with predictions of mild and cold periods for the coming month, and in some cases with a more extended forecast, such as the general weather of a season ahead. For example, one of his typical reports sent out in August to clients in a group of

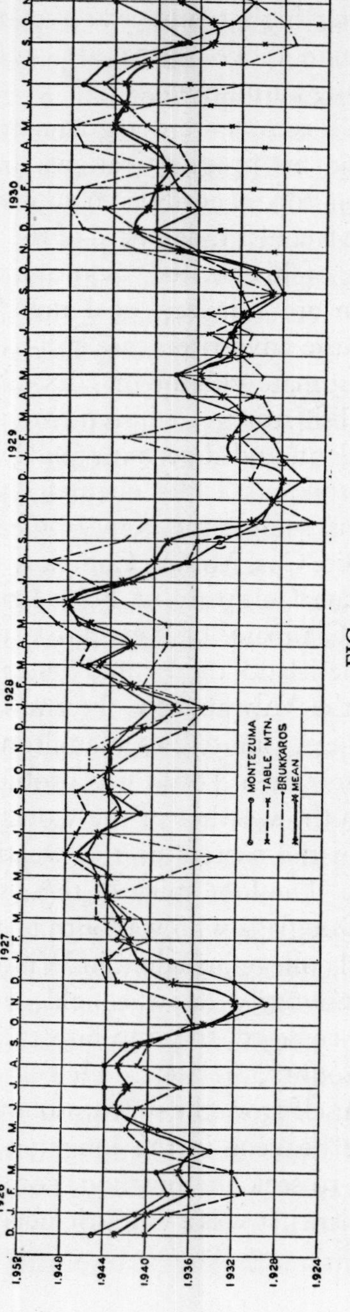

FIG. 29

This chart shows (superimposed in the form of ten-day means) the *solar constant* results obtained at Mt. Montezuma in Chile, Table Mountain in California, and Mt. Brukkaros in Africa for 1926–30. The three stations agree in showing certain trends in common, and thereby indicate a real variation of the sun. (Courtesy, Smithsonian Institution) states in the North Atlantic or Great Lake region reads, "The solar conditions forming high temperatures continue, so that temperature averages high above normal are expected for September and the remaining autumn months."

Of course Clayton's forecasts are not guaranteed, but he has been more successful in his prognostications than the official weather staff at Washington, according to an investigation undertaken in 1927 by the Retail Trade Board of the Boston Chamber of Commerce, one of his clients. Some of his early subscribers, among whom are retailers, coal merchants, electric light companies, and large advertisers, are still using his service which helps them to estimate volume of sales, plan the buying of raw materials, establish storage requirements, outline selling and advertising campaigns, and determine possible risks in numerous business undertakings. His clientele included many successful business firms, such as the New England Coke Company, the Berwind White Coal Mining Company of New York, the Interwoven Stocking Company of New Brunswick, New Jersey, the Knox Hat Company of New York, the Providence Gas Company of Rhode Island, the United States Rubber Company of Connecticut, the Milwaukee Coke and Gas Company, and the Canadian Canners, Limited, of Hamilton, Canada.

During all these years when Abbot was probing the sun and Clayton was spying on the weather of the world, another altogether novel attack on the secrets of the weather was being launched in the West. The lone spirit of these singular events was Andrew Ellicott Douglass, who was born in 1867, son of an Episcopal preacher and college president in Windsor, Vermont. In 1902 Douglass temporarily left the field of astronomy in which he had become engaged, to jump into the arena of local politics in Coconino County, Arizona. He felt at that time an urgent need to free himself from the sort of isolation which constant watching of the heavens in the long lonely nights had forced upon him, and to seek the bustling, companionable life of a small town politician. It was a fantastic change, yet understandable.

The " environment of a name," as in the case of Abbot and so many other eminent men of science, had caused Andrew Ellicott Douglass to study science in his boyhood. He was named after his great-grandfather who had been a distinguished astronomer, and also as a geographer had helped in determining the boundaries of many of the original thirteen colonies. His grandfather had been professor of engineering at West Point. Douglass had inherited the astronomical apparatus which had been handed down in the family, and before long had chosen astronomy as a career. In 1889 he was graduated from Trinity College where he taught both astronomy and physics in his senior year, and became an assistant in the Harvard College Observatory. The following year W. H. Pickering took him to Peru for some astronomical work, and Douglass found time to investigate the movement of sand dunes. At twenty-seven he went with Percival Lowell, a man of abundant energy, imagination, and private means, to build a new observatory at Flagstaff, Arizona. Seven years later came that sudden determination to mix in politics. Although not a lawyer, he ran for the office of County Probate Judge and was elected.

During the early days of his judgeship, Douglass took a summer trip in a buckboard into the great forests of yellow pines near the great " Rim " of the Colorado Plateau. It was this six-hundred-mile journey into the woodlands of Arizona which suggested to Douglass the clue that was to uncover that third line of attack on the weather. Here began his first investigations which brought the study of tree rings to the aid of astronomy, and the two to the partial solution of the mystery of weather. This original investigation of Douglass, apparently so remote from its final contribution, resulted, however, in some interesting scientific findings. The history of pure science, like that of political science, is often unpredictable.

Douglass had originally pondered over the relation between sunspot cycles and weather cycles which Eduard Brückner had reported in 1887. This Swiss professor had found that when sunspots were numerous the weather on earth was quite the reverse of what it was when sunspots were few. Furthermore, the number of sunspots increased over a period of seventeen or eighteen years, after which they decreased in number over a similar period. The seventeen-year cycle of sunspot activity corresponded to a seventeen-year period of cold or warm weather on earth. Brückner, in his classical investigation of European weather data gathered from century-old weather journals, diaries, and literary references to floods, droughts, unusually cold winters and hot summers, had also made use of records of the rise and fall of lake and river levels and the abundance and dearth of harvests. The announcement of this discovery of a thirty-five-year weather cycle recalled to some that Francis Bacon had evidently heard about this three hundred years earlier, for among his writings we find, " They say it is observed in the Low Countries that every five and thirty years the same kind of weather comes about again, as great frosts, wet, droughts, warm winters, summers with little heat, and the like."

Perhaps, thought Douglass, the yellow pine trees of Arizona, some of which were known to be more than a thousand years old, might offer information to correlate the abundance of sunspots with weather changes on earth. Perhaps tree rings, records of the passage of the years and an unfailing date book of history, might hold the secret of the weather of the past when no written records were kept. Douglass reasoned that since the rings of trees measure their food supply, which to a large degree is dependent upon the moisture available, they ought thus to give data of the rainfall of hundreds of years ago. He argued that a rainy year would show up in a rich thick ring, while a dry one would give rise to a thin, meager ring. This would be especially true in a cool dry climate like that of northern Arizona, where the absence of other competing vegetation, of a widely fluctuating water supply in the soil, and of insect pests would minimize any interference from these factors.

First Douglass attempted to get records of rainfall of this district as far back as possible, to test the correlation of moisture and the thickness of tree rings. Fortunately, temperature and rainfall measurements had been made and recorded at Whipple Barracks to the south of Flagstaff since 1867, and they were made available for his study. Then, in January, 1904, he visited the lumber yards of the Arizona Lumber and Timber Company and spent hours in the snow measuring the rings of many of their oldest trees. The president of the company became interested in the singular pastime of this strange hybrid of astronomer and politician, and had sections cut from the ends of scores of logs and stumps sent to Douglass for analysis. These pieces were carefully scraped with razor blades and brushed with kerosene for examination under the microscope. Every ring from the

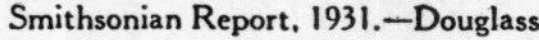

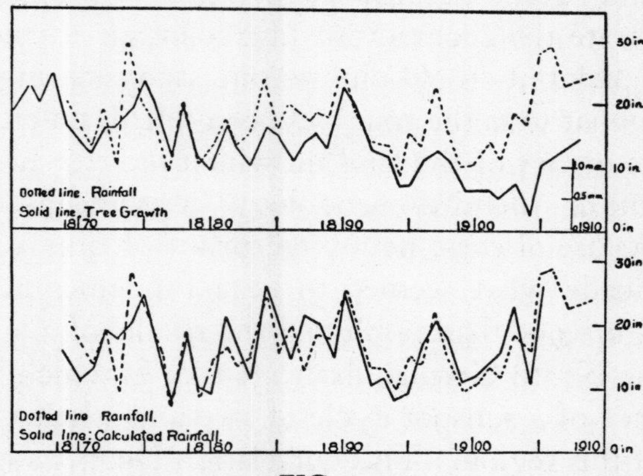

FIG. 30

Top: The *dotted* line represents the rainfall which had been recorded back to 1867. The *solid* line represents the tree growths as shown by the tree rings of that same period.

Bottom: The *dotted* line represents, as above, the rainfall recorded since 1867. The *solid* line represents the rainfall of the same region as calculated from the tree rings.

(Courtesy, Smithsonian Institution)

center of the tree to its bark was scrupulously scrutinized. To facilitate the dating of the rings, Douglass would make one pin prick to mark the last year of each decade, two to mark the middle year of each century, and three for the century year. Those cross sections which contained more than a thousand rings had an additional four pin pricks at the thousand-year tree-ring position. Douglass made tens of thousands of measurements, tabulated the data, drew curves and graphs, and as the average age of his trees was 348 years, he was able to draw conclusions regarding the rainfall and tree-ring appearance of periods hundreds of years back.

Douglass found a striking correlation between tree growth and the recorded rainfall of the region. So accurate were his measurements and so apparently reliable his method that any marked peculiarity of any year could be identified with surprising ease and clarity in trees which often had grown more than four hundred miles apart. For example, the yellow pine ring of 1851 is small in trees which grew in regions between Santa Fé and Fresno because it represents a drought year. He could illustrate the accuracy of his technique in another way. He would pick out an old pine stump, study its rings, and then declare in what year the tree had been felled, much to the surprise of the owner of the land on which the tree had been cut. His tree time or " dendro-chronology " was uncannily accurate.

With the use of these new fingerprints of time and weather, Douglass made what seemed to be a fundamental discovery. Hellmann, in 1906, had published the results of a study he had made of the North German drainage area in which he reported the influence of a sunspot cycle of five and a half years on the weather of this region. This correlation Douglass had also observed in the yellow pines of the Flagstaff-Prescott region, but, he said, it " was presumably an eleven-year cycle." In other words, there was a relationship not only between tree-ring growth and rainfall, but also between both of these and the sunspot cycle. Douglass was back again where he had started — back to an astronomy, which, however, required neither telescope nor observatory.

Finding cycles or periods in the abundance of sunspots on the solar disk was nothing new. This was first recorded in 1843 by Schwabe after an investigation which had lasted a score of years. Even before that date an Italian observer wrote in 1651 that when sunspots were few, high temperatures prevailed on earth.

Another investigator, too, reported the same phenomenon after a life-long study of the records of one hundred million individual observations made over a period of a century. The relations between an eleven-year sunspot activity cycle and rainfall, terrestrial temperature, storms, the rise and fall of the surface of lakes in Africa and Australia, the growth of peat bogs, and the formation of varves had been discussed almost perennially.

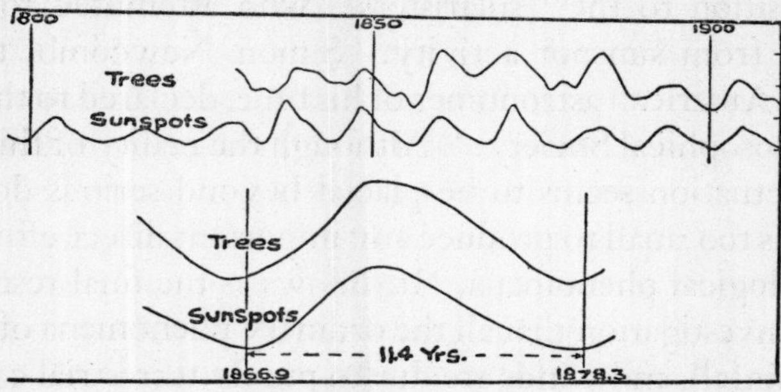

FIG. 31

Two top curves: Correlation between tree growth in northern Europe and sunspot cycles covering a period of almost a hundred years.

Two lower curves: The 11.4-year sunspot cycle of 1866.9–1878.3 compared with the weather cycles as shown by tree-ring growth over the same period. (Courtesy, A. E. Douglass)

Varves are bands or layers of clay alternating with layers of sand laid down by the melting of the ice sheets several thousand years ago during the Ice Ages. A pair of such layers of varying thickness was laid down each year by the retreating glaciers. They were first studied by Baron de Geer, a Swedish geologist, who by counting them was able to show that the glaciers in southern Sweden started to melt over 13,500 years ago. Ernst Antevs, using this same method, was able to unfold the story of the retreating glaciers in the Connecticut River Valley. He found that it took 4300 years for the glacier in this section of the world to retreat 185 miles. Since greater solar activity means more melting of ice, and since more melting gives a thicker varve, a study of these layers has also been able to indicate cycles of weather. It turned out that these cycles clearly correlated with the eleven-year sunspot cycle.

Business booms and depressions, the outbreak of wars, the abundance and scarcity of crops, birth and suicide rates, and (according to J. B. S. Haldane) even the number of rabbits and hares in Canada also seemed to follow the sunspot cycle. So the announcement by Douglass of some causal relationship between terrestrial climatic conditions and sunspots added very little in the way of novelty, except to bring more publicity and plenty of opposition to the "solaristers" who attempted to foretell weather from sunspot activity. Simon Newcomb, the most eminent American astronomer of his time, declared to the American Philosophical Society: "Although the reality of this eleven-year fluctuation seems to be placed beyond serious doubt, the amount is too small to produce any important direct effects upon meteorological phenomena. It follows as the final result of the present investigation that all the ordinary phenomena of temperature, rainfall, and winds are due to purely terrestrial causes and that no changes occur in the sun's radiation which have any influence upon them." This opinion expressed more than a generation ago was echoed by Hann, a European authority on climatic conditions, as well as by many other eminent men of science since that time.

But Douglass, like Abbot and Clayton, was not completely convinced that he was altogether wrong. Just about this time, Ellsworth Huntington came to California from Yale University with the *Pulse of Asia* which he had written in 1907. He had heard of the tree-ring investigations of Douglass. They fitted in very neatly with a theory he had developed from a hunch that came to him one glowing day as he was leading a caravan of exploration into a desert in Asia. He saw in his mind's eye how fluctuations of climate throughout the ages might easily have shaped the course of history. To him history appeared as a series of pulsations. He had seen a close correlation between the rise and fall of lake levels caused by a rhythmic change of climate, and the rise and fall of dynasties. Perhaps in the trees of California he might see even more than Douglass had perceived. Perhaps the big sequoias would add further testimony to the tie-up of weather and hoary historical happenings. He went into the great forests and studied almost half a thousand trees by the method Douglass had introduced. From the data thus collected he drew climatic curves of California and compared them with those of the Old World. Some of the trees under investigation were so old that in one of them, for example, Huntington thought he made out the picture of a drought period which corresponded with the plague period of Egypt back in 1230 B.C. — the tree had 3210 rings. Other trees seemed to tell him that Greek philosophy had thrived during the rainy period of 400 B.C. More rings hinted that the decline of the Roman Empire was synchronous with the decline of rainfall in that center of the world.

Douglass, too, had not given up the quest of the secrets that tree rings might be hiding. The sequoia tree-ring investigations were not quite as conclusive as those of the Arizona pines. Even many of his pines were giving him trouble. For some scores of years a number of them failed to show those regular periodic pulsations he expected. Near the year 1700 the tree-ring story seemed to break down altogether, so much so that he admitted years later that he "very nearly gave up the work." But he did not abandon it. Perhaps E. E. Free was right when he wrote: "Weather cycles might be thought of as a great many clocks ticking at once. Some tick every second, some every eleven seconds, some every thirty-five seconds, and so on. On first hearing, such tickings would seem to constitute an unsortable chaos. Sometimes the ticks would coincide, sometimes they would not. No rhythm or regularity would be apparent. But by careful listening it would be possible to figure out the periods at which various of the clocks were ticking." Perhaps, thought Douglass, by listening to the tickings of other "tree-ring clocks" he could make out the grand symphony. In 1913 he went to Europe to make a study of the most important tree-ring collections in several centers of the old world. At Fleet near London, at Eberswalde near Berlin, in the forest of Sopteland in Norway, and in other places in south Sweden, Vienna, Munich, and Dresden he found the eleven-year cycle verified in many of these foreign trees.

Soon after, several organizations such as the National Geographic Society, the Museum of Northern Arizona, and the American Museum of Natural History made grants to permit him to continue his researches in this field. The giant sequoias which had lured Huntington also beckoned Douglass. Before long he was in the great forests of California collecting dozens of radial pieces cut from the stumps of the giant sequoias. For study of these in the laboratory, he was equipped with a new instrument of his own design and construction. It was an ingenious machine, the first and only one of its kind in existence, made possible by funds supplied by Clarence G. White of Redlands, California. This machine, first called the optical periodograph and later the *cyclograph*, was built in order to cut down the labor and minimize the errors involved in the tedious routine of finding rhythms or cycles in the growth of those ancient trees some of which had thousands of rings.

He tried this method of analysis on tens of thousands of trees. Every minute that he could steal from his multiple duties at the University of Arizona as professor of astronomy and director of the Steward Observatory was spent in drawing up and analyzing charts which he had pinned to the walls of the attic of one of the university buildings at Tucson. Other specimens of wood and numberless graphs were filed away in the basement of the university gymnasium. So accurate was his procedure that when discrepancies between poor specimens indicated what seemed to show a missing tree ring in several of his oldest trees (each over two thousand years old), Douglass obtained twelve clearer specimens of this group of trees and found the missing ring present.

Yet even with his machine inconsistencies occasionally bobbed up. The most serious one concerned several tree rings which he had dated as belonging to a period between 1670 and 1720. When interpreted in relation to the expected sunspot cycle of that half century they represented a flattening of the sunspot curve of that time which was totally unexplainable. This disturbing element bothered Douglass greatly until one day early in 1922 when he received a letter from Professor E. Walter Maunder of the Royal Observatory at Greenwich, England. The letter called attention to a prolonged dearth of sunspots between 1645 and 1715 which the Englishman had dug out of some old records. Maunder suggested that if there were really any definite connection between solar activity and tree growth this extended minimum ought to show up in the tree-ring studies. He had not known of Douglass' difficulties with exactly this period, and when the latter read the letter he was convinced that here was the explanation of the inconsistency which had almost ended his tree-ring studies among the Arizona pines. This still unexplained dearth of sunspots which Maunder had discovered coincided exactly with the failure of his trees to mirror the expected sunspot cycle. It was a remarkable vindication of the validity of his working hypothesis, based on more than a quarter of a million measurements, which correlated sunspot activity with weather and tree-ring formation.

Incidentally, this method of dating by tree-ring analysis has enabled Douglass to determine the dates of the establishment of nearly a hundred prehistoric villages in the Chaco Canyon region of New Mexico. It is based on a method known as *cross-dating*. Studies are made of the tree-ring arrangement of beams or even bits of charcoal picked up in the ruins of old pueblos. The relative widths of the tree rings are indicated by lines — long lines representing narrow rings and short lines, wide rings (see next page). Two strips of cross-section paper containing these lines derived from two trees, one of which has already been dated, are compared. If the lines match, the two pieces of timber crossdate, that is, were growing at the same time. By this ingenious method Douglass found that the village of Oraibi is five hundred years old, that the Pueblo Bonito, the largest of them, was built between 919 and 950 A.D., and that the oldest of these sites goes back to 643 A.D. This chronology, dating back almost thirteen hundred years, is quite accurate.

Douglass' data seem to show definitely that tree growth varies according to cycles with lengths bearing simple ratios to the sunspot cycle. In addition, his researches indicate that the growth of tree rings in arid regions is proportional to rainfall with an

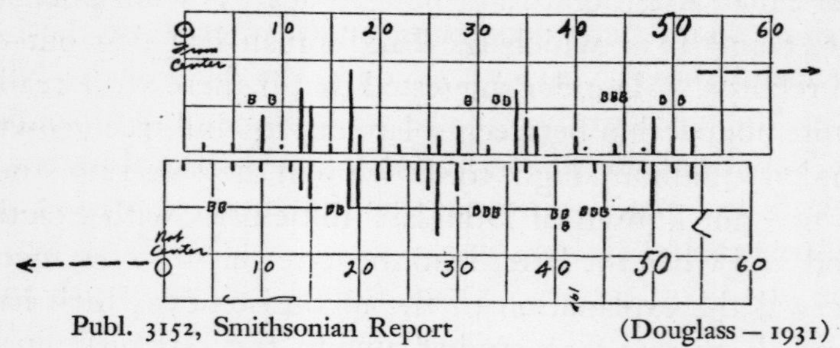

Publ. 3152, Smithsonian Report (Douglass – 1931)

FIG. 32

Crossdating between a Betatakin Douglas fir (above) and a Pueblo Bonito pine (below) to illustrate chronology building. The upper specimen extends a century later (to right) and the lower extends nearly as much earlier (to left). Thus the two are joined into one continuous chronology.

accuracy of about eighty per cent. In this way he has learned much of the weather cycles of the past which may offer a clue to the weather cycles of the future. Through the help of the Carnegie Institution of Washington, he has lately been enabled to give all of his time to this important work.

Abbot, too, with the aid of data from the various solar observatories, is finding that the curves representing changing solar radiation, terrestrial temperatures and sunspot numbers resemble each other too closely to be coincidental. He, like Douglass, is getting pulsation or cycle effects of solar radiation. He obtained his solar radiation cycles by means of his cycle-analyzing machine or *periodometer*, which he used since 1918. After unscrambling the apparent disharmony of the solar constant figures, he drew the following conclusions in 1935:

1. The solar variation comprises twelve or more regular periodicities which support successful predictions of solar changes for years in advance.
2. The periodicities of solar variation are integral submultiples of twenty-three years.

3. Solar changes influence weather since the periodicities occur in departures from normal temperatures and precipitations at numerous terrestrial localities.
4. Weather tends to repeat itself at intervals of twenty-three years.
5. Various phenomena depending on weather show the influence of the 23-year cycle such as the level of the Nile River, the levels of the Great Lakes, the rainfall of southern New England, the widths of tree rings, the abundance of cod and mackerel, and the thickness of varves of Pleistocene and Eocene ages.

"I have a vivid conviction," wrote Abbot, "of the truth and importance of these conclusions which is shared by my colleagues and friends who are most conversant with the evidence."

Abbot ascribes the long cycle of twenty-three years which dominates the sun to some such phenomenon as this. For some yet unexplainable reasons, violently burning material from the interior of the sun pushes its way to the surface. This increases the sun's radiation which reaches the earth. "It is to be regarded," wrote Abbot, "like the stirring of a fire with a poker, which brings up from below the hotter materials, and throws out temporarily a greater radiation in our rooms." As this fresh material from the sun's interior burns itself out, the high solar radiation is followed by a period of relatively low radiation.

The influence of solar radiation on the weather of the earth as shown by numerous cycle correlations has recently been found for other planets, also. An astronomer at the Astrophysical Observatory at Potsdam studied the brightness of Mars, Jupiter, Saturn, and Neptune from photographic and other records dating as far back as 1840. He found that variations in the brightness of these planets which shine by the reflected light from the sun recurred in rhythms of time similar to those found for terrestrial weather conditions. Jupiter showed a gradual change in brightness recurring every 11.6 years, while Neptune showed a similar change in brightness over periods of twenty-three years.

While the interpretation of the story of the tree rings, the data of solar constant measurements, and the figures gathered from a study of world weather is still only partially understood, it seems fairly certain that the three separate investigations of Abbot, Clayton, and Douglass have at last met to strengthen each other. Other scientists are more skeptical. Charles F. Talman wrote late in 1934: " The sun's output of heat undoubtedly varies, but whether its variations produce identifiable effects upon the weather of the earth is an unsettled question. . . . No connection has been demonstrated," according to this well-known meteorologist, " between a particular state of the sun and a particular drought, hot summer, or cold winter on our planet." He, of course, does not accept such correlations as that announced by Clayton in 1935 between solar constant changes and the destructive drought which burned up the West the previous year. Sir William Napier Shaw, sometime president of the International Meteorological Committee, believes that " so long as we are not fully cognizant of the action of the drama of weather, or as Clark Maxwell expressed it, of the real ' go ' of things, such predictions are like the ancient Greek oracles or the prophecies of the Sibyls. It takes a wiser man to appreciate them at their real values than it does to make them."

To be sure, neither Abbot, Clayton, nor Douglass is dogmatic in his claims for any clear-cut applications of the findings in this infant science. Speaking before the National Academy of Sciences, Abbot said: " We have not yet tried the bold venture of long-range forecasting that might even enable meteorologists to forecast long in advance the fat years and the lean years as Joseph is said to have done in Egypt. We expect to discover by a little more research whether we have real cause and effect in these relationships." He is too clear-headed a scientist to insist upon the validity of a theory which deals with so complex a phenomenon as weather. Atmospheric circulation, clouds, water vapor, ozone, and other variables characteristic of the atmosphere on the one hand, and differences of the nature and conformations of the earth's surface on the other, introduce secondary modifying influences which result in great inequalities in weather changes in different localities. "For analogy, let us consider the tides which are caused by the attraction of the moon and the sun," he writes. "On the open ocean the tides are very low, but when they rush into landlocked inlets they rise many feet. Similarly, conditions associated with prevailing winds, mountain chains, oceans and deserts may magnify effects of solar variation on weather." In short, he is not unaware of the possibility that in the realm of solar weather control indirect effects may often overpower direct ones. Yet he concludes that he cannot but feel that a promising step has been taken toward general forecasts covering a number of years in advance. He believes the method may yet be greatly improved, and that future long-range weather forecasting will be based on the periodic fluctuations of the solar radiation which, according to him, is the arbiter of terrestrial temperatures.

Still another method of attack on this problem has been launched at the Scripps Institute of Oceanography at La Jolla, California. Here George F. McEwen is at work on a system of weather forecasting based upon a correlation between offshore water temperatures and the amount of rainfall over the Pacific seaboard. He has discovered that apparently when the Pacific waters near the coast have higher than average temperatures in the summer, the following winter is drier than usual. Although this is still on a purely empirical basis, he claims a "hit right" frequency of almost seventy-five per cent. And while he continues to probe into the physics of ocean waters to enhance the value of this method, he is ready, he says, "to make any use of the extensive work on solar radiation and sunspots that we find to be of help."

A somewhat similar study has been made during the past five years by Charles F. Brooks, director of the Blue Hill Meteorological Observatory. Thermographs were attached on commercial steamships sailing the Atlantic, chiefly between New York and Bermuda, and analyzed for some correlation between the temperature of the ocean water and weather changes along the Atlantic coast of the United States. Brooks' report, issued near the close of the year 1934, claimed that low sea temperatures were followed by warmer weather on land, and vice versa. This relationship was found to predominate rather consistently.

In several sections of the world, meanwhile, long-range weather forecasts are being officially issued for the average weather to be expected over large agricultural areas. Many of these are based at least in part upon the pioneer researches of Abbot and Clayton. For example, in India, where in 1876 the failure of the moisture-laden monsoons to appear resulted in a famine which took the lives of five millions, attempts were made many years ago to find some way of predicting the behavior of coming monsoon seasons. After a long and careful study of the rainfall, temperature, pressure, and wind direction of both nearby and distant regions, certain correlations were discovered. These appeared to be capable of application to the foretelling of seasonal weather conditions months in advance. It was found, for instance, that abundant Indian rains tend to be associated with low pressures in India, Java, Australia, and South Africa, and at the same time with high pressure in Samoa, Honolulu, Chile, and Argentina. If the reverse of these conditions prevailed, an Indian drought might be expected. Rain in India seemed also to follow previous scanty rainfall in Java, Zanzibar, and southern Rhodesia, and to be correlated, strangely enough, with previous low temperature in the Aleutian Islands thousands of miles away. This information, too, could be used as a basis for forecasting weather in India months in advance. Under the directorship of Sir Gilbert Walker, "foreshadowings" by seasons became a regular function of the meteorological office at Simla. This method has been sufficiently successful to warrant the continuation of the service. In southern Rhodesia seasonal rainfall, and in northeastern Brazil floods and droughts, are predicted with some degree of accuracy on a similar basis of world weather correlation formulas in which all of this information is used.

In our own country the Weather Bureau has thus far not undertaken any such forecasts. Charles F. Marvin, former chief of the Bureau, who in 1934 retired after fifty years of service, was frankly and deliberately conservative in this difficult field. He attributed the findings of Abbot to errors of observation and actually ascribed the weather curves of Abbot and Clayton to the natural operation of the laws of chance. Under his directorship the Bureau discouraged long-range weather forecasting projects. However, the Science Advisory Board created in 1933 by an executive order of President Franklin D. Roosevelt included in its first report of suggested science projects a study of air masses to further weather predictions. In this way the character and motions of the great continental air masses might be studied and their future behavior predicted with much greater certainty than at present. It also recommended the extension of climatological work looking toward long-range weather forecasting by planning the cooperation of the meteorological services of other countries, including Canada, Mexico, Norway, and Russia. Already, under the direction of Willis R. Gregg, the new chief of the United States Weather Bureau, temperature, pressure, moisture, and wind velocity data are being collected in various parts of the country by a score of army, navy, and commercial fliers equipped with meteorographs taken daily to altitudes as high as twenty thousand feet; and later, also, it is planned to go to higher regions of the stratosphere. The data thus collected will be analyzed for possible clues and, in conjunction with the findings of Abbot, Clayton, and Douglass, will be used in the attempt to extend the time range of weather forecasts.

There is still very much that is indefinite in all this work. The field is still almost virgin. Possibly all of its devotees are partly correct in their conclusions. There may be "nine-and-sixty ways to construct weather lays," every one of them right. Perhaps experiments in this field represent man's presumption in thinking he can solve an insoluble problem. In any case, the work goes on. Data are still coming in. Clayton continues to edit his *World Weather Records* for the Smithsonian Institution. More meteorological observers are traveling to the most inaccessible places of the earth, from Little America to the frigid wastes of the North Polar regions, to gather information on winds and other air conditions. Radio signal devices are being employed in an effort to find some relation between air pressures and the density of the various layers of ionized gases above the earth's atmosphere. Daily solar measurements, also, are still being made with pyrheliometers at many stations in various sections of the world. Solar constant determinations continue to be made by Smithsonian observers.

To the list of stations which have been built and operated under the direction of Abbot, another has been recently added. About ten miles from the summit of that mountain where Moses is said to have communed with God, on Mount St. Catherine, the highest and dryest of spots rising 8450 feet above the Sinai Desert, men are keeping vigil, holding the sun steady with tools of our science laboratories, even as Joshua is said to have held it with prayer and supplication. Here, while the monks of the neighborhood chant their psalms, men of science call out measurements.

In *Reason in Science*, George Santayana expressed the thought that "the lands that science is discovering have not yet been circumnavigated." Surely he might have been thinking of the realm of long-range weather forecasting, for scarcely has its ship left port on its long, uncertain voyage.

CHAPTER THIRTEEN

GALAXIES

NEW WORLDS BUILT OF SPECTRAL LINES AND MATHEMATICAL SYMBOLS

Dealing especially with the observational data collected by Hubble and Humason and the new interpretations of Richard C. Tolman

MAN IS EARTHBOUND to an insignificant speck of dust with "a superficial whiff of atmosphere, a splash of ocean, and a smear of biology." Though powerless to rise far above it, he has tried to fathom its mysteries. In the early days of his mental gropings, led by mystic and religious formulas he reveled in speculations. During those primitive strivings which go back to the dim dawn of history he set up many and strange systems of the heavens. To Thales the earth was a circular disk floating in an ocean of water. The world was flat and at the center of the universe, said Anaximander, and the sun but a hole in a solid dome of sky through which the fire of the Gods was visible. Anaximenes painted a different picture. Looking up from the flat surface of the earth, he saw the stars as silvery nails driven into the solid vault above.

Slowly these ancient ideas crumbled as the watchers of the sky increased in number and the motions of the stars and planets gave strange clues to the architecture of the universe. Pythagoras taught his disciples that the earth was a sphere which revolved around the sun, but men did not listen. About 250 B.C. Aristarchus of Samos saw the sun as the center of the universe and attempted to estimate its distance from the earth which revolved around it. Again men would not heed. Almost two thousand years passed. Then modern astronomy was born. On May 24, 1543, *On the Revolution of the Heavenly Bodies*, dedicated to Pope Paul III, was brought to the deathbed of its author, Nicholaus Copernicus, a Pole. The earth was indeed a globe, he declared, not stationary as Ptolemy the Egyptian had insisted, but a moving ball revolving around the sun as Pythagoras had believed.

The universe of Copernicus was still very small, not much larger than the limits of the outermost planets. Aristarchus thought the stars were quite remote but few, and even Ptolemy, their first cataloguer, could chart only slightly more than a thousand. By the seventeenth century a burst of scientific accomplishment brought with it the invention of the telescope and, in the hands of Galileo Galilei, astronomy was at last equipped with a tool which could reach beyond the clearest eye and hold the mind in check. Half a million stars appeared, and men began to realize that " the sun is but a private in the host of heaven." Astronomy was reborn; celestial horizons continued to recede, exposing further spaces spangled with new points of light. Then came Isaac Newton, posthumous son of an English farmer, who, while secluded outside of London during the Great Plague, in 1665, discovered the universal Law of Gravitation which explained the mysterious movements of heavenly bodies that even the genius of Galileo failed to understand.

Then began a feverish activity to study the myriad stars that blinked beyond the orbit of the farthermost planet. The positions of thousands of them were laboriously determined. Among the most prodigious workers in this virgin field was an erstwhile oboe player in a Hanover regiment. After his first battle William Herschel had fled to England to escape the tumult of war and, while teaching music to keep alive, had, at the age of thirty-five, turned to astronomy. He might have remained an amateur stargazer for the rest of his life had he not on the night of March 13, 1781, discovered a new planet, Uranus, a feat which brought him both the attention of the King and a wealthy wife.

Herschel built larger mirrors which he himself ground, never taking his fingers off the disks as he polished them for hours at a stretch while his sister Caroline fed him. With a nineteen-inch reflecting telescope of his own construction he swept the heavens, and hundreds of new stars revealed themselves in a great concourse of points of light. This Milky Way, he told the Royal Society in 1784, was " a most extensive stratum of stars of which our Sun and the solar system was but a part." The observer on earth sees the Milky Way as a thing apart, but in reality he is near the center of it. Herschel figured that the sun was a little away from the center of this Milky Way which was a huge flattened disk or watch-shaped system of star groups with a diameter roughly about six times the magnitude of its thickness. This patch of light Thomas Wright of England had called a luminous girdle around the sky — indeed, he was the first to correctly interpret this phenomenon. When Herschel died science inscribed over his grave " *Coelorum perrupit claustra* " — " He broke through the heavens."

For a while astronomy tarried. The mantle of Galileo, Copernicus, and Herschel was waiting to fall upon the shoulders of a new explorer who could venture beyond the Milky Way. But first it was necessary to know with some degree of astronomical accuracy the distances of the stars from the earth. This was not a simple matter. Herschel had attempted to measure stellar distances but had failed. Today the nearest star we know is *Proxima Centauri*, which is about twenty-five trillion miles away from us as compared with a mere ninety-three million miles, the distance of the sun from the earth. Light travelling at the speed of 186,000 miles a second can cover six trillion miles in a year. Hence it takes light 4.2 years to cover the distance from Proxima Centauri to the earth. (We say that this star is 4.2 *light years* away from us.) On the same basis light can reach us from the sun in only eight minutes. Yet this is our *nearest* star.

William Herschel was dead but sixteen years when another milestone in astronomy was reached. His son John, walking in the footsteps of his father, was cataloguing more stars from among the Magellanic Clouds visible in the Southern sky when in 1838 he received a letter from Frederick W. Bessel. This astronomer had determined the distance of *Cygni 61*, by a new method known as trigonometric parallax. The enormous distances of stars from a terrestrial observer are so great that they appear fixed in position. Constant and careful watching, however, revealed the fact that they did not appear fixed in space when located with reference to other stars still more remote. The farther away the star actually was, the smaller the angle through which it appeared to move. By measuring the angle between the relative positions of two stars as viewed from two different points on the earth, or from one place on the earth's surface which changed as our sphere revolved around the sun, it was possible by trigonometry to compute the distance of the nearer star from us.

Bessel measured the distance of Cygni 61 by this method and found this star to be 60,000,000,000,000 miles from the earth. A few months later Thomas Henderson, a Scot, announced from his observatory on the Cape of Good Hope that he had determined the distance of *Alpha Centauri* to be 25,000,000,000,000 miles (4.3 light years), and by the same method of parallax Struve, the great-grandfather of the present director of the Yerkes Observatory, had found the distance of *Alpha Lyrae*. The method was extremely difficult, so that by 1900 the distances of only sixty out of the millions of stars had been determined. Only thirteen stars were found within eleven light years from the earth. The annual average of accomplishment was only a single stellar distance, in spite of the work of numerous astronomers. The parallax method meant "measuring the size of a pinhead two miles away," equivalent according to Jeans to the apparent distance in the sky that a star at a hundred light years moves. Fancy measuring such a distance!

Yet parallax measurement was assiduously pursued and improvements in technique were discovered and applied. The Yerkes Observatory began in 1903 a photographic method of observation which increased its accuracy. At the Mt. Wilson Observatory, Walter S. Adams, its present director, devised a spectroscopic method of determining stellar parallaxes based upon peculiarities of the intensity of the light as shown in the spectral lines of certain types of stars, which by giving information about their brightness gave some clue to their distance as well. Within the five years preceding 1921, this method enabled Adams and his coworkers to determine the distances from the earth of two thousand stars. Adriaan van Maanen made some brilliant contributions in this field, and Henry N. Russell and Harlow Shapley devised still another method by the study of eclipsing variable stars. But in spite of these brilliant achievements, the number of stars of which the distances were determined was but nothing in the vast ocean of celestial space.

Our universe including the sun and, of course, the earth is the Milky Way or galactic system. Beyond our own galactic system there seemed to be other patches of light. Were they other universes? As early as 1750 the existence of such structures was suspected. Emmanuel Kant became enamored of this picture, and built in his mind a succession of celestial systems of increasing order without end. Spinoza, too, spoke and wrote of an infinite number of worlds beyond the horizon of our own.

As science halted on the rim of the Milky Way she gathered new recruits, surveyed the space already conquered, and reinforced her lines for a new and deeper offensive. Then with new techniques, new devices, and new leviathans of the heavens she broke through once more in a colossal surge that carried man's vision outside the Milky Way or galactic system to within the borders of the extragalactic nebulae. By 1782 Messier, a Frenchman, had found and listed a hundred and three cloudy spots in the sky called nebulae. Some were like planetary disks and others like wispy clouds. Then in 1848 Lord Rosse, equipped with a six-foot-diameter telescope, fifty feet long, slung in chains between two high walls of masonry, noticed for the first time the spiral form of some of them. Twenty years later Sir William Huggins was the first to use the spectroscope to learn the nature of these nebulae. Were they aggregations of stars? he wondered. " I directed the spectroscope," he wrote in 1867, " to one of these small nebulae. The reader may now be able to picture the feeling of excited suspense, mingled with a degree of awe, with which, after a few moments of hesitation, I put my eye to the spectroscope. No continuous spectrum such as is given off by the sun and other stars and such as I had expected! A single bright green line only such as is given off by a luminous gas!" But that was not the complete story of the nebulae. For later it was found that most of them give continuous spectra like the sun. These "island universes," as William Herschel had called them, were found to contain large numbers of stars since they gave continuous spectra such as are given by clusters of stars. Some, however, consist, not of aggregations of stars, but of large masses of luminous gas.

These nebulae were evidently too remote for any method yet devised to determine their distance. Stellar parallax determinations of bodies beyond the fringe of our galactic system were out of the question. At distances greater than a hundred light years parallax was powerless to give any information. Some other method based on an entirely different principle was wanted. For a century astronomers kept vigil for a new technique which was finally found. Its discovery is one of the classics of science.

Among the numerous types of stars that dot the heavens, one of the strangest and least understood of all is the *Cepheid variable* star, so named after its prototype *Delta Cephei* located in the constellation Cepheus. Long ago it had been observed that certain fairly faint stars suddenly flared up, increased in brightness, reached a peak of light intensity, and then gradually grew faint again. This fluctuation or pulsation of the Cepheid variable has been likened by Jeans to the blaze that appears as fresh heaps of coal are thrown at regular intervals into a dying fire. To Eddington, another master of the life history of stars, "Cepheid pulsation is a kind of distemper which happens to stars at a certain youthful period; after passing through it they burn steadily. There may be another attack of disease later in life." Their period of fluctuation of brightness varies usually from a few days to as long as a month or even fifty days.

In 1912 Miss Henrietta Leavitt, a graduate of Radcliffe College working in the Harvard Observatory, made a capital dis-

Edwin Powell Hubble

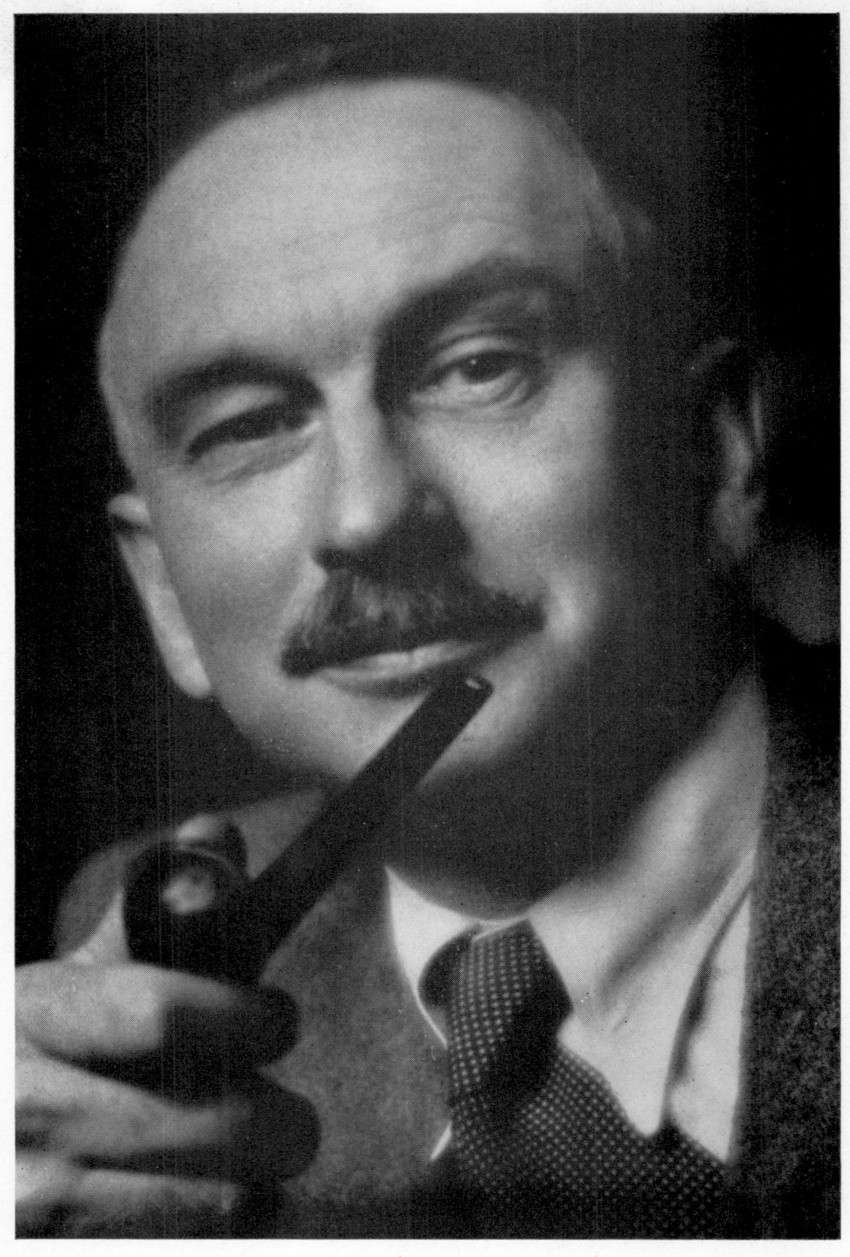

Richard Chace Tolman

covery. For years she had been studying photographic plates exposed to various portions of the skies to learn more about the nature of stars and stellar aggregations. While examining some photographs of a cluster of stars out near the boundary of the Milky Way in which many Cepheids had been reported, her trained eye came across an unusual phenomenon. In these pictures taken of the Lesser Magellanic Cloud at the Harvard University Observatory at Arequipa, Peru, she discovered that the large, brighter Cepheids, among its hundreds of thousands of stars, fluctuated more slowly than the fainter, smaller ones. The brighter Cepheids took a longer time to reach their greatest luminosity and then die down. Other eyes had undoubtedly seen similar pictures, but had missed the story which was revealed to this woman. In 1880 Henry Draper had introduced the photographic study of nebulae, and large numbers of such photographs had accumulated all over the world. Miss Leavitt began a thorough investigation of hundreds of these photographs. From this available data she was confirmed in her belief that the period of pulsation of a Cepheid was definitely related to its brightness.

Miss Leavitt then announced her discovery of the *period-luminosity law* which others before her had completely missed. The period of fluctuation of a Cepheid was directly proportional, she said, to its real brightness or candlepower. Now the *apparent* brightness of a star is not always its real or *intrinsic* brightness, because the observed brightness of a star depends upon its distance from the observer — the farther away the star, the dimmer it appears. Hence if the fluctuation of one Cepheid was more rapid than that of another Cepheid star at the same distance from the earth, then its intrinsic brightness was less than that of its neighbor Cepheid.

The value of the discovery of this law was clear. If it were universally true, it could be used as a key to the problem of stellar distances. Assume the presence of two Cepheids of the same period of pulsation that is, it takes them the same time to pass from their greatest brightness to dimness. Assume further that one of them appears a hundred times brighter than the other. Then one must be ten times farther than the other since luminosity of a source of light, as every schoolboy knows, varies inversely as the square of its distance ($100 = 10^2$). Furthermore, if one of these Cepheids occurred in a system such as the Milky Way of a known distance from the earth, then the other distance could be calculated. And finally the distance of this other star system would be the same as the distance of its Cepheid, of which the period of fluctuation and brightness were observable. Here indeed was an entirely new method for the use of stellar astronomy. Another measuring rod had been prepared, and with it another veil was to be lifted by man groping with a problem that seemed insoluble.

The discovery of this unsought phenomenon is another example of how strangely research advances into new fields, and how avidly science grasps at any straw which appears in the surrounding whirlpool of ignorance. The work of Miss Leavitt reached the famous Leyden Observatory where the first successful attempt to apply it toward determining the location of the Lesser Magellanic Cloud was made. At about the same time a former zoologist and newspaper man who had turned to astronomical research was working with the sixty-inch telescope on Mt. Wilson. Harlow Shapley was studying dozens of groups or *globular clusters* of stars which seemed to be isolated systems yet to belong to our own Milky Way. Some of these clusters which his telescope resolved consisted of as many as 35,000 stars. When the importance of Cepheids was shown by Miss Leavitt's work, Shapley made a hunt for them among these clusters and found many of them. After a number of investigations he succeeded in working out the period-luminosity law, so that actual distances could be determined from Cepheids. Previously only relative distances were known. Thus he found that the cluster of Hercules with its 35,000 stars was about 36,000 light years away, and hence within the Milky Way, the diameter of which is about 100,000 light years. By the same method he found nearly a hundred globular clusters; the farthest, NGC 7006, was about 220,000 light years from the earth. Shapley was now able to generalize the law that Miss Leavitt had discovered. To clear his mind from those staggering figures of thousands of stars many of them larger than the sun, situated hundreds of thousands of light years away, he would now and then turn to his entomological hobby. He would appear before the National Academy of Sciences to illuminate its members on such insect topics as *Pterergates in Pogonomyrmex Californicus* or the *Thermokinetics of Liometopum Apiculatum Mava.*

Shapley was fumbling with universes only a quarter of a million light years away. For 1925 this distance was altogether too close. Other universes were scattered through space — great beacons which beckoned to any explorer who was ready to leave the shores of the then known continents and venture out into the endless seas of dark interstellar space. The astronomical Columbus who was to lead an expedition into the new worlds was Edwin P. Hubble. Born in Marshfield, Missouri, Hubble later came to Chicago where his father was engaged in the insurance business. At the University of Chicago he came under the influence of Millikan, his teacher of physics, and Hale, his inspirational guide. Astronomy interested him far more than any other subject, and mathematics was a second love. His keen mind brought him at twenty-one to Oxford University as a Rhodes scholar from Illinois. Here Hubble, who came of English stock, read law and went so far in that direction as to be admitted to the bar in Louisville, Kentucky. Then, having had enough jurisprudence, like Tycho Brahe he suddenly turned again to the laws of the heavens as a research worker at the Yerkes Observatory. George Ellery Hale soon asked him to work at Mt. Wilson and in 1919 he came to California.

At once Hubble began an extended study of the thousands of nebulae which were already known. He had already in 1917 made a systematic photographic study of them, and he wondered if they belonged to our own system of stars. The nearest of these nebulae were visible as faint patches somewhat larger than the moon. He concentrated his attention on Messier 31, the great spiral nebula in the constellation called Andromeda, first referred to by Al Sufi, a Persian, in 905 A.D., and on Messier 33, another celestial pinwheel in Triangulum. Messier 31 appeared many times fainter than other bodies of known distance from the earth. But that gave no clue to its intrinsic brightness. Hubble successfully searched for Cepheid variables and found a dozen of them with fluctuating periods similar to some in the Milky Way. Then with the aid of the period-luminosity law he calculated their intrinsic luminosities and found them to be four thousand times greater than that of the sun, member of our own Milky Way. From this figure he was safe in declaring that Messier 31 was about 900,000 light years away, far from our own galaxy of stars and hence of extragalactic location. Further work resulted in an excellent analysis of the Andromeda nebula which turned out to be similar to the Milky Way both in size and composition.

Messier 33 was also searched for Cepheids and again the observation of these telltale bodies opened up sealed pages and told the story that this nebula, too, was beyond the celestial girdle, an external galaxy, a remote island universe in the ocean of space, somewhat less than one million light years from us. Hubble's ship was well on its way into the new uncharted seas. He had definitely shown that there were universes far beyond our own galaxy and pointed to the possibility of the existence of thousands of other systems inhabiting space. The theory of island universes, once contemplated and later rejected, had returned and was now an established fact.

There followed from this one of the most amazing chapters in the history of astronomical exploration. Once the way had been shown, there was a feverish rush to chart the new universes of extragalactic space beyond the Milky Way. The hundred-inch and the sixty-inch and other large telescopes went hunting for the new universes. Hundreds of nebulae were resolved into stars, gases, clouds of dust, and larger particles made visible by near by stars, "primeval chaos of shining fluid," as Herschel had described them. Among them were frequently found Cepheids and even novae, those odd points of glaring light that suddenly rise seemingly out of nowhere, take a look at the firmament, and then die of exhaustion never to reappear. Many of these novae were recorded by the Chinese, and tradition has it that Hipparchus made his great catalogue of stars because he once saw a nova and, inspired by it, wanted to learn if it was a rare or a frequent phenomenon. The first of these novae to arouse great interest in Europe was reported by Tycho Brahe in 1572 in Casseopeia. It was so bright that it could be seen in broad daylight, and lasted for six months. Another was discovered late in 1934 in the constellation Hercules. It expanded at the rate of ten thousand miles per minute and in one month increased in brightness a hundred thousand times. Before it disappeared from sight it was more brilliant than the North Star. Only forty-six of these rare stars have been reported in history since 1572; the star of Bethlehem may have been one of them. Their origin is not understood. Some think they result from the collision of a star with another hidden, dark star, or from the sudden release of pent-up energies in certain stars. Novae also help to determine distances of nebulae, for it has been found that the maximum brightness of a nova indicates roughly the general order of its distance from the earth.

The data kept piling up. No one knew where the calculations would lead. Suddenly out of these fresh researches appeared a most startling discovery — a discovery which may yet rank among the six greatest in the history of science. The entire family of extragalactic universes, as far as the telescopic eye aided by the photographic plate could reach, seemed to be racing away from the speck of dust upon which mortal observers were perched. Moving away, speeding along at terrific velocities which kept accelerating with increase in distance, racing away into the farthermost limits of the heavens, zooming through space went all of the nebulae. Like a huge soap bubble the supergalaxy kept expanding, fleeing the earth as if it were a leper, increasing in size at a rate which would double its diameter every fourteen hundred million years. This revelation came upon the world with lightning rapidity and found science unprepared to meet it with a universally accepted explanation. It was fantastic, awe-inspiring, alarming, almost ominous.

Hubble was the leader in this new development. His chief lieutenant was Milton L. Humason, who had joined the ranks of astronomers in an unusual way. He had finished grammar school at fourteen, and although the son of a California banker, this completed his formal education. He disliked school. From the streets of Pasadena the top of Mt. Wilson beckoned to Humason, and so he climbed the mountain to work in the hotel near the Observatory. That view from the peak of the neighboring mountains, the San Gabriel Valley, Pasadena, Los Angeles, and the Pacific Ocean captivated him. The mountain fever got him, and he stayed doing odd jobs at the hotel, driving a mule team which pulled supplies and machinery up the mountain for the Observatory, working in the great clockroom of the telescope, helping with the routine photographic work in the laboratory up in the clouds. Humason later married the daughter of one of the observatory staff, and soon after went at astronomy seriously. Many of the workers of the Observatory began to call upon him, as a skilled stellar photographer, for aid. So valuable did he become that in 1922 he was made a member of the official staff and given a chance at the big telescopes. He had graduated from the position of " night assistant " and now dressed in polar costume, with a woolen hood over his head and short flowing jacket to protect him from the long cold nights, he would shout his own instructions from the top of the telescope to younger " night assistants " in the darkness fifty feet below him.

Soon after Hubbel first showed definitely that there existed galaxies beyond our own, he and Humason turned their attention to a problem which had been presented by another astronomer working at the Lowell Observatory at Flagstaff, Arizona. Vesto M. Slipher had been studying by means of spectroscopic analysis the motions of spiral-shaped nebulae. The method of parallax had failed to give any clear data. The analysis of the spectra of moving bodies was more promising. The discovery of the use of this newer method goes back to a day in 1841 when Christian Doppler of Prague discovered what is now known as the "Doppler effect." After establishing the fact that the pitch of a sound rises as the source of the sound moves toward the listener (because more sound waves crowd in upon him) he proved that this same "Doppler effect" or change in frequency also applied to light. Color in light is analogous to pitch in sound. Red light has the lowest frequency (largest wave length) of visible light. Violet, at the other end of the spectrum of visible light, has the highest frequency (smallest wave length). Hence a luminous object moving toward the observer would change to a higher frequency, in other words, it would shift from the red end to the violet end of the spectrum. Thus if a red light source, for example, is moving toward the observer, more light waves per second reach him, the light increases in frequency and appears orange, yellow, green, blue, or violet depending upon the velocity of approach. Similarly, if a violet light is moving away from the observer it changes in frequency in the direction of the red end of the spectrum. The faster the light is moving the greater will be the change in frequency, and hence the greater the shift in color.

The amount of this shift could thus be used as a measure of the velocity of approach or recession of a light source. The first to apply this principle to a study of the movements of luminous bodies in the sky was Sir William Huggins, soon after the invention of the spectroscope. Huggins identified the spectrum lines of certain elements in various luminous bodies in the sky and then compared their positions with the spectral lines of the same stationary elements obtained on earth. He noticed a slight lack of coincidence or shift of the spectrum lines, which he attributed to motion of the light source. When the account of this method of research was printed by the Englishman in 1868, it was greeted with skepticism. Not until this technique was repeated and his results confirmed did astronomers realize the importance of this new approach.

By the use of the same method, Slipher had found that some

spiral nebulae were whirling at great speeds, one end approaching the earth and the other retreating. By 1928 his data on the movements of forty-three of the nearest nebulae indicated also that in general all of the spirals were rapidly moving away from the earth. He did not grasp the significance of his figures. Hubble, however, found a curious relationship between the velocities of recession of these nebulae and the distances of these moving nebulae from the earth. The California astronomer discovered that the velocity of recession as shown by the red shift of their spectral lines increased with the distance of the nebulae from the earth. The more distant nebulae were moving away faster than the nearer ones. Was this velocity-distance relationship a fundamental one? Was it applicable to regions beyond the six million light years that had already been plumbed? Were all the nebulae rushing away from the earth?

It appeared to Hubble imperative to test this relationship at once, not only within the entire range of extragalactic nebulae which he had picked out of more and more remote space, but also to extend these observations as far into extragalactic space as his instruments would permit. First it was necessary to discover the distances of the extragalactic nebulae with the aid of new methods based on the data furnished by Cepheid variables. This was Hubble's job. Then it was necessary to determine by means of the spectrograph the shift, if any, of their spectral lines to the red. This was the work assigned to Humason. The hundred-inch telescope was made available to them and the project was started in 1928.

Obtaining spectra of the very distant nebulae was a tremendously difficult undertaking. Humason had to keep a nebula, little more than a point of light among thousands of others all around it, steadily fixed over the slit of a spectrograph attached to the telescope. All through the night the spot of light in the heavens had to be watched constantly for many reasons. For example, although the wheel which kept the hundred-inch telescope focussed on that spot is approximately correct, its speed varies slightly with changes of temperature. Then just as the night ended and the first light of dawn appeared, the photographic plate had to be shielded until the following night when again it was exposed to the same spot of the same nebula. A complete exposure of one nebula often took as long as seventy-five hours, which frequently meant eight to ten whole nights. Watching points of light over a narrow slit would have broken almost any astronomer. Yet after a long lonely vigil his colleagues would often find Humason tired but still steady.

The photographic film was then carefully developed at the mountain observatory. The spectrum of the nebula was compared with that of the sun, and any shifts in the position of certain well-known spectrum lines, such as those of calcium or helium, were recorded. This was a very delicate job, for Humason was working with a picture only one-tenth of an inch long and one-thirty-second wide, containing closely placed lines imprinted by light which had left its nebular source as much as a hundred million years ago. Often nothing very clear could be made out of the negative and the entire photographing process had to be repeated. At other times the lines were not quite so faint and Humason was able to record a shift of the lines toward the red end of the spectrum. The film was then brought down to the Observatory Office at 813 Santa Barbara Street in Pasadena, where further studies of it could be made. The time at the hundred-inch telescope had to be so carefully divided among the various astronomers at Mt. Wilson, for there were so many projects under way that Humason was forced to remain at the foot of the mountain the greater part of each month. During this time he would make additional measurements of the spectrum shift from the film, and calculate the velocity this represented.

Hubble would now determine the distance which this red shift indicated for the position of the nebula. Then he would study this position of the nebula from the earth with relation to the velocity with which it was moving. This was much more than routine work. It was exciting. The men waited breathlessly for the figures to shape themselves. "We never knew," said Humason, "but what we would get results that did not follow the others. There was the same excitement in the laboratory as when new planets were discovered." But each picture showed the lines were moved toward the red. The nebulae were all receding from the earth. There was no exception. Moreover, the velocity-distance relation held even way out in the deepest extragalactic space. The farther away the nebula, the faster it was receding (see List of Illustrations).

As they kept piercing the heavens to more and more remote distances, Hubble and Humason placed their observational figures on graph paper. N.G.C. 385, a nebula in Pegasus, twenty-three million light years away, was receding at a velocity of 2400 miles per second. There were other nebulae which had flown higher than Pegasus. N.G.C. 2562 in the Cancer cluster, 29.5 million light years distant, was racing away at a speed of 3000 miles per second. Nebulae in Perseus, thirty-six million light years from the sun, were hurrying along at 3200 miles per second. N.G.C. 4884, a spot of light forty-five million light years away in the Coma Bereniceo cluster of stars, was leaving us behind at the speed of 4700 miles a second. The Ursa Major Cluster discovered by Walter Baade only a few years before, and estimated to be eighty-five million light years from the terrestrial observer, was dashing madly away at the even greater speed of 9500 miles per second. When the Leo Cluster was discovered in 1930, one hundred and five million light years out in space, it was found that it was ripping away from us at the stupendous speed of 12,000 miles per second. The Gemini Cluster bodies, one hundred thirty-five million light years away, was roaring through space at 15,000 miles per second. And a nebula in a cluster in Boötes situated at the farthest outposts thus far measured (two hundred and twenty million light years away) seemed to be moving even faster — at a superexplosive speed estimated at 24,000 miles per second (a speed equal to twice the velocity of alpha rays expelled by radium).

The probable error of the figures obtained was calculated and found to be not more than about ten per cent — an exceedingly

Clusters of nebulae	Distance in million light years	Velocity in miles per second	Number of nebulae observed in each cluster
Virgo	6.	700	23
Pegasus	23.5	2,400	4
Pisces.............	24	2,900	4
Cancer	29.5	3,000	2
Perseus	36	3,200	4
Coma Bereniceo....	45	4,700	8
Ursa Major........	85	9,500	1
Leo...............	105	12,000	1
Corona Borealis ...	120	13,500	1
Gemini	135	15,000	2
Boötes	220	24,000	1

accurate result for this type of astronomical investigation. Both the accuracy of this method of analysis and the extreme range to which it was applicable were due in no small measure to the introduction of a new camera lens. During the course of Hubble's and Humason's amazing exploration into the heavens, they had been handicapped by the slowness of the lens they were forced to use. The nebulae which they wished to photograph were so far away and so faint that extremely long exposures had to be made to get sufficient light. These long exposures often meant blurred pictures. What was therefore needed was a much faster lens, that is, one of smaller focus which would give pictures in less exposure time and hence of greater clarity.

Dr. W. B. Rayton, who had been making and improving lenses for a quarter of a century at the Bausch and Lomb Company in New York, was asked to make a short-focus spectrographic objective for the men at Mt. Wilson. Before long Humason received an eightfold enlargement of a microscopic objective with a focal length of 32 mm. and an aperture of 50 mm., or a ratio of f/0.6, which Rayton had made from his own design. Humason tried it out. It was a wonder. It had high speed, gave excellent definition, and cut the time of exposure to one-third. It was far superior to any even from Germany which until then had been leading the world in the field of optical instruments.

By 1934 the Hubble-Humason team had produced the undisputed observational results described above. They were based upon the period-luminosity law for distances of the extragalactic nebulae, and upon the red shift as shown by photographs for the velocities of recession. The straight line on Hubble's graph

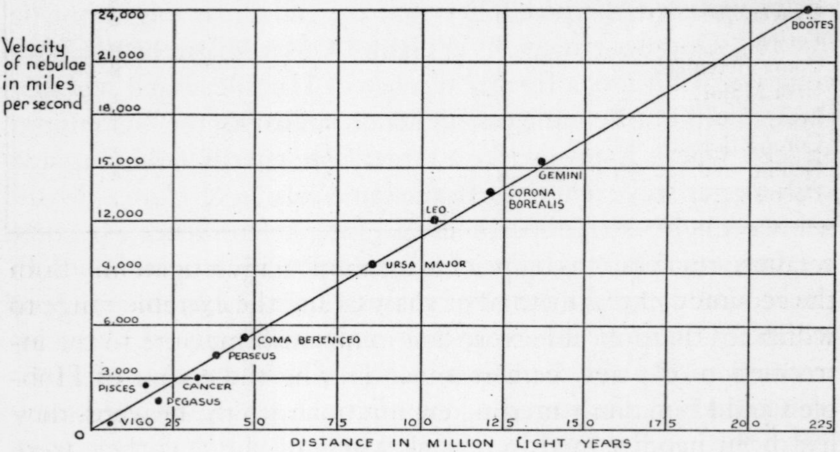

FIG. 33

Graph showing the *Velocity-Distance Relationship* of some of the extragalactic nebulae as found by Hubble and Humason.

indicated that there was a regular increase of about one hundred miles per second for each additional million light years of distance from the observer. These facts seemed well established. They were the conclusions of two of the most competent astronomical observers of all time, equipped with the most powerful instruments in existence.

Seldom had a discovery started such a world-wide discussion. The nature and extent of the physical universe had always been one of the fundamental problems over which science had debated. Many theories had been advanced, but the lack of sufficient data had been a stumbling block to the acceptance of any one of them. Now here was a new theory — one that postulated an ever expanding sky-rocketing universe with all the nebulae rushing away from the earth.

Eddington, the Quaker astronomer of England, was moved to

call it " so preposterous that I feel almost an indignation that anyone should believe in it except myself." Perhaps the red shift of the spectral lines of the nebulae did not necessarily mean that the nebulae were moving away from the earth. Zwicky, Hubble's colleague at the California Institute of Technology, seriously discussed the possibility that the red shifts might not be due to " Doppler effects." William D. MacMillan of the University of Chicago, a former teacher of Hubble, asked whether there might not be some phenomenon similar to the " Compton effect " where X-rays strike a target, lose energy, and reappear with longer wave lengths. In the same way light from a distant nebula might strike particles in interstellar space, become weaker, and appear as light with a greater wave length. Such an effect would explain the observational data of Hubble without ascribing them to an expanding super-universe. Others attempted to explain the phenomenon which the California astronomers had discovered as due not to an actual outward moving of the nebulae but to a property of light which coming from great distances loses energy by the gravitational effects of material particles strewn through intergalactic space.

Another interesting point was raised. Perhaps, some said, our measurements indicate that a hundred and thirty-five million years ago nebulae were rushing away at a speed of 15,000 miles a second, while forty-five million years ago they were moving away with a velocity of only 4700 miles a second, and today the expansion of the universe has in reality stopped, since some of the nearest galaxies seem actually to be stationary with respect to the earth. And while Einstein declares that " it is reasonable to attribute this displacement or red shift to a velocity effect," Hubble himself hopes to determine by further investigation whether the motion is real or apparent. In April, 1934, he told the National Academy of Sciences: " Red shifts are due either to actual motion or to some hitherto unrecognized principle of physics. The cautious observer refrains from committing himself to the present interpretation and employs the colorless term *apparent velocity*."

Hubble continued to study the imprints of the light of the past on the photographic plates attached to his telescope. New and more remote nebulae revealed themselves. To gain some clearer idea of the extent and anatomy of the physical universe he followed the plan of J. C. Kapteyn of Groningen, Holland. Kapteyn a generation before had inaugurated a statistical study of the stars by concentrating research on certain selected areas and then from the data thus collected attempting to arrive at a general conclusion as to the nature of the whole heavens. Hubble made 1283 photographs of a small portion of the sky observable on Mt. Wilson. Penetrating to the farthest space thus far probed, his pictures showed 44,000 separate nebulae. This number, he computed, corresponded to a total of about seventy-five million island universes within the range of the hundred-inch telescope sweeping but a small fraction of the sky. Since the total region observable from Mt. Wilson was in turn but a fraction of one per cent of the complete universe, the probable number of universes was estimated to be about 500,000,000,000,000. This staggering number of nebulae was distributed fairly uniformly through a finite space of which he estimated the radius of curvature to be three billion light years.

Hubble estimated that the average distance between any two nebulae was about a million and a half light years. Each nebula contained enough matter to make a thousand million stars. The average luminosity of each nebula was eighty million times that of our sun. He also found the mean density of matter in space to be about 10^{-30} grams per cubic centimeter. That is, the relation between the mass of the universe and the space it occupied was infinitesimally small — comparable, in fact, to one grain of sand inside a volume equivalent to that of the earth. According to this figure the universe is almost wholly empty space, even though it contains billions of nebulae. The most perfect vacuum we can produce in our laboratories is still very dense in comparison with the emptiness of the entire universe.

All of the above estimates are of course highly problematical. They are based on the assumption that the portion of space which the 100-inch telescope made available to the astronomer was a fair sample of the whole extragalactic system. "We must make the assumption of the observable region being a fair sample of the universe," said Hubble, "or dream." And while this structure of the superuniverse which Hubble has painted is still very vague, he reminds us that "in our generation for the first time, the structure of the universe is being investigated by direct observations."

Hubble had sculptured a new universe out of the cold, hard granite of observational data. It was of course a more acceptable one than theologians had furnished mankind. And now other universe-builders were busy painting pictures of the cosmos with the stuff of mathematical symbols and involved equations. Had not Pythagoras said that "God geometrizes"? Perhaps in the language of mathematics, which Galileo had declared was that in which nature's great book was written, could be found a description of the universe. Hampered by a lack of observational data, men had hunted for new mathematical symbols with which to fashion new universes.

Many years before Hubble's achievements the great Einstein himself had also incidentally tried his hand at this game of picturing the universe. He had reached a model of a *static universe* — a universe which never changed. It was a difficult picture to accept. But the days of accepting theories only when they could be converted into buildable mechanical models were gone. The universe of Einstein was indeed one which could scarcely be visualized except by a pure mathematician, and then only in terms of strange symbols picked presumably out of thin air. But then Einstein holds that, in a certain sense, pure thought is competent to comprehend the real, even as the ancients believed.

Einstein's equation of a static universe appeared in 1917. Toward the close of the same year Willem de Sitter, director of the astronomical observatory at Leyden, Holland, joined the ranks of the universe-builders. De Sitter had been among the first to understand and appreciate Einstein. After a thorough study of the relativity theory he attempted to apply it to astronomy and the architecture of the universe. Like Einstein, this man went back to pure mathematics and obtained a picture of a different universe. Einstein's equation showed a universe filled with matter and at a standstill. De Sitter postulated a universe that was practically empty, but in which there might be some mutually receding particles of matter. Neither of these older models, however, agreed with the observational data collected by Hubble. De Sitter's model failed because, strictly taken, it contained no matter at all, and Einstein's because the matter in it stayed at rest and showed no red-shift phenomenon unearthed at Mt. Wilson. Einstein was ready with one terrific hammer blow to smash his static universe to smithereens in the face of the findings of the California astronomers. There was nothing sacred about his equations, admitted this greatest of all living mathematical physicists. Mathematics was not a golden image that had to be worshipped, nor was the world required to serve offerings to authorities.

There was an urgent and immediate need for a revamping of cosmological models. It was only natural that some redeemer might be found in Pasadena where Hubble, Hale, Millikan, and other luminaries in theoretical as well as experimental science had often gathered to thresh out the implications of Hubble's bewildering discovery. Among the scientists who engaged in these endless discussions was Richard Chace Tolman, professor of physical chemistry and mathematical physics at the California Institute of Technology, one of the men who " with a philosophical taste that is delightful makes this place so livable."

Tolman had already had a distinguished career. After studying chemical engineering at the Massachusetts Institute of Technology, he attended technical schools in Germany where he worked with dyes and artificial silk. His father, president of the Samson Cordage Works in Shirley, Massachusetts, was interested in the cotton industry, and this technical experience which his son was getting abroad was looked upon with great favor. But Richard was too much interested in theoretical science to enter his father's business. He returned to America to study under A. A. Noyes several difficult problems connected with the

The largest telescope in the world. The 100-inch reflector of the Mt. Wilson Observatory showing the interior of the Dome, Cassagrain observing platform, etc., as seen from the west. *(Courtesy, G. E. Hale)*

THE VELOCITY-DISTANCE RELATION FOR EXTRA-GALACTIC NEBULAE

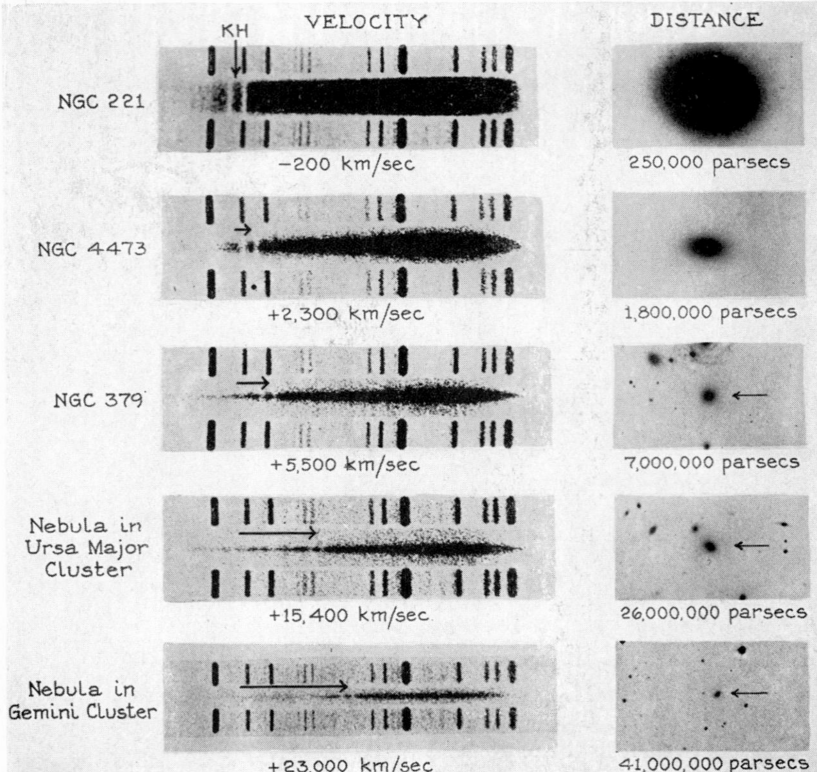

The arrows above the nebular spectra point to the H and K lines of calcium and show the amounts these lines are displaced toward the red end of the spectra. The comparison spectra are of helium.

The direct photographs (on the same scale and with approximately the same exposure times) illustrate the decrease in size and brightness with increasing velocity or red-shift.

NGC 4473 is a member of the Virgo cluster and NGC 379 is a member of a group of nebulae in Pisces.

1 parsec = 3.26 light years.

The red end of the spectrum in the above photographs is to the right.

Note how the farther away the nebula is, the greater is the shift of the calcium lines of the spectrum. *(Courtesy, M. L. Humason)*

MILTON L. HUMASON

theory of ionization. Except for interludes in the Chemical Warfare Service and as director of the Fixed Nitrogen Laboratory, he has been an impractical theoretical man ever since.

As early as 1907 he became enmeshed in the attractive web of Einstein's special theory of relativity, and ten years later published *The Theory of the Relativity of Motion.* He showed that he could handle highly abstract and theoretical problems like a master, and declared that "The days of adventurous discovery have not passed forever." At this time he added his testimony "to the growing conviction that the conceptual space and time of science are not God-given and should be altered whenever the discovery of new facts makes such a change pragmatic." In 1927 appeared his *Statistical Mechanics* devised to investigate the laws that describe the gross behavior of systems containing many molecules if we cannot follow or predict the exact behavior of individual elements. The years that followed found him increasingly immersed in relativistic thermodynamics.

The delicacy of the astronomical discovery of Hubble and Humason on the mountain interested Tolman from the very start. The experimental discovery and measurements of small effects had always given him real esthetic satisfaction, and he liked to discuss the details of the actual experiments which finally culminated in the discovery of the recession of the extragalactic nebulae. The implications of the discovery were equally important to him. He had faith in the value of theory as a tool of discovery. "We must admire Galileo," he said, "for insisting on observational facts as the ultimate arbiter and thus breaking away from a decadent Aristotelian tradition. But we must not let this just admiration blind us to the power and skill of those other theoretical physicists who obtain the suggestion for physical principles from the inner workings of the mind and then present their conclusions to the arbitrament of experimental test."

Tolman undertook a reinvestigation of the problem of the structure of the universe. Locked in Room 5 in the basement of the Gates Chemical Laboratory of California "Tech," shrouded in the thick smoke of his ever puffing pipe, Tolman set to work with pencil and paper. He had the difficult problem of finding the pattern of a whole universe. Tolman is not simply a pure mathematician. He is a brilliant mathematical physicist who was wrestling with the problem of getting a clear picture of a physical situation and then shaping it into a mathematical equation. His method was very much like Einstein's. He first jotted down a long equation on one of the sheets of paper that cluttered his desk. That equation represented an idealized picture of the physical universe. Partly because of the mathematical difficulties involved and partly because of the limited range of observational data available, his equation represented only a highly idealized model of the superuniverse. He kept changing his equations. When necessary he would supplement Einstein's principles of relativistic mechanics with those furnished by his own development of relativistic thermodynamics. Now he would add another symbol, remove still another, change the sign or exponent of a letter, and keep juggling the formulas as new obstacles or new interpretations reached his mind. With every stroke of his pencil a different universe appeared, with every crumpling of a whole sheet of formulas many universes were destroyed. In the morning he built, in the evening, he tore down. He was like a god and a demon building and destroying worlds in his den.

Some men are guided by psychic intuitions but most great ideas have come after long travail with numerous worthless ones. This is true of Tolman. In 1929 out of his self-imposed seclusion Tolman finally emerged. He had witnessed the lifting of a veil. He had obtained a new picture of a new non-static universe based on the observational data of Hubble. It was not a spectacle of myriads of stars, cepheids, novae, comets, planets, giant clusters, vacuous expanses of interstellar space, dust and chaos. It was a bold condensation of a single mathematical equation.

$$ds^2 = \frac{e^{g(t)}}{(1 + \frac{r^2}{4} R^2)^2} (dx^2 + dy^2 + dz^2) + dt^2$$

This equation (or line element) did not look very different from the equations of either Einstein or De Sitter. The same symbols were used. But there was in that equation enough of a variation to give a universe which could change with the time factor instead of remaining static like Einstein's and which contained matter instead of being empty like De Sitter's.

Tolman had read a great deal on the many attempts to fashion new universes mathematically. But, as is rather common in science, he too had overlooked some important papers. Just a few months before his own paper was read before the National Academy of Sciences, an equation entirely equivalent to his own had been derived by H. P. Robertson of Princeton University. And seven years before, a brilliant Russian mathematician, A. Friedman, had made the first deliberate attempt to investigate line elements for a non-static universe. To be sure, both these men had derived their equations from general geometric considerations rather than, as Tolman had done, from actual observational data furnished by Hubble. Yet when after the publication of his own more important findings the work of these men was brought to his attention, Tolman quickly dug up the papers and acknowledged their priority. After studying them he wrote that Friedman, " in spite of the lack of attention that has been paid to his article, should receive credit as the originator of the new chapter in cosmology." Tolman is no scientific prima donna.

The first attempt to apply such mathematical equations to actual phenomena was made in 1927 by a young Belgian priest, Abbé Georges Lemaître, of the University of Louvain. This young man had at the age of nine decided to be a scientist and at the same time a Catholic priest, since his family history called for one. He took the usual seminary courses leading to the priesthood. Later through a scholarship created by the Commission for the Relief of Belgium, he was enabled to study at Harvard University the application of the theory of relativity to astronomy. To him the search for salvation and the search for scientific truth were not incompatible, and " seeking truth was a service to God." Lemaître investigated Friedman's equation and applied his non-static line element to actual astronomical data. He made the important discovery that the apparent red shift of the light from the nearest galaxies could be interpreted with the help of the concept of an expanding universe. As his results were published in a rather inaccessible journal, however, they remained unknown until Eddington called them to the attention of the world in 1930. This was after Tolman had advanced his own cosmological model based on a mass of fresh data which was not available to Lemaître.

Einstein's mathematical model had failed to do very much for it lacked observational evidence. With Tolman's new concept of a dynamic universe based on a fair amount of observational data, the cosmological world began to hum. Einstein was excited and declared that Tolman's work has given an original and especially illuminating mathematical equation. At the invitation of Millikan and Hale, Einstein came to Pasadena to discuss this all-absorbing question. Both in 1931 and in 1932 he sat as a schoolboy in the lecture room of the California Institute of Technology while Hubble graphically described the observational data behind his discovery of the velocity-distance relationship, and Humason showed those uncanny spectral pictures of " light howling down the spectral scale " toward the red end, and Tolman hammered out the details of his new dynamic universe built from the bricks and mortar of the new discoveries. Einstein made no secret of his amazement at the work of this American triumvirate. More than once during the course of these discussions he would rise from his seat, go to the blackboard in front of the room and add his interpretations and suggestions which Tolman would then translate into English to the assembled scientists.

The open season for universe-builders had arrived. It seemed that everybody capable of handling extremely involved equations took a hand. Eddington showed that Einstein's original static model would be unstable, liable to expansion or contraction if once disturbed from its original state, and hence really a special case of the now generally accepted expanding-universe model. De Sitter in Holland, Laue and Heckmann in Germany, McRae and McVittie in England, and many others presented their favorites. Silberstein fashioned a universe out of nothing but radiation. Takeuchi, a Japanese, was the first Oriental to advance a mathematical model of the universe. No mechanical set-ups were demanded or invoked to give visual clarity to the worlds of the pure mathematicians. And Jeans was led to declare, " We can understand the universe today only if we think of it as the creation of a pure mathematician in terms of pure thought. It becomes a bewildering paradox as soon as we try to grasp it in terms of a mechanical model." Bertrand Russell was more critical, almost unkind. " It is the privilege of pure mathematicians," he said, " not to know what they are talking about."

The implications of the new discoveries which emerged from Pasadena were many and profound. For one thing, they heralded what came perilously near to being a recrudesence of those philosophical discussions reminiscent of the days of Kepler and Copernicus. Were it not for the background of scientific data which the exponents of the various schools occasionally evoked to strengthen their points of view, these discussions of the ultimate future of the universe, the teleological or purposeful aspects of creation, and the existence of a pristine power in whose hands the cosmic machine wound up billions of years ago was slowly unwinding, might have done justice to the great metaphysicians who centuries ago filled the air with pompous words trumpeting high sounding hypotheses. Science which centuries before had broken away from abstruse metaphysics seemed once again to be clothing itself in the raiments of pure philosophy to such an extent that it became at times indistinguishable from philosophy.

This eternally expanding universe was dreadful to contemplate. This ever inflating rubber balloon might burst and end in the chaos from which it started. Why, in fact, had it not already burst? Tolman thought of this and saw the danger to science. " In studying the problem of cosmology," he said, " we are immediately aware that the future fate of man is involved in the issue, and we must hence be particularly careful to keep our judgments uninfected by the demands of religion and unswerved by human hopes and fears. The problem must be approached with the keen, balanced, critical and skeptical objectivity of the scientist."

Tolman thought of other possible cosmological equations which might keep intact the observational fact of the outer nebulae rushing away from the earth and at the same time not result in a final state of expansion. A number of such models proved possible. These, according to his extension of thermodynamics to relativity, could undergo a continual succession of identical expansions and contractions without ever coming to a state of rest. These postulated perpetually moving accordion-like universes. This in spite of an equilibrium demanded by the classical thermodynamics which predicted the sun and stars cold and all of creation dead and lifeless.

In addition to Hubble's and Tolman's ideas of the changing structure of the universe there was a third — much older than these. There were thus three concepts of the universe around which men rallied. The oldest was that of a universe which was constantly getting colder with all the stars radiating their heat far into space. The universe was running down, unable to maintain its status quo, because of the classical form of the second law of thermodynamics. According to this law, heat and other forms of energy always pass on the whole from regions of higher intensity to regions of lower intensity. This would eventually result in a uniform distribution of heat throughout space. Extreme cold, stagnation and death would follow, since the amount of energy would be infinitesimally small when evenly distributed throughout the colossal volume of the universe. This was the gloomy picture which until a few years ago was the orthodox model of most scientists. Jeans and Eddington today are still the spokesmen of this concept of the degradation of matter — modern Jeremiahs who prophesy doom and regard the " hope of unlimited progress for human civilization to be an exploded myth." The second concept, that of Hubble, was hardly less pessimistic. The ever expanding universe would some day have to end in the nothingness of complete expansion.

Against these two pictures the newer physics and astronomy aligned themselves with Tolman's third concept. They were armed with the weapons of a relativistic thermodynamics whose equations insisted that it was possible for a universe to expand and contract forever without coming to a state of rest (maximum entropy where free energy would cease to exist). It was now possible to believe at least in a hypothetical universe which continuously regained its birth — a perpetually living universe which alternately expanded and shrank. Millikan, Smuts, and the mathematician, Bishop C. W. Barnes, stand at the head of the phalanx which sees this view strengthened by the partially demonstrated phenomenon of radiation changing back again into matter just as matter is definitely known to change into radiation. Radiation, by some mechanism still very little understood, is believed to be replenishing the lost matter of the universe. This interpretation banishes completely not only the first gloomy picture of a decaying universe but also that of an expanding universe thinning out into nothingness. It holds out the hope of saving mankind from an otherwise inexorable extinction.

But these concepts were, after all, based to a great extent on pure speculation. None of the adherents are dogmatists. They, too, have their deep doubts. Tolman, awed by the immensity of space and exulted by the temerity of the human spirit in attempting a solution of such a fundamental problem, reminds us that, "We do not have sufficient data so that we could assign the actual universe to any one model." His highly simplified pictures of the universe, he never fails to tell us, are analogous to the rigid, weightless levers of simple mechanics or to the spherical, rigid yet, at the same time, perfectly elastic molecules of the physicist. Hence we must be very careful in interpreting the actual universe in terms of conclusions that we may draw as to the behavior of our conceptual models. Yet, rather than appeal to special acts of creation as a way out of the dilemma of the structure of the universe, he is ready to skate on thin, speculative ice. "The chief duty and glory of theoretical science," he believes, " is to extrapolate — as cautiously and wisely as may be — into regions yet unexplored."

The new developments in the field of cosmology have revived the question of the age of the universe. As Hubble has pointed out, every exploration into extragalactic space is an investigation not only of the size but also the age of the universe. These recent discoveries have played havoc with the more or less generally accepted old ideas. For the age of the cosmos, scientists had spoken of hundreds of billions of years, based on evidences furnished by radioactivity, saltiness of the sea, depth of rock strata, and other similar data. But as the newer horizons spread out they synchronously crowded the years into shorter epochs. An expanding universe must have started within much more recent times, or by now it would have been scattered more widely or have completely thinned out before it could start to shrink again. This pulsating universe could not have been on its expanding journey more than about two or three billion years instead of the two or three hundred billion years previously suggested.

Yet all evidences seemed to indicate that many of the stars are much older than a mere few billion years. Some of the double stars, for example, seemed to be at least two hundred billion years old, as indicated by the shape of their orbits. Here we had a situation in which the stars appeared much older than the universe itself. Could it really be that the offspring was older than its parent? That was a riddle until Eddington stepped in and, in his characteristic fashion, offered a solution. " Cuts are in fashion now," said Eddington, " and if the theory of an expanding universe is right, it looks as if we were in for a cut of about 99 per cent in our time scale. That naturally causes a great deal of concern to the department affected; namely, the department of stellar evolution." Perhaps, he reminded science, our ideas of the time that it took stars to pass through their many evolutionary stages from birth to the present are very inaccurate. We may have miscalculated the speed of evolution of stars which may have passed through their life cycles in much shorter time than we had supposed. They might, in fact, be very much younger than we ever dreamed — much younger, in fact, than the universe. Jeans, on the other hand, on the basis of the work done in 1935 on binary stars by Robert G. Aitken, director of the Lick Observatory in California, placed the age of the universe at 10,000 billion years.

Lemaître goes even further and speaks boldly of an instantaneous creation of the whole universe. In December, 1932, he told an audience in Pasadena, " It was ten thousand million years ago that a lone atom, with mass equal to that of the universe, burst. Then the millions of island universes began to take shape for the race through space. This terrific flight is still on — a flight witnessed by the earth itself which is part of this colossal atom. (The most recent estimate of the age of the earth made by Edith Kroupa of Vienna in 1934 is 1800 million years. It is based on the radioactive decay of certain minerals.) This is the poetic picture of a priest who cannot reject the idea of an expanding universe and its implications simply because it does not coincide with the biblical story of creation. For, at the same time, it does not exclude the belief in some divine Force or Creator who set the whole drama in action. Perhaps this " Universe Egg " which Lemaître laid has much in common with the vaporings of those churchmen who ordered Galileo to recite for years the seven penitential psalms for daring to teach that the earth revolved around the sun. Perhaps, on the other hand, this conception is just as meaningful as that of any of the mathematical physicists who have attempted the ambitious task of picturing a universe for us.

Will further observational data clear up the cosmological muddle? Hubble believes they will. " I believe," he wrote in 1932, " the 200-inch telescope will definitely answer the question of the interpretation of red shifts, whether or not they represent actual motion, and if they do represent motion — if the universe is expanding — may indicate the particular type of expansion." Perhaps out of this boiling cosmological pot will come fundamental answers to more than one perplexing question. And just as likely, perhaps not. Harlow Shapley has taken exception to some of the findings of Hubble such as the uniformity in the distribution of the nebulae in the universe and the general movement of recession of *all parts* of the universe. He has said that " although in the last twenty years our knowledge of the sidereal world has more than doubled, the list of things we want to know has trebled or quadrupled, leaving us relatively more ignorant than heretofore." And he has advised that strangely ambitious colloidal aggregate which we know as man not to hope with its incipient mind and meager grasp to interpret the whole of the metagalactic system.

Perhaps we should not. But we will, even though all of our fundamental strivings must end, as Poincaré said, " not with a period but with a question mark."

SOURCES AND REFERENCE MATERIAL

CHAPTER ONE

Genetics

CASTLE, W. E., Genetics and Eugenics (4th Ed.). *Harvard University Press, Cambridge, Mass., 1930.*

CONKLIN, E. G., Heredity and Environment (6th Ed.). *Princeton University Press, Princeton, N. J., 1929.*

EAST, E. M., Biology in Human Affairs. *McGraw-Hill Publishing Co., New York, 1931.*

HOGBEN, L., Genetic Principles in Medicine and Social Science. *Alfred A. Knopf, New York, 1932.*

HURST, C. C., The Mechanism of Creative Evolution. *The Macmillan Company, New York, 1932.*

HURST, C. C., Heredity and the Ascent of Man. *The Macmillan Company, New York, 1935.*

HUXLEY, ALDOUS, Brave New World. *Doubleday, Doran, Garden City, L. I., 1932.*

ILTIS, HUGO, Life of Mendel. *W. W. Norton & Co., New York, 1932.*

JENNINGS, H. S., The Biological Basis of Human Nature. *W. W. Norton & Co., New York, 1930.*

MORGAN, THOMAS HUNT, The Scientific Basis of Evolution (2nd Ed.). *W. W. Norton & Co., New York, 1935.*

MORGAN, THOMAS HUNT, Embryology and Genetics. *Columbia University Press, New York, 1934.*

MORGAN, THOMAS HUNT, The Theory of the Gene. *Yale University Press, New Haven, Conn., 1926.*

MORGAN, BRIDGES, STURTEVANT, The Genetics of Drosophila. *Carnegie Institution, Washington, D. C., 1919.*

MORGAN, STURTEVANT, MULLER, BRIDGES, The Mechanism of Mendelian Heredity. *Henry Holt & Co., New York, 1926.*

NEWMAN, H. H., Evolution, Genetics and Eugenics. *University of Chicago Press, Chicago, Ill., 1932.*

SHARP, L. W., Introduction to Cytology (3rd Ed.). *McGraw-Hill Publishing Co., New York, 1933.*

Singer, C., The Story of Living Things. *Harper & Bros., New York, 1931.*

Sinnott and Dunn, Principles of Genetics (2nd Ed.). *McGraw-Hill Publishing Co., New York, 1932.*

Stockard, C. R., The Physical Basis of Personality. *W. W. Norton & Co., New York, 1931.*

CHAPTER TWO

Anthropology

Boaz, F., Anthropology and Modern Life. *W. W. Norton & Co., New York, 1932.*

Boule, M., Fossil Men. *Gurney & Jackson, London, England, 1923.*

Gregory, W. K., Our Face from Fish to Man. *G. P. Putnam's Sons, New York, 1929.*

Hooton, A. E., Up From the Ape. *The Macmillan Co., New York, 1931.*

Hrdlička, Aleš, The Old Americans. *Williams & Wilkins Co., Baltimore, Md., 1925.*

Hrdlička, Aleš, Children Who Run On All Fours. *McGraw-Hill Publishing Co., New York, 1931.*

Hrdlička, Aleš, The Skeletal Remains of Ancient Man. *Smithsonian Institution, Washington, D. C., 1930.*

Keith, Sir Arthur, New Discoveries Relating to the Antiquity of Man. *W. W. Norton & Co., New York, 1931.*

Kroeber and Waterman, Source Book in Anthropology. *Harcourt, Brace & Co., New York, 1931.*

Loomis, F. B., The Evolution of the Horse. *Marshall Jones Co., Boston, Mass., 1926.*

MacCurdy, G. G., Human Origins. *Appleton-Century Co., New York, 1934.*

Osborn, H. F., Men of the Old Stone Age. *Charles Scribner's Sons, New York, 1921.*

Peake and Fleure, The Corridors of Time (Vol. 1). *Yale University Press, New Haven, Conn., 1927.*

Radin, Paul, The Racial Myth. *McGraw-Hill Publishing Co., New York, 1934.*

Richarz, S., Age of the Human Race in the Light of Geology. *Smithsonian Institution, Washington, D. C., 1930.*

SMITH, G. ELLIOT, The Evolution of Man. *Oxford University Press, New York, 1924.*

SOLLAS, W. J., Ancient Hunters and their Modern Representatives. *The Macmillan Co., New York, 1924.*

TILNEY, F., The Master of Destiny. *Doubleday, Doran, Garden City, L. I., 1930.*

ZUCKERMAN, S., Functional Affinities of Man, Monkeys, and Apes. *Harcourt, Brace & Co., New York, 1933.*

CHAPTER THREE

Physical Disease

BEN MEYR, B., Your Germs and Mine. *Doubleday, Doran, Garden City, L. I., 1934.*

CLENDENNING, L., The Human Body. *Alfred A. Knopf, New York, 1927.*

DE KRUIF, P., Men Against Death. *Harcourt, Brace & Co., New York, 1932.*

DIBLE, J. H., Recent Advances in Bacteriology (2nd Ed.). *P. Blakiston's Son & Co., New York, 1932.*

ECKSTEIN, G., Noguchi. *Harper & Bros., New York, 1931.*

GARRISON, H. F., Introduction to the History of Medicine (4th Ed.). *W. B. Saunders Co., Philadelphia, Pa., 1929.*

HAGGARD, H. W., Devils, Drugs and Doctors. *Harper & Bros., New York, 1930.*

D'HERELLE, F., Bacteriophage and Its Behavior. *Williams & Wilkins Co., Baltimore, Md., 1926.*

JORDAN AND FALK, Newer Knowledge of Bacteriology and Immunology. *University of Chicago Press, Chicago, Ill., 1928.*

KENDALL, A. I., Civilization and the Microbe. *Houghton, Mifflin Co., New York, 1923.*

MOHR, O. L., Heredity and Disease. *W. W. Norton & Co., New York, 1934.*

PACKARD, F. A., History of Medicine in the U. S. *Paul B. Hoeber, New York, 1931.*

PARK, W. H., AND WILLIAMS, A. W., Who's Who Among the Microbes. *Appleton-Century Co., New York, 1929.*

PEARL, RAYMOND, Ancestry of the Long Lived. *Johns Hopkins Press, Baltimore, Md., 1934.*

PEARL, RAYMOND, The Biology of Death. *Scientific Monthly, New York, 1921.*

REID, E. G., The Great Physician (Wm. Osler). *Oxford University Press, New York, 1931.*

RIVERS, T. M., Filterable Viruses. *Williams & Wilkins Co., Philadelphia, Pa., 1928.*

ROSENAU, M. J., Preventive Medicine and Hygiene. *Appleton-Century Co., New York, 1927.*

SIGERIST, H. E., American Medicine. *W. W. Norton & Co., New York, 1934.*

SIGERIST, H. E., The Great Doctors. *W. W. Norton & Co., New York, 1933.*

SMITH, THEOBALD, Parasitism and Disease. *Princeton University Press, Princeton, N. J., 1934.*

STIEGLITZ, J. O. (Ed.), Chemistry in Medicine. *The Chemical Foundation, New York, 1928.*

WELCH, WILLIAM H., Papers and Addresses of W. H. Welch (3 vols.). *Johns Hopkins University Press, Baltimore, Md., 1920.*

ZINSSER, HANS, Rats, Lice and History. *Little, Brown & Co., New York, 1935.*

CHAPTER FOUR
Cancer

BAUR, FISCHER AND LENZ, Human Heredity. *The Macmillan Co., New York, 1931.*

EWING, JAMES, Neoplastic Diseases. *W. B. Saunders Co., Philadelphia, Pa., 1928.*

HOLMES, BARBARA, Cancer and Scientific Research. *The Macmillan Co., New York, 1931.*

OSTERHOUT, W. J. V., The Nature of Life. *Henry Holt & Co., New York, 1924.*

ROUS, PEYTON, The Modern Dance of Life. *The Macmillan Co., New York, 1929.*

SLYE, MAUD, Songs and Solaces. *The Stratford Company, Boston, Mass., 1934.*

SLYE, MAUD, 33 Papers on Cancer Research. *American Journal of Cancer, Annals of Surgery, Journal of Cancer Research, Journal of the A. M. A., 1914–35.*

TOBEY, J. A., Cancer. *Alfred A. Knopf, New York, 1932.*

WARBURG, OTTO, The Metabolism of Tumors. *Constable & Co., London, England, 1930.*

International Symposium on Cancer Control; Lake Mohonk Conference, New York. *The Surgical Publishing Co. of Chicago, Ill., 1927.*

CHAPTER FIVE

Glands

ALLEN, E. (ED.), Sex and Internal Secretions. *Williams & Wilkins Co., Baltimore, Md., 1933.*

CAMERON, A. T., Advances in Endocrinology. *P. Blakiston's Son & Co., Philadelphia, Pa., 1934.*

CAMERON, A. T., Textbook of Biochemistry (4th Ed.). *The Macmillan Co., New York, 1933.*

CANNON, W. B., Bodily Changes in Pain, Hunger, Fear and Rage. *Appleton-Century Co., New York, 1920.*

CANNON, W. B., The Wisdom of the Body. *W. W. Norton & Co., New York, 1932.*

CHITTENDEN, R. H., Development of Physiological Chemistry in America. *Reinhold Publishing Corp., New York, 1930.*

COBB, I. G., The Glands of Destiny. *The Macmillan Co., New York, 1928.*

CREW, F. A. E., Sex Determination. *Methuen & Co., London, England, 1933.*

CUSHING, HARVEY, Pituitary Body and Its Disorders. *B. Lippincott Co., Philadelphia, Pa., 1912.*

HOSKINS, R. G., The Tides of Life. *W. W. Norton & Co., New York, 1933.*

KENDALL, E. C., Thyroxin. *The Chemical Catalogue Co., New York, 1929.*

STIEGLITZ, J. O. (Ed.), Chemistry in Medicine. *The Chemical Foundation, New York, 1928.*

VORONOFF, S., The Conquest of Life. *Brentano's, New York, 1928.*

WELLS, HUXLEY AND WELLS, The Science of Life. *Doubleday, Doran, Garden City, L. I., 1931.*

CHAPTER SIX

Mental Diseases

BEERS, CLIFFORD W., A Mind That Found Itself. *Longmans, Green & Co., New York, 1908.*

BENTLEY AND COWDRY, Problem of Mental Disorder. *McGraw-Hill Publishing Co., New York, 1934.*

CAMPBELL, C. M., Toward Mental Health. *Harvard University Press, Cambridge, Mass., 1933.*

COTTON, H. A., The Defective, Delinquent and Insane. *Princeton University Press, Princeton, N. J., 1922.*

COX, C. M., Early Mental Traits of 300 Geniuses. *Stanford University Press, Palo Alto, Cal., 1926.*

FREUD, ANNA, Psychoanalysis for Teachers and Parents. *Emerson Books, N. Y., 1935.*

FREUD, SIGMUND, New Lectures on Psychoanalysis. *W. W. Norton & Co., New York, 1932.*

HART, BERNARD, Psychopathology. *The Macmillan Co., New York, 1927.*

HOGBEN, L., Nature and Nurture. *W. W. Norton & Co., New York, 1933.*

JASTROW, J., The House That Freud Built. *Greenberg, Publisher Inc., New York, 1932.*

KRETSCHMER, E., Physique and Character. *Harcourt, Brace & Co., New York, 1925.*

LANDMAN, H. J., Human Sterilization. *The Macmillan Co., New York, 1933.*

LANGE, J., Crime and Destiny. *Albert and Charles Boni, New York, 1930.*

LORIMER, F. AND OSBORN, Dynamics of Population. *The Macmillan Co., New York, 1935.*

MENNINGER, K. A., The Human Mind. *Alfred A. Knopf, New York, 1930.*

POPENOE AND JOHNSON, Applied Eugenics. *The Macmillan Co., New York, 1934.*

TAYLOR, W. S., Readings in Abnormal Psychology. *Appleton-Century Co., New York, 1926.*

WHITE AND JELLIFFE, Modern Treatment of Nervous and Mental Diseases. *Lea and Febiger, Philadelphia, Pa., 1923.*

WHITE, WILLIAM A., Forty Years of Psychiatry. *Nervous & Mental Disease Publishing Co., New York, 1933.*

ZWEIG, S., Mental Healers. *Viking Press, New York, 1931.*

CHAPTER SEVEN

Vitamins

BERMAN, LOUIS, Food and Character. *Houghton, Mifflin Co., New York, 1932.*

BODANSKY, M., Introduction to Physiological Chemistry. *John Wiley & Sons, New York, 1927.*

DE KRUIF, PAUL, Hunger Fighters. *Harcourt, Brace & Co., New York, 1928.*

FUNK, CASIMIR, The Vitamines. *Williams & Wilkins Co., Baltimore, Md., 1922.*

LUSK, G., Elements of the Science of Nutrition (4th Ed.). *W. B. Saunders Co., Philadelphia, Pa., 1928.*

MCCOLLUM AND SIMMONDS, The Newer Knowledge of Nutrition (4th Ed.). *The Macmillan Co., New York, 1929.*

MENDEL, LAFAYETTE B. ET AL, The Vitamins. *Journal of the American Medical Association, Chicago, Ill., 1932.*

SHERMAN, HENRY C., The Vitamins (2nd Ed.). *Reinhold Publishing Corp., New York, 1931.*

SHERMAN, HENRY C., Food and Health. *The Macmillan Co., New York, 1934.*

SHURE, BARNETT, The Vitamins in Health and Disease. *Appleton-Century Co., New York, 1933.*

Vitamins, A Survey of Present Knowledge. *Medical Research Council, London, England, 1932.*

CHAPTER EIGHT

Insects

BOUVIER, E. L. (transl. Howard), The Psychic Life of Insects. *Appleton-Century Co., New York, 1922.*

DE KRUIF, PAUL, Microbe Hunters. *Harcourt, Brace & Co., New York, 1926.*

ESSIG, E. O., A History of Entomology. *The Macmillan Co., New York, 1931.*

FABRE, J. H., Social Life in the Insect World. *Appleton-Century Co., New York, 1914.*

FABRE, J. H., Book of Insects. *Dodd, Mead & Co., New York, 1932.*

FERNALD, H. T., Applied Entomology (3rd Ed.). *McGraw-Hill Publishing Co., New York, 1935.*

FLINT, W. P., Insects; Man's Competitor. *Williams & Wilkins Co., New York, 1933.*

HINGSTON, R. W., Problems of Instinct and Intelligence. *The Macmillan Co., New York, 1930.*

HOWARD, L. O., A History of Applied Entomology. *Smithsonian Institution, Washington, D. C., 1930.*

HOWARD, L. O., The Insect Menace. *Appleton-Century Co., New York, 1931.*

HOWARD, L. O., Fighting the Insects. *The Macmillan Co., New York, 1932.*

HUXLEY, JULIAN, Ants. *J. Cape & H. Smith, New York, 1930.*

IMMS, A. D., Recent Advances in Entomology. *P. Blakiston's Son & Co., Philadelphia, Pa., 1931.*

LUTZ, F. E., Fieldbook of Insects. *G. P. Putnam's Sons, New York, 1921.*

METCALF AND FLINT, Fundamentals of Insect Life. *McGraw-Hill Publishing Co., New York, 1932.*

PECKHAM, G. W. AND E. G., Wasps, Social and Solitary. *Houghton, Mifflin Co., New York, 1905.*

RILEY AND JOHANNSEN, Medical Entomology. *McGraw-Hill Publishing Co., New York, 1932.*

WHEELER, W. M., Demons of the Dust. *W. W. Norton & Co., New York, 1930.*

CHAPTER NINE

Matter

ASTON, F. W., Mass Spectra and Isotopes. *Longmans Green & Co., New York, 1933.*

DARROW, K. K., Introduction to Contemporary Physics. *D. Van Nostrand Co., New York, 1926.*

DE BROGLIE, L. V., Wave Mechanics. *E. P. Dutton & Company, New York, 1930.*

DIRAC, P. A. M., Quantum Mechanics. *Oxford University Press, New York, 1930.*

EDDINGTON, A. S., The Nature of the Physical Universe. *Cambridge University Press, New York, 1929.*

FARKAS, A., Ortho, Para and Heavy Hydrogen. *Cambridge University Press, New York, 1935.*

GAMOW, G., Constitution of Atomic Nuclei. *Oxford University Press, New York, 1931.*

GREGORY, J. C., A Short History of Atomism. *The Macmillan Co., New York, 1931.*

HEYL, P. R., New Frontiers of Physics. *Appleton-Century Co., New York, 1930.*

JAFFE, BERNARD, Crucibles; The Lives and Achievements of the Great Chemists. *Simon & Schuster, New York, 1930.*

LEMON, H. B., From Galileo to Cosmic Rays. *Chicago University Press, Chicago, Ill., 1934.*

MAGIE, W. F., A Source Book in Physics. *McGraw-Hill Publishing Company, New York, 1935.*

MILLIKAN, R. A., Time, Matter and Values. *University of North Carolina Press, Chapel Hill, N. C., 1932.*

MILLIKAN, R. A., The Electron. *University of Chicago Press, Chicago, Ill., 1917.*

MILLIKAN, R. A., Science and The New Civilization. *Charles Scribner's Sons, New York, 1930.*

NOYES AND NOYES, Modern Alchemy. *Charles C. Thomas, Springfield, Ill., 1932.*

RUTHERFORD, CHADWICK AND ELLIS, Radiations from Radioactive Substances. *The Macmillan Co., New York, 1932.*

SCHROEDINGER, E., Science and the Human Temperament. *W. W. Norton & Co., New York, 1935.*

SODDY, FREDERICK, The Interpretation of the Atom. *G. P. Putnam's Sons, New York, 1932.*

CHAPTER TEN

Radiation

BAVINK, B., The Natural Sciences. *Appleton-Century Co., New York, 1932.*

BOHR, NIELS, Atomic Theory and Description of Nature. *The Macmillan Co., New York, 1934.*

BRAGG, WILLIAM, Concerning the Nature of Things. *Harper & Bros., New York, 1925.*

BRAGG, WILLIAM, The Universe of Light. *The Macmillan Co., New York, 1932.*

CHASE, C. T., The History of Experimental Physics. *D. Van Nostrand & Co., New York, 1932.*

CREW, H., The Rise of Modern Physics (2nd Ed.). *Williams & Wilkins Co., Baltimore, Md., 1935.*

LANGDON-DAVIES, J., Inside the Atom. *Harper & Bros., New York, 1932.*

LENARD, P., Great Men of Science. *The Macmillan Co., New York, 1933.*

MAGIE, WM. F., A Source Book in Physics. *McGraw-Hill Publishing Co., New York, 1935.*

MILLIKAN, R. A., Electrons (+ and —), Protons, Photons, Neutrons and Cosmic Rays. *University of Chicago Press, Chicago, Ill., 1935.*

PLANCK, MAX, Where is Science Going? *W. W. Norton & Co., New York, 1932.*

CHAPTER ELEVEN

Astrophysics

EDDINGTON, A. S., Atoms and Stars. *Yale University Press, New Haven, Conn., 1927.*

HALE, GEORGE E., The New Heavens. *Charles Scribner's Sons, New York, 1922.*

HALE, GEORGE E., The Depths of the Universe. *Charles Scribner's Sons, New York, 1924.*

HALE, GEORGE E., Beyond the Milky Way. *Charles Scribner's Sons, New York, 1926.*

HALE, GEORGE E., Signals from the Stars. *Charles Scribner's Sons, New York, 1932.*

JEANS, JAMES, The Stars in Their Courses. *The Macmillan Company, New York, 1930.*

JEANS, JAMES, The Universe Around Us. *The Macmillan Company, New York, 1929.*

JEANS, JAMES, The Mysterious Universe. *The Macmillan Company, New York, 1930.*

Jeans, James, Through Space and Time. *The Macmillan Company, New York, 1933.*

Russell, Henry Norris, Composition of the Stars. *Oxford University Press, New York, 1933.*

Russell, Henry Norris, The Solar System and Its Origin. *The Macmillan Company, New York, 1935.*

Stetson, H. T., Man and the Stars. *McGraw-Hill Publishing Company, New York, 1930.*

CHAPTER TWELVE

Weather

Abbot, C. G., Solar Radiation and Weather Studies. *Smithsonian Institution, Washington, D. C., 1935.*

Abbot, C. G., Annals of the Smithsonian Astrophysical Observatory (4 vols.). *Smithsonian Institution, Washington, D. C.*

Abbot, C. G., The Earth and The Stars. *D. Van Nostrand & Co., New York, 1925.*

Abbot, C. G., The Sun and the Welfare of Man. *Smithsonian Institution, Washington, D. C., 1929.*

Abbot, C. G., 25 Years of Solar Radiation Study. *Smithsonian Institution, Washington, D. C., 1931.*

Brooks, C. E. P., Climate Through the Ages. *Ernest Benn, London, England, 1926.*

Brooks, C. F., Why the Weather? *Harcourt, Brace & Co., New York, 1935.*

Clayton, H. H., World Weather. *The Macmillan Co., New York, 1923.*

Clayton, H. H., World Weather and Solar Activity. *Smithsonian Institution, Washington, D. C., 1934.*

Douglass, A. E., Climatic Cycles and Tree Growth. *Carnegie Institution, Washington, D. C., 1919–1928.*

Douglass, A. E., The Secret of the Southwest. *National Geographic Magazine, Washington, D. C., Dec. 1929.*

Free, E. E. and Hoke, Weather. *Robert M. McBride & Co., New York, 1928.*

Humphreys, W. J., Rainmaking. *Williams & Wilkins Co., Baltimore, Md., 1926.*

Huntington, E., The Climatic Factor (No. 192). *Carnegie Institution, Washington, D. C., 1914.*

HUNTINGTON, E., Pulse of Asia. *Houghton, Mifflin Co., New York, 1907.*

HUNTINGTON, E., Earth and Sun. *Yale University Press, New Haven, Conn., 1923.*

SHAW, WM. N., Forecasting Weather. *Constable & Company, London, England, 1923.*

SHAW, WM. N., The Drama of Weather. *The Macmillan Co., New York, 1933.*

TALMAN, C. F., The Realm of the Air. *Bobbs-Merrill Co., New York, 1931.*

CHAPTER THIRTEEN

Galaxies

AITKEN, Robert G., The Binary Stars (2nd Ed.). *McGraw-Hill Publishing Company, New York, 1935.*

COLLIER, K. B., Cosmogonies of Our Fathers. *Columbia University Press, New York, 1935.*

DE SITTER, WM., Kosmos. *Harvard University Press, Cambridge, Mass., 1932.*

EDDINGTON, A. S., The Expanding Universe. *The Macmillan Co., New York, 1932.*

HUBBLE, EDWIN, Red Shifts in Spectra of Nebulae. *Oxford University Press, New York, 1934.*

JEANS, JAMES, The New Background of Science. *The Macmillan Co., New York, 1932.*

MACPHERSON, H. C., Modern Cosmologies. *Oxford University Press, New York, 1929.*

MACPHERSON, H. C., Makers of Astronomy. *Oxford University Press, New York, 1933.*

MILNE, E. A., Relativity, Gravitation and World Structure. *Oxford University Press, New York, 1935.*

REICHENSTEIN, D., Albert Einstein. *E. Gladston, Ltd., London, England, 1935.*

SHAPLEY, HARLOW, Flights from Chaos. *McGraw-Hill Publishing Company, New York, 1930.*

SWANN, W. F. G., Architecture of the Universe. *The Macmillan Co., New York, 1934.*

Tolman, R. C., Theory of Relativity of Motion. *University of California Press, Berkeley, Cal., 1917.*

Tolman, R. C., Statistical Mechanics. *Reinhold Publishing Corp., New York, 1927.*

Tolman, R. C., Relativity, Thermodynamics and Cosmology. *Oxford University Press, New York, 1934.*

Annual Reports of the Director of the Mt. Wilson Observatory, 1919–1935.

INDEX

ABOUT THE AUTHOR

BERNARD JAFFE *was born in New York City in 1896. He received his Bachelor of Science degree from the College of the City of New York and his Master of Arts degree from Columbia University. After one year with the A.E.F. as a private in the 108th Infantry, 27th Division, he turned to teaching. He taught chemistry in various New York City high schools, rising steadily in his profession until in 1931 he was appointed chairman of the Physical Science Department of the Bushwick High School in Brooklyn, a post he still holds. He has published two successful textbooks:* CHEMICAL CALCULATIONS *and his recent* NEW WORLD OF CHEMISTRY. *In 1930 his* CRUCIBLES, *an account of the lives and achievements of the great chemists, won the Francis Bacon Award for the Humanizing of Knowledge. To the making of* OUTPOSTS OF SCIENCE *have gone four years of research and travel, involving visits to the laboratories of over fifty American scientists.*

from THE INNER SANCTUM *of*
SIMON *and* SCHUSTER
Publishers · 386 Fourth Avenue · *New York*

Date Due
